AUDITING
Standards and Procedures

THE WILLARD J. GRAHAM SERIES IN ACCOUNTING

Consulting Editor

Robert N. Anthony   *Harvard University*

AUDITING
Standards and Procedures

ARTHUR W. HOLMES, C.P.A.
Professor of Accounting

WAYNE S. OVERMYER, C.P.A.
Professor of Accounting

Both of the University of Cincinnati

1975

 Eighth Edition

RICHARD D. IRWIN, INC. Homewood, Illinois 60430
Irwin-Dorsey International London, England WC2H 9NJ
Irwin-Dorsey Limited Georgetown, Ontario L7G 4B3

Eighth Edition

First Printing, April 1975

ISBN 0-256-01641-0
Library of Congress Catalog Card No. 74-25805
Printed in the United States of America

Preface

Auditing: Standards and Procedures is a totally modernized and comprehensive text in auditing standards and procedures designed for the student and the practitioner. Its purpose is to offer a thorough knowledge of auditing through the application of auditing standards and adherence to auditing procedures. Although accounting theory is closely related to auditing applications, it is introduced only in those cases where it is deemed advisable to enter into theoretical accounting concepts and the application of accounting principles so that auditing standards and procedures might be clarified and emphasized. Like its predecessors, this eighth edition is not specialized; it is devoted to auditing practices applicable both to manufacturing and to nonmanufacturing business organizations in general.

Consideration of legal responsibility, with all of its modern implications, has been expanded and emphasized. Those familiar with the preceding editions will recognize that while the underlying pattern of the book remains fundamentally unchanged, the eighth edition represents a thorough revision and modernization. Internal control and modern reliance upon internal control are additionally emphasized in order to reduce detailed audit work. Pronouncements of the American Institute of Certified Public Accountants, opinions of the former Accounting Principles Board, opinions of the Financial Accounting Standards Board, pronouncements of the American Accounting Association, and regulations of the Securities and Exchange Commission have been woven into the presentation throughout the book.

The use of the computer in the audit process has been expanded and emphasized. Chapters have been expanded on Internal Control: Electronic Systems; Internal Auditing; Statistical Sampling; and Examination of Records: Electronic Systems.

Audit programs are broken into components and distributed throughout the book. An audit program—subject to variations for any particular examination—follows the related internal control questionnaire for each item or related group of items to be examined; the procedures to be followed and the reasons for the procedures are discussed in similar sequence in each chapter. It has been proved that by this form of organization the reader is more effectively aided in acquiring a knowledge of the philosophy of auditing, the reasons for auditing, and how the conduct of an audit is facilitated in a proper and logical manner and with proper understanding of and regard for auditing standards and procedures. Financial statement considerations are set forth in the various sections of each chapter, or are presented at the conclusion of each chapter, in accordance with modern financial reporting.

Within the book, materials used for illustrative purposes have been designed to stand out sharply so that a standard or procedure is tied closely in the reader's mind with a clearly presented example. At the end of each chapter, questions and problems have been separately classified, and new questions and problems have been added. The working time of the majority of the problems has been reduced, and time-consuming arithmetical computations have been drastically curtailed. The illustrative audit and its work papers have been revised.

Chapters 10 and 11 present discussions of raw data needed as a sample for each section of an audit, both for manual systems and for electronic systems. The text has been designed to afford a faster start for a course in auditing. As stated, increased emphasis has been placed on automation and the examination of electronically prepared records and upon sampling.

The short audit problem *Metalcraft, Incorporated* by Holmes and Kiefer, separately issued together with all necessary material, has been totally revised and shortened. Again, this separate production is issued in order to meet the widespread demand for a short manufacturing case. Also, the Holmes and Moore *Audit Case* has been totally revised and the working time drastically shortened.

We deeply appreciate the continued universal acceptance of this book and wish to thank sincerely all persons and institutions throughout the world who have adopted or read it. Also, we are indebted to the accounting profession, to all accounting professors, to the personnel of all accounting firms, and to other readers who have offered constructive comments and criticisms that have aided materially in the compilation of preceding editions and this edition.

Special gratitude could be expressed to a legion of individuals—both educators and professional persons—but lack of space makes that pleasant undertaking impossible. We hope it will be realized that within a preface it is not possible to acknowledge the appreciation due to hundreds of institutions and to professional firms.

March 1975   Arthur W. Holmes
                                                Wayne S. Overmyer

Contents

ix

Section IV: Miscellaneous Current Liabilities: *Accrued Expenses. Amounts Withheld. Declared Dividends. Unclaimed Wages.* Long-Term Liabilities Currently Payable: *Deposits.* Section V: Revenues Received in Advance: *Audit Objectives. Rent Received in Advance. Interest Received in Advance. Deferred Gross Profit on Installment Sales. Collection in Advance on Contracts and on Sales. Redeemable Tickets and Coupons. Subscription Received in Advance.* Section VI: Contingencies: *Audit Program for Contingencies. Liability Certificate.* Section VII: Financial Statement Considerations.

1
Auditing Concepts

Auditing is a private profession rendering a public service. Consequently, in financial reporting and in the administration of financial practices, professional accounting has a more commanding voice and more influence than any other group associated with the reporting of economic activity. Business organizations report to their stockholders, creditors, labor organizations, certain governmental agencies, the news media, financial analysts, and others through the medium of an independently prepared audit report which *includes* related financial statements. It would be meaningless for a company to report upon itself without the attestation of an independent party because the company would be acting both as litigant and judge. In the audit report, an opinion is expressed by an independent accountant—normally a certified public accountant—regarding the fairness of the presentation of the financial statements. Over the past years, the functions of certified public accountants have rapidly expanded beyond the realm of an audit only. Within this book, it will be demonstrated that due to improvements in modern internal control, automatically compiled financial records, electronic data processing, quantitative and qualitative analyses, management sciences, the application of statistical analysis techniques to business problems, and statistical applications in the selection and analysis of audit samples, an auditor is available to engage in activities in the fields of management advisory services, operations research, and financial and operating services.

SECTION I: INDEPENDENT AUDITS

Independent Auditing

Auditing is not a branch of accounting; it is an independent discipline which relies upon the results of accounting and other functional operations and data. Auditing does not measure and communicate financial and business data because those are the functions of accounting. Auditing

1

reviews and reports on the propriety or impropriety of management's measurements and communication of financial operations. Traditionally, auditing is an attest function involving the objective examination of financial statements prepared by management. In his examination of the financial statements of a client, an auditor relies upon the examination of internal controls, records, transactions and their underlying evidence for authority and validity, other financial and legal records and documents, and evidence obtained from outside sources. Thus, it is discernible that the basis for any audit decision must be based upon *evidence*. An audit is performed in order to ascertain the fairness, integrity, and authenticity of management's financial statements. An audit is conducted with the intention of rendering an opinion of the fairness of the presentation of the financial statements. The financial statements should be prepared in accordance with the application of generally accepted accounting principles consistently applied from period to period.

More broadly defined than in the preceding paragraph, auditing embraces the traditional concept, plus the examination and evaluation of all information-gathering functions and all phases of management functions and activities, in order to acertain if operations are conducted in an effective and efficient manner. This is known as *management auditing* or *operational auditing*. Today, the majority of CPA firms simultaneously conduct a financial audit and a management audit in order to protect management, stockholders, creditors and so forth. Normally, a small client needs more management advice than does a large, well-organized corporation. The future professional accountant must be able to understand and comprehend the entire management information system.

While the immediate objectives of an audit are to ascertain the reliability of financial statements, the long-range objectives of an audit should be to serve as a guide to management's future decisions in all financial matters, such as controlling, forecasting, analyzing, and reporting. These objectives have as their purposes the improvement of performances.

Because an independent audit is intended to determine the reliability of management's representations of its stewardship, the audit should be performed by persons who are *independent* of management. The independent auditor should be professionally competent, so that there may be rendered a professionally expert and impartial opinion of the results of the audit. A professional auditor is a critic—and his function is critical appraisal.

Examination procedures will vary from one audit to another. An auditor must be guided by the exigencies of each situation as it arises. Exact procedural rules cannot be formulated which will be applicable to every audit. Therefore, the scope of an audit will vary to fit the requirements of a particular case. There is only *one audit:* that which satisfies the requirements of an engagement, judged from professional standards of performance. In all circumstances, a combination of a thorough knowledge of principles and procedures, sound judgment, adequate education, proper professional training, and an open mind designates the successful professional accountant.

Evidence. As stated, any audit conclusion is based upon evidence. The evidence may be submitted by a client, obtained from outsiders, or may be generated by the auditor. Necessary audit evidence may be in existence at the time an audit is started, or it may be created during the course of an audit, or it may be the result of logical deduction. On the approximate basis of audit sequence—audit evidence may be classified as follows:

A. Adequate internal control procedures.
B. All accounting and financial records.
C. Documents: internally prepared and externally prepared, and automatically available for substantiation. This would include such items as stock certificates and bonds owned, and notes receivable.
D. Information obtained from independent outsiders: written or oral, and created during the course of an audit.
E. Physical assets: e.g., cash on hand, inventories, fixed assets.
F. Authoritative client representations: written and oral.
G. Auditor's computations or calculations, including comparisons with client-prepared data.

The various types of evidence will be discussed in depth as this book develops. It must be remembered that in judging the reliability of evidence, classification is only a means to an end, and that end is a valid audit conclusion. Chapter 6 of *Statements on Auditing Procedure No. 33*, issued by the American Institute of Certified Public Accountants, recognizes the importance of evidential materials; certain other *Statements on Auditing Procedure* treat other evidential matters.

Internal Auditing

At this point only brief consideration is given to internal auditing; the subject will be treated more fully in Chapter 6. While independent audits are conducted by professional public accountants, internal audits are conducted by regular employees of a company. As will be explained, there are vast differences and also many similarities in the nature of the work performed by external and internal auditors. Internal auditing is a staff function. The internal auditor appraises financial and operating procedures, reviews financial records and accounting and operating procedures, evaluates the system of internal control, periodically summarizes the results of the continuous investigation, prepares recommendations for better procedures, and reports the results of his findings to top management—the president or the board of directors. The transmission of information to top management must emphasize the future effect of plans and decisions.

An internal auditor does not engage in accounting activities or any other line activity. As indicated, his work emphasizes appraisal, analysis, and reporting upon the policies and methods of operation. The work of an internal auditor incorporates studying the efficiency of such functions as purchasing, receiving, storing, requisitioning, producing, cost accounting, sales procedures, general accounting, controlling receivables and payables, receiving and disbursing cash, and many others. After evaluating the system of internal control in operation and after studying the operational methods prescribed by management, the internal auditor is in a position to determine the efficiency of the system of internal control and the operational methods in force, and to report his findings and recommendations for improvements.

Thus it is discernible that the objectives, type of work, and covered work areas of the independent auditor and the internal auditor are different. When an audit is conducted by independent professional public accountants, the opinion of an impartial expert is a distinct advantage to the organization and a protection of the interests of stockholders, creditors, and others. Complete impartiality and independence are not possible for the internal auditor because he cannot divorce himself completely from management.

In a large company, the internal audit staff may be made up of many people. In a small company, it may not be economically sound to maintain such a separate staff; consequently, the accounting work must be divided between personnel so that no one person is in complete charge of a transaction.

Public Accountancy

Accounting is an academically based discipline which involves the correct analysis and recording of business transactions, the construction of financial statements from the summarized results of the business transactions, and the analysis and interpretation of those financial statements and related statistical data. Accounting in this sense is constructive and is performed by management; the results are the representations of management. As stated earlier, auditing is analytical and is carried out *independently of management*—in order to judge management's performance.

The profession of public accountancy offers the following principal types of services:

1. *Auditing*, which is the objective examination of financial statements, accompanied by the expression of a competent opinion concerning the fairness of the presentation of those financial statements.
2. *Management advisory services*, consisting of services to clients on

matters of accounting, financial planning and control systems, management information systems, mechanization of data processing, EDP systems, quantitative decision systems, operation research techniques, inventory control systems, business policies, organization procedures, product costs, distribution, and many other phases of business conduct and operation.

3. *Investigation service*, for such matters as the purchase and sale of a business, sales analyses, the preparation of budgets, an investigation of systems of internal control, a detailed examination of cash transactions in the event of suspected fraud, and many others.

4. *Representation services*, which arise when a client requires representation in tax matters, security registrations, union negotiations, contract termination, and so forth.

5. *Assistance*, which varies from indicating accounting entries, installing accounting systems, changing accounting procedures, preparing tax returns, and assisting with internal control.

Modern business is involved and complicated in its financial ramifications. Apparently, specialization is an outstanding manifestation of our economic life. As the principles and conduct of business have advanced and as financial operations and ramifications have become more involved in the past several decades, the work of the professional public accountant now covers an increasingly wider scope of activities. These activities correspond to the services of the profession of public accountancy, indicated above. Scientifically, the present-day auditor must be a well-trained individual so that he can keep pace with the business field and aid in leading business to a stage of profitable and sound operation.

Auditor. In order to distinguish between a client's internal accountant as a constructionalist and a public auditor as an independent analyst, this text frequently will use the term "auditor" in a sense of a professional certified public accountant.

Development of Auditing

The profession of public accountancy has become a social force because of the reliance by stockholders, creditors, management, and others upon the auditor's representations. Public accountancy is one of the younger professions, and the progress of the profession is at an accelerating rate. Professional standing is the result of public concession, and the profession of public accountancy is on a par with other professions with respect to ethical conduct and on an approximate par in most states with respect to education and experience required for admission to public practice at a certified level. Educational requirements are constantly being properly raised in the majority of the jurisdictions of the United States.

Accounting in a very rudimentary form was practiced as soon as civilization developed to a stage where business transactions took place between people. Accounting developed in keeping with economic theory and business practice during the 16th, 17th, and 18th centuries. Late in the 18th century, men established themselves as public accountants; they quite commonly were little more than copyists and letter writers. In the 19th century, the "expert" bookkeeper came into existence. His chief function was to trace fraudulent transactions and to locate errors. Late in the 19th century and early in the 20th century, accounting treatises and texts began to make their appearance; and together with the increased size of business units and multiplicity of transactions, accounting theory and practice developed rapidly until today, when we find the competent certified public accountant well educated and well trained for professional work.

Over approximately the last three decades, the activities of public accounting have emerged from detailed audits to today's modern examination of financial statements (and their underlying transactional data) and the accompanying expression of opinion of those statements. Paralleling the shift in audit emphasis has been a greatly increased range in the activities of professional certified public accountants. As previously listed in the section "Public Accountancy," some of these activities include tax services, surveys for a multitude of purposes, services in connection with normal business operations, services in connection with mergers, receiverships, corporate reorganizations, governmental bureau activities, services related to regulations over securities issuances, management advisory services, and many others. And the new fields demanding the services of the professional certified public accountant will be greatly expanded with the increased demands of the world of business.

Internal Control Review

Internal control has been defined by the Committee on Auditing Procedure of the American Institute of Certified Public Accountants as follows:

Internal control comprises the plan of organization and all of the coordinate methods and measures adopted within a business to safeguard its assets, check the accuracy and reliability of its accounting data, promote operational efficiency, and encourage adherence to prescribed managerial policies. This definition possibly is broader than the meaning sometimes attributed to the term. It recognizes that a "system" of internal control extends beyond those matters which relate directly to the functions of the accounting and financial departments.

Stated differently, and in the narrower sense of accounting and financial operations, internal control is a function of management operated in order to safeguard assets, to guard against improper fund disbursements, and to offer assurance that unauthorized obligations cannot be incurred. These objectives are to be accomplished through the internal company procedural controls and verification of the clerical accuracy involved.

ILLUSTRATION. Improper internal control would exist if one person could (1) count cash sales money, (2) deposit the money in the bank, and (3) record the cash receipts in the accounting records. That person would be placed in a position that could lead to theft by recording and placing in the bank an amount less than the total cash receipts.

The independent auditor relies upon the system of internal control in deciding upon the extent of detailed examination and in deciding upon the reliability of financial statements. These concepts of the reliability of internal control will be developed as the book progresses. In starting any audit, the best place is to begin with a review of operations accompanied by an examination of the system of internal control in operation.

As will be demonstrated, an audit is dependent upon the examination of evidential data leading to figures for the financial statements.

Management Control Review

In addition to a review of accounting and financial operations in connection with a review of internal control in the narrower sense, the auditor today extends the audit function into all management areas. A review of management controls is commonly known as "management auditing," as discussed earlier in this section. The purpose of a management audit is to identify management practices which require improvement and to evaluate the operations of a total system. The emphasis is on the location of problem areas within management. In a management control review, the major areas examined will include company objectives, policies, organization, personnel behavior, employee compensation and benefits, financial management, systems, procedures, and various tax accounting methods, and marketing policies and practices.

SECTION II: THE AUDIT REPORT

The audit report is the document in which the professional public accountant sets forth the scope and nature of his examination and in which he expresses his independent expert opinion concerning the client's financial statements accompanying the report.

So far as persons outside the managerial or directive ranks are concerned—stockholders, creditors, and so forth—the tangible evidences of an audit are expressed only in the financial statements and the accompanying report of the examination. In order to develop early a concept of the expected terminal result, there is submitted below the standard short-form audit report (or certificate) recommended by the Committee on Auditing Procedure of the American Institute of Certified Public Accountants.

SHORT-FORM AUDIT REPORT OR CERTIFICATE

Date

To the Stockholders and the Board of Directors of the ABC Company:

We have examined the balance sheet of the ABC Company as of December 31, 1975, and the related statements of income and retained earnings for the year then ended. Our examination was made in accordance with generally accepted auditing standards, and accordingly included such tests of the accounting records and such other auditing procedures as we considered necessary in the circumstances.

In our opinion, the accompanying balance sheet and statements of income and retained earnings present fairly the financial position of the ABC Company at December 31, 1975, and the results of its operations for the year then ended, in conformity with generally accepted accounting principles applied on a basis consistent with that of the preceding year.

(Signed)   X, Y, and Z
Certified Public Accountants

The scope section (first paragraph) of the report is factual. The opinion section (second paragraph) represents the considered judgment of the auditor. The report may be expanded by inserting explanatory material between the first and second paragraphs. If the auditing standards and procedures to be described are not followed, the opinion cannot be rendered in the terms set forth in the illustrative report just given.

If additional major financial statements—such as the *statement of changes in financial position*—are rendered in addition to the balance sheet, income statement, and statement of retained earnings, they should be indicated in both the scope section and the opinion section.

Today, the statement of changes in financial position is considered to be a major financial statement. Therefore, the scope section should be stated as follows: "We have examined the balance sheet of the ABC Company as of December 31, 1975, and the related statements of income and retained earnings and changes in financial position for the year then ended. Our examination was . . . . Because financial statements normally are rendered in comparative form, the opinion section of the report would appear as follows: "In our opinion, the preceding financial statements fairly present the financial position of the ABC Company as of December 31, 1975 and 1974, and the results of its operations and the changes in its financial position for the years then ended, in conformity with generally accepted accounting principles applied on a consistent basis."

The form of the report is not necessarily used inflexibly, since circumstances of each engagement may cause variations in its phrasing, as will be pointed out in subsequent sections of this chapter and in Chapters 2 and 28. It is not possible to use one form of report in all engagements, but the standard short report constitutes the basis upon which to build the report required in the circumstances.

Some accounting firms use a "modified" short audit report. The modified short form normally contains all of the elements of the recommended short form but opens with the opinion section, as follows:

MODIFIED SHORT-FORM AUDIT REPORT

In our opinion, the accompanying balance sheet, statement of income and retained earnings and statement of changes in financial position present fairly the financial condition of the Hark Corporation at December 31, 1975, and the results of its operations for the year then ended, in conformity with generally accepted accounting principles applied on a basis consistent with that of the preceding year. Our examination of these statements was made in accordance with generally accepted auditing standards, and accordingly included such tests of the accounting records and such other auditing procedures as we considered necessary in the circumstances.

The short-form audit report and the modified short-form audit report may be expanded by the Institute in the near future.

SECTION III: PROFESSIONAL ORGANIZATIONS

In this early stage of the study of auditing, it is advisable that the student possess an introductory knowledge of professional accounting organizations. There are many accounting organizations and societies, and each is devoted to the fulfillment of its functions and objectives. All are interested in the advancement of accounting and auditing. As this book progresses, material in addition to that set forth in this section will be presented which pertains to each organization. To attempt an in-depth study of each organization and society would require a total book.

The American Institute of Certified Public Accountants. The American Institute of Certified Public Accountants is the only national organization of certified public accountants. It was established in 1887 under the name of The American Association of Public Accountants. In 1916, it changed its name to The American Institute of Accountants; and in 1936, it merged with the American Society of Certified Public Accountants. On June 3, 1957, the name was changed to The American Institute of Certified Public Accountants. (AICPA) Briefly, the objectives of the Institute are to unite the certified public accountants in the United States; to promote and maintain high professional standards of practice; to assist in the maintenance of standards for entry into the profession; to promote the interests of CPAs; to develop and improve accounting education; and to encourage cordial relations between CPAs in the United States and professional accountants in other countries.

To be eligible for membership in the Institute, the applicant must be in possession of a valid and unrevoked certified public accountant's certificate issued by the legally constituted authority of one of the jurisdictions of the United States, and must have passed an examination in accounting and other related subjects satisfactory to the Board of Directors of the Institute.

The AICPA cooperates with the state societies of certified public accountants in order to promote a united profession; formulates and follows a position on state and national legislation affecting accounting practice; prepares uniform certified public accountant examinations; cooperates with teachers of accounting in raising the standards of accounting education; and establishes and enforces rules of professional ethics. These topics will receive additional attention in Chapters 2 and 3.

The Accounting Principles Board (APB) which was in existence from 1959 to 1973, issued 31 Opinions (certain of which were revised in part or in whole) dealing with accounting and reporting standards. They were issued in order to promote uniformity in the application of principles and in order to narrow the differences in the areas of financial reporting. The Opinions issued by the APB are binding on members of the Institute. The APB had 18 non-paid, part-time members, and was a senior committee of the AICPA. All members were CPAs. The APB was declared out of existence in 1973, and was replaced by the *Financial Accounting Standards Board* (FASB) described in the following paragraphs.

In 1972, as a result of the recommendations of the report titled *Establishing Financial Accounting Standards*, the *Financial Accounting Foundation* (FAF) was incorporated as an entity apart from all existing professional bodies. It has nine trustees, whose principal duties are to appoint the members of the *Financial Accounting Standards Board* (below) and to raise funds for the operation of that Board (FASB). Of the nine trustees of the FAF, one is the president of the Institute, and the remaining eight are appointed by the Board of Directors of the Institute for three-year terms (after initial staggering). Four trustees are CPAs in public practice, two are financial executives, one is a financial analyst, and one is an accounting educator. The last four are chosen, respectively, from names submitted by the following: the Financial Executives Institute, the National Association of Accountants, and the American Accounting Association.

The Financial Accounting Standards Board has the function of establishing standards of financial accounting and reporting. The Board has seven full-time salaried members. Each serves for a term of five years, with a possible additional five-year renewal period. While on the Board, no member may have any other business affiliation. The FASB is independent of any other organization. Four of the FASB members are CPAs from public practice. The remaining three need not be CPAs, but must be experienced in financial reporting. At least five of the seven members of the FASB must approve a standard before it is issued in finalized form.

The Board of Trustees of the FAF also established a Financial Accounting Standards Council, made up of about 30 members who serve the FASB in an advisory capacity. The chairman of the FASB is the ex-officio chairman of the Advisory Council. Members of the Advisory Council are appointed for one year, with indefinite renewal. Not more than 25 percent of the members of the Advisory Council may be chosen from any one field of activity.

It is to be noted that the word "standards"—not "principles"—is used, and this is good because a search for principles involves concepts and not *reality*, with which auditing is concerned.

Prior to the issuance of a Standard by the FASB, public hearings are held on it. This is done so that interested parties may express their views. Proposed Statements must be available for public comment, normally for a 60-day period. Responses are submitted to all Board members. After the FASB has officially issued a statement, the Board may issue formal interpretations of it, and to do this five affirmative Board member votes are required.

It must be remembered that the Opinions of the former Accounting Principles Board remain in effect and will be effective unless changed and superseded by Statements of the FASB.

In December 1973, Statement of Financial Accounting Standards No. 1 was issued; it treats of the disclosure of foreign currency transaction information. It was adopted by the unanimous vote of the FASB. At the present time approximately 15 other topics are on the agenda of the Board. It is recommended that the reader remain abreast of the activities of the FASB.

The attitude of the Securities and Exchange Commission is to the effect that it endorses the establishment of the FASB. The SEC has issued Accounting Series Release No 150, indicating that it will look to the FASB for the private sector in improving financial reporting standards.

Another senior committee of the AICPA is the *Committee on Auditing Procedure*, which at this date has issued 54 Statements on Auditing Procedure. Certain Statements change portions of certain other preceding Statements, and a few Statements supersede certain other Statements. As this book progresses, proper consideration will be given to many of these Statements—because this is a book on auditing standards and procedures. The Committee on Auditing Procedure maintains jurisdiction over matters pertaining to auditing and an audit report; however, close cooperation between the FASB and the Committee on Auditing Procedure is of vital importance to professional accounting.

There are many other Institute committees and boards, as indicated in the by laws of the Institute, some of which will be referred to in this book.

In February, 1974, the Board of Directors of the AICPA authorized the appointment of a commission to do an in-depth study of the functions of auditors. The majority of the commission will not be CPAs. The commission "is expected to develop recommendations on the future responsibilities of independent auditors in terms of increasing public expectations and the feasibility of meeting them." Some of the items to be considered are the responsibility of an auditor for detecting fraud, the monitoring of financial information releases to the public, the changing of the standard short-form audit report, the action of the profession to reduce the risks of misunderstanding regarding its role, and several other items.

State Societies of Certified Public Accountants. Within each state, certified public accountants have organized state societies. In general, the objectives of a state society are as follows: elevation of the profession of public accounting, maintenance of high professional standards for obtaining a certificate of certified public accountant, cultivation of the spirit of professional cooperation, encouragement of proper education, and advancement of the interests of members.

The AICPA, many state societies, and many organizations briefed in the following paragraphs have programs for continuing education. The subject of continuing education is considered in Chapter 2.

The Financial Executives Institute. This organization is of high quality and is devoted to the furtherance of the functions of controllership, financial management, and financial reporting.

The National Association of Accountants. This important association is active in the development of an increasing knowledge of accounting practices, methods, and cost accounting, and through research, it develops a better understanding of the nature, purposes, and uses of accounting as applied to all types of economic endeavor. Local chapters promote educational cooperation with universities in an excellent manner. The Institute of Management Accounting of the NAA awards a Certificate in Management Accounting to candidates who successfully complete all five parts of an annual examination within a consecutive three-year period. The five parts are (1) Economics and Business Finance, (2) Organization and Behavior, (3) Public Reporting Standards, Auditing and Taxes, (4) Periodic Reporting for Internal and External Purposes, and (5) Decision Analysis, Including Modeling and Information Systems.

The American Accounting Association. The American Accounting Association is the national organization whose activities are devoted primarily to accounting and related research, the development of accounting principles, and the improvement of the teaching of accounting. The original organization was founded in 1916 and in 1935 the present name was adopted. Its membership includes teachers of accounting and related subjects, and accountants at both the noncertified and certified levels who are privately and publicly employed.

American Woman's Society of Certified Public Accountants. This society was formed in 1933 to advance the professional interest of women certified public accountants. In 1938 the American Woman's Society of Certified Public Accountants organized an affiliate, the American Society of Women Accountants, which provides membership for women engaged in any phase of accounting.

The Institute of Internal Auditors. The Institute of Internal Auditors was incorporated in 1941. The objectives of internal auditing are to protect the interests of an organization by ascertaining the reliability of the accounting and statistical data; by ascertaining the extent to which assets are properly accounted for; and by ascertaining the extent of compliance with established policies, plans, and procedures.

The National Society of Public Accountants was organized in November, 1945. It has a strong program in education and is constantly trying to raise standards.

The National Society for Business Budgeting was incorporated in 1951; it has as a part of its objectives the fostering of an understanding of budgetary planning and control, and cooperation with educational institutions in improving the quality of courses in budgeting.

The Federal Government Accountants Association. This association is a national professional organization and most of the members are primarily engaged in Government accounting, auditing, budgeting, and related financial management activities. The membership also is represented by industrial, educational, and private personal service organizations interested in Government programs. This Association, like the AICPA, the various State Societies, and others, also has a code of professional ethics.

The major objectives of the FGAA are as follows:

(1) Unite professional financial managers in Government service to perform more efficiently for their own development and for the benefit of the Government.
(2) Encourage and provide an effective means for interchange of work-related and professional ideas.
(3) Aid in improving financial management techniques and concepts.
(4) Improve financial management education in the Government and universities.

SECTION IV: UNITED STATES GOVERNMENT SERVICES ORGANIZATION

At this point, brief consideration is given to auditing operations of some of the organizations and offices existing in the framework of the U.S. Government.

The United States General Accounting Office. The General Accounting Office (GAO) was created by the Congress of the United States over 50 years ago. It has an extremely wide range of audit authority for governmental contracts with private business organizations—particularly those connected with national defense. As time passes, the efforts of the GAO are particularly directed to evaluating the cost and benefit results of government programs. The GAO is responsible to the Comptroller General of the United States.

The GAO has a new code (1972) of audit standards titled "Standards for Audit of Governmental Organizations, Programs, Activities and Federal Institutions." The GAO has the legal responsibility to approve federal agency accounting systems for both civil and defense agencies. There are approximately 325 systems in the federal government. Because of the many changes in various laws, agencies are constantly changing their systems—after which they must be approved by the GAO. On May 9, 1973, the Comptroller General of the U.S. stated: "This (system design and system change projects) is an area where CPA firms can provide the government with a valuable service and some have done so in the past."

The Cost Accounting Standards Board. This board (the CASB) is an independent agency in the legislative branch of the Federal Government. It began its operations in February, 1971. By law (an amendment to the Defense Production Act of 1950, which authorized the creation of the Board) the Board is directed to develop cost accounting standards (rules of measurement or anything established by custom or authority) for national defense contractors and subcontractors. These standards are used in the pricing, administration, and settlement of negotiated defense contracts in excess of $100,000 except where the negotiated price is based on established market or catalogue prices of similar items sold in large quantities to the public, or prices established by law or regulation. The work of the CASB formerly was performed by the GAO. Early in 1975, Congress raised the $100,000 to $500,000.

The Comptroller General of the United States serves as Chairman of the Board. He appoints four additional Board members, whose background and experience represents government, industry, the academic accounting community, and professional accounting. The Board is responsible to the Congress of the United States, and is charged to promulgate cost accounting standards designed to achieve uniformity and consistency in the cost accounting principles followed by defense contractors and subcontractors.

The executive secretary of the Board is a permanent employee. The Board is served by a full-time staff of 20 to 25 experienced accountants and lawyers. Currently, there are 23 professional staff members, of which 15 are CPAs and 6 are lawyers. The staff represents the same diversity of backgrounds as the Board members; the staff is supported by an administrative staff. Each professional staff member is assigned responsibility for a major research project and the research projects are coordinated by a group of four project directors. Each member of the professional staff participates in policy determination for all staff activities.

The AICPA, the National Association of Accountants, the Financial Executives Institute, and the FGAA have established committees to work with the CASB—thus lending much varied professionalism to the Board. The Management Accounting Practices Committee of the NAA started the development of a statement of concepts for contract costing. Since the development of that statement, the CASB has evolved policies concerning many of the issues of interest to contractors. In 1973 the Board published "A Statement of Operating Policies, Procedures and Objectives."

As of this date the CASB has promulgated five cost accounting standards, dealing with the following:

(1) Consistency between estimating, accumulating, and reporting of costs.
(2) Consistency in the allocation of direct and indirect costs.
(3) Allocation of corporate home office expenses into segments—such as sales, divisions, and plants.
(4) The capitalization of tangible assets.
(5) Accounting for unallowable costs.

Briefly, the procedure of the Board is to accept or reject a new subject for study; the proposal for a new study-subject is presented by the staff in writing. If the Board accepts the proposal, the staff starts with library research, a study of Armed Services Board of Contract Appeal cases, and Court of Claims cases. Staff members then visit contractors in order to determine the possibility of establishing a standard for the selected subject. Frequently, additional data are obtained from other contractors, professional accounting associations, business consultants, trade associations, Government agencies and the academic community. Then the staff drafts a standard which is sent to several contractors for their reaction. Thus far, the Board has not actively participated—other than to approve the item for study. When the staff has drafted a proposed standard, it is sent to the Board, and if the executive secretary of the Board so recommends, the proposed standard is published in the *Federal Register*. After study, the Board will either approve the standard or reject it. If approved, the standard is published in the *Federal Register* for the second time, together with a detailed explanation of the reaction of the Board to comments received as the result of the first publication in the *Register*. The proposed standards are sent to Congress for a period of 60 days. If Congress does not comment within the 60-day period the standard is effective.

SECTION V: AUDITING STANDARDS AND PROCEDURES

Relationship of Accounting and Auditing

In accounting, the proper determination of periodic net income is of fundamental importance. Net income has many definitions. Here, net income may be thought of as the increase in *net* assets, measured by the excess of periodic revenues over periodic costs and expenses.

In order properly to determine periodic net income, there must be a proper matching of revenues and the related costs of obtaining those revenues. Therefore, in the conduct of an audit, resulting in the preparation of financial statements that present fairly the results of operations for a period, the proper determination of periodic net income is of primary importance; and in order properly to determine periodic net income, the audit must be competently conducted. Financial statements must be presented on the premise that there has been consistency in the application of accounting principles from year to year. However, changes in price levels may invalidate comparisons even when consistency in statement preparation has prevailed.

Accounting principles and auditing standards and procedures are interrelated and integrated. In the related fields of accounting principle application and auditing, the concepts of *disclosure, consistency, materiality,* and *conservatism* have emerged. At this point, *brief* consideration is granted each concept. The concepts should serve as guides in the application of accounting principles, in the preparation of financial statements, and in the performance of an audit.

Disclosure.   Financial data must be translated into meaningful and useful reports, the financial statements must adequately disclose the results of managerial stewardship. If adequate disclosure of all material data is not given in financial statements, there exists a withholding of data and information from persons interested in those financial statements. To state fixed assets at their net amount would not offer disclosure of original cost or the accumulated provision for depreciation. To fail to disclose adequate information regarding long-term leases would constitute substandard reporting. To combine all expenses into one income statement total would result in failing to disclose important cost data. To include the loss in a lawsuit of a considerable sum as "miscellaneous expense" would constitute failure to disclose pertinent information. To charge cash dividend payments to a Paid-In Capital account without explanation would withhold pertinent information.

Preferably and properly for the benefit of users of financial statements, adequate disclosure should appear *within* the financial statements, and voluminous footnotes which may tend to becloud adequate disclosures should be avoided. Footnotes to financial statements are important, but they should always add to or supplement information appearing in the statements; footnotes should not repeat or contradict information appearing in the financial statements.

Consistency.   Consistency (the comparability of data from period to period) in financial statement preparation implies that the same basis of applying accounting principles has been followed in the current year as in the prior year. For example, inconsistency would result if in 1974 the statements were prepared on the cash basis of accounting and if in 1975 the accrual method was followed. Inconsistency would prevail if a building was depreciated 2 percent in year 1, 10 percent in year 2, and 3 percent in the next year. If extraordinary gains or losses resulting from the sale of securities (or any other asset) were credited or debited to Retained Earnings in 1974 and were credited or debited to income in 1975, inconsistency would prevail.

Changes in accounting methods resulting in a lack of consistency from year to year should be pointed out in footnotes to the financial statements or in the audit report in order to avoid distortion in reporting net income and other financial data. If properly examined, an approved change in accounting methods would not lead to a qualification or disclaimer of opinion.

Materiality. Much has been written about materiality, but not much has been done about it, simply because materiality is elusive. It cannot be universally quantified. Judgment must be used in each individual case, after establishing guidelines for that case. Materiality is on the agenda of the Financial Accounting Standards Board—and the accounting profession should establish standards for materiality—if they can be established. As used in accounting, materiality implies importance—relative or absolute—and the materiality of an item may be dependent upon its nature or its size, or both. The method of recording used by an accountant may depend upon the materiality of an item. Also, the procedures used by an auditor may depend upon item materiality. The problem of determining the boundary line between material and immaterial is immediately imposed. Most people will agree that any item should be considered as being material if a reason exists that knowledge of it would influence decisions of management, stockholders, creditors, and so forth. An amount considered material by one person may be considered as immaterial by another person. The concept of materiality has the two following criteria: (1) the relative size of the amount, and (2) the importance of the amount to third parties. In the case of *Charles A. Howard, et al.* (1 SEC 6), the Securities and Exchange Commission stated that materiality is "a fact which if it had been correctly stated or disclosed would have deterred or tended to deter the average prudent investor from purchasing the securities in question." Rule 2.02 (c) of the Securities and Exchange Commission's Regulation S–X states: "The accountant's certificate shall state the opinion of the accountant as to any material changes in accounting principles or practices. . . ." Rule 3.02 states: "If the amount which would otherwise be required to be shown with respect to any item is not material, it need not be separately set forth."

In judging materiality, both an actual quantitative dollar amount and a relative dollar amount must be considered. Is 10 percent of a net income of $1,000 material? Is 10 percent of a net income of $1,000,000 material? Assume that $20,000 of expense is not accrued as of December 31, 1974, in which year a net income of $175,000 was reported. In 1975, this same company reported a net loss of $5,000. If the 1974 expense had been properly accrued, the net income for 1975 would have been $15,000. This may indicate a material situation to a credit grantor. In the *BarChris* case, (Chapter 3) the judge ruled that the 15.7 percent difference in net income was not material!

In an audit, adjustments sometimes may not be made for nonmaterial errors; nonmaterial expense or income items may be combined into a single account; and small differences between cost and market price for inventory totals may be ignored. There are many other examples, each of which must be judged individually and in total for the effect on financial statements. Of course, many nonmaterial items (or errors) may become a material amount in total.

Materiality must also be judged on the basis of a given company and a given set of circumstances—as exemplified by companies in the "start up" stage, those whose net income is relatively stable annually per dollar of sales, those with widely fluctuating net incomes, and those whose net incomes are consistently low per sales dollar.

Materiality also refers to unusual items of revenue or expense of a large amount and of a nonrecurring nature. Materiality must be judged both on the basis of one item and on the basis of the net amount of several small items of nonrecurring revenues and expenses. Materiality should be judged in relationship to the total of the income exclusive of the nonrecurring items. A nonrecurring expense or revenue of material amount may distort normal net income if it is placed in the income statement and if it is not properly disclosed and explained. If all nonrecurring items of expense and revenue are properly placed in the income statement, full disclosure prevails, and there is no attempt to levelize periodic net income by burying these items in the statement of retained earnings.

The Accountants' International Study Group published its study on *Materiality in Accounting in* 1973. It was prepared by the U.S. delegation and discusses the attitudes and practices in Canada, the U.K. and the U.S. Among its general conclusions are:

(1)   Materiality is essentially a matter of judgment. An item should be deemed material if it could reasonably be expected to have an influence on the users of financial statements.

(2)   Size alone is not the sole determinant of a material item. Whether the nature of the item is a factor in the determination of net income, unusual or contingent, must be considered. Also, the relationships of the amount to the financial statements taken as a whole, to related items, and to corresponding amounts in previous years or amounts expected in the future are important factors.

(3)   A reasonable approach for quantitative guidelines, when compared

to an appropriate base, is that 10 percent or more would be considered material, under five percent immaterial. Items between this range should be considered individually in light of all relevant factors. Lower quantitative limits should be applied with respect to certain transactions such as those with directors and officers.

It is interesting to note that the British Companies Act in 1895, quoted from the *Lord Davey Report:* "Every contract or fact is material which would influence the judgment of a prudent investor in determining whether he would subscribe for the shares of debentures offered by the prospectus." (*The Lord Davey Report,* 1895, Cmd. 7779 (1895) par. 14[5]). Thus the British brought the concept of materiality to the United States based upon British common law involving cases of deceit and misrepresentation.

Conservatism. Practical conservatism does not properly match periodic revenues and related expenses. "Conservatism" probably is the most overworked word in accounting, and the word has developed an implication similar to pessimism or understatement. Conservatism is no justification for the understatement of any item in the financial statements. Obviously, conservatism in financial reporting deals with the future. The doctrine of conservatism is that when two or more reasonable conclusions exist, conservatism dictates the choice of the one that results in the least favorable *immediate* showing. Conservatism only defers the favorable effect because understatement in one period leads to overstatement in a subsequent period. A few examples of the practice of conservatism would include the use of Lifo costing compared with Fifo, the charging of research and development costs to expense upon incurrence, recording accelerated depreciation in the accounts, and so forth. As *formerly* practiced in accounting, conservatism might be summarized in terms of the following illustrations: Always record an unrealized loss, but never record an unrealized profit. If in any doubt, charge capital expenditures to expense, even though the item purchased will survive one accounting period! In times of rising prices, use Lifo as the method of pricing inventory. Write off intangible asset costs as soon as possible—even though they are revenue-producing assets! Many of these illustrations are old concepts, but some of them still persist.

To be conservative in accounting should mean to be "within safe bounds, or moderate, or adhering to sound principles," as stated in Webster's *New International Dictionary*. Therefore, assets and revenues should not be understated to a point below their net realizable cash amount, and liabilities and expenses should not be overstated. Conservatism should mean the middle ground between understatement and overstatement—that is, the proper statement of costs, expenses, revenues, assets, and liabilities. If the old concept of "conservatism" is followed, management and owners are not presented with reliable financial data—and net capital and periodic net incomes are understated; such understatements result in premature deferred cost allocation.

Accounting Principles

According to Webster's *New International Dictionary*, a *principle* is a fundamental truth; a primary or basic law or doctrine; a settled rule of action.

Principles of *accounting* developed in courses in accounting theory are assumed to be understood by the reader. Briefly, principles of accounting are not fundamental truths as expressed in the preceding paragraph. Rather, they are rules derived from experience which serve as guides in the transmission of accounting data and information for those who use the data and information for decision-making purposes. Progress in the development of principles results from urging a change in practice, based on the assumption that the premise is sound though not universally accepted at that time.

As applied to auditing, applied accounting principles are the basic data which indicate the objectives of auditing and suggest the manner in which the objectives of an audit are accomplished. The applied accounting principles must stand the test of scientific investigation. In auditing, basic concepts are commonly referred to as "standards."

Auditing Standards

Webster's *New International Dictionary* defines a standard as "that which is set up and established by authority as a rule for the measurement of quantity, weight, extent, value, or quality. That which is established by authority, custom, or general consent, as a model or example. Criterion. Test."

As applied to auditing, a standard is a measurement of performance—set up by professional authority and consent. Standards connote similarity of the quality of performance.

The conformance of financial statements to the application of generally accepted principles must be determined in the light of objective standards and not in accordance with what the accountant or his client happens to consider acceptable. Auditing *procedures* are the acts to be performed during the course of an examination; they are not principles or standards but simply involve the methodology followed.

Fundamentally, auditing *standards* control the nature and extent of the evidence to be obtained by means of auditing *procedures*. In other words, a standard is a measuring device of applied procedures resulting in general acceptability of the results of the performance. Both applied accounting principles and auditing standards directly influence each audit program.

In *Statements on Auditing Procedure No. 33*, the American Institute of Certified Public Accountants has set forth the following standards.

AICPA AUDITING STANDARDS

GENERAL STANDARDS

1. The examination is to be performed by a person or persons having adequate technical training and proficiency as an auditor.
2. In all matters relating to the assignment an independence in mental attitude is to be maintained by the auditor or auditors.
3. Due professional care is to be exercised in the performance of the examination and in the preparation of the report.

STANDARDS OF FIELD WORK

1. The work is to be adequately planned and assistants, if any, are to be properly supervised.
2. There is to be a proper study and evaluation of the existing internal control as a basis for reliance thereon and for the determination of the resultant extent of the tests to which auditing procedures are to be restricted.
3. Sufficient competent evidential matter is to be obtained through inspection, observation, inquiries, and confirmations to afford a reasonable basis for an opinion regarding the financial statements under examination.

STANDARDS OF REPORTING

1. The report shall state whether the financial statements are presented in accordance with generally accepted principles of accounting.
2. The report shall state whether such principles have been consistently observed in the current period in relation to the preceding period.
3. Informative disclosures in the financial statements are to be regarded as reasonably adequate unless otherwise stated in the report.
4. The report shall contain either an expression of opinion regarding the financial statements, taken as a whole, or an assertion to the effect that an opinion cannot be expressed. When an overall opinion cannot be expressed, the reasons therefor should be stated. In all cases where an auditor's name is associated with financial statements the report should contain a clear-cut indication of the character of the auditor's examination, if any, and the degree of responsibility he is taking.

Thus, auditing *standards* are measuring devices or models to which the audit *must* conform. The preceding standards should be expanded in the near future.

At this point, it is to be noted that the U.S. General Accounting Office has a new (1972) set of audit standards titled "Standards for Audit of Governmental Organizations, Programs, Activities and Functions."

Audit Procedures

Procedures are acts to be performed during the course of an examination. Audit *procedures* are based on professional judgment applicable in the circumstances. The procedures result in fulfillment of any stated standard. Proper procedures lead to proof of accuracy of the records and the fairness of the presentation of financial statements. Audit procedures constitute the course of action available in determining the validity of audit standards and the application of accounting principles. At this point, the procedures used during the course of an audit are summarized in order to give the reader a general picture of the work to be done prior to the presentation of audit reports. The results of the procedures must measure up to all auditing standards. In every audit, there must be review and observation, inspection and count, evidence proof, accuracy proof, and reconciliation. (See Numbers 2 and 3 under "Standards of Field Work," previously discussed under "Auditing Standards.") Naturally, there must be a reason for each procedure. With these requirements in mind, audit procedures may be briefed as follows:

1. *Test control systems.* As EDP systems tend to condense data, data tests will depend upon control tests. Even if EDP is not in operation, control systems must be adequately examined.

2. *Review operational activities.* Review such matters as the preparation and routing of invoices, payroll methods, insurance coverage, and depreciation methods.

3. *Inspect and count.* Inspection and count procedures represent the competent examination of a client's assets—cash, inventories, investment securities, machinery, and others.

4. *Obtain evidence proof.* There must be proof of the existence, legitimacy, and accuracy of evidence which resulted in entries in the client's records. The majority of accounting entries normally are evidenced by a document available for examination. The following are a few examples of documents that constitute evidence proof:

   a) Documents in support of assets and revenues: an independent certification from the bank, notes receivable, inventory count sheets, bills of lading, creditors' invoices, sales orders, sales invoices, shipping records, consignment contracts and records, confirmations from customers, deeds or titles of abstract for real property, tax bills, and contracts.

   b) Documents in support of liabilities and expenses: purchase requisitions, purchase orders, creditors' invoices, receiving records, disbursement records; copies of mortgages, contracts, and confirmations.

   c) Documents in support of activities and agreements: partnership agreements, corporate charters, code of regulations, minutes of directors' and stockholders' meetings, reports on activities of regulatory commissions, laws of a governmental body, budget appropriations; resolutions for retained earnings appropriations, asset pledging, loan agreements, and dividend declarations.

d) Documents in support of internal and interdivision transactions: employment records, earnings records, payroll certifications, production orders, cost accumulations by departments or by products, depreciation analyses; interdivision purchase orders, cash transfers, and approved general journal entry transactions.

5. *Obtain accuracy proof.* There must be proof of the accuracy of entries in accounting records; the evidence proofs are traced to the records on the basis of sampling and testing for manual, mechanical, and EDP systems.

6. *Prepare reconciliations.* This involves comparing a client's records with data obtained from independent sources. For example, the bank balance is reconciled to the Cash ledger account balance; the total of sales invoices for a period may be reconciled with the total charges to customers for the same period.

Procedures vary between audit engagements. If procedures are improper, the audit will fall below recognized standards of performance. In each audit, a plan of action is devised based upon the application of *accounting principles;* the plan must conform to *audit standards; audit procedures* are adopted, and the procedures are applied to obtain satisfaction regarding all financial data.

Audit procedures should be tailored to fit each circumstance, and they must be streamlined to avoid waste motion and unnecessary audit operations—as exemplified by the use of a computer.

SECTION VI: AUDITING IN GENERAL; SELECTION OF AN AUDITOR

Conduct of an Audit

When an auditor visits a client frequently during a fiscal period (and this is common) and at the time of his visits brings up to date all audit work since his preceding visit, the audit is referred to as being on a "continuous" or an "interim" basis. When the audit is performed on a continuous or interim basis, the client should be given reports stating the progress made during the course of the work, the situations requiring correction, and any other matters of interest to the client. These reports are not similar to a formal audit report, normally contain no opinion, and accompanying financial statements may contain a disclaimer of opinion.

When an auditor performs his work annually, semiannually, or sometimes quarterly, the audit is referred to as a "periodic" audit. Formal audit reports may be prepared annually only, with progress reports being used at the other intervals.

The only disadvantage of interim auditing is the rather remote possibility of record alteration after an interim visit and prior to the final examination for the year. However, if an auditor exercises care in the use of continuous trial balances, work papers, and distinctive code marks, this possible disadvantage is effectively eliminated. Today, most auditing firms are in frequent contact with the majority of their clients.

There are many advantages to be derived—by the client and by the auditor—from the adoption of continuous or interim audit work, a few of which are as follows:

1. The work of the audit staff is spread more evenly throughout the year.
2. The audit and the annual report may be completed earlier.
3. The client is induced to keep all accounting on a current basis.
4. Errors are allocated to short periods.
5. Fraud may be detected earlier and stopped promptly.
6. The auditor has time available for more intensive investigation.
7. The client is currently informed as to financial and operating matters.
8. Assets, liabilities, revenues, and expenses may be reconciled, confirmed, and tested more frequently and at other than peak work-load times.

Advantages of Audits

The modern auditor is one of the persons upon whom the entire financial community focuses attention. A businessman cannot hope to maintain all of the various phases of his business at his immediate command at all times. He depends upon his associates and employees to advise him and to consult with him in many matters of daily operation. He relies upon a disinterested professional outsider to advise him upon his financial and management problems. This person is the auditor, whose duty it is to bring to his client fresh, sound advice, comment, and analyses, and to present the financial statements of the client on an impartial basis. Through the auditor, the businessman receives data, ideas, and reactions that otherwise would be lost to him for the more efficient operation of his business. The auditor also frequently causes the employees of a client to put forth their best efforts for accuracy and efficiency.

In summary form, and not in any sequential order of importance, the advantages of an audit may be expressed in terms of the following uses:

1. To supply owners, management, and others with financial statements, certified by an independent authority.
2. To serve as the basis for the extension of credit.
3. To supply credit-rating agencies with required information.
4. To serve as the basis for the preparation of tax returns.

5. To assist government examiners in their examinations as required by state and federal laws for building and loan associations, banks, and many other business organizations.
6. To establish the amounts of losses from fire, theft, burglary, and so forth.
7. To enable fiscal agents to obtain surety.
8. To curtail fraud.
9. To determine amounts receivable or payable under (*a*) agreements for bonuses based on profits, (*b*) contracts for sharing expenses, and (*c*) cost-plus contracts.
10. To serve as a basis for rewarding deserving employees.
11. To assist in patent litigation and licensing agreements.
12. To provide data for a proposed change in financial structure.
13. To serve as the basis for changes in accounting and operating practices.
14. To protect the public through compliance with registration and reporting requirements of the Securities and Exchange Commission.
15. To serve as a basis for answering questionnairs for stock exchanges, government bureaus, and others.
16. To serve the investing public.
17. To serve as a basis for action in bankruptcy and insolvency cases.
18. To determine proper execution of trust agreements and partnership agreements.
19. To supply both buyer and seller with proper financial data in the event of a proposed sale and purchase of a business or in the event of a merger.
20. To furnish estates of decreased persons (particularly partners or-stockholders in closed corporations) with information in order to obtain proper settlements and avoid possible costly litigation.
21. To indicate the general financial stewardship of the client.
22. To assist in the correction of causes of fluctuations in profits and losses.
23. To establish and/or improve systems of internal control.

General Discussion of an Audit

Each audit engagement has its own individual characteristics and peculiarities. Regardless of individual peculiarities and lack of similarity, each audit must measure up to the general standards, the standards of fieldwork, and the standards of reporting set forth under "Auditing Standards" above.

In the early days of independent examinations, audits were classified into several types or "classes," such as the balance sheet audit, the balance sheet audit with a review of revenues and expenses, the detailed audit, and others. Although the precise purpose of an audit may vary with the circumstances, "classes" of audits do not exist today. The modern audit has acquired the name of "general audit," which means that there is an examination of financial condition as of a given date and an examination of revenue and expense operations for a given period ending on the balance sheet date. In accordance with the effectiveness of internal control and internal auditing, the examination of underlying data, transactions, evidences, and so forth, will be curtailed or extended to the point of reliance upon or rejection of the data by the auditor.

In nonsequential outline form, a general audit includes the following:

1. Examination of organization agreements, such as the corporate charter and amendments thereto, or partnership contracts, or trust agreements; examination of minutes of the meetings of stockholders and the board of directors, and contracts.
2. Examination of the system of internal control.
3. Examination of the operation of the accounting system.
4. Establishment of the ownership of assets.
5. Proof that all proper assets owned are included in accordance with accepted principles of accounting.
6. Proof that all liabilities are included in correct amount.
7. Evidence for the conclusion that capital stock issues are properly authorized and are of proper amount.
8. Evidence for the conclusion that capital reserves are properly authorized and are of proper amount.
9. An analysis of charges and credits to Retained Earnings and other Noncapital Stock Capital accounts to assure their propriety for inclusion.
10. Determination of proper periodic net income, which involves testing of expense and revenue transactions to the extent necessary to permit an expression of opinion of the statement of income and retained earnings. The tests are made on the premise that a proper sample will result in acceptance reliability.
11. Examination of adjusting and closing entries and of any other nonroutine entries necessary to the production of the financial statements.

As stated earlier, evidence is the basis for any audit conclusion. In order to arrive at a conclusion regarding financial condition and the results of operations for a period, it obviously would be ridiculous to examine each bit of evidence in existence. Therefore, tests of transactions and underlying data will be made, and the results of these tests will form the basis for the overall audit conclusion. The extensiveness of the tests to be applied during an audit is dependent on (1) the adequacy of the system of internal control in operation, (2) the purpose of the audit, (3) the condition of the records, (4) the effectiveness of the accounting procedures, (5) any particular emphasis desired, and (6) the necessity of obtaining certain information on one engagement which is not important in another and which may cause a shift in emphasis between engagements.

ILLUSTRATION. The terms of an agreement are for the performance of an audit and the rendition of an opinion. If it is discovered that certain transactions, data, and so forth have been handled in a manner that would make it impossible to certify to the statements without extending normal investigation, the auditor should discuss with the client the necessity for extending the audit procedures so that reporting standards may be met. As a converse situation, an auditor might discover that the system of internal control in operation is so effective that a detailed review of a given area of activity would be a waste of time and an unnecessary expense to the client. In such a situation, the auditor should reduce the detailed work. The majority of clients normally leave the amount of work to the discretion of the auditor, realizing that he is best equipped to make the decision.

A satisfactory system of internal control is of major assistance in an audit. If the system of internal control is inadequate, the auditor must perform additional work in order to satisfy himself of the accuracy of revenues, expenses, assets, liabilities, and capital. The effect of an adequate system of internal control is to eliminate a vast amount of work in connection with the discovery of incorrectly recorded and omitted transactions; in addition, both the auditor and the client are given greater assurance that net income, assets, liabilities, and capital are properly stated.

Although certain verifications may be in the form of tests, the verifications must be of sufficient magnitude to satisfy the auditor of the propriety of the transactions as a whole. The auditor must be certain that all transactions which should be recorded are entered, and that none are entered that should not be recorded, so that irregularities may not exist. Again, the system of internal control will be a determining factor in the decision of the auditor concerning the amount of detailed work to be done. *The less efficient the system of internal control, the greater the detail of the audit.*

The operating procedure followed in each audit may differ from that in each other audit; each audit must be handled in a manner that fits the particular situation. In many instances, there arise unforseen conditions which cause the auditor to depart from a scheduled plan. However, the purposes listed above in "Advantages of Audits" should be accomplished in every case.

The auditor gathers material for his report by means of the examination of evidence, which may be documentary and supplied by the client or by outsiders; it may be oral, consisting of information furnished by client personnel; or it may be circumstantial, which indicates reliance upon the system of internal control. Oral and circumstantial evidence does not constitute irrefutable proof; therefore, the auditor supplements this type of evidence with satisfactory auditing procedures. In certain cases, only one line of evidence is necessary to validate a transaction; in certain other cases, the auditor may investigate all evidences as a prerequisite to his expression of judgment.

It is not the function of an auditor to appraise physical properties. Competent specialists are qualified for work of this nature. However, if he feels assured that real and personal properties are carried at fair figures, an auditor can determine the adequacy of insurance coverage, distinguish between capital and revenue expenditures *as indicated by the client*, and account for all financial matters concerning the assets.

In any audit, the underlying procedures of conduct are the same; the differences lie in the degree of intensive investigation of individual transactions. The requirements of each engagement will determine the amount of work to be done, and the emphasis must be on the practical realities of the case in hand and not upon automatic procedures.

Under extraordinary circumstances, it is conceivable that procedures may be extended to the point where verification is made of *all* transactions and *all* records with respect to mathematical accuracy, accountability, and the proper application of principles of accounting. In such a case, the auditor must verify the ownership and existence of all assets; verify all revenues, expenses, cash receipts and cash disbursements; prove records of original entry; verify postings to acquisitions, and disbursements, and trace them to the original records; compare sales orders with shipping records and trace them to the original entries; analyze and compare expenses; and substantiate all liabilities. This would constitute a detailed examination—a rarity because any reasonable internal control usually makes such detail unnecessary.

Special Examinations or Investigations

A special examination is the result of a special objective and is not for the verification of financial condition and operating results. Because investigations are made with the objective of ascertaining specific information concerning some particular phase of a business or its activities, the auditor will frequently work in conjunction with lawyers, engineers, insurance companies, appraisers, and others. Some of the objectives for which investigations are made are as follows:

1. For the determination of rights in patent infringement litigation.
2. For the purchase and sale of a business or for a merger.
3. For the advisability of installing electronic data processing systems.
4. For the use of EDP in sales analysis; payroll systems; home office cost allocations to subsidiaries, divisions, plants, and/or products.
5. For factory overhead distribution methods.
6. For the verification of the results of a purchase or sales contract.
7. For a study of depreciation methods and rates.

8. For a study of the efficiency of fixed equipment.
9. For cost analyses of products.
10. For the computation of losses from fire, burglary, or other casualty.
11. For a study of the adequacy of working capital or total capital.
12. For the determination of proper internal organization and reorganization.
13. For the determination of action in cases of insolvency and bankruptcy.
14. For the approval of actions of administrators, trustees, and executors.

The reports prepared for investigations differ from audit reports. The service is more that of a business consultant and is often one of the most valuable services an accountant can offer. The investigations do not so much involve a verification of the accuracy as they entail analyses of the adequacy of existing records and methods, which analyses will be used for management advice and recommendations for action.

The Selection of an Auditor

As a result of proposals by the New York Stock Exchange in 1939, and the Securities and Exchange Commission in 1940, the methods of selecting corporation auditors have come to occupy a prominent place in the minds of the public, stockholders, creditors, financial analysts, and others. The interest of the public and other groups in corporate affairs has increased, and the desirability of a competent independent audit as an opinion of the stewardship of management is now widely recognized. In 1972, the Securities and Exchange Commission recommended the establishment of audit commmittees for companies subject the SEC registration and in 1973 the New York Stock Exchange recommended that listed companies establish audit committees.

The question arises: How should the auditors be appointed? Some corporations delegate the selection to the board of directors. Some have the board of directors nominate the auditors, followed by stockholder election from the nominations. Some provide for the appointment of an audit committee from the board of directors; this committee makes all arrangements with the accountant selected. If the board of directors elects the auditors, the nominations should be made by a committee of nonemployee directors. The Securities and Exchange Commission—which regulates security selling in the United States—has recommended that the stockholders elect the auditors from nominations made by a committee of nonemployee board members.

The Investment Company Act of 1940 provides that auditors of registered investment companies shall be nominated by a committee of nonemployee directors; the selection of the committee of the board of directors must be submitted to the stockholders for ratification or rejection. At a meeting called for that purpose, the services of an auditor may be terminated without penalty by a majority vote of the outstanding voting securities. The audit report must be addressed both to the board of directors and to the security holders.

The professional public accountant recognizes his public duty; the only question, therefore, is whether it is best to select the auditor (1) by stockholder nomination and approval, (2) by stockholder ratification of the choice of the board of directors or a portion of the board, (3) by direct selection of the entire board of directors, or (4) by direct selection of a committee of nonemployee directors. If the stockholders elect him, the auditor is placed in a position of public recognition. If one active officer holds a large portion of the voting stock, that officer alone may elect the auditor, thus defeating the purpose of stockholder selection. Voting by proxy could have the same effect of defeating the purpose of stockholder selection. If nominations of auditors were from the floor at a meeting of the stockholders and if no one group controlled a voting majority, rotation of auditors might result, which could be disadvantageous to the corporation; also, in such cases, the auditor would be subjected to selection almost on the basis of a lottery. In the United States where corporate shares are widely distributed and where stockholders are relatively inactive, the theory of stockholder selection of auditors may outweigh its practical advantages.

One national CPA firm which conducted an extensive investigation of audit committees, found that the biggest reason given for establishing such committees was the suggestion of the CPA, and that the most common method of selecting the committee members was selection by the board of directors. For this same firm, clients using audit committees exceeds 70 percent.

An ideal method of selection might be along the lines of the following:

1. An audit committee composed of nonofficer and nonemployee directors is elected annually by the board of directors. This committee submits for action by the board of directors as a whole recommendations for appointment of auditors. The committee meets with the chosen CPAs before the beginning of the audit and also after the audit is completed.
2. The auditors are chosen by the board as a whole, and in most cases the appointment is presented to the stockholders at the annual stockholders' meeting for approval or rejection.
3. When the audit is completed, the auditors appear at a meeting of the auditing committee of the board, or at a meeting of the entire board of directors, to answer questions pertaining to the audit.
4. The audit report covering the examination of the company is addressed to the stockholders and frequently also to the board of directors.
5. The auditors (or a member of the firm) attend the annual meeting

of the stockholders to answer questions concerning the report and the examination. The auditors also are given the right to make any statement or explanation they desire with respect to the examination.

In all cases, regardless of the method of selection, the choice of the auditor should be made early in the fiscal year so that the work may be performed, in part, prior to the close of the year. Normally, the auditor is selected at the annual meeting of the stockholders. The auditor should be invited to attend meetings of the directors (and stockholders) so that persons present may ask questions and so that the auditor may maintain current relationships with the affairs of the client.

In the past few years, certain groups have appeared, who contend that corporate auditors should be rotated. Each member of these groups normally owns a very few shares of stock; the groups are extremely vociferous, and evidently want auditors changed just for their own satisfaction—and for no valid business reason. They do not understand corporate management, fiscal policies, auditing—or anything else. Little do they realize that the auditor serves as a constant watchdog over the corporation, and an authoritative adviser to it in fiscal and other policies. Also, they probably do not know that many corporations have engaged the same CPA firms for decades, and they also probably do not know that many large companies maintain members of their CPA firm in their home office on a year-round basis. This same group also objects to corporate contributions to philantropic educational, research, and scientific organizations.

QUESTIONS

1. Why is an independent audit of the financial statements of a business organization considered to be vitally important in our modern society?

2. What are the differences between (*a*) independent auditing, (*b*) internal auditing, and (*c*) public accountancy in general?

3. How much evidence should be examined to arrive at an opinion of the fairness of the presentation of a client's financial statements?

4. Why are client internal controls important to an auditor?

5. Which of the following is the primary objective of a CPA when he reviews internal control: (*a*) The safeguarding of assets, verifying the reliability of the accounting data, promotion of operating efficiency, determination of the adherence to management policies, (*b*) reasonable protection against fraud, (*c*) to serve as the basis for suggestions for improving the accounting system, or (*d*) to serve as the basis for reliance on the system of internal control and determining the scope of other audit procedures?

6. In what respects do the *functions* of an independent CPA differ from the functions (*a*) of an internal accountant and (*b*) of an internal auditor?

7. In an examination of financial statements, an auditor is interested in the accumulation and examination of accounting and other financial evidence.

   a) What is the objective of the auditor's accumulation and examination of accounting and other financial evidence during the course of his audit?

   b) The source of evidence is of primary importance in the auditor's evaluation of its quality. Evidence may be classified according to its source; for example, one class (assume bank checks) originates with the client, passes through third parties, and is returned to the client where it may be examined by the auditor. List the classifications of accounting evidence according to source and briefly discuss the effect of the source on the reliability of the evidence.

   (AICPA, adapted)

8. How can a CPA determine if the accounting practices of a client are in conformity with generally accepted accounting practices?

9. What criteria may be used to determine materiality?

10. What are the possible uses of certified financial statements?

11. In which one of the following instances will the concept of materiality be of least importance to a CPA? (*a*) the scope of the audit of specific assets, (*b*) specific transactions which should be reviewed, (*c*) effects of audit exceptions upon an opinion, (*d*) effects upon the CPA's independence of his direct interest in the capital stock of his client.

12. *a*) From your knowledge of financial reporting, why are footnotes to financial statements sometimes desirable or necessary?

   b) Prepare a list of several different examples of information which might be disclosed in footnotes to financial statements.

   c) Prepare a list of several different examples of information which might be contained in an audit report which probably would not appear in the financial statements or footnotes thereto.

13. On a first audit, how can a CPA express an opinion on the consistency of the application of generally accepted accounting principles?

14. You are engaged in the audit of the financial statements of Kidd, Inc., which opened in its first branch in 1975. During the audit, Kidd's president raises the question of the accounting treatment of the branch operating loss for its first year, which is material in amount.

   The president proposes to capitalize the operating loss as a "startup" expense to be amortized over a five-year period. He states that branches of other companies engaged in the same business normally suffer a first-year loss which is invariably capitalized, and you are aware of this practice. He argues, therefore, that the loss should be capitalized so that the accounting will be "conservative"; further, he argues that the accounting must be "consistent" with established industry practice.

   a) Discuss the president's use of the words "conservative" and "consistent" from the standpoint of accounting terminology. Discuss the accounting treatment you would recommend.

   b) What disclosure, if any, would be required in the financial statement?

   (AICPA, adapted)

15. If an auditor receives the major portion of his income from one client, can he be considered to be independent?

16. What purposes might be served by a special examination of cash transactions? In preparing a report of such an examination, should the auditor point out the limitations of the examination?

17. For 10 consecutive years you have performed the annual audit for the Moose Company. Standard short-form reports always have been issued. Early in 1975 you recommended that the company change from Fifo to Lifo for purposes of costing sales and valuing inventories. Your recommendation immediately was placed in operation. What effect, if any, would this change have upon the audit report for the year ended December 31, 1975?

18. Management advisory services constitute one of the principal operating areas of the professional certified public accountant. How could the professional CPA be of service in determining the advisability of a proposed capital expenditure for the expansion of a client's operations?

19. How would you recommend that an auditor be selected by (*a*) a partnership and (*b*) a corporation?

20. During the course of an audit, it was noted that certain cash disbursements were charged to Promotion Expense. There was no substantiating evidence, but the disbursement vouchers were approved by the president of the company. The related checks, made payable to the order of "Cash," were signed by the treasurer, countersigned by the secretary, and endorsed by the treasurer. The officers refuse to furnish additional information. As auditor, what course of action would you follow? Why?

21. During the course of an audit for the year ended December 31, 1974, you discovered that factory maintenance expense for 1974 had declined by 50 percent of its average for the past five years and that it was 30 percent below the 1973 amount. All other expenses and all revenues were approximately the same in 1974 and 1973. What procedure should be followed after making this discovery?

22. Companies 1, 2, and 3 allow their customers a discount of 3 percent of sales price when accounts are paid within 10 days of the date of the invoice.

    In its accounts, Company 1 debits its customers for 97 percent of the gross amount billed and credits Sales for the same amount. If payment is made within the 10-day period for the gross amount less 3 percent, the customer is credited with the amount paid. If payment is made after the 10-day period for the full amount billed, the customer is credited with 97 percent of the amount paid, the remaining 3 percent of the amount received being credited to Sales Discount Not Taken and shown on the income statement as an item of "other income."

    Company 2 debits Accounts Receivable for the full amount billed. When payment is made within the 10-day period for 97 percent of the amount billed, the customer is credited with the full amount billed, the 3 percent not remitted being charged to Discounts on Sales and shown on the income statement as a deduction from sales.

    The procedure of Company 3 is the same as that of Company 2;

but in the income statement, the "discounts on sales" item is treated as an element of administrative expense.

Discuss the theory underlying each of the preceding treatments of sales discounts. State which method you prefer, indicating your reasons therefor.

PROBLEMS

1. Part A: The internal accountant for the Grad Company (which uses the calendar year as its fiscal year) made the following errors of omission or commission:

   a) A $2,000 collection from an accounts receivable customer, received December 28, 1974, was not recorded until it was deposited in the bank on January 2, 1975.

   b) A vendor's invoice for $3,200 for inventory received in December 1974 was not recorded as a purchase until January 1975. Based on physical count and pricing, inventories were properly stated as of December 31, 1974.

   c) Depreciation for 1974 was understated $1,800.

   d) In October 1974, an invoice for $400 for office supplies was charged to travel expense. The office supplies were totally used in 1974.

   e) The December 31, 1974 sales on account, amounting to $6,000, were recorded in January 1975.

   As the CPA for the Grad Company, and assuming that no other errors were made, and ignoring all taxes, answer the following:

   Net income for 1974 was: (1) understated $1,000, (2) understated $4,200, (3) overstated $5,000, (4) correct, or (5) none of the preceding.

   Part B: Assume the same facts as in Part A, and answer the following:

   Working capital as of December 31, 1974 was: (1) understated $6,000, (2) understated $1,000, (3) understated $2,800, (4) correct, or (5) none of the preceding.

2. When preparing his opinion of a client's financial statements, a CPA must comply with the generally accepted standards of reporting. One of the reporting standards relates to consistency.

   a) Discuss the statement regarding consistency that a CPA is required to include in his opinion. What is the objective of requiring a CPA to write a statement about consistency?

   b) Discuss what statement, if any, regarding consistency, a CPA must make in his opinion relating to his first audit of the financial statements for: (1) a newly organized company ending its first fiscal year and (2) a company established for several years.

   c) Discuss why the changes described in each of the following cases would or would not require recognition in a CPA's opinion regarding consistency, assuming that the amounts are material.

      (1) The company disposed of one of its three subsidiaries that had been included in its consolidated statements in prior years.

      (2) After two years of computing depreciation under the declining-balance method for income tax purposes and under the

straight-line method for reporting purposes, the declining-balance method was adopted for reporting progress.

(3) The estimated remaining useful life of plant property was reduced because of obsolescence.

(AICPA adapted)

3. Annual income statements for two consecutive years are presented for Hitch, Inc. After examining the statements, answer the following questions:

a) Is full disclosure of all material data set forth in both statements?

b) Are the statements prepared on the basis of consistency?

c) Do you consider the items marked with an asterisk to be material in amount?

d) Are the income statements properly prepared in accordance with modern practice? This is in addition to your answers to (*a*), (*b*), and (*c*).

In each case, set forth specifically the reasons for your answer.

HITCH, INC.

Income Statement for the Years Ended December 31

	1975	1974
Net sales	$3,600,000	$2,800,000
Cost of sales	1,980,000	1,500,000
Gross profit	$1,620,000	$1,300,000
Selling and administrative expenses, including 1975 loss of $100,000* on sale of obsolete inventory	$1,000,000	$ 740,000
Net operating income	$ 620,000	$ 560,000
Other expense, net	20,000	50,000
Net income before extraneous items	$ 600,000	$ 510,000
Organization costs written off	20,000	
	$ 580,000	
Profit on sale of fixed assets (net of taxes)		40,000
		$ 550,000
Refund (or assessment) of prior years' taxes	−50,000	10,000
Net income before federal income tax	$ 530,000	$ 560,000
Federal income tax	260,000	280,000
Net income for the year	$ 270,000	$ 280,000
Retained earnings, January 1	$1,080,000	$1,096,000
	$1,350,000	$1,376,000
Organization costs amortized		6,000
		$1,370,000
Add (or deduct): Profit or loss on sales of investment securities (net of taxes)	$ 140,000	−20,000
Retained Earnings, December 31	$1,490,000	$1,350,000

4. One of your clients has the opportunity of selling to a new customer, Ferris, Inc., which has been in business for four months. Your client requested financial statements and advice in order to judge the risk involved in extending credit.

Your client received the following financial data and then requested that you prepare (*a*) an income statement, (*b*) a balance sheet, and (*c*) a list of points that might bear further investigation if credit is to be extended. Ignore depreciation and income taxes.

FERRIS, INC.

Financial Data at End of Four Months, April 30, 1975

Cash deposited in bank from:

Sale of common stock of $80,000 par value.	$ 88,000
Collection of accounts receivable	72,000
Note payable to bank	8,000

Cash withdrawn from bank for:

Operating expenses	24,000
Inventory purchased	40,000
Payment of store equipment (50 percent of total cost)	20,000

Inventory:

Sold (all sales are on account; total net sales at cost plus 50 percent) . . .	120,000
Purchased	96,000
Paid for	40,000

5. In order to prepare a modern income statement, from the following information, what audit adjustments would you prepare as of December 31, 1974. Explain the reason for each adjustment. Consider each item to be *material* in amount. The accounts have not been closed for the year ended December 31, 1974. The corporation began operations January 2, 1971. The financial statements have never been audited, but adjusting entries have been made through December 31, 1973. You have been retained to audit the records of the corporation for the year ended December 31, 1974; the accounts have not been adjusted or closed.

During the course of your examination, the following data are discovered:

a) Office equipment, purchased January 2, 1971, at a cost of $22,000, having an estimated salvage value of $2,000 and an estimated life of five years, now is reestimated to have a total life of 10 years from January 2, 1971; the estimated salvage remains unchanged. The straight-line method of depreciation is used.

b) Interest deducted in advance on notes payable amounts to $5,000. The Interest Expense account has a debit balance of $7,500. The company failed to record interest deducted in advance at the end of 1972, $3,000; and at the end of 1973, $3,100. All original entries were made to the Interest Expense account.

c) Merchandise in transit, December 31, 1973, F.O.B. shipping point, of $15,000 was not included in the inventory as of December 31, 1973, but was entered in the Purchases account in 1973.

d) Merchandise costing $6,000 was included in the inventory as of December 31, 1973, but was not entered in the Purchases account until January 10, 1974.

e) On July 1, 1973, a three-year insurance policy was purchased for $3,600. Prepaid expenses did not appear on the December 31, 1973, balance sheet.

f) Depreciation on certain equipment was not entered in 1972 and 1973. The equipment was purchased September 1, 1972, at a cost of $22,400, and it has an estimated useful life of 10 years and an estimated salvage value of $3,200. The company uses the straight-line method of depreciation.

6. You are attempting to audit the single-entry records of Henry Miles, a sole proprietor. The following substantiated data are obtained, from which you are to prepare a balance sheet as of December 31, 1975, and an income statement for the year then ended. Show the calculations necessary to support the statements.

Your analysis of the cash transactions for the year ended December 31, 1975, is as follows:

Cash balance, January 1, 1975	$ 9,000

Cash receipts for the year ended December 31, 1975, from:

Cash sales	19,440
Accounts receivable	86,400
Interest on notes receivable	180
Rents	9,000
Bank loan	7,200
Notes receivable	3,600
	$134,820

Cash disbursements for the year ended December 31, 1975, for:

Accounts payable	$ 72,000
Operating expenses	30,600
Personal withdrawals	21,600
	$124,200

Other pertinent data follows:

	1/1/75	12/31/75
Trade accounts receivable	$10,800	$ 9,000
Trade notes receivable	10,800	7,200
Interest earned and not received	540	540
Merchandise inventory	57,600	54,000
Expenses paid in advance	1,980	720
Unpaid expenses	2,880	864
Accounts payable	12,600	11,520
Rent received in advance	720	900
Noninterest-bearing note payable	0	7,200

2

Short-Form Reports; Education; The CPA Examination; Staff Organization

SECTION I: SHORT-FORM AUDIT REPORTS

It is important that a concept of the ultimate objectives of an audit be obtained early in the study of the subject in order to realize the implication, ramifications, and responsibilities of the work of auditing and reporting. In Chapter 1, standard short-form audit reports were illustrated and additional report material is now presented. Through the medium of the report, interested and proper persons are advised of the audit, its scope, and the conclusions reached. The standards of reporting set forth in Chapter 1 will be developed in this chapter.

Objectives of the Short-Form Report

The short-form audit report sets forth the scope of the examination in relation to generally accepted auditing standards and contains an expression of opinion of the fairness of the financial statements, *which are representations of management*. The report also expresses an opinion as to whether the representations of management are in conformity with generally accepted accounting principles applied on a basis consistent with the practices of the preceding year. Both the scope and the opinion sections of the standard audit report set forth the essential aspects of a professional engagement and govern the responsibility of the accountant.

In many audits, two reports are prepared, as follows:

1. *The short-form report*, accompanied by appropriate footnotes.
2. *The long-form audit report*, including appropriate footnotes, com-

ments on the financial statements, operations, ratio studies, other information material, statistical data, and other matters (Chapter 28).

A short-form audit report, including the financial statements and appropriate footnotes, both of which are an integral part of the report, is prepared if the report is to be submitted to stockholders as a portion of a company's annual report. A long-form report—if prepared—is issued to management and may or may not be issued to stockholders, creditors, regulatory agencies such as the SEC, and others.

"Opinion" versus "Certificate"

In past years, the audit report commonly was referred to as a "certificate," and it is still commonly referred to as such. The change to the use of the term "report" has been prompted by the relationship commonly—though erroneously—considered to exist between the words "to certify" and "to guarantee." Webster's *New International Dictionary* defines "to certify" as "to give certain information of, to verify, to attest authoritatively"; however, words often are used in violation of their proper meaning.

An audit report is always an expression of opinion and is not a guaranty. Since a report is an expression of opinion, modern practice has discarded the use of the word "certify" in connection with the expressed opinion of the fairness generally—because the word "certify" may be interpreted as a guaranty—and has substituted the expression "in our opinion." Of course, if all material under certification is a statement of fact, there can be no objection to an unqualified use of the word "certify"; for example, if an accountant were asked simply to copy an income statement, he would state: "I hereby certify that this is a copy of the income statement as rendered by the ABC Company"; the statement that in his opinion the income statement was a copy could readily be interpreted to mean that the auditor was not certain that he had correctly copied the statement.

By using the term "in our opinion," the auditor in no way lessens his responsibility; but he is protected by the statement that he is rendering only his opinion, *expertly*, on the basis both of facts and of conclusions reached by work adequately performed in accordance with accepted auditing standards and procedures.

All statements are statements of opinion so far as certain items are concerned; therefore, the opinion is determined by the adherence to proper standards of reporting, good judgment, and professional skill. However, if an auditor renders a statement as his opinion without having reasonable grounds to support that opinion or without himself believing it to be true, he may be adjudged guilty of fraud and may be held liable to those injured by relying on such statements. If an accountant makes a statement of fact which implies the *correctness* of a financial statement, he may be held for deceit, or a tort based on fraud, in the event that the statement was false. Consequently, if a financial statement is certified as a statement of fact and if that statement is false, the liability of the auditor is extended to injured third persons who are not parties to the audit contract.

Standard Short-Form Report Contents

All audit reports must conform to the "Standards of Reporting" shown in Chapter 1, Section III. If descriptions and comments are desirable or necessary, they are inserted between the scope paragraph and the opinion section. Although the short-form report should not contain detailed comments, it should be designed and drafted with perfect clarity, so that there is not the remotest possibility of misinterpretation on the part of the reader.

Dating the Report.   In accordance with material to be developed later, an auditor should report on events of significance occurring after the close of the period under examination. The report cannot be drafted and dated until the audit is completed; and after the audit is finished, the auditor is not in a position of obtain information concerning subsequent developments. Therefore, the report should be drafted, dated, and delivered without delay after completion of the fieldwork so that the auditor may not be accused of possessing knowledge concerning events subsequent to the field work and prior to the drafting of the report.

Addressing the Report.   The report should be addressed to the client. If the auditor is appointed by the stockholders,—and this is normal for a larger company—address the report to "The Stockholders of the ABC Company."

Signing the Report.   It is customary practice to manually sign reports with the full firm name. If the auditor is a sole practitioner, only his name would be used. No reference is made to any one member of the firm, unless it is a specific requirement—private or in accordance with the regulations of a governmental agency.

Assumptions of the Report.   The following assumptions are basic to every audit report: (1) that the auditor is holding himself forth as one skilled in auditing, and is qualified to render the reports; (2) that the auditor has performed the type of examination that would be made by a skilled professional; (3) that the auditor is assuming the responsibility for his expression of opinion; (4) that there are recognized principles of accounting which are applicable to the company under audit; and (5) that the application of the principles results in financial statements which fairly reflect the financial position and the operating results of the company on a basis consistent with that of the preceding year.

The Scope-of-Examination Section.   Within the scope section of the report, there is the statement: "We have examined the balance sheet of the ABC Company as of December 31, 1975, and the related statements of income, retained earnings and changes in financial position for the year then ended." This is a statement concerning the examination in general and indicates the dates and period covered; it is factual.

Next follows the statement: "Our examination was made in accordance with generally accepted auditing standards, and accordingly included such tests of the accounting records and such other auditing procedures as we considered necessary in the circumstances." This statement further elaborates the scope of the examination. The statement indicates that the accountant is professionally skilled and that he could judge fairly the extent of the tests considered necessary in the circumstances. It also indicates that not only the financial records but also other evidences were examined and procedures followed to the extent expertly considered necessary. The statement also implies that the auditor has followed all procedures required in a particular engagement, and not that all procedures are equally applicable to all examinations.

The Opinion Section.   The opinion section of the report opens with the statement: "In our opinion, the accompanying balance sheet, statements of income, retained earnings and changes in financial position present fairly the financial position of the ABC Company at December 31, 1975, and the results of its operations for the year then ended. . . ." This section expresses the *opinion* of the auditor with respect to the financial statements of the client and is the most important section of the report. The auditor is rendering his opinion as to the fair presentation of the financial statements. There is no statement as to correctness, since it is well recognized that only financial statements prepared at the termination of a business are correct.

The opinion concludes with the statement: ". . . in conformity with generally accepted accounting principles applied on a basis consistent with that of the preceding year." This section should not be included if it is not true; all significance would be lost (1) because the principles have not been generally accepted or (2) because they were not maintained on a basis consistent with that of the preceding year.

Consistency of application of principles from year to year is of fundamental importance if comparative data and analyses are to be of value, and if owners and other interested groups are not to be misled.

ILLUSTRATION. In a given year, a company may follow the policy of charging all small tools to expense as they are acquired, and the practice may be consistent during the entire year. In the succeeding year, it may consistently follow the policy of capitalizing all small tools acquired. Consistency has been maintained in both years, but there has been no consistency *between* years.

Changes in accounting principles or accounting practices adopted by the client for the year under examination must be fully disclosed and the effect shown. If the application of accounting principles is not consistent from year to year, a report becomes meaningless for comparative purposes; and full comment must be made as to deviations in the application of principles. Likewise, departures from the application of *accepted* principles should be described and either a qualified opinion or an adverse opinion is necessary. Any departure from opinions of the Accounting Principles Board and the FASB which have a material effect *must* be disclosed; if they are not disclosed, the reporting is substandard.

Accounting principles are evolutionary, and there is disagreement as to certain of the principles and their application. What might constitute an accepted principle of accounting in one industry might not constitute an accepted principle in another industry. When the expression "in conformity with generally accepted accounting principles applied on a basis consistent with that of the preceding year" is used, the understanding should be that the principles are commonly followed in application for similar businesses within the industry and that they have been followed consistently; otherwise, the expression should be altered to suit the exact situation. If the principles followed by any particular industry differ from the principles followed in all industries generally, an explanation of those differences should be presented.

Short-Form Report Variations

If an audit report is not rendered in standard form, it may contain:

1. Explanations.
2. Expansions.
3. Qualifications of the opinion.
4. A disclaimer of opinion.
5. An adverse opinion.

An audit report will contain an *unqualified* (positive, or good) opinion if the auditor has no reservations concerning the financial statements.

An audit report will contain a *qualified* (partially good) opinion if the auditor takes exception to certain current-period accounting applications of the client.

An audit report will contain a *disclaimer of opinion* (no opinion) if the auditor has been so restricted that he cannot render an opinion; he should set forth his reasons for disclaiming an opinion. As an example of a disclaimer of opinion, assume that the auditor did not audit the financial statements. "The accompanying balance sheet of the ABC Company as of December 31, 1975, and the related statement of income and retained earnings for the year then ended were not audited by us and accordingly we disclaim an opinion of them."

An audit report will contain an *adverse* (unfavorable) opinion when, for example, the auditor believes that the financial statements are misleading, or do not reflect the application of generally accepted accounting principles.

Report Explanations

Explanations which do not qualify or disclaim an opinion *may* be made in the scope or opinion section, preferably may be separately stated in a middle paragraph, or may be worked in throughout the report. Because of variations in the conditions surrounding each audit, it is often necessary to change the standard phraseology of a report by inserting explanations. The precise wording of each report must be carefully studied so that all conditions are exactly stated, so that a true reflection of the scope and results is presented, and so that any deviations from acceptable procedures are specified. Nothing should be left for imaginative distortion.

A few examples of report explanations and alterations within the scope and/or opinion paragraphs follow:

1. *Reliance upon Reports of Other Accountants.*   In Illustration 2–1, the report contains a statement regarding the audit reports of the accountants who examined the records of subsidiary companies; the subsidiary company assets, sales, and net income are also indicated. It is to be noted that the reference to the reports of other accountants is contained in both the scope section and the opinion section.

With regard to reliance upon the work of other accountants, Rules 201, 202, and 203 of the *Code of Professional Ethics* of the AICPA should be studied.

Rule 2–05 of Regulation S–X of the Securities and Exchange Commission is as follows:

If, with respect to the certification of the financial statements of any person, the principal accountant relies on an examination made by another independent public accountant of certain of the accounts of such person or its subsidiaries, the certificate of such other accountant shall be filed (and the provisions of Rules 201, 202, and 203 shall be applicable thereto); however, the certificate of such other accountant need not be filed (*a*) if no reference is made directly or indirectly to such other accountant's examination in the principal accountant's certificate, or (*b*) if, having referred to such other accountant's examination, the principal accountant states in his certificate that he assumes responsibility for such other accountant's examination in the same manner as if it had been made by him.

Rules 201, 202, and 203 just mentioned, refer to the requirements as to accountants' competence, auditing standards, and accounting principles.

2. *Changes in Accounting Practices.*   Changes in accounting practices should be set forth if the effect is to alter consistency of application

of principles. Briefly, in the report presented in Illustration 2–2, the effect of a change in accounting practice is set forth, and the certifying accountant approves the change in the application of principles.

ILLUSTRATION 2–1

ACCOUNTANTS' REPORT

Example of Reliance upon Other Accountants

March 1, 1975

To the Share Owners of the American Company:

We have examined the consolidated balance sheet of American Company and its subsidiaries as of December 31, 1974 and the related statements of income and reinvested earnings and changes in financial position for the year then ended. Our examination was made in accordance with generally accepted auditing standards, and accordingly included such tests of the accounting records and such other auditing procedures as we considered necessary in the circumstances. We previously examined and reported upon the consolidated financial statements of the Company and its subsidiaries for the year 1973. The financial statements of two subsidiaries included in the consolidated financial statements (constituting total assets of $9.5 million and $8.6 million and total operating revenues of $3.7 million and $3.2 million included in the consolidated totals for 1974 and 1973, respectively) were examined by other auditors. The consolidated financial statements of Eastern Company, Incorporated, the Company's nonconsolidated subsidiary (the investment in and net income of which are disclosed in the accompanying financial statements) were also examined by other auditors. The reports of other auditors have been furnished to us and our opinion expressed herein, insofar as it relates to the amounts included in the consolidated financial statements for subsidiaries examined by them, is based solely upon such reports.

In our opinion, based upon our examination and the reports of other auditors, the consolidated financial statements accompanying present fairly the consolidated financial position at December 31, 1974 and 1973, the consolidated results of operations and the consolidated changes in financial position for the years then ended of American Company and its subsidiaries, in conformity with generally accepted accounting principles applied on a consistent basis.

Lane and Lane

ILLUSTRATION 2–2

ACCOUNTANTS' REPORT

Example of Change in Procedure

March 3, 1975

To the Board of Directors and Stockholders, the Blue Bird Company:

We have examined the balance sheet of the Blue Bird Company as of December 31, 1974, the related statements of income and retained earnings, and the statement of changes in financial position for the year then ended.

Our examination was made in accordance with generally accepted auditing standards, and accordingly included such tests of the accounting records and such other auditing procedures as we considered necessary in the circumstances.

As a result of a change in accounting practices, employees' vacation pay expense in the amount of $210,000 has been accrued to the year ended December 31, 1974. This change resulted in the accrual of vacation pay in the period in which vacations were earned rather than in the period in which they were taken.

In our opinion, the accompanying balance sheet, related statements of income and retained earnings, and the statement of changes in financial position present fairly the financial position of the Blue Bird Company as of December 31, 1974, and the results of its operations for the year then ended, in conformity with generally accepted accounting principles applied on a basis consistent with that of the preceding year, except for the accrual of vacation pay expense as described in the preceding paragraph, in which change we concur.

3. *Changes in Pricing Policies.* Changes in pricing policies which have material effects upon the financial statements should be set forth in a middle paragraph.

ILLUSTRATION. As of January 1, 1975, the company adopted the last-in, first-out method of pricing inventories. This change in the basis of pricing resulted in a reduction of approximately $400,000 in inventories and $200,000 in net income after taxes below the amount which would have resulted from continued use of the former methods of pricing.

In our opinion, the accompanying balance sheet and statements of income and retained earnings and the statement of changes in financial position, present fairly the financial position of the company at December 31, 1975, and the results of its operations for the year then ended, in conformity with generally accepted accounting principles applied on a basis consistent with that of the preceding year, except for the change made in the basis of pricing inventories referred to in the preceding paragraph, which change we approve.

Report Expansion

When the short-form report is expanded, it normally is divided into three sections: (1) the scope of the audit, (2) comments, and (3) the opinion paragraph. For example, see Illustration 2–2.

If desired, the short-form report may be expanded to include comments and analyses, although the more universal—and proper—practice is to keep the short-form certification as concise as possible and to include other comments in footnotes to the financial statements or in the long-form audit report.

The following illustration sets forth some items which are exemplary of the information commonly found in footnotes to the financial statements. Purposely, this illustration is briefed at this early stage.

ILLUSTRATION: NOTES TO THE FINANCIAL STATEMENTS (IN PART)

Summary of Significant Accounting Policies: The company's accounting policies conform to generally accepted accounting principles. A summary of significant accounting policies is presented below.

Principles of Consolidation: The accounts of all subsidiaries in which the company directly or indirectly owns more than 50 percent of the voting stock are included in the consolidated financial statements. Investments in unconsolidated subsidiaries and in other companies in which less than a majority interest is held are accounted for by use of the equity method.

Translation of Foreign Currencies: The procedures followed in translating items recorded in foreign currencies into United States dollars are in general: (1) current assets and current liabilities at rates of exchange in effect at the year-end, (2) investments, properties, and long-term debt at historical rates, and (3) income and expenses at average rates of exchange during the period, except depreciation and amortization which are based on the dollar costs of the properties. Gains and losses resulting from such translations and any gains or losses on forward exchange contracts are reflected in income as they occur, and have not been material. In the accompanying balance sheets, foreign currency long-term receivables and long-term debt have been translated at historical rates. Translation of such items at the rates of exchange in effect at the balance sheet dates would not materially change the reported amounts.

Inventories: Inventories are priced at the lower of cost or market, determined mainly on a Lifo basis. Inventories of materials and supplies are valued at the lower of average cost or market.

Depreciation, Depletion, and Amortization: In general, depreciation of plant and equipment is computed on a straight-line basis over the estimated useful business life of the facilities. Depletion of producing properties and amortization of intangible costs applicable to production are computed on the unit-of-production method, based on estimated net recoverable inventory reserves. Costs of non-producing property are capitalized and amortized over projected holding periods based on past experience.

Exploration Expenses: Exploration costs incurred in connection with the acquisition or retention of acreage are capitalized, and the other costs are charged against income. Lease rental expense and non-production exploration expense are charged against income as incurred.

Research and Development Costs: Expenditures for research and development activities are charged to income as incurred.

Income Taxes: Provision is made in the accounts to reflect the federal income tax effects of certain transactions included in financial results in a period different from the period in which they are included for income tax purposes, except that no such provision is made for statutory depletion and intangible development costs, which, for income tax purposes, are expensed as incurred. Investment tax credits are reflected in income as realized.

Net Income per Share: Net income per share is computed based on the weighted average number of shares outstanding during each year. Fully

diluted net income per share computations are based on the assumed conversion of all outstanding convertible debentures, after giving effect to the elimination of related interest expense, net of taxes, applicable to those convertible debentures.

In addition to the disclosures in the preceding illustration, additional disclosures—when necessary—would include: (*a*) changes in the application of accounting principles, (*b*) accounting policies unique to the industry, (*c*) departures from in-force Opinions of the APB and departures from Statements of the FASB, (*d*) changes resulting from mergers and divestitures, (*e*) major changes in the conduct of the business, and (*f*) major events occurring after the end of the fiscal year.

Report Qualifications

The dangerous subject of qualifications of opinions is prefaced by the following statement: *All qualifications should be set forth in a separate paragraph between the scope section and the opinion,* followed by an overriding opinion paragraph.

A qualification is the rendition of an audit report opinion in a form which involves reservations or exceptions concerning the financial statements. A reservation or exception may be a disagreement with the application of a recognized principle, standard, or procedure, and it results in an uncertainty. When qualifications are necessary, only the opinion is qualified—not the scope section. To qualify the scope section of a report would indicate that the auditor was remiss in his duties.

To summarize, qualifications arise because of (1) minor limitations placed on the scope of the audit, (2) the failure of a client to apply generally accepted accounting principles, (3) the failure to apply accounting principles consistently, (4) a difference of opinion between the auditor and a client, in which case the auditor believes the financial statements should be adjusted, (5) the uncertainty of an item or its status, and (6) an uncertainty of position because the eventual outcome of a matter cannot be established. It is possible that the exceptions taken by an auditor are sufficiently significant to preclude the rendition of *any* opinion concerning the fairness of the financial statements.

The scope section of an audit report may contain certain statements (not qualifications) if all normally recognized standards and procedures are not followed in the course of an examination, and the opinion may remain unqualified. The next illustration is presented as an example of a scope explanation and an unqualified opinion.

ILLUSTRATION. Our examination was made in accordance with generally accepted auditing standards, and accordingly included such tests of the accounting records and such other auditing procedures as we considered necessary in the circumstances; however, it was not practicable to confirm accounts receivable from governmental agencies; by other auditing procedures, we have satisfied ourselves of the validity, amount, and collectibility of these receivables.

In our opinion, the accompanying balance sheet and statements of income and retained earnings present fairly the. . . .

As example of a normal scope section and a qualified opinion, the following illustration is presented.

ILLUSTRATION.   Our examination was made in accordance with generally accepted auditing standards, and accordingly included such tests of the accounting records and such other auditing procedures as we considered necessary in the circumstances.

Except as to adjustments which may result from final determination of the litigation explained in Note 1, in our opinion the accompanying balance sheet and statements of income and retained earnings present fairly the. . . .

The AICPA has done much to lead to confusion in the area of qualifications and disclaimers of opinion. For example, *Statement on Auditing Procedure No. 33*, Chapter 10, paragraph 3 interprets the fourth standard of reporting as follows:

"This standard does not preclude the expression of separate opinions on financial position and results of operations." In other words, the auditor may express one type of opinion on the income statement and another type of opinion on the balance sheet.

This could hold for a first audit only, as shown in the Illustration in Item 4, below. Rules 202 and 203 of the *Code of Professional Ethics* of the AICPA sets forth the responsibility of the auditor for adhering to generally accepted accounting principles and for following accepted auditing standards applicable in the circumstances. In addition, Rule 2–02 of Regulation S–X of the Securities and Exchange Commission contains the following: "Any matters to which the accountant takes exception shall be clearly identified, the exception thereto specifically and clearly stated, and, to the extent practicable, the effect of such exception on the related financial statements given."

As stated, all qualifications should be described in a middle paragraph of the report—that is, between the scope section and the opinion section. The auditor should not condone exceptions to sound procedure and fail to comment upon the exceptions in his report, and then attempt to justify an unsatisfactory situation by footnote explanations to the financial statements. Financial statement footnotes are purely explanatory. If proper delineation between exceptions, qualifications, and explanations is observed, unjustifiable assumptions as to the scope of the audit or as to the opinion conclusions are prevented.

Exceptions taken by the auditor may be expressed or implied, and may be positive or negative. Preferably, all exceptions resulting in qualification should be expressed and positive because implied exceptions have the effect of leaving an element of doubt. As an example of an expressed exception: "We are of the opinion that fixed assets should be stated at cost." As an example of an implied exception: "We verified the inventory for clerical accuracy"; the implication is that inventories were not physically tested and that the inventory-taking was not observed. As an example of a positive exception: "Additions to fixed assets were verified, but related expense accounts were not examined." As an example of a negative exception: "The inventory of the company was certified by the treasurer as being taken under his supervision"; in this case, the auditor is stating that he did not observe the taking of the inventory and did not test it. The implication is that the accountant did examine inventory computations for clerical accuracy; if he did examine them, he should so state. A negation should state the work not performed, leaving the implication that all other procedures were followed. As an example of a combination of both a positive and a negative exception: "We did not observe the taking of the physical inventory; but we did examine inventory prices, computations, and summaries"; in this case, the procedures followed and those not followed are both explained.

Several examples of exceptions and resulting report qualifications are:

1. *Auditing Procedure Omitted*. If a recognized auditing procedure has been omitted, or if the scope of the examination has been satisfactory for all items except one of material amount, an unqualified opinion *may* be rendered, *provided* that full disclosure is set forth. In addition, the auditor should state that he has satisfied himself by means of other auditing procedures—if he is to render an unqualified opinion.

ILLUSTRATION. Our examination was made in accordance with generally accepted auditing standards, and accordingly included such tests of the accounting records and such other auditing procedures as we considered necessary in the circumstances; however, it was not practicable to observe the taking of the immaterial physical inventory, as to which we have satisfied ourselves by means of other auditing procedures.

If the auditor believed that an unqualified opinion could *not* be rendered, the scope section would appear as is the preceding illustration. The opinion section might be illustrated as follows:

ILLUSTRATION. With the preceding exception, which precludes the rendition of an opinion of the financial statements in entirety, in our opinion the accompanying balance sheet, statements of income and retained earnings, and changes in financial position present fairly the financial position (except inventory) of the X Company at December 31, 1975, and the results of operations (cost of sales excepted) for the year then ended, in conformity with generally accepted accounting principles applied on a basis consistent with that of the preceding year.

This is known as a "piecemeal" opinion—*and it should never be used*, simply because an auditing procedure should *not* be omitted. To some people the inventory might be considered material. Also the auditor *did not have an opinion of the statements as a whole.*

2. Uncertainty of One Item.   If the examination results in uncertainty with respect to one item of material amount, the uncertainty and a necessary qualified opinion might be stated as shown in the following illustration, in a middle paragraph, provided an opinion can be rendered.

ILLUSTRATION.   At the date of the balance sheet and at the date appended to this report, the company is involved as defendant to a patent infringement suit in the amount of $300,000, which amount is material when considered from the point of view of the net assets as expressed in the accompanying balance sheet and when considered from the point of view of the earning capacity of the company as reflected in the patent revenues in the accompanying statement of income.

With the exception noted in the preceding paragraph, in our opinion. . . .

3. Uncertainty of Position.   It occasionally becomes necessary to qualify an opinion because of uncertain circumstances, particularly those revolving about a controversy as exemplified by differences existing between the client and a taxing authority. A contingency might be footnoted to the balance sheet; and at the same time, the auditor might consider it necessary to qualify his opinion.

ILLUSTRATION.   Except for the possibility of an additional assessment for federal income taxes, in our opinion the accompanying balance sheet and statements of income and retained earnings fairly present the. . . .

4. Records Not Available.   If, for example, *in a first audit*, it is not possible to substantiate the year-opening balance of an account and if an opinion is possible in all other respects, the exception and the opinion might be stated as follows:

ILLUSTRATION.   Our examination was made in accordance with generally accepted auditing standards, and accordingly included such tests of the accounting records and such other auditing procedures as we considered necessary in the circumstances, except that owing to the fact that all detailed inventory records as of January 1, 1975, have been destroyed, it is not otherwise possible to establish an inventory as of that date.

In our opinion, the accompanying balance sheet fairly presents the financial position of the X Company at December 31, 1975, in conformity with generally accepted accounting principles. With the exception of the inability to establish an inventory as of January 1, 1975, which may affect cost of sales and final net income, it is our opinion that the accompanying statements of income and retained earnings otherwise present fairly the results of operations for the year then ended.

This illustration follows the line of thought expressed in Statement on Auditing Procedure No. 43, paragraph 20, issued by the AICPA. Many CPAs would consider a disclaimer to be in order.

5. Disagreement with Respect to the Application of Accounting Principles. If the auditor cannot approve the client's application of accounting principles, exceptions might be stated as follows:

ILLUSTRATION.   As of April 1, 1975, the company reflected an adjustment of its fixed properties by a charge to Additional Capital. In our opinion, the preferable treatment would be represented by a charge to Retained Earnings of that portion of the adjustment which would have exhausted the balance in Retained Earnings at that date.

Except as stated above, in our opinion. . . .

Again, many accountants would issue a disclaimer.

6. Disapproval of Change in Principle.   This example represents the disapproval by the auditor of a client's change in principle application:

ILLUSTRATION.   At December 31, 1975, inventories are stated at cost, which is $50,000 in excess of current replacement cost at that date. In our opinion, proper accounting principles require that inventory be stated at the lower of cost or market, because the company consistently followed that method of pricing inventories in all past years.

At June 30, 1975, remaining unamortized bond premium on the bonds outstanding was credited to income.

With the exceptions stated in the two preceding paragraphs, in our opinion. . . .

Disclaimer of Opinion

If the auditor's exceptions or qualifications are of a magnitude sufficient to negate an opinion, an opinion should *not* be rendered. An auditor cannot make the ridiculous statement to the effect that "our examination was restricted with respect to confirmation of receivables, title verification, inventory tests, and examination of trust indentures; but subject to these exceptions, in our opinion the financial statements are presented fairly."

When conditions brought about by restrictions, forced deviations from accepted auditing standards, or failure to be consistent, warrant no opinion, the auditor should specifically state that he must disclaim an opinion on the financial statements; and he should present his reasons for that action—in the scope of his report.

Report Examples with Opinion Disclaimed.   Illustrative suggestions are presented for report rendition when an opinion is not possible.

Referring back to 2. Uncertainty of One Item. If the one item is of sufficient materiality to preclude the rendition of an opinion, the opinion section may be changed to read as follows: "Because of the materiality of the amount involved in the current patent infringement suit, the financial position and the results of operations for the year ended December 31, 1975, cannot be presented fairly until the case is concluded, and we hereby disclaim an opinion of the financial statements as a whole."

As previously noted in 4 and 5 above there are exceptions, and these might be considered sufficient to disclaim an opinion. Also, a disclaimer should always be used if limitations are placed (by management) on the scope of the examination.

When the terms of the engagement excluded the confirmation of receivables and the testing of inventories, but when all other auditing procedures were proper, the opinion section might be stated as indicated in the following illustration.

ILLUSTRATION. As indicated in the opening paragraph, the terms of our engagement excluded confirmation of receivables and the testing of inventories. Because of the materiality of these items and the required omission of auditing procedures necessary to satisfy ourselves with respect to them, it is not possible for us to render an opinion as to the fairness of the financial statements as a whole, and therefore we disclaim any opinion regarding the fairness of the financial statements.

If the reader is interested further in the area of uncertainties, he is referred to the following: (*a*) *Statement on Auditing Procedure No. 33*, Chapter 10, paragraphs 45–47; (*b*) *Accounting Principles Board Opinion No. 9*, paragraph 23–26; (*c*) *SEC Accounting Series Release No. 115*, dealing with the doubt that a business may continue; (*d*) *APB Opinion No. 20*, dealing with error correction; (*e*) *SAP No. 47*, treating of events taking place after the end of the accounting period.

Adverse Opinion

An adverse (bad) opinion is one which states that the financial statements do not present fairly the financial position or the results of operations in conformity with the application of generally accepted accounting principles. The fairness of presentation are so material that in the judgment of the auditor, neither a qualified opinion nor a disclaimer can be justified. A disclaimer of opinion would not be appropriate because the auditor has formed an opinion regarding the lack of fairness of presentation. When an adverse opinion is rendered, the auditor should set forth—usually in a middle paragraph—the reasons for the adverse opinion.

ILLUSTRATION. Due to the materiality of the amount of understated inventories as described in the preceding paragraph, we are of the opinion that the financial statements do not present fairly the financial position of the ABC Company as of December 31, 1975, or the results of its operations for the year then ended in conformity with the application of generally accepted accounting principles.

It is the firm belief of the authors that all audit reports should be either: (*a*) *Unqualified*, or (*b*) *Disclaimed*, or (*c*) *Adverse*. This would eliminate qualifications, exceptions, and all other uncertainties which lead not only to confusion, but also to legal trouble, as shown in Chapter 3.

Unaudited Financial Statements

During the past few years, the spot-light subject of unaudited financial statements has received much attention in the literature—perhaps too much. This focus of attention has been brought about by (1) improperly worded engagement letters (also known as a contract letter, a proposal, a letter of understanding, and so forth), (2) no engagement letter, (3) legal cases, (4) fright, and/or (5) a desire on the part of one who imagines he has been injured to complain about something.

Financial statements are either audited, partially audited, or unaudited. Unaudited financial statements should be accompanied by a total disclaimer of opinion. The Auditing Standards Division of the AICPA has issued a guide attempting to clarify the provision of Sec. 516 of *Statement on Auditing Standards No. 1*, which had incorporated SAP No. 38, *Unaudited Financial Statements*. SAP No. 38 states that a CPA has no responsibility to apply any audit procedures to unaudited financial statements. However, in litigation, this contention has not always held up.

If financial statements are not audited, an accountant *should have no responsibility* for the fairness of the presentation of those statements, and a disclaimer of opinion should be issued. An engagement letter is of great importance when unaudited financial statements are to be prepared. The engagement letter addressed to the client should clearly state that the financial statements will be prepared without audit, and a client-signed copy of the letter should be retained by the accountant. One form of an engagement letter is shown in Illustration 2–3. In certain cases, *some* audit work is performed, but not enough to enable to rendition of even a qualified opinion; in other words, the financial statements as a whole have not been audited, and a disclaimer is in order.

When financial statements are prepared from the records without audit, some accountants place a statement similar to the following illustration at the bottom of each financial statement.

ILLUSTRATION. In accordance with the terms of our agreement, this financial statement was prepared from the records without audit, and we hereby disclaim any opinion regarding it.

Interim Financial Statements

Frequently, interim financial statements are prepared for a client, at dates when only a partial audit is performed. With respect to the submission of an opinion, the same policy should be followed for interim financial statements as for those prepared at the end of a fiscal year—if that is possible. If it is not possible to render an opinion, the auditor should disclaim; if a qualified opinion can be rendered, it is proper to do so. If the interim statements are prepared on the stationery of the auditor and if only partial audit work is performed, each sheet should bear the

ILLUSTRATION 2–3

ENGAGEMENT LETTER FOR UNAUDITED STATEMENTS

Dear _____ :

The purpose of this letter is to obtain your confirmation of our engagement concerning the extent and nature of the services we will perform with regard to the preparation of unaudited financial statements for your company. Because this engagement does not include an audit of your company's financial statements, you are not to record this as an audit engagement in the minutes of meetings of the board of directors, or any committees, or elsewhere in your records.

In accordance with this agreement, our services will not satisfy the requirements for an audit required by any stock exchange, and those services will not satisfy the requirements for an audit in accordance with generally accepted auditing standards.

Our engagement will provide the following services: (1) The discussion of recommendations regarding your company's accounting methods and financial affairs in general, (2) recommendations for periodic adjusting entries, (3) the preparation of all federal and state tax returns from the records as prepared by you, the preparation—without audit—of financial statements for your use. To the unaudited financial statements, we will attach our report, as follows:

Disclaimer of Opinion

The accompanying balance sheet of the ABC Company as of December 31, 1975, and the related statements of income, retained earnings, and changes in financial position for the year then ended were not audited by us, and, we disclaim an opinion on them.

Signature and Date

Accepted for the ABC Company

_____
                Name

_____
                Title

_____
                Date

notation: "Prepared from the Records without Complete Audit. An opinion is hereby disclaimed." An illustration of an interim report is presented.

ILLUSTRATION. We submit herewith financial statements of the XYZ Company for the three months ended March 31, 1976. Certain phases of our annual examination are conducted on an interim basis throughout the year, but only at the close of the company's fiscal year, December 31, is our examination sufficient in scope to permit us to express an opinion of the financial statements of the company. Therefore, we disclaim an opinion regarding the fairness of the presentation of the accompanying financial statements.

SECTION II: AN AUDITOR'S EDUCATION

Formal Preliminary Education

At the collegiate level, the education of a person who plans to obtain a CPA certificate must be broad, liberal, and scientific. In addition to the courses necessary to fulfill the requirements for a major in accounting, a properly educated accountant should have proficiency in the following: A mastery of English so that he may speak and write properly, interestingly, and forcefully. He should take courses in mathematics, through advanced calculus and dfferential equations, including statistics and probability. For decision-making purposes, he must be quantitatively oriented. He should have studied the humanities, including philosophy and logic; the behavioral sciences; and the physical sciences. He should have courses in economics and finance, business management, production, marketing, and business law.

In this educational area, a book titled *Horizons for a Profession*, by Roy and MacNiell, published by the American Institute of Certified Public Accountants is recommended reading. One part of this book—"The Common Body of Knowledge for Certified Public Accountants"—is widely approved in professional literature and in educational circles.

Every CPA should possess at least an undergraduate college degree; graduate school degrees are recommended. Almost all large CPA firms hire only college graduates, and the tendency is to offer a higher starting salary to those who have advanced degrees. The subject of continuing education (after the collegiate degree level) is treated later in this section.

At this early point, it must be emphasized that formal education is the basis for the ability to pass the CPA examination. Many areas of professional education will require further development before an ideal educational goal can be attained.

Requirements for Certified Public Accountant's Certificates

State Requirements. The 50 states, the Virgin Islands, Puerto Rico, Guam, and the District of Columbia have enacted laws that set forth the requirements for obtaining a certificate of certified public accountant. The law of each jurisdiction is administered by a board of accountancy. The first law establishing the title of certified public accountant was passed by the state of New York on April 17, 1896.

Requirements for admission to the examination differ in the various states and jurisdictions. At the present time (1974), most states require that each candidate for examination be a college graduate. Some states permit a college graduate to take all or a part of the examination and confer the certificate after the candidate has acquired his experience and fulfilled any remaining examination requirements. As of the end of 1974, eleven jurisdictions do not require experience of a candidate who is a college graduate with a major in accounting. Several states have enacted legislation requiring a college degree as of a future date.

Upon the successful completion of the examination and after fulfilling the experience requirements (if any) of a given jurisdiction, the candidate receives the certificate of certified public accountant and may then use the title of *Certified Public Accountant*. Illegal use of this title constitutes a misdemeanor in all jurisdictions.

The public accountancy laws of the jurisdictions contain reciprocity clauses whereby a person who has received his certified public accountant's certificate in one state may use the title in another state by complying with the reciprocity clause of the law of that state.

The CPA examinations are offered in May and in November. The examination is given under the auspices of the jurisdictional board of accountancy. Normally, a candidate has the privilege of retaking those sections of the examination in which he was unsuccessful, provided he submits himself for reexamination within a specified period. If the prescribed time elapses before satisfactory completion of the entire examination, the full examination must be taken again.

The Board of Examiners of the AICPA prepares the examination for the 54 jurisdictions. The sections of the examination are as follows: (1) accounting theory, (2) accounting practice, (3) auditing, and (4) commercial law. All 54 jurisdictions use the Advisory Grading Service of the American Institute of Certified Public Accountants. Several states now require that a candidate be examined on the AICPA's *Code of Professional Ethics*.

Jurisdictional Educational Requirements.   This section considers *only* the jurisdictional educational requirements and not necessarily the requirements for a well-educated person. Although state laws are not uniform in the requirements for admission to the examination for certification, the profession would be distinctly benefited if state educational requirements were uniform. Some states now accept the college degree, with a major in accounting, in fulfillment of the experience requirements. At present, public experience requirements vary from none to five years. Any experience requirement should be abolished if a candidate has completed a satisfactory college course with a major in accounting. The accounting profession steadily has strengthened its requirements for the CPA certificate; however, if the highest plane of professional excellence is to be attained, progressive evolution must be continuous. This evolution has led to stricter requirements as to higher education and toward state legislation calling for the registration and licensing of all persons who practice public accounting. If the legislation applies only to those who have adequate collegiate education and who have satisfactorily passed adequate examinations, the profession of accountancy will be placed on a par with the professions of law and medicine so far as public practice is concerned.

State Legislation.   At this time, the subject of state legislation with respect to public accounting practice purposely will be given only brief consideration; however, the reader should follow closely the current developments in the various jurisdictions.

State legislation is of two types: (1) nonregulatory or permissive and

(2) regulatory. Nonregulatory laws constitute the earlier type of legislation; this is the type of legislation still in effect in some jurisdictions. Regulatory legislation is predominant, and it should be universal. Under the nonregulatory laws, there is no attempt to confine the public practice of accounting to certified public accountants; and any person, whether certified or not, may engage regularly or partially in public practice.

Regulatory legislation is the more recent type and is approved by the AICPA, and the profession as a whole. A majority of the jurisdictions now have such regulatory laws embracing two classes of practitioners—certified public accountants and public accountants. However, there is no uniformity of regulation among the jurisdictions. States with regulatory two-class legislation confine the practice of public accounting to those persons who have fulfilled state requirements and are licensed as certified public accountants or as public accountants. Certified public accountants qualify by the customary examination. In general, regulatory legislation takes the following forms: (1) the continuation of a state board of accountancy, with authority to give CPA examinations; (2) the prohibition of the use of the title of certified public accountant by those not qualifying by state board examination; (3) the required registration of noncertified public accountants before a definite date and prohibition of registration after that date; (4) an annual permit fee; and (5) the prescription of a code of ethics by the state board of accountancy.

Regulation with high standards is desirable. The justification for regulation must be the protection of public and other interests by competent personnel. There should be no dilution of the certified public accountant's certificate by waiver or other immunity grant; there should be no "subsidizing" or "leveling" of those not presently qualified to meet existing standards.

Many states have enacted legislation permitting the incorporation of professional service organizations—including accountants. Incorporation is as proper for accountants as it is for lawyers, physicians, and architects who are permitted to incorporate by their professional societies.

Continuing Professional Education.   Every professional person—in any profession—has always continued to study as his life progressed. If he did not do so, he realized he could not advance professionally—and would fade into obscurity. Because of the expanding scope of professional accounting, the necessity for continuing education after obtaining a CPA certificate and, (if state-required) a license to practice publicly, *finally* was openly recognized by the AICPA and many State Societies of CPAs.

In 1969 the AICPA appointed an *ad hoc* committee on continuing education, and in 1971, Council of the Institute urged all states, either by regulation or legislation, to adopt a continuing education requirement for CPAs in order to remain in practice as a CPA.

As of December 1974, 14 states have required programs of continuing professional education, and five states have voluntary programs of continuing education. The forms of continuing professional education include special university class attendance, the AICPA and the NAA continuing education programs, technical sessions at meetings of the AICPA and the state societies, state sponsored seminars, work-shops, CPA self-study units, the in-firm programs of national CPA firms, and individual study programs. Normally, each state society of CPAs grants credit for class-room programs at the rate of one credit for each eight hours of successful study. The original proposal for continuing education suggested 40 hours per year; however, this is now a matter to be decided by each state society.

In the continuing education programs, the subjects include auditing, accounting, taxation, management advisory services, practice administration, EDP, fair-value accounting, planning, control, estate accounting, pension costs, cost accounting, fiduciary accounting, all phases of real estate accounting, SEC filings, IRS audit techniques, staff training, corporate liquidation, and many other subjects.

The authors are of the opinion that a top-quality CPA does not need to be forced to follow a mandatory program of training—he will automatically continue his education. If the marginal CPA follows a mandatory program, he probably will continue with his certification—but he will not change for the better.

Personal Qualifications of an Auditor

To be highly qualified as an auditor, a person must possess the following personal and technical attributes:

1. *Idealism.* Professional success originally is built upon the idealism in which the profession was founded.
2. *Culture.* The word is used in its broad sense.
3. *Leadership.* Without this quality, professional status is not attainable.
4. *Personality.* The auditor must possess a pleasing personality, tact, judgment, resourcefulness, self-control, and dignity.
5. *Character.* Any person of professional status must be honest, possess high moral standards, be industrious, and possess good work and play habits.
6. *Mental capacity and alertness.* The auditor—through education and professional experience—must develop the mental capacity to analyze every situation which arises in a business. Otherwise, the most important phase of auditing—its analytical aspect—is lost.
7. *Constructive and analytical ability.* As an adviser on the general phases of business operations, the auditor must construct systems, reports, and analyses so that they will be helpful to the client who relies upon them.

8. *A mastery of modern auditing procedures and practices.* Auditing is becoming more exact in its procedures and reporting.
9. *An excellent knowledge of accounting theory.* This knowledge is the basis upon which rests all future professional progress.
10. *A thorough knowledge of the operation of modern accounting practice.* Electronic data processing must be studied and understood.
11. *Training in federal, state, and local taxation procedures.*
12. *A comprehensive knowledge of cost accounting, budget preparation and control, government accounting procedure, and commercial law.* The laws of sales, contracts, agency, negotiable instruments, insolvency, and bankruptcy are interwoven with auditing.
13. *The ability to install accounting systems and office operating systems.*
14. *A sound knowledge of business organization and operation.* Advice as to the form of business organization, incorporation procedure, purchasing, and sales procedure requires this knowledge.

Specialization is growing in the field of professional accounting. It is common to find in the offices of a CPA firm specialists in certain fields: taxation, data processing, system design and installation, management advisory services, and so on. Regardless of the specialization, the foregoing qualifications are necessary for complete professional competence. Naturally, the auditor must also have sound common sense. He is a professional person; and his personal attributes coupled with his ability, education, and experience will determine in great measure the extent of his success.

SECTION III: STAFF ORGANIZATION OF PUBLIC ACCOUNTANTS

Public accounting firms may be organized as partnerships, corporations, or single proprietorships. For efficient operation, the office of a firm of public accountants must be well organized. For occupational-level purposes, professional accountants are commonly classified according to responsibility and experience. Many public accounting firms of at least moderate size usually have the following occupational levels among their personnel:

Partners. Firm partners are persons of top-level authority. The duties of partners vary with the size of the firm. The majority of professional engagements are obtained through the contacts of these men, who also maintain client relationships. In most cases, local partners report to national office partners. The partners select the staff, lead and plan staff training, and determine office operating policies. Audit reports are approved by partners, and prior to closing an engagement, they are discussed with them by managers (or sometimes with supervisors), to determine if all audit work was properly performed in accordance with the terms of the engagement, if it was performed in accordance with accepted auditing standards, and if the results of the audit fairly present financial condition and operating results.

Leadership and participation in professional and business societies and organizations are expected of partners. These persons are the members of the firm who most frequently act in business advisory capacities, in special investigations, and in representation services. Many firms will have an in-charge partner, a partner in charge of personnel recruitment, a partner in charge of taxes, a partner in charge of management advisory service, and so forth.

Managers.   Managers are responsible to partners and relieve the latter of many administrative duties by assuming charge of engagements. In a large office, a manager performs many of the functions of a partner or acts as a liaison officer between partners and other members of the staff. He may manage many engagements concurrently, he directs supervisors and senior accountants, and he reviews work papers and drafts of audit reports already prepared and passes judgment on the audit procedures followed.

If an item of discussion is of material significance, after approval by the partners, a manager may settle accounting problems with the client. A manager normally discusses the report and results of the audit with the client. Because of the managerial nature of his duties, he must have the capacity to transcend detail and watch for large issues. He must be fully informed on current accounting literature, electronic data processing, new auditing procedures, taxes, and requirements of regulatory bodies. He must possess the point of view of an executive. Managers often are in direct charge of staff training.

Supervisors.   Supervisors constitute a category between a manager and a senior. In large firms, the category of supervisor commonly exists, while in small firms the categories of manager and supervisor may be combined. When managers are used, supervisors normally report to them in all matters. Supervisors are placed in field charge of many engagements, and report to their manager, but a supervisor does not extensively engage in liason work, SEC filings, management advisory services, or in audit areas requiring specialized knowledge.

Senior Accountants.   There are several grades within the senior classification. These grades normally are measured by such factors as the quality of the work; the difficulty of the assignments; and the ability to supervise others, to cooperate with staff members, supervisors, managers, and the partners, the ability to transfer from one assignment to another, to adhere to a time budget, and to produce (or at least initiate) reports. A senior usually is in immediate field charge of each audit engagement, and he is active both in the field and in the office. He may concurrently be in charge of several engagements. The senior should be able to plan an audit, to assign and supervise semiseniors and staff accountants, to direct their work, and to assume responsibility for the completion of the audit in the field—all in accordance with firm policy or instructions delegated by a partner or manager. He must coordinate work papers prepared by staff accountants, and he should inform them how their work fits into a coordinated unit. In the field, the senior performs the more important audit procedures such as examining the capital structure, determining the propriety of the basis of asset valuation, and gathering data for tax returns. The original drafts of audit reports frequently are prepared by seniors. A senior is responsible directly to a supervisor, a manager or a partner and must discuss material matters with his supervisors before making commitments.

A senior accountant should be a college graduate and a certified public accountant. It is the senior who is responsible for much of the field training of the staff accountants; he must possess initiative and be resourceful and tactful for the direction of staff accountants and for the benefit of the client. It is at the senior level that specialization usually starts; the senior may show, for example, an interest and proficiency in taxes, budget, systems, retail stores, public utilities, or electronic data processing applications.

Semisenior Accountants.   When this category is used, these are persons who although they are not quite as advanced as the senior accountants have demonstrated the ability to conduct an audit or a section thereof with a minimum amount of supervision. Preferably, semiseniors should be college graduates who have obtained or are obtaining their designations as certified public accountants. This classification may be omitted in smaller firms.

The semisenior must be able to visualize the interrelationships of the various parts of an audit in the unified whole in order to realize the importance of his phase of an engagement. He must advance his powers of concentration and perception above those of a staff accountant. He must demonstrate leadership, since he expects to become a senior. He must consult with his senior whenever necessary.

Staff Accountants.   The staff (or junior) accountant takes care of detailed work on an engagement, commonly under the direct supervision of a senior—or a person of still higher level. His initial responsibilities are limited; however, his work is of importance to his firm and to the client. He need have no prior experience but should have a good formal college education in schools offering recognized courses in accounting and related subjects. The present tendency of accounting firms is to select college graduates on the basis of faculty recommendations, tests offered by the AICPA, and selections made by personnel directors of accounting firms. In general, the statement can be made that the fieldwork of a staff accountant will—to mention only a few of the duties—consist of the verification of footings, extensions, and postings; he will trace original evidences into the records, prepare analyses and schedules, and prepare bank reconciliations. The staff accountant must report errors and unusual items and circumstances directly to his senior—*and to no other person.*

The qualities possessed by a staff accountant and those developed within him constitute his foundation for future success. Although his assignments are often monotonous, he must realize that familiarity with such tasks is a necessary prerequisite to success. A staff accountant must work in close association with men of experience and mature judgment; he must train himself not to divulge information to a client or to a client's employees; he must not be opinionated; he must have a good attitude toward his work and must be energetic, industrious, conscientious, and patient; he must be curious; he must possess the capacity to grow; and he is expected to enhance the dignity of the profession, of his firm, and of his superiors.

When a staff accountant is first employed, he may be kept in the office for several weeks, during which time he will study the audit manuals of his firm which outline the procedure for the conduct of an audit, the preparation of work papers, internal controls, report contents, and so forth. He also may be required to proofread typed reports against the manuscripts, to prove all computations in the manuscript reports, and to attend lectures given by partners and managers.

In smaller accounting firms, the six occupational levels outlined may be telescoped in the ranks of *staff accountant, senior accountant,* and *partner.* There are variations from the preceding personnel outlines, of course, due to differences in size of organizations, branch office distribution, and type and number of clients.

A definite line of demarcation does not exist between the duties and responsibilities of the various occupational levels; rather, the duties shade into each other and overlap at many points.

SECTION IV: STAFF TRAINING OF PUBLIC ACCOUNTANTS

The profession of accountancy can be no stronger than the ability of its personnel. The profession must maintain a position whereby it will be able to attract capable men and women, select the best, further their education, and train them for professional recognition. In the past several years, educational institutions, the various state societies, and the national societies, working separately and together, have done much to advance the standards of personnel selection. The Committee on Accounting Personnel of the American Institute of Certified Public Accountants has developed tests intended to indicate whether an individual has the ability, the vocational interest, and the general aptitude necessary for the successful practice of accounting. These tests are now used widely in universities throughout the United States. Additional material on education appears in Chapter 3.

Staff training begins after employment. The staff training is a combination of self-training and training by the employer. The staff accountant should realize that his professional progress and monetary advancement usually are in direct relationship to his efforts and ability.

The self-training of an individual involves obtaining an adequate collegiate academic education, solving new accounting problems, securing a complete understanding of the functioning of his firm, acquiring a knowledge of the operations of each client's business, obtaining his certification, perusing constantly the current literature in accounting, and perfecting his ability to analyze accounting and related situations. Academically, self-training should extend beyond formal accounting, in the narrow sense, into the allied fields set forth in "Formal Preliminary Education," in Section II above.

As distinguished from self-training, employer training follows various patterns, depending upon the preferences of the individual firm. Each new employee is in need of a bridge between his academic training and his work for a client. Certain firms require that a prospective employee successfully pass an examination as a prerequisite to employment.

Once employment is an established fact, the method of employer training again will vary. One plan of training is to retain a new employee in the office of the firm until he has become acquainted with internal office procedures. Another plan of training is to supplement the preceding system with organized staff training in the firm's office and/or in area or regional classes for firm personnel. Partners and/or, managers may conduct lectures and seminars; assign, discuss, and grade specialized problems; demonstrate audit procedures and the reasons for those procedures; discuss current accounting thought; discuss the problems of clients; discuss new laws affecting accounting; demonstrate the preparation of work papers; and illustrate the preparation of reports. The instructional staff may be rotated so that the burden is not placed on one man and so that new employees may obtain the advantage of the views of all firm members.

QUESTIONS

1. What are the objectives of a short-form audit report?
2. Name the types of variations that may be made to a standard short-form audit report. Do not illustrate the variations.
3. In general, what are the occurrences in the course of an audit which might lead to report qualifications?
4. Under what conditions should an opinion be disclaimed in an audit report?

5. Is it possible to qualify an audit report without also invalidating the financial statements?

6. *a*) Under which of the following circumstances should an adverse opinion be rendered?
    (1) The examination scope was limited by the client.
    (2) Sufficient auditing procedures were not performed to form an opinion of the financial statements as a whole.
    (3) Exceptions to the fairness of presentation of the financial statements are so great that a qualified opinion is not justified.

    b) An unqualified short-form report implies or states which of the following statements?
    (1) States that disclosure is adequate in the financial statements and accompanying footnotes.
    (2) States that all material items have been disclosed in conformity with the application of generally accepted accounting principles.
    (3) Implies that only items disclosed in the financial statements and accompanying footnotes are properly presented and assumes no position on the adequacy of disclosure.
    (4) Implies that disclosure is adequate in the financial statements and accompanying footnotes.

    (AICPA, adapted)

7. *a*) If reference to an explanatory comment appears in the opinion paragraph of an audit report, is a qualification of opinion implied?
    b) Should the scope section of an audit report ever be qualified? Present the reason for your answer.

8. Upon completion of the examination of his client's financial statements the CPA in his report must either express an opinion or disclaim an opinion on the statements taken as a whole. His opinion may be unqualified, qualified, or adverse.
    a) Under what general conditions may a CPA express an unqualified opinion of his client's financial statements?
    b) Define and distinguish between (1) a qualified opinion, (2) an adverse opinion, and (3) disclaimer of opinion on the statements taken as a whole.

9. What opinion should be rendered to the financial statements of a corporation which showed (*a*) treasury stock classified as an investment asset, (*b*) dividends on treasury stock as other income, and (*c*) profit on the sale of treasury stock as other income?

10. A client maintains several branch sales offices throughout the country. The accounts receivable ledgers for each branch office are kept at each branch. Accounts receivable represent a material proportion of the total assets of the company. An internal auditing staff regularly examines the branch office accounts and confirms the receivables.

    The company is well managed; in the past, its financial records have been properly maintained. From the work prepared at the head office, there is no reason to question the accuracy of the reports of the internal auditors. The client proposes that you limit your examination to the head office records and rely on the internal auditors' reports as to the accounts receivable maintained at the branches.

State in what way you would amend the standard short-form audit report in this case and set forth your reasons for any amendment.

11. Alden, Inc., your client (year ending December 31, 1975) informs you on December 18, 1975, that it has a serious shortage of working capital because of operating losses incurred since October 1, 1975. Application has been made to a bank for a loan, and the bank has required financial statements.

Indicate the type of opinion you would render under each of the following independent sets of circumstances. Give the reasons for your decision.

a) Alden asks that you save time by auditing the financial statements prepared by its chief accountant as of September 30, 1975. The scope of your audit would not be limited in any way.

b) Alden asks that you conduct an audit as of December 15, 1975. The scope of your audit would not be limited in any way.

c) Alden asks that you conduct an audit as of December 31, 1975, and render a report by January 16. To save time and reduce the cost of the audit, it is requested that your examination not include circularization of accounts receivable or observation of the taking of inventory.

12. Based upon the following audit report (a) prepare a list of criticisms and (b) draft a proper report:

To Seleco, Inc:

We have audited the accounts of the company as of September 30, 1975, and we have tested the records and accounts and the accounting methods and procedures employed by the company.

We reviewed the report of Gull and Company, CPAs, Honolulu, who audited the records of the subsidiary company located in that city.

Accounts receivable were not confirmed. We verified inventory summaries for clerical accuracy, and the board of directors certified that the inventories are valued at not in excess of replacement cost. In accordance with the accounting records, all liabilities are in the balance sheet.

In our opinion, the accompanying balance sheet and income statement correctly present financial condition and operating results as of September 30, 1975.

13. Criticize the following report from the standpoint of (a) the adequacy and propriety of the report and (b) the liability of the accountant.

We have examined the records of the ABC Company for the year ended December 31, 1975, and hereby certify that the accompanying balance sheet is in accordance therewith. We further certify that the statement, in our opinion, truly and correctly presents the financial condition of the company at December 31, 1975.

14. During the audit of the records of the Doggit Company for the year ended December 31, 1975, the following resolution appears in the minutes of the directors for the December, 1975, meeting:

As of January 1, 1976, fixed tangible asset values are to be reduced 20 percent; related accumulations for depreciation are to be reduced in the same ratio; Retained Earnings is to be charged with the net devaluation. This resolution is based upon the report of the Happy Appraisal Company.

In the annual report to the stockholders for the year ended December 31, 1975, the president will refer to the proposed devaluation.

a)   How would you treat this matter in the 1975 financial statements and audit report?

b)   In 1976 and 1977, how would you deal with the situation?

15.   A corporation has consistently priced its inventories on the Fifo basis. At the close of the year under examination, it changed to the Lifo method of determining inventory values. As a result of the change, the net income and the federal income tax were substantially reduced.

How should the change be disclosed in the audit report?

16.   Your client, the Chucker Company, is a closely held manufacturing corporation. A full-time accountant maintains all the records and prepares statements each month. You are retained to perform a December 31, 1975, year-end audit which the client states will be *used only by management.*

Perpetual inventory records are not maintained. Management supervises the physical inventory and states that you need not observe the taking of the inventory or test inventory quantities. As a matter of customer relations, management is of the opinion that you should not confirm receivables. Accordingly, the terms of your engagement call for a customary annual audit except for confirming receivables, observing the physical inventory, or testing inventory counts.

In the course of the audit, you find no exceptions to the consistent application of acceptable accounting principles

a)   Draft a short-form audit report to be submitted for this engagement.

b)   Explain why your short-form audit report varies or does not vary from the customary form.

17.   In your state (jurisdiction) what are the requirements for eligibility for the CPA examination?

18.   Inquire from a member of a firm of CPAs as to the differences in the organization of the staff of that firm compared with the staff organization presented in this text.

19.   An engagement letter represents a written agreement between a CPA and a client regarding an examination of the client's financial statements.

a)   What are the objectives of an engagement letter?

b)   Who should prepare and sign an engagement letter?

c)   When should an engagement letter be sent to a client?

d)   Why should an engagement letter be periodically renewed?

(AICPA, adapted)

20.   At the conclusion of an audit a CPA should not express the opinion that the financial statements present fairly the position of the company and the results of its operations, in conformity with generally accepted accounting principles (1) when his exceptions are such as to negate the opinion, or (2) when the examination has been less in scope than

he considers necessary to express an opinion on the statements taken as a whole.

a) Describe fully a situation in which an auditor cannot express an opinion because his exceptions are such as to negate the opinion. Present a full explanation of the criteria applicable in making this decision.

b) Describe fully a situation in which an auditor cannot express an opinion because his examination has been less in scope than he considers necessary. Explain why you think no opinion should be expressed in the situation which you describe.

c) Draft an appropriate short-form audit report which an auditor might submit in the situation given in your answer to (b).

(AICPA, adapted)

3

Professional Ethics and Legal Responsibilities

SECTION I: PROFESSIONAL ETHICS AND INDEPENDENCE

The Professional Attitude of Accountancy

The professional attitude of accountancy is expressed in its competence, its independence, and its moral integrity. This chapter will develop the concepts of competence, ethics, independence, moral integrity, and legal responsibility. Independent auditing has become so much a matter of public interest in modern financial activities that individuals and groups other than owners must be satisfied with the accuracy, clarity, and unequivocality of financial statements and audit reports. These other-than-owner groups rely upon opinions rendered by competent persons of independence and high moral integrity, and today if the opinions are considered to be unreliable, it is almost a certainty that a lawsuit will follow.

The auditor is responsible *for his opinion of* the financial statements. The financial statements are the representations of the client, but the opinion rendered is that of the auditor. The opinion must carry the weight of professional competence and integrity; and it must be expressed independently and without concession.

Ethics of Professional Accounting

Ethics constitutes ideal human characteristics of self-discipline in excess of the requirements of the law. For professional accountants, ethics involves a system of moral principles and the observance of rules to govern relationships with clients, the public, and other accountants. Ethics relates to the independence, self-discipline, and moral integrity of the professional person. The ethics of a profession as practiced by the professional

68

personnel constitutes its greatness of stature and its bulwark against decadence. Ethical rules are formulated as standards of moral suasion and as the tangible basis for disciplinary actions. Disciplinary actions may be taken by the trial board of the American Institute, by the State Boards of Accountancy, and by the courts. The justification for rules of ethical conduct lies in the increased respect and esteem with which the profession and its work will be regarded by the public.

The codified ethical rules of a profession are either mandatory or advisory. Whether rules of ethical conduct should be mandatory or advisory is a matter of personal opinion. In any event, the terminal results of the practice of ethical codes are objective independence, self-discipline, and moral integrity. Written rules do not raise professional standards; the practice of the profession results in a demand for codification of standards. The public then may realize the existence of code and may judge the profession; the aspirant to the profession possesses a guide; the practitioner possesses a standard of measurement.

Codes of ethics apply only to the members of the organization establishing the code. Clients prefer accountants who are subjected to the disciplinary action of an organization that enforces a rigid code of ethics rather than employ accountants who are wholly nonregulated—either by law or by the rules of a professionay society. The American Institute of Certified Public Accountants has formulated a mandatory *Code of Professional Ethics* for members of the Institute, and the Rules of Conduct follow.

AMERICAN INSTITUTE OF CERTIFIED PUBLIC ACCOUNTANTS

CODE OF PROFESSIONAL ETHICS

Rules of Conduct
March 1, 1973

DEFINITIONS

The following definitions of terminology are applicable wherever such terminology is used in the rules and interpretations.

Client. The person(s) or entity which retains a member or his firm, engaged in the practice of public accounting, for the performance of professional services.

Council. The Council of the American Institute of Certified Public Accountants.

Enterprise. Any person(s) or entity, whether organized for profit or not, for which a CPA provides services.

Firm. A proprietorship, partnership or professional corporation or association engaged in the practice of public accounting, including individual partners or shareholders thereof.

Financial statements. Statements and footnotes related thereto that purport to show financial position which relates to a point in time or changes in financial position which relate to a period of time, and statements which use a cash or other incomplete basis of accounting. Balance sheets, statements of income, statements of retained earnings, statements of changes in financial position and statements of changes in owners' equity are financial statements.

Incidental financial data included in management advisory services reports to support recommendations to a client, and tax returns and supporting schedules do not, for this purpose, constitute financial statements; and the statement, affidavit or signature of preparers required on tax returns neither constitutes an opinion on financial statements nor requires a disclaimer of such opinion.

Institute.   The American Institute of Certified Public Accountants.

Interpretations of Rules of Conduct.   Pronouncements issued by the Division of Professional Ethics to provide guidelines as to the scope and application of the Rules of Conduct.

Member.   A member, associate member or international associate of the American Institute of Certified Public Accountants.

Practice of public accounting.   Holding out to be a CPA or public accountant and at the same time performing for a client one or more types of services rendered by public accountants. The term shall not be limited by a more restrictive definition which might be found in the accountancy law under which a member practices.

Professional services.   One or more types of services performed in the practice of public accounting.

APPLICABILITY OF RULES

The Institute's Code of Professional Ethics derives its authority from the bylaws of the Institute which provide that the Trial Board may, after a hearing, admonish, suspend or expel a member who is found guilty of infringing any of the bylaws or any provisions of the Rules of Conduct.

The Rules of Conduct which follow apply to all services performed in the practice of public accounting including tax and management advisory services except (a) where the wording of the rule indicates otherwise and (b) that a member who is practicing outside the United States will not be subject to discipline for departing from any of the rules stated herein so long as his conduct is in accord with the rules of the organized accounting profession in the country in which he is practicing. However, where a member's name is associated with financial statements in such a manner as to imply that he is acting as an independent public accountant and under circumstances that would entitle the reader to assume that United States practices were followed, he must comply with the requirements of Rules 202 and 203.

A member may be held responsible for compliance with the Rules of Conduct by all persons associated with him in the practice of public accounting who are either under his supervision or are his partners or shareholders in the practice.

A member engaged in the practice of public accounting must observe all the Rules of Conduct. A member not engaged in the practice of public accounting must observe only Rules 102 and 501 since all other Rules of Conduct relate solely to the practice of public accounting.

A member shall not permit others to carry out on his behalf, either with or without compensation, acts which, if carried out by the member, would place him in violation of the Rules of Conduct. (See Opinion No. 2)

INDEPENDENCE, INTEGRITY, AND OBJECTIVITY

Rule 101—Independence. A member or a firm of which he is a partner or shareholder shall not express an opinion on financial statements of an enterprise unless he and his firm are independent with respect to such enterprise. Independence will be considered to be impaired if, for example:

A. During the period of his professional engagement, or at the time of expressing his opinion, he or his firm

1. Had or was committed to acquire any direct or material indirect financial interest in the enterprise; or
2. Had any joint closely held business investment with the enterprise or any officer, director or principal stockholder thereof which was material in relation to his or his firm's net worth; or
3. Had any loan to or from the enterprise or any officer, director or principal stockholder thereof. This latter proscription does not apply to the following loans from a financial institution when made under normal lending procedures, terms and requirements:
   a. Loans obtained by a member or his firm which are not material in in relation to the net worth of such borrower.
   b. Home mortgages.
   c. Other secured loans, except loans guaranteed by a member's firm which are otherwise unsecured.

B. During the period covered by the financial statements, during the period of the professional engagement or at the time of expressing an opinion, he or his firm

1. Was connected with the enterprise as a promoter, underwriter or voting trustee, a director or officer or in any capacity equivalent to that of a member of management or of an employee; or
2. Was a trustee of any trust or executor or administrator of any estate if such trust or estate had a direct or material indirect financial interest in the enterprise; or was a trustee for any pension or profitsharing trust of the enterprise.

The above examples are not intended to be all-inclusive.

Rule 102—Integrity and objectivity. A member shall not knowingly misrepresent facts, and when engaged in the practice of public accounting, including the rendering of tax and management advisory services, shall not subordinate his judgment to others. In tax practice, a member may resolve doubt in favor of his client as long as there is reasonable support for his position.

COMPETENCE AND TECHNICAL STANDARDS

Rule 201—Competence. A member shall not undertake any engagement which he or his firm cannot reasonably expect to complete with professional competence.

Rule 202—Auditing standards. A member shall not permit his name to be associated with financial statements in such a manner as to imply that he is acting as an independent public accountant unless he has complied with the applicable generally accepted auditing standards promulgated by the Institute. Statements on Auditing Procedure issued by the Institute's committee on auditing procedure are, for purposes of this rule, considered to be interpretations of the generally accepted auditing standards, and departures from such statements must be justified by those who do not follow them.

Rule 203—Accounting principles. A member shall not express an opinion that financial statements are presented in conformity with generally accepted accounting principles if such statements contain any departure from an accounting principle promulgated by the body designated by Council to establish such principles which has a material effect on the statements taken as a whole, unless the member can demonstrate that due to unusual circumstances the financial statements would otherwise have been misleading. In such cases his report must describe the departure, the approximate effects thereof, if practicable, and the reasons why compliance with the principle would result in a misleading statement.

Rule 204—Forecasts. A member shall not permit his name to be used in conjunction with any forecast of future transactions in a manner which may lead to the belief that the member vouches for the achievability of the forecast.

RESPONSIBILITIES TO CLIENTS

Rule 301—Confidential client information. A member shall not disclose any confidential information obtained in the course of a professional engagement except with the consent of the client.

This rule shall not be construed (a) to relieve a member of his obligation under Rules 202 and 203, (b) to affect in any way his compliance with a validly issued subpoena or summons enforceable by order of a court, (c) to prohibit review of a member's professional practices as a part of voluntary quality review under Institute authorization or (d) to preclude a member from responding to any inquiry made by the ethics division or Trial Board of the Institute, by a duly constituted investigative or disciplinary body of a state CPA society, or under state statutes.

Members of the ethics division and Trial Board of the Institute and professional practice reviewers under Institute authorization shall not disclose any confidential client information which comes to their attention from members in disciplinary proceedings or otherwise in carrying out their official responsibilities. However, this prohibition shall not restrict the exchange of information with an aforementioned duly constituted investigative or disciplinary body.

Rule 302—Contingent fees. Professional services shall not be offered or rendered under an arrangement whereby no fee will be charged unless a specified finding or result is attained, or where the fee is otherwise contingent upon the findings or results of such services. However, a member's fees may vary depending, for example, on the complexity of the service rendered.

Fees are not regarded as being contingent if fixed by courts or other public authorities or, in tax matters, if determined based on the results of judicial proceedings or the findings of governmental agencies.

RESPONSIBILITIES TO COLLEAGUES

Rule 401—Encroachment. A member shall not endeavor to provide a person or entity with a professional service which is currently provided by another public accountant except:

1. He may respond to a request for a proposal to render services and may furnish service to those who request it. However, if an audit client of another independent public accountant requests a member to provide professional advice on accounting or auditing matters in connection with an expression of opinion on financial statements, the member must first consult with the other accountant to ascertain that the member is aware of all the available relevant facts.

2. Where a member is required to express an opinion on combined or consolidated financial statements which include a subsidiary, branch or other component audited by another independent public accountant, he may insist on auditing any such component which in his judgment is necessary to warrant the expression of his opinion.

A member who receives an engagement for services by referral from another public accountant shall not accept the client's request to extend his service beyond the specific engagement without first notifying the referring accountant, nor shall he seek to obtain any additional engagement from the client.

Rule 402—Offers of employment. A member in public practice shall not make a direct or indirect offer of employment to an employee of another public accountant on his own behalf or that of his client without first informing such accountant. This rule shall not apply if the employee of his own initiative or in response to a public advertisement applies for employment.

OTHER RESPONSIBILITIES AND PRACTICES

Rule 501—Acts discreditable. A member shall not commit an act discreditable to the profession.

Rule 502—Solicitation and advertising. A member shall not seek to obtain clients by solicitation. Advertising is a form of solicitation and is prohibited.

Rule 503—Commissions. A member shall not pay a commission to obtain a client, nor shall he accept a commission for a referral to a client of products or services of others. This rule shall not prohibit payments for the purchase of an accounting practice or retirement payments to individuals formerly engaged in the practice of public accounting or payments to their heirs or estates.

Rule 504—Incompatible occupations. A member who is engaged in the practice of public accounting shall not concurrently engage in any business or occupation which impairs his objectivity in rendering professional services or serves as a feeder to his practice.

Rule 505—Form of practice and name. A member may practice public accounting, whether as an owner or employee, only in the form of a proprietorship, a partnership or a professional corporation whose characteristics conform to resolutions of Council.

A member shall not practice under a firm name which includes any fictitious name, indicates specialization or is misleading as to the type of organization (proprietorship, partnership or corporation). However, names of one or more past partners or shareholders may be included in the firm name of a successor partnership or corporation. Also, a partner surviving the death or withdrawal of all other partners may continue to practice under the partnership name for up to two years after becoming a sole practitioner.

A firm may not designate itself as "Members of the American Institute of Certified Public Accountants" unless all of its partners or shareholders are members of the Institute.

If the reader will refer back to Rule 505, he will note that the practice of public accounting by a corporation organized for that purpose is permissible. This has been true since 1969, whereas prior to that time the form of organization (for AICPA members) had to be a partnership or a single proprietorship. However, Council of the Institute resolved that stockholders of professional CPA corporations shall be jointly and severally liable for the acts of the corporation or its employees—except where professional liability insurance is carried, or capitalization is maintained in amounts considered to be adequate to offer adequate protection to the public.

The Division of Professional Ethics of the AICPA also has issued its *Interpretations of the Rules of Conduct,* as follows:

INTERPRETATIONS OF RULES OF CONDUCT

Interpretations under Rule 101—Independence

101–1—Directorships. Members are often asked to lend the prestige of their name as a director of a charitable, religious, civic or other similar type of nonprofit organization whose board is large and representative of the community's leadership. An auditor who permits his name to be used in this manner would not be considered lacking in independence under Rule 101 so long as he does not perform or give advice on management functions, and the board itself is sufficiently large that a third party would conclude that his membership was honorary.

101–2—Retired partners and firm independence. A retired partner having a relationship of a type specified in Rule 101 with a client of his former firm would not be considered as impairing the firm's independence with respect to the client provided that he is no longer active in the firm, that the fees received from such client do not have a material effect on his retirement benefits and that he is not held out as being associated with his former partnership.

101–3—Accounting services. Members in public practice are sometimes asked to provide manual or automated bookkeeping or data processing services to clients who are of insufficient size to employ an adequate internal accounting staff. Computer systems design and programming assistance are also rendered by members either in conjunction with data processing services or as a separate engagement. Members who perform such services and who are engaged in the practice of public accounting are subject to the bylaws and Rules of Conduct.

On occasion members also rent "block time" on their computers to their clients but are not involved in the processing of transactions or maintaining the client's accounting records. In such cases the sale of block time constitutes a business rather than a professional relationship and must be considered together with all other relationships, between the member and his client to determine if their aggregate impact is such as to impair the member's independence.

When a member performs manual or automated bookkeeping services, concern may arise whether the performance of such services would impair his audit independence—that the performance of such basic accounting services would cause his audit to be lacking in a review of mechanical accuracy or that the accounting judgments made by him in recording transactions may somehow be less reliable than if made by him in connection with the subsequent audit.

Members are skilled in, and well accustomed to, applying techniques to control mechanical accuracy, and the performance of the record-keeping function should have no effect on application of such techniques. With regard to accounting judgments, if third parties have confidence in a member's judgment in performing an audit, it is difficult to contend that they would have less confidence where the same judgment is applied in the aproces of preparing the underlying accounting records.

Nevertheless, a member performing accounting services for an audit client must meet the following requirements to retain the appearance that he is not virtually an employee and therefore lacking in independence in the eyes of a reasonable observer.

1. The CPA must not have any relationship or combination of relationships with the client or any conflict of interest which would impair his integrity and objectivity.

2. The client must accept the responsibility for the financial statements as his own. A small client may not have anyone in his employ to maintain accounting records and may rely on the CPA for this purpose. Nevertheless, the client must be sufficiently knowledgeable of the enterprise's activities and financial condition and the applicable accounting principles so that he can reasonably accept such responsibility, including, specifically, fairness of valuation and presentation and adequacy of disclosure. When necessary, the CPA must discuss accounting matters with the client to be sure that the client has the required degree of understanding.

3. The CPA must not assume the role of employee or of management conducting the operations of an enterprise. For example, the CPA shall not consumate transactions, have custody of assets or exercise authority on behalf of the client. The client must prepare the source documents on all transactions in sufficient detail to identify clearly the nature and amount of such transactions and maintain an accounting control over data processed by the CPA such as control totals and document counts. The CPA should not make changes in such basic data without the concurrence of the client.

4. The CPA, in making an examination of financial statements prepared from books and records which he has maintained completely or in part, must conform to generally accepted auditing standards. The fact that he has processed or maintained certain records does not eliminate the need to make sufficient audit tests.

When a client's securities become subject to regulation by the Securities and Exchange Commission or other federal or state regulatory body, responsibility for maintenance of the accounting records, including accounting classification decisions, must be assumed by accounting personnel employed by the client. The assumption of this responsibility must commence with the first fiscal year after which the client's securities qualify for such regulation.

Interpretation under Rule 201—Competence

201–1—Competence. A member who accepts a professional engagement implies that he has the necessary competence to complete the engagement according to professional standards, applying his knowledge and skill with reasonable care and diligence, but he does not assume a responsibility for infalibility of knowledge or judgment.

Competence in the practice of public accounting involves both the technical qualifications of the member and his staff and his ability to supervise and evaluate the quality of the work performed. Competence relates both to knowledge of the profession's standards, techniques and the technical subject matter involved, and to the capability to exercise sound judgment in applying such knowledge to each engagement.

The member may have the knowledge required to complete an engagement professionally before undertaking it. In many cases, however, additional research or consultation with others may be necessary during the course of the engagement. This does not ordinarily represent a lack of competence, but rather is a normal part of the professional conduct of an engagement.

However, if a CPA is unable to gain sufficient competence through these means, he should suggest, in fairness to his client and the public, the engagement of someone competent to perform the needed service, either independently or as an associate.

Interpretation under Rule 203—Accounting principles

203–1—Departures from established accounting principles. Rule 203 was adopted to require compliance with accounting principles promulgated by the body designated by Council to establish such principles. There is a strong presumption that adherence to officially established accounting principles would in nearly all instances result in financial statements that are not misleading.

However, in the establishment of accounting principles it is difficult to anticipate all of the circumstances to which such principles might be applied. The rule therefore recognizes that upon occasion there may be unusual circumstances where the literal application of pronouncements on accounting principles would have the effect of rendering financial statements misleading. In such cases, the proper accounting treatment is that which will render the financial statements not misleading.

The question of what constitutes unusual circumstances as referred to in Rule 203 is a matter of professional judgment involving the ability to support the position that adherence to a promulgated principle would be regarded generally by reasonable men as producing a misleading result.

Examples of events which may justify departures from a principle are new legislation or the evolution of a new form of business transaction. An unusual degree of materiality of the existence of conflicting industry practices are examples of circumstances which would not ordinarily be regarded as unusual in the context of Rule 203.

Interpretation under Rule 204—Forecasts

204–1—Forecasts.   Rule 204 does not prohibit a member from preparing, or assisting a client in the preparation of, forecasts of the results of future transactions. When a member's name is associated with such forecasts, there shall be the presumption that such data may be used by parties other than the client. Therefore, full disclosure must be made of the sources of the information used and the major assumptions made in the preparation of the statements and analyses, the character of the work performed by the member, and the degree of the responsibility he is taking.

Interpretation under Rule 301—Confidential client information

301–1—Confidential information and technical standards.   The prohibition against disclosure of confidential information obtained in the course of a professional engagement does not apply to disclosure of such information when required to properly discharge the member's responsibility according to the profession's standards. The prohibition would not apply, for example, to disclosure, as required by Statement on Auditing Procedure No. 41, of subsequent discovery of facts existing at the date of the auditor's report which would have affected the auditor's report had he been aware of such facts.

Interpretations under Rule 401—Encroachment

401–1—Relations with clients also served by other public accountants.   The unsolicited sending to clients of firm literature or invitations to seminars which cover services that are currently being rendered to the client by another public accountant is considered a violation of Rule 401.

401–2—Reliance on work of others.   Rule 401–2 makes clear that it is not improper for a member expressing his opinion on combined or consolidated financial statements to insist on auditing such components as in his judgment are necessary to warrant the expression of his opinion. However, the auditor's exercise of judgment in this regard is subject to review. For example, insistence upon auditing an unreasonably large percentage of consolidated net assets or net income may lead to the conclusion that the auditor's judgment had been made as part of a plan or design to solicit an engagement, which action would be a violation of the rule against encroachment.

Interpretations under Rule 502—Solicitation and advertising

502–1—Announcements.   Publication in a newspaper, magazine or similar medium of an announcement or what is technically known as a "card" is prohibited. Also prohibited is the issuance of a press release regarding firm mergers, opening of new offices, change of address or admission of new partners.

Announcements of such changes may be mailed to clients and individuals with whom professional contacts are maintained, such as lawyers and bankers. Such announcements should be dignified and should not refer to fields of specialization.

502–2—Office premises.   Listing of the firm name in lobby directories of office buildings and on entrance doors solely for the purpose of enabling interested parties to locate an office is permissible. The listing should be in good taste and modest in size. The indication of a specialty such as "income tax" in such listing constitutes advertising.

502–3—Directories: telephone, classified and trade association. A listing in a telephone, trade association, membership or other classified directory shall not:

1. Appear in a box or other form of display, or in a type of style which differentiates it from other listings in the same directory.

2. Appear in more than one place in the same classified directory.

3. Appear under a heading other than "Certified Public Accountant" or "Public Accountant" where the directory is classified by type of business occupation or service.

4. Be included in the yellow pages or business section of a telephone directory unless the member maintains a bona fide office in the geographic area covered. Determination of what constitutes an "area" shall be made by referring to the positions taken by state CPA societies in the light of local conditions. Such listings may:

1. Include the firm name, partners' names, professional title (CPA), address and telephone number.

2. Be included under both the geographical and alphabetical section where the directory includes such sections.

502–4—Business stationery. A member's stationery should be in keeping with the dignity of the profession and not list any specialty.

The stationery may include the firm name, address and telephone number, names of partners, names of deceased partners and their years of service, names of professional staff when preceded by a line to separate them from the partners, and cities in which other offices and correspondents or associates are located. Membership in the Institute or state CPA society or associated group of CPA firms whose name does not indicate a specialty may also be shown. In the case of multi-office firms, it is suggested that the words "offices in other principal cities" (or other appropriate wording) be used instead of a full list of offices. Also, it is preferable to list only the names of partners resident in the office for which the stationery is used.

502–5—Business cards. Business cards may be used by partners, sole practitioners and staff members. They should be in good taste and should be limited to the name of the person presenting the card, his firm name, address and telephone number(s), the words "Certified Public Accountant(s)," or "CPA" and such words as "partner," "manager" or "consultant" but without any specialty designation.

Members not in the practice of public accounting may use the title "Certified Public Accountant" or "CPA" but shall not do so when engaged in sales promotion, selling or similar activities.

502–6—Help wanted advertisements. A member shall not include his name in help-wanted or situations-wanted display advertising on his own behalf or that of others in any publication. In display advertising, the use of a telephone number, address, or newspaper box number is permissible.

In classified advertisements other than display, the member's name should not appear in boldface type, capital letters or in any other manner which tends to distinguish the name from the body of the advertisement.

502–7—Firm publications. Newsletters, bulletins, house organs, recruiting brochures and other firm literature on accounting and related business subjects prepared and distributed by a firm for the information of its staff and clients serve a useful purpose. The distribution of such material outside the firm must be properly controlled and should be restricted to clients and individuals with whom professional contacts are maintained, such as lawyers and bankers. Copies may also be supplied to job applicants, to students considering employment interviews, to nonclients who specifically request them and to educational institutions.

If requests for multiple copies are received and granted, the member and his firm are responsible for any distribution by the party to whom they are issued.

502–8—Newsletters and publications prepared by others. A member shall not permit newsletters, tax booklets or similar publications to be imprinted with his firm's name if they have not been prepared by his firm.

502–9—Responsibility for publisher's promotional efforts. It is the responsibility of a member to see that the publisher or others who promote distribution of his writing, observe the boundaries of professional dignity and make no claims that are not truthful and in good taste. The promotion may indicate the author's background including, for example, his education, professional society affiliations and the name of his firm, the title of his position and principal activities therein. However, a general designation referring to any specialty, such as "tax expert" or "tax consultant" may not be used.

502–10—Statements and information to the public press. A member shall not directly or indirectly cultivate publicity which advertises his or his firm's professional attainments or services. He may respond factually when approached by the press for information concerning his firm, but he should not use press inquiries as a means of aggrandizing himself or his firm or of advertising professional attainments or services. When interviewed by a writer or reporter, he is charged with the knowledge that he cannot control the journalistic use of any information he may give and should notify the reporter of the limitations imposed by professional ethics.

Releases and statements made by members on subjects of public interest which may be reported by the news media, and publicity not initiated by a member such as that which may result from public service activities, are not considered advertising. However, press releases concerning internal matters in a member's firm are prohibited.

502–11—Participation in education seminars. Participation by members in programs of educational seminars, either in person or through audiovisual techniques, on matters within the field of competence of CPAs is in the public interest and is to be encouraged. Such seminars should not be used as a means of soliciting clients. Therefore, certain restraints must be observed to avoid violation of the spirit of Rule 502 which prohibits solicitation and advertising. For example, a member or his firm should not:

1. Send announcements of a seminar to nonclients or invite them to attend. However, educators may be invited to attend to further their education.

2. Sponsor, or convey the impression that he is sponsoring, a seminar which will be attended by nonclients. However, a member of his firm may

conduct educational seminars solely for clients and those serving his clients in a professional capacity, such as bankers and lawyers.

In addition, when a seminar is sponsored by others and attended by non-clients, a member or his firm should not:

1. Solicit the opportunity to appear on the program.

2. Permit the distribution of publicity relating to the member or his firm in connection with the seminar except as permitted under Interpretation 502–9.

3. Distribute firm literature which is not directly relevant to a subject being presented on the program by the member or persons connected with his firm.

502–12—Solicitation of former clients. Offers by a member to provide services after a client relationship has been clearly terminated, either by completion of a nonrecurring engagement or by direct action of the client, constitute a violation of Rule 502 prohibiting solicitation.

502–13—Soliciting work from other practitioners. Rule 502 does not prohibit a member in the practice of public accounting from informing other practitioners of his availability to provide them or their clients with professional services. Because advertising comes to the attention of the public, such offers to other practitioners must be made in letter form or by personal contact.

502–14—Fees and professional standards. The following statement is required to be published with the Code of Professional Ethics pursuant to the Final Judgment in the court decision referred to below:

The former provision of the Code of Professional Ethics prohibiting competitive bidding, Rule 3.03, was declared null and void by the United States District Court for the District of Columbia in a consent judgment entered on July 6, 1972, in a civil antitrust suit brought by the United States against the American Institute. In consequence, no provision of the Code of Professional Ethics now prohibits the submission of price quotations for accounting services to persons seeking such services; and such submission of price quotations is not an unethical practice under any policy of the Institute. To avoid misunderstanding it is important to note that otherwise unethical conduct (e.g., advertising, solicitation, or substandard work) is subject to disciplinary sanctions regardless of whether or not such unethical conduct is preceded by, associated with, or followed by a submission of price quotations for accounting services. Members of the Institute should also be aware that neither the foregoing judgment nor any policy of the Institute affects the obligation of a certified public accountant to obey applicable laws, regulations or rules of any state or other governmental authority.

Interpretation under Rule 503—Commissions

503–1—Fees in payment for services. Rule 503, which prohibits payment of a commission to obtain a client, was adopted to avoid a client's having to pay fees for which he did not receive commensurate services. However, payment of fees to a referring public accountant for professional services to the successor firm or to the client in connection with the engagement is not prohibited.

Interpretation under Rule 505—Form of practice and name

505-1—Investment in commercial accounting corporation. A member in the practice of public accounting may have a financial interest in a commercial corporation which performs for the public services of a type performed by public accountants and whose characteristics do not conform to resolutions of Council, provided such interest is not material to the corporation's net worth, and the member's interest in and relation to the corporation is solely that of an investor.

Any rule in the code is subject to change, and the reader should maintain current knowledge of all changes. The *Code of Professional Ethics* represents a philosophy of professional behavior and not merely a set of rules.

Members of the American Institute of Certified Public Accountants may be tried and punished by the Trial Board of the Institute (or a subtrial board) in accordance with the bylaws of the Institute. With the *Code of Professional Ethics* of the Institute as a guide, with the code of ethics of his state society of certified public accountants as additional assistance, with an adequate concept of moral responsibility, and with a good sense of professional conduct, effective safeguards are established for the interests of the professional activities of the accountant subject to ethical regulation, and for the interests and welfare of those who rely upon that accountant.

In the states having legally enforceable rules of conduct, if the rules set forth by the state board of accountancy are violated, upon conviction by the state board, the certificate of the certified public accountant may be revoked.

Because of the growth, both in size and in activity, of the Federal Government Accountants Association, its code of ethics (and official interpretations), which not presented here, are recommended reading.

The Independence of the Auditor

The backbone of the profession of public accountancy is the independence of the auditor. Independence should be thought of as freedom from persuasion, influence, or control by an *audit* client. In other words, if an auditor followed the wishes of management, his audit opinion would be of no value. Present-day concepts of independence are critical, and the standards by which independence is judged are rigorous. An independence in action and in mental attitude must be maintained by an auditor at all times.

The concept of independence is a dual one: (1) independence is the adherence to objective standards or rules describing certain relationships, and (2) independence is a state of mind and a manifestation of integrity to be challenged only for specific cause, such as failure to make full disclosure, as indicated in Rules 101 and 102 of the *Code of Professional Ethics* of the AICPA. If his independence—either because of violation of rules or because of an improper state of mind—is questioned or questionable, a public accountant may not remain in demand, and he may be subjected to actions of the Trial Board of the Institute. His independence initially has been assumed voluntarily and is one of his most cherished possessions. In addition to the *Code of Professional Ethics*, the concept of independence has been further intensified by the Securities and Exchange Commission.

With respect to independence, the Securities and Exchange Commission adopted Rule 2–01, as follows:

REGULATION S-X RULE 2–01: QUALIFICATIONS OF ACCOUNTANTS

a. The Commission will not recognize any person as a certified public accountant who is not duly registered and in good standing as such under the laws of the place of his residence or principal office. The Commission will not recognize any person as a public accountant who is not in good standing and entitled to practice as such under the laws of the place of his residence or principal office.

b. (As amended) The Commission will consider an accountant not independent with respect to any person or any of its parents, its subsidiaries, or other affiliates (1) in which, during the period of his professional engagement or at the date of his report, he or his firm or a member thereof, had, or was committed to acquire, any direct financial interest or any material indirect financial interest; or (2) with which, during the period of his professional engagement, at the date of his report or during the period covered by the financial statements, he or his firm or a member thereof, was connected as a promoter, underwriter, voting trustee, director, officer, or employee.

c. In determining whether an accountant is in fact independent with respect to a particular registrant, the Commission will give appropriate consideration to all relevant circumstances including evidence bearing on all relationships between the accountant and that registrant, or any affiliate thereof, and will not confine itself to the relationships existing in connection with the filing of reports with the Commission.

Under Rule (2*e*) the Commission may deny, temporarily or permanently, the privilege of appearing or practicing before it in any way to any person who is found by the Commission after notice of and opportunity for hearing in the matter (*i*) not to possess the requisite qualifications to represent others, or (*ii*) to be lacking in character or integrity or to have engaged in unethical or improper professional conduct, or (*iii*) to have willfully violated, or willfully aided and abetted the violation of any provision of the federal securities laws, or the rules and regulations thereunder.

SEC Accounting Series Release No. 126 (July 5, 1972) was issued for the purpose of resolving various questions of independence that come before the Commission. Release No. 126 does not supersede Release No.

47, or No. 81, but it does further implement the policies regarding those releases.

The *Rules of Practice* of the Commission place that body in a position to enable it to enforce its regulations with respect to the qualifications of accountants certifying to financial statements filed with the Commission. Specific additional requirements of the Securities and Exchange Commission with respect to independence are detailed in periodic releases of the Commission.

Thus, independence is based upon any accountant-client relationship which in any manner detracts from the objective independence of the auditor. Independence will be lacking in the following instances: if the auditor owns an interest in his client's business, if he serves as director and auditor, if he serves as a voting trustee, if disclosure is not full and proper, if he subordinates his opinion to that of his client, if he is associated with another accountant who owns an interest in the business of his client, if the client indemnifies the accountant against loss, if the accountant serves as promoter, if family relationships exist, and perhaps if he receives a substantial percentage of his total professional income from one client.

Independence and Tax Practice

In the majority of audit engagements, the CPA will prepare tax returns for a client. Does the preparation of tax returns for an audit client impair independence? Independence is not impaired if the tax service is limited to assistance and advice and does not involve decision-making processes. This is true because an audit is one operation and the preparation of tax returns is separate from the attest function. Opinions No. 12 and No. 13 of the Committee on Professional Ethics concur with this idea. To quote from Opinion No. 13: "In tax practice, a member or associate must observe the same standards of truthfulness and integrity as he is required to observe in any other professional work. This does not mean, however, that a member or associate may not resolve doubt in favor of his client as long as there is reasonable support for his position." Through 1973, the Division of Federal Taxation of the AICPA has issued nine Statements or Responsibilities in Tax Practice. The legal liability of tax practitioners is treated in Section III of this chapter.

Professional Conduct

The professional reputation of an auditor is based upon his competence, upon his soundness of judgment, upon his honesty, and upon his independence—of which his honesty is an integral part.

The ethical professional conduct of an auditor falls naturally into three general divisions, some of which overlap: the relationship of the auditor

(1) to his client, (2) to other accountants, and (3) to the public and to specialized and business groups.

Relationship to the Client

With respect to the relationship of the auditor to his client, the question of the identity of the client immediately arises. In a single proprietorship, the proprietor is the client, unless a creditor or a prospective purchaser of the business requested an audit. In the case of a corporation, where the auditor is appointed by the stockholders or by the board of directors, the corporation as a separate legal entity evidently is the client but the responsibility of the auditor extends to the management and to the stockholders. The relationship existing between an auditor and his client is both legal and moral. The client may rightfully expect the highest degree of professional skill directed toward the competent performance of the activities involved in the audit. Each audit engagement is a contract in which the auditor agrees to exert his best efforts, to accept responsibility for his work, and to safeguard the interests of the client to the best of his ability.

Unforeseen conditions often cause an auditor to diverge from his original approach or to perform work in addition to that originally planned. If the client does not agree to the proposed additional work, the auditor has relieved himself—insofar as the client is concerned—of responsibility for damage that might result because the work is not performed.

Contingent Fees.   The *Code of Professional Ethics* of The American Institute prohibits the rendering of service for a contingent fee (Rule 302). A contingent fee is one based on the results of a finding. If the fee is contingent, independent judgment might be swayed in a human attempt to win an award. The rule does not apply where the fees are determined or are to be determined by courts or other public authorities, or in tax matters, if determined, based on the results of judicial proceedings or the findings of government agencies.

The Auditor as a Director.   Because of the risk of loss of independence, a person should not serve simultaneously as auditor and as a member of the board of directors of a client corporation. In addition, no member of an accounting firm should be on the board of directors of a corporation if another member of the firm conducts the audit. It is the duty of a board of directors to supervise the management of a company, and an auditor would find it extremely difficult to maintain two points of view at one time—one of management and one of independent survey. The Securities and Exchange Commission specifically denies the evidence of an auditor who also serves as a director of a registrant.

Public accountants frequently are requested by nonprofit civic and philanthropic organizations to serve as auditor and as a member of the board of directors. Each individual nonprofit organization case should be decided on its own merits; opinions differ as to the propriety of an accountant's serving as auditor and as a member of the board of directors. If an auditor-director is closely connected with the administration of the organization's funds, his position is untenable. If the auditor-director and the other directors of such a nonprofit organization are removed from administrative duties, many believe that there is no objection to the auditor's serving on the board of directors, providing the auditor does offer advice on or perform management functions. The question of the propriety of serving in such a dual capacity must be considered from the point of view of the auditor, the organization, and the sources of the funds of the organization. Regardless of the seeming propriety of a dual-service capacity, the accountant should bear constantly in mind the fact that he is serving in such dual capacity. See Rules 101 and 504 of the *Code of Professional Ethics.*

Auditor's Responsibility to Stockholders. When an auditor is appointed by the board of directors of a corporation (without stockholder ratification) the corporate entity is the client so far as the contract of the accountant is concerned. As stated above, the auditor has a responsibility to the stockholders of the corporation. The legal position of the auditor with respect to the stockholders apparently—and this will be expanded later in the chapter—is in the area somewhere between the client and the public, but close to the public insofar as legal liability is concerned. If the auditor is guilty of negligence construed to constitute fraud toward third parties, the accountant may be held liable for damages by the stockholders. Even if the auditor is not appointed directly by the stockholders, it is the ethical duty of the auditor to protect their interests, since the stockholders are the residual owners of the entity being examined.

Responsibility for Audit Reports. Financial statements are those of the client. The auditor has his responsibility in the determination of the accuracy of the recording of the data underlying their preparation, in the form of their presentation, and in his opinion of the statements. If the auditor is guilty of negligence, he is responsible for his negligence and for improper financial statements resulting therefrom. Thus, the responsibility is borne in part by management and in part by the auditor. If an auditor does not—or cannot—render an opinion, he assumes only the responsibility of explaining why no opinion has been given.

The Securities and Exchange Commission has held that the *primary* responsibility for the accuracy of financial information filed with it rests with management and not with the auditor; the client, therefore, must understand that the auditor is not assuming managerial responsibilities.

The business affairs of a client must be held inviolate. The auditor should expect the client to submit adequate evidence so that sound conclusions may be reached. At the conclusion of every audit, the client receives a report, a portion of which will be the financial statements of the client, footnotes to the financial statements, comments on the audit, and the opinion of the auditor or the reasons why an opinion cannot be rendered. All data contained in the report are strictly confidential. The report should be presented to the client only.

Relationship to Other Accountants

The relationship of the auditor to other accountants should be such that fellow members are dealt with in an honest and honorable manner. Personal criticism of other accountants should be strictly avoided. The general responsibility of the auditor to other accountants is of a moral nature. Today, public accounting firms are working together to an extent undreamed of a few years ago.

Young men and women in the profession of accountancy are entitled to an opportunity to improve themselves professionally. Rule 402 of the *Code of Professional Ethics* of the American Institute grants this opportunity with respect to employment and relationships with other accountants.

Relationship to the Public and Others

The auditor's ethical responsibilities to the nonprofessional public should be such that the public or a particularly interested section of a business community is not misled as to the condition of a business through the medium of an audit report. If an auditor does not safeguard his moral responsibility toward the public, his good reputation will soon be lost. If he fails to safeguard his legal responsibilities, he may incur legal liability.

An auditor should not be a party holding a financial interest in the business under scrutiny; he should be an independent, disinterested outsider. The auditors should not take advantage of data obtained in an audit by passing that information along to others, thereby enabling them to profit. Such acts are violations of ethical responsibility toward both the public and the client. The auditor is not an insurer or guarantor; but if he exercises the care, diligence, and skill normally expected of a professional man, he is giving to the public all that can be expected in the general category of sound professional judgment. As the field of accountancy broadens, the auditor must be prepared to accept and to discharge the new responsibilities expected by the public.

It is desirable that the auditor be present when his report is discussed with creditors of the client; in many instances, a creditor will indicate in advance the type of information it desires and the manner in which it prefers that the information be presented.

Federal, state, and local tax authorities commonly deal with the auditor in the course of their normal operations and in the conferences that follow their examination.

SECTION II: LEGAL RESPONSIBILITIES

Legal Liabilities of the Public Accountant

Under existing rules of law, the liabilities of public accountants may be divided as follows:

1. Liability for breach of contract.
2. Liability for negligence.
3. Liability for fraud.
4. Liability under the various Federal Securities Acts.

It must be remembered that the lines of demarcation between the four divisions may be shadowy and indefinite; one division often merges into, and overlaps, another.

Legal responsibilities of public accountants are great, and have been increasing. That fact, however, should not constitute a signal to panic, and writers who attempt to frighten accountants by expressing non-constructive views are to be highly criticized. It is true that the possibility of error and resultant liability is fraught with greater danger to the fortune and reputation of the public accountant than to any other class of professional person—because the public accountant is directly or indirectly associated with a larger portion of the population and with the financial activities of the country than are the members of any other profession. In addition, public accountants do not possess the right of privileged communication enjoyed by lawyers, medical doctors, and clergymen. British and Canadian courts have been much less severe than the courts of the United States in their interpretation of the liability of an accountant and have held to the concept of privity of contract between the auditor and his client. However, the 1963 decision of the British House of Lords in the case of *Hedley Byrne & Co., Ltd.* v. *Heller & Partners Ltd.*, had the effect of rejecting the decision in the *Ultramares* case (below) and extending the accountant's liability to third parties, but if the auditor has expressed appropriate reservations in notes to the financial statements, this can constitute a disclaimer, and it may be effective against action brought by third parties.

Naturally, the accounting profession as an entity realizes that wrongs committed by an individual should be punished; the profession makes no attempt to shield a guilty party. But the accounting profession also is interested in protecting its personnel against unwarranted charges of negligence, fraud, and breach of contract. Unwarranted charges generally arise through some person with inadequate knowledge who suffered investment losses after relying upon an auditor's statement which he was not competent to understand. The honest and capable auditor must institute protective action in order to establish the rights normally accorded professional status. The qualified auditor willingly shoulders full responsibility for his acts; but he should not be forced to assume management's responsibilities, because he is a check against management and not a part of it.

Liability for Breach of Contract.   Under the general laws of contracts, liability to a client exists if the auditor breaches the contract. If the subject matter of a contract between an auditor and his client is illegal, a valid contract does not exist. An auditor must not disclose the affairs of a client to third persons. An auditor must not withhold information from a client.

At this point it is to be emphasized that the liability of public accountants is not a new concept for any of the divisions of liabilities set forth earlier in this section. One of the earliest cases (and this dealt with breach of contract in 1854) was the English case of *Hadley* v. *Baxendale, 156 Eng. Rep. 145* (Ex. 1854). In 1905 the New York State Appellate Division, in the case of *Smith* v. *Jordan Assur. Corp.* 109 App. Div. 882, 96 N.Y.S. 820, established the liability of public accountants to their clients and quoted from Cooley, *Torts,* 2d ed., as follows: "Every man who offers his services to another and is employed assumes the duty to exercise in the employment such skill as he possesses with reasonable care and diligence. . . ." There are many other early cases involving breach of duty as a tort, and breach of duty as a breach of contract.

Liability for Negligence and Fraud.   The subjects of negligence and fraud are not separated into two distinct categories—simply because based on court decisions—they are not separable at this time. Negligence is failure to do that which a reasonable and careful person ordinarily would have done under similar circumstances, or it is the performance of an act which a reasonable and careful person would not have done under similar circumstances. The professional auditor is holding himself forth as an expert. Ignorance of his duties does not constitute a defense against action; there must be no pretense to knowledge when knowledge does not exist. The auditor must exercise the same degree of prudent skill expected of any other professional person. He is not expected to possess a "super" skill but simply that of a competent professional man. Difficulty occasionally arises because what amounts to lack of skill in one case may be of no consequence in another case. The auditor must discover whether or not the financial records represent actual conditions and not merely determine that they are mathematically correct. He is under legal obligation to show accurate conditions commensurate with the exercise of reasonable professional skill. A legal obligation is not necessarily incurred if he exercises reasonable skill and true conditions are not disclosed; in a lawsuit, the accountant must convince the court of the exercise of reasonable skill.

In the past, the liability for negligence generally was restricted to the client with whom the auditor had a contract; however, under recent court cases and under the Securities Acts, to be discussed later, negligence may be extended to a third party—normally, a stockholder. The purposes of an audit and the extension of audit procedures may limit or extend the contractual obligation existing between the auditor and the client, and thereby assist in fixing the degree of legal responsibility. To be liable for ordinary negligence under a contract, the auditor (1) must owe a duty to the client plaintiff, (2) must have violated or breached that duty, (3) must have caused an injury to the plaintiff resulting directly from the negligence, or (4) must have caused the injury by ignoring contributory negligence on the part of the client. Contributory negligence is not a defense if it has not contributed to the accountant's failure to perform and report.

At this point, it is well to emphasize that charges of negligence, fraud, and fraud with intent to deceive are not new concepts—or allegations. They have existed since at least 1854 in England, and since 1905 in the United States. In the 1930s, the McKesson Robbins case exploded; at one time in the late 1960s, approximately 100 cases were open against auditors; and in 1973 the gigantic Equity Funding case was exposed, and this case may require years before it is finalized. The accounting profession should not panic—it has no cause to do so; the media are always looking for sensationalism.

In the preceding paragraphs, negligence has been construed as "ordinary" negligence; the auditor customarily is liable only to his client for ordinary negligence. However, if the negligence is construed to be "gross" negligence, it may be held to be *constructive or technical fraud*. In fraud, there is deceit; negligence does not include deceit. Gross negligence may be described as flagrant or reckless departure from the standards of competence and due care in performing or reporting on professional engagements; intentional concealment or misstatement need not be present. In the Ultramares case (*Ultramares Corporation* v. *Touche*, 74 A.L.R. 1139; 255 N.Y. 170; 174 N.E. 441) (1931) the late Justice Cardozo created the concept that gross negligence resulted in constructive or technical fraud; and if fraud is present, a right of action for damages is open to *anyone* who suffered because he relied upon the accountant's report and opinion. In order to establish fraud, there need be no contract between the accountant and third parties whom the accountant has never seen and whom he does not know. Evidently, if it is possible to demonstrate to the satisfaction of the court that there existed a misstatement of an essential fact or if there is an omission of an essential fact and if a third person suffered because of such misstatement or omission, the auditor may be held liable to those third persons regardless of his competency, carefulness, and caution. Thus, an inexcusable error constitutes neglect toward the client; and it may be construed as fraud toward injured third persons. In the Ultramares case, the court held that test and sampling were proper but that failure to detect fictitious receivables, inflated inventories, and errors in accounts payable, and failure to discover that the same receivables were pledged at several banks, constituted negligence, and that the jury should decide whether the offense was ordinary negligence or gross negligence amounting to fraud.

Several additional legal cases are briefly set forth at this point; in a text of this nature, it is necessary to brief each case.

ILLUSTRATION. On April 13, 1965, the Supreme Court of New York County, in the case of *Stanley L. Bloch, Inc.,* v. *Klein,* 258 N.T.S. 2d 501, found that the defendants who are certified public accountants are not relieved of liability solely on the ground that the balance sheet in question merely purported to reflect the condition of plaintiff's books. The plaintiff was attempting to recover $140,000 allegedly sustained by the issuance of a balance sheet containing substantial errors in inventories and retained earnings.

ILLUSTRATION. Another case is that of *Commercial Investment Trust Financial Corporation* v. *P. W. R. Glover et al.,* in which C.I.T. lent money to Manufacturers Trading Corporation. C.I.T. relied on Manufacturers Trading Corporation's certified public accountants' reports of examination in making and continuing to make loans to Manufacturers Trading Corporation. C.I.T. was not a client of the certified public accountants involved but was a creditor of the accountants' client. C.I.T. contended that Manufacturers Trading Corporation's receivables were worthless and uncollectible, or did not exist; that required collateral did not exist or was insufficient to cover the loans; and that the provision for bad debts was inadequate. The plaintiff, C.I.T., attempted to prove that the defendant accountants' audit report representations were materially false and misleading. The defendant accountants claimed a denial of opinion of the receivables and underlying collateral, which appeared in the audit report. Had the plaintiff won, the effect of the case could have been an extension of the concept of the Ultramares case—involving liability to third parties for fraud—to liability to third parties for mere negligence. The plaintiff did not prove ordinary negligence to the satisfaction of the courts. The decision of the lower court for the defendants was upheld by the United States Court of Appeals. The Court of Appeals stated that "we do not believe we should attempt to go beyond the standards of the market place, as reflected in current judicial decisions." Evidently, the references were to the Ultramares case and to that of *O'Connor* v. *Ludlam* (92F.[2d]50).

ILLUSTRATION. Several months after the verdict in the C.I.T. case, arose the case of *The First National Bank and Trust Company of South Bend* v. *Small et al.* In this suit, the bank claimed it had relied upon the accountants' audit reports in renewing a $100,000 loan to Manufacturers Trading Corporation of Cleveland, Ohio. The jury, by a vote of 11 to 1, found for the plaintiff. The audit reports were the same as in the C.I.T. case. Thus, the concept of negligence is still confused.

In the past, an auditor was liable only to the client for ordinary negligence; at the present time, the courts may or may not decide that even ordinary negligence gives the right of action to third persons, as that privilege exists under the Securities Act. The Ultramares case, the case of *Lawrence* v. *Fox*, and other recent cases have narrowed the area between negligence and fraud, and have caused fraud to be much easier to establish. If fraud is proved, privity of contract is no defense to the suit. Legal cases are on record where the purchaser of a commodity has sued and recovered directly from a manufacturer for damages caused by defective manufacture, even when the purchaser obtained the product from a dealer. A slight extension of these cases to the field of public accounting would render an auditor more directly liable to third persons for what a court might consider to be ordinary negligence. In the State Street Trust Company case (278 N.Y. 104), which finally was settled out of court, one court placed the accountant under direct responsibility to third persons who relied upon the accountant's statements, even without proof of gross negligence amounting to fraud, as established in the Ultramares case. In the State Street Trust Company case, the plaintiff had loaned money to the accountant's client prior to the receipt of the accountant's statements.

At the present time, if an error is one of judgment not accompanied by negligence, no penalties have been imposed. However, it is obvious that the concept of *caveat emptor* is breaking down and may become a concept of the past. The trend is toward the concept of *vendor emptor*.

ILLUSTRATION. In the Yale Express case of *Stephen Fischer, et al.*, v. *Michael Kletz, et al.*, U.S.D.C. Southern District of New York, 65 Civ. 787, growing out of the bankruptcy of Yale Express System, Inc., the court ruled that the case should go to trial because there were so many questions involved for which there were no provisions of law or no clear precedents.

ILLUSTRATION. In the BarChris case (*Escott* v. *BarChris Construction Corp.*, 283 F. Supp. 643, 701 [S.D.N.Y. 1968]) the plaintiffs were purchasers of convertible subordinated debentures; the defendants included those who signed an SEC registration statement, the underwriters, and the independent CPA firm. By argument of all parties involved, the judge decided the questions of fact. The court concluded that earnings had been overstated, that the current ratio was materially overstated, that a loan was recorded as a sale, that a sale-leaseback was recorded as a sale, that the accounts receivable contained large sums from a subsidiary, that the footnotes to the financial statements materially understated contingent liabilities, that the registration statement was false in many respects, and so forth.

ILLUSTRATION. In the Continental Vending Machine Corporation case, two partners and a manager of a CPA firm were federally indicted on charges of conspiring to defraud! While the three persons were named defendants, the firm as a whole was named as a co-conspirator—not as a defendant. The defendants were found guilty, even though the charges of conspiring to defraud and fraud were both ridiculous. The case centered on the reporting of loans made by Continental to an affiliate, and both companies were ruled by the president of Continental, who borrowed millions from Continental and used his Continental stock as collateral. The president of Continental, his brother, and an administrative assistant pleaded guilty, and were placed on probation for 3 years after serving 6 months of an 18 month term.

ILLUSTRATION. In the Westec Corp. case (*Carpenter* v. *Hall*, Complaint, C.A. No. 68-H-738, S.D. Texas, Houston, 1968) there were 93 defendants, including a CPA firm. The complaints directed against the CPA firm included negligence for breach of contract, fraud under the 1933 Securities Act, superficial examination, failure to detect the sale of a plant, failure to detect the fictitious sale of oil properties, deliberately concealing the materiality of earnings brought about by pooling acquisitions, and others.

ILLUSTRATION. In the Rhode Island Hospital Trust decision (*Rhode Island Hospital Trust National Bank* v. *Swartz, Bresenoff, Yavner, Jacobs and others, U.S.C.A., Fourth Circuit*, No. 71-1284, Norfolk, Va., 1971) the Court of Appeals ruled negligence in the audit of the financial statements of International Trading Corporation and related companies, resulting in a loan loss to the plaintiff bank in excess of $100,000. Although the lower district court concluded that the evidence failed to show "fraud or collusion on the part of Accountants, any lack of good faith, misrepresentation, breach of duty, negligence, or failure to use reasonable care in the preparation and issuance of financial statements," and dismissed the case, the Court of Appeals disagreed with regard to negligence—and reversed the decision. International Trading borrowed from the Rhode Island Bank by pledging inventories and accounts receivable. The Court of Appeals held that the borrower, by changing its method of handling its unloading of inventories from bag to bulk necessitated facilities changes. In 1963, over $212,000 allegedly was spent by International to improve its leasehold improvements in Florida, Georgia, and Rhode Island. The Court of Appeals ruled that the improvements were fictitious. The accountants issued the audit report, in which reservations were expressed regarding their fairness, such as "our examination included a general review of the accounting procedures and such tests of the accounting records as we were permitted to make." In addition, the report also pointed out that the work on warehouse improvements, including the installation of machinery, was done by company employees. "Fully detailed cost records were not kept of these capital improvements and no exact determination could be made as to the exact cost of said improvements." A disclaimer of opinion was rendered. Then one of the partners of the accounting firm died. His work papers showed that International Trading treated labor costs connected with the improvements as an expense—which the accountant attempted to segregate—but the work papers allegedly showed that no material cost had been recorded. This case illustrates at least the following points: (1) An accountant should use strong language in a disclaimer (2) he should render an adverse opinion when client-imposed restrictions cause doubt, (3) in rendering a disclaimer of opinion or an adverse opinion, he should use a short-form report, or (4) he should not accept the client. Also, it might have been a good idea if the lending bank watched the actions of its borrowers—the bank assumed the initial risk, and then wanted to pass the responsibility for the performance of the borrower to others.

ILLUSTRATION.   In the case of *Gold* v. *DCL, Incorporated* (SDNY para. 94,036), lost by the plaintiff, a third party attempted to hold the accountants liable for loss when the market price of DCL's stock fell, even though the auditing firm had informed DCL that it intended to qualify its opinion as "subject to the ability of DCL to fully recover the cost of its computer equipment by lease renewals, by new leases and by sale of equipment." The plaintiff held that the duty to disclose arose from the auditor's status, making it responsible "to all persons relying on its figures." The court disagreed, stating that "there is, however, no basis in principle of authority for extending an auditor's duty to disclose beyond cases where the auditor is giving or has given some representation or certification . . ." "In this case, the auditor issued no public opinion, rendered no certification, and in no way invited the public to rely on its financial judgment . . ."

ILLUSTRATION.   In 1973, the Georgia Court of Appeals in the case of *MacNerland* v. *Barnes,* involving the purchase of stock in Continental Rent-A-Car of Georgia by a plaintiff. The court was asked to rule on whether common law liability for negligent misrepresentation would be governed by the relatively narrow rules of the Ultramares case on the broader rules in certain recent cases, such as the Rhode Island Trust case, above. The court followed Ultramares, and the Georgia Supreme Court would not review the decision of the Court of Appeals, which held (a) "An accountant is not liable for negligence in the preparation and issuance of an uncertified financial statement, containing an express disclaimer of opinion, to third parties, not in privity, even though their reliance on such statement is known or could be anticipated, and (b) an accountant may be liable to such third parties if he agrees to verify certain figures contained in a statement and negligently fails to do so." The decision also recognizes a disclaimer of opinion, and also cited SAP No. 38 of the AICPA. The following is quoted from the case: "*Ultramares* has been under attack by various text writers and periodicals. It has also been criticized in certain cases cited by the appellant. *Ryan* v. *Kanne* (1969, Iowa) 170 NW2d 395; *Rusch Factors, Inc.* v. *Levin* (1968, DC RI) 284 F Supp. 85; *Rhode Island Hospital Trust Nat. Bank* v. *Swartz, Bresenoff, Yavner & Jacobs* (1972, CA4 Va) 455 F2d 847; *Shatterproof Glass Corp.* v. *James* (1971, Tex. Civ. App.) 466 SW2d 873, 46 ALR3d 968.

"We have, nevertheless, found no persuasive authority upholding liability where there was both lack of privity and an uncertified statement or more particularly an express disclaimer. *Ultramares* stands as the major rule and we see no reason to depart from its rationale.

Support for this view is found, inter alia, in two fairly recent decisions. The Tenth Circuit, *Stephens Industries, Inc.* v. *Haskins and Sells,* 438 F2d 357, in applying Colorado law has held that a public accountant may be liable for damages to his client resulting from either fraud or negligence but as to third parties, even those who the accountant knew or should have known were relying on his audit, liability can be found and only upon fraudulent conduct, and proof of mere negligence will not suffice. The Florida Court of Appeals has held that even though there was a certified statement made that the accountant was not liable for mere negligence to third parties with whom there was no privity of contract. *Investment Corp. of Fla.* v. *Buchman*, 208 So.2d 291.

Where as here there is a written disclaimer, the accountant would not be liable to third parties for mere negligence in the preparation of a financial statement."

ILLUSTRATION. In the *Stephens Industries* case, mentioned above, the U.S. Court of Appeals (10th cir.) January 1971 Term, No. 229–70, the Court was aware of the limitations placed on the auditor by the client in determining the collectibility of certain receivables. The Court stated that the accountants "followed the scope of the audit as outlined by their clients and carefully limited their work product results to coincide exactly with the understanding." This case indicates that a CPA's engagement, starting with an engagement letter and working through to the preparation of a report which follows the terms of the engagement letter will stand the test of sophisticated court examination.

ILLUSTRATION. The sharp focus on unaudited financial statements was brought to public attention in the case of 1136 *Tenants' Corporation* v. *Max Rothenberg & Company*, Index 10575/1965, New York County, Trial Term, Part VII (1970). In this case the annual accounting fee was $600, and the judgment was for $237,278. On April 8, 1971, the Appelate Division of the Supreme Court of the State of New York (the highest court in the state) upheld the July 1, 1970 decision of the Supreme Court of New York County (a trial court). The plaintiff was a corporation which owned a cooperative apartment building, and the defendants were CPAs who—according to the Trial Court—were engaged not only for purposes of write–up–work, but also to audit; one of the senior partners admitted that some audit work was performed. The building was managed by Riker & Company, management agents, which collected maintenance charges from the building occupants, deposited the collections in its own bank account, and paid bills from that account. Each month Riker & Company sent the plaintiff a statement in which it supposedly set forth income and expenses. The defendants entered the data from these statements on the records of the plaintiff. Evidently, not all incomes and expenses were set forth in the monthly statements. The CPA firm had no connection or business with Riker & Company other than being hired by Riker personally, who was the head of Riker & Company. Riker & Company allegedly appropriated some of the collections and did not pay all bills, thereby causing loss to the plaintiff. This case resulted in the AICPA and the New York State County of CPA's filing a brief *amicus curiae* with the Court of Appeals of the State of New York. Briefed, the "statement of the case" follows: "From November 1963 to March 1965, the defendant accounting firm was orally retained by plaintiff, an incorporated apartment cooperative owned by its stockholder-tenants and managed by a separate realty agent Riker & Co., to perform services leading to the preparation of corporate financial statements and letters containing information for the stockholders' tax records. Defendant was to receive $600 per year for these services.

The accountants submitted to plaintiff financial statements for the year 1963 and for the first six months of 1964. In each case, the statements were accompanied by a letter of transmittal which began as follows: "Pursuant to our engagement, we have reviewed and summarized the statements of your managing agent and other data submitted to us by Riker & Co., Inc. (the agent), pertaining to 1136 Tenants' Corporation (the client-cooperative). . . ." and concluded:

The following statements were prepared from the books and records of the Corporation. No independent verifications were undertaken thereon . . ."

The financial statements themselves were marked with a legend which read, "Subject to comments in letter of transmittal."

The financial statements and letters did not reveal that I. Jerome Riker, the agent's principal officer had assertedly diverted funds of the cooperative to his own purpose, or had failed to pay mortgage installments, taxes or municipal service charges as they became due. Any such diversions were unknown to the accountants. The dispute at trial with which this brief is concerned was as to whether the accountants had undertaken or were otherwise obliged to perform auditing procedures which would have uncovered the asserted defaults. (*The Journal of Accountancy,* November 1971).

Regardless of who was right or who was wrong in this particular lawsuit, and the decision (or decisions to come) of the courts, and all the furor appearing in the professional literature, the case definitely points up (1) the necessity for a properly worded engagement letter, or contract, (2) the necessity for investigation of underlying—or even hidden—evidence, and (3) the insistence upon rendering a total disclaimer of opinion when doubt exists.

ILLUSTRATION. Finally, there exists the multitudinous Equity Funding Corp. of America affair, which broke into public view early in 1973, even though it is alleged that the fraud or frauds extended over at least a decade. The parent company was organized in 1960, and Equity Funding became bankrupt April 5, 1973; evidently bogus insurance policies were issued and were sold to other related companies, thus creating at least $120 million of non-existent assets, and the sale of $2 billion is fictitious life insurance policies. Also, it was reported that there was stated to be $2 million in negotiable bonds supposedly held for Equity Funding by a Chicago bank, which, according to the bank were never there. At least three accounting firms have been mentioned as being connected to the audits of Equity Funding and its subsidiaries. In 1964, Equity Funding went public, and one firm audited the parent company prior to that year, and in 1972 the same firm assumed the audit of the life insurance subsidiary, also. One man was in charge of the Equity Funding audit for four years—and during that time he was not certified—which is most unusual; he finally became certified in 1972. The general thought is that this man was more of an insider than an independent outsider.

Eight former officers of Equity have been indicted in connection with the sale of $2.2 billion of fraudulent insurance policies. They were charged with filing false statements with the Illinois Secretary of State. This brought to 25 the number of former executives indicted for criminal fraud. As of February 23, 1974, 5 of the 25 changed their original plea to that of guilty.

The trustee of Equity Funding had identified and eliminated from the company's records $143.4 million of fictitious assets as of February 22, 1974. Also, it is reported that $80 million cash received by the company from borrowing cannot be accounted for. Net total writedowns of nonexistent assets have been reported as $185.4 million. The report of the trustee stated that the fraud was of three types: the creation and inflation of fictitious assets, the failure to record liabilities for borrowed money, and the creation of false insurance policies that were sold to co-insurers. In this examination by the trustee, approximately 50 accountants from one national CPA firm were used, together with many lawyers and governmental agencies, and many members of the trustee's staff. *This case may be in the courts for years.*

In a book of this nature, space naturally does not permit a full discussion and analysis of all cases. For additional study, the reader is referred to such cases as *Otis McAllister, Continental Vending, Texas Gulf, Palsgraf* v. *Long Island R. Co.*, (1928), *State Street Trust Co.*, (1938), *Investment Corp. of Florida* v. *Buchman*, (1968), *Drake* v. *Thor Power Tool Co.*, (1968 and 1971), many others, and various SEC cases.

In summary, in order to establish fraud other than that arising from gross negligence, there must be fraudulent intent. The auditor may be liable for fraud (1) if he is guilty of making a statement known to be untrue or without reasonable grounds for believing it to be true or with utter disregard for the truth, made with the intent that another person shall act thereon; (2) if that person acts thereon; and (3) if the act causes injury to the person acting thereon. No legal obligation normally is incurred by the auditor if the client sets up restrictions that have the effect of not enabling the auditor to disclose fraud and these restrictions are disclosed by the auditor in the audit report, to the SEC, and to the public; suspicions of fraud must be disclosed to avoid liability, and a total disclaimer of opinion, or an adverse opinion, should be rendered. The auditor is not responsible for carefully laid fraudulent plans if reasonable skill would not discover them. Unintentional mistakes of inconsequential nature have not resulted in legal liability. Departure from recognized professional practice must be reported.

Audit reports and accompanying financial statements often get into the hands of third parties when the original intention was that the data were not to be available to such third parties. There is no denying the fact that in certain small audits, all auditing procedures are not followed because all procedures are not considered necessary and because third parties did not exist—*at that time*. Then a third party develops. Many third parties do not possess technical skill but they claim injury because of their reliance on the auditor's report. In such instances, in his report, (1) the auditor should clearly indicate omitted standard procedures; (2) he should clearly set forth his reasons for such omission; (3) he should limit his report to a statement of his findings; and (4) normally, he should disclaim an opinion.

One of the most infamous legal procedures occasionally used against the accountancy profession is the "strike-out." The objective of the plaintiff in such a suit is to extort money from the defendant, forcing him to purchase freedom from publicity for acts of which he is not guilty. The procedure in a strike-out suit is as follows: A bond issue may be in default, and bankruptcy proceedings may follow. Copies of the accountant's statements issued prior to the bond default or the bankruptcy are obtained. "Experts" are obtained who will offer false testimony concerning the statements to the effect that the independent accountant was guilty of negligence or fraud. The "expert" witness is in no danger of perjury because his testimony is presented as his opinion, and convictions rarely are made for opinion testimony.

Liability under the Federal Securities Acts. In addition to adhering to professional society and state codes of professional ethics, accountants who express opinions on financial statements of companies whose securities are registered with the Securities and Exchange Commission must meet the rigid tests of independence established by the Commission.

The various laws that grant the Securities and Exchange Commission authority in the matters of issuing securities and dealing in the securities of registered companies grant the Commission the privilege of requiring certification of financial statements filed with it. Rule 11 of the rules of practice of the Securities and Exchange Commission is as follows:

e) The Commission may disqualify, and deny, temporarily or permanently, the privilege of appearing or practicing before it in any way to any person who is found by the Commission after hearing in the matter
 (1) Not to possess the requisite qualifications to represent others or
 (2) To be lacking in character or integrity or to have engaged in unethical or improper professional conduct.

As administered by the Securities and Exchange Commission, the Securities Act of 1933, the Securities Exchange Act of 1934, the Public Utility Holding Company Act of 1935, the Trust Indenture Act of 1939, the Investment Advisers Act of 1940, and the Investment Company Act of 1940 have gone farther in establishing clearly definable liability for a public accountant than has the common law.

Essentially, the Securities Act of 1933, as amended, is a disclosure act. It provides for the disclosure of data and information pertinent to a registrant company's business and securities, offered for sale. The data and information must be available to potential investors in deciding whether or not to acquire securities of that company. The securities must be registered with (and approved by) the Commission before they can be sold to the public. The Act also is designed to prevent misrepresentation, deceit, and fraud in the sale of securities. The Commission is not required to pass judgment on the merit of the securities, and the Commission neither approves nor disapproves a security offering. *However*, in Accounting Series Release No. 115, issued in 1970, the SEC practically stops a company from "going public" if uncertainty exists regarding its status as a going concern. Release No. 115 does not concern itself with the scope of an audit, as does Release No. 90, but only with financial condition. Perhaps the SEC overstepped the 1933 act in this case.

The Securities Act of 1933 provides that financial statements required to be filed with the Commission shall be certified by an independent public accountant. The concepts of independence, as outlined in Chapter 1, Section 1, are rigid.

ILLUSTRATION. The SEC holds that a certified public accountant who has performed some service such as journalizing and posting a client's transactions is not in fact independent. His opinion of the financial statements in these cases will not be accepted by the SEC. The Commission contends that such activities place the accountant in the category of an employee of the client.

In July 1972, the SEC published Accounting Series Release No. 126 involving the independence of auditors; this release did not supersede ASR No. 47, of 1944, or ASR No. 81, of 1958, but is supposed to complement them. To quote from ASR No. 126;

"The primary purpose of this release is to set forth presently existing guidelines employed by the Commission in resolving the various independence questions that come before it," the SEC said, and added:

"The critical distinction which must be recognized at the outset is that the concept of independence is more easily defined than applied. As a result, the guidelines and illustrations presented in these releases cannot be, nor are they intended to be, definitive answers on any aspect of this subject. Rather, they are designed to apprise the practitioner of typical situations which have involved loss of independence, whether in appearance or in fact, and by so doing to place him on notice of these and similar potential threats to his independence."

The Securities Act has made the accountant liable to third-party investors not only for fraud but also for innocent, though negligent misrepresentation. A major requirement of the Securities Act is that a registration statement must be filed with the Commission prior to the issuance of securities for sale in interstate commerce—if the issue exceeds a defined amount. Minute detail is required in the registration statement, including a complete economic history of the registrant company. If an accountant "prepared or certified" the financial statements of the registrant, the written consent of the accountant is necessary to use his name in connection with those statements; then a civil liability may be imposed on the accountant. If statements submitted are not prepared in accordance with recognized principles of accounting, the Commission presumes that such statements are misleading or inaccurate, even though footnotes are appended to the statements.

After proper filing of the registration statement, 20 days elapse before the obligations and rights of the act become effective. After the effective registration date, a security purchaser may decide to sue the certifying accountant for misrepresentation of a material fact or for the omission of a material fact in the statements used for registration purposes. In order to recover, the plaintiff must prove loss; but he is not required to prove that the loss resulted from the misrepresentation. If the plaintiff purchased the securities after one year following the registration date and after more recent financial statements were available to that plaintiff, he must prove that the loss resulted from misrepresentation in the statements submitted for registration.

The defenses of the accountant against such action are as follows: (1) proof that the financial statements filed with the Commission were not fair copies of the statements prepared by the accountant; (2) proof that prior to the registration date, written notice was given the Commission by the accountant that he would not be responsible for the financial statements filed with the registration statement; (3) proof that the statements were true and proper and that they contained no omission or mis-statement; (4) proof that the financial statements were used with the registration statements without the knowledge of the accountant and that upon learning of the use of the statements, the accountant gave public notice to the situation and also notified the Commission to withdraw his authority for the propriety of the statements; (5) proof that the plaintiff investor possessed knowledge of incorrectness in the statements at the time the securities were purchased; (6) proof that the loss of the investor was caused by reasons other than the accountant's error; (7) proof that the accountant acted in good faith in conformity with a regulation of the Commission; (8) proof that the accountant relied upon a technical expert for some phase of the financial statements and that the accountant had no reason to question the accuracy of the figures of that technician; (9) proof that action by the plaintiff was brought subsequent to three years from the date on which the security was offered to the public in accordance with the act; and (10) proof that action by the plaintiff was brought subsequent to one year from the date the plaintiff learned of the accountant's misrepresentation.

In accordance with the act, the recovery of the plaintiff is limited to the difference between the price paid for the security (not in excess of the public offering price) and (1) the value at the date the suit was instigated, or (2) the price at which the plaintiff sold the security before he filed his suit, or (3) the price at which the plaintiff sold the security after filing his suit but before judgment.

The burden of proof is placed upon the accountant, and he must defend as many suits as are instituted against him by disgruntled security holders. The liability of the accountant attaches to prospectuses issued in connection with a proposed security sale as well as to the registration statements.

The Liability Committee of the AICPA attempts to obtain relief from the liability burdens placed on public accountants by the Securities Act of 1933 as amended, by having the SEC shift the burden of proof from the defendant accountant to the plaintiff. Also, the SEC was requested to shorten the "reliance period" following the effective date of the registration statement within which a securities buyer is presumed to have relied on the alleged untruth in the registration statement, change the stated standard of care to that applicable to the accounting profession, and provide a statutory limit to the liability of an accountant.

The Securities Exchange Act of 1934 relates to securities exchanges and securities listed on exchanges, over-the-counter markets, and brokers dealing in securities. The general purposes of the Securities Exchange Act are to protect the investing public by curtailing speculation, to prevent the manipulation of stock prices, and to review the annual reports of companies subject to registration. The Securities Exchange Act has placed additional responsibilities on the accountant. It must be emphasized at this point that the Commission does not view the accountant as the *originator* of the financial statements of a registrant; rather, the Commission looks upon him as an expert lending his opinion.

SECTION III: CURRENT LEGAL AND SEC HIGHLIGHTS

At this time, the American Law Institute is preparing a draft of the codification of federal securities laws, in which limits are provided with respect to the liability of an auditor. One SEC commissioner stated that the SEC is sympathetic to the pleas of the AICPA to limit the liabilities of auditors, on the basis that it is absurd to expose them to liability for the entire amount of an offering while each underwriter was responsible only for his participation. This is sensible and proper.

A pressing current question is: Will the SEC develop and enforce the application of accounting principles, or will the FASB (and the AICPA as a whole) lead in that area? The FASB *should* lead, and in a logical manner; it should not jump from one area or topic to another unrelated area or topic. Also, neither the FASB nor the AICPA should compromise its position on any proposed standard when the attempt is made by special-interest groups (in the business world and in the government) to alter a proposed Standard for its own selfish interests.

If the FASB does not move in a rapid and logical manner, it will receive not only non-compliance from its pronouncements, but it will be forced to cope with governmental bodies—principally the SEC. The SEC has the power of law behind it, but it has expressed a *willingness* for the FASB and the profession as a whole to promulgate financial reporting and accounting thought.

For both non-SEC areas and SEC areas, professional accounting should and *must* take the lead, and professional literature should *not* take a fearful attitude. There has been far too much negative thinking and unwarranted pessimism in recent literature.

Another aggravating area that leads many people (professional and non-professional) into a labyrinth of confusion and doubt is the news and other media, and their insinuations and installations of doubt in the minds of readers and viewers. An example is a front page headline appearing in *The Wall Street Journal*, April 4, 1973, as follows: *Inside and Outside. Why Didn't Auditors Find Something Wrong with Equity Funding? Some Say the Usual Checking Isn't Designed for Frauds: But Were Parties Too Cozy? When a Factory Goes Astray.* While this paper is highly respected, it would be much more appropriate not to act in a manner that caused a reader to draw correct or incorrect conclusions prior to the finalization of a happening on a case.

The SEC, in the reporting requirements of the revised Form 10–K, found it necessary to issue an interpretative release in order to assist those preparing the form. The revised 10–K was issued as a surprise to the accounting profession, demands much more information than its predecessor; and the filing deadline was reduced from 120 days to 90 days following the end of a fiscal year. Because so many companies use the calendar year as their fiscal year, the last week in March is jokingly referred to as "10–K week" in the accounting profession. Form 10–K now requires disclosure by lines of business, products or services, research and development costs, competitive position, sources of raw materials, number of employees, and order backlogs. In addition, Form 10–K, as revised, calls for the past five-year breakdown of sales and incomes under certain conditions. Form 10–K now is composed of two parts: Part I must be filed by all registrants required to file, together with necessary financial statements, supporting schedules, and exhibits. Part II may be omitted if the registrant has filed with the SEC a definitive proxy that involves the election of directors, or if the registrant files such a statement not later than 120 days after the close of a fiscal year. SEC proxy rules must be followed for items relating to management, remuneration, and transactions with insiders, such as indebtedness of insiders to the registrant or its subsidiaries; pension, retirement, and savings plans of the registrant, its parent, or its subsidiaries; pending legal actions must be disclosed; also, there must be disclosed the names and ages of all executive officers and any family relationship between them, and criminal convictions, bankruptcy proceedings, and other information involving directors. *Certified* comparative financial statements are now required for the last *two* years. Then there is the new quarterly Form 10–Q; it replaced Form 9–K, which was filed annually. Form 10–Q is an expansion of income statement data formerly incorporated in Form 9–K, together with new disclosures regarding capitalization and stockholders' equity. Also, the SEC requires a monthly Form 8–K when specified transactions or events occur. Thus, it is obvious that legal responsibilities are increasing—in these cases as required by the SEC, whether or not the Securities Acts, as amended, so intended.

Late in 1973, one national accounting firm brought suit to stop the SEC from interpreting certain sections of APB No. 16 dealing with business combinations. Briefly, the SEC had earlier ruled that a company must have owned treasury stock for a period at at least two years before that stock was used to effect a business combination! In other words, a company could not currently acquire some of its own outstanding shares and then immediately (or within two years) use those shares to acquire an interest in another company. The SEC was attempting to formulate accounting principles by interpreting APB Opinions which it had never adopted! The complaint of the accounting firm held that the SEC violated the Administrative Procedures Act, in that it failed to give public notice of its interest, thus stopping public comment. The SEC changed its position and withdrew its ruling; then the CPA firm withdrew its suit. It is time that CPA firms took such aggressive action, and the firm took commendable action. CPA firms should take more legal actions, not only against regulatory agencies, but against creditors and stockholders who do not attend to their affairs properly and then try to find a scapegoat. The SEC should not assume the part of an activist in the publication of accounting doctrines; that is *not* the purpose for which the SEC was established!

Legal Liability of Tax Practitioners

The tax work of certified public accountants not only involves the preparation of returns but tax advice, tax planning, and representation before taxing authorities and in the courts. As in the case of civil liability, similar rules of law exist for tax practice—that is, the CPA may be found guilty of breach of contract or for negligence in the preparation of tax returns. Because third parties do not rely on tax returns prepared by a CPA, gross negligence evidently does not exist. However, a CPA may be accused of preparing fraudulent tax returns.

ILLUSTRATION. A CPA filed *tentative* tax returns for a client for two consecutive years. When he filed the final returns, they were exactly the same as the tentative returns; and the CPA had not examined the client's records. Because proper and timely returns had not been filed, the Internal Revenue Service brought action against the taxpayer, who settled the tax deficiencies. Then the taxpayer sued the CPA for the amount of the tax deficiency plus legal fees and won the suit on the basis that there was a breach of contract because the CPA failed to perform properly. The defendant appealed and won, and the case went to the Supreme Court of the state, which reversed the Appellate Court. If the CPA had advised his client of the possible consequences resulting from late filing and had permitted the client to do the "decision making," liability could have been avoided.

In advising clients on tax matters, the CPA should insist that after advice is rendered, the client make decisions and should always indicate to the client—in writing—that he is advising and not guaranteeing. Because tax advice does not enter the area of the attest function, the CPA must always keep the benefits to his clients foremost in his mind. As the preparer of any tax return requiring the signature of the preparer, the CPA must sign it. If a CPA is asked to review a return prepared by a taxpayer, at his discretion the CPA may sign it; however, he should sign it only if in the course of his review, he obtains information equivalent to the knowledge he would have obtained if he prepared the return.

QUESTIONS

1. *a*) What information may appear on the cover of a book written by a member of the AICPA?
    b) An auditor has been asked to perform the functions in (*a*), (*b*), and (*c*), listed below, for a creditors' committee which is in control of a debtor corporation. The corporation will continue to operate under its present management subject to extension agreements.
    a) Cosign checks issued by the debtor corporation.
    b) Cosign purchase orders in excess of established amounts.
    c) Exercise general supervision to insure compliance with the budgetary controls and pricing formulas established by management, with the consent of the creditors, as part of an overall program aimed at the liquidation of deferred indebtedness.
    Would the auditor be considered independent for the purpose of expressing his opinion on the debtor's financial statements?

2. *a*) May an AICPA member, without violating confidential information, use an outside service bureau for the processing of client's tax returns? Assume that the CPA will control the input data and that the computer service will perform the mathematical calculations and print the returns.
    b) An AICPA member performed the following services for a corporation client: Write-up, work, adjusting entries, and financial statement preparation. The financial statements prepared under these circumstances are acceptable to the state of incorporation's Secretary of Commerce Securities Commission, and to the State Attorney General. Is the auditor independent? Present reasons for your answer.

c) A CPA firm accepted 10-year, interest-bearing debentures in settlement of audit fees. The client was in financial difficulties, and a plan of reorganization had been approved by a U.S. District Court. If a market exists, the CPA firm plans to sell the debentures as soon as possible after they are issued. Did the CPA firm violate the rules of independence? Present reasons for your answers.

3. Refer to Rule 101 of the *Code of Professional Ethics* of the AICPA. The rule concerns the expression of an opinion and concerns discreditable acts. Prepare a list of imaginary situations—one each for *(a)* through *(e)*—which would constitute discreditable acts.

4. Rule 302 of the Code of Professional Ethics prohibits contingent fees except in certain cases. What justification exists for this rule?

5. A certified public accountant enters into an agreement with a client that the audit fee will depend on the number of days required to complete the engagement.
   a) What is the essence of the rule of professional ethics dealing with contingent fees?
   b) What are the reasons for the rule?
   c) In your opinion, did the auditor violate the rule?

6. For each of the following cases, state whether you believe the proposed action would be proper or improper according to the *Code of Professional Ethics* of the AICPA. Justify your decisions.
   a) A firm of certified public accountants is considering the use of an outside mailing service to handle confirmations of the accounts receivable of clients upon whose financial statements the firm is to render an opinion. The mailing service would mail the requests, receive the replies, remove the replies from the envelopes, and return them to the accountants.
   b) A certified public accountant, now on the staff of a firm of certified public accounts but contemplating public practice in his own name, plans to send announcements of his establishment in practice to clients of the firm by which he is now employed, as well as to friends and acquaintances. Some such clients have indicated that they would like him to continue with them; they are not yet aware of his decision to enter upon practice for himself.
   c) In the sale of his entire practice to another certified practitioner, a certified public accountant proposes to turn over to the latter all of his work papers and business correspondence.
   d) A CPA plans to initiate discussions with an accountant who is at present employed on the staff of another public accounting firm with a view to persuading the accountant to come to work for him.

7. Rule 502 of the *Code of Professional Ethics* of the AICPA states "A member shall not endeavor to obtain clients by solicitation. Advertising is a form of solicitation and is prohibited."
   a) Discuss the reasons for the rule prohibiting advertising
   b) When a CPA establishes his own practice, how can he ethically obtain new clients?

8. State four circumstances under which a certified public accountant in expressing his opinion on financial statements as the result of an audit may have acted in a manner discreditable to the profession.

9. *a*) You have audited the financial statements of the Bock, Inc., in accordance with generally accepted auditing standards and were satisfied with your findings. If the Bock, Inc. had a loan of a material amount payable to a finance company of which your brother was the principal stockholder have any effect on your audit opinion? Discuss.

   b) Your 16-year-old son owns 200 of the 200,000 shares of the common stock of the Bock, Inc. Would this fact have any effect on your audit opinion? Discuss.

10. As auditor, your are requested by a client corporation to sign published statements of anticipated earnings. What position would you take with respect to this request? What are the reasons for your answer?

11. What are the primary differences, between the *Code of Professional Ethics* of the AICPA and the *Code of Ethics* of the Federal Government Accountants Association?

12. What are the legal responsibilities of a public accountant with respect to the work done by him as a professional auditor? Discuss in general.

13. Without consulting its CPA, a client has changed its accounting practices so that they are not in accordance with generally accepted accounting principles. During the regular audit engagement, the CPA discovers that the statements are so misleading that they might be considered fraudulent.

   a) Discuss the specific action to be taken by the CPA.

   b) In this situation, what obligation does the CPA have to outsiders if he is replaced? Discuss briefly.

   c) In this situation, what obligations does the CPA have to a new auditor if he is replaced? Discuss briefly.

   (AICPA, adapted)

14. Frequently, an auditor requests that the client supply him with a certification of (*a*) inventory quantity, pricing, and condition; (*b*) receivables, particularly with respect to their collectibility; and (*c*) capital assets, particularly when appraised amounts are used in the accounts.

   To what extent may an auditor use these certifications as safeguards against charges of negligence and at the same time assume full responsibility for the engagement?

15. Facts discovered during the course of an audit are regarded as professional secrets. Name the conditions under which professional secrecy may be abrogated.

16. A client is indebted to the First National Bank, its regular depositary and source of borrowed funds. The client submits a copy of your annual audit report to the bank. The bank requests additional information from you. State the course you would follow, and present your reasons.

17. The auditor of the Canon Company completed his examination of the financial statements of the company and then prepared the company's federal income tax return. He made a mathematical error in preparing

the return. Several months later, the Internal Revenue Service advised the Canon Company of the error and assessed an additional tax of $2,460, including interest. If you were the auditor, what position would you take?

18. You are the auditor for the Vine Company. Mr. Grape, a member of the board of directors, owns all of the capital stock of the Plum, Inc., which you also audit. The Vine Company buys all of its raw materials from Plum, Inc. Grape is the only member of the board of the Vine Company who knows that you audit the records of the Plum, Inc. In the report of your examination of the Vine Company, what would you indicate with respect to this situation?

19. What is the difference between negligence and fraud?

20. What are the liabilities of the independent auditor under the federal securities acts?

21. What are the rules of the Securities and Exchange Commission with regard to audit reports?

22. How have the Securities Acts made the independent auditor liable to third-party investors?

23. The A Company purchased $50,000 of merchandise from the B Company. Because of an error in a decimal point, the B Company billed the A Company for $5,000. The A Company recorded the purchase at $5,000 and sent its check to the B Company for that amount. No objection was received from the B Company. During your annual audit of the A Company, you discovered the error, which the company admitted but refused to correct, stating that it was not interested in keeping books for the B Company. Later, you were engaged to audit the records of the B Company; remembering the incident, you investigated and found that the B Company had entered the receivable at $5,000 and had accepted the A Company's check in full settlement.

 In each examination, what course would you follow?

24. Base your answers to the following questions on the *Code of Professional Ethics* of the AICPA. Assume that each of the accountants in the cases below is a CPA and is subject to the Code of the Institute. In each case, present a reason for your conclusion.

 a) Garland was in the process of establishing his practice in Boston. He prepared a small brochure showing the advantages of the services of his public accounting firm and sent a copy of that brochure to each prospective client in the immediate area. Is this action permissible?

 b) Heckman is practicing on his own account and has audited the financial statements of Eaton Inc., for many years. Due to a press of duties, this year he is able to spend only enough time to read the statements prepared by the treasurer and the chief accountant of the Eaton, Inc. Due to his many years of work for this client during which time no fraud was discovered, he believes that is sufficient to permit him to give an unqualified opinion on this year's statements. Is this permissible?

 c) Downy expresses an unqualified opinion of the financial statements of the Lux Company in which statements the basis of valuation of the fixed assets is not shown. He is aware of the fact that the fixed assets are valued on the statements at appraisal value, which is substantially above cost. He feels it is not his duty to divulge this information so long as he does not state any basis for the fixed assets. Is he correct?

d) Sims contends that he is not violating the code of ethics of the AICPA by expressing an unqualified opinion on the financial statements of the Gee Company, despite the fact that they were examined by Herman Beely, an employee of his firm. Is he correct?

e) An announcement of the affiliation of Harold Waters with the accounting firm of Kent and Co. was made in the *Washington News*. Kent contends that this is entirely proper, as the announcement was made in a very small conventional-type notice. Is he correct?

(AICPA, adapted)

4

Internal Control: Manual Systems; Fraud

SECTION I: INTRODUCTION

Internal Auditing

The function of internal auditing is becoming increasingly important as companies expand and as accounting systems become more complex. All companies should be encouraged and educated to realize the importance of internal auditing and internal control. The maintenance of good client relations is only one of the advantages of making suggestions in these areas to clients, not only at a fiscal year-end, but throughout the year. The implementation of suggested changes must be followed up by the auditor in order to assure success for the client.

Internal auditing, which is conducted by employees of an organization, is the verification and appraisal of procedures, recorded data, and performance under the policies and plans of the organization. It is a major function of the modern business entity used in controlling and directing its activities.

The Institute of Internal Auditors issued the following *Statement of the Responsibilities of the Internal Auditor:*

Internal auditing is the independent appraisal activity within an organization for the review of the accounting, financial, and other operations as a basis for protective and constructive service to management. It is a type of control which functions by measuring and evaluating the effectiveness of other types of control. It deals primarily with accounting and financial matters but it may also properly deal with matters of an operating nature.

The overall objective auditing is to assist management in achieving the most efficient administration of the operations of the organization. This total objective has two major phases, as follows:

(1) The protection of the interests of the organization, including the pointing out of existing deficiencies to provide a basis for appropriate corrective action. The attainment of this objective involves such activities of the internal auditor as:

a) Ascertaining the degree of reliability of the accounting and statistical data developed within the organization.

b) Ascertaining the extent to which company assets are properly accounted for and safeguarded from losses of all kinds.

c) Ascertaining the extent of compliances with established policies, plans, and procedures.

(2) The furtherance of the interests of the organization, including the recommendation of changes for the improvement of the various phases of the operations. The attainment of this objective involves such activities of the internal auditor as:

a) Reviewing and appraising the policies and plans of the organization in the light of the related data and other evidence.

b) Reviewing and appraising the internal records and procedures of the organization in terms of their adequacy and effectiveness.

c) Reviewing and appraising performance under the policies, plans, and procedures.

Internal auditing is a staff or advisory function rather than a line or operating function. Therefore the internal auditor does not exercise direct authority over other persons in the organization.

The internal auditor should be free to review and appraise policies, plans, and procedures but his review and appraisal does not in any way relieve other persons in the organization of the primary responsibilities assigned to them.

Independence is basic to the effectiveness of the internal auditing program. This independence has two major aspects, as follows:

(1) The head of the internal auditing department should be made responsible to an officer of sufficient rank in the organization as will assure adequate consideration and action on the findings or recommendations. The organizational status of the internal auditor and the support accorded to him by management are major determinants of the range and value of the services which management will obtain from the internal auditing function.

(2) Internal auditing should not include responsibilities for procedures which are essentially a part of the regular operations of a complete and adequate accounting system or of a properly organized operating department. In some instances management may assign current operating responsibilities to the internal auditing department, but in such cases the execution of the current operating responsibilities should be performed by a separate personnel and be subjected to the same review and appraisal as is accorded other operations.

Some of the distinctive objectives of internal auditing may be summarized as follows:

1. To assist management in attaining the most efficient administration of company operations by establishing procedures for adherence to company operating policies.

2. To determine the reliability of the financial data produced and the effectiveness of the internal procedures.

3. To reveal and correct inefficient operations.

4. To recommend necessary changes in the various phases of the operations.
5. To ascertain the extent of the protection of, accounting for, and safeguarding of company assets against losses of any kind or description.
6. To determine the degree of coordination attained among the policies set forth by management.

Internal auditing extends beyond the routine of a detailed verification of a transaction as it is reflected in an accounting entry into the realm of a complete periodic survey and analysis of the business operations. In a small business organization, management is in a position to remain abreast of current operations. In a large business organization, management is so far removed from current detail that it must delegate authority for the execution of operations and procedures; at the same time, it must be in a position whereby the validity of financial and statistical data is in no way questionable. Management formulates policies, orders the policies placed in effect, and then relies upon answers submitted by personnel charged with proper responsibility and given proper executive authority. In order to ascertain that formulated policies are properly administered and executed, there must be an internal examination of the data resulting from the execution of the policies. If the independent auditor were to perform these duties for a large company, his entire time might be expended with one client—and he might no longer remain independent.

ILLUSTRATIONS. A few examples of the necessity for internal auditing may be cited: There may be one person in each department of a large department store who is responsible for approving sales returns for cash refunds. Internal auditing is necessary because there must be control of cash and inventories. Another example of the necessity for internal auditing rests in the activities of a pegboard payroll procedure. Operations should be verified as to the existence of the person being paid, proper pay scale, deductions, and accumulation of earnings. Further internal auditing of the payroll as to the allocation of costs as well as performance is vitally necessary. Another example of the necessity for internal auditing may be cited in an order-filling department of a wholesale hardware outlet, where the activities would be analyzed to determine that accounts receivable are correctly recorded as well as inventory being properly controlled.

While the internal auditor is performing work of an auditing nature, he cooperates with—and does not compete with—the independent auditor. He must of necessity possess the point of view of management, and he cannot be expected to possess the disinterested objectivity of the independent accountant. Receiving his power from management, the internal auditor must retain the point of view and the objectives of management; and at the same time, he must have sufficient independence for effective operation. He attains a knowledge of functions, operations, personnel, and organization vital to the guidance of the business which could not be obtained by the independent auditor; the function of the latter is to analyze constructively the business operations and to render an expert opinion thereon.

The internal auditor must report to management; therefore, he must be certain that all data are correct and reliable for interpretation into policy-forming functions of management. To the extent of the ascertainment of the reliability of data, the work of the internal auditor parallels that of the independent auditor. The internal auditor's duties have continued to expand and in many instances include the auditing of management policies.

The functions of the internal auditor must be expressed in terms of specific auditing operations. The auditing operations, drafted and organized in the form of an internal audit program, constitute a procedural manual for the guidance of the internal auditor. The composition of the program is dependent upon such factors as:

1. The centralization or decentralization of operations.
2. The nature of company activities, as expressed, for example, in many small products versus a few large products.
3. The effectiveness of the accounting system in its ability properly to collect accounting data and other financial data so that they are presented in an understandable and usable form.
4. The effectiveness of the system of internal control.
5. The efficiency of personnel.
6. The opportunity for errors and irregularities.
7. The provision for review and updating the gathering of needed information. This is particularly true in manual systems where pegboards and accounting machines are involved in recording financial transactions.

When the internal auditor performs his examining operations, he has an immediate twofold objective: (1) the verification of the accuracy of recorded data; and (2) an appraisal of the accounting, financial, and operating procedures.

The first objective—the verification of the accuracy of recorded data—is also one of the objectives of the independent auditor. In order to accomplish this objective, the program of internal audit should be designed around the three phases of:

1. *Responsibility*—charging the proper person with providing data.
2. *Accountability*—the invocation of the principle of charge and discharge.
3. *Publicity*—the dissemination of information.

The second objective—an appraisal of the accounting, financial, and operating procedures—must be measured in terms of the results shown by the answers obtained in the first objective.

As will be emphasized through the text, the independent auditor depends upon internal auditing in its operation through the system of internal control. The independent auditor depends upon the system of internal control to function so effectively that he is not forced into unnecessary detailed examinations.

Internal auditing assists the operations of the independent auditor. With the proved satisfaction of the system of internal control and with a satisfactory internal auditing department, an independent auditor is in a much better position to render an authoritative opinion of financial condition and the results of operations.

As one of his functions, the independent auditor must ascertain that, although a part of management, the internal auditor is sufficiently independent to render impartial opinions. The independent auditor also must study and review the practices of the internal auditor. In addition, work papers and reports of the internal auditor must be reviewed. Additional material on internal auditing appears in Chapter 6.

SECTION II: INTERNAL CONTROL: MANUAL SYSTEMS

Internal control constitutes the methods followed by a company (1) to protect assets, (2) to protect against improper asset disbursements, (3) to protect against the incurrence of improper liabilities, (4) to assure the accuracy and dependability of all financial and operating information, (5) to judge operating efficiency, and (6) to measure adherence to company-established policies. Internal control may be administrative or financial. Administrative internal control normally pertains to activities which are not directly financial in nature, as exemplified by a company policy that each of its traveling salesmen must prepare and send to the home office a daily report indicating calls made, orders received, rejections and the reasons therefor. Financial internal control pertains to financial activities [(2), (3), and (4), above] and may be exemplified by the separation of the duties of personnel in disbursing cash and recording related cash transactions.

In many cases financial and administrative internal control interweave—there are no mutually exclusive boundaries. Internal control exists throughout all levels of authority and is not centralized at any one point; but here, primary interest will be focused on financial internal control. Proper financial internal control is accomplished by management's verification of financial transactions and financial recording. In an audit, the independent auditor is more concerned with financial internal control than with administrative internal control. In a nonaudit, engagement involving management advisory services, the independent auditor may be more interested in administrative internal control than in financial internal control.

The proper and effective operation of a system of financial internal control depends (1) on the establishment of accountabilities; (2) on well-planned accounting and financial records and the proper operation of them; and (3) on the effective segregation of the duties of company personnel. In the perfect segregation of duties, the monetary accountability and work of one employee is automatically verified by another employee; each employee operates independently and does not duplicate the work of another; and each employee facilitates the logical conclusion of the work. Internal control might be termed integrated "work-and-data" processing. The subdivision of the work is so planned that no person has complete control of one transaction through all of its phases; for example, no one person has complete control of cash receipts, cash disbursements, payroll, expenses, or sales. Different persons arrive at the same results, thereby proving the reliability of the accounting and assisting in the prevention of fraud and errors.

ILLUSTRATION. One person may write the checks while another person will code the disbursement and a third person will record the disbursement. Thus, accountabilities are charged and discharged with a minimum of lost effort and time, and a maximum degree of internal control is insured.

ILLUSTRATION. One person may count the cash from the cash registers, while another person independently adds the sales invoices or controls the cash register tapes, and a third person records the cash. The accountabilities are charged and discharged with a minimum of lost effort and time.

Management's Function

Internal control is a function of management. As business organizations have grown in physical size, as operations have expanded in complexity, and as transactions have increased in number, it has become imperative that management supply itself promptly with reliable data based on the objectives of asset preservation, error elimination, and income determination, plus means of evaluating company policy. Business data and accounting information must be prepared effectively and economically, so that the cost of obtaining them is less than the benefits derived—just as it is imperative to manufacture and sell a product at a profit in a competitive market.

Principles of Financial Internal Control

Internal control procedures vary with each individual company; there is no one universal system that is applicable to all business entities. Also, it must be remembered that the benefits of proper internal control applications may not be immediately apparent, and that those benefits may not be rapidly measured. Due to the fact that effective financial internal control is based upon the concept of charge and discharge of responsibility and duty, the cardinal principles of internal control may be stated as follows:

1. Responsibility for the performance of each duty must be fixed. Without the proper charge of responsibility, the quality of the control will be inefficient.
2. Accounting and financial operations must be separated. An employee should not be in a position in which he has control of the records

and at the same time control of the operations giving rise to entries in the records. For example, the person in charge of the general ledger should not have access to the cash or the records of cash sales.

3. Proofs of accuracy should be utilized in order to assure correctness of operation and accounting. For example, sales for a day should be totaled and proved against the sum of released merchandise tags, if a retail system of inventory is used.

4. No one person should be in complete charge of a business transaction. Any person purposely or inadvertently will commit errors, but the probability is that an error will be discovered if the handling of a transaction is separated between persons.

5. Employees must be carefully selected and trained. Careful training results in better performance, reduced costs, and more alert employees.

6. Employees should be bonded. Bonding is a protection to the employer and it serves as a psychological deterrent to a tempted employee.

7. Employees should be rotated on a job, if possible; vacations for those in positions of trust should be enforced. Rotation reduces the opportunity for fraud, points to the adaptability of an employee, and often results in new ideas for the organization.

8. Operating instructions for each position should be reduced to writing. Manuals of procedure promote efficiency and prevent misunderstanding.

9. The protective advantages of a double-entry system of accounting should not be exaggerated. A double-entry system is *not* a substitute for internal control. Errors are made under double entry; and the system alone will not prove omission, incorrect entry, or dishonesty.

10. Controlling accounts should be used as extensively as possible. Controlling accounts serve as a proof of accuracy between account balances and between duty-segregated employees.

11. Mechanical and/or electronic equipment should be used, if feasible. Although error and manipulation must be watched even when mechanical and/or electronic equipment is used, operating procedures are facilitated, the division of labor is promoted, and internal control may be strengthened.

Reliance upon the System of Internal Control

An auditor must measure the degree of the effectiveness of internal control in order to arrive at justifiable decisions. Careless financial control, careless management, and careless accounting make an audit difficult and costly and limit its reliability. A recognized auditing standard provides for a review of and reliance upon the system of internal control as an indicative guide to the necessary amount of verification. Consequently, the auditor examines the procedures employed and the data produced by the client to judge the accuracy of the client's representations and thus determines the extent of the examination detail.

In addition to professional recognition of the standard of reliance upon the system of internal control, the Securities and Exchange Commission has recognized the importance of the system of financial internal control in its relationship to the amount of testing in an audit. Regulation S–X Rule 2.02 (*b*), requires the accountant, in the determination of the scope of the audit made for the purpose of reporting on financial statements filed with the Commission, "to consider the adequacy of the system of internal check and control" and "to consider the internal system of audit regularly maintained by means of auditors employed by the registrant's staff." The Subcommittee on Audits and Audit Procedure of the New York Stock Exchange also recognizes the dependence of the independent auditor on the system of internal control.

A system of financial internal control is not difficult to operate; a good system saves the auditor much time in conducting his examination and assures him of the reliability of the recorded data. A proper system of internal control is simply an integral part of any well-managed business. Reasonable financial internal control can be installed regardless of the size of a business organization. Of course, if collusion exists between two or more dishonest employees, the system of financial internal control can be manipulated. Responsibility must be fixed to the greatest possible extent and at every level of authority.

An Auditor's Review of the System of Internal Control

The purposes of the auditor's review of the system of internal control (particularly of the system of financial internal control) may be expressed as follows:

1. To measure the adequacy of the system as one of the bases for the expression of an opinion concerning the financial statements.
2. To serve as a basis of proof of weakness or strength in internal operations.
3. To serve as a guide to the scope of the detailed audit work necessary.
4. To serve as a basis for possible recommendations for improving the system of internal control.

In his review, the auditor may follow any plan consistent with the determination of these four purposes and applied in accordance with good professional judgment. For example, he may obtain oral statements of procedure, examine organization charts and work-flow charts, examine procedure manuals and written instructions, and watch the system in its operation by following transactions through their routines. Another plan is to review selected portions of the system of internal control at one time and other portions at other times. For a new client, still another plan is to review the system of internal control at a date preceding formal work on the audit. An audit program is then designed; and for succeeding audits, the system is periodically reviewed. In an initial survey of a system of internal control, it is advisable to approach the review from a transaction point of view in order to determine the flow of work and the accountabilities of the persons engaged in the work. This may be accomplished by preparing flow charts and by studying their application to actual operations.

ILLUSTRATION. The J & S Company is owned and operated by two men, Jones and Smith. There is also one clerk on the staff. As a part of your audit, you have requested that a flow chart be prepared for the procedure for paying purchase invoices. In discussing the need for the flow chart you learn that most of the purchases are made by Jones. Below is the prepared flow chart.

PROCEDURES	CLERK	JONES	SMITH
1. Two copies of the vendor's invoice are received.	◯		
2. One copy of invoice is sent to Jones.		◯	
3. Mathematical accuracy is checked.		▢	
4. Invoice is sent to Smith.			◯
5. Invoice is filed in unpaid invoice file.			▽
6. On date payment is due, the invoice is pulled and a check is drawn and signed.			◯
7. Remittance invoice and check are sent to Jones.		◯	
8. Invoice and check are inspected and check is countersigned.		▢	
9. Invoice and check are sent to clerk, who mails check.	◯		
10. Paid invoice is filed.	▽		

The following weaknesses can be detected in the system:

1. Invoice is not checked against merchandise received. This should be done by Smith as Jones does most of the buying.
2. The clerk should not mail the checks since all invoices are received through the clerk.
3. Voucher-checks are not used and should be.

ILLUSTRATION. On page 110 an illustration was presented of the need for internal auditing in a large department store. This illustration now is extended in order to point up the internal control features upon which the independent auditor may rely to reduce the risk of misstatements and to reduce the amount of transaction examination.

A large department store has many departments handling distinctly different products. Sales returns are made by individuals who have purchased these items for cash or on credit terms. It is not feasible to verify all of these various types of returns. The auditor must rely upon the system of internal control and its dependability in determining the extent of his audit. How will he do this and feel safe that control and honesty exist throughout the store? If refunds are made or credit given for merchandise that is not returned, then the inventory would be too small and would result in an error in gross profit. The auditor will test these various types of returns by comparing the return sales document with that particular inventory record to determine whether or not the item had actually been returned. In addition, he would make certain that the person responsible for approving sales returns, particularly in the case of cash refunds, is properly bonded. Further, if the inventory is kept at retail, any discrepancies between physical and book inventories mean that either merchandise or cash is being stolen.

In all cases, the ability of the independent auditor is of greater importance than the review method followed. The review may take the form of prepared questionnaires, or it may be designed as a reminder list. In all cases, the review must be coordinated with the audit. Financial internal control questionnaires are presented in each of the following chapters for a review of the internal control applicable to each item under discussion.

Coordination of Independent Auditors and Internal Auditors

The effect of internal auditing is to give the independent auditor greater reliance upon the system of internal control than he would have if internal auditing did not exist—provided he is satisfied with the system of internal control and the results of the internal auditing procedures.

As in the case of internal control, it must be remembered that an adequate internal audit does not imply that the work of the independent auditor is performed for him—he does not accept the results of internal auditing in lieu of his own examination; he merely relies upon the results after examination to affect his verification. Independent auditing is a matter of evidence verification, and the verification of that evidence includes tests of work performed by the internal audit staff.

As business units have grown in size, as the number and complexity of transactions have increased, and as systems of internal control have become more effective, the independent auditor—by recognized standards—relies more and more upon data collected by management. In order to reduce the work of the independent auditor, there must be coordination of effort between the independent auditor and the internal auditor.

Sound bases for the promotion of coordination of the two separate groups are established by mutuality of interests, the establishment of financial statement reliability, and professional recognition of reliance on systems of internal control. In order to coordinate the efforts of the two groups effectively, the following situations must exist: each group must retain its separate identity; the independent auditor must test the adequacy of the work of the internal auditor and the results of internal control; the independent auditor must not divulge in advance what activities of the system of internal control or of internal audit he will examine, or the extent of his examination.

Thus, the coordination between the two groups culminates (1) in satisfaction of the independent auditor, based upon his review; and (2) in the direct use of data prepared for the independent auditor by a client's staff.

ILLUSTRATIONS. A few instances of the results of coordination are cited: (1) The independent auditor may request that the client prepare an aging schedule of accounts receivable. The independent auditor will examine the schedule, but time is saved because it was prepared for him; in order properly to express his opinion, he must be satisfied with it to the same extent as if he had prepared it himself. (2) The indepndent auditor may request the client to prepare schedules of fixed asset acquisitions. (3) The internal auditor may have confirmed accounts receivable; the independent auditor may then restrict his confirmation to a smaller percentage of the receivables or to accounts of selected amounts. (4) The work of inventory examination may be reduced if the internal auditing staff has performed its duties to the satisfaction of the independent auditor. (5) The independent auditor may have assisted in establishing the system of internal control and in training the personnel; he may thus possess additional confidence in the system.

Further coordination between the two groups could constitute a review of prepared questionnaires or reminder lists that the internal audit department uses to check the various phases of the accounting function.

SECTION III: ERROR CLASSIFICATION; FRAUD

While computerized fraud appears in bold-face type in the headlines, plain old garden-variety fraud still probably accounts for most of the $1.5 billion that American businesses are estimated to lose each year through fraud and embezzlement. One recent survey found that 72 percent of the annual toll is carried out through manipulations of cash disbursements, 15 percent through inventory, and 13 percent through cash receipts and other operations. It is a problem for all businessmen whether or not his operations are computerized, and regardless of whether his operations are large or small. Owners of smaller firms have one advantage: they can readily survey their situation and tighten internal controls where necessary.

Error Classification

In order to understand the installation and operation of a system of internal control, the forms of accounting mismanagement and fraud which may be encountered and which should be prevented must be understood. All accounting errors are either (1) intentional or (2) unintentional. Either an intentional or an unintentional error may result in (1) errors of principle, (2) errors of omission, or (3) errors of commission.

An *intentional* error of principle, omission, or commission arises from deliberate planning, usually involving a dishonest person. An *intentional* error may become the basis of legal action.

An *unintentional* error of principle, omission, or commission is a mistake. It arises from carelessness or a lack of adequate knowledge.

An error of principle application results in incorrect records and statements.

An error of omission is a failure to make an accounting entry which should be made and results in incorrect records and statements. Errors of omission may be difficult to detect, since an entry does not exist for examination. Detection of errors of omission is accomplished largely by tracing original evidences of transactions.

An error of commission usually is the result of carelessness or deliberation and results in incorrect records and statements.

Miscellaneous Legal Considerations

In order to understand the requirements for an adequate system of internal control, an auditor must be familiar with certain legal terminology.

Crime. A crime is made up of (1) a criminal intention and (2) a criminal act. The intention and the act must both occur, since the intention without the act or the act without the intention does not constitute a crime. A crime is the omission of an act that is required or the commission of an act forbidden by the state that affects the rights of the public. A crime is punishable by the state. A tort is a wrong in which the omission or commission of an act affects the rights of an individual and therefore affects organized society. Consequently, an act or its omission may be both a tort and a crime.

Fraud. Fraud is a deceitful and dishonest act. As applied to account-ing, fraud constitutes any act or omission to act of a deceitful and there-fore dishonest nature, or negligence so gross as to constitute fraud. The result is to take property from its owner without the permission or knowl-edge of the owner or to misstate a situation, either knowingly or by negligence. Fraud may constitute a felony or a misdemeanor.

As applied to accounting in general and to internal control in particu-lar, the prevention of fraud through proper internal control is much more desirable than the detection of fraud. "Defalcation" and "misappro-priation" are terms popularly used to designate fraud; but legally, there are no such acts.

Larceny. Larceny is a crime in which personal property of another is fraudulently taken away. In larceny, there must be trespass, not neces-sarily into the owner's property but of that particular part of the owner's property stolen. The trespass must be without consent or authority. Cri-minal intent is necessary; the accidental misplacing of an asset by an employee, for instance, does not constitute larceny. The property must be removed from its normal or regular abode. In larceny, the property must have an owner (as most property does); but the offending persons need not necessarily recognize this fact.

Embezzlement. In embezzlement, there need be no trespass, and the property taken need not be removed from its regular abode. Embezzle-ment is punishable only by statutory law.

To summarize: fraud may constitute embezzlement or larceny, or both; it may be a misdemeanor or a felony; and it is always a crime or a tort. Legal action may originate by the state or its subdivisions or by an injured person.

"Reasons" for Fraud

Although detection of fraud is not one of the objectives of an audit and although many persons view the word "fraud" with abhorence and astonishment, it still exists. It is true that large frauds are rare enough to rate news headlines; but if all the little fraudulent acts were totalized, the sum would be staggering. In large companies, internal control and check are fraud preventatives. In small companies, close supervision by the owners provides protection against fraud by employees. On page 2 of *Statement on Auditing Standards*, issued by the AICPA, the follow-ing statement appears: "However, the ordinary examination devoted to the expression of an opinion respecting financial statements is not pri-marily or specifically designed, and cannot be relied upon, to disclose defalcations and other similar irregularities, although their discovery may result." This statement does not mean that the auditor is not alert to the detection of fraud. The statement merely means, in effect, that the auditor should not be held responsible for undetected fraud. By the definition of internal control, an auditor makes his examination to determine that a company safeguards its assets, and he tests the accuracy and reliability of accounting data. Reliance for the prevention and detection of fraud should be placed principally upon an adequate accounting system, adequately supervised, with closely related and proper internal control.

The analysis of the underlying reasons for fraud falls within the province of the psychiatrist. The determination of the methods used constitutes one of the problems of the auditor. *The best control over fraud is to place the possibility of the act beyond the reach of every person who may be tempted.* Prevention or the subsequent detection of fraud depends upon the technique of internal control and the examination by the independent auditor. The first "reason" for fraudulent accounting methods or entries is to cover larceny or embezzlement. The second excuse for fraudulent entries or failure to make entries lies in the utterance of a false position—particularly those positions of financial condition and financial operation which will have the effect of misleading stockholders, creditors, or other interested parties. The primary responsibility of the auditor is centered in this type—financial statement fraud. A system of internal control is not necessarily effective in preventing or eliminating fraud arising from the second reason. Honest management and capable, independent auditors constitute the best preventative in such circumstances.

Forms of Fraud

In order to control fraud, one must be familiar with the forms it takes and the methods used by the criminal. In this discussion of the forms of fraud, no attempt is made to consider fully the remedies. The next section of this chapter, entitled "Installation of a System of Internal Control," treats of the remedial phase. As reflected in thefts of assets, the common forms of fraud are as follows:

1. Thefts of assets other than cash.
2. Thefts of cash by failure to account for cash receipts.
3. Thefts of cash by the execution of fraudulent disbursements.

1. *Thefts of Assets Other than Cash.* Merchandise thefts occasionally are negotiated over a long period without detection, especially if the inventory control system is inadequate and if the individual thefts are small. This type of operation may be discouraged if parcels carried by employees are checked in and out of the premises. Periodic physical inventory should be taken by personnel other than the regular custodians of the inventory. Another form of merchandise theft arises through the execution of false sales orders, accompanied by the shipment of goods to fictitious customers and the subsequent pickup of the merchandise

at the quarters of a confederate or at the fictitious address. (For proper internal control, see the section entitled "Sales.")

Thefts of securities may not be discovered until long after perpetration. The theft of securities registered as to principal requires forgery in order to liquidate them.

Thefts of supplies and small tools are common; centralized control and proper issuance procedure curb such thefts. (For proper internal control, see the sections of this chapter entitled "Internal Control of Investments" and "Internal Control of Fixed assets.")

2. *Thefts of Cash by Failure to Account for Cash Receipts.* In the theft of cash by failure to account for cash receipts, a variety of methods exist. A few of the common methods are as follows:

a. The theft of cash sales money, without recording the sales on a cash register or entering them on a sales invoice. This type of theft may be difficult to detect because records do not exist. In some instances, only a part of a total sale is rung on the register or entered on a sales invoice; and the difference is pocketed immediately or when the opportunity arises. There should be separation of receiving cash and selling. Cash may be taken and never recorded when it is received from such sources as income from investments in the form of coupons or checks, interest on notes receivable, and casual sale of capital assets and scrap material. (See the section entitled "Sales.")

b. The abstraction of cash from cash sales or accounts receivable collections, entering the correct amount of cash, followed by underfooting the total Cash debits and either the Sales or Accounts Receivable credit column in the cash receipts record, so that the Cash ledger account balance agrees with the reconciled bank statement balance. A variation of this procedure is to carry a Cash debit column total and a Sales or Accounts Receivable credit column total forward to the succeeding page at lower figures than the correct totals. If checks received from customers are abstracted, forgery is necessary to convert the checks into cash. The underfooted column totals are posted in order to bring about an equilibrium of debits and credits. This form of fraud may be disclosed by proving the accuracy of the footings. The functions of receiving cash and accounting for it should be separated. (See the section of this chapter entitled "Receipt of Cash.")

ILLUSTRATION. Theft of cash by underfooting receipts may be exemplified as follows: The cash collections from sales and accounts receivable were as indicated in the cash receipts record below:

Date	Cash Dr.	Accounts Receivable Cr.	Cash Sales Cr.
July 1–15	$ 6,880	$ 4,280	$ 2,600
16–31	26,832	9,448	17,384
	$33,512	$13,728	$19,784

The cashier-accountant entered the Cash debits, Accounts Receivable credits, and Cash Sales credits at the correct figures; he then underfooted the Cash column $200 and the Cash Sales column $200. This enabled him to extract $200 in cash and at the same time have the Cash ledger account agree with the reconciled bank balance.

c. Overstating sales discounts allowed a customer. The difference between the correct discount and the recorded overstated discount is stolen. This method operates effectively when cash is available; manipulation and forgery are necessary if discounts are overstated and a check stolen, an endorsement forged, and the check then cashed. The method of operation is simple, and detection is avoided unless the auditor examines discount entries and compares the check detail of the duplicate bank deposit slips with the amount of the checks recorded in the cash receipts record. (See the section entitled "Receipt of Cash.")

d. Debiting some account other than Cash when money is received from a customer. Expense accounts are favorites, since they are least subject to complete verification and the customer receives proper credit in his account. The auditor may find an entry charging Bad Debts and crediting Accounts Receivable; a purported correcting entry charging one customer (fictitious) and crediting a real customer; or a debit to Supplies, Sales Returns, or Sales Allowances, and so on.

e. Writing off good accounts as uncollectible and not recording the receipt of cash when the customer remits. A variation of this is the stealing of cash from the later liquidation of an account thought actually to be uncollectible. (See the section entitled "Receipt of Cash.")

f. Setting up a fictitious customer account in the records and charging the account for sales to a legitimate customer. Collection from the legitimate customer will never be recorded because he has no account receivable on the records. Later, the fictitious account is charged to Bad Debts. Confirmation of accounts receivable is an aid in detecting this form of fraud, since the confirmation request will be returned to the sender. (See the section entitled "Receipt of Cash.")

g. Undercharging a customer *on the records*, and when the customer remits, stealing the difference between the amount charged and the amount received from the customer. Securing confirmation of accounts receivable is an aid, as is the comparison of duplicate bank deposit slips with the cash records. (See the section entitled "Receipt of Cash.")

h. Lapping involves the withholding of current cash receipts without an entry being made; at the time of a subsequent cash receipt, the entry for the first cash receipt is made and the later receipt is not recorded.

ILLUSTRATION. An example of lapping follows: Customer A remits $100 on account. The cashier or bookkeeper retains the $100 and makes no entry. A few days later, Customer B remits $150. Customer A is now credited with $100 and B with $50. The shortage remains at $100, the theft of the $100 from A's remittance is covered, and a shortage of $100 exists in the account of B. A few days later, Customer C remits $400 on account. Customer B is then credited with $100, C receives no credit, and the resultant shortage is $400.

These manipulations may go on indefinitely. Safeguards against lapping include a proper system of internal control, the matching of cash receipts with credits to customers' accounts, confirmation of accounts receivable, comparison of bank deposits against controlled duplicate deposit tickets, and review of bank statements for prior months to determine that inter-bank transfers did not involve "kiting," an act frequently necessary to cover lapping, as discussed on page 123.

i. Failure to account for returned and unclaimed dividend and payroll checks, and cashing these checks with forged endorsements. Someone other than the accountant or the cashier should open all returned mail in order to prevent this practice.

The theft of cash receipts may take many other forms, but in operating principle they are the same as those presented here; the circumstances of any one case may alter the specific method of manipulation.

3. Thefts of Cash by the Execution of Fraudulent Disbursements. In the theft of cash by the execution of fraudulent disbursements, numerous methods are used. The internal control remedies designed to prevent fraud through cash disbursements are discussed in the section of this chapter entitled "Installation of a System of Internal Control." Illustrations of several forms of fraudulent disbursements follows:

a. The theft of money from petty and other cash funds. Petty cash vouchers bearing forged approvals, incorrectly prepared vouchers with correct approvals, and used vouchers with altered dates are placed in the cash fund to cover the amount stolen. As an aid in the detection of this type of fraud, the auditor should permanently mark the used cash vouchers. Control of unused cash fund vouchers should not be vested in the fund cashier.

b. Forging checks, cashing them, and destroying them when they are returned by the bank. The cashier should not be given access to the returned paid checks, and all checks must be accounted for by the auditor. This form of fraud is practiced most successfully if checks other than the regularly used checks are obtained. In order to cover the fraud, cash disbursements posting totals must be raised; or unrecorded receipts must be deposited in the bank.

c. Raising the amounts of paid checks returned by the bank. Original record entries may be altered afterward, or they may be incorrectly stated before the check is prepared, for an amount in excess of the check mailed to a creditor. The fraudulent practitioner then abstracts the amount of cash representing the difference between the entry and the check. The cashier should not have access to returned checks, the checks must be examined for alterations.

d. Altering the date on a paid disbursements voucher and presenting it again for payment. The official signing the check should compare it with the voucher and should deface the voucher so that it cannot be presented again for payment. The date of payment should be ineradicably placed upon the voucher.

e. Preparing false vouchers for fictitious expenses and purchases, making false entries in the records of original entry, and preparing checks for the false payments. Usually, the vouchers and checks are prepared in favor of fictitious creditors, an accomplice accepts the check, or forgery is practiced by the employee. If the voucher and check are prepared in favor of a bona fide creditor, endorsements must be forged. Officials approving vouchers should be familiar with the creditors, and the auditor should have a knowledge of them. In addition, checks should be mailed directly by the last individual who signs them.

f. Kiting. Kiting occurs when a check on one bank (A) is deposited in another bank (B) and the amount of the check is not shown as a deduction from the balance in Bank A at the date of the transfer. This always occurs near the end of an accounting period. No entry is made, but the check deposited in Bank B covers the cash shortage and has the effect of increasing the balance of the cash in banks per the records at the end of the period, since the check has not cleared against Bank A. Kiting is practiced to cover the theft of cash and sometimes to pad a cash position. If it is practiced to pad a cash position, a false credit entry is made to income to equal the debit to Cash. Check-signing officials should be careful in signing checks toward the end of an accounting period. Kiting may be practiced with one bank alone or with many. The composition of cash deposits at the end of an accounting period must be watched, and returned paid checks for the first part of the next accounting period must be scrutinized.

g. Omitting merchandise purchase returns and allowances, thereby overstating the net purchases. Cash equal to the amount of the return is abstracted; or two checks are presented for approval at different times, one for the correct net purchase and the other for the return. The latter will bear forged endorsements. The preparation of vouchers must not be in the hands of the disburser of checks if this opportunity for fraud is to be closed.

h. Purchase discounts may be understated, underfooted, or apparently not taken, and the discount abstracted from cash. The auditor must compare purchase invoice terms with the disbursements records and the checks and must verify footings.

i. Overfooting cash disbursements credit totals in order to cover a straight cash theft. Some other total must also be overfooted.

j. Payroll manipulation is a fertile field for the criminally inclined. Fraud may be perpetrated through this source (1) by padding the earnings of employees, (2) by overfooting the payroll records, (3) by padding the payroll with fictitious employees, (4) by leaving ex-employees on the payroll, (5) by keeping unclaimed wages, and (6) by failing to record deductions from employees' wages. There are a multitude of other possibilities, but all are variations of the six mentioned.

Clever criminals constantly are at work devising new schemes to defraud employers and others. The auditor must be on guard at all times in order to frustrate criminal practices. There is no accounting system which cannot be manipulated by someone, either working alone or in collusion with another person. Both the independent auditor and the employer are more interested in preventing fraud than in tracing it after it has occurred. Prevention of any crime is much better than loss and subsequent prosecution and punishment of the criminal. A criminal intent is often forgotten if the temptation leading to its execution is removed by placing successful execution beyond all reasonable reach. In every business, then, there should be in operation a system of financial internal control which is efficient in safeguarding assets and in its sound business procedure. In the following discussion of the installation of such a system, the reader will note that most forms of fraud are prevented. Certain methods of executing fraud cannot be prevented completely by an internal control system; the auditor must be cognizant of these possibilities.

SECTION IV: INSTALLATION OF A SYSTEM OF INTERNAL CONTROL

Devoted to auditing in general, this text will not attempt a full discussion and demonstration of the procedures involved in the installation of a system of internal control under all possible operating conditions. The general procedures and the common safeguards applicable to the conditions usually found in business organizations will be considered.

In designing a system of internal control, the personnel should be segregated by functions into (1) those who initiate or authorize transactions; (2) those who execute the transactions; and (3) those who have responsibility for the asset, liability, expense, or revenue resulting from the transaction.

The system should adhere to the "Principles of Financial Internal Control" set forth in Section II of this chapter. Once installed, the system must be watched and controlled constantly—*it will not operate without supervision.*

From the standpoint of internal control, business transactions may be divided into the following classes: (1) purchase of assets and services, (2) sales of assets and services, (3) receipt of cash, (4) disbursement of cash, and (5) internal transactions.

Purchases of Assets and Services

General. Proper internal control over acquisition procedures demands that purchasing be segregated from receiving, from recording of the purchase, and from payment. The purchasing department of every company should have exclusive power to place properly authorized orders for all assets required by the organization. Purchases of services, such as labor, originate in and are authorized by the personnel department. The acquisition of professional services and of fixed assets is usually a power granted executive offices or vested in the board of directors. All routine purchases made by the purchasing department should bear the approval of a major executive. In small concerns, where a separate purchasing department cannot be maintained, one person in the organization should have exclusive power to initiate all purchases, and his purchases should receive the approval of another person.

Steps Involved. Each purchase made by a concern involves (1) the request for an item, arising in some department; (2) placing of the purchase order with a vendor; (3) receipt of the goods or services; and (4) approval of the invoice.

The Purchase Requisition. The department requesting assets or services sends a properly approved, written requisition to the purchasing department. The requisition is prepared with a sufficient number of copies to satisfy the requirements of the system; the original is sent to the purchasing department, and a copy is retained in the place of origin. The purchase requisition sets the purchasing department into operation for the instigation of the purchase.

The Purchase Order. The purchasing department should receive bids for the article requisitioned. The order is placed in conformity with the policy of the company as to such items as quality, quantity, price, packing, shipping, and so forth. The purchase order is issued after proper approval. The original copy is sent to the vendor; when accepted, this constitutes a contractual commitment. The number of additional copies will vary, depending upon the practices of the company. Copies may be sent to the requisitioning department, to the receiving department, to the accounting or treasury department, to the budget department, to the officer who approved the purchase order, and to the storekeeper. One copy is retained by the purchasing department and filed in an Orders Placed file. The copy to the requisitioning department serves as notice that the request is honored. In many concerns, the copy sent to the receiving department does not show quantities—thus properly forcing the receiving department to count and inspect the goods received. The copy to the accounting department places that department on notice concerning future cash disbursements. The copy to the budget department serves as the basis for appropriation reduction and as an indication of adherence to predetermined policy. The storekeeper's copy advises him of the fact that space must be provided for the material. When filing the purchase order, the purchasing department should attach its copy of the purchase requisition. If a purchase order is canceled by the company or if it is not accepted by the supplier, all copies thereof should be recalled and filed, because all purchase order numbers should be accounted for.

Receiving.   When received, the goods are weighed, counted, or measured, and inspected for quality and specification. The receiving department prepares its receiving report in quadruplicate at least; one copy is sent to the purchasing department, one to the storekeeper, one to the accounting department to be attached to the vendor's invoice, and one attached to the receiving department's copy of the purchase order and filed. The receiving department should be permitted to accept nothing as "received" unless a purchase order is on hand.

Invoice Procedure.   Invoices should not be approved until the goods have been inspected, counted, and approved. Invoices should be routed to the purhcasing department first, where they are stamped with the purchase order number, date of receipt, and verification of receipts. After the receiving report is accepted by the purchasing department, that department's copy of the purchase order is removed from the Orders Placed file and transferred to the Orders Filled file. The purchasing department approves the invoice, compares it with the receiving report, and forwards it to the accounting department, preferably with a copy of the receiving report. The accounting department compares the invoice with its copy of the purchase order and receiving report, and verifies extensions and footings; the invoice is then ready for payment. At payment, the invoice is stamped "Paid," together with the date; and the invoice and the accounting department's copy of the purchase order are filed. All invoices and vouchers must be approved by the proper disbursing officer.

This written review is frequently supported by a systems flow chart either maintained by the client or prepared by the CPA as part of his internal control review program.

Sales of Assets and Services

Cash Sales.   For cash sales, good internal control requires that one person makes the sale, to be verified by another person who receives payment and attends to the change making. The salesperson records the sale on a sales ticket. The total of the sales tickets prepared each day must equal the total of the cash received. A variation of this is to have the wrapper of the parcel check the sales slip against the price marked on the merchandise. Time is required to prepare cash sales tickets, and the modern trend is to have the salesman ring a cash register which ejects a slip recording the amount of the sale and which also accumulates the sales totals within the register. Each customer then pays a central cashier. The total money received by the central cashier must be in agreement with the total sales register accumulations. When it is not possible to have both salesmen and cashiers, cash registers with a visible sales record should be ued, together with the ejection of a slip showing the total of the sale, which is given to the customer. This tends to eliminate the possibility of not ringing or of underringing a sale.

Every business making sales for cash has a different problem to be solved. A good system of inventory control is an aid in correct accounting for cash sales. If the inventory is kept at retail, any discrepancies between physical and book inventories mean that either merchandise or cash is being stolen. Further control over the cash receipts is discussed in the next section entitled, "Receipt of Cash."

Credit Sales. Credit sales involve (1) receiving and preparing the sales order, (2) shipping the order, (3) charging and billing the customer, and (4) receiving payment from the customer. Credit sales procedures vary greatly for different concerns. General procedures are outlined here for a typical company interested in good control.

Preparing the Sales Order. When an order is received from a customer it is approved by the sales department and the credit division. After approval by the credit department, one copy is sent to the shipping department if the company manufactures in advance of orders received. The order serves as a notice of release from the storeroom. If the company manufactures on contract, one copy of the order is prepared for the manufacture of goods.

Shipping. Someone other than the person who gathers the order must check the merchandise against the order. In some cases, the shipping copy of the order is routed directly to the storeroom, where one employee calls the items and another gathers them, the calling employee making notations for deductions from the inventory records. Then, the goods and the shipping copy of the order are sent to the shipping room for final checking and shipment. The shipping department makes any alterations necessary, such as added transportation charges, and returns its copy of the order to the billing department.

Charging and Billing. The billing department changes other copies of the sales order to agree with the shipping department's copy for goods actually shipped. Sales invoices are then prepared by the billing department. The original sales invoice is sent to the customer; the duplicate is filed with the customer's order; the triplicate is sent to the accounting department; the quadruplicate is sent to the sales department, where the salesman is notified of shipment to his customer. When company truck deliveries are made, one or two copies accompany the truck driver, who has the customer sign as a delivery receipt. In some variations of the foregoing, all orders are copied onto an order sheet; and in some instances, a copy of the sales order serves as an invoice.

It is the duty of the sales and credit departments to be certain that orders are not fictitious. In department stores where charge accounts are maintained, the procedure is simpler and different in operation; but it is the same in principle. The salesclerk prepares a sales invoice in duplicate, giving the original to the customer and sending the duplicate to the accounting department, where it serves as the basis for a charge to Accounts Receivable, a credit to Sales, and a credit to Inventory.

In any situation, the accounting department's copy of the invoice is the original datum authorizing a charge to a customer. This function is exclusively that of the accounting department; it should not be given to the sales department and should not be handled by a cashier who later records the receipt of cash from the customer.

Sales Returns and Allowances.   A credit memorandum for sales returns and sales allowances should be executed and approved by a person who is not the accountant and not the cashier. Since returned merchandise should be routed to the receiving department (or to an adjustment desk), any questionable sales returns memorandums are traceable. False credit memorandums result in cash embezzlements or collusion with a customer and subsequent loss of accounts receivable. The credit memorandum for returned goods must be accompanied by authorization to the receiving department or the storeroom to accept the goods and place them on the inventory records again.

ILLUSTRATION.   During your audit of the XYZ Corporation, you note that a problem seems to exist in the credit sales area. In order to obtain more information, you have followed the document flow through the sales, billing and shpping procedures. The client had prepared a flow chart of the procedures as shown on page 131.

After review of the client's flow chart, you determined that the following weaknesses existed in the sales procedure of the XYZ Corporation:

(1) The sales department should not file part five of the Sales Invoice. This should be mailed to the customer as an acknowledgement of receipt of the order.

(2) The credit department should not file part six. The credit check should be made immediately and then returned with the "OK" to the sales department. In addition, the sales department should not route the other invoices to warehouse and shipping until it receives this credit approval. Under the present procedure, the merchandise is being shipped without credit approval.

(3) In shipping, the merchandise should be compared with the description on the "Mdse. Request 2." This is not being done.

(4) The "packing slip 4" should not be filed by shipping. It should be sent with the merchandise to the customer.

(5) A system should be initiated to cover the procedure if the goods are not available for shipment. The sales department should be notified.

(6) Numerical sequence of the "Mdse. Requests 2" should be accounted for by Billing at the time they are filed.

(7) In the accounting department, before the tape is discarded, the "Sales Invoice 3" file should be balanced to the general ledger sales control account.

Flowchart of Sales Procedure

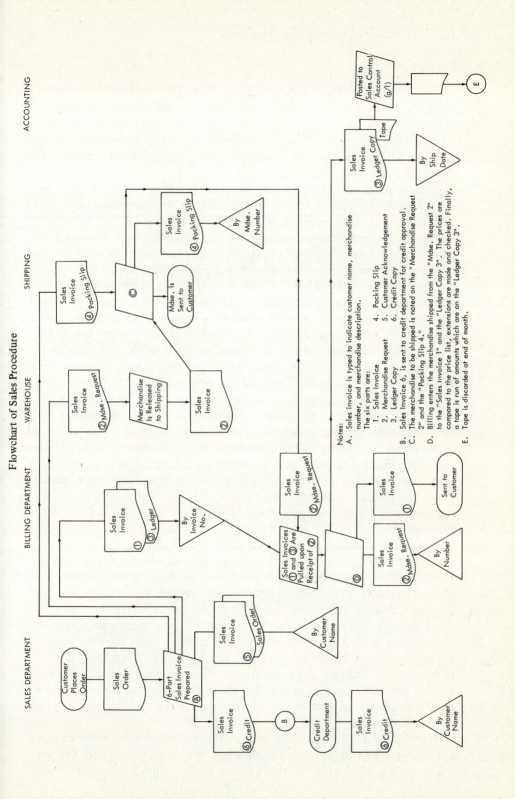

SALES DEPARTMENT   BILLING DEPARTMENT   WAREHOUSE   SHIPPING   ACCOUNTING

Notes:

A. Sales Invoice is typed to indicate customer name, merchandise number, and merchandise description.

The six parts are:

1. Sales Invoice   4. Packing Slip
2. Merchandise Request   5. Customer Acknowledgement
3. Ledger Copy   6. Credit Copy

B. Sales Invoice 6, is sent to credit department for credit approval.

C. The merchandise to be shipped is noted on the "Merchandise Request 2" and the "Packing Slip 4."

D. Billing enters the merchandise shipped from the "Mdse. Request 2" to the "Sales Invoice 1" and the "Ledger Copy 3". The prices are compared to the price list, extensions are made and checked. Finally, a tape is run of amounts which are on the "Ledger Copy 3".

E. Tape is discarded at end of month.

Receipt of Cash

Problems Involved. The operation of a system of internal control for cash receipts must result in assurance that all cash receipts are recorded as such as they are received and that all cash which should be received is received. Cash stolen before a record is made of its receipt is more difficult to trace than cash received and recorded, followed by a theft and manipulation of the records.

Certain procedures for the assurance of the proper original recording of cash receipts were discussed in this chapter in connection with cash and credit sales. In the section of this chapter entitled "Forms of Fraud," methods used in failing to account for cash receipts were discussed, together with certain steps necessary for their detection. In addition, the following internal control procedures must be established and enforced.

Cash Received by Mail. Cashiers should not open incoming mail, since this would give them access to cash and the opportunity for record manipulation. The mail must be opened by someone not connected with the cashier's office who does not have access to the formal accounting records and who does not have access to cash funds. All remittances received should be listed in detail, one copy being sent to the cashier for entry in the cash records and for the preparation of the bank deposit, another to the accounting department for entry in the receivable ledgers and the general ledger, and another to the treasurer for comparison with the controlled duplicate deposit tickets. The remittance list serves as a deterrent to lapping. The controlled duplicate deposit ticket shows any discrepancy between the true source of a bank deposit and the false source recorded on the records. The cash is sent directly to the treasurer, since the cashier need not even see it. Before depositing the money, the treasurer should compare the cash with the duplicate deposit ticket for amounts.

Interbank transfers of funds must be specifically approved in order to prevent kiting. The treasurer is properly controlled because both the cashier and the bookkeeper have their records of the money turned over to the treasurer. After the treasurer has verified the receipts and the duplicate deposit tickets, he should approve the deposit tickets and forward them to the internal auditing department for comparison with the records and with the subsequent bank statement. The internal auditing department must retain all data for the independent auditor; if there is no internal auditing department, the treasurer should retain the controlled duplicate deposit tickets for the independent auditor. The controlled duplicate deposit ticket affords the auditor a check against bank statement deposits.

If the person who opens the mail abstracts cash, the remitting customers can be relied upon to complain when they receive requests for payments previously made. If the cashier steals money, his records must be altered, thus making him eligible for detection by the auditor. Overstating sales discounts will be of no avail to a ledger clerk unless collusion exists between that clerk and the cashier. Cashiers must never have access to customers' accounts, since this opens the way to fraud and concealment made possible under the variety of forms discussed earlier in this chapter. If the foregoing procedures are followed, lapping and kiting are impossible unless collusion exists between employees.

Cash Clearing Point. All cash receipts should be cleared through one point in an organization. If there are branches where cash is collected, it may be locally deposited by the branch, with proper advice to the home office. The branch should not be permitted to make disbursements from its receipts.

The Receipt and Recording of Cash Should Be Separated. If two or more persons perform different duties in connection with cash receipts and the related accounting records, the possibilities of fraud will be reduced. The person receiving cash should not have access to the accounting records—subsidiary or control. In a retail store, one person should count the cash and prepare it for deposit; another person should compare the cash count with the sum of independently controlled cash register tapes, sales tickets, or adding machine tapes—depending upon the system in operation. The Sales and Accounts Receivable credit totals must be reconciled with the Cash Receipts debits and Sales Discounts and other debits.

Deposit Cash Intact. Cash should be deposited in the bank as it is received. Disbursements should not be made from receipt money but should be made by check or from specific funds established for that purpose.

Instructions to Customers and to Banks. Invoices and statements should show to whose order remittance checks should be made payable. Checks made payable to the order of "Cash," "Bearer," or a third party are easier to cash than checks made payable directly to the order of the properly named payee.

Depositary banks should be instructed in writing—by proper authorization of the board of directors in the case of corporations—to accept checks and other cash items for deposit only, thereby limiting the negotiability of the instruments.

Disbursements of Cash

Problems Involved. Satisfactory evidence must exist for the establishment of the validity of each cash disbursement. In order properly to control the disbursement of cash, it is necessary that there be separation of the activities of invoice approval (see the section of this chapter entitled "Purchases"), recording of the payables, preparing the checks in payment of invoices, and controlling the checks.

Petty Cash. Petty cash disbursements should be limited to established small-maximum amounts. Petty cash vouchers, used and unused, must be controlled. The petty cash voucher should be prepared in ink. It should be signed by the petty cash custodian and the payee, and it should be approved by a third person. After reimbursement, the vouchers should be canceled by someone other than the fund custodian, and before the petty cash custodian has access to them.

The Bank. Commercial account disbursements should be supported by filing with the depositary banks a resolution passed by the board of directors indicating those persons authorized to sign checks. All disbursements should be by check, since a receipt is thereby obtained automatically. Checks should not be prepared payable to the order of "Cash" or "Bearer."

The Voucher and Other Evidence. Properly authorized and properly approved vouchers should be the basis for check preparation. Once paid, a voucher must be so controlled that it cannot be presented again for payment; this control is effected by proper stamping or perforation. In addition, approved invoices and all other papers related to the voucher must be attached to it and stamped or perforated. Also, all unused voucher forms must be controlled in order to prevent false preparation. Purchase returns and allowances must be verified to be certain that the payment is not for an excess amount. Purchase discounts taken must be verified to ascertain that they are properly computed and that the payment check is not for an amount smaller than the voucher, thereby opening the way for the extraction of an equivalent sum from cash receipts.

The Check. The person who disburses the check should have no connection with the preparation or the approval of the underlying voucher. If checks bear more than one signature, neither signature should be that of the cashier. Checks should be mailed directly by the last person signing them, who should detach all vouchers and papers and return them to the accounting department.

In order to prevent check substitution and manipulation, returned paid check should be sent to some person other than the cashier or the accounting department. *After* reconciliation of the bank statements, the paid checks may be released to the accountant. All checks must be accounted for; paid checks must be examined for alteration and substitution by comparing them with original evidences such as invoices and vouchers. Checks that are spoiled and completed, but unused, must be voided immediately in order to prevent their possible misuse by depositing them as cash receipts, extracting an equivalent amount for cash receipts, and overstating the debit to an account—probably an expense.

Payroll Control

A discussion of payroll procedure could be placed with purchases or with cash disbursements. It is treated here independently and should be read carefully and also tied in with the section of this chapter entitled "Disbursements of Cash."

The Problems.   Payroll procedure involves (1) hiring; (2) keeping a record for each employee of the time worked and not worked; (3) computing the periodic pay, individually and in total; (4) paying the employee; and (5) termination of employment. See paragraph (*j*), item 3 under "Forms of Fraud" above which discusses possible methods of manipulating a payroll. Payroll manipulation may be accomplished by one person alone if precautions are not taken. Even with proper safeguards, the collusion of two or more employees makes fraud comparatively easy.

Separation of Duties.   In establishing proper internal control over payrolls, the duties of hiring, payroll computation, and payment of employees should be separated. The objectives of such separation are to prevent collusion, to avoid payroll padding, and to facilitate the work of the various persons charged with payroll duties toward the proper computation of the payroll. Of course, too much separation without proper reconciliation can lead to the fraud it is supposed to prevent.

Personnel Records.   If there is a personnel department, employees should be hired by that department on the basis of written requests from operating departments. The personnel department should maintain a record of each active employee, his name, address, social security number, original application, references, experience, date of employment, department, rate of pay, changes in pay rates and the effective dates thereof, and separation notices. The data are necessary not only for the employer but are required under the Fair Labor Standards Act and under the various Social Security Acts. Notification must be received by the personnel department when an employee terminates his employment, either voluntarily or by dismissal. The active personnel file should not be made available to payroll clerks, cashiers, or the paymaster.

Payroll Records.   Payroll records usually are made up of timecards or other original evidence of time worked, an individual earnings record, and a payroll journal or summary. In some medium-sized organizations, pegboard systems are frequently used to insure accuracy and internal control by providing for the preparation of the payroll journal, the employee's earnings record, and the writing of the payroll check in one operation.

In keeping the time record of an employee, a time-recording clock system is best; but the punching of the cards must be supervised, so that the cards of absentees are not rung in and out by fellow workers, time clerks, or foremen. The foremen should turn in daily reports for each man for his time spent on jobs, operations, idle time, and so forth. These reports are compared with the timecards by the payroll clerks; theoretically, the total hours and minutes worked per the report of time spent on jobs, operations, idle time, and so forth, should equal the elapsed time per the clock cards. If clock cards are not used, someone must be charged with the duty of reporting absences and time off for which payment is not to be made. As of the end of each day or the end of each pay period, the timecards, absentee reports, and late reports are inspected, and the necessary data—usually the time paid for—recorded on the earnings record of each employee. This work must be performed by a person who is not connected with the distribution of the pay to the employees.

The accumulation of the payroll should be prepared by a person not connected with the preparation of the currency or checks or with the distribution of the pay. Each individual's earnings record, per payroll period, should show the regular time worked, overtime, time lost, deductions for FICA benefits, unemployment insurance, hospital care, union dues, pension benefits, income taxes withheld, and other items, and the net cash to be paid. This same information must also be summarized into the total payroll for the period. When the individual earnings records and the payroll journal are prepared, the names of employees listed thereon must be compared with the active employment records of the personnel department. An employee of the accounting department must test-check the earnings records and the payroll journal and, in addition, must verify extensions and footings. The total of the checks or the total cash drawn must be verified against the proved total of the payroll. If the employees are paid in cash, the pay envelopes are prepared and sealed, after the cash has been counted and verified. When payment is by check, it is advisable to maintain a separate payroll account at the bank and to reimburse this account each pay period with the exact amount of the net cash to be distributed.

Paying the Employees. As far as internal control is concerned, it is almost immaterial whether the payment is made by check or cash. Wage payment by check is preferable, however. Payment by cash has many disadvantages, as follows:

1. Unclaimed wages are more easily appropriated by improper parties, since forgery is not necessary, except when employees must sign a receipt.
2. Payroll robbery may occur.
3. It is easier for the paymaster to withhold amounts that have been refunded from overpayments or to deduct amounts from an envelope where earnings have been overcomputed and to change the envelope to indicate the smaller amount. The receipts from the employee may then be raised by the paymaster to the figure appearing in the payroll journal.
4. It is easier to divert funds by padding the payroll.

The paymaster—not a member of the accounting department and not the person who originally computed the payroll—should pay the employees. The work of the paymaster is verified by an accompanying employee. Each employee is identified as he is paid; if he is paid in cash, the employee should sign a receipt for his wages. Identification takes many forms, from personal acquaintance, through identification tokens, to fingerprinting; but personal acquaintance is the best, since the other methods are cumbersome and costly and not always foolproof. The employee must be given a statement of his gross earnings, deductions, and net cash or check received. Later, if payment has been in cash, receipt signatures are compared with the signatures originally obtained for that purpose. Unclaimed envelopes are returned to the accounting department, and the paymaster or a payroll clerk retains the unsigned receipts until the wages are claimed or are returned to general cash or to a specific fund.

An annual verification of some value for the wages paid may be obtained by the controlled independent mailing of the federal W–2 forms by the auditor, with instructions that all complaints be addressed directly to him. If there has been payroll padding, the W–2 form would indicate more than was actually received; and an employee could be relied upon to complain, since he would be subject to a greater income tax based upon the W–2 form than would be due based upon his actual wage.

If the duties of the various employees are not segregated, payroll manipulation may be extremely easy. If one person prepares the earnings records and the payroll journal without verification by another person of the employment records and the time worked, he can pad the earnings of employees or place fictitious employees on the payroll and remove the excess amounts from the envelopes before giving them to the employees. Or if an accounting department employee prepares the payroll, he can pad the amounts or add fictitious names and pocket the difference when he prepares the pay envelopes. The payroll clerk (or the accounting department employee or the paymaster) could overfoot the payroll journal and abstract the amount of the overfooting if his work is performed alone or is not verified. If the payroll clerk pays the employees and if his records are not compared with employment department records, he could permit the names of ex-employees to remain on the payroll and retain the money; or he could fail to make payroll deductions on the payroll record, remembering, of course, to make the deductions in the pay envelopes.

Employment, timekeeping, and earnings record procedure and payment must be completely segregated from one another in order to assure accuracy and correctness of payroll procedure.

Inventory Control

Inventories are as important as money. The purposes and objectives of inventory control are to prevent theft and misuse, to serve as a guide in a purchasing program, and to expedite production orders and sales orders by insuring that proper items and quantities are in stock. It is necessary that the working capital cycle from cash through inventories and back to cash be properly controlled and guided. Small losses along a production line can become staggering in total.

A perpetual inventory system should be in operation, and general ledger controlling accounts should be maintained. A perpetual inventory system may be under the control of a stores clerk, or it may be maintained in the accounting department. If possible, one person should be made responsible for all materials received by and issued from the storerooms. This person should sign for all items received. A controlling account record of the receipts, issues, and inventory balances should be kept in the accounting department; periodically, this department will make its entries in summary form—not in detail. Thus, the perpetual subsidiary account totals are verified by a department that does not have access to the materials. The records of the storekeeper—in summary form—and the records of the accounting department should agree. Where differences exist, a record of the reconciliation must be maintained for review by the auditor.

Materials should leave the storeroom only upon receipt of written materials requisitions, properly authorized and executed. A duplicate requisition should remain in the requisitioning department for later comparison with the copy in the storeroom. The requisition received by the storekeeper serves as his authority to issue material and credit his accounts. His accounts may be formal, or they may be simply bin tags. The cost and general accounting departments are notified of the issuance by the storekeeper so that the proper order or department may be charged and the controlling inventory accounts (and duplicate perpetual inventory accounts, if they are kept) credited. The controlling accounts, the sum of the perpetual inventory accounts, and the results of a physical inventory should be in agreement. Fraud can arise through improper requisitions, theft, or collusion. If the materials and their records are separated and if receipts and issues are traced, theft is the only method of fraud possible, and it should be discoverable. In a concern that uses the unit retail inventory method of accounting control, the sales tickets or tags removed from merchandise serve as inventory credit data. Storage facilities should be studied so that items scattered in several places may not be missed, misplaced, or misused.

Control of Office and Sales Department Supplies.   The best plan of control for these items is to place them on the same basis of accountability as that established for inventories. However, it is a fact to be faced that many concerns do *not* control office and sales department supplies in that manner. If the inventory control system as outlined is not used, a central storage point—locked—should be selected for supplies. One person should be responsible for issuance, on the basis of a requisition by the person or department requiring supplies. Occasionally, a review should be made to determine if the requisitions of a person or a department are out of line with normal requirements.

Internal Control of Accounts Receivable

An account receivable can be credited when cash is received; a note receivable substituted; merchandise returned for credit; an allowance or discount granted; the account charged off as uncollectible; the correction for an overcharge; or the correction of an error where the wrong account was charged for a sale.

When statements are mailed to customers, the statements should be compared with the account receivable balances by a person other than the one who prepared the statements and not one who has a relationship to the routine duties of the accounts receivable clerk or the duties of the cashier. The person who compares the statements with the accounts should mail them; and the returned, undelivered statements should be routed directly—and unopened—to that person.

When cash is received from a customer, the procedures for internal control over cash prevail. Credits to Accounts Receivable arising from sales returns should be traced through the receiving department just as a purchase is traced. Credits to accounts receivable raising from sales allowances and uncollectible accounts should be supported by proper written authorizations. Credits arising from sales discounts should be reconciled with the cash receipts.

Internal Control of Investment Securities

Investments should be purchased and sold only upon proper authorization, the evidence of which should be examined by the auditor. Such evidence may be found in the actions of the board of directors, of finance committees, or of a person properly empowered to buy and sell. A detailed list or subsidiary ledger record of each security should be maintained independently of the person or persons exercising physical control of the securities. Investment securities should be kept in a safe-deposit box, and access to the box should be forbidden to any one person alone. Security registration should be in the name of the client. In some cases, where the title is vested in a nominee, the securities should bear blank endorsements in order to clear the title.

Internal Control of Fixed Assets

Fixed assets should be controlled not only physically but on the basis of a controlling account for each asset group, supported by subsidiary plant ledger accounts. Fixed assets should be acquired only upon proper requisition and authorization. Retirements of fixed assets should be by proper authorization, and a notice of retirement should be sent to the accounting department for proper account entries. In addition to controlling the acquisition and disposition of fixed assets, accounting for the proper handling of the investment credit must be provided for.

Many fixed assets are small but individually costly. They should be closely guarded against theft and frequently compared with the property inventory records.

ILLUSTRATION. Seven cash registers were busily ringing up sales at the Evanston, Ill., branch of a big Midwestern supermarket chain. Every night the register stubs checked out, usually to the penny. There was only one thing wrong; the chain had equipped the store with but six registers. The seventh was the idea and personal property of the store manager and his assistant who had set up their own private checkout counter. This scheme defied detection for 27 months. Meanwhile, more than $70,000 went through the extra register into the two conspirators' pockets.

Internal Control of Liabilities

The internal control procedures indicated for purchases and cash disbursements are applicable to liabilities also, since a liability results from the acquisition of an asset, the incurrence of an expense, or the conversion of another liability, and since the usual eventual liquidation of the liability is by the payment of cash or the amortization of the advance receipt.

The principle of internal control for liabilities should be to the effect that a liability cannot be incurred without proper authorization. Another principle is that liabilities should be handled so that they will be liquidated at the proper time in order to take advantage of discounts; to maintain a good credit rating; to comply with laws—such as the payment of income taxes withheld, social security taxes, and others; and to meet the legal requirements of contracts with respect to interest payments, bid deposits, and principal payments, or as in the case of advance receipts to make certain that income earned is recorded in the proper period.

Financial Internal Control for a Small Organization

The preceding discussion of internal control has been predicated on the assumption that the number of office employees is large enough to segregate accountabilities, duties, and authorities. In some cases, it may well be imagined that the organization must be of tremendous proportions to use an adequate system of internal control effectively.

There are more small concerns than large companies, and the part played by internal control is just as important to the small concern as to the large one. Assume a single proprietorship, consisting of the owner, and only one office employee, and a few salesclerks. The office employee performs all the accounting and other office work. Let it also be assumed that the one office employee is interested in maintaining his honesty—both with regard to his self-respect and with regard to the attitude of his employer toward him.

In order to effect reasonable internal control in the circumstances set forth, the duties of the *owner only*—without technical accounting knowledge—may be set forth as follows:

1. Purchases
   a) Maintain a sequentially prenumbered list of all purchase orders placed.
   b) As the goods and invoices from each purchase order are received, note the receipt on the proper purchase order.
2. Sales
   a) Keep all cash registers locked.
   b) Remove the cash register tapes, and/or
   c) Keep a record of all prenumbered sales tickets.
   d) Compare adding machine tapes of sales tickets with the tickets, with the Cash debit for the day, and with cash deposited in the bank.
3. Cash receipts
   a) Reconcile cash with sales tickets or cash register tapes (see 2, above).
   b) Open all mail.
   c) List remittances and *retain one copy of the list.*
   d) Deposit all cash *daily.*
   e) Compare bank deposit and Cash Receipts debit.
4. Cash disbursements
   a) Disburse by prenumbered and controlled checks.
   b) When paying invoices, stamp them "Paid," and tick off on the purchase order in item 1 (*a*), above.
   c) Add check disbursements daily or weekly, and compare with bookkeeper's Cash credit.
   d) Maintain a petty cash fund, and sign each petty cash voucher.
   e) Review (or prepare) the bank reconciliation.
5. Payroll
   a) Examine the payroll list, or the payroll journal, *noting the employees'* names, authorized gross pay, deductions, and net cash.
   b) *Add the payroll.*
6. Inventories
   a) Use retail system or other unit control, if possible.
   b) Supervise or personally count the inventory periodically.
7. Accounts receivable
   a) Test sales tickets, invoices, and so forth, against the statements.
   b) Personally mail the statements.
   c) Compare the statements with the accounts receivable ledger.

8. General
    a) Obtain an explanation of general journal entries.
    b) Become personally acquainted with the one office employee.
    c) Engage a competent independent auditor for a periodic audit, with interim visits.

QUESTIONS

1. Crampton Financing Inc. opened four personal loan offices in neighboring cities on January 2, 1975. Small loans are made to borrowers who repay the principal with interest in monthly installments over a period not exceeding two years. John Crampton, president of the Company, uses one of the offices as a central office and visits the other offices periodically for supervision and internal auditing purposes.

    Mr. Crampton is concerned about the honesty of his employees. He came to your office in December 1975 and stated, "I want to engage you to install a system to prohibit employees from embezzling cash." He also stated, "Until I went into business for myself I worked for a nationwide loan company with 500 offices and I am familiar with that company's system of accounting and internal control. I want to describe that system so you can install it for me because it will absolutely prevent fraud."

    a) How would you advise Crampton regarding his request that you install the large company's system of accounting and internal control for his firm? Discuss.
    b) How would you respond to the suggestion that the new system would prevent embezzlement? Discuss.

    (AICPA, adapted)

2. Adherence to generally accepted auditing standards requires, among other things, a proper study and evaluation of the existing internal control. The most common approaches of reviewing the system of internal control include the use of a questionnaire, preparation of a memorandum, preparation of a flow chart, and combinations of these methods.

    a) What is the objective of a CPA in reviewing internal control for an opinion audit?
    b) Discuss the advantages to a CPA of reviewing internal control by using:
        (1) An internal control questionnaire.
        (2) The memorandum approach.
        (3) A flow chart.
    c) If he is satisfied after completing his evaluation of internal control for an opinion audit that no material weaknesses in the client's internal control system exist, is it necessary for the CPA to test transactions? Explain.

    (AICPA, adapted)

3. a) At the outset of an audit, you reviewed the client's internal audit procedures and found them to be excellent. Does this indicate that a portion of your work is completed?

b)   How does internal auditing assist the independent auditor?

c)   Name several distinctive features of internal auditing.

4.   Internal controls may be characterized as being either administrative or financial.

a)   What are administrative internal controls?

b)   What are financial internal controls?

c)   What is the effect of administrative and financial internal controls on work of an independent auditor?

5.   An internal control questionnaire includes the items listed below. For each item, explain what is accomplished by the existence of the controls involved.

a)   Are costs and expenses under budgetary control?

b)   Is a postage-meter machine used?

c)   Are statements of account mailed to all customers once each month?

d)   Has the depositary bank been instructed not to cash checks made payable to the order of the company?

6.   Describe fully a good system of internal control which will minimize fraudulent possibilities for the following:

a)   Purchase of raw materials.

b)   Payroll for a company with (1) 4,000 employees and (2) 20 employees.

c)   Credit sales for a manufacturing company receiving its orders through the mail and also from field salesmen.

d)   Cash sales in general.

e)   Cash receipts from accounts receivable.

f)   Cash disbursements to creditors.

g)   Inventory receipts and issuance.

h)   Dividends received.

i)   Shipping department.

j)   Petty cash.

7.   You are auditing the records of a medium sized corporation that retails men's suits. Sales are made by five salesmen to approximately 1,500 charge customers. Because of his familiarity with retail men shops, the sales manager has been asked to approve each sale before it is written up. In the case of past-due accounts, it will also be his responsibility to determine whether additional credit can be extended. Further he will recommend the write-off of uncollectible accounts. One bookkeeper and two billing clerks handle the accounting records. As an independent auditor, in what way is your audit program affected by the credit procedures of your client?

8.   *a)*   Why does a CPA review the system of internal control of a client, and to what major questions does he seek answers in undertaking the review?

b)   Compare the extent of an auditor's review of internal control for the first examination of a new client with the review of the system of a client whose records he has examined regularly over a period of years.

9. Blankets, Inc., a new audit client, processes its sales and cash receipts documents in the following manner:

   (1) *Payment on account.* The mail is opened daily by a mail clerk in the sales department. The mail clerk prepares a remittance advice (showing customer and amount paid). The checks and remittance advice are then forwarded to the sales department supervisor who reviews each check and forwards the checks and remittance advice to the head of the accounting department.

   The accounting department head, who also acts as credit manager in approving new credit, reviews all checks for payments on past due accounts and then forwards the checks and remittance advices to the accounts receivable clerk. The remittance advices are posted directly to the accounts receivable ledger cards. The checks are endorsed by stamp and totaled. The total is posted to cash receipts. The remittance advices are filed chronologically.

   After receiving the cash from the previous day's cash sales, the accounts receivable clerk prepares the daily deposit slip in triplicate. The third copy of the slip is filed by date and the second copy and the original accompany the bank deposit.

   (2) *Sales.* Sales clerks prepare sales invoices in triplicate. The original and second copy are presented to the cashier. The third copy is retained by the sales clerk in the sales book. When the sale is for cash, the customer pays the sales clerk who presents the money to the cashier with the invoice copies.

   A credit sale is approved by the cashier from an approved credit list after the sales clerk prepares the three-part invoice. After receiving the cash or approving the invoice, the cashier validates the original copy of the sales invoice and gives it to the customer. At the end of each day the cashier recaps the sales and cash received and forwards the cash and the second copy of all sales invoices to the accounts receivable clerk.

   The accounts receivable clerk balances the cash received with cash sales invoices and prepares a daily sales summary. The credit sales invoices are posted to the accounts receivable ledger and then all invoices are sent to the inventory control clerk in the sales department for posting to the inventory control cards. After posting, the inventory clerk files all invoices numerically. The accounts receivable clerk posts the daily sales summary to the cash receipts and sales journals and files the sales summaries by date.

   The cash from cash sales is combined with the cash received on account to comprise the daily bank deposit.

   (3) *Bank deposits.* The bank validates the deposit slip and returns the second copy to the accounting department where it is filed by date by the accounts receivable clerk.

   Monthly bank statements are reconciled promptly by the accounting department supervisor and filed by date.

   You recognize that there are weaknesses in the existing system and believe a chart of information and document flows would be beneficial in evaluating this client's internal control in preparing for your examination of the financial statements. Complete the flow chart given below, for sales and cash receipts of Blankets, Inc. by labeling the appropriate symbols and indicating information flows. The chart is complete as to symbols and document flows. The symbols shown in the illustration are used.

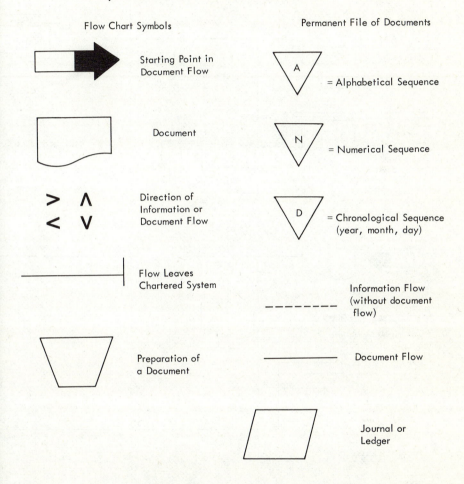

Flow Chart Symbols

Starting Point in Document Flow

Document

Direction of Information or Document Flow

Flow Leaves Chartered System

Preparation of a Document

Permanent File of Documents

A = Alphabetical Sequence

N = Numerical Sequence

D = Chronological Sequence (year, month, day)

Information Flow (without document flow)

Document Flow

Journal or Ledger

10. *a*) The policy of a client is that the pegboard payroll and supporting timecards accompany all payroll checks presented to the treasurer for his signature. The treasurer insists that the timecards be dated, marked paid, and the check number be placed on the timecards before he will review and sign the checks. The objective of the treasurer is to preclude the submission of fictitious timecards or the resubmission of timecards for which checks have already been drawn. Do you consider this procedure effective? Explain.

b) Why should the function of the payroll department and the regular disbursing activities be separated?

BLANKETS, INC.

Flow Chart for Sales and Cash Receipts

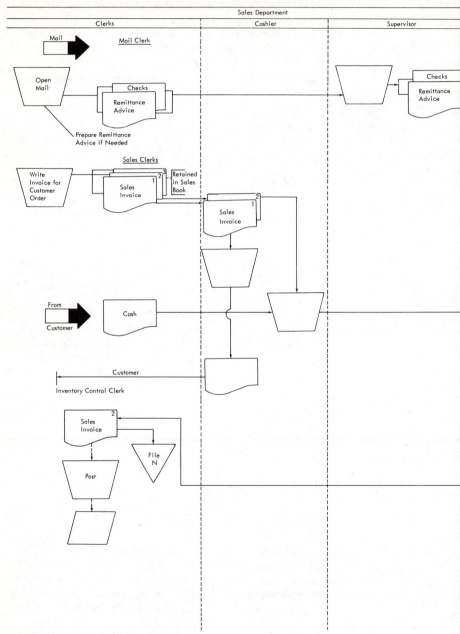

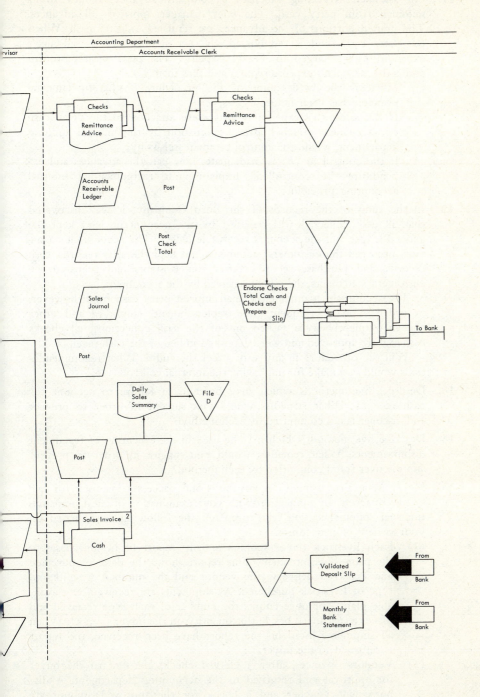

11. For salesmen's traveling expenses, a company advances money to its salesmen from petty cash. The sales manager approves all advances. The unused portions of the advances are returned to petty cash. When the petty cash fund is reimbursed, the net amount of the salesmen's expenditures is charged to Travel Expense. The petty cash custodian audits the salesmen's expense reports and files them.

    a) What is the weak point of the procedure? What fundamental principle has been ignored?

    b) If the salesmen's expense reports were attached to the petty cash reimbursement voucher after examination by the internal auditing department, would the control be adequate? Why?

    c) If the control in (*b*) is inadequate, how can the advances and expenditures be controlled? Explain your recommended internal accounting procedure.

12. In the audit of the records of the Burd Company, it was discovered that all cash collected was received by the accountant who kept the general ledger and the accounts receivable ledger. The accountant's assistants prepared the customers' statements and kept the sales records, cash records, and purchase records. After the assistants had prepared the customers' statements, they were received by the accountant.

    The accountant maintained a small imprest petty cash fund; however, in order to avoid frequent fund replenishment, employee and other checks frequently were cashed out of the cash collections; all checks cashed were approved and were deposited in lieu of the cash receipts.

    Will the procedure in any way affect the audit? What recommendations would you make for improving the internal control?

13. Describe five methods which may be used in failure to account for cash receipts. What remedies would you suggest in order to prevent and discover fraud committed by each method?

14. Describe five methods which may be used in the execution of fraudulent disbursements. What remedies would you suggest in order to prevent and discover fraud committed by each method?

15. Meyer Meat Processing Company buys and processes livestock for sale to supermarkets. In connection with your examination of the Company's financial statements, you have prepared the following notes based on your review of procedures:

    (1) Each livestock buyer submits a daily report of his purchases to the plant superintendent. This report shows the dates of purchase and expected delivery, the vendor and the number, weights and type of livestock purchased. As shipments are received, any available plant employee counts the number of each type received and places a tick mark beside this quantity on the buyer's report. When all shipments listed on the report have been received, the report is returned to the buyer.

    (2) Vendors' invoices, after a clerical check, are sent to the buyer for approval and returned to the accounting department. A disbursement voucher and a check for the approved amount are

prepared in the accounting department. Checks are forwarded to the treasurer for his signature. The treasurer's office sends signed checks directly to the buyer for delivery to the vendor.

(3) Livestock carcasses are processed by lots. Each lot is assigned a number. At the end of each day a tally sheet reporting the lots processed, the number and type of animals in each lot, and the carcass weight is sent to the accounting department, where a perpetual inventory record of processed carcasses and their weights is maintained.

(4) Processed carcasses are stored in a refrigerated cooler located in a small building adjacent to the employee parking lot. The cooler is locked when the plant is not open, and a Company guard is on duty when the employees report for work and leave at the end of their shifts. Supermarket truck drivers wishing to pick up their orders have been instructed to contact someone in the plant if no one is in the cooler.

(5) Substantial quantities of by-products are produced and stored, either in the cooler or elsewhere in the plant. By-products are initially accounted for as they are sold. At this time the sales manager prepares a two-part form; one copy serves as authorization to transfer the goods to the customer and the other becomes the basis for billing the customer.

For each of the numbered notes 1 to 5 above state:

a) What the specific internal control objective(s) should be at the stage of the operating cycle described by the note.

b) The control weaknesses in the present procedures, if any, and suggestions for improvement, if any.

(AICPA, adapted)

16. *a)* State several methods which may be used in the falsification of sales records.

b) Outline the procedure you would follow in order to detect falsification of those records.

17. Describe a suitable distribution of duties among the accounting department, the treasurer's department, and any other department to provide adequate protection of disbursements by check.

18. List five different methods to which dishonest employees may resort in manipulating payrolls. Do not give variations of the same method.

19. State at least four essential points which should be considered in the installation of an adequate system of internal control in a large manufacturing concern for (*a*) inventories and (*b*) payrolls.

20. Outline the steps necessary for a system of internal control for cash receipts for the following:

a) A theater.

b) A hamburger drive-in.

c) A hotel dining room.

d) A chain grocery store.

e) A franchised pizza parlor.

    f) A women's specialty shop selling for cash and credit.

    g) Income from bonds and stocks.

    h) A TV sales and service store.

21. A stockroom maintains individual inventory records. In such a situation, how would you be certain that an employee did not take goods home and simply credit his inventory accounts for the thefts?

22. One manufacturing company has 25,000 customers and 10 office employees. Another company manufacturing the same product has 250 customers and 2 office employees. Sales are proportionate, that is 100 to 1. For each company, outline a system of internal control for cash receipts and disbursements.

23. Enumerate five important items which should be considered by an auditor in the evaluation of the nature and extent of the internal control relating to accounts receivable of a merchandising company.

24. *a*) A medium-sized manufacturing company requests an evaluation of its system of internal control. What are some of the factors and procedures to look for in determining the effectiveness of the operation of a system of internal control?

    b) Your client is the sole owner of a small business. He mistakenly believes that because he has few employees, a system of internal control is not practicable for his business. List 10 control measures which can be instituted in such a situation to provide reasonable internal control.

(AICPA, adapted)

25. A medium-sized manufacturing concern requests an outline of the duties of its office employees, so that a good system of internal accounting control may be effected. The employees, four in number, are as follows: an officer, a cashier, a bookkeeper, and a clerk.

26. Three people (A, B, and C) constitute the accounting staff of a small wholesale dry goods company. In addition to the three persons in the accounting department, two men are in the warehouse and two more are drivers of the company's delivery trucks. The two men in the warehouse handle all goods coming in as well as assist the drivers in loading their trucks to make daily deliveries. In some instances, the drivers make collections before deliveries are permitted to be made. Outline a satisfactory system of internal control for cash. The cash receipts and disbursements are approximately $750,000 per year.

PROBLEMS

1. The Harmony Loan Company has 100 branch loan offices. Each office has a manager and four or five subordinates who are employed by the manager. Branch managers prepare the weekly payroll, including their own salaries, and pay employees from cash on hand. Each employee signs a payroll sheet signifying receipt of his salary. Hours worked by hourly personnel are inserted on the payroll sheet from timecards prepared by the employees and approved by the manager.

    The weekly payroll sheets are sent to the home office together with other accounting statements and reports. The home office compiles the employees' earnings records and prepares all federal and state salary reports from the weekly payroll sheets.

Salaries are established by home office job-evaluation schedules. Salary adjustments, promotions, and transfers of full-time employees are approved by a home office salary committee based upon the recommendations of branch managers and area supervisors. Branch managers advise the salary committee of new full-time employees and terminations. Part-time and temporary employees are hired without referral to the salary committee.

a) Based upon your review of the payroll system, how might funds for payroll be diverted?

b) Prepare a payroll program to be used in the home office to audit the branch office payrolls of the Harmony Loan Company.

(AICPA)

2. The following eight functions are to be performed by three clerical employees of a client:

a) Maintain the general ledger.

b) Maintain the accounts payable ledger.

c) Maintain the accounts receivable ledger.

d) Prepare checks for signature.

e) Maintain the cash disbursements records.

f) Issue credits for returns and allowances.

g) Reconcile the bank account.

h) Handle and deposit cash receipts.

There is no problem regarding the ability of the three employees. You are requested to assign the listed functions to the three employees in a manner to achieve the highest degree of internal control. The three employees will perform no accounting functions other than those listed; accounting functions not listed will be performed by other client personnel.

a) How would you distribute the listed functions among the three employees? Assume that with the exception of the preparation of bank reconciliations and the issuance of credits for returns and allowances, all functions require an equal amount of time.

b) What are four unsatisfactory combinations of the listed functions?

(AICPA, adapted)

3. The board of trustees of a local church requests you to review its accounting procedures. As a part of this review you have prepared the following comments relating to the collections made at weekly services and record-keeping for members' pledges and contributions:

a) The board of trustees has delegated responsibility for financial management and audit of the financial records to the finance committee. This group prepares the annual budget and approves major disbursements but is not involved in collections or record-keeping. No audit has been considered necessary in recent years because the same trusted employee has kept church records and served as financial secretary for 15 years.

b) The collection at the weekly service is taken by a team of ushers. The head usher counts the collection in the church office following each service. He then places the collection and a notation of the amount counted in the church safe. Next morning the financial secretary opens the safe and recounts the collection. He withholds $100 to meet cash expenditures during the coming week and deposits the remainder of the collection intact. In order to facilitate the deposit, members who contribute by check are asked to draw their checks to "cash."

c) At their request a few members are furnished prenumbered predated envelopes in which to insert their weekly contributions. The head usher removes the cash from the envelopes to be counted with the loose cash included in the collection and discards the envelopes. No record is maintained of issuance or return of the envelopes, and the envelope system is not encouraged.

d) Each member is asked to prepare a contribution pledge card annually. The pledge is regarded as a moral commitment by the member to contribute a stated weekly amount. Based upon the amounts shown on the pledge cards, the financial secretary furnishes a letter to requesting members to support the tax deductibility of their contributions.

Describe the weaknesses and recommend improvements in procedures for

a) Collections made at weekly services.

b) Record-keeping for members' pledges and contributions.

(AICPA, adapted)

4. Indicate by number and letter the best answer for each of the following items which relate to internal control. Choose only one answer for each item.

(1) From the standpoint of good procedural control, distributing payroll checks to employees is best handled by the
   a) Treasury department.
   b) Personnel department.
   c) Payroll accounting section.
   d) Departmental supervisors.

(2) To minimize the opportunity for fraud, unclaimed salary checks should be
   a) Deposited in a special bank account.
   b) Kept in the payroll department.
   c) Left with the employee's supervisor.
   d) Held for the employee in the personnel department.

(3) A responsibility that should be assigned to a specific employee and not shared jointly is that of
   a) Access to the company's safe deposit box.
   b) Placing orders and maintaining relationships with a prime supplier.
   c) Attempting to collect a delinquent account.
   d) Custodianship of the cash working fund.

(4) For control purposes the quantities of materials ordered may be omitted from the copy of the purchase order which is
   a) Forwarded to the accounting department.
   b) Retained in the purchasing department's files.

     c)   Returned to the requisitioner.

     d)   Forwarded to the receiving department.

 (5) Jones Co. has an inventory of raw materials and parts consisting of thousands of different items which are of small value individually but significant in total. A fundamental control requirement of Jones Co.'s inventory system is that

     a)   Perpetual inventory records be maintained for all inventory items.

     b)   The taking of physical inventories be conducted on a cycle basis rather than at year-end.

     c)   The storekeeping function not be combined with the production and inventory record-keeping functions.

     d)   Materials requisitions be approved by an officer of the Company.

 (6) The sales department bookkeeper has been crediting house-account sales to her brother-in-law, an outside salesman. Commissions are paid on outside sales but not on house-account sales. This might have been prevented by requiring that

     a)   Sales order forms be prenumbered and accounted for by the sales department bookkeeper.

     b)   Sales commission statements be supported by sales order forms and approved by the sales manager.

     c)   Aggregate sales entries be prepared by the general accounting department.

     d)   Disbursement vouchers for sales commissions be reviewed by the internal audit department and checked to sales commission statements.

                                (AICPA, adapted)

5. Indicate by number and letter the best answer for each of the following items which relate to internal control. Choose only one answer for each item.

 (1) The best statement of the CPA's primary objective in reviewing internal control is that the review is intended to provide

     a)   Reasonable protection against client fraud and defalcations by client employees.

     b)   A basis for reliance on the system and determining the scope of other auditing procedures.

     c)   A basis for constructive suggestions to the client for improving his accounting system.

     d)   A method for safeguarding assets, checking the accuracy and reliability of accounting data, promoting operational efficiency, and encouraging adherence to prescribed managerial policies.

 (2) A company holds bearer bonds as a short-term investment. Custody of these bonds and submission of coupons for interest payments normally is the responsibility of the

     a)   Treasury department.

     b)   Legal counsel.

     c)   General-accounting department.

     d)   Internal-audit department.

(3)   Operating control of the check-signing machine normally should be the responsibility of the

    a)   General-accounting department.

    b)   Treasury department.

    c)   Legal counsel.

    d)   Internal-audit department.

(4)   Matching a supplier's invoice, the purchase order, and the receiving report normally should be the responsibility of the

    a)   Warehouse-receiving department.

    b)   Purchasing department.

    c)   General-accounting department.

    d)   Treasury department.

(5)   A CPA learns that his client has paid a vendor twice for the same shipment, once based upon the original invoice and once based upon the monthly statement. A control procedure that should have prevented this duplicate payment is

    a)   Attachment of the receiving report to the disbursement support.

    b)   Prenumbering of disbursement vouchers.

    c)   Use of a limit or reasonableness test.

    d)   Prenumbering of receiving reports.

(AICPA, adapted)

6.   Two separate features of the operating methods of the Frampton Company are described below. You are to point out (*a*) any existing weaknesses in internal control, including an explanation of possible errors or manipulations that might occur because of each weakness; and (*b*) recommendations for changes in procedure for the correction of each weakness.

a)   When materials are ordered, a duplicate of the purchase order is sent to the receiving department. Upon receipt of the materials, the receiving clerk records the receipt on the duplicate of the purchase order and sends it to the accounting department to support the accounting entry. The materials are then taken to the storeroom where the quantity is entered on bin tags.

b)   A sales branch of the company has an office force consisting of the branch manager and one assistant. The branch has a local bank account from which branch expenses are paid. The account is in the name of "Frampton Company, Special Account." Checks drawn on the account require the signature of either the branch manager or the company treasurer. Bank statements and paid checks are returned by the bank to the branch manager who reconciles the account and retains all materials in his files. Disbursement reports are prepared by the branch manager and submitted to the home office on scheduled dates.

(AICPA, adapted)

7.   The Curtainwall Company carries a fidelity bond covering its branch manager, located in Jackson City. The coverage under the policy was $10,000 to December 31, 1975; as of that date, the coverage was increased to $20,000, because of increased business.

    On August 3, 1976, the branch manager disappeared. He wrote to the home office stating that he was short to the extent of $24,000, that he was hopelessly involved, and that he was leaving the country.

The branch manager had been in charge of all branch transactions. Each day, he remitted to the home office a report setting forth the quantities of each item sold and received, and stating the daily opening and closing inventories. The report also detailed charge sales and cash sales; cash receipts also were detailed by cash sales and accounts receivable collections. Branch cash receipts were deposited in a bank account, subject to withdrawal only by the home office. The home office compared the bank statements with the reports of the branch manager; they were in agreement. At the end of each month, a home office representative visited the branch and counted the inventory; he then compared his count with the end-of-the-month branch report.

After the manager had announced his shortage, the Curtainwall Company requested that its certified public accountants verify the shortage. With the consent of the company, the accountants circularized all receivables and received confirmations to the extent of 80 percent of the total of the receivable dollars. A summary of the examination showed that the claim against the insurance company consisted of 100 account names, totaling $24,000.

You are employed by the insurance company and are requested to accept the results of the circularization of the company accountants after reviewing their work; the company accountants willingly cooperate with you; this cooperation avoids the necessity of another request for confirmation.

Explain (*a*) the method of embezzlement used by the manager and (*b*) the steps you would take in your investigation of the $24,000 claim.

8. The Jetson Corporation became your client in 1975 when its former CPA died. You have completed your initial examination of Jetson Corporation's financial statements for the year ended December 31, 1975, and have prepared a draft of your audit report containing your unqualified opinion which was addressed to the board of directors according to instructions. In addition, you have drafted a special report in letter form outlining deficiencies in the system of internal control noted in the course of your examination and your recommendations for the correction of these deficiencies.

When you reviewed the drafts of these reports with Jetson's president, he instructed you not to render the internal control letter. The president stated that he was aware the deficiencies existed and would give them his personal attention. Because he felt the board of directors should be concerned with major policy decisions and not with day-to-day management problems, the president believed the board should not be burdened with such matters.

a)   What factors would you consider before deciding whether or not you should render the internal control letter?

b)   If you decide to render the internal control letter to Jetson Corporation, should it be rendered to the board of directors or the president?

(AICPA, adapted)

5

Internal Control: Electronic Systems

SECTION I: INTRODUCTION

In a book devoted to the audit function, it is not feasible or practical to enter into an in-depth treatise on computer programming or computer operating procedures; these basics belong in other texts and other courses of study.

The responsibilities set forth in the preceding chapter relating to internal control for manual systems are also applicable where electronic systems are used for all or some of the phases of financial record keeping. There are many instances where the internal auditor's duties and responsibilities are even further emphasized when electronic systems (EDP) are used for data processing because of the possible loss of data due to "erase" instructions being erroneously or improperly given and also because of improper storage of data which may cause them to be erased.

SECTION II: INTERNAL CONTROL:
ELECTRONIC SYSTEMS

In order for an EDP system to function at its best, clear lines of authority and responsibility must be established. The functional responsibilities should provide for the separation of initiation and authorization of a transaction and the recording of the transaction. Further separation is desired in establishing responsibility for the protection of the assets. If such separation is built into an EDP system, efficiencies from specialization will result and it will also be possible to make cross-checks that promote accuracy without duplication of effort. As a result of EDP systems, there has been made possible much centralization of processing of financial transactions.

Under manual systems it was not uncommon to have separate departments for order filling, production, marketing, budgeting, and many others. Today, however, the data processing center is performing most or all of these functions and a greater coordination of effort is possible. Reports can now be generated that will permit more accurate evaluation of how a department is functioning and its effect on the operation of the entire organization. For example, analyzed sales reports reveal that sales of a particular product are increasing at a faster rate than budgeted. Determination of the rate can be made, and this information would be made immediately available to the production department so that the material as well as production facility needs can be arranged. Also, it can be determined what effect this will have on the organization's financial needs. The extent of analysis will determine the degrees of integration of the entire organization and the effectiveness of the internal control that exists. If there is good integration of the financial and organizational activities, reports can be prepared for many departments from a single record of each business transaction.

Reliance upon the System of Internal Control

Since the data processing is carried out in one department, importance of control cannot be overemphasized. Keeping in mind that there must be separation between people who authorize transactions, record transactions, and are responsible for the safeguarding of the company's assets, satisfactory internal control can only be maintained if adequate procedures are provided. In an EDP system, just as in a manual system, we must keep in mind the requirements of such groups as the Securities and Exchange Commission, the American Institute of Certified Public Accountants, and the New York Stock Exchange. The independent auditor must satisfy himself as to the adequacy of the system of internal control. For example, if a salesman sends in an order to be filled and after inspecting it for description manually the order is processed by a computer system, the auditor must be able to determine the integrity of the system by determining that the authorization of the transaction was properly executed, that the recording function was properly executed, and that the information storing function has been properly executed. To insure these major aspects of internal control there would have to be physical as well as operational segregation of the tapes or disk packs and the scheduling of personnel from machine room operations.

Control by the Department Originating Data (Input Control)

How much control the department originating the data to be processed has is largely dependent upon the size of the company. Where large companies are involved, one will find many using departments, and this requires extensive internal control. Frequently the final coordinating of the material is through someone outside the data processing department. For example, a large company has established a sales control group. The company maintains sales records on its disk packs for its 15,000 customers. This sales control group performs the following internal control functions:

1. Reviews all changes in the sales records—such as change in territory, change in salesman, and changes in terms of sale.
2. Compares the sales on reports from the territory sales to the total sales and to other sales reports.
3. Reviews the exceptions and differences to determine what action must be taken to adjust these exceptions.

Point 3, above, may be described as the editing function. In order for this function to be properly performed by the computer, programmed checks must be built into the instructions or program. For example, the auditor wants the program to detect the loss of data. This would be accomplished for salesmen's orders taken by assigning each salesman a number and assigning each week of the year a number. His record would show a report for each week, or if not, the computer would print out the fact that a certain week was missing. Also, it would prevent the sending in of two reports for a week as the machine would reject the second report. Another programmed check would be the arithmetic function. For example, if a salesman is to charge $10 per unit for a product and he would make a calculation at $8 per unit, the machine would reject his calculation. Another programmed check would be one to determine that all transactions are posted to the proper record. If the auditor wanted to determine whether or not a salesman has been paid all the commissions he is entitled to for the sales he has made, this could be verified by giving the computer a print-out instruction, and the recorded commissions would be printed out. When compared with the sales department's records, this would provide the verification.

Programmed controls to detect and correct errors are vitally important in any EDP system. In order to insure internal control of these procedures, immediate handling of all errors should be taken care of by the program. In this way errors will be handled separately and in such a manner that the audit trail will be maintained and that the corrections will be properly reentered into the system.

Output Controls

Even though great care may be taken in developing programmed controls, output controls must be provided for. Comparisons of control totals of data processed with totals independently arrived at by departments responsible for original source data are mandatory if a satisfactory system of internal control is to be maintained. A definite sampling program of individual items processed will also provide another means of output controls. By breaking the sampling procedures down among the several interested groups or departments, the inaccuracies that frequently develop, with routine sampling, are eliminated.

Administrative Controls

In order for an EDP system to provide maximum internal control, administrative controls are absolutely necessary. Complete documentation of systems design and programming must be maintained so that the system can be evaluated and modified when necessary. Lack of documentation can and will create chaos in an EDP system. Data system survey, data systems study, and programming must be provided if an EDP system is to operate with any degree of reliability.

Accurate computer programming cannot be overemphasized. The preparation of flow charts, program listings, and computer operating instructions must be complete in every detail. The computer will do no more than it is instructed to do. Since more and more users of EDP equipment are using off-premises facilities, a tight control of all phases of the program must be maintained. At the very least a programming manual should be set up and currently maintained. This should consist of a written record of all policies, procedures, and techniques that are to be standard throughout the departments that are using the computers. This would insure well-formulated and well-documented procedure changes, and thus should prevent the manipulation of the system by unauthorized persons.

Summary of Internal Computer Controls

1. Whenever changes are made in memory records such as the fixed asset control account or payroll and inventory records, the change should be initiated by persons other than those immediately involved with the change. For example, the personnel department should initiate the information regarding a person joining or leaving the firm; the superintendent or division head should not initiate this information.
2. Serially prenumbered documents should be used, whenever possible, authorizing changes to master records. This prenumbered document should be recorded at the point of issue and again in the data processing department where authorization for this change should be verified.
3. Computer operating personnel should at no time be permitted to check and record the receipt and distribution of input, output, and traffic between the program and the machine steps. In addition, computer programming personnel should *not be permitted* to use the computer.
4. Batch totals, number of documents or total dollars, or hash totals,

adding of invoice numbers, and so forth, would assist in providing suitable controls for master records. In this manner control information is maintained independently of the computer for each type of master data. For example, control accounts should be maintained for each type of deduction from a numerical or financial item.

5. Accurate records should be kept on all data file maintenance and its updating. The original notifications should be kept on file in the data processing department and it should also contain a copy of the notification of the updating that was sent to the point of issue.

6. To assume that source data is being verified, master file data should be printed out periodically.

7. The following records of movement of data should be accurately maintained by the data processing control group:

    a)   A receipt indicating the source of data.

    b)   A log indicating when the data were processed by the computer.

    c)   A log indicating when the data was returned from being processed, and a receipt indicating the return of the data to the source.

    d)   A log listing all output records and reports received from processing.

    e)   A log detailing the distribution of output records and reports.

8. Input controls are essential and the records control group in data processing should possess the following:

    a)   A document count.

    b)   Control totals for hours, rates, dollars, units, pounds, voucher numbers, and so forth.

    c)   Batch controls consisting of document count and control totals.

    d)   Batch summary totals run daily, weekly, or on some other cycle which will provide the necessary check.

    e)   Finally, a system summary total which will control the tremendous variety of document batches involving the total system. For example all the facets of accounting for a payroll.

9. Output controls are essential and the records control group in data processing should have the following:

    a)   All columnar totals.

    b)   Hash totals, like totals of voucher numbers in a batch so that it can be determined that all data have been included.

    c)   Record counts which clearly relate to the number of specific records involved in a transaction or an account balance, or the total system balance.

    d)   Complete cross footings to verify columnar total or totals.

    e)   Limit checks. These are instructions which cause the computer to reject listings of any data not within the programmed limits.

f) During processing, check points should be established which will provide a means of locating errors early and quickly thereby making it unnecessary to rerun an entire program when an error is discovered.

g) The establishing of a zero balance is desirable to prove accuracy of computations within a known total.

10. A parity check, which assures that proper sequence of data is maintained, should be built into the computer program.

11. Preauthorization of *all* computer usage, especially overtime, should be required and a record maintained. Also contained in this preauthorization of usage would be the operating instructions, programs to be used, reference files to be drawn from the data processing library, and planned start and stop time of the run.

12. To complement the preauthorization of computer use, computer operators should maintain operating logs which would include estimate versus actual run time.

13. Whenever possible, no operator should be permitted to operate the computer alone. A second person should be present and both initial the operating log.

14. Whenever errors are made, a register of errors should be maintained supported by a printout of the error, action taken, and record of the manual intervention. It is highly desirable to maintain a printout record of all manual interventions.

15. When control totals are programmed, they should be checked by someone other than the computer operator. An even more desirable procedure would be to have the program build up and check its own controls against the input data. Certainly no output should leave the data processing department without passing through the records control group for their verification.

16. Magnetic tapes or disks should be kept in a library and someone other than the programmers or computer operators should be responsible for their safekeeping. That person should:

a) Maintain a written record of each tape or disk with the history of its use, including content, updating, run numbers, number of passes, reference label and any other information needed to identify the reel or disk.

b) Definitely tie in tape or disk usage with the preauthorization procedure so that no tape or disk can be issued without proper preauthorization.

c) Use a follow up or trailer label with control totals of selected items updated during processing. In addition, the record control group should maintain similar but independent controls for comparison.

d) Not permit any reference or master tape or disk to be over-written during an amending or updating process. A new tape or an updated disk should be written so that generation identification can be maintained.

e) Provide different locations for security for master tapes or disks of exceptional importance. In addition, it would be desirable to keep the supporting documents.

f) Provide a safe file for disks and tapes at point-of-use.

17. Data processing operations should include a register of all changes regardless of their nature and cross-reference to other programs which might be affected by the change should be noted. Changes or new programs should not be allowed in operation until they have been tested and approved by the head of data processing.

18. If at all possible, only one person should be responsible for an operation at any one time. There must be a division between the employees who authorize a transaction and produce the input, as well as those who process the data and those who use the data.

19. Employees should be rotated within the data processing group. As can be seen, this should prevent an employee from so dominating an area of operations that losses from fraud or error are not detected.

20. In addition to rotating personnel, it is desirable to bond key personnel. This will impress the persons involved with their responsibilities and should prompt a review of a firm's internal control of its computer operations by the insurance company.

Internal Control Illustrated

An example of how internal control is developed and maintained for an EDP system follows. The case deals with a market research firm that has independent research individuals and supervisors conducting surveys in many cities. In each city there is a supervisor who coordinates the research and sends in the reports at designated intervals. In addition, each supervisor submits a report of each researcher's activity which include the time spent, miles traveled, and incidental expenses necessary to the performance of his duties. When these reports are received by the research firm, they are compared with a master program of studies maintained by the Field Coordinator. After determining the validity of the report, it is turned over to the accounting department for proof of calculations. When a study is started the Field Director is responsible for informing the Field Coordinator as to vital statistics of the field representatives and their supervisors. It will then be the responsibility of the Field Coordinator to prepare the necessary card input forms so that when the mathematical accuracy of the field representative's reports has been verified, the voucher record can be prepared and the necessary checks written by the computer. The accounting department will then verify the accuracy of the voucher register and written checks and mail them, together with a correct copy of the report, to the proper person.

The duties and responsibilities of the various individuals and departments involved in this program are as follows:

COMPUTER PROGRAMMING DEPARTMENT:
1. Develop program and test to determine its ability to meet the controller's instructions.
2. Acts in a consulting capacity when problems arise or changes needed to be made in the program.
3. Will not have any duties related to verifying mathematical accuracy of reports of field representatives and supervisors.
4. Will not participate in the preparation and running of the card input information.
5. Will not participate in the preparation and running of the summary card edit which is needed to prepare the invoice record.
6. Physical facilities and supervision are completely separate from all other persons and departments involved in this program.

FIELD DIRECTOR:
1. Organizes market research projects and obtains the necessary field representatives and supervisors to perform the market research work.
2. Completes written authorization for payment of researchers, stating the vital statistics of the individuals as well as the rates of pay.
3. Is responsible for informing the Field Coordinator in writing as to additions or deletions of field representatives and supervisors as well as changes in pay rates.

FIELD COORDINATOR:
1. Maintains an up-to-date master list of all studies and their location as well as the field representatives and supervisors engaged to perform the market research work.
2. Maintains up-to-date rate file and payment dates.
3. Upon the written instruction of the Field Director, card input forms will be completed which identify the field representative and supervisor together with the various rates for the activities required.
4. Prepares print-out and/or delete instructions when a field representative or supervisor is no longer performing any services.
5. Is completely separate as to physical facilities and supervision in relation to all other persons and departments involved in this program.

CONTROLLER OF THE ACCOUNTING DEPARTMENT:
1. Responsible for determining mathematical accuracy and completeness of coding of field representatives' and supervisors' reports.
2. Submits report to computer department for card punching and preparation of summary card edit report making sure that the parity

bit is provided for so that the transfer of the information to the disk pack can be confirmed.

3. Compares all rejected items with respective reports and makes necessary corrections on reports.

4. Has the computer department cut new cards from corrected reports and preparation of corrected summary card edit report.

5. Upon preparation of correct summary card edit report, the computer will then run the invoice register.

6. A final comparison of field representatives' and supervisors' reports is made with the invoice register before the computer writes the checks.

7. The checks are then written by the computer and a summary of the various charges is also pointed out. In addition a hash total is created consisting of the total of the hours worked.

8. This distribution is compared with the invoice register and any errors are corrected.

9. The approved checks with the supporting report are then mailed to the designated person.

10. At no time will the accounting department have anything to do with the authorizing of persons to be paid in this manner.

11. At no time will the accounting department have anything to do with assigning identifying numbers or rates of pay.

12. At all times the physical facilities as well as supervision will be completely separated from all other persons and departments involved in this program.

SECTION III: AUDITING ELECTRONIC SYSTEMS

Compared to old-fashioned fraud, computer fraud may appear to be very elusive. However, there are methods of guarding a computerized business operation from embezzlers.

Businesses that rely on data processing are vulnerable in two general areas—on-premises with their own computers, and off-premises with their data processing provided by a service bureau. With the advent of small, relatively inexpensive, and very powerful computers, the on-premises problems have grown at an ever-increasing rate. However, most large CPA firms now are advising and assisting their clients in designing their data processing system and making it operational. They take care in counseling their clients as to the importance of (1) careful screening and testing of data processing employees, (2) making certain that there is limited access to the computer and the file library, and (3) developing a sound recovery plan in an event that operations are disrupted.

The off-premises problem is very different. Once it was commonly thought that off-premises EDP services bore all the responsibility of auditing the records they processed for their various users. Since that is no longer the case, new standards are being and have been developed for the audit of off-premises EDP services.

It is quite easy for a computer crook to fool an auditor who does not understand data processing. There is no short cut to the proper training of the auditor in the uses—and abuses—of a computer system. However, valuable aids have been developed for conducting a thorough and efficient audit of computerized records. All large CPA firms have developed satisfactory programs for auditing both on-premises and off-premises computerized records.

Using the case set forth in the preceding section for a market research firm, consideration is now given to the auditing procedures that might be used by an independent accountant.

1. Study the programs that have been written. Most programs not only have the machine language but the instructions are written clearly and can be readily understood.
2. Review the flow chart to determine application of the program.
3. Select an adequate number of field representative and supervisor reports and review them as to proper preparation and correction.
4. Compare reports selected with the invoice register.
5. Compare canceled checks with invoice register.

The foregoing procedure would be considered as auditing "around" the computer. In order for the auditor to more satisfactorily complete his audit, he should audit through the computer as well.

The following steps are illustrative of what the auditor should do to satisfy himself as to the validity of the computer programs.

1. Obtain an unused disk pack so that there is no possibility of putting test information into the client's system.
2. Prepare card input forms or "test deck" that will:
    a) Select the correct stored program.
    b) Set up initial file load and creation of the pack for each city.
    c) Determine limits of program as it applies to field representative and supervisor numbers.
    d) See if the program will accept numbers beyond the program limits.
    e) Test the program for the verification of initial file load and creation of the pack for each city.
    f) Attempt to run the summary card edit with an incorrect date.
    g) Run the summary card edit programs.
    h) Attempt to pay a field representative for a period for which he has already received payment.
    i) Attempt to pay a field representative at a different rate than that stored in the program.

j)   Verify the computational errors on the field representative's report that have not been corrected by the accounting department.

k)   Attempt to put a field representative already in city 1 in city 2 where he could not possibly be doing any work.

l)   Pick up possible key punch errors by making several erroneous corrections.

m)   Make the necessary corrections and have the computer verify the corrections.

n)   Print the invoice register with allocations.

o)   Examine the instruction for a "dummy" check.

p)   Attempt to pay field representative in city 1 at the time city 2 checks are due.

q)   Attempt to pay supervisor 2 when there is only supervisor 1.

r)   Attempt to pay each field representative separately when the program states that one check will be made payable to the supervisor for all work performed.

s)   Put in a fictitious field representative's name and keep all other vital statistics the same as that of a legitimate field representative.

t)   Instruct the computer to prepare a check payable to this fictitious field representative.

u)   Remove the fictitious field representative's name from the system.

v)   Put in the legitimate field representative's name.

w)   Instruct the computer to print out all accumulated information and reset for new year.

The preceding steps will permit the auditor to perform his audit function as well as evaluate the stated system of internal control.

Where a client does not have a computer on his premises but has some one else do the work elsewhere or has facilities for shared-time usage of an EDP system, the auditor has added responsibilities in determining the adequacy of internal control. Not only would he have to satisfy himself as to the operational features of the system but he would also have to determine the possibility of improper use by other parties. Needless to say the use of a computer of another person or shared-time of distant EDP system can cause considerable problems if original source documents are not maintained in *complete* detail and for a long period of time.

QUESTIONS

1.   The audit of the financial statements of a client that utilizes the services of a computer for accounting functions compels the CPA to understand the operation of his client's electronic data processing (EDP) system.

   a)   The first requirement of an effective system of internal control is a satisfactory plan of organization. List the characteristics of a satisfactory plan of organization for an EDP department, including the relationship between the department and the rest of the organization.

b) An effective system of internal control also requires a sound system of records control of operations and transactions (source data and its flow) and of classification of data within the accounts. For an EDP system, these controls include input controls, processing controls, and output controls. (Confine your comments to a batch-controlled system employing punched cards and to the steps that occur prior to the processing of the input cards in the computer.)

(AICPA, adapted)

2. Walt Lammert, a CPA, is examining the financial statements of the Buxton Sales Corporation, which recently installed an off-line electronic computer. The following comments have been extracted from Lammert's notes on computer operations and the processing and control of shipping notices and customer invoices:

a) To minimize inconvenience Buxton converted without change its existing data processing system, which utilized tabulating equipment. The computer company supervised the conversion and has provided training to all computer department employees (except key punch operators) in systems design, operations and programming.

b) Each computer run is assigned to a specific employee, who is responsible for making program changes, running the program and answering questions. This procedure has the advantage of eliminating the need for records of computer operations because each employee is responsible for his own computer runs.

c) At least one computer department employee remains in the computer room during office hours, and only computer department employees have keys to the computer room.

d) System documentation consists of those materials furnished by the computer company—a set of record formats and program listings. These and the tape library are kept in a corner of the computer department.

e) The Company considered the desirability of programmed controls but decided to retain the manual controls from its existing system.

f) Company products are shipped directly from public warehouses which forward shipping notices to the general accounting department. There a billing clerk enters the price of the item and accounts for the numerical sequence of shipping notices from each warehouse. The billing clerk also prepares daily adding machine tapes ("control tapes") of the units shipped and the unit prices.

g) Shipping notices and control tapes are forwarded to the computer department for key punching and processing. Extensions are made on the computer. Output consists of invoices (six copies) and a daily sales register. The daily sales register shows the aggregate totals of units shipped and unit prices which the computer operator compares with the control tapes.

h) All copies of the invoice are returned to the billing clerk. The clerk mails three copies to the customer, forwards one copy to the warehouse, maintains one copy in a numerical file and retains one copy in an open invoice file that serves as a detail account receivable record.

Describe weaknesses in internal control over information and data flows and the procedures for processing shipping notices and customer invoices and recommend improvements in these controls and processing procedures. Organize your answer sheets with *Weakness* listed on the left side of the sheets and *Recommended Improvement* in juxtaposition on the right.

(AICPA, adapted)

3. The eight following items contain examples of internal control deficiencies observed by a CPA in his client's computer data processing system. For each of these conditions or situations, select from the list of control features or procedures given the one which, if properly utilized, would have been *most* useful in either preventing the error or in ensuring its immediate and prompt correction.

a) The night operator understood more about programming than anyone realized. Working through the console, he made a change in a payroll program to alter the rate of pay for an accomplice in an operating department. The fraud was discovered accidentally after it had been going on for several months. The best control procedure would be

   (1)   Review of console log for unauthorized intervention.

   (2)   Payroll review and distribution controls outside of data processing.

   (3)   Audit trail use of payroll journal output.

   (4)   Control total review.

b) A customer payment recorded legibly on the remittance advice as $20.50 was entered into the computer from punched cards as $2,050.00. The best control procedure would be

   (1)   A limit test.

   (2)   A valid field test.

   (3)   Keypunch verification.

   (4)   A check digit.

c) A program for the analysis of sales provided questionable results and data processing personnel were unable to explain how the program operated. The programmer who wrote the program no longer works for the company. The best control procedure would be

   (1)   A run manual.

   (2)   Operator instructions.

   (3)   Layouts.

   (4)   Assembly run checking.

d) Due to a program error which had never happened before, the accounts receivable updating run did not process three transactions. The error was not noted by the operator because he was busy working on a card punch malfunction. There were control totals for the file which were printed out. An examination of the console printout would have disclosed the error. The best control procedure would be

   (1)   An error message requiring operator response before processing continues.

      (2)   Reconciliation of control totals by control clerk.

      (3)   Internal audit review of console log.

      (4)   Label checking by next computer program.

e)   A new computer program to process accounts payable was unreliable and would not handle the most common exceptions. The best control procedure would be

      (1)   Test data.

      (2)   Documentation.

      (3)   An error report.

      (4)   Assembly run error printouts.

f)   A batch of cards was next to the computer waiting for processing. The personnel manager, showing some visitors through the installation, pulled a card from the batch to show the visitors what it looked like. He absentmindedly put the card into his pocket rather than back into the batch. The missing card was not detected when the batch was processed. The best control procedure would be a

      (1)   Trailer label.

      (2)   Transmittal control log.

      (3)   Control total.

      (4)   Missing data check.

g)   An apparent error in input data describing an inventory item received was referred back to the originating department for correction. A week later the department complained that the inventory in question was incorrect. Data processing could not easily determine whether or not the item had been processed by the computer. The best control procedure would be

      (1)   Input edit checks.

      (2)   Missing data validity check.

      (3)   Transmittal control.

      (4)   An error log.

h)   The master inventory file, contained on a removable magnetic disk, was destroyed by a small fire next to the area where it was stored. The company had to take a special complete inventory in order to reestablish the file. The best control procedure would be

      (1)   Fire insurance.

      (2)   Data processing insurance.

      (3)   A copy of the disk.

      (4)   Remote storage of a copy of the disk and the transactions since the disk was copied.

                                 (AICPA, adapted)

4.   What are the divisions of functional responsibilities where an EDP system is in use?

5.   What factors must be kept in mind when developing a satisfactory system of internal control?

6.   How can the auditor satisfy himself as to the adequacy of a system of internal control relating to purchases of raw materials?

7.   What is the editing function? What must be done to insure that this function is performed?

8.   How can programmed controls assist the auditor in performing his audit?

9. Why are output controls necessary for a system of internal control?

10. What are administrative controls?

11. Discuss the reasons for physical and organizational segregation between systems and programming, personnel, computer operators, and disk pack librarians.

12. What controls can be employed to safeguard against the computer operator's manipulation of records?

13. The independent auditor must evaluate the EDP system used by his clients. What steps would be involved in this evaluation?

14. Who should initiate changes in memory records?

15. What internal control procedures would assist in providing suitable controls for master records?

16. What records of movement of data should be accurately maintained by the data processing control group?

17. What input controls are essential and must be maintained by the records control group?

18. What output controls are essential and must be maintained by the data processing group?

19. What is involved in the preauthorization of computer usage?

20. What must be done whenever errors are made?

21. Who is responsible and what must this person do who is in charge of magnetic tapes or disk packs?

22. CPAs may audit "around" or "through" computers in the examination of the financial statements of clients who utilize computers to process accounting data.

    a) Describe the auditing approach referred to as auditing "around" the computer.

    b) Under what conditions does the CPA decide to audit "through" the the computer instead of "around" the computer?

    (AICPA, adapted)

23. When auditing an electronic data processing system the CPA must be aware of the different types of controls built into the equipment. The controls built into the equipment fall into two groups: those incorporated by the user in his program, and those built into the equipment by the manufacturer.

    a) Why are accuracy checks on system components or peripheral equipment necessary?

    b) Define and give the purpose of each of the following program checks and controls:

        (1)   Record counts.

        (2)   Limit check.

        (3)   Reverse multiplication.

        (4)   Sequence check.

        (5)   Hash totals.

    c) Most electronic data processing equipment manufacturers have built-in checks to ensure that information is correctly read, processed, transferred within the system and recorded. One of these built-in checks is the parity bit.

    (1)   What is the parity bit?

    (2)   When would the parity bit control be used?

  d) When computers are used the CPA has to be familiar with the information stored on tapes, disk packs, and so forth. A common form of retention employs the grandfather-father-son principle.

    (1)   Define the grandfather-father-son principle.

    (2)   Why are grandfather-father-son tapes usually stored at different locations?

                                   (AICPA, adapted)

24. What procedure would you follow in determining the adequacy of a client's system of internal control as it relates to the accounts receivable program that is on their computer?

6
Internal Auditing

SECTION I: INTRODUCTION

The internal audit function was briefly set forth in Chapter 4. This chapter will expand that topic; however, in a book of this nature, no attempt will be made to exhaustively discuss the subject.

The continuing explosive growth in size and diversification of businesses today through mergers, consolidations, pooling of interests, and natural growth has created many complex problems for the internal auditor. This has been particularly true where accounting systems and systems of management control have not been found to be compatible. In other instances the lack of understanding of the objectives sought by the internal auditor have led to unnecessary confusion. No longer is the internal auditing staff performing principally a number-checking function. The Institute of Internal Auditors describes the internal audit function as follows:

Internal auditing is a series of processes and techniques through which an organization's own employees ascertain for the management, by means of firsthand, on-the-job observation, whether: established management controls are adequate and are effectively maintained; records and reports—financial, accounting and otherwise—reflect actual operations and results accurately and promptly; and each division, department or other unit is carrying out the plans, policies and procedures for which it is responsible.

Thus it is discernible that internal auditing has developed into a management tool which should function by appraising all corporate activities, the objectives being to promote the efficient attainment of all corporate objectives. If internal auditing does not provide this required service, the independent auditor's work load would be increased tremendously and in many instances almost impossible to perform. As indicated in Chapters 4 and 5, the internal auditor and independent auditor have distinct functions to perform in order for a company to secure maximum benefit from their services. In order to insure that maximum benefit is provided the client, the independent auditor will develop an extensive check list whereby the internal functions of the client's operations can be accurately evaluated.

SECTION II: INTERNAL AUDITING FUNCTION

Depending on size, rate of development, and management's ability to use information, internal auditing practices will vary greatly from one company to another. However, certain objectives must be kept in mind regardless of size, rate of development, and management's ability to use information. First, the internal auditor must determine the adequacy of internal control. This, for example, not only relates to seeing that the proper persons are handling cash but would also involve determining whether or not sound accounting principles are being followed in the recording of cash receipts and disbursements. Second, he would be responsible for determining whether or not there is compliance with company policies and procedures, noting any variances so that a determination can be made as to whether a policy should be changed. As an example, the company may have a sales policy relating to discounts given on certain sizes of orders. The internal auditor discovers that this policy is not being followed by one salesman. Full documentation of the variances should be made so that the sales executive can objectively evaluate the situation and make an intelligent decision. Another objective would be the verification of the existence of assets. This involves establishing proper safeguards for assets and preventing and discovering fraud. An illustration of this objective would be the establishment of a system of inventory control which would insure that all units produced would go to the finished goods stock room and not into the employees' lunch boxes. Still another objective would be for the internal auditor to verify and evaluate the reliability of the accounting and reporting system. Here, for example, the internal auditor would be interested in determining whether figures presented are comparable. This may involve recommending that the company maintain its records on a 13-month rather than a 12-month basis; or, as more and more firms are doing, changing to a fiscal year rather than a calendar year basis for reporting results from operations. Investigating to determine that the reports are timely is a must. With EDP systems in operation today, the internal auditor will find many reports being prepared that no longer have application. Another desirable objective is for the internal auditor to objectively report his findings to management and recommend corrective action where necessary. This undoubtedly is the most crucial of all of the objectives. If the internal auditor cannot communicate his findings clearly and follow them up to objectively evaluate the results, then he is not assisting management in promoting the efficient attainment of all corporate objectives. Thus, it can be seen from these objectives that the internal audit staff of a company is in a highly responsible position. An internal audit staff which is recognized not only as its company's expert on internal control but which also provides a broader type of appraisal service will demand and realize proper recognition. Further, it will supplement the work of the independent auditors and facilitate cooperation with them on the annual audit.

SECTION III: EXECUTIVES AND DIRECTORS IN THE INTERNAL AUDIT FUNCTION

A system of internal audit which functions properly can be of assistance in pinpointing areas of revenue improvement and cost reduction, and the following points may serve as a basic guide of internal audit procedures to be used by executives and directors.

Organization Guides
1. The audit committee of the board of directors should approve the internal audit program (or schedule) and ascertain the coordination between the internal and external audit operations.
2. The person in charge of internal auditing should report to a top executive who is in a position to see that deficiencies are eliminated and that corrective action is taken.
3. In consultation with the company's independent auditors, an internal audit schedule should be established each year.

Qualification Guides
1. Internal audit staff appointments should be made on the basis of capacity and the probability of advancement to higher positions.
2. Every internal auditor should engage in continuing education, continuing training, and self-improvement.
3. All internal auditors should be permitted to maintain independence in all work and data they review.

Performance Guides
1. Internal auditors should submit periodic reports to top management in order to evaluate progress as specified by an established schedule.
2. Internal auditors should have total access to all necessary work areas of the company.
3. No internal auditor should be over-burdened with routine duties.
4. Inventories of physical facilities should be taken on a cyclical basis, in accordance with a preestablished schedule.
5. A written program should serve as a guide to internal audit work, and the audit programs should be changed with changing conditions.
6. Internal audit work papers should include proper documentation of all tests—setting forth the data examined, procedures followed, results, conclusions, and so forth.
7. Internal audit programs should be "signed off" to indicate completion of all requirements.
8. Examination results should be set forth in a written report directed

to top management, and the report should contain follow-through recommendations, and the recommendations should provide for deficiency corrections.

SECTION IV: INTERNAL AUDITING DEPARTMENT

As a general rule, the organizational level at which an internal auditor will find himself to a very great extent depends upon his ability and effectiveness. In most instances, the head of the internal auditing staff reports to the controller—or similar financial executive. The philosophy supporting this is that the controller understands the audit function and can provide direction and supervision. The controller is also well versed in company affairs and sufficiently independent to view the internal audit department's responsibilities with objectivity.

There are those who disagree with the preceding reasoning and believe the head of the internal auditing staff may report to a nonfinancial executive or even directly to the board of directors. The philosophy supporting this positioning of the internal auditor points out that independent verification of financial records is a basic duty of the internal auditor. How can the internal auditor be truly independent when he reports to an executive whose work he is examining? It would seem, therefore, that if some basic principles are followed, the internal auditor should function effectively at all levels in an organization. One basic principle that should be established is that the internal auditor is a member of the management team. Even though he will work in an independent manner, a proper working climate must be developed so that he will be able to make his views heard and understood among executives who are in a position to implement his recommendations, as indicated in the preceding section.

Another basic principle is the improving of the image of the internal auditor to all employees of the company. There is probably no other job in the organization that has as much varied information and knowledge about the entire company as that of the internal auditor. Further, there must be a reconciliation of desired objectives. If the internal auditor and operating management realize that they are both striving for the same objectives, the suggestions and recommendations of the internal auditor will be reasonably considered. Another basic principle that must be emphasized is that the internal auditor is a staff man and as such is committed to a role of assistance, advice, and council to the operating personnel. Again, with his comprehensive knowledge, the internal auditor is well qualified to give this assistance and direction at all operating and administrative levels. Finally he must be able to communicate his findings. This frequently will involve discussing the purpose of his work before he even starts his audit. As the audit progresses it would be desirable to discuss his findings within the limits established by management, so that their relevancy can be evaluated. At the termination of the audit, he should discuss his findings with the operating personnel within the limits established by management.

As stated earlier, the explosive growth of business today has created many complex problems for the internal auditor. However, his ability to solve these problems to management's satisfaction will largely determine his organizational position. The internal auditing staff will really find its place in the organization only when they show they are a constructive force.

SECTION V: INTERNAL AUDITING ACTIVITIES

A closer examination of what the internal auditor is expected to accomplish will illustrate the importance of his work to his employer and also to the independent auditor.

Internal auditing activities fall into two major categories: (1) financial and (2) operational or management auditing.

Financial auditing attempts to verify the existence of assets and to ascertain that proper safeguards are maintained for them as well as prevent and discover fraud. It is also involved in checking the reliability of the accounting and reporting system including a review of the system of internal control. Verifying the existence of assets would involve such work as the review and testing of procedure in connection with receiving and disbursing cash; verification of inventories by taking or observing physical counts, verification of the accuracy of pricing procedures, and reviews of cost accounting records; reviews of liabilities to determine that all obligations are recorded and to ascertain that prescribed payment procedures are followed; reviews of revenues and expenses regarding propriety and regarding allocation to proper accounting classifications and to the appropriate accounting periods; tests of the effectiveness of accounting systems and procedures, particularly in respect to internal control.

In order to assist in establishing the accuracy of the balances of receivables and payables, an internal auditing department may send confirmation requests for balances due from customers and due to creditors. The requests for confirmation may be either on a test basis, or all customers and creditors may be circularized. When an internal auditing department sends requests for confirmation of account balances, that department prepares the requests totally independent of the accounting department, controls the mailing, opens replies received from debtors and creditors, and independently investigates all reported differences. If the internal auditing department and the independent auditor work closely with each other in requesting confirmations, much independent audit time (and cost) can be saved, as will be pointed out in Chapter 13 where confirmations are treated fully. Illustration 6–1 presents one form of confirmation request to be used by an internal auditing department.

ILLUSTRATION 6–1
CONFIRMATION REQUEST

COLONIAL COMPANY
Internal Auditing Department
Deer Park, Ohio

Date_____

To: _____
_____
_____

No. _____

THIS IS NOT A REQUEST FOR PAYMENT

In connection with the examination of our records, your account shows an unpaid

balance of $ _____ due $\begin{Bmatrix} us \\ you \end{Bmatrix}$ on _____ .

Please compare this amount with your records as of the date above, If <u>correct</u>, please sign below; if <u>not</u> correct, state the unpaid amount according to your records, supplying full information on the reverse side of this request.

We would also appreciate a confirmation of all notes due $\begin{Bmatrix} us \\ you \end{Bmatrix}$ on _____ , as follows:

Date of Note	Date Due	Interest Rate	Interest Paid to:	Amount of Note	Collateral or Guaranties, or State "None"
_____	_____	_____	_____	_____	_____
_____	_____	_____	_____	_____	_____
_____	_____	_____	_____	_____	_____

This request is made in the usual course of our regular examination for the purpose of verifying your account. This is not a bill or a statement. An addressed envelope is enclosed for furnishing the desired information promptly. Thank you.

Very truly yours,

Internal Auditing Department
COLONIAL COMPANY

The above statement is _____ correct. (List any differences on the reverse side of this form.)

Company Name _____
Signed by _____

Date _____

* Fill in same date as filled in above.

Operational or management auditing involves the extension of internal auditing to all operations of a business and does not confine itself to the financial and accounting areas. Since financial and accounting activities touch almost every activity of an organization, operational or management auditing is an extension of conventional auditing beyond the financial and accounting areas. An example would be making an appraisal of a company's inventory levels and the adequacy of warehousing facilities at the same time that the accuracy of the inventory is verified. Additional examples would be studying the profitability of leasing operations, investigating a decline in productivity, checking alternative methods of transportation and related charges, a review of policies relating to the maintenance of plant and equipment. Other operational areas into which the internal auditor is moving are those related to personnel, compliance with laws and regulations, and conflict of interest of company executives. Needless to say great care must be exercised by the internal auditor in performing the operational or management audit as he must not presume to take on responsibilities that he is not equipped to handle. Also, he should not do any second guessing in regard to decisions previously taken by operating managers. He must further guard against criticism of a purely technical nature, such as engineering and research operations, as they are beyond his competence.

As can be ascertained from the preceding discussion, the duties and responsibilities of the internal auditor are set forth. This will undoubtedly assist the independent auditor in performing his audit.

To give further recognition to the importance of the duties and responsibilities assumed by internal auditors, a certification program has been recently established. An individual meeting the established requirements and satisfactorily passing a comprehensive examination will become a Certified Internal Auditor.

SECTION VI: AUDIT OF GOVERNMENT ORGANIZATIONS, PROGRAMS AND ACTIVITIES

There have been profound changes in our social, political, and economic order that have demanded new and better service from our governmental bodies. In order to provide these new services, there must be cooperation among Federal, state, and local governments. Everyone interested must know whether government funds are handled properly and in compliance with existing laws. However, this is not enough as it must also be determined whether these programs are being conducted efficiently and economically. Interested parties must have this information provided by someone who is not a part of the program but is independent and objective. Recognizing the need for independence, governments have developed internal audit staffs which report to the highest practicable echelon within their governmental body and are organizationally located outside the line-management function of the entity under audit.

The best example of this trend is the General Accounting Office which is responsible to Congress and therefore is in a position to audit *any* phase of Federal government activity. To assist in this audit area, each Federal department has an internal audit staff which reports to the Secretary of that Federal government department. This approach is being followed in most States and large local governments. With the increasing need for information, many CPAs are being retained to perform this internal audit function. It should be mentioned here that many audits that are performed on Federal Government projects require the signing of an agency-prepared opinion specifically designed for the type of audit performed. For example, the following opinion is for the audit of the Federal agencies indicated:

The financial statements of the Federal Home Loan Bank Board, the Federal Home Loan Banks, and the Federal Savings and Loan Insurance Corporation present fairly the financial position at December 31, 1974, and the results of their operations and changes in their financial position for the year then ended, in conformity with the principles and standards of accounting prescribed by the Comptroller General, applied on a basis consistent with that of the preceding year.

Ethical Principles

The Federal Government Accountants Association has developed a Code of Ethics in order to foster the highest professional standards and behavior which will insure exemplary service to the Federal Government. The following are taken from the Association's Code of Ethics:

1. A member shall adhere to the Standards of Conduct promulgated by his employer.
2. A member shall not engage in acts or be associated with activities which are contrary to the public interest or discreditable to the Federal Government Accountants Association.
3. A member shall not engage in private employment or hold himself out as an independent practitioner except with the consent of his employer, if required.
4. A member shall not purposefully transmit or use confidential information obtained in his professional work for personal gain or other advantage.
5. A member shall strive to perform the duties of his position and supervise the work of his subordinates with the highest degree of professional care.
6. A member shall continually seek to increase his professional knowledge and skills and thus to improve his service to employers, associates and fellow members.
7. A member shall render opinions, observations, or conclusions for official purposes only after appropriate professional consideration of the pertinent facts.
8. A member shall exercise diligence, objectivity, and honesty in his professional activities and be aware of his responsibility to identify improprieties that come to his attention.

9. A member shall be aware of and strive to apply requirements and standards prescribed by authorized Government agencies which may be applicable to his work.

10. In the performance of any assignment, a member shall consider the public interest to be paramount.

11. A member shall not engage in any activity or relationship which creates or gives the appearance of a conflict with his responsibilities to his employer.

12. In speaking engagements or writings for publications, a member shall identify personal opinions which may differ from official position of his employer.

Auditing Standards

On October 1, 1968, the General Accounting Office issued a statement entitled "Internal Auditing in Federal Agencies." This publication set forth the basic principles and concepts for developing and operating internal audit staffs for Federal agencies. In June 1972, standards which amended the 1968 publication were published and have expanded the duties and responsibilities for internal auditing. These standards provide for a scope of audit that is concerned with legal requirements and financial compliance as well as auditing for economy, efficiency, and achievement of desired results.

Definitions of these three elements of such an audit are as follows:

a) *Financial and compliance*—determines (a) whether financial operations are properly conducted, (b) whether the financial reports of an audited entity are presented fairly, and (c) whether the entity has complied with applicable laws and regulations.

b) *Economy and efficiency*—determines whether the entity is managing or utilizing its resources (personnel, property, space, and so forth) in an economical and efficient manner and the causes of any inefficiencies or uneconomical practices, including inadequacies in management information systems, administrative procedures, or organizational structure.

c) *Program results*—determines whether the desired results or benefits are being achieved, whether the objectives established by the legislature or other authorizing body are being met, and whether the agency has considered alternatives which might yield desired results at a lower cost.

A study of the following standards illustrates that each of the three elements of audit can be performed separately if this is considered desirable. They are forward-looking standards and include some concepts and areas of audit coverage which are still evolving.

General Standards

1. The full scope of an audit of a governmental program, function, activity, or organization should encompass:

    a) An examination of financial transactions, accounts, and reports, including an evaluation of compliance with applicable laws and regulations.

    b) A review of efficiency and economy in the use of resources.

    c) A review to determine whether desired results are achieved.

2. The auditors assigned to the audit must collectively possess adequate professional proficiency for the tasks required.

3. In all matters relating to the audit work, the audit organization and the individual auditors shall maintain an independent attitude.

4. Due professional care is to be used in conducting the audit and in preparing related reports.

Examination and Evaluation Standards

1. Work is to be adequately planned.

2. Assistants are to be properly supervised.

3. A review is to be made of compliance with legal and regulatory requirements.

4. An evaluation is to be made of the system of internal control to assess the extent it can be relied upon to ensure accurate information, to ensure compliance with laws and regulations, and to provide for efficient and effective operations.

5. Sufficient, competent, and relevant evidence is to be obtained to afford a reasonable basis for the auditor's opinions, judgments, conclusions, and recommendations.

Reporting Standards

1. Written audit reports are to be submitted to the appropriate officials of the organizations requiring the audits. Copies of the reports should be sent to other officials who may be responsible for taking action on audit findings and recommendations and to others responsible or authorized to receive such reports. Copies should be made available for public inspection.

2. Reports are to be issued on or before the dates specified by law, regulation, or other arrangement and, in any event, as promptly as possible so as to make the information available for timely use by management and by legislative officials.

3. Each report shall:

    a) Be as concise as possible but, at the same time, clear and complete enough to be understood by the users.

    b) Present factual matter accurately, completely, and fairly.

    c) Present findings and conclusions objectively and in language as clear and simple as the subject matter permits.

    d) Include only factual information, findings, and conclusions that are adequately supported by enough evidence in the auditor's work papers to demonstrate or prove, when called upon, the bases for the matters reported and their correctness and reasonableness. Detailed supporting information should be included in the report to the extent necessary.

e) Include, when possible, the auditor's recommendations for actions to effect improvements in problem areas noted in his audit and to otherwise make improvements in operations. Information on underlying causes of problems reported should be included to assist in implementing or devising corrective actions.

f) Place primary emphasis on improvement rather than on criticism of the past; critical comments should be presented in balanced perspective, recognizing any unusual difficulties or circumstances faced by the operating officials concerned.

g) Identify and explain issues and questions needing further study and consideration by the auditor or others.

h) Include recognition of noteworthy accomplishments, particularly when management improvements in one program or activity may be applicable elsewhere.

i) Include recognition of the views of responsible officials of the organization, program, function, or activity audited on the auditor's findings, conclusions, and recommendations. Except where the possibility of fraud or other compelling reason may require different treatment, the auditor's tentative findings and conclusions should be reviewed with such officials. When possible, without undue delay, their views should be obtained in writing and objectively considered and presented in preparing the final report.

j) Clearly explain the scope and objectives of the audit.

k) State whether any pertinent information has been omitted because it is deemed privileged or confidential. The nature of such information should be described, and the law or other basis under which it is withheld should be stated.

4. Each audit report containing financial reports shall:

a) Contain an expression of the auditor's opinion on whether the information contained in the financial reports is presented fairly. If the auditor cannot express an opinion, the reasons therefore should be stated in the audit report.

b) State whether the financial reports have been prepared in accordance with generally accepted or prescribed accounting principles applicable to the organization, program, function, or activity audited and on a consistent basis from one period to the next. Material changes in accounting policies and procedures and their effect on the financial reports are to be explained in the audit report.

c) Contain appropriate supplementary explanatory information about the contents of the financial reports as may be necessary for full and informative disclosure about the financial operations of the organization, program, function, or activity audited. Violations of legal or other regulatory requirements, including instances of noncompliance, shall be explained in the audit report.

Of particular importance to all accountants is the expansion of the audit function to encompass the social measurement of government programs. Since social measurements are an appraisal of the end process of government, specific audit techniques may vary, but the measuring process is similar to other performance auditing. Social measurement is intensifying a problem long familiar to auditors and that is: How much evidence is enough? Arriving at a good supportable opinion is even more difficult to obtain where social measurement is involved. A unique feature of determining social measurements of government programs is the fact that while auditors normally examine activities on which the accounting has been done by someone else, in many cases the auditors must attempt to first perform the necessary accounting. The auditors of the General Accounting Office have been well aware of this unique situation and do not feel that performing the initial accounting is compatible with the auditor's responsibilities. Therefore, they are strongly pushing the development of the social accounting concept within the agencies and departments. Consequently, if the agencies and departments do their own social measurement and reporting, the auditors can revert to their original role of independent examination and appraisal. The problems faced in performing such an audit can be illustrated by the following situation.

ILLUSTRATION. A city has developed a program for training unemployed individuals as truck drivers. The proposal is presented showing that if funds in the amount of $150,000 are available, 100 individuals can be trained as truck drivers. The program is approved and the funds spent. An audit is performed and all funds have been found to be properly spent. However, the audit was expanded to determine, if possible what was accomplished. It was determined that only 60 persons signed up for the course; that 50 completed the course; that 8 persons were hired as truck drivers; that 32 persons obtained jobs unrelated to the program; and 10 could not be located. Questions still unanswered were:
(1) How many positions were available when the program was proposed, (2) What effect, if any, was there on those who completed the course, and could not obtain a position, and (3) Was there some other project that could have been of more social significance?

As the standards and preceding illustration so clearly set forth, the internal audit function for governmental organizations, programs, and activities uniquely supplements routine management checks through its independent approach and methods of review.

QUESTIONS

1. What factors have caused the internal auditor to face an increasingly more difficult job?

2. Regardless of the size of an organization, where internal auditing is performed certain objectives must be established. What are these objectives?

3. What steps should an internal auditor take when he discovers that a company policy is not being followed?

4. What is the philosophy of those companies which have the internal auditor reporting to the controller?

5. What is the philosophy of those companies which have the internal auditor reporting to a nonfinancial executive?

6. What basic principles should the internal auditor use to insure success of his work?

7. Regardless of where the internal auditor may appear on the organization chart of a company, what will determine his position?

8. Into what categories would you place the internal auditor's activities?

9. Present some examples of financial auditing that would be performed by the internal auditor.

10. Present some examples of operational or management auditing that would be performed by the internal auditor.

11. In addition to knowing that government funds have been properly handled, what other approaches might be made by a government internal auditor?

12. What primary requirements must be met if a government internal auditor's report is to be objective?

13. The FGAA Code of Ethics states: "In the performance of any assignment, a member shall consider the public interest to be paramount." Explain.

14. What should the full scope of an audit of a governmental program, function or activity encompass?

15. If it is impossible for the auditor to be sufficiently independent to produce unbiased opinions, conclusions, and judgments, relating to the agency being audited, what would you recommend he do?

7
Starting an Audit

SECTION I: PRE-AUDIT ARRANGEMENTS

Preliminary

Preliminary audit arrangements with a client—particularly with a new one—are of vital importance both to the client and to the auditor. This was strongly indicated in Chapter 3. This chapter will consider (*a*) the preliminary arrangements to be made with a new client; (*b*) the preliminary arrangements to be made with a continuing client with whom the auditor does not have frequent contact (for example, if the contact is only once a year); (*c*) distinctive auditing terminology; and (*d*) the audit personnel to be used, and charging a client.

Throughout the entire study and practice of auditing, it should be constantly borne in mind that (*a*) the audit work to be performed is dependent upon the evaluation of the system of internal control; (*b*) the most widely used audit tool is transactional testing and item (or quantity) testing; and (*c*) the cost of an audit is a function of time and quality of effort.

In any audit—for a new client or for a continuing client—the ideal audit approach· is that in which the cost of obtaining a specified level of the quality assurance of data is at a minimum and where the substitution of an alternative procedure for the one used would either increase the total cost or reduce the level of quality assurance of the accuracy of data.

Arrangements with a Client

When negotiations between a new client and an auditor are in the first stages, the auditor should obtain as much information as possible to assist him during the course of the examination. During the preliminary arrangement stage, most clients desire to answer questions and to conduct the auditor through the premises. The auditor thus has an excellent opportunity to meet personnel and to note for himself the organization and general operation of the company. A satisfactory introductory visit with a new client often will save much time and work later. The client has a better understanding of his business than the auditor, but the auditor has a better knowledge of auditing than the client. An auditor must listen to his client, but he should not follow the directions of a client with the result that when the client receives the audit report, he has nothing more than a written analysis of verbal information supplied by himself, substantiated by proper examination.

For the most effective results, all audit work should be properly planned in advance and then be adequately supervised, following the examination and evaluation of the system of internal control. The general layout of the client's company and its operations must be thoroughly surveyed and studied before the auditor engages in active examination work. Thus, in a preliminary way the auditor familiarizes himself with the client's problems; and his ability to assist the client is thereby increased. Because of the differences between engagements, the auditor must call forth all his ingenuity in order to give the client the best possible results.

Today, in the majority of cases, the visit of an auditor is carefully planned. The broad business service and the analytical nature of the work performed by an auditor make necessary certain preliminary arrangements with the client so that the latter's routine will not be affected and so that the auditor may perform his work in the minimum of time commensurate with good practice. If an auditor is careful, he can in most cases detect irregularities just as effectively in an arranged visit as in a surprise visit.

The auditor formerly made many of his visits to a client in the nature of a surprise, so that the client's employees would be caught unawares if they were in arrears with their work, if they had made errors that they had not taken time to locate, or if they were guilty of malpractices. Today, surprise visits normally exist only when required by law, by a regulation, or by client request.

In a repeat engagement, a telephone conversation frequently constitutes the only preliminary arrangement. A new engagement letter may be used, or the prior engagement letter may be brought up to date. When the audit is performed by the same firm member who conducted it in the past, he should refer to the office files for the work papers of prior periods and review them. When the audit is a repeat engagement but is made by a member of the firm who did not formerly conduct that particular engagement, work papers of former years should be studied and necessary correspondence with the client should be reviewed. In addition, the firm member who is to conduct the audit should confer with the man formerly in charge of the engagement, if he is still available.

First Audit Considerations.   When an audit is to be performed for the first time, particular care should be exercised in the preliminary arrangements so that there is agreement between the auditor and the client.

In a first audit, the following points must be covered; some of them must be covered on a repeat engagement:

1. Study the client's business and obtain organization charts and work-flow charts.
2. Evaluate the client's system of internal control and internal audit.
3. Ascertain the purpose of the audit.
4. Ascertain the period to be covered.
5. Clear the testing of entries.
6. Clear the confirmation of receivables, securities, liabilities, and so forth.
7. Investigate the accounting system in operation.
8. Arrange the time of starting the examination.
9. Agree upon the fees to be charged.
10. Arrange for the number of people to be used in the audit.
11. Ascertain whether or not the client's records are to be closed (or in balance) prior to the start of the audit.

Internal Control and Internal Audit.   In order to discover—in part at this early stage of preliminary negotiations—the effectiveness of the system of internal control in operation and the adequacy of internal auditing, the auditor will address many questions to executive personnel. A *few* of these questions are as follows:

1. Does one employee function in more than one of the following capacities?
    a) Cashier.
    b) Accountant.
    c) Accounts receivable or accounts payable clerk.
    d) Shipping or receiving clerk.
    e) Payroll clerk.
    If one employee does occupy more than one of the preceding positions, the auditor is immediately notified that internal control might be improved; and the amount of audit work will be increased over the amount that would be necessary if such dual capacities did not exist. Obviously, in a small concern, all of these functions cannot be segregated; consequently, the fewer the number of employees charged with financial accountabilities, the more extensive must be the examination.
2. Are all cash receipts deposited intact daily? Failure to deposit all receipts daily—and intact—opens possibilities for fraudulent practices,

places temptation before employees, and adds to the work of the audit because the ability to trace receipts to the bank is lessened.

3. Who may authorize cash disbursements? If this responsibility is not centralized, unauthorized disbursements may be possible.

4. How are inventories controlled? Failure to control them properly is serious both from the standpoint of poor control and from the standpoint of additional audit work.

5. In your opinion, is any employee dishonest? One of two answers will be forthcoming. If no one is suspected of dishonesty, the auditor must watch for inadvertent temptations placed before employees. If some person's honesty is doubted, the auditor subsequently must attempt to prove or disprove the suspicion.

Purpose of the Audit. During preliminary negotiations with a new client, the auditor should determine the purpose for which an audit is to be performed. It may be made for purposes of general financial reporting, for credit purposes, for the prospective sale of the business, because of a suspicion of fraud, or for any of the other purposes presented in Chapter 1.

The Period to Be Covered. On a new engagement, the auditor must understand the length of the audit period. He must also ascertain when the last audit was made and by whom, since a lapse of time without an audit will have an effect not only on the scope of the examination but also on the opinion rendered. Many business concerns have audits made for interim periods; or if an examination is made for a specific purpose, it may include a period of more or less than one year.

Testing of Entries. After the auditor has examined and evaluated the system of internal control in operation, he is in a position to start formulating his plans concerning the necessary extent of detailed verification.

The majority of examinations involve tests of data and transactions. The purpose of testing is to prove or disprove the accuracy of the data, the validity of transactions, and the records as an entirety. An auditor must be satisfied that the transactions are legitimate and that the accounting for them is proper so that financial statements are not affected.

The necessary amount of testing will be developed as each specific section of an audit is developed. The amount of testing by classes of data and transactions is treated in Chapters 10 and 11. Testing must satisfy the auditor that the items examined are correct to a high degree of probability—or that the results of the tests are unsatisfactory. If the results are not adequate or conclusive, additional testing must be performed, or certain data must be verified in detail.

At this point in the preliminary arrangements, the client must be induced to realize the necessity for testing transactions and data. The auditor must also make clear to the client the fact that as the examination progresses, more or less testing may be required than had originally been planned. After the tests of transactions have indicated their accuracy reliability, the auditor will also scrutinize additional transactions of a similar nature.

An auditor does not indicate to a client the specific transactions and data he will examine, since such information might pave the way for the covering of irregularities.

Confirmation of Receivables. Requesting confirmations of receivables should be settled before an audit begins. Recognized auditing procedure dictates that receivables be confirmed whenever it is feasible and reasonable to do so. Internal auditing departments frequently confirm receivable balances. If an independent auditor is satisfied with the system of internal control and with the results obtained by the internal auditing department, he may decide to limit his confirmation requests to selected accounts—for example, those with a balance in excess of a specified dollar amount.

Investigate the Accounting System. Prior to active work on an engagement, the auditor should familiarize himself with the operation of the accounting system in use. He cannot hope to perform a competent audit, instruct assistant staff members, budget time, and give advice as to the requirements of the audit if he does not possess a good knowledge of the system in operation. Although the principles of accounting are universally the same, the adoption of peculiar techniques may be brought about by local conditions and requirements and by variations in operating systems.

Most clients are anxious to have the auditor investigate their accounting system and advise them of any desirable changes in procedures. Well-qualified employees usually are willing to point out phases of the system which are obsolete or not operating satisfactorily.

The auditor must understand or become familiar with the client's use of electronic data processing equipment.

Time of Starting an Audit. The time of starting an audit must be settled. If possible, it is advisable to perform certain preliminary work far in advance of the close of the fiscal period, thus relieving pressure at a later date. The client naturally desires to know when the audit will be started so that he can have all records in readiness for the auditor.

Fees to Be Charged. Fees must be arranged before an audit is begun. Most auditors prefer a per diem rate because it is seldom possible to estimate exactly the total fee in advance of the work. Most clients prefer a flat fee, since they then know the exact cost involved. Good professional men are honest and efficient; if the client realizes that fact, he also realizes that the auditor will render his services in the minimum time consistent with good work. If the auditor accepts a flat fee, he is almost certain to liberalize his estimate as mere protection. If his flat fee estimate is too high, the auditor may be placed in the position of attempting to explain the high estimate. If the estimate is too low, the auditor suffers, since he must not accelerate the pace of his work beyond the speed at which the best results are obtained. If per diem rates are accepted, the client usually wants an approximate idea of the time to be spent. Most auditors have a fairly clear idea of the time required for any engagement if the preliminary survey is adequate and if unforeseen conditions do not develop.

It is well to have an understanding with the client as to the meaning of a day's work. In busy seasons, the auditor frequently works 12 or more hours per day, but 7 hours is considered a normal day's work. Therefore, the charge for one man for one calendar day will not necessarily be the per diem charge but rather the per diem rate for a 7-hour day applied to the total hours worked per day.

Number of People. The number of people to be assigned to the engagement should be discussed with the client, together with the grade of each person. The client usually leaves this matter to the discretion of the accounting firm, but the firm member arranging for the engagement should express his intentions. With the personnel established in advance, the client is familiar with his approximate total daily cost.

Closing (or Balancing) the Records. It is not the normal duty of the auditor to balance or close the records of a client. In a new engagement, the auditor should make his position clear on this point because if a ledger is out of balance, many hours might be spent searching for errors. Normally, an auditor requests a balanced trial balance or a completed period-end work sheet. If the auditor has given a client an estimate of the time required for an audit, the client may be dissatisfied with additional hours required to do the work that should have been done by his own employees.

Engagement Confirmation Letter

After all preliminary arrangements have been made with either a new client or a continuing client, a letter confirming the arrangements should be sent to the client; and it should be accepted in writing by the client. The practice of sending an engagement confirmation letter represents good professional practice. This letter should set forth the conditions of the audit, its scope, any limitations imposed, date of report delivery, and any other pertinent matters. Illustration 7–1 presents an engagement confirmation letter. The letter of confirmation should contain a space for acceptance by the client, and the signal duplicate should be returned to the auditor.

This paragraph contains some—not all—of the reasons for sending a client an engagement confirmation letter. There is a total written agreement which should add legal protection in the event of claims and lawsuits. If properly drafted, the engagement letter can overcome any misunderstanding on the part of the client regarding the services he expects

ILLUSTRATION 7–1

ENGAGEMENT CONFIRMATION LETTER

CORBIN, DRAKE AND COMPANY
Certified Public Accountants
University Building
Cincinnati, Ohio 45221

January 11, 1975

Mr. Richard W. Hess, President
Ohio Manufacturing Company
8959 Blue Ash Road
Cincinnati, Ohio 45242

Dear Mr. Hess:

This letter is in confirmation of our conversation of today regarding the examination of the financial statements of the Ohio Manufacturing Company.

For the year ended December 31, 1975, the examination will be made in accordance with generally accepted auditing standards and will include all procedures considered necessary for the rendition of an opinion regarding the financial statements. We will prepare the annual federal income tax return. In addition, we will visit the company at interims and will prepare unaudited financial statements as of the end of each of the first three quarters of the year, for which statements we will not provide an opinion.

Our examination will include (1) a study and evaluation of the system of internal control, (2) proper tests of the accounting records and other financial records to the extent considered necessary, and (3) a review of the accounting system in operation. The audit will not include a detailed examination of all transactions, because an audit is not specifically designed to disclose defalcations, although their discovery may result from a normal audit. As stated, our examination of the annual financial statements of management will be made in accordance with generally accepted auditing standards, and this examination does not imply the accuracy of particular figures, but it does imply the fairness of the presentation of management's financial statements taken as a whole.

Our services will be rendered at our regular per diem rates given to you today, and the maximum fee for 1975 will not exceed $xx,xxx plus out-of-pocket expenses, unless unforeseen circumstances develop during the course of our examination, or unless you request additional services. In either of the two latter events, the situation will be discussed with you, and if we are to proceed, we are to be reimbursed separately for these additional services.

We will send management letters to you if during the course of our work it is our opinoin that (1) improvement should be made in internal control, (2) your application of accounting principles does not have general acceptance, (3) the accounting system could be improved, and (4) any other matters require comment or attention.

ILLUSTRATION 7–1 (*Continued*)

We estimate that the engagement will require approximately twenty days for one manager, one senior and two staff accountants, and approximately two days for the services of a partner, unless unforeseen circumstances develop.

In accordance with our agreement, you are to have customer statements ready for mailing on the morning of January 5, 1976; we will insert our confirmation requests and control the mailing. Also, you are to prepare a general ledger trial balance not later than February 1, 1976, together with schedules of prepaid insurance, fixed assets and related accumulated depreciation.

If the contents of this letter are acceptable to you, please acknowledge by signing the duplicate copy in the space provided and return to us.

Sincerely yours,

CORBIN, DRAKE AND COMPANY

WFC:db

Accepted by: _____
                Ohio Manufacturing Company

Date: _____

to be rendered; frequently, smaller clients are not knowledgeable regarding the services they want or expect. For an audit client, the engagement letter should point out that the examination will be made in accordance with generally accepted auditing standards of a scope adequate (normally) for the rendition of an unqualified opinion. The client may be of the belief that the primary purpose of an audit is to disclose asset defalcation; consequently, the letter should be drafted to dispel this idea. The client must be made to understand that the audited financial statements are his—not the auditor's. Engagement letters should clear ambiguity regarding fees to be charged. The engagement letter should point out the fact that financial statements are unaudited unless the examination was made in accordance with generally accepted auditing standards. The client's attention should be called to the fact that certain accounting practices are not generally acceptable but may be acceptable to various taxing authorities.

Engagement Memorandum

After obtaining an engagement, the auditor prepares an engagement memorandum, which is retained in the firm's permanent file. Illustration 7–2 presents one form of engagement memorandum. The purpose of the memorandum is to cover the points discussed with the client, to guide firm personnel, and to set in motion the machinery for preparation for the engagement. For repeat engagements, details may be omitted from the memorandum, due to familiarity with the nature of the engagement.

If the firm member who made preparatory negotiations with a new client is a partner or manager who will not perform the audit, he should discuss the engagement with the accountant who will be in immediate charge. For further information, the in-charge person refers to the engagement memorandum and to the duplicate letter of confirmation (or contract), and to any other papers and correspondence in the office files.

Preparation for the Audit by the Client's Staff

Normally, there is a vast amount of pre-audit work which can be performed by a client's staff before the auditor's visit. This work is usually indicated by the auditor, and it constitutes an internal function and not an external audit procedure. The following list is indicative of the schedules and data that at the request of the auditor, clients may prepare prior to his visit:

1. Trial balances
    a) General ledger, factory ledger, private ledger
    b) Accounts receivable and accounts payable

ILLUSTRATION 7–2

CORBIN, DRAKE AND COMPANY	Case No.: 12345
	Prepared by: W.F. Corbin
Engagement Memorandum	Date: January 14, 1975

1. Name of Client	Ohio Manufacturing Company
2. Places of Business: Main Office	8959 Blue Ash Road, Cincinnati, Ohio 45242
Other	None
3. Telephone	791–8888
4. Type of Business	Manufacturing of automotive accessories
5. Conference with	Richard W. Hess, President
6. Date and Place of Conference	January 11, 1975, at company's offices
7. Representatives of Corbin, Drake & Co.	William F. Corbin
8. Confirmation Letter Sent	January 11, 1975
9. Report to Be Addressed to	Board of Directors and Stockholders
10. Statements to Be Prepared	Balance sheet at December 31, 1975; related statements of income, retained earnings, and statement of changes in financial position for year ended December 31, 1975; federal income tax return. Also, unaudited state-ments at the end of each of the first three quarters.
11. Report Copies	12
12. Account to Be Charged	Ohio Manufacturing Company
13. Fee Basis: 7–Hour Day	Regular. Total, without extras, $xx,xxx. See engage-ment confirmation letter.
14. Estimated Man–Hours	300
15. Audit Locale	8959 Blue Ash Road, Cincinnati, Ohio 45242
16. Name of Person in Charge of Records	Robert P. McMann
17. Starting Date	January 5, 1976. At our choice, preliminary work may start any time.
18. Report to Be Finished	April 18, 1976; annual meeting of stockholders
19. Type of Audit	Regular
20. Period to Be Covered	January 1, 1975–December 31, 1975
21. Former Auditors	Arlington and Deekin
22. Type of Organization	Corporation—Ohio
23. Comments	Electronic data processing for sales, payroll, and payables
24. Assigned to: Partner	William F. Corbin
Manager	James Denny
Senior	Harold S. Pace
Staff	Russell Edwards, James Waters

2. Cash
    a) Returned bank checks arranged in accordance with request of auditor
    b) Bank reconciliations
    c) Schedules of cash items in transit
    d) Confirmation requests to be mailed by auditor
3. Receivables
    a) Statements to debtors, to be verified and mailed by auditor

  b) Aging schedules for receivables
  c) Schedules of notes receivable, together with notes
4. Investments
  a) Schedules of investments, indicating type, interest received, and interest accrued, dividends, stock splits, conversions, and so forth
  b) Investment purchases and sales transactions during year
5. Inventories
  a) Original inventory-count data
  b) Summaries of inventories by classes, locations, and so forth
  c) Inventory price schedules
  d) Sales price schedules for finished goods
6. Prepaid expenses
  a) Insurance schedules
  b) Other prepayments scheduled in accordance with auditor's instructions
7. Fixed assets
  a) Schedule showing agreement of control with plant ledgers
  b) Schedules of additions to capital assets with supporting vouchers
  c) Schedules of deductions from capital assets
  d) Analysis of accumulated depreciation showing credits and charges
  e) Analysis of repair accounts showing detail
8. Accounts and notes payable
  a) Statements from creditors
  b) Schedules of notes payable and any collateral given
9. Bonds and mortgages payable
  a) List of owners if there is no trustee
  b) Copies of bond indentures
  c) Schedules of premium or discount amortization
  d) Schedules of interest payments and accruals
  e) Canceled bonds which have been retired during the period
10. Corporate proprietorship
  a) Schedules of ownership of capital stock by name and number of shares if there is no transfer agent
  b) Analysis of charges and credits made during year to each non-capital stock proprietorship account
11. Revenues and expenses
  a) Labor summaries and overhead distribution summaries
  b) Lists of actual manufacturing expenses
  c) Schedules of tax payments
  d) Analysis of expenses and revenues, as indicated by auditor
12. Miscellaneous
  a) Copies of contracts, leases, royalty agreements, and so forth
  b) Other papers arranged in accordance with auditor's request

In many audits, certain data just indicated is not required. In some audits, the client prefers that the auditor prepare all schedules.

When the staff of a client prepares schedules for the auditor, they become a part of his file of work papers accumulated on the engagement. The accuracy of the data will be verified by the auditor. At the beginning of each fiscal period, many companies open an Audit file, accumulating therein all data and correspondence pertaining to the audit for that fiscal period.

Distinctive Auditing Terminology

At this point, certain distinctive auditing terms are introduced. Accountants commonly employ these distinctive terms to designate a function related to auditing.

Analyze. The transitive verb "to analyze" means to resolve into elements or parts and to separate the parts in relation to the whole or to one another. Consequently, the analysis of an account involves separating the entries into a systematic classification, together with explanations, in order to obtain accuracy.

Check. As a noun, the work "check" is used quite loosely in accounting; it may mean control or supervision in order to secure accuracy. As a transitive verb, "check" may mean the placing of a mark against an item, *after verification.* "Checking" may be used to indicate a comparison of the same number or numbers in two or more places. The words "check" and "checking" should be avoided in order to prevent ambiguity.

Compare. The transitive verb "to compare" means noting the similarity or dissimilarity of individual items, subtotals, or totals in a series of data—such as the comparison of a series of financial statements, or the comparison of two or more numbers, or of the same number in two or more places, as on a sales invoice and in a sales journal.

Confirm. "To confirm" means to obtain additional proof from a source other than the client or his records—for example, by obtaining from a bank an independent statement of the amount of cash on deposit, or by obtaining directly from customers, statements indicating the amounts owed by them.

Examine. The transitive verb "to examine" means to investigate, to inspect, or to test by appropriate method and in accordance with accepted standards.

Foot. To "foot" means to verify the accuracy of vertical subtotals and totals. "Crossfoot" means the verification of the accuracy of horizontal subtotals and totals.

Inspect. The transitive verb "to inspect" means to review critically or to investigate. "Inspect," "scan," and "scrutinize" may be used synonymously—all to the effect that entries are reviewed by inspection without complete verification, because complete verification would result in unwarranted work. Frequently, certain parts of the total entries are verified or vouched and the remainder are examined by inspection.

Reconcile.   This refers to bringing two separate and independent sets of related figures into agreement—for example, to reconcile the cash balance according to the ledger with the cash balance according to the bank statement.

Testing.   Testing refers to the verification of a *portion* of the accounting transactions. Testing is acceptable practice in internal and independent auditing. The assumption is that if the results of the tests are satisfactory, other similar data—although untested—will contain the same percentage of reliability.

Trace.   "To trace" is to determine if an item is properly disposed of in accordance with its original authority.

Verify.   To verify is to prove truth or accuracy. The term is used in the overall sense of proving the accuracy of footings, extensions, and postings; the existence and ownership of assets; depreciation charges; stockholders' ledger balances; and innumerable other items.

Vouch.   The transitive verb "to vouch" means to answer for or to warrant. Vouching is the examination of the underlying evidence which is in support of the accuracy of a transaction. The process of vouching is intended to substantiate an entry by proving authority, ownership, existence, and accuracy.

Voucher.   A voucher is any documentary evidence in support of a transaction. A voucher may be a paid check, a receipted invoice, a requisition for the withdrawal of materials from a storeroom, an authorization to place a new employee on the payroll, or a request for repairs. Frequently, a voucher is viewed as an authorization to disburse money; this concept is not all-inclusive.

Starting an Audit

Initial Audit Actions.   Each engagement will be under the control of a partner, a manager, or a firm supervisor. When he is assigned to a new client, the auditor in field charge should obtain a letter of introduction to the client from the person who arranged the engagement. The person in charge should study the engagement memorandum and all available correspondence. If he is not familiar with the industry of which the client's business is a part, he should inform himself through libraries, trade journals, and other staff members.

If the audit is a repeat engagement, the in-charge member of the accounting firm should take from the office files a copy of the preceding report and work papers, the necessary data from the permanent file, and the audit program for the past year and the year under audit. Upon arrival at a client's office, the auditor in charge of the engagement should set his staff to work. It does not particularly matter what is done first; so long as a well-controlled plan of examination is followed and the audit staff is properly guided. One of the first convenient tasks is to count cash, reconcile bank balances, and control and reconcile all negotiable securities; this is particularly true if the audit is being made promptly at the close of the accounting period or if fraud is suspected. Otherwise, each member of the audit staff may be assigned to any one of a variety of duties.

It is advisable for the in-charge auditor to devote a sufficient amount of the first day's time to visiting key personnel, reviewing significant events for the year and, in general, obtaining information of importance not necessarily available in the financial records.

Division of Duties among Staff.   On any audit, the duties of all audit personnel must be well defined by the in-charge auditor in order to avoid duplication of work and in order to secure the most effective audit results. The in-charge auditor should fully instruct his staff concerning the form and content of the work papers so that all papers will be prepared in accordance with the policies of the firm. If such instructions are not given, the work papers of each person on an engagement may differ in form and content, which will result in a waste of time, since the in-charge auditor may be forced to revise the schedules. The in-charge auditor—in accordance with firm policy—advises the staff members as to the methods to be followed in the routine progress of the audit.

ILLUSTRATION.   If the mechanical accuracy of postings is to be verified, the in-charge person will decide whether such verification shall be done (1) from the journals to the accounts or (2) from the accounts to the journals, and whether one person will do the verification or whether two shall be used—one to call entries and the other to tick them. The in-charge person also will indicate the extent of the testing; for example, he might instruct a member to verify sales in detail for a selected month; and if all transactions are in order, he might reasonably assume that the sales for the remaining 11 months are in order.

It is not unusual for the person in charge to extract (or verify the extraction of) the general ledger trial balance, since he must be familiar with the accounting system as a whole. Matters brought to the attention of that person by staff accountants which warrant discussion with the client should be handled by the in-charge person, never by another person—without authorization. The person in charge extracts information from the minutes; and he examines the charter and amendments thereto, the code of regulations, and copies of trust indentures and mortgages.

As indicated in Chapter 2, staff accountants vary from young persons on their first engagement to people who serve as seniors on certain audits and as staff accountants on others. A new staff accountant usually will be assigned to such duties as verifying extensions, footings, and postings; counting and reconciling cash balances; aging accounts receivable; verifying the balances of accounts receivable; vouching security transactions; proving the clerical accuracy of inventory sheets; verifying additions to and deductions from fixed assets; proving the proper balance of prepaid expenses; verifying the balances of notes and accounts payable accounts; verifying interest expense, prepaid interest, and accrued interest; and analyzing sales and expenses. Many other duties are normally assigned to staff accountants.

After the staff accountants have been assigned their initial tasks and after a superior has reviewed important events with key personnel, the in-charge accountant may perform any of the following duties, not necessarily in the order named:

1. *If the audit is for a new client:*
   a) Prepare a schedule of all books, records, and data storage media, and become familiar with the operation of the accounting system.
   b) Examine the system of internal control.
   c) Examine the articles of incorporation and amendments thereto (or the articles of copartnership).
   d) Examine the code of regulations (bylaws).
   e) Examine the minutes of the meetings of the board of directors (and committees of the board) and the stockholders (or the minutes of partners' meetings).
   f) Prepare a general ledger trial balance.
2. *If the audit is a repeat engagement:*
   a) Examine the minutes for the current year.
   b) Examine changes in the charter (or articles of copartnership).
   c) Examine alterations to the code of regulations (bylaws).
   d) Prepare a general ledger trial balance (or review it if prepared by another audit team member).

SECTION II: CHARGING AND PERSONNEL

Methods of Charging a Client

There are three common methods of charging a client:

1. *The Per Diem Basis.* Under this method, the charges are on the basis of time spent by partners, managers, supervisors, seniors, staff members, and office help. The rates are agreed upon with the client prior to the start of the engagement. Practices vary among accounting firms as to the number of working hours which constitute a day; a seven-hour day is considered normal. Per diem rates vary among accounting firms; and within one firm, the same rate is not necessarily used for all clients.

As a variation of a straight per diem rate, there is a growing tendency to use the per diem rate as only one factor of the total charge; other factors are results accomplished and importance or responsible nature of the work. Another variation is to charge a client at two or three times the salary rate of the firm personnel.

2. The Flat Fee Basis.   Under this method, a prearranged sum is agreed upon for the entire assignment, provided unforeseen circumstances which were not anticipated in advance do not arise during the course of the work. Some accountants charge a flat sum per month or per quarter, in accordance with the periodicity of the visits with the client.

3. The Maximum Fee Basis.   Under this method, per diem rates are used, with the understanding that the engagement is not to exceed a maximum sum. For self-protection, the auditor should insert an "escape" clause in his agreement in the event of unforeseen conditions which might develop during the course of the work.

Time Reports

A daily time report should be kept by each accountant or by one person for all members of a crew working on one assignment. The time reports are turned in to the accounting firm's office periodically—daily, biweekly, or once each month. The time report for each accountant will include not only his hours worked for each client but details of the type of work performed, as shown in Illustration 7–3. This report may be used as a measure of individual fee income productivity.

The time report of each accountant is transcribed into a record of *hours for each client.* The record of hours serves as a time and cost ledger for each client, segregated into each type of work performed on the engagement. Expense reports are kept for each accountant for travel and other costs chargeable to each job.

Billing a Client

Time and expense reports constitute one base used in billing a client and are directly or indirectly related to the methods of charging, unless the work is performed for a flat fee or for an agreed periodic charge.

Within one firm, practices may vary among clients. Some clients want to complete detail of charges; others do not. Invoices may be brief, indicating only the amount billed; or they may indicate the type of work

ILLUSTRATION 7–3
TIME REPORT (front)

				Week Ended	February 10, 1976		
Date	Case No.	Description	Hours	Date	Case No.	Description	Hours
2-5	428	Accounts receivable		2-8	428	Prepaid items	6
		confirmations	9		336	Conferences re: taxes	2
2-6	428	Accounts receivable			434	Contingencies	1
		aging	3				
	42	Office cash	2	2-9	428	Confirmations	2
	434	Minutes	2		282	Management ser-	
						vices	4
2-7	121	Investments	3			Unassigned	1
	121	Notes payable	2	2-10	42	General ledger	4
	282	Management ser-			336	Cash in bank	2
		vices	3				
					434	Liabilities	2
							48

TIME REPORT (reverse)

		TIME REPORT								

Name Harold S. Pace   Week Ended February 10, 1976

Case No.	Name of Client	Dates: 1976						Total	Office Only	
		2-5	2-6	2-7	2-8	2-9	2-10		Date	Amount
428	Ohio Manufacturing Co.	9	3		6	2		20		
121	The Carpet House			5				5		
42	R.S. Parnell, Inc.		2				4	6		
336	Molitor Corp.				2		2	4		
434	Evanston Co.		2		1		2	5		
282	Middle Motors			3		4		7		
	Unassigned					1		1		
	Total	9	7	8	9	7	8	48		

Approved W.F.C.

performed; or they may indicate the class of firm personnel used, with or without a description of the type of work performed.

Personnel Records

Many accounting firms have the auditor in charge of the engagement rate the assistants. These ratings are used when questions arise concerning promotions in rank, pay, and responsibility.

QUESTIONS

1. Why is it necessary to make preliminary audit arrangements with a client—particularly a new one?

2. When a CPA accepts an audit engagement from a new client who is a manufacturer, it is customary for the CPA to tour the client's plant and notes the plant facilities and the manufacturing operations.

   Discuss the ways in which the observations and note-taking would be of help to an auditor as he plans and conducts the audit.

   (AICPA, adapted)

3. The New York Stock Exchange requires each member brokerage firm which conducts business with the public to enter into a contract with a firm of independent public accountants for an audit annually without notice to the brokerage firm. The auditors are required to agree to conduct the audit in accordance with the regulations of the Exchange, to notify the Committee on Member Firms as soon as the audit is started, to fill in the Committee's financial questionnaire, and to submit signed reports to the Committee. The member firms are required to notify the Committee of the Exchange not later than April 1 of each year of the accounting firm selected and to file copies of the contract.

   What are the advantages and disadvantages of a surprise audit of this nature?

4. Draft an engagement letter for a proposed audit under the simple and incomplete conditions set forth below. Prepare your letter in a form different from the illustration in the text. Make any assumptions you wish.

   You have just returned to your office from a conference with the president of the Apple Company, a new client. You have made all preliminary arrangements with the client; the records of the company have never been examined by a CPA. Sales for the current year are $7,000,000.

5. Draft an engagement memorandum for the situation set forth in your answer to Question 4. Do not follow the form shown in the text.

6. An auditor has completed all preliminary arrangements with a new client. Why would the auditor be interested in the client's adjusted trial balance at the beginning of the period under examination?

7. *a*) During the early stages of an audit, the auditor asked for the minutes of the meetings of the board of directors. His request was refused. If you were the auditor, what course would you pursue?

   b) If the request for the minutes were refused, as in (*a*), but if you were offered a certified copy of all resolutions pertaining to accounting matters, what course would you pursue?

8. *a*) In addition to the work to be performed by a client's staff, what preliminary arrangements should be made with a new client prior to accepting an audit engagement?

   b) Before accepting a repeat engagement, what preliminary arrangements (other than the work to be performed by the client's staff) should be made with a client whose records you audited one year ago?

9. *a*) Upon his initial visit to a client, the auditor found that the asset, liability, and capital accounts had been ruled and balanced and that the revenue and expense accounts had been closed at the end of the period to be examined. In this case, the auditor desired to extract a preadjusted trial balance. How should he proceed so that he could do the work rapidly and be free from error?

   b) What entries should a professional public accountant normally make on the accounting records of an audit client?

10. On July 31, 1976 a business was converted from a partnership to a corporation. You have regularly audited the financial statements of this business as of December 31 of each year and are requested again to examine them for the year 1976. As compared with the auditing procedures followed in the examinations of prior financial statements, state what procedures you would eliminate or add for purposes of the latter examination.

11. On November 1, 1976, a client corporation of long standing acquired a 100 percent interest in Farn, Inc. The records of Farn, Inc. have been regularly audited in the past by a reliable firm of CPAs. You were called upon to audit the records of both companies for the year ended December 31, 1976. Consolidated financial statements are to be prepared.

    To what extent would you examine the records of Farn, Inc. for years prior to 1976.

12. You are the auditor of a large retail department store. The fiscal year ends June 30, 1976. What would you do first:

    a) If you could not start the audit until August 1, 1976?

    b) If you began the audit on July 1, 1976?

PROBLEMS

1. The statements in (*a*) and (*b*) below represent the opinions and attitudes sometimes encountered by CPAs:

   a) The modern audit emphasizes testing. This is dangerous because testing is dependent upon the judgment of the auditor, which may be defective. If every transaction is verified, only then can an audit be relied upon.

   b) It is important to read footnotes to the financial statements, even though they are often presented in technical language and may be incomprehensible. An auditor may reduce his exposure to third-party liability by stating something in the footnotes that contradicts his presentation in the financial statements.

You are to evaluate each of the preceding statements and set forth:

(1)   Areas of agreement with the statement—if any.

(2)   Areas of misconception, incompleteness, or fallacious reasoning included in the statement—if any.

(AICPA, adapted)

2.   High Finance, Inc. opened four loan offices in neighboring cities on January 2, 1975. Small cash loans are made to borrowers who repay the principal with interest in monthly installments over a period not exceeding two years. Uppton High, president of the Company, uses one of the offices as a central office and visits the other offices periodically for supervision and internal auditing purposes.

High is concerned about the honesty of his employees. He came to your office in December 1975 and stated that he wanted to engage you to install a system to prohibit his employees from embezzling cash. He also stated that until he went into business for himself he worked for a nationwide loan company with 500 offices and that he was familiar with that company's system of accounting and internal control. He stated, "I want to describe that system so you can install it for me because it will absolutely prevent fraud."

a)   How would you advise Mr. High regarding his request that you install the large company's system of accounting and internal control for his firm? Discuss.

b)   How would you respond to the suggestion that the new system would prevent embezzlement?

c)   Assume that in addition to undertaking the systems engagement in 1976, you agreed to examine High Finance's financial statements for the year ended December 31, 1975. No limitations were imposed.

(1)   How would you determine the scope necessary to satisfactorily complete your examination?

(2)   Would you be responsible for the discovery of fraud in this examination? Discuss.

(AICPA, adapted)

3.   Capitol, a single proprietor, intends to form a partnership with Hill. Capitol did not keep records and he cannot offer Hill financial statements to serve as a basis for determining the capital interests of the two men. Therefore, both men agree that Capitol shall continue to operate as a single entity until December 31, 1975. Capitol is to keep proper accounting records to serve as the basis for drafting a partnership contract.

On December 10, 1975, you are engaged to establish a starting point in the accounting retroactive to December 1, 1975.

From the following data, prepare a columnar work sheet setting forth the assets, liabilities, and capital of Capitol as of December 1, 1975; the transactions for the period December 1–10, 1975; income statement figures for the period December 1–10, 1975; and the balance sheet figures as of December 10, 1975. Show necessary computations.

You ascertain the following facts with regard to balances on pertinent dates and transactions during the 10-day period:

a) As of December 1, 1975:

(1) Cash balance per bank, November 30, 1975. . . . . $ 9,130
Outstanding checks, determined from checkbook:

No. 171 . . . . $ 670
178   290
193   340   1,300

(2) Accounts receivable from invoice copies:

A 1,600
B 1,000
C 1,200   3,800

(3) Accounts payable, from creditors' statements:

L $2,340
M 1,240
N   200   3,780

b) Transactions, December 1–10 inclusive:

(1) Sales on account to:

D, merchandise (cost $180) delivered December 4 . . . . $ 280
E, merchandise (cost $350) delivered December 7   500
F, merchandise (cost $300) delivered December 12,
and purchased from L, below   640   1,420

(2) Purchases of inventory on account from:

L, ordered December 1, received December 2. . . . . . . $1,180
N, ordered December 4, received December 8.   600
P, ordered December 10, received December 13   500   2,280

(3) Cash receipts:

Dec. 2 Cash sales (cost, $1,250). $1,720
5 A   800
7 Cash sales (cost, $640)   970
9 B   600
10 C (deposited December 11, 1975) 1,200   5,290

(4) Cash disbursements:

Dec. 1 December rent (Check No. 194) . . . . $ 450
5 M (Check No. 195) 1,000
9 L (Check No. 196) 1,000
9 Capitol, withdrawal (Check No. 197).   700   3,150

(5) December 4, receipt of credit memorandum for return
of inventory to M; goods received November 28
and returned November 30   240
December 9, allowance on invoice to B; November 24,
caused by an error in pricing   160

c) Balances, December 10, 1975:

(1) Cash balance per bank statement, December 10,
1975   10,110
Outstanding checks:

No. 193   340
196   1,000

(2) Inventory, physical count, priced at lower of cost
or market; all salable   6,400

(AICPA, adapted)

4. Small, Inc., a new client, prepared the trial balance set forth below as of December 31, 1975, the close of its second fiscal year. You were requested to examine the records. The examination resulted in the necessity of applying the entries indicated in the additional data below.

Prepare the audit adjustments and an eight-column work sheet for the year ended December 31, 1975. Ignore federal income taxes.

SMALL, INC.

Trial Balance, December 31, 1975

	Debits	Credits
Cash	$ 164,000	
Accounts receivable, net	200,000	
Inventories, December 31, 1974	223,000	
Unexpired insurance, December 31, 1974	6,000	
Land	220,000	
Buildings	330,000	
Accumulated depreciation, buildings		$ 6,600
Machinery	148,000	
Accumulated depreciation, machinery		15,000
Sinking fund assets	25,000	
Unamortized bond discount	25,000	
Treasury stock, common	35,000	
Accounts payable		189,000
Bond interest accrued		3,750
First-mortgage, 6 percent sinking fund bonds		226,500
Common stock		500,000
Premium on common stock		50,000
Stock donation		60,000
Retained earnings, December 31, 1974		74,150
Sales, net		875,000
Purchases of inventories	283,500	
Payroll	169,000	
Factory operating expenses	121,500	
Administrative expenses	35,000	
Bond interest	15,000	
	$2,000,000	$2,000,000

(AICPA, adapted)

ADDITIONAL DATA:

(1)   The $5000,000 common stock was issued at a 10 percent premium to the vendors of the land and buildings on December 31, 1973, the date of organization. Stock of a par value of $60,000 was donated back by the vendors and was recorded by a debit of $60,000 to Treasury Stock and a credit to Stock Donation. It was donated because the proceeds from its subsequent sale were to be considered as an allowance on the purchase price of land and buildings in proportion to their values as first recorded. The treasury stock was sold in 1975 for $25,000, which was credited to Treasury Stock.

(2)   On December 31, 1975, a machine costing $5,000 when the business started was removed. The removed machine had been depreciated at 10 percent during the first year. The only entry made was one crediting the Machinery account with its sales price of $2,000.

(3)   Depreciation is to be provided on the straight-line basis, as follows: buildings, two percent of cost; machinery, 10 percent of cost. Ignore salvage.

(4)   Inventories December 31, 1975, $175,000.

(5)   Three years' insurance is carried on buildings and machinery; and a premium of $9,000 had been paid on December 31, 1973.

(6)   The first-mortgage, six percent sinking fund bonds, par value of $250,000, mature in 10 years from January 1, 1974, with interest

payable on April 1 and October 1. They were sold on January 1, 1974, at 90; the discount is to be amortized over the life of the bonds on a straight-line basis.

(7) A sinking fund is built up on the straight-line basis, with a provision that installments after the first shall be decreased by the amount of the annual six percent interest, which interest is to be added to the fund.

The records disclose that the proper installment to the sinking fund was paid by the company on December 31, 1975, but that the amount was charged in error to the First-Mortgage, 6 Percent Sinking Fund Bonds account.

(8) The sinking fund trustee reported an addition of $1,500 interest to the fund on December 31, 1975. This had not been recorded by the company.

5. You are meeting with executives of Fall, Inc., to arrange your firm's engagement to examine the company's financial statements for the year ending December 31, 1975. One company executive suggested that the audit work be divided among three audit staff members so that one man would examine asset accounts, a second would examine liability and capital accounts, and the third would examine revenue and expense accounts in order to minimize time, avoid duplication of staff effort, and reduce interference with company operations.

Advertising is the company's largest expense, and the advertising manager suggested that a member of your staff whose uncle owns the advertising agency which handles the company's advertising be assigned to examine the Advertising Expense account. The staff member has a thorough knowledge of the complex contract between the company and the advertising agency on which the company's advertising costs are based.

a) To what extent should a CPA follow a client's suggestion for the conduct of an audit? Discuss.

b) List and discuss the reasons why audit work should not be assigned solely according to asset, liability and capital, and revenue and expense categories.

(AICPA, adapted)

6. You have been engaged to examine the financial statements of Kalb, Inc., for the year ended December 31, 1975. The former CPA firm declined to accept the engagement because a son of one of the CPA firm's partners received a material amount of Kalb common stock in exchange for engineering services rendered to Kalb, Inc., in 1975. The CPA firm's partner whose son received the stock had not participated in the Kalb examination in past years. Another of the CPA firm's 20 partners would have been in charge of this engagement.

In the past the audit report was considered and discussed at the annual meeting of the stockholders. Because of the shortage of time before the stockholders' meeting early in 1976, Kalb directors are willing to accept (*a*) your report containing unaudited financial statements and (*b*) your final report after the audit is completed. At a later date the client would like to receive (*c*) a report containing a forecast of the Corporation's operations for 1976 and 1977.

a) Should the former CPA firm of Kalb, Inc., have declined the examination of the financial statements for the year ended December 31, 1975? Discuss.

b) Discuss the issues involved in the client's request that you render unaudited financial statements prior to the rendition of your final audit report.

c) What are the issues involved for a CPA in rendering a report containing forecasts of a client's future operations? Discuss.

(AICPA, adapted)

PRACTICE MATERIAL ASSIGNMENTS

Metalcraft, Incorporated: Audit Problem:
  Read General Instructions and Miscellaneous Information.
Colby, Gears, Inc.: Holmes and Moore Audit Case:
  Introductions for Parts I, II, III, and IV.

8

Audit Programs and Audit Work Papers

SECTION I: AUDIT PROGRAMS

Discussion of an Audit Program

In order to understand, report, and render an opinion, an auditor must inquire, examine, and authenticate. As an aid to inquiry, examination, and authentication, an auditor prepares a logically planned program of audit procedures for each examination. Audit programs are of two general types, as follows:

1. A planned and predetermined scheduling for the conduct of each audit, or
2. A skeleton or progressive form setting forth briefly the scope, character, objectives, and limitations of the audit.

Each audit program should be streamlined so that the procedures developed for each audit are in accordance with the circumstances of that examination. The auditor must be efficient in planning each audit; unnecessary procedures must *not* be included. Every procedure set forth in an audit program must be useful and necessary in the circumstances. Any one particular procedure must not be applied simply because it has always been applied.

In preparing an audit program, full advantage must be taken of the knowledge and judgement of experienced firm personnel so that all procedures in the program are proper. Each audit step must be justifiable as being an efficient method of obtaining information necessary for an expression of opinion. Audit programs must be so planned and procedures must be adopted which will result in reasonable assurance that all financial statement figures are properly recorded and included in accordance with accepted principles of accounting. The representations of management must be supported by evidence, and the internal control and accounting procedures in effect must be reviewed.

Imagination and initiative must be used effectively during the course of an audit, regardless of the care exercised in planning an audit program, because all conceivable contingencies for each individual examination cannot be reduced to writing prior to the examination.

The purpose of a planned and predetermined audit program is (1) to serve as a procedural guide during the course of the audit or (2) to serve as a check-off list as the audit progresses and successive phases of the work are completed in order that no verification or procedure may be overlooked. Each method of operating a planned audit program has its advantages and disadvantages. A planned audit program should not be rigid; it must be flexible to meet changing conditions. A planned audit program should suggest; it should not stifle thought.

The planned audit program for any one client must be revised periodically in conformity with changing conditions of the client's operations and in accordance with changes in auditing, standards, and procedures. each of which has an important role in shaping the program.

ILLUSTRATION. One national accounting firm *completely* rewrites the audit program of each client once every three years; for the intervening two years, the program is revised annually as required.

During the course of an examination, the entire audit program for a client will be completed. Each section of an audit program is signed by the accountant responsible for that particular section of the examination.

Advantages of a Planned Audit Program. The advantages of a planned audit program may be set forth as follows:

1. It places responsibility for each audit procedure.
2. It promotes the division of work over the audit staff in an organized manner.
3. It results in proper audit routine and saves time.
4. It emphasizes the essential procedures for each client.
5. It serves as a guide in succeeding years.
6. It facilitates the review by a manager and/or partner.
7. It assures adherence to auditing standards and the application of generally accepted accounting principles.

Disadvantages of a Planned Audit Program. Disadvantages claimed by opponents of a predetermined audit program are as follows:

1. The responsibility of the in-charge auditor is limited to the program.
2. Independent, constructive thinking is deterred.
3. The audit becomes "automatic."

These claims are to the effect that if a predetermined audit program is used, the person in charge will not assume proper responsibility, he will not think independently, and the audit will follow the lines of least resistance. If this situation exists, evidently the staff members are inefficient and would be so under any circumstances. A General Information section of an audit program appears in Illustration 8–1, in part.

ILLUSTRATION 8–1

```
                              AUDIT PROGRAM
                             General Information


Prepared by_____
Date_____
Reviewed by_____
Date_____

 1.  Name of Client_____
 2.  Address_____
 3.  Fiscal Year Ends_____
 4.  Name and Address of Branches and Subsidiaries_____
 5.  Audit:  To Start_____  To Be Finished_____
 6.  Estimated Man-Hours_____
 7.  Personnel Assigned:  Partner_____  Manager_____
                          Supervisor_____  Senior_____
                          Staff Accountants_____
 8.  Describe the Audit_____
 9.  Number of Reports:_____Complete_____Short_____
10.  Reports to Be Addressed to: _____
11.  Tax Returns:_____ Federal_____ State_____ Other_____
12.  Securities Listed:_____ Exchange(s)_____
13.  Capital Stock:_____ Registrar_____ Transfer Agent___
14.  Corporation_____Partnership_____Single Proprietorship____Estate____Other___
15.  Date Organized_____ State_____
16.  Other States in Which Authorized to Do Business_____
17.  Officers, Directors, Employees (Place a "D" after Directors):
         President_____  Internal Auditor_____
         Vice President(s)_____  Office Manager_____
         Secretary_____  Bookkeeper(s)_____
         Treasurer_____  Cashier(s)_____
         Controller_____  Other_____
18.  Attorneys_____
19.  Bonds and Other Debt Securities_____
20.  Describe Any Intercompany Relationships or Affiliations and the Extent and Nature Thereof_____
21.  Retirement Pension Plan Description_____
22.  Banks:  Name of:_____
             Type of Account:_____
             Required Signature(s)_____Title(s)_____
23.  Special Comments_____
     _____
     _____
```

Internal Control Questionnaire

As stated in prior chapters, an auditor relies upon the system of internal control in effect to serve as a guide regarding the amount of detailed examination work to be performed during the course of an audit. There fore, in order to obtain adequate information for the evaluation of the adequacy of a client's system of internal control, an internal control questionnaire is prepared. For a new client, the internal control questionnaire (see Illustration 8–2) should be completed in full; in a repeat engagement, the internal control questionnaire should be reviewed and compared with the operational policies of the client. Periodically, the internal control questionnaire should be revised in accordance with changes in the operational policies of a client and in accordance with changes in the accounting system.

Developing an Audit Program and Internal Control Questionnaire

In developing an audit program and an internal control questionnaire, an auditor must include all procedures and questions considered adequate for the engagement. Procedures and questions of a nature that are petty under the circumstances of the engagement should be excluded. The line of demarcation between inclusion and exclusion may be difficult to determine; therefore the program and the questionnaire must be flexible. Adequacy of inclusion and exclusion may be entirely different between clients. When developing a specific audit program and internal control questionnaire, the auditor must study all of the aspects and operations of a new client; for a repeat-engagement client, the auditor studies changes in operations, products, personnel, and client procedures.

Internal control questionnaires must be integrated with each operation and with the functional organization of the client. In the development of an audit program and internal control questionnaire, time budgets for staff members may be prepared, as exemplified by one accounting firm which posts assignments for several months in advance, by date, client, and individual members of the firm.

Many accounting firms use a standard preprinted audit program and internal control questionnaire. When used, applicable and nonapplicable items must be noted for each client. Preprinted programs and internal control questionnaires may have the disadvantage of too much standardization for a varied clientele.

Audit Program and Internal Control Questionnaire Illustrated

Starting with Chapter 12 at the beginning of *each succeeding chapter* there will be presented (1) that portion of an audit program applicable to the standards and procedures to be followed; and (2) the applicable section of the internal control questionnaire. This material, assembled from all chapters, constitutes a complete illustrative audit program and a complete internal control questionnaire. *These programs and questionnaires are only generally suggested examples.* In the illustrations, and "Yes," "No," and "Not Applicable" type of questionnaire is used. In many instances, spelled-out answers are preferable, but this is not feasible in a book.

A suggested part of the general information section of the audit program and the internal control questionnaire may appear as indicated in Illustrations 8–1 and 8–2, respectively. In many respects, the general information section of an audit program is similar to an engagement memorandum; changed where necessary, an engagement memorandum may be prepared to serve the purpose of the general information section of the audit program.

ILLUSTRATION 8–2

INTERNAL CONTROL QUESTIONNAIRE General Information				
Company_____ Period Covered_____	Yes	No	Not Appli- cable	Remarks
1. Do we have the latest organization chart?	____	____	____	_____
2. Are the duties of officers and employees fixed as to responsibility?	____	____	____	_____
3. Are accounting manuals in use?	____	____	____	_____
4. Is the accounting department function completely divorced from:				
a) Selling?	____	____	____	_____
b) Purchasing?	____	____	____	_____
c) Manufacturing?	____	____	____	_____
d) Credit granting?	____	____	____	_____
e) Cash receipts?	____	____	____	_____
f) Cash disbursements?	____	____	____	_____
5. Does the client have a controller or the equivalent?	____	____	____	_____
6. Does the client have an internal auditor or the equivalent?	____	____	____	_____
7. Does the internal auditor:				
a) Follow written programs? Are such programs designed to test internal control?	____	____	____	_____
b) Issue reports covering his examination?	____	____	____	_____
8. Are accounting employees' duties rotated?	____	____	____	_____
9. Are all employees required to take vacations?	____	____	____	_____
10. Are employees in positions of trust bonded?	____	____	____	_____
11. Are the bonds adequate in amount and character?	____	____	____	_____
12. Is collusion improbable between relatives who are employees?	____	____	____	_____
13. Are the accounting records adequate for the business?	____	____	____	_____
14. Are internal reports to management adequate to disclose abnormal financial figures?	____	____	____	_____
15. Are expenses under budgetary control?	____	____	____	_____
16. Is adequate control exercised over branch operations?	____	____	____	_____
17. If any officers are also executives of other organizations (other than known affiliates) with which the client does business:				
a) Are transactions with those enterprises subject to the same routines as transactions with regular vendors and customers?	____	____	____	_____
b) Are duties of those officials such that irregular transactions are improbable?	____	____	____	_____
Prepared by_____ Date_____		Reviewed by_____ Date_____		

Petty Cash Section. A suggested illustrative portion of an audit program and internal control questionnaire for a cash fund is shown in Illustration 8–3 and 8–4.

ILLUSTRATION 8–3

AUDIT PROGRAM (IN PART)

Company_____

Period Covered_____   Petty Cash (or Any Cash Fund)

1. Count and list all items in the fund._____

2. Reconcile with Cash Fund general ledger account._____

3. Trace all checks in the fund to subsequent deposit tickets and to the bank statements._____

4. Test–trace the fund vouchers to the reimbursement voucher; inspect distributions, approval, and original evidence._____

(See Chapter 12 for complete audit program for cash funds.)

ILLUSTRATION 8–4

INTERNAL CONTROL QUESTIONNAIRE
(IN PART)
Petty Cash (or any Cash Fund)

Company_____ Period Covered_____	Yes	No	Not Appli-cable	Remarks
1. Is the imprest system used?	____	____	____	_____
2. Is responsibility for each fund vested in one person?	____	____	____	_____
3. Are fund cash vouchers:				
a) Required for each fund disbursement?	____	____	____	_____
b) Prenumbered by the printer?	____	____	____	_____
c) Signed by the recipient of the cash disbursed?				
d) Executed in ink?	____	____	____	_____
e) Executed with amounts written in numerals and spelled out?	____	____	____	_____
f) Approved by a responsible person?	____	____	____	_____
g) Canceled, together with supporting documents, so that they cannot be misused thereafter?	____	____	____	_____

(See Chapter 12 for complete internal control questionnaire for cash funds.)

Prepared by_____   Reviewed by_____
Date_____   Date_____

Filing the Audit Program and the Internal Control Questionnaire.
Practices of filing an audit program and an internal control questionnaire
vary among accounting firms.

ILLUSTRATION. One national firm of accountants files the internal control questionnaire *as a unit* at the beginning of the work papers and files
each section of the audit program with the work papers for that section.
Another firm files both the program and the questionnaire as a unit at the
beginning of the work papers.

If the completed audit program and internal control questionnaire are
filed as a unit with the client's permanent records, they are valuable—as
a unit—in assisting memory in the future and in giving members of
the firm who are visiting a repeat client for the first time a preliminary
idea of procedures followed in the past. Filing an audit program and
internal control questionnaire with the work papers interspersed at each
section forces a review of the work papers. If desired, all work papers
can be indexed to a designated space on the audit program and each
section of the audit program indexed to the applicable work papers.

The Effect of EDP on Internal Control and on an Audit Program

Automation is the performance of control functions by machinery.
When an electronic data processing system is in operation, the work
of employees is performed by machines. The personnel who operate
the EDP equipment do not originate transactions or accumulate data—
they merely process the transactions and data furnished by the various
departments of a business. Internal controls must be established so that
there is a counterbalancing verification between those persons who originate transactions and accumulate data and those persons who process
the transactions and data through the electronic equipment into the form
of storage and printout of—for example—sales by dates, products, salesmen; accounts receivable; classified expenses; payroll analyses; and so
forth.

Proper internal control demands that the personnel operating the electronic data processing machines are not afforded the opportunity to tam-
per with the input data. Therefore, proper internal control may be
effected by establishing a separate group whose duty it is to verify the
accuracy of the data processing center. To illustrate: In the accumulation
of its payroll, a large manufacturer of electrical goods and aircraft engines
has a battery of comptometer operators who predetermine the payroll
figures for each employee, and in total. These data then are electronically
processed and stored at the data processing center, and the payroll checks
are printed. The totals of the comptometer operators—by items—must
be in agreement with the totals of the processing center. Thus, internal
control is effected, and errors and manipulation are prevented. As a part

of his audit program, the auditor might decide to compare a printout of a payroll with personnel and payroll department records for such items as names, pay rates, hours worked, deductions, etc.

Due to the flexibility of the uses of EDP equipment and due to the variety of types of equipment, an auditor may find it necessary to prepare a new and individual internal control questionnaire for each client using electronic data processing equipment.

Additional effects of electronic data processing on internal control questionnaires and audit programs are discussed in Chapters 5, 11, and in subsequent chapters.

SECTION II: AUDIT WORK PAPERS

Importance of Work Papers

A review of recent court cases involving the liability of CPAs for negligence, fraud, and conspiracy to defraud, and a review of the advice of legal counsel and the Institute and that of other attorneys definitely will indicate the importance of proper work paper preparation.

Also, informative work papers accumulated during an engagement are important because they support the audit report. The work papers reflect the adherence to accepted auditing standards, the auditing procedures employed, and the conclusions reached during an engagement.

Following a well-designed audit program and internal control questionnaire, the preparation of proper audit work papers develops logical thought in the procedural conduct of an audit. Audit work papers include all data compiled during the course of an examination—a pencil draft of the report, trial balance work sheets, schedules, analyses, confirmations, comments; a copy of the articles of incorporation and amendments thereto; excerpts from bylaws; copies of leases, contracts, and minutes of meetings of the board of directors (and committees within the board) and the stockholders; and all other papers collected during the course of an audit which are in support of the procedures followed and the standards adhered to in the examination. Copies of the original records of a client do not fall within the concept of work papers; but with the consent of the client, they become work papers.

Work papers, per se, do not include correspondence, audit programs, internal control questionnaires, and procedural memoranda; but if the audit work is attacked, the defendent will want such material.

A Complete Set of Work Papers

In a separate binder accompanying this text, there is presented a complete set of work papers for an Illustrative Audit. These are the papers normally necessary for the examination of the records of a medium-sized manufacturing concern. Examples involving alternative forms of work papers are presented throughout the text. The purpose of the Illustrative Audit work papers accompanying the text is to serve as a guide in proper technical preparation, arrangement, fullness of content, and method of indexing. Among accountants there will be variations in the preferred forms of work papers. There are many variations necessary in the content of work papers for different types of industries and for business concerns within those industries. However, the general rules governing the preparation of all work papers are the same under any operating conditions.

Purpose of Audit Work Papers

Validity of Records. In his work papers, an auditor compiles all data, analyses, notes, schedules, excerpts, confirmations, and other materials pertaining to the audit. From these papers and the completed audit program and internal control questionnaire, he extracts the materials for the audit report submitted to the client. The client is not necessarily concerned with the procedures used by the auditor; but the client is interested in the audit report, and the *audit work papers constitute the only tangible connecting link between the records of the client and the report.*

Review of Internal Control. Audit work papers should indicate the results of the review of client internal control. These results may be evidenced in the internal control questionnaire, but comments on the internal control of specific items may appear in each of the appropriate work papers.

Data Reference. Work papers serve the auditor as one source of information for his advice in discussing business matters with the client. They also aid an auditor in the solution of questions involving taxes with the various taxing units. In addition, they serve to assist in the preparation of reports to the Securities and Exchange Commission, and other governmental commissions and bureaus. Work papers may be used for reference many years after the completion of an audit.

Position Defense. Properly prepared audit work papers assist the auditor in justifying his position against criticism, in offering court testimony, and in defending himself in the event of legal attack. When offered as testimony or when serving as the basis of the opinion of witnesses, properly prepared work papers frequently are the best protection of the professional integrity of the auditor.

Audit Review. Complete work papers constitute the best aid to personnel who review the work of the fieldmen, and for the review of the audit report. The purpose of reviewing work papers and the report by a superior is to ascertain that all statements and schedules have been properly prepared and are correctly supported; that procedural technique has been suitable and adequate; that comments are appropriate; and that all necessary comments have been included.

In an accounting firm, the following steps may be normal for the review of work performed by field personnel: (1) the person in field-charge of an engagement prepares the audit report, (2) a manager reviews the work papers and the report, and (3) a partner then reviews all work. The interest of the partner in the review is prompted by good business practice and by the fact that he is primarily responsible for the work. With proper review, the Ultramares case might never have existed.

Future Reference. Audit work papers serve as a guide for subsequent audits of the same client. This does not mean that the form and content should be followed without change; but peculiarities of the examination will be set forth, there is a basis for follow-up and action, and a reminder is available when changes in procedure are contemplated. If the records of a client are stolen, lost, altered, or burned, complete work papers will prove of value in reconstruction.

Principles of Audit Work Paper Preparation

Care in Preparation. Work papers must be carefully prepared, and it is impossible to formulate invariable rules of preparation. Audit work papers must be so designed and prepared that managers and partners can effectively review an audit with the assurance (1) that the audit program has been fulfilled; (2) that the examination was made in accordance with generally accepted auditing standards applicable in the circumstances; and (3) that the financial statements have been prepared in accordance with accepted principles of accounting, consistently applied.

In work papers, *do not* recopy information available in a client's records but include only summarized material. The auditor preparing a work paper should state his conclusions therein in order to expedite the audit and in order to set forth his understanding of the audit objectives.

If the auditor will ask himself the following questions and if he can satisfactorily answer them, he soon will be able to make those fine discriminations necessary for the preparation of good work papers:

1. Are these data necessary to the report?
2. Are these data necessary to the support of any item in the report?
3. Are these data necessary in the event of a future investigation?
4. Are these data necessary for the verification of the correctness of the records and the transactions?
5. Will the omission of these data have material consequences?

The ability and skill of an auditor frequently can be judged by his work papers. When an auditor has adhered to all applicable auditing standards and accounting principles, followed all necessary procedures, completed his engagement, and submitted the work papers to a superior, and if the latter can write a report from the work papers submitted without asking questions, the papers have withstood the test of excellent preparation. Another test of good work papers occurs when it becomes necessary for one accountant to leave a partially completed engagement and turn over its completion to another member. If the latter can proceed without confusion to himself or to the staff of the client, the work papers are good.

In order to construct adequate work papers, it is necessary to plan carefully the course of the audit and the papers required in its consummation. If the work papers are properly planned, it is unnecessary to rewrite schedules. Normally, only one item or account analysis is placed on each work paper. The only exception to this procedure occurs when related accounts are analyzed—for example, notes payable, interest expense, and accrued interest on the notes. If several accounts or sets of data are placed on one sheet, it is impossible to index the schedules correctly, to arrange the work papers in accordance with the audit program, or to arrange them properly for the drafting of the report in an orderly and rapid fashion. All pertinent data must be reduced in writing, and the memory must be relied upon only to the extent that it can be substantiated by evidence.

Physical Aspects.   Broadly construed, work papers include all data collected during the course of an audit, with the result that the content and the form of the work papers are of paramount importance. The content must be full and explicit. The form must be impeccable from the standpoint of neatness and arrangement, so that the character, thoroughness, and exactness of the auditor are reflected.

The major expense of operating a firm of public accountants is the cost of personnel. Therefore, it is only logical to offer firm personnel adequate facilities in order to promote their efficient operation, both for the firm and for the client. High-grade paper is excellent economy when measured in terms of the benefits derived, and the paper should absorb, not reflect, light. Rulings on the paper should never be crowded, since figure legibility is important to the auditor and to the stenographic staff.

Control of Work Papers.   All work papers must be protected during the course of an audit. Responsibility for each work paper must be established both during and after the audit.

In order to promote what might be termed the "internal operating control" of work papers, many auditors follow a plan somewhat along the following lines: In the preparation of a general ledger trial balance, the individual items are marked with an "S" if they are to be separately scheduled or with an "A" for an analysis, when such additional procedures are to be followed. A Remarks column is used on the trial balance work paper for explanations available or desirable at the time the trial balance is taken. Immediately after completing the trial balance, work sheets are headed for each indicated schedule and analysis. These headed schedules are placed in an Incomplete file. As the audit work is assigned, the firm members would receive the work papers from the Incomplete file. The completed work papers are then placed in a Completed file, arranged in the sequence of the trial balance.

Superscribing the Work Papers. Each completed work paper should be signed and dated by the person performing the work in order to establish responsibility of action. At the top of each sheet must be placed the name of the client, the account name and number, or a title for the data contained in the paper, and the period of the audit.

Deficiencies in Work Papers. Work papers should be free of deficiencies, a *few* of which are set forth below:

1. Lack of evidence that the system of internal control was investigated and was found to be adequate or inadequate.
2. Failure to note the final clearance of points raised earlier in the audit.
3. Failure to describe the review of accounts not analyzed.
4. Negligence in indicating the auditing procedures followed.
5. Failure to cross-reference audit adjustments.
6. Incomplete data for the preparation of the report.
7. Pricing bases omitted for assets.
8. Overall depreciation policies not surveyed.
9. Certificates not obtained for inventories, liabilities, etc.
10. Failure to include statements of work performed concerning post-balance-sheet-date transactions.
11. Failure to include statements regarding the closing of tax matters of prior years.
12. Failure to spell out fully names of securities.
13. Failure to compare original cost price and current market replacement cost for assets—when necessary.
14. Failure to indicate the investigation of inventory controls, cost systems, and obsolete inventories.
15. Failure to clear cash funds of noncash items.
16. Failure to assemble and analyze confirmation request replies.

Ownership of Work Papers

Work papers accumulated by an auditor are his property. In the cash of *Ipswich Mills* v. *Dillion and Son*, 260 Mass. 453, the decision was that the client has no right to work papers prepared by an auditor. The case was decided in 1927, and it relieved much uncertainty concerning the ownership of work papers. It also appears that federal revenue agents have no direct access to auditor's work papers but must refer to original records and data. There is nothing, of course, to prevent an auditor from showing his work papers to the client or revenue agent, or from giving the client a copy of them.

In a court case, work papers may be offered by an auditor in evidence to establish the fairness of his opinion and the propriety of his audit. Also, they may be offered in evidence by a plaintiff to support his allegations. A court order can force an auditor to divulge the contents of his work papers. Several jurisdictions have statutory laws specifically vesting work paper ownership in the accountant.

Audit Code Legend

In preparing work papers, an auditor will use many tick-marks of various shapes and colors, both in the records of the client and in his work papers. In order to assist his memory as to the meaning of each symbol and in order to allow another firm member to understand the meaning of each, a legend should be prepared. The following list partially illustrates an audit code legend.

√   Place this symbol in records of original entry to indicate comparison with an original document, such as an invoice.

Ⅵ   Place under vertical totals to indicate footing.

W   Place opposite amounts in ledger accounts to indicate the tracing of postings from records of original entry.

Λ   Use this inverted check mark to show that a comment has been investigated and accepted, or adjusted and accepted.

—   This hyphen under an amount in a record that has been examined indicates the last item of the current period.

=   Two parallel hyphens are used beneath the grand total of a footed column to indicate its agreement with the sum of the distribution totals.

●   In the check record, place beside each outstanding check, and the amount is to be listed in the bank reconciliation.

⊙   A circled dot is placed beside each item in the check record, indicating comparison with the paid check. The same legend may be placed on the paid check.

S   Use in the trial balance to indicate that a schedule is to be prepared.

$ A slant line is drawn through the "S" to indicate the completion of the schedule.

∅   This symbol placed on a duplicate deposit ticket indicates the comparison of that document with an entry in the cash receipts record.

There are many additional audit code legends. More than one code legend often may be used in connection with one number in one place—for example, √, Ⅵ, and W .

Illustrative Work Papers

A few work papers are illustrated at this point. Additional work papers appear in succeeding chapters and in the Illustrative Audit.

Trial Balance Work Papers. General ledger trial balance work papers should be prepared early in the audit in order to promote familiarity with the accounts and to serve as a guide during the examination. There are many forms of general ledger trial balance work papers. Normally, the general ledger trial balance is drawn in the order in which the accounts appear in the ledger—which order should follow the arrangement of the financial statements.

A convenient arrangement is to place all balance sheet accounts on one work paper and all revenue and expense accounts on another paper. Where there are many accounts, the balance sheet accounts and the revenue and expense accounts may be further subdivided into at least one sheet for each of the following groups: assets, liabilities, proprietorship accounts, revenues, and expenses. This type of segregation of the accounts facilitates comparisons, directs attention to the points of the audit requiring special emphasis, and permits more than one person to use the trial balance papers.

Illustration 8–5 presents one form of trial balance work paper.

In the Work Paper Number column, there will be placed the number or numbers of the individual work papers accumulated during the course of the audit which have reference to and are in support of the particular item in the trial balance. As each individual audit work paper is completed and its number placed in the trial balance work papers, the number of the work paper in the trial balance may be circled to indicate that all work on that item is completed.

If the Trial Balance columns are prepared in comparative form—one for the preceding year and one for the current year—figure comparison is facilitated; and accounts are set forth which require investigation due to major changes or due to peculiarities. See the Illustration Audit.

The Adjustments columns contain all audit adjustments, and are made as their necessity is discovered during the course of the examination. Audit adjustments are recorded as follows:

1. On the individual work paper for the account adjusted.
2. On a work paper entitled "Audit Adjustments," where all adjustments are placed in chronological order, together with full explanations.
3. On the trial balance work sheet.

A copy of the audit adjustments is presented to the client at the conclusion of the audit so that he may post to his records. Some auditors will not issue a report unless the client takes up the adjustments, since the auditor is rendering his opinion of the client's representations.

ILLUSTRATION 8-5

THE HILL CORPORATION
Trial Balance Work Paper, Year Ended December 31, 1975

		Prepared By	Approved By	Initials	Date

Work Paper No.	Acct. No.	Account Name	General Ledger Trial Balance December 31, 1975		Audit Adjustments		Income Statement		Balance Sheet December 31, 1975		Report Reclassification Data and Remarks
			Debit	Credit	Debit	Credit	Debit	Credit	Debit	Credit	
1	1	Cash in bank	106,000			(1) 500			105,500		Cash on hand and in bank, $106,300
2	2	Petty cash fund	1,000			(6) 200			800		
3	3	Accounts and notes receivable	194,000						194,000		Notes: $25,000; Accounts, $169,000
4	3A	Allowance for doubtful items		5,000		(2) 3,000				8,000	Doubtful accounts, $8,000; Notes: None
5	4	Marketable securities	85,000						85,000		
6	5	Inventories	95,000						95,000		Raw, $50,000; In process, $30,000: Finished, $15,000
7	9	Prepaid insurance	3,000		(3) 300				3,300		
8	21	Machinery	102,000		(4) 800				102,800		
9	21A	Accumulated depreciation—machinery		19,000	(5) 300					18,700	Net, $84,100
10	22	Office equipment	30,000						30,000		
11	22A	Accumulated depreciation—office equipment		7,200						7,200	Net, $22,800
12	31	Accounts and notes payable		49,000						49,000	Notes, $10,000; Accounts $39,000
13	32	Taxes withheld		4,000						4,000	
14	33	Accrued items		2,500		(7) 400				2,900	
15	34	Federal income tax liability, 1975									(See below)
16	51	Common stock		300,000						300,000	Issued, 300,000 shares; par $1.00 per share
17	52	Retained earnings		147,000						147,000	Retained earnings, $194,892
18	70	Sales		985,000				985,000			See sales analysis
19	71	Cost of goods sold	696,000		(6) 200	(5) 300 / (4) 800	695,100				
20	81	Selling expense	98,000		(1) 500		98,500				
21	91	Administrative expenses	111,000		(2) 3,000	(3) 300	113,700				
22	96	Other revenues		5,300				5,300			
23	97	Other expenses	3,000		(7) 400		3,400				
			1,524,000	1,524,000	5,500	5,000	910,700	990,300	616,400	536,800	
							79,600			79,600	
							990,300	990,300	616,400	616,400	
15	34	Federal income tax, 1975					31,708 AJE8			31,708 AJE8	See Audit Adjustments WP.
		Net income retained after taxes					47,892			47,892	
							79,600			79,600	

Notes: Many auditors include the December 31, 1974 (prior year), adjusted trial balance immediately before the December 31, 1975, company Trial Balance columns.

See the trial balance work papers in the Illustrative Audit for a larger illustration.

There are many forms of trial balance work papers.

The Reclassification column in Illustration 8–5 is used to reclassify the accounts for purposes of preparing financial statements. Such reclassification promotes ease of operation and saves time in preparing the statements on a basis consistent with the practice of the preceding period. Reclassification of accounts for financial statement purposes frequently has the effect of combining related items, thus relieving the statements of unnecessary detail. As an example of a reclassification entry, credit balances of significant amount in accounts receivable should be segregated for balance sheet purposes, but they need not be segregated in the records of the client. Another example of a reclassification entry would be the segregation of affiliated company receivables from trade receivables.

The Remarks normally pertain to comments relating to the preparation of financial statements, although they may be for guidance during the course of the examination.

The degree of complication of accounts often will influence an auditor on preparing his working trial balance. For simple audits of small enterprises, one method of work paper preparation may be used; whereas, for involved accounting structures and EDP systems, another method may be adopted in order to allow space for greater detail and analysis and to save time in balancing out the work papers.

Audit Adjustments Work Papers. Adjustments made by the auditor are recorded in full on separate work papers entitled "Audit Adjustments." Each adjustment should be accompanied by a complete and clear explanation. Account titles should not be abbreviated. Each adjustment should be fully cross-indexed to the related work papers where the entry originated and to the control and subsidary accounts. Audit adjustments should be numbered consecutively, and the same number should appear in the Adjustment column of the trial balance work papers and in all leading and supporting schedules.

The Illustrative Audit contains complete audit adjustment work papers. See also Illustration 8–6.

Leading Schedules. Any schedule is prepared so that desired information may be developed. A leading schedule—or summary schedule or top schedule—is one that classifies and summarizes similar or related items. The total of each leading schedule becomes the balance sheet class total or the income statement class total to be used in the financial statements. For example, in Illustration 8–7, a leading schedule is shown for fixed assets and the related accumulated depreciation. The adjusted fixed asset total and the adjusted accumulated depreciation total will agree with the balance sheet totals for these two items.

Supporting Schedules. Supporting schedules and analyses are prepared in substantiation of items in a leading schedule. The supporting schedules carry the detail of the periodic debits, credits, and adjustments. A supporting schedule for machinery is shown in Illustration 8–8. An analysis of sales is presented in Illustration 8–9. On each supporting sched-

ILLUSTRATION 8–6

THE HILL CORPORATION
Audit Adjustment
For the Year Ended December 31, 1975

	Initials	Date
Prepared By		
Approved By		

Acct. No.	Audit Adjustments	Debit	Credit
	AJE 1 (1)		
81	Selling Expenses (Store Supplies Expense).	500	
1	Cash in Bank.		
	Check No. 1822, issued to Store Supplies, Inc., December 30, 1975, not recorded.		
	AJE 2 (4)		
91	Administrative Expenses (Doubtful Accounts)	3,000	
3A	Allowance for Doubtful Items		3,000
	To increase the allowance for doubtful items to $8,000, on the basis of the aging schedule.		
	AJE 3 (7)		
8	Prepaid Insurance	300	
91	Administrative Expenses (Insurance)		300
	To adjust prepaid insurance; see schedule.		
	AJE 4 (8)		
21	Machinery	800	
71	Cost of Goods Sold (Factory Operating Expense) . .		800
	Machinery purchased December 28, 1975, charged to expense.		
	AJE 5 (9)		
21A	Accumulated Depreciation--Machinery.	300	
71	Cost of Goods Sold (Depreciation of Machinery) . .		300
	Amount to be depreciated $97,000 X 0.10. $ 9,700 1975 company provision . . . . $10,000 Overdepreciation . . . . $ 300		
	AJE 6 (2)		
71	Cost of Goods Sold (Factory Supplies)	200	
2	Petty Cash		200
	Factory expense vouchers in petty cash fund.		
	AJE 7 (23)		
97	Other Expense (Interest)	400	
33	Accrued Items		400
	Interest accrued on notes payable.		
	AJE 8 (30)		
99	Federal Income Taxes	31,708	
34	Federal Income Tax Liability		31,708
	1975 federal income tax provision.		

ule, there must be recorded all of the work performed in connection with the verification and analysis of the scheduled item, the methods of verification employed, the questions raised during the examination of each item, and the answers to the questions. A supporting schedule must also contain conclusions reached and the methods used to arrive at those conclusions. A brief summary of all work performed usually accomplishes this purpose. If the summary is inadequate, the reviewers will not be in a position to judge the thoroughness of the procedures or the maintenance of proper auditing standards.

Agenda or Audit Notes. A work paper entitled "Agenda" or "Audit Notes" is developed during the course of an audit. It will contain notes and reminders for points that cannot be settled the moment they arise,

ILLUSTRATION 8-7
LEADING SCHEDULE

THE HILL CORPORATION
Fixed Assets and Accumulated Depreciation, December 31, 1975

			Prepared By	Approved By
Initials				
Date				

Work Paper No.	Account No.	Account Name	Fixed Assets at Cost				Annual Rate SL	Accumulated Depreciation				Book Value	
			Balance 12-31-74	Additions 1975	Deductions 1975	Balance 12-31-75		Balance 12-31-74	Additions 1975	Deductions 1975	Balance 12-31-75	12-31-74	12-31-75
8	21	Machinery and	107,000	7,800	12,000	102,800*							
9	21 A	Accumulated Depr.					10%	11,000	9,700	2,000	18,700	96,000	84,100
10	22	Office Equipment and	30,000	4,000	4,000	30,000**							
11	22 A	Accumulated Depr.					10%	5,200	2,800	800	7,200	24,800	22,800
			137,000	11,800	16,000	132,800		16,200	12,500	2,800	25,900	120,800	106,900

* Estimated salvage, $5,800.
** Estimated salvage, $2,000.
Note: The investment tax credit was purposely ignored, due to any possible legal changes.

but which must be disposed of prior to concluding the examination. The notes and reminders may pertain to verifications, conversations with officers, unsettled items, and other matters. The reviewing auditor uses this sheet to determine that all points therein have been settled and all related work performed at the close of the audit. The items on the agenda sheet may or may not be cross-indexed to the corresponding item in the audit program. Upon the final disposition of each item on the agenda sheet, it should be ticked off. All items not cleared by the in-charge auditor should be referred to a manager or partner for final disposition.

ILLUSTRATION 8–8

SUPPORTING SCHEDULE

THE HILL CORPORATION		Initials	Date
Analysis of Machinery Account (Acct. No. 21) — Prepared By			
For the Year Ended December 31, 1975 — Approved By			

12-31-74	Balance per general ledger and audit		$107,000
	Additions, 1975:		
1-6-75	V 2346. Carlton Machine Co., 1 radial drill	$3,200√	
2-10-75	V 2562. Cincinnati Machinery, Inc., 1 Logan		
	bed lathe	2,300√	
3-8-75	V 2884. Western Company, 1 shear press	1,500√	
	Total additions		7,000
			$114,000
	Deductions, 1975:		
3-8-75	CR 86. Sold 1 De Land screw machine (cost). . . .	$7,800Tz	
3-19-75	CR 92. Sold 1 automatic turret boring mill		
	(cost).	4,200Tz	
	Total deductions		12,000
4-31-75	Balance per general ledger		$102,000
2-20-75	AJE 4 V 3262. Duracraft Products, Inc., 1		
	balancing machine charged to		
	Factory Expense.		800
12-31-75	Adjusted Balance		$102,800

	AJE 4		
	Machinery	800	
	Cost of Goods Sold (Factory Operating Expense) . .		800
	One balancing machine charged to Factory		
	Operating Expense.		

√ = Vouchers examined.
T = Traced to cash receipts.
z = Approval of sale examined.

Indexing Work Papers

Work papers are indexed, subindexed, and cross-indexed, either during the audit or at its conclusion. Work papers must be completely indexed so that ready reference to any account, analysis, or section of an audit is easily available and so that reference to any schedule may be made rapidly at any time. A few of the several satisfactory methods of indexing are presented in Illustration 8–10. The items in Illustration 8–10 and their

ILLUSTRATION 8–9

THE HILL CORPORATION
Analysis of Sales Account (Acct. No. 70)
for the Year Ended December 31, 1975

	Prepared By	Approved By
Initials		
Date		

Month, 1975	Porta Files	Graters	Slicers	Coffee Mill Housings	Medicine Cabinets	Rigid Staks	Box No. 16	Box No. 30	Box No. 40	Total
January	$ 12,570	$ 7,406	$ 6,246	$ 18,620	$ 9,648	$ 1,460	$ 7,502	$ 3,489	$ 2,754	$ 69,695
February	10,281	9,888	8,920	19,408	10,246	2,675	6,210	5,209	6,565	79,402
March	13,246	7,100	7,746	11,289	11,704	1,990	7,420	6,363	8,260	75,118
April	11,895	11,923	13,462	17,505	9,860	2,785	8,210	5,666	7,058	88,364
May	12,775	10,241	11,313	13,131	10,267	7,121	8,672	3,110	5,810	82,440
June	15,688	9,460	10,946	15,282	11,416	4,686	7,215	5,569	8,020	88,282
July	14,045	10,821	14,685	19,314	8,749	5,480	7,921	6,586	5,774	93,375
August	13,160	10,046	13,721	17,665	9,568	6,840	6,725	6,741	8,020	92,486
September	15,928	10,313	11,348	15,208	8,486	6,211	7,218	5,708	5,690	86,110
October	19,302	8,142	9,875	16,408	7,214	3,941	8,868	4,960	8,515	87,225
November	16,582	6,321	10,440	14,622	5,720	3,662	7,340	4,108	6,621	75,416
December	14,100	6,105	9,641	12,480	6,946	2,741	8,269	5,348	6,457	72,087
Total for 1975	$169,572	$107,766	$128,343	$190,932	$109,824	$49,592	$91,570	$62,857	$79,544	$990,000TB
Less: Sales returns:										
January			$ 86	$ 40		$ 63	$ 32	$ 195	$ 23	$ 250
April	$ 150	$ 260		409			195			1,310
July	87		115		$ 78		124	241	125	1,015
October	627			349	462	257	100	270		1,728
December	12	205	210				380			697
	$ 349	$ 1,092	$ 411	$ 798	$ 540	$ 320	$ 636	$ 706	$ 148	$ 5,000TB
Net Sales, 1975	$169,223	$106,674	$127,932	$190,134	$109,284	$49,272	$90,934	$62,151	$79,396	$985,000

ILLUSTRATION 8–10

METHODS OF INDEXING WORK PAPERS

Method				*Audit Report and Financial Statements*
I	*II*	*III*	*IV*	
1	A	AA	1	Audit Program and Internal Control Questionnaire
2	B	BB	2	Agenda
3	C	CC	3	Abstract of Minutes
4	D	DD	4	Trial Balance Work Papers
5	E	EE	5	Audit Adjustments (Sheet 1)
5–1	E–1	EE–1	6	Audit Adjustments (Sheet 2)
5–2	E–2	EE–2	7	Audit Adjustments (Sheet 3)
6	F	101	8	Cash Summary
6–1	F–1	101A	9	Cash in Bank (First National)
6–2	F–2	101B	10	Bank Confirmation(s)
6–3	F–3	101C	11	Petty Cash Fund(s)
6–4	F–4	101D	12	Payroll Fund(s)
7	G	102	13	Accounts and Notes Receivable and Related Allowances
7–1	G–1	102A	14	Accounts Receivable
7–2	G–2	102B	15	Notes Receivable
7–3	G–3	102C	16	Allowance for Doubtful Accounts
7–4	G–4	102D	17	Confirmation Data
8	H	103	18	Inventory Summary
8–1	H–1	103A	19	Raw Materials
8–2	H–2	103B	20	Work in Process
8–3	H–3	103C	21	Finished Goods
8–4	H–4	103D	22	Inventory Certificate
8–5	H–5	103E	23	Inventory Test Schedule
8–6	H–6	103F	24	Inventory Pricing Schedule
9	I	104	25	Prepaid Expense Summary
9–1	I–1	104A	26	Prepaid Insurance
9–2	I–2	104B	27	Interest Paid in Advance
10	J	105	28	Long-Term Investment Summary
10–1	J–1	105A	29	Bonds
10–2	J–2	105B	30	Stocks
11	K	106	31	Fixed Asset Summary
11–1	K–1	106A	32	Office Equipment
11–2	K–2	106B	33	Factory Equipment
12	L	107	34	Accumulated Depreciation Summary
12–1	L–1	107A	35	Accumulated Depreciation, Office Equipment
12–2	L–2	107B	36	Accumulated Depreciation, Factory Equipment
13	M	108	37	Intangible Assets Summary
13–1	M–1	108A	38	Patents
14	N	201	39	Current Liability Summary
14–1	N–1	201A	40	Accounts Payable
14–2	N–2	201B	41	Taxes Withheld
14–3	N–3	201C	42	Federal Income Taxes
14–4	N–4	201D	43	Certificate of Liabilities
15	O	251	44	Bonds Payable
15–1	O–1	251A	45	Letter to Trustee
15–2	O–2	251B	46	Trustee's Certificate
16	P	276	47	Capital Summary
16–1	P–1	276A	48	Common Stock
16–2	P–2	276B	49	Paid-In Capital–Excess over Stated or Par Value
16–3	P–3	276C	50	Retained Earnings
17	Q	301	51	Sales and Sales Returns

ILLUSTRATION 8–10 (*Continued*)

Method				
I	*II*	*III*	*IV*	*Audit Report and Financial Statements*
17–1	Q–1	301A	52	Sales and Sales Returns, Product 1 (Store 1)
17–2	Q–2	301B	53	Sales and Sales Returns, Product 2 (Outside Salesmen)
18	*R*	*401*	54	Direct Material Cost
19	*S*	*501*	55	Direct Labor Payroll Summary
19–1	S–1	501A	56	Direct Labor, Department 1
19–2	S–2	501B	57	Direct Labor, Department 2
20	*T*	*601*	58	Manufacturing Overhead Summary
20–1	T–1	601A	59	Supervision
20–2	T–2	601B	60	Factory Taxes
20–3	T–3	601C	61	Rent
20–4	T–4	601D, etc.	62	Etc.
21	*U*	*701*	63	Selling Expense Summary
21–1	U–1	701A	64	Salesmen's Commissions
21–2	U–2	701B	65	Traveling Expense
21–3	U–3	701C	66	Sales Office Expense
21–4	U–4	701D, etc.	67	Etc.
22	*V*	*801*	68	Administrative Expense Summary
22–1	V–1	801A	69	Officers' and Office Salaries
22–2	V–2	801B	70	Depreciation of Office Equipment
23	*W*	*901*	71	Other Expense Summary
23–1	W–1	901A	72	Interest Expense
23–2	W–2	901B	73	Sales Discount
24	*X*	*951*	74	Other Revenue Summary
24–1	X–1	951A	75	Interest and Dividend Revenue
24–2	X–2	951B	76	Miscellaneous

corresponding numbers and letters are not complete. Only enough is given so that the system may be understood.

Method I.   Method I assigns a number to each main work paper and to each leading schedule. Supporting schedules carry the number of the leading schedule, followed by a sequential subnumber. Method I is adaptable to indefinite expansion.

Method II.   Method II uses a letter of the alphabet to designate leading schedules, followed by numbers for supporting schedules. If leading schedules exhaust the alphabet, double letters may be used.

Method III.   Method III indexes on the basis of double letters for all nonfinancial schedules. Financial schedules and their accompanying data are indexed on the basis of a unit of one hundred, followed by letters for subsidiary data.

If more than one sheet is used for an item, a letter is suffixed, as shown for cash reconciliations and the cash-in-bank confirmations. If 10 sheets were used for cash, the 10th would be numbered 101J.

Method IV.   This method—*and much can be said in its favor*—simply starts with the number 1 and numbers each succeeding sheet consecutively.

General Comments on Indexing. Each auditor has his individual preferences regarding work paper indexing. Each work paper must have its index number in an upper or a lower corner. Entries in supporting schedules which are transferred to leading schedules are cross-indexed with the page of the leading schedule, and vice versa. Totals on supporting schedules transferred to leading schedules are indexed to the leading schedule. Confirmation replies, adding machine tapes, EDP printouts, and so forth are not assigned a number unless they are attached to an indexed work paper. Audit adjustments in the schedules and on the audit adjustments work paper are cross-referenced completely by showing the schedule number from which the adjustment is obtained and the schedule number to which it is transferred. Balances on schedules which are to be used in the financial statements are cross-indexed to the trial balance work sheet. Cross-indexing may also be done between the audit program and the work papers; then, the work paper index number is placed in front of the item on the audit program.

Cross-indexing is important, since it locks the work papers together. Pencil of a color different from that used in the body of the schedule may be used for indexing in order to make the references stand out.

One document can be filed in only one place, but it may support two or more items. For example, the customary bank confirmation contains data for notes payable to the bank; the confirmation should be indexed to both the cash work papers and the notes payable work papers; on the cash work papers and the notes payable work papers, the references should be back to the bank confirmation, which probably will be filed under "Cash." On the trial balance work paper—notes payable line—the reference would be to the work papers for cash and notes payable.

Filing of Work Papers

Filing systems for work papers vary among accounting firms, but normally, the filing is divided into:

1. *The permanent file:* permanent data and work papers retained more than two years.
2. *The current file:* current and prior-year work papers and audit data.

The Permanent File. The purposes of the permanent file are to provide a financial history of the business of each client: to provide a reference for continuous and recurring items; to reduce the annual preparation of new work papers for items with no change; and to organize specialized data for future audits, for tax investigations, for proposals to change capital structure, and for other purposes.

The permanent file may contain the following:

1. An information sheet similar to Illustration 8–1.
2. A copy of the articles of incorporating and amendments thereto, and the code of regulations of a corporation; a copy of the articles of copartnership for a partnership.
3. Copies of deeds of trust.
4. A copy of stock-listing applications, if listed.
5. Excerpts or copies of important minutes of meetings of the board of directors, and stockholders, and important committees of the board.
6. Copies of contracts, pension plans, labor agreements, and so forth.
7. Samples of stock certificates and bonds.
8. Copies of engagement memorandums.
9. A chart of accounts.
10. A copy of the client's accounting manual and/or memorandum on the system of operation.
11. Audit programs for several years.
12. Internal control questionnaires for several years.
13. Organization charts.
14. Personnel and their duties, indexed to items 9 and 12.
15. Copies of authorized signatures.
16. Copies of tax returns—federal, state, and local.
17. Copies of data filed with the Securities and Exchange Commission.
18. Lists of plants, offices, stores, and so forth.
19. Schedules of noncurrent accounts—for example, the cumulative depreciation schedule.
20. Copies of audit reports.

The Current File. The current file consists of the work papers prepared during the course of the last audit and all papers, data, and correspondence accumulated during the dates intervening between the last and the current fiscal periods. To this will be added the work papers for the current audit. A complete set of papers for an average audit may be composed of the following:

1. Engagement memoranda—current and next engagement.
2. Internal control questionnaire and audit program—current year.
3. Correspondence.
4. Copies of minutes, new leases, new contracts, charter changes, etc.
5. Agenda sheets.
6. Audit report—typed copy and manuscript copy.
7. Financial statements and tax returns.
8. The trial balance work sheet.
9. Audit adjustments, and perhaps closing and reversing entries.
10. Leading schedules.
11. Supporting schedules, following the proper leading schedules.

12. Time and expense reports, if they are not retained by the firm office manager.

Periodically, in accordance with the policy of the firm, material in the current file is transferred to the permanent file. As shown in the following section, the word "permanent" does not mean perpetual retention.

Preservation of Audit Records

When should audit records be destroyed? The answer to the question of preservation and demolition of materials accumulated on an audit may be summarized as indicated below. Among auditing firms there is no particular uniformity of agreement with respect to these points. Old work papers for noncumulative and nonhistorical items are seldom referred to by the auditor. Some auditors destroy work papers when the period of legal liability has expired; if this practice is followed, local and federal statues of limitations should be consulted. For variations in practice, see *Management of an Accounting Practice* (MAP 19) issued by the American Institute.

The following suggestions represent the demolition practices of one firm of certified public accountants for a continuing client:

1. Retain permanently:
   a) A typed copy of each audit report.
   b) The up-to-date internal control questionnaire and audit program.
   c) Permanent work papers necessary to trace financial statements.
   d) Summaries of existing fixed assets and related depreciation provisions.
   e) Analyses of all capital accounts.
   f) Tax returns and supporting important data (many firms destroy all tax material after examination and final clearance with the taxing authorities; clearance notices should be retained).
   g) Data filed with the Securities and Exchange Commission.
   h) Correspondence of a permanent nature.
   i) Active contracts and trust deeds.
   j) Up-to-date lists of key personnel and their duties.
   k) The current accounting manual.
   l) Active chart of accounts, plant lists, current organization chart, and so forth.
   m) Articles of incorporation and amendments thereto.
   n) Samples of stock certificates and active bonds.
2. Retain for 10 years:
   a) Detailed analyses of fixed assets.
   b) Detailed analyses of revenue and expense accounts.
   c) Expired contracts.

    d) Reports prepared by affiliated accountants which can be duplicated.

    e) Excerpts of minutes.

3. Retain for five years:

    a) Agenda sheets.

    b) Engagement memoranda, time and expense reports.

    c) Bank reconciliations and the related confirmation requests replies.

    d) Trial balances of receivables and payables.

    e) Confirmation replies for receivables and payables.

    f) Analyses of prepaid expenses and deferred credits.

    g) Inventory data.

4. Retain for two years:

    a) Routine correspondence.

    b) Extra copies of typed reports.

    c) Rough-draft report.

Summary of Standards of Work Paper Preparation

The points of technical importance in connection with the adherence to preparation standards for audit work papers may be summarized as follows:

1. Place the name of the client at the top of each work paper.
2. Below the name of the client, place the name of the statement item treated in the work paper. If desired, 1 and 2 may be reversed.
3. Below item 2, place the fiscal period date of the audit.
4. Place the index number in an agreed corner of each work paper.
5. Cross-index each work paper to the sheet to which it is transferred and to the sheet from which it is obtained.
6. Use only one side of each sheet.
7. Be certain that each supporting schedule has its own separate sheet of work paper, with the exception of coordinated items such as notes receivable and interest received and accrued thereon.
8. On each schedule, state the method of verification used for the item under examination and the conclusions reached.
9. Obtain reproductions—do not copy—of minutes, contracts, and other items readily supplied by the client.
10. Each work paper must be signed and dated.
11. Use audit code ticks whenever they are necessary.
12. Prepare each work paper in an orderly, neat, and legible manner.
13. Be certain that there are no arithmetical errors.
14. Do not include or copy insignificant or irrelevant material.
15. The adjusted balance of each item on the work papers must agree with the corresponding adjusted trial balance figure.

QUESTIONS

1. *a*) What are the advantages (if any) of a planned audit program?
    b) If properly prepared, what are the disadvantages of a planned audit program?

2. Of which of the following two statements do you approve? What are the reasons for your answer?
    a) For any one firm of CPAs, internal control questionnaires should be standardized—that is, a uniform questionnaire should be used for all clients.
    b) An internal control questionnaire should be separately designed and prepared for each client.

3. In order to adhere to generally accepted auditing standards, a proper study and evaluation must be made of the system of internal control. Common approaches used by a CPA in his review of a system of internal control include the use of a questionnaire, the preparation of memorandum, the preparation of a flow chart—and combinations of these methods.
    a) Discuss the advantage to a CPA of reviewing internal control by using:
        1. An internal control questionnaire.
        2. A memorandum.
        3. A flow chart.
    b) After evaluating the system of internal control for an opinion audit, and if he is satisfied that no material weakness exist, is it necessary to test transactions? Explain.

4. An internal control questionnaire included the items listed below. For each item, explain what is accomplished by the existence of the controls involved.
    a) Are expenses under budgetary control?
    b) Is a postage-meter machine used?
    c) Are statements mailed to all customers once each month?

5. A manufacturing company has 400 employees. A portion of your accounting firm's internal control questionnaire for payroll follows:

Question	*Answer*
a) Who prepares the payroll?	Payroll clerk
b) Who prepares payroll checks?	Payroll clerk
c) Who approves the payroll?	Chief accountant
d) Who signs payroll checks?	Assistant treasurer
e) Who distributes paychecks?	Department foreman
f) Who authorizes pay rates?	Plant superintendent
g) Who reconciles the payroll account?	Chief accountant
h) Who controls unclaimed checks?	Chief accountant

What additional questions should be included in the questionnaire to permit an appraisal of the effectiveness of the internal control over payroll? Explain why each of the additional questions is necessary.

(AICPA)

6. You are assigned to the regular annual audit of a small manufacturing company having 40 employees. Prepare a list of the records, reports,

and other data for the personnel and their compensation that would be of interest to you, as auditor, and that you would expect to find. State briefly, the purposes for which these records, reports, and data would be used in an audit.

7. *a*)   In the course of an audit, a CPA obtains data from several sources. These data and other details are incorporated in the work papers. List several general classifications of the content of work papers which are normally prepared in connection with an audit, and give an example of each classification. In classifying the content, consider the source of evidence and the auditor's activities.

   b)   Prepare a list of types of work papers that you would expect to find in an ordinary annual audit.

(AICPA, adapted)

8. Are all audit adjustments prepared by the auditor submitted to the client for transcription into his records?

9. *a*)   In an audit work paper, why is a brief recital of the work performed of importance?

   b)   What are the purposes of a work paper entitled "Notes to be Cleared"?

10. Design a system of work paper indexing which will differ from the examples presented in the text.

11. A medium-sized manufacturing corporation is your client. Describe a method of filing your work papers, taking into consideration everything from your formal report to the most insignificant—but necessary—memorandum.

12. At the conclusion of an audit, you submitted to your client a work paper containing all audit adjustments, which you considered necessary. The client admitted their correctness but refused to record them in his accounts. What would be the effect of his refusal *a*) upon the audit report and *b*) upon the suceeding audit?

13. Prepare audit papers covering the following unrelated items.
   a)   Office buildings and accumulated depreciation.
   b)   Factory manager's profit-sharing bonus.
   c)   Royalty income.
   d)   Sales and cost of sales of building lots sold by a real estate development.

   Assume your own figures. The work papers may be concise but should be sufficiently informative to enable your supervisor to verify the report during your absence and thereby satisfy himself with respect to auditing procedures. Neatness and form of presentation are important. Illustrations should be sufficiently complex to involve other than extremely simple situations.

14. The records of Play, Inc., are to be audited for the year ended December 31, 1975. The company manufactures children's toys. The company was incorporated January 3, 1968. The records have never been examined by an independent public accountant.

   For the accounts listed below, prepare an outline of the work you would prepare with respect to the balances of those accounts at January 1, 1975, based upon recognized principles of accounting, properly applied.

The accounts are as follows:

a) Provision for Doubtful Accounts.

b) Inventories.

c) Machinery and the related Accumulated Depreciation.

d) Trade Accounts Payable.

e) Common Stock Issued and Outstanding.

15. For the cases below, state whether the expenditures should be capitalized or charged to an expense account. Present reasons for your answers. If you consider that there are alternative procedures which might be followed, state the conditions under which each would be appropriate.

a) Installation of a new machine, $1,000.

b) Inward transportation charges on the machine in (a), $100.

c) Revision of shop layout, $2,000.

16. During a preliminary audit discussion with a new client, the following information is disclosed:

a) All sales are made on open account. Terms are net cash in 30 days. Sales invoices are prenumbered and are entered in the accounting records as each sale is made. Invoices are placed in an open file until the customer remits, when they are marked "paid" and filed alphabetically by customer. The entry for the receipt of cash is made as each customer remits.

b) All inventory purchases are made on open account; and the accounts are paid by the 15th day of the following month. Entries for purchases are made from the check record as each invoice is paid, thereby eliminating accounts payable from the accounts.

c) The inventory is taken of all goods in the warehouse plus all goods in transit to the customer, provided that a sales invoice has not been prepared.

Do you consider the foregoing procedures to be proper? Present reasons for your answers. What suggestions might you offer for the client's system?

17. Name the *informational* categories which should be maintained in the permanent file of work papers rather than in the file of work papers for the current annual examination of the records of a corporation.

18. In 1975, Pink Inc. developed a new product. The Red Company was engaged to develop a manufacturing process for the product. Pink advanced $200,000 to Red on October 1, 1975, to cover estimated development costs. The costs were defined as direct labor and direct material, plus 25 percent of these direct costs to cover overhead. During the development stage, no profit was allowed Red; but when a successful manufacturing process is developed, the Red Company is to be licensed to manufacture the product.

The Red Company is to submit monthly progress reports and a monthly statement of the costs charged against the advance. Officials of Red have abided by the terms of the development process contract. Because the officials believed the $200,000 advance was not an asset of

Red, it was deposited in a special account in a bank which was not the regular depositary; no entry was made on the records of the Red Company.

At the end of each month, timecards and material requisitions were analyzed, and the costs applicable to the contract were accumulated on the required monthly statement, but no entry was made on the Red records. A check was then drawn on the special bank account and deposited to the regular Cash account as a cash sale for the amount shown on the statement.

At December 31, 1975, the unexpended balance of the special account was $87,400, but the check for December costs of $40,000 was not drawn until January 5, 1976. On January 10, 1976, you started the audit of the Red Company for the year ended December 31, 1975.

a) State the procedures by which you might discover the existence of the contract.

b) How should the information regarding balances or transactions in connection with the contract be shown on the December 31, 1975 balance sheet?

PROBLEMS

1. You have been engaged to examine the financial statements of Olympia, Inc. for the year 1976. The accountant who maintains the financial records has prepared all of the financial statements since the organization of the company, January 2, 1974. You discover numerous errors in these statements. The client has asked you to compute the correct income for the three years 1974 through 1976 and to prepare a corrected balance sheet as of December 31, 1976.

In the course of your examination you discover the following:

(1) Sales taxes collected from customers is included in the Sales account. When sales tax collections for a month are remitted to the taxing authority on the 15th of the following month, the Sales Tax Expense account is charged. All sales are subject to a 3 percent tax. Total sales plus sales taxes for 1974 through 1976 were $495,430, $762,200 and $924,940, respectively. The totals for the Sales Tax Expense account for the three years were $12,300, $21,780 and 26,640.

(2) Furniture and fixtures were purchased on January 2, 1974 for $12,000 but no portion of the cost has been charged to depreciation. The Corporation wishes to use the straight-line method for these assets which have been estimated to have a life of 10 years and no salvage value.

(3) In January 1974 installation costs of $5,700 on new machinery were charged to Repairs Expense. Other costs of this machinery of $30,000 were correctly recorded and have been depreciated using the straight-line method with the estimated life of 10 years and no salvage value. Current estimates are that the machinery has a life of 20 years, a salvage value of $4,200 and that the sum-of-the-years-digits depreciation method would be most appropriate.

(4)   An account payable of $8,000 for inventory purchased on December 23, 1974 was recorded in January 1975. This merchandise was not included in inventory at December 31, 1974.

(5)   Inventory costing $6,550 was not included in the December 31, 1975 inventory, and merchandise costing $2,180 was included twice in the December 31, 1976 inventory. The periodic inventory method is used.

(6)   A check for $1,895 from a customer to apply on account was received December 30, 1974, but was not recorded until January 2, 1975.

(7)   Dividends of $2,500 have been declared near the end of each calendar quarter since the Corporation was organized. The company accountant has consistently followed the practice of recording all dividends at the date of payment which is the 15th of the month following the month of declaration.

(8)   At December 31, 1974 sales catalogues advertising a special January 1975 sale were on hand but their cost of $1,360 was included in Advertising Expense for 1974.

(9)   When the 500 shares of outstanding stock having a par value of $100 were initially issued on January 2, 1974, the $55,000 cash received was credited to the Common Stock Account.

(10)   The Corporation has used the direct writeoff method for bad debts. Accounts written off during each of the three years amount of $1,745, $2,200, and $5,625, respectively. The Corporation has decided that the allowance method would be more appropriate. The estimated balances for the Allowance for Doubtful Accounts at the end of each of the three years are: $6,100, $8,350 and $9,150.

(11)   On January 2, 1975, $100,000 of 6 percent 20-year bonds were issued for $98,000. The $2,000 discount was charged to Interest Expense. The company records interest only on the interest payment dates of January 2 and July 1.

(12)   A pension plan adopted January 2, 1976, includes a provision for a pension fund to be administered by a trustee. The employees who joined the Corporation in 1974 and 1975, were given credit for their past service. A payment of $25,000 for the full amount of these past service costs was made into the fund immediately. A second payment of $15,000 was made into the fund near the end of 1976. However, actuarial computations indicate that pension costs attributable to 1976 are $16,600. The only entries applicable to the pension fund made during 1976 were debits to Pension Expense and credits to Cash. The Corporation wishes to make the maximum annual provision for pension cost in accordance with generally accepted accounting principles.

Prepare a work paper showing the computation of the effects of the errors upon income for 1974, 1975 and 1976 and upon the balance sheet as of December 31, 1976. The work sheet analysis should be presented in the same order as the facts are given with corresponding numbers. Use the columnar headings appearing below for your work paper.

Explanation	Income						Balance Sheet Corrections		
	1974		*1975*		*1976*		*December 31, 1976*		
	Dr.	*Cr.*	*Dr.*	*Cr.*	*Dr.*	*Cr.*	*Debit*	*Credit*	*Amount*

(AICPA, adapted)

2. You have been assigned to complete the examination of the 1975 financial statements of a client company because the senior and an inexperienced staff accountant who started the engagement were hospitalized. The engagement is about one-half completed, and the audit report must be delivered in three weeks in accordance with your firm's agreement with the client. You estimate that by utilizing the client's staff to the greatest possible extent you can complete the engagement in five weeks. Your firm cannot assign an assistant to you.

The work papers show the following status of work on the audit:

(1) *Completed:* Cash, fixed assets, depreciation, mortgage payable, and stockholders' equity.

(2) *Completed except as noted later:* Inventories, accounts payable, tests of purchase transactions, and payrolls.

(3) *Nothing done:* Trade accounts receivable, inventory receiving cutoff, price testing, accrued expenses, unrecorded liability test, tests of sales transactions, payroll deduction tests, observation of payroll distribution, review of operations, preliminary audit report, internal control investigation, internal control letter, minutes, tax returns, procedural recommendations for management, subsequent events, supervision and review.

Your review discloses that the staff accountant's work papers are incomplete and were not reviewed by the senior. For example, the inventory work papers contain only incomplete notations, incomplete explanations, and no cross-references.

a) What standards of fieldwork were violated by the senior who preceded you? Explain why the fieldwork standards you list have been violated.

b) In planning your work to complete this engagement, you should examine work papers and schedule certain work as soon as possible and also identify work which may be postponed until after the audit report is submitted to the client.

(1) List the areas on which you should work first, that is for your first week of work, and for each item explain why it deserves early attention.

(2) State which work could be postponed until after the report is rendered to the client and present reasons why the work may be postponed.

(AICPA, adapted)

3. You are to audit the financial statements of Rehab. Inc., a contractor specializing in rehabilitating real properties. The company accountant prepared the following trial balance.

REHAB, INC.

Trial Balance

December 31, 1975

	Dr.	Cr.
Cash, commercial account	$ 23,900	
Cash, payroll account	1,000	
Supplies, January 1, 1975	2,500	
Trucks and equipment	24,800	
Accumulated depreciation, trucks and equipment		$ 10,100
Suspense		10,350
Common stock		5,000
Retained earnings		11,550
Sales		363,000
Supplies	75,000	
Subcontractors	9,800	
Labor	210,000	
Payroll taxes	8,500	
Other salaries	28,000	
Other expenses	16,500	
	$400,000	$400,000

Your examination as of December 31, 1975, disclosed the following:

(1) The records are generally maintained on a cash basis, and financial statements are prepared on an accrual basis. For financial reporting purposes the completed-contract method of accounting is used.

(2) The company's bank reconciliations showed outstanding checks of $1,400 for the Commercial account and none for the Payroll account. The Payroll account is operated on the imprest basis with $1,000 as the fixed amount. The only other reconciling items arose from the company's method of treating payroll taxes.

At the end of each payroll period a check is deposited in the Payroll Cash account for the amount of the payroll taxes withheld from the employees and the employer's portion of the payroll taxes. The employer's portion is charged to expenses when the check to be deposited is drawn. The accountant draws checks on the payroll account to pay the payroll taxes when they are due, either monthly, quarterly, or annually. The following amounts, which you determined to be correct from your audit of the payroll and related taxes, are on deposit in the Payroll account:

a) $1,100 for December F.I.C.A. Taxes.
b) $2,100 for December federal tax withheld.
c) $900 for fourth quarter state unemployment tax.
d) $800 for 1975 federal unemployment tax.

In addition the company has on hand depositary receipts totaling $6,300 covering October and November F.I.C.A. and federal taxes withheld from employees.

(3) The company maintains a cost and analysis job record. The records for December jobs follow:

Job No.	Status	Contract Price	Paid Billings	Unpaid Billings	Supplies Used	Direct Labor Charged	Sub-contracts Charged
602 . . .	Closed	$17,000	$3,500	$13,500	$1,850	$11,800	$700
603 . . .	Open	15,800	3,700	2,500	700	4,200	500
604 . . .	Closed	4,500	4,500	–	550	2,450	–

Your audit disclosed there are no other "open" jobs. The amount shown as "Subcontracts Charged" is the subcontractor's billing. For estimating purposes, your client adds 10 percent to a subcontractor's estimate. The subcontractor's invoice for Job No. 602 in the amount of $700 had not been paid at year-end. In addition the subcontractor's invoice for $200 for Job No. 603 had not been received.

The company has consistently considered expenses such as insurance, payroll taxes, and administrative expenses as period costs.

(4)   The physical inventory of supplies amounted to $3,000. The prior years' experience has been that one-third of the supplies on hand at year-end becomes obsolete and is discarded during the following year.

(5)   The company paid country club expenses of $1,600 for the company president, in accordance with an action of the board of directors. These expenditures were charged to Other Expenses. The president has kept records which show that 40 percent of his country club expenses were for business purposes.

(6)   To obtain additional working capital, the company president borrowed $10,000 from his life insurance company by taking advantage of the loan provision of his life insurance policy and turned the proceeds over to the company as a loan. The company does not pay the premiums on the policy. The company recorded the transaction in the Suspense account.

(7)   The following schedule was extracted from the company's income tax return for 1974. The books and the tax return were in agreement.

Description	Date Acquired	Cost	Prior Depreciation	Life	Depreciation This Year
Truck No. 1	1/1/71	$ 3,000	$1,500	6 yrs.	$ 500
Truck No. 2	7/1/72	3,600	900	6 yrs.	600
Misc. equipment.	1/1/70	12,000	3,600	10 yrs.	1,200
Office equipment	1/1/70	2,000	1,600	10 yrs.	200
		$20,600	$7,600		$2,500

You determined the following:

a)   Truck No. 1 was sold to an employee on July 1 for $350 cash. The proceeds were applied to the purchase of a new truck, No. 3, which was invoiced by a dealer at a price of $4,200. The company paid cash for the new truck. The sale of Truck No. 1

was placed in Suspense. The new truck has an estimated life of six years.

b) All depreciation is computed by the straight-line method. The company has not recorded any depreciation for 1975.

Prepare a work sheet and separate audit adjustments to determine the financial statements that will accompany your report. Supporting computations should be in good form. Ignore federal income taxes.

(AICPA, adapted)

4. You have been engaged to prepare corrected financial statement figures for The Willis Co. The records are in agreement with the following balance sheet;

THE WILLIS CO.

Balance Sheet

December 31, 1975

Assets		*Liabilities and Capital*	
Cash	$11,000	Accounts payable	$10,000
Accounts receivable	11,000	Notes payable	3,000
Notes receivable	13,000	Common stock	20,000
Inventory	25,000	Retained earnings	27,000
	$60,000		$60,000

A review of the records of the corporation indicates that the following errors and omissions had not been corrected during the applicable years:

December 31	*Inventory Overstated*	*Inventory Understated*	*Prepaid Expense*	*Prepaid Income*	*Accrued Expense*
1972	$ –	$6,000	$900	$ –	$200
1973	7,000	–	700	400	75
1974	8,000	–	500	–	100
1975	–	9,000	600	300	50

The net income according to the records is: 1973, $7,500; 1974, $6,500; and 1975, $5,500. No dividends were declared during these years, and no adjustments were made to retained earnings.

Prepare a work sheet to develop the corrected net income for the years 1973, 1974, and 1975 and the adjusted balance sheet items as of December 31, 1975. (Ignore income taxes.)

(AICPA, adapted)

5. Jerry Deets, a retailer, kept poor records. You are asked to prepare an income statement for the year ended December 31, 1975. Support your statement with the necessary work papers and computations. Use the accrual method.

Inventory purchases were paid for by check, but the costs of most other items were paid out of cash receipts. No record was kept of cash in bank or of sales. Accounts receivable were recorded only by keeping a copy of each invoice, and this copy was destroyed when the customer paid his account. Weekly, all cash on hand was deposited in the bank.

Deets started business January 2, 1975, with $10,000 cash and a building which cost $27,000 of which $6,000 was the value of the land. The building had an estimated useful life of 25 years and an estimated salvage value of $1,000. By analyzing the bank statements, it was possible to ascertain the following information:

Total deposits, $163,400 (excluding original investment).

Bank balance, December 31, 1975, $12,100.

Checks paid by the bank in January, 1976, but dated in December, 1975, amounted to $3,400. Cash on hand, December 31, 1975, $1,590.

An inventory of merchandise, taken on December 31, 1975, showed $18,000 at cost. Unliquidated customers' invoices totaled $1,270, but $170 of that amount is not collectable. Unpaid suppliers' invoices for merchandise amounted to $5,500. During the year, Deets borrowed $10,000 from his bank but repaid by check $5,100, including $5,000 principal. He had taken $9,600 from the cash collections to cover personal expenses. Business expenses paid in cash were as follows:

Advertising.	$ 500
Part-time help	3,600
Supplies	925
Utilities.	680
Taxes.	675

Store fixtures with a list price of $7,000 were purchased on January 5, 1975, on an installment basis. During the year, checks for the down payment of $1,000 and all maturing installments totaled $5,700. At December 31, 1975, the final installment of $1,500 remained unpaid, plus interest of $50. The fixtures have an estimated useful life of 10 years and an estimated salvage value of $1,000. Use a full year in computations for depreciation; the straight-line method is to be followed for all assets.

PRACTICAL MATERIAL ASSIGNMENTS

Metalcraft, Incorporated: Audit Problem:
  Assignment 1: Trial Balance
Colby Gears, Inc.: Holmes and Moore Audit Case:
  Trial Balance Preparation

9
Statistical Sampling

SECTION I: INTRODUCTION

Sound sampling procedures must be established early if the auditor wishes to attain his objective of determining the propriety of the financial statements and their preparation in compliance with the application of generally accepted accounting principles.

A modern auditor is qualified to make logical deductions from a relatively small portion of a large body of data. Therefore, he should use statistical sampling techniques without fear or uncertainty.

Historically, sampling procedures became necessary when large-scale enterprises developed, making it impractical, as well as impossible, to perform a total audit of a client's accounting records. During their growth, large-scale enterprises were developing satisfactory systems of internal control. Today, adequate systems of internal control are effectively operative and thus permit an auditor to make tests of transactions and the documentation supporting those transactions so that an opinion can be rendered. Scientific sampling techniques have developed rapidly within the past 25 years; however, only recently have these techniques been applied to any extent by the independent auditor.

Because an auditor is able to project the results of sampling so that the size and value of a financial statement item can be determined, frequency of clerical errors, the non-duplication of steps in internal control procedures, and so forth, facilitate the auditor in determining the reasonableness of dollar values reflected in the financial statements.

Under no circumstances, however, should statistical sampling techniques be used to replace good judgment. Needless to say, good judgment is needed to determine the nature and extent of statistical sampling as well as to evaluate the results. The auditor normally will not place total reliance on the results of a single sample but will perform a variety of other tests on related records and procedures to determine their impact on the accuracy of the financial statements. The auditor's judgment is the final determining factor in any specific sampling instance.

In general, if judgment or accounting principles are involved, statistical sampling is not applicable. The impropriety of statistical sampling may be illustrated in the case of the examination of general journal entries for corrections, adjustments, and nonrepetitive transactions which are outside the system of internal control. A borderline case of the propriety-impropriety concept of statistical sampling may be illustrated by the random selection of entries from a ledger account for plant repairs and maintenance, or the random selection of entries from a fixed tangible asset account, even where the entries are numerous. The propriety of random sampling may be illustrated in the case of a company maintaining 200 bank accounts, ranging from small to large, wherein some are active and others are not very active. A random sample of 20 bank accounts should in all probability result in a representation of the quality of the 200 accounts; however, the auditor is running the risk—also a probability—that his random sample of 20 accounts might produce only small and inactive accounts.

As set forth in the Statement on Auditing Standards No. 1 by the AICPA, three standards of field work (Chapter 1) relate directly to statistical sampling.

The first standard simply means that if statistical sampling is to be used in any phase of an audit, careful planning and supervision must be provided. In addition, problems of designing, selecting, and evaluating samples must consider the reliability and precision of the results. This greatly assists in the significance of the sample in its relation to other information obtained during the audit as well.

The second standard, relating to the evaluation of internal control, discussed in Chapter 4, involves a thorough knowledge of the procedures and methods practiced by the client and a reasonable degree of assurance that they are being carried out. This standard also recognizes the extent to which an auditor can rely on internal control and his audit procedures to provide a reasonable basis for his opinion. Thus, statistical sampling may be applied to test compliance with internal control procedures that leave an audit trail in the form of documentary evidence of compliance. Generally, statistical sampling is not applicable where internal control procedures depend upon segregation of duties which leave no audit trail.

The third standard recognizes that there is some degree of uncertainty in the concept of a reasonable basis for rendering an opinion. Therefore, "precision" and "reliability" must be carefully evaluated in relation to the statistical sampling procedures that might be adopted. If these terms are to be meaningful, the auditor should relate precision to materiality and reliability to the reasonableness of the basis for his opinion.

Some basic mathematical terms must be understood so that any statistical sampling used in carrying out the audit program will be meaningful. The *arithmetic mean* is the "point of central tendency" of the values of the universe. Simply stated, it is the sum of all the values in the universe divided by the number of the items in the universe. There is also a need for understanding that there is some indicator which will set forth how much the individual values depart from the average. This indicator is a *measure of dispersion*. Measures of dispersion are: (a) the range of values and (b) the standard deviation. The range of values gives only the highest and lowest values of the universe. The standard deviation will indicate more about the spread of all values about the arithmetic mean. The standard deviation is the square root of the average of the squares of the differences between the individual values and their mean. This statement can be expresses as follows:

$$\sigma = \sqrt{\frac{\Sigma(X - \bar{X})^2}{n}}$$

σ = Standard deviation
Σ = Sum of
$(X - \bar{X})$ = Distance of each value from the mean.
n = Number of items in the universe.

Value (x)	n	Total
~~25~~	~~1~~	Exclude
50	1	50
60	3	180
70	5	350
80	6	480
95	2	190
100	1	100
	18	1,350

Mean = 's 1350 ÷ 18 = 75 ($\bar{X}$)
(Value 25 would be excluded as it varies too widely from the mean.)

Applying the formula:
Deviation

$(X - \bar{X})$	$(X - \bar{X})^2$	n	$\Sigma(X - \bar{X})^2$
-25	625	1	625
-15	225	3	675
$- 5$	25	5	125
5	25	6	150
20	400	2	800
25	625	1	625
		18	3,000

$$\sigma = \sqrt{\frac{3,000}{18}}$$
$$\sigma = \sqrt{166.67}$$
$$\sigma = 12.9$$

To apply the results of this calculation, we must use the following statistical data which indicates the certain given number (t) of standard deviations:

$t(x\sigma)$	Percent of items included
±1.00	68.62%
±1.65	90.00%
±1.96	95.00%
±2.58	99.00%

Therefore, if a confidence level of 90 percent is desired:

$$
\begin{array}{ll}
12.9 & (\sigma) \\
\underline{1.65} & (t) \\
\overline{21.285} & \text{standard deviation}
\end{array}
$$

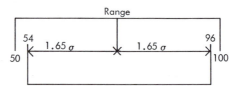

It can be further stated that 90 percent of all values will be between 54 and 96. (75-mean-21 standard deviation rounded = ′s 54; 75 + mean + 21-standard deviation rounded = ′s 96)

Basis of Sampling and Testing

Sampling is based on the theory of probabilities. Sampling is not an automatic tool. The judgment of the accountant and the effectiveness of internal auditing and internal control, all affect the sample, its quality, and the interpretive results of the sample tested. In using statistically designed samples, the auditor must exercise judgment in defining and establishing the areas of accounts, entries, or documents from which he will select his samples. Statistical techniques do not supplant the judgment and decision of the auditor—they supplement his judgment and decisions.

Auditors have used sampling processes for many decades. However, the selection of the sample often has been arbitrarily chosen. Statistical procedures for the selection of the samples to be examined and the evaluation of the results of the sample examinations have reached a logical pattern.

The laws of probability will control the results of statistical sampling, and the results then are measurable on the basis of preestablished levels for acceptance or rejection of the data in the universe. If less than a 100 percent test is applied to an area, sampling risks are incurred. Sample results will be precisely the same as the results obtained by a 100 percent examination by pure coincidence only. However, if the results of sample examination are satisfactory, the quality of the universe may be accepted as satisfactory, provided the sample was selected without bias or prejudice. The conclusions drawn from any sample are based on the theory that the same conclusions would be reached if additional samples were drawn and examined. The estimate of the results of examining a sample is called the *estimated precision* of the sample.

This question immediately arises: What is the extent of the examination necessary for entries in journals, ledger accounts, the proof of ledger account balances, invoices, cash receipts data, paid checks, and other data and vouchers? Before proceeding with the extent of the examination for these and all other data, a general discussion of sampling and testing is presented.

This chapter will attempt to crystallize the generalities of sampling and testing into terms of specific guidance. Auditing problems involve the exercise of competent judgment in arriving at decisions concerning their solution, and there is nothing in a statistical approach to stop an auditor from performing any type of work he considers necessary in the circumstances, or to alter the actions to be taken in connection with the tests.

Before a statistical problem can be solved, the problem must be posed in a manner lending itself to statistical analysis. What is a proper sample? A proper sample is one in which the percentage (or amount) of error or correctness in the sample is the same as in the population. Generally, the *assumption* is that if the error in the sample is acceptable, the remaining data of that population are acceptable. It should be remembered, however, that in auditing, if 20 or 30 or 40 of the accounts receivable balances out of a total of 100 accounts are correct, this constitutes evidence—not proof—that the remaining 60 or 70 or 80 balances are correct; but of course, this is true of any other similar statistical problem.

Within *very* broad limits, the size of the sample is independent of the size of the population. To illustrate: If 1,000 is an adequate sample for a population of 10,000, then 1,000 is an adequate sample for an *identical* population of 100,000. In one case, this is 10 percent; and in the other case, it is one percent. However, in auditing, identical populations seldom are encountered.

The following statement must be remembered: Before statistical sampling can be used effectively, the audit problem must be such that it can be solved statistically—and satisfaction with the results of a statistical test does not constitute irrefutable proof of the same level of accuracy of remaining data within the area sampled and tested.

Characteristics of a Sample. Every sample must possess the following characteristics: (1) it must be adequate, (2) it must be representative, and (3) it must show stability.

An adequate sample contains a sufficient number of items to show the same results which would be found in the selection of another sample of the same size from the same population (in other words, the sample must not be so small that it offers distortion). Also, a sample is adequate when each individual item has the same probability of inclusion as all other items of that particular population.

A representative sample possesses characteristics similar to all of the data in the population. In sampling, the proportion of good and bad in the population must be constant; and with respect to auditing, there can be no assurance that a sample will definitely show the same characteristics as the particular population; but in line with the theory of probability, if the sample has been selected at random, it assumedly should be sufficiently representative of the population.

A sample shows stability when the results of examining the sample remain the same regardless of the increase in the size of the sample.

In determining the size of a sample, three problems arise: (1) the extent of error to be allowed in the results of the sample test (this is decision based upon judgment—and judgment may be influenced by statistics, or statistics may be influenced by judgment); (2) the precision desired in estimating the extent of error through the sampling process; and (3) the risk the auditor is willing to assume of being misled by the sample data.

Sample Selection and Testing

To test is to examine the quality of data. Sampling is the selection of a part of a totality of similar or homogeneous material, which part is to be representative of the totality. Commonly, the *totality* is termed the *whole*, the *population*, or the *universe*. Sampling and testing may be described as the selection and the examination of parts from which conclusions are available concerning the population.

In auditing, all items of one type form that population—for example, all sales invoices constitute a population, and the specifically selected sales invoices to be examined constitute the sample.

Whether the independent auditor uses judgment or statistical sampling in performing the audit, certain decisions must be made so that his test will be properly executed. The decisions that must be made are as follows:

1. The population or universe to be sampled must be defined.
2. The information to be obtained from the sample must be established so that the method of sampling can be accurately selected.
3. The desired precision must be decided upon so that the amount of sampling can be specifically outlined.
4. The desired reliability must be assured so that the sample results will be relevant to the audit.

Statistical sampling formalizes many of the rules of action and criteria which accountants have developed in the past for the measurement of data quality without the benefits of statistical methods. The basic concepts of statistical sampling, coupled with objective analysis, are analogous to the processes and terminal objectives of judgment sampling procedures. Statistical applications add nonbiased sample selection methods and methods of measuring the results of the examined samples.

Statistical (scientific) sample selection is accomplished by the application of four stages to the examination process; each is independent of the other. The four stages of statistical sampling are as follows:

1. *Design stage.* The outlining or development of the sample approach, based upon the effectiveness of the internal control, the type of data, the importance of the data, and the desired tightness of inspection.
2. *Drawing the sample.* Statisticians prefer random samples on the basis that a random sample enjoys a good probability of being representative of the population.
3. *Statistical evaluation.* This is the mathematical evaluation of the sample(s) examined. Based upon the homogeneity of items in the population, the expected reliability and precision of the sample should fall within the forecast limits.
4. *Determining the adequacy of the sample results.* This has nothing to do with mathematics but is in answer to this question: Did the sample results provide adequate estimates to serve as the basis of measuring and judging the universe in terms of recognized standards of the accounting profession?

SECTION II: TYPES OF STATISTICAL SAMPLES

There are several types of statistical samples, as follows:

1. Unrestricted random sample with replacement.
2. Sampling for attributes.
3. Discovery sampling.
4. Stratified random sampling.
5. Systematic sample.
6. Cluster sample.

Unrestricted Random Sample

An unrestricted random sample with replacement is one in which each item in the universe has the same equal chance of being a part of the sample selected. All remaining items have an equal chance of being chosen as the second item in the sample, and so on, until the total sample is accumulated. When an unrestricted random sample is selected, there must be no preference or lack of preference which would tend to include or exclude any datum in the universe. No individual has any control over the items to be selected out of a universe. An unrestricted random sample is a good sample if the accounting data are subject to random item selection; and many accounting data are eligible for random sample selection. However, an unrestricted random sample may not *automatically* be a good and representative sample. The random method of selection of a sample may be used for verification of inventory count-and-price sheets, for paid checks to be examined, for sales invoices to be examined, and for many other items. It is also used appropriately when each item in the universe is proportionately equal to each other item, as exemplified by the selection of accounts receivable of approximately similar balances.

Only unrestricted random samples can be used for statistical analysis because the limits of error in making final decisions can be computed statistically. Unrestricted random selection is not synonymous to haphazard selection because in random selection, each item in the population has a determinable probability of being chosen. Because randomness is related to the laws of probabilities, a known behavior pattern is provided. For example, if 10 percent of the records of a population contain errors, it can be predicted that approximately 10 percent of the sample records will contain similar errors. Of course, acceptable and unacceptable error limits must be established in advance in order to determine the acceptance or rejection of the results of the sample. If the examination results of the sample are not satisfactory, additional samples may be selected until an acceptance or rejection level is reached. Perhaps the prejudgment was poor.

In order to apply mathematical formulas to a sample, that sample must be random, it must be free from predetermined prejudice or suspicion and it must be selected as being entirely representative of the population being examined. Therefore, all items in a population must be homogeneous and the sample taken from the population must be representative. This basic principle can be applied to the majority of accounting data and transactions; there are exceptions, as indicated by the inconclusive results emanating from a random sample of general journal entries, and in the confirmation of accounts receivable where neither the authenticity of the account receivable nor the effectiveness of tht internal accounting controls can be established. In order to apply the basic principles of drawing a conclusion from a representative sample drawn from a homogeneous population, it would be necessary to confirm accounts receivable each month—obviously an unreasonable procedure.

Selecting a Random Sample.   In auditing, random numbers for a sample may be selected by various methods. One method of selection is to use a published table of random numbers, such as the Table of 105,000 Random Decimal Digits, prepared by the Interstate Commerce Commission. An extract from the table is reproduced in Illustration 9–1. The randomness of this table may be illustrated by noting that each digit—0 through 9—appears an equal number of times. A very comprehensive and reliable table of random numbers can be found in the *Hand-*

ILLUSTRATION 9–1

RANDOM NUMBER TABLE

Line	(1)	(2)	(3)	(4)	(5)	(6)
1	10480	15011	01536	02011	81647	91646
2	22368	46573	25595	85393	30995	89198
3	24130	48360	22527	97265	76393	64809
4	42167	93093	06243	61680	07856	16376
5	37570	39975	81837	16656	06121	91782
6	77921	06907	11008	42751	27756	53498
7	99562	72905	56420	69994	98872	31016
8	96301	91977	05463	07972	18876	20922
9	89579	14342	63661	10281	17453	18103
10	85475	36857	53342	53988	53060	59533
11	28918	69578	88231	33276	70997	79936
12	63553	40961	48235	03427	49626	69445
13	09429	93969	52636	92737	88974	33488
14	10365	61129	87529	85689	48237	52267
15	07119	97336	71048	08178	77233	13916
16	51085	12765	51821	51259	77452	16308
17	02368	21382	52404	60268	89368	19885
18	01011	54092	33362	94904	31273	04146
19	52162	53916	46369	58586	23216	14513
20	07056	97628	33787	09998	42698	06691
21	48663	91245	85828	14346	09172	30168
22	54164	58492	22421	74103	47070	25306
23	32639	32363	05597	24200	13363	38005
24	29334	27001	87637	87308	58731	00256
25	02488	33062	28834	07351	19731	92420
26	81525	72295	04839	96423	24878	82651
27	29676	20591	68086	26432	46901	20849
28	00742	57392	39064	66432	84673	40027
29	05366	04213	25669	26422	44407	44048
30	91921	26418	64117	94305	26766	25940
31	00582	04711	87917	77341	42206	35126
32	00725	69884	62797	56170	86324	88072
33	69011	65795	95876	55293	18988	27354
34	25976	57948	29888	88604	67917	48708
35	09763	83473	73577	12908	30883	18317
36	91567	42595	27958	30134	04024	86385
37	17955	56349	90999	49127	20044	59931
38	46503	18584	18845	49618	02304	51038
39	92157	89634	94824	78171	84610	82834
40	14577	62765	35605	81263	39667	47358
41	98427	07523	33362	64270	01638	92477
42	34914	63976	88720	82765	34476	17032
43	70060	28277	39475	46473	23219	53416
44	53976	54914	06990	67245	68350	82948
45	76072	29515	40980	07391	58745	25774
46	90725	52210	83974	29992	65831	38857
47	64364	67412	33339	31926	14883	24413
48	08962	00358	31662	25388	61642	34072
49	95012	68379	93526	70765	10592	04542
50	15664	10493	20492	38391	91132	21999

book of Sampling for Auditing and Accounting Methods (Vol. 1) by Herbert Arkin, 1963, McGraw-Hill Book Company, Inc.

When selecting a sample from a table of random numbers, it is necessary that the items in the population be numbered so that any and all items are available for possible selection. In many cases, the items in the population already bear serial numbers—as exemplified by prenumbered checks. A beginning number in the random number table then is selected as a starting point; and in accordance with the predetermined number of items to be selected, the random numbers necessary to complete the sample are determined. The random numbers may be selected from the random number table in any order and in any direction within the table—consecutively, every second number, every third number, crosswise, or in any other predetermined systematic pattern. Because of the quantity of numbers in a random number table, there exists an almost infinite number of ways of determining a sample. Therefore, even if a client knew that a certain random number table was to be used by the auditor, he could not anticipate the pattern of the sample to be selected.

ILLUSTRATION.   For the year under examination a client has used 5,000 consecutively numbered (3,681–8,680) checks. It is predetermined by decision that five percent, or 250 checks, will be audited in detail for payee, amount, signature, endorsement, proper original record entry, and classification of charges. A starting point is selected in the random number table (Illustration 9–1) by the "random stab" method. Thus, the digits that determine the starting point would be selected by closing your eyes and making a "blind stab" at the table. Since the "blind stab" will rarely land on a specific number, you might specify that the starting point will be the "first four digits in the line above" or the "last four digits in the line below" the "blind stab." The point thus selected is 30,134 which is in line 36, column 4. On the basis that the random number table is to be used vertically and consecutively and proceeding down the column using the last four numbers of the digit, the first check that will be selected for audit is 8,171. Proceeding according to plan, you would skip the next number as it is below the number of the items in the universe, selecting digit 4,270 as the next check to be audited. Since 250 numbers are to be selected, the numbers in columns 4, 5, and 6 will be used and you would proceed to columns 1, 2, 3 and the unused part of 4 to complete the selection.

Another possible use to which the independent auditor can apply the random number table is the determining of dollar value. Having discussed the principles of unrestricted random sampling and having seen in the preceding illustration how the random number table helps achieve randomness, it is desirable to see if this procedure has any application to accounting data that have dollar values.

ILLUSTRATION.   We want to estimate the total inventory purchases of a client for a particular month as represented by the 300 invoices issued, based on a random sample of 30 of them. The first step in preparing to use the random number table is to establish correspondence between the elements of the universe and the digits in the table by assigning the invoices the numbers 001 through 300, ignoring 000 and all other numbers above 300. The correspondence scheme should be specified in writing before the sample is selected. The next procedure to be specified in writing is the route to be taken through the table. This is determined to be the first three digits in the first usable line starting at the bottom of column 5 and moving upward. This establishes the starting point and route. The results would be as follows:

105	$ 2,000
148	1,800
232	1,600
016	1,400
023	2,000
200	20,000
040	1,000
189	2,400
267	1,800
248	1,600
197	2,000
133	2,200
091	1,400
232	1,600
174	1,200
188	2,400
277	1,600
061	2,000
078	2,200
219	1,000
045	1,000
244	1,600
257	2,000
170	1,200
183	2,400
273	1,600
259	2,000
208	1,200
002	1,800
253	1,000
	$69,000

The total month's purchases would therefore be $690,000 (10 × $69,000).

Several interesting observations can be made from this list:

1. There is one exceptional item, digit 200.
2. Without this one exception, all of the figures fall within a relevant range, $1,000 to $2,400. By far the large majority of the items vary by only a few hundred dollars.
3. One three-digit number, 232, appears twice.

In evaluating these observations, it would appear that digit 200 so distorts the sample that the auditor should throw this sample out and start all over again by re-defining the sampling objectives. However, with by far the majority of the items falling within a relevant range, it would seem desirable to substitute another invoice for 200. This might also be considered desirable because of the repetition of 232.

Upon more careful study of the situation the independent auditor would find that a thorough review of all 300 invoices prior to taking the sample would have caused him to exclude the extreme values and thus assure a valid sample. He should not even consider eliminating the exceptional invoice from the present sample, and substituting another invoice at random as this violates the very basis of unrestricted random sampling. The purpose of an unrestricted random sampling plan is to eliminate subjective bias of any kind, even if it seems that by so doing the distortion has been eliminated.

It is not unusual to have the same usable digit, 232, appear twice in a sample. As illustrated in the calculation, the value will be counted twice, just as if it were two items. The final result is only 29 different invoices, but invoices are not being counted; however, the number of "sampling elements" are being counted. This procedure is known as "replacement." After selecting the number 232 the first time it was not eliminated. Thus, in unrestricted random sampling, a random number and its corresponding element are selected and counted as often as they happen to appear. If sampling without replacement were involved, it would be necessary to perform several extra computations as correction factors to compensate for interfering with the chance workings of the unrestricted random process.

Sampling for Attributes

Sampling for attributes attempts to measure the frequency or rate of occurrence of an event or type of item, such as an error.

A variable is a characteristic which may vary within a range of values and would probably be represented numerically. A client's accounts receivable control account balance would be an example of a variable. Attributes are usually associated with the rate of occurrences of certain specific characteristics of a population. The percentage of the client's sales invoices that contain extension errors is an example of an attribute.

ILLUSTRATION. The auditor has defined his sampling objective as determining the percentage of the client's sales invoices that contain extension errors. The next step is to determine the desirable sample size. Based upon prior experience with this client's invoices, the auditor determined that the records contain 10 percent errors and he wishes to determine with 95 percent reliability that the occurrence rate of extension errors in the universe does not exceed 5 percent. One method used to satisfactorily answer this problem is to use tables found in *Supplementary Section 2—Sampling for Attributes* as published by the American Institute of Certified Public Accountants. Illustrations 9–2, 9–3, 9–4, and 9–5 are available for use in answering such auditing problems. To find the required sample size, he would select Illustration 9–3 which provides reliability or confidence level of 95 percent. Next would be selected the precision or upper limit percentage corresponding to his determination of errors, 5 percent. He would then proceed down that column until he reached the value of his estimated occurrence rate of 10 percent. Then following that line to the left, he would arrive at a sample size of 120 sales invoices.

As the illustration points out, certain definite steps must be followed in order to sample attributes successfully:

1. The auditor must define his sampling objectives.
2. He must determine the size of the sample.

Illustrations 9–2, 9–3, 9–4, and 9–5 are so constructed that they represent cumulative binomial distribution and assume that an unrestricted random sample will be drawn with replacement. If these tables are to be used by the auditor, he will be required to be precise in the definition of the sampling problem. He must therefore establish the upper precision limit, the required confidence level, and the estimate of the sample occurrence rate if he is to arrive at a satisfactory sample size through the use of tables already illustrated.

Looking at Illustrations 9–2 through 9–5 more closely, it can be seen that round numbers are infrequent in the precision limit percentages. Since the auditor would think in round numbers, he would select the number closest to his set precision limit percentage which would give him the more conservative results. For example, using the 95 percent confidence level table and desiring a five percent precision limit and a three percent occurrence rate, he would select the 3.3 percent as his occurrence rate and a sample size of 460. Thus, if the occurrence rate selected does not appear in the table, he would move down to the next higher value.

ILLUSTRATION. To continue with the preceding sales invoice problem where a sample size of 120 sales invoices was established, the auditor would now use an unrestricted random sample procedure to select the 120 sales invoices to be audited for extension errors. His audit of these sales invoices reveals the following extension errors:

Invoice No. S6321 – 10 items @ $10.00 = $110.00
5 items @ 20.00 = 110.00
Invoice No. S7943 – 5 items @ 20.00 = 10.00

Since the auditor is seeking to determine the percentage of sales invoices containing errors, he has found two invoices that contain errors. As far as sampling the attribute of sales invoices containing errors is concerned, he is not interested with the size or value of the error in this procedure. The auditor must now evaluate the results to determine whether or not he can state with 95 percent confidence, that the population does not contain an occurrence rate of sales invoices containing extension errors in excess of five percent.

Illustrations 9–6, 9–7, 9–8, and 9–9 are available to answer this problem. These tables can be found in *Supplementary Section 2—Sampling for Attributes* as published by the AICPA.

ILLUSTRATION 9–2

DETERMINATION OF SAMPLE SIZE

Percentage of Occurrences in Sample
Reliability (confidence level): 99%

Sample Size	1	2	3	4	5	6	7	8	9	10	12	14	16	18	20	25	30	35	40	45	50
																Precision (Upper Limit) Percentage					
50								0	0	0	0	2.0	4.0	4.0	6.0	10.0	14.0	18.0	22.0	26.0	32.0
60								0	0	0	1.7	3.3	5.0	5.0	6.7	11.7	15.0	20.0	23.3	28.3	33.3
70						0	0	0		1.4	2.9	4.3	5.7	7.1	8.6	12.9	15.7	20.0	25.7	30.0	34.3
80									1.2			5.0	6.2	7.5	8.8		17.5	21.2	26.2	31.2	36.2
90				0	0			1.1		2.2	3.3	5.6	6.7	7.8	10.0	13.3	17.8	22.2	26.7	32.2	36.7
120			0	0	.6	.8	1.7	1.7	2.5	3.3	5.0	6.7	7.5	9.2	10.8	15.0	20.0	24.2	29.2	33.3	38.3
160						1.2	1.9	3.1	3.8	4.4	5.6	7.5	8.8	10.6	12.5	16.9	21.2	25.6	30.6	35.0	40.0
240		0	.4	.8	1.7	2.5	2.9	3.8	4.6	5.4	7.1	8.8	10.4	12.1	13.8	18.3	22.9	27.5	32.5	37.1	42.1
340		.3	.9	1.5	2.1	2.9	3.8	4.4	5.3	6.2	7.6	9.4	11.2	12.9	14.7	19.4	24.1	28.8	33.5	38.5	43.5
460	0	.4	1.1	1.7	2.6	3.3	4.1	5.0	5.9	6.7	8.5	10.2	12.0	13.7	15.7	20.2	24.8	29.6	34.6	39.3	44.3
1000	.2	.9	1.7	2.5	3.4	4.2	5.1	6.0	6.9	7.8	9.6	11.4	13.3	15.1	17.0	21.8	26.6	31.4	36.3	41.2	46.2

ILLUSTRATION 9–3

DETERMINATION OF SAMPLE SIZE

Percentage of Occurrences in Sample
Reliability (confidence level): 95%

Sample Size	__	__	__	__	__	__	__	__	__	__	__	__	__	__	__	__	__	__	__	__	__
												Precision (Upper Limit) Percentage									
	1	2	3	4	5	6	7	8	9	10	12	14	16	18	20	25	30	35	40	45	50
50					0	0	0	0	0	2.0		4.0	6.0	8.0	10.0	14.0	18.0	22.0	26.0	32.0	36.0
60					0	0	0	1.7	1.7		3.3	5.0	6.7	8.3	10.0	15.0	18.3	23.3	28.3	33.3	38.3
70					0	0	1.4		2.9	2.9	4.3	5.7	7.1	10.0	11.4	15.7	20.0	24.3	28.6	34.3	38.6
80				0	0	1.2		2.5		3.8	5.0	6.2	8.8	10.0		16.2	20.0	25.0	30.0	35.0	40.0
90				0	0		2.2	3.3	3.3	4.4	5.6	6.7	8.9	10.0	12.2	16.7	21.1	25.6	30.0	35.6	40.0
120			0	.8	.8	1.7	2.5	3.3	4.2	5.0	6.7	8.3	10.0	11.7	13.3	17.5	22.5	27.5	31.7	36.7	41.7
160		0	.6	1.2	1.9	2.5	3.1	3.8	5.0	5.6	7.5	8.8	10.6	12.5	14.4	18.8	23.8	28.1	33.1	38.1	43.1
240		.4	.8	1.7	2.5	3.3	4.2	5.0	5.8	6.7	8.3	10.0	11.7	13.8	15.4	20.0	24.6	29.6	34.6	39.2	44.2
340	0	.6	1.2	2.1	2.9	3.5	4.4	5.3	6.2	7.1	8.8	10.6	12.4	14.4	16.2	20.9	25.6	30.6	35.3	40.3	45.3
460	0	.9	1.5	2.4	3.3	3.9	4.8	5.7	6.7	7.6	9.3	11.1	13.0	14.8	16.7	21.5	26.3	31.1	36.1	40.9	45.9
1000	.4	1.2	2.0	2.9	3.8	4.7	5.6	6.5	7.4	8.4	10.2	12.1	14.0	15.9	17.8	22.7	27.5	32.4	37.4	42.3	47.5

ILLUSTRATION 9–4

DETERMINATION OF SAMPLE SIZE

Percentage of Occurrences in Sample
Reliability (confidence level): 90%

Sample Size	Precision (Upper Limit) Percentage																				
	1	2	3	4	5	6	7	8	9	10	12	14	16	18	20	25	30	35	40	45	50
50					0	0	0	2.0	2.0		4.0	6.0	8.0	10.0	10.0	16.0	20.0	24.0	30.0	34.0	38.0
60				0	0	0	1.7		3.3	3.3	5.0	6.7	8.3	10.0	11.7	16.7	21.7	25.0	30.0	35.0	40.0
70				0	0	1.4		2.9		4.3	5.7	7.1	8.6	11.4	12.9	17.1	21.4	25.7	31.4	35.7	41.4
80			0	0	1.2		2.5		3.8	5.0	6.2	7.5	10.0			17.5	22.5	27.5		36.2	
90			0	0		2.2	3.3	3.3	4.4		6.7	7.8	10.0	12.2	13.3	17.8	22.2	27.8	32.2	36.7	42.2
120		0	0	.8	1.7	2.5	3.3	4.2	5.0	5.8	7.5	9.2	10.8	12.5	14.2	19.2	24.2	28.3	33.3	38.3	43.3
160		0	.6	1.2	2.5	3.1	3.8	5.0	5.6	6.2	8.1	10.0	11.9	13.8	15.6	20.0	25.0	29.4	34.4	39.4	44.4
240	0	.4	1.2	2.1	2.9	3.8	4.6	5.4	6.2	7.1	8.8	10.8	12.5	14.6	16.2	20.8	25.8	30.8	35.4	40.4	45.4
340	0	.9	1.5	2.4	3.2	4.1	5.0	5.9	6.8	7.6	9.4	11.2	13.2	15.0	17.1	21.8	26.5	31.5	36.2	41.2	46.2
460	.2	.9	1.7	2.6	3.5	4.3	5.2	6.1	7.2	8.0	9.8	11.7	13.7	15.4	17.4	22.2	27.0	32.0	37.0	41.7	46.7
1000	.5	1.3	2.2	3.1	4.0	4.9	5.9	6.8	7.7	8.7	10.6	12.5	14.4	16.4	18.3	23.2	28.0	33.0	37.9	42.9	47.9

ILLUSTRATION 9–5

DETERMINATION OF SAMPLE SIZE

Percentage of Occurrences in Sample
Reliability (confidence level): 85%

Sample Size	Precision (Upper Limit) Percentage																				
	1	2	3	4	5	6	7	8	9	10	12	14	16	18	20	25	30	35	40	45	50
50			0	0	0	0	2.0	2.0	2.0	4.0	6.0	6.0	8.0	10.0	12.0	16.0	22.0	26.0	30.0	34.0	40.0
60				0		1.7		3.3	3.3	5.0	6.7	8.3	10.0	11.7	13.3	18.3		26.7	31.7	36.7	41.7
70			0	0	1.4		2.9		4.3		7.1	8.6	10.0		14.3	18.6	22.9	27.1	32.9	37.1	42.9
80			0	0		2.5		3.8	5.0	5.0	7.5	8.8	10.0	12.5		18.8	23.8	28.8		37.5	
90			0	1.1			3.3	4.4		5.6	7.8	8.9	11.1		14.4	18.9	24.4	28.9	33.3	38.9	43.3
120	0	0	.8	1.7	2.5	3.3	4.2	5.0	5.8	6.7	8.3	10.0	11.7	13.3	15.0	20.0	25.0	30.0	34.2	39.2	44.2
160	0		1.3	1.9	2.5	3.8	4.4	5.0	6.3	6.9	8.8	10.6	12.5	14.4	16.3	20.6	25.6	30.6	35.6	40.0	45.0
240	0	.8	1.3	2.1	3.3	4.2	5.0	5.8	6.7	7.5	9.6	11.3	13.3	15.0	17.1	21.7	26.7	31.3	36.3	41.3	46.3
340	.3	.9	1.8	2.6	3.5	4.4	5.3	6.2	7.1	7.9	10.0	11.8	13.5	15.6	17.4	22.4	27.1	32.1	37.1	41.8	46.8
460		1.1	2.0	2.8	3.7	4.6	5.7	6.5	7.4	8.3	10.2	12.2	13.9	15.9	17.8	22.6	27.6	32.4	37.4	42.4	47.1
1000	.6	1.4	2.3	3.3	4.2	5.1	6.1	7.0	8.0	8.9	10.8	12.8	14.7	16.6	18.6	23.5	28.4	33.3	38.3	43.3	48.3

ILLUSTRATION 9-6

EVALUATION OF RESULTS

Number of Occurrences in Sample
Reliability (confidence level): 99%

Sample Size	Precision (Upper Limit) Percentage																				
	1	2	3	4	5	6	7	8	9	10	12	14	16	18	20	25	30	35	40	45	50
50									0			1	2		3	5	7	9	11	13	16
60								0			1	2	3		4	7	9	12	14	17	20
70							0			1	2	3	4	5	6	9	11	14	18	21	24
80						0			1		2	4	5	6	7	10	14	17	21	25	29
90					0			1		2	3	5	6	7	9	12	16	20	24	29	33
120				0		1	2		3	4	6	8	9	11	13	18	24	29	35	40	46
160			0		1	2	3	5	6	7	9	12	14	17	20	27	34	41	49	56	64
240		0	1	2	4	6	7	9	11	13	17	21	25	29	33	44	55	66	78	89	101
340		1	3	5	7	10	13	15	18	21	26	32	38	44	50	66	82	98	114	131	148
460	0	2	5	8	12	15	19	23	27	31	39	47	55	63	72	93	114	136	159	181	204
1000	2	9	17	25	34	42	51	60	69	78	96	114	133	151	170	218	266	314	363	412	462

ILLUSTRATION 9–7

EVALUATION OF RESULTS

Number of Occurrences in Sample
Reliability (confidence level): 95%

Sample Size	Precision (Upper Limit) Percentage																				
	1	2	3	4	5	6	7	8	9	10	12	14	16	18	20	25	30	35	40	45	50
50						0				1		2	3	4	5	7	9	11	13	16	18
60					0			1			2	3	4	5	6	9	11	14	17	20	23
70					0		1		2		3	4	5	7	8	11	14	17	20	24	27
80				0				2		3	4	5	7	8	9	13	16	20	24	28	32
90				0			2		3	4	5	6	8	9	11	15	19	23	27	32	36
120			0			2	3	4	5	6	8	10	12	14	16	21	27	33	38	44	50
160		0	1	2	3	4	5	6	8	9	12	14	17	20	23	30	38	45	53	61	69
240		1	2	4	6	8	10	12	14	16	20	24	28	33	37	48	59	71	83	94	106
340	0	2	4	7	10	12	15	18	21	24	30	36	42	49	55	71	87	104	120	137	154
460	0	4	7	11	15	18	22	26	31	35	43	51	60	68	77	99	121	143	166	188	211
1000	4	12	20	29	38	47	56	65	74	84	102	121	140	159	178	227	275	324	374	423	473

ILLUSTRATION 9–8

EVALUATION OF RESULTS

Number of Occurrences in Sample
Reliability (confidence level): 90%

Sample Size	| Precision (Upper Limit) Percentage																				
	1	2	3	4	5	6	7	8	9	10	12	14	16	18	20	25	30	35	40	45	50
50					0			1			2	3	4	5	7	8	10	12	15	17	19
60				0			1		2		3	4	5	6	9	10	13	15	18	21	24
70				0		1		2		3	4	5	6	8	10	12	15	18	22	25	29
80			0		1		2		3		5	6	8	9	12	14	18	22	25	29	33
90			0		1	2		3		4	6	7	9	11	14	16	20	25	29	33	38
120		0		1	2	3	4	5	6	7	9	11	13	15	17	23	29	34	40	46	52
160		0	1	2	4	5	6	8	9	10	13	16	19	22	25	32	40	47	55	63	71
240	0	1	3	5	7	9	11	13	15	17	21	26	30	35	39	50	62	74	85	97	109
340	0	3	5	8	11	14	17	20	23	26	32	38	45	51	58	74	90	107	123	140	157
460	1	4	8	12	16	20	24	28	33	37	45	54	63	71	80	102	124	147	170	192	215
1000	5	13	22	31	40	49	59	68	77	87	106	125	144	164	183	232	280	330	379	429	479

ILLUSTRATION 9–9

EVALUATION OF RESULTS

Number of Occurrences in Sample
Reliability (confidence level): 85%

Sample Size								Precision (Upper Limit) Percentage													
	1	2	3	4	5	6	7	8	9	10	12	14	16	18	20	25	30	35	40	45	50
50				0		1	1			2	3		4	5	6	8	11	13	15	18	20
60				0		1		2		3	4	5	6	7	8	11	13	16	19	22	25
70			0		1		2		3		5	6	7	8	10	13	16	19	23	26	30
80			0	1	1	2	3	3	4		6	7	8	10	11	15	19	23	26	30	34
90			0			2	3	4		5	7	8	10	11	13	17	22	26	30	35	39
120		0	1	2	3	4	5	6	7	8	10	12	14	16	18	24	30	36	41	47	53
160		0	2	3	4	6	7	8	10	11	14	17	20	23	26	33	41	49	57	64	72
240	0	2	3	5	8	10	12	14	16	18	23	27	32	36	41	52	64	75	87	99	111
340	1	3	6	9	12	15	18	21	24	27	34	40	46	53	59	76	92	109	126	142	159
460	1	5	9	13	17	21	26	30	34	38	47	56	64	73	82	104	127	149	172	195	218
1000	6	14	23	33	42	51	61	70	80	89	108	128	147	166	186	235	284	333	383	433	483

Taking Illustration 9–7 and going down the Sample Size column to 120 and across the page to the 10 percent Precision (Upper Limit. Percentage column, it will be seen that a number of sales invoices (6) could contain errors. Since two invoices were found to contain errors, the auditor can state with confidence that the population does not contain an occurrence rate of sales invoices containing errors in excess of five percent.

Discovery Sampling

Discovery sampling may be considered as a special case of attribute sampling. This is true when the auditor's knowledge of the population to be sampled is such that he would expect the occurrence rate of a particular characteristic to be zero percent or near zero percent. If the auditor is unfamiliar with the population being sampled or reasonably expects an occurrence rate of three percent or more, he should use attribute sampling. Therefore, it can be said that if the auditor is looking for a characteristic that might indicate widespread irregularities or serious errors in the financial statements, discovery sampling would be a desirable procedure as it would indicate the need for more extensive tests. Discovery sampling will give the auditor assurance that errors do not exceed a certain rate and should eliminate the need for a 100 percent examination of the population. In drawing up the procedures to be followed, the auditor should:

1. Describe the characteristics to be evaluated.
2. Clearly define the population as to its nature and size.
3. State the specified degree of reliability to be accepted.
4. Establish the maximum occurrence rate in the population so that a specified level is not exceeded.
5. Determine the sample size.
6. State the occurrences in the sample and their nature.

ILLUSTRATION. As part of his annual audit of Finney Company, the auditor is preparing to examine the postings of vouchers payable. Since postings to balance sheet accounts, which should properly be posted to income statement accounts and vice versa, could cause a major misstatement of income, the auditor is concerned with improper postings and their occurrence rate. The total number of vouchers payable is 14,000. After a review of the voucher register, the auditor determines that he will examine all vouchers over $1,000. There are 720 such vouchers. For the remaining vouchers, he decides to use discovery sampling to determine, with 95 percent confidence, that improper postings do not occur in over one percent of the vouchers. The auditor found the following posting errors:

1. No. 800, repairs to building, were charged to repairs of machinery and equipment.

2. No. 750 paid for a major overhaul of a punch press which extended its life by two years had been charged to repairs and maintenance.
3. No. 500 paid for a new lathe had been charged to office equipment.
4. No. 50 for purchase of parts to repair a large press were charged to factory machinery.

One method to use to assist in answering this problem is to use tables found in Supplementary Section 4—Discovery Sampling as published by the American Institute of Certified Public Accountants.

Today many CPA firms have computer programs developed which assist in more rapidly selecting the unrestricted random numbers, determine the sample size, offer a choice of confidence levels, accept selected error rate in the universe, recognize the desirable sample reliability selected, and immediately indicate the sample size plus print out the unrestricted random numbers that should be used in performing the audit.

Stratified Random Sampling

In many respects, stratified random sampling is similar to the technique of unrestricted random sampling. The primary difference is that the population is divided into two or more groups, each of which is sampled separately and then combined to give an estimate of the total population value.

ILLUSTRATION. Your client is a manufacturer of sewing machines and it has been decided to take a stratified random sample to estimate the total inventory in the hands of the franchised dealers. It is desired to have a precision of 8,000 sewing machines at the 95 percent confidence level. On the basis of data obtained from the prior audit, the following information is developed:

Stratum	Number of Dealers	Amount of Variance from Mean
1 (1 to 9 sewing machines)	10,000	16
2 (10 to 19 sewing machines)	1,500	49
3 (20 to 29 sewing machines)	500	81
4 (30 to 39 sewing machines)	300	144

The auditor desires the greatest precision in this situation so he chooses the optimum sampling method. (Proportional sampling method could be used, but this would require more samples.)

The first step is to determine the total number of dealers whose inventory will be taken. This may be illustrated as follows:

Σ = sum of
n = total sample size
Nh = number of dealers in specific stratum
Sh^2 = variance from mean in each stratum in the past
V = desired total variance $(4,000)^2$
nh = number of dealers in each stratum that will be audited

$$n = \frac{(\Sigma Nh \cdot Sh)^2}{V + (\Sigma Nh \cdot Sh^2)}$$

Nh	$Sh = \sqrt{Sh^2}$		$Nh \cdot Sh$
10,000	$\sqrt{16}$ =	4	40,000
1,500	$\sqrt{49}$ =	7	10,500
500	$\sqrt{81}$ =	9	4,500
300	$\sqrt{144}$ =	12	3,600
12,300			58,600

Nh	Sh^2	$Nh \cdot Sh^2$
10,000	16	160,000
1,500	49	73,500
520	81	40,500
300	144	43,200
12,300		317,200

$$n = \frac{(58,600)^2}{(4,000)^2 + 317,200} = \frac{3,433,960,000}{16,317,200} = 211 \text{ dealers}$$

After determining the size of the dealer sample, the auditor must calculate the number of dealers that will be audited in each stratum nh. This is done as follows:

$$nh = \frac{Nh \cdot Sh}{58,600} \times 211$$

$Nh \cdot Sh$			nh
40,000	$\dfrac{40,000}{58,600}$ =	68% × 211 =	143
10,500	$\dfrac{10,500}{58,600}$ =	18% × 211 =	38
4,500	$\dfrac{4,500}{58,600}$ =	8% × 211 =	17
3,600	$\dfrac{3,600}{58,600}$ =	6% × 211 =	13
58,600			211

The inventory was then taken, based upon an unrestricted random selection of the dealers in each stratum, and the following results were obtained.

Stratum	Mean Sewing Machines per Dealer in Each Stratum	Actual Sewing Machine Variance from Mean in Each Stratum
1	4	14
2	9	38
3	25	85
4	36	130

New symbols must now be established for determining actual audit results.

Yh = mean sewing machines per dealer in each stratum.
Si^2 = actual sewing machines variance from mean in each stratum.
N = total inventory.

The estimate of the total sewing machine inventory would be calculated as follows:

$$N = Yh \cdot Nh$$

Stratum	yh	Nh	N
1	4	10,000	40,000
2	9	1,500	13,500
3	25	500	12,500
4	36	300	10,800
			76,800

It is now desirable to determine the precision attained, in other words $\sqrt{V}$ must be calculated.

$$V = \Sigma Nh \cdot (Nh - nh) \cdot \frac{Si^2}{nh}$$

$$\sqrt{V} = \text{precision obtained}$$

Stratum	Nh	nh	Si²	Nh − nh	$\frac{Si^2}{nh}$	$Nh \cdot (Nh - nh) \cdot \frac{Si^2}{nh}$
1	10,000	143	14	9,857	.10	9,857,000
2	1,500	38	38	1,462	1.00	2,193,000
3	500	17	85	483	5.00	1,207,500
4	300	13	130	287	10.00	861,000
	12,300	211				14,118,500

$$V = 14,118,500$$
$$\sqrt{V} = 3,757$$

It can be seen that the requirements of 95 percent confidence level of 8,000 sewing machines, ± 4,000, were met.

The final requirement would be to determine if the auditor over or under sampled. The following calculation must be made so that the auditor can be assured the inventory figure arrived at is reliable.

Therefore,

$$n = \frac{(\Sigma Nh \cdot Si)^2}{V + (\Sigma Nh \cdot Si^2)}$$

Stratum	Nh	Si^2	$Si = \sqrt{Si^2}$	$Nh \cdot Si$	$Nh \cdot Si^2$
1	10,000	14	3.74	37,400	14,000
2	1,500	38	6.16	9,240	57,000
3	500	85	9.21	4,605	42,500
4	300	130	11.40	3,420	39,000
				54,665	152,500

$$n = \frac{(54,665)^2}{(4,000)^2 + 152,500} = \frac{2,988,262,225}{16,152,500} = 185$$

The auditor could have sampled 185 dealers rather than 211, or he has oversampled by 12+ percent.

Systematic Sample

A systematic sample is made by selecting every nth item beginning with a random start. This procedure does not require a sample of a given size nor does it require that every possible sample of that size is equally likely to be drawn. The auditor can also vary the sample interval if he so desires. The auditor's knowledge of the population being sampled would be a significant factor in using this sampling technique upon which he would express an opinion.

Cluster Sample

Instead of drawing individual sample items, the auditor would select groups of contiguous sample items. For example, using a random number table, select two pages within the check register and audit all checks on those pages. A possible disadvantage to this method is that a group of contiguous checks might be for similar expenditures and therefore the sample may not provide adequate coverage of the range of expenditures.

SECTION III: HOW MUCH STATISTICAL SAMPLING?

The amount of statistical sampling is dependent upon the system of internal control, extent of the internal audit program, the relative importance and size of the item, and the predetermined acceptance quality levels plus the auditor's professional judgment. The independent auditor must arrange the audit program so that the sample will be sufficient to serve the purpose of the audit and will not extend it to a point at which the cost of selecting a sample and examining it exceeds its worth.

After a sample has been selected for audit, the discovery of more errors or the finding that the sample is not representative of the population may justify increasing the sample to 100 percent of the data. Or the size of the sample may be increased in quantity or in amount if discovered errors are material. The auditor can tolerate small, insignificant errors; he is not so much concerned with them as he is with errors that distort fair presentation of the financial statements.

QUESTIONS

1. Under what circumstances should statistical sampling techniques be used to replace good judgment?
2. What is a proper sample?
3. What determines the size of the sample?
4. Whether the independent auditor uses judgment or statistical sampling, what decisions must be made so that the tests will be properly executed?
5. What is the definition of:
   a) Unrestricted random sample?
   b) Sampling for attributes?
   c) Discovery sampling?
   d) Stratified random sampling?
6. The use of statistical sampling techniques in an examination of financial statements does not eliminate judgmental decisions.
   a) Identify and explain the areas where judgment may be exercised by a CPA in planning a statistical sampling test.
   b) Assume that a CPA's sample shows an unacceptable error rate. Describe the various actions that he may take based upon this finding.
   c) A nonstratified sample of 80 accounts payable vouchers is to be selected from a population of 3,200. The vouchers are numbered consecutively from 1 to 3,200 and are listed, 40 to a page, in the voucher register. Describe four different techniques for selecting a random sample of vouchers for review.

   (AICPA, adapted)
7. What procedure would you follow in preparing the following items for sampling through the use of a random number table?
   a) A job order cost inventory which identifies individual jobs as follows: A43R2, B67C1, C42R5, D54K3.
   b) Individual accounts in an accounts receivable subsidiary ledger identified as follows: Cin 26BB, Day 42CC, Cleve 66DD, Tol 83EE.
8. The following statements apply to unrestricted random sampling with replacement, a sampling technique which may be employed by an auditor under proper circumstances. Answer them as being true or false.
   a) The auditor's prior knowledge of the materiality of the items to be tested may negate the need for random selection.
   b) A rigid definition of the population of accounts receivable must specify that only active accounts with balances be included.
   c) If a population consists mostly of accounts with large balances, it is

acceptable to exclude accounts with small balances from the population to be sampled because the error in a small balance could not be material.

d) Excluding extremely large items from the definition of the population and evaluating them separately so that they have no chance of being included in the sample would violate the definition of unrestricted random sampling.

e) To be random a sample must be completely unbiased and its selection governed completely by chance.

f) If there is great variability in the number of entries on each item to be sampled, the population could be defined first to select a random sample of items (such as invoices) and then to select a random sample of one entry (quantity and/or price and/or amount) from each item selected.

g) The precision of an estimate of a population mean from a sample mean increases as the degree of confidence in the estimate increases.

h) It is likely that five different random samples from the same population would produce five different estimates of the true population mean.

i) A 100 percent sample would have to be taken to attain a precision range of ± $0 with 100 percent reliability.

j) The standard deviation can be used to predict the probable range of difference between a sample mean and the population mean.

(AICPA, adapted)

9. J. Byer, CPA, is in the process of examining the financial statements of Summit Appliance Repair Company for the year ended June 30, 1975. His client has a large fleet of identically stocked repair trucks. The client establishes the total quantities of materials and supplies on these repair trucks at year-end by physically inventorying a random sample of trucks.

Byer is evaluating the statistical validity of his client's 1975 sample. He knows that there were 74 trucks in the 1974 required sample. Assumptions about the size, variability, specified precision (confidence interval), and specified reliability (confidence level) for the 1975 sample are given in each of the following five items. You are to indicate in each case the effect upon the size of the 1975 sample as compared to the 1974 sample. Each of the five cases is independent of the other four and is to be considered separately. Your answer choice should be selected from the following responses:

a) Larger than the 1974 sample size.

b) Equal to the 1974 sample size.

c) Smaller than the 1974 sample size.

d) Of a size that is indeterminate based upon the assumptions given.

(1) Summit has the same number of trucks in 1975, but supplies are replenished more often, meaning that there is less variability in the quantity of supplies stored on each truck. The specified precision and specified reliability remain the same. Under these assumptions what should be the required sample size for 1975?

(2) Summit has the same number of trucks; supplies are replenished less often (greater variability): Summit specifies the same precision but decides to change the specified reliability from 95 percent to 90 percent. Under these assumptions, what should be the required sample size for 1975?

(3) Summit has more trucks in 1975. Variability and specified reliability remain the same, but with Byer's concurrence Summit decides upon a wider specified precision. Under these assumptions, what should be the required sample size for 1975?

(4) The number of trucks and variability remain the same, but with Byer's concurrence Summit decides upon a wider specified precision and a specified reliability of 90 percent rather than 95 percent. Under these assumptions, what should be the required sample size for 1975?

(5) The number of trucks increases, as does the variability of quantities stored on each truck. The specified reliability remains the same, but the specified precision is narrowed. Under these assumptions, what should be the required sample size for 1975?

(AICPA, adapted)

10. In prior years, the independent auditor had used judgment sampling in selecting purchase vouchers to be audited. This year he decided to take several samples using a random number table. If the desired reliability of his estimate is to be 90 percent, approximately how many times out of every 10 samples drawn would he expect the actual value to be exactly the same as the estimated value?

11. If the desired precision is set at ± $2,000 for an inventory value and the difference obtained is $1,500, is the estimate satisfactory or unsatisfactory? Why?

12. In order to increase the reliability of an estimate that has set ± $5,000 as its desired precision, would you increase or decrease the ± $5,000 desired precision limit? Why?

13. Basically every estimate made by the independent auditor is either of a quantity or of a rate of occurrence. What are the statistical terms that best describe these estimates? Give an example of each.

14. What are the three basic steps that must be followed when using a random number table to select an unbiased sample?

15. While variables are defined as quantitative characteristics of a universe, attributes are most commonly associated with the rate of occurrence of qualitative characteristics of a universe. In each of the following items, indicate whether variable or attribute would best describe the desired results.

a) Percentage of freight bills containing errors.
b) Total dollar value of the freight bills.
c) Total number of units in the raw material inventory.
d) Total number of material requisitions used in June.
e) The number of customers' statements having errors in them.
f) The number of sales invoices having extension errors of $10 or more.

16. An auditor examines a random sample drawn from a universe of 20,000 records. He determines that the rate of error occurrence in his sample is 5 percent. Which of the following statements could he make regarding the rate of error occurrence in the universe? Why?
     a) Exactly 5 percent.
     b) Within some range around 5 percent.
     c) Likely to be contained within some range around 5 percent.

17. The term reliability is synonymous with what other term?

18. What difference is there between unrestricted random sampling and stratified random sampling?

19. In the examination of a particular account, the independent auditor must test certain items within a finite population to form an opinion of the reliability of the account as a whole. In a judgment sample the auditor commonly tests most of the large dollar-amount items and a smaller proportion of lesser dollar-amount items. A random stratified sample makes the same type of selection, but it is said to be superior to the judgment sample.
     a) For each of the following define the terms and explain how the selection process could be applied to a test of accounts receivable:
         (1) A judgment sample.
         (2) A stratum in a finite population.
         (3) A systematic random stratified sample.
     b) Explain why a random stratified sample is superior to a judgment sample.

                                                (AICPA, adapted)

20. You are now conducting your third annual audit of the financial statements of Elite Corporation for the year ended December 31, 1975. You decide to employ unrestricted random number statistical sampling techniques in testing the effectiveness of the company's internal control procedures relating to sales invoices, which are all serially numbered. In prior years, after selecting one representative two-week period during the year, you tested all invoices issued during that period and resolved all of the errors which were found to your satisfaction.
     a) Explain the statistical procedures you would use to determine the size of the sample of sales invoices to be examined.
     b) Once the sample size has been determined, how would you select the individual invoices to be included in the sample? Explain.
     c) Would the use of statistical sampling procedures improve the examination of sales invoices as compared with the selection procedure used in prior years? Discuss.
     d) Assume that the company issued 50,000 sales invoices during the year and the auditor specified a confidence level of 95 percent with a precision range of plus or minus 2 percent.
         (1) Does this mean that the auditor would be willing to accept the reliability of the sales invoice data if errors are found on no more than 4 sales invoices out of every 95 invoices examined? Discuss.
         (2) If the auditor specified a precision range of plus or minus 1

percent, would the confidence level be higher or lower than 95 percent assuming that the size of the sample remains constant? Why?

(AICPA, adapted)

21. The following nine items apply primarily to discovery sampling, a sampling technique often employed in transaction testing. Assuming that all samples are to be drawn from large populations, select the best answer to each of the following items.

(1) Discovery sampling is concerned with the occurrence rate of a characteristic and therefore may be considered a special case of
   a) Random sampling.
   b) Sampling for attributes.
   c) Sampling for variables.
   d) Stratified sampling.

(2) A CPA using discovery sampling is looking for a characteristic which, if discovered in his sample, might be indicative of more widespread irregularities or serious errors in the financial statements being examined. If a CPA discovers one such error while using a discovery sampling plan, the CPA
   a) Is satisfied.
   b) Must test more extensively.
   c) Must expand his testing to 100 percent.
   d) May not use any sampling plan.

(3) A CPA who believes the occurrence rate of a certain characteristic in a population being examined is 3 percent and who has established a maximum acceptable occurrence rate at 5 percent should use (a) (an)
   a) Attribute sampling plan.
   b) Discovery sampling plan.
   c) Stratified sampling plan.
   d) Variable sampling plan.

(4) Discovery sampling should not be used if a CPA estimates that the occurrence rate of a certain characteristic in a population being examined exceeds approximately
   a) 20 percent.
   b) 10 percent.
   c) 5 percent.
   d) 0 percent.

(5) The statement, "A CPA tests disbursement vouchers to determine whether or not compliance deviations exceed 0.2 percent," omits which of the following necessary elements of a discovery sampling plan?
   a) Characteristic being evaluated.
   b) Definition of the population.
   c) Maximum tolerable occurrence rate.
   d) Specified reliability.

(6) To determine the proper sample size in a discovery sampling plan, a CPA need not know the
   a) Estimated occurrence rate in the population.

    b) Maximum tolerable occurrence rate.

    c) Population size.

    d) Specified reliability of the sample.

(7) As the specified reliability is increased in a discovery sampling plan for any given population and maximum occurrence rate, the required sample size

    a) Remains the same.

    b) Decreases.

    c) Increases.

    d) Cannot be determined.

(8) Discovery sampling is to be applied to several populations at the same specified reliability and maximum tolerable occurrence rate. If each population being sampled is twice as large as the preceding population tested, the percentage of each succeeding population tested would

    a) Remain the same.

    b) Decrease.

    c) Increase.

    d) Not be determinable.

(9) Discovery sampling should be used to estimate whether a population contains

    a) Errors of any kind.

    b) Noncritical errors.

    c) Critical errors.

    d) No errors.

(AICPA, adapted)

PROBLEMS

1. For the year under audit, a client has 20,000 consecutively numbered (1,382–21,381) sales invoices. It is determined by decision, based on past experience, that one percent, or 200 invoices, will be audited in detail for correctness of extensions, charge to subsidiary account, classification as to type of sales, and commission classification. Since Illustration 9–1 is to be used in preparing your answer, you will use the last four digits of the random number when random number selected is under 10,000. After the starting point is selected, you will continue vertically and consecutively down the page and proceed in this manner until the 200 sales invoices are selected. The "random stab" method is used, and the digit so selected is 04839 which is line 26, column 3. List the remaining 199 digits.

2. Over the year under audit, your client has made 2,000 sales to its most important type of customer, department stores. The auditor wishes to evaluate the "importance" of this customer type and determine that by taking a random sample of two percent of these invoices, their importance can be determined. By assigning consecutive numbers (1–1,999) to these invoices and using a random number table, the following invoices and their values are determined:

011...	$ 1,000	578...	$3,000	1245...	$1,600	711...	$2,000
573...	2,000	961...	2,800	492...	2,800	884...	1,000
360...	1,500	969...	2,400	363...	1,400	795...	2,200
093...	1,800	1129...	1,800	001...	3,000	948...	1,400
975...	1,200	336...	1,300	062...	1,100	473...	2,600
907...	125,000	765...	2,200	295...	1,100	595...	1,800
905...	1,300	1382...	1,700	591...	2,500	349...	2,800
1977...	2,200	092...	1,000	392...	2,300	584...	3,000
342...	1,700	916...	1,100	213...	1,600	634...	1,200
857...	1,400	628...	1,500	418...	1,300	765...	1,100

a) What is the total of the sample?

b) What is the average value of the sample invoices?

c) What is the estimate of the total value of the 2,000 invoices?

d) The total sales for the company to all customers was $850,000. It is further determined that the year-to-year sales to the customer represented by digit 907 has always been in this range. Do you believe a good sample has been selected? Why or why not?

e) Is there any procedure that can be followed so that the auditor can sample these customer invoices and arrive at an acceptable sales figure for this class of customer?

3. The eight following items apply to random sampling for attributes, a sampling technique often employed in transaction testing. Assume that all samples are to be drawn from large populations.

(1) A CPA wishes to determine the percentage of items in his client's inventory with annual sales of less than 50 percent of the units on hand at the inventory date. Which of the following exhibits the characteristic the CPA is measuring?

	Item	Units in Inventory	Units Sold This Year
a.	Firs	251	525
b.	Furs	243	124
c.	Friezes	198	98
d.	Furzes	144	92

(2) A CPA specifies that a sample shall have a confidence level of 90 percent. The specified confidence level assures him of:

a) A true estimate of the population characteristic being measured.

b) An estimate that is at least 90 percent correct.

c) A measured precision for his estimate.

d) How reasonably he can estimate the population characteristic being measured.

(3) A CPA specifies that a sample shall have a precision of 5 percent. The specified precision assures him of:

a) A precise measure of the population characteristic being measured.

b) An estimate that is at least 5 percent correct.

c) A measured reliability for his estimate.

d) The range within which the population characteristic being measured is likely to be.

(4) If all other factors specified in a sampling plan remain constant, changing the specified reliability from 90 percent to 95 percent would cause the required sample size to:

a) Increase.

b) Remain the same.

c) Decrease.

d) Become indeterminate.

(5) If all other factors specified in a sampling plan remain constant, changing the specified precision from 8 percent to 12 percent would cause the required sample size to:

a) Increase.

b) Remain the same.

c) Decrease.

d) Become indeterminate.

(6) If all other factors specified in a sampling plan remain constant, changing the estimated occurrence rate from 2 percent to 4 percent would cause the required sample size to:

a) Increase.

b) Remain the same.

c) Decrease.

d) Become indeterminate.

(7) In the evaluation of the results of a sample of a specified reliability and precision, the fact that the occurrence rate in the sample was 2 percent rather than the estimated occurrence rate of 4 percent would cause the required sample size to:

a) Increase.

b) Remain the same.

c) Decrease.

d) Become indeterminate.

(8) In the evaluation of the results of a sample of a specified reliability and precision, the fact that the occurrence rate in the sample was the same as the estimated occurrence rate would cause the reliability of the sample estimate to:

a) Increase.

b) Remain the same.

c) Decrease.

d) Become indeterminate.

(AICPA, adapted)

4. A CPA's client is considering the adoption of statistical sampling techniques. Accordingly, he has asked the CPA to discuss these techniques at a meeting of client employees. In connection with this presentation the CPA prepared the following table which shows the comparative characteristics of two populations and the samples to be drawn from each. (For example, in Case 1 the variability of population 1 is smaller than that of population 2 whereas the populations are of equal size and the samples to be drawn from them have equal specified confidence intervals and specified confidence levels.)

	Population 1 Relative to Population 2		Sample from Population 1 Relative to Sample from Population 2	
	Size	*Variability*	*Specified Precision*	*Specified Reliability*
Case 1	Equal	Smaller	Equal	Equal
Case 2	Smaller	Equal	Equal	Higher
Case 3	Equal	Equal	Wider	Equal
Case 4	Larger	Equal	Narrower	Equal
Case 5	Equal	Greater	Equal	Higher

Using the table and the technique of unrestricted random sampling with replacement, meeting participants are to be asked to determine the relative required sample sizes to be drawn from the two populations. Each of the five cases is independent and is to be considered separately.

(1) The required sample size from population 1 in case 1 is:
   a) Larger than the required sample size from population 2.
   b) Equal to the required sample size from population 2.
   c) Smaller than the required sample size from population 2.
   d) Indeterminate relative to the required sample size from population 2.

(2) The required sample size from population 1 in case 2 is:
   a) Larger than the required sample size from population 2.
   b) Equal to the required sample size from population 2.
   c) Smaller than the required sample size from population 2.
   d) Indeterminate relative to the required sample size from population 2.

(3) The required sample size from population 1 in case 3 is:
   a) Larger than the required sample size from population 2.
   b) Equal to the required sample size from population 2.
   c) Smaller than the required sample size from population 2.
   d) Indeterminate relative to the required sample size from population 2.

(4) The required sample size from population 1 in case 4 is:
   a) Larger than the required sample size from population 2.
   b) Equal to the required sample size from population 2.
   c) Smaller than the required sample size from population 2.
   d) Indeterminate relative to the required sample size from population 2.

(5) The required sample size from population 1 in case 5 is:
   a) Larger than the required sample size from population 2.
   b) Equal to the required sample size from population 2.
   c) Smaller than the required sample size from population 2.
   d) Indeterminate relative to the required sample size from population 2.

(AICPA, adapted)

5. In any statistical sampling situations, the desired precision is usually specified before any information is obtained. Precision obtained through

sampling is usually expressed as a numerical quantity or as a percentage of the estimate. Thus-

a) If the estimate is $300,000 and the precision of this estimate is ± two percent, the true value is expected to be no less than _____ and no more than _____.

b) If the estimate is $500,000 and the precision limits are $475,000 and $525,000, the precision is ±$_____ or ±_____ percent.

c) If the estimate is $220,000 and the precision of this estimate is ±$10,000, the precision limits are _____ and _____.

d) If the estimate is $400,000 and the precision of this estimate is ± three percent, the precision limits are _____ and _____.

e) If the estimate is $50,000 and the precision limits are $48,000 and $52,000, the precision is $_____ or _____ percent.

6. When an auditor is sampling for attributes, it is usually expressed as a percentage. Also, he expresses his precision limits of his estimates as a percentage. In his auditing of different clients he has found it desirable to set extension error occurrence rates at certain determined levels. Determine the true error occurrence rate of the entire population for each of the following:

a) An error occurrence rate of four percent ± one percent.

b) An error occurrence rate of three percent ±1½ percent.

c) An error occurrence rate of six percent ± three percent.

7. What does an auditor mean when he says that in a certain universe there is a 90 percent probability that the error occurrence rate is five percent ± two percent?

8. In using Illustrations 9–2 through 9–5 an auditor can determine the required sample size.

a) Describe how the required sample size is determined.

b) Determine the required sample size under each of the following conditions.

	Client 1	Client 2	Client 3	Client 4
Reliability	99%	95%	90%	85%
Upper precision limit	18	25	14	30
Estimated occurrence rate	9	17	9	25
Sample size	?	?	?	?

c) Determine the required sample size under each of the following conditions. What conclusion can you draw from your answers?

	A	B	C	D
Confidence level	99%	95%	90%	85%
Estimated occurrence rate	10	10	10	10
Upper precision limit	16	16	16	16
Sample size	?	?	?	?

d) Determine the required sample size under each of the following conditions. What conclusions can you draw from your answers?

	W	X	Y	Z
Confidence level.	95%	95%	95%	95%
Estimated occurrence rate	6	6	6	6
Upper precision limit	10	12	14	16
Sample size	?	?	?	?

9. Illustrations 9–6 through 9–9 provide the auditor with a means of determining whether or not he can state with a definite degree of confidence that the population does not contain more than a certain predetermined percent of errors. Using Illustrations 9–6 through 9–9 provide the answers for the following situations.

(a)	Client 1	Client 2	Client 3	Client 4
Confidence level.	99%	95%	90%	85%
Number of errors	18	16	32	17
Sample size	340	120	460	160
Upper precision limit	?	?	?	?

(b)	A	B	C	D
Number of errors	16	17	17	17
Sample size	240	240	240	240
Upper precision limit	9%	12%	10%	16%
Confidence level.	?	?	?	?

(c)	W	X	Y	Z
Sample size	160	160	160	160
Upper precision limit	14%	12%	12%	12%
Confidence level.	99%	95%	90%	85%
Number of errors	?	?	?	?

10. While examining the internal control procedure for the make-up and issuance of payroll checks, the auditor becomes concerned over the possibility of posting errors and defalcations. He has determined that posting errors represent non-critical errors while defalcations are critical. There are 6,000 payroll checks issued monthly. The estimated occurrence rate of non-critical errors is two percent and the auditor desires 90 percent assurance that the actual frequency of these errors does not exceed five percent, and defalcations do not exceed 0.5 percent.

a) What type of sampling techniques should the auditor employ?

b) What sample size or sizes should be drawn?

c) Assume 11 posting errors were discovered and no defalcations were noted in the sample. What conclusions can the auditor reach from these results?

11. In his examination of financial statements, a CPA generally finds numerous opportunities for using statistical sampling. Select the correct answer for each of the different situations which follow.

(1)   In an examination of financial statements a CPA generally will find stratified random sampling techniques to be most applicable to
   a)   Recomputing net wage and salary payments to employees.
   b)   Tracing hours worked from the payroll summary back to the individual time cards.
   c)   Confirming accounts receivable for residential customers at a large electric utility.
   d)   Reviewing supporting documentation for additions to plant and equipment.

(2)   A client maintains perpetual inventory records. In the past all inventory items have been counted on a cycle basis at least once during the year and physical inventory differences have been minor. The client now wishes to minimize costs of conducting the physical inventory by changing to a sampling method in which many inventory items will not be counted during a given year. For purposes of expressing an opinion on his client's financial statements an auditor will accept the sampling method only if:
   a)   The sampling method has statistical validity.
   b)   A stratified sampling plan is used.
   c)   The client is willing to accept an opinion qualification in the auditor's report.
   d)   The client is willing to accept a scope qualification in the auditor's report.

(3)   In an examination of financial statements a CPA would not find use of statistical sampling techniques to be generally acceptable if:
   a)   The population were large.
   b)   Absolute precision of measurement were required.
   c)   None of the items were individually significant.
   d)   The population were not normally distributed.

(4)   In connection with his examination of the financial statements of Melons, Inc. a CPA is testing the effectiveness of the Company's inspection system for purchases from melon growers. For one lot of 2,000, Company inspectors found the bad melon rate to be 4 percent. If the CPA wishes to sample from this lot with a confidence level of 90 percent and a precision (confidence interval) of ±2 percent, the required sample size is 230. If the precision is changed to ±1 percent and other specifications remain the same, the required sample size is:
   a)   684
   b)   251
   c)   209
   d)   63

(AICPA, adapted)

12.   Select the decision a CPA should make as he examines the financial statements of Olympia, Inc.
   (1)   In connection with his review of charges to the plant maintenance account, the CPA is undecided as to whether to use probability sampling or judgment sampling. As compared to probability sampling, judgment sampling has the primary advantage of:

   a)   Providing no known method for making statistical inferences about the population solely from the results of the sample.
   b)   Not allowing the auditor to select those accounts which he believes should be selected.
   c)   Requiring that a complete list of all the population elements be compiled.
   d)   Not permitting the auditor to know which types of items will be included in the sample before the actual selection is made.

(2) The CPA believes that the error occurrence rate of charging capital items to expense is 2 percent, which will have an immaterial effect upon the financial statements. The maximum acceptable occurrence rate is 3 percent. Under these circumstances the CPA should select a plan of:
   a)   Discovery sampling.
   b)   Attribute sampling.
   c)   Variable sampling.
   d)   Stratified sampling.

(3) The CPA reviewed a random sample of 40 maintenance job orders and determined in each the dollar amount of capital items improperly charged to expense. He wishes to estimate this amount for all maintenance job orders with a 95 percent level of confidence. The 95 percent refers to the probability that the true population value will fall within the limits thus established for:
   a)   Only this sample.
   b)   All samples selected from this population.
   c)   All samples of this size selected from this population.
   d)   All samples of this size selected from any population.

(4) The CPA has estimated with 95 percent confidence that the total dollar amount of capital items improperly expensed is $43,200 ± $9,216. If he reduces the interval estimate from ± $9,216 to ± $4,608 without sampling further, his confidence level changes from 95 percent to:
   a)   99.3 percent.
   b)   90 percent.
   c)   68 percent.
   d)   47.5 percent.

(5) Olympia had two billing clerks during the year. Snow worked three months and White worked nine months. The CPA wishes to use discovery sampling to test clerical accuracy during the tenure of each clerk. If the quantity of bills per month is constant and the same specified reliability and maximum tolerable occurrence rate is specified for each population, the ratio of the sample drawn from White's bills to the sample drawn from Snow's bills would be:
   a)   More than 3:1.
   b)   3:1.
   c)   More than 1:1 but less than 3:1.
   d)   1:1.

(AICPA, adapted)

13. The following situations apply to an examination of the Cherry Company which is being conducted by Grant Moore, CPA. Moore plans to select sufficient inventory items for test counts and pricing tests so that he can roughly estimate the total inventory cost.

(1) The size of Moore's statistical sample is influenced by the degree of variability in the cost of the items being sampled. The standard deviation, a basic measure of variation, is the:

    a) Average of the absolute differences between the individual values and their mean.

    b) Square root of the average of the absolute differences between the individual values and their mean.

    c) Average of the squared differences between the individual values and their mean.

    d) Square root of the average of the squares of the differences between the individual values and their mean.

(2) The greater the variability in the cost of the items being sampled (as measured by population standard deviation) the:

    a) Greater the usefulness of a table of random numbers in selecting a sample.

    b) Larger the sample size required to make reliable statements with a given precision.

    c) Greater should be the level of confidence required when establishing the estimate.

    d) More likely that an interval estimate made from sample data will be correct.

(3) Moore does not know the standard deviation of the cost of the items in Cherry's inventory. He can assume that the standard deviation computed from his sample is an adequate estimate of the population standard deviation if the sample:

    a) Is randomly selected, regardless of the number of items in the sample.

    b) Is randomly selected and contains at least 30 items.

    c) Contains at least 30 items, even if not randomly selected.

    d) Either is randomly selected or contains at least 30 items.

(4) Moore decides to use stratified sampling. The basic reason for using stratified sampling rather than unrestricted random sampling is to:

    a) Reduce as much as possible the degree of variability in the overall population.

    b) Give every element in the population an equal chance of being included in the sample.

    c) Allow the person selecting the sample to use his own judgment in deciding which elements should be included in the sample.

    d) Reduce the required sample size from a nonhomogeneous population.

(5) Cherry also asks its CPA's assistance in estimating the proportion of its active 30-day charge account customers who also have an active installment credit account. The CPA takes an unrestricted

random sample of 100 accounts from the 6,000 active 30-day charge accounts. Of the accounts selected, ten also have active installment credit accounts. If the CPA decides to estimate with 95 percent confidence, the estimate is that:

a) At most 10 percent of the active 30-day charge account customers also have active installment credit accounts.

b) At least 10 percent of the active 30-day charge account customers also have active installment credit accounts.

c) Between 7 percent and 13 percent of the active 30-day charge account customers also have active installment credit accounts.

d) Between 4 percent and 16 percent of the active 30-day charge account customers also have active installment credit accounts.

(6) The assistance of the auditor is requested in estimating the average gross value of the 5,000 invoices processed during June 1975. The auditor estimates the population standard deviation to be $8. If he wishes to achieve a precision of ± $2 with a 95 percent level of confidence, he should draw an unrestricted random sample of:

a) 404 elements.

b) 101 elements.

c) 96 elements.

d) 62 elements.

(AICPA, adapted)

14. The eight following items apply to random sampling for attributes, a sampling technique often employed in transaction testing. Assume that all samples are to be drawn from large populations.

(1) Which of the following is an application of sampling for attributes?

a) Estimating the total dollar value of accounts receivable.

b) Estimating the reliability of a sample estimate.

c) Estimating the precision of a sample estimate.

d) Estimating the percentage of sales invoices with totals of less than $10.

(2) In a random sample of 1,000 records a CPA determines that the rate of occurrence of errors is 2 percent. He can state that the error rate in the population is:

a) Not more than 3 percent.

b) Not less than 2 percent.

c) Probably about 2 percent.

d) Not less than 1 percent.

(3) From a random sample of items listed from a client's inventory count an auditor estimates with 90 percent confidence that the error occurrence rate is between 4 percent and 6 percent. The auditor's major concern is that there is one chance in twenty that the true error rate in the population is:

a) More than 6 percent.

b) Less than 6 percent.

c) More than 4 percent.

d) Less than 4 percent.

(4) If from a particular random sample a person can state with 90

percent confidence that the occurrence rate in the population does not exceed 20 percent, he can state that the occurrence rate does not exceed 25 percent with:

a) 95 percent confidence.

b) Greater reliability on his sample.

c) The same reliability on his sample.

d) Less reliability on his sample.

(5) If a CPA wishes to select a random sample which must have a 90 percent confidence level and an upper precision limit of 10 percent, the size of the sample he must select will decrease as his estimate of the:

a) Occurrence rate increases.

b) Occurrence rate decreases.

c) Population size increases.

d) Reliability of the sample decreases.

(6) If a CPA selects a random sample for which he specified a confidence level of 99 percent and upper precision limit of five percent and subsequently changes the confidence level to 90 percent, the sample will produce an estimate which is:

a) More reliable and more precise.

b) More reliable and less precise.

c) Less reliable and more precise.

d) Less reliable and less precise.

(7) If the result obtained from a particular sample will be critical, e.g., an unqualified opinion could not be rendered, which of the following is the most important to the auditor?

a) Size of the population.

b) Estimated occurrence rate.

c) Specified upper precision limit.

d) Specified confidence level.

(8) Which of the following need not be known to evaluate the results of a sample for a particular attribute?

a) Occurrence rate in the population.

b) Size of the sample.

c) Reliability of the sample.

d) Occurrences in the sample.

15. A client manufacturers typewriters, and it has been decided to take a stratified sample to estimate the total inventory in the hands of his dealers. It is desired to have a precision of 16,000 typewriters at the 95 percent confidence level. On the basis of data obtained from the prior audit, the following information is developed:

Stratum	Number of Dealers	Amount of Variance from Mean
1 (1 to 9 typewriters)	20,000	35
2 (10 to 19 typewriters)	3,000	92
3 (20 to 29 typewriters)	1,000	174
4 (30 to 39 typewriters)	600	320

a) Using the optimum sampling method, determine the sample size of dealers to be audited.

b) Determine the number of dealers in each stratum who will be audited.

c) The following results were obtained as a result of random selection of dealers and the taking of their inventory:

Stratum	Mean Typewriters per Dealer in Each Stratum	Actual Typewriter Variance from Mean in Each Stratum
1	4	25
2	13	85
3	25	170
4	40	300

(1) Determine the estimate of the total inventory.

(2) Determine the precision attained.

(3) Was the sample adequate?

10

Examination of Evidence and Original Records: Manual Systems

SECTION I: INTRODUCTION

Original Records

One of the bases for the formulation of an audit opinion is the reliance upon transactional and other evidence obtained from a client and from outside sources. The evidence of a client lies in both *nonfinancial* and *financial* original records. The types, quantities and quality of evidence to be examined will be developed in this chapter and in Chapter 11, together with the auditing standards and procedures to be adhered to in the examination of the evidence.

It must be remembered that this book is not "specialized" as to any one type of business. The auditing procedures developed and described are applicable basically to all types of business organizations. Naturally, the mechanical accounting procedures of one business entity will differ from those of another; a company may not use a formal cash disbursements record or a voucher register, but it will use a similar medium for recording money spent and for recording assets purchased and expenses incurred. In other words, the auditing standards and procedures developed are based upon the underlying application of proper accounting theory, consistently applied.

Nonfinancial Records

The nonfinancial records to be considered are the articles of incorporation, the articles of copartnership, the code of regulations, the minutes of the stockholders, the minutes of the executive committee, contracts, leases, pension plans, labor agreements, and any other records that might result in or directly influence financial transactions.

The examination of the nonfinancial records preferably should be performed early in the course of the audit (or prior to starting the audit), for the reason that these records may disclose information necessary for proper guidance during the course of the examination of the financial records. In addition, an auditor must verify the fact that the transactions recorded have authority based upon actions of the owners and directors and also have authority granted by public governing bodies.

The examination of nonfinancial records is a function of the in-charge accountant, since he has authority to decide if recorded transactions fall within the range of the nonfinancial records.

An Audit Program for Nonfinancial Records

In any audit, an auditor should review all nonfinancial records in order to ascertain that authorized transactions are properly recorded and that recorded transactions were properly approved.

An audit program for the nonfinancial records may be summarized as follows:

Examine (or obtain a copy of) and excerpt (or note) pertinent information from each of the following:

1. The articles of incorporation and any amendments thereto (or the articles of copartnership).
2. The provisions of the code of regulations (bylaws) that affect the audit and the operations of the company.
3. The minutes of the meetings of the board of directors and the stockholders.
4. The minutes of the meetings of the executive committee and other policy-forming committees.
5. Contracts, leases, agreements, pension plans, profit-sharing arrangements, union contracts, and so forth.

The audit procedures to be followed for the preceding nonfinancial records are described in the following subsections.

Examine the Articles of Incorporation and Any Amendments Thereto and Excerpt Pertinent Financial Provision. The following points are to be included:

a) The exact name and address of the company.
b) The date of incorporation and charter number.
c) The classes of authorized capital stock, the number of authorized shares of each class, and their respective par, no-par, or stated values.
d) Dividend provisions for preferred stock.
e) Preferred stock: cumulative and noncumulative features, participat-

ing and nonparticipating features, voting privileges, liquidation and redemption features, and conversion provisions.

f) The purpose clause.

g) The principal place of business.

h) The name and address of the corporation's fiscal agent.

i) Bank designated as depository.

The preceding data will be placed in the permanent file. On succeeding engagements, the file will be placed in current condition by any necessary changes.

In the examination of the articles of copartnership, the following points should be included:

a) The names of the partners.

b) The type of each partner—that is, general, limited, silent, and so forth.

c) The capital requirements of each partner.

d) Agreements with respect to drawings.

e) Profit-sharing agreements.

f) The treatment of interest on drawing accounts and capital accounts.

g) Salaries, if any, and their accounting treatment.

h) Termination procedures in the event of death, and so forth.

On a repeat engagement, amendments to the articles should be noted.

Examine the Code of Regulations and Excerpt Regulations that Affect the Audit and the Operations of the Company. The following points are to be included:

a) The date, place, and quorum requirements of the annual stockholders' meeting.

b) The requirements for special meetings of the stockholders. Meetings held in nonconformity with the provisions of (*a*) and (*b*) would constitute unauthorized procedure.

c) The procedure for the selection of the auditors.

d) The provisions and methods for the election of directors.

e) The methods of filling vacancies on the board of directors.

f) The duties of the directors.

g) The policies of the board of directors in the selection of executive officers.

h) Dividend policy provisions, if any.

i) The order of business in a meeting of the board of directors or of the stockholders.

j) The method of voting and results of the voting.

k) The methods of amending the code of regulations.

This material will become a part of the permanent file. On succeeding audits, an examination should be made of any amendments to the code of regulations.

Examine the Minutes of the Meetings of the Board of Directors and Note All Pertinent Actions. The following points are to be included:

a) The proper dating and signing of the minutes of the meetings of the board of directors.

b) The compensation of officers and directors.

c) Bonus, profit-sharing, and stock option agreements.

d) Pension agreements.

e) Contracts with executives, including deferred compensation plans.

f) Union contracts.

g) Dividend declarations.

h) Authorizations for capital stock increases and decreases to be considered by the stockholders.

i) Treasury stock purchases and sales.

j) Stock subscription forfeitures.

k) Authorizations for bond issues.

l) Authorization for the cancellation of treasury bonds.

m) Authorization for the construction or purchase of capital assets.

n) Authorization for the purchase and sale of investment securities.

o) Material-purchase contracts and their provisions.

p) Sales contracts and their provisions.

q) Budget appropriation actions.

r) Appropriations of retained earnings.

s) Depreciation policies.

t) Surety bonds.

u) Method of electing officers.

v) Authorized depositaries and authorized signatures for checks and borrowings.

w) Home office instructions to branches.

x) Comments on expansion plans needed to support accumulation of retained earnings.

y) Approval of employee fringe benefit plans, such as insurance and stock purchase.

z) Selection of the auditors.

If the minutes are not in satisfactory condition, the attention of the client should be directed to that fact. In extracting notes from the minutes, the auditor must learn to distinguish relevant from irrelevant data. Matters of interest to an auditor in the minutes are those that affect the audit and those that bear upon company operations in accordance with authorization by the board of directors.

An authorization by the board of directors usually results in an action to be taken. For example, the auditor must insist that surety bonds be purchased in accordance with board action. If authorizations by the board of directors have not been properly followed or recorded, the auditor must insist on compliance or qualify his report.

Examine the Minutes of Meetings of the Stockholders and Note All Pertinent Actions.   The following points are to be included:

a)   Authorizations for capital stock issuance and retirement.
b)   Authorizations for the sale or merger of the business.
c)   The method of electing directors.
d)   The time, place, and quorum requirements of meetings.
e)   The method of voting the shares of stock.
f)   Approval of stock option plans.

In examining the minutes of meetings of the stockholders, the auditor must be certain that actions taken by the stockholders are properly followed by the board of directors and officers of the corporation.

In small close corporations, the stockholders, directors, and officers may be the same persons. The auditor must distinguish between the actions of these persons in their capacities as officers, directors, and stockholders.

Examine All Contracts, Leases, Agreements, Pension Plans, Profit-sharing Arrangements, Union Contracts, and so forth, and Excerpt Important Provisions.   In the examination of each of these miscellaneous items, the primary objective is to determine that the provisions of each of the items have been adhered to, not only in terms of the documents involved but also from the point of view of the accounting and financial requirements involved. At this time it would also be desirable to develop the perpetual record of a client's various governmental agency reporting numbers.

SECTION II: ROUTINE ASPECTS OF AUDITING

Commonly Accepted Routine Aspects of Auditing

There are certain routine or transactional duties which are necessary in every audit and which have as their objectives the proof of accuracy and the obtaining of reliable evidence. The transactional and routine phases of an audit deal fundamentally with the examination of transaction data and the recording of those data in the financial records. The routine or transactional features primarily involve the following:

1.   *Proof of extension accuracy* on invoices and other vouchers.
2.   *Proof of footing accuracy* on invoices, other vouchers, ledger accounts, and journals.
3.   *Proof of posting accuracy* from journals to ledger accounts.
4.   *Vouching and verification of transactions* of all descriptions.
5.   *Preparation of reconciliations* between related—but independent—figures.
6.   *Analysis of accounts.*

The amount of detailed examination to be performed on each audit in connection with each of the preceding six items depends upon:

1. The system of internal control and extent of internal auditing.
2. The probability that major or serious errors will be discovered with the use of a partial verification of the transactions.
3. The contractual arrangements with the client.
4. The number of errors discovered and their materiality.

Suggestions regarding the amount of detailed examination are set forth in Section III of this chapter and in Chapter 11.

Proof of Extension Accuracy.   Extensions involve multiplications on invoices, payroll records, inventory-count-and-price sheets, and various other data. Normally, the proof of extension accuracy is performed in accordance with the plan of testing devised for the examination and in accordance with the test sample selected. The objective of proof of extension accuracy should be that the largest possible dollar accuracy is proved with a minimum of work.

Proof of Footing Accuracy.   Footings result from vertical or horizontal additions. There is no substitute for proof of footing accuracy; and if a dishonest employee realizes that the auditor will foot the original records for only certain months, he may risk the practice of fraud in other months, with the hope that his practices will not be discovered. Consequently, an auditor should not indicate the pages or periods footed.

ILLUSTRATION.   The necessity of the proof of footing accuracy may be exemplified as follows: If the cash disbursements record were overfooted, a theft of cash could be committed for the amount of the overfooting of the Cash credits. Or if the cash receipts record were underfooted, cash could be extracted to the amount of the underfooting of the Cash debits.

When a client submits adding machine tapes to the auditor, the latter should verify the submitted tapes. If the total of an adding machine tape prepared by the auditor does not agree with the total in the record being footed, figure comparisons must be made and if necessary a new adding machine tape must be prepared. An adding machine tape affords evidential proof of the work done. In the proof of footing accuracy, it frequently happens that the auditor must release the records to a member of the client's staff for the performance of routine work before the footing process is completed. When this occurs, the auditor must make a notation of his temporary stopping place and the totals to that point.

Suggestions regarding the amount of proof of footing accuracy for ledger accounts and the various journals are discussed later in this chapter.

Proof of Posting Accuracy.   An auditor traces the posting of entries from the records of original entry to the ledger accounts in accordance with the selected testing plan. When postings are being verified, the entries are traced from the journals to the ledger accounts.

The work of proving posting accuracy is facilitated if two persons are used. A specific order of procedure is naturally established in the verification of posting accuracy. A quite standard order follows:

Accountant with Journal	*Account with Ledger*
1. Calls the ledger folio.	1. Locates the account.
2. Name and number of the account.	2. Verifies the name and number of the account.
3. Calls the date of the transaction.	3. Verifies the date of the transaction.
4. Indicates a debit or a credit.	4. Verifies a debit or a credit.
5. Calls the amount; places a tick mark in the journal.	5. Verifies the amount; places a tick mark after the entry.
6. Calls the page of the journal.	6. Verifies the journal page.

In verifying postings, the auditor must be certain (1) that he understands the journal entry, (2) that the entry is accurate from the standpoint of correct debits and credits, (3) that the entry is posted to the proper accounts, (4) that necessary subsidiary ledger postings are made, (5) that a debit is posted as a debit and a credit as a credit, and (6) that transpositions and slides do not exist.

Corrections of postings are placed on the audit work papers—on the audit adjustments sheet. If the accounts have been closed by the client, posting corrections involving small amounts are ignored by many accountants on the basis that the small amounts will have no significant effect upon the net income or the classification of expenses, revenues, assets, or liabilities. If there are many small errors in posting, the aggregate may be large, in which case these errors cannot be ignored. Exactly where a small amount stops and a large amount starts is a question of materiality to be judged by the factors in each case. Whenever there is a question as to the advisability of accepting or correcting an improper posting, *correct it.*

Vouching and Verification of Transactions.   Vouching is the examination and authentication of underlying evidential papers and data which are in support of the accuracy of transactions; verification is the proof of accuracy of extensions, footings, postings, ownership, and existence.

Vouching and verification of transactions rest upon the documents offering proof of the validity of recorded transactions; examples of such documents would include purchase invoices, sales invoices, paid checks, duplicates of cash receipts, and contracts.

The purposes of examining the underlying evidences of transactions—commonly called vouchers—are to ascertain (1) that the voucher is authorized by the proper persons, (2) that the voucher is for a proper expenditure, (3) that the amount of the voucher is correct, (4) that the voucher has been properly entered in the records, and (5) properly filed for future reference.

It occasionally happens that original vouchers are lost or inadvertently destroyed. If they cannot be located, alternative procedures such as correspondence, receiving room reports, requisitions, purchase orders, and other data may be used.

Preparation of Reconciliations. Another routine feature of auditing is the obtaining of reconcilements between two groups of related, but independent, figures. As examples, a reconciliation is prepared for cash per the bank statement and the balance according to the Cash ledger account; reconcilements are prepared for various accounts on the records of a subsidiary company and its parent company; the subsidiary accounts receivable are reconciled with the controlling account for accounts receivable.

Analysis of Accounts. It may be necessary to analyze an account (1) in order to detail its composition into its component parts on a classified basis or (2) in order to detail the individual charges and credits in the account in chronological order. Type (1), above, is exemplified by the analysis of the Sales account, Illustration 8–9; type (2), above, by the analysis of the Machinery account, Illustration 8–8.

Use of Audit Code Legends. An auditor should not deface the records of his client. The auditor must use tick marks which are small, legible, and consistent as to meaning throughout the examination. Each auditor may devise his personally preferred tick marks, and he may vary them from audit to audit, unless standard tick marks are required by his firm. Each different tick mark must indicate that a specific operation has been performed in connection with the engagement. The material in Chapter 8 should be reviewed at this point, and the code legend in the Illustrative Audit should be studied. An accountant may use a personalized rubber stamp to indicate loose-paper examination. A rubber stamp effectively prevents the duplicate presentation of the same paper evidence.

SECTION III: SAMPLE SELECTION; RECORD TESTING

Errors

In Chapter 4, errors were classified as (1) errors of principle, (2) errors of omission, and (3) errors of commission. These classifications were subdivided into intentional or unintentional errors. Errors made in the application of accounting principles normally result in dollar amount errors and are as serious as any other type of error. Appropriate tests and auditing procedures must be applied to business transactions to assure their genuineness—evidenced by legal and company authority—and to remove from the financial statements the possibility of doubt for reliability. At this point, additional consideration is devoted to errors as an introduction to the adequate determination of statistical and non-statistical samples for testing the accuracy of each area of operational and financial records and data.

Material Errors. A "material" or "serious" or "substantive" error is defined as one that is "considerable in amount or numbers; it is substantial, firm, or solid." A material error is one that affects the financial statements to the point where the auditor cannot tolerate the error unless it is corrected. Another concept of a material error is to the effect that the error is so significant that the person who uses the resulting financial statement probably will have his judgment or decisions influenced.

If material errors in a sample exceed a predetermined percentage of the items or transactions or dollars in the sample, the entire whole (of which the sample is a part) may be rejected as unsatisfactory, or the testing may be extended—perhaps to the point of a 100 percent examination. The decision to accept or extend the sampling is necessary in order finally to accept as satisfactory the body of data being examined, or to reject the body of data as unsatisfactory. In this manner, objectivity of sample examination then finally assures proper presentation of the financial statements in accordance with accepted auditing standards and accounting principles.

The percentage, or dollar amounts, or number of errors acceptable in an audit area under examination will be dependent upon the importance of the data in relationship to other related data, to the financial statements, and to the decision concerning the rendition of an opinion of the statements. At the present time, there can be no uniformity of opinion regarding universally acceptable error limits because each area of an audit differs from every other area, each audit differs from every other audit, and finally because decisions must be made in the determination of the adequacy—for the purpose involved—of sample results.

Minor Errors. A minor error is one that will not influence judgment concerning financial statements and one that the auditor is *willing* to accept without correction. A minor error in one area of the records may be a material error in another area. For example, an error of $100 in the operation of a petty cash fund may be serious, whereas an error of $100 in an inventory might be minor. Therefore, in each audit and in each area of every audit, material and minor errors must be defined in advance of examination.

Error Correction. If a client has prepared his financial statements prior to audit, it is common practice for the auditor not to adjust errors which in his opinion are insignificant. While this is common practice, it is not a preferred practice because there could develop the human tendency to increase neglect or to decrease the concept of seriousness. If the financial statements of a client have not been prepared prior to independent examination, no reason exists for failure to correct all errors—material or minor. Thus, while the results of examining a sample may be acceptable, logically, if all discovered errors are corrected, the financial statements will be more proper than if corrections were not made and the carry-over effect into the next year will be eliminated.

Pre-Audit Concepts of Error Definition and Decision

Acceptable and unacceptable errors for each area should be defined prior to the examination in order to establish the acceptability or rejection of an item, an area, or a total. In this way, prejudice and bias are eliminated, and objectivity is established.

ILLUSTRATION. In the examination of the records of Company A, the pre-audit decision is reached that (1) an error of not more than $0.10 in a petty cash voucher will be ignored; (2) an error of not more than $10 in an inventory subclass total will be ignored; (3) a date error on any document will be ignored; (4) all errors in accounting postings will be corrected; (5) an error of not more than $1 in any payroll computation, individual or otherwise, will be ignored.

In the examination of the records of Company B, the decision is reached in advance of the audit that (1) all errors discovered in cash disbursements will be corrected, (2) all errors discovered in cash receipts will be corrected, (3) all discovered date errors will be corrected, (4) any error of more than $0.50 in payroll computations will be corrected.

In defining an error, there must be included a definition of an acceptable minor error, an acceptable or unacceptable minor error total within a data area being examined, and a major or material error. A material error will demand correction if financial statements are to be submitted without qualification. A predefined minor error (or the sum of minor errors) may not *demand* correction. Minor errors, however, could not exist in "material" numbers without leading to the rejection of the sample of the data examined from any area.

If judgment or statistical sampling methods are to be employed with ease and success in the examination of accounting data and records, it is necessary that a pre-audit definition of *each type* of error in *each area* of the accounting activity be established. This is necessary in order to determine if an item, a document, a transaction, an entry, an amount, etc., is correct or incorrect. Also, it is necessary to predefine each type of error in each area in order to determine if the results of the sampling are acceptable or unacceptable. If the results of the sampling are unacceptable, the testing would be extended (1) until the auditor was satisfied or (2) until it was determined that the entire area must be rejected—to be followed by (*a*) corrections, or (*b*) a restriction of opinion, or (*c*) a disclaimer of opinion.

In any area of examination, if a percentage of incorrect *items* (one percent, two percent, five percent, and so forth) is to be used as the basis of acceptance or rejection, the predefinition of minor errors and material errors must be precisely delineated so that personal bias or prejudice will *not* enter decisions.

Examination of Original Financial Data and Records

Auditing procedures applicable to original financial data and to original accounting record entries are now considered. Sample sizes depend upon the effectiveness of internal control, the extent of internal auditing, the importance of the data, the desired tightness of inspection, and the sampling tables used. In general, the larger the mass of data, the smaller will be the sample in proportion to the universe. The sample sizes suggested in this chapter are based on an effective system of internal control, and the sample sizes may be decreased if internal control is excellent, and should be increased if internal control is not satisfactory or if defined errors exceed specifications set forth in an adopted sampling plan.

Vouchers and Their Examination

The purposes of examining original evidential papers and data-supporting transactions are as follows:

1. To determine that the vouchers are properly authorized and approved.
2. To determine that the vouchers are for proper purposes.
3. To determine that the amounts of the vouchers are correct.
4. To determine that the vouchers are properly entered in the records and filed.

In the examination of vouchers and all underlying documents, the objective of the auditor is to verify the largest possible dollar amount of any set of data. Even though he will not examine all of the vouchers, the auditor should request access to all vouchers of each class.

The following schedule shows the various types of vouchers and the normally related records of original accounting entry:

Vouchers	*Probable Record of Original Entry*
Journal voucher	General journal
Minutes	General journal; cash records
Sales invoices	Sales journals
Customers' credit memoranda	Sales returns journals
Duplicate bank deposit tickets and/or customer remittance lists	Cash receipts records; bank statements
Creditors' invoices	Purchase record; voucher register
Creditors' debit memoranda	Purchase return records; voucher register
Paid bank checks	Cash disbursements records; expense distribution records
Payroll checks	Payroll record
Payroll summary	Cash disbursements records; labor distribution schedules or journals
Expense reports	Cash disbursements records; expense distribution records
Petty cash vouchers	Cash disbursements records; expense distribution records
Stores requisitions	Requisition summary or the equivalent of a work-in-process record

Audit Program for Voucher Examination

An audit program for the examination of original evidential papers may be introduced as follows:

1. Account for all numbers for consecutively prenumbered documents.
2. Examine the system of filing each class of voucher.
3. Decide upon a sample in accordance with the data to be examined—their type, quality, importance, and filing.
4. Draw the sample and all related data.
5. Compare the date, name, and amount of each sample voucher with the corresponding date, name, and amount appearing in the original accounting record.
6. Verify the correctness of computations on the sample vouchers.
7. Verify approval for accounting record entry, payment, receipt of goods, or other purpose.
8. Examine the distribution of the vouchers for correct department or account classification.
9. Investigate "duplicate" vouchers in order to determine that duplicate accounting entries were not made.
10. Reconcile the minutes of the board of directors, major committees, and so forth with the accounting entries arising therefrom, in accordance with the vouchers.
11. Trace each document in the sample to its record of original accounting entry—individually or summarized—and tick off.
12. Prepare necessary work papers setting forth all procedures followed and the findings.

The preceding program is applicable to any type of original documentary (voucher) evidence—sales invoices, vendors' invoices, cash receipts data, petty cash disbursements vouchers, and so forth—to be discussed in the following pages.

As stated previously, sample size depends upon the effectiveness of internal control, extent of internal auditing, the importance of the data, the rigidity of inspection desired, and upon the statistical sampling plan being used. Sample size also depends upon the type of business and the relative importance of one item—for example, each sale of an aircraft manufacturer versus each sale in a chain of retail drugstores. Sample size cannot be set forth specifically for universal adoption; in each audit, judgment must be exercised, based upon the desired tightness of inspection. Recognized sample plan tables preferably should be used by an auditor. The level of tightness of inspection must be developed in accordance with the requirements of the audit.

Important Points in Voucher Examination. For the sample selected, several points of importance in the examination of any type of voucher are presented on the following page.

The auditor must obtain the names of all persons properly authorized to approve vouchers for sales, sales returns and allowances, cash receipts, purchases of assets, purchase returns and allowances, receipt of goods, cash disbursements, and all others. Then, armed with the samples of the vouchers of each type, the auditor is ready to proceed with the examination and authentication (vouching) of the vouchers and any related data, and the tracing of the items into the original accounting records—the cash receipts record, the cash disbursements record, the invoice or voucher register, the payroll record, the sales record, and all others.

Voucher examination should be undertaken in a systematic manner. Many types of vouchers are serially numbered, thus facilitating the selection of random samples. The auditor should have access to all vouchers of a particular type, even though he will not examine each one. Accessibility to all items of a type prevents bias from entering into the selection of a random sample. Voucher examination is a necessary phase of an audit, but it is a lengthy process; therefore, based upon the effectiveness of internal control, an adequate and representative sample is necessary—and at the same time, the sample should not be excessive, thereby unnecessarily increasing audit cost.

Any type of voucher may be filed numerically or chronologically (as exemplified by the frequent practice of filing paid checks by months); or they may be filed alphabetically by (say) creditors. Regardless of the filing method used, the auditor must place his code legend on the examined vouchers so that the same voucher may not be selected or presented a second time—perhaps with an altered date. If a client insists that the vouchers are not be marked, the auditor must prepare a list of those examined. After examination and authentication, the auditor will return the vouchers to the client as they were presented to him or drawn by him.

It must be remembered that vouching of transactions, alone, is not sufficient evidence to assure the auditor that each transaction is fundamentally correct and authoritatively recorded. The evidence may *appear* to be correct and in order, but a knowledge of the operating conditions of the business may show that evidence in the form of vouchers is not authentic. The system of internal control and audit in operation must be investigated to satisfy the auditor that a voucher for the purchase of materials, for example, constitutes a voucher for the purchase of materials for the business and not for an employee. In other words, the auditor must assure himself not only that the transactions are correctly recorded but also that the transactions recorded are proper business transactions.

In the examination of any voucher involving count and price, the auditor must be certain that unit prices are given in correct terms for the unit of count indicated on the voucher; otherwise, the extension, although mathematically correct, would be incorrect in total actual valuation.

Sample Selection

Solely for illustrative purposes, assume that a test program requires an examination of approximately 17 percent (2 months out of 12) of one type of voucher—for example, sales invoices. If internal control is satisfactory, a 17 percent examination of routine transactions is *extremely* high; but some assumption must be used, and these illustrative sample sizes are not intended for universal use. It is then decided that:

1. If a block sample is to be used:
   Select the vouchers of two nonconsecutive months. The two months may be selected at random, or the last month of the fiscal year may be used and the other month drawn at random. Then examine and authenticate the sample items in accordance with items 5–11, page 299.
2. If a random sample is to be used:
   Draw a random sample of 17 (exactly 16⅔) percent of the vouchers based upon a table of random numbers. Then examine and authenticate the sample items in accordance with items 5–11, page 299.
3. If a combination block and random sample is to be used:
   Select the vouchers for one month (assume the last) of the period, plus a random sample of 8 percent of the vouchers from the remaining 11 months. Then examine and authenticate the sample items in accordance with items 5–11, page 299.

If the results of the examination of the sample are within the established limits of acceptance, the universe may be accepted as satisfactory. If the results of the examination of the sample are below the acceptance limits, the universe should be rejected as being of unsatisfactory quality, or the decision may be to continue sampling until a conclusion is available.

The techniques of the preceding methods of sample selection are applicable to *any type of original documentary data.* The client is *not* informed of the sample selected, and the auditor consequently locates all documents of a particular type from which the sample will be drawn.

ILLUSTRATION. In this illustration, an extensive test is made of the accuracy of inventory extensions. In the verification of the clerical accuracy of inventory count-and-price sheets, the examination plan is established as follows, on the overall basis of proof of accuracy of extensions of 10 percent of the inventory cost:

1. Three randomly selected extensions (quantity times unit cost) on each sheet of 30 lines involving page totals of less than $500 are to be proved to the nearest $1. All discovered errors are to be corrected. If the dollar errors accumulate to more than 5 percent of the sheet total as shown by the client, the extension selection plan is to be continued

until three consecutive samples result in errors of less than 5 percent of the sheet total.

2.   Ten randomly selected extensions on *all* sheets whose totals are between $500 and $1,000 are to be proved. All discovered errors are to be corrected. If the dollar errors accumulate to more than 2 percent of the sheet total as shown by the client, the extension selection plan is to be continued until four consecutive samples result in errors of less than 3 percent of the sheet total.

3.   *All* extensions on *all* sheets whose totals exceed $1,000 are to be proved. If the dollar errors accumulate to more than 1 percent of the sheet total as shown by the client, the extension plan is to be continued until five consecutive samples result in errors of less than 1 percent of the sheet total.

4.   The sampling and testing in paragraphs 1 and 2 are to be continued if necessary until the required 10 percent quota is filled. The items examined on the inventory count-and-price sheets are to be compared with original inventory-count cards; the inventory prices used in extending are to be compared with the latest invoices.

Individualistic features of various types of vouchers will be presented, together with the transactional audit examination objectives applicable to the records of original accounting entry into which the various types of vouchers are transferred—individually or summarized.

Examination of Sales and Sales Returns Data

The major objective in connection with the examination of cash and credit sales data is to be certain that all sales revenue has been recorded and has been received or is receivable. If sales are made on the basis of orders received, shipping records usually are available so that the auditor may compare these records with duplicate copies of the invoices and with the entries in the sales journals. If sales slips or tickets are used or if cash registers accumulating daily totals are used, these will be available for examination and comparison with the original accounting records.

During the examination of the documentary sales data, copies of the sales invoices should be controlled. In order to easily draw a random sample, the copies of the sales invoices should be sequentially numbered, and all vouchers should be accounted for by the billing department. The sales invoices or related papers should bear evidence of the date of shipment, evidence of prices and extensions, and evidence of credit approval. In accordance with the proof of footing and posting accuracy, the accuracy of sales distributions to departments, products, and so forth, should be proved.

In connection with sales returns, the procedure of the client should be to the effect that duplicate credit memoranda are properly approved prior to entry to the credit of the customers' accounts receivable. The credit memoranda should be examined in the same manner as sales invoices, but with reverse effect.

In vouching sales and sales returns, the following points are important:

1. Unshipped but recorded end-of-the-period sales must not be included in inventory.
2. Sales returns and allowances credit memorandums must be properly authorized, approved, and recorded.
3. Sales record entries must be supported by customers' orders, cash register tapes, duplicate sales slips, or duplicate copies of recorded invoices.
4. Customers must be genuine in order to avoid inventory thefts.
5. Money from cash sales should be recorded as received and deposited daily.
6. Sales records must be promptly closed at the end of the period.
7. All orders received should be filled; if they are not, revenue is lost.
8. Customers should be charged with applicable transportation costs.
9. Invoices must be properly controlled and sequentially numbered.

If a statistical plan with specified tightness of inspection levels is not available, a random sample of sales invoices *not* in excess of approximately 8 percent of the dollar sales should normally be adequate to judge the quality of the data in the universe. If a block sample is used, approximately one month's sales or four nonconsecutive weeks' sales are adequate if internal control is satisfactory.

Examination of Cash Receipts and Related Data

In vouching cash receipts and their related data, the problem of the auditor is to ascertain that all cash receipts have been properly accounted for, that all cash that has been received has been recorded, and that all cash that should have been received was received and recorded. Cash receipts arise mainly from cash sales and from collections of receivables. In vouching cash receipts, the auditor should obtain the daily remittance lists prepared by the person who opens the mail (see Chapters 4 and 5); and he should obtain the cash register tapes and duplicate sales invoices—in accordance with his sample plan.

On the basis of the selected sample of original remittance lists, paid invoice copies, and cash register tape totals, the corresponding cash receipts should be traced to the cash receipts record. The same receipts should be traced to the duplicate bank deposit tickets and to the bank statement; totals of duplicate deposit tickets may be compared with total bank deposits, or total cash credits to accounts receivable plus cash credits to other accounts may be compared with total bank deposits.

Cash receipts records may be divided into original vouchers and entries in cash receipts records where there are no original vouchers. Limits for the examination and authentication of cash receipts vary in accordance with the importance of cash and the internal control exercised over it. Normally, the vouching of approximately 8± percent of cash receipts is adequate to judge the quality of the totality of the receipts.

Cash and checks received should be listed and deposited in the composition in which they are received. If customers send remittance advices with their checks, additional evidence of cash receipts is available—if the remittance advices are on hand—and independent vouchers may thus be used for proving the accuracy of postings to subsidiary ledger accounts. Additional consideration is given cash receipts in Chapter 12.

ILLUSTRATION. An examination plan for cash receipts for a certain audit was established as follows:

1. Prove the footing and posting accuracy of the cash receipts journal for December plus three randomly selected nonconsecutive months.

2. Vouch all cash receipts for two months—December plus one month drawn at random from the other three months in paragraph 1; assume the random month to be June. The footing and posting accuracy of June and December has been proved as a part of the four months' proof.

3. Vouch cash receipts from original data to the cash receipts journal for the other 10 months, as follows:

Customers' Names Beginning with:*	Vouch for Months of:†
A	January and July
E	February and August
J	March and September
O	April and October
S	May and November

* A, E, J, O, and S were drawn at random from the alphabet.
† Months drawn at random from 10 months, except remaining May and November.

Examination of Creditors' Invoices and Related Data

The major objectives in the examination and authentication of invoices from creditors, and related internally prepared vouchers for items purchased, are to determine that:

1. Purchase orders are properly originated and approved and placed in accordance with company policy.
2. Invoices are correct as to unit price, quantity, extensions, and totals.
3. Invoices and related vouchers are properly approved for payment.
4. Items purchased are received.
5. Available discounts are taken.
6. Distributions are made to proper accounts.
7. Revenue and capital expenditures are properly distinguished.
8. All items and services purchased are for company use.

For purposes of identification, examined vouchers should be ticked off in the record of original entry. Checks in payment of paid invoices should be compared with the invoices and internally prepared vouchers and ticked off in the voucher record and in the cash disbursements record. Normally an examination of from 2 to 10 percent of the invoices should determine the quality of the universe.

Creditors' debit memoranda should be investigated to determine that proper distinction is made between returned goods and allowances for such items as transportation and defective goods not returned. The proper end-of-the-period cutoff time for debit memoranda and for inventory inclusion or exclusion should be established.

Examination of Cash Disbursements and Related Data

Cash disbursements may have been examined and authenticated in connection with the examination of vouchers payable and/or paid checks. In the examination of cash disbursements when a voucher register or invoice record is used to record the original liability, the cash disbursements record probably will be merely a check register. The procedure for examination of vouchers in support of expenditures will follow that of the sections titled "Examination of Creditors' Invoices and Related Data" in the preceding section and "Examination of Paid Checks" below.

If a voucher register system is not used, the cash disbursements record may carry the distribution of the disbursements for expenses and assets purchased; in this situation, the procedure will follow that outlined for the examination of creditors' invoices, synchronized with the examination of the actual cash disbursements and paid checks. In the examination and authentication of cash disbursements when a voucher system is not in operation, the auditor must examine invoices particularly. This is necessary because invoices may not be recorded in one organized place; as a result, there may be less rigid internal control over payables. Invoice distribution must be examined to ascertain the propriety of the accounts charged. If one check is issued in payment of more than one invoice, the total of any one check in the check sample should be compared with the total of the invoices paid; this may necessitate an extension of the invoice sample to correspond to the checks.

The vouching of cash disbursements should parallel the examination of invoices, varied for invoices open at the beginning of the period but paid in the period and for invoices unpaid at the close of the period.

Examination of Paid Checks

The sample pattern for paid check examination and authentication may be parallel to the vouching of invoices and related vouchers for payables and to the examination of the record of cash disbursements (above). If this procedure is followed, there is systematic correlation between the examination of the cleared checks and the paid payables. A "systematic-unsystematic" sample may be drawn, made up of some (or all) of the paid checks in support of the audited payables and other checks outside the sample of the payables vouchers. For integration purposes, a systematic sample is recommended. Systematic sampling avoids duplicate or cross-examination between the checks and the payables data and records.

Regardless of the sample and test pattern, the points set forth below are applicable to all examined paid checks. These points are discussed in more detail in Chapter 12.

1. Examine paid checks which were outstanding at the beginning of the period and tick off on the prior work papers.
2. Obtain access to all paid checks, arranged in proper order.
3. Account for all checks issued during the current period.
4. The date of the check must agree with the corresponding disbursements data.
5. The name of the payee must agree with the name in the cash disbursements record and in the voucher register, invoice record, and so forth.
6. The amount of the check must agree with the amount in the cash disbursements record, the voucher register or invoice record, and the bank statement.
7. Checks must bear authorized signatures.
8. Endorsements must be proper. Today, endorsements are not given much attention unless a nonpayroll check is made payable to the order of an employee.
9. Outstanding checks must be listed and must be of proper total (*a*) for the bank reconciliation and (*b*) because the end of the accounting period is a timely moment to attempt to cover fraud.
10. If fraud is suspected, bank paid dates must be watched in order to detect possible resubmission of the checks and to prove that checks written were properly recorded.
11. Checks made payable to the order of "Cash" or "Bearer" must be investigated.

The decision may be reached to initiate the examination and authentication of items purchased and cash disbursements by way of paid checks. In this case, the paid checks for the year under audit should be arranged in numerical sequence for ease of drawing the sample. Based upon a table of random numbers, the sample of paid checks is drawn.

The items in the check sample then are:

1. Compared with the related invoice or invoices and with the related payables data, which in turn are examined for quantities, prices, totals,

authorizations to purchase, authorizations to spend money, receipt of goods, and the propriety of the names of creditors.

2. Traced to corresponding entries in the voucher register or invoice record.
3. Traced to the cash disbursements records.
4. Examined for proper dates, signatures, and endorsements.

As the selected checks are investigated, each check is ticked by the auditor and each corresponding entry in the cash disbursements is ticked.

In all check examinations, if there is a lack of supporting vouchers or invoices, the auditor cannot be assured that the expenditure was proper for the business. The auditor should consider that busy executives sometimes sign or authorize the signing of checks as a routine matter and may not be interested in or have knowledge of the purpose for which a check is being written.

Examination of Petty Cash Disbursements

Petty cash (or any cash-fund) disbursements should be—but are not always—operated under the imprest system, with the preparation of a voucher for each such disbursement. Each petty cash voucher should be indelibly dated, contain an explanation of the expenditure, indicate the account to be charged at the time of fund reimbursement, show the amount of the expenditure (numerically and spelled out), be properly approved, and be signed by the person receiving the money and the person disbursing the money. Whenever expedient, all cash-fund vouchers should be supported by original invoices.

The examination procedure for petty cash disbursements (or any cash-fund disbursements) may be outlined as follows:

1. Select a block or random sample of the reimbursement vouchers and the accompanying individual expenditure vouchers. The size of the sample is dependent upon the importance of the size and activity of the fund compared with other assets and/or other operations and upon the internal control of the fund and its activities.
2. Prove the accuracy of extensions and footings on the reimbursement vouchers in the sample.
3. Prove the total of the individual expenditure vouchers with the total of each reimbursement voucher selected.
4. Trace reimbursement voucher data to the cash disbursements record.
5. Examine each selected individual expenditure voucher for date, approval, and amount.
6. Examine the propriety of ledger account distributions as indicated by the selected reimbursement vouchers.

Some writers in the field of accounting have expressed an opinion that fraud is of no significance; one publication stated that "the auditor expects to find no errors." Obviously, recent court cases should be examined! Regardless of the hopefulness of these statements, an auditor should attempt to determine whether the cash fund is properly used. An auditor must watch petty cash disbursements because they often are the source of petty thefts or of unauthorized private financing. One method for the auditor to reveal such undesirable operations is to recount the cash fund in a surprise visit or to watch the amount of the reimbursement checks and to investigate if they are regularly of an amount materially below the amount of the fund. If there is any unauthorized use of the cash fund, the attention of the client should be directed to the existing state of affairs.

Examination of Payroll Records and Related Data

Original payroll data and periodically accumulated payroll records assume a variety of forms. The vouching of payroll records is given additional consideration in Chapter 22. On the basis that certain payroll data constitute original evidences, at this point brief consideration is given payroll data. A proper sample of original payroll data—timecards, earnings records, and related personnel data—should be drawn, and the items in the sample verified for employee wage rate, hours worked, gross pay, taxes withheld, hospitalization, union dues, and other items; the result will be the net take-home pay.

Payroll data such as timecards may be block- or random-sampled. If timecards are not sequentially numbered, a table of random sample numbers cannot be used unless the timecards are numbered by the client or the auditor. In a given case, it may be decided—based upon sample size and desired inspection level—to examine 5 percent of the unnumbered timecards. The auditor decided to start with a randomly drawn number from 1–20 (assume number 8 was drawn). Then, on the basis of 5 percent—one out of 20—the auditor selected the timecard that was 8th in the file, then the 28th, 48th, etc., until the sample was completed. This plan would be practicable only if employee turnover was rapid; if there was no employee turnover and if the timecards were filed alphabetically, the same employee's timecard would be produced on each draw. If a block sample is used, all employees would be covered in the examination of the sample.

Each item in the sample would be authenticated and traced through such media as the payroll journal and the cash disbursements record. If a payroll journal is in use, the examination of that journal for footings, postings, and distributions would follow the plan set forth in "Audit of Any Special Journal" The examination of the paid payroll checks will follow the system outlined previously in this chapter under "Examination of Paid Checks." Payroll checks must be authenticated for name of employee, date, and amount. Because of the ease with which payroll checks are cashed, more than one endorsement is common. Payroll checks are not original vouchers, but they are similar to cash or petty cash receipts; they support disbursements based upon payroll journals, earnings records, and timecards. If a revolving payroll fund is used, the procedure for examination and authentication is precisely the same as that followed for petty cash when related vouchers are used, with the payroll checks taking the place of the petty cash vouchers.

Audit of the General Journal

General journal entries may be examined in total, or a sample may be chosen and examined. Some accountants favor an examination of all general journal entries; others are satisfied if the results of the examination of a sample are satisfactory. Whether a complete examination or a sample examination of general journal entries should be made is dependent upon the internal control and the extent of the operational functions of the general journal. When a sample plan is used, it is recommended that general journal entries not examined be read in order to detect any existing peculiarities.

Complete Examination. If the function of the general journal is limited to correcting entries, period-end adjusting entries, closing entries, and nonrepetitive and nonroutine transactions, and if an examination of all entries is desired, the audit program may be developed as follows:

1. *Obtain Access to All Documents Supporting and Authorizing Entries in the General Journal.* Entries in the general journal may be unsupported; or they may be supported by independent vouchers, minutes actions, correspondence with collection agencies, contractual agreements, requests from company officials, and other sources.

When journal vouchers are used, they may serve as the journal, or they may serve as support for the formal journal entries. In the first case, posting may be directly from the journal vouchers, or the journal vouchers may be summarized and posted at the end of each month. Good accounting practice dictates written *authority for* and *proper approval of* each journal voucher or each general journal entry of a nonroutine nature. Full explanations should accompany each entry.

2. *Trace Amounts Appearing on All Documents to the General Journal.* The auditor should obtain all documents—formal authorizations from actions of the board of directors, written informal authority, data from collection agency correspondence, contracts, etc.—and trace the items and amounts to the entries in the general journal or the journal vouchers in order to ascertain that each entry conforms to the underlying authorization and approval. Based upon the authorizations, an auditor may detect irregularities by reading the journal entries. Errors of principle frequently appear in the general journal or on journal vouchers.

As each document is examined and its accounting contents traced to the journal or the voucher, the auditor must place his code legend on the document so that it cannot be used again. A tick mark also must be placed opposite the corresponding journal entry.

3. *Determine the Equity of Debits and Credits.* Entries in the general journal and on journal vouchers should be examined for correct elements of debits and credits, and for mathematical equality of debits and credits. When compound entries appear, each entry should be footed for equality. For simple entries accompanied by several detailed items forming a part of that entry, the detail of the several items should be footed. A situation such as the following may be detected:

Accrued Interest Receivable $2,000	
Interest Income.	2,000
Interest accrued on the following bonds:	
Education Bond . . . . $ 500	
New Department Store 900	
Research Corporation 700	
$2,000	

A proof of the footing will result in $2,100. The error may or may not be inadvertent.

If the general journal is a multicolumn arrangement, all columns should be crossfooted and footed for equality of debits and credits. The auditor must watch for and investigate all general journal or journal voucher entries which reduce asset account balances.

ILLUSTRATION. A check is received from a customer for the full amount of his account. The bookkeeper deposits the check in the bank but abstracts currency from the bank deposit in an amount equal to the customer check; he then prepares a general journal entry charging Sales Returns for the amount stolen. An examination of the entry and the authority for it should disclose the fraud.

4. *Prove the Posting Accuracy of All General Journal Entries.* Proof of posting accuracy should be ascertained for all general journal—or journal voucher—entries by tracing to the ledger accounts involved in order to assist in determining the propriety of ledger account balances.

Sample Examination. If the general journal contains repetitive entries, the entries may be sequentially numbered by the auditor; or if journal vouchers are used, they either have been or can be numbered. In accordance with the effectiveness of internal control and the size of the universe, and based upon an acceptable sampling plan, a random sample may be drawn and examined together with the related underlying evidence. For the general journal or journal vouchers, a very tight level of inspection is recommended. Then—limited to the sample—the four steps outlined in the preceding paragraphs should be followed.

If the results of examining the sample are satisfactory, the totality of the general journal entries or the journal vouchers may be accepted as of satisfactory quality. If the results of the examination of the sample fall in the rejection level, the discovered errors should be corrected and another sample or samples drawn from the remaining entries or vouchers until a decision is reached for universe acceptance or rejection. If prepared sampling plans are not available, every *n*th general journal entry or journal voucher may be selected on the basis of a random start.

Audit of Any Special Journal or Record

The following suggested audit program applies to the examination of *any* original specialized journal or record. The objectives of the examination of any special journal—sales, cash receipts, voucher register, invoice record, cash disbursements, payroll, and so forth—are (1) to ascertain the mechanical accuracy of the equality of debits and credits, the proper distribution of entries, correct footings and crossfootings, and the proper inclusion of all items; and (2) to ascertain the correctness of the transfer of the original data—in detail or summarized—to the original accounting journal. If the original documentary evidences already have been examined and authenticated (vouched) on the basis of the examination of a sample and a conclusion reached regarding their quality, only the first objective of proving mechanical accuracy remains to be accomplished.

In the examination of the entries in any specialized original record, either a block or a random sample may be chosen, or the sample may be partially blocked and partially random.

An audit program for the examination of any specialized original record, by itself, assuming original documentary data have been tested and traced to that specialized record, may be developed as indicated in the following paragraphs. If a block sample of any original specialized record is to be used, and if a block is considered to be the special journal entries for one month, and if the examination of the system of internal control and the audit of the original documentary evidence has proved to be satisfactory, then normally and generally:

1. Prove the accuracy of footings for a selected number (assume two) of nonconsecutive months of the year, including the last; vary the other month each year. The two months are on the basis of a decision to adopt a sample of approximately 17 percent of the universe in accordance with the effectiveness of internal control.
2. Prove the accuracy of crossfootings for the months footed in order to integrate the data in the selected block. Some auditors foot only the "key" columns—for example, cash debits in the cash receipts record, voucher credits in the voucher register—then crossfoot totals.
3. Prove the accuracy of postings for the months footed and crossfooted in order to complete the verification of the data flow from the original data or records to the ledger.

If original documents such as cash register tapes, bank deposit data, vendors' invoices, and remittance list data *have not* already been tested and traced to the original specialized record, the three preceding steps should be followed, plus the authentication and tracing of original documentary data to the specialized record, as indicated in paragraph 1 or 2, below.

1. *Block sample.* If a block sample of original documents is selected, authenticate the original documentary data and trace to the record of original accounting entry for the selected number of nonconsecutive months of the period, including the last; vary the other months each year on the basis of a random selection of the other months.
2. *Random sample.* If a random sample of original documents is selected in accordance with the size of the universe and the desired level of tightness of inspection according to the adopted sampling plan, authenticate and trace the items in the sample to the original accounting record.

   For either a block or a random sample, accept or reject the universe in accordance with the acceptance and rejection levels of the adopted plan; or continue sampling, authenticating and tracing until a decision is available.
3. *Combination block and random sample.* The auditor may desire to examine a block (say, one week or one month) of original data, plus a random sample selected from the transactions for the remainder of the period. The total items in the block plus the items in the random sample would equal the sample size required in accordance with the adopted sampling plan, its tightness of inspection, and its acceptance and rejection levels.

The auditor may desire to start with the original accounting journal or record and trace entries therein back to the original documentary evidences. In this case, in order to select a random sample, each journal—record—page and each line of each page should be numbered. Then, based on a random number table, a random sample of page line numbers is drawn and the entries traced back to the original documentary evidences.

Footings of and Postings from Special Journals or Records

If a block sample of original documents is used, the extent of the proof of accuracy of footings of the original journals and postings therefrom should correspond approximately with the sample examination and the vouching of the original documentary evidences to the original journals involved.

If accuracy proof of footings and postings is on a block basis and when original documentary data are selected at random, the pattern for the test of the vouching of original documentary evidences will be on a "systematic-unsystematic" basis. For example, assume that three nonconsecutive months (extremely high) are chosen for proof of accuracy of footings and postings; a part of a random sample of original data drawn for verifying cash receipts, for example, may fall within the three months, and a part may fall outside those three months. The following illustration should be studied for sample plan:

ILLUSTRATION. Each page of a sales journal is 40 lines deep; 54 pages were used for the year. On the basis of 2,160 entries, the sampling plan called for the examination of 40 items. If the results of the examination of the 40 items are not conclusive, another 40 items are to be selected, and so on, until a decision can be reached. Also, the plan called for proof of footing and posting accuracy of the sales journal for two months selected at random.

From the Sales Journal for All Pages Ending in:	Authenticate Items	Alternate Authentication†
Digit:* 2	1 through 10	10 selected at random
4	11 through 20	10 selected at random
7	21 through 30	10 selected at random
9	31 through 40	10 selected at random

    * Digits drawn at random from 1 through 10.
    † Depending upon availability and cost of drawing.

General Ledger Examination

An audit program for the mechanical phases of the examination of a general ledger may be developed as follows:

1. Prepare and prove the mechanical accuracy of a general ledger trial balance at the beginning and at the end of the period (post-closing).
2. Prove the accuracy of postings to the general ledger from records of original entry:
   a) In accordance with the pattern followed for the examination and authentication of the records or journals of original entry set forth in the preceding pages.
   b) For the number of nonconsecutive months—including the last month of the period—selected for proof of accuracy of footings and postings of the original records.
3. Prove the accuracy of footings and *balances of all accounts not analyzed.*
4. If there are private or subsidiary ledgers in addition to the general ledger, the preceding program should be followed, but the proof of posting accuracy should be extended on the basis of (assume) an inspection level tightness applicable to the situation.

A discussion of the audit program and the purely mechanical phases of the examination of a general ledger is now presented.

A trial balance at the beginning and at the end of the period is taken for purposes of facilitating comparisons. If the audit is a repeat engagement, the auditor has a trial balance of the preceding period which he should compare with the ledger account balances of the client in order to determine that the audit adjustments of the prior period were recorded and so that comparative statements will be consistently prepared. If the audit is for a new client and if the report of a preceding auditor is available, the financial statement figures in the report should be compared with the trial balance of the preceding period. It may be discovered that the audit adjustments of the former auditor were not entered in the ledger or that they were entered in the period now under examination; in the latter case, the adjustments applicable to the preceding period should be removed from the current period.

Prior to preparing a trial balance, the auditor should determine that all postings have been made for the current period. This precaution saves time and prevents the significance of possible alteration after the ledger has been released to the client. In order to eliminate the possibility of undetected additional postings after the trial balance has been prepared and the ledger released to the client, the auditor should tick the last item at the stopping point for postings from all records of original entry. Possible additional postings might not be reflected in the financial statements, and they might be the result of various types of attempted manipulation.

ILLUSTRATION. The general ledger of the Blank Company was maintained by the accountant, with the exception of the Cash account, which was kept by the president. The accountant would prepare a trial balance and advise the president of the difference between the total of the trial balance debits and credits; theoretically, this difference should have been the cash balance. Alone in his control of the cash, the president would instruct the accountant to charge Traveling Expense for a certain amount; and he would credit his Cash account for the same amount, which he already had stolen. An analysis of the Traveling Expense account proved that there was no authentic support for 40 percent of the traveling expense. One entry appeared after the tick mark indicating the last posting from the cash disbursements journal, and that one entry led to the discovery of the fraud.

In proving the accuracy of postings to the general ledger, an attempt should be made to control all records of original entry at one time. As the proof of posting accuracy is completed from each original record, there is no objection to releasing that record to the client's staff.

In the proof of posting accuracy, alertness is necessary in the face of a monotonous task. An undetected posting can be the one that resulted from an unauthorized transaction—for example, an inventory theft with an undetected credit in the Inventory account.

In proving the accuracy of the footing of the general ledger accounts, following the proof of posting accuracy, prepared adding machine tapes for each account footed may be retained until the audit is completed.

If an account is to be analyzed, its final balance will be set forth in the analysis. This amount is then compared with the trial balance amount of that account; therefore, it is not necessary to foot that account during the footing stage. When the trial balance is being prepared, or immediately after it has been prepared, the in-charge auditor will indicate the accounts to be analyzed. In accordance with this indication and the footing sample plan, the auditor will know which accounts to foot.

A private ledger may be maintained for the purpose of restricting confidential information from employees. The restricted information is usually composed of executive salaries and bonuses, dividends in closely held corporations, investment security transactions, sometimes inventories, and the final net income or loss. In the examination of a private ledger, it is important that evidence be available in support of *all* entries. Generally, when there is a private ledger, there is a private checking account.

Original Record Examination for Events Subsequent to the Balance Sheet Date. It is entirely possible that events may occur after the balance sheet date and prior to the closing of the audit which have an effect on the fairness of the financial statements. As a result of this possibility, the auditor must examine selected transactions taking place in that interim. A few examples are presented here as an introduction to the problem.

ILLUSTRATIONS. (1) Cash transactions subsequent to the balance sheet date must be examined to detect irregularities arising from checks deposited on the last day of the period and later returned marked "N.S.F." A check may have been fictitious and deposited to cover a cash shortage temporarily. (2) Sales entries may be excessive early in the new period, indicating that sales of the final month were held over. (3) Minutes must be examined to ascertain if actions taken by the board of directors in the new period have an effect on the financial statements for the period under review. (4) Large charges to uncollectible accounts or to the Sales Allowances account many appear early in the new period, which entries should have been made applicable to the period under examination. (5) A fire or other casualty may have occurred which will have a serious effect on earnings or capital assets. Such a situation should be mentioned in the audit report or in financial statement footnotes.

Proper Closing Time

In examining records of original entry, an auditor must be certain (1) that all entries for the period under audit are recorded and (2) that entries applicable to the subsequent period are not recorded in the period under audit. Therefore, the proper stopping points—or "cutoffs"—for entries in each record of original entry are presented below.

General Journal. The proper cutoff is for the last authorized entry before closing. The auditor should examine minutes records for the authorization of transactions resulting in accounting entries near the end of the period to determine if entries have been made in accordance with the authorizations; also, he must examine entries made early in the subsequent period to determine if they are applicable to that period.

Cash Receipts Records. The cutoff for cash receipts should be the final cash received on the last day of the period. The auditor must compare cash receipts entries for the last few days of the period under examination and the first few days of the subsequent period to determine if the cutoff was made at the proper time. Cash receipts entries must be compared with the bank statement to determine if cash deposited early in the new period was a cash receipt of the period under review or of the subsequent period. Remittance lists must be compared with cash receipts entries, particularly as to dates, to ascertain that entries and deposits of the period under review were not held over to the subsequent period.

Cash Disbursements Records. The cutoff for cash disbursements should be at the point of the last check written *and mailed* in the period under review. The auditor must ascertain that checks were not prepared, entered, and held (not mailed) at the end of the period in order to reduce payables by amounts not due until early in the subsequent period.

Voucher Register Entries. The cutoff should be for all acquisitions through the last day of the period on the basis of receiving records, invoices and their dates, passage of title, and inventory in transit.

Sales and Sales Returns Records. The sales cutoff point should be for sales made through the last day of the period under examination. Normally, a sale is made when merchandise is shipped or services are rendered. Therefore, for several days prior to the close of the period under review and for several days of the subsequent period, sales invoice dates should be compared with shipping records, bills of lading, and credits to inventory accounts.

Analysis of an Account

As illustrated in Chapter 8, an auditor analyzes certain accounts and traces the entries appearing in the accounts back to the records of original entry. The purpose of analyzing an account is to prove the correctness and propriety of the entries made therein during the year under audit and to determine the correctness of the account balance for presentation in the financial statements.

In a chronological analysis of an account, the details of the charges, credits, and explanations are transcribed from the ledger to the work papers; and the account entries are traced to the original documentary data and to the records of original entry (see Illustration 8–9, Chapter 8). The records of original entry already have had their accuracy proved from the point of view of mechanical verification. If errors are discovered in the account being analyzed, the analysis proceeds as if no errors were made; and the auditor works toward the final balance shown by the accounts of the client. Then, the auditor adjusts the ledger balance as shown on his work sheet to conform to correct conditions by listing all errors in an appropriate space on the schedule and preparing the audit adjustments—one entry for total errors of the same type.

ILLUSTRATION 10–1

METAL CORPORATION

Analysis of Insurance Expense (Acct. No. 222)
Year ended December 31, 1975

Explanation	Build-ings	Factory Equip-ment	Office Equip-ment	Inventory	Medical	Accident	Total
Debits: 1975							
January.........		$ 200		$ 2,000	$ 800	$1,000	$ 4,000
February.........	$2,200		$1,200	1,600	800	1,200	7,000
March		600		2,600	400	800	4,400
April			600	1,800	400	800	3,600
May...........	1,700	200	400	2,000			4,300
June		800	400	1,000	1,200	800	4,200
July...........		800	800	1,600	600		3,800
August.........	200		400	1,400	600	200	2,800
September.......				2,400			2,400
October	400	200	600	2,400	1,200		4,800
				1,000*			
November	880		600	3,400	1,800	1,200	8,880
December				3,000	1,000		4,000
Totals	$5,380	$2,800	$5,000	$26,200	$8,800	$6,000	$54,180
(Credits): 1975							
April..........					$ (300)		$ (300)
July...........			$ (400)			$ (480)	(880)
December						(400)	(400)
Totals			$ (400)		$ (300)	$ (880)	$(1,580)
Net: 12/31/75.......	$5,380	$2,800	$4,600	$26,200	$8,500	$5,120	$51,600
Deduct: AJE24*				(1,000)			(1,000)
Audit Balance 12/31/75.........	$5,380∧	$2,800∧	$4,600∧	$25,200√	$8,500√	$5,120∧	$51,600

AJE 24 (36)
Telephone and Telegraph
Expense............... 1,000
Insurance Expense........   1,000
Telephone Expense for November,
1975, charged to Insurance
Expense in error.

* Error needing adjustment.
√ Examined all insurance premium notices and confirmed policies and rates with insurance company.
∧ Examined premium notices only.

When corrections are given to the client—and if the client has closed his accounts—the corrections are necessarily made *after* the end of the fiscal period. Such a situation could mean that on a subsequent audit, the client's ledger account balances are out of agreement with the auditor's adjusted amounts, and that the accounts and the prior year's audit report must be reconciled. This is accomplished by picking up the client's figures in the auditor's analyses and entering his own adjustments, thereby reconciling the audited beginning balance of the second year with the adjusted balance at the end of the first year. If the client has not closed his accounts—and that is the usual situation—and has entered the auditor's adjustments prior to closing, the book balances will automatically agree with those of the auditor; proof of this is afforded by taking a trial balance at the beginning of the current audit period and comparing it with the completed audit work papers of the prior period.

The Illustrative Audit presents account analyses in addition to the analysis set forth in Illustration 10–1 and in Chapter 8.

QUESTIONS

1. Whether it is the first audit or a continuing audit of a corporation, what nonfinancial records must be carefully reviewed and summarized by the independent auditor?

2. In any audit, why should the auditor review all nonfinancial records?

3. What are the audit procedures to be followed when auditing nonfinancial records?

4. In an examination of the articles of incorporation and the amendments thereto, what significant provisions should be noted by the auditor?

5. In a first audit of the records of a corporation, why is the auditor interested in the code of regulations (bylaws)?

6. As auditor, what information would you expect to obtain from the minutes of the:
   a)   Annual stockholders' meeting.
   b)   Board of directors' meetings.

7. An auditor customarily makes inquiries of responsible employees and nonaccounting officers. State five separate items about which an auditor might inquire that are not primarily concerned with internal control. For each of the five items, explain the purpose of the inquiry.

8. In each audit, what are the determining factors in deciding upon the amount of detailed examination?

9. What is the basic difference between a material error and a minor error?

10. Why is it necessary to define an error prior to examining data?

11. For detailed examination an auditor customarily selects a sample (in series or at random) of items entered in a voucher register.
    a)   What are the audit purposes of this type of vouching test?
    b)   List the items for which each voucher should be examined.

12. An audit report normally includes the following statement: ". . . and accordingly included such tests of the accounting records as we considered necessary in the circumstances."

    How does the accountant determine what tests of the accounting records are necessary and the extent of their testing?

    (AICPA, adapted)

13. Briefly state those routine duties which are necessary to every audit and which have as their objectives the proof of accuracy and the obtaining of reliable evidence.

14. State what you would accept as satisfactory documentary evidence, such as sales invoices, vendors' invoices, or other original records, in support of entries in each of the following:

    a) Sales register.
    b) Sales returns register.
    c) Voucher register or invoice register.
    d) Payroll journal.
    e) Check register.

15. State briefly how you would proceed to detect errors (*a*) in a detailed list of accounts payable, (*b*) in a detailed list of accounts receivable, and (*c*) in a trial balance.

16. During the examination of a voucher register used to record invoices from all creditors, you could not locate 20 internally prepared vouchers in support of entries and check payments. In such a situation, what procedure would you follow?

17. A client insisted that you refrain from stamping or marking in any manner the business vouchers you had examined and traced into the original records. What suggestions have you to offer for the elimination of all possibilities for duplicate presentation of these documents?

18. If a transaction can be traced through all of its phases, starting with the original voucher evidences, is it necessarily correct? Present reasons for your answer.

19. A sales journal contained one column for details of sales and one column for weekly summaries of sales. The accountant footed the weekly summaries and assumed that all sales entry procedure was proper. Was the correct procedure followed by the accountant?

20. Describe a sales cutoff and indicate the auditing steps you would follow in verifying a sales cutoff.

21. The cash receipts register of a company contains columns with the following headings: Cash, Dr.; Sales Discount, Dr.; Accounts Receivable, Cr.; and Miscellaneous, Cr.

    In an audit, explain the nature and extent of your examination with respect to amounts in the Sales Discount column, with reasons for your procedure.

22. Describe a method of verifying petty cash disbursements.

23. You were instructed to audit the check record for the fiscal period. A voucher system was in operation, and all checks were sequentially

numbered. State exactly your audit procedure and present reasons for each step.

24. Your client keeps his records on the accrual basis and maintains an invoice register in which invoices are entered when they become liabilities. What procedure would you follow in examining this register and the supporting records for a selected month?

25. What are the points of importance in auditing the entries in a general journal?

26. List at least six points of which an auditor must be certain in verifying the accuracy of postings?

27. Why is it necessary to test the accuracy of the footings of the various journals and to prove the accuracy of the postings to the general ledger accounts involved, even though there is a trend away from these procedures? What irregularities may be detected through this procedure?

28. Assume that you were auditing the records of a company for the first time. How could you assure yourself that there were no liens upon the assets other than those disclosed by statements from officers and employees and those disclosed by an examination of the accounts?

29. What purposes are served by analyzing selected accounts?

30. An auditor is interested in verifying transactions occurring between the balance sheet date and the date of completing his examination.
    a) Present specific examples of auditing steps to be followed and the reasons for them.
    b) As a result of matters disclosed by this additional auditing, what might be some of the effects on the audit period-end financial statements?

31. An annual audit includes a review of transactions and events which occurred or are recorded after the balance sheet date.

    In connection with the audit of each of the following, state a significant auditing procedure involving transactions or events which occurred after the balance sheet date. Briefly state the reason for each procedure you give.
    a) Cash in bank.
    b) Accounts receivable.
    c) Merchandise inventory.
    d) Accounts payable.

32. You are meeting with executives of Oil Rich Corporation to arrange your firm's engagement to examine the corporation's financial statements for the year ending December 31, 1975. One executive suggested that the audit work be divided among three audit staff members so one man would examine asset accounts, a second would examine liability accounts, and the third would examine income and expense accounts to minimize audit time, avoid duplication of staff effort, and curtail interference with company operations.

    Advertising is the corporation's largest expense, and the advertising manager suggested that a staff member of your firm whose uncle owns the advertising agency which handles the corporation's advertising be assigned to examine the Advertising Expense account. The staff member has a thorough knowledge of the rather complex contract between Cooper Cosmetics and the advertising agency on which Cooper's advertising costs are based.

a) To what extent should a CPA follow his client's suggestions for the conduct of an audit? Discuss.

b) List and discuss the reasons why audit work should not be assigned solely according to asset, liability, and income and expense categories.

c) Should the staff member of your CPA firm whose uncle owns the advertising agency be assigned to examine advertising costs? Discuss.

(AICPA, adapted)

PROBLEMS

1. In many companies, labor cost represents a substantial percentage of total dollars expended in any one accounting period. One of the auditor's primary means of verifying payroll transactions is by an adequate payroll test.

    You are conducting the annual examination of the financial statements of Hess, Inc., a medium-sized manufacturing company. You have selected the records of a number of hourly employees for a detailed payroll test. The following work sheet outline has been prepared:

Column Number	Column Heading
1	Employee number
2	Employee name
3	Job classification
	Hours worked
4	Straight time
5	Premium time
6	Hourly rate
7	Gross earnings
	Deductions
8	F.I.C.A. withheld
9	F.I.T. withheld
10	Union dues
11	Hospitalization
12	Amount of check
13	Check and check number
14	Account number charged
15	Description of account

    a) What factors should the auditor consider in selecting his sample of employees to be included in any payroll test?

    b) Using the column numbers above as a reference, state the principal way(s) that the information in each column would be verified.

    c) In addition to the payroll test, the auditor employs a number of other audit procedures in the verification of payroll transactions.

    List three additional procedures which may be employed.

    (AICPA, adapted)

2. In connection with his examination of the financial statements of D O Wholesalers, Inc. for the year ended June 30, 1975; a CPA performs several cutoff tests.

a) 1. What is a cutoff test?
2. Why must cutoff tests be performed for both the beginning and the end of the audit period?
b) The CPA wishes to test D O's sales cutoff at June 30, 1975. Briefly describe the steps that he should include in this test.
c) The CPA obtains a July 10, 1975 bank statement directly from the bank. Explain how he will use this cutoff bank statement in his review of the June 30, 1975 bank reconciliation.

(AICPA, adapted)

3. You are engaged to audit the records of the Wissel Company and its subsidiary, the Wade Company, for the year ended December 31, 1975. During the course of the audit, it is discovered that the balance of the intercompany accounts do not agree.

The Wissel Company manufactures an item, which it sells to its subsidiary company at cost plus 20 percent. The subsidiary company then sells the items to retail stores. Following is a copy of part of the intercompany ledger accounts:

ACCOUNT IN THE WISSEL COMPANY GENERAL LEDGER
Intercompany Account—Wade Company

Date	Reference	Amount	Date	Reference	Amount
1975	Total forwarded	78,933	1975	Total forwarded	24,117
Dec. 26	SR 877	1,950	Dec. 26	CR 48	3,567
Dec. 27	SR 878	1,194	Dec. 29	CR 49	31,127
Dec. 28	SR 879	2,183	Dec. 31	Balance	28,189
Dec. 29	SR 880	849			
Dec. 31	SR 882	1,891			
		87,000			87,000

ACCOUNT IN THE WADE COMPANY GENERAL LEDGER
Intercompany Account—Wissel Company

Date	Reference	Amount	Date	Reference	Amount
1975	Total forwarded	27,449	1975	Total forwarded	76,523
Dec. 28	CD 62	31,127	Dec. 26	VR 876	2,175
Dec. 31	CD 63	19,777	Dec. 28	VR 877	1,950
Dec. 31	RG 74	2,329	Dec. 29	VR 878	1,194
Dec. 31	Balance	6,318	Dec. 31	VR 881	3,647
			Dec. 31	VR 883	1,511
		87,000			87,000

The following explanations are for references in the ledger accounts:
SR = Sales register and invoice number.
CR = Cash receipts record.

CD = Cash disbursements record.
VR = Voucher register and invoice number.
RG = Returned goods register and debit memorandum number.

A review of the inventory observation work papers discloses the following information:

Observation at Wissel Company on December 31, 1975:

(1) Last shipment prior to the physical inventory was billed on invoice No. 882, dated December 31, 1975.

(2) No returned merchandise was received from the Wade Company during the month of December, 1975.

(3) The last receiving report used in December, 1975, was No. 742, dated December 30, 1975.

Observation at Wade Company on December 31, 1975.

(1) Last shipment prior to the physical inventory was billed on invoice No. 843, dated December 31, 1975.

(2) The last shipment of merchandise returned to the Wissel Company in December, 1975, was entered on debit memorandum No. 74, dated December 31, 1975.

(3) The last receiving report used in December, 1975, was No. 337; it was dated December 31, 1975, and was for merchandise billed on Wissel invoice No. 879.

You are to prepare:

a) A reconciliation of the intercompany accounts.

b) The journal entries required by each company to:

    (1) Adjust the intercompany accounts.

    (2) Adjust the inventories which are based on physical inventories taken on December 31, 1975, and priced by each company at its cost.

(AICPA, adapted)

4. Fox Run, Inc., was organized on January 2, 1975, with a paid-in-cash capital of $400,000, consisting of 4,000 shares of no-par common stock, stated value $100 per share. The purpose of the corporation is to acquire unimproved land and subdivide it into building lot sites.

The 1975 transactions of the corporation are summarized as follows:

(1) The corporation paid $96,000 cash for 120 acres of unimproved land. The land was divided into building lots 100 feet wide and 120 feet deep, resulting in 310 lots. The remaining land was devoted to streets, play areas, and other general purposes.

(2) According to location, the lots were priced for sale as follows:

Lot Section	Sales Price (Each)	Number of Lots
Indian Hill	$3,000	80
Price Hill	2,000	100
Mt. Adams	1,600	130

(3)   Costs and expenses of 1975, all paid, were as follows:

Fees for surveying	$ 9,000
Title clearance fees	3,000
Utilities installations	56,620
Grading and trees	45,000
Street paving	75,500
Cost of model home—to be offered for sale	27,000
Advertising	14,600
General office expense of which 25 percent is to be applied to 1975 income	48,000
Salary of sales manager	18,000
Sales commissions	5,272

(4)   Sales of lots in 1975, all at list price.

Indian Hill	26 lots
Price Hill	32 lots
Mt. Adams	12 lots

All lots were sold with a 25 percent down payment, except six of the Indian Hill lots, which were sold for cash in full. Noninterest-bearing notes were taken for the unpaid balances. The notes were payable in three equal installments, starting one year from the date of sale.

(5)   The corporation is to recognize gross profits on the sale of the lots—after deducting commissions payable to salesmen—in the proportion that cash collected each year bears to the sales price.

You were requested by the corporation to prepare work papers in good form for:

a)   Sales for 1975.

b)   Cost of lots sold in 1975.

c)   Cost of remaining lots.

d)   An income statement for 1975.

e)   A balance sheet at December 31, 1975.

f)   An analysis of the Cash account for the year 1975.

5.   A bank balance at the beginning of the period was $20,000. Audited cash receipts for the period amounted to $52,000 and were so recorded; however, only $48,000 was deposited in the bank and no cash was on hand or in transit. Audited cash disbursements for the period were $42,000. According to the cashier, the bank balance at the end of the period was $15,000; the bank statement at the end of the period was $36,000. Also, according to the cashier, the outstanding checks at the end of the period were $10,000. Obviously, the cashier failed to deposit $4,000. How did he attempt to cover his fraud? Show calculations.

6.   Your client, James Cameron, is the sole owner of the Cameron Variety Store. Cameron did not maintain formal accounting records. From your examination of his records, you have established the accuracy of the data shown below:

On the basis of the data, prepare:

a)   A work sheet, setting forth in summary form the transactions for the year ended December 31, 1975.

b)   An income statement for the year ended December 31, 1975.

c)   A balance sheet as of December 31, 1975.

Pertinent Data

a) Assets, liabilities, and capital at December 31, 1974:

Cash in bank	$ 7,000
Accounts receivable	10,550
Provision for doubtful accounts	800
Merchandise inventory	16,300
Prepaid supplies	300
Store equipment	4,000
Accumulated depreciation, store equipment	1,500
Accounts payable	4,250
Accrued miscellaneous expenses	400
Notes payable	5,000
James Cameron, capital	26,200

b) A summary of the transactions for 1975, as recorded in Cameron's checkbook, follows:

Deposits for the year (including the redeposit of $325 of checks charged back by the bank)	83,185
Checks issued during the year	83,990
Customers' checks charged back by the bank	325

c) The following information is available for accounts payable:

Merchandise purchased on account during the year	57,790
Merchandise purchases returned to accounts payable vendor	1,410
Payments of accounts by check	55,460

d) The following information is available for accounts receivable:

Accounts written off	810
Accounts collected	43,080
Accounts receivable balance, December 31, 1975 (of this balance, $710 is estimated to be uncollectible)	11,920

e) The following items are included among the checks drawn during the year:

Salaries	$10,000
Rent	3,600
Heat, light, and telephone	400
Supplies	620
Taxes and licenses	1,020
Drawings of James Cameron	6,140
Merchandise purchased for cash	2,080
Miscellaneous	770
Note payable	3,000
	$28,530

f) Merchandise inventory, December 31, 1975, was $17,900.
g) Supplies inventory at December 31, 1975, was $235.
h) Accrued expenses at December 31, 1975, amount to a total of $290.
i) Cash sales for 1975 are assumed to account for all cash received other than that collected on accounts receivable.
j) Store equipment is to be depreciated at the rate of 10 percent per year.

(AICPA, adapted)

7. Your client, Fromway, Inc., operates a small hardware store but has not maintained a formal set of records. From various tax returns, bank statements, check stubs, cash register tapes, and invoices, you have established the accuracy of the following data.

From this information prepare:

a) A work sheet, setting forth in summary form the transactions for the year ended December 31, 1975.

b) A combined income and retained earnings statement for the year ended December 31, 1975.

c) A balance sheet as of December 31, 1975.

Information Collected

a) Assets, liabilities, and capital at December 31, 1975:

Cash in bank	$ 14,000
Accounts receivable	21,100
Provision for doubtful accounts	1,600
Merchandise inventory	32,600
Supplies on hand	600
Store equipment	8,000
Accumulated depreciation, store equipment	3,000
Accounts payable	8,500
Accrued expenses	800
Notes payable	10,000
No-par common stock	50,000
Retained earnings	2,400

b) A summary of cash receipt and disbursement transactions is as follows:

Deposits for the year (including the redeposit of $650 of NSF checks which cleared)	$166,370
Checks issued during the year	167,980
Customers; NSF checks charged back by bank	650

c) Information gathered relating to accounts receivable:

Uncollectible accounts written off	1,620
Cash collected from accounts receivable	86,160
Accounts receivable balance, December 31, 1975, (of this balance, $1,400 is definitely uncollectible)	23,840

d) Information gathered relating to accounts payable:

Purchases of merchandise on account	115,580
Merchandise purchases returned to creditors	2,820
Cash payments received from creditors	110,920

e) Other 1975 cash disbursements by check:

Salaries	34,080
Rent	7,200
Utilities	800
Supplies used	1,240
Taxes, licenses, and insurance	2,040
Cash purchases of merchandise	4,160
Miscellaneous expenses	1,540
Notes payable	6,000
	$ 57,060

f) Merchandise inventory at December 31, 1975, is $35,800.

g) Supplies inventory at December 31, 1975 is $470.

h) Accrued expenses at December 31, 1975, is $580.

i) Cash sales for 1975 account for all cash received other than that collected on accounts receivable.

j) Store equipment rate of annual depreciation is 10 percent.

Suggestion: Prepare your calculations in orderly sequence and prepare journal entries in abbreviated form, being sure to tie the entries with the work sheet.

PRACTICE MATERIAL ASSIGNMENTS

Metalcraft, Incorporated: Audit Problem:
Complete Assignment 1.

Colby Gears, Inc.: Holmes and Moore Audit Case:
Complete Original Records and Their Examination.

11

Examination of Evidence and Records: Electronic Systems

SECTION I: INTRODUCTION

Automation may be described as the performance of control functions by machinery. The auditing standards applicable to records produced by electronic equipment are the same as those applicable to records maintained in ink, journalizing and posting machines equipped with programming bars, and by punched card equipment. Thus, the objectives of audit and control do not change. For the audit of electronically produced data and records, only the examination procedures will be altered—and in the majority of instances, these alterations will not be too great. The "storage unit" constitutes one of the greatest changes. The auditor should not be surprised if he asked to see the accounts payable file and was handed a magnetic tape, a disk pack, or informed that the information requested is stored in a computer many miles away.

In general, data processing has advanced in the following stages:

1. Readable hard-copy original data are prepared, converted to machine-sensible form, and then processed.
2. Readable hard-copy original data and the machine-sensible form data are prepared simultaneously. This may be illustrated by the typing of a sales invoice and the simultaneous paper-tape punching of the sales invoice data for machine processing.
3. Readable hard copy will not exist, and the original data are prepared only in machine-sensible form. This may be illustrated by the insertion of an employee's key in a time clock, with the time transfer being made directly on magnetic tape.

At the present time, hard-copy originating data are frequently available, from which the auditor may proceed to test and follow through the processing to the printout point; or he may work from the printout point back to the available hard copy.

The auditor must remember that the five component parts of electronic data processing equipment are input, storage, arithmetic processing, control, and output. If an audit program is designed with these points, functions, and operations in mind, an auditor should experience no more difficulty than in an examination running from original documents, to a journal, to a ledger, to a trial balance, to the financial statements.

Auditing procedures are affected by the presence of a computer, in terms of the two following major phases of an audit examination: (1) the evaluation of the system of internal control and (2) the evaluation of the records produced by the EDP system.

If the auditor is to deal effectively with EDP systems, he should have computer knowledge and capability at two levels: (1) a basic working knowledge of computers and computer-based data processing sufficient to adequately review the system of internal control, to conduct proper tests of the system he is auditing, and to objectively evaluate the quality of the records produced; and (2) the ability to use the computer, when necessary, in making the tests desired.

SECTION II: AUDITING EDP SYSTEMS AND RECORDS

Internal Control Examination

Basic to an audit of the records and data prepared with electronic equipment is the assurance of adequate internal control; the first intensive work of the auditor will constitute a review of the control procedures. In his study of internal control, the auditor should investigate (1) the controls established outside tht data processing center and (2) the controls built into the equipment. System designers will prepare flow diagrams which show the basic operations to be performed; these should be studied for internal control features.

Electronic data processing equipment strengthens internal control, because it normally provides for internal control features built into the equipment by the manufacturer, and at the programming stage and in the form of self-proof devices and automatic stoppage of the equipment if an error is found. The theory, purpose, and results of internal control do not change, but the mechanics of examining the system of internal control do change to parallel the programming and the work flow through the equipment.

There are several types of program controls—or checks—built into or incorporated in every data processing program. The auditor should ascertain that his client is availing himself of the opportunity effectively to use these controls and checks. Also, the auditor should make use of these controls and checks in his examination of the operation of the system. A few of the controls and checks incorporated in a data processing program are proof figures, sequence checks, self-checking numbers, check points, cross-footing balance checks, limit check, reverse multiplication, record count, and hash totals. When duplicate arithmetic circuits are in operation, all arithmetic computations are prepared twice—simultaneously and independently. In the course of an audit, the results may be compared for proof of accuracy.

The effectiveness of the controls within the equipment may be tested by following through a series of transaction data; or a comprehensive understanding and testing of the program itself should be obtained.

Flow chart diagrams normally show the type of information recorded at the input stage, its progress through each procedure, and the contents of the output—all of which may be held on magnetic tape, punch cards, disk pack, or storage facilities of a remote service center. The determination of the extent to which controls are built into the computer programs and the testing through the use of test decks to determine if they are operative will require different techniques depending on the circumstances.

Flow diagrams normally show the type of information recorded at the input stage, its progress through each procedure, and the contents of the output—all of which may be held on magnetic tape, punch cards, disk pack, or storage facilities of a remote service center. The determination of the extent to which controls are built into the computer programs and the testing to determine if they are operative will require different techniques depending on the circumstances.

It has been a common practice for an organization making changes in data processing methods to seek the help of its auditing firm in designing the changes. In this way the auditor can review the control features and point out probable weaknesses in the controls and, in addition, provide for audit trails and the safeguarding of files.

Internal control of electronic equipment may be further illustrated by using accounts receivable and related sales procedures somewhat as follows:

1. The computer center should account for the serial numbers of all sales invoicers. These should be verified by the accounts receivables department.
2. Copies of all invoices should be routed directly to the accounts receivable department.
3. Summarized invoice totals should be submitted to the accounting department by the computer center without routing through the accounts receivable department.
4. There should be independent internal investigation to determine that all sales orders shipped are billed.
5. If perpetual inventories are maintained, the computer center should prepare inventory control credits for inventory sold and inventory control debits for returned inventory.

6. Master tape changes for product prices should be independently approved by the sales department.
7. The computer center should produce a printed record of all changes in prices, item numbers, and item descriptions, which should be authorized by and verified by the sales department.
8. An authorized person outside the data processing center should verify a printout of the master register for changes.
9. Exceptions to master tape prices should be followed up by a person outside the computing center.
10. If shipments are made to customers who do not appear on the master tape, an outside person should follow up the transactions for propriety.

Audit tests should be made of all items and procedures set forth above, plus the testing of other control features peculiar to the operations of any given client. Each section of the investigation should be repeated each year because with the advances in electronic data processing, controls and procedures may change rapidly. An auditor cannot assume that a control or procedure currently in effect will not be altered in the near future.

Internal control can be greatly improved through the separation of duties of individuals. Recognizing the principle of separation would require the data processing functions to be divided as follows: (1) system analysis and design, (2) programming, (3) computer operation, and (4) internal audit or control section.

A Client's Documentation of the Data Processing System

Also basic to an audit of the records and data prepared with EDP equipment is the assurance that the client has adequate documentation of the data processing system. Documentation consists of documents and records which clearly set forth the system and procedures for carrying out the data processing tasks. It is the means of communicating the essential elements of the EDP system and the logic built into the computer programs. The auditor should determine whether or not the client's documentation will at least serve the following purposes:

1. Provide a valid basis for a satisfactory evaluation of internal control.
2. Supply the computer operator with complete and current operating instructions.
3. Provide answers to all questions relating to the operation of the computer program.
4. Serve as a good basis for review of present system and evaluation of proposed system expansion.
5. Be so complete that revisions can be easily performed.
6. Provide the best instruction for new personnel.

A careful examination of the preceding points clearly illustrates why the examination of a client's documentation is vital to the successful completion of an EDP system audit.

Since the computer run is the basic unit on which documentation is based, the run manual must be inspected in detail so that the auditor has a complete understanding of the runs and their interrelationship. The run manual is prepared by the system analyst and/or programmer and consists of the complete description of the program or programs used for a data processing run. This manual is an important corporate record and should be given fireproof storage. In order to prevent its loss or alteration, a control copy should be stored outside the data processing center. Further auditing should reveal that access to the run manual is restricted to the systems and programming personnel and under no condition should the machine operators have access to this manual.

The following should be found in the run manual and inspected in detail by the auditor:

1. *Problem definition*—should present formally and clearly the problem to be solved. In addition, it should set forth the part this program is in relation to the overall data processing system.

2. *System description*—should support the problem definition by clearly indicating the general outline of the program computer and noncomputer, and how it relates to the EDP system flow charts, the record formats, the activity codes, and how the control function, if involved, is to be handled.

3. *Program description*—covers the details which document the computer program portion of the system only. This is one of the most important sections of the run manual as it consists of the program flow charts; decision tables used in testing the program together with a complete description of these tables; a listing of all working storage areas; sense switches, if any, which permit alteration of the program flow; a complete description of program modification or "patches"; and program listing which serves as a backup in case the source deck or disk pack is lost or destroyed.

4. *Operating instructions*—contains all information required to run the program by the computer operator including any and all changes which are listed as separate instructions.

5. *Listing of controls*—summarizes the controls, inside and outside, and the procedures associated with a program. Such things as checking the accuracy of input data, checking on batch controls, programmed error detection, and checks on the accuracy of output are provided for in this section of the run manual.

6. *Acceptance record*—consists of copies of input and output test data as it relates to the original test and any subsequent changes. Here the auditor would also find who was responsible for initiating the change as well as the person responsible for making the change.

Proper documentation can be invaluable to the auditor when a review of internal control and methods of testing indicates that he should use computer-based tests. Further, it can eliminate much of the detailed work associated with writing a program or developing test data. He will also find that the time he needs in developing his audit approach will be reduced.

Equipment Malfunctions. It is desirable for the auditor to have a general understanding of built-in hardware control features. This will aid him in understanding the working of the equipment, why it is reliable, and to evaluate the effectiveness of machine checks.

Since a computer system consists of both electronic elements and mechanical parts, there can be a malfunction of either a mechanical part or an electronic element. Electronic elements are controlled by electrical pulses and failure of an electronic element, such as a transitor, may lead to an error. A mechanical part failure may occur when there is a malfunction of the read/write units that are most frequently associated with input/output and file storage equipment. Warped cards or an improperly balanced disk pack can cause mechanical errors.

Equipment Controls. A redundant character check is frequently used for the sole purpose of detecting an error that may occur. This type of check involves the addition of a character to determine whether or not an error has taken place when moving of data in the system is involved. It assists in determining whether the transfer has been correctly made by repeating the redundant character.

A duplicate process check is sometimes used to eliminate errors. This involves having the same process performed twice, usually at different times, and then compare the results.

If the auditor wishes to verify whether or not the equipment has been activated without testing the actual results, he will perform an echo check. This may involve sending a command to activate an input or output device to perform an operation and the device responding that the command is being followed.

Another equipment check is the validity check. This may involve an instruction of increasing the pay rate for a certain class of employee before the memory system has been updated.

One other step may be taken by the auditor to determine the extent of a client's equipment controls, and that is to perform an equipment check. This involves checking the computer to see whether or not it is operating properly without checking the results of operations. This is not a positive check as the equipment may be functioning properly, but incorrect information could be processed and the results obtained would be meaningless.

The auditor may find it necessary to develop equipment controls dealing with specific pieces of the EDP system. Such controls might involve the central processor, card reader, card punch, printer, direct access storage devices, and any other hardware of the EDP system.

Operating reports and computer logs will greatly aid the auditor in determining to what extent he will be concerned about the possible existence of errors in the data processing equipment. Because the auditor can usually place considerable reliance upon the equipment and the hardware controls for detecting errors, he should devote more attention to the procedures for handling errors and making certain that they have been handled properly.

Input/Output Controls and the Audit. Of primary importance to the auditor is realizing the importance of input errors and how they can occur. One of the most common errors is incorrectly recording data at the point of inception. When (*a*) raw material is requisitioned for processing, (*b*) raw material is recorded as being requisitioned. An error can be created when a keypunch operator is converting data to machine-readable form. Because of difficulty in reading a 7,000 figure, the keypunch operator punches 9,000. A source document may be lost in handling. The bank may lose a deposit ticket and it cannot be determined to whom the overage belongs. Finally, there may be errors in processing the data by the computer. A wrong program used to process the data may run, but the results are completely incorrect. Very frequently the auditor can locate the input errors by reviewing the output and comparing it to source documents. This would involve the auditor in carefully inspecting error corrections in order to eliminate the introduction of new errors or the accumulation of uncorrected errors in an error correction account. The frequency and type of errors that an auditor encounters at the point of input and output will aid greatly in determining the nature and extent of his audit work.

SECTION III: AUDIT RETRIEVAL PACKAGES

Because of the expanding automated environment, the computer is becoming increasingly involved in the overall audit process. With more material being processed, files are becoming larger and processing is becoming more sophisticated. Therefore, these data bases are being extensively used for internal decision-making as well as facilitating the audit process.

In the not-too-distant past, the auditor was presented information as a result of the client's programs or it was obtained for him through specially-written programs. Under such unfavorable conditions the auditor would frequently receive more information than he needed or the special programs were difficult to justify economically.

It is therefore clear that an auditor needed a retrieval package that would provide him with a means, on short notice, whereby he could retrieve a wide variety of specific information from computerized records and enable him to perform the needed audit procedures.

As a result, all large CPA firms have developed audit retrieval packages which usually consist of prewritten computer programs that can be linked together and accurately adapted by the auditor to the requirements of his audit program. Such names as Auditionic 16, Audassist, Auditape and several others are examples of these retrieval packages.

These retrieval packages are used to:

1. Perform mathematical computations.
2. Select samples.
3. Search and retrieve items that have audit significance from a large mass of data.
4. Make file comparisons and at the same time merge and/or sort data.
5. Summarize and report selected data.
6. Print and/or punch out results in the required audit format.

In order for the preceding results to be obtained, these retrieval packages recognize the complexity of design and the magnitude of computer systems configurations. All of these retrieval packages therefore have certain common objectives as follows:

1. To provide computer-based audit independence for the auditor.
2. To provide immediate access to data generated and stored by a variety of computer systems and at various locations.
3. By specifically utilizing the speed and accuracy of a computer system, the routine clerical analyses can be reduced.
4. To permit the execution of major segments of an audit through the computer.
5. To increase and improve the range of statistical and analytical techniques necessary for comprehensive auditing.
6. To minimize the requirements for a high degree of computer-technological expertise on the part of the auditor.
7. To direct the auditor's time and talents into more advanced auditing techniques.

The following examples will demonstrate the basic applications of these retrieval packages.

1. The client has an inventory of 50,000 items and the auditor needed to know the structure of this inventory. Therefore, the auditor's program has certain criteria established, such as: slow turnover (units), unusual cost/selling price relationship (dollar value), last purchase/requisition date (obsolescence). This program would therefore provide the auditor with several types of materials necessary for the proper valuation of inventory.
2. The client has used 100,000 purchase vouchers during the year. Since all vouchers were prenumbered, the auditor can generate a random number basis of selection rapidly, determine a satisfactory sample size, establish the desired statistical confidence level, and print out the desired voucher information in numerical sequence.

3. The client has used 25,000 sales invoices during the year and each invoice has a minimum of 20 extensions. The auditor would follow procedure 2, above and satisfy himself as to the accuracy of the client's sales invoices.

4. In observing a physical inventory, an auditor will make test counts of selected inventory items. The next step in the audit is to compare these selected items with the client's inventory records in order to identify discrepancies. To facilitate this comparison, the auditor will punch his information into cards or tape and then, using the retrieval package, match his findings against the client's complete file. Quantity differences, cost and price extensions will be printed out at the same time. If the auditor has set his precision limits, the print-out will be listed for the auditor's further examination. This same basic retrieval package, with minor adjustments, could be used for comparing current and prior-years expense accounts and for comparing account payable confirmation replies against the account payable subsidiary accounts.

All of these retrieval packages are aimed at harnessing the speed and accuracy of the computer as an aid to an auditor in improving the quality of his audit work and also to require less time. In addition, an auditor will achieve greater reliability in certain aspects of an audit, thus giving him greater confidence in his audit work and reporting.

SECTION IV: AUDITING PROBLEMS RELATING TO COMPUTER SERVICE CENTERS

Many small to medium-sized organizations need certain phases of their accounting activity to be handled by a computer. However, it is not economically feasible for them to own the needed equipment, so they contract for services of a computer which is used by many firms. All of these computer service centers have many programs already prepared or have qualified personnel that can be hired to prepare the necessary programs to meet a particular requirement. The main problem the auditor faces here is that an outside organization enters into the client's scheme of processing, internal control, and record retention. However, since there is separation of persons, deliberate manipulation of these records is quite unlikely to take place. Because of this arm's-length relationship, errors in data processing are likely to be detected. Certain audit procedures must be followed by the auditor under these circumstances. The auditor must first assure himself that his client has proper control over data transmitted to the processing center. This involves document count, transaction count, and a control total such as the total of employee identification numbers. The auditor must then make certain that his client has a means of verifying the details processed by the service center such as a pre-list of the amount of all account receivable invoices turned over for processing. The auditor would then determine the center's control over the master file and changes thereto plus the control over error correction and resubmission. This is extremely important as the issuance of instructions and data to the service center must be restricted to authorized persons. This same care must be exercised in the return of the data to the client's personnel responsible for maintaining controls. The carrying out of these functions can be determined by the auditor through the inspection of error printouts, error log maintained by the client, and the signatures of the persons receiving the input data at the service center and output data in the client's office. Certainly the auditor should observe the operations at the service center noting the manner in which the data are processed and inspecting the record security procedures. The final step in his audit program would be to examine for accuracy a sample of transactions processed at the service center.

Time-sharing computer service centers are now extensively used for the processing of accounting information. Here the client will have an input/output device in his own office, usually a teletypewriter with special features that adapt it to the central computer frequently located in some other city. In this way each user operates from his terminal as if he were the sole user of the central computer. The client will have an identification number that only he has access to and will use this number to identify the files he wishes to use.

The system is so designed that it prevents one user from gaining unauthorized access to the files of another. Frequently the client will not only have his own data files but all firms providing this service have developed many programs, such as a random numbers selection program that a client has access to at a very nominal cost. It is evident that the on-line processing method used in time-sharing service is distinctly different from the method of batching data and sending it to a service center for processing as described earlier. Since the auditor is seldom able to audit the control programs of the time-sharing center, a client should make certain that the information required for audit purposes can be made available. In addition, the auditor must assure himself that the time-sharing service center has controls and protections that will produce the desired results.

The auditor must satisfy himself that the time-sharing center provides protection against unauthorized alteration or destruction of the client's program and that there is provision for file reconstruction if something should happen. Further, there must be control against unauthorized use of the client's file as well as any proprietary programs. Finally, there must be complete provision for recovery from equipment failure as well as inaccurate transmission of input/output data. Having satisfied himself as to the time-sharing center's controls, he must then determine the adequacy of his client's controls over input data and the control totals, record count, and any other measures taken to insure accurate input. Since it is impractical for the auditor to obtain satisfaction about the computer center's time-sharing system by direct examination, records maintained at the service center may be tested by using printouts of the file or by running audit routines. An audit routine would involve testing a certain series or set of transactions or the development of simulated transactions which would determine the accuracy of operation of the program.

SECTION V: THE AUDIT TRAIL AND AUDIT PROCEDURES

The skepticism with which an auditor greeted the introduction of the computer to the field of accounting has been replaced by the determination to use this device for improving his services to his clients. Early programs were indeed unsatisfactory largely due to the lack of knowledge on the part of programmers and system designers. However, management's need of inquiry trails for reference purposes and the auditor's insistence upon maintaining adequate audit trails and procedures have completely changed the unacceptable conditions that existed originally.

Most clients have sufficient printed records, detailed journals, and source documents so that audit trail conditions have not changed enough to require significantly different audit procedures from those used in non-EDP systems. Undoubtedly the best way the auditor can assure himself as to the existence of satisfactory audit trails and audit procedures is through the development of special audit computer programs; see Section III, above. This is being widely done today so that the auditor uses the computer to develop audit criteria and procedures for analysis and selection of records for audit as well as to analyze the transaction and master files. The auditor will not only successfully accomplish the objective of his audit but will insure management against a system that will not provide them with the information needed to operate the business satisfactorily.

QUESTIONS

1. How has data processing advanced over the past 15 years?
2. If an audit program is designed properly, an auditor should experience very little difficulty in performing his audit. What are these points of design?
3. What are the major phases of an audit examination that are affected by the presence of a computer in the accounting system?
4. What basic knowledge is required to effectively audit EDP systems?
5. How does electronic data processing equipment strengthen internal control?

6. What are some of the controls and checks incorporated in a data processing program?

7. How can the effectiveness of controls within the equipment be tested?

8. Why is it desirable for the auditor to assist his client in developing and changing his EDP system?

9. How frequently should the auditor review his client's system of controls?

10. In order for internal control to be effective in an EDP system, how would you divide the processing function?

11. What is meant by adequate documentation of the data processing system?

12. Of what importance is the "run manual" to the auditor?

13. How can proper documentation assist the auditor?

14. What types of equipment malfunctions are possible in an EDP system?

15. When would a redundant character check be used?

16. What will assist an auditor in determining the extent of errors in the data processing equipment?

17. What gave rise to the need for audit retrieval packages?

18. What is a retrieval package?

19. Under what conditions could an auditor advantageously use a retrieval package?

20. Briefly discuss the objectives of retrieval packages?

21. Describe how a retrieval package would be used in the audit of inventory.

22. Describe how retrieval packages will assist the auditor in performing an audit.

23. What problems does an auditor face when a client uses a computer center for processing his data?

24. What distinct differences are there between a computer service center and time-sharing computer service?

25. How can a user of time-sharing computer service be assured of proper access to his information?

26. What must an auditor do to satisfy himself as to the validity of the time-sharing computer service?

27. Examine, comment on, criticize, and evaluate the following computer installation.

This description outlines a computer installation for payroll. The computer installation incorporates the maintenance of earnings records for each employee, and in total, itemized and totaled deductions, payroll check writing, and payroll distribution to accounts or departments or products. Basic data are time-clock cards, and/or job or operation time-cards; these data, plus the necessary payroll data, such as pay rates and deductions, are initially recorded on punched cards, and then transferred to magnetic tapes (or by use of a keyboard, the information originally may be placed on magnetic tape), ready for input into the electronic computer.

A master magnetic tape carries data for each employee, such as social security number, clock number, name, rate of pay, income tax withheld, and itemized other deductions. Another magnetic tape is used daily or for each pay period to enter changes in fixed data. Another magnetic tape is used to enter data as to current (daily, weekly) hours worked and accounts to be charged.

An output connection from the computer is to a magnetic tape used to prepare the equivalent of a payroll journal, listing each payroll check, deductions itemized, net pay, and so forth. Another output tape is used to prepare the payroll distribution by account number and amount. This tape is used for direct posting of the ledger and to distribution summaries which are held on magnetic tape, and it is processed through a printer for sight reading.

A new master magnetic tape is prepared to carry forward the fixed information and new account balances; this new tape is a part of the input for the next pay period. The computer then records information from the various input tapes, processes the information for earnings computations, updates the master tape, and prepares the several new output tapes. The printer is connected directly to the computer in order to write checks—or the printer may be used separately. A separate program and tape are used for the preparation of periodic tax reports.

12

Cash and Cash Transactions

SECTION I: AUDIT CONSIDERATIONS

Approach to an Audit

An audit primarily constitutes the examination of past events with the objective of rendering an opinion regarding a client's financial statements. However, all audits should be performed with the thought in mind of the future operations and financial condition of a business organization. Past history cannot be changed.

In the communication and measurement of financial operating data, income statements may be of greater importance than balance sheets. Therefore, it may *appear* to be logical to approach an audit from a revenue and expense point of view. However, all revenue and expense transactions terminate in assets and their acquisition or disbursement, and/or in liabilities and their incurrence or liquidation.

Logically and properly, balance sheet items normally are considered initially because to do so automatically integrates the examination of assets, revenues, liabilities, and expenses. When examining an asset or a liability, all related items will be examined along with the activity of the asset or liability. As an example, when auditing notes receivables, there will be a correlated examination of the transactions which gave rise to the notes, interest income, interest accrued, notes receivable discounted, and the related discounting expense. Of course, an audit can be approached by initially examining revenue and expense transactions and tying those transactions into the related assets or liabilities, but this procedure is awkward and time-consuming.

Cash Audit Objectives

The objectives of auditing cash transactions, cash funds, and cash bank balances are to establish the validity and propriety of the cash transactions and to properly set forth the cash position for purposes of financial statement presentation. While cash is no more valuable than any other asset of equal current market price, the examination of cash transactions, funds, and bank balances is important because of the reasons set forth in the following subsection.

Importance of the Audit of Cash

The scope of the examination of cash and cash transactions should be maintained in harmony with the examination of any other asset. When good cash controls are built into a company's operating system, cash transactions may be tested on the same basis as noncash transactions.

The audit of cash and cash transactions is of importance for several reasons, among which are the following:

1. The majority of business transactions involve the Cash account or terminate it. Although a transaction may have no immediate effect upon cash, all assets purchased and sold and all expenses incurred and liquidated will finally affect cash.
2. Cash is a favorite source of fraudulent transactions.
3. Credits to receivables commonly are posted from the cash receipts records; therefore, if cash debits from customer collections are incorrect, one or more customers' accounts probably are incorrect.
4. Charges to payables commonly are posted from disbursements records.
5. Errors in the cash accounts may indicate that errors were made elsewhere.

Cash balances and cash transactions commonly are verified early in an audit in order to prevent the necessity of working backward to a balance at a financial statement date. Cash balances may be large, or they may be small; and cash transactions may be few or voluminous. In accordance with the system of internal control in effect and the requirements of the engagement, the extent of the examination of cash transactions—as expressed in the original accounting records and underlying documents—must be decided by the auditor in accordance with the procedure set forth in Chapters 10 and 11.

ILLUSTRATION. An auditor may decide to foot cash receipts and disbursements records, to trace postings therefrom, and to vouch cash receipts and disbursements for a selected block sample. Regardless of the decision reached with respect to the proof of footing and posting accuracy and with respect to the vouching of transactions, certain procedures are required in every audit, so that the cash balance and its composition may be verified as of the audit date, and so that cash transactions may be verified in sufficient detail for the rendition of a considered opinion.

Cash assumes many forms, such as cash in bank; cash on hand; undeposited checks, money orders, and drafts; petty cash funds; change funds;

payroll funds; unclaimed wages, etc.—all in accordance with the peculiarities of each company.

In this chapter, cash funds are considered first, followed by the audit considerations necessary for cash on hand and in banks, and cash receipts and disbursements.

SECTION II: INTERNAL CONTROL OF CASH FUNDS

The internal control features of any cash fund should be to the effect that the fund is safeguarded, that unauthorized disbursements cannot be made, and that responsibility for fund control is centered in one person.

ILLUSTRATION 12–1

INTERNAL CONTROL QUESTIONNAIRE
Cash Funds

	Yes	No	Not Applicable	Remarks
Company_____ Period Covered_____				
1. Is the imprest system used?	___	___	___	_____
2. Is responsibility for each fund vested in one person?	___	___	___	_____
3. Are cash fund vouchers:				
a) Prenumbered by the printer?	___	___	___	_____
b) Required for each fund disbursement?	___	___	___	_____
c) Signed by the person who receives the cash?	___	___	___	_____
d) Filled in with numerals and spelled-out amounts?	___	___	___	_____
e) Approved by a responsible person?	___	___	___	_____
f) Properly canceled, together with supporting documents, so that they cannot be used again?	___	___	___	_____
4. Does the fund custodian have access to cash receipts?	___	___	___	_____
5. Does the fund custodian have access to general accounting records?	___	___	___	_____
6. Are reimbursement checks made payable to the order of the fund custodian?	___	___	___	_____
7. Are personnel advances from the fund properly approved?	___	___	___	_____
8. Are checks cashed from the fund deposited promptly?	___	___	___	_____
9. Are postdated checks in the fund?	___	___	___	_____
10. When the fund is reimbursed, are the cash vouchers internally audited?	___	___	___	_____
11. Is there a surprise internal audit of each cash fund?	___	___	___	_____
12. Is each fund reasonable in amount?	___	___	___	_____

Prepared by_____   Reviewed by_____
Date_____   Date_____

Internal Control Questionnaire for Cash Funds

An internal control questionnaire for any cash fund (Illustration 12–1) may be completed at the termination of the examination or at an earlier time. Even if it is possible to conclude that the internal control is satisfactory, that conclusion is no assurance that errors do not exist or that fraud has not been committed. The internal control questionnaire, Illustration 12–1, indicates the standards of satisfactory control applicable to cash funds.

SECTION III: CASH FUND AUDIT PROGRAM

There are innumerable methods of operating cash funds. The following audit program for the examination of a cash fund is based on the assumptions (1) that an imprest system is in operation and that the total composition of the fund is equal to the general ledger account balance; (2) that cash vouchers are used; and (3) that summaries of the vouchers are prepared at each reimbursement of the fund.

The following suggested audit program may be expanded, contracted, or rearranged in accordance with the requirements of each engagement. Items inapplicable to a particular audit should be ignored. The order of presentation in the following paragraphs is flexible—not rigid.

Simultaneously Control All Cash and All Negotiable Securities. The simultaneous control of each fund, all undeposited cash, and all negotiable securities is necessary in order to prevent transfers from fund to fund, from cash to securities, or from securities to cash during the course of the examination of cash. Therefore, all safes, cashboxes, securities files, and so forth should be sealed at one time. After counting and recording the contents of each safe, and so forth, each item may be released.

Count and List All Items in the Fund. If possible, in order to avoid confusion and to save time, the cash, securities, and notes preferably should be counted either after the close of business hours or prior to opening for the day. The cash count should not be announced in advance, since a shortage might thus be temporarily covered.

Salary advances, loans, and similar items are frequently found in a cash fund; they are not a part of a fund; they are receivables.

The auditor usually will count the currency and coin, and list and total these items in his work papers. It is not necessary to open rolled coin packages unless the auditor suspects that the packages are short or have been stuffed. Checks in the fund must be listed. The auditor should compare checks in the fund with his work papers of the preceding period to ascertain if someone is permanently borrowing from the fund.

Cash expense vouchers in a fund should be tabulated. The auditor should examine the vouchers for date, amount, purpose, signature of the fund custodian, underlying evidence, and approval of a proper officer.

One form of work paper for a cash fund is presented in the Illustrative Audit; another form is shown in Illustration 12–2.

Obtain the Signature of the Fund Custodian, Acknowledging Return of the Fund Items.   The auditor should insist that his count of a cash fund be witnessed so that he cannot be accused of malpractices if a shortage exists. After the count, the auditor should obtain a receipt from the fund custodian for the intact return of the fund. Another view is that the auditor should merely indicate on his work papers the name of the person in whose presence the fund was counted, since obtaining a receipt from the fund custodian implies that the fund was out of that person's custody.

Obtain Responsible Written Approval for Expense Vouchers, Receivables, and Employees' Checks in the Fund.   Even though the preceding items appear to be regular and are evidently properly supported, the insistence upon written approval is a precaution that should not be overlooked.

ILLUSTRATION.   The composition of a cash fund appeared to be in good order. The auditor requested the treasurer to approve the fund composition. The fund contained several employee IOU's; the treasurer examined the IOU's and noted one IOU for $75, ostensibly from an office employee in the treasurer's department. The treasurer stated that he remembered that the employee had borrowed $75. The treasurer also recalled that the employee had repaid the $75 directly to him and that he had turned the amount over to the fund custodian. Further investigation proved the date of the original cash voucher was 2/6/75; the fund custodian had removed the original cash voucher, changed the date to 12/6/75, and altered the cash voucher number to one of current usage.

Reconcile the Fund with the General Ledger Amount Balance at the Date of the Balance Sheet.   After the total of the fund has been obtained, it should be compared with the general ledger account balance in order to determine that the two balances are in agreement.

ILLUSTRATION.   A staff accountant examined a cash fund, listed all items, and obtained a fund total of $1,000; however, he failed to compare the $1,000 figure with the general ledger account balance, which was $1,100. Later, the supervisor in charge noted the $100 discrepancy. The fund custodian—unable to place $100 in the fund due to an unannounced count—had assumed the risk of nondiscovery of the theft of $100, and the shortage almost missed detection.

Trace All Checks in the Fund to the Bank Statement.   Checks in the fund dated prior to the fund cash count should be deposited, under the control of the auditor; and the auditor should examine the succeeding bank statement to ascertain that they cleared. If the checks did not clear, they must be treated as uncollectible items or as advances, in accordance with the circumstances. If approved postdated checks and other checks for nondeposit are in the fund at the audit date, they are considered

ILLUSTRATION 12–2

						Initials	Date
		KINKAID COMPANY			Prepared By		
		Cash Fund No. 1					
		December 31, 1975			Approved By		

		Denomination	Number	Amount	Total
Money:	Currency:	$5.00	34	$170.00	
		1.00	132	132.00	
		0.25	45	11.25	
	Coin:	0.10	30	3.00	
		0.05	55	2.75	$ 319.00

	Date	Maker	Bank	Amount	
Cashed Checks:					
	Dec. 27, 1975	John Bulow	Central	$140.00*	
	Dec. 31, 1975	E. H. Jones	First	120.00*	260.00
Total cash and cash items . . . . $ 579.00					

Approved Expense Vouchers:

Number	Date	Distribution	Amount	
812	12-23-75	Entertainment	$ 62.49 ø	
813	12-27-75	Office Supplies	13.10 ø	
814	12-27-75	Travel	23.12 ø	

Not approved:
(Jan. 2, 1976)

815	12-30-75	Supper money	21.29 ø	
				120.00

Advances to Employees:

Date		Name	Amount	
Dec. 10, 1975		James Muskie	$250.00 ⅴ	
Dec. 20, 1975		James Drew	50.00 ⅴ	
				300.00

Total . . . . $ 999.00

Shortage (AJE 9) approved by treasurer, B. Kile, and charged to Office Operating   1.00

Total . . . . $1,000.00#

Count witnessed by _____

Return of fund acknowledged by _____

* Cashed at bank, under our control.

ⅴ Reviewed with and approved by treasurer, B. Kile.

ø Checked to general ledger (AJE 9), and reversed as of January 1, 1976.

Agrees with general ledger.

Examined reimbursement vouchers No. 846, 962, and 1641 (10 percent). No errors.

AJE 9

Entertainment.	62.49	
Office Supplies	13.10	
Travel Expense	23.12	
Office Operating Expense (Supper Money)	21.29	
Office Operating Expense (Shortage)	1.00	
Cash Fund No. 1		121.00

To clear the cash fund of expense items as of December 31, 1975.
This entry is to be reversed as of Jan. 1, 1976, in order to offset 1976 charges
when the fund is reimbursed.

as receivables as of the balance sheet date, and should be cleared by audit adjustment.

ILLUSTRATION. On July 3, 1975, the office manager exchanged his personal check of $200 for cash from a petty cash fund and asked that his check not be deposited in the bank. On December 31, 1975, he issued a new check in exchange for the check of July 3, 1975. On January 2, 1976; the auditor counted the petty cash and directed that the check of the office manager be deposited; it was returned marked "N.S.F." The auditor then requested that the treasurer approve the $200 "loan"; the treasurer refused, and the $200 was deducted from the salary of the office manager on January 31, 1976.

Examine Original Evidence and Compare the Cash Fund Vouchers with the Covering Reimbursement Voucher; Inspect Distributions and Approvals. The auditor should select an appropriate sample of the cash fund reimbursement vouchers. With satisfactory internal control, 10 percent of the reimbursement vouchers should be totally adequate. The individual cash vouchers in each examined reimbursement summary should be examined for date, purpose, approval, amount, and account to be charged. Original evidence should be examined for alterations. The vouchers should be totaled and compared with the amount of the reimbursement check. Distributions to expense accounts should be scrutinized for accuracy.

ILLUSTRATION. A cash fund of a company was reimbursed regularly every other Friday. The auditor selected four reimbursements for examination. His adding machine tapes for *approved* cash fund expense vouchers in each reimbursement were $30 short of the distribution in the voucher summary and in the voucher register in each instance. He extended his test to 100 percent, and every reimbursement was $30 in excess of the sum of the approved vouchers. There were 25 reimbursement vouchers (the fund had not been reimbursed at the end of the period), or a total shortage of $750, which was equally charged to travel and to entertainment.

Verify Footings and Crossfootings of the Reimbursement Vouchers. The proof of accuracy of footings and crossfootings of the selected reimbursement vouchers should be determined, as a fraud prevention.

ILLUSTRATION. Each approved fund voucher in each reimbursement agreed with the distribution entries in the reimbursement summary. In footing the reimbursement summaries, it was discovered that they were overfooted $160 for the year, and an equivalent amount had been extracted from the cash fund.

Trace Reimbursement Vouchers to the Voucher Register, Disbursements Record, or Other Medium. The distribution of cash fund vouchers as expressed in each selected reimbursement voucher should be traced to the original accounting record where the debits are recorded, in order to be certain that the final distribution to the accounts is proper.

ILLUSTRATIONS. (1) The reimbursement voucher shows $100 charged to Postage Expense. When carried to the voucher register, the $100 appeared in Advertising Expense—inadvertently. (2) A reimbursement voucher shows $175 as entertainment expense. Purposely, because total entertainment expense was considered to be excessive, the $175 has been carried to the voucher register as factory maintenance expense.

Obtain from a Responsible Official Written Acceptance and Approval of Any Shortage in the Funds. Such approval should be obtained even though the fund custodian makes up the shortage at the time of the count. The effect of the request is to approve shortages if they are the result of honest errors and to place an official on notice that a shortage exists.

Obtain Confirmation Direct from Company Personnel of the Amount of Cash—from the Fund—Held by Them at the End of the Fiscal Period. The purpose here is not so much to discover how much cash the employees have as it is to find out if they originally received the cash in the amounts indicated.

ILLUSTRATION. A confirmation states that a salesman received $200 for traveling expense on December 28, 1975; the voucher was for $300.

If funds exist at distant locations—branch stores, for example—and if the auditor cannot visit those distant locations, caution must be exercised. The materiality of the amount of each such fund, the system of internal control, and the system of internal audit will guide the auditor in his decision either to accept or reject the fund composition. The best procedure to follow is to insist that funds that cannot be counted be reimbursed by the main office as of the close of business on the last day of the year. He also should insist that all distant fund vouchers be sent to the main office for examination.

If the Examination Takes Place after the End of the Fiscal Period, Reconcile the Account Back to the Fiscal Period Ending Date. Frequently, it is not possible to count the fund cash exactly at the close of the year. When a fund is verified after the close of the period, the work papers must be designed so that the fund is worked back to the closing date of the period. This is accomplished by showing the fund composition at the date of the actual count and by showing the summarized transactions between the date of the count and the end of the period. The resultant figure will be the total of the fund at the close of the fiscal period, as shown below:

Fund cash, February 10, 1976	$1,800
Add: Cash vouchers, January 1–February 10, 1976	400
	$2,200
Deduct: Reimbursement cash, January 1–February 10, 1976	200
Fund balance, December 31, 1975	$2,000

Verify Special Funds. A client may maintain many special funds. a few of which are as follows:

a) Petty cash and change funds.

b) Travel expense funds.

c) Payroll funds—in the office and/or in separate bank accounts.

d) Employee savings funds.

e) Dividend funds, against which dividend checks are issued.

f) Interest funds, against which interest checks are cashed.

g) Sinking funds—if under control of the client.

h) Funds held in trust (1) from the collection of income from the fund assets; (2) from the collection of rents; and (3) from the sale of merchandise under guaranty, refund, and other, contracts.

i) Restricted funds arising from the assignment of receivables.

j) Funds that have not been segregated on the client's records, but legally or contractually are separable.

If special funds have been intermingled with other funds or with general cash on the records of the client, each fund should be segregated for audit purposes.

In isolated instances, there may be hidden funds for which there is no accounting record. When such funds exist, they usually arise from such sources as quantity rebates, refunds, and sales of scrap. An examination of underlying contracts, letters, and other data, and casual conversation and questions usually reveal these hidden funds, which the auditor must take up in his records, and which he should insist that the client take up if an unqualified report is to be rendered.

SECTION IV: INTERNAL CONTROL OF CASH ON HAND AND IN BANKS, AND CASH TRANSACTIONS

Proper internal control dictates that cash receipts be deposited intact— that is, as they are received; that all cash which should be received was received; that only authorized disbursements are made; that all disbursements be made by check; that both receipts and disbursements are properly accounted for in the records; and that account distributions are proper. Adequate internal control also demands the separation of personnel duties for receiving cash, recording receipts, depositing, reconciling, authorizing disbursements, and disbursing.

Internal control questionnaires for cash are shown in Illustrations 12–3 and 12–4.

SECTION V: AUDIT PROGRAM FOR CASH AND CASH TRANSACTIONS

Because of the fact that the large majority of sales are made on credit, this chapter purposely deemphasizes the audit of revenues, which are

ILLUSTRATION 12–3

INTERNAL CONTROL QUESTIONNAIRE
Cash Receipts

	Yes	No	Not Appli- cable	Remarks
Company_____ Period Covered_____				
1. Are bank accounts properly authorized by the board of directors?	___	___	___	_____
2. Is the mail opened by a person:				
a) Who does not prepare the bank deposit?	___	___	___	_____
b) Who does not have access to accounts receivable or the general ledger?	___	___	___	_____
3. Does the person who opens the mail list the receipts in detail?	___	___	___	_____
4. Are the listed mail receipts compared with the accounting records by an independent person?	___	___	___	_____
5. Are cash receipts deposited daily and intact?	___	___	___	_____
6. Is cash sales money proved against the totals of invoices, cash register tapes, inventory release tickets, etc.?	___	___	___	_____
7. Is the proof in Question 6 prepared by a person who does not have access to the cash?	___	___	___	_____
8. Are cash receipts from miscellaneous sources independently controlled?	___	___	___	_____
9. Does a person other than the person who prepares the bank deposit make the deposit?	___	___	___	_____
10. Is the bank–stamped duplicate deposit ticket returned to a person other than the one who prepared the deposit?	___	___	___	_____
11. Are bank–stamped duplicate deposit tickets compared with the cash receipts record?	___	___	___	_____
12. Are all persons bonded who handle cash or cash transactions?	___	___	___	_____
13. Are returned customer checks delivered to a person other than the one who prepared the bank deposit?	___	___	___	_____
14. Is it impossible for employees to redeem dishonored customer checks?	___	___	___	_____
15. Are noncash negotiable securities in the custody of a person other than the one responsible for cash receipts?	___	___	___	_____
16. Does any person in the cashier's department (answer "No" for proper control):				
a) Prepare sales invoices?	___	___	___	_____
b) Maintain the sales record?	___	___	___	_____
c) Have access to the accounts receivable ledger?	___	___	___	_____
d) Have access to customers' statements?	___	___	___	_____
e) Authorize credit extention?	___	___	___	_____
f) Approve discounts, returns, or allowances?	___	___	___	_____
g) Sign notes payable?	___	___	___	_____
h) Participate in collection duties?	___	___	___	_____
i) Prepare, sign, or mail checks?	___	___	___	_____

Prepared by_____   Reviewed by_____
Date_____   Date_____

ILLUSTRATION 12–4

INTERNAL CONTROL QUESTIONNAIRE
Cash Disbursements (Except Payroll)

Company_____

Period Covered_____

	Yes	No	Not Appli- cable	Remarks

1. Are all checks prenumbered by the printer?
2. Are spoiled checks retained and properly filed?
3. Are voided checks mutilated to avoid reuse?
4. Are unused checks properly controlled?
5. Is a check protector used?
6. Are all checks made payable to a person or a company?
7. Are persons who sign checks prohibited to:
    a) Have access to petty (or other) cash funds?
    b) Approve cash disbursements?
    c) Record cash receipts?
    d) Post to the ledger accounts?
8. If used, are signature machines properly controlled?
9. Are persons who sign checks properly authorized to do so?
10. Have banks been instructed not to cash checks payable to the order of the company?
11. Are all checks signed only after they are prepared?
12. When checks are presented for signatures, are accompanying invoices and other necessary papers also submitted?
13. Are invoices and other accompanying papers stamped "Paid" at the time the accompanying checks are signed?
14. Is it impossible to present an invoice or voucher for payment two or more times?
15. Do two different persons prepare checks and approve invoices?
16. Are bank accounts reconciled at least once each month?
17. Are bank statements and paid checks delivered directly to the person who prepares the reconciliation:
18. Is the person preparing the reconciliation:
    a) Prevented from signing checks?
    b) Prevented from handling cash?
    c) Prevented from recording cash transactions?
19. Does the person preparing the reconciliation:
    a) Account for all check numbers?
    b) Examine signatures?
    c) Examine endorsements?
    d) Examine payee's name?
20. Are interbank fund transfers promptly recorded?
21. Are improperly endorsed checks returned to the bank for correction?
22. Are long-outstanding checks properly followed and controlled?

Prepared by_____ Reviewed by_____

Date_____ Date_____

treated in Chapter 13, which also includes an internal control question-naire for revenues. If revenues primarily are derived from cash transac-tions, the reader should refer to Chapter 13, Section III, for the examina-tion of revenues and related items.

If possible, the most convenient time to audit cash on hand is immedi-ately after the close of, or preceding the opening of, a business day. So far as procedure is concerned, it is immaterial when cash is examined. The extent of the examination of cash receipts, revenues, cash disburse-ments, and related expenses is dependent upon the system of internal control, the methods of accounting, and the discoveries made during the course of the audit—all in accordance with the results of the samples tested.

The validity of the balance of cash on hand and in banks is dependent upon the accuracy of the accounting for cash receipts and cash disburse-ments. Therefore, the audit program for cash suggested in the following subsections includes performance standards and auditing procedures for cash on hand and in banks and for receipts and disbursements, in addition to the features of original record examination presented in Chapters 10 and 11. In general, the audit program follows the sequence of reconcilia-tions, receipts, related revenues, disbursements, and related expenses, as presented in the following subsections. It should be realized that variations in sequence of procedure may be necessary in order to suit each auditor and to facilitate the operations of any particular engagement.

Confirm Bank Balances.   Confirmation of amounts on deposit should be obtained as of the closing date of the fiscal period. It will be pointed out below that it may be necessary to prepare a second reconciliation if the date of the cash examination is subsequent to the closing date. Confirmation requests should be prepared by the client at the direction of the auditor and mailed by the auditor; in order to avoid alteration, they should be returned directly to the auditor by the bank.

ILLUSTRATION. The necessity of obtaining direct confirmations may be exemplified as follows: Confirmation requests were placed in the client's outgoing mail by the auditor. The treasurer of the client company extracted one confirmation request, opened it, wrote in the December 31 bank balance as $1,486, and mailed it back to the auditor. This request was for a payroll account balance which had been transferred to another bank; but $1,486 had been left in the first bank, since that represented the amount of uncashed and unclaimed payroll checks issued to terminated employees. The treasurer had taken the unclaimed payroll checks and cashed them at various stores and had issued orders that all ex-employees calling for their past wages be referred to him. During the course of the audit, an ex-employee called in person for his check; the fraud was discovered due to the absence of the treasurer from his office and the presence of the ex-employee's check among those returned by the bank at the time the account was closed.

Requests for confirmation should be mailed to *all* banks with which the client has conducted business since the last audit, in order to prevent missing an existing bank balance. Preferably, the requests should be mailed in advance of the audit so that replies will be available when the auditor starts his examination.

The request to a bank is so framed that it not only requests the amounts on deposit to the credit of the client but also asks the bank to list all primary and secondary obligations of the client and to show any collateral of the client held by the bank. A request to the bank and a confirmation from the bank are shown in the Illustrative Audit, in a form different from that of Illustration 12–5.

When confirmation request replies are received by the auditor from the bank, he must compare each balance with the bank statements and with his work papers for the items, in order to assure agreement or disagreement.

If possible, the auditor should compare the detail of cash receipts as shown by the cash receipts record with the *detail* of the confirmed duplicate deposit tickets for the last few days of the audit period and the first few days of the subsequent period. He may mail these duplicate deposit tickets to the bank and request direct confirmation of the *detail* appearing therein, or he may include this request as a part of the confirmation procedure, as indicated oin Illustration 12–5.

Today, the majority of banks do not compare the detail of deposit tickets with the items deposited; most banks total the items deposited and compare that total with the total of the deposit tickets. Therefore, the comparison of details is a practice of the past. Because a bank cannot be expected to allot excessive time to examining the duplicate deposit tickets of its customers—in this case, the client of the auditor—the client should carefully control its duplicate deposit tickets by not permitting them to be returned to the cashier or the accountant. Duplicate deposit tickets are easily altered.

Deposits in transit must be traced to the next bank statement, or direct confirmation of deposits should be obtained from the bank. Items in transit should reach the bank in a few days at the maximum. If more than normal time elapses, it may indicate that cash has been received and charged on the records of the client and temporarily borrowed by an employee by a system of lapping. Occasionally, when a cash receipt is not deposited, the cashier will make the statement that advances for salaries or travel expenses were made from the receipts and that the cashier is waiting for reimbursement for those items before making the deposit. Even if the excuse is the truth, the attention of the client should be called to this undesirable practice.

Cash deposits made by branches on the last day of the year, but not taken up by the home office on the same day owing to transportation, should be considered as home office receipts as of the last day of the

ILLUSTRATION 12–5

REQUEST TO BANK FOR CONFIRMATION OF BALANCES

(mailed to bank in duplicate)

JANUARY 7, 1976

NATIONAL BANK
CINCINNATI, OHIO   45201

GENTLEMEN:

Please complete this report and mail it directly to our auditors, Corbin and Drake, Certified Public Accountants, in the accompanying envelope.

Very truly yours,
·THE STANLEY COMPANY
Allen J. Reid, Treasurer

. . . .

Corbin and Drake
Certified Public Accountants
Cincinnati, Ohio   45230

DUPLICATE
To be retained by bank

GENTLEMEN:

In connection with your audit of
THE STANLEY COMPANY   , we report that:

1. Our records show balance(s) to the credit of the above named, in the account(s) and on the date(s) indicated, as follows:

Name of Account	At Close of Business		Amount
Checking	December 31	75	$ 45,228
Payroll	December 31	75	$ 6,721
			$

2. At the close of business on __December 31 19 75__, our records show liabilities of the above named, direct (or as maker, endorser, or guarantor of loans, notes, acceptances, or other accounts or contracts), as follows:

(If none, please so state.)

Description of Obligation	Date of Loan or Discount	Amount	Maturity Date	Int. Rate	Description of Collateral or Security
Unsecured note loan	11/15/75	$20,000	2/15/76	7%	None Interest paid to February 15, 1976

3. Letters of credit, drafts, trust agreements, open contracts for the purchase and sale of foreign exchange, security agreements under the Uniform Commercial Code, etc.:   None

4. Authenticated copies of deposit slips are enclosed for deposits indicated below:

Date		Amount	Date		Amount
Dec. 29	19 75	$ 6,784	Jan. 2	19 76	$ 1,721
Dec. 30	19 75	$ 3,428	Jan. 2	19 76	$ 4,625
Dec. 31	19 75	$ 1,927	Jan. 4	19 76	$ 3,751

5. This report covers our principal office and all branches unless otherwise stated.

NATIONAL BANK
Name of Institution

Date __January 8, 19 76__   By___ James B. Dunn ___

period. Transit items, if not traced by the auditor, may cover fraud through kiting. Some companies carry a Cash in Transit account which is charged with cash on its way to the home office and credited when the money is received. If a customer notifies the company that he is paying a bill, no entries should be made until the cash is received.

Obtain Bank Statements, Duplicate Deposit Tickets, and Paid Checks. In order to assure proper cash transactions and balance verification, the auditor must obtain (or have access to) all bank statements, bank deposit receipts, or duplicate deposit tickets, paid checks, and the last bank reconciliation prepared by the client.

When cash is counted and reconciled *after* the closing date, the auditor should have the bank send him directly the bank statement and the paid checks to the date of the bank statement. By obtaining the subsequent bank statement and the paid checks directly, kiting may be detected.

ILLUSTRATION. On December 31, 1975, a deposit was made in Bank A prior to the auditor's visit; the detail of the deposit agrees with the entries in the cash receipts record. On February 1, 1976, the auditor receives directly from Bank A the January 31, 1976, bank statement and the checks paid from January 1, 1976, through January 31, 1976. One check for $2,000 was a company check on Bank B, entered as a receipt (agreeing with the entries in the cash receipts record and the credits to Accounts Receivable); but it had not been entered as a credit to Cash in the disbursements record.

Count and List Cash and Cash Items. Cash on hand may contain currency; undeposited checks, money orders, and drafts; matured and cashed bond coupons; unclaimed wages; and, perhaps, expenditure vouchers. Such items as expenditure vouchers, loans, and advances should be cleared from cash by audit adjustments.

If it is not convenient to simultaneously count all cash, cash items, and negotiable securities such as notes, bonds, certificates of deposit, warehouse receipts, and so forth, each item must be sealed by the auditor in order to prevent transfers. Such control is also necessary so that money may not be temporarily borrowed on securities in order to cover a cash shortage existing between the cash on hand and in the bank and the cash balances shown in the accounts. When shortages are thus concealed, the counted cash may be taken later to reclaim the securities for the inspection by the auditor. After the count—for his own protection—the auditor preferably should obtain a receipt from the cash custodian indicating the return of all items. A work paper for the count and record reconciliation of cash is presented in Illustration 12–6; in this illustration, the weakness of permitting disbursements from current receipts should be noted.

ILLUSTRATION 12–6

COUNT OF GENERAL CASH AND BOOK RECONCILIATION

ALEXANDER COMPANY
Cash Count and Book Reconciliation
December 31, 1975

	Initials	Date
Prepared By		
Approved By		

	Denomination	Number	Subtotals	Totals
Currency:	$10.00	24	$ 240.00	
	5.00	7	35.00	
	1.00	62	62.00	$ 337.00
Coin:	0.50	4	$ 2.00	
	0.10	8	.80	2.80
Checks: Maker	Bank	Date		
Berning Co.	Southern	1-14-76	$ 450.00 (1) (5)	
Jamestown Co.	Provident	12-23-75	150.00 (2)	
Salem Supply Co.	Norwood	12-31-75	1,210.70 (3)	1,810.70
Postal Money Orders:				
Cross Store		12-30-75		119.30 (3)
Notes: In client's cash:				
Gerald Hock, foreman				50.00 (4)
Approved Vouchers: In the client's cash:				
No. 86 Transportation-In		12-31-75	25.28 (5)	
No. 87 Advance, Traveling		12-31-75	100.00 (5)	125.28
				$ 2,445.08
Add: Cash in Bank, per general ledger				12,682.01
				$ 15,127.09
Deduct: Audit Adjustment 10 (below)				575.28
Total cash available				$ 14,551.81
Cash record receipts				$465,282.19
Less: Cash record disbursements				460,357.12
				4,925.07
Plus: Balance, January 1, 1975				10,202.02
Balance per books, December 31, 1975				15,127.09

Counted January 2, 1976, at 8:30 A.M.
Returned to (Henry Davenport), Cashier

(1) Postdated check.
(2) Returned by bank, 12-30-75, N.S.F. Redeposited, 1-2-76—cleared.
(3) Entered in cash records, 12-31-75. Cleared in January, 1976.
(4) Note redeemed 1-2-76, considered as cash on hand.
(5) AJE 10

Trade Accounts Receivable	450.00	
Transportation-In · · · · · · · · · · · · · · · · · ·	25.28	
Advances for Travel	100.00	
Cash		575.28
To correct the December 31, 1975 cash balance.		

Prepare Bank Reconciliations. A bank reconciliation may be prepared for each bank account at this point or earlier in the audit procedures. An auditor should prepare at least one independent reconciliation:

a) At the balance sheet date, or

b) At a date prior to the balance sheet date, or

c) At a date subsequent to the balance sheet date.

A separate confirmation request should be used for each date (if more than one confirmation is prepared) unless both dates are past, or unless one is in the past and one at the present time.

a) *Reconciliation at the Balance Sheet Date.* In preparing a bank reconciliation at the balance sheet date, it is advisable to start with the bank balance and work toward the client's ledger balance, since the client's records are being proved and not the records of the bank. The adjusted balance is then proved by working from the records of the client to the adjusted bank balance. This type of reconciliation is presented in Illustration 12–7.

All cash on deposit and in transit should be verified as of the same date in order to detect unrecorded fund transfers. Deposits in transit

ILLUSTRATION 12–7

BANK RECONCILIATION

THE STANLEY COMPANY Bank Reconciliation–First National Bank December 31, 1975			Initials	Date
	Prepared By			
	Approved By			

Balance per bank certificate, December 31, 1975 . . . . $45,228
Add: Receipts, December 31, 1975, deposited January
　　　3, 1976# 3,928
　　　　　　　　　　　　　　　　　　　　　　　　　　　$49,156
Deduct: Outstanding Checks:

Number	Date	Paid by Bank (1)	Amount
19,946	11- 1-75		$ 190
20,150	12-18-75		9,000 CC
20,162	12-28-75	1-4-76	1,468
20,167	12-29-75	1-5-76	1,281
20,180	12-29-75	Voided; on file	
20,194	12-31-75	1-6-76	1,131
20,195∗	12-31-75	1-6-76	47
			$13,117

　　　Less: Certified check outstanding
　　　　　(CC above): 20,150 . . . . 9,000　　　4,117
Adjusted Bank Balance, December 31, 1975 . . . .　　$45,039
Balance per books, December 31, 1975 . . . .　　$38,066
Add: Note collected (2) . . . .$ 7,000
　　　Less: Collection charges (3) . . . .　4　　6,996
　　　　　　　　　　　　　　　　　　　　　　　　　　　$45,062
Deduct: Exchange charges (4)　　　　　　　　　　　　　　　　　23
Adjusted Book Balance, December 31, 1975　　　　　　　　　　$45,039
　　(1) Dates from the 1-31-76,
　　　　Bank Statement
　　(2) AJE 11
　　　　Cash in Bank 7,000.00
　　　　　　Notes Receivable . . . .　　　　7,000.00
　　(3) AJE 12
　　　　Collection Charges . . . .　4.00
　　　　　　Cash in Bank . . . .　　　　　4.00
　　(4) AJE 13
　　　　Exchange Charges. . . . .　23.00
　　　　　　Cash in Bank . . . .　　　　　23.00
　　　#Confirmed by bank.
　　　∗Last check.

must be added to the balance as shown by the bank statement on the basis that the cash charges were proper additions to the cash receipts for the period under examination.

Unreturned certified checks should be included in the list of outstanding checks; the bank charge should then be deducted to effect the reconciliation. In this way, the fact that these checks were outstanding will be brought to attention. When the certified checks are paid, they will be eliminated from the reconciliation. The bank charge slip for the certified check should not be accepted in lieu of the check, but only as evidence that a certified check is outstanding.

ILLUSTRATION.   A check for $29,000 was certified for payment. In preparing the bank reconciliation at the end of the month, an office employee found the bank charge slip and ticked it off as a paid item, thereby eliminating it from the list of outstanding checks. The fact was that the certified check had been sent to an attorney for delivery to the creditor, but the attorney misplaced the check for several months. The creditor then exercised his privilege of penalty infliction for nonpayment. If the office employee had included the certified check as outstanding and then deducted the bank charge, the fact that the certified check had not been cleared would have been revealed.

b) Reconciliation at a Date Prior to the Balance Sheet.   If the system of internal control is adequate—that is, (1) if the client prepares a reconciliation at least once each month, (2) if the bank statement and paid checks are sent direct by the bank to the person who prepares the reconciliation, and (3) if employees signing checks have no connection with the accounting or cash-handling duties—it is considered acceptable practice to review the client's reconciliations, prepare a reconciliation at a date prior to the balance sheet date, and then confirm the bank balance and review cash receipts and disbursements transactions from the reconciliation date (1) to the balance sheet date and (2) to a cutoff date, if necessary.

ILLUSTRATION.   The balance sheet date is December 31, 1975; the reconciliation date is November 30, 1975. The auditor should proceed as follows: Obtain direct from the bank the November 30, 1975, bank statement and paid checks, and prepare a reconciliation as of November 30, 1975. Examine the client's reconciliation as of October 31. Compare the balances per banks and per books on the two reconciliations with the bank statements and the Cash ledger account balances. Verify the checks outstanding at October 31 by examining those enclosed with the November 30 bank statement and tick them off in the October 31 client reconciliation. Substantiate deposits in transit, other credits, and bank charges as of October 31 by comparison with the November 30 bank statement. If necessary, next obtain directly from the bank at a cutoff date—assume January 10, 1976—the bank statement as of that date and the paid checks to that date. (See the comment on page 354, with regard to cut-off statements.) For the period from November 30, 1975, to January 10, 1976, compare paid checks with the cash disbursements record and with the client's list of outstanding checks at November 30 and December 31, 1975; also compare the January 10, 1976, bank statement with the cash receipts records for deposits. Next, trace all fund transfers between banks from November 30, 1975; to the cutoff date—January 10, 1976. In this way, the client's reconciliation at December 31, 1975, is proved.

c) Reconciliation at a Date Subsequent to the Balance Sheet. This is a variation of (*b*), above, and is easy to perform in those cases where the audit is started after the balance sheet date.

ILLUSTRATION. Again, assume that December 31, 1975, is the balance sheet date. The auditor should verify the client's reconciliation as of December 31, 1975. At a cutoff date—assume January 10, 1976—the auditor should obtain directly from the bank the bank statement and paid checks to that date, and he should prepare a reconciliation. The transactions between December 31, 1975, and January 10, 1976, should be reviewed and substantiated to prove the accuracy of the December 31, 1975, balance. He would then proceed as indicated at the asterisk (*) in (b), above; but the review period would be from December 31, not November 30.

ILLUSTRATION 12–8

THE STANLEY COMPANY

Bank Reconciliation—First National Bank, December 31, 1975
Prepared January 10, 1976

Explanation	*Client Balance, Dec. 31, 1975*	*Verified Receipts*	*Verified Disbursements*	*Auditor Balance, Jan. 10, 1976†*
Per bank statement and certificate	$45,228	$15,620	$10,500	$50,348
Deposits in transit:				
December 31, 1975.	3,928	− 3,928		
January 10, 1976.		5,000		5,000
Checks outstanding:				
December 31, 1975.	− 4,117		− 4,117	
January 10, 1976.			2,462	− 2,462
Unrecorded bank charges and credits:*				
Note collected by bank on January 8, 1976, entered by client on January 11, 1976.		− 3,000		− 3,000
Collection charges			− 12	12
Per Client Records	$45,039	$13,692	$ 8,833	$49,898

* When compared with Illustration 12-7, the assumption is that the client's records had been adjusted as of December 31, 1975.

† Or other later date.

A convenient form of bank reconciliation for balance, receipts, and disbursements, when the independent reconciliation is prepared initially at a date subsequent to the balance sheet date, is shown in Illustration 12–8. In this reconciliation, it is assumed that the client's December 31, 1975, reconciliation was reviewed and proved by preparing a reconciliation at January 10, 1976.

d) Miscellaneous Considerations in the Preparation of Reconciliations. It is only in cases of suspected fraud, unlocated error, or ineffective internal control that paid checks returned by the bank are compared with the bank statement. Bank statements should be reviewed for attempted alterations, particularly alterations of error corrections—"EC"—made by the bank. If the persons preparing accounting entries have access to unused checks, the comparison of paid checks to bank statement debits must be made.

ILLUSTRATION. Fraud through bank statement manipulation may be illustrated as follows: The bookkeeper, who was empowered to sign checks, drew a check payable to the order of a creditor for $1,900. He then used another check, marked the related stub "sample," made the check payable to the order of the client company for $1,000, cashed it, and did not make an entry for it. When the checks were returned by the bank, the bookkeeper destroyed the check for $1,000, raised the $1,900 check to $2,900, and placed an "EC" in the bank statement opposite the $1,000 item to effect the raising of the $1,900 check to $2,900. In the cash disbursements record, he charged Accounts Payable and credited Cash for $2,900, and posted $1,900 to the debit of Accounts Payable (subsidiary and control), $1,000 to the debit of Supplies Expense, and $2,900 to the credit of Cash. Investigation of the "EC" on the bank statement led to the discovery of the manipulation.

All checks and cash items on hand at the date when a bank reconciliation is prepared should be traced to subsequent deposit tickets and to the next bank statement. Such items should be deposited—under the control of the auditor—with a request for direct advice of protest for uncollectible items. The auditor should request that the client obtain signed duplicate deposit tickets for the amount deposited. In his work papers, the auditor should prepare any necessary notes pertaining to such items. Undeposited checks may represent customer collections and checks cashed as accommodation for employees and others. If some of the undeposited checks on hand are from employees, the auditor must be positive of their collection; otherwise, the indication might be that rather permanent borrowing was taking place or that a shortage existed and was covered by placing a fictitious check among those to be deposited.

In order to prove the total of checks cleared during a period (below, the assumption is for one year), approved practice is as follows:

Proof of checks cleared:

Balance, per bank statement, January 1, 1975		$ 77,869
Add: Deposits per bank statements, footed . . . .(1)		441,802
		$519,671
Less: Balance per bank statement, December 31, 1975		45,228
Checks and other debits cleared by the bank during 1975,		
per bank statements, footed. . . . .(2)		$474,443
Outstanding checks, January 1, 1975, list footed.		$ 2,408
Add: Disbursements during 1975 per cash record, footed		476,152
		$478,560
Less: Outstanding checks, December 31, 1975, per reconciliation . .		4,117
Checks and other debits cleared during 1975—agrees with (2) above.		$474,443

Reconciliation of receipts and deposits:

Receipts during 1975 per cash record, footed.	$443,720
Add: Deposits in transit, January 1, 1975	2,010
	$445,730
Less: Deposits in transit, December 31, 1975	3,928
Deposits per bank statement during 1975—agrees with (1) above. . .	$441,802

When a bank reconciliation—as originally prepared—does not agree with the records of the client, after taking the necessary adjustments into consideration, the auditor need not devote time immediately to the location of discrepancies. These discrepancies probably will be discovered as paid checks—for other than the last month of the period—are compared with the disbursements record and as cash receipts are compared with deposits.

If Necessary, Prepare a Second Reconciliation at a Subsequent Date. Auditors are in general agreement that a second—cutoff—reconciliation should be prepared at least on the partial basis of following through the year-end reconciliation to a cutoff date; in this case, cash is not recounted.

The procedure in preparing a cutoff reconciliation is as follows: At a date after the balance sheet date, request *direct* return of the cutoff bank statement, together with the accompanying paid checks. Many banks object to the request for a cutoff statement, or refuse to prepare one due to the interruption of computer operations; in this event, the auditor must wait until the bank's subsequent period ends and have the bank statement for that period mailed directly to him, together with the paid checks. He may then select any date within the new period as a cutoff date. Without preparing another complete count and reconciliation, and using the cutoff bank statement date and paid checks:

a) Trace year-end deposits in transit to the cutoff date.

b) Compare paid checks returned with the cutoff statement with the outstanding check list at the end of the year.

c) Investigate entries for all balance sheet date checks not cleared and all customers' checks returned.

d) Examine returned checks to be certain that the proper checks were listed as outstanding at the end of the year. A check may have been outstanding at the end of the year but not recorded as a disbursement.

e)   Account for any other items affecting the balance sheet date reconciliation.

Checks drawn to the order of a bank—indicating fund transfers—should be traced to the Cash debit and credit to detect kiting.

If the foregoing procedure is followed, all items necessary to effect a reconciliation at the cutoff date have been traced.

Prior to closing the audit, it may be required or advisable to count the cash again, and prepare a second and complete reconciliation. This is on the basis that the year-end reconciliation has not been or could not be followed through to the subsequent cutoff date. A second reconciliation should not be announced in advance.

If a surety policy specifies a second *count and reconciliation,* or if the audit is conducted according to the requirements of the New York Stock Exchange, the procedures in (*a*) to (*e*), above, should be followed; and, in addition:

f)   Control and count the cash and prepare a complete second reconciliation.

Use the Paid Check Examination Procedure.   Checks outstanding at the end of the preceding audit should be ticked off on the preceding bank reconciliation. Unticked items in the preceding reconciliation would indicate that those checks are still outstanding.

Access should be obtained to all paid, voided, and canceled checks written during the period, even though the examination of them will be on a test basis. When checks have been paid by a bank, they should not be returned to the company cashier or to anyone else in the organization who has access to unused checks. If they were returned to the cashier, he could remove a fraudulently executed check made payable to himself or to a fictitious person and thus hide a fraud covered by depositing cash receipts and failing to enter the receipt, or by overfooting the disbursements record, or by creating a fictitious purchase. The extent to which checks should be traced into the check record will depend upon the conditions set forth in Chapters 10 and 11. The check sample will be selected on a block or a random basis, or a combination of both.

All checks issued during the period should be accounted for, including those that are voided and spoiled. The voided and spoiled checks should be so mutilated that they cannot be used again and should be filed numerically with the paid checks. Checks with altered numbers should be investigated; usually, there is no reason for the alteration of check numbers. When a check is spoiled, or prepared and voided, a notation to that effect should be made in the cash disbursements record, so that all check numbers are recorded therein. On his work papers, it is common practice for the auditor to list the number of the last check of the period; this indicates to him the starting point on a succeeding audit. It is also necessary to account for all checks in order to prevent the cashing of fraudulently prepared checks, with the subsequent overfooting of the check record in order to force bank balances into agreement with account balances. Checks of higher than next-of-sequence number should not be used, and unused checks must be safeguarded by management. Under a properly controlled EDP system, checks of higher than next-of-sequence cannot be used.

Check dates and bank "Paid" dates sometimes must be compared for checks written during the final week of a fiscal period, in order to determine if checks were written and not mailed. The date of the check must agree with the date in the check register; this is necessary in order to prevent submission of old checks, which might mean that fictitious purchases were recorded and the money stolen, although the name of a regular creditor had been used in the voucher record and in the check record.

The name of the payee must be the same on the check, in the check record, and in the voucher record. If the name of the payee is not the same in these three places, an outside associate of an employee might be receiving money under false pretenses on the basis of false invoices; also, it might indicate that some other creditor has been overpaid.

As checks are traced to the disbursements record, each entry in the record should be ticked. In addition, the checks must be ticked to indicate their examination and to prevent later re-representation. Not only must the auditor determine that all listed outstanding checks were of proper amount, but he must also determine that there were no checks outstanding which were not listed at any time and which have been presented since. This is done before the engagement is closed and after the checks have cleared at the cutoff date.

If a check is for less than a check record entry, the cashier has a bank balance in excess of his book balance and is in a position whereby the writing of an unrecordecd check will correct the discrepancy but will result in embezzlement if the check is written to himself, or is made payable to a fictitious creditor, or if an endorsement is forged by the cashier.

The auditor must be familiar with the names and signature of persons delegated to sign checks. An auditor is not responsible for the detection of forged checks; if signatures clearly are improper, the attention of the client should be directed to that fact.

If the audit is started after the close of the period, disbursements for the interim between the end of the fiscal period and the date of the audit should be verified to be certain of the balance at the end of the fiscal period and to ascertain that a period-end shortage did not exist.

Where the client is both a debtor and a creditor with respect to one party, a net check may be issued for the balance of the contratrans-actions. In these cases, the auditor must compare the paid check with the disbursements record and must also reconcile the related entries in the cash receipts records to ascertain the correct amount of the check.

Proper endorsement implies that a transaction has been completed in the intended manner. Endorsements should be test-examined, and questionable endorsements should be investigated. In those instances where paid checks are not endorsed or are improperly endorsed, they should be returned to the bank for correction. There is disagreement as to the advisability of attempting to review endorsements, on the basis that all endorsements are guaranteed by the banks involved. However, there are many instances where the examination of endorsements has led to the conclusion that such examination was worth the effort. The majority of checks are endorsed for deposit, and the auditor should satisfy himself of the propriety of the disbursement if endorsements are for other than deposit—as exemplified by small retailers when they pay wholesalers.

Double endorsements should be examined, particularly when the checks are made payable to individuals and the second endorsement is that of a company employee. It is most unusual for business firms to endorse checks received to another party; a check may be issued in the name of a regular creditor for the payment of a fictitious invoice or in duplicate payment of a legitimate invoice. If a check is endorsed in blank with a rubber stamp, or if it is endorsed to another party, both endorsements should be investigated and supporting evidence of the underlying transaction examined; the fact that there is more than one endorsement should place the auditor on the alert. If checks are issued in the name of two parties, both endorsements must be present.

ILLUSTRATION. Grain growers often have crop-mortgage loans with credit-granting agencies. A flour mill issues grain-purchase drafts. One grain-purchase draft was issued to a producer *and* to the Farm Security Administration; it passed through two banks without the Farm Security Administration endorsement. Investigation showed that the producer had intentionally by-passed the Farm Security Administration. The first bank handling the draft was forced to pay the Farm Security Administration $2,000. Eventually, the bank collected from the producer, but with considerable expense and inconvenience.

To summarize, paid checks must be examined for consecutive numbering, dates, payee, signatures, bank paid dates, and endorsements. This usually is done at the time the checks are traced to the disbursements records, where payee, dates, and amounts must agree.

Determine Proper Receipts and Disbursements Cutoff. An auditor must ascertain that all cash received and disbursed up to the end of the fiscal period has been entered in the cash records before they are closed for the period. Cash receipts entered on remittance lists and held until the succeeding period will be disclosed when bank reconciliations are prepared. Cash receipt and disbursement transactions made after the close of the fiscal year must not be shown as transactions of the year under examination if financial statements are to be proper for that year.

Some companies will hold open the cash receipts and disbursements records, or either of them, for a few days after the end of the period. The intent in such instances is to present a more favorable cash position, or a larger net income, or a smaller accounts payable position. In some cases, checks are prepared payable to creditors and entered as cash disbursements, with no intention of mailing the checks for several days after the end of the period; the auditor should reverse these entries.

Cash investments made at the close of the year by proprietors have the effect of increasing current assets and capital. If these investments are withdrawn immediately after the beginning of the new year, the intent is obviously one of "window dressing" the balance sheet, and the auditor must correct the period-end statements. The auditor also must watch current ratios and their manipulation, especially when bond indentures require the maintenance of specified minimum ratios. In his work papers and in the financial statements, the auditor will show the true cash position at the close of the period, just as though the cash records had been promptly closed and no transactions entered which had as their objective the alteration of the statements.

Compare Daily Receipts Entries with Duplicate Deposit Tickets, Bank Statements, Invoices, Cash Register Tapes, Sales Slips, and so forth. Assuming that all cash receipts are deposited in daily total received, selected duplicate deposit tickets are compared with the total of corresponding sales slips (or corrected cash register tapes, or duplicate copies of paid invoices, or with controlled remittance lists) and with the entries in the cash receipts record and sales record and with the bank statement. An important point to be remembered is that the entries in the cash receipts record might agree with the bank statement credits, but the cash deposited might be short of the amount received. Duplicate deposit tickets should be footed unless they are definitely controlled, since they might be underfooted to agree with an understated Cash Receipts debit, thus leaving a bank balance in excess of the ledger balance and thereby paving the way for the execution of an authorized disbursement.

If a cash register is used to record sales, cash register tapes are compared with the daily (or weekly or monthly) entries in the sales records—on a test basis. The sales should be recorded as the corrected total of the register tapes, shortages or overages being charged or credited to a Cash Short or Over account. The system of internal control must be watched in order to judge its effectiveness.

The auditor must be certain that cash deposited (according to the records) on the last day of the fiscal period actually was deposited in the bank if the bank has not credited the deposit according to the bank statement. If fraud exists in the manipulation of cash receipts, receipts will be deposited without recording them in the cash records; thus, a shortage is covered by bringing the cash in the bank into agreement with the cash according to the records. Therefore, duplicate deposit tickets for the last several days of the period should be compared with the bank statement and compared with the entries in the cash receipts record to ascertain that all receipts agree with deposits and to ascertain the existence or nonexistence of lapping. A lapse of more than one day plus holidays may lead to the discovery of lapping. When receipts are banked and not recorded toward the close of the period in order to cover a shortage, they will be recorded early in the following period, thus subsequently leaving short the cash balance in the bank.

All receipts for several days after the end of the period should be traced into the bank. If cash receipts are entered as of the end of the year but were received in the new year, the auditor should reverse the entries; otherwise, an inflated year-end cash position is shown.

ILLUSTRATION.   The bookkeeper held the cash receipts record open to January 5, 1976, and recorded all receipts through that date as December 31, 1975 receipts. The bookkeeper claimed that he was so pressed for time that he did not have the opportunity to bank the receipts until January 6, 1976. A confirmation of the receivables proved that all receipts recorded to January 5, 1976, were open at December 31, 1975. The auditor reversed the entries and showed a bank overdraft of $18,000 at December 31, 1975.

The test period for tracing deposits into the bank depends upon the circumstances of the audit and the effective control over cash receipts. Normally, approximately one month's transactions should be traced. For additional months, the auditor should compare total monthly receipts with the total deposits on the bank statements. It must be remembered that the comparison of the monthly total receipts of the footed cash record with the deposits as shown in the bank statement shows only that the two sets of figures either are in agreement or are not in agreement.

In auditing receipts by tracing accounts receivable credit postings, a systematic test pattern must be developed which may be followed from year to year. Either a block of the accounts may be selected or the test may be on a random sample basis. If a verification is made of a selected block of the accounts in one year, the pattern might be so developed that all accounts receivable in the ledger will be verified over a few years.

In tests of this nature, many auditors believe that it is advisable not to tick ledger and cash records entries so that employees of the client will not realize which sections were tested—either on a block or any other sample basis. The view is based on the assumption that if a dishonest employee realized which sections were tested and if he expected that different sections would be tested in succeeding audits, he would operate his false entries through the sections recently tested. However, if the test is on a random sample basis, an employee could not possibly guess where the test would fall; therefore, there is no objection to ticking the tested items. The audit code legend need not be divulged to the client, so that the employees would not know the meaning of the particular markings used in the accounts receivable and cash records.

In accordance with the examination of original records, the cash receipts and disbursements records should be footed and the postings traced to the general ledger and the subsidiary ledger accounts. Distributions of cash receipts and cash disbursements to proper revenue, receivable, expense, payable, and other accounts should be verified.

Examine the Treatment of Customers' Checks Returned by Banks. When a check of a customer, deposited in a bank, is returned by the bank to the depositor with an attached notation "Account Closed," "Not Sufficient Funds," or "No Such Account," that check should serve as the basis of an accounting entry charging Accounts Receivable and crediting Cash. Some companies use a special account—Checks Returned by Bank—for returned checks so that the items may be closely followed. The maker of a returned check should be notified at once of the action of the bank. Improper treatment may lead to confusion or to fraud.

ILLUSTRATION.   A bank returned a check to a depositor with the notation N.S.F. The depositor's accountant charged Accounts Receivable and credited Cash; he then called the maker, who told him to redeposit the check in five days. In the interval, the accountant extracted an equal amount from cash receipts; he then redeposited the check but made no entry. Later, he charged the account receivable to the allowance for doubtful accounts. The auditor traced the transaction and called for the N.S.F. check but was told that it had been destroyed. A request to the marker and the tracing of the entries on the bank statement disclosed the fraud.

The auditor should request his client that the banks notify him directly of all unpaid checks from the balance sheet date to the conclusion of the audit. This is necessary not only to examine the treatment of returned unpaid checks but also to detect kiting.

Compare Undeposited Checks with Data from Cash Remittance Lists and with Entries in the Cash Receipts Record. In order to ascertain the validity of the checks on hand, undeposited checks must be compared with the current remittance lists—if remittance lists are used.

ILLUSTRATION.   Among the checks on hand is one of current date for $500, apparently from a customer. A comparison of the checks with the remittance lists fails to disclose receipt of this check. It had been prepared by the cashier to cover a shortage. The cashier had intended to destroy it when it was returned by the bank and to substitute another fictitious check for it.

Cash receipts records must be examined to ascertain that undeposited company collection checks have been recorded as cash receipts. If they are not recorded, they may have been used to cover a shortage.

ILLUSTRATION. A company did not prepare remittance lists. A comparison of the checks on hand with the entries in the cash receipts record fails to disclose entry for a check of $900. The cashier was hopeful that the shortage of $900 would not be discovered if he purposely failed to record the receipt.

An auditor must be certain that all cash available for deposit at the end of the period actually is deposited; this is accomplished by comparing the subsequent bank statement and the bank-stamped duplicate deposit tickets with the cash receipts entries and the cash to be deposited. In examining the bank statement, the auditor must watch for deposits subsequently charged back by the bank. If false cash receipts entries were made to "window dress" a cash position and sales, supported by the deposit of a fictitious check, or if the cashier had misappropriated customer remittances and had placed a covering fictitious check in the bank, and if the fictitious checks were drawn on banks located at distant points, several days might elapse before the checks were charged back to the depositing client.

Occasionally, when the cash is counted, an amount in excess of the required amount appears. This may be the result of failure to record a receipt, or it may be intentional. In any event, the cause of the excess amount should be determined.

ILLUSTRATION. A tabulation of the cash on hand indicated an overage of $200. Matching the cash receipts with the entries in the cash receipts record failed to show the source of the $200, and all checks on hand matched entries in the cash receipts record. Therefore, before a bank reconciliation had been prepared, the cash was proved out of balance by $200. Later, when accounts receivable confirmations were requested, one customer replied that he had paid $200 and agreed to send a photo-copy of his paid check. The cashier intended to extract $200 cash but was surprised before he could do so.

List Checks Payable to the Order of Cash, Bearer, Payroll, Banks, Officers, and Unusual Creditors. All checks made payable to the order of the above listed—known and unknown—should be listed and investigated, endorsements examined, and the purpose for which the checks were issued fully vouched into the records.

There is no reason for preparing a check payable to the order of "Cash" or "Bearer"; however, checks *are* so prepared, especially when funds are advanced on the personal accounts of officers, who then cash them from available funds. The proper accounting procedure is to make the check payable to the officer, have him endorse it, and then cash it. When cash is given officers and charged to their personal accounts, the auditor should have each officer examine his account and approve it in ink.

ILLUSTRATION.   The vice-president in charge of sales travels extensively; he maintains a Personal account which has no relationship to the traveling expenses incurred; the balance of this account is offset against his bonus at the end of each year. When he requisitions money for personal use, he orders that the checks be drawn to "Cash," cashed out of available funds, and charged to his Personal account. When he travels, he follows the same procedure but orders the withdrawn money charged to the Travel Expense account. A voucher is given him for each personal withdrawal; he places these vouchers in his desk. The auditor examined all checks drawn to the order of "Cash" for the vice-president's personal use and for his traveling expenses; the checks charged to his Personal account were compared with the vouchers given the vice-president. Three vouchers were issued at dates when the vice-president was traveling at distant points. The cashier-bookkeeper admitted that he had withdrawn money for himself and had placed the vouchers in the vice-president's desk; the total involved was $1,200.

Checks drawn for payroll should be compared with the periodic net cash payroll, as expressed in the original payroll record. If a fund is maintained for paying terminated employees, one of two situations may prevail: (*a*) the fund may be separately reimbursed; or (*b*) the net cash payroll may include the amount already paid terminated employees, in which case the auditor must ascertain that the excess in the payroll check was transferred to the fund for terminated employees.

ILLUSTRATION.   A company maintains a fund for payroll advances and for the payment of terminated personnel. Employee No. 144 severed his employment and was paid the wages due him from this fund. At the next regular payroll date, Employee No. 144 was included in the regular payroll; a check was prepared for him. Later, the fund custodian obtained this final check, forged an endorsement, cashed it at a grocery store, and—in reimbursing the fund—charged the wages of Employee No. 144 to an expense account.

In connection with non-payroll checks made payable to the order of employees, the auditor must exercise care in the examination of the records for the first several days of the period after the balance sheet date. Occasionally, when employees are indebted to a company, they will issue their personal checks to eliminate their indebtedness at the end of the period. Immediately after the opening of the new period, they will reinstate their loan by drawing a company check. Where the intent is obviously to misstate a true situation, the auditor should reverse the year-end entries and in the financial statements show the loan or advance as a receivable.

List and Investigate Checks Long Outstanding.   Checks outstanding for more than two months should be separately listed by the auditor and reported to the proper officer of the client. The payees of long-out-standing checks should be notified of their nonpresentation. If a duplicate check is issued, payment must be stopped on the original check; the auditor must be certain that accounting entries were not duplicated when the duplicate check was issued.

If checks are outstanding for a considerable time and if payment is stopped at the bank and a duplicate check not issued, the checks should be written back into the accounts by a debit to Cash and a credit to a liability account or to an income account. Some accountants prefer one credit, some another. The authors prefer a credit to nonoperating income, because usually the sums involved are not large and a special liability therefore need not be created; also, an income usually is realized. In some instances, however, an investigation of outstanding checks proves that the checks never were mailed; therefore, a liability exists.

ILLUSTRATION. The importance of investigating long-outstanding checks may be exemplified as follows: Among the outstanding checks at October 31, 1976 were three checks issued as follows:

January 10, 1976	$18.60
February 18, 1976	24.30
April 9, 1976	13.20
Total.	$56.10

The cashier decided to appropriate the $56.10; he eliminated the three checks from the outstanding list, which placed his bank balance $56.10 above the Cash ledger account balance. He then prepared a check payable to "Cash" for that amount, cashed it from available funds, marked the check "Void" in the cash disbursements record, and then claimed that the check must have been destroyed in the office. The auditor followed the reconciliation procedure illustrated on page 358 and was out of balance $56.10; he then compared checks with the bank statement and discovered one bank statement debit for $56.10.

Verify Cash in Foreign Banks and Branches. Cash in foreign banks, and branches should be converted to domestic dollars at the balance sheet date, using the current rate of exchange at that date. If the domestic dollar is not at par at the balance sheet date, it will be at a premium, or it will be at a discount. If the dollar is at a premium, the loss should be shown as "other" expense in the income statement (or charged to the allowance, below). If the dollar is at a discount with the result that the dollar value of the foreign funds is greater than the book value, the appreciation should not be shown as income but should be credited to an account entitled Allowance for Foreign Exchange Fluctuations.

Investigate Bank Overdrafts. Occasionally, bank overdrafts occur at the end of the period. The overdraft may actually exist in the bank, or it may only be an apparent overdraft on the records of the client; in the latter case, it is the result of liquidating liabilities in anticipation of cash receipts to be deposited in time to cover the checks issued in payment of the liabilities. If the checks have not been mailed, the auditor should charge Cash and credit the proper liability; if the checks have been mailed, they must be treated as outstanding, whether or not a true overdraft is thereby created.

Test Discounts. As indicated in Chapters 10 and 11, the auditor should test the cash receipts records to determine that sales discounts and transportation allowances are not overstated and that cash has not been removed from cash receipts to cover the overstated discount.

ILLUSTRATION. The sales discount terms of a company are uniformly 2/10, n/30. An examination of the cash receipts record leads to the investigation of the following discounts:

Item	Cash Dr.	Sales Discount Dr.	Accounts Receivable Cr.
1	$1,184.46	$ 62.34	$1,246.80
2	829.44	34.56	864.00
3	3,317.50	102.60	3,420.10

Remittance lists are compared with the Cash debit entries; and the discovery is made that item 1 was paid at a two percent discount but recorded as five percent, that item 2 was paid at a two percent discount but recorded as four percent, and that item 3 was paid at a two percent discount but recorded as three percent. The total of the recorded discounts is $199.50, and the discounts taken are $110.61; the theft of $88.89 was covered by extracting cash from cash receipts.

A discount taken in excess of the regularly granted amount does not necessarily indicate theft if the customer exceeded his privilege and if the client permitted the excessive discount. In such instances, the auditor should request an official approval of these excess discounts. If customers take discounts after the discount period and if the client does not object to the procedure, there is no action to be taken. It is simply an abused privilege.

Discounts earned by the client must be investigated for the possibility of deliberate understatement compared with the amount earned and the extraction of cash of equal amount from cash receipts.

Test for Lapping. Evidences of lapping may be watched for in connection with the audit of cash or of accounts receivable. As pointed out, lapping is practiced in connection with the accounting for customer remittances. When lapping is practiced, the guilty person normally exercises special care to be certain that the cash bank balances agree with the cash ledger balances so that a surprise count will not uncover a discrepancy between the two. The guilty person, therefore, always is certain that each deposit ticket *in total* equals the recorded receipts *in total*.

If the amount of a lapping shortage is to be reduced, either currency or a personal check of the defaulting person must be deposited. If a remittance deposited is greater than the amount of the lapping shortage, the difference must be stolen—or an account other than Accounts Receivable credited—or the ledger balance and the bank balance will again be out of agreement.

To detect lapping, bank deposit tickets in their *detail* must be matched with entries in the cash receipts record. Failure to record a bank deposit in the cash receipts record is indicative of the lapping process. Later, there will be an entry in the cash receipts record and no matching amount on a deposit ticket. From Illustration 12–9, the reader will ascertain that a matching of deposit tickets with cash receipts entries would reveal the irregularities.

Test for Kiting. Kiting was explained in Chapter 4. The auditor must be certain that paid checks and checks returned because of insufficient funds have not been made accessible to any employee who had the opportunity to overstate a bank balance temporarily through the deposit of a fictitious check.

Checks representing interbank transfers of funds should be investigated in order to detect the possibility of kiting. When a check is drawn on one bank and deposited in another bank, the entry crediting the bank on which the check is drawn will be omitted if kiting exists. Therefore, when there is a transfer of funds, the Cash credit portion of the entry must be examined and matched with the offsetting bank deposit.

ILLUSTRATION. On December 31, 1975, the cashier deposits in the City Bank a check for $10,000; the check was drawn on the State Bank in another city. No entry is made for the deposit or for the withdrawal until late in January, 1976. Because the check did not clear the State Bank until January 3, 1976, and because the bank balances actually were $10,000 short, the bank balances at December 31, 1975, are brought into agreement with the ledger account balances.

To detect kiting, the auditor should compare end-of-the-period deposits—according to the bank statement—with cash charges and credits in the client's records. A surprise count and reconciliation of cash at a date later than the end of the period also will reveal the practice.

It is possible that management may be involved in kiting. If management desired to present a padded cash balance and a padded Sales account, it could order that a check be drawn on one bank and deposited in another bank, and that the accounting department charges the Cash account and credits the Sales (or some other revenue) account, but that no entry be made crediting any Cash account. If this occurs, it will be very close to the end of a period when financial statements are to be prepared.

ILLUSTRATION 12–9
LAPPING DEMONSTRATION

Date	Composition	Customer	Actual Collection	Cash Receipts Record Entry		Deposit Ticket	
May 1	Currency............	A	$ 300.00				
	Check..............	B	246.21	B	$ 246.21	B	$ 246.21
	Check..............	C	195.30	C	195.30	C	195.30
	Total, May 1		$ 741.51		$ 441.51		$ 441.51
2	Currency............	D	$ 150.00				
	Check..............	E	247.10	E	$ 247.10	E	$ 247.10
	Check..............	F	869.20	F	869.20	F	869.20
	Total, May 2		$1,266.30		$1,116.30		$1,116.30
3	Currency............	G	$ 249.00			G	$ 128.85
	Check..............	H	321.15			H	321.15
	No collection			A	$ 300.00		
	No collection			E	150.00		
	Total, May 3		$ 570.15		$ 450.00		$ 450.00
4	Currency............	I	$ 198.00			I	$ 10.81
	Check..............	J	465.18			J	465.18
	Check..............	K	111.11	K	$ 111.11	K	$ 111.11
	Check..............	L	94.16			L	94.16
	No collection			G	249.00		
	No collection			H	$ 321.15		
	Total, May 4		$ 868.45		$ 681.26		$ 681.26

The misappropriated amounts may be summarized as follows:

Date	Collections	Receipts Entered	Misappro-priated
May 1............	$ 741.51	$ 441.51	$300.00
May 2............	1,266.30	1,116.30	150.00
May 3............	570.15	450.00	120.15
May 4............	868.45	681.26	187.19
			$757.34

Examine Cash Receipts for Bona Fide Nature. In the verification of cash receipts and disbursements, in addition to the procedures discussed in Chapter 10 and in this chapter, care must be exercised to ascertain that the recorded receipts are actual receipts. If the control over cash is inadequate or if currency disbursements are made from cash receipts, the audit of the receipts is more difficult; and the proof of posting accuracy should be conducted with extreme care, since the objective is to discover account credits which are not supported by cash debits.

Cash from extraneous sources must be examined because of the possibility of stealing money from nonrecurring transactions, and to be certain of the proper account distribution for the credits.

Vouch Disbursements in Cash Records for Debits to Accounts Other than Accounts Payable. When the system of accounting is such that entries other than debits to Accounts Payable are recorded in the cash disbursements records, the other disbursements should be examined for authenticity of invoice, approval for payment, and correctness of recorded amount in order to ascertain the validity of the transactions.

The procedures for the verification of cash disbursements were discussed in Chapter 10. A summary of the proof of disbursements may be prepared as shown below:

	Debit	Credit
Vouchers payable at beginning of period, per ledger . . .		$ 10,000
Credit to Vouchers Payable for period		100,000
Deduct: Amount due as debtor in settlement of amount		
due as creditor	$ 3,000	
Vouchers settled by notes	5,000	
Purchase discounts taken	2,000	
Unpaid vouchers at close of period, as shown by		
reconciliation of vouchers payable with balance		
per general ledger	8,000	
Cash disbursements for period, per ledger	· 92,000	
	$110,000	$110,000

SECTION VI: COMPENSATING BALANCES ARRANGEMENTS

Compensating balances, and other credit arrangements involve the dual role of cash in bank and an amount owed to the same bank. Compensating balances arrangements between a borrower and a lending bank come into existence when money is borrowed or a line of credit is established at a bank. Normally, the terms of such an arrangement are to the effect that the borrower must maintain a cash balance at least equal to an agreed percentage of the amount borrowed, or a cash balance of an agreed upon dollar amount. In accordance with the agreement, the cash balance may be in a checking account, savings account(s), or certificate(s) of deposit.

While compensating balances arrangements affect both assets and liabilities, the subject is treated at this point because (1) confirmation requests to a bank are necessary—in a form different than that shown in Illustration 12–5, (2) the confirmation request must be sent to the lending officer (or other designated official) of the bank and (3) the SEC in Accounting Series Release No. 148 (which is an amendment to Regulations S–X) now requires that financial statements filed with the SEC disclose compensating balances arrangements and short-term borrowing arrangements.

Accounting Series Release No. 148 suggests that the confirmation of credit arrangements be made separately from the customary bank confirmation because normally this confirmation of credit arrangements cannot be processed by bank personnel who handle a standard bank confirmation request. The confirmation letter (See Illustration 12–10 for an example) should be sent to the proper officer of the lending bank. All information should be supplied by the borrower to the bank prior to mailing the confirmation request. The confirmation request should be *verified by the auditor and be mailed by him*. The letter should be sent on the client's stationery, because the client must sign the letter.

In a balance sheet, only those amounts of compensating balances which

ILLUSTRATION 12–10
BANK CREDIT ARRANGEMENT CONFIRMATION LETTER

PATTON, INC.
Cincinnati, Ohio 45202

January 5, 1976

Mr. Harry Haver, Vice President--Loans
Eighth National Bank
Cincinnati, Ohio 45202

Dear Mr. Haver:

Financial statements filed with the Securities and Exchange Commission now must contain disclosure of certain information regarding credit arrangements, including compensating balances. Accounting Series Release No. 148, issued by the SEC contains the following:

> "A compensating balance is defined as that portion of any demand deposit (or any time deposit or certificate of deposit) maintained by a corporation (or by any other person on behalf of the corporation) which constitutes support for existing borrowing arrangements of the corporation (or any other person) with a lending institution. Such arrangements should include both outstanding borrowings and the assurance of future credit availability."

In connection with the periodic audit of the financial statements of Patton, Inc., as of December 31, 1975, please confirm the following information as of the dates indicated by signing and mailing the attached copy of this letter directly to our auditor, Morton and Town, Certified Public Accountants, Carew Central Towers, Cincinnati, Ohio 45202.

A. LINES OF CREDIT

   1. The Company has available at your Bank a line of credit totaling $50,000,000, the terms of which are set forth in a communication of June 3, 1975. This line is withdrawable at the option of the Bank.

ILLUSTRATION 12–10 (*Continued*)

2. Related debt outstanding at the close of business December 31, 1975 is $30,000,000.
3. The amount of the unused line of credit at December 31, 1975 is $20,000,000.
4. The rate of interest at the close of business December 31, 1975 is 9.5% per year.
5. The arrangement does not state that this line of credit supports commercial paper or other borrowing agreements.

B. COMMITMENTS

1. The Company has a commitment from the Bank for $80,000,000 in borrowed money, and the terms of the commitment are set forth in the agreement dated September 23, 1975.
2. Related debt outstanding December 31, 1975: None.
3. Amount of this unused commitment December 31, 1975: $80,000,000.
4. Interest rate December 31, 1975: Not applicable.
5. Other related fees or commitment: $\frac{1}{2}$ of 1% per year on the average daily unused amount.

C. COMPENSATING BALANCE ARRANGEMENTS

1. There were (or were not) compensating balance arrangements under the line of credit as of December 31, 1975.
2. Withdrawal of the compensating balances was not legally restricted at December 31, 1975.
3. The terms of the compensating balances arrangements December 31, 1975 were as follows:
   The Company is expected to maintain an average compensating balance of 20% of the debt outstanding under its line of credit as determined from the bank records, adjusted for the estimated average uncollected funds.
4. The Company uses a factor of 1.5 business days for uncollected funds in determining its compliance with compensating balances requirements.
5. There were no changes in the compensating balances arrangements during 1975 and through the date of this letter.

D. COMPENSATING BALANCES ARRANGEMENTS BY OR FOR OTHERS

1. During 1975 and through the date of this letter, no compensating balances were maintained by the Company at the bank on behalf of an affiliate or any other third party and no third party maintained compensating balances at the Bank on behalf of the Company.

E. OTHER DEBT TO THE BANK

1. On December 31, 1975 no other debt was owed by the Company to the Bank.
   Sincerely yours,

By:_____

William M. Shell

ILLUSTRATION 12–10 (*Concluded*)

CONFIRMATION

Date: January 16, 1976

Morton and Town
Certified Public Accountants
Carew Central Towers
Cincinnati, Ohio 45202

Gentlemen:

The terms of the credit arrangements with this Bank, as set forth in the preceding Bank Credit Arrangements Confirmation Letter are in agreement with
the understanding of this Bank, except as noted below.

No exceptions _____

_____

_____

Eighth National Bank

By: _____

Harry Haver, Vice President–Loans

---

are legally restricted under the terms of a credit arrangement are to
be segregated; other compensating balance arrangements are to be disclosed by financial statement footnotes. The following must also be disclosed: (1) rate of interest, (2) maximum amount of short-term borrowing outstanding at any month-end, and (3) the amount and terms of
unsecured lines of credit for short-term borrowing. Illustration 12–10
is modeled from a suggestion of the AICPA. Starting January, 1974 detailed footnotes *must* be appended to Form 10–K of the SEC explaining
all compensating balance arrangements.

SECTION VII: FINANCIAL STATEMENT CONSIDERATIONS

Cash in the Balance Sheet

For proper balance sheet presentation, under the caption of "cash on
hand and in banks" there should be included only unrestricted and freely
withdrawable deposits, cash and cash items on hand awaiting deposit,
and the cash balances in cash funds. The net cash balances in unrestricted

cash funds may be shown separately, but acceptable practice is to combine these items with the cash on hand and in the banks.

Cash in foreign banks and branches may be included in the "cash on hand and in banks" among the current assets, at the rate of exchange prevailing at the balance sheet date, if the funds are unrestricted either by the depositor or by governmental action.

If bank funds are restricted from freedom of withdrawal brought about by deposits in closed banks, rendered judgments, bid deposits, rent deposits, deposits on contracts, funds in escrow, trust funds balances, compensating balances arrangements, and so forth, the funds should not be included in the balance sheet under the caption of "cash on hand and in banks." Each restricted amount should be shown in its proper classification in the balance sheet, with a statement of such restriction appearing as a balance sheet footnote, when necessary.

An overdraft may actually exist in a bank, or it may be only an apparent overdraft on the records of the client. If the latter, it probably is the result of paying liabilities in anticipation of cash collections to be deposited before the issued checks have cleared. If the prepared checks have not been mailed, the auditor should prepare an audit adjustment, debiting Cash and crediting Accounts Payable as of the balance sheet date.

An actual bank overdraft should be shown as a current liability. If accounts are maintained in at least two banks, an overdraft in one bank theoretically should not be offset in the balance sheet by balances in other banks. In practice, it is customary to use the principle of offset, provided the balances are freely transferable from one bank to another.

QUESTIONS

1. You have audited the financial statements of a company for several consecutive years. All petty cash vouchers and original data supporting them for 1975 were destroyed in a fire on December 31, 1975. Interim audit work had not been performed. In connection with the destroyed vouchers and data, and assuming that all other records and data were intact and that the imprest amount of the fund was $5,000, how would you proceed in your examination?

2. The Rusk Company, opens a branch in Rover, a city several hundred miles from the home office. A large petty cash fund will be required at the branch. Because of the danger involved in retaining a large cash fund at the branch, it is decided to establish the fund in a bank account in Rover. The fund is to be established in the name of the corporation, and the bank is authorized to cash checks drawn against the account by the branch cashier. Disbursements from the fund are to be supported by proper receipt and are to be sent to the home office for approval, as a basis for fund reimbursement. Do you consider this procedure proper?

3. A company employs seven salesmen. Advances for travel expenses are made to the salesmen from a cash fund after proper approval by the sales manager. When a salesman returns from a trip, the cash not spent is returned to the fund custodian, who reviews the expense reports of the salesmen and files them. When the fund is in need of reimbursement, expenditures are classified and entered in a voucher register, a check is prepared for the net cash disbursed, and the fund is replenished.

    a)   Wherein is the procedure at fault?
    b)   What principle of cash fund control has been violated?
    c)   Would the procedure be proper if the salesmen's expense reports were attached to the reimbursement voucher?
    d)   Suggest a system that would afford proper control.

4. In an examination of cash a CPA watches for signs of "lapping" and "kiting."

    a)   Define (1) "lapping" and (2) "kiting."
    b)   List the audit procedures that would uncover (1) lapping and (2) kiting.
    c)   In his examination of financial statements a CPA evaluates the quality of the accounting evidence available to him. An audit procedure that *may* be employed in the examination of cash is to submit duplicate deposit slips to the depository banks to be authenticated.
    (1)   Discuss the reliability of authenticated duplicate deposit slips as accounting evidence.
    (2)   What additional audit procedures are avaliable to a CPA to verify the detail of deposits?

                                                       (AICPA, adapted)

5. In his examination of the financial statements of Kurby, Inc. for the year ended June 30, 1976, an auditor performed several cutoff tests.

    a)   (1)   What is meant by a "cutoff test"?
           (2)   Why must cutoff tests be made for both the beginning and the end of the audit period?
    b)   The auditor obtains a July 10, 1976 Kurby, Inc., bank statement directly from the bank. How will he use this cutoff statement:
           (1)   In his examination of the June 30, 1976 bank reconciliation?
           (2)   To obtain other information for the audit?

6. *a*)   Under what circumstances might valuation problems arise in connection with the audit of cash in general?
    b)   Realized and/or unrealized gains and losses may arise in connection with cash—especially for international corporations. Ignore price-level changes, and explain the nature of these unrealized and/or realized gains and losses in connection with cash.

7. The fiscal year of the Nile Company is June 30. On June 26, the company received a large check from one of its regular customers in an amount equal to 20 percent of Nile's total assets and 40 percent of its total current assets. On June 27, Nile mailed the check to its bank for deposit. The check never reached the bank. On July 15, the customer stopped payment on the check and issued a duplicate check; this check was traced to the bank by the auditor.

By confirmation and inquiry, the auditor for Nile satisfied himself that the original check had been received and was mailed to the bank. It was impossible to determine at what point in the transmission the check was lost. Would you carry the amount of the lost check as a part of the June 30 cash in bank balance or would you consider it to be a portion of the accounts receivable balance? Present reasons for your answer.

8. In the audit of cash, what significance would you attribute to each of the following:
   a) An unentered bank check for $10,000, drawn December 31, 1975, on the First National Bank, and a deposit of the same amount on the same day in the Second National Bank?
   b) Offsetting items appearing on a bank statement but not appearing in the cash records?
   c) A bank statement charge for a check but no corresponding paid check?

9. A fidelity bonding company asks you to perform a cash audit for one of its insured customers for the three-year period ended, June 30, 1976. You discover a disbursement for "Rent, June, 1973, $2,500," on July 6, 1973. As a voucher, you are shown a check dated July 6, 1973, payable to the order of the landlord for $2,500, endorsed with a rubber stamp and stamped "Paid" by the client's bank. One rental payment of $2,500 is to be made each month.

   State, with your reasons, whether you would accept this check as adequate evidence that the payment was made as recorded; and if not, what course would you adopt?

   (AICPA, adapted)

10. A company operates retail sales stores in several cities. Each store collects its own receivables, and each store maintains a local bank account in which all cash sales money and all cash from the collection of receivables is deposited intact daily. On Monday of each week, the banked collections of the preceding week are transferred to the home office by a check drawn on the local bank; no other checks are drawn on this account. Cash receipts and disbursements records are maintained and copies are retained by each store; all other original accounting records are maintained at the home office.

    As a part of your periodic audit, you will include an examination of cash transfers betwen the stores and the home office. All stores will be visited.
    a) List the purposes of the audit of cash transfers.
    b) Name the audit procedures necessary for an examination of the cash transfers only, from each store to the home office.

11. During the course of an audit of a small company, you were working in the office of the treasurer, who had sole control over cash receipts and disbursements. While you were counting the cash and examining the related records, the treasurer watched you and several times asked if he might be of assistance.

    You discovered that the cash receipts record had been underfooted and that several receipts had not been deposited. What action would you take? What are the reasons for your answer?

12. A company has bank accounts in New York, Cincinnati, and Los Angeles. Transfers of funds between these banks are common, depending upon where the cash balances are plentiful and where they are low. If you were in Los Angeles, how would you proceed to verify the balances at a given date?

13. In tracing checks to the cash disbursements record, you found a series of 10 checks unentered in the last month of the year under review, none of which has been returned by the bank. Inquiry reveals that these checks were signed in blank by the treasurer and given to a vice-president who was making a business trip which ended two weeks after the close of the fiscal year. He had requested the signed checks, which would then only require his countersignature, to avoid carrying a large amount of cash customarily expended on such trips for traveling expenses.

Outline or briefly explain the following:

a) Additional auditing procedures to be followed in view of this practice, and

b) Recommendations you would make to your client to accommodate the vice-president in an acceptable accounting manner.

14. A client presented the cash reconciliation shown below. How should it be verified?

Cash per client records		$200,000
Cash, per bank.	$188,000	
Undeposited checks.	30,000	
	$218,000	
Deduct: Checks outstanding.	20,000	
	$198,000	
Add: Cash in registers	2,000	$200,000

15. In connection with the examination of cash and cash transactions, outline a test audit procedure of cash records to reveal the following irregularities:

a) Improper cash borrowing during the period under review which have been restored before the close of the period, and

b) Misappropriation of accounts receivable collections at the close of the period by kiting or by overlapping receipts.

16. You have prepared bank reconciliations. They agree with those prepared by the client. You compared all checks with the check register. No checks were outstanding at the reconciliation date. You decided not to trace cash receipts according to the cash receipts records into the bank statement because the cashier knew of the audit in advance. Other than abstracting cash and underfooting his cash receipts records, what might the cashier have done to conceal a shortage of $1,000 at the end of the period?

17. In an audit of the records of a manufacturing company, what documentary evidences (a) of authorization for acquisition or payment and (b)

of correctness of amount would constitute satisfactory evidence in the following instances?

a) A buliding purchased for cash.

b) Commissions paid to salesmen.

c) Wages paid to factory employees.

d) Raw material inventories purchased.

18. The Lexon Company maintains bank accounts in Boston and San Diego. All payrolls, vouchers, and invoices must be approved by proper departmental heads for payment; they are again approved by the treasurer, who turns them over to the cashier for check preparation. All checks require the signatures of the cashier and the treasurer. At the end of each month, the cashier obtains the bank statements and prepares the bank reconciliations. He then gives the reconciliations, bank statements, paid checks, and other data to the treasurer, who reviews and approves the reconciliations. All checks are serially numbered.

The cashier embezzled $25,000 on December 17, 1975, by drawing a check payable to his own order on the Boston Bank; the countersignature of the treasurer was forged by the cashier. The cashier did not enter the check in the disbursements record. On December 31, 1975, the cashier drew a check for $25,000 on the San Diego bank, payable to the order of the Boston bank; the treasurer's signature was obtained by the explanation that funds were being transferred. The cashier then deposited the check in the Boston bank on December 31, 1975. No entries were made in the records.

When the cashier obtained the December bank statement and the paid checks from the Boston bank, he removed and destroyed the check payable to himself. The treasurer did not discover the shortage.

During the course of your audit of the company for the year 1975, which you started on January 31, 1976, you discover the embezzlement.

Describe three methods of verifying cash transactions and balances by the use of which this type of fraud should be discovered.

19. A client has several accounts in one bank. One of these accounts is restricted to weekly payroll disbursements and is operated on an imprest basis. The account should always reconcile to a zero balance; and for this reason, your client has not reconciled the account at any time during the year under review. The account does not appear in the general ledger.

In the course of the audit of the payroll, you examine all paid checks returned by the bank during the eight weeks following the balance sheet date. Included among these are checks totaling $2,600, all of which are dated prior to the balance sheet date. The paymaster also has on hand unclaimed payroll checks for $200 dated prior to the balance sheet. The bank statement shows a balance of $2,300 at the balance sheet date.

Assuming that there is no fraud involved and that no errors in footing have been made, present three possible explanations of the situation indicated by the figures. For each explanation, set forth the procedures you would follow to determine if the explanation is correct.

(AICPA)

20. A buys its raw material from B. After purchases reach $10,000 each month, B rebates 10 percent of the net purchase price to all of its customers, including A. B mails the rebate checks on the 10th of the following month. A's purchases have exceeded the base figure in every month of the past year. You, as auditor for A, can find no record of the receipt of the cash rebates. The cashier informs you that the treasurer deposits these checks each month in "A, Private" bank account and that no entries are made in the records of the company for the rebate. The confirmation you have received from the bank shows "A, Private, $32,000," which agrees with your computation of the discount. What will you do?

21. You were engaged to audit the financial statements of a client that does not deposit its receipts intact and that pays some expenses out of cash receipts. You found it impossible to visit the client's offices until January 20, 1976. However, you had requested the client to prepare a bank reconciliation as of the balance sheet date, December 31, 1975; but the client had not complied with your request. In fact, the client had not prepared a reconciliation since December 31, 1974.

    On the morning of January 20, 1976, you counted the cash on hand, which was $4,000; and you obtained directly a bank statement as of that date, which showed a balance of $16,520; there were no outstanding checks. The balance of the Cash ledger account, after work sheet posting of the receipts and disbursements from January 1 to January 20, 1976, was $22,000, thus resulting in a discrepancy of $1,480.

    a) How would you proceed to account for this difference?

    b) As to procedure in the future, what suggestions would you offer?

22. Explain fully your understanding of compensating balances.

PROBLEMS

1. As auditor for Loom, Inc., you examined the office operating cash fund immediately after the close of business, June 30, 1976, the end of the company's fiscal year and arrived at the following fund composition:

Currency and coin	$ 552
Fund vouchers:	
Office supplies expense	288
Travel expense	120
Office equipment repairs	85
Loans to office employees.	200
A check drawn by Loom Inc., payable to the order of Gary Tret, fund custodian	600
An employee's check, returned by bank and stamped NSF	115
A sheet of paper bearing the signatures of several office employees, together with their contributions (total, $100) for a gift for a departing employee. Attached to the sheet of paper is currency of.	100
	$2,060

The Office Operating Fund general ledger account has an imprest balance of $2,000.

a) What audit adjustments should be prepared as of June 30, 1976?

b) At what amount should the cash fund be shown in the balance sheet as of June 30, 1976?

2. A surprise count of the Small Company's imprest cash fund, carried on its records at $10,000, was made on December 10, 1975.

The company acts as agent for an express company in the sale of money orders. Blank money orders are held by the Small cashier for issuance to customers upon payment of the designated amounts. Settlement with the express company is made weekly with its representative, who calls at the Small office. At that time, he collects for orders issued, accounts for unissued orders, and leaves additional blank money orders, serially numbered.

The items presented by the cashier as composing the fund follows:

Currency.		$6,950
Cashed checks.		1,000
Vouchers (made out in pencil and signed by recipients)		500
N.S.F. checks (dated July 10 and 15, 1975).		250
Copy of cash fund receipt vouchers:		
Return of traveling expense advance	$200	
Sale of money orders (Nos. 1015–21)	100	300
Blank money orders—claimed to have been purchased for $100		
each from the express company (Nos. 1022–27)		600

At the time of the count, there were also on hand unissued money orders, Nos. 1028-37.

The following day, the custodian of the fund produced vouchers aggregating $400 and explained that these vouchers had been misplaced the previous day. They were for wage advances to employees.

a) Show the proper composition of the fund as of December 10, 1975.

b) State the audit procedures necessary for the verification of the items in the fund.

3. The June bank statement of Witch Inc., showed an ending balance of $187,387. During June the bank charged back NSF checks totaling $3,056, of which $1,856 had been redeposited by June 30. Deposits in transit on June 30 were $20,400. Outstanding checks on June 30 were $60,645, including a $10,000 check which the bank had certified on June 28. On June 14, the bank charged the Witch account against the account of Walsh Inc.; the bank did not detect the error. During June, the bank collected foreign items for Witch; the proceeds were $8,684 and bank charges for this service were $19. On June 30, the adjusted cash in bank of Witch, Inc. is:

a) $149,442.

b) $159,442.

c) $147,142.

d) $158,242.

e) None of the above.

(AICPA, adapted)

4. Mr. James Coal recently acquired a controlling interest in Imports, Inc., importers. In his review of the duties of employees, Coal became aware of loose practices in check signing and the operation of a special cash fund.

    You have been engaged as the company's CPA, and Coal's first request is that you suggest a system of sound practices for the signing of checks and the operation of the special cash fund. Coal prefers not to acquire a check-signing machine.

    In addition to Coal, who is the company president, there are 20 employees including four officers. About 300 checks are drawn each month. The special cash fund has a working balance of about $500 and about $1,000 is expended from the fund each month.

    Prepare a letter to Coal, setting forth your recommendations for good internal control procedure for:

    a) Signing checks. (Coal does not want to be drawn into routine check signing duties. Assume that you decided to recommend two signatures on each check.)

    b) Operation of the special fund.

    (AICPA, adapted)

5. Nuclear Power, Inc., issues books of sight drafts to the formen of its 10 field crews. The foremen use the drafts to pay the overnight expenses of the field crews when they are away on field duty.

    The drafts are prenumbered and are limited (in printing) to expenditures not in excess of $300. The foremen prepare the drafts in duplicate and send the duplicates, and accompanying expense reports, to the general office.

    The draft duplicates are accumulated at the general office, and a voucher is prepared when there are two or three duplicates in the office. The voucher is the authority for issuing a company check for deposit in an imprest fund of $5,000 maintained at a local bank to meet the drafts as they are presented for payment. The company maintains a separate general ledger account for the fund.

    The audit of the voucher register and the cash disbursements disclosed the following information regarding sight drafts and the reimbursement of the imprest fund:

    (1) Voucher No. 10524 dated 12/31/75, paid by Check No. 10524 dated 12/31/75, for the following drafts:

Draft No.	Date	Crew No.	Explanation	Amount
6001	12/24/75	3	Expenses, 12/22–24	$160
2372	12/28/75	6	Expenses, 12/26–28	310
5304	12/30/75	7	Advance to foreman	340
Vouchers total				$810

    (2) Voucher No. 10531 dated 12/31/75, paid by Check No. 10531 dated 1/3/76, for the following drafts:

Draft No.	Date	Crew No.	Explanation	Amount
4060. . . . . .12/29/75		1	Expenses, 12/27–29	$150
1816. . . . . . 1/3/76		4	Expenses, 1/1–3	560
Voucher total.				$710

(3) Voucher No. 23 dated 1/8/76, paid by Check No. 23 dated 1/8/76, for the following vouchers:

Draft No.	Date	Crew No.	Explanation	Amount
1000. . . . . .12/31/75		9	Expenses, 12/28–31	$270
2918. . . . . .1/3/76		10	Expenses, 12/28–31	190
4061. . . . . .1/7/76		1	Expenses, 1/4–6	210
Voucher total.				$670

(4) All of the preceding vouchers were charged to Travel Expense.

(5) Examination of the imprest fund bank statement for December, the January cutoff bank statement and accompanying drafts presented for payment disclosed the following information:

   (*a*) Reimbursement Check No. 10524 was not credited on the December bank statement.

   (*b*) The bank honored Draft No. 2372 at the established maximum authorized amount.

   (*c*) Original 1975 drafts drawn by foremen but not presented to the client's bank for payment by 12/31/75 totaled $1,200. This total included all 1975 drafts itemized above except No. 4060 and No. 2372, which were deducted by the bank in December.

   a) Prepare the audit adjustment as of December 31, 1975. The December 31, 1974 bank statement shows a balance of $5,730. A supporting work paper analyzing the required adjustments should be prepared.

   b) Prepare a reconciliation of the bank statement and the financial statement figure for the imprest cash account. The first figure in your reconciliation should be the bank statement balance.

(AICPA, adapted)

6. Uniform, Inc. did not exercise adequate internal control over its cash transactions. During an audit, you found the following data concerning the cash position as of June 30, 1976. On the company's records the balance of cash on hand and in bank was $17,350. A credit of $250 for a note collected by the bank does not appear on the company's records. The bank statement balance is $13,500. Outstanding checks are as follows:

Number	Amount
1972	$520
1973	360
1974	408
1975	346

The cashier prepared the following reconciliation:

Balance per bank statement		$13,500
Deduct: Outstanding checks:		
No. 1973	$360	
No. 1974	408	
No. 1975	346	1,014
		$12,486
Add: Unrecorded credit		250
		$12,736
Add: Cash on hand (this count is correct)		4,614
Cash per company records, June 30, 1976		$17,350

a) Prepare a correct reconciliation.
b) Indicate the amount of the shortage.
c) How did the cashier attempt to conceal the shortage?

7. You started the examination of the financial statements of the Doll Company on January 20, 1976, for the year ended December 31, 1975. The Cash account balance as of December 31, 1975, is $49,440.

The cashier's December 31, 1975, cash reconciliation contained the following items:

Cash per ledger, December 31, 1975	$49,440
Cash per bank, December 31, 1975	52,819
Checks outstanding	5,065
Check of Dodd, Inc., charged by bank error on December 20, 1975; corrected by bank on January 7, 1976	150
Cash in transit, credited by bank on January 2, 1976	700

From January 2, 1976, to January 20, 1976, the date of your cash count, total cash receipts appearing in the cash records were $10,700. According to the bank statement for the period from January 2, 1976, through January 20, 1976, total deposits were $9,593.

The count of the cash and cash items on hand at the close of business on January 20, 1976, was as follows:

Currency	$485
Expense vouchers	75
Checks of customers in payment of accounts	190
	$750

After further investigation, you discover the following:

(1) On July 5, 1975, cash of $800 was received on account from a customer; the Provision for Doubtful accounts was charged and Accounts Receivable credited.

(2) On December 5, 1975, cash of $600 was received on account from a customer; Inventory was charged and Accounts Receivable credited.

(3) Cash of $700 received during 1975 was not recorded.

(4) Checks received from customers from January 2, 1976, to January 20, 1976, totaling $400, were not recorded but were deposited in the bank.

(5) In the cashier's desk, there were receipts for bills paid by customers on January 14, 1976, totaling $900; these were unrecorded and undeposited.

    a) Prepare the necessary audit adjustments for (1) through (5).
    b) Compute the correct bank balance as of December 31, 1975.
    c) Compute the cash shortage as of December 31, 1975, and up to January 20, 1976.

8. King Towers, Inc., owns an apartment complex and rents to tenants. In your audit for the year ended December 31, 1975, you verified the following data:

Prepaid rent, January 1, 1975	$ 5,000
Delinquent rent, December 31, 1975	2,000
Gross available rent for the year 1975	775,000
Space occupied by King, Inc., for its own offices	30,000
Vacancies	75,000
Uncollectible rents, 1975	1,500
Prepaid rent, December 31, 1975	7,500
Delinquent rent, January 1, 1975	3,250
Prerental deposits forfeited	1,250
Refunds to tenants	750

In order to reconcile the preceding date with the cash receipts for the year 1975, you are to prepare a schedule of cash collections for the year.

9. In connection with an audit of the financial statements of the Bell Company for the year ended December 31, 1975, the following information regarding cash has been obtained:

	Nov. 30, 1975	*Dec. 31, 1975*
(1) Balance per bank	$185,700	$193,674
(2) Balance per company records	154,826	167,598
(3) Outstanding checks	63,524	75,046

  (4) Receipts for December, 1975, according to the bank, amounted to $1,350,450; according to company records, $2,335,445.

  (5) Dishonored checks are recorded as a reduction of cash receipts, and when such checks are later redeposited, they are recorded as a regular cash receipt. Dishonored checks returned by the bank and recorded by the company amounted to $6,250 in December, 1975, and according to company records, $5,000 were redeposited. Dishonored checks recorded on the bank statements, but not on the company records until the following months, were $250 at November 30, 1975, and $2,300 at December 31, 1975.

  (6) On December 31, 1975, a $2,323 check of Ball, Inc., was charged to the Bell Company account in error.

  (7) Proceeds of a note of the King Company collected by the bank on December 10, 1975 were not entered by Bell:

Principal	$2,000
Interest	20
	$2,020
Bank collection charge	5
Net proceeds	$2,015

  (8) The company has hypothecated its accounts receivable with the bank under an agreement whereby the bank lends the company

80 percent on the hypothecated receivables. Accounting for and collecting the accounts are performed by the company, and adjustments of the loan are made from daily sales reports and daily deposits.

The bank credits the Bell account and increases the amount of the loan for 80 percent of the reported sales. Sales reports are forwarded by the company to the bank on the day following the date of sales. The bank allocates each deposit 80 percent to the payment of the loan and 20 percent to the Bell account. Thus, only 80 percent of each day's sales and 20 percent of each collection deposit are entered on the bank statement.

The company records the hypothecation of new accounts receivable (80 percent of sales) as a debit to Cash and a credit to the bank loan as of the date of sales. One hundred percent of the receivables collections is recorded as a cash receipt; 80 percent of the collections is recorded in the cash disbursements record as a payment on the loan.

In connection with the hypothecation the following facts were determined:

a) Included in the deposits in transit is cash from the hypothecation of receivables. Sales were $40,500 on November 30, 1975, and $42,250 on December 31, 1975. The balance of the deposit in transit December 31, 1975, was made up from collections of $32,110 which were entered by the company in the manner indicated above.

b) Collections on accounts receivable deposited in December other than deposits in transit totaled $1,200,000.

c) Sales for December totaled $1,450,000.

(9) Interest on the bank loan for the month of December, charged by the bank but not recorded by the company, was $6,140.

From the preceding information:

a) Prepare bank reconciliations as of November 30 and December 31, 1975, and reconciliations of cash receipts and disbursements per bank with cash receipts and disbursements according to company records for the month of December, 1975. Assume that you have satisfied yourself of the propriety of the preceding information.

b) Prepare audit adjustments to correct the Cash account as of December 31, 1975.

(AICPA, adapted)

10. During the audit of the financial statements of Rivers, Inc., for the year ended December 31, 1975, the following bank reconciliation was submitted to you by an employee of the company:

Balance per bank statement	$122,136
Outstanding checks	171,024
	$ 48,888
Deposits in transit	151,424
Balance per company records	$102,536

From the bank, you obtained the bank statement and the paid checks on January 15, 1976, for all bank transactions through January 14, 1976. According to the records of the company, checks issued from January 1, 1976, to January 15, 1976, amounted to $89,928. Checks returned by the bank on January 15 totaled $233,752. Of the checks outstanding at December 31, 1975, $38,400 were not returned by the bank with the bank statement of January 15, 1976; and of those issued, according to the records of the company, in January, 1976, $28,800 were not returned by the bank.

a)   Prepare a schedule for the preceding date.

b)   Suggest four possible explanations for the existing conditions. In each case, state your reaction, and include any appropriate audit adjustment.

(AICPA, adapted)

11.   At a year-end, bank activity for all bank accounts may be reconciled with the records for several days prior to the end of the year and for several days after the year-end in order to detect kiting. If such a reconciliation can be prepared, many detailed comparisons can be avoided.

a)   Using the data in the problem, prepare a work paper to determine kiting; and reconcile on the work paper the bank balances at the *three dates shown*, and show the bank activity for the period from December 1, 1975, to January 12, 1976.

b)   For each time on your work paper, show, by number, and separately describe, the procedures necessary to complete the audit.

c)   Prepare audit adjustments necessary at December 31, 1975.

THE OXIDE COMPANY

	November 30, 1975	December 31, 1975	January 12, 1976
Balance, bank statement	$34,442	$27,502	$36,633
Balance, company records	28,332	32,807	
Outstanding checks	8,824	9,731	4,672
Deposits in transit	3,500	4,000	2,500

	December 1–31, 1975	January 1–12, 1976
Receipts, cash record	$ 96,323	$29,250
Credits, bank statement	94,101	32,149
Disbursements, cash record	100,848	17,757
Charges, bank statement	101,041	23,018

The client obtained bank statements for November 30 and December 31, 1975, and reconciled the balances. Directly you obtained the statement of January 12, 1976, and the necessary confirmations. You have found that there are no errors in adddition or subtraction in the client's records. The following information also was obtained:

(1)   Check No. 89 for $34 cleared the bank in December as $134. This was found in proving the bank statement. The bank made the correction on January 8, 1976.

(2)   A note of $2,000, sent to the bank for collection on November

15, 1975, was collected and credited to the account on November 28, 1975, net of a collection fee of $8. The note was recorded in the cash receipts on December 21, 1975, at which date the collection fee was entered as a disbursement.

(3) The client records returned checks in red in the cash receipts record. The following checks were returned by the bank:

Customer	Amount	Returned	Recorded	Redeposited
M	$327	Dec. 6, 1975	No entries	Dec. 8, 1975
N	673	Dec. 27, 1975	Jan. 3, 1976	Jan. 15, 1976

(4) Two payroll checks for employee's vacations totaling $550 were drawn on January 3, 1976, and cleared the bank on January 8, 1976. These checks were not entered in the client's records because semimonthly payroll summaries are entered only on the 15th and the last day of each month.

(AICPA, adapted)

12. From the information presented in the problem:

 a) Prepare a reconciliation of the Bear Company's bank account as of December 31, 1975.

 b) Prepare one journal entry to adjust the Bear Company's records to reflect the correct bank balances at December 31, 1975. In auditing the records of Bear, you obtained the bank statement, paid checks, and other memoranda relating to the company's bank account, for December, 1975, directly from the bank. In reconciling the bank balance at December 31, 1975, you observed the following facts:

(1) Balance per bank statement, 12/31/75 . . . . $146,580
(2) Balance per Cash account, 12/31/75 91,140
(3) Outstanding checks, 12/31/75 62,475
(4) Receipts of 12/31/75, deposited 1/2/76 9,555
(5) Proceeds of bank loan, 12/15/75, discounted for three months at 10 percent per year, omitted from records 19,500
(6) Deposit of 12/23/75, omitted from bank statement 5,300
(7) Check No. 917 of Barr Company, charged by bank in error to Bear Company . . . . $ 8,210
(8) Proceeds of note of Van Company, collected by bank, 12/10/75 not entered in cash record:

    Principal . . . . $ 4,000
    Interest 40

                         $ 4,040
    Less: Collection charge 10   4,030

(9) Erroneous debit memorandum of 12/31/75, to charge company's account with settlement of bank loan, which was paid by Check No. 714 on same date 10,000
(10) Deposit of Barr Company of 12/6/75, credited in error to Bear Company 2,500

13. The following is a summary of the cash receipts and disbursements of Cutter, Inc., for the last six months of 1975.

Month	Receipts	Disbursements
July.	$ 26,742	$ 23,102
August	19,003	33,594
September	30,740	30,138
October	49,163	46,811
November	56,688	40,389
December	68,159	56,739
	$248,855	$233,788

The bank balance on July 1, 1975, was $58,050, and on December 31, 1975, it is $76,717. No checks were outstanding on July 1. Checks outstanding on December 31, 1975, were $8,100. Undeposited checks, December 31, 1975, are $4,500, which are included in the December receipts. Bank deposits for the year totaled $241,340.

a) What is the total shortage; how was it accomplished?

b) Start with the July 1, 1975, bank balance; prepare statements showing how the cashier of Cutter, Inc., made his reconciliation appear to be perfect.

14. In the following problem, sales are made on open account, and the terms are 2/20, n/30, which terms are *strictly enforced.*

What is the shortage arising from:

a) Stating discounts in excess of actual discounts taken?

b) The theft of discounts when a customer did not take a discount?

c) Accounting entry and posting manipulation?

d) Total manipulation?

Sales Record

Date		Explanation	Accounts Receivable Dr.	Sales Cr.
Dec.	1	Amber Company	1,925.00	1,925.00
	2	Barton Company	1,637.54	1,637.54
	3	Clark Company	2,800.00	2,800.00
	4	Barton Company	1,450.60	1,450.60
	7	Dome Company	1,880.50	1,880.50
	8	Amber Company	1,534.84	1,534.84
	10	Ethyl Company	1,670.40	1,670.40
	13	Amber Company	5,600.00	5,600.00
	15	Ethyl Company	6,257.80	6,257.80
	16	Barton Company	1,103.60	1,103.60
	18	Barton Company	3,598.20	3,598.20
	21	Dome Company	808.74	808.74
	22	Amber Company	2,612.00	2,612.00
	23	Dome Company	4,936.48	4,936.48
	27	Ethyl Company	3,987.00	3,987.00
	30	Clark Company	2,667.84	2,667.84
	31	Barton Company	920.00	920.00
			44,990.54	44,990.54

Cash Receipts Record

Date		Explanation	Cash Dr.	Sales Dr. Discount	Accounts Receivable Cr.
Dec.	1	Amber Company	3,377.08	79.12	3,456.20
	3	Amber Company	604.00	12.32	616.32
	7	Ethyl Company	9,525.60	194.40	9,720.00
	9	Barton Company	2,964.62	123.52	3,088.14
	10	Amber Company	1,886.50	38.50	1,925.00
	16	Dome Company	1,822.90	57.60	1,880.50
	20	Ethyl Company	1,637.00	33.40	1,670.40
	22	Clark Company	6,052.40	127.60	6,180.00
	23	Ethyl Company	5,932.66	125.14	6,057.80
	29	Amber Company	6,992.14	142.70	7,134.84
	30	Dome Company	776.42	32.32	808.74
			41,571.32	966.62	42,537.94

Amber Company

Date		Explanation	Debit	Credit	Balance
Nov.	15	Merchandise	3,456.20		3,456.20
	24	Merchandise	616.32		4,072.52
Dec.	1	Cash		3,456.20	616.32
	1	Merchandise	1,925.00		2,541.32
	3	Cash		616.32	1,925.00
	8	Merchandise	1,534.84		3,459.84
	10	Cash		1,925.00	1,534.84
	13	Merchandise	5,600.00		7,134.84
	22	Merchandise	2,612.00		9,746.84
	29	Cash		7,134.84	2,612.00

Barton Company

Date		Explanation	Debit	Credit	Balance
Nov.	1	Balance			1,840.00
	3	Merchandise	2,000.00		3,840.00
	5	Merchandise	1,600.00		5,440.00
	28	Merchandise	400.00		5,840.00
	29	Cash		5,840.00	
Dec.	2	Merchandise	1,637.54		1,637.54
	4	Merchandise	1,450.60		3,088.14
	9	Cash		3,018.14	
	16	Merchandise	1,103.60		1,103.60
	18	Merchandise	3,598.20		4,701.80
	31	Merchandise	920.00		5,621.80

Clark Company

Date		Explanation	Debit	Credit	Balance
Oct.	28	Merchandise	1,612.00		1,612.00
Nov.	15	Merchandise	428.00		2,040.00
	29	Merchandise	1,540.00		3,580.00
Dec.	3	Merchandise	2,800.00		6,180.00
	22	Cash		6,180.00	
	30	Merchandise	2,667.84		2,667.84

Dome Company

Date		Explanation	Debit	Credit	Balance
Dec.	7	Merchandise	1,808.50		1,808.50
	16	Cash		1,808.50	
	21	Merchandise	808.74		808.74
	23	Merchandise	4,936.48		5,745.22
	30	Cash		808.74	4,936.48

Ethyl Company

Date		Explanation	Debit	Credit	Balance
Nov.	30	Merchandise	9,720.00		9,720.00
Dec.	7	Cash		9,720.00	
	10	Merchandise	1,670.40		1,670.40
	15	Merchandise	6,257.80		7,728.20
	20	Cash		1,670.40	6,057.80
	23	Cash		6,057.80	
	27	Merchandise	3,897.00		3,897.00

PRACTICE SET ASSIGNMENTS

Metalcraft, Incorporated: Audit Problem:
    Assignment 2, Section A: Petty Cash.
    Assignment 2, Section B: Cash in Bank.
    Assignment 2, Section C: Payroll Fund.
Colby Gears, Inc.: Holmes and Moore Audit Case:
    Cash in Bank. Petty Cash.

13

Accounts Receivable; Related Revenues; Credit Losses

Audit Objectives

Some of the objectives in the examination of accounts receivable are the determination of their *accuracy of amount*, their *validity*, their *collectibility*, and their proper presentation in the balance sheet at cash collectible amounts. In every audit of accounts receivable, a minimum of work is necessary in order to arrive at a conclusion concerning the four objectives. The exact procedures followed in arriving at this conclusion and the manner in which they are applied will differ between engagements. The *major* objective of the examination is to simultaneously determine the accuracy of revenues, revenue deductions, and credit losses. Without a sale (other than for cash) there would be no receivables.

Preface to Accounts Receivable, Revenues, and Credit Losses

Trade accounts receivable arise in the normal course of selling the regularly offered product or service; nontrade accounts receivable arise from sources other than sales. Regarding accounts receivable, most auditors generally refer to trade accounts; and accounts receivable, revenues, and credit losses are so treated here, with the understanding that the prescribed auditing procedures are the same for all classes of receivables. Before proceeding with an examination of accounts receivable, the auditor must be familiar with any peculiar conditions surrounding the business of the client, the organization and efficiency of the client's sales department and credit department, the nature of the products sold, the sales policies, the credit terms granted, and internal control over accounts receivable and sales. The scope of the examination of accounts receivable depends upon these factors.

Care must be exercised in auditing accounts receivable because normal liquidation of an account receivable results in a cash receipt and because fraud is possible by the manipulation of receivables. Fraud will result from lapping; receivables (and sales) may not be entered in the ledgers; they may be understated; credits to receivables may be fictitious; an account may be fictitious. The methods used to cover fraud from these sources were discussed in Chapters 4 and 12. In the credit-oriented world of business existing today, the audit of receivables, related revenues, and credit losses must be emphasized.

Revenue realizations are events which involve transactions with assets and liabilities. Balance sheet assets, liabilities, and retained earnings are residuals emanating from the revenue-expense-net income cycle. Therefore, the examination of revenue items is of primary importance if residual balance sheet amounts are to be properly stated. As indicated in Chapter 12, from the point of view of conducting an audit, it is proper and logical normally to start with the examination of a named balance sheet item and its related activities, as exemplified by correlating the examination of accounts receivable with sales, sales returns, and bad debts expense.

The majority of revenue accounts are examined when original records are audited, or when assets and liabilities related to specific revenues are audited. In accordance with the effectivenss of internal control and internal auditing, the extent of the verification of revenues and expenses may be extended or curtailed. If properly applied, internal control procedures and internal auditing procedures, as set forth in other chapters up to this point are an aid in reducing the detailed work necessary in any examination other than one involving fraud.

The verification of revenues is based upon tests, scrutiny, and comparisons, with detailed analyses of selected items for either the entire period, a portion of the period, or selected entries within the records. The examination of revenues should be sufficiently extensive to satisfy the auditor that the transactions are genuine, that they are accurately recorded, and that account classification is proper. Also, the materiality of each revenue is a guiding factor in determining the extent of its examination. The extent of the testing is determined by the effectiveness of the system of internal control and the findings in a particular engagement (see Chapters 9 and 10). Systems of internal control may not be found in small businesses for reasons of economy and because of limited personnel. In those cases the auditor may encounter as much detailed work as in the audit of larger concerns where detailed work is less necessary because of the existence of effective systems of internal control.

The final result of any business transaction comes to rest in capital accounts. At first glance, it might appear that retained earnings and consequently revenues and expenses have been verified, if all balance sheet accounts have been verified. It is possible, however, that errors still exist and that overstatements and/or understatements of both expense and revenue might be missed. Therefore, it is necessary to examine revenues and expenses in order to ascertain that assets and liabilities are properly stated.

The presentation of a proper income statement is equally as important as the presentation of a proper balance sheet; if one statement is inaccurate, so is the other statement. If a balance sheet is to be accurate, the related income statement must be free from error; and if the latter statement is to be accurate, revenues and expenses must not only be correct in amount but there must be proper allocation of revenues and expenses with respect to fiscal periods.

Briefly, and without invoking the arguments involved, for revenue realization the passage of title accompanied by a sale constitutes a reasonable test. Decisions of the Tax Court of the United States have lent much weight to the passage of legal title as the principal factor. However, the passing of legal title is not a good measure of the impact on income of a going concern. The passage of title is dependent upon such factors as possession; *the intention of the parties*—including deferred payments, shipments on approval, C.I.F. (cost including insurance and freight) contracts, F.O.B. (free on board) contracts, sale by sample, the Uniform Commercial Code, and down payments. In the event of approval, title remains with the seller until the buyer approves. If not from a legal point of view in all cases at least from an accounting point of view any consideration received in exchange in the sale is considered as revenue; the receipt of cash is not necessary.

The receipt of a sales order is the first in a chain of events leading to the recognition of revenue; the receipt of the order itself is not an event of revenue realization, since the order must be followed by production, delivery, transfer of title, and finally the recognition of the revenue. If other than cash—that is, accounts receivable, notes receivable, and so forth—the assets received in exchange are not immediately available for use in the business process but normally will be converted to a useful medium; the acquisition of assets other than cash in exchange is not a bar to the recognition of revenue.

Audit of Revenues

Work papers for the analyses of revenues must be designed with the idea of setting forth the desired information in the most enlightening manner.

The Illustrative Audit Papers accompanying the text should be reviewed. Additional illustrations of work papers for revenues appear at other points throughout the text.

If during the course of an audit, original entries have been examined and verified in accordance with the procedures of Chapters 10 and 11 and succeeding chapters, to that extent the revenues have been verified. In any examination, the auditor must perform sufficient work to assure himself that the financial statements fairly present financial condition and the results of operations. The amount of verification of the individual items of revenue will be tempered by several conditions, primary among which are the following:

1. The effectiveness of the system of internal control.
2. The condition and accuracy of the account classifications, and the recording of the accounting and statistical data.
3. The size and extensiveness of the business of the client.
4. Any restrictive arrangements imposed during the stages preliminary to the audit.

If adequate tests have been made of original documentary evidences, original record entries, and account postings, accompanied by proper verification in accordance with the sample selections set forth in the examination of original records, and if the system of internal control is satisfactory, only those income statement items which have a direct relationship to assets and liabilities need receive additional attention. Examples of such items are uncollectible account expense, unusual sales, and selected others.

If the percentage of error is within the limits of established satisfaction for the test, it may reasonably be concluded that the same percentage applies to the remaining untested items in the data array. Where the percentage of error is close to the established limits of satisfaction or if the nature of the errors is serious, additional audit work is necessary if any assurance is to be offered of the propriety of the financial statements.

An auditor can render a valuable service to a client by a careful analysis of revenues and by suggestions for increasing revenues. This work will include the following.

1. The examination of revenue accounts.
2. The investigation of all pronounced fluctuations.
3. A percentage comparison of each expense with net sales or gross profit.
4. A percentage comparison of gross profits with sales for the purpose of determining causes of fluctuation.

It is impossible, of course, to draw a program in detail for revenue verification because of strictly local conditions surrounding each audit.

SECTION I: INTERNAL CONTROL OF ACCOUNTS RECEIVABLE

Internal control over receivables starts with an accepted sales order, thereby bringing into existence evidence for the formation of an audit trail. Internal control of receivables and credit losses has as primary objectives the approval of sales orders, the approval of credit granting, proper shipment, billing the customer, invoice verification, the recording of the receivables in proper amount, the collection of the receivables, accounting and control of cash receipts, and the controlled banking of the proper cash receipts. Proper internal control of receivables also requires the approval of returned sales and the proper accounting for the return and the returned merchandise, and the approved charge-off of uncollectible items. Periodically the receivables should be aged in order to determine the actions and efficiency of the credit department and the collection division.

ILLUSTRATION 13–1

INTERNAL CONTROL QUESTIONNAIRE
Accounts Receivable

	Yes	No	Not Applicable	Remarks
Company_____ Period Covered_____				
1. Are subsidiary ledgers regularly balanced with the controlling accounts?	___	___	___	_____
2. Does the client periodically age the accounts?	___	___	___	_____
3. Are delinquent accounts periodically reviewed by a proper official?	___	___	___	_____
4. Are adequate doubtful account allowances set up?	___	___	___	_____
5. Are uncollectible account write-offs properly approved?	___	___	___	_____
6. After an account has been written off as uncollectible, is proper control exercised in the event of future collection?	___	___	___	_____
7. Are credit adjustments approved by a proper official?	___	___	___	_____
8. Are credit memorandums sequentially numbered?	___	___	___	_____
9. Are all credit memorandum numbers accounted for?	___	___	___	_____
10. Are monthly statements sent to all customers?	___	___	___	_____
11. Are the statements prepared or verified by someone not having access to the cash receipts records or the accounts receivable credits?	___	___	___	_____
12. Are statements mailed by someone other than the accounts receivable department?	___	___	___	_____
13. Are statements controlled to prevent interception prior to mailing?	___	___	___	_____
14. Does the client confirm accounts receivable balances by a person independent of: a) The cashier? b) The accounts receivable department? c) The credit manager?	___ ___ ___	___ ___ ___	___ ___ ___	_____ _____ _____
15. Is the credit department separated from the accounts receivable record keeping?	___	___	___	_____
16. Are disputed items and differences reported by customers handled by a person other than the cashier or the accounts receivable department?	___	___	___	_____
17. Are unusual discounts and allowances approved by a responsible person?	___	___	___	_____
18. Are the duties of the accounts receivable personnel separated from all cash receipts and disbursements functions?	___	___	___	_____

ILLUSTRATION 13–1 (*Continued*)

	Yes	No	Not Appli- cable	Remarks
19. To pay an account receivable credit balance, is proper official approval required?	____	____	____	_____
20. Are accounts receivable personnel rotated on their jobs?	____	____	____	_____
21. Are all shipments represented by invoices?	____	____	____	_____
22. Does the cash collection division operate as a verification of the work of the accounts receivable department?	____	____	____	_____
23. Does the credit division, in passing on credit terms and limits, have any connection with:				
a) The sales department?	____	____	____	_____
b) The accounts receivable bookkeeper?	____	____	____	_____
24. Are customer credit limits adhered to?	____	____	____	_____
25. If customers are charged in advance of shipment, is the proper account credited?	____	____	____	_____
26. Are consignments-out carried in accounts receivable?	____	____	____	_____
27. Are any balances carried as trade accounts receivable, other than trade accounts receivable?	____	____	____	_____
28. If accounts receivable are pledged as loan security, is the accounting treatment proper?	____	____	____	_____

Prepared by_____   Reviewed by_____
Date_____   Date_____

In order to effect proper internal control over receivables, (1) sales must be separated from accounting for them; (2) accounting for sales must be separated from the receipt of cash arising from the receivables; and (3) returns, allowances, discounts, and uncollectible charge-offs must be properly approved and separated from the cash receipts function.

A client may or may not operate an internal auditing division; in either event, the auditor must review the system of internal control and be satisfied with it, or extend his examination beyond the test limits set forth in Chapters 10 and 11 and the proposals to be established in this chapter.

An internal control questionnaire for accounts receivable is shown in Illustration 13–1, and one for sales and other revenues is shown in Illustration 13–2.

SECTION II: INTERNAL CONTROL OF REVENUES

The objectives of an audit of revenues may be summarized as follows:

1. To determine the adequacy of internal controls over all revenues.
2. To ascertain that all revenues earned have been recorded and that all recorded revenues have been earned.
3. To analyze and interpret trends in the various revenue categories by studying management-prepared comparisons, or by preparing, analyzing, and interpreting comparisons.

ILLUSTRATION 13–2

INTERNAL CONTROL QUESTIONNAIRE
Sales and Other Revenues

Company_____

Period Covered _____

	Yes	No	Not Appli-cable	Remarks

1. Are sales orders properly controlled?
2. Are orders from customers approved by the sales department?
3. Are orders from customers approved by the credit department?
4. Is the credit department independent of the sales department?
5. Are sales orders consecutively prenumbered by the printer?
6. Are all sales orders accounted for?
7. Are sales orders matched with sales invoices?
8. Are back orders properly controlled?
9. Are shipments made on proper authority?
   a) Are shipping advices prenumbered?
   b) Are shipping advices matched with the items of sales invoices?
   c) Does the billing department receive a copy of the shipping advice directly from the shipping department?
10. Is there simultaneous preparation of the following:
    a) Invoice?
    b) Shipping advice?
    c) Inventory requisition?
11. Are sales invoices consecutively prenumbered by the printer?
12. Are voided sales invoices retained?
13. Are all sales invoices accounted for?
14. Are sales invoices examined for:
    a) Credit terms granted?
    b) Quantities billed versus quantities shipped?
    c) Prices, extensions, and footings?
15. Are sales proved independently of the accounting department?
16. Is merchandise from returned sales promptly handled:
    a) In the receiving department?
    b) In the inventory records?
    c) In the accounts receivable records?
17. Are receiving reports prepared for sales returns?
18. If receiving reports are prepared, are they matched with credit memorandums?
19. Is the preparation of credit memorandums properly controlled to prevent unauthorized sales returns debits and accounts receivable credits?
20. Are the classes of sales indicated below controlled and recorded in the same manner as regular charge sales:
    a) Cash sales?
    b) C.O.D. sales?
    c) Sales to employees?
    d) Scrap sales?
21. Is it possible to match unit sales with inventory record credits:
    a) By the use of a perpetual inventory for a manufacturer?
    b) By the use of the retail method for a nonmanufacturer?
22. Is there an adequate check on transportation allowances:
    a) By reference to terms of sale?
    b) By comparison with rate schedules and transportation bills?
23. Are revenues from interest and dividends properly accounted for?

Prepared by_____   Reviewed by_____

Date _____   Date _____

SECTION III: AUDIT PROGRAM FOR ACCOUNTS RECEIVABLE

The following audit program is typical of the procedures to be followed in the examination of accounts receivable.

Compare an Accounts Receivable Trial Balance with the Balance of the Controlling Account.   The auditor should prepare or obtain from the client a trial balance of the subsidiary accounts receivable. This trial balance may be in the form of an adding machine tape or it may be in printed form from data processing equipment. Time is saved if the auditor requests that the client prepare a trial balance of the accounts receivable in the form of an aging schedule. If accounts receivable other than trade accounts are included in the client's trial balance, they should be segregated as shown in Illustration 13–3, so that a proper trade account receivable position is shown. The *net* total of the footed trial balance is then compared with the controlling account balance. Individual balances in the trial balance are then compared with the account balances as shown in subsidiary ledgers.

The footings and balances of customers' accounts in subsidiary ledgers are then proved on a test basis; normally, this test would not exceed 10 percent of the accounts.

If the balance of the controlling account is out of agreement with the sum of the subsidiary account balances, the client should be requested to locate the difference; this is a function of the client, unless the auditor is requested to locate differences. If the client cannot locate discrepancies and if the auditor is not retained to do so, the differences may be set forth in the audit report. If the auditor is to locate differences between the controlling account balance and the balance of the sum of the related subsidiary accounts, he should—from the date the differences appeared—prove the footing accuracy of *all* applicable records of original entry, unless the error obviously is of a mathematical nature. He also must verify posting accuracy both to control and to subsidiary accounts for discovered errors. An alternative procedure sometimes used is to analyze the controlling account and at the same time trace entries from the ledgers to the records of original entry.

The client should reconcile controlling accounts and subsidiary account balances at least each month. Errors can then be allocated to a certain period and time is saved in effecting a reconciliation. When controlling account balances are greater than the sum of the subsidiary accounts, the possibilities of fraud are present, as illustrated by posting to a controlling account and not to a subsidiary account; then when Cash should be charged, a fictitious debit would be passed to another account, probably an expense. Money to be received depends upon subsidiary accounts and not upon controlling account balances, even though our modern accounting systems and effective systems of internal control are dependent upon the controlling account principle. If it becomes necessary to adjust the controlling and subsidiary accounts to agreement—in the rare instance where errors cannot be located—the controlling account should be brought into agreement with the sum of the subsidiary accounts.

Age the Accounts Receivable. Aging involves an analysis of the accounts receivable made for the purpose of ascertaining their probable collectibility or uncollectibility and of ascertaining the efficiency of a credit and collection department. The aging process assists in the establishment of the amount necessary for the provision for doubtful accounts and thereby leads directly to the balance sheet valuation of the receivables. Aging is accomplished by segregating the unpaid accounts, either on the basis of the dates of maturity or on the basis of the dates of billing, and classifying the past-due amounts from either date.

An aging schedule based upon maturity is presented in Illustration 13–3. This aging schedule is an extension of an accounts receivable trial balance, and it also segregates nontrade receivables including the controlling account. In a concern with only a few accounts, this form is satisfactory. In a company with many accounts, it would be unnecessary for the auditor to include in the aging schedule accounts *not* due; only past-due accounts and nontrade accounts would be placed in the schedule. When a client prepared the aging schedule, normally *all* accounts are included, as in Illustration 13–3, for the guidance of the credit and collection departments.

The results of aging can be used effectively in the audit report by classifying the totals of each time-interval past due.

In business concerns having a large number of accounts receivable, each with a relatively small balance, auditing practice permits test of the aging schedule, assuming that the schedule has been prepared by the client. Therefore, sampling techniques are applied in the examination of aging schedules of large department stores, public utility corporations, large bakeries, and others.

ILLUSTRATION.   A bakery has 100,000 accounts receivable from grocery stores, the majority of which are 30-day accounts. Ten thousand of the accounts are to be selected for detailed aging. The customers' accounts are in trays, 1,000 accounts in each of 100 trays, and the accounts are filed alphabetically. At random, management selected 10 trays for individual aging, plus all accounts with balances in excess of $2,000.

The balance of each account under $2,000 included in the sample is classified into past-due categories as follows: 0–2 months; 2–4 months; 4–6 months; over 6 months. The proportion of total dollars of the sampled accounts falling into each age category is estimated to apply to the remaining 90 percent of the unsampled accounts which are under $2,000.

On the basis of past experience, loss expectancy rates are applied to each age category aged in detail and the results are multiplied by 10 in order to cover the 90 percent not scheduled.

On the basis of the preceding illustration, an auditor might examine the aging of 10 percent (1,000) of the client's accounts with balances under $2,000 and 10 percent of all accounts with balances of more than $2,000. On the basis of examining the aging of 1,000 out of 100,000 accounts (1 percent), the auditor might reject the sample if he discovered errors in age category classifications of more than 1 percent of the total dollars in each category.

During the process of examining a prepared aging schedule, the following points must be borne in mind:

a) Segregate other-than-trade accounts receivable.
b) Watch payment promptness from customers with large balances.
c) Investigate reasons for credit balances.
d) Be certain the bad debt provisions are adequate but not too large.
e) See that postdated invoices are not placed in the past-due accounts.
f) Watch for past-due balances which constantly increase; this can mean that the customer should be cut off, or it may indicate that a customer has paid his account and that the money has been misappropriated.

In an aging analysis, the credit terms determine the time intervals to be used in aging the accounts. If normal credit terms are 2/10, n/30, in Illustration 13–3, then $444 of the account of A was overdue at December 31, 1975. It should be noted that the account of P, falling in three time intervals, was paid on January 10, 1976, and that the payment was noted in the work papers. The auditor should examine accounts receivable entries after the balance sheet date to determine if evidence of collectibility is thereby affected. The Remarks column should contain reference to any incompleteness of data and to all other items pertinent to the audit of the accounts receivable.

ILLUSTRATION. Long-overdue accounts may appear in the analysis; investigation may prove that the account is being slowly liquidated, or it may happen that an item is in dispute; such situations are exemplified in the accounts of D and J. Items in dispute should be discussed with the client in order to attempt to determine their probable collectibility.

While an auditor is examining credits to any account receivable, he must watch noncash credits because of possible fraud, as pointed out in Chapters 4, 5, and 12. He must be especially watchful of credits to accounts placed in a suspense ledger, if one is used, and to all old accounts previously considered uncollectible, if a suspense ledger is not used. Non-cash credits should be supported by proper authorizations.

Credit balances in accounts receivable should be investigated to determine their legitimacy, since credit balances may arise through postings to incorrect accounts; also, a credit balance represents a liability—which may be due and payable, as exemplified by account I in Illustration 13–3.

ILLUSTRATION 13–3

COOK COMPANY

Trial Balance and Analysis of Accounts Receivable, December 31, 1975

No.	Customer		Balance Dr.	Balance Cr.	Items Not Due	Past-Due—Days 1/30	31/60	61/90	91/120	121/180	Over 180	Charge-Off
1	A	√	444			200	100	50	50	44		444
2	B	√	2,461		2,461							
3	C	√		43								
4	D	√	1,218		1,000			218				
5	E	√	500									
6	F	√	1,700						1,700			
7	G	√	77							27	50	77
8	H	√	750									
9	I	√			105							
10	J	√	110		100						10	10
11	K	√	300		75	25	50	50	25	50	25	150
12	L	√	5,000									
13	M	√	216					100	100	16		
14	N	√	48		48							
15	O	√	400		200		150	50				
16	P	√	375				175	100	100			
17	Q	√	75									75
18	R	√	83								83	
19	S	√	620									
20	T	√	3,200		3,200							
21	U	√	1,000		600							
22	V	√	2,400		2,400							
23	W	√	100									
24	X	√	20						20			20
25	Y	√	300						300			
26	Z	√	360		260	100						
			21,757	148	10,344	325	475	888	1,975	137	168	776
			148									

Control account balance 21,609

Deduct:

Direct charge-off	776	
Personnel	100	
Consigned	900	
Branches.	750	
Subsidiary	5,000	
Miscellaneous . .	620	8,146

Adjusted Control

Balance.   13,463

COOK COMPANY

Trial Balance and Analysis of Accounts Receivable, December 31, 1975

| Provide Allowance | Last Payment | | Accounts with | | | | | Remarks |
	Date	Amt.	Company Personnel	Consignees	Branches	Subsidiary Companies	Miscellaneous	
	6/15/75	10						Correspondence is to the effect that there will be no additional collections.
								Merchandise returned; account active.
1,700	4/8/75	300		AJE 500				Good, but always slow. Adjust out.
								Doubtful; put on a C.O.D. basis
	3/18/75	100			AJE 750			In receivership; no dividends expected.
								This is an advance; adjust.
								Returned merchandise. Send check.
150	None							In dispute; client willing to accede.
								Doubtful; see credit department for accumulation.
						AJE 5,000		Subsidiary company advance.
108	7/12/75	50						50 percent doubtful.
	10/16/75	300						Always good, but about 90 days late.
	1/10/76	375						Paid in full.
								Loan to former employee. Not collectible.
83	1/7/76	350						Customer claims he will pay—in 1976
							AJE 620	Sale of used factory machinery—O.K.
				AJE 400				Adjust $400 out. Set up two accounts.
			AJE 100					Loan to private secretary—good.
	None							Customer moved—no trace.
	8/6/75	750						Always fast to this time; will pay in February, 1976; see correspondence.
								Good.
2,041			100	900	750	5,000	620	

√ Compared with subsidiary ledger.

Installment Account Analysis. Today installment sales are common—too common—for many companies, buyers, and the general economy. In the audit of receivables where merchandise is sold on a deferred payment plan, the method of verifying the validity and balance of an account follows the same plan as that used for any trade receivable. In addition, the auditor must be familiar with the form of the installment sales contract to ascertain that payment agreements are being fulfilled. Installment accounts may be supported by installment notes. In installment sales, title may pass; or it may pass with a mortgage being given by the creditor; or the seller may retain title until the installment collections have been liquidated.

The auditor must watch for delinquent installments and report upon them. If governmental regulatory requirements are in effect, the auditor must ascertain that those requirements are being met with respect to credit terms granted. In addition, the provisions of the Truth in Lending Law must be followed. The accounting methods used in the handling of foreclosures of chattel mortgages and repossessions must be investigated; the method used in pricing repossessed goods must be verified, and the auditor must be certain that installment receivable balances have been reduced when goods are repossessed. In order to judge effectively the collectibility of installment accounts receivable, the cash collections for each year divided by the average receivables for that year will result in a ratio that indicates whether the collections for any one year are progressing or regressing as compared with another preceding or subsequent year.

When installment accounts receivables are aged, the time intervals in the aging schedules should be set up in accordance with one of the two following plans: (*a*) one installment past due, two installments past due, and so forth; or (*b*) by months of the current year and by months of subsequent years. If the client sells under different payment plans, an aging schedule should be prepared for each such plan. For management purposes delinquent installations should be set forth in the audit report.

One method of handling installment sales is to record as profits only the gross profit proportion of the total collections made, thereby deferring the gross profits on uncollected amounts from sales of the current year. While the installment sales method is acceptable for tax purposes, it is not ordinarily a good basis for recognizing income, except in rare cases where risk, collection costs, and losses on repossessions are extremely high and largely immeasurable.

Confirm Accounts Receivable. In order that the auditor may express his opinion as to the fairness of the financial statements in a clear and unequivocal manner, it is necessary to confirm accounts receivable in those examinations where it is practicable and reasonable to do so.

Confirmation of accounts receivable on a test basis is an established and recognized audit procedure and is a required procedure on a 100 percent basis for brokers' customer accounts under the Securities and Exchange Commission's Rule X–17A–5.

The direct objective of confirmation of receivables is to verify the balances of the accounts. In arriving at a decision concerning the extent of the requests for confirmations, several factors must be considered. If internal control over cash and receivables is not satisfactory, or if fraud is suspected, or if the persons handling cash or receivables have permission to grant sales allowances or to charge off doubtful accounts, *all* debtors should be circularized. If internal control is satisfactory and if the receivables are few in number, but if their aggregate dollar total represents a material portion of the current assets or all assets, *all* debtors should be sent confirmation requests. If the internal control system is satisfactory, if the number of receivables is large, and if each account is relatively small, the selection of a representative sample, as set forth in Chapters 9, 10, and 11, normally should result in satisfactory assurance of accuracy.

Sample confirmation requests sent to debtors should include:

a)   Accounts large and small, active and inactive, selected at random.
b)   Accounts of customers who are in financial difficulty.
c)   Accounts in which debits are large at the year-end.
d)   Accounts turned over to collection agencies.
e)   Accounts in dispute between the client and the debtor.
f)   Accounts charged off during the year.
g)   Accounts with credit balances.

The sample to be circularized is drawn by the auditor. If the client requests that certain customers be omitted from the list to be circularized, the auditor should investigate those accounts, extend his audit procedures, and comment upon them.

There are two methods of confirming receivables by direct communication with debtors:

a)   The *positive method*, in which a communication is addressed to the debtor, requesting him to confirm directly to the auditor the accuracy or inaccuracy of the balance shown.
b)   The *negative method*, in which a communication is addressed to the debtor, asking him to advise the auditor *only* in case of disagreement with the stated amount.

If there is a suspected condition of dispute, inaccuracy, or irregularity, the positive method of confirmation is desirable; this method is preferable if the client sells only to a few large customers.

The negative method of confirmation is proper in the majority of instances, especially for those concerns with a large number of small accounts, as exemplified by department stores, installment houses, chain stores, public utilities, and others dealing with the ultimate consumer.

In many audits of retail department stores, installment houses, chain stores, public utilities, and others doing business with the final consumer, receivables are due in a stated time after billing; if the auditor controls cash receipts after the close of the period and traces the cash receipts to *proved* customers' account balances, he has attained a result as good as a negative confirmation. Accounts showing balances due after the due date can then be confirmed. Therefore, confirmation requests in negative form can be limited to approximately 2 percent of the small mass receivables if approximately 98 percent have been collected and if internal control is satisfactory.

Confirmation requests take many forms, ranging from a rubber-stamp imprint on a monthly statement for a negative confirmation to a formal letter requesting a reply for a positive confirmation request. There is no denying the fact that a reply would always be desirable, since evidence of attention to the request is thereby secured; but the cost and time involved and the percentage of replies received generally lead to the conclusion that the negative form is satisfactory.

In the audit of companies where confirmation requests are sent primarily to nonbusiness personnel, the negative form is advantageous, because the customer receives a notice that the records of the creditor show a given balance, which is assumed to be correct if no reply is received. This relieves the debtor of the necessity of answering a confirmation request, unless there is a discrepancy. Strictly speaking, a negative confirmation is not a confirmation, since no knowledge is received from the debtor unless discrepancies do exist.

With respect to positive confirmations, the following comments are offered. As stated, direct confirmation is the best way of verifying account balances and of detecting errors. However, after obtaining replies to positive confirmation requests, it is still possible that there have been errors in the confirmed accounts, that the ledger account balances are incorrect, that a confirmation reply is not genuine, and that an account may be uncollectible. In spite of these possibilities, the confirmation procedure should effectively relieve the auditor of further responsibility after he has exercised professional care. Objectives to the positive method of confirmation are the time and expense involved and the relatively low percentage of replies received. Another objection sometimes offered to positive confirmation requests is the reaction of customers, because some of them imagine they are receiving a special request for payment.

In preparing to send confirmation requests, the staff of the client should be requested to prepare the statements to be mailed for confirmation. Account balances only may be placed on the statements or the entire account activity may be shown. The auditor should compare the account balance on the statements with the amount in his accounts receivable trial balance, which he already has compared with the ledger balance. The auditor should mark the accounts for which confirmations are requested.

Confirmations may be requested as of the end of the fiscal period or at interim dates. A list of confirmation requests may be prepared, or copies of the requests may be preferable, in order to save time.

The confirmation request is then attached to the statement. The auditor personally should mail the requests directly to the debtors in his own envelopes, enclosing an envelope for reply if the positive method is used. If an employee of the client were to mail the requests—positive or negative—he might abstract a fictitious statement, approve it, and return it to the auditor, who would be ignorant of the circumstances.

Upon their return directly to the auditor, the replies must be compared with the list of accounts receivable, and all differences noted and investigated; amounts in agreement with the list should be ticked.

ILLUSTRATION. One type of noted difference may be illustrated as follows: A debtor claims his account balance to be $5,000 less than the statement sent him for confirmation, stating that he mailed the remittance on December 26, 1975—and the statement to be confirmed was dated December 31, 1975. The remittance was not entered in the customer's account until January 4, 1976; and entries on the bank statement did not match entries in the cash receipts record. Thus, a shortage has been covered by lapping.

If positive confirmations are sent and if a reply is not received within a reasonable time, a second request should be sent if the account has not been liquidated in the interim. If desirable a third request may be sent by registered mail in those audits—brokerage firms, for example—where confirmations are required. Normally, if a reply is not received after the second request, the auditor may reasonably assume that there are no differences between the balance according to the client and that according to the debtor; however, this assumption does not excuse the auditor from an examination of the composition of the accounts, an investigation of the bona fide nature of the unconfirmed accounts, or a review of the transactions affecting the accounts.

When differences exist between the client and a debtor, they usually take the form of:

a) Charges for items shipped at the end of the period, which items were not received by the debtor until after the close of the period.
b) Cash payments made by the debtor and not received by the client until after the close of the period.
c) Returned items either not received or not credited until after the close of the period.
d) Disputed items, such as allowances, damaged goods, and questionable return privileges.
e) Manipulation of the accounts on the records of the client.

All differences between debtor and creditor balances must be investigated to determine the existence of errors and fraud. The differences should be discussed with the client in order to arrive at the correct accounts receivable balance. If positive confirmations were used under a sampling process and if the number of replies received was not satisfactory or if discrepancies were great, the sampling should be extended.

Illustration 13–4 persents a negative type of confirmation request. Illustration 13–5 shows a positive type of confirmation request.

ILLUSTRATION 13–4

CONFIRMATION REQUEST: NEGATIVE TYPE

IMPORTANT

In connection with the periodic audit of our records, the enclosed statement indicates the balance of your account at the date stated thereon. If, after examining your account, you do not agree with this balance, please explain any differences directly to our auditors: Hale and Jackson, Certified Public Accountants, Carew Tower, Cincinnati, Ohio 45202

If a reply is not received by our auditors WITHIN TEN DAYS, it will be assumed that the statement is correct. Remittances are NOT to be sent to the auditors.

As stated earlier, confirmation requests should be mailed to accounts with credit balances. Credit balances may be the result of loans or deposits required with orders, in which case they are not true credit balances in accounts receivable. They also may be the result of overpayments, merchandise returned, allowances, or accounting errors.

The extent of the examination of receivables and the extent of the confirmation results may be set forth in the audit report somewhat as follows:

Explanation	Number of Accounts	Per-centages	Amounts	Per-centages
December 31	600	60	$65,600	82
November 30	250	25	9,600	12
October 31.	100	10	4,000	5
Prior	50	5	800	1
Totals	1,000	100	$80,000	100

If receivables are not confirmed by correspondence, it is the recognized duty of the auditor so to state in his report, with the reasons for non-confirmation. This is necessary in order to adhere to accepted auditing standards. The auditor should mention *all* procedures omitted in each engagement (and the reasons therefor) in order to avoid being charged with negligence. An auditor will at all times endeavor to obtain the best possible evidence in substantiation of the accuracy and collectibility of the receivables. If accounts receivable were not confirmed, a typical

ILLUSTRATION 13–5

CONFIRMATION REQUEST: POSITIVE TYPE

Date_____

To:_____
_____
_____

Gentlemen:

Please advise our auditors, Hale and Jackson, Certified Public Accountants, Carew Tower, Cincinnati, Ohio 45202, on the attached form, of the correctness of the balance of your account as shown by our records at the date and in the amount stated below, or of any exceptions you may take thereto. An addressed envelope for your reply is enclosed. Your prompt attention will be appreciated.

Very truly yours,

_____
Name of Client

(This is a request for confirmation, not for remittance.)

· ·

Hale and Jackson
Certified Public Accountants
Carew Tower   No._____
Cincinnati, Ohio 45202

    We confirm the correctness of the balance of $_____ in our account on the records of_____ as of_____ 197__, with the exceptions noted below.

Business Name_____
Signed by_____

Exceptions (please state differences in detail, giving all pertinent dates and amounts):

_____
_____
_____

(Use other side if necessary.)

section of the report might read as follows: "Auditing tests of records regarding accounts receivable have been made; but at the request of the client, we did not follow the generally accepted procedure of communicating directly with debtors."

If receivables are not confirmed, the review of internal control should be extended for sales, shipments, billing, collections, and bank deposits. Also, the number of sales transactions verified should be extended. Cash collections should be identified with individual debits to accounts receivable by controlling incoming checks and by following them through the cash receipts records to the bank.

Determine Accounts Receivable Validity. The attempt of the auditor is to determine that the accounts are those of bona fide customers, not fictitious items to be writtten off later, with the consequent appropriation of cash or inventory. Confirmation requests assist in determining validity and accuracy. The auditor should examine the system of handling receivables and the general sales procedure, and he should note any changes in procedure from period to period which may affect the system of internal control. In order to establish accounts receivable validity—in addition to confirming balances—it is necessary to proceed on a *test* basis, as follows:

a) Account for, or be certain of the accounting for, all invoices, sales tickets, cash register tapes, and so forth. As indicated in Chapters 10 and 11, all these items must be controlled, even though the audit is on a test basis. If sales invoices are not consecutively prenumbered, there is always present the opportunity to not record an item and retain the cash. Therefore, the objectives of the auditor in controlling *all* items are to afford him control over accounts receivable activities.

b) Prove the posting accuracy to controlling and subsidiary accounts, either at this point or in connection with the examination of the original records.

c) Verify prices billed to customers, and the extensions and footings on invoices, and compare with entries in the sales record. If the sales record entries are smaller in amount than the invoiced amounts, cash may be diverted.

d) Compare sales invoices in (*c*) with shipping records. If sales orders or customer purchase orders are available, they should be compared with the invoices, for items and amounts, and with the shipping records. This is necessary to determine fictitious accounts or billings in advance of orders. This procedure should be followed for at least several days prior to and after the close of the period. Shipping records must be examined to ascertain that all goods shipped were billed to customers.

ILLUSTRATION. Invoices totaling $57,800 were prepared and entered as sales on December 30, 1975. There were no sales orders, no shipping records, and no reductions of inventory. This is an example of "window dressing."

e) Examine debit entries which give rise to accounts receivable credits in order to be certain that accounts have not been charged off without proper authorization. Entries charging bad debts (allowance or expense) returns, and allowances *have* been made either in collusion with customers or by employees of the seller alone.

f) Receiving records must be examined for goods returned to the seller; and the auditor must ascertain that the credit has been passed to the proper receivable in order to prevent overstatement of receivables.

The preceding actions, involving the testing of the accuracy of the sales records, were discussed in Chapters 10 and 11.

Determine Proper Cutoff of Sales Records. Sales records and cash records may be kept open in order to present a more desirable financial condition and an increased sales figure. This practice is commonly known as "window dressing," a form of management fraud. In order to attempt to solidify the action, invoices may be dated back. If shipping records are compared with duplicate invoices, the practice of holding the sales records open usually is disclosed. Credits to accounts receivable made after the close of the periods, when the cash receipts record has been held open, will have been discovered in the audit of cash. If sales were entered and the customers were charged but if the inventory *was not* reduced at the close of the period because shipment was not made, a padded net income would be shown to the extent of the entire sales figure; the intention may have been to bolster a weak financial condition. The auditor should reverse the sales entries. However, if the sale was entered and the inventory *was* reduced but if shipment did not take place, the auditor should reduce the sales and the receivables and restore the inventory. In cases of this nature, revenue of one period is incorrectly shown in another period. In those cases where inventory has been reduced, investigation may prove that the sales were actually made in the period under audit and that shipment was deferred at the request of the customer.

Verify Collection-on-Delivery Accounts. Collection-on-delivery accounts arise when such terms are granted a customer or when a regular customer becomes negligent in his payments and is placed on that basis. Normally, receipts from C.O.D. sales are received within a few days after shipment; if any other condition exists, the auditor should investigate the circumstances of delay. Title to goods shipped on a C.O.D. basis may remain with the seller until delivery to the customer or payment by him.

Depending upon custom, the seller may record the sale either at the time of shipment or upon collection. If the sale is recorded at the shipment date, the amounts due are trade accounts receivable at the balance sheet date. If the sale is not recorded until payment is received, the goods shipped must be included in inventory at the balance sheet date, even though this is not in compliance with the Uniform Commercial Code. In order to adhere to the Uniform Commercial Code and in order properly to control inventory under the retail inventory method or under a nonretail perpetual inventory method, it is better to record the sale at the date of shipment.

Test Discounts. In examining accounts receivable, tests must be made of discounts taken by customers; this may be done when cash transactions are audited. Cash discounts may be overstated in the records and the cash misappropriated. This type of fraud is brought to light by testing the discounts (and, if possible, by matching the *detail* of the cash receipts with authenticated copies of deposit tickets when cash receipts are in the form of checks). The sample chosen for the testing of discounts may be selected from the same selected for confirmation, or it may be from the nonconfirmed accounts.

Commonly, any discount in excess of 2 or 3 percent is viewed as a trade discount; occasionally, discounts higher than this are treated as cash discounts. The auditor must investigate trade and client practices and discuss procedure with the client. A good determinant of a trade discount is as follows: If the discount is allowed if the debtor pays beyond the limit stated in the agreement for payment, and/or if it exceeds 2 or 3 percent, it probably is a trade discount. The test of a valid cash discount should include time as well as percentage. For example, 2/10, n/30 is less valid than 3/10, n/60. Also, the risk of noncollectibility is a factor. For example, 1 percent in a nonrisk situation is less valid than 3 to 5 percent in an extremely risky situation.

Test Returns and Allowances and Related Credit Memoranda. In examining sales returns and allowances, all credit memoranda issued should be sequentially numbered and accounted for, and authoritatively signed. As in the case of discounts, the entry of unauthorized returns and allowances probably is indicative of fraud; therefore, proper authorization is of fundamental importance. The total of the credit memoranda for returned goods and for allowances should agree with the general ledger control entries for returned goods and for allowances. The prices, extensions, and footings on credit memoranda should be tested and credit memoranda for sales returns compared with receiving records. Then, the returned goods should be traced to the inventory records.

If credit memoranda involving material amounts are issued to customers after the balance sheet date, the memoranda should be examined for several weeks to ascertain if the original charges were recorded in order to inflate sales or receivables for the period under examination. Large and extraordinary returns made during several weeks after the balance sheet date should be examined for the propriety of the proper period of original sales entry. If impropriety exists, the credit memoranda should be adjusted as of the balance sheet date by a credit to Accounts Receivable and a charge to Sales; if the "sales" were costed as they were recorded, an audit adjustment charging Inventory and crediting Cost of Sales also must be made. If the credit memoranda issued after the balance sheet date are legitimate and in the regular course of business, they would be entered in the period subsequent to the balance sheet date.

Sales returns and allowances may offer the auditor excellent clues to defective merchandise; to labor and inspection failures; and to such practices as fictitious sales, shipping to customers without a purchase order, and returns and allowances authorized by improper personnel. Because there is no return on merchandise in a sales allowance and consequently no receiving report, the auditor must use extreme care and examine correspondence files for possible differences of opinion between client and debtor, and for differences between agreed allowances and recorded allowances. Sales allowances should be approved by someone who does not have access to cash or inventory.

Reclassify Consignment Accounts, if Applicable. Merchandise out on consignment grants the consignee the privilege of deferring payment until the merchandise is sold. If merchandise is out on consignment, consignment records should be maintained. Today, many companies treat consignments-out as sales at the time of consignment. The consigned inventories are owned by the consignor and should be included in his inventory at the close of a period, regardless of the method of accounting at the time of consignment. The auditor must examine consignment contracts and records and must examine the accounts receivable to ascertain if consignments-out accounts are included therein. One good indication as to whether an account represents an outward consignment exists where the account shows large debits and small irregular or periodic payment credits. The auditor may not realize that an account is a consignment unless he looks for small credits, or confirms the accounts, or examines correspondence, or watches for consignment reports accompanying customer remittances. It may be necessary to wait several days after the period-end in order to obtain the year-end consignment report of a consignee.

When goods are consigned out, profit should not be recognized until the goods are sold by the consignee. The auditor should obtain year-end confirmations from consignees for goods sold to the year-end and for remaining inventory at that date. Consignment sales profits may be reduced by certain expenses allowed consignees in addition to commissions, all in accordance with the agreement between the consignor and the consignee. If the consignor has billed goods shipped to the consignee at a price above cost, the remaining inventory must be reduced—at least to cost.

Under any given circumstance of handling goods consigned in and/or out, the auditor must:

1. Ascertain that remaining inventories appear on the records of a client consignor at no more than cost.
2. Ascertain that remaining goods do not appear as inventory on the records of a client consignee.
3. Ascertain that a client consignor has taken up all profits on out-consigned goods sold by consignees through the last day of the period.
4. Ascertain that a client consignor has reduced his profits by agreed expenses allowed the consignees.
5 Ascertain that a client consignee has recorded all profits on in-consigned goods sold through the last day of the period.

6. Ascertain that a client consignee has deducted allowable expenses from his remittances to consignors.

In the schedule of accounts receivable in Illustration 13-3, space is provided for the segregation of consignment accounts which might be included in receivables. An audit adjustment should be made as follows:

```
Sales . . . . . . . . . . . . . . . . . . . . . . . . . . . . . . . .   1,000
Inventory. . . . . . . . . . . . . . . . . . . . . . . . . . . . . .     700
    Cost of Sales . . . . . . . . . . . . . . . . . . . . . . . . .           700
    Accounts Receivable . . . . . . . . . . . . . . . . . . . . .             1,000
    To restore to inventory the cost of consigned goods, and
    to relieve trade accounts receivable of the sales price of
    consigned goods.
```

If consigned goods were sold at the balance sheet date, as indicated by a consignment report, but if the consignee had not remitted, the account receivable should be included as such and the sale recorded.

Examine Accounts Receivable from Affiliated Companies. In preparing an analysis of accounts receivable (see Illustration 13-3), the "accounts receivable" of subsidiary and otherwise affiliated companies may be found to represent sales, merchandise transfers, advances of assets, or expenses paid. Each such receivable must be analyzed to determine if the account is a current or noncurrent asset; the classification depends upon the nature of the account and the intention behind the transactions.

In a consolidated balance sheet, accounts receivable from subsidiary companies are eliminated against the related accounts payable on the statements of the subsidiary companies; and all other intercompany accounts are eliminated. If a consolidated balance sheet is not prepared, accounts receivable from subsidiary companies are shown in the balance sheet. Credits to subsidiary company accounts for returns and allowances made subsequent to the close of the period must be investigated, since the possibilities for management fraud exist in this connection.

Determine Proper Treatment of Branch Accounts. The examination of trade accounts receivable of domestic branches follows the same procedure as that adopted in the examination of any trade receivable. A branch may keep its own accounts receivable, or they may be kept at the home office. If a branch does not keep its accounts receivable, the auditor must investigate to be certain that the accounts receivable do not include accounts reciprocal at the home office; if reciprocal accounts are so maintained, they must be eliminated from the trade receivables.

ILLUSTRATION. A summarized analysis of an "account receivable" with a sales branch is as follows:

```
Receivable from branch customers . . . . . . . . . . . $2,000
Cash advance to branch . . . . . . . . . . . . . . . . .    500
Expenses paid for branch . . . . . . . . . . . . . . . .    100
    Total . . . . . . . . . . . . . . . . . . . . . . . . . . . $2,600
```

Only the receivables from branch customers are current assets.

Concerns with foreign branches frequently operate each branch as a separate organization. It is normal procedure to maintain the accounts in the home office, although many large companies use one account with each branch, in which case each foreign branch carries a complete set of records, plus its reciprocal account with the home office. If the records are kept at the home office, amounts may be stated in home office currency or both home office and foreign country currencies. At the branch, it is normal procedure to carry amounts in the currency of the country in which the branch is located.

If the foreign branch is audited by a recognized accountant of the foreign country, the domestic auditor will accept his report—after proper examination—and then consolidate the accepted financial statements of the foreign branch with those of his domestic client. Amounts stated in foreign currencies should be converted to domestic currencies at the balance sheet date so that financial statements may be prepared with a common denominator.

If funds in foreign branches are in any way restricted, the consolidated balance sheet should clearly show such restriction.

Examine the Treatment of Foreign Receivables. Sales are often made to customers in foreign countries directly from the domestic home office. If sales to customers in foreign countries are made against open drafts, it is always possible that a draft will not be honored. In such cases, an account receivable should not appear; the transaction should be handled on a basis similar to that of a consignment, and the goods should be included in the inventory of the client-exporter. If payment has been received preceding shipment, this situation will not exist; and the auditor must examine the records to be certain that the money received and the inventory are not both included. When foreign accounts receivable exist, original orders and shipping records must be examined to determine validity; and investigation must prove that the merchandise is in the hands of a foreign customer and not a foreign sales agent.

ILLUSTRATION. Diversion of funds from foreign customers and other sources may be exemplified as follows: When the bookkeeper was absent from the office, the president noticed that a check in the amount of $2,500, remitted by a foreign customer, had been credited to the accounts of six domestic customers. For years, the bookkeeper had been misappropriating C.O.D. cash and covering the diversions by depositing foreign remittances and crediting the C.O.D. accounts.

Segregate Nontrade Receivables from Officers, Directors, and Stockholders. Amounts due from officers, directors, and stockhollders must be carefully investigated. The client may keep such items in his accounts receivable ledger, or they may be kept separately; in the former instance, they should be separated in the accounts receivable schedule (Illustration 13–3). The accounts must be analyzed, even if there is no balance at the balance sheet date, in order to determine the reason for their existence, to determine that credits are proper, and to determine proper balance sheet presentation. The audit report may carry the detail of these items; in many cases, these "accounts receivable" are not current assets.

If any of the items are loans to client personnel, the corporation's code of regulations should be examined to determine if the action is permissible. Also, the auditor should obtain direct confirmation of all open and closed loans.

Analyze and Segregate Other Nontrade Receivables. In addition to nontrade accounts receivable already mentioned, there are many other nontrade receivables which should be segregated from trade accounts receivable in the balance sheet. Many nontrade accounts receivable are not current assets. A few nontrade receivables are indicated at this point. Care must also be exercised in discovering improper credits to nontrade accounts receivable.

Uncollected subscriptions to capital stock of the client corporation may or may not be evidenced by notes. The account balance should be verified by confirmation and inspection of contracts, and their collectibility determined in a manner similar to that for any receivable.

Deposits may be on contracts, on open bids, on public utility facilities, for faith of performance, and so forth. In certain cases, the deposits should be confirmed; in other cases—as exemplified by deposits with public utilities—correspondence and receipts should be inspected.

Claims against transportation companies, insurance companies, and others should be examined by oral investigation, inspection of correspondence, and copies of claims filed and approved. Proofs of loss must be examined.

Determine Pledged Accounts and Determine Customers' Equity. The auditor may discover that a client is being partially financed as follows:

a) By pledging accounts receivable as bank loan security.
b) By assigning accounts receivable to financing companies.
c) By factoring.

When accounts receivable are pledged or hypothecated as loan security with a bank or a finance company, the lien should be disclosed in the records; and the balance sheet should contain a statement, parenthetically or by footnote, of the total dollar amount of the pledged receivables. The loan would appear as a liability. The pledged receivables should be confirmed by the bank or finance company for the amount of the loan and for the total of the uncollected balances of the receivables pledged.

When a loan is obtained by pledging selected receivables, there are two methods of granting the loan:

a) *The substitution plan.* In this plan, the borrower who has pledged the receivables accepted by the bank is permitted to use all cash received from customers whose accounts were pledged, provided he can substitute other acceptable accounts receivable of equal amount; if this cannot be done, the loan must be reduced.

b) *The nonsubstitution plan.* Under this method, customers will remit either directly to the bank or directly to the borrrower, in accordance with the agreement with the bank. If remittance is made to the borrower, the borrower then remits to the bank daily or weekly for all collections from pledged receivables of that day or week. The bank holds such remittances in escrow in the name of the borrower.

In either plan, a loan agreement will exist between the bank and the borrower which must be investigated in order to determine the accounts pledged. The listing of the pledged accounts must be compared with the indicated items in the accounts receivable ledger.

In the accounts receivable ledger, each pledged account should be coded to indicate that it is pledged by stamping the account entry; and underlying invoice copies should be so stamped, even if the agreement does not require it.

The *assignment* of accounts receivable differs in procedure from pledging as loan collateral. When accounts receivable are assigned, the assignment agreement with the finance company may or may not require that all invoices and periodic statements sent to customers bear a notice of the assignment. If the notice of assignment on invoices and statements directs that the debtor remit to the assignee, that is called the "notification" plan. If notice of assignment is not required, the debtor remits to the borrower; that is known as the "nonnotification" plan.

Normally, the assignment of accounts receivable is accompanied by a guaranty by the assignor that the accounts either will be collected or replaced by collectible accounts. In infrequent cases, the accounts are assigned without guaranty. In such cases, the customers' ledger accounts should be closed to indicate the completion of the transaction. In cases of assignment without guaranty, there is no remaining equity for the assignor. However, if an auditor discovers closed accounts as the result of an assignment, he should investigate before concluding that the assignment was outright, without guaranty; the client may have recorded the entries incorrectly. In order to establish proof of no guaranty, a confirmation to that effect must be obtained from the assignee.

If accounts receivable have been assigned in the customary manner, accompanied by a guaranty of collection by the assignor, the assignee normally will advance only a portion of the face value, retaining the balance in support of the guaranty. In the ledger, the accounts assigned (and related specific invoices) should be marked to show that they have been assigned together with the name of the assignee.

When accounts receivable have been thus assigned, the auditor should read the contract to ascertain that all conditions have been fulfilled. He should then obtain a confirmation from the assignee setting forth (*a*) the balance of the uncollected assigned accounts; (*b*) the amount advanced by the assignee; and (*c*) the amount withheld by the assignee—that is, the guaranty fund. The assignee normally requires a schedule of the invoices assigned and reasonable proof of shipment. The schedule is supported by copies of the invoices rendered customers, to which are attached the formal account, properly signed by the designated person.

The accounting for assigned accounts receivable is similar to that for notes receivable discounted. When accounts receivable are assigned, the usual entries are as follows:

```
Cash ..................................  13,400
Equity in Assigned Receivables ...............   6,000
Discount Expense.......................     600
    Accounts Receivable Assigned .............          20,000
```

The balance sheet of the conditional assignor should show the assigned accounts. There are several methods of portraying the assignment in the balance sheet, one of which is as follows:

```
Accounts receivable. ....................               $62,750
    Less: Assigned accounts ...............  $20,000
    Amount withheld.....................    6,000    14,000
                                                      $48,750
```

Since the assignor may become liable for the amount of the guaranty, this fact should be expressed on the balance sheet, as above, or as a footnote. Merely to show the accounts receivable at $48,750 hides the contingency of $20,000 and the fact of assignment. The provision for doubtful accounts would be subtracted from the $48,750 remaining equity, and the provision should be large enough to cover losses on *all* accounts receivable.

The auditor should examine the accounting records for several weeks after the close of the fiscal period in order to ascertain if any of the accounts assigned at the balance sheet date were reacquired. Such reacquisition may be the result of an uncollectible item, in which case the auditor is better enabled to value the assigned accounts as of the close of the period. In addition to the foregoing reasons for the examination of the records after the balance sheet date, it may be that the assignment was made shortly before the close of the period in order to strengthen the cash position, with reacquisition of the receivables immediately after the close of the period. In conditions of this nature, made for the obvious purpose of "window dressing" the balance sheet, full disclosure of the reacquisition should be made in the report.

The *factor* is a modern manifestation of specialization and has become increasingly prominent in certain industries. Briefly, the services rendered by the factor include, among others, granting credit, billing the customer, and collecting the accounts receivable. The effect is to eliminate the credit, billing, and collection departments of a manufacturer, jobber, or merchant. The factor guarantees payment of all accounts approved by him, since he has approved all sales; if the factor rejects an account, the factoring merchant has the privilege of assuming it. The records of the factoring merchant will show only one account with the factor and no accepted customer accounts receivable.

The auditor must obtain confirmation from the factor of the amount due from him or to him, advances by the factor, and collateral held, if any; he must read the factoring agreement and verify charges for interest, discount, allowances, and transportation.

Determine Account Collectibility.   Collection constitutes proof of collectibility. Confirmations and other auditing procedures attempt to establish proof of the existence and accuracy of the accounts. However, an account may be confirmed, it may be correct, it may be valid—and it may never be collected. Therefore, the auditor must attempt to determine the collectibility of the accounts receivable, so that financial statements may be properly prepared and so that an adequate expression of opinion may be rendered in the audit report. One method of determining collectibility is to investigate the accounts, noting all evidences of possible uncollectible items. The procedure under this plan would be somewhat as follows: The total of the debit balances must be compared with the credit sales for the credit period.

ILLUSTRATION. If the credit terms are 2/10, n/30, and all discounts are normally taken, and if the credit sales for the 30-day period preceding the date of the examination amounted to $250,000, the balance of the accounts receivable should not be more than about $85,000; if the balance is $350,000, at least $100,000 is past due, even if no discounts have been taken. The collection experience of the current year should be compared with that of the preceding year. It is also possible that certain customers were granted special terms; this should be investigated and abuse of the credit-terms privilege directed to the attention of management.

The next step would involve a discussion of the receivables and their collectibility with credit department personnel. If a company has many customers and a major portion of the business is not conducted with any one customer, that company in general may be in a better collection position than a company with a few large customers. An examination should then be made of the losses of preceding periods and of the uncollectible accounts charged off in the current period, to determine if the bad debt rate is increasing and if uncollectible account charge-offs are properly approved. Finally, correspondence would be examined for indications of bad debts and probable future uncollectible accounts.

List Past-Due Accounts Not Paid at the Completion of the Audit.
Payments on past-due accounts made prior to closing an engagement
should be indicated in the work papers, since such payments might affect
the provisions for doubtful accounts.

***Determine the Adequacy of the Provision (Allowance) for Doubtful
Accounts.*** As shown in Illustration 13–3, accounts considered doubtful
should be provided for in the Provision for Doubtful Accounts; and
all accounts considered to be uncollectible should be charged to Bad
Debts Expense or to the provision therefor. In deciding whether an account is *doubtful*, judgment must be used. That judgment may be formulated affirmatively if the following conditions exist:

a) If notes have been accepted for past-due accounts receivable.

b) If accounts are in the hands of collection agencies or lawyers.

c) If a customer is in receivership.

d) If a customer is on a C.O.D. basis but has an unpaid previous balance
in open receivables.

e) If periodic charges to receivables exceed periodic credits and
balances continue to increase.

f) If a customer is no longer charging and is liquidating his balance in
round amounts.

g) When answers are not received to collection letters.

In deciding if an account is beyond the doubtful stage and in the
category of an *uncollectible* account, the guides to uncollectibility may
be expressed as follows:

a) If a customer has been discharged from bankruptcy and there are no
dividends.

b) If a customer has disappeared, is out of business, or is deceased.

c) When collection is barred by the statute of limitations.

d) If there is a long-standing balance and there has been no reply to
payment requests.

e) If a collection agency indicates inability to collect.

f) If there are disputed items which the client is willing to settle.

If the direct charge-off method of handling doubtful accounts is not
used, then a provision for doubtful accounts must be created. The creation
of an allowance merely suspends the credit to Accounts Receivable to
the time of proved uncollectibility. The annual charge to Bad Debts
Expense is based upon total sales, charge sales, or the balance of accounts
receivable, or is created as a result of aging the accounts receivable.
In setting up a provision for doubtful accounts, the collection experience
of the client must be taken into consideration. Whatever method is used,
the auditor should review it and watch its effectiveness. Doubtful accounts should be discussed with the client before the auditor adjusts
a provision. Some companies set up an allowance for doubtful accounts

separately for each fiscal year; if this procedure has been followed, the auditor may more easily determine its adequacy than if a blanket allowance for all past years is used. If separate annual provisions are employed and if the credit sales for each year are divided into the accounts receivable written off each year, a useful ratio is obtained. The average of this ratio for several years, applied to the credit sales of the current year, should result in a test of the adequacy of the current year's provision.

An auditor must ascertain that receivables written off as uncollectible have been properly authorized, preferably by the credit department and another executive or the legal department, if one is maintained; unauthorized charge-offs should not be permitted and the attention of the client should be called to any such charge-offs. The auditor also should examine all correspondence connected with the charge-off of any account receivable. He also must investigate the method of controlling the accounts charged off so that a future recovery may be properly handled. If correspondence indicates a good credit rating, the auditor should investigate for fraud in connection with recoveries of accounts charged off. If the client has a mixture of small and large accounts receivable and if he employs a percentage method to create the allowance, the auditor should inspect the accounts with large balances, since the loss of one of these might eliminate the provision.

If notes are taken for doubtful accounts, the full amount of the note probably should be provided for in the allowance. Notes charged off should be returned to the Accounts' Receivable account and charged off from there in order to complete the credit record. If charge-offs are recovered, the recovery should be passed through Accounts Receivable in order to add to the credit record. Such recoveries must be traced to the bank.

It sometimes happens that a debtor may be constantly paying on an account; at the same time, the balance may be continually increasing. This is a danger signal; in providing for the allowance the auditor must realize that there is the probability of sudden termination of payments. Arrangements may be made to place this type of customer on a C.O.D. basis.

Companies selling on the installment plan—and using the deferred gross profits method of taking up income—have no justification for creating *any* allowance for doubtful accounts, collection expenses, or losses on repossessions, unless these losses and expenses are likely to exceed the amount of the gross profit deferred. A proper matching of revenues and expenses prohibits the charging of expenses prior to the recognition of related revenue, particularly when the revenue deferred is far in excess of the estimated expenses to be incurred in the realization of the revenue.

Companies that recognize income on installment sales at the time of sale should provide adequate allowances for doubtful accounts, for losses on repossessions, and even for collection expenses. In such cases, a separate allowance may be set up for each year's sales. For example, if a 1975 account proves uncollectible in 1977, the 1975 allowance would be charged—that is, the auditor must ascertain that the allowance for the correct year has been charged. He must also determine the adequacy of the remaining allowance for each year; if all accounts from any one year have been collected, any remaining balance must be transferred to income.

In the work papers, the summary of the aging of the installment receivables and the percentage and amount of the related allowance may be illustrated as follows:

Accounts with:	Account Totals	Allowance Percentage	Allowance Amount
No delinquent installments	$101,000	5 percent	$ 5,050
One delinquent installment	30,000	10 percent	3,000
Two delinquent installments.	22,000	30 percent	6,600
Three delinquent installments	14,000	40 percent	5,600
Four delinquent installments	7,000	60 percent	4,200
Five delinquent installments.	2,000	70 percent	1,400
Over five delinquent installments	500	100 percent	500
Total Installment Accounts	$176,500		$26,350

In verifying installment accounts and notes receivable and the related provision for doubtful items, the auditor may discover that the client holds chattel mortgages against the items sold. When such a situation exists, a provision for doubtful accounts *may* not be necessary; however, adequate provisions for repossession losses should be created. If provisions for repossession losses have been set up, the auditor must verify their computation and determine their adequacy on the basis of past experience and anticipated conditions. If the client will not follow the practice of using such provisions or allowances; the auditor may comment to that effect in his report.

Other Provisions or Allowances. A few companies create allowances for sales rebates, discounts other than cash, and transportation charges to be deducted. The auditor should verify sales allowances on the basis of past experience. Allowances for discounts other than cash should be verified on the basis of available discounts in the balance of the accounts receivable at the close of the period. Normally, the charges creating such allowances are to be deducted from Sales and should not be considered as expenses in the income statement. Allowances for transportation should be estimated on the basis of merchandise sold F.O.B. destination, wherein the customer pays the transportation charge and deducts it from his remittance to the seller. Where there are allowances of the nature outlined, the auditor must satisfy himself concerning their adequacy and consistency from year to year.

Written Representations Obtained from the Client

If an auditor requests from the client his written representations covering accounts and notes receivable, the certificate thus obtained should be signed by the treasurer and the credit manager. The representations should be somewhat as follows:

1. Trade accounts and trade notes receivable represent valid claims against customers of the company.
2. Nontrade receivables from officers, directors, stockholders, and controlled companies are correctly and properly set forth in the balance sheet.
3. Consignments are excluded from the receivables.
4. The accounts receivable balance contains no charges for merchandise shipped after the balance sheet date.
5. All assigned receivables are properly indicated in the records.
6. All notes receivable discounted are properly indicated in the balance sheet.
7. The balance of the accounts and notes receivable is not subject to allowances for price adjustments, liens, transportation deduction, or discounts in excess of the customary cash discount.
8. All known uncollectible notes and accounts receivable have been charged off at the balance date.
9. The allowance for doubtful accounts of $_____, in the opinion of undersigned, is adequate to provide for all losses in the receivables at the balance sheet date which may result from uncollectibility.

Management Reports

Management requires periodic reports of accounts receivable in order to be certain that all work relating to them is being performed in accordance with company policy. The required reports include:

1. An aged trial balance of the receivables. The dollar amount in each age classification should be expressed as a percentage of the total receivables. This report focuses immediate attention upon the quality of the receivables from report date to report date and in comparison with the same report date of the prior year. This report also furnishes management with information regarding the effectiveness of the collection program.

2. Analyses of requests for credit, classified into those approved and those rejected. Decisions then may be made regarding the credit policy of the company—it may be proper, or too lenient, or too rigorous—and the resultant effect on profitable operations.

3. An analysis of accounts charged off as uncollectible. If the causes of bad debts can be determined, decisions may be made regarding the effectiveness of credit and collection policies. Also, such analysis and

proper follow-up discourages fraudulent charge-offs and premature charge-offs.

SECTION IV: FINANCIAL STATEMENT CONSIDERATIONS

Presentation of Accounts Receivable

In the balance sheet, accounts receivable should be divided between trade and nontrade. If nontrade accounts receivable are material in amount (assume 5 percent of the total), they should be segregated as to their nontrade sources—for example, receivables from officers, directors, stockholders, affiliated companies, capital stock subscriptions, contract prepayments, bid deposits, and so forth. This segregation is necessary due to the relationship of these persons to the corporate entity, the responsibility to owners, and the possibilities of personal interest. If the items are strictly insignificant in amount, they may be shown in one total as "other accounts receivable."

Receivables from affiliated companies should be segregated on the basis of presenting intercompany data as distinct from trade data and on the basis that a receivable may represent or be converted to a long-term advance. The question of treating affiliated company receivables as current asset in the balance sheet depends upon expected cash collectibility.

Receivables from capital stock subscriptions should be segregated in the balance sheet, due to the relationship of the receivable to the capital structure. Capital stock subscriptions are treated as current assets if collection is anticipated and reasonably certain and if the cash to be received is to be used for working capital purposes. If collection is uncertain or not contemplated, the items should be subtracted from the proper Capital Stock—or Capital Stock Subscribed—account, since assets will not be realized.

Receivables of significant amount from foreign customers preferably should be segregated in the balance sheet if the collection time is longer than that for normal domestic receivables.

Trade accounts receivable should be stated at their *gross* debit total. If credit balances occur in any of the accounts receivable and cannot be offset by a debit balance in the same account, these balances actually are accounts payable and should be shown separately among the current liabilities, if material in amount. If the total of the credit balances is small, it may be shown with the miscellaneous accounts payable. Credit balances in accounts receivable may be liquidated, or they may be eliminated by future sales; but for balance sheet purposes, they should not be deducted from the gross debit balance of the accounts receivable.

The presentation of assigned accounts receivable was illustrated earlier. If accounts receivable are pledged as loan collateral, the fact of hypothecation should be stated parenthetically.

Allowances for doubtfull accounts discounts, transportation charges to be deducted, and rebates should be subtracted in the balance sheet from the gross total of the trade accounts receivable and the balance of the receivables shown net. If an allowance for doubtful accounts is not used—or is not necessary—the balance sheet should point to that fact. If accounts receivable are not properly subdivided, creditors and investors may be misled; and it might be alleged that the auditor was negligent in his duties.

Relating to the classification of assets as current or other than current, Rule 3–13 of Regulation S–X of the Securities and Exchange Commission states:

Items classed as current assets shall be generally realizable within one year. However, generally recognized trade practices may be followed with respect to items such as installment receivables or inventories long in process, provided an appropriate explanation of the circumstances is made and, if practicable, an estimate is given of the amount not realizable within one year.

Thus, in preparing financial statements in conformity with the requirements of the Securities and Exchange Commission, the segregation indicated in the rule must be followed.

SECTION V: ADDITIONAL REVENUE CONSIDERATIONS

Revenues

Assurance that all revenues earned have been recorded is an important phase of any audit. The balance sheet is an excellent guide in determining all possible sources of revenue. Assets that usually produce revenue may appear, and investigation may prove that no revenue or insufficient revenue is being received, or that revenue is being received and not recorded. This is an immediate notice that the auditor may be of constructive service in suggesting more profitable investments or in tracing revenue that is not finding its way to the client.

Sales

All sales are either for cash or on credit. Ignoring fraud, errors in recording sales result in an overstatement on an understatement of revenues. Errors that result in an overstatement of sales and that the auditor must detect are:

1. Proper credits to other accounts, passed to the sales accounts in error.
2. Crediting Sales for orders taken when goods have not been shipped.
3. Crediting some account other than Sales for sales made.
4. Making errors in computing invoices.
5. Closing the sales records prematurely in the preceding period

The errors resulting in understatements of sales are:

1. Errors in computing invoices.
2. Failure to take up profits on consignment sales actually consummated.
3. Crediting some account other than Sales for sales made.
4. Failure to record sales.
5. Holding the sales records open beyond the end of the preceding period, which reduces sales figures for the current period.
6. Prematurely closing the sales records for the current period.

The vouching of the original evidence of sales at the time original documentary and accounting evidence is examined normally is the first step in the sales audit program and is conducted on the basis of samples.

If internal control and the recording system are satisfactory, sales *record totals* should be proved for one or two months, and the totals should be compared with charges to receivables and to cash. If internal control and the recording system are not satisfactory, sales transactions should be examined in greater detail and the failures of the system should be reported. Sales *ostensibly* made but not delivered do not constitute real sales, should not be anticipated, and therefore should be excluded from sales. An expected sale may be canceled at any time; and even though a sales order may lead to the collection of the profit on the cancellation, that does not constitute justification for recording such anticipation. The only justification for taking up profits on uncompleted work exists in industries in which the construction period overlaps the accounting period. Cases of this nature are exemplified almost exclusively in the heavy construction industries. In such businesses, care must be exercised to determine the validity and accuracy of the degree of completion of the contracts; otherwise, net income will be distorted between accounting periods.

In comparing sales of the current year with sales of the preceding year or years, the auditor must ascertain that the Sales account includes only those items held forth for sale in the regular course of business operations. Pronounced fluctuations in sales should be investigated for cause and effect. Common causes of increase or decrease in product sales include the following: general business conditions; price policy changes; style changes; changes caused by product emphasis or de-emphasis; interruptions to business caused by strikes, fires, or other events; the use of substitute products; changes in managerial efficiency; and employee dishonesty. Illustrations are presented in Chapter 28 showing dollar and percentage increases or decreases from the preceding year.

For a manufacturing concern, sales should be classified by products; for a mercantile concern, they should be classified by departments and in some cases by products according to departments. Many other classifications are possible; those indicated in Illustrations 13–6 and 13–7 and in Chapter 28 are of assistance to an auditor in order properly to analyze the sales transactions of a business and advise the client.

ILLUSTRATION 13–6

B COMPANY

Product Sales Analysis, December 31, 1975

1975	Venetian Blinds	Traverse Rods	U-Do-It Kits	Awnings	Repair Work	Total
January	$ 15,342	$ 1,721	$ 956	$ 255	$ 565	$ 18,839
February	10,161	950	433	368	712	12,624
March	22,840 √ϕ	2,482 √ϕ	1,121 √ϕ	985 √ϕ	625 √ϕ	27,693
April	37,246	3,247	1,432	2,347	969	45,241
May	62,357 ∧	5,960 ∧	3,006 ∧	4,691 ∧	1,475 ∧	77,489 ∧
June	85,135	8,146	3,927	7,211	1,322	105,741
July	71,468 √ϕ	6,912 √ϕ	3,941 √ϕ	8,928 √ϕ	1,140 √ϕ	92,389
August	40,860	4,111	2,103	6,402	982	54,458
September	23,682	2,428	1,116	3,195	741	31,162
October	35,849	3,610	1,927	850	1,069	43,305
November	26,489	2,728	1,408	205	542	31,372
December	19,712 –√ϕ	1,847 –√ϕ	989 –√ϕ	182 –√ϕ	767 –√ϕ	23,497
Total	$451,141 ⊙	$44,142 ⊙	$22,359 ⊙	$35,529 ⊙	$10,909 ⊙	$564,080 ⊙

√ Priced, extended, and totaled 240 duplicate invoices. Error: $48.63 in 7 invoices. Ignore.
∧ Tested sales account distributions. O.K.
ϕ Tested 10 percent of the postings to customers'·accounts.
⊙ Footings agree with postings to the general ledger sales accounts.
– Compared invoices and shipping records for December 20–31. Cutoff proper.

Comparison with 1974:

1974 sales	$380,752	$46,976	$24,202	$42,727	$11,264	$505,921

Increase (+) or decrease (–)

| 1975 over 1974 | +70,389 | –2,834 | –1,843 | –7,198 | –355 | +58,159 |

Shipping records are examined as valid evidence of shipping dates; hence, they serve as the guide for the proper closing of the sales records. A comparison of the sales invoices with shipping records also might reveal a pronounced increase or decrease in sales toward the end or in the beginning of a period, thereby possibly indicating late or premature closing of the sales records. For the last several days of the accounting period and for the first few days of the subsequent period, the auditor should compare the orders received and the sales invoices against the sales records to determine that all are recorded, and he should examine subsidiary ledgers to ascertain that proper customers were charged. If an order was received before the close of the period, was not shipped or only partially shipped at the close of the period, and was recorded in total as a sale, both accounts receivable and sales are overstated. Also, if orders were received and shipments made before the end of the period and if the sales are recorded as of the new period, sales and receivables are understated for the period under audit. The sales figures shown should

ILLUSTRATION 13–7

B COMPANY

Proof of Venetian Blind Sales Accuracy, December 31, 1975

Inventory, January 1, 1975	$ 28,746
Purchases	156,752 √
Labor	95,325 ∧
Overhead.	66,392 ⌀
	$347,215
Inventory, December 31, 1975	31,416
Cost of blinds sold:	$315,799
Cost of blinds sold is 70 percent of net sales	$315,799
Add gross profit—actual	135,210
	$451,009
Difference (ignore)	$ 132

√ Traced to test-months' invoices.
∧ Distribution verified.
⌀ Allocation to products examined.

represent net sales prices—that is, the gross sales price less such items as trade discounts, quantity discounts, and freight charged to customers. Cash discounts may or may not be deducted, depending upon the cash discount policy of the seller.

It is sometimes possible to verify roughly the accuracy of sales figures by computing the number of product units sold and multiplying by the unit sales price. This is usually possible only if commodities are few in number and if unit inventory records are properly reduced upon shipment. The formula for such a test is as follows: Units of inventory at beginning of period, plus units manufactured or purchased, minus units in ending inventory, equals units sold during period.

Miscellaneous Sales Considerations

Invoice Examination. Invoice examination loses some of its importance when accounts receivable are confirmed, because the confirmation replies tend to reveal fictitious billings. As stated before, sales orders must be compared with sales entries and shipping records in order to determine that orders received were shipped, that proper entries were made, and to ascertain that shipments were made only for orders received. If sales orders exist and if there is no record of the related sales, the auditor should trace the reason for nonshipment in order to be certain that the sale was not recorded and the proceeds diverted. If shipment is made and no order exists, the shipment may have been made as a theft of goods through collusion with an outside party; or the shipment may have been made near the end of the period, in order to overstate sales, since the goods could not be returned until the following period. If sales are evidenced by the release of tags or tickets from merchandise, the auditor must ascertain that all such evidence is retained as carefully as cash register tapes or invoices. Sales must be test-traced to the sales accounts, to the cash accounts and to the bank, and to the accounts receivable accounts—both control and subsidiary.

Sales by Field Agents. In certain industries, sales are made by field agents; the reports of these representatives are treated by the auditor as though they were original invoices, with proper verification of sales made and collections received. If field representatives are selling tangible merchandise and if the merchandise is charged to them at retail, the agent is accountable for the total charged to him, either in the form of cash or merchandise, or both. In terms of the quantity of product sold, sales should be reconciled with the beginning inventory plus purchases (or production figures) minus the ending inventory, in order to determine the correctness of quantities sold. When multiplied by the prices, the quantities will equal the total sales dollars.

By-Product Sales. Two theories of almost equal merit are followed in connection with by-product sales. One theory provides for treatment of by-product sales as a reduction of the cost of the main product, whereas the other advocates treatment of the by-product sales as a separate sales item. In many industries, the sales of by-products constitute an important source of revenue; in those cases, the auditor must ascertain that by-product sales are correctly and consistently treated. By-products are frequently sold at a loss, unknown to the producer, whereas a change in price policy and a more rigid cost allocation might result in producing a profit on these sales. The verification of by-product sales follows the same audit path as the verification of any sale. In some cases, by-products are scrapped completely, whereas a little processing of the product would result in an increased net income; in other cases, by-products are processed and sold, whereas the net income would be increased if the by-product, unprocessed, were given away.

Sales of Scrap Material. The same general remarks apply to sales of scrap material as to sales of by-products. Sales of scrap may be treated as (1) sales, (2) cost reductions, or (3) other revenue. The auditor should inquire as to the disposal of scrap and should verify scrap sales in the regular manner. Cost of handling scrap must be weighed against the revenue obtainable, and the proper disposition must be judged by the possibility of the maximum net income which can be produced. The auditor must be careful to detect cases of unrecorded scrap sales, which means that income is being diverted from its correct channels.

Revenues Received in Advance. The auditor must analyze original records in order to determine the proper division between the realized revenue and the amount of the revenue received in advance. In the rendering of a service, the discounting of commercial paper, the taking of subscriptions for future delivery, or the sale of tickets for future use, this situation will occur. Comparisons should be made of the volume of orders for future delivery on hand at the end of the current year and of the preceding year. If fluctuations are pronounced or if the future contracts will result in sales at a lowered profit because of rising costs, management's attention should be directed to the situation.

When revenue is received from subscriptions, the possibilities for performing a satisfactory audit do not always exist. Subscriptions may be the result of regular solicitations by authorized personnel, in which case duplicate and serially numbered subscription blanks may be available. The retained duplicate serves the auditor as his evidence of the probability of revenue; but it is possible, of course, to prepare the duplicate for an amount different from the original left with the subscriber. If the subscriptions are for magazines, mailing lists may be used as the basis of determining the amount of revenue that should be or has been received. Differences between the mailing list data or other available data and the accounting information shown in the original records should be reconciled in order to make certain that all revenue received has been recorded.

The subscription or other records serve as the basis of computation of the amount of revenue received in advance as well as the amount earned. Since there is no uniformity of method in the recording of subscriptions, there can be no uniformity in the method of auditing revenues from such sources; the auditor must use his own ingenuity in each case and conduct his work so that proper net income results are shown. Systems of internal control should be devised so that the persons receiving money do not have access to any other records and so that the persons responsible for the subscription records never come in contact with the cash receipts.

Dues for clubs, associations, and other membership organizations are verified by an examination of membership lists which have been approved by responsible officers, and by an examination of the secretary's records for admission of new members and resignations within the fiscal year. The periodic amount of the dues for varying classes of members is determined; and from the data obtained, the total revenue is computed. The auditor must trace dues received to the records to be certain that all revenue has been recorded.

Rental Revenue.   Rental revenues are verified in accordance with the terms of the lease, if one exists. The auditor should obtain or prepare a schedule of rentals by properties, tenants, and periodic rentals. A schedule of occupancy and vacancy should be requested from someone not responsible for collections or the recording of cash receipts. From the schedule of occupancy and vacancy, and from the rental schedule, the auditor should compute the total rent which should be received and verify the cash receipts and the rent accounts to determine that the proper amounts were received. The system of internal control should be adequate to protect the owner against the possibility of rent being received and diverted. All changes in rentals should be authorized by someone not concerned with collections, and the rental schedules should be changed accordingly. Vacancies, which mean the termination of revenue, should be properly authorized. The auditor should indicate all rentals in arrears and inquire into collection attempts in progress. If advance rental payments have been received, they should be prorated between periodic revenue and amounts received in advance. In the audit report, occupancy and vacancy figures should be submitted for study.

It frequently happens that cash or other deposits are required of the lessee as a protection against default. In some cases, the cash deposits apply to the last rental periods; in others, interest on the deposit is paid the lessee by the lessor. Deposits are indicated in the rental contract, and the auditor must verify the existence and correct treatment of such deposits.

Royalties.   In certain types of machinery-manufacturing companies and patent-holding companies, royalties constitute a major revenue. The auditor should examine the royalty contracts, noting particularly the royalty rates and the method and the time of settlement. Statements received from the licensee should be examined in order to determine the correctness of the amounts remitted. Then, the accounts are examined to ascertain that the correct amounts are recorded.

Profits on Long-Term Construction Contracts.   Because many long-term construction periods overlap accounting periods, profits frequently are taken up on the percentage-of-completion method. In the percentage-of-completion method, profit is recorded in the ratio of the actual cost of the partially completed project to the total *estimated* cost of the entire contract.

ILLUSTRATION.   Profit computation on uncompleted construction may be exemplified as follows: Assume that a contract is for $308,000, that the work finished to date has cost $100,000, and that the estimated cost to complete is $120,000.

Contract price		$308,000
Less: Cost to date	$100,000	
Cost to complete (estimated)	120,000	220,000
Estimated profit		$ 88,000

Of the total estimated profit of $88,000, 100/220, or $40,000, represents the amount earned in the current period.

If a contract is on a cost-plus basis, current-period profit can be determined with much greater accuracy than if the contract is for a flat price. In flat-price contracts, many companies originally estimate the gross profit on the contract, and by using the estimated gross profit percentage figure, bring into the records as of the end of the accounting period the estimated gross profit earned on the contract to that date.

If the "completed-contract" method is used, the excess of accumulated costs over current billings should be shown as a current asset. An excess of accumulated billings over corresponding costs is a current liability.

Profits taken up on uncompleted contracts should be verified by the auditor. Mature judgment is necessary to determine (1) the validity of the profits taken up and (2) the cost to complete the contract. If amounts are withheld by the customer—for contingencies or workmanship—the auditor must confirm the amounts, ascertain if the amounts withheld are in agreement with the terms of the contract, and attempt to ascertain the probabilities of contingencies for which the amounts were withheld.

Revenue Examination Summary

Presented below is a brief summary for the examination of sales and other revenues.

a) Investigate the system of internal control.
b) Verify revenues through the audit of original records, and the examination of assets.
c) Audit by comparison.
d) Verify invoice prices, extensions, footings, and discounts.
e) Trace sales from invoices to the sales records.
f) Foot sales records and trace to the ledger accounts.
g) Verify postings to customers' accounts and to inventory records.
h) For a few days before and after the close of the period, compare sales records and shipping records.
i) Examine the accounting for prepaid transportation charges.
j) Examine the treatment of cash from C.O.D. sales.
k) Investigate the accounting for consignment sales.
l) Examine the accuracy of the accounting for installment sales.
m) Test for inventory debits arising from sales returns.
n) Verify interest and dividend revenues.
o) Analyze sales of fixed assets and other nonrecurring revenue-producing items, and ascertain the correctness of recorded net gains or losses from these sources.
p) Examine selected revenue accounts to determine the accuracy of related assets.
q) By reference to the type of business, prove selected revenue accounts.
r) Watch for revenue not recorded.

QUESTIONS

1. You have been engaged to examine the financial statements of Rite, Inc. for the year ended December 31, 1975, you have started the audit. Discuss the following questions relating to your examination:
   a) Several accounts receivable confirmations have been returned with the notation that "verifications of vendors' statements are no longer

possible because of our data processing system." What alternative audit procedures could be used to verify these accounts receivable?

b) You are considering obtaining written representations from the client concerning the financial statements and matters pertinent to them.

(1) What are the reasons for obtaining written representations from the client?

(2) What reliance may the auditor place upon written representations from (*a*) the client, (*b*), independent experts, and (*c*) debtors?

(AICPA, adapted)

2. In your first audit of the financial statements of a large retail store, what procedures should be followed in the examination of accounts receivable?

3. If you consider internal control over the accounts receivable of a client to be proper and if the client uses EDP equipment, what are your reasons for not accepting a print-out, made under your supervision, of the accounts receivable trial balance?

4. In reviewing the individual balances in an accounts receivable trial balance, the auditor must watch for certain factors which will influence his judgment regarding the proper segregation and description of those items for balance sheet purposes. What are these factors and what is the significance of each?

5. a) On engagements where receivables are not confirmed, what criteria does an auditor use to determine whether to express an unqalified opinion, a qualified opinion, or render a disclaimer of opinion?

b) What steps should be taken if 85 percent of a client's debtors (no debtor is any agency of the federal government) refused to confirm accounts receivable balances?

c) Do you consider it necessary to obtain confirmations of accounts receivable paid prior to the completion of an audit? Discuss.

6. You are verifying accounts receivable by positive confirmation. Prepare a list of columnar headings of work papers for the control of confirmation requests sent out and the replies received.

7. Outline a system for the selection for confirmation of five percent of the total of the accounts receivable of a client where individual balances vary from $5 to $5,000. There are 10,000 accounts receivable.

8. Your examination of the financial statements of the City Department Store disclosed the following information:

(1) The store has 30,000 retail accounts which are billed each month on a cycle basis. There are 20 billing cycle divisions of the accounts receivable ledger, and accounts are apportioned alphabetically to the divisions.

(2) All charge sales tickets (prenumbered by the printer) are microfilmed for the sales of each day. The sales tickets are then sorted into their respective cycle divisions, and adding machine tapes are prepared to arrive at the total daily sales for each division. The daily total for the divisions are then combined for comparison with the grand total daily charge sales from cash register readings.

When the totals are balanced, the daily sales tickets are filed behind the related customer account cards in the proper cycle divisions. Cycle control accounts for each division are maintained by posting of the tapes of daily sales.

(3)   At the cycle billing date, all of the customers' transactions are posted to the accounts in the individual cycle. The billing machine automatically accumulates six separate totals: old balance, purchases, returns, payments, new balances, and overdue balances. After posting, the documents and the customers' statements are microfilmed and the statements mailed to the customer.

(4)   Within each division a trial balance of the accounts in the cycle, obtained as a by-product of the posting operation, is compared with the cycle control account.

(5)   Credit terms are net cash within 10 days of receipt of the statement. A credit limit of $300 is set for all accounts.

(6)   Before the statements are mailed they are reviewed to determine which are past due. Accounts are considered past due if the full balance of the prior month has not been paid. Past-due accounts are noted for subsequent collection effort by the credit department.

   a)   What audit procedures would you apply in an audit of the accounts comprising one billing cycle division. Confine your procedures to the sales tickets and charges to the accounts and to the verification of account balances.

   b)   Assume that the group of accounts selected in part (*a*) was in the cycle division billed on January 19. List the additional audit procedures you would apply to satisfy yourself of the reasonableness of the total balance of accounts receivable on January 31, 1975, the fiscal year-end.

(AICPA, adapted)

9.   The Amelia Dairy Company purchases raw milk from farmers, processes the milk, and delivers it to retail customers. You are engaged in auditing the accounts receivable of the company and determine the following:

(1)   The company has 50 retail routes; each route consists of 100 to 200 accounts, the number that can be serviced by a driver in a day.

(2)   The driver enters cash collections from the day's deliveries to each customer directly on a statement form in record books maintained for each route. Mail remittances are posted in the route record books by office personnel. At the end of the month the statements are priced, extended, and footed. Photocopies of the statements are prepared and left in the customers' milk boxes with the next milk delivery.

(3)   The statements are reviewed by the office manager, who prepares a list for each route of accounts with 90-day balances or older. The list is used for intensive collection action.

(4)   The audit program used in prior audits for the selection of retail accounts receivable for confirmation stated: "Select two accounts from each route, one to be chosen by opening the route book at random and the other as the third item on each list of 90-day or older accounts."

Your review of the accounts receivable leads you to conclude that statistical sampling techniques may be applied to their examination.

a) Since statistical sampling techniques do not relieve the CPA of his responsibilities in the exercise of his professional judgment, of what benefit are they to the CPA? Discuss.

b) Give the reasons why the audit procedure previously used for selection of accounts receivable for confirmation (as given in 4 above) would not produce a valid statistical sample.

c) What are the audit objectives or purposes in selecting 90-day accounts for confirmation? Can the application of statistical sampling techniques help in attaining these objectives or purposes? Discuss.

d) Assume that the company has 10,000 accounts receivable and that your statistical sampling disclosed six errors in a sample of 200 accounts. Is it reasonable to assume that 300 accounts in the entire. population are in error? Explain.

(AICPA, adapted)

10. During the examination of accounts receivable, a client asked that you do not request confirmations from certain debtors who do not want their identities revealed to anyone. In this situation, what steps would you follow?

11. A corporation manufactures electronic equipment and sells exclusively to 50 distributors located in major cities in the United States. At the financial statement date, June 30, 1976 receivables from distributors totaled $3,000,000. Total current assets were $6,300,000.

In examining the receivables, the procedures followed were:

(1) A review of the system of internal control proved it to be excellent.

(2) The subsidiary receivables total agreed with the balance of the controlling account as of June 30, 1976.

(3) The receivables were aged, and none was past due.

(4) For the months of January and May, 1976, a detailed examination was made of sales and collections.

(5) Positive confirmations were obtained from the 50 distributors as to the amount of their balances as of June 30, 1976.

You are to criticize the completeness or incompleteness of the preceding audit program. State the reasons for your recommendations concerning the addition or the elimination of any of the procedures outlined.

12. Your client has 50,000 active trade accounts receivable. As of November 30, 1975, a month preceding the close of the fiscal period, trial balances of the accounts receivable were prepared for you by the client. You compared the items on the trial balance with the individual account balances and footed the trial balance. The total was then reconciled with the general ledger controlling account.

At November 30, 1975, accounts receivable confirmation was requested on the following basis: Accounts in excess of $200 (1,000 accounts, aggregating 60 percent of the dollar amount of the receivables) were circularized, with a request for a direct reply; negative confirmations were sent to all other customers. Differences reported had been satisfactorily reconciled.

Ignoring the question of uncollectible and past-due accounts, what additional audit procedures would you recommend in connection with the accounts receivable at the end of the calendar year 1975?

13. In response to a request for positive confirmation of its outstanding receivables, one of your client's customers—a large wholesaler whose debit balance represents approximately 50 percent of the total accounts receivable and 20 percent of the total current assets of the client—replies that its records are not maintained in a manner permitting confirmation.

   a) State the additional audit procedures, if any, which should be followed.

   b) State the disclosures, if any, which should be made in the financial statements or in footnotes thereto.

   c) State the qualifications, comments, or references, if any, you should include in a short-form report in addition to the items in (*b*), above.

14. A client had assigned $2,000,000 of its accounts receivable in order to secure a loan.

   a) How should the assignment be shown in the balance sheet?

   b) If the client failed before the loan was liquidated, how would the claims of other creditors be affected?

15. During the audit of the records of the owner of a large office building, it was noted that the receivables included overdue rentals of 10 percent of the total annual rent. The cashier acts as the accountant; the building manager verifies the rental collections by a comparison of the list of rents receivable furnished by the accountant. The rent rolls are kept by a clerk responsible to the accountant; the clerk prepares the monthly bills and submits them to the accountant, who mails them.

   In order thoroughly to test the rental revenue, what audit procedure would you follow?

16. During the course of an investigation made for the purpose of preparing approximate figures for a proposed sale of a company, you were instructed not to age, analyze, or confirm the accounts receivable. How might you proceed in order to be reasonably certain that the provision for doubtful accounts is adequate? Credit terms are 2/10, n/30.

17. You were retained by the stockholders of a manufacturing company to audit its financial statements. Several of the stockholders believe that net income might be overstated. The basis for their suspicion lies in an arrangement whereby certain officers receive, in addition to their salaries, bonuses based upon a percentage of the net income before federal taxes.

   a) List the steps that the officers could take in order to overstate net income.

   b) List the procedures you would follow to reveal the overstatements.

18. During the audit of the records of a retail store, your computations showed a gross profit of 45 percent of net sales. An examination of the inventory records, kept under the retail inventory method, showed that no item is originally marked to sell at a gross profit in excess of 40 percent of sales prices. What procedure should be followed?

19. During the audit of a hotel that operates several large dining rooms, time did not permit comparing the guest checks in detail with the food

sales accounts. What procedure might you follow in order to be relatively certain that major discrepancies were not present? Ignore any existing system of internal control.

20. A large manufacturer has several manufacturing and selling branches. All bills are rendered by the home office, and all collections for products sold are made by the home office. In the audit of the company, the branches are not to be visited. What procedure should be followed in verifying the sales and the expenses of the various branches?

PROBLEMS

1. Your client, the Valley Shopping Center, has 30 store tenants. All leases with the tenants provide for a fixed rent plus a percentage of net sales, in excess of a fixed dollar amount computed on an annual basis. Each lease also provides that the landlord may engage a CPA to audit all records of the tenant for assurance that sales are being properly reported.

   You have been requested by your client to audit the financial statements of the Western Steak Restaurant to determine that the sales totaling $634,000 for the year ended December 31, 1975 have been properly reported to the landlord. The restaurant and the Shopping Center entered into a 5-year lease on January 1, 1975. The restaurant offers only table service. No liquor is served. During meal times there are four or five waitresses in attendance who prepare handwritten prenumbered restaurant checks for the customers. As customers leave, payment is made at a cash register, attended by the proprietor. All sales are for cash. The proprietor also is the accountant. Complete files are kept of restaurant checks and cash register tapes. A daily sales record and general ledger are also maintained.

   a) List the auditing procedures that you would employ to verify the total annual sales of the restaurant.

   (AICPA, adapted)

2. The Parks Company manufactures hospital supplies, and has the following system for billing and recording accounts receivable:

   (1) A customer's order is received in the order department and a clerk prepares a prenumbered sales order in which is inserted pertinent information, such as the customer's name, address, account number, quantity, and items ordered. After the sales order form has been prepared, the customer's order is attached.

   (2) The sales order form is then passed to the credit department for approval. Approximations of the billing values are made in the credit department for those accounts on which credit limitations are imposed. After investigation, approval of credit is noted on the form.

   (3) The sales order form then is passed to the billing department where a clerk types the customer's invoice on a billing machine that multiplies the number of items and the unit price, then adds the automatically extended amounts for the total of the invoice. The billing clerk determines the unit prices for the items from a price list.

   The billing machine has registers that accumulate daily totals of customer account numbers and invoice amounts to provide "hash" totals and control amounts. These totals, which are inserted in a daily record, serve as predetermined batch totals for verification of computer inputs.

The billing is done on prenumbered, continuous, multi-copy forms having the following designations:

a) "Customer's copy."

b) "Sales department copy," for information purposes.

c) "File copy."

d) "Shipping department copy," which serves as a shipping order. Bills of lading are also prepared as by-products of the invoicing procedure.

(4)   The shipping department copy of the invoice and the bills of lading are then sent to the shipping department. After the order has been shipped, copies of the bill of lading are returned to the billing department. The shipping department copy of the invoice is filed in the shipping department.

(5)   In the billing department one copy of the bill of lading is attached to the customer's copy of the invoice and both are mailed to the customer. The other copy of the bill of lading, and the sales order form, are stapled to the invoice file copy and filed in invoice numerical order.

(6)   A key punch machine is connected to the billing machine so that punched cards are created during the preparation of the invoices. The punched cards become the means by which the sales data are transmitted to a computer. The cards are fed to the computer in batches. One day's accumulation of cards comprises a batch. After the punched cards have been processed by the computer, they are placed in files and held for two years.

What procedures would a CPA employ in his examination of selected audit samples of the company's

a) Typed invoices, including the source documents.

b) Punched cards.

(The procedures should be limited to the verification of the sales data being fed into the computer. Do not carry the procedures beyond the point at which the cards are ready to be fed to the computer.)

(AICPA, adapted)

3.   Easy-Operate, Inc., was formed July 31, 1974, and sells household appliances at retail on installment contracts. The following information was taken from the accounts of the company at fiscal year-ends:

	July 31	
	1976	1975
Installment contracts receivable:		
1975 contracts	$ 8,000	$126,000
1976 contracts	160,000	
Sales	500,000	300,000
Inventory, new, at cost	84,500	64,500
Purchases of inventory	310,000	
Selling and administrative expenses	140,000	
Loss on defaulted contracts	17,100	1,000
Allowance for defaulted contracts	9,000	9,000

The CPA's audit as of July 31, 1976, disclosed the following:

(1) When a contract is in default the merchandise is repossessed and the contract written off to Loss on Defaulted Contracts. Information regarding repossessed items is kept on a memo basis and is not entered in the records. Any income derived from the sale of this merchandise is credited to Loss on Defaulted Contracts. No repossessed goods were sold in 1975 or 1976 for more than the unpaid balance of the original contract. An analysis of the Loss on Defaulted Contracts account follows:

Contracts written off:		
1975 contracts		$15,000
1976 contracts		6,000
		$21,000
Less sale of repossessed merchandise:		
1975 contracts	$3,200	
1976 contracts	700	3,900
Balance.		$17,100

The market value of the repossessed inventory on hand at July 31, 1976, was $800 all of which was repossessed from 1975 contracts. There was no merchandise repossessed during the year ended July 31, 1975.

The $8,000 balance of 1975 installment contracts receivable is considered collectible.

(2) The gross profit ratio for 1975 was 40 percent.

(3) The company's financial statements are prepared on the accrual basis, and the installment method of reporting income is used for income tax purposes. The company is on the charge-off method for losses on defaulted contracts for income tax purposes.

a) Prepare a schedule to compute the adjustment to the balance of Allowance for Defaulted Contracts account that the CPA would suggest at July 31, 1976. The rate of bad debt losses for 1976 is expected to be the same as the experience rate for 1975 based on sales.

(AICPA, adapted)

4. You are auditing the financial statements of Colonial, Inc., a wholesale office supply company, for the year ended September 30, 1976. Your internal control review points out many weaknesses. In examining the accounts receivable, the following information is available as of September 30, 1976.

(1) The Accounts Receivable general ledger debit balance is $780,430, and the Provision for Doubtful Accounts general ledger debit balance is $470. The total of the accounts receivable in the subsidiary ledger is $768,594.

(2) In preparing to confirm accounts receivable you discover that the accounts vary greatly in dollar amount, and you therefore decide to use a three-strata procedure, as follows: (*a*) negative confirmation requests for accounts under $200; (*b*) positive confirmation requests, unrestricted random sampling and the technique of estimation sampling for variables for accounts of $200 to

$2,000; and (*c*) positive confirmation requests for all accounts of $2,000 or more.

(3) Your review of accounts receivable and discussions with the client disclose that the following items are included in the accounts receivable (both control and the subsidiary):

a) Accounts with credit balances total $1,746.
b) Receivables from officers total $8,500.
c) Advances to employees total $1,411.
d) Accounts that are definitely uncollectible total $1,187.

(4) Uncollectible accounts are estimated to be ½ percent of the year's net credit sales of $15,750,000.

(5) The confirmations and analysis of the subsidiary ledger provide the following information:

(a) The 1,270 subsidiary ledger accounts with balances of less than $200 total $120,004. Twenty-seven confirmations show a net overstatement of $970. The client agrees that these errors were made.

(b) The 625 subsidiary ledger accounts with balances of $200 to $2,000 total $559,875. The following errors were reported in the replies received from the random sample of 50 positive confirmation requests (the appropriateness of a sample of 50 items was determined statistically based upon desired levels of precision and reliability and investigation established that the customers were correct):

	Balance per Client	Correct Balance
Customer #471	$ 847	$ 827
Customer #701	500	400
Customer #202	1,900	2,100
Customer #415	206	196
Customer #911	1,400	1,250
Customer #544	400	–
Customer #939	1,700	1,300
Customer #481	557	597
	$7,510	$6,670

Subsidiary ledger balances of $37,280 were confirmed in the replies to all of the remaining 42 positive confirmation requests.

(c) The 28 accounts with balances of $2,000 and over comprise the remainder of the accounts receivable subsidiary ledger. Investigation established that errors existed in five of these accounts and that the net overstatement is $4,570.

a) Prepare journal entries necessary (1) to reclassify items which are not trade accounts receivable, (2) to write off uncollectible accounts and (3) to adjust the provision for doubtful accounts.

b) Using the arithmetic mean of the sample as a basis, prepare a schedule computing an estimate of the dollar amount of the middle stratum of accounts receivable at September 30, 1976.

c) Assuming that the net adjustment of accounts receivable computed in part (*a*) was $10,000 and that the estimate of the middle stratum in part (*b*) was $600,000, prepare a schedule computing an estimate of total trade accounts receivable at September 30, 1976.

(AICPA, adapted)

5. The Lamb Company, showed a balance in its Accounts Receivable control of $21,530 as of December 31, 1975. The subsidiary ledger accounts of the company appear below. Credit terms are 60 days net.

Account No.	Date	Debit	Credit	Balance
1.	May 31	500		500
	July 1		300	200
	7	500		700
	Sept. 1		300	400
	25	800		1,200
	Nov. 1		300	900
	Dec. 10	300		1,200
2.	Aug. 8	840		840
	Oct. 4		840	0
	Nov. 25	2,200		2,200
3. (Two-month, 6 percent note)	Jan. 1	12,000		12,000
	Mar. 1		12,120	120 Cr.
	Dec. 1	10,000		9,880
4. (" " " " ")	Feb. 3	1,000		1,000
	Aug. 3	1,000		2,000
5.	Feb. 10	3,000		3,000
	Apr. 9		3,000	0
	May 4	4,000		4,000
	July 2		4,000	0
	Sept. 6	5,278		5,278
	Nov. 26	222		5,500
6.	July 17	500		500
	Aug. 16	444		944
	Sept. 30 (open)	750		1,694
	Oct. 15		944	750
	18	600		1,350
	Dec. 20		600	750

The Provision for Doubtful Accounts, before audit, has a credit balance of $500. The Provision for Doubtful Accounts is to be adjusted to a balance determined as follows:

Accounts not due. . . . . ½ of 1 percent
Accounts 1–60 days past due . . . . 2 percent
Accounts 61–120 days past due. . . . . 5 percent
Accounts over 120 days past due . . . . 50 percent

The provision is to be based only on the trade accounts. Except where payments are earmarked, the oldest items are paid first.

From the information presented:

a) Prepare work papers for aging the accounts receivable. In your schedule, show also the disposition and any remarks which you, as the auditor, would note.

b) Show the adjustments necessary for the provision and also any other necessary adjustments.

6. From the bonds in the following list, prepare work papers illustrating how it would be possible to verify the total interest earned during the year 1975 without computing the income from each individual bond. All bonds were purchased at par, at issuance date, and those sold were sold at par plus accrued interest.

Bond	Rate %	Date Acquired	Date Sold	Par Each	Total Cost
A	6.0	2/10/75		$1,000	$12,000
B	6.0	3/8/75	12/9/75	1,000	14,000
C	7.0	4/3/75	11/6/75	1,000	16,000
D	7.0	4/29/75		1,000	18,000
E	7.0	6/15/75	12/20/75	1,000	20,000

7. You are auditing the financial statements of Miles, Inc. for the year ended December 31, 1975. Your examination of the accounts receivable proves that the data presented below represent typical operations for sales, sales returns, uncollectible items, and receivables balances. Cash receipts are applied to the oldest billings. Credit terms are net cash in 60 days.
From the data:

a) Prepare an aging schedule, based upon the number of days past the transaction date.

b) Prepare the entry to charge off accounts and amounts which in your opinion are uncollectible.

c) On the assumption that there is no balance in the Allowance for Doubtful Accounts, what are your suggestions for the establishment for an allowance? What are the reasons for your suggestions? Annual sales are approximately $12,000,000.

Account No.	Dates (1975) and Transactions	Balance Dec. 31, 1975
1	Nov. 15, $6,000 sale, Nov. 25, $1,000 return Dec. 17, $15,000 sale.	$20,000 Dr.
2	June 10, $2,000 sale. July 10, $2,000 sale. Aug. 10, $2,000 sale. Aug. 25, $2,000 cash. Sept. 10, $2,000 sale. Sept. 25, $1,000 cash. Nov. 10, $2,000 sale. Dec. 10, $2,000 sale.	9,000 Dr.
3	Dec. 20, $6,000 sale. Dec. 31, $14,000 return arising from sale of Nov. 15.	8,000 Cr.
4	Oct. 10, $7,000 advance to branch office.	7,000 Dr.
5	June 10, $12,000 sale. Customer has been paying $1,000 per month.	6,000 Dr.
6	Feb. 10, $10,000 sale. Apr. 10, $10,000 cash. July 10, $2,000 allowance for defective goods. Has agreed to send check January 2, 1976.	2,000 Cr.
7	Jan. 4, $1,000 sale. Customer totally bankrupt.	1,000 Dr.
8	Sept. 5, $12,000 sale. Nov. 12, $11,000 cash.	1,000 Dr.

8. You are examining the financial statements of the Howard Company for the year ended December 31, 1975. During the audit of the accounts receivable and other related accounts, certain information was obtained, from which you are to prepare:

   a) Audit work papers for the accounts receivable and the allowance for doubtful accounts as of December 31, 1975.

   b) Audit adjustments, based upon your work papers. New account titles may be used.

   The December 31, 1975, debit balance in the Accounts Receivable control account is $197,000.

   The only entries in the Bad Debts Expense account were: A credit for $324 on December 1, 1975, because Company X remitted in full for the account charged off October 31, 1975, and a debit on December 31 for the amount of the credit to the Allowance for Doubtful accounts.

   The Allowance for Doubtful accounts is presented below:

	Debit	Credit	Balance
January 1, 1975			3,658
October 31, 1975. Uncollectible: Co. X, $324; Co. Y, $820; Co. Z, $564	1,508		2,150
December 31, 1975, 5 percent of $197,000		9,850	12,000

An aging schedule of the accounts receivable as of December 31, 1975, and the decisions are as follows:

Age	Net Debit Balance	Amount to Which the Allowance Is To Be Adjusted after Adjustments and Corrections Have Been Made
0–1 month	$ 93,240	1 percent
1–3 months	76,820	2 percent
3–6 months	22,180	3 percent
Over 6 months	6,000	Definitely uncollectible, $1,000; $2,000 is considered 50 percent uncollectible; the remainder is estimated to be 80 percent collectible.
	$198,240	

There is a credit balance in one account receivable (0–1 month) of $2,000; it represents an advance on a sales contract; also, there is a credit balance in one of the 1–3 months' accounts receivable of $500 for which merchandise will be accepted by the customer.

The ledger accounts have not been closed as of December 31, 1975.

The Accounts Receivable control account is not in agreement with the subsidiary ledger. The differences cannot be located, and the auditor decides to adjust the control to the sum of the subsidiaries after any corrections are made.

9. From the following information based upon an examination of the records of a new client, prepare a schedule setting forth the sales, cost of goods sold, and gross profit for 1974, 1975, 1976, and in total for the three years. The schedule should be supported by necessary computations.

The client has not prepared financial statements for 1974, 1975, or 1976; during these years, no accounts have been written off as uncollectible; the rate of gross profit on sales has remained constant for each of the three years.

Prior to January 1, 1974, the client used the accrual method of accounting. From January 1, 1974, to December 31, 1976, only cash receipts and disbursements records were maintained. When sales on account were made, they were entered in the subsidiary accounts receivable ledger. No general ledger postings have been made since December 31, 1973.

As a result of your examination, the following correct data are available:

	12/31/73	12/31/76
Accounts receivable balances:		
Less than one year old	$15,400	$28,200
One to two years old	1,200	1,800
Two to three years old		800
Over three years old		2,200
	$16,600	$33,000
Inventories	$11,600	$18,800
Accounts payable for inventory purchased	$ 5,000	$11,000

Cash received on accounts receivable in	1974	1975	1976
Applied to:			
Current year collections	$148,800	$161,800	$208,800
Accounts of the prior year	13,400	15,000	16,800
Accounts of two years prior	600	400	2,000
Total	$162,800	$177,200	$227,600
Cash sales	$ 17,000	$ 26,000	$ 31,200
Cash disbursements for inventory purchased	$125,000	$141,200	$173,800

PRACTICE MATERIAL ASSIGNMENTS

Metalcraft, Incorporated: Audit Problem:
    Assignment 3, Section A: Trade Accounts Receivable.
    Assignment 3, Section B: Provision for Doubtful Accounts.
Colby Gears, Inc.: Holmes and Moore Audit Case:
    Trade Accounts Receivable. Accounts Receivable from Subsidiary.
    Officer and Employee Receivables. Provision for Doubtful Accounts.

14

Notes and Acceptances Receivable and Related Revenue

Audit Objectives

The audit objectives of examining notes and acceptances receivable are to determine validity, accuracy of amount, propriety of related revenues, and proper valuation for financial statement presentation.

Preface to Notes and Acceptances Receivable

All classes of notes and acceptances receivable are included in the procedures to be developed in the examination of these assets and their related revenues. Notes and acceptances may be classified as follows:

Notes Receivable. (1) Trade notes, (2) nontrade notes, (3) employees' notes (other than loans or advances), (4) note of stockholders, and (5) notes of affiliated companies (other than loans or advances).

Acceptances Receivable. (1) Trade acceptances and (2) bills of exchange.

Notes receivable may be secured with collateral or chattel, or they may be unsecured. Trade notes are considered a more desirable asset than accounts receivable by some persons and a less desirable asset by others. If a note results from the conversion of an open account which was past due, that note would be a less desirable asset than a good account. The fact that a note represents an unconditional promise to pay a specified sum of money is meaningless if the debtor cannot liquidate his indebtedness; a businessman is not particularly interested in instituting proceedings for note collection or in disposing of collateral held as security. If a note or acceptance is taken in the customary course of business and if it is not an open account conversion, then it is at least as good an asset as an account receivable, since it is a written evidence of indebtedness. Notes are more reasonably discounted than are accounts receivable in the event that borrowing is necessary. Industries differ in the extent to which they employ notes and acceptances as opposed to open accounts.

Trade acceptances are bills of exchange drawn by the seller on the purchaser of goods and accepted by such purchaser. In order to attain negotiability, trade acceptances must be made payable to the order of a definite person or company. Trade acceptances thus offer the seller the opportunity to finance himself by the ready discount of the paper. Trade acceptances (and notes received in the sale of merchandise) are eligible for rediscount at a Federal Reserve bank.

Bankers' acceptances are drafts, the acceptor of which is a bank or trust company. A bank thus extends credit to buyers, usually upon the presentation of satisfactory security. Bankers' acceptances are not used as frequently as notes and trade acceptances. They are used principally in the financing of extremely large transactions; in foreign trade; and in sales and purchases of commodities such as cotton, grain, and copper.

SECTION I: INTERNAL CONTROL OF NOTES AND ACCEPTANCES RECEIVABLE

The general pattern of intenral control of notes and acceptances receivable follows that for accounts receivable. After approval for the acceptance of notes receivable, there must be proper control of the notes and properly safeguarded collection. Proper internal control further demands (1) that the notes receivable custodian does not have access to cash or to the accounting records; (2) that a responsible official who does have access to the notes approves note renewals in writing; (3) that charge-offs of defaulted notes be approved in writing by a responsible official who does not have access to cash or notes; and (4) that proper procedures be adopted for the follow-up of defaulted notes.

The remarks appearing in Chapter 13 concerning the internal control over receivables are applicable to notes and acceptances receivable.

An internal control questionnaire for notes and acceptances receivable is shown in Illustration 14–1.

SECTION II: AUDIT PROGRAM FOR NOTES AND ACCEPTANCES RECEIVABLE

Normally, interest is verified at the time of the examination of the revenue-producing receivables. The following audit program for notes and acceptances receivable and related revenue may be expanded or contracted in accordance with the requirements of each engagement. The procedures to be followed for notes and acceptances receivable and related revenue are developed in the following subsections.

ILLUSTRATION 14–1

INTERNAL CONTROL QUESTIONNAIRE
Notes and Acceptances Receivable

	Yes	No	Not Applicable	Remarks
Company_____ Period Covered_____				
1. Are individual notes regularly proved with the controlling account balance?	___	___	___	_____
2. Is a detailed record maintained for the notes receivable?	___	___	___	_____
3. Prior to their acceptance, are all notes properly approved?	___	___	___	_____
4. Are the amounts of partial payments noted on the reverse side of the notes?	___	___	___	_____
5. Is a contingency record carried for discounted notes receivable?	___	___	___	_____
6. Does the client periodically confirm notes receivable balances?	___	___	___	_____
7. Are unpaid notes properly followed?	___	___	___	_____
8. Are past–due notes charged back either to Accounts Receivable or to a Dishonored Notes account?	___	___	___	_____
9. Does proper approval exist for the write–off of uncollectible notes?	___	___	___	_____
10. Is proper control exercised over future collections of notes charged off?	___	___	___	_____
11. Does the custodian of the notes receivable have access to:				
a) Cash receipts records?	___	___	___	_____
b) Notes receivable records?	___	___	___	_____
c) General ledger accounts?	___	___	___	_____
12. If negotiable collateral is held against the notes, does the custodian have access to:				
a) Cash receipts and disbursements records?	___	___	___	_____
b) Notes receivable records?	___	___	___	_____
c) General ledger accounts?	___	___	___	_____
13. Are notes receivable and related collateral kept under proper control?	___	___	___	_____
14. Is more than one person required to be present when access to notes and related collateral is necessary?	___	___	___	_____
15. Is notes receivable collateral adequate?	___	___	___	_____
16. Is proper internal control maintained over revenue from notes receivable?	___	___	___	_____

Prepared by_____   Reviewed by_____
Date_____   Date_____

Prepare or Obtain a Schedule of the Items. It is desirable, although not necessary, to examine notes and acceptances receivable early in an engagement. Preferably, these receivables should be examined simultaneously with cash in order to detect the covering of possible shortages brought about by borrowing on notes and acceptances and using the cash therefrom to cover the shortages.

An auditor should prepare or obtain from the client a list of notes and acceptances receivable as of the close of the fiscal period. The list should show the name of the makers or acceptors, the names of endorsers or drawers, note dates, due dates, the amount of the notes, interest rates, discount rates (if discounted), interest collected in the period, interest accrued and/or prepaid, payments made on the principal, the balance due, and any collateral held. If the auditor obtains a schedule from the client, he should match the *detail* of the items in the schedule with the corresponding instrument—provided it has not been discounted. Data presented by the client and verified by the auditor should be placed in the audit work papers. Illustration 14–2 presents a notes receivable schedule; see also the Illustrative Audit.

Reconcile Controlling and Subsidiary Account Balances. The footing of the notes receivable listing (trial balance) must be verified in order to prove the agreement of the controlling account and the sum of the subsidiary balances. If the subsidiary account balance totals and the controlling account balance are not in agreement, the discrepancy must be located.

Postings to subsidiary ledgers and controlling accounts should be test-proved as to accuracy so that the test will result in reliability.

The balance of the notes receivable subsidiary accounts should be test-proved, and the composition of each individual account must be in agreement with the items in the listing. The balance of the controlling account must be verified after proof of posting accuracy.

ILLUSTRATION. The necessity for reconciling subsidiary account balances in total against the proved balance of the controlling account may be illustrated as follows: The auditor extracted the balance of each subsidiary account, totaled the subsidiary accounts, and compared this total with the client's controlling account balance, as expressed in the trial balance; the two totals agreed. However, one note of $1,500 in the subsidiary ledger had not been posted to the controlling account, since the entry charging Notes Receivable and crediting Sales for $1,500 had not been made when the note was taken. The bookkeeper had overfooted the ledger accounts for Notes Receivable and for Sales by $1,500. His intention was to retain the $1,500 when the note was paid and then remove the subsidiary ledger account.

Inspect Items on Hand. Notes receivable will be (*a*) on hand; (*b*) out for collection; (*c*) discounted; (*d*) pledged as collateral; or (*e*) returned to the maker if paid after the balance sheet date and prior to the audit.

If only a few notes are on hand, they should be inspected for proper preparation, amounts, witnessing when required, notarizing, and signatures in order to determine their apparent authenticity. If the note volume is large, a sample should be drawn; and the auditor must be satisfied with the results of the sample, or the sample must be extended. If irregu-

ILLUSTRATION 14–2

FOX COMPANY

Notes Receivable Schedule, December 31, 1975

Name of Maker	Date of Note	Due Date	Amount of Note	Interest Rate %	Interest Prepaid 12/31/75	Interest Accrued 12/31/75	Interest Income 1975	Collateral Description	Collateral Value	Remarks
Acorn Co. ⊙	9/1/75	2/1/76	$ 5,000 √=	6	–0–	(4) $100	$ 100	None		
Barley Co. ⊙	10/1/75	3/1/76	3,000 √	6	–0–	(2) 45	45	None		
Calumet Co. ⊙	10/15/75	4/1/76	6,000 √	6	–0–	(2.5) 75	75	100 shares X Co., Common	$7,500 #	Stock certificates examined
Diamond Co. ⊙	11/1/75	3/1/76	1,000 √	6	–0–	(2) 10	10	None		
Elkhart Co. ⊙	11/1/75	4/1/76	8,000 √	6	–0–	(2) 80	80	200 shares Y Co., Common	9,300 #	Stock certificates examined
Fable Co. ⊙	12/1/75	3/1/76	4,000 √	6	–0–	(1) 20	20	None		
General Co. ⊙	12/15/75	4/15/76	6,000 √	6	–0–	(0.5) 15	15	None		
Hammond Co. ⊙	12/31/75	5/31/76	14,000 √	6	–0–	(0) 0	0	None		Endorsed by W. C. Hammond
			$47,000 ⋀				$ 345			
Interest earned on notes paid in 1975							876 ×			
Total note interest, 1975							$1,221			

⊙ Examined for dates, amounts, and signatures.
√ Confirmed—directly.
⋀ Agrees with control account balance.
= Paid Feb. 1, 1976, plus interest. Traced to cash receipts.
× Verified.
Market quote, 1/2/76, *The Wall Street Journal.*
Prepared by client, at our request.
None of the notes represent renewals.
All notes are for normal product sales.

larities appear in signatures and/or related collateral, the attention of the client should be directed to the matter and the situation corrected. The notes should then be compared with the prepared lists on the assumption that the lists already have been compared with the subsidiary accounts and with the notes receivable records. The objective in examining the notes on hand is to obtain original evidence, data for private entries, and information for future cash collections.

In the examination of notes, an auditor must watch endorsements, and he may desire information concerning the credit ratings of makers *and* endorsers. An auditor is not responsible for the validity of signatures and endorsements; but the client should be informed if irregularities appear. All former credit and collection experience with the maker of a note should be investigated to ascertain whether the present experience may result in an uncollectible note. If the notes are demand notes, the auditor should investigate and indicate on his work papers the arrangements for the payment of the principal. The payee of a note is the client, and the note should be made payable to him or endorsed to him.

Confirm Notes and Acceptances Receivable. The most valuable evidence of the ownership and existence of a note receivable is obtained from the confirmation of the maker and from the confirmation from holders when the notes are not in the possession of the client. Recognized auditing practice dictates that notes receivable should be confirmed if it is possible to obtain the confirmation on a reasonable and practicable basis. If the system of internal accounting control is sound, an auditor may limit his requests for confirmations to tests. For many industrial concerns, notes do not constitute a material proportion of the current assets; in financial organizations, notes may constitute the principal asset.

The accounting transactions for notes for which confirmations were requested but not received should be verified back through the original transactions giving rise to the notes, such as sales orders, inventory credits, shipping records, and invoices.

ILLUSTRATION.   Failure to confirm notes may be illustrated as follows: A partial payment may be made on a note, the cash stolen, and a partial-payment notation omitted on the reverse of the note and in the cash receipts records. Confirmation would reveal the discrepancy.

Confirmations from note makers must always be obtained for notes receivable out as collateral, for notes receivable discounted, and for notes out for collection, because the auditor otherwise does not possess knowledge of the existence of the notes. Information concerning notes receivable discounted at banks and notes pledged as loan collateral with the banks will appear in the certification obtained from the bank at the time cash is verified if the bank confirmation request is designed to include such items. When note confirmations are requested, the requests are mailed under the control of the auditor and the replies must be returned directly to the auditor. Note confirmation requests should provide for the verification of collateral held as security for the note. The confirmation replies become a part of the work papers (see Illustration 14–3 and the confirmations illustrated in Chapter 13). Illustration 14–3 presents a summary of the confirmation statistics.

ILLUSTRATION 14–3

KAMOY COMPANY

Notes Receivable Confirmation Summary, December 31, 1975

Confirmation No.	Maker	Balance	Not Con-firmed	Confirmed Exceptions None	Some	Remarks
1	A	$ 8,000		$ 8,000		
2	B	2,500		2,500		
3	C	4,000	$4,000			
4	D	10,000		1,000		
5	E	500		500		
6	F	5,000		5,000		
7	G	7,500		7,500		
8	H	2,500		2,500		
9	I	3,000		3,000		
10	J	10,000			$10,000	Paid 12/31/75 ⊖
Total Circularized		$ 44,000	$4,000	$30,000	$10,000	
		100%	9%	68%	23%	
Total Notes Receivable		$110,000				
Percentage Circularized		40%				

⊖ Received on 1/3/76.

In his report, the auditor should indicate nonconfirmation of notes receivable, together with his reasons for departing from normally accepted procedure; and he should present an explanation of his satisfaction with the accuracy of the notes. If the auditor is not permitted to correspond with note debtors, he should obtain a written statement from the client to that effect and at least qualify his report. If notes receivable are discounted, out of the offices as loan collateral, or in the hands of collectors, they must be verified by obtaining written confirmation from the holders. If the notes are out for collection, the opinion of the collection agent concerning the possibilities of collection should be obtained as a guide for provisions for uncollectibility.

Determine the Disposition of Past-Due Notes. Note dates must be properly segregated. When notes, drafts, and acceptances are dishonored at maturity, good accounting treatment dictates that the dishonored instrument be charged to Accounts Receivable, or to Notes Receivable Dishonored, together with accrued interest, protest fees, and collection costs. The complete entry to recognize immediate dishonor should be as follows:

```
Notes Receivable Dishonored (or Accounts Receivable) . . . . . 10,050
    Cash (for protest, and so forth). . . . . . . . . . . . . . . .            50
    Notes Receivable . . . . . . . . . . . . . . . . . . . . . . . .       10,000
```

In order to complete their credit files, many companies first charge past-due dishonored notes to the Accounts Receivable account and then immediately transfer the item to Notes Receivable Dishonored.

Past-due notes have lost their negotiability; they are similar to past-due accounts receivable, except that the notes still exist as evidences of indebtedness. As soon as uncollectibility is established, the past-due note should be charged to expense or to an allowance provided for that purpose. It sometimes happens that a due note is uncollected at the balance sheet date but is collected before the completion of the audit. The collection of the note constitutes proof of its collectibility; however, in the balance sheet where the note due at the balance sheet date existed, it should be shown as a note. All notes collected after the balance sheet date and prior to closing the engagement should be traced to the cash receipts records and to the bank deposits, and noted in the audit work papers.

Verify Note Collateral. If the client has taken collateral as security for the notes, it should be examined by the auditor and listed in accordance with debtor notes held. The auditor should verify the value of the collateral and include pertinent comments in his work papers.

When confirming notes, it is advisable to obtain confirmation of any existing collateral from the owner who pledged it in order to ascertain that all collateral is present. Equally as important as the confirmation of the collateral is the verification of its value because the worth of the underlying note may be dependent upon the value of the collateral. The collateral should be priced at market at the balance sheet date, and this price may be stated parenthetically in the balance sheet. The market price of the collateral is particularly important if held against notes that appear to be doubtful. It may be necessary to reexamine the market price of collateral prior to closing an audit, particularly if collateral market prices have declined between the balance sheet date and the date of closing the audit. Collateral may take the form of trust receipts, warehouse receipts, stocks, bonds, notes, insurance policies, and liens against tangible assets. The auditor must determine that the collateral is properly endorsed and/or accompanied by a properly executed power of attorney. When required by state law, the genuineness of chattel and the registration of the mortgage might be investigated in order to determine the adequacy of the security when necessary. Collateral notes are common in bank examinations and finance company examinations; they may or may not be common in audits of mercantile and manufacturing companies.

Verify Note Genuineness.   In addition to obtaining confirmations of notes, the auditor should sufficiently investigate and understand the sources of the notes to be convinced that they are genuine. Therefore, he must trace contra-entries for notes receivable debits and notes receivable credits.

If the number of notes is small and the number of note transactions also small, transactions resulting in notes receivable debits and notes receivable credits should be traced from sales orders, invoices, shipping records, loan applications, and accounting entries to the debtors' accounts. If the number of notes is large, as in the case of loan companies, finance companies, and banks, the transactions giving rise to the notes receivable should be tested.

In its discounting operations, a bank may purchase notes in large volume from note brokers who have discounted them for original holders. Therefore, the bank owning the notes may not have knowledge of the makers; in such instances, it is common practice for the client's bank to advise the auditor to accept the items, and the auditor then qualifies his report to that effect.

In the examination of the records of financial institutions, payments made by individual debtors during the course of the audit should be witnessed, as an additional verification of the accuracy of the balances and the propriety of the accounting. This type of verification frequently serves in lieu of note confirmation wherein payments were made during the course of the audit.

If an audit is started after the close of the fiscal period, note transactions for the interim period should be verified in the records of original entry and traced to the ledger accounts; the transactions will involve either full payment, partial payment, discounting, or renewal. If full payment has been received, or if the notes were discounted, they will not be present; and entries in the cash receipts records must be examined for the interim between the date of the balance sheet and the date of the examination. The reason for the verification of interim transactions is to prevent the improper use of such notes to replace stolen cash or securities. By verifying all interim note transactions, the balance sheet date balance also is verified.

Investigate Renewed Notes.   Renewed notes should be investigated and their collection possibilities discussed with the client. A renewal of a note may be an indication of its ultimate uncollectibility, and the auditor must be certain that allowances for doubtful items are sufficiently large to absorb collection failure. Notes receivable discounted must also be discussed with the client with respect to their collection possibilities. Trade acceptances are not renewable but are eligible for discount.

Methods of accounting for notes may or may not reflect the fact of renewal. Consequently, an auditor must be alert to detect renewals. When the method of accounting for notes receivable does not satisfactorily reflect renewals, a recommendation from the auditor usually will be followed. Upon renewal, either a full explanation should be placed in the debtor's Note account, or a debit and a credit should be passed to the Notes Receivable account.

Determine Collectibility.   This is accomplished by investigating the credit standing of the makers of the notes. Confirmation and other procedures are no indication of the collectibility of notes, drafts, or trade acceptances. Of course, the majority of such instruments are collected in the normal course of business conduct; but that fact does not deter the auditor from investigating the credit standing of debtors so that asset values will be properly set forth in the financial statements.

The credit standing of debtors rendering notes of large amounts and notes of small amounts should be investigated on an adequate test basis. The test may be of the notes confirmed or of the notes not confirmed, or it may be spread over both in accordance with the selection of the sample. In all probability, the test will be restricted to unsecured notes.

In investigating credit standings, particular attention will be devoted to the following:

a)   Notes of other than trade debtors.

b)   Demand notes, and whether demand has been made and rejected.

c)   Client's endorsements on the reverse side of notes. Was the note offered for discount and rejected by the bank?

d)   Reasons for past-due notes.

e)   If the client is not the payee, investigation of the credit standing of the payee *and* the endorser. Why did the client acquire this note? Is it the primary obligation of an affiliated company?

The collectibility of notes—those on hand, discounted, and out for collection—should be discussed with management in order to obtain a complete opinion concerning collectibility.

Trace Receipts from Discounted Notes.   Notes receivable discounted indicate transactions that are to be reviewed by the auditor in order to ascertain that correct accounting procedure has been followed. Cash received from discounted notes should be traced to the cash receipts records in the same manner as cash received from direct loans.

When the payee of a note, draft, or acceptance endorses and discounts the instrument, he becomes secondarily liable; that is, if the original maker does not take up the instrument at maturity, the payee who discounted the instrument must remit to the bank. The possibility that the maker may not pay thus creates a contingency to the payee who has discounted the instrument.

When notes, drafts, or acceptances are discounted, the contingency should be shown as such on the records and must be clearly set forth in the financial statements. When a note receivable is discounted, Cash and Discount (Interest) Expense are charged and the Notes Receivable Discounted account is credited. The creation of the latter account thus reveals the contingency.

If after the balance sheet date but prior to closing the audit, a discounted instrument is dishonored, recognized accounting practice is that a direct current liability should be set up.

If the maker of a note remits directly to the bank at maturity, the discounting company charges Notes Receivable Discounted and credits Notes Receivable. If the maker remits to the payee (which probably will not happen, because the payee cannot deliver the paid instrument), the latter should charge Cash and credit Notes Receivable; then he must charge Notes Receivable Discounted and credit Cash to record the reduction of his bank balance made by the bank.

If a note, draft, or acceptance receivable is given to a creditor instead of being discounted, the accounting treatment is the same as that presented in the foregoing paragraphs. The only condition under which the Notes Receivable account should be credited directly upon the discount of a note is in the event of endorsement "without recourse."

When discounted receivables are dishonored at maturity, the complete accounting entry to reflect the dishonor should be as follows:

Notes Receivable Dishonored (or Accounts Receivable)	10,140	
Notes Receivable Discounted	10,000	
Cash (for protest fees, interest, and face of note)		10,140
Notes Receivable		10,000

Obtain Approval of Notes Charged Off as Uncollectible. Notes charged off as uncollectible should bear written executive approval. The notes should be inspected by the auditor, all correspondence and actions examined and confirmation obtained.

ILLUSTRATION. The necessity of examining note charge-offs may be exemplified as follows: The treasurer approved the charge-off to Bad Debts Expense of a $1,000 note and explained to the auditor that the note had been misplaced. The auditor examined all correspondence, which was to the effect that the maker would be unable to pay the note; in addition, the auditor was satisfied that the credit standing of the maker was poor. However, the auditor decided to investigate further and wrote to the maker, discovering that the treasurer had settled the note for $600—which he had kept—and had returned the note to the maker.

Review Allowance Provided for Notes. Companies engaged in a business in which note transactions are voluminous normally set up a separate allowance for doubtful notes, drafts, and acceptances. Companies accepting only a few notes normally provide an amount in the allowance for doubtful accounts to take care of possible note losses.

When notes, drafts, and acceptances are examined, the possible uncollectible items which should be adequately provided for in the allowance will include past-due notes, notes frequently renewed, serial notes accepted for a former note of doubtful collectibility, notes of debtors in insolvency, and notes on which payments have been irregular.

Verify Interest: Revenue, Accrued, and Prepaid. The auditor must compute or verify accrued and prepaid interest, interest revenue, and in the event of notes receivable discounted, interest expense. Most notes bear interest; trade acceptances do not bear interest. Interest accumulation on demand notes must be verified. When demand notes are due to a bank, the bank will submit periodic invoices for the interest. Interest accrues daily on all interest-bearing notes; in bank audits, an analysis of the interest accounts is of utmost importance.

Interest revenue credits, interest expense debits, prepaid interest debits and credits, and accrued interest receivable debits and credits must be definitely "tied in" with the interest-bearing instruments.

Separate Other-than-Customer Notes. These include notes from employees, accommodation notes, and so forth, and should be examined and traced to the records not only for accuracy of entry but for the purpose and legitimacy of issuance. These notes should be segregated in the balance sheet, since they may not represent current items.

In smaller companies not conducting extensive note business, postdated checks may be found along with—or in lieu of—notes of this type. Such postdated checks should be separately scheduled in the work papers and their subsequent collection noted. In all probability, an accounting entry will not be made when a postdated check is received; the check is merely held for future possible collection.

SECTION III: FINANCIAL STATEMENT CONSIDERATIONS

Notes, drafts, and acceptances receivable should be shown at an amount not in excess of their cash collectible worth. In the balance sheet of a client, the auditor must follow accepted accounting standards of disclosure in the presentation of notes, drafts, and acceptances receivable, and of items discounted. If the term "notes receivable" is used without qualification in a balance sheet, the understanding should be that the item represents only trade notes of current maturity. Trade notes and trade acceptances of current maturity may be shown separately or together as current assets.

Trade notes receivable not due should be considered as current assets if the collection terms fall within the cycle of operations of the business. If a trade note is past due, it should be transferred to an Account Receivable or to a Notes Receivable Dishonored account, since it has lost its negotiability. Adequate allowances should be provided for all classes of past-due notes and acceptances.

Nontrade notes should be shown separately from trade notes, either as current or as noncurrent assets, depending upon their nature and the circumstances of the case. Most concerns use one allowance to include all receivables. If only one allowance for doubtful items is carried, it should be deducted from the sum of the notes, drafts, acceptances, and accounts receivable in the balance sheet. If the provision for doubtful items is created *only* for doubtful accounts receivable, losses on other items must be charged directly to expense.

With respect to the balance sheet presentation of notes receivable discounted, there are two commonly accepted ways in which the situation may be expressed:

1. The notes receivable may be shown at (assume) a net $150,000 (out of a total of $200,000) in the current asset section. If this method is followed, a footnote must be appended to the balance sheet, as follows: "The company, at December 31, 1975, had discounted $50,000 of trade notes receivable." This method is most extensively used.
2. The discounted items may be shown as a deduction from the notes (or drafts or acceptances) receivable on the asset side of the balance sheet. A reason for showing gross notes receivable on the balance sheet is in case notes are obtained for past-due accounts and an analyst is determining days' sales outstanding. These notes, whether discounted or not, are uncollected sales and should be used in finding the days of uncollected sales.

Client Representations

In order to adhere to recognized standards in the examination of receivables, an auditor should obtain signed written representations from the client for all receivables. The client's certificate of these representations for notes will include the following points:

1. Trade notes receivable represent valid claims.
2. Trade notes receivable do not contain charges for goods shipped after the balance sheet date.
3. The balances of the trade notes receivable are not subject to adjustment of price, terms, transportation allowances, and discounts in excess of customary terms of the company.
4. Nontrade notes receivable are separately set forth, properly classified.
5. Contingencies for discounted items are properly reflected in the records.

6. All known uncollectible items have been charged off.
7. In our opinion the allowance for doubtful receivables is adequate to provide for all possible losses in all receivables at the balance sheet date which may prove to be uncollectible in the future.

The signed certificate is one of the auditor's work papers. The representations of the client do not reduce the responsibility of the auditor in his examination of receivables. Rather, the representations serve as a deterrent to a false statement, and they serve as some measure of protection for the auditor.

QUESTIONS

1. You are in charge of the annual examination of the financial statements of the Duster Corporation, a distributor of mining equipment. Duster's sales are either for cash or a combination of a substantial cash payment and one or two 60- or 90-day nonrenewable interest-bearing notes for the balance. Title to the equipment passes to the customer when the initial cash payment is made. The notes, some of which are secured by the customer, are dated when the cash payment is made (the day the equipment is delivered). If the customer prefers to purchase the equipment under an installment plan, Duster arranges for the customer to obtain such financing from a bank.

   You began to examine the December 31, 1975, financial statements on January 5, 1976, knowing that you must leave temporarily on January 7, 1976, after outlining the audit program for your assistant. Before leaving, you inquire about the assistant's progress in his examination of notes receivable. Among other things, he shows you a work paper listing the makers' names, the due dates, the interest rates, and amounts of 20 outstanding notes receivable totaling $500,000. The work paper contains the following notations:
   (1) Reviewed system of internal control and found it to be satisfactory.
   (2) Total of $500,000 agrees with general ledger control.
   (3) Traced listing of notes to sales records.
   The assistant also informs you that he is preparing to request positive confirmation of the amounts of all outstanding notes and that no other audit work has been performed in the examination of notes and interest arising from equipment sales. There were no outstanding accounts receivable for equipment sales at the end of the year.
   a) What additional audit procedures should the assistant apply in his audit of the Notes Receivable account. Duster has no other notes. A subsidiary ledger is not maintained.
   b) Prior to leaving you ask your assistant to examine all notes receivable on hand. He returns in 30 minutes from the office safe where the notes are kept and states that 1975 notes on hand total $400,000.
   List the possible explanations that you might expect from the client for the $100,000 difference. Eliminate fraud from consideration. After

each explanation indicate the audit procedures you would apply to determine if each explanation is proper.

(AICPA, adapted)

2. In your audit of the Long, Inc., you prepared a schedule of notes receivable as shown below. The company, a manufacturer, does not have many notes receivable. All notes have resulted from sales to customers.

Column Number	Column Heading
1	Name of maker
2	Names of endorsers
3	Date of note
4	Due date
5	Principal
6	Interest rate
	Discounted
7	Date
8	Rate
9	Amount of discount
	Interest
10	Collected
11	Accrued
12	Prepaid
13	Payment on principal
14	Balance due
15	Collateral held

Draw a line down the middle of a lined sheet of paper.

a) On the left of the line state the specific source or sources of information to be entered in each column and, where required, how data of preceding columns are combined.

b) On the right of the line state the principal way or ways that such information would be verified.

(AICPA, adapted)

3. Your client is engaged in the small-loan business. With respect to customer notes receivable, (*a*) do you consider it necessary to verify the notes by confirmation; or (*b*) do you consider comparison of the passbooks (at the time payments are made) with the ledger cards to be satisfactory?

   If you were to decide upon verification by direct correspondence, what would constitute a satisfactory test?

   If you were to decide upon verification by a comparison of passbooks and ledger cards, what would constitute a satisfactory test?

4. You were engaged to audit the financial statements of the Mixit Company for the year ended December 31, 1975. You cannot start the audit until January 15, 1976. The cashier has complete control of all cash, cash records, and negotiable securities. The following items were in the trial balance as of December 31, 1975:

Cash, Wells Fargo Bank, San Francisco.	$108,000
Cash, American Bank & Trust Company, Chicago.	84,000
Cash, Chase Manhattan, New York .	196,000
Petty cash .	20,000
Common stock, Upp Company .	150,000
Preferred stock, Down Company .	100,000
U.S. Treasury notes.	125,000
Trade notes receivable .	195,000

a)   How might the cashier manipulate his records in order to conceal a shortage in cash as of December 31, 1975?

b)   Outline the steps you would follow to detect the manipulation.

5.   You are examining the statements of True, Inc., for the first time. The company has many installment notes receivable. When an installment sale is made, the entire finance or carrying charge, which is included in the amount billed to the customer, is credited to a revenue account. In response to your recommendation that an allowance for the unearned portion of such charges be maintained, the controller states that the company has always considered the finance charge an addition to the sales price. He also states that there are very few balances settled before maturity, with an allowance being made on carrying charges, and that the doubtful note allowance is large enough to cover a shrinkage in the accounts equal to the unearned portion of the finance or carrying charges.

a)   Briefly state your arguments in favor of the creation of an Allowance for Unearned Finance Charges.

b)   If an Allowance for Unearned Finance Charges were not to be established, would this constitute grounds for an exception in your report? If so, on what basis would you make this exception?

c)   If the allowance were established, state whether it should be shown on the liability side of the balance sheet or as a deduction from the notes receivables.

6.   An export company located in the United States shipped merchandise, against open drafts, in October, 1975, to a customer in a foreign country. Owing to adverse financial conditions, the foreign customer refused the goods. In the course of your audit of the export company early in January, 1976, you found a December 31, 1975, account receivable of the foreign customer for $80,000, made up of the sales price of the merchandise, $75,000 and $5,000 for transportation charges. The cost of the goods to the export company was $42,000; and the December 31, 1975, market price is the same. There is no other foreign market for the goods. The export company insists that the customer will accept the goods within two weeks (after completing your audit).

In preparing a balance sheet for the exporter, as of December 31, 1975, how would you treat this receivable?

7.   A client discounted $250,000 of its notes receivable on December 28, 1975. You started your audit early in January, 1976. The Notes Receivable account had been directly credited when the receivables were discounted. The president of the company told you that the notes receivable would not be reclaimed by the company. For these reasons, you did not show the receivables discounted in your statements, made no comment in your report, and rendered an unqualified opinion. The remaining notes receivable of the client appeared to be current and collectible.

The client took your report to the City Bank on January 21, where an account was maintained, and received a loan of $300,000. The company then took up the $250,000 of notes receivable from the First National Bank, where they had been discounted. The City Bank learned of this repurchase and called you in and asked why you did not show the situation as it existed on December 31, 1975. Reply to the banker.

PROBLEMS

1. You are examining the financial statements of Burn, Inc., for the year ended December 31, 1975. Your analysis of the 1975 entries in the Notes Receivable account follows:

BURN, INC.

Analysis of Notes Receivable

For the Year Ended December 31, 1975

Date 1975		Trade Notes Receivable	
		Debit	Credit
Jan. 1	Balance forward	$118,000	
	Received $25,000 6% note due 10/29/75 from Dale whose trade account was past due		
Feb. 29	Discounted Dale note at 6%		$ 24,960
Mar. 29	Received noninterest-bearing demand note from Hedge, the corporation's treasurer for a loan	6,200	
Aug. 30	Received principal and interest due from Alley and in accordance with agreement, two principal payments in advance		34,200
Sept. 4	Paid protest fee on note dishonored by Cole	5	
Nov. 1	Received check dated 2/1/76 in settlement of Bailey note. The check was included in cash on hand 12/31/75		8,120
Nov. 4	Paid protest fee and maturity value of Dale note to bank. Note discounted 2/29/75 was dishonored	26,031	
Dec. 27	Accepted furniture and fixtures with a fair market value of $24,000 in full settlement from Dale		24,000
Dec. 31	Received check dated 1/3/76 from Hedge in Payment of 3/29/75 note. (The check was included in petty cash until 1/2/76 when it was returned to Hedge in exchange for a new demand note of the same amount.)		6,200
Dec. 31	Received principal and interest on Cole note		42,437
Dec. 31	Accrued interest on Alley note	1,200	
		$151,436	$139,917

The following information is available:

(1) Balances at January 1, 1975, were a debit of $1,400 in the Accrued Interest Receivable account and a credit of $400 in the Unearned Interest Income account. The $118,000 debit balance in the Notes Receivable account consisted of the following three notes:

Alley note of 8/31/71 payable in annual installments of $10,000 principal plus accrued interest at 6% each August 31. . . . . $70,000
Bailey note discounted to Dunlop at 6% on 11/1/74 due 11/1/75 8,000
Cole note for $40,000 plus 6% interest dated 12/31/74 due on 9/1/75. 40,000

(2) No entries were made during 1975 to the Accrued Interest Receivable or the Unearned Interest Income account and only one

entry for a credit of $1,200 on December 31 appeared in the Interest Income account.

(3)   All notes were from trade customers unless otherwise indicated.

(4)   Debits and credits offsetting Notes Receivable debit and credit entries were correctly recorded unless the facts indicate otherwise.

Prepare a work sheet to adjust each entry to correct or properly reclassify it, if necessary. Enter your adjustments in the proper columns to correspond with the date of each entry. Do not combine related entries for different dates. Your completed work sheet will provide the basis for one compound journal entry to correct all entries to Notes Receivable and related accounts for 1975. Formal journal entries are not required.

2.   The Cliff Company regularly purchases materials from the Mount Company and remits on the day materials are received.

On July 1, 1975, the Mount Company borrowed $500,000 from the Cliff Company and gave its six-month negotiable note. By agreement, the note was not to be liquidated by applying Mount Company billings against it. The Cliff Company discounted the note, and made no entries at the time of extending the loan.

In preparing the financial statements of the Cliff Company as of December 31, 1976, how would you present the situation if the Mount Company had paid $400,000 of the loan in accordance with the agreement? Ignore interest and discount. Also prepare the audit adjustments necessary for the records of the Cliff Company.

3.   Treet, Inc., is on a calendar year basis. On June 30, 1971, the company paid $440,000 cash for certain business property. The land was valued at $40,000 and the building at $400,000. The estimated life of the building is 50 years, with an estimated salvage value of $40,000. Depreciation has been accumulated by the straight-line method.

On June 30, 1975, the property was sold for $640,000, for which payment was received as follows:

Cash of $160,000 and the four following noninterest-bearing notes:

Due June 30, 1976 . . . . $128,000
Due June 30, 1977 . . . . $128,000
Due June 30, 1978 . . . . $160,000
Due June 30, 1979 . . . . $ 64,000

The seller elected to record the gain on the sale on the installment method because the collection of the receivable is not assured.

a)   Prepare computations and entries to record the sale on June 30, 1975.

b)   Prepare computations and entries to record the collections of the notes at their maturity dates.

c)   As of December 31, 1975, in which sections of the balance sheet should the account balances be shown?

(AICPA, adapted)

4.   During the course of the audit of the financial statements of Marker, Inc., for the year ended December 31, 1975, you examined the notes receivable represented by the following items:

*Item
No.*

1. A four-month note dated November 30, 1975, from the Avon Company, $10,000; interest rate, 6 percent; discounted on November 30, 1975, at 6 percent.
2. A draft drawn payable 30 days after date for $15,000 by the Bark Company on the Carew Company in favor of the Gusto Company, endorsed to Marker, Inc., on December 2, 1975, and accepted on December 4, 1975.
3. A 90-day note dated November 1, 1975, from J. C. Cline, $25,000; interest at 6 percent; the note is for subscriptions to 250 shares of the preferred stock of Marker, Inc., at $100 per share.
4. A 60-day note dated May 3, 1975, from the First Company, $3,000; interest rate, 6 percent; dishonored at maturity; judgment obtained on October 10, 1975. Collection doubtful. (No interest after maturity.)
5. A 90-day note dated January 4, 1975, from the president of Marker, $8,000; no interest; note not renewed; president confirmed.
6. A 120-day note dated September 14, 1975, from the Stocker Company, $6,000; interest rate, 6 percent; note is held by bank as collateral.

When the company discounted a note, Interest Expense was debited for the discount cost and Interest Income was credited for the revenue.

From the information presented, prepare the following:

a) A work sheet for the notes receivable as of December 31, 1975.
b) All necessary audit adjustments, including entries for interest accrued and prepaid.
c) A presentation of the notes receivable in the balance sheet as of December 31, 1975.

(Note: In computing interest, the first day is omitted and the maturity date day is included.)

5. Hessby, Inc. manufactures special-order limousines, ambulances, and hearses. Every order is different, with regard to armor plate, television, telephones, oxygen equipment, color, guns, and many other items. Its Notes Receivable account at December 31, 1975, follows:

Date	Explanation	Debit	Credit	Balance
Oct. 1, 1974	A, distributor; 2 years; 6%; payable one eighth each 3 months	32,000		32,000
Nov. 15, 1974	B, distributor; 6 months; 6%	5,000		37,000
Jan. 1, 1975	A, principal payment		4,000	33,000
Feb. 1, 1975	C, distributor; 2 years; 6%	8,000		41,000
Apr. 1, 1975	A, principal payment		4,000	37,000
Apr. 9, 1975	D, distributor; 8 months; 6%	20,000		57,000
Apr. 9, 1975	D, note discounted at 6%		20,000	37,000
Apr. 15, 1975	E, distributor; 6 months; 6%	8,000		45,000
May 15, 1975	B, plus interest		5,000	40,000
July 1, 1975	A, principal payment		4,000	36,000
Oct. 1, 1975	Keck; 1 year; 6%	5,000		41,000
Oct. 1, 1975	A, principal payment		4,000	37,000
Oct. 15, 1975	E, plus interest		8,000	29,000
Oct. 15, 1975	E, distributor; 6 months; 6%	8,000		37,000

During the course of the audit, examination of the Notes Receivable account, of the notes, and of allied information revealed the following:

(1) Interest earned on all notes taken in 1975 was recorded as it was re-

ceived. Interest was received on all notes fully or partially liquidated or renewed. Interest on the notes taken in 1974 was properly accrued at December 31, 1974, and the entry reversed at January 1, 1975.

(2)   Keck is vice president of the company.

(3)   The E note of October 15, 1975, was a renewal of the original note of April 15, 1975. E has always been a good credit risk.

(4)   The bank notified Hessby that the note of D was paid at maturity.

On the basis of the information presented, prepare the following:

a)   Work papers for the Notes Receivable, together with interest accrued, earned, and received in 1975.

b)   Audit adjustments necessary at December 31, 1975, including the entry for accrued interest.

The company computes interest on the basis of 12 months per year. Note transactions occurring between the first of months are computed on the basis of a half month. You accept this procedure.

PRACTICE MATERIAL ASSIGNMENTS

Colby Gears, Inc.: Holmes and Moore Audit Case:
Accrued Interest Receivable.

15

Inventories and Cost of Sales

SECTION I: IMPORTANCE AND OBJECTIVES OF AN INVENTORY AUDIT

The propriety of periodic net income is determined in large measure by the proper accounting for inventories and the cost of goods sold. Proper accounting for inventories also determines the accuracy of the matching of periodic revenues and related expenses and serves as the basis for future management decisions. Accounting for and auditing of inventories are important considerations in the determination of periodic net income, because the income statement is inaccurate if the inventories are improperly charged to cost of goods sold during the period and if the remaining inventories are improperly stated. Assets and proprietorship are also incorrect if the inventories are improperly stated as to total amounts. The method of inventory pricing should be consistent from period to period in order to reflect net income in a consistent manner. If the basis of pricing an inventory has been changed from one year to the next year, the accounting policies are altered—and full disclosure of such changes should be reflected in the audit report. If full disclosure is not given, it is misleading, and someone may allege injury.

Inventories frequently constitute the largest current asset of a business organization—and one of material importance compared with the total of all assets. Currently, business is inventory-conscious, a condition promoted by advanced discussion and application of various methods of costing sales and pricing inventory in order to allocate net incomes more accurately to their proper accounting periods. This condition has been accelerated by better accounting procedures, keener competition, the universally growing desire for useful costs, and the requirements of federal income tax legislation and the tax legislation of the various states.

Auditor's Responsibility for Inventories

The responsibilities of an auditor for inventories may be divided into (1) his professional responsibilities, which are the outgrowth of the requirements necessary to the rendition of a sound professional opinion, based upon an adequate examination of the inventory and the inventory records, and the method of costing sales; and (2) his legal responsibilities (Chapter 16), arising from an act or a failure to act under the responsibilities falling within the sphere of accounting and auditing. Legal responsibilities have been established under common law and under the requirements of the Securities and Exchange Commission.

Professional responsibilities are composed of (1) a study and evaluation of the system of internal control for inventories, (2) observation of the taking of the inventories, (3) testing of inventory counts, and (4) the examination and proof of accuracy of the inventories in terms of prices in order to set forth properly the inventories and the related cost of sales.

In attempting to meet and to discharge these professional responsibilities, the auditor will employ certain procedures and tests. The extent of these procedures and tests depends upon the client's internal control over inventories, upon the inventory records, and upon the care exercised by a client in taking a physical inventory.

The audit report must disclose omitted procedures, together with reasons for the omissions. In order to avoid qualification of an audit opinion, a sufficient amount of work should be performed. It must be clearly understood that an auditor is not a guarantor of inventory prices, quality, or quantity; neither is he an expert in materials. If the opinion of the auditor is unqualified, the assumption should be that he has followed all procedures necessary to convince him of the accuracy of the inventory and the propriety of costing sales.

It is the opinion of the authors that in the face of more stringent auditing procedures—and regardless of whether individual auditors have been declared negligent by courts and regulatory bodies—there should never be regimented standardized practices for the audit of inventories— or any other item. Each company differs in its operations, accounting applications, and internal control; and the requirements of each audit engagement vary in accordance with the findings of the engagement.

Prior to developing internal control techniques and audit procedures applicable to inventories, a few comments—approximately paralleling the professional responsibilities of the auditor—of a general nature are offered for consideration.

Inventory Taking and Observation

Although the actual taking of a physical inventory does not fall within the province of the auditor's work, he should nevertheless be familiar with the procedure and work necessary to take an inventory in a systematic, accurate, and efficient manner. Auditors are constantly called upon to draft the plans and instructions to be followed when an inventory is to be taken. An auditor should participate in the preparation for taking the inventory and should observe the actual process in order to assure himself of the fairness of the presentation of the financial statements.

Inventory-taking procedures cannot be described for all possible types of companies, but the procedures set forth here should cover the problems and outline the procedures for at least 80 percent of the mercantile and manufacturing companies. Naturally, variations in the procedures should be made whenever such a step becomes necessary for the best interests of the client and for the most efficient completion of the inventory taking; such changes in the described procedures will vary with the size and nature of the inventory and with the system of internal control.

Definite plans should be developed concerning the date of the physical inventory, who is to supervise the count, the personnel of the counters and checkers, and the sequence of the counting. A set of written instructions should be prepared, to be studied by each person connected with the taking of the inventory. The inventories should be arranged for efficient and fast work. Inventory tags should be serially prenumbered and prepared in duplicate or with a perforation separating the top and bottom sections of the tag. The inventory crew should count, weigh, or measure the inventory; place the name of the inventory item, its code number, its location, the item count or weight or measurement on the tag; and after signing the tag, attach it to the goods. A second crew may verify the first count; or the original count may not be placed with the goods, and the second crew may again count and independently record the count. In the meantime, inventory sheets should be prepared so that the data on the tags may be transferred, priced, extended, and totaled. Upon the completion of the process of taking the inventory, the original tags, or the half below the perforation, or the count tags of the second crew should be taken from the inventory items, collected, and turned over to the person in charge of the inventory procedure for transfer to the inventory summary sheets. A grand summary of all of the inventory sheets may be prepared. The duplicates, or top portions of the tags, may be left attached to the goods until the inventory summary is completed or until such time as the person in charge is certain that he will have no reason to recheck any item. Original tags should be kept, together with summary sheets, until the auditor has completed verification of the inventory.

There are many variations of the procedure just described, all of which are equally effective. For example, instead of using a tag system, inventory sheets may be prepared by departments. One person may call the items, codes, description, and count, while a second person records the data. Also, inventory records may be kept on punch cards or on magnetic tape, in which case a print-out of the data should be tested against computations made by the auditor.

Points which must be kept in mind while the inventory taking is being conducted are as follows: (1) withdrawals from inventory and additions to inventory must be recorded on the count tags or sheets during the time of taking the inventory; and (2) all discrepancies between physical and book inventories must be recorded and the book inventories corrected.

Most companies have a natural business year, at the end of which production is at a minimum and inventories are low. If the natural business year were chosen as the fiscal year, the inventory problem would be greatly simplified. Many concerns do not use a natural business year but, instead, maintain the fiscal year which was originally established when the company was small and when the choice of the accounting period was an unimportant matter. For most concerns, unfortunately, the fiscal year is the calendar year, whether or not it is the natural business year.

With modern inventory control methods, many concerns rotate the counting of inventory; that is, certain items of inventory are counted each month (or each week) and the perpetual inventory records brought into agreement with the count. In this way, the inventory is completely counted at least once a year without serious disruption of activity. Mercantile concerns which keep their inventory records by the retail method simply reduce the total of their inventory by the amount of the net markup and use the resultant figures for monthly income statements. The gross profits method of computing inventory is also used extensively in the preparation of interim statements.

ILLUSTRATION.   The following is an example of minimum inventory observation instructions that would be used as an audit guide:
1.   Obtain copy of client's physical inventory instructions. Observe that instructions are being followed. Any deviations should be noted and discussed with management.
2.   Survey the entire plant area. Inquire and note slow-moving, obsolete, or damaged items. These conditions should be noted on the inventory tags. Visit shipping and receiving areas and observe the propriety of cut-off. Inspect common carriers on the premises and check adeqacy of handling for inventory purposes.
3.   Test inventory quantities from inventory tickets on a selected sampling basis. Trace-test counts to final inventory listing.
4.   Test client's tag controls; account for all tags, including those unused and voided.
5.   Complete and review inventory observation work papers.

Inventory Pricing

By "inventory pricing" is meant the dollar amount of inventory to be used for statement purposes at the end of a period, which amount will be carried forward as a charge to cost of sales in the succeeding period. Inventory pricing is a direct result of the method used in costing periodic sales. Inventories may be priced:

1. At cost [the cost may be (*a*) identified cost or (*b*) a derived cost, such as Fifo, Lifo, an average cost, the base-stock method, or a standard cost].
2. At market—replacement cost at the balance sheet date.
3. At the lower of cost or market.
4. At sales price, which may be below cost or market.
5. Under the gross profits method.
6. Under the retail inventory method.
7. Dollar value Lifo.

An auditor is responsible for ascertaining the accuracy of pricing an inventory in accordance with the method used to cost periodic sales and, in accordance with the application of accepted accounting principles. Inventory pricing is a problem in which consideration must be given (1) to the method of costing periodic sales, (2) to the goods to be included in the inventory, and (3) to the unit costs to be used in pricing the inventory and for net income determination.

In accordance with recognized principles, the primary *basis of accounting* for inventories is cost—which is net acquisition price. In the matching of revenues and periodic costs and expenses, initial inventory cost should be the invoice price plus transportation, receiving, testing, insurance, and purchasing costs—less cash and trade discounts. There is no justification for recording inventories at amounts greater than their net cash outlays.

By "market" is meant the current replacement cost of the quantity on hand, except that (1) the market price should not exceed the established sales price, less reasonable costs of completion and distribution this tends to prevent the showing of a loss when the goods are finally sold; and (2) the market price should be no less than the net realizable amount reduced by a normal profit margin.

When cash discounts are lost, should the discount lost be a period charge, or should it be added to inventory? A period charge appears to be proper because future periods should not be burdened with cost expenditures resulting from deferment caused by a weak financial condition.

If inventory cost is derived, if sales have been costed throughout the period on a derived cost basis, and if the market at the end of the year is below this derived cost for the year-end inventory, for balance sheet purposes, the inventory preferably should be reduced to market price, unless Lifo is being used.

If actual cost of goods sold is to be shown as the cost of sales, the inventories *must* be stated at cost, either identified or derived. The variation between cost and a lower market—if the lower of cost or market rule is followed—*should* then be shown as "other expense" prior to the determination of the net income for the period.

Due to the effect on cost of sales and periodic net income determination, methods of determining an ending inventory—on other than an identified or derived cost basis—are necessary and desirable when the usefulness of the inventory is no longer as great as its cost. This utility decline may be due to physical deterioration, obsolescence, price changes, or other causes; and in conformity with the adoption of the rule of the lower of cost or market, the decline below cost would be recognized as a loss of the current period.

The majority of accountants still agree that inventories should generally be stated in the balance sheet at the lower of cost or market. Those accountants who disapprove of this method do so on the basis of the fact that the write-down of an inventory from cost (identified or derived, except Lifo) to a new, lower market price transfers the loss into the period of the price decline and not to the period in which the goods are sold. This is true; but most accountants, bankers, and businessmen believe in recognizing a loss upon discovery. Other objections are these: A devaluation may be required, even if there is no change in sales price. If devaluation in the subsequent period, the net income for the subsequent period would be inflated; if some of the goods are still on hand at the later date after the market price has recovered, they may be priced at a higher figure than before and thus reflect an unrealized gain, though customary procedure avoids such an unrealized inventory profit by continuing to use the former lower market figure as "cost."

The rule of "cost or market, whichever is lower," may be applied either to each item or to the total of each class of inventory, whichever method more clearly reflects net income.

There is no one method of costing sales or of pricing inventory which is universally applicable to all companies; however, consistency of method should be followed from year to year so that net incomes are not distorted between fiscal periods. *Since this is a text in auditing, a discussion of valuation principles and methods is not included.*

ILLUSTRATION.   The following is an example of inventory pricing instructions that could be used as an audit guide:

1. Confirm inventory in hands of others.
2. Clerical testing: Foot all pages totaling over $15,000 and every tenth page. Add all pages to arrive at this total inventory. Manually test all extensions over $5,000. Sight test the remainder of extensions. Summarize the results of testing.
3. Trace-test physical counts to inventory listing.

4. Test of standard labor rates: Using factory summary schedules maintained by the client, obtain hours and wages for a three-month period. Calculate an average rate per hour for both manufacturing and assembly. Compare the results to the standard manufacturing and assembly rates used to price the inventory. Test the factory summary schedule by reconciling with the payroll distribution. Examine employee time cards for one week and accumulate the total to compare with the factory summary. Cross reference the rates used to the verification of rates per our payroll test.

5. Test of manufacturing overhead: Compute rate and compare it to the rate used in pricing the inventory.

6. Pricing—Raw Material: Select approximately 25 percent of the dollar value of inventory items, and obtain most recent vendors' invoices. Substantiate unit prices used by reference to the invoices.

7. Pricing—Work in Process: Select approximately 15 to 20 percent of the dollar value of inventory items. Substantiate material unit costs by reference to raw material inventory listing. Substantiate material quantities by reference to blueprints. Substantiate labor cost by reference to the client's listing of labor operations stated in hours-per-hundred pieces. Test overhead extensions by applying overhead rate to direct labor.

8. Pricing—Finished Goods: Select approximately 15 to 20 percent of the dollar value of inventory items. Substantiate material unit cost by reference to raw material inventory listing. Substantiate material quantities by reference to blueprints. Substantiate labor cost by reference to client's listing of labor operations stated in hours-per-hundred pieces. Test labor dollar extensions by applying standard labor rates to schedule of hours-per-hundred pieces. Test overhead extensions by applying overhead rate to direct labor.

9. Compare curernt year gross profit percentage with that of the preceding year.

10. Schedule unrecorded receiving reports and goods in transit, if any.

11. Compile and review work papers, including those relating to inventory observation. Draw conclusions as to their adequacy.

12. Obtain an inventory certification from the client.

Clerical Record Accuracy

The auditor's responsibility for verification of the clerical accuracy of the inventory records dictates that he must adequately test the clerical work performed in connection with the inventory to assure himself that extensions, footings, and summarizations of the inventory are proper. The amount of clerical accuracy verification to be performed is dependent upon such factors as the internal control over inventory, the total size and materiality of the inventory, the quality—condition—of the inventory records, and its physical composition. These factors will be discussed later.

With punch card or electronic data processing equipment, total clerical accuracy may be verified by an independent running of the cards or the magnetic tapes.

General Responsibilities

The general responsibilities of the auditor involve the reasonableness of scrap procedure, the determination of the adequacy of insurance coverage, an audit by comparison, determination of proper cutoff dates, obtaining inventory certificates from the client, and proper balance sheet presentation of the inventories—all to be considered later in this chapter.

Inventory Reports for Management

Inventory reports—normally internally prepared—for top management in the areas of finance, purchasing, production, and sales are a "must" because through inventory control, usage, and sale, working capital properly is used or misused and a periodic net income or net loss is produced. Financial management is interested in maintaining inventories at a minimum coordinate with anticipated near-future sales; thus, there will not be an overinvestment in inventories—particularly if short-term bank credit is desired. Purchasing, sales, and production executives are interested in qualities of raw materials, work in process, and finished goods in stock so that shortages will not develop and interrupt normal production schedules and so that information is available with regard to slow-moving items.

Thus, a variety of internally prepared inventory reports should be available for the auditor to review and appraise. These reports will include: (1) inventory usage, (2) a list of purchase commitments, (3) short-term and long-term inventory requirements, (4) obsolete items, (5) inventory on markdown, (6) book inventory versus physical counts, (7) cost versus current replacement cost, and many others.

If management does not properly respond to a cyclical change in demand for its products, an excess or a deficiency in inventories will result. If inventories are excessive, liquidity is reduced and obsolescence risks increase. If inventories are deficient in amount, supplies may be at a premium and customers may be lost.

SECTION II: INTERNAL CONTROL OF INVENTORIES

Adequate internal control of inventories is directly related to purchasing, manufacture, and accounting for the goods and products. Proper internal control over inventories dictates that the goods be properly ordered, received, controlled, segregated, requisitioned, and used, and that the remaining inventories be properly counted, priced, extended, and totaled. Each element of internal control, above, should be independent of each other element so that total inventories will result in the proper reflection of cost of goods sold and net income. Also, proper internal control over manufactured goods includes the addition of direct labor and factory overhead in proper amounts at the work-in-process stages. The internal controls for purchasing and receiving and for purchase returns were set forth in Chapter 4.

An internal control questionnaire for inventory is shown in Illustration 15–1. An internal control questionaire for the acquisition of inventories appears in Chapter 16. To further satisfy himself as to the adequacy of internal control, the auditor should review any procedure manuals the client might have relating to his program of inventory control. If these procedure manuals are not in good form or not kept up to date, the auditor may find it desirable to flow-chart several of the critical phases of internal control.

ILLUSTRATION. As a part of his review of the inventory on hand the auditor finds that several items in the inventory are considerably in excess of these same items in the two prior years. Further investigation reveals that prior years' amounts were desirable levels and that the current year's balances, although correct, are excessive. In his efforts to determine the reason for this undesirable situation, he learns that the client has no formal procedure established for the handling of purchase requisitions. Using the following symbols, the auditor prepares a flow chart for the handling of a purchase requisition.

Activity relating to the initiation of the purchase requisition.

Additional data is recorded on the purchase requisition.

The purchase requisition is filed in a closed file until a purchase order is prepared.

The purchase requisition is being inspected by the people responsible for its validity.

Indicates the handling of the purchase requisition by responsible parties.

Transfer of purchase requisition to location outside the scope of this flow chart.

THE SOUTHERN COMPANY

Flow Chart of Purchase Requisition – Copy #1	Department Head	Purchasing Department		
		Clerk	Purchasing Agent	Buyer
1. Purchase requisition is prepared in duplicate by department head on set of prenumbered forms. Keeps Copy #2 in current reference file.				
2. Copy 1 is sent to purchasing department.				
3. A clerk in the purchasing department stamps the date of receipt on the purchase requisition and enters requisition number and date on master list.				
4. Copy is reviewed by purchasing agent and checked against perpetual inventory record. He approves requisition by initialling.				
5. The copy is checked against the economic order quantity requirement by the clerk.				
6. Copy 1 is turned over to the responsible buyer.				
7. The copy is reviewed by the buyer to determine its proper completion and validity.				
8. If found in order, the buyer will determine that current prices are available and approves by initialling.				
9. Current prices and supplier's name are entered on the purchase requisition by the clerk.				
10. Purchasing agent inspects requisition to determine if he can approve. He then approves by initialling.				
11. A prenumbered purchase order form is selected and its number placed on the requisition by the clerk.				
12. The purchase requisition is filed by supplier.				

It is conceivable that alternate procedures could be required if certain steps cannot be promptly completed, such as current prices not being available. The auditor should prepare separate flow charts for these alternatives. Such flow charts will greatly assist the auditor in determining the adequacy of the client's system of internal control.

ILLUSTRATION.   In the process of verifying unit costs of the inventory, the auditor encounters difficulties in locating the necessary purchase invoices.

A further investigation reveals that the client has changed his data processing procedures and his flow chart is no longer applicable to his practices. The auditor prepares the following flow chart as a means of assisting his client as well as facilitating hi own review of the system of internal control. (An IBM Flowcharting Template is used in preparing the flow chart.)

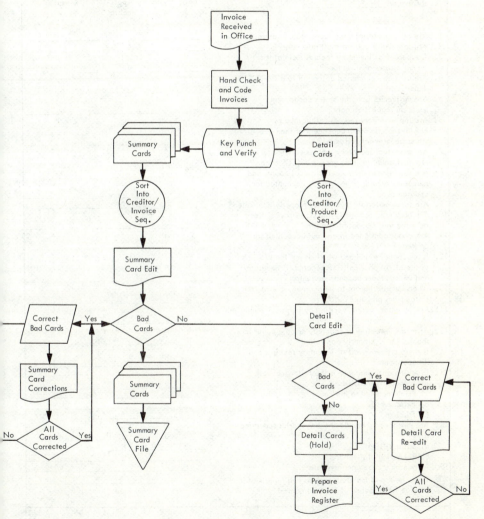

SECTION III: AUDIT PROGRAM FOR INVENTORIES

An audit program to be followed for inventories is developed in the following subsections.

Observe the Taking of the Physical Inventory and Test Quantity Counts. Recognized auditing procedures include the observation of the taking of the physical inventory, the testing of inventory quantities, and

ILLUSTRATION 15-1

INTERNAL CONTROL QUESTIONNAIRE
Inventories

Company_____ Period Covered_____	Yes	No	Not Appli-cable	Remarks
1. Are all inventories under centralized control?	____	____	____	_____
2. Are safeguards against theft adequate?	____	____	____	_____
3. Are perpetual inventory records maintained for all classes of inventory?	____	____	____	_____
4. Are all items purchased delivered to a stores department?	____	____	____	_____
5. Are deliveries from the stores department made on requisition only?	____	____	____	_____
6. Are the inventory records maintained by employees who are independent of the stores department personnel?	____	____	____	_____
7. Are perpetual inventory records verified by physical count at least once every 12 months?	____	____	____	_____
8. Are discrepancies between physical counts and perpetual records investigated, accounted for, and approved?	____	____	____	_____
9. Are scrap materials inventories properly controlled?	____	____	____	_____
10. Are obsolete, damaged, and slow-moving items reported to a responsible person?	____	____	____	_____
11. Are goods consigned in and out accounted for properly?	____	____	____	_____
12. Is merchandise on hand which is not the property of the client physically segregated (if necessary) and under proper accounting control?	____	____	____	_____
13. When inventories are to be counted, are written instructions prepared?	____	____	____	_____
14. Are inventory counts verified by persons independent of those in charge of the inventory records?	____	____	____	_____
15. After the inventory is counted, are the count tags, sheets, etc., properly controlled?	____	____	____	_____
16. Is there proper cutoff of inventory receipts and disbursements?	____	____	____	_____
17. In taking an inventory, is the following work independently verified:				
a) Prices applied to the count?	____	____	____	_____
b) Extensions?	____	____	____	_____
c) Footings?	____	____	____	_____
18. Are persons who handle the inventories separated from:				
a) Sales billings?	____	____	____	_____
b) Recording of purchases?	____	____	____	_____
19. Is insurance coverage adequate?	____	____	____	_____
20. Does the client maintain records and reports which provide for a review of internal control?	____	____	____	_____

Prepared by_____   Reviewed by_____
Date_____   Date_____

testing the accuracy of inventory records. Inventories that are incorrect as to quantity, pricing, and clerical accuracy may be the result of unintentional mistakes—but are mistakes, nevertheless—and the auditor therefore must exert himself to show accurate inventories.

From client personnel an auditor must ascertain the methods employed in counting, weighing, or measuring the inventories; he is obligated to satisfy himself that the quantities shown by the records actually were present.

The observation of the inventory taking and the physical tests of the inventory may be made at interim dates, followed by working client records forward to the date of the financial statements. This saves audit time during busy seasons and saves client time during periods of unusual inventory activity.

Recognized auditing procedure includes an adequate test of the inventory quantities, if it is reasonable and practicable to do so. If it is neither reasonable nor practicable for the auditor or an independent specialist to observe the taking of the inventory and to test the quantities, such omission *must* be set forth in the audit report, together with the reasons for departure from recognized practice.

The auditor should familiarize himself with client procedure for ordering, receiving, recording, and issuing materials, so that he may judge the reliability of the internal control. He should read the inventory-taking instructions of the client in order to determine the adequacy of the inventory-taking procedure.

In determining the accuracy of the physical inventory quantity, consideration must be given to such factors as the system of internal control over the inventory, the accuracy of the inventory records, the effectiveness of the method of taking the physical inventory, and the frequency with which the client verifies the physical inventories and corrects the inventory records. In order to prevent alterations, the inventory records should be controlled in the interval between the time of testing the inventory quantities and the time of converting quantities to dollars for statement purposes.

If the audit is subsequent to the closing date, the auditor should start with the quantity on hand at the date of his examination, add the quantity sold, and subtract the quantity purchased or produced since the closing date in order to work back to the correct balance at the period-closing date.

In testing the count of the physical inventory and comparing it with the recorded count of the client, the objective is to prove the accuracy of the client's inventory recording. Discrepancies should be adjusted to the satisfaction of the auditor. The testing of the inventory should be representative of a sufficient sample so that the audit report may be rendered without qualification. The normal quantity test may vary between 5 percent and 10 percent of the items, in accordance with the desired tightness of inspection level and the test results of the selected sample.

While testing inventory quantities, the auditor must watch for items that are obsolete or slow moving. This must be done if the inventories are to be properly priced at an amount not in excess of sales price less profit and disposition costs. The determination of obsolete and slow-moving items is more easily accomplished while testing physical quantities

ILLUSTRATION 15–2

HAMLEN COMPANY

Test of Inventory Quantity and Prices
Purchased Items, December 31, 1975

| | | Prepared By | | Initials | Date |
| | | Approved By | | | |

| | Purchases | | | | | Inventory | | | | Inventory Short (over) |
Description	Quantity	Cost	Invoice Amount	Vendor	Date of Invoice	Quantity 12/31/75	Cost §	Amount	Inventory	
Corner beads	61,500 ft.	$ 9.35 M	$ 575.02	Inland Steel Co.	11/5/70*	150,000 ft.†	$ 9.35 M	$1,402.50	$ 1,402.50	—
Casing beads	83,750 ft.	16.90 M	1,415.38	Inland Steel Co.	1/22/71*	32,500 ft.	16.90 M	380.25	380.25	—
Picture mold	85,500 ft.	10.35 M	884.92	Inland Steel Co.	11/5/70*	105,000 ft.‡	10.35 M	1,086.75	1,086.75	—
Double faced tape	6,395 bxs.	12.10 bx.	1,149.50	Inland Steel Co.	12/23/70*	5 bxs.	12.10 bx.	60.50	60.50	—
Floor track	63½ gr.	15.41 gr.	978.53	Creative Tapes, Inc.	10/22/70*	3 gr.	15.41 gr.	45.90	45.90	—
Base screed	7,784 ft.	10.50 C'	817.32	Northern Steel Co.	12/6/70*	2,160 ft.	10.50 C'	226.80	226.80	—
Self-furring lath	9,456 ft.	8.30 C'	784.85	Northern Steel Co.	12/6/70*	5,400 ft.	8.30 C'	448.20	448.20	—
Flat rib lath	7,872 ft.	11.58 C'	911.57	Inland Steel Co.	11/23/70*	4,320 ft.	11.58 C'	50.03	50.03	—
Inventory tested			$7,517.09						$ 3,700.93	
Total inventory-dollar value									$18,500.00	
Percentage tested									20%	

* Invoice examined.
† Total items tested–quantity . . . . 150,000 ft.
   Total items purchased . . . . 500,000 ft.
   Percentage tested 30%
‡ Total items tested–quantity . . . . 105,000 ft.
   Total items purchased . . . . 525,000 ft.
   Percentage tested 20%
§ In all cases, cost was not in excess of market.

and reconciling the physical inventory with the recorded inventory than at any other time. Slow-moving items may be detected by preparing schedules that show the number of months' purchases (or production) in the inventory and by comparing the results with the turnover of selected items of inventory. A valuable source of information is employees who aid in checking the inventory; they often disclose obsolete or unsalable items.

If perpetual inventory records are maintained and if the perpetual records are used in lieu of an actual full count at the balance sheet date, the auditor should be satisfied with the frequency with which the perpetual records and physical inventories are reconciled.

Work Papers. Several types of work papers are accumulated during the examination of inventories. These schedules must show clearly the amount and kind of work performed in connection with the inventory and must also contain written descriptions of the work, as well as general comments of client personnel made during the course of the audit. A few work papers are presented in Illustrations 15–2, and 15–3. Additional papers appear in the Illustrative Audit.

ILLUSTRATION 15–3

TEST OF INVENTORY PRICES

P & B COMPANY Inventory Price Tests Manufactured Items December 31, 1975		Initials	Date
	Prepared By		
	Approved By		

			Client Price 12/31/75				Market Price 12/31/75				Inventory Price Changes
Item	Quan-tity	Unit	Ma-terial	Labor	Over-head	Total	Ma-terial	Labor	Over-head	Total	
210	10,000	Ea.	$4.00	$2.00	$4.00	$10.00	$4.00	$1.40	$2.80	$ 8.20	Deduct $12,000
211	2,000	Ea.	6.00	4.00	8.00	18.00	7.00	4.00	8.00	19.00	
212	12,000	Ea.	2.00	2.00	4.00	8.00	2.00	2.20	4.40	8.60	
213	8,000	Ea.	3.00	1.75	3.50	8.25	3.00	1.75	3.50	8.25	
214	5,000	Ea.	7.00	2.00	4.00	13.00	8.00	1.50	3.00	12.50	Deduct $2,500
	37,000						√	∧	⊙		

√ Compared with vendors' last invoices.
∧ Compared with labor reports.
⊙ Compared with overhead distributions rate calculated report dated 1/1/75.

Inventory price of items tested . . . . $ 342,500
Inventory price of total items   1,490,000
Percentage tested 23%

The work papers demonstrated may be prepared in connection with the audit of an inventory. Those presented are only suggested forms, since each individual audit must be provided for according to the requirements of the engagement, the types of inventories, and the amount of work to be done. On some audits, certain of the work papers shown here and in the Illustrative Audit may not be used.

Compare Original Count Data with Inventory Summaries. The auditor should obtain the tags or sheets upon which the original inventory count was recorded and verify the accuracy of the transcriptions therefrom to existing inventory summaries. In this comparison, the auditor must be certain that quantities—dozens, reams, hundreds, and so forth— are stated in the same unit on the original data and on the summary sheets where the prices will be applied.

This comparison is in the nature of a test in all but extremely small audits. Normally, a comparison of *not more* than 25 percent of the items should serve to satisfy the auditor of the clerical accuracy of the transcription and the quality of the universe. If data processing cards or tapes are used for count transfer purposes, the cards or tapes may be selected at random or by blocks of similar inventory items.

The auditor must ascertain that inventory tags, cards, count sheets, and final summaries have been signed or initialed by the persons responsible for their compilation. This is necessary in order to establish responsibility in the event of errors.

Verify Extensions, Footings, and Total Summaries. The auditor should test the accuracy of extensions, footings, and totals on inventory sheets. Quantities and unit prices must be stated in correct units: dozens, price per dozen; tons, price per ton; and so forth.

ILLUSTRATION. An original inventory sheet showed 1,000 dozens, and the summary transcription showed 1,000 items; the unit cost was $1.50 each; the inventory was understated $16,500.

The verification of extensions and footings will be by test of a predetermined sample. The auditor must decide upon the extent of this testing (set forth below), and his decision should be based upon the quality of the methods employed in taking the inventory and the accuracy of the results. As a rule, the larger quantities of inventory should be verified in greater detail than the smaller quantities because a greater number of dollars may be tied up in the larger quantities. It must always be remembered, however, that an error might result in grossly understating a large item, thus making it appear small. Consequently, a test of small items must not be ignored. Frequently, large errors may be detected by scrutiny.

Some persons are of the opinion that if an inventory is small in value, *all* extensions and footings should be verified. However, if the inventory is small in value, it evidently is not material and does not require an extensive testing as in circumstances where an inventory is material in amount.

If inventories are maintained on punch cards or on magnetic media, trays of cards or tapes may be selected at random for similar items of inventory, processed through the print-out stage, and compared with the similar print-out of the client. Also, if the auditor is satisfied with the internal control over both the inventories and the data processing equipment, he may accept the client's original print-out and scrutinize it for accuracy, and/or test a sample of the items in the print-out.

Compare Inventory Summaries with Subsidiary and Controlling Accounts. If subsidiary inventory records are maintained, the balances should be compared with count data—and price data if the subsidiary records contain prices. Also, subsidiary inventory accounts should be compared with receiving records as an accuracy verification and as a determinant of proper cutoff. Subsidiary records should be adjusted to proper count and price in accordance with the taking of the inventory. If kept in terms of prices, a trial balance of the subsidiary accounts should be compared with the Inventory controlling account. If it is possible, differences should be accounted for; otherwise, the controls should be adjusted to the sum of the corrected subsidiary accounts, *after* physical quantity and price tests have proved the accuracy of the subsidiary records.

Test Inventory Pricing. The prices applied to the inventory by the client must be tested by the auditor to be certain that the inventory is fairly presented for financial statement purposes. The auditor should study the client's inventory instructions, if any, with respect to pricing. A discussion of specific items and the applicable procedures is presented in the following subsections.

Raw Material; Merchandise; Supplies. The inventory price used should be compared with the invoice cost and with current market price. Normally, the test should be for *not more* than 40 percent of the inventory dollars of raw materials and merchandise, or the test should be in accordance with the acceptance or rejection limits established for the quality of the sample.

Raw materials constitute the original materials purchased for manufacture. Merchandise inventory is the term used by mercantile concerns for stock in trade. Supplies are used by manufacturing, mercantile, and service organizations. The auditing procedures for quantities and prices are the same for these three classes of inventories. Where supplies are not significant in amount, they may be inventoried by estimate and inspection rather than inventoried, by physical count, weight, or measurement.

There must be a clear understanding of what constitutes the true original cost of raw materials and merchandise. As stated, that cost is composed of the invoice price, transportation-in charges, duties, and transportation insurance; cash and trade discounts are proper reductions of invoice price. As pointed out in a preceding section, the bases of pricing the raw material or merchandise inventory are identified cost; market; the lower of cost or market; last cost; replacement cost; Fifo; Lifo; weighted average cost; and base stock. It is not within the field of an auditing text go into a full discussion of the theories, advantages, and disadvantages of the various methods of pricing. Each method has its adherents and its opponents; the auditor must be familiar with all methods. Regardless of the method used to arrive at inventory prices, it must be borne in mind that the principal objective of inventory pricing is the determination of the proper periodic cost of sales and net income or loss for a fiscal period through the process of properly matching revenues and related expenses. *In addition, the basis of pricing should be consistent from period to period; and if a change in basis is adopted, it should be explained.* Also, the auditor should insist that a client adopt a method of costing sales and determining the value of the residual inventory which will appropriately reflect net income.

In the pricing of purchased items of inventory, invoices constitute the source of information for cost data; and in the testing of prices used against invoice costs, transportation and other charges must be verified. Current market prices should be obtained from papers, trade journals, and the purchasing department. The items of transportation, duties, and insurance, which are added to cost, must also be added to replacement bid prices in the comparison of the two prices. If a client is buying at prices above the market, an unusual situation exists which should be investigated.

Certain raw materials, merchandise, and supplies do not lend themselves readily to counting, weighing, or measurement. If book inventories are relied on, they must be supported by a competent test of physical quantity. In many instances, technical experts are employed to verify specialized inventories.

The inventory work papers in the Illustrative Audit accompanying this text should be examined, along with Illustrations 15–2, and 15–3.

Work in Process. Work in process is in a state of development—and therefore may be difficult to audit. An audit program for work-in-process inventories will vary according to the accounting system and the nature of the processes and operations. The auditor must familiarize himself with the cost system in operation before verifying the work-in-process inventories. In many cost systems, there are three elements of factory cost which are placed in process: (*a*) direct material cost, (*b*) direct factory labor cost, and (*c*) manufacturing overhead.

If the cost system is an integral part of the general accounting system, the inventories of work in process can be accurately verified for the three elements of cost, as follows:

1. Test charges to Work in Process for raw materials transferred.
2. Test labor charges to Work in Process.
3. Test the propriety of the distribution of overhead to Work in Process.

If the cost system is not related to the general records, it may be possible to obtain accurate costs for work-in-process inventories—but it is improbable that the cost records are accurate. If there is no cost system, it may be difficult to audit work in process as of the balance sheet date at a later date. With no cost system, the auditor may be forced to rely—in part—upon the estimates of employees and available specifications, and prior-year costs. The following illustration presents one method of approximating work-in-process inventory:

ILLUSTRATION.   A rough verification for work-in-process inventory:

January 1, 1975, inventories:			
Raw material		$ 10,000	
Work in process		35,000	
Finished goods		45,000	$ 90,000
Cost, 1975:			
Materials purchased		$300,000	
Labor		400,000	
Overhead		200,000	900,000
			$990,000
Cost of items sold in 1975 (from available cost specifications and estimates, or from 1974 unit costs)			880,000
December 31, 1975, inventories in total			$110,000
Deduct: Raw material inventory, counted and priced		$ 14,000	
Finished goods inventory, counted and priced		54,000	68,000
Remainder: Work in Process, December 31, 1975			$ 42,000

In auditing work-in-process records, footings and extensions should be tested, just as for any other inventory. Shop orders—or job tickets or production orders or departmental costs—are totaled and compared with the Work in Process controlling account. The subsidiary work-in-process records must be tested to ascertain that raw materials are charged to work in process at correct amounts; incorrect amounts mean that the work-in-process inventory is incorrect or that the figure for finished goods or cost of sales is incorrect if the product has reached the finished goods stage or has been sold. If raw material inventories are priced, for example, at the lower of cost or market, then the raw material cost, direct labor cost, and manufacturing overhead cost in work in process likewise should be priced at the lower of cost or market. Consistency should be maintained in this direction.

Production orders for work in process may also be tested to determine the accuracy of the cost of the labor in process. This is accomplished by comparing labor cost records with the subsidiary work-in-process records. If standard costs are used, variance accounts may be examined to ascertain undercharges and overcharges based on standard cost and actual cost.

Factory overhead is distributed to production on many different bases. Regardless of the method in operation, the auditor must examine the distribution of the overhead into work-in-process records to determine the accuracy of distribution and the correct dollar amount of the work-in-process inventory. The auditor must also verify the items constituting factory overhead to be certain that selling, administrative, and nonoperating costs are not included. If different distribution bases for overhead are used in different departments and divisions of a company, the auditor must be certain that an equitable distribution has been achieved.

In distributing factory overhead to product cost, a normal overhead rate should be established; that is, the overhead should be distributed so that normal costs are established rather than actual costs. This procedure levels out the cost to manufacture products and makes necessary Underabsorbed Overhead and Overabsorbed Overhead accounts. The auditor must ascertain that these accounts do not become an addition to Work in Process for underabsorbed overhead and a deduction from Work in Process for overabsorbed overhead; any balances in these accounts should be charged or credited directly to Cost of Sales, or distributed between Work in Process, Finished Goods, and Cost of Sales accounts.

Work-in-process records should be examined to be certain that shipped production has been cleared therefrom. An examination of the sales records and their comparison with the work-in-process records should disclose this situation. If the cost system is not tied in with the general records, this situation may easily exist; if the cost records are correct and if they do tie in with the general records, the condition can exist only through failure to transfer work in process to finished goods inventory, followed by failure to cost the sale at the time the sale was made.

Finished Goods; Finished Parts. If finished goods and finished parts are purchased, pricing and audit procedure follow the principles discussed under "Raw Material; Merchandise; Supplies." If the finished goods and finished parts were manufactured, the procedure follows that for work in process, already described, plus some additional work. Inventory records should be tested against the physical count; and the inventory may be worked back to the closing date if necessary. Discrepancies should be explained to the satisfaction of the auditor. Shipping records for the last few days or weeks of the period under audit must be compared with invoices and inventory records to be certain that there have not been included in inventory items which have been billed or shipped, or both. If a sale has been charged to a customer on the client's records and not billed or shipped, Sales should be decreased and Inventory increased, since the inventories are still owned by the client.

If certain customers purchase under special contracts giving them lower prices than are normally granted, the sales prices in such cases should be compared with production costs plus selling expenses in order to determine whether or not the contracts are profitable; if they are not, such work-in-process inventories should be reduced from cost to sales price less cost of selling.

Inactive stock item cards should be inspected to be certain that the goods have not become obsolete so far as pricing is concerned, with a resulting loss for which provision has not been made. These items should be discussed with the client.

Determine Proper Cutoff for Acquisitions of Inventories.   In order to arrive at a proper figure for a remaining inventory and for the periodic cost of sales, proper purchases and sales cutoff must exist at the end of the period. Customary procedure for inventory purchase cutoff follows receipt of the goods, except that at the end of the fiscal period, items in transit for which the buyer has a liability for payment should be added to the inventory in order to parallel the sale on the records of the supplier. All goods received up to the close of the period (or in transit F.O.B. vendor at the close of the period) must be included in inventory. Even if a delayed billing is received in the subsequent period, these items received or in transit must be taken into the inventory and into payables. In order that the propriety of the cutoff may be determined, invoices, receiving records, and inventory records must be compared. This comparison should be made for a few days or weeks preceding the end of the period in order to ascertain that all billings and receipts of goods were included in the inventory. The same records for a few days or weeks subsequent to the end of the year should be examined to determine that all billings and receipts of goods recorded in the new period are applicable thereto.

ILLUSTRATION.   The detection of fraud by the comparison of receiving reports, invoices, and inventory records may be exemplified as follows: X was department manager and a buyer of valuable oriental merchandise. He personally rented space in an office under an assumed name as a dealer in oriental merchandise. As buyer, X would order a large quantity of oriental rugs and tapestries. He had an accomplice deliver a small quantity to his employer's receiving department, thus obtaining the receiving department's receipt of shipment. X would then increase on the receipt the quantity of merchandise received and requisition a check for the increased amount. The check would be issued payable to the assumed-name dealer, and X would then receive and cash it. The auditor checked inventory records against the invoices for a period prior to and subsequent to the balance sheet date and disclosed the fraud.

Determine Proper Sales Cutoff.   Normally, sales and receivables are recorded as such upon delivery to a customer or to a delivery service. Departures from this custom may arise for C.O.D. sales, and they do exist for sight draft sales and F.O.B. destination sales. The sale may be recorded when shipment is made, although title may not pass until the goods are available to the buyer. Thus, the usual test for the conversion of inventory into receivables is delivery, with the exceptions just noted, and with the exception of certain construction contracts wherein interim billings take place, or for installment sales where the privileges and obligations of a purchaser are acquired in advance of title.

As a general rule, goods should be included in the inventories of the person holding legal title, who normally is the person liable for payment.

Customers must be charged for all goods shipped to the end of the period with the consequent reduction of the book inventory, even though the customer requests a delayed billing.

Goods billed to customers prior to the close of the period but shipped after the close of the period should be excluded from the inventory *only* if title has passed and if the seller is warehousing the goods for the buyer. To verify delayed shipments, compare sales invoices with shipping records for a few days preceding the close of the period and subsequent thereto. If title has not passed, the sales entry should be reversed and the goods included in the inventory. While the "legal title" rule is stressed in tax administration and as a proper criterion for inventory inclusion, the "legal title" rule is not always followed as a practical solution to many inventory problems.

In the examination and comparison of sales records, orders, sales invoices, and shipping records for the last few days of the period under audit and for the first several days of the subsequent period are examined, to ascertain that the sales and consequent inventory reductions are in the correct period; the auditor must determine that there are no fictitious billings accompanied by fictitious shipping records and made with the objective of inflating net income. The confirmation of accounts receivable is of assistance in this detection; also, entries for large returns in the subsequent period may offer a clue to this practice.

Ascertain the Propriety of the Treatment of Goods in Transit. As indicated, goods in transit to the client should be included in the inventory if title has passed and if the buyer possesses knowledge that the goods are in transit. If title has not passed for the in-transit items, entries charging Inventory and crediting Accounts Payable should be reversed.

Goods in transit at the end of the period naturally cannot be inspected. Work papers should be prepared for goods in transit, listing the shipments. A separate ledger account for items in transit may be set up in order to record the unreceived purchases if title has passed, so that total inventories may be brought up to the correct figure.

Shipment conditions must be investigated to determine title. If goods are shipped F.O.B. shipping point, the assumption is that title passes when the goods are placed with a common carrier for shipment. In such cases, the goods must be in the inventory of goods in transit. If shipment is F.O.B. point of destination, title does not pass to the purchaser, and the goods are not considered in transit until the purchaser is notified of arrival. Such a situation makes necessary the reversal of a recorded purchases entry if notification of arrival has not been received at the closing date.

Examine the Treatment of Goods Consigned In and Out. Goods out on consignment should be included in inventory and excluded from accounts receivable. Goods held on consignment should be excluded from inventory. Today, many companies treat consignments-out as sales and consignments-in as purchases, particularly where returns and other losses are not more than on ordinary sales and purchases. If consigned merchandise has been recorded as a debit to Accounts Receivable and a credit to Sales, the entries *preferably* should be reversed on the records of the consignor, and the inventory in the hands of the consignee should be included in the consignor's inventory.

In the audit of consigned-out goods, examination should be made of correspondence, shipping records, and consignment reports, supplemented by obtaining confirmation of merchandise-out. The auditor should examine the consignment contract and note its provisions with respect to remittances, guaranties, established sales price, credit extensions by the consignee, the treatment of transportation and insurance, the method of computing the consignee's commission, and other items of importance.

The auditor should obtain confirmation from consignees for merchandise held as of the balance sheet date, its sales price, the balance of cash due the consignor, accounts receivable held by the consignee if the consignor is to receive cash therefrom, accrued commissions if the consignor is to remit to the consignee, and expenses paid by the consignee to be deducted when he remits.

Goods held on consignment should be record-segregated from the inventory owned. Records for consignments-in should be maintained for the items held and for the commissions earned. In examining consignments-in and the records with respect to them, the auditor should:

a) Examine consignment contracts, correspondence, and reports for the audit period.

b) Obtain a list of the goods held.

c) Test the quantities of the items on hand and reconcile these with the records of the consignee.

d) Obtain confirmations from the consignors and compare them with the quantity tests; confirmations should be requested even if no consigned merchandise is on hand at the balance sheet date in order to prove that contention and to establish claims or amounts payable.

e) Verify the consignors' confirmations with respect to unremitted cash from sales, any contingencies, and other items.

Confirm Merchandise in Warehouses. When goods are stored in public warehouses, the auditor should inspect the warehouse receipts. In the event that warehouse certificates are pledged as loan collateral, the auditor should obtain confirmation from the pledgee. Pledged merchandise must be so indicated on the balance sheet. Warehouse certificates must be surrendered when goods are released. Consequently, under normal conditions, it is only necessary to obtain confirmation of the existence of the goods in warehouses; it is not usually necessary to examine the goods. However, the Allied Crude Vegetable Oil Refining Corporation case should not be forgotten.

If the auditor suspects that goods were withdrawn without certificate surrender, or if the goods stored represented a major proportion of the total inventories, current assets, or total assets, the auditor should match warehouse receipts with confirmations; and if it is practicable, he should visit the storage quarters and examine and test the inventories for quantity and condition. In the *Statement on Auditing Procedure No. 37* issued by the Committee on Auditing Procedure of the AICPA, the following specific recommendations are made that the auditor of the warehouseman must perform:

a) Make a study and evaluation of the effectiveness of both the accounting controls and the administrative controls.

b) Test the warehouseman's records relating to accountability for all goods placed in his custody.

c) Test the warehouseman's accountability under recorded outstanding warehouse receipts.

d) Wherever practicable and reasonable, observe physical counts of the goods in custody and reconcile his tests of such counts with records of goods stored.

e) Confirm accountability (to extent considered necessary) by direct communications with the holders of warehouse receipts.

These recommendations are also set forth in *Statement on Auditing Standards No. 1*, Section 332.

The auditor should apply any other procedures he considers necessary in the circumstances.

Segregate Items Other Than Inventory. In examining inventories, the auditor must ascertain that equipment purchases and raw materials and work in process destined to become fixed assets are not included in the inventory. The inventory should be composed only of raw materials, work in process, finished parts, and finished goods and supplies.

Examine Purchase Commitments. Purchase commitment contracts should be examined and work papers prepared which contain full data relative to the contracts. Confirmations from the suppliers should be requested for partial deliveries. If market prices have fallen to a point below the purchase commitment contract price, provisions for accrued net loss should be made, unless a complementary sales contract offers adequate protection. If advances of money were made to vendors on purchase commitments, the advances should be shown separately among the current assets as "advances on purchase contracts." The charges should be vouched to be certain that they represent advances. Debit balances in accounts payable should be investigated to determine whether any of them should be classified as advances on purchases. Because of the possibility of future loss, extraordinary purchase commitments in excess of reasonable requirements for the immediate future should be mentioned as a balance sheet footnote.

Compare Inventory Prices and Sales Prices. After testing a client's pricing of inventories, the auditor should compare inventories ready for sale with related estimated sales price in order to form an opinion concerning the probable future gross profit rate and its comparison with the gross profit rate of the current year and of past years. If a profit is to be realized, not only must the cost of the inventories be normal but the cost of selling and administration must be normal. If the conclusion is reached that a satisfactory profit margin will not be forthcoming, it is possible that for a manufactured inventory, finished goods and perhaps the inventory of work in process are overpriced at the balance sheet date. If Lifo is used, it is possible that remaining inventory is grossly underpriced.

Eliminate Inventory Profits. As a matter of good accounting, a profit margin should not be added to inventories. If interdepartment, interdivision, or intercompany profits have been taken into inventory, they should be eliminated.

In the uncompleted contract work-in-process inventory of a manufacturing company, if a profit has been added to the inventory, it should be eliminated so that the inventory will not be stated in excess of cost and so that a profit will not be recorded before it is earned.

In the case of construction companies, where the construction period extends over more than one fiscal period, it is recognized practice to include the estimated profit on the completed portion of the existing contracts in income for federal income tax purposes. If the client is a construction company and if the in-process contracts contain an estimated profit, the auditor should obtain a certification from architects and engineers of the percentage of the work completed and the estimated cost to complete the project. The total cost to date plus the estimated cost to complete must then be compared with the contract price in order to determine the propriety of the included profit; the exception to this comparison would be in the event of cost-plus contracts. The auditor should investigate to be certain that the profit or loss on all contracts completed in the year under examination has been taken into income. If completed contract accounts are open at the balance sheet date, the auditor must investigate to ascertain the reason why they have not been closed. It may develop that the customer refused acceptance, or there may be a lawsuit in process, or the intention may be to shift profits to another year.

ILLUSTRATION. Failure to bill customers for $600,000 of completed construction in 1975 resulted in shifting $72,000 of net income to 1976.

If work under a contract is guaranteed, the auditor must investigate the adequacy of repair warranties created for the purpose of meeting the guaranties. He should ascertain that the expense charges represent expectations that will be recovered in the contract price.

Segregate Pledged Inventories. When inventories are verified, the auditor must watch for evidences of inventories assigned or pledged as loan security and for evidences of other liens on the inventories. Inventories assigned or pledged as loan security at banks should be verified when confirming the bank balances. Other liens on inventories may be detected if insurance policies are endorsed to another as beneficiary under the policy. An inventory certificate obtained from the client should set forth inventory pledged as loan security and all other liens against the inventory.

If inventories are purchased under letters of credit, the goods withdrawn under the trust agreement should be segregated from owned inventory as property of the bank that holds the agreement. The auditor must investigate to be certain that goods withdrawn under trust agreements are not again used as security for a loan at another bank.

Apply the Gross Profits Test. The calculation of the inventory by the application of the gross profits test serves as a rough check on the reasonableness of the ending inventory. The test is based on the assumption that the rate of gross profit in the current year is approximately the same as the average rate for several preceding years. If gross profit rates fluctuate from year to year, the test is not of much value. When the gross profits test is used, it must be remembered that it constitutes only a *test* of the general accuracy of the ending inventory.

The test is of value in retail stores and wholesale organizations which maintain uniform gross profit margins. In a manufacturing company, the inventories must be separated for the three elements of cost—raw material, labor, and overhead; in this manner, errors must be ascertained.

If the gross profits test discloses *major* discrepancies between the calculated inventory and the priced inventory, an inquiry *may* reveal one of the following situations:

a) Fictitious sales may have been recorded.
b) Figures for goods purchased may have been inflated.
c) Quantities and/or prices may have been incorrectly stated in the priced inventory.
d) Purchases and sales cutoffs may have been improper.
e) Sales prices may have been materially increased or decreased without corresponding increases and decreases in purchase costs.
f) The basis of pricing the ending and beginning inventories may have varied.

The best use of the gross profits method to arrive at an inventory is in the event of thefts, fires, and improper conversions.

Examine Inventory Quality. Inventories of poor quality, items that are obsolete, and slow-moving items may be determined in the examination of the individual inventory records if returned sales are large and if items are not sold in accordance with management's expectations when the inventories were purchased or manufactured. These inventories should never be carried at a price in excess of possible realization. In order to determine obsolete items, after inspecting the inventory, the auditor must discuss inventories with the client. The auditor should obtain data pertaining to obsolete items from the perpetual inventory records on the basis of nonmovement; a comparison of sales price and inventory price often leads to the discovery of obsolescence. Also, a decreasing rate of turnover may serve as a guide to the detection of obsolescence. When obsolescence is established, the inventory may be written down directly or an allowance of sufficient size to cover the loss may be provided.

In similar manner, slow-moving and defective items must not be priced in excess of possible realization. These items eventually might be sold at a price below cost, and the possible loss should be provided for as soon as a suspicion of loss arises.

ILLUSTRATION. In connection with its studies of inventory management, one national accounting firm found for several clients that slow-moving or obsolete goods ranged to more than 40 percent of the inventory on hand.

The auditor is responsible in a general way for ascertaining that the quality of the goods is satisfactory for resale or productive purposes. The ascertainment of proper quality affects the pricing of the inventory; and from the standpoint of correct pricing, the auditor is concerned. At no time should the auditor be considered a specialist in determining the quality of the client's inventory. The certificate of inventories (Illustration 15–4) should contain a client statement concerning quality.

Compute Inventory Turnover. Computation of the rate of inventory turnover is often an aid (*a*) in determining growing quantities of obsolete and unsalable goods and (*b*) in determining the tendency to buy in advance of requirements.

Inventory turnover is determined by dividing the cost of sales by the average inventory; the greater the number of subperiods in the average, the more accurate will be the rate of turnover. If the normal rate of gross profit for a business is small, turnover will be more rapid than in a company where gross profit rates are high. The auditor must be acquainted with normal turnovers for various types of industries and businesses. Turnover may be affected (*a*) by quantity and (*b*) by the method of pricing the inventory. To determine the cause of a change in turnover, unit costs must be compared with those of previous periods.

Examine Scrap Materials Procedure.   Proceeds from scrap materials often constitute a large dollar amount of revenue, even though the amount is not significant in comparison with total revenues. Many companies do not maintain inventory records of scrap, by-products, and other waste. In many instances, records of these items should be kept—at least in terms of quantity—particularly if the quantities are large or if the material is valuable, as in the case of filings in precisious-metal operations.

When records are kept, the auditor should test the clerical accuracy of the records, just as in the case of any inventory; he also should test quantities (whether or not quantity records are kept), and he must be careful of the pricing of the items. Scrap materials should be reasonably priced at all times at a price not in excess of final realization. Revenues from the sale of scrap materials should be properly recorded either as sales, as other revenues, or as a reduction of cost of sales.

Examine Spoiled Work Reports.   Spoiled work results in an expense that may be absorbed in the cost of the completed units; however, it is more properly taken up by a credit to Work in Process or Finished Goods and a charge to some special account, such as Spoiled Work, which is treated as a manufacturing overhead expense. Of course, this treatment results in the finished product ultimately absorbing the cost of the spoiled and defective work, but normal unit costs are not drastically distorted. The auditor must investigate the method of treating spoiled work and ascertain that the treatment is in accord with sound practice so that proper costs are shown. Production must be credited for the cost of the spoilage, including material, labor, and overhead in the product. Unreasonable amounts of spoiled work may be called to management's attention and must be considered in the light of the type of product manufactured. Some industries have extremely high spoiled-work costs, as exemplified by the clay products industries, the knitting industries, and certain food products industries.

Determine the Propriety and Adequacy of Insurance Coverage.   There are many types of loss protection insurance obtainable upon inventory. The type of inventory in large measure determines the type of insurance to be carried. Fire and extended coverage, theft, and burglary insurance are needed for small-item merchandise. Fire insurance only might be sufficient for large items of metal—sheet steel, bar stock, and so forth.

In examining the propriety and adequacy of the insurance coverage, the auditor must be certain of the following points:

a)   Wherever located, the inventory must be covered.
b)   The beneficiary under the insurance policy should be the client or the owner of a lien against the inventory.

c) The operation of coinsurance clauses must be analyzed.

d) Policy expiration dates must be noted; insurance brokers usually can be relied upon to reinsure, but the auditor should not rely on others.

e) If the policy is originally issued on a "provisional" basis, premium refunds should be verified.

f) Premium refunds should be credited to the proper accounts.

g) When "specific" insurance coverage is purchased on increasing and decreasing inventories, the auditor must ascertain that interim inventory reports have been properly and promptly submitted to the insurance brokers. This procedure is necessary so that insurance at all times will be adequate but not excessive. The auditor must not judge the adequacy of the insurance coverage by comparing inventories with the face of the policy. Modern policies are designed so that the face of the policy shows a minimum amount of insurance; as inventories increase, additional specific amounts are purchased. If the average of the inventory for the year is less than the average insurance in force, premium refunds will be made.

Audit the Inventories by Comparison. A comparison of items with similar items of preceding periods often discloses slow-moving items, obsolete goods, and unnecessary quantity variations—particularly increases that result from buying in advance of requirements, with the consequent harmful effect on working capital. This comparative study may be made as follows:

	Quantity, December 31			Total Cost, December 31			Dollar Increase (Decrease*)	
Item	*1975*	*1974*	*1973*	*1975*	*1974*	*1973*	*1975-74*	*1974-73*
804	10,000	7,000	6,000	$10,000	$ 7,700	$ 5,400	$ 2,300	$ 2,300
904	100	9,000	12,000	1,000	90,000	100,000	89,000*	10,000*
999	400	420	450	800	820	900	20*	80*

Item 804: Sales are increasing. Cost prices are decreasing.
Item 904: Large demand. Short supply.
Item 999: Obsolete. No purchases since 1971.

In making these comparisons in terms of raw materials, work in process, finished goods, and supplies, the auditor should determine that the prices of the inventories at the beginning of each year are in agreement with (*a*) the client's records, (*b*) his work papers, (*c*) tax returns, and (*d*) financial statements. Any variations must be investigated and disclosed in the report of the examination.

Obtain an Inventory Certificate. Auditors ordinarily obtain from the client a written representation concerning the inventories. Normally, this certification is drafted by the auditor and signed by the client. If a satisfactory certification cannot be obtained, the probabilities are that the audit report must be at least qualified. While an inventory certification does not relieve the auditor of any responsibility, it does emphasize the fact that the financial statements are those of management. To be included in the inventory certification are representations concerning ownership, quality, quantity, pricing methods, total amounts, obsolete goods, purchase commitments, and pledged items.

Illustration 15–4 presents one form of inventory certificate. In each

ILLUSTRATION 15–4

CERTIFICATE OF INVENTORIES

Name of Client __The Lyons Company__

Period Ended ___December 31, 1975___

Dayton and Piqua, Certified Public Accountants
Cincinnati, Ohio

Gentlemen:

We believe the following statements to be accurate representations of the inventories at the close of the accounting period stated above. The inventories are classified as follows:

Raw Materials	$155,000.00
Work in Process	45,000.00
Finished Goods	75,000.00
Supplies	10,000.00
Total	$285,000.00

The preceding total is represented by the following:

Physical inventories	$198,000.00
Book inventories	87,000.00
Total	$285,000.00

1. All inventories were included in the preceding total.
2. All physical inventories were taken by actual count, weight, or measurement.
3. For book inventories, all quantities are based upon physical inventories taken at November 30, 1975, and worked forward from that date to December 31, 1975, on the basis of purchases and sales records.
4. Raw materials, supplies, and purchased merchandise were priced at the lower of cost or market, as applied to each item in the inventory. Costs were determined by Fifo. Market price is considered as the lower of replacement cost or net realizable amount, loss all costs of carrying, selling, and profit.
5. Work in process and finished manufactured product has been priced at manufacturing cost, except obsolete and unsalable items, which were priced at net realizable amount.
6. The basis of pricing the inventories is consistent with the methods followed at the close of the preceding period.
7. Purchase commitments are not in excess of current market price at the balance sheet date.
8. Sales commitments do not exist below inventory prices.
9. All items included are the property of the company.
10. There are no hypothecated inventories.
11. The liabilities for all items included in the inventories have been recorded as of the closing date, above.
12. No items are included which were billed or shipped prior to the closing date.
13. When discrepancies occurred between physical and book inventory figures, the book figures were adjusted to the physical count.
14. All inventory is salable and in good condition.
15. The following exceptions to the printed statements are noted:
       No exceptions

Date __January 25, 1976__   THE LYONS COMPANY
                                   James Lyons, President
                                   John Ebel, Treasurer

engagement, the certificate should be designed to suit the existing circumstances.

QUESTIONS

1. Explain the effect of each of the following errors in the December 31, inventory of your client:
   a) Incorrectly excluded 100 units of Product W, valued at $1 per unit, from the ending inventory; purchase was not recorded.
   b) Incorrectly excluded 200 units of Product X, valued at $2 per unit, from the ending inventory; purchase was recorded.
   c) Incorrectly included 300 units of Product Y, valued at $3 per unit in the ending inventory; the purchase had not been recorded.
   d) Incorrectly excluded 400 units of Product Z, valued at $4 per unit, in the ending inventory; the purchase had not been recorded.

2. Describe and briefly discuss the responsibilities of an auditor for inventories he observes.

3. What should an auditor do if he has omitted required audit procedures?

4. Why is it necessary for the auditor to participate in the preparation for the taking of a clients inventory?

5. What are the minimum inventory observation instructions that would be used as an audit guide?

6. What inventory pricing problems does the auditor face when valuing ending inventory?

7. What inventory pricing instructions would an auditor use as an audit guide?

8. Why is it important for management to receive periodic inventory reports?

9. What areas of internal control are essential to an audit of inventories?

10. What factors does an auditor consider when determining the accuracy of the physical inventory quantity?

11. Set up the headings of a work paper, that could be used to test the quantity and prices of inventory of a dry goods wholesaler.

12. What constitutes the true original cost of raw materials and merchandise?

13. As relating to inventory, what does a proper "cutoff" date refer to?

14. For the past five years a CPA has audited the financial statements of a manufacturing company. During this period, the examination scope was limited by the client regarding the observation of the annual physical inventory. Since the CPA considered the inventories to be of material amount and he was not able to express an unqualified opinion on the financial statements in each of the five years.

    The CPA was allowed to observe physical inventories for the current year ended December 31, 1975, because the client's banker would no longer accept the audit reports. In the interest of economy the client requested the CPA not to extend his audit procedures to the inventory as of January 1, 1975.

    What should the CPA mention in his short-form report?

15. Late in December, 1975, your CPA firm accepted an audit engagement at Quality Jewelers, Inc., a corporation which deals largely in diamonds. The corporation has retail jewelry stores in several Eastern cities and a diamond wholesale store in New York City. The wholesale store also sets the diamonds in rings and in other quality jewelry.

The retail stores place orders for diamond jewelry with the wholesale store in New York City. A buyer employed by the wholesale store purchases diamonds in the New York diamond market, and the wholesale store then fills orders from the retail stores and from independent customers and maintains a substantial inventory of diamonds. The corporation values its inventory by the specific identification cost method.

Assume that at the inventory date you are satisfied that Quality Jewelers, Inc., has no items left by customers for repair or sale on consignment and that no inventory owned by the corporation is in the possession of outsiders.

a) Discuss the problems the auditor should anticipate in planning for the observation of the physical inventory on this engagement because of the—

   (1) Different locations of the inventories.
   (2) Nature of the inventory.

b) (1) Explain how your audit program for this inventory would be different from that used for most other inventories.

   (2) Prepare an audit program for the verification of the corporation's diamond and diamond jewelry inventories, identifying any steps which you would apply only to the retail stores or to the wholesale store.

c) Assume that a shipment of diamond rings was in transit by corporation messenger from the wholesale store to a retail store on the inventory date. What additional audit steps would you take to satisfy yourself as to the gems which were in transit from the wholesale store on the inventory date?

(AICPA, adapted)

16. *a*) How is it possible to ascertain the existence of slow-moving items of inventory?

b) How should slow-moving and obsolete inventory items be priced for balance sheet purposes?

17. Wherever practicable and reasonable, auditing standards require that the auditor be present at the taking of an inventory and that he satisfy himself by suitable observation and inquiry as to the effectiveness of the methods of taking the inventory and as to the reliance which may be placed upon the client's representations regarding the inventories and the inventory records.

The Rose Company has been in operation for several years. You are requested to audit the financial statements for the year ended December 31, 1975. This is your first examination of the company's records.

What procedures would you consider necessary to satisfy yourself of the accuracy of the January 1, 1975 inventory so that an unqualified opinion could be rendered to the financial statements? The inventory was an item of material amount at January 1, 1975, and December 31, 1975.

18. What special procedures should an auditor adopt in the observance of inventory taking where large quantities of packaged materials are stacked in solid formation?

19. Your client is a toy manufacturer. The company closes its records annually each December 31. Perpetual inventory records are maintained in terms of quantities and prices. A complete physical inventory is taken each November 30. At November 30, 1975 you observed the taking of the physical inventory and were satisfied with the procedures followed. By testing the counts you were satisfied with the accuracy of the client's counts.

There were differences between the client's count and the perpetual records for about 30 percent of the items. Before adjusting the inventory records for the larger differences, of which there were about 10, the records were verified and the items were recounted. Typical examples of adjustments for the larger differences are:

Description of Item	Perpetual Record before Adjustment	Perpetual Record after Adjustment
Red paint (gallons)	662	657
Cotter pins (dozens)	2,260	2,120
Wheels	6,901	6,883

The company did not make additional physical tests of inventories during 1975. For the year ended December 31, 1975, the company used inventory quantities shown by the perpetual inventory records.

In outline form, prepare an audit program setting forth the essential procedures to be followed in your audit of inventories as of December 31, 1975. Do not include procedures unless you believe them to be essential under the conditions as stated.

(AICPA, adapted)

20. When examining the sales of a company, the auditor in charge of the engagement advised you that it would be necessary to devote attention to the company's shipping records (*a*) for the period under examination, and (*b*) particularly for several days preceding the close of the audit period, and (*c*) particularly for several days subsequent to the close of the audit period. For (*a*), (*b*), and (*c*), why is such attention necessary?

21. A new client engaged in a nonmanufacturing business requests an audit of its records for the fiscal year ended June 30, 1976. Certified statements are to be prepared. Inventory records have been improperly maintained. In order to be certain of the income statement, the correct inventory at June 30, 1976, is essential. Sales records and inventory purchases records have been properly maintained. Describe the procedure to be followed in order to be certain that the income statement will present fairly

the net income for the year ended June 30, 1976. Assume that prior audit reports are not available.

22. Explain under what conditions an auditor would be justified in accepting the pricing of an inventory on each of the following bases:
    a) Cost price.
    b) Market price.
    c) Lower of cost or market.
    d) Standard cost.

    The inventories have been consistently priced from year to year; and the auditor has properly observed the taking of the inventory and has properly tested for clerical accuracy, price, and quantity.

23. In examining the records of a company engaged in wholesaling goods, you discover that a substantial part of the inventory of merchandise is on consignment to customers in other cities and a substantial part is in independent warehouses in other cities.

    State the procedures you would follow in the verification of the inventory on consignment and in the warehouses.

24. During an audit of the records of a brewery, it is discovered that barrel deposits are billed to customers as a part of the total sales price, with no indication in the billing that the deposits will be refunded upon the surrender of the barrels. When a customer returns barrels, in order to obtain the total sales price, the brewery redeems them for the same amount originally added and records the return as a purchase. The inventory of the barrels on hand is carried as a current asset. In such a situation, what advice would you offer a client?

25. If an auditor had followed all accepted auditing procedures for the verification of inventories, if he were convinced that the inventories were correct, and if he considered himself to be in a position whereby he could render an unqualified opinion would it be advisable for him to request an inventory certificate from the client? Why or why not?

26. A manufacturer of farm equipment has a fiscal year ending June 30. The useful life of its product is not over 10 years. New models are introduced each year. An inventory of repair parts is maintained; and a price list of parts, which shows prices to dealers and retail sales prices, is published annually.

    Perpetual inventory records of repair parts are maintained in quantities, and an annual physical inventory is taken. For statement purposes, the inventory is extended at current list prices to dealers and reduced to cost by application of a computed gross profit percentage figure.

    You are a new CPA in charge of the annual audit of the company as of June 30, 1976. When the audit is finished, your work will be reviewed and you will be questioned about each phase of the audit. In connection with the audit of the repair parts inventory, for example, you will be asked if that inventory is included in the inventory certificate obtained from the client.

    In connection with the audit of the repair parts inventory, what additional questions might you expect to be asked when your work is reviewed?

27. A company owns and operates 50 retail furniture stores. Perpetual inventory records are maintained at the central office and are kept in terms of quantity, units and unit cost, total cost, and store or company warehouse location. Store and warehouse inventories are taken by company employees on serially numbered tags. The inventory crews work in teams of two: one employee enters the description and count of the items on a perforated inventory tag; the second employee verifies the description and count and removes the lower portion of the count tag.

   The removed portions of the tags are returned to the central office, where the descriptions and count are transferred to "item" inventory punch cards; the items then are priced at the lower of cost or market, or reduced for damaged merchandise and obsolete items, and by the use of data processing equipment are extended and summarized. Several weeks before the close of the fiscal period, the central office sends a copy of the inventory instructions to the auditors.

   What procedure would you follow to verify the inventory under the circumstances outlined?

28. Your client, a manufacturer with a large and active inventory, takes his inventory as of the close of business on December 31 and "cuts off" as of that date. However, the inventory taking is not completed until the following January 8. Describe the auditing procedures you would follow with regard to inventories received and shipped during inventory taking.

(AICPA, adapted)

PROBLEMS

1. The information presented below relates to the final inventory of paper taken in your audit of Market Research, Inc. on December 31, 1975.

		Per Ream	
Inventory Classification	Quantity	Cost	Market
Report Grade:	(Reams)		
Grade 1	100	$6.00	$6.60
2	30	5.00	4.60
3	20	4.80	4.80
Letter Stock (watermark)			
Grade 101	40	1.40	1.30
102	20	1.20	1.25
103	10	1.60	1.60
104	6	2.50	2.00
105	8	2.00	1.75
106	6	3.50	3.00
107	12	1.50	1.50
Letter Stock (80% rag content)			
Grade 201	16	1.50	1.00
202	8	2.00	1.75
203	14	2.00	2.50
204	6	1.50	1.50
205	10	1.60	1.40

Using the data presented above, prepare the necessary work papers setting forth the valuation of the inventory at the lower of cost or market assuming application (*a*) by item, (*b*) by classification, and (*c*) total inventory. (Prepare a separate work paper for each application).

2. The Jamison Company year ends December 31. You have completed the audit and have found a number of errors. The company had taken, under your careful observation, a physical inventory. The following data were found during your audit:

   a) Goods shipped F.O.B. shipping point by a supplier, in the amount of $9,000, had been excluded from the inventory, and further testing revealed that the purchase had not been recorded.

   b) A purchase of $6,000 had been received and recorded as purchased. However, upon your inspection the goods were found not to meet specifications of the order and would be immediately returned.

   c) Materials costing $20,000 and having a selling price of $22,000, had been segregated in the warehouse for shipment to a customer. The materials had been excluded from inventory even though a signed purchase order had been received from the customer. Terms F.O.B. destination.

   d) Materials costing $6,000 was out on consignment with Tarboro, Inc. Since the monthly statement from Tarboro, Inc. listed these materials on hand, the items had been included in the final inventory.

   e) The sale of $14,000 worth of materials and costing $10,000 had been shipped F.O.B. point of shipment on December 31. However, this inventory was found to be included in the final inventory.

   f) Materials costing $5,000 and selling for $6,000 had been segregated, but not shipped at December 31, and were not included in the inventory. A review of the customer's purchase order set forth terms as F.O.B. destination. The sale had not been recorded.

   g) Your client has an invoice from a supplier, terms F.O.B. destination, but the goods had not arrived as yet. However, these materials costing $13,000 had been included in the inventory count, but no entry had been made for their purchase.

   h) Merchandise costing $15,000 had been recorded even though the merchandise had not arrived. Terms of Sale are F.O.B. shipping point according to the suppliers invoice which had arrived by December 31.

   Further inspection of the client's records revealed the following December 31 balances: inventory, $50,000; Accounts receivable, $42,000; accounts payable, $27,000; sales, $330,000; purchases, $150,000; net income, $24,000.

   Using the preceding indicated account balances as starting points, prepare an audit work paper showing the corrections and the correct balances.

3. In connection with his examination of the financial statements of Moellman Products Co., an assembler of home appliances, for the year ended May 31, 1976, Ray Dooley, CPA, is reviewing with Moellman's controller the plans for a physical inventory at the Company warehouse on May

31, 1976. Note: In answering the two parts of this problem do not discuss procedures for the physical inventory of work in process, inventory pricing or other audit steps not directly related to the physical inventory taking.

Part A. Finished appliances, unassembled parts and supplies are stored in the warehouse, which is attached to Moellman's assembly plant. The plant will operate during the count. On May 30, the warehouse will deliver to the plant the estimated quantities of unassembled parts and supplies required for May 31 production, but there may be emergency requisitions on May 31. During the count the warehouse will continue to receive parts and supplies and to ship finished appliances. However, appliances completed on May 31 will be held in the plant until after the physical inventory.

> What procedures should the Company establish in order to be certain that the inventory count includes all items that should be included and that nothing is counted twice?

Part B. Warehouse employees will join with accounting department employees in counting the inventory. The inventory-takers will use a tag system.

> What instruction should the Company give to the inventory takers?

(AICPA, adapted)

4. As a part of the initial audit of the records of the Calhoun Company for the year ended December 31, 1975, you are to examine the inventories. The company was organized in January, 1973, and for the years 1973 and 1974 prepared its own unaudited statements.

The inventory audit resulted in the accumulation of the following information.

A physical inventory of all material on the premises was taken December 31, 1975, and was priced at $500,000 (raw materials, $200,000; work in process, $200,000; finished goods, $100,000), based on the lower of cost or market. Materials in transit costing $15,000 were not included in the physical inventory as of December 31, 1975, but the liability had been recorded properly prior to the year-end. Material consigned by the Nelson Company was on hand and was included in the raw materials inventory of the Calhoun Company at the consigned cost of $35,000.

The audit of the raw materials inventory revealed errors of (*a*) items duplicated, $26,000; (*b*) items missed in counting, $4,000; and (*c*) extension footing errors, $10,000 overvaluation.

Work-in-process inventory included $100,000 applicable to a single contract which was 50 percent completed as to both labor and material. The contract calls for a completed price of $208,000, plus applicable selling and administrative expenses.

Prepare the necessary audit adjustments. Indicate the effect of the examination on your audit report. Show all calculations.

5. From the following information for the Green Company: (*a*) prepare work papers for the inventories, setting forth, in detail and in total, the proper amount of the inventory at December 31, 1975; and (*b*) prepare the necessary audit adjustment to correct the client's inventory.

Under your observation company personnel counted the inventory after the close of business on December 31, 1975, the date of the annual examination. You tested the counts, which were recorded on inventory tags attached to the items. From the count tags, the client prepared the summary presented below and gave it to you for verification, after having adjusted the Inventory control account to the total shown below:

Item	Quantity	Cost	Market	Total
A-510	720 units	$ 3.60 dozen	$ 3.64 dozen	$ 2,592.00
A-520	48 units	4.70 each	4.80 each	252.60
A-530	164 units	16.50 each	16.50 each	2,706.00
A-540	68 units	5.15 each	5.20 each	353.60
A-550	80 units	9.10 each	8.10 each	7,280.00
A-560	140 dozen	2.00 each	2.00 each	280.00
A-570	190 gross	144.00 gross	132.00 gross	27,360.00
				$40,824.20

As you compared the correct tag quantities with the summary, you noted that item A-530 was for 146 units and that item A-540 was for 86 units.

6. On December 15, 1975, under your observation, your client took a complete physical inventory and adjusted the Perpetual Inventory controlling account to agree with the physical inventory.

As of December 31, 1975, you decided to accept the balance of the controlling account after reflecting transactions recorded in that account from December 16 to December 31. The audit was for the year ended December 31, 1975.

In your examination of the sales cutoff as of December 15 and December 31, the following items not considered earlier were disclosed:

Item	Cost Price	Sales Price	Date Shipped	Date Billed	Inventory Control Credited
A	$300	$400	12/14/75	12/16/75	12/16/75
B	400	550	12/10/75	12/19/75	12/10/75
C	200	275	1/2/76	12/31/75	12/31/75

What audit adjustments if any, should be made for each item?

(AICPA, adapted)

7. You are auditing the records of the Jamesway Company for the fiscal year ended October 31, 1975. You have observed the taking of the physical inventory on that date and you have tested the count.

All merchandise received up to and including October 30, 1975, has been included in the physical count. The following lists of invoices are for purchases of merchandise and are entered in the voucher register for the months of October and November, 1975, respectively:

Amount	*F.O.B.*	*Date of Invoice*	*Date Merchandise Received*
October, 1975:			
$ 3,000	Destination	Oct. 20	Oct. 22
2,200	Destination	Oct. 21	Oct. 23
925	Shipping point	Oct. 20	Oct. 30
3,975	Shipping point	Oct. 26	Nov. 5
2,500	Destination	Nov. 3	Oct. 29
1,025	Shipping point	Oct. 26	Oct. 30
8,600	Shipping point	Oct. 26	Oct. 30
10,251	Destination	Oct. 21	Oct. 30
3,457	Destination	Oct. 28	Oct. 30
November, 1975:			
$ 1,000	Destination	Oct. 29	Nov. 5
3,120	Destination	Oct. 30	Oct. 31
5,350	Shipping point	Oct. 28	Oct. 30
4,500	Shipping point	Nov. 1	Oct. 30
6,040	Shipping point	Oct. 26	Nov. 5
7,530	Shipping point	Oct. 28	Nov. 4
5,000	Destination	Oct. 28	Nov. 4

Perpetual inventory records are not maintained, and the physical inventory is to be used as a basis for the financial statements.

a) What audit adjustments would you suggest in view of the facts?

b) What adjustments would you suggest to the physical inventory as originally taken? Show all calculations.

8. On July 31, 1976, fire destroyed a portion of the finished goods inventory of Narson Inc. Under a fire insurance policy containing an 80 percent coinsurance clause, the company's inventory is insured for $120,000. Inventory costing $70,000 was not damaged by the fire.

At the close of each calendar year, a physical inventory is taken of raw materials, work in process, and finished goods. At December 31, 1974, and 1975, the inventories were $175,000 and $189,500, respectively. Examination of the selected ledger accounts below shows the following as of July 31, 1976.

(1) Raw material at a cost of $20,000 in transit to the company had not been recorded.

(2) The company had been billed (F.O.B. shipping point) for $10,000 of raw material that was not received; the $10,000 had been charged to Purchases of Raw Materials.

Selected Ledger Account Balances

Explanation	Dec. 31, 1975	July 31, 1976
Trade accounts receivable	$150,000	$175,000
Inventories.	189,500	?
Trade accounts payable	75,000	80,000
Administrative expense.	310,000	168,000
Depreciation of factory equipment	12,000	8,000
Direct factory labor	124,000	85,000
Factory supplies expense	7,000	4,000
Manufacturing expenses	12,000	7,500
Purchases of raw materials.	264,000	193,000
Purchase discounts	5,500	3,000
Sales	600,000	282,000
Sales returns.	30,000	2,000

As the auditor for the company, you are requested to prepare necessary calculations to:

a)   Determine the inventory prior to the fire on July 31, 1976.

b)   Determine the loss recovery from the insurance company.

9.   You are engaged in the annual audit of the records of the Dry Hole Company, a manufacturer of oil field equipment and related parts. At the end of the current fiscal year, May 31, 1976, the finished goods inventory is stated in the records of the company at $750,200. The company priced the inventory at moving average manufacturing cost. In the test of the net realizable value of the inventory, you selected items totaling $344,235 (less than 15 percent for selling expenses). Included in the test were four parts which have comparable value relationships:

Part No.	Per May 31, 1976, Inventory		May 31, 1976 Most Recent Cost to Produce	Latest Net Sales Price
	Units	Unit Price		
1132	6	$4,425	$4,154	$3,904.41
1134	2	3,180		
1136	3	7,250		
1138	1	5,435		

On all other items included in your test (except for two items requiring special attention, and detailed below) you determined that the inventory was stated in excess of net realizable value by $46,938.55.

The two items not included in the preceding test and requiring special attention are as follows:

a)   One drawworks priced in the inventory at $55,000. This item was manufactured at a cost of $140,000 and was written down to $55,000 on May 31, 1975. The company expects to sell this item for $96,000, and your examination of correspondence with a prospective buyer supports this contention.

b)   One slush pump priced in the inventory at its cost, $40,000. This is the first pump of this type produced by the company, and the company expects to sell it for $38,000 less a 25 percent discount.

Assuming that your inventory test is representative and is valid, and taking into consideration the two special items, compute the amount of the inventory write-down in order to state the May 31, 1976, inventory at net realizable value.

(AICPA, adapted)

10. Your client, Central Appliances, Inc. operates a retail store in the center of town. Because of lack of storage space, Central keeps inventory that is not display in a public warehouse outside of town. The warehouseman receives inventory from suppliers and, on request from your client by a shipping advice or telephone call, delivers merchandise to customers or to the retail outlet.

The accounts are maintained at the retail store by a bookkeeper. Each month the warehouseman sends to the bookkeeper a quantity report indicating opening balance, receipts, deliveries and ending balance. The bookkeeper compares book quantities on hand at month end with the warehouseman's report and adjusts his books to agree with the report. No physical counts of the merchandise at the warehouse were made by your client during the year.

You are now preparing for your examination of the current year's financial statements in this recurring engagement. Last year you rendered an unqualified opinion.

a) Prepare an audit program for the observation of the physical inventory of Central Appliances, Inc. (1) at the retail outlet and (2) at the warehouse.

b) As part of your examination would you verify inventory quantities at the warehouse by means of

(1) A warehouse confirmation? Why?

(2) Test counts of inventory at the warehouse? Why?

c) Since the bookkeeper adjusts the records to quantities shown on the warehouseman's report each month, what significance would you attach to the year-end adjustments if they were substantial? Discuss.

d) Assume you are unable to satisfy yourself as to the inventory at the audit date of Central Appliances, Inc. Could you render an unqualified opinion? Why?

(AICPA, adapted)

16

Inventories and Cost of Sales (Concluded)

SECTION I: COST OF SALES

If gross profits are inadequate over the long-run, a company cannot hope to survive. Today, the media attempt to make the public believe that profits are in the category of a sin. If there are no profits, there would be no business organizations—and therefore there would be no method of capital expansion and no way to support the critics in the various media.

The key to the maintenance of an adequate gross profit lies in the proper and consistent costing of sales, the pricing of the residual inventory, and in the maintenance of proper sales prices. This chapter will complete the examination for inventories and the cost of goods sold. The emphasis is directed to internal control over inventory acquisitions and the audit procedures necessary for the items purchased, cost of sales, and inventory reductions.

The verification of inventories—presented in Chapter 15—takes care of the materials element of the cost of the goods sold. The inventories stated in the balance sheet should conform to those shown in the income statement, unless losses are recorded when the market price of the period-end inventories is below their cost. Such losses should be shown not as a part of the cost of sales but as other expenses, because the gross profit percentage figures are distorted if they are treated otherwise, and because the ending inventories are on hand and have not been sold.

Labor and manufacturing overhead charges, which properly belong in cost of sales for a manufacturing company, are for convenience discussed in Chapter 15. The cost of sales figure is of prime importance because of its necessity in gross profit determination. The maintenance of an adequate gross profit margin means that with proper control of selling and administrative expenses, a net income can be realized. When gross profit figures depart from a normal condition, the auditor must investigate all causes of the change and perhaps comment upon them. Departures might be the result of changes in price policy, in sales volume, in raw material costs, in labor costs, or in manufacturing overhead charges; quantity or pricing errors in inventories; a "price-profit" squeeze; errors in the purchase records; a loss on inventory price decline erroneously included in cost of sales; or, possibly, an improper diversion of inventory, involving fraud.

Cost systems must be studied with a view toward determining the accuracy of the figures for manufacturing costs resulting from the method of cost accumulation in force. Inventory requisition summaries should be inspected and the quantities traced to the credits on inventory records on a test basis. Quantities shown on the requisitions must agree with the quantities shown on the inventory records as disbursements. If disbursements for which requisitions have not been issued are shown on inventory records, there is evidence of inventory manipulation. Authorizations to sign inventory requisitions should be compared with the signatures appearing on the requisitions. If it is discovered that control in this area is loose, the auditor can render a valuable service to the client by pointing out the necessity and the value of strict inventory control.

Unit prices placed on requisitions for determination of the cost charged to Work in Process must be test-compared with the cost of the items issued. Extensions must be verified and traced to the work-in-process ledger. The auditor will find differing opinions as to what cost should be used—for example, weighted average; moving average; Fifo; Lifo; base stock, standard cost; and so forth. Each system has its advantage and disadvantages, and the auditor should be interested in ascertaining that whichever method has been chosen, it is followed consistently and results in proper net income determination.

Ratio analysis figures should be developed, analyzed, and presented in the audit report. Labor charges, both direct and indirect, must be analyzed so that the accuracy of distribution to departments and to products is ascertained; this verification must be performed in accordance with the method of distribution employed in each individual case.

In order adequately to confirm the accuracy of cost of goods sold—to be developed in this chapter—inventory acquisitions must be verified on sample basis. Authority for inventory acquisitions should be investigated and compared with creditors' invoices. Creditors' invoices are verified for price, quantity, extensions, and footings; the acquisition is traced to the receiving and inventory records, and then traced to the payment records; paid checks should be compared with the invoices and with the entries. Examination of dates is important in order to eliminate the inclusion of old and paid invoices. Postings to subsidiary inventory records and to subsidiary records for accounts payable must be verified in conjunction with this phase of the work; then, the sum of the balances of the subsidiary accounts payable is proved with the balance of the control account. Common errors in recording acquisitions of inventories are as follows:

1. Failure to include items in inventory when vendor invoices have been received and recorded.
2. Omission of invoices from both the records and also omission of the related inventory.

ILLUSTRATION 16–1

INTERNAL CONTROL QUESTIONNAIRE
Inventory Acquisitions and Related Items

	Yes	No	Not Appli-cable	Remarks
Company_____				
Period Covered_____				
1. Is there an organized purchasing department?				
2. Is the purchasing department independent of:				
a) The receiving department?				
b) The shipping department?				
c) The accounting department?				
3. Are all purchase orders executed in writing?				
4. Are all purchase orders sequentially prenumbered?				
5. Are purchase orders properly approved for:				
a) Price?				
b) Quantity?				
c) Supplier?				
6. Does the accounting department receive directly:				
a) A copy of the purchase order?				
b) A copy of the receiving report?				
7. Does the accounting department match invoices with:				
a) Purchase orders?				
b) Receiving reports?				
c) Expense items?				
8. Are returned purchases routed through the shipping department?				
9. Does the receiving department obtain copies of purchase orders for authority to accept incoming items?				
10. Are receiving reports sequentially numbered and controlled?				
11. Is the sequence of numbers checked by the accounting department?				
12. Does the receiving department retain a copy of receiving report?				
13. Does the purchasing department receive a copy of the receiving report?				
14. Is the accounting department notified of returns to vendors?				
15. Are shipping reports prepared for items returned to vendors?				
16. Are the shipping reports in Question 15 matched with credit memorandums from vendors?				
17. Does the accounting department match invoices with:				
a) Purchase orders?				
b) Receiving reports?				
18. Are invoices entered by persons who do not have access to cash and/or inventories?				

ILLUSTRATION 16–1 (*Continued*)

	Yes	No	Not Applicable	Remarks
19. Are invoices properly approved:				
a) Prices?				
b) Extensions and footings?				
c) Transportation charges?				
d) Payment?				
20. Are shortages and damaged goods properly reported?				
21. Are invoices adequately stamped to prevent duplicate payment?				
22. Do nonmaterial purchase orders originate in one place?				
23. Are nonmaterial invoices properly approved prior to payment?				
24. Are invoices received from creditors compared with open accounts by the accounting department?				
25. Are all vouchers, supporting documents, and expense distributions received and signed by a properly authorized person prior to the authorization for payment?				
26. Prior to approval for payment, are all related documents for an invoice assembled in one place?				
27. Is a postage meter used for outgoing mail?				
28. Are items purchased for the convenience of employees routed in the regular manner?				
29. Where applicable, have inventories been valued for specified situations according to the requirements of the:				
a) Cost Accounting Standards Board?				
b) Internal Revenue Service?				
30. Have material changes been made in:				
a) Method of counting inventory?				
b) Method of valuing inventory?				

Prepared by_____   Reviewed by_____
Date_____   Date_____

3. Inclusion of items in inventory and failure to record the vendor invoice.
4. Omission of items from inventory when they are returned to the vendor and failure to take up the related credit memorandum because it probably has not been received.
5. Errors in card or tape punching.

Internal Control of Inventory Acquisitions

Adequate internal control over inventory acquisitions involves authorized ordering and the separation of the function of ordering from receiving, shipping, and accounting. All purchase orders should be in writing, properly authorized and approved. Only required items should be purchased, and the system must prevent unauthorized and unrequired items.

After ordering and upon receipt of the goods, the goods and the related invoices, receiving reports, and purchase orders must be properly controlled to prevent misuse of the items and to prevent improper payment.

Payment to creditors must be controlled on the basis of proper accounting for items purchased and on the basis of preventing duplicate payments.

An internal control questionnaire for inventory acquisitions is shown in Illustration 16–1.

An audit program for inventory acquisitions is developed in the following subsections.

Examine the System of Internal Control. If the system of internal control over purchased inventory is adequate, as indicated in the internal control questionnaire shown in Illustration 16–1, and if the auditor is satisfied with the operations of the system, his examination may be limited to a test of the data, as indicated in Chapters 9, 10, and 11. On the basis of random sample selection of the purchases data, a test of not more than 10 percent of the data should normally result in a quality assurance, or rejection of the entire purchases data population. Many auditors use a block of one month. Proper internal control over purchases of inventories was set forth in Chapters 4 and 5.

SECTION II: AUDIT PROGRAM FOR INVENTORY ACQUISITIONS

Audit Program for Inventory Acquisitions

Acquisitions of inventories were discussed in Chapters 10 and 13. Methods of accounting for purchased inventories are subject to a wide variation of practice, ranging through the use of data processing equipment, a voucher register, a purchase journal, the practice of making no entry until payment is made, the treatment of discounts as cost price reductions, the treatment of purchase discounts as other revenue, the classification of items purchased, the use of perpetual subsidiary inventory accounts, and so on, down to the point where no organized and reliable records are maintained.

If inventory acquisitions are not correctly recorded and are not properly audited, the cost of sales, gross profit on sales, and net income are incorrect, and the balance sheet is improper. Errors resulting in an understatement of inventory acquisitions are as follows: (1) charging some account other than Purchases or Inventory; (2) entering the acquisition at too low a figure; (3) failing to enter a purchase; and (4) holding the purchase record open at the end of the preceding period. Errors resulting in an overstatement of inventory acquisitions are as follows: (1) charging expenses or capital assets to Purchases; (2) failing to credit Returns and Allowances; (3) charging Inventory or Purchases when no inventory is bought or received; (4) overstating the acquisition price; (5) recording invoices more than once; and (6) holding the purchase record open at the end of the current period.

Examine and Compare Purchase Orders, Receiving Records, Related Invoices, and Accounting Entries. In the verification of the correctness of purchases of inventories, the system of purchasing used by the client must be understood, followed by the examination of the purchase orders for such data as supplier, dates, quantities, prices, extensions, footings, approvals, order numbers, and receiving report numbers—if the receiving report is not attached to the purchase order. In connection with the purchase order, all contracts should be examined to determine that the orders were placed in accordance with contract terms.

The selected sample of invoices should then be compared with the purchase orders and all differences noted. Then, the related receiving records are examined and compared with the invoices. The auditor must determine that all records bear proper approval. The purchase requisition should be compared with the purchase order. If requisitions for orders placed are not available, a further investigation should be made to determine if the purchasing department is making unauthorized purchases.

In order to establish the accuracy of the accounting, the selected sample of invoices should be tested for prices, extensions, and footings, and the invoices compared with the entries in the inventory acquisition record.

Receiving records should be examined for six or seven days prior to and after the close of the period, to be assured of proper cutoff, and to be certain that receiving records agree with invoice quantities.

Normally, with a satisfactory system of internal control, the preceding comparisons may be limited to not more than a 10 percent or a one-month test; the test should be extended if the initial results are not satisfactory.

Examine Back Orders. Back orders and the method of handling them should be examined in order to ascertain the effectiveness of the system of internal control over back orders. A back order is really a delayed portion of a purchase order, and if the delay is too long, the client may be accepting goods no longer needed. Also, the receipt of goods under a back order should follow the same receiving, approval, entry, and payment procedure as a filled purchase order.

Examine the Treatment of Transportation Costs. Transportation-in is a part of the cost of the inventories purchased. If a client is the vendee and if he pays transportation charges and deducts them from the invoice price and remits net to the vendor, the transportation is prepaid and does not appear as a transportation-in expense but should be charged to the creditor when the carrying charges are paid. The auditor must examine transportation payments of this nature to ascertain their correctness. He also must verify all other transportation-in charges by vouching bills of lading and transportation bills to the expense accounts and tracing them through the disbursements records into the accounts. Enormous sums have been recovered for clients through a verification of transportation bills, not only by examination of the mathematical accuracy of the statements but particularly by examination of shipment classifications and rate charges.

Examine Payment Data. The auditor must always be satisfied that purchased inventories are legitimate and the payments for them are correct. Payments for purchased inventories are traced through cash disbursements by the examination of invoices and related internally prepared vouchers. Invoices and vouchers selected in the sample indicated above are compared with disbursement entries; the auditor must note the approval for payment, based upon receipt of the goods, and the approval of prices and totals. Checks must be matched with the invoices and related vouchers and with the entries in the disbursements records. Precautions should be taken so that an invoice cannot be paid twice. As indicated in Chapters 9, 10, and 11, discounts must be verified.

Normally, the comparison of the disbursements entries with the related payment checks and invoices may be limited to not more than 10 percent or one month's transactions; if the internal control is not satisfactory, the test should be extended.

Compare Subsidiary Inventory Accounts with Receiving Reports, Invoices, and Requisitions. This comparison is necessary to be certain that the subsidiary inventory accounts are properly charged with correct quantities—and costs, if costs are used in the subsidiary inventory records. Receiving department reports also are compared with inventory records in order to test the accuracy of the inventory records and to be certain that all material received is actually sent to the storerooms. Normally, this test may be not more than 5 percent of the invoices.

Stock requisition summaries should be inspected and traced to stockroom inventory records and to work-in-process records in order to ascertain further that stock records are properly kept and that the work in process is correctly charged for materials placed in process.

Verify Postings. Postings from the inventory acquisition records to the general ledger accounts may be traced as follows: for one, or not more than two, nonconsecutive months, if the system of internal control is satisfactory; if the internal control is not satisfactory, the test should be extended, assuming that satisfaction is obtained with the results. Additional material concerning the verification of posting accuracy appears in Chapters 10 and 11.

Examine the Distribution of Items Purchased. The auditor should examine inventory acquisition records in order to determine distribution to proper accounts.

Inventory acquisitions should be analyzed by product classification and summarized by amounts per month in order to determine the gross profit on each product sold. Major variations in price and quantity should be pointed out, together with the causes of the change. Inventory cost includes not only the invoice price of the items purchased but also all incidental costs, such as transportation-in, storage, handling charges, duties, and any other costs necessary to place the goods in condition for use. Although these items are considered a part of the cost of the inventory, separate ledger accounts may be maintained for each. The entire cost is shown in the cost of sales section of the income statement.

When more than one type of inventory is purchased in one shipment, the incidental costs theoretically should be prorated over the various inventories; however, expense considerations often prohibit such distribution.

Foot the Inventory Acquisition Record. In accordance with the test plan set forth in Chapters 7 and 8, the inventory acquisition record should be footed and crossfooted for one or two nonconsecutive months. If the system of internal control is not satisfactory or if the results of the tests are not satisfactory, the proof of footing accuracy should be extended to the point where satisfaction is obtained or the universe is rejected.

Verify Items Returned. Inventories returned to vendors must be verified in order to determine that accounts payable have been charged and that inventory accounts have been reduced. The failure to record a return could lead the way to the theft of cash; if a return was not recorded, the creditor's account payable balance would be in excess of the amount owed. If the creditor was paid the proper amount, the remainder could be credited to Cash—followed by the preparation of a false check or the abstraction of the amount from cash receipts.

When items purchased are returned, the auditor must verify the returns by examining proper documentary credit memoranda and must vouch the return entries into the original records and to both controlling and subsidiary accounts payable. Vendors' recent statements must be compared with ledger account balances to determine that proper credit has been granted the returning buyer; this verification often discloses discrepancies caused by disputed items. Returns are handled in a variety of ways, and the auditor must investigate the method used to ascertain the correctness of the results and the ease or difficulty of obtaining the results. Some companies use a return record, some write returns in red in the purchase record, and others wait until all inventories purchased are inspected and approved before making an entry in the inventory acquisition record; in this situation, there will be no record of the return. In the latter case, the auditor must include all end-of-the-period acquisitions; rigid invoice and receiving record examination will be helpful. The method is good if properly used since it saves work.

SECTION III: MISCELLANEOUS INVENTORY CONSIDERATIONS

Inventory Loss Provisions

As stated in the preceding chapter, allowances *may* be created for losses on obsolete inventories and for possible losses on purchase commitments. In addition, an allowance may be created for the difference between cost and market if Inventory is not credited directly when the market price at the balance sheet date is below cost. A reserve for anticipated losses in the new accounting period may be provided from retained earnings when it is expected that market prices may continue to decline—but this reserve is *not* commonly used, simply because management normally will protect retained earnings. The first type is a valuation allowance created by a charge to Loss on Inventory Decline and a credit to Allowance for Loss on Inventory Decline. The charge is an expense, to be shown in the "other expense" section of the income statement; and in the balance sheet, the allowance is subtracted from the cost of the inventory. It is *perfectly* permissible to credit the Inventory account directly and not create the valuation allowance. Of course, if inventories are priced at the lower of cost or market and if periodic inventory procedures are in force, neither the inventory credit nor the allowance will appear.

In the rare event that a reserve has been created from retained earnings for future anticipated declines and if the decrease in replacement cost takes place in the succeeding accounting period, the expense account—Loss on Inventory Decline—should be charged, with an offsetting credit to the Inventory account. The Reserve for Anticipated Future Declines in Inventory account should *not* be charged when a loss occurs because such a procedure would result in failure to disclose the loss as an expense of the proper period. After the Reserve for Anticipated Future Declines in Inventory account has fulfilled its purpose, it should be returned to Retained Earnings, not to a revenue account.

Auditor's Legal Responsibility for Inventories

With respect to legal responsibilities, British courts have held that if the auditor obtained an inventory certificate from the client and reported the submission of such a certificate in the balance sheet, he was not responsible for the inventory. This ruling was established in the Kingston Cotton Mill Company case, in which the evidence disclosed that the inventory prices and quantities were overstated. The court held the auditors not to be negligent on the basis of the certification obtained from the client. At this point, the reader is referred to Chapter 3, for additional material on legal liability.

Under common law in the United States, it has been generally held that accountants are liable to third parties for the practice of fraud; liability for negligence normally was limited to the client, based upon the privity of contract between the auditor and his client. The following cases and court decisions set forth these general rules.

In the case of *Landell* v. *Lybrand* (264 Pa. 406, 107 Atl. 783, 8 A.L.R. 461), the plaintiff purchased capital stock in a company whose records had been audited by the defendants. The report of the auditor had been shown the plaintiff by an outside party, and the plaintiff had relied upon that report. In his suit, the plaintiff charged the accountants with negligence and carelessness. The Supreme Court of Pennsylvania ruled that the accountants had no liability to the plaintiff because there was no contract between them.

In the case of *Ultramares* v. *Touche* (255 N.Y. 170, 174 N.E. 441), the plaintiff was a third party who had relied upon the report of the auditors. The case was based upon misrepresentation of accounts receivable, but the case would be no different had the alleged misrepresentations involved inventories. There were two charges: (1) misrepresentations that were the result of negligence and (2) misrepresentations that were alleged to be fraudulent. The certified balance sheets in the case were used for credit purposes. From the following excerpt quoted from the court decision, it is apparent that the liability of the accountant was limited to the client for negligence, but that the accountant may be held liable to third parties for fraud. The excerpt from the court decision is as follows:

To creditors and investors to whom the employer [client] exhibited the certificate, the defendants owed a like duty to make it without fraud, since there was notice in the circumstances of its making that the employer did not intend to keep it to himself. A different question develops when we ask whether they [the defendants] owed a duty to the creditors and investors to make it without negligence. If liability for negligence exists, a thoughtless slip or blunder, the failure to detect a theft or forgery beneath the cover of deceptive entries, may expose accountants to a liability in an indeterminate amount for an indeterminate time to an indeterminate class.

The court went on to say that the opinion of an expert may be fraudulent if the basis of the opinion is such that there was no sound belief in support of the opinion; also, if there was a statement of fact in the certificate, whether believed to be true or untrue, the accountants are liable for deceit—that is, fraud—in the event that the statement of fact is false.

In the case of the *State Street Trust Company* v. *Ernst* (278 N.Y. 104, 704, 15 N.E. [2d] 416, 16 N.E. [2d] 851, 120, A.L.R. 1250), the same rules were followed. A quotation from the court follows:

We have held that in the absence of contractual relationship or its equivalent, accountants cannot be held liable for ordinary negligence in preparing a certified balance sheet even though they are aware that the balance sheet will be used to obtain credit. Accountants, however, may be liable to third parties, even where there is lacking deliberate or active fraud. A representation certified as true to the knowledge of the accountants, when knowledge there is none, a reckless misstatement, or an opinion based on grounds so flimsy as to lead to the conclusion that there was no genuine belief in its truth, are all sufficient upon which to base liability. A refusal to see the obvious, a failure to investigate the doubtful, if sufficiently gross, may furnish evidence leading to an inference of fraud so as to impose liability for losses suffered by those who rely on the balance sheet.

Under the Securities Act of 1933 as amended and the Securities Exchange Act of 1934, the liabilities of the auditor are greater than in preceding cases at common law, if it is later proved that negligence prevailed when the statements were prepared—with respect to inventories or any other item.

The Securities Act makes the following provision:

In case any part of the registration statement, when such part becomes effective, contained an untrue statement of a material fact or omitted to state a material fact required to be stated therein or necessary to make the statements therein not misleading, any person acquiring such security (unless it is proved that at the time of such acquisition he knew of such untruth or omission), either at law or in equity, in any court of competent jurisdiction, sue. . . .

The Securities Act also provides that the burden of proof is upon the auditor to show that "he had, after reasonable investigation, reasonable grounds to believe and did believe, at the time such part of the registration statement became effective, that the statements therein were true and that there was no omission to state a material fact required to be stated therein or necessary to make the statements therein not misleading."

With respect to the recovery of damages, the Securities Exchange Act provides that if the accountant "proves that any portion or all of such damages represents other than the depreciation in value of such security resulting from such part of the registration statement, with respect to which his liability is asserted, not being true or omitting to state a material fact required to be stated therein or necessary to make the statements therein not misleading, such portion of or all such damages shall not be recoverable."

The Securities Exchange Act sets forth the liability for statements which may prove to be misleading, as follows:

Any person who shall make or cause to be made any statement in any application, report, or document filed pursuant to this title or any rule or regulation thereunder or any undertaking contained in a registration statement as provided in subsection (d) of section 15 of this title [Title I, Sec. 18], which statement was at the time and in the light of circumstances under which it was made false or misleading with respect to any material fact, shall be liable to any person (not knowing that such statement was false or misleading) who, in reliance upon such statement, shall have purchased or sold a security at a price which was affected by such statement, for damages caused by such reliance, unless the person sued shall prove that he acted in good faith and had no knowledge that such statement was false or misleading. A person seeking to enforce such liability may sue at law or in equity in any court of competent jurisdiction. In such suit the court may, in its discretion, require an undertaking for the costs of such suit and assess reasonable costs, including reasonable attorney's fees, against either party litigant.

Thus, the legal hazards of the profession are ever increasing, with a constantly disappearing line of demarcation between liability for fraud and liability for negligence.

SECTION IV: FINANCIAL STATEMENT CONSIDERATIONS

Inventory Comments in the Audit Report

In order to issue an unqualified report, the auditor must adhere to all recognized auditing standards, and must follow all acceptable audit procedures. With respect to inventories, the issuance of an unqualified report would mean that the auditor has observed the taking of the inventory, tested quantities, examined inventory records for clerical accuracy, compared the records with physical amounts, and examined the pricing. Any deviations from recommended procedures should be specifically set forth in the scope section of the audit report, followed by any necessary opinion qualification or disclaimer.

If the auditor includes no exceptions in his report, the assumption should be that he has performed all work necessary and all work considered to be acceptable practice. If exceptions are included, they must be clearly expressed as such and must be clearly distinguished from informative comments; normally a disclaimer of opinion is then in order.

ILLUSTRATION. (Scope paragraph)
"Our examination was conducted in accordance with generally accepted auditing procedures, except:
"Auditing tests of inventory records have been made; but, upon instructions of the company, we have not applied the generally accepted auditing procedures of attendance at the physical count of the inventories; nor were we permitted physically to test inventories."

If the basis of pricing the inventory has been changed during the year, such changes and their effect upon income should be explained.

ILLUSTRATION. (Middle paragraph)
"During the year ended December 31, 1975, the company adopted the Lifo method of costing sales and determining the cost of the inventory. As a result, net income for the year 1975 was $100,000 less than it would have been had the change from Fifo to Lifo not been made. In our opinion, the change is justified, based upon the fact that by the use of this method, cost of sales figures will reflect current market prices for raw material usage."

If all accepted auditing procedures have been followed in connection with the examination of the inventories, it may be considered desirable to describe the scope of the inventory examination in a separate paragraph of the report. The following illustration would not lead to a disclaimer of opinion.

ILLUSTRATION.   (Middle paragraph)

"We have tested quantities, prices, and the clerical accuracy of inventory computations; we have obtained written representations from responsible officials of the company as to title, quality, quantity, and pricing. The inventories were taken under our observation, and we are satisfied that the inventory prices expressed in the financial statements are fair and proper."

When a client places restrictions on the auditor's scope of inventory examination the "AICPA'S Statement on Auditing Standards No. 1" has set forth some guidelines.

ILLUSTRATION.   (Scope paragraph)

". . . and such other auditing procedures as we considered necessary in the circumstances, except that in accordance with your instructions we were not in attendance at the taking of the physical inventory as of November 30, 19 . . . . ."

(Opinion paragraph)

"Because the inventory as of November 30, 19, . . . enters materially into the determination of financial position, results of operations, and changes in financial position, we do not express an opinion on the aforementioned financial statements taken as a whole."

Where a qualified opinion must be rendered because the scope of examination was restricted, the qualification should directly relate to the items in the statements on which an unqualified opinion cannot be expressed rather than to the restriction.

In addition, if the auditor has not satisfied himself by alternative means on other auditing procedures with respect to opening inventories, he should either disclaim an opinion on the statement of income or qualify his opinion thereon, depending on the degree of materiality of the amounts involved.

ILLUSTRATION

"We have examined the balance sheet of X Company as of December 31, 1975 and the related statements of income and retained earnings and changes in financial position for the year then ended. Our examination was made in accordance with generally accepted auditing standards, and accordingly included such tests of the accounting records and such other auditing procedures as we considered necessary in the circumstances, except as stated in the following paragraph.

"Because we were not engaged as auditors until after December 31, 1975, we were not present to observe the physical inventory taken at that date and we have not been able to satisfy ourselves by alternate means concerning inventory quantities. The amount of the inventory at December 31, 1974, enters materially into the determination of the results of operations and changes in financial position for the year ended December 31, 1975. Therefore, we do not express an opinion on the accompanying statements of income and retained earnings and changes in financial position for the year ended December 31, 1975."

Quotations from selected portions of Rules 2–02 and 3–07 of Regulation S–X of the Securities and Exchange Commission are presented. The reader will readily determine their relationship to inventory procedure requirements.

Rule 2–02: Accountants' Certificates

b)   Representations as to the audit
The accountant's certificate (i) shall state whether the audit was made in accordance with generally accepted auditing standards; and (ii) shall designate any auditing procedures generally recognized as normal and deemed necessary by the accountant under the circumstances of a particular case, which have been omitted, and the reason for their omission.

Nothing in this rule shall be construed to imply authority for the omission of any procedure which independent accountants would ordinarily employ in the course of an audit made for the purpose of expressing the opinions required by paragraph (*c*) of this rule.

c)   Opinions to be expressed
The accountant's certificate shall state clearly:
  (i)   the opinion of the accountant in respect of the financial statements covered by the certificate and the accounting principles and practices reflected therein;
 (ii)   the opinion of the accountant as to any material changes in accounting principles or practices, or adjustments of the accounts, required to be set forth by Rule 3–07; and
(iii)   the nature of, and the opinion of the accountant as to, any material differences between the accounting principles and practices reflected in the financial statements and those reflected in the accounts after the entry of adjustments for the period under review.

d)   Exceptions
Any matters to which the accountant takes exception shall be clearly identified, and the exception thereto specifically and clearly stated, and, to the extent practicable, the effect of each such exception on the related financial statements given.

Rule 3–07: Changes in Accounting Principles and Practices

Any change in accounting principle or practice, or in the method of applying any accounting principle or practice made during any period for which financial statements are filed which affects comparability of such financial statements with those of prior or future periods, and the effect thereof upon the net income for each period for which financial statements are filed, shall be disclosed in a note to the appropriate financial statements.

Other Federal Governmental agencies are issuing regulations which if followed by a client, would have material impact on financial statements. The Cost Accounting Standards Board, dealing primarily with contractors, recognizes the uses of standards and standard costs. In addition, it sets forth how variances must be handled so that costs and services are matched.

ILLUSTRATION.
   a) Variances, irrespective of the materiality of their amount, are allocated directly to applicable cost objectives.
   b) Variances, where their amount is immaterial, are included in appropriate indirect cost pools for subsequent allocation to applicable cost objectives, and when their amount ceases to be immaterial, are allocated directly to applicable cost objectives.
   (Materiality is defined as variances in excess of five percent of the cost group).

The reader can readily visualize the impact this will have on financial statements of contractors and related companies. No longer will clients be able to arbitrarily write off variances to Cost of Sales.

For Federal income tax purposes, full absorption costing now is mandatory in valuing the inventories of all manufacturers. The regulations divide indirect production costs into three categories:

a) Those which must enter into the computation of inventoriable costs regardless of their treatment by the taxpayer in his financial reports.
b) Those which are not required to enter into the computation of inventoriable costs regardless of their treatment by the taxpayer in his financial reports.
c) Those which may be included or excluded from inventoriable costs depending upon their treatment in the taxpayer's financial reports, provided such treatment is not inconsistent with generally accepted accounting principles.

Even though specific guidelines are set for direct material and direct labor, in the preceding definition and handling of indirect production costs, the auditor may have future difficulties in attempting to value inventories to meet all of these various required situations.

Financial Statement Presentation

Inventories are classified as current assets in the balance sheet. Supplies are sometimes treated as prepaid expenses and, more normally, as inventory, particularly if the supplies are used in manufacturing. If inventories are to be used after the normal operating cycle—as exemplified by heavy construction industry materials of significant amount—they should be removed from the current asset category. Preferably, for manufacturing companies, in the financial statements or in footnotes to the financial statements, inventories should be divided into raw materials, work in process, and finished goods—and not combined into one title.

Original cost is the starting point in pricing an inventory. Because differences in pricing methods result in different total dollar amounts, and also because the determination of total inventory amounts requires judgment, the basis of pricing the inventories—Fifo, Lifo, and so forth—should be clearly set forth in the balance sheet. When the method of pricing the inventory has been changed, the financial statements should disclose and explain the change and indicate the effect of the change—if material—on net income for the period. See also *Restatement and Revision of Accounting Research Bulletin No. 43*, chapter 4.

When financial statements are filed with the Securities and Exchange Commission, the method of determining cost and market must be disclosed (Rule 5–02, 6 [*b*], Regulation S–X); in other than SEC practices, this disclosure is not considered necessary.

Securities and Exchange Commission Requirements. Regulation S–X, in the section pertaining to inventories in the statements of registrants, requires the following: "The basis of determining the amounts shown in the balance sheet shall be stated. If a basis such as 'cost,' 'market,' or 'cost or market, whichever is lower,' is given, there shall also be given, to the extent applicable, a general indication of the method of determining the 'cost' or 'market': for example, 'average cost' or 'first-in, first-out.' "

New York Stock Exchange Requirements. In the preparation for listing applications, the instructions of the New York Stock Exchange contain the following regulations for the pricing of inventories and the methods of computing the cost of sales:

Indicate the practice followed in adjusting inventories to the lower of cost or market; that is, whether on a basis of specific items, groups or classes, or entire inventory.

State whether "market" is considered

a) as replacement market, and whether in that event allowance is made for any decline in price of basic commodities in finished goods and work in process, or,

b) as selling market, and whether in that event allowance is made for selling expense and normal margin of profit.

State the company's practice if (*a*) and (*b*) are followed in respect of different parts of the inventory.

Describe treatment of intercompany profit on goods included in inventory.

State general method of computing cost of goods sold; that is, whether computed on basis of "average cost," "last-in, first out," "first-in, first-out,"—other.

When money is borrowed and inventory pledged as security, the amount of inventory pledged should be stated in the balance sheet, and the loan will appear as a liability. The amount borrowed on the inventory may take the form of loans or advances.

If inventories are written down from a higher cost to a lower replacement market and if an allowance is employed to show inventory reductions, the allowance may or may not be shown in the balance sheet; common practice is not to show it but to present the inventory at the net figure. However, if the valuation allowance happens to be based on judgment and not on actual computation, the allowance should not be set forth.

Reductions from cost to market should be shown in the "other expense" section of the income statement so that the cost of sales is accurately presented. Some auditors believe that this procedure should be followed only if the reduction is significant and if it is nonrecurring.

Gross profit increase and decrease should be compared on an annual basis, and the percentage of gross profit earned on net sales should be computed and compared with that of prior years. A complete study should be made to determine the causes of fluctuations in gross profit and in gross profit percentage, so that causes of increased or decreased profits may be pointed out, and so that possible remedial measures may be instituted for correction of an unfavorable trend or for promotion of a desirable trend. The audit report should contain a description of the causes and effects of changes in gross profit.

It may be of interest to note here that the American Institute of Certified Public Accountant and the American Accounting Association differ in the basis that each would consider in the choice of method for assigning costs to inventory values. The AICPA in its *Accounting Research Bulletin No. 43*, chapter 4, entitled "Inventory Pricing," "*Statement Auditing Procedure No. 43*, and *Statement on Auditing Standards No. 1*" agree that:

Cost for inventory purposes may be determined under any one of several assumptions as to the flow of cost factors (such as first-in first-out, average, and last-in first-out); the major objective in selecting a method should be to choose the one which, under the circumstances, most clearly reflects periodic income.

However, The American Accounting Association in its *Accounting and Reporting Standards for Corporate Financial Statements and Preceding Statements and Supplements, Supplementary Statement No. 6*, "Inventory Pricing and Changes in Price Levels" stipulates that:

(1)   Ideally, the measurement of accounting profit involves the matching precisely of the identified costs of specific units of product with the sales revenues derived therefrom.

(2)   Where conditions are such that precise matching of identified costs with revenues is impractical, identified cost matching may be simulated by the adoption of an assumed flow of costs.

(3) A flow assumption can be realistic, in that it reflects the dominant characteristics of the actual flow of goods; thus it may reflect the actual dominance of first-in first-out (FIFO), average, or last-in first-out (LIFO) movement. A flow assumption can be artificial, on the other hand, in that it premises a flow of costs that is clearly in contrast with actual physical movement.

(4) The LIFO flow assumption now has wide usage although in very few, if any, instances of its application can the assumption be justified on the ground that it corresponds even approximately with the actual flow of goods. Artificial LIFO has appeal to some during periods of markedly changing price levels as a means of approaching a matching of current cost (dollar costs adjudged to reflect changes in the general purchasing power of the monetary unit) with current revenue; however, grave doubt exists as to whether the accuracy of such artificial matching is sufficient to justify the resultant departure from realism. Present use of the method should be considered a transitory step which may be ultimately supplanted by better methods of accomplishing the intended results.

QUESTIONS

1. You are completing an examination of the financial statements of The Nu-Style Co. for the fiscal year ended February 28, 1976. Nu-Style's financial statements have not been examined previously. The controller has given you the following draft of proposed footnotes to the financial statements:

THE NU-STYLE CO.
Notes to Financial Statements
Year Ended February 28, 1976

Note 1. Because we were not engaged as auditors until after February 28, 1976, we were unable to observe the taking of the physical inventory at February 28, 1976 by alternative procedures.

Note 2. With the approval of the Commissioner of Internal Revenue, the Company changed its method of accounting for inventories from the First-in first-out to the last-in first-out method on March 1, 1975. In the opinion of the Company the effects of this change on the pricing of inventories and cost of goods manufactured were not material in the current year but are expected to be material in future years.

For each note discuss:

a) The note's adequacy and needed revisions, if any, of the financial statements or the note.

b) The necessary disclosure in, or opinion modification of the auditor's report. (For this requirement assume the revisions you suggest in part, *a*, if any, have been made). Complete your discussion of each note (both parts *a* and *b*) before beginning discussion of the next note.

(AICPA, adapted)

2. *a*)   What criteria might be adopted for inventory valuation?

   b)   Why is so much importance attached to the satisfactory valuation of inventories by the CPA?

3. State how a CPA would report each of the following items in a balance sheet for his client:

   a)   Defective goods requiring further processing.

   b)   Finished goods in hands of agents and brokers.

   c)   Raw materials received but without supporting invoices.

   d)   Merchandise on hand received on a consignment basis.

   e)   Finished goods in hands of customers on an approval basis.

4. State the effect of each of the following errors made by Stateside, Inc., upon the income statement and the balance sheet of the (1) current period and (2) succeeding period:

   a)   Goods being held on a consignment basis were included in the ending inventory.

   b)   1,000 actual units in inventory were listed as 100.

   c)   A purchase of inventory was not recorded, and even though they were on hand at the inventory date, they were not counted.

   d)   A purchase of inventory was not recorded but were correctly included in the inventory count.

   e)   Goods sold to a customer were not recorded as a sale. However, since they were in the warehouse they were included in the inventory count.

   f)   Goods sold to a customer were not recorded as a sale. However, they were correctly excluded from the inventory count.

5. Listed *below* are errors that are frequently made when taking inventories. By using the letter *H* to indicate an item is too high, the letter *L* to indicate an item is too low; and the letter *N* to indicate no effect, tell what effect each of the following errors has on the financial statements of your client for the years 1975 and 1976 for the statement sections listed.

     A.   Total Assets

     B.   Total Liabilities

     C.   Cost of Goods Sold

     D.   Net Income

   a)   Goods bought in 1975 were included in 12/31/1975 inventory but purchase and liability not recorded until January 1976.

   b)   Goods bought in 1976 were included in 12/31/1975 inventory and the purchase was recorded in 1975.

   c)   Goods were bought in 1975 and the purchase was recorded in that year. However, the goods were erroneously omitted from the 1975 inventory.

   d)   Goods bought in 1975 were excluded from 12/31/1975 inventory and the purchase was recorded in January 1976.

6. Annual earnings for Gregg, Inc. for the period 1971–1975 are presented below. However, a review of the records for the company reveals the listed inventory misstatements. Calculate the correct net earnings for each year.

Detail	1971	1972	1973	1974	1975
Reported net income (loss)	$39,000	$40,000	$4,000	($9,000)	$30,000
Inventory understatement, end of year. . .				8,000	
Inventory overstatement, end of year. . .	3,000		5,600		3,200

7. Cite certain instances in which estimates of inventory values are necessary or appropriate and describe what procedure would be followed in developing satisfactory estimates for such inventory costs.

8. An auditor finds that a client has the accounts listed below on his records. How should they be reported in the client's year-end financial statements?
   a) Customer Materials on Hand for Processing.
   b) Advance Payments on Purchase Commitments.
   c) Raw Materials for Building Rehabilitation.
   d) Allowance for Reduction in Inventory Value—Cost to Market.

9. In examining the purchase discounts of a company for the year ended December 31, 1975, describe the procedure to be followed if—
   a) The amount of the discounts shown on the records is $24,000, and
   b) Purchases of merchandise during 1975 amounted to $1,800,000, all subject to uniform discounts of 2 percent if paid within 10 days.

10. Clermont, Inc., is engaged in the construction of large office buildings and justifiably takes up profits each year on uncompleted contracts in the process of construction at the end of each year.
   How should the auditor for the company verify the accuracy of the profit included on partially completed contracts, assuming that all contracts are for a fixed sum?

11. On December 1, 1975, the board of directors of Newhope Co. requests that you audit the records of the corporation for the year ended December 31, 1975. The company operates a chain of 40 retail stores: the total assets of the corporation are $3,600,000 and the total sales for 1975 will be approximately $16,000,000. This is the first audit of the records.
   In your examination of company internal control and in your discussion with corporate executives—prior to December 31, 1975, the following information is ascertained:
   As of December 31, 1975, the cost price of the inventory will be approximately $2,000,000. The company does not use the retail inventory method, but all merchandise is marked accurately with both retail and coded-cost prices. The company's inventory policy, which has been consistent for years, is as follows: A representative from the head office visits each store on or about December 31. The store manager calls off the items in stock to the representative from the head office, stating the quantity of each item on hand and the unit cost, or an arbitrary figure which is below the marked cost. When an arbitrary figure is given, it represents the manager's opinion of the market price. Quantities and unit prices are listed on an adding machine tape, not accompanied

by a description. Items to which no value is assigned are not listed. Tapes are returned to the head office, where they are extended and totaled. The total for each store is reduced by 15 percent. The resulting store totals are summaried, and the adding machine tapes are destroyed.

a) Set forth your recommendations for company procedure in order to enable the expression of an unqualified opinion of the financial statements. Assume that other phases of the audit do not indicate any report exceptions.

b) As to inventory, state the general program you would follow.

c) State your position in the event that your proposals as to inventory procedures are not accepted.

12. In an audit for the year ended December 31, 1975, you discovered the following transactions, all of which occurred near the closing date.

(1) Merchandise costing $2,000 was received on January 3, 1976. The related invoice was received and recorded on January 5, 1976. The invoice showed the shipment was made by the vendor, F.O.B. destination, on December 28, 1975.

(2) Merchandise with a cost price of $600 was received on December 28, 1975, and the invoice was not recorded. It was located in the office of the purchasing agent, and it was stamped "On Consignment."

(3) A packing case containing products regularly manufactured by the client and costing $800 to manufacture was in the shipping room when the physical inventory was taken. It was not included in the inventory because it was stamped "Hold for Shipping Instruction." Investigation disclosed that the customer's order was dated December 18, 1975. The products were shipped, and the customer was billed on January 10, 1976.

(4) Merchandise received on January 6, 1976, costing $700, was entered in the invoice register on the same day. Shipment was made F.O.B. vendor's plant on December 31, 1975. It was not included in the client's inventory because it was not received as of December 31, 1975.

(5) A product, manufactured to the special order of a customer, was finished and in the shipping room on December 31, 1975. The customer was billed on that date; and the merchandise was excluded from the December 31, 1975, inventory, although the item was not shipped until January 5, 1976.

State whether each item should be included in or excluded from inventory at December 31, 1976, together with the reason for your decision in each of the five cases.

(AICPA, adapted)

13. The Porous Company had a debit balance in its Applied Overhead account. When the accounts were closed for the year 1975, the balance of this account was closed to Work in Process and to Finished Goods, in the proportion of each to the total. Do you consider the procedure to be correct or incorrect?

14. Name several common errors which may be revealed by an audit of raw material purchases.

15. The Strong Company of Delaware received a shipment of goods and an accompanying invoice from London on December 26, 1975, and recorded the inventory and the liability therefor as of that date. The invoice was paid on January 15, 1976; because of exchange rate fluctuations, the account was liquidated for $2,000 less than the recorded liability. The exchange rate began fluctuating on January 2, 1976; and the audit of the company was started on January 4, 1976. What provisions should be made in the December 31, 1975, statements for possible exchange fluctuations? What changes should be made in the valuation of the inventory?

16. Assuming that a perpetual inventory system is maintained, describe an effective *test* for the general accuracy of the original purchase records maintained for purchases of raw materials. When inventory was acquired it was charged to the Purchases account.

17. During the audit of the records of a company, you examined purchase orders and creditors' invoices, computed the extensions and footings on all examined invoices, traced these invoices to the invoice register, examined the vouchers supporting the payment of the invoices and compared them therewith, traced the vouchers to the check register, and compared the paid checks with the entries in the check register. Were the audit procedures adequate? Should additional operations have been performed?

18. A client is considering changing his method of inventory pricing from Fifo to Lifo. What advice might you offer with respect to the following:

a) If the change in method is to be made as of January 1, what change is required in the pricing of the inventory at that date?

b) If the Lifo method of inventory pricing is used during the year, what values attach to the quantities in the inventory at December 31, which are in excess of the quantities in the inventory at January 1?

c) How may the December 31 inventory be priced for financial statement purposes if the market price at that date is lower than Lifo cost?

19. State how you would obtain a substantial verification of the inventory record balance of the physical quantities of inventories in each of the following cases:

a) A large, outdoor pile of coal.

b) Grain in an elevator.

c) A large quantity of nails, dumped in a bin, the inventory being carried in pounds.

Record balances are obtained by maintaining a continuous record of receipts, withdrawals, and arithmetically computed balances.

20. Retail chain grocery companies commonly charge inventory to each store at retail and credit cash sales to each store. Periodically, main office men take a physical inventory of the stores in order to verify the accuracy of the store managers and the inventories. How would you audit the store inventories of a chain grocery company?

21. During the course of the audit of the Torch Company for the fiscal year ended June 30, 1976, the following situation was revealed:

On June 19, 1976, the Torch Company placed a purchase order with the Sound Company for merchandise at a cost of $200,000. The merchandise was not manufactured to a special order but was standard merchandise normally available for sale by the Sound Company. The merchandise had not been received by the Torch Company at June 30, 1976.

a) Under what conditions should the Torch Company show the $200,000 as a liability on its balance sheet as of June 30, 1976?

b) Under what circumstances is it proper for the Torch Company to omit the $200,000 as a liability as of June 30, 1976?

c) How should the $200,000 be treated, if at all, on the balance sheet of the Torch Company as of June 30, 1976, if it is not shown as a liability? Present reasons for your answers to each part of the question.

22. Briefly discuss the impact on inventory valuation as required by the Cost Accounting Standards Board and the Internal Revenue Service.

PROBLEMS

1. You have been working with the auditor in charge of the examination of the Blue Rock Department Store financial statements. As a means of reviewing prior years' ending inventory, and testing the value of the current year's ending inventory, the in-charge auditor supplies the following information.

Beginning Inventory in 1974 is $140,000.

For 1974...... Sales $300,000	Purchases	$220,000
For 1975...... Sales $320,000	Purchases	$240,000
For 1976...... Sales $400,000	Purchases	$320,000

The average rate of gross profit is 20 percent of sales: Prepare the necessary work paper setting forth the ending inventories for 1974, 1975, and 1976.

2. On January 15, 1975, your client, Jonathan, Inc., purchased the entire inventory of a men's suit manufacturing concern for $200,000. He has requested that you allocate the cost to the various categories of items purchased. The physical count and expected selling price is as follows:

Item	Quantity	Selling Price
Two pants—wool	3,000	$50
Two pants—knit	10,000	40
Two pants—rayon	4,000	30
Sport coats.........	6,000	20
Separate pants.......	1,000	10

Prepare a work paper which will allocate the cost based on their relative expected sales price.

3. The Stratified Company buys merchandise on the following terms from The Raudona Company: 20 percent trade discount: 2/10, n/30 cash discount.

What would be the entries under the following unrelated situations if Stratified Company purchased 200 items at $12.50 each.

a) Purchases are recorded at invoice price, and discounts lost are summarized in the accounts. Invoice paid within the discount period.

b) Purchases are recorded net, and discounts lost are summarized in the accounts. Invoice not paid within discount period.

c) Purchases are recorded at invoice price, and discounts earned are summarized in the accounts. Invoice paid within discount period.

If the Stratified Company values its inventory at cost, what would be the per unit inventory valuation basis under each of the above conditions?

4. In performing the audit for 1975, an auditor finds the following situations that existed in 1975. Assuming that the records for 1975 have been closed, what entries, if any, should be made for each of the following:

a) A sale on account of $2,400 was not recorded when made on December 28, 1975, but was recorded when the cash was received in January, 1976. These items had not been included in the 1975 ending inventory.

b) Inventory in the amount of $3,600 was missed when taking the physical inventory at December 31, 1975.

c) Raw material purchases in the amount of $4,000 were erroneously charged to Machinery and Equipment on July 1, 1975. Machinery and Equipment is being depreciated on a straight-line basis using a 10-year life.

d) Although the client correctly included $2,000 of merchandise purchased in his inventory at December 31, 1975, the invoice was not recorded. Payment has not been made to date.

5. The Bimel Realty Company acquired a tract of undeveloped land for $600,000. Installation of streets, sewage system, water and gas lines cost an additional $300,000. As a result of a survey, the land is divided into the following lots at their respective sales values:

Type	No. of Lots	Sales Price per Lot
Select.	40	$10,000
Choice	80	7,500
Standard	100	5,000

a) What is the cost of each lot to the company, assuming that the costs are to be allocated on the basis of their relative sales value?

b) During 1975 the company sold five select lots, 10 choice lots, and 20 standard lots. What is the inventory value of the remaining lots at December 31, 1975?

6. O'Neil, Inc., took its annual physical inventory on December 20, 1975, which showed an inventory at a cost of $200,000. The company prepares its financial statements on a calendar year basis; therefore the auditor must establish the inventory at that date. Through the audit of the client's accounts, the following information is obtained for the period December 20–31, 1975:

Sales discounts: Allowance to customers for invoice payments
made within discount period . . . . $ 300
Purchases on account: Goods placed in stock   48,000
Sales allowances: Allowances to customers for goods received
by them in damaged condition   800
Purchases: Goods in transit as of 12/31, shipped by supplier
F.O.B. shipping point   6,000
Purchase returns: Goods returned to supplier but credit memo
not received   2,400
Sales returns: Goods returned to O'Neil, Inc., original
selling price   4,000
Sales made to customers (markup, 125 percent of cost)   66,000

Calculate the inventory value for financial statement purposes at December 31, 1975.

7. Based upon the following data, do you consider the December 31, 1975 inventory to be reasonable? Show all calculations to support your opinions.

Inventory, January 1, 1975 . . . . $250,000
Inventory, December 31, 1975   150,000
Purchases, 1975   400,000
Sales, 1975   600,000

Average gross profit rate is 40 percent of sales.

8. Prepare the necessary adjustments for the following conditions on the records of the Judd Company as of December 31, 1975.
   a) Goods that cost $4,000 were included in the December 31, 1975, inventory and were included in the accounts payable of that date. The goods were received on January 6, 1976; $1,000 of the goods were returned on January 7, 1976.
   b) Goods that cost $6,000 were received on December 31, 1975, and were included in the ending inventory. No entry was made for purchases or accounts payable.
   c) Merchandise that cost $8,000 had been shipped to the Judd Company, F.O.B. shipping point. The invoice was received on December 31, 1975. No entries appeared, and the merchandise was not received on December 31, 1975.

9. You are engaged in audit of the financial statements of the Squire Manufacturing Company as of December 31, 1975. You are verifying the pricing of the inventory of work in process and finished goods which appear on the company records as follows:

Finished goods inventory, 110,000 units. $504,900
Work-in-process inventory, 90,000 units, 50 percent completed   330,480

The company follows the practice of pricing these inventories at the lower of cost or market on a first-in, first-out method. Raw materials are placed in production at the start of the process, and overhead is applied to the product at the rate of 75 percent based on direct labor dollars. You learn that the market value of the finished goods and the work-in-process inventories is greater than the amounts shown above, with the exception of the defective units in the ending inventory of finished goods, the market value of which is $1 per unit.

A review of the company's cost records reveals the following information:

	Units	Materials	Labor
Inventory, January 1, 1975, 80 percent completed	100,000	$100,000	$160,000
Additional units started in 1975	500,000		
Material costs incurred		550,000	
Labor costs incurred			997,500
Units completed in 1975:			
Good	500,000		
Defective	10,000		

Finished goods inventory, December 31, 1975, includes 10,000 defective units.

You also learn the defective units are found to be defective at the point of final inspection.

a) From the preceding information, you are to prepare schedules showing:

   (1)   The effective or equivalent production.

   (2)   Unit costs of production for materials, labor, and overhead.

   (3)   The pricing of the inventories of finished goods, defective units, and work in process.

b) Prepare the necessary work papers and audit adjustment or adjustments, if any, to correctly state the inventory valuation of finished goods and work in process. The accounts have not been closed. Ignore federal income taxes.

(AICPA, adapted)

10.   You are auditing the records of Metal, Inc., which priced its finished goods inventory on the basis of average yearly production cost and its raw material inventory on the basis of first-in, first-out cost. Because of continuous fluctuation in the market price of the basic raw material used, management proposes to change its inventory valuations from the cost basis to the basis of the lower of cost or market.

The company inventories, at January 1 and December 31, 1975, were as follows:

Explanation	Jan. 1	Dec. 31
Raw materials:		
Tons on hand	2,000	1,000
Book value on Fifo basis.	$53,000	$22,500
Market price per ton	$ 20	$ 30
Finished goods:		
Tons on hand	750	900
Book value, at average yearly cost	$38,000	$36,000
Market price per ton	$ 50	$ 55

Costs other than raw materials have remained constant throughout the year. In 1975, 19,000 tons of raw material were purchased at a total cost if $400,000. Shrinkage and waste in the manufacturing process amount to 25 percent of the materials used.

Management requests that you show the result of changing from one basis to the other.

Prepare a comparative statement showing (*a*) the present and revised inventory costs and cost of goods sold and the effect of the proposed change upon the balance sheet at December 31, 1975; and (*b*) prepare the entry to bring the records into agreement with the new plan, if adopted.

11. During the audit of the records of the Troy Company for the year ended December 31, 1975, the following facts were disclosed:

Raw material inventory, January 1, 1975	$ 14,404
Raw material purchases	104,656
Direct labor	126,000
Manufacturing overhead applied (150 percent of direct labor)	189,000
Finished goods inventory, January 1, 1975	24,800
Selling expenses.	162,456
Administrative expenses	147,544

Your examination discloses the following additional information:

a) Purchases of raw materials were as follows:

Month	Units	Unit Price	Amount
January–February.	1,100	$17.76	$ 19,536
March–April	900	20.00	18,000
May–June	500	19.60	9,800
July–August	700	20.00	14,000
September–October	900	20.40	18,360
November–December.	1,200	20.80	24,960
			$104,656

b) Data with respect to quantities are as follows:

	Units	
Explanation	1/1/75	12/31/75
Raw material	700	Note A
Work in process (80 percent completed).	0	500
Finished goods	300	800
Sales, 4,100 units.		

Note A: Raw materials are issued at the beginning of the manufacturing process. During the year, no returns, spoilage, or waste occurred. Each unit of finished goods contains one unit of raw material.

From the preceding information, you are to prepare a statement of cost of goods manufactured and sold. In the preparation of this statement, inventories are to be stated at cost as follows: raw materials, according to the Fifo method; direct labor, at an average rate determined by correlating total direct labor cost with effective production during the period;

and manufacturing overhead, at an applied rate of 150 percent of direct labor cost.

12. Your client operates a retail store. The data for one department for the month of March are as follows:

Purchases at cost, net.	$ 64,000
Additional markups	1,000
Initial inventory, at cost	10,000
Transportation-in	1,000
Gross markdowns.	7,250
Gross sales	106,000
Initial inventory, at retail	15,000
Markdown cancellation	750
Purchases, at retail	109,000
Returns from customers	6,000
Ending physical inventory, at retail.	18,000
Cash discounts earned	200
Department expenses.	30,000
Transfers-in from other departments (cost $1,000), at retail	1,200
Transfers-out to other departments, at retail	1,000

As the auditor, you are asked to find the following:
a) The cost of the merchandise sold.
b) The gross margin in dollars and in percentage.
c) Expense percentage.
d) The stock shortage in dollars and in percentage.
e) Net income in dollars and percentage.
f) Stock turnover for March.

13. The Shebesta Corporation manufactures a highly flammable cleaning fluid. On May 31, 1976, a fire completely destroyed the work-in-process inventory.

After the fire, a physical inventory was taken, as follows:

Raw materials	$30,000
Finished goods	60,000
Supplies	5,000

As of January 1, 1976, the inventories were as follows:

Raw materials	$ 15,000
Work in process	50,000
Finished goods	70,000
Supplies	2,000
	$137,000

A review of the records showed that sales and gross profit for the past five years were as follows:

	Sales	Gross Profit
1971	$300,000	$ 86,200
1972	320,000	102,400
1973	330,000	108,900
1974	250,000	62,500
1975	280,000	84,000

Sales for the first five months of 1976 were $150,000. Raw material purchases were $50,000. Freight on purchases was $5,000. Direct labor for the five months was $40,000. For the past five years manufacturing overhead was 50 percent of direct labor cost.

Insurance on inventories was carried with three different companies. Each policy contained an 80 percent coinsurance clause. The amount of the insurance carried on the inventories was as follows: Company A, $38,000; Company B, $35,000; and Company C, $35,000.

a)   Compute the value of the destroyed inventory.

b)   Compute the expected recovery from each insurance company.

(AICPA, adapted)

14.   You are conducting the audit of the University. Bookstore for the fiscal year ended May 31, 1976. The University Bookstore uses the retail method of accounting for its inventory. The following classifications are used:

Classification No.	Items Included
1	Stationery (paper)
2	Pens
3	Athletic goods
4	Pennants (cloth and paper insignia)
5	Drawing and scientific equipment
6	Supplies (pencils, paints, and so forth)
7	Books
8	Candy and tobacco
9	Jewelry
10	Leather goods
11	Markdown goods

The inventory was taken at retail on the night of May 31, 1976. The auditor was present and observed the work as it progressed; in certain instances, set forth later, he made his own independent counts and recorded them independently of the count and recording of the inventory crew.

An inventory summary prepared by store employees, was as follows:

Sheet Nos., Incl.	Classi- fication No.	Items	Retail	Percent- age of Markup on Retail	Cost
1– 50	1	Stationery	$ 11,451.18	45%	$ 6,298.15
51– 58	2	Pens	1,115.75	40	669.45
59– 85	3	Athletic goods	2,420.10	35	1,573.07
86– 92	4	Pennants	751.50	50	375.75
93–107	5	Drawing and scientific equipment	35,775.50	40	21,465.30
108–120	6	Supplies	6,111.60	45	3,361.38
121–170	7	Books	78,721.85	20	62,977.48
171–177	7a	Consigned-in books	8,348.00	20	6,678.40
178–190	8	Candy and tobacco	1,166.10	40	699.66
191–194	9	Jewelry	3,460.90	40	2,076.54
195–199	10	Leather goods	2,861.40	50	1,430.70
200–205	11	Markdown goods	1,555.20	0	2,555.20
			$153,739.08	28.4%	$110,161.08

Errors discovered when the individual retail inventory sheet extensions and footings were verified are as follows:

Extension Errors

Sheet No.	Line No.	Extended as:	Correct Extension
88	10	$ 4.00	$ 14.00
122	7	320.00	230.00
179	18	47.00	52.50
192	3	36.80	80.63
196	19	216.00	274.20

Footing Errors

Sheet No.	Footed as:	Correct Footing
2	$ 115.20	$ 215.20
52	86.00	68.00
142	2,426.50	3,206.80
180	26.70	22.20
193	842.70	886.20

As a result of the testing of selected items of inventory by the auditor, the following information was obtained:

Sheet No.	Name of Item	Sheet Count	Correct Count	Retail per Unit
55	Pens	19	29	$19.75
60	Insignia sweaters	60	48	12.50
94	Drawing sets	24	20	32.50
122	*Anthology*	10	6	7.50
131	*Cost Accounting*	150	120	5.00
197	Brief cases	18	21	20.00

In addition, the following information was obtained:

(1) An examination of pennants shows that 20 percent of the retail inventory was not salable, due to out-of-date dated items (for example, "Class of 1970), and torn and shopworn paper items.

(2) All items in classification 7a were at the Medical College branch store and were held by the Bookstore on consignment.

(3) Markdown goods constitute discontinued titles and other items priced to sell at cost or less to the store, depending upon the possibilities for sale. In the store's retail inventory records and cost records, these items are carried properly at zero value. In the inventory listing, above, the items are priced (retail) at May 31, 1976, sales prices, which are considered reasonable.

(4) In the stock room of the store, there were two boxes of textbooks to be returned to a publisher under the 20 percent return privilege in effect with most publishing companies. These books were not included in the inventory count; their retail price was $300.

From the information presented:

a) Prepare audit work papers for the inventory, setting forth the proper items for inclusion in and exclusion from the inventory; proper retail prices; and proper cost prices, by classifications and in total.

b) Prepare all necessary audit adjustments.

PRACTICE MATERIAL ASSIGNMENTS

Metalcraft, Incorporated: Audit Problem:
  Assignment 5: Inventory of Raw Material.
  Assignment 5: Inventory of Work in Process.
  Assignment 5: Inventory of Finished Goods.

Colby Gears, Inc.: Holmes and Moore Audit Case:
  Inventories and Cost of Sales.
  Expense Accounts, other than those covered in prior assignments.

17

Investments and Related Revenues

Audit Objectives

The audit objectives in the examination of investments is sixfold. The auditor is interested in (1) the evidence of existence, (2) the evidence of ownership, (3) the cost or other basic acquisition figure, (4) determining that their values are being stated on a basis that conforms with generally accepted accounting principles, (5) proper revenue determination, and (6) whether the related disclosures in the audited financial statements are adequate.

As pointed out in Chapter 12, cash and all securities must be controlled simultaneously by the auditor in order to prevent the covering of discrepancies in either cash or securities.

Preface to Investments

Investments may be securities or other assets not used directly in productive operations. Investments are classified as (1) temporary marketable securities (current assets) or (2) long-term investments (noncurrent).

Temporary marketable securities and long-term investments are considered together because the auditing procedures are the same for both classes, although they appear in different sections of the balance sheet, and although different principles of pricing apply to each class. The form, the marketability, and the maturity of an investment are not necessarily the final indication of its classification as temporary or long term.

Temporary Marketable Securities. Temporary marketable securities are represented by high-grade marketable securities acquired because there is available cash in excess of current business requirements, or by securities acquired as a fund for emergencies. A temporary investment frequently takes the form of high-grade government certificates, notes, and other modern obligations. When temporary marketable securities are purchased, the normal intention is to sell them when cash is required for operating purposes. In all instances, a temporary investment must be liquid—that is, readily marketable at a definite price.

Temporary investments are classified as current assets because they represent the temporary conversion of presently unrequired cash. Quick liquidity with no loss is highly desirable in temporary cash conversions. If temporary investments have lost their marketability they should be removed from the current asset classification, since they lack the liquidity necessary for current assets.

Long-Term Investments.   Long-term investments are acquired for one or more of the following purposes:

1.   To exercise partial or full control of subsidiary or affiliated companies.
2.   To yield a relatively permanent other revenue.
3.   To establish business relationships.
4.   To create specific funds.

Long-term investments usually result from management decisions concerning long-run business policies, and temporary investments are usually the result of excess cash balances. The long-term investment may or may not be readily marketable; marketability is not a prerequisite for a long-term investment.

Thus the primary distinction between temporary investments and long-term investments lies in the purpose for which the investment originally was made. Of course, what is originally a temporary investment may become a long-term investment if the cash is not needed when normally expected and the investment is retained. In this case, the intention and purpose have changed. Similarly, it may be decided to convert a long-term investment to cash for working capital purposes, or for other reasons. In the balance sheet, long-term investments are classed separately.

Forms of Long-Term Investments.   Long-term investments may take the following forms:

1.   Capital stock of other companies, representing a controlling interest or a minority interest.
2.   Bonds of controlled or noncontrolled companies.
3.   Mortgages—chattel or real estate.
4.   Notes.
5.   Loans or advances to subsidiary companies.
6.   Special funds—bond retirement, stock redemption, endowment, pension, building, insurance, or other funds.
7.   Fixed assets not used directly in the business.
8.   Cash values of life insurance policies on employees, the company being the beneficiary.
9.   Investments in partnerships or other nonstock enterprises.
10.   Certificates of deposit (may be long-term or short-term.)

Reports to Management

In many instances, it is desirable periodically to submit to top management—for example, the board of directors—reports setting forth the securities portfolio and its activities to date from the date of the last report. Such a report should set forth the cost of each security, its current market price, the rate of return being earned on cost and on current market price, purchases and sales of securities, gains and losses on sales, and any other important and desired data. Based upon a periodic report of this nature, management may arrive at decisions regarding investment policies and practices.

SECTION I: INTERNAL CONTROL OF INVESTMENTS

Policies with regard to investments normally originate with the board of directors of a corporation. The auditor must be familiar with these policies and observe the actions of the board. Proper internal control over investments dictates that the custodianship of investment securities and the accounting for the securities be separated; that the securities be properly controlled physically in order to prevent unauthorized usage; that the securities be registered in the name of the owner; and that purchases and sales be made upon proper authorization. Access to securities should not be vested in one person only. Revenue received from investments periodically should be reconciled with the amounts that should be received.

An internal control questionnaire for investment securities is shown in Illustration 17–1.

SECTION II: AUDIT PROGRAMS FOR INVESTMENTS; INVESTMENTS IN CAPITAL STOCKS OF OTHER COMPANIES

Audit Program for Investments in Capital Stocks

The procedures to be followed for investments in capital stocks are developed in the following subsections.

List and Examine Stock Certificates.   After obtaining control of all cash and all securities, the auditor should prepare or obtain a schedule listing the stock certificates. The listing should be compared with the ledger accounts to ascertain that the two records are in agreement. This comparison should "tie in" the certificates with the composition of the account balance, both as to amounts and as to specific items.

ILLUSTRATION.   Stock certificates indicating 1,000 shares of the common stock of the Harvey Company are on hand, and the ledger account indicates

ILLUSTRATION 17-1

INTERNAL CONTROL QUESTIONNAIRE
Investment Securities: Temporary and Long Term

	Yes	No	Not Appli-cable	Remarks
Company_____ Period Covered_____				
1. Are all investment documents under the control of a custodian?	____	____	____	_____
2. Is the custodian adequately bonded?	____	____	____	_____
3. Is an independent custodian employed?	____	____	____	_____
4. Are investment documents kept in a safe-deposit box?	____	____	____	_____
5. To open the box, must more than one person be present?	____	____	____	_____
6. Are investment documents periodically inspected and reconciled with the accounting records?	____	____	____	_____
7. Does the securities custodian have access to the accounting records?	____	____	____	_____
8. Are registered securities held in the name of the client?	____	____	____	_____
9. If registered securities are not in the name of the client, are they properly endorsed in blank, or in the name of a custodian, or in the name of a nominee, or is a power of attorney attached?	____	____	____	_____
10. Are securities held as collateral, or securities held for safekeeping for other parties, properly segregated—in the records and physically?	____	____	____	_____
11. Does the accounting department maintain an independent record of each investment security?	____	____	____	_____
12. Is there proper accounting for all investment income?	____	____	____	_____
13. Are puchases and sales of investments properly authorized?	____	____	____	_____
14. Do board of director minutes authorize acquisition of the securities of other companies?	____	____	____	_____
15. Are adequate records maintained where a controlling interest, either by purchase or a pooling of interests, has been secured?	____	____	____	_____
16. Is proper control exercised over securities written down to zero?	____	____	____	_____
17. Are all insurance and fidelity bonds adequate?	____	____	____	_____

Prepared by_____   Reviewed by_____
Date_____   Date_____

1,000 shares of the common stock of the Data Company. Investigation proves that originally 1,000 shares of Data Company stock were purchased at $90 per share and later sold at $88 per share; with part of the proceeds, 1,000 shares of Harvey Company stock were purchased at $60 per share. No entries were ever made. The cash shortage was $28,000.

While the operation of listing stock certificates and comparing them with the ledger accounts is being performed, the auditor will obtain an impression of the valuation methods used in connection with the securities. Controlling and subsidiary accounts may or may not exist in the records of the client; if they do exist, they must be reconciled.

Work papers should be prepared in a manner to effect adequate analysis and proper detail. It is advisable to use separate work papers for capital stocks, bonds, mortgages, and so on, for each of the security classes. Work papers for capital stock certificates are shown in Illustration 17–2 and in the Illustrative Audit. If desired, a separate work sheet might be prepared to determine profits and losses on sales; then the work sheet in Illustration 17–2 would be merely a list of the securities on hand at the end of the year to support the analysis of the account as it appears in the ledger. This is advisable if there are only a few securities.

During the listing and examination of stock certificates and other securities, a representative of the client should be present. In audits of trust companies, investment companies, brokerage firms, and banks, where it is impossible to complete the securities count and tabulation within a few hours because of the size of the portfolio, the securities must be broken into groups, sealed, and then examined and tabulated. Withdrawals from and additions to any group during the audit must be made in the presence of the auditor, who reseals the packages and makes notations on his work papers in accordance with the changes. In those concerns maintaining large portfolios of marketable securities, the auditor attempts to complete the count and tabulation rapidly as of the balance sheet date by assigning adequate staff personnel to the task in order to effect better control of the situation and in order to avoid disrupting normal operations of the client.

If internal control over the securities is weak and if a cutoff bank reconciliation is prepared after the balance sheet date, the auditor must control all cash, securities, notes, undeposited cash items, and other negotiable paper in order to prevent substitution.

ILLUSTRATION. Improper contról may be exemplified as follows: At a cutoff date, the auditor examined and tabulated the securities, released them, and requested the cash on hand and a bank statement. The company treasurer, who was in charge of cash and securities, immediately went to the bank for the bank statement. While at the bank, he borrowed $2,000 in the name of the company, giving as collateral a stock certificate released by the auditor. The $2,000 was credited to the company account; at the same time, he cashed a company check for $2,000. The $2,000 cash thus obtained was placed in undeposited cash receipts, since it represented the amount of prior cash receipts taken from this source by the treasurer. He then presented to the auditor the bank statement, the petty cash funds, and the undeposited receipts; in this manner, the bank reconciliation agreed with the Cash ledger accounts. Later, when the auditor requested an independent bank confirmation, the $2,000 loan appeared with the notation of the collateral.

ILLUSTRATION 17–2

GRAPHITE COMPANY

Capital Stock Investments, Acct. #110
December 31, 1975

Name of Stock	Cer- tificate No.	Com- mon or Pre- ferred	Balance, December 31, 1974			1975 Purchases			1975 Sales		
			Shares	Cost per Share	Total Cost	Shares	Cost per Share	Total Cost	Shares	Sales Price per Share	Total Sales Price
Action, Inc.	C2740	C	100	60	$ 6,000√						
Brake, Co.	71247	C	200	74	14,800√				100	$68	$ 6,800σ
Casper, Inc.	C1030	C	300	48	14,400√				200	80	16,000σ
Dragnet, Inc.	23562	C				100	$56	$5,600⊙			
					$35,200√			$5,600			$22,800A

√ Agrees with 1974 work papers.
⊙ Brokers' invoices inspected.
√ Market price from *The Wall Street Journal,* 1/2/76.
σ Dividends verified from *Standard and Poor's Stock Guide.*
A Traced to cash receipts.
∧ Traced to ledger accounts and to cash records.
∅ Confirmed.
All certificates are in the name of the Graphite Company.
Examination witnessed by James Joseph.
Received above securities from auditor—1/21/76
   (Signed)   James Joseph
            Custodian

   The auditor should obtain a receipt upon the return of the securities; his work papers should note the date of the count and the names of the witnesses. In examining securities, the auditor must ascertain that they are unqualifiedly available to the client. Securities should be registered in the name of the client or his nominee, endorsed to the client, or endorsed in blank; or they should have a power of attorney, signed and witnessed, authorizing the transfer, attached to the security if it is carried in the name of some other party. If stocks are not fully paid, a liability must exist for the unpaid balance.

   In security examination and analysis, care must be exercised to avoid errors of denomination—for example, by recording a bond of a par value of $1,000 as $100 or $10,000. Care also must be exercised that the name of the issuing company is accurately recorded in the work papers and in the client's records and that stock certificate numbers agree on the certificate, the work papers, and the client's records.

   In the case of an audit for a stockbroker, certificates are pledged

	Initials	Date
Prepared By		
Approved By		

1975 Gain or Loss	Balance, December 31, 1975			Market Price, December 31, 1975		Dividends Received 1975	Held by Others		
	Shares	Cost per Share	Total Cost	Per Share	Total		Name of Holder	No. of Shares	Reason Held
	100	$60	$ 6,000	$84✓	$ 8,400	$ 240σ			
L $ 600∧	100	74	7,400	72✓	7,200	300σ			
G 6,400∧	100	48	4,800	88✓	8,800	800σ			
	100	56	5,600	64✓	6,400	300σ	West & Co.	100	Sold 1/5/76∅
G $5,800			$23,800		$30,800	$1,640F			

as collateral for money borrowed by the broker on his own securities; customer securities are also pledged with the broker for customer margin requirements. Brokers actively pledge margin stocks as call loan collateral for loans from bankers. In these cases, the bank may be asked to prepare a collateral list, or the auditor may send to the bank a list of securities pledged and ask the bank to verify and confirm or disaffirm it. The auditor must determine the proportions between money borrowed by the broker and the market price of the pledged securities. Most banks require $120 of securities as collateral for $100 of loan, unless state or federal regulations require a higher margin. The $20 or more spread must be maintained in the event of a decline in security prices.

Confirm Stock Certificates Held by Others. Stock certificates not available for examination should be confirmed directly to the auditor by the party holding them. Confirmation requests for securities should be followed until an adequate answer is obtained or until the securities are otherwise accounted for to the satisfaction of the auditor, based upon sample selection and quality level acceptance or rejection. Confirmation data should be set forth in the work papers for capital stock.

a) They may be pledged, hypothecated, or assigned as loan collateral.
b) They may be awaiting transfer and registration.
c) They may be held by brokers, awaiting delivery, or on loan.
d) They may be held by a custodian for safekeeping.
e) They may be deposited as a performance guaranty.

If a security is out of the client's possession for any reason other than those listed above, the auditor should obtain the certificate and examine it—at the time when other securities are examined and before they are released to the security custodian. The auditor should not release securities in his possession and then call for confirmations, because such procedure would allow time for released securities to be placed in the hands of the confirming party.

Obtain Market Prices and Compare with Cost or Other Price Basis. Market prices should be obtained as of the balance sheet date; entered on the work papers, as shown in Illustration 17–2; and totaled and compared with the cost or other basic figure. Market price may or may not be used to adjust cost for financial statement purposes.

Market prices are easily obtained for exchange-listed securities which are actively traded. Market quotations for securities traded over the counter and for close corporations often are difficult to obtain and are not particularly reliable, unless a recent purchase and sale have been made in that security. If a fair market price is not available, the auditor should so indicate in his work papers. For securities with an inactive market, the use of the bid price is safer than the average of bid-ask prices.

Vouch Purchases and Sales. Normally, authorization for the purchase and sale of securities should be recorded in the minutes of the board of directors. Security purchases and sales should be vouched for the period under audit in order to determine the profit or loss from security sales, the proper pricing of the securities purchased and account relief for securities sold, the correctness of the accounting data, and the composition of the balance at the end of the period.

When purchases and sales of capital stocks are vouched, brokers' invoices are traced to the client's records and to the individual ledger accounts involved. In preparing to vouch security purchases and sales, the auditor may start with the capital stock investment portfolio as of the close of the preceding year, add the cost of the stocks purchased, and deduct the securities sold (at cost), thus arriving at the protfolio composition as of the end of the year, as shown in Illustration 17–2. The opening and closing inventories may be verified by confirmation from brokers for those securities in their custody.

The cost of capital stock is the market price, plus commissions, plus applicable taxes, plus postage and insurance added by the broker. The sales price is commonly considered to be the net proceeds realized after deducting commissions and transfer taxes.

The Investment account must be examined to ascertain that it is credited for the number of shares indicated on the statement of the broker and that the credit is for the carrying value of the securities. The profit or loss on disposition is shown as such in the income statement.

If when stocks are sold, they can be identified as to purchase price, the Investment accounts are credited in accordance with the cost of the lots sold. If stocks sold are not identifiable because the owner earlier surrendered several certificates and received one certificate therefor, then the profits or losses must be computed on the basis of the first-in, first-out method for federal income tax purposes. Sales of stocks and the resultant profit or loss are most easily verified at the time of auditing the investment accounts and may be scheduled on the work papers for investments, as shown in Illustration 17–2, or scheduled separately.

If the audit is conducted after the close of the accounting period, sales and purchases of securities taking place after the closing date must also be verified and traced to the records involved in order to determine account composition at the end of the year under examination.

Verify Dividends from Stocks. The most appropriate time to verify dividends from capital stock investments is at the time of analyzing the stock investment accounts and preparing the work papers. The Dividend account should be analyzed and "tied in" with the stocks owned within the year, as shown in Illustration 17–2. Dividends paid by a company may be verified by reference to investment services, or by a correspondence directly with the company involved if it is small or "close." If the stock is held in a "street" name, dividends will be received directly from the broker in whose name the stock is held. It may happen that the broker has been instructed to retain the dividends in order to build up the client's balance. In this event, the auditor must compare the statements of position rendered by the broker with the records of the client to be certain that the client has properly taken up the dividend by a charge to a receivable.

Frequently, dividends receivable are not entered on the records of a recipient; where dividends receivable are recorded, the date-of-stock-record method should be followed in order to avoid showing a revenue that may not be received because of sale of the capital stock.

When asset dividends are received on capital stock investments in noncontrolled companies, all dividends are taken directly to revenue accounts, which the auditor must verify by referring to the dividend actions of the issuing companies and tracing the dividends through the cash accounts into the banks.

If capital stock investments represent controlling interests, the method of treating dividends received depends on whether the investor carries the investment at cost or at cost adjusted for subsidiary profits, losses, and dividends. If the profits of a subsidiary company are taken into the parent company's records as a charge to the proper Investment account, the records of the subsidiary company should be examined (or the report of another auditor accepted) to determine the correctness of the profits. If the profits of a subsidiary company are not taken up in the records of the parent company, then the subsidiary company may declare (*a*) dividends that reduce the subsidiary company's retained earnings below the amount on its records at the time of acquisition or (*b*) dividends that do not reduce the subsidiary company's retained earnings below the amount at the time of acquisition. If dividends reduce the retained earnings of the subsidiary company below the acquisition figure, the reduction should be credited to the Investment account and not to revenue. The auditor must verify dividend actions of subsidiary companies in order to determine the amounts the investor should receive and in order to verify the distribution between revenue and a return of capital.

If a company pays stock dividends, the dividend received by an investor may be in the same class of capital stock owned or in a different class. A stock dividend received in the same class of capital stock results in no additional wealth to the stockholder; he still has his former proportionate ownership, now represented by a larger number of shares, with a consequent smaller base per share and the same total cost as before; therefore, only the number of shares is changed. The auditor must note the recording of the additional shares in the investor's records in order to reflect properly the number of shares held after receipt of the stock dividend, the adjusted cost per share, and the total cost. Gain or loss on the subsequent sale of any of the shares is determined on the basis of the adjusted cost price of all shares owned, including those received as a dividend.

When a stock dividend is received in a class of shares different from those originally held, (*a*) the dividend may be treated as revenue, in accordance with income tax regulations; or (*b*) the cost of the original shares may be apportioned over the original shares and the dividend shares on the basis of the market price of the shares at the date the dividend is paid.

In verifying dividends received from companies engaged in wasting-asset activities, or from investment fund companies, care must be exercised to segregate returns of capital from income for wasting-asset companies and properly to segregate capital gains and normal income for investment companies. This segregation may be verified by reference to investment services; by notices sent to shareholders by the companies; or by the determination of the United States Treasury Department, based upon annual statements filed with it.

Separate Securities Held as Collateral or Otherwise. When securities are held as collateral for loans granted, they are examined in order to be certain that proper securities are held and that contingent title rests with the transferee. These collateral securities should be set forth in separate work papers and should be separated from the client's property. In addition, the auditor should satisfy himself as to the value of the collateral as it is an important factor in determining collectibility.

Watch for Evidence of Affiliation and Prepare Consolidated Financial Statements When Necessary. Investments in and advances to affiliated companies must be shown as a separate item in a nonconsolidated balance sheet.

If the investment is in a controlled company, the auditor must verify the cost or other basic acquisition figure of the investment. If affiliated or controlled companies are audited and consolidated balance sheets rendered, the assets and liabilities of those companies are substituted for the stock owned by the parent company. In such cases, the audit procedures relative to verification of assets and liabilities of the subsidiary companies are followed.

Frequently, a balance sheet will show an item as an "investment" when a more accurate picture would be shown by a consolidated balance sheet. When the control is complete, or nearly so, a parent-subsidiary relationship exists. When the stock ownership in a company is a controlling interest and when there is at the same time a fairly large floating supply of stock, the company commonly is spoken of as an "affiliate." Investments in controlled companies, either subsidiaries or affiliates, should not be classed as current assets because of the lack of future intention to convert to cash.

The Accounting Principles Board, in *Opinion No. 16, Business Combinations* and *in Opinion No. 18, The Equity Method of Accounting for Investments in Common Stock*, has set forth guidelines for presentation of these types of investments in the financial statements.

One point of view is that in almost all business combinations, one company acquires another company and therefore the *purchase* method should be used to recognize this combination. Those favoring this method reason that a business combination is a bargained transaction regardless of the nature of the consideration. The stock that is issued on such an occasion would take into consideration all assets and liabilities which comprise the cost of the acquired company which would include those items not previously shown on the acquired company's financial statements. An all-inclusive approach is a basic consideration of this method. One problem of this method is that available stock values may not be a reliable indicator of the value of the stock, and the resultant goodwill, if any, is stated only by coincidence and not determined by direct valuation.

Another viewpoint would have business combinations use the pooling of interest method. Those following this viewpoint believe that where common stock is issued to effect a combination, no corporate assets are distributed to stockholders and the net assets of the issuing corporation are increased by the net assets of the acquired company. In some instances both groups of stockholders surrender their stock and receive stock of a new corporation. One important problem of this method is that this combination does not accurately reflect the economic substance of the business combination transaction. Financial statement presentation for a business combination using the pooling of interest method should reflect operations as if they had been combined at the beginning of the period.

There are those who would record the initial investment at cost, but would adjust the carrying amount of the investment to recognize the share of the investor's earnings or losses of the investee after the date of acquisition. The financial statement presentation would also include adjustments similar to those made in preparing consolidated statements. The APB recommends that when an investment of 20 percent or more of the voting stock of an investee is acquired, that the equity method is appropriate. Therefore, financial statements should be consolidated and in parent-company financial statements prepared for issuance to stock-holders, this combination should be effected.

When accounts of affiliated or controlled companies cannot be audited or consolidated financial statements cannot be rendered—with or without audit—book valuations of stocks should be examined. If under such circumstances it cannot be determined that book valuations are realistic, the opinion of the report should be at least qualified.

In some cases involving long-term investments, the floating supply of stock is so small, owing to a large percentage of ownership by one company, that market prices are not a true indication of the value of the security as a whole. Also, a controlling interest may be more valuable per share than the minority stock, because profits of the subsidiary company may be absorbed by the parent company by the arbitrary pricing of transactions between the parent and the subsidiary. In such cases, the auditor may price the securities at book value, stating that method of valuation in his report; he may examine the financial statements of the affiliated companies if a consolidated balance sheet is not prepared; or he may examine the records of the affiliates if consolidated financial statements are prepared.

Of interest to accountants is a ruling of the Securities and Exchange Commission, under the Investment Company Act. This rule pertains to securities of registered management investment companies which have been placed in the custody of a company that is a member of a national securities exchange, as defined by the Securities Exchange Act. The custodian company may accept such securities only upon a written contract with the investment company; the securities must be completely segregated from securities of the custodian or of any customer. The segregation must be both physical and separately identified in the records of the custodian. The custodian may not assign, hypothecate, or otherwise dispose of such securities, except upon the direction of and for the account of the registered management investment company. Such securities must be verified by physical examination by an independent public accountant retained by the management investment company at the end of each annual and semiannual fiscal period, and also must be examined by the accountant at least one other time during the fiscal period, which time shall be selected by the accountant. The accountant must render a certificate to the Commission in which he must state that he made the examination and in which he must describe the examination; the securities are subject to examination by the Commission at all times.

Realizing the complex situations an auditor may find when auditing a parent-subsidiary company situation, The American Institute of Certified Public Accountants, in its *Statements on Auditing Procedure No. 34* entitled *Long-Term Investments* sets forth its recommendations as to types of reports that may be rendered by the auditor.

. . . when there are restrictions on the scope of his examination or uncertainties as to future developments with respect to investments:

A. There may be situations where sufficient evidential matter is not made available to the independent auditor or where he is not permitted to examine a sufficient number of subsidiaries of a holding company so that there is an effective limitation on the scope of his examination. In these circumstances an exception is required in the scope representation of the independent auditor's report, and a qualified opinion or a disclaimer of opinion is required, as contemplated in section 332 of Statement on Auditing Standards No. 1.

B. There may be situations in which the independent auditor has examined the available evidential matter but finds that because of existing conditions there is uncertainty about the ultimate realization of long-term investments. In such circumstances the independent auditor should either qualify his opinion or disclaim an opinion on the financial statements taken as a whole, depending on the materiality of the investments. Examples of these types of reports are as follows:

Qualified Opinion

(Middle paragraph)

Investments described in Note 1 are in companies whose financial statements indicate they are in the promotional and development stage (or other wording descriptive of the facts). Accordingly, the ultimate realization of these investments depends on circumstances which cannot be evaluated currently.

(Opinion paragraph)

In our opinion, subject to the realization of the carrying values of investments referred to in the preceding paragraph, ...

Disclaimer of Opinion
(Same scope and middle paragraphs as above)

(Opinion paragraph)

Because the investments referred to in the preceding paragraph enter materially into the determination of financial position and results of operations, we do not express an opinion on the accompanying financial statements taken as a whole.

BONDS OF CONTROLLED OR NONCONTROLLED COMPANIES

Audit procedures for bonds held as investments vary only in minor respects from the procedures set forth for the examination of investments in capital stocks. Therefore, in the development of the audit procedures for bond investments, procedures that are the same as those for capital stock investments are *not* repeated.

Bonds may represent (1) stock in trade, (2) temporary investments, or (3) long-term investments. Bonds may be (1) coupon or (2) registered. Registered bonds may be registered (*a*) as to principal only or (*b*) as to principal and interest—in which case the interest is paid by check. Currently, there is a trend away from the use of corporate coupon bonds, due to the fact that coupons are bulky, and because corporations are interested in knowing the identity of their bondholders, and because interest to bondholders must be reported to Internal Revenue Service.

The auditor must be familiar with all types of bonds: land development, real estate mortgage, collateral trust, equipment trust, income, and debenture; serial, participating, and convertible; and the various types of government bonds.

Audit Program for Investments in Bonds

The procedures to be followed by investments in bonds are described in the following subsections.

List and Examine the Bonds. Bond investments should be listed in a work paper; or the client should prepare a listing in advance, in accordance with the auditor's instructions. The listing should be compared with the ledger accounts and reconciled with the composition of the accounts, just as for capital stock certificates.

Illustration 17–3 presents a work paper for the scheduling of bonds. In the Remarks column should be placed such data as the following:

a) Warrants attached to the bonds.
b) Extension of maturity date with bondholder approval.
c) Reduction of interest rates with bondholder approval.
d) Tax-free covenants.
e) Reasons for pledging.
f) Subsequent coupons attached.

Separate work papers may, if necessary, be prepared for the extraction of data from trust indentures.

Serial numbers of the bonds should be stated in the work papers to aid the auditor in the succeeding year in vouching purchases and sales. Serial numbers of bonds on hand at the examination date should be compared with the serial numbers of the same bonds appearing in the work papers for the preceding examination in order to detect unauthorized activities.

ILLUSTRATION. The advantage of recording bond numbers in the work papers may be illustrated as follows: "Bearer" bonds of the X Company were listed in the December 31, 1974, work papers with the numbers 8G462–8G471, inclusive. At December 31, 1975, there are 10 bearer bonds of the X Company on hand, which amount agrees with the work papers of December 31, 1974. However, the serial numbers of the bonds on hand at December 31, 1975, are 8D521–8D530, inclusive. The bond custodian had sold the bonds in February, 1975, used the proceeds to purchase an apartment building, sold the building at a profit, and then purchased the new bonds and returned them to the portfolio. At the interest dates of the original bonds, he gave the cashier a memorandum of the proper interest, explaining that he had deposited the coupons at the bank when he went to the safe-deposit box.

The same care and the same procedures should be followed in the examination of bonds as for the examination of capital stock investments. If the bond interest is payable by coupon, the auditor must determine that the coupons payable after the audit date are attached to the bonds. The work papers should indicate the presence or absence of future coupons. The auditor also must determine the presence of matured but uncashed coupons. If matured coupons are attached to the bonds, (*a*) the interest may be in default, (*b*) the debtor corporation may be in the process of reorganization, or (*c*) the coupons may have been overlooked by the owner. All irregularities should be brought to the attention of the client. If interest has been accrued at the end of the preceding period and if that interest was not collected due to default, the accrued interest entry should be reversed. Interest that is uncollectible or doubtful should be entered in the Interest—Doubtful column, and subsequent interest actions should be followed.

If corporate treasury bonds exist, they should be inspected by the auditor at the time bonds held as investments are examined. Treasury bonds should be shown as a deduction from the proper bond liability account. Treasury bonds must be safeguarded so that they cannot be used improperly.

The minutes of the board of directors and/or other groups must be examined for evidence of authority to acquire bonds. All relevant data from these sources and from trust indentures must be placed in the work papers.

Confirm Bonds Held by Others. The same procedures as those set forth for the confirmation of capital stock investments should be followed for bond investments held by others.

Obtain Market Prices and Compare with Cost or Other Price Basis. The same procedure should be followed as for obtaining market prices for capital stocks. It must be remembered that bonds usually are quoted

ILLUSTRATION 17–3

PERRY COMPANY

Bond Investments, Acct. No. 86
December 31, 1975

Bond Nos. Incl.	Name of Issuer	Type of Bond	Maturity Date	Balance, 12/31/74			Purchases in 1975			Sales in 1975		
				No.	Par Each	Total Cost	No.	Par Each	Total Cost	Par	Cost	Sales Price
198-202√ˣ	A Co.	Debenture	July 1, 1990	5	$1,000	$ 4,500√						
17-26√ˣ	B Co.	First mtg.	April 1, 1999				10	$1,000	$10,000⊙ /\			
118-127	C Co.	First mtg.	July 1, 1979	10	1,000	9,000√				$10,000	9,000	$9,500⊙ /\
119-138√ˣ	D Co.	Debenture	July 1, 1985	10 10	1,000	10,800√	10	1,000	10,200⊙ /\			
						$24,300√			$20,200		$9,000	$9,500

√ Agrees with 1974 work papers and general ledger.
⊙ Brokers' statements inspected.
√ Market price from *The Wall Street Journal*, 1/3/76.
σ Interest verified from Moody's *Annual Bond Record*.
/\ Traced to cash and ledger accounts.
∧ Calculations verified.
√ˣ Examined and confirmed.
    All bonds are registered in the name of the client.
    Examination witnessed by Gene Willis.
    Received above securities from auditor.
       (Signed)   Gene Willis   1/21/76
                 Custodian

as a percentage of par rather than in dollars. The *Wall Street Journal* quotes on a 100 basis; United States Government bonds are quoted in terms of a thirty-second of a dollar (for example, 102.4 means $102\frac{4}{32}$); the auditor must convert to the proper denomination.

Vouch Purchases and Sales. The vouching of bond purchases and bond sales follows the same procedures as those set forth for the purchases and sales of investments in capital stocks. When a bond is purchased, it may be bought at the prevailing market price plus interest accrued. The purchase of the accrued interest is not a part of the permanent cost of the bond and will be returned to the purchaser at the succeeding interest date.

Verify Bond Revenue. The Bond Interest Income account should

			Initials	Date
	Prepared By			
	Approved By			

Balance, 12/31/75		Market, 12/31/75		Interest					Profit or Loss on Sale	
Par	Amount	Each	Total	Rates	Dates	Received	Accrued	Doubt-ful		Remarks
$ 5,000	$ 4,500	$ 930✓	$ 4,650	6%	7/1 1/1	$ 300σ	$ 150			In safe deposit
10,000	10,000				7/1	300σ	150			In safe
		1,000✓	10,000	6%	1/1					deposit
—	—	—	—		10/1	800σ			P$500	Sold July
				8%	4/1					1, 1975
20,000	21,000	1,007✓	20,140		7/1	400σ	800			10 in safe
				8%	1/1					deposit,
	$35,500		$34,790			$1,800	$1,100∧		$500	10 held by broker; request delivery.

be analyzed and reconciled with the interest that should have been earned on the bonds owned during the year; then the amount received is traced to cash receipts. The bond interest received may be entered in the appropriate section of the bond schedule, or a separate schedule may be prepared for the interest received. If a separate schedule is prepared, it might take the form shown in Illustration 17–4.

Registered bonds, for which interest is paid by check, are examined, and the interest rates and dates noted; for coupon bonds—registered or unregistered as to principal—the amount of the interest is stated on each coupon. The interest on income bonds may or may not have been received, since payment is contingent upon the interest earned; if the records indicate that no interest has been received on this type of bond, confirmation of the lack of interest payments should be obtained from the issuing company. If interest on any type of bond is in default, a notation to that effect should appear as a footnote to the financial statements, together with the amount of the default.

While verifying bond interest earned, the auditor must watch for the correct treatment of interest accruals at the time of purchase and at the time of disposal in order to be certain that revenues are not understated or overstated and that the asset values are correctly reflected in the records. Statements of brokers for security sales and purchases will contain data pertaining to interest accruals.

ILLUSTRATION 17–4

SCHEDULE OF INTEREST RECEIVED

| Bond Name | Par Held | % Rate | Annual Interest | Interest | | | | | | | Total Received |
				Jan.	Feb.	Mar.	May	July	Sept.	Oct.	
A Co.	$10,000	6	$600			$300			$300		$ 600
B Co.	5,000	8	400	$200			$200				400
C Co.	10,000	5	500							$250*	250
D Co.	4,000	6	240		$120		$60†				180
											$1,430

* Purchased in August.
† Sold in May.

Certain bonds issued by the United States government are discount bonds, sold at the present value of the principal sum to be paid at maturity, without the payment of current interest; the price of the bond accumulates to par at maturity. In this type of bond, the interest accumulation preferably should be brought into the records periodically.

Verify Accrued Bond Interest, and the Amortization of Premiums and Discounts. The auditor must verify interest accruals at the end of the accounting period and determine that the amounts are in asset accounts and income accounts. Bond interest accrued may be placed in the appropriate column of Illustration 17–3, or a column may be added in the schedule of interest received (Illustration 17–4); or the accrued interest may be separately calculated. In accruing interest, the exact number of days should be used, based upon a 360-day year.

The auditor must verify computations for the amortization of premiums and discounts if amortization procedures are followed.

INVESTMENTS IN MORTGAGES

A mortgage is a conditional deed transferring conditional title to the mortgagee. The mortgage serves as evidence of security for the debt. A bond or note may be executed at the time a mortgage is taken and is evidence of debt under a mortgage. The two instruments—the mortgage and the note—ordinarily constitute the evidence of a complete mortgage transaction. A mortgage may be a real estate mortgage, a chattel mortgage, or a purchase money mortgage received in partial payment for property sold. Normally, mortgages are not current assets unless they are to be liquidated in a short time or unless the audit is for a building and loan company, a bank, or an insurance company. For an investor in mortgages who maintains adequate records, there will normally exist for audit the following records:

1. One or more general ledger controlling accounts.
2. A subsidiary ledger account with each mortgage, setting forth the original amount of the loan, principal and interest payments, loan data, interest rates, insurance coverage, principal payment terms, interest and/or principal payments in arrears, and so forth.
3. The mortgage, filed in accordance with the filing system used—usually numerically.
4. Mortgage notes.
5. Insurance policies covering the property.
6. Correspondence from attorneys pertaining to title examination.
7. Appraisal reports.
8. Abstracts.

Audit Program for Investments in Mortgages

The procedures to be followed for investments in mortgages are developed in the following subsections.

List and Examine the Mortgages. The auditor should prepare or request a schedule of the mortgages. The total amount due on the mortgages is obtained from the schedule and compared with the general ledger accounts. Discrepancies must be investigated and located.

ILLUSTRATION. Interest of $300 paid by a mortgagor was credited to principal on the subsidiary ledger but was properly credited to Interest Income in the controlling account.

A schedule for mortgages owned appears in Illustration 17–5. In preparing the schedule, all data cannot be supplied from one source. Information will be taken from the mortgage, from ledger cards for principal and interest, from insurance policies, from appraisal reports, and so forth. In order to reduce detail work, the schedule may be made "progressive" by using the original schedule, eliminating paid mortgage loans, adding new loans, and adding a new column for the principal balance due.

The auditor should examine the mortgages to ascertain that they are properly signed and sealed. The auditor also must ascertain that each mortgage indicates recording on the public records; the mortgage should show the book and page number of the county recording and the name of the recording clerk. This information need not be copied into the work papers, since that would constitute unnecessary work; a suitable rubber stamp may be used on the mortgages. The auditor should examine each mortgage for the correctness of the name of the mortgagor by comparing it with the client's records. If the client is not the mortgagee, the auditor must search for an assignment of ownership. If the mortgage

ILLUSTRATION 17–5

BROOKVILLE CORPORATION

Schedule of Mortgages Owned, Acct. #92
December 31, 1975

Mortgagor	Location of Property	Property Appraisal		Original Mortgage	Type or Mortgage	% Rate	Interest Dates	Maturity Date	Required Installments	
		Date	Amount						Dates	Amount
Duncan Co., Lincoln St., Cincinnati	Same	10/10/74	$ 75,000	$ 20,000	Second	8	12/31; 6/30	Dec. 31, 1984	Dec. 31; June 30	$ 2,000
Ebner Co., Locust St., Detroit	Ninth St.	8/6/75	30,000	10,000	First	7	5/1; 11/1	May 1, 1979	May 1	1,000
New Products, Albany, N.Y.	Hudson St.	8/9/72	88,000	20,000	First	7½	6/30; 12/31	Jan. 1, 1991	June 30	2,000
Hudson Apts., Chicago	Same	11/14/74	345,000	90,000	First	8	5/1; 11/1	May 1, 1993	May 1	5,000
Wahl Co., Park Ave., Cincinnati	On premises	7/6/75	6,000	2,000	Chattel	9	12/31	Dec. 31, 1979	Dec. 31	500
				$142,000					Total Required . .	$10,500
Less: Principal payments prior to 1975				13,500					Less: Unpaid . . .	1,000
				$128,500					Received	$ 9,500
Less: Principal payments, 1975				9,500						
Balance, December 31, 1975				$119,000						

Examined on January 10, 1976, in the office of J. C. Parker, Treasurer.
Mortgage balance agrees with general ledger balance.
Mortgages properly signed and sealed.
See file letter from C. R. Bern, Attorney, to the effect that all mortgages are properly recorded.
Insurance appears adequate.
Principal and interest payments vouched to cash records and traced to accounts.
All taxes paid to proper dates; no delinquencies.
Notes on Duncan Company Mortgage:

Appraisal	$75,000
First Mortgage.	25,000
Remaining equity.	$50,000
Second mortgage (above)	20,000
Margin of safety.	$30,000

Audit Adjustment

Accrued Interest Receivable.	$1,316.67	
Interest Income		$1,316.67

	Initials	Date
Prepared By		
Approved By		

Mort-gages Exam-ined	In-surance Cover-age	Interest			Cash Received, 1975		Taxes Paid to	Mortgage Balance Due	Remarks
		Paid to	Accrued	Ar-rears	Prin-cipal	Interest			
Yes	$20,000	12/31/75	0	0	$2,000	$ 1,600	12/31/75	$ 18,000	Interest on reducing balance.
Yes	10,000	11/1/75	116.67	0	0	700	12/31/75	7,500	Principal payment, due on
Yes	30,000	12/31/75	0	0	2,000	1,500	12/31/75	12,000	May 1, 1975, in
Yes	90,000	11/1/75	1,200.00	0	5,000	7,200	12/31/75	80,000	arrears.
Yes	5,000	12/31/75	0	0	500	180	—	1,500	Mortgage is on laundry machinery.
			$1,316.67		$9,500	$11,180		$119,000	
			AJE						

portfolio is large, a section of the total of the mortgages may be examined annually.

In the event of second or subsequent mortgages, prior claims must be deducted from the property value in order to arrive at the remaining equity. See Illustration 17–5.

If a participation agreement exists in place of an original mortgage, the senior participant holds the mortgage and receives the entire interest and principal payments. The junior participant will be reimbursed for his proportionate part by the senior participant. In such cases, the auditor must verify the agreement and trace interest and principal payments received in order to be certain that the agreement has been maintained.

Examine for Assignment. As stated above, if the client is not the mortgagee named in the original mortgage, there should be attached to the mortgage on file an assignment or a series of assignments. Although mortgage assignments are not common, if they do exist, the auditor should ascertain (*a*) that the assignment data are in agreement with similar data in the mortgage, and that the assignment is not for another document; (*b*) that the assignment is issued by the original mortgagee, and that his rights are unconditionally transferred; and (*c*) that the assignment was properly recorded in the public records, by examining the assignment for the county clerk's stamp for record number, page number, date, and signature.

Study the Search of Title. The auditor should examine the letter of title search from the client's attorney. Title search papers usually contain a description of the property and its location as to street, lot number, subdivision name, and so forth. A column for title search papers may be placed in the work papers. The auditor may rubber-stamp the letter, so that the same letter will not be read again on a subsequent audit. Abstracts and deeds should be examined in a similar manner.

Examine Insurance Policies, Appraisal Reports, and Assessed Valuations. Insurance policies on mortgaged properties should be examined to ascertain the adequacy of the protection of the loan. It is customary practice for the mortgagor to carry fire and extended coverage insurance equal to the original amount of the mortgage. The policies should be in the possession of the mortgagee and assigned to him. If the policies are not on hand, the auditor should confirm the insurance through a broker. Policy amounts should be matched with the mortgage amounts in the schedule of mortgages owned. It is not necessary to confirm insurance policies on hand.

Prior to lending money on real or personal property, the lending institution customarily appraises the property pledged as security. If the loan is made by a bank or building and loan company, laws usually require an appraisal. The appraisal is made (*a*) to determine the adequacy of the margin of safety between the current market price of the property and the amount of the loan and (*b*) to determine that not more than the legal percentage of appraisal value is loaned.

The majority of lending institutions do not appraise properties at a date subsequent to that of granting the loan. If the auditor believes that appraisal values are overstated—in order to grant the loan, or if the loan principal payments have been slow in a declining market—he should call for an independent appraisal of such properties. If the loan has been paid down to a point where the present amount due is below the legal loan limit based upon a current appraisal, he may conclude that the mortgagee's equity is adequate. However, in his report, he may point out the original overappraisal.

Examine Evidences of Tax Payments. The auditor must obtain adequate information concerning tax payments by mortgagors. Receipted tax bills may be obtained if the mortgagee holds them, or county records may be examined by test. In some cases, mortgagors remit to the mortgagee, who then pays the taxes and thus directly obtains the receipted tax bills.

Confirm Balances with Mortgagors. Balances due from mortgagors should be confirmed directly to the auditor, together with the interest rates, insurance coverage, and tax payments. This confirmation should be on the basis of not more than a 15 percent sample if the number of loan accounts is large; as the number of loans decreases, the size of the sample should increase. The sample may be drawn at random, or by alphabetical or numerical block.

ILLUSTRATION. The necessity of obtaining confirmations of interest rates may be illustrated as follows: The secretary of a loan company had charged a borrower interest at the rate of 8 percent but had entered interest at the rate of 6 percent and abstracted the difference from cash receipts; similar activities extended over 30 separate loans.

Confirmation should be obtained for *all* loans which are delinquent as to principal payments or interest payments.

Confirm Mortgages and Notes Held by Others. Confirmations should be obtained for all mortgages and mortgage notes not presented for examination. The mortgage may be deposited as loan collateral; it may be in the hands of an attorney for collection, cancellation, completion, or foreclosure proceedings; or it may be held in escrow for specific performance or pending a lawsuit.

ILLUSTRATION. The necessity for confirming mortgages held by others may be exemplified as follows: In the examination of the building and loan company cited earlier, the auditor found—for one account—the appraisal report, the title examination letter, and the insurance policies; a mortgage was not present, since the loan ostensibly was made two weeks prior to the close of the period. The auditor was informed that the mortgage was in the hands of the attorney, who would return it by mail upon its completion. The confirmation request reply from the attorney stated that he did not have the mortgage in question. Investigation proved that the secretary of the loan company had written checks to a fictitious person, cashed the checks, filed an appraisal report, forged a title letter, and purchased insurance policies.

Vouch Principal and Interest Receipts; Vouch Disbursements. Principal and interest payments made by mortgagors are vouched to the original records and traced to the ledger accounts in order to determine the propriety of account balances and in order to avoid misappropriation of receipts. The size of the sample will be dependent upon internal control and the size of the portfolio.

If mortgage notes exist in connection with a mortgage, the auditor should ascertain that partial payments are endorsed on the notes.

In vouching disbursements made on mortgage loans, the auditor must examine the minutes of the board of directors, or the minutes of the proper committee, for authority for the loan, its amount, name of the mortgagor, etc., and trace the amounts to the disbursements records, being certain that the disbursement checks were drawn payable to the order of the proper borrower.

If the client is not regularly engaged in the business of investing in mortgages, the auditor must examine state and/or federal laws, the corporate charter, and the code of regulations to determine if restrictions exist on the investment of company funds in mortgages. If the auditor is examining the records of an estate or a trust and if specific instructions are not set forth in the will or trust agreement, he should follow the laws of the state in which the estate or trust is established.

Perhaps Compare Mortgage Data with Public Records. In addition to examining the mortgages for the data set forth earlier, the auditor may decide to test a number of the mortgages by comparison with the public records. This test may be necessary in order that he may be assured of the genuineness of the mortgages and assignments and their proper recording. In examining county records, the auditor should watch for liens, assessment levies, and unpaid taxes; the data obtained are compared with the confirmation request replies obtained from the borrowers.

Verify Interest and Delinquent Interest. The schedule of mortgages (Illustration 17–5) provides space for interest received, accrued, and delinquent. The data for interest received originates in the receipts data.

ILLUSTRATIONS.   The testing of the interest income many be illustrated as follows: The auditor decided to test interest income by selecting two months. He obtained all payment tickets for those months, added the interest received, compared the total with the Interest Income account, and compared the total with the cash receipts records. He then traced each ticket to the corresponding subsidiary ledger account and examined the subsidiary ledger further for interest credits therein which might not be supported by individual tickets.

Depending upon the accounting system used by the mortgagee, interest may or may not be accrued at the balance sheet date. If interest is accrued, the computation should be verified.

Delinquent interest should be verified from the client's computations or computed from the records. In at least one state, in the financial statements prepared for the Department of Commerce of that state, delinquent interest must be set forth as a balance sheet footnote.

Confirm Sinking Funds. If a mortgage provides for the establishment of a sinking fund, the auditor should obtain confirmation from the sinking fund trustee in order to be certain that sinking fund provisions are being fulfilled. If the provisions have not been followed, the situation should be mentioned in the audit report. See the following section.

INVESTMENT IN FUNDS

Funds may be created for any conceivable purpose, including pension funds, sinking funds, endowment funds, building funds, and funds for redemption of certain capital stock. Pension funds and sinking funds for the retirement of bond issues are the two most commonly found. Funds may be in the form of cash or securities, or both, and may be under the jurisdiction of the company establishing the fund or under the care of a trustee. Sinking funds are commonly held by a trustee; pension funds are commonly administered by an insurance company or a trust company.

Audit Program for Investments in Funds

The procedures to be followed for investments in funds are developed in the following subsections.

Examine Authorization for the Fund. The authorization usually will be found in the minutes of the board of directors or of the stockholders. If an employee pension fund exists, examination should be made of the approval of the Commissioner of Internal Revenue, if it is a qualified plan for federal income tax purposes. Pertinent features of the fund and its operation should be extracted for the permanent file, or a copy obtained from the client.

From the Fund Trustee, Obtain Confirmation of the Fund Assets. The composition of a fund according to the records of the client should be compared with the confirmation of that fund composition as obtained from the trustee. The contributions should be supported by the trustee's report covering not only the composition of the fund but also its activity with respect to expenses, securities purchased and sold, interest and dividends received, and cash receipts. If the trustee has purchased for the fund and canceled some of the company's outstanding bonds, the canceled bonds should be examined and entries verified for the reduction of the bond liability account.

If the fund is not under the jurisdiction of a trustee, the composition of the fund must be examined according to the procedures involved in any cash and securities examination. In the event of sinking funds for extractive industries companies, the auditor must verify annual production, since in many extractive industries, a certain amount per unit of production is set aside for bond or capital stock redemption.

Verify Fund Revenues. If a sinking fund trustee is not used, amounts earned by the fund must be verified in the same manner as for interest on bonds and dividends on capital stock.

Determine That the Trust Agreement Is Observed. The major point in determining that the trust agreement is being observed is to prevent the violation of a contract. It may be necessary that the legal counsel and the auditor confer in this connection.

ILLUSTRATION 17–6

THE PROCESSING COMPANY

Pension Fund, Acct. #90
December 31, 1975

Explanation	1972	1973	1974	1975
Balance, January 1	0	$ 76,125	$125,808	$172,632
Additions:				
Company expense charges	$50,000	30,000	35,000	40,000
Employees' contributions	25,000	30,000	35,000	40,000
Interest: 3% of average balance	1,125	3,183	4,824	6,378
	$76,125	$139,308	$200,632	$259,010
Deductions:				
Benefits paid (below)	0	$ 12,000	$ 23,600	$ 36,700
Refunds to employees	0	1,500	4,400	3,700
	0	13,500	28,000	40,400
Balance, December 31	$76,125	$125,808	$172,632	$218,610

Benefits Paid To	Date	Type	1973	1974	1975
Jones	Mar. 1, 1972	Annuity	$ 3,000	$ 3,600	$ 3,600
Smith	July 1, 1972	Death	9,000	0	0
Cartier	Mar. 1, 1973	Annuity		12,000	14,400
Flynn	May 1, 1973	Annuity		8,000	9,600
Sprang	July 1, 1974	Annuity			600
Grant	Aug. 1, 1974	Death			3,100
Swartzel	Sept. 1, 1974	Annuity			800
Sells	Oct. 1, 1974	Annuity			900
Stierwalt	May 1, 1975	Annuity			1,600
Avers	June 1, 1975	Annuity			2,100
			$12,000	$23,600	$36,700

Trace Final Disposition of the Fund. The final disposition of all funds should be examined and traced to the records, and it must be in agreement with the provisions for establishing the fund.

For work papers for pension funds and sinking funds, see Illustrations 17–6 and 17–7.

ILLUSTRATION 17–7

THE PROCESSING COMPANY	Prepared by _____
	Date _____
Sinking Fund Investments, Acct. #91	Reviewed by _____
December 31, 1975	Date _____

Under the terms of the bond issue, dated January 1, 1969, in a total amount of $500,000, bonds in a total of $50,000 are to be retired each July 1.

At December 31, 1975, $200,000 of bonds are outstanding.

The bond indenture provides that the company shall set aside $50,000 each six months starting July 1, 1969 (in addition to the $50,000 retirement at July 1, 1969), for the purpose of establishing a sinking fund for future retirements. Interest earned is to be added to the fund. The fund is under company control.

Balance, December 31, 1974		$ 56,525
Added to the fund, 1975:		
January 1	$50,000	
July 1	50,000	100,000
		$156,525
Bonds retired and canceled, 1975:		
January 1	$50,000	
July 1	50,000	100,000
		$ 56,525
Interest earned, 1975.		1,725
Balance, December 31, 1975		$ 58,250

INVESTMENTS IN LIFE INSURANCE

The purpose of acquiring life insurance as an investment usually is either to enable the beneficiary business organization to recover losses of business income which may result upon the death of the insured, who is economically valuable to the organization, or to supply funds to the organization to liquidate the ownership of the deceased person— usually a partner or a stockholder of a close corporation. In determining the amount of the insurance for asset purposes, some auditors use cash surrender values at the end of the insurance anniversary date or at the balance sheet date; others use loan values at the beginning of a policy year. While there is no uniformity of practice, apparently there is a tendency to use loan values at the beginning of a policy year.

In answer to the question as to whether cash surrender values at the last premium date or at the balance sheet date should be used, it may be stated that the differences in values normally are not material—but consistency must prevail. In policies involving dividend allocations or other circumstances where differences might be material, it is advisable to request from the insurance company the cash surrender value or loan value as of the balance sheet date.

Audit Program for Investments in Life Insurance

The procedures to be followed for investments in life insurance are developed in the following subsections.

Examine the Policies.   The objectives of the auditor in examining the policies are to understand their contents and terms, to be certain that the policies are in force and that the client is the beneficiary, and to ascertain that loan values and cash surrender values and accumulated dividends and interest are properly and consistently recorded.

The auditor should prepare work papers for life insurance, setting forth at least the following data:

a) Name of insurance company
b) Policy number
c) Date of policy
d) Name of insured
e) Name of beneficiary
f) Type of insurance   } Obtained from the policies
g) Amount of insurance
h) Annual premium
i) Premium payment date
j) Cash surrender value or loan value

k) Prepaid premiums—over one year
l) Accumulated dividends and interest   } Obtained from the client's records and from insurance
m) Loans outstanding on the policies   company confirmations
    and terms of the loans

Determine Cash Surrender Values or Loan Values.   Insurance premiums represent advance payments. In the majority of instances, before a policy accumulates a cash surrender value or a loan value one or two annual premium payments must be made. The cash surrender value is the amount for which the policy may be liquidated if surrendered and canceled, either by the insured or by one acquiring the policy by assignment. The loan value is the amount which may be borrowed on the policy.

Determination of cash surrender values or loan values is directly related to the proper determination of periodic expense and prepaid expenses at the year-end. After an annual premium has been paid, cash surrender values and loan values increase. The current cash surrender value or loan value stated in a policy normally is the amount available at the next premium date. However, most insurance companies today are equipped to supply the auditor with this information at the client's balance sheet date. If a policy is borrowed on or redeemed at an earlier date, a discount factor—usually five or six percent per year and a prorata reduction of the last premium paid—is involved. Consequently, the cash surrender value or loan value immediately after the payment of an annual premium is the stated amount as of the succeeding premium date, less the discount and the prorata reduction for the remainder of the policy year. At the end of each month during the year, the discount period is reduced, and the cash surrender value or loan value is increased until, at the end of the policy year, the cash surrender or loan value agrees with the amount stated in the policy.

That portion of the premium which is not added to the policy loan value or cash surrender value may be treated as a prepaid expense and should be prorated to expense equally over the year. The discount and fractional-year elements involved in a cash surrender value or a loan value may also be considered as prepaid expense until the appropriate time arrives to add them to the cash surrender or loan value.

Loan and cash surrender values in insurance policies usually are stated in terms of $1,000 of insurance. Upon request, insurance companies prepare an "analysis of policy" setting forth elapsed years, annual premiums, dividends, cash values exclusive of dividends, and certain other data not pertinent to the discussion here. An analysis is presented below for the cash surrender values for a $10,000 policy, based upon a given age and on the assumption of 20-pay life, and on the assumption that the policy anniversary date coincides with the owner's balance sheet date.

Year	Premium	Dividends	Surrender Value at End of Year
1973	$762.40	0	0
1974	762.40	$60.00	0
1975	762.40	64.20	$ 970.00
1976	762.40	66.70	1,580.00
1977	762.40	69.30	2,281.00

Upon the payment of the third premium, a cash surrender value starts to accumulate and is the cash surrender value at the end of that premium period; if the policy were cashed between the premium dates of 1975 and 1976, the cash surrender value would be reduced by the amount of the premium for the number of months between the date of surrender and the next premium date.

The question arises concerning the proper treatment of premiums paid prior to the accumulation of a cash surrender value: (*a*) Should premiums paid in the first two years be expensed in total? Or (*b*) should premiums paid in the first two years be prorated between expense and investment values, on the assumption that the policies *will* be retained until a cash surrender value exists?

If (*a*), above, is followed, the balance sheet is correct, since the policy *does not possess* a cash surrender value at that time. Therefore, the entry for the first and second annual premiums would be as follows:

Life Insurance Expense (or Prepaid Life Insurance). 762.40
   Cash in Bank 762.40

The prepaid life insurance would be prorated over the year.

If (*b*), above, is followed, the balance sheet is not correct for the first two years and should be footnoted. However, the proration of the annual expense is stated with greater accuracy. The following entry could be made in each of the first two years:

```
Contingent Cash Surrender Value of Life Insurance . . . . . . .  323.33
Life Insurance Expense (or Prepaid Life Insurance) . . . . . . .  439.07
    Cash in Bank . . . . . . . . . . . . . . . . . . . . . . . . . . . . .         762.40
```

The debit to Contingent Cash Surrender Value of Life Insurance assumes an equal annual accumulation of the cash surrender value.

Upon the payment of the third premium, the entry is as follows, if (*a*) is used:

```
Cash Surrender Value of Life Insurance . . . . . . . . . . . . .  970.00
Life Insurance Expense (or Prepaid Life Insurance). . . . . . . .  762.40
    Miscellaneous Income . . . . . . . . . . . . . . . . . . . . . .         970.00
    Cash in Bank . . . . . . . . . . . . . . . . . . . . . . . . . . . . .         762.40
```

If (*b*) is used, the following entry will be made:

```
Cash Surrender Value of Life Insurance . . . . . . . . . . . . .  970.00
Life Insurance Expense (or Prepaid Life Insurance). . . . . . . .  439.06
    Contingent Cash Surrender Value of Life Insurance . . . . .         646.66
    Cash in Bank . . . . . . . . . . . . . . . . . . . . . . . . . . . . .         762.40
```

A work paper for investments in life insurance appears in the Illustrative Audit.

Determine Accumulated Dividends and Interest. Dividends on life insurance policies may be applied as a reduction of premiums, or may be left with the insurance company to accumulate at interest, or applied to the purchase of additional insurance. If the dividends are used to reduce periodic premiums, the term "premiums" is construed to mean "net premiums after dividends." Dividends are based on the earnings of the insurance company.

Examination should be made of the premium receipts and the related ledger records to determine that proper entries have been made. Premium receipts set forth not only the annual premiums but also the total accumulated dividends and interest at the beginning of the year (if left to accumulate), and interest and dividends to be added upon payment of the annual premium. If interest and dividends are left to accumulate, the value of the policy is thereby increased. The accumulated dividends and interest may be set forth in a separate account or may be added to the cash surrender value or loan value of the policy. This accumulation on the client's records should be in agreement with the amounts confirmed by the insurance company. Dividend accumulations do not constitute income because they represent premium reductions; interest on the accumulated dividends represent income—which is taxable.

Confirm Policies and Their Status. The auditor should obtain confirmations from the insurance companies for all life insurance in force, requesting such information as the following for each policy, described by policy number:

a)   Cash surrender values or loan values—at the desired dates.
b)   Total accumulated dividends and interest.
c)   Amount of loans on the policies.
d)   Interest on the loans.
e)   Date to which premiums are paid.
f)   Name of party paying the premiums.
g)   Name of the beneficiary.
h)   If the policy is assigned, to whom?

The auditor must ascertain that loans made on the policies have been properly recorded in the records of the client. In most instances, the insurance companies retain the policies when loans are made on them.

Extract Policy Agreements Affecting Proceeds.   There are many types of insurance policies written to protect business income for a period following the death of a key person and to enable either the company or another person to purchase the business interest of a deceased owner. Deferred compensation plans are frequently provided for through life insurance policies. The two most commonly used types of insurance are ordinary life and the stated-number-of-payments type. Regardless of the type of insurance purchased, the auditor must be familiar with the agreements in the policies which affect the use of the proceeds of the insurance.

ILLUSTRATION.   The Lueckman Company carried two life insurance policies on its president, one in the amount of $100,000 to be used to acquire the company stock owned by the president and the other in the amount of $50,000 to meet the requirements of a deferred compensation plan for his widow. Upon the president's death, the company, being the beneficiary, received the $150,000. It used the $100,000 to purchase the deceased president's stock and the $50,000 was used to pay the widow $10,000 a year for five years as agreed in the deferred compensation contract. No income tax was paid on the proceeds of the policies, and the company can claim a $10,000 deduction for each of the five years for income tax purposes.

If the auditor believes that statements contained in the policies are not in accord with the intention of the parties involved or if he considers the insurance to be inadequate to fulfill the objectives when it was originally purchased, the situation should be called to the client's attention. He might also recommend that a qualified certified life underwriter be consulted to review the insurance program.

Premiums on life insurance of the types under consideration are not deductible expenses for federal income tax purposes; the proceeds are not taxable unless the policy was acquired by assignment for a consideration, in which case the proceeds are taxable to the extent that they exceed the consideration for assignment plus the nondeductible premiums paid.

If the life of an employee is insured by the employer and if the named beneficiary is not the employer, the premiums paid by the employer constitute taxable income to the employee—except premiums paid under a group insurance plan.

SECTION III: FINANCIAL STATEMENT CONSIDERATIONS

Valuation of Investment Securities

The balance sheet should disclose fully the basis used in the valuation of investments in all securities.

Temporary Marketable Securities Held by Industrial and Commercial Concerns. Temporary marketable securities, classed as current assets, may be priced at the lower of cost or market, with the higher of the two figures stated parenthetically. The lower of cost or market is usually for the entire portfolio of temporary investments rather than for individual items. Today, most companies carry their temporary marketable securities at cost—even if cost is above current market—with a parenthetical notation of the lower market price. This method has the advantage of permitting the ledger accounts to remain at the same level as that required for income tax purposes and still affords full disclosure in the balance sheet. This method is often followed when there is no intention of disposing of the securities in the immediate future and when objection is raised to adjusting the records for what might prove to be a temporary condition at the balance sheet date.

The preceding paragraph does not prohibit the establishment of an allowance for declines when market price is materially below cost.

ILLUSTRATION. The establishment of an allowance for decline in temporary investments may be illustrated as follows: Assume that temporary marketable securities which cost $200,000 on March 1, 1975, have a market price of $168,000 on December 31, 1975. An allowance may be established, as follows:

Unrealized Loss from Temporary Investment Declines. 32,000
   Allowance for Decline in Temporary Investments   32,000

The Unrealized Loss from Temporary Investments account is closed to the Profit and Loss account and appears in the "other expense" section of the income statement. The allowance for decline in temporary investments may appear in the balance sheet as a deduction from the securities, at cost; or the securities may be stated at market, with the cost appearing parenthetically. If, in 1976, the securities are sold for $160,000, the 1976 income statement would show a loss of $8,000 for income tax purposes, the 1976 loss would be $40,000.

Securities of Dealers. Securities held as stock in trade may be priced at cost, market, or the lower of cost or market. Normally, security dealers carry their securities at the lower of cost or market, with a parenthetical notation of the higher figure.

In the balance sheets of brokerage firms, securities in trading accounts and investments accounts, including short-position securities, are commonly carried at market, without indicating cost or the sales proceeds of short-position securities. If securities are carried at market, which price is in excess of cost, provision should be made for income taxes on the unrealized profit; or the market price should be reduced by the applicable taxes, with full disclosure given the situation.

Securities of Investment Companies. For balance sheet purposes, marketable securities of investment companies may be carried at cost, with market price stated parenthetically, or at market, with cost stated parenthetically. The balance sheet of an investment company should be supported by the detail of the investments. In addition, Regulation S–X, Rule 6.02–9, of the Securities and Exchange Commission, with respect to management investment companies and the applicable federal income taxes, states:

Appropriate provision shall be made, on the basis of the applicable tax laws, for federal income taxes that it is reasonably believed are, or will become, payable in respect of (a) current net income, (b) realized gains on investments, and (c) unrealized appreciation on investments. The company's status as a "regulated investment company" as defined in Supplement Q of the Internal Revenue Code as amended shall be stated in a note referred to in the appropriate statements. Such note shall also indicate briefly the principal assumptions on which the company has relied in making or not making provisions for such taxes.

Long-Term Investments. The underlying basis for the valuation of long-term stock investments is cost. In the event that long-term stock investments have declined materially in price since the date of acquisition and over a long period of time, the extent of the decline should be reflected parenthetically in the balance sheet. Long-term stock investments in noncontrolled companies normally are required for income purposes, and the return on cost is the true indication of real productivity; therefore, current market fluctuations are of less importance. Today, stock investments in subsidiary companies commonly are carried at cost adjusted for profits, losses, and dividends—the equity method.

Consideration must be given to advances to subsidiary companies, since they usually constitute parent company investments. The form of the advances might be represented by notes, bonds, or stocks; but regardless of the form, an investment exists. If the investment is carried at cost, the auditor should analyze the retained earnings and other equity accounts of the subsidiary company since the date of acquisition to be certain that those accounts of the subsidiary company have not been used to "window dress" the balance sheet of the parent company. If the investments in subsidiary company stocks were originally recorded at a price other than cost, there should be an item of goodwill or capital surplus involved.

Long-term investments in bonds may be carried at original cost plus amortized discount, or minus amortized premium, but commonly are carried at cost.

Mortgages should be shown separately from bonds, and allowances for doubtful collection should be established, where necessary.

Investments in funds should be set forth in accordance with the intention of establishing the funds. For example, bond retirement funds and nontrusteed pension funds are not current assets.

Life Insurance. Under the purpose test, the cash surrender value or the loan value of life insurance, wherein the company is the beneficiary, should be shown as a long-term investment of the beneficiary company.

If a policy is pledged with the insurance company as security for a loan, the amount of the loan may be deducted from the cash surrender or loan value of the policy and the net remaining cash values shown in the balance sheet. The report should disclose the loan, since borrowing against the policy tends to defeat the purpose for which the insurance was written. In the balance sheet, the subtraction of the loan from the cash value is permissible on the basis that the loan is not against the borrower but against the policy. If a loan on a policy is not paid prior to policy cancellation or maturity, the amount of the loan is deducted by the insurance company and the net amount due paid to the beneficiary.

If the policy is pledged with any lender other than the insurance company, the loan is an obligation of the borrower and should be shown as a liability—current or other, depending upon the loan agreement; the cash surrender value or the loan value of the policy should be shown gross in this case, in the long-term investment section of the balance sheet.

Miscellaneous

Assume that a corporation owns some of its capital stock as treasury stock. If the corporation declares and pays *capital stock* dividends, a proper number of dividend shares should be issued to the corporate treasury. In this way, the corporation would maintain the same—and proper—ratio of treasury shares to total shares issued and outstanding after the stock dividended as existed before the stock dividend. The same number of dollars of retained earnings per dividend share should be capitalized for the dividend shares issued to the treasury stock and to the stock outstanding. The balance sheet should indicate the additional shares held in the treasury—and the treasury shares should be shown at original acquisition cost, in order to indicate the restriction on retained earnings.

QUESTIONS

1. You are engaged in the examination of the financial statements of Goings, Inc. and its recently acquired subsidiary, Gone Corporation. In acquiring Gone Corporation, during 1974, Goings, Inc. exchanged a large number of its shares of common stock for 90 percent of the outstanding common stock of Gone Corporation in a transaction that was accounted for as a pooling of interests. Goings, Inc. is now preparing the annual report to shareholders and proposes to include in the report combined financial statements for the year ended December 31, 1975 with a footnote describing its exchange of stock for that of Gone Corporation. Goings, Inc. also proposes to include in its report the financial statements of the previous year as they appeared in Goings, 1974 annual report along with a five-year financial summary from Goings' prior annual reports, all of which had been accompanied by your unqualified audit opinion.

   Discuss the objectives or purposes of the standard of reporting which requires that the auditor's report state whether generally accepted accounting principles have been consistently observed over the past two periods.

   (AICPA, adapted)

2. A CPA is examining the financial statements of the Norwood Corporation for the year ended June 30, 1976. Approximately 95 percent of the assets of the Norwood Corporation consist of investments in the stocks of subsidiary companies. None of these stocks is actively traded. The CPA has satisfied himself that investments are properly stated at cost and that the equity in the underlying assets of the subsidiaries, which is to be shown in a footnote, has been properly computed based upon the unaudited financial statements of the subsidiaries. Under these circumstances what type of opinion should the CPA render on the financial statements of the Norwood Corporation be?

   (AICPA, adapted)

3. How should each of the following be classified on the balance sheet?
   a) Bonds acquired July 1, 1975, for $107,000, and which mature April 1, 1984, for $100,000.
   b) A bond redemption fund administered by three trustees under a trust indenture agreement.
   c) Listed stock rights that are to be sold.
   d) Stock that is intended to be transferred to a supplier in cancellation of trade account payable.
   e) Cash surrender value of officers' life insurance with the company being the beneficiary.
   f) Cash surrender value of officers' life insurance whose premiums are paid by the company but the officers' spouses are the beneficiaries.
   g) Stock held for purposes of controlling the activities of a subsidiary.
   h) Parking lot for customers' convenience.
   i) Land acquired for an expansion program at least five years from now.
   j) Advances to a subsidiary company.
   k) United States Treasury Bills acquired to provide income for idle cash during the slack season.

    l)   A company's own bonds in a bond retirement fund.

    m) Accrued interest on company's own bonds held in the bond retirement fund.

    n)   A fund to be used to pay current bond interest.

    o)   A preferred stock redemption fund.

    p)   A profit sharing plan whose beneficiaries are the salaried employees of the company administered by three company-appointed trustees.

4. On April 1, 1975, the Bridge Company invested some of its plant expansion fund cash in bonds issued by the local school district. The corporation paid $95,000 for one hundred $1,000, six percent bonds due in 10 years. Interest is paid semiannually on April 1 and October 1. Show how the bonds should be presented on the company's balance sheet at the end of 1975.

5. What type of an opinion should a CPA render under the following circumstances? Do not consider any other conditions or circumstances.

    a)   Woof, Inc. owns properties which have substantially appreciated in value since purchase. The properties were appraised by competent appraisers and are reported in the balance sheet at the appraised values with full disclosure. The CPA believes that the values reported in the balance sheet are reasonable.

    b)   Kitty Corporation has material investments in stocks of subsidiary companies. Stocks of the subsidiary companies are not actively traded in the market, and the CPA's engagement does not extend to any subsidiary company. The CPA is able to satisfy himself that all investments are carried at original cost, and he has no reason to suspect that the amounts are not stated fairly.

    c)   Growl, Inc. has large investments in stocks of subsidiary companies, but the investments are not material in relation to the financial position and results of operations of Growl. Stocks of the subsidiary companies are not actively traded in the market, and the CPA's engagement does not extend to any subsidiary company. The CPA is able to satisfy himself that all investments are carried at original cost, and he has no reason to suspect that the amounts are not fairly stated.

    d)   Meow Corporation has material investments in stocks of subsidiary companies. Stocks of the subsidiary companies are actively traded in the market, but the CPA's engagement does not extend to any subsidiary. Management insists that all investments shall be carried at cost, and the CPA is satisfied that the original costs are fairly presented. The CPA believes that the client will never ultimately realize a substantial portion of the investments, but there is no disclosure to this effect in the financial statements.

                                                      (AICPA, adapted)

6. Public accounting firms often develop and use a questionnaire to investigate and record their inquiries into a client's internal control system in order to determine if there are weaknesses in internal control.

    Prepare an internal control questionnaire pertaining to securities (short-term and long-term investments) held by a medium-sized manufacturing company.

                                                             (AICPA)

7. In the audit of any investment security, state six requisites that would lead to the rendition of an unqualified opinion regarding the investment securities.

8. Prepare an audit program setting forth the procedures you would follow in an examination in which one of the most important phases involves investment securities of material amounts in stocks, bonds, and mortgages. Do *not* copy the audit program of the text.

9. A corporation temporarily invested some of its excess funds in government securities. In the course of your preliminary audit work, you ascertain that all the securities were acquired at various dates during the year under examination through a brokerage firm and that the securities are in the name of the client corporation but are being held in safekeeping by the brokerage firm. The corporation does not maintain an investment ledger.

   Outline the audit procedures for the bonds and the revenue therefrom, as reflected in the records of the corporation.

10. Prepare a list of columnar headings for work papers, and the source or sources of information from which you would enter data in each column, for (*a*) short-term investments in bonds and (*b*) long-term investments in stocks.

11. Why is it necessary that an auditor devote attention to bond numbers and stock certificate numbers when examining investment securities?

12. *a*) On December 31, 1975, the Tab Company mailed stock rights to all shareholders. You were auditing the records of the company as of that date. What is the effect of the issued rights on the December 31, 1975, balance sheet?

    b) On December 31, 1975, the Bat Company received $75,000 of subscriptions brought about by the issuance of stock rights on December 15, 1975. You were auditing the records of the Bat Company as of December 31, 1975. What is the effect of the subscriptions on the balance sheet? How would you audit the subscriptions?

13. You were auditing the records of John Crow as of December 31, 1975. One account was with a stock brokerage firm. The account showed (*a*) margin stocks, $500,000; and (*b*) due to the broker, $200,000. The market price of the stock was $600,000. How would you show this situation in the balance sheet of Crow? Crow intimated that he would like to have the balance sheet reflect an equity in the stocks of the difference between market price and the amount due to the broker.

14. Your client is a trader in securities. On December 31, 1975, the client was "long" in the market to the extent of $232,000 in one stock as of November 30, 1975, quotations. He was "short" in another stock to the extent of $154,000 as of the same date. As of December 31, 1975 the market price of the long stock was $236,000; the market price of the short stock was $156,000. How should this situation be reflected in the client's balance sheet?

15. *a*) To what extent should an auditor investigate a client's ownership of real estate and mortgages?

b) Why should fire insurance policies covering mortgaged properties be examined when a client holds the mortgage?

16. Finance, Inc., one of your clients, is engaged—in part—in the purchase of mortgage notes. During the current examination year, you find that the company has purchased from the City Bank mortgage notes from several individuals. Of the notes, some were purchased at par, some at a premium, and others at a discount. Each note purchased requires equal payments each month to cover both principal and interest. By agreement, each mortgagor pays fixed monthly amounts to cover insurance and property taxes. The seller of the mortgage notes continues to service them, remitting each month to Finance, Inc., the payments received for principal and interest; the seller retains the payments for taxes and insurance in escrow until the tax bills and insurance invoices are received for payment.
   a) Name the documents that should be on hand in support of your client's investment.
   b) Outline the steps you would take in the audit of the transactions, covering both principal and interest features.

17. In 1965, James Moser established a large philanthropic fund, incorporated in a certain state. The fund assets are composed of high-grade investment securities donated by Moser. Under the terms of the fund, the State Trust Company was to appoint an Executive Committee charged with supervision of the investment activities and the operating activities of the fund. General operations are administered by a general manager.

   Of the fund revenue, approximately 10 percent is required for administration; remaining revenue is donated to assist in the erection of medical colleges for universities. Final approval for contributions rests with the Executive Committee; it is not necessary that the annual revenue be distributed in the year of earning. The beneficiary of a contribution is required to donate a certain portion of the construction costs of the project, and the contribution from the fund is contingent upon the approval of construction plans by its medical staff and the submission of architects' certificates for work complete.

   In connection with the audit of the fund for the year ended December 31, 1975:
   a) Describe four operations which should be performed in the verification of the investments and the investment revenue.
   b) Describe four operations for the verification of donation disbursements.

   (AICPA, adapted)

18. A building and loan company holds a large number of mortgages on real estate. How should these mortgages be examined every six months, at which dates reports must be filed with the Department of Commerce of the state of incorporation? How should the mortgage revenue be verified?

19. Present procedures for the verification of transactions in a sinking fund for the redemption of bonds when the fund is in the custody of an independent trustee.

PROBLEMS

1. During your audit of the 1975 financial statements of Cranston, Inc., you discover a new account titled "Miscellaneous Assets." Your examination reveals that in 1975 Cranston, Inc., began investing excess cash in marketable securities and the corporation's accountant entered all transactions he believed related to investments in this account. Information summarized from the account appears below:

CRANSTON, INC.

Information Summarized from
The Miscellaneous Assets Account
For the Year Ended December 31, 1975

Date 1975		Folio	Debit	Credit
	Compudata common stock:			
Mar. 31	Purchased 500 shares @ 48		$24,000	
July 31	Received cash dividend of $2 per share			$ 1,000
July 31	Sold 100 shares @ 60			6,000
Nov. 15	Pledged 100 shares as security for $4,000 bank loan payable February 15, 1976			4,000
Nov. 30	Received 150 shares by donation from stockholder whose cost in 1968 was $10 per share		1,500	
	Standard Atomic common stock:			
Mar. 31	Purchased 900 shares @ 26		23,400	
June 30	Received dividend ($0.25 per share in cash and one share Standard Atomic preferred for each five shares common owned)			225
	Standard Atomic preferred stock:			
June 30	Received 180 shares as stock dividend on Standard Atomic common			
July 31	Sold 80 shares @ 17			1,360
	Interstate Airlines bonds (due November 30, 1985, with interest at 6% payable May 31 and November 30):			
June 30	Purchased 25 $1,000 bonds @ 102		25,625	
Nov. 30	Received interest due			750
Nov. 30	Accumulated amortization			25
Nov. 30	Sold 25 bonds @ 101			25,250
	Other:			
July 31	Sold 40 shares of Evanston, Inc., treasury stock: @ 82 (purchased in 1973 at $80 per share—carried at cost).			3,280
Dec. 29	Paid 1976 rental charge on safe deposit box used for investments		35	
			$74,560	$41,890

All purchases include brokers' fees and sales are net of brokers' fees and taxes when applicable. The fair market values (net of brokers' fees and taxes) for each security as of the 1975 date of each transaction were:

Security	3/31	6/30	7/31	11/15	11/30
Compudata common	48		60	61¼	62
Standard Atomic common.	26	30			
Standard Atomic preferred		16⅔	17		
Interstate Airlines bonds		102			101
Cranston, Inc., common			82		

Prepare a work sheet to distribute or correct each of the transactions entered in the Miscellaneous Assets account. Ignore income taxes. Prepare separate entries for each transaction. Combine adjustments in one formal entry. The following column heading are recommended for your work sheet, plus those in the problem.

ADJUSTMENTS TO DISTRIBUTE AND CORRECT ITEMS IN THE MISCELLANEOUS ASSETS ACCOUNT

Miscellaneous Assets Debit (Credit)	Investments Debit (Credit)	(Gain) Loss from Sale of Investments	(Income) from Dividends and Interest	Other Accounts Name of Account	Debit (Credit)

(AICPA, adapted)

2. Snorkel, Inc., has various long-term investments and maintains its records on the accrual basis. The records for the year ended December 31, 1975, have not been closed. An analysis of the Investment account for the year follows:

SNORKEL, INC.

Analysis of Investment Account
Year Ended December 31, 1975

1975	Transactions	Account per Client Debit	Credit
Jan. 3	5,000 shares Backand Oil Co.	$ 5,000	
	1,000 shares General Corp.	33,500	
	50 shares, 6% Pfd. Grey Steel	6,000	
	$100,000 4% bonds, Martin Co.	10,225	
Feb. 10	Purchased 5,000 shares, Wash Motors	15,000	
Mar. 1	Cash dividend, Grey Steel		$ 300
Apr. 1	Interest, Martin Co. bonds		200
May 15	Sold 800 rights, General Corp.		1,200
May 16	Exercised 200 rights, General Corp. to purchase		
	50 shares, General Corp.	2,250	
Aug. 5	Sold 200 shares, Wash Motors		2,500
Oct. 1	Sold 100 shares, General Corp.		3,350
Sept. 18	Interest, Martin Co. bonds		200
		$71,975	$7,750

Your work papers for the year ended December 31, 1974, show the following securities in the Investment account:

Date of Acquisition	Number of Shares or Face Value of Bonds	Type of Security	Name of Issuer	Amount
Jan. 2, 1967	5,000	Common stock, no par value	Backand Oil Co.	$ 5,000
Apr. 1, 1968.	1,000	Common stock, $100 par value	General Corp.	33,500
Nov. 15, 1968. . . .	50	6% preferred stock, par value $100	Grey Steel	6,000
Oct. 1, 1973	$10,000	4% bonds	Martin Co.	10,225
				$54,725

After inquiry the following additional data were obtained:

(1) The General Corporation on May 12 issued warrants representing the right to purchase, at $45 per share, one share for every four shares held. On May 12 the market value of the stock rights-on was $50 and ex-rights was $49. Snorkel, Inc. sold 800 rights on May 15 when the market price of the stock was $51. On May 16, 200 rights were exercised.

(2) On June 30 Wash Motors declared a reverse stock split of one for five. One share of new $0.50 par value common was exchanged for five shares of old $0.10 par value common.

(3) Snorkel, Inc. acquired the Martin Company bonds, which are due September 30, 1978, for $10,300. Interest: April 1 and October 1.

(4) The sale of 100 shares of General Corporation stock was from the 1,000 shares purchased April 1, 1968. The stock was sold for $65 per share.

(5) The government of Backand in early 1975 confiscated the assets of the Backand Oil Company and nationalized it. Despite the protest of the United States, the Backand government has refused to recognize any claims of the stockholders or management of the Backand Oil Company.

Prepare a work sheet showing the adjustments to arrive at the correct Investment account balance at December 31, 1975. The work sheet should include the names of other accounts affected by the adjustments or reclassifications. (Formal journal entries are required. Supporting computations should be in good form.)

(AICPA, adapted)

3. Your client, who uses the accrual basis of accounting, owns stock in the Cogent Investment Trust. In the process of auditing his records for the year ended December 31, 1975, you prepared the following Dividends Received account; all amounts are cash receipts.

Dividends Received

February 29	$ 6.72
April 25	354.31
July 25	322.10
October 25	.45
Balance per records, December 31, 1975	$683.58

During 1975, your client did not purchase or sell any shares. It was established by confirmation from the client's broker that 3,183 shares of this stock were owned by the client on December 31, 1974, and 3,245 shares were owned on December 31, 1975.

By referring to a national financial reporting service, you accumulated the following information:

COGENT INVESTMENT TRUST

Dividend Data: 1975

Declared: February 12, to stockholders of record February 19, payable February 26, a capital gain dividend of $0.14 per share payable in cash or, at option of stockholder, in paid-up shares at $11.55 per share; any fractional shares are payable in cash.

Declared: April 1, to stockholders of record April 8, payable April 22, a regular dividend of $0.11 per share.

Declared: October 7, to stockholders of record October 14, payable October 24, a capital gain dividend of $0.09 per share payable in cash, or at option of stockholder, in paid-up shares at $12.06 per share; any fractional shares are payable in cash.

Declared: December 9, to stockholders of record December 16, payable January 3, 1976, a regular dividend of $0.11 per share.

a) Prepare an analysis setting forth the number of Standard Investment Trust shares held by your client on January 1 and December 31, 1975, and accounting for the changes. Show your computations.

b) Prepare an analysis of your client's revenue from the trust shares, distinguishing between capital gains and dividend revenues.

c) Prepare any audit adjustments necessary as of December 31, 1975.

(AICPA, adapted)

4. John Guide uses a fiscal year ending March 31. A summary of his transactions in the capital stocks of the X Company is presented below, except for several cash dividends that have no bearing upon the situation. In all transactions, Guide uses the specific stock certificate identification method.

Guide was confused for the year ended March 31, 1976, and summons you to prepare schedules showing the computations of the following:

a) The remaining cost of the X Company common shares owned on March 31, 1976.

b) The gain or loss on sales of the stock and rights of the X Company for the year ended March 31, 1976.

The transactions in X Company common stock are as follows:

1969

June 6   Purchased 50 shares of X common, par $100 per share, at a total cost of $4,850.

1972

Apr. 15 Converted 50 shares of X preferred stock into 50 shares of X common, in accordance with the conversion privilege. The preferred shares originally cost $4,900, and the market price at conversion date was $96 per share. The market price of the common stock at April 15, 1972, was $101 per share.

1974

May 7 Received additional shares of X common in a two-for-one stock split, in which the par value was reduced from $100 to $50 per share.

June 6 Purchased 100 shares of X common at a total cost of $5,300.

Nov. 4 Exercised the option to receive one share of common stock for each 10 shares held, in lieu of a cash dividend of $5.40 for each share held. The market price of a share was $54.

1975

Nov. 2 Received stock dividend equal to 20 percent of the common shares held.

1976

Jan. 4 Received warrants representing the right to purchase at par one share of X common for each 10 shares of common owned. On the date of the issuance of the warrants, the market price of the stock ex-rights was $58, and the market price of the rights was $2 each.

Jan. 15 Guide exercised the 100 rights applicable to the block of shares purchased on June 6, 1974, and sold all remaining rights. The net proceeds from the sale of the rights amounted to $1.80 per right.

Mar. 12 Sold 60 shares of X common for $3,240 net. The shares were identified as 50 of those purchased on June 6, 1974, and 10 of those purchased on January 15, 1976.

(AICPA adapted)

5. From the following information:

   a) Prepare a work sheet analyzing the Investment account for the period January 1, 1975, to September 30, 1975, showing transactions, adjustments, and final balance as of September 30, 1975.

   b) Prepare the necessary audit adjustments to correct the following Investment account as of September 30, 1975, appearing in the records of the Paint Company:

Date		Explanation	Debit	Credit
1975				
Jan.	1	Balance	188,300	
	31	Sold Red stock		21,364
Mar.	31	Bought White common	12,125	
June	30	Dividend on Blue common	10,000	
July	31	Sold Blue common		8,750
Aug.	31	Sold Green bonds		22,500
Sept.	30	Interest on Brown mortgage		500

The audit work papers of the preceding year show that the account balance as of January 1, 1975, consisted of the following:

Red Company common:

1,000 shares, purchased in June, 1967, @ $20 per share	$ 20,000
2,000 shares, purchased in August, 1969, @ $16 per share.	32,000
1,500 shares, purchased in May, 1972, @ $22 per share	33,000

White Company common:

2,000 shares, purchased in January, 1973, @ $33 per share	66,000

Blue Company common:

100 shares, purchased in August, 1968, @ $73 per share (par $100)	7,300

Green Company 5 percent bonds:

20 bonds, $1,000 each, purchased in July, 1971, @ par (interest dates February and August 1)	20,000

Brown Company chattel mortgage on machinery:

5 percent, $10,000 mortgage taken in September, 1974, in settlement of a receivable	10,000
	$188,300

Your examination discloses the following:

(1) In January, 1975, 1,000 shares of the Red Company common stock purchased in May, 1972, were sold for $21,364, net of brokerage.

(2) In March, 1975, 500 shares of White Company common stock were purchased at $24 per share plus brokerage, for $12,125.

(3) In June, 1975, the Blue Company paid a 100 percent stock dividend—common on common.

(4) In July, 1975, the Paint Company sold to its president, for $125 per share, 100 shares of Blue Company common stock, for which the president gave his check for $8,750 and a letter in which he agreed to pay the balance upon demand of the treasurer of the company.

(5) On August 1, 1975, the Green Company redeemed its five percent bonds at 110 plus accrued interest.

(6) In September, 1975, the Paint Company received one year's interest on the $10,000 chattel mortgage of the Brown Company which it holds.

6. As auditor for the Adams Company, you are to prepare the following:

   a) Work papers for the securities and for security transactions for the year ended December 31, 1975, including columns for the following:

     (1) Securities inventory at December 31, 1974, divided into security name, number of shares, cost, and average cost per share.

     (2) Security purchases in 1975, divided into date, shares, and amount.

     (3) Security sales in 1975, divided into date, shares, amount, average cost of shares sold, and profit or loss on sales.

     (4) Securities inventory at December 31, 1975, divided into name of security, shares, and cost.

     (5) Dividends received in 1975.

   b) Audit adjustment for all security transactions.

Marketable securities owned by the Adams Company at December 31, 1974:

Security A, 1,500 shares, at a cost of.	$120,000
Security B, 1,200 shares, at a cost of.	84,000
Security C, 1,000 shares, at a cost of.	130,000
Security D, 800 shares, at a cost of.	85,000
Security E, 1,000 shares, at a cost of.	70,000
	$489,000

Security transactions for 1975 are as shown in the two tables following:

Purchases	Shares	Cost
April 15	500 A	$50,000
April 25	200 F	15,000
July 15.	300 G	40,000
July 25.	200 D	20,000
August 15	200 D	25,000
September 15	1,000 G	90,000

Sales	Shares	Cost
March 10.	200 C	$ 30,000
April 10	1,200 B	110,000
June 15	300 C	50,000
August 20	1,000 E	30,000
September 15	1,000 A	125,000

Other data are as follows:
(1) Cash dividends received, 1975: A, $12,000; C, $6,000; D, $5,000; and F, $1,000.
(2) Stock dividend received on June 15, 1975; E, 100 percent.
(3) Market price of securities at December 31, 1975: $565,000.

(AICPA, adapted)

7. Camp Right, Inc. completed the following transactions relative to its acquisition of stocks to be held as permanent investments:
January 10, 1975
Purchased 100 shares of Knives Corp. Class A common stock at $70 plus brokerage fees and transfer commissions in the amount of $300.
March 6, 1975
Purchased for a lump sum of $75,000, the following stocks of Bars, Inc.

Stock	Number of Shares	Market Price at Date of Purchase
Preferred, $100 par	200	$ 90
Class A, Common, $50 par	200	60
Class B, No-par common	200	150

April 15, 1975
Purchased 300 additional shares of Knives Corp. Class A common at $80 per share plus brokerage fees and transfer commissions in the amount of $1,020.
June 30, 1975
Received a share for share stock dividend on the Knives Corp, common stock.
August 15, 1975
Sold 400 shares of Knives Corp, Class A common stock at $45 per share (Use the FIFO method in recording the sale).
September 30, 1975
Received a two-for-one stock split on the common stock of Bars, Inc.

November 30, 1975
　　Received the following cash dividends:
　　　　Knives Corp. common stock—$5.00 per share.
　　　　Bars, Inc. preferred—6%
　　　Bars, Inc. Class A Common—$3.00 per share
　　　　Bars, Inc. Class B no-par common—$1.00 per share.
　a)　Prepare entries for Camp Right, Inc. for the above transactions. Pre-
　　　pare calculations for explanations to your entries. Use cost method
　　　and FIFO method for disposition of stock.
　b)　Prepare an audit work paper showing the composition of the long-
　　　term investments at December 31, 1975.

8.　From broker's invoices and communications received by your client, you
　　determine that the following investment transactions have taken place
　　during 1975:

Feb. 21　Purchased 500 shares of Geographic Industries at 80½ plus
　　　　brokerage charge of $250.
July 1　Received a 50 percent stock dividend.
Oct. 1　Received stock rights permitting the purchase of one share at
　　　　$60 for every 4 shares held. On this date rights were being
　　　　traded at $3 each and stock was being traded at $72 per share.
Nov. 15　Exercised 500 rights which pertained to the stock acquired on
　　　　February 21, and sold remaining rights at 2½ less brokerage
　　　　charges of $10.
Dec. 27　Sold 200 shares from the holdings acquired on February 21 at
　　　　70½ less brokerage charges of $100.

　a)　Prepare the necessary journal entries to record the foregoing transac-
　　　tions. (Be sure and support your entries with computations.)
　b)　Prepare the investment account balance on December 31, 1975, show-
　　　ing the shares and costs making up the balance.

PRACTICE MATERIAL ASSIGNMENTS

Metalcraft, Incorporated: Audit Problem:
　Assignment 4: Marketable Securities and Related Revenue.
　Assignment 7: Section B: Sinking Fund Investment.
Colby Gears, Inc.: Holmes and Moore Audit Case:
　Marketable Securities. Investment in Subsidiary.

18
Prepaid Expenses, Deferred Charges, and Matching Expenses

Audit Objectives

The objectives of the auditor are to ascertain that the dollar amounts of prepaid expenses and deferred charges are determined in accordance with generally accepted accounting principles and that their amounts are reasonable when viewed from the standpoint of future benefits to be derived, and that they have been properly authorized.

SECTION I: PREPAID EXPENSES AND DEFERRED CHARGES

The proper determination of periodic net income involves the matching of revenues and related expenses by properly timing the charging of prepaid items to expense. Accurate income statements include that portion of prepaid items chargeable against the revenues of the current period. Accurate balance sheet disclosure of prepaid items is a result of determining the portion of the prepaid items chargeable against the revenues of future periods.

Prepaid expenses and deferred charges are considered in the same chapter, although prepaid expenses are classed as current assets and deferred charges are separately set forth. By documentary evidence and by record examination, the auditor must determine that amounts carried forward as prepaid expenses or deferred charges actually are chargeable to the operations of future periods, and that the methods of amortization of the respective items are in accordance with accepted accounting principles.

585

Prepaid Expenses

Short-term prepaid items are classified as current assets in accordance with recognized accounting principles. Current assets include those that will be consumed during the normal business operating cycle. Short-term prepaid expenses usually represent expenditures for services and supplies acquired prior to the balance sheet date but not consumed at that date, and which are properly chargeable against the revenues of subsequent periods, and which will be consumed in the normal operating cycle. If an amount paid in advance did not exist, cash for the services or supplies would be required in the subsequent period at the time of converting products or services into receivables and cash. Selling prices include *not only* inventory costs but all other expired costs—including the absorbed portion of prepaid items and the write-off of deferred charges and depreciation. But *if the "turnover" is within the normal operating cycle*, the item is classified as a current asset.

Prepaid expenses represent working capital, they may have a going-concern realizable value, and they usually constitute items that will be converted into expenses in a short time.

Deferred Charges

Long-term deferred charges arise from services and items that have been acquired but that will be converted into expenses only over a period of time longer than the normal operating cycle. Compared with prepaid expenses, deferred charges usually represent long-term intangible items not possessing going-concern conversion values, as exemplified by plant rearrangement costs, future business costs, research and development costs, leasehold premiums, unamortized bond discounts, stock issuance underwriting costs, long-term advance contract costs, suspense debits, and other similar items for which a future period will derive income benefit. Income should be realized from the use of a deferred charge; and by the time the benefits cease, the entire cost of the deferred charge should be charged against revenues derived.

Thus, for both prepaid expenses and deferred charges, it is necessary to allocate used portions to current expense—on the basis of expiration and derived revenue usage, and to establish as assets the currently unused portions of the items which will benefit future periods.

Methods of Allocating Short-Term Prepayments and Long-Term Deferred Charges

The method of allocating short-term prepaid expenses and long-term deferred charges to expense is generally dependent upon the characteristics and use of each item. Three methods of allocation follow:

1. *The time basis,* where the item expires exactly or approximately in proportion to elapsed time.
   a) *Prepaid expenses.*
      (1) Unexpired insurance premiums.
      (2) Prepaid rent and lease costs.
      (3) Taxes paid in advance.
      (4) Interest deducted in advance.
   b) *Deferred charges.*
      (1) Unamortized bond discount and issuance costs.
      (2) Plant rearrangement and moving costs—or 2 (*b*) (4), below.
      (3) Stock issuance underwriting costs.
      (4) Long-time advance contract costs.
      (5) Public utility service deposits.
      (6) Last month rent deposit.
2. *The revenue basis,* where the item expires in proportion to revenue produced by its use.
   a) *Prepaid expenses.*
      (1) Currently unused prepaid advertising.
      (2) Prepaid selling expenses—sometimes 2 (*b*) (3), below.
      (3) Commissions paid in advance.
      (4) Unused royalties.
      (5) Salary advances.
      (6) Subscriptions and dues paid in advance.
   b) *Deferred charges.*
      (1) Research and development costs.
      (2) Experimental costs.
      (3) Promotion expense.
      (4) Plant rearrangement and moving costs—or 1 (*b*) (2), above.
3. *The inventory basis,* where the items are charged to expense on a usage basis.
   a) *Prepaid expenses.*
      (1) Unused office supplies and factory supplies.
   b) *Deferred charges.*
      (1) Performance bond costs.

Occasionally, the circumstances surrounding any particular prepaid expense or deferred charge cause it to shift from one basis of allocation to another. In those instances where the benefits to be derived cannot be precisely correlated to specific time periods, or to usage, or to sales revenue or production, but where at the same time it is quite certain that future periods will benefit, generally accepted accounting practice dictates that the prepaid expense or deferred charge be written off as rapidly as is reasonable in the circumstances.

If doubt exists as to the future benefit of a prepaid expense or a deferred charge, it should be written off in entirety, so that net income and assets are not overstated. The tendency today is toward rapid or immediate write-off of questionable prepaid expenses and deferred charges provided that income and assets are not *understated.*

ILLUSTRATION. A deficit should not be hidden by failure to absorb
   expenses improperly deferred, as brought forth in the case of a company
   which did not amortize prepaid expenses and deferred charges during the
   first five years of its six-year existence.

Certain development costs of early years of operation sometimes are set up as deferred charges to be written off in subsequent years as revenues are produced. However, these items should not be permanently capitalized, and their nature should be revealed in financial statement footnotes, and necessary comments should be made in the audit report. The items should not be capitalized merely to show a net income in early years.

Comments on the Examination of Prepaid Expenses and Deferred Charges

Normally, prepaid expenses and deferred charges are not of material amount when compared with current or total assets. Also, the expense portion of prepaid expenses and deferred charges charged off normally is not material when compared with sales, cost of goods sold, or net income.

The examination of prepaid expenses is primarily one involving the calculation of amounts prepaid and amounts to be charged to expense in the current period, or the test verification of client calculations.

Casualty insurance expenses commonly are examined during the course of the audit of prepaid expenses. Workmen's compensation insurance should be prorated to manufacturing, selling, and administration on the basis of the rates applicable to the payrolls involved; and all other types of insurance expense likewise must be properly prorated. The various types of insurance expense should be compared with the same expense of the prior year; major variations should be investigated.

The examination of deferred charges often requires mature judgment in the proper allocation of costs to expense, as opposed to routine calculations or verifications for the majority of prepaid expenses.

Work papers should be prepared for each item in a manner so that reference to them at a later date will reveal adequate information. Upon completion of the work papers, both the results therein and the methods used should be reviewed with the proper client personnel so that all data are clear to all parties concerned.

Mathematical computations of *material* amounts should be verified in order to assure the propriety of asset and expense elements. Documentary evidences of original acquisition are examined, and the transactions traced to the accounts for amounts and items of consequence. Confirmations should be obtained for rental, service, and similar deposits. The policies of a client with respect to the amortization of prepaid expenses and deferred charges should be discussed and understood. The amounts of prepaid expenses at the beginning and at the close of a fiscal period should be compared to determine the effect on working capital of increases or decreases in the items.

Management Reports

For prepaid expenses and long-term deferred charges, internally prepared reports for management purposes are of importance primarily in connection with prepaid insurance, and deferred research and development expenses. Normally, other prepaid items and deferred charges are either immaterial in amount or are so automatically necessary or are so obvious that report preparation is not necessary; reporting for these items is in the realm of expense and authorization control.

Reports submitted to management concerning insurance are necessary so that decisions may be made regarding the propriety and adequacy of insurance coverage in the light of changing price levels and changing operating conditions within a company. With regard to deferred development and research expenses, management should decide upon the amounts period over which such items are to be amortized.

SECTION II: INTERNAL CONTROL OF PREPAID EXPENSES AND DEFERRED CHARGES

Proper internal control over prepaid expenses demands that they be currently reviewed to determine that they are in force and that they are neither overstated nor understated. If refunds are available, internal control should determine that the refunds are properly controlled and deposited in a bank.

Proper internal control over deferred charges is to the effect that a periodic review of the items be made to determine that they are stated in proper amount and to determine that amortizable amounts still remain. Long-term deferred charges should be established only by authority of the board of directors, or executive committee, or other top-level authority.

An internal control questionnaire for prepaid expenses and deferred charges is shown in Illustration 18–1.

ILLUSTRATION 18–1

INTERNAL CONTROL QUESTIONNAIRE
Prepaid Expenses and Deferred Charges

Company_____

Period Covered_____   Yes   No   Not Appli- cable   Remarks

1. Are capitalized items properly authorized?
2. Is amortization properly authorized or otherwise supported?
3. Are lump-sum charge-offs properly authorized?
4. When prepaid items are purchased, is the company policy uniform with regard to charges to assets and charges to expenses?
5. Is the insurance program reviewed periodically to determine:
   a) That the insurance is in force?
   b) That the insurance is adequate?
   c) That premiums are correct?
6. Is all insurance carried through one broker?
7. Are insurance premium payments compared with insurance policies and brokers' bills?
8. Are all insurance policies under the control of a person who does not have access to cash disbursements?
9. Are premium refunds and claims properly accounted for?
10. Do all insurance policies name the company as beneficiary?
11. Are all assets, for which the Company is responsible, covered by insurance?
12. Do you consider amortization to be proper for:
    a) Prepaid expenses?
    b) Deferred charges?
13. Are original debits to deferred charge accounts proper items to be deferred?
14. Do you consider deferred charges in the balance sheet to be of proper amount?

Prepared by_____   Reviewed by_____

Date_____   Date_____

SECTION III: AUDIT PROGRAM FOR PREPAID EXPENSES AND DEFERRED CHARGES

The following audit program applies to a variety of prepaid expenses and deferred charges considered in this chapter.

PREPAID EXPENSES

1. Prepaid insurance premiums:
   a)   Schedule and examine the policies.
   b)   Compare the prepaid insurance premiums and insurance expense.

   c) Examine refunds and claims.

   d) Determine the adequacy of the insurance.

2. Prepaid rent and lease costs:

   a) Verify rental payments rent agreements.

   b) Schedule prepaid rent.

   c) If appropriate, prorate deposits.

3. Taxes paid in advance:

   a) Schedule each type of tax.

   b) Compute or verify prepaid amounts.

4. Interest deducted in advance:

   a) Schedule the notes or other indebtedness.

   b) Calculate or verify the prepaid amount.

5. Commissions paid in advance:

   a) Investigate existing agreements.

   b) Confirm the advances.

   c) Verify the prepaid amounts from sales or other base.

   d) Charge off unrecoverable advances.

6. Advances to employees:

   a) Confirm, if necessary.

7. Prepaid selling expense:

   a) Schedule each item.

   b) Determine the applicability of each item to the future.

8. Dues and subscriptions paid in advance:

   a) Schedule and defer, if material.

9. Supplies inventories:

   a) Test quantities and prices.

   b) Test mathematical computations.

   c) Eliminate obsolete items.

DEFERRED CHARGES

10. Plant rearrangement costs:

   a) Verify costs.

   b) Examine the deferred charge for future benefits.

   c) Amortize properly.

11. Research and development, experimental, and promotional costs:

   a) Vouch costs.

   b) Determine future benefits.

   c) Amortize properly.

12. Public utility service deposits:

   a) Confirm.

   b) Determine the propriety of carrying forward.

13. Unamortized bond discount and expense:

   a) Analyze the account for correctness of amount.

   b) Verify the amortization.

   c) Remove unamortized amounts on partial debt retirements.

SHORT-TERM PREPAID EXPENSES

Prepaid Insurance Premiums

Common types of insurance involving prepayments are fire, burglary, theft, sprinkler, plate glass, messenger, boiler, tornado and windstorm, liability, holdup, elevator, fidelity, check forgery, use and occupancy, and workmen's compensation insurance.

Schedule and Examine the Policies and Invoices. Insurance policies should be scheduled either by the auditor or by the client, so that each policy is listed; for an example, see Illustration 18–2. The auditor should obtain the original policies and compare them with the insurance invoices. During the course of scheduling the policies (or verifying the client's schedule) and comparing them with the insurance invoices, the auditor should refer to his schedule of the last prior audit and note policy cancellations and new policies purchased. This is necessary in order to obtain a clue as to losses, policy cancellations, and the issuance of new policies.

Each policy should be written with the client as the sole beneficiary, or with a mortgagee as the beneficiary (in which case the policy will be in the hands of the mortgagee), or with the client as beneficiary with an endorsement to the mortgagee. If a policy is not drawn in favor of the client, or if a policy is recorded in an insurance register and is not on hand, or if paid checks indicate premium payments and the policy cannot be produced, a clue is immediately given that a liability should be on the records, since it is probable that a lien exists against the insured assets. If from the policies presented or from the insurance register, the auditor is doubtful of the insurance in force, he should obtain direct confirmation thereof from the broker of the insurance company.

When scheduled, the debit entries in the various insurance accounts should be vouched from the policies or the register, using insurance receipts and paid checks as payment evidence. In scheduling the policies, the auditor should be certain that all policies are submitted for examination. In order to accomplish this, he must (*a*) trace premium payments for the period if the internal control is poor or if there is reason to believe that all policies are not submitted; or (*b*) test premium payments sufficiently to prove that all policies are submitted.

ILLUSTRATION. A client insured his inventory for $325,000 under one fire insurance policy, which is submitted to the auditor. The auditor discovers an entry in the cash disbursements record for an additional premium payment covering the inventory, but a policy is not submitted. Upon inquiry, the broker confirmed the $325,000 of coverage *plus* an additional $100,000 of "specific" coverage based upon the monthly fluctuations in the inventory. The client did not submit the "specific" policy due to the fact that the insurance company had made certain refunds to the client under the specific coverage, which the client diverted to his private use.

Compute or Verify the Prepaid Insurance Premiums.   Insurance expense ordinarily is prorated over the life of the policy on a straight-line basis. The short-rate cancellation method is not used for an operating concern due to the normal expectation of continuing the insurance in force. In the event of bankruptcy and the preparation of a statement of affairs, cancellation values are used.

After work paper computation or verification of the amount of prepaid insurance and insurance expense, the auditor must, of course, compare these amounts with the amounts as shown by the client's records for both prepaid amounts and expenses.

In connection with workmen's compensation and liability insurance, it is entirely possible that a liability for additional premiums rather than a prepaid amount may exist at the balance sheet date. Payrolls are the basis for liability and compensation insurance; and in some states, an advance deposit is required. In order that the auditor may determine the existence of an unrecorded liability of this nature, he should proceed as follows: Take the total payroll from the policy date to the balance sheet date and multiply by the insurance rate; from this total, subtract the premiums paid in order to ascertain the existence of any additional liability. Excess premium payments are carried forward as prepaid expenses.

When insurance is carried with mutual insurance companies, the insured may be called upon for an additional premium payment if the mutual company operates at a loss. This possibility is so remote, however, that accepted practice is to the effect that there is no necessity for footnoting the balance sheet for such a contingency.

Examine Refunds and Claims.   Credits to insurance accounts are the result of policy cancellations and refunds for excess specific coverage. Data for these items appear in the cash receipts records, in policy endorsements, and in correspondence from the insurance broker.

If claims for reimbursement under policy protection have been filed with the insurance companies, those claims should be reflected in the financial statements of the client.

Determine the Adequacy of the Insurance.   In connection with the examination of insurance, one of the most important points is to ascertain that insurance coverage is adequate for all risks insured. Coinsurance clauses should be examined because they provide that the insured shall maintain insurance of at least 80 percent (assuming an 80 percent coinsurance clause) of the present sound value of the property and that failing to do so, the insured becomes a coinsurer to the extent of all amounts below 80 percent and to that extent must bear the proportionate loss. If the insurance carried is over 80 percent of the actual cash value, the coinsurance clause is automatically nonoperative and the insurance company is liable for the entire loss up to the face of the policy. In his report, the auditor should state his opinion concerning the adequacy of the insurance in force. By examination of insurance policies, the auditor frequently obtains indirectly information about changes in property values, disposition of assets, retirement of assets not disposed of, title to properties, and existence of liens and mortgages.

Inventories constantly fluctuate in volume and in total cost. In order to obtain adequate insurance for this fluctuating value—and yet not be overinsured—some firms carry a policy wherein the premium is based upon the average cost of the inventory, computed upon the submission of inventory figures to the insurance company each month.

Fidelity bond insurance should be compared with authorizations of the board of directors. In addition, the adequacy of the amount of the fidelity bond insurance should be reviewed from the standpoint of the requirements of the existing code of regulations of a corporation. If necessary, the auditor might suggest an appraisal of the fidelity bond in view of changes in the operations of the client or changes in specific personnel.

Deferred Compensation Plans

Many corporations today have deferred compensation plans that are covered by insurance policies. Under these plans the corporation will carry life insurance on its key executives and the company will be the beneficiary. However, these policies will furnish the funds to pay the designated parties in the deferred compensation plan agreement for the designated number of years. Since the company is the beneficiary, the premiums paid are charged to an expense account (or to Retained Earnings), and upon receipt of the value of the policy, the liability for the deferred compensation plan will be set up. Under these conditions, payments under the agreement will be charged to the liability account. However, this is a deductible expense for federal income tax purposes and will be so recognized.

In order for the tax return and the company records to be reconciled, the Retained Earnings reconciliation on the tax return will show the amount of deferred compensation plan agreement paid each year. Since this type of policy as well as other life insurance policies having the company the beneficiary are significant, the auditor must review these policies and prepare schedules for them similar to the other policies in Illustration 18–2. It would also be desirable to directly confirm the existence of such policies as shown in Illustration 18–3. Particular attention must be given to the designated beneficiaries on such policies. If someone other than the company itself is the beneficiary, premium payments must be considered as an additional compensation to the employee. If the employee designates someone other than the company to be the beneficiary,

ILLUSTRATION 18-2

WORDEN COMPANY
Prepaid Insurance at December 31, 1975

					Initials	Date
Prepared By						
Approved By						

Company	Policy Number	Type of Coverage	Dollar Coverage	Policy Years	Policy Dates From	Policy Dates To	Premium	Expense 1975	Months Prepaid	Prepaid 12/31/75
United	U10FT	Fire and extended—buildings	$840,000.00	3	2/1/74	2/1/77	$6,480.00	$2,160.00√	13	$2,340.00√
Brentwood	B11FT	Fire and extended—machinery and fixtures	650,000.00	3	4/1/74	4/1/77	4,968.00	1,656.00√	15	2,070.00√
Brentwood	N12FT	Fire and extended—inventories—90% coinsurance	600,000.00	1	9/30/75	9/30/76	1,104.00∧	276.00√	9	828.00√
Superior	S13UF	Use and occupancy	100,000.00	1	7/1/75	7/1/76	216.00∧	108.00√	6	108.00√
Superior	S14MF	Money and securities	40,000.00	3	5/1/75	5/1/78	1,152.00∧	256.00√	28	896.00√
Brentwood	B1500	Open-stock burglary	30,000.00	3	4/1/74	4/1/77	1,512.00	504.00√	15	630.00√
Anderson	AX16PT	Auto liability	200,000.00	1	5/1/75	5/1/76	192.00∧	128.00	4	64.00√
Beech	BF17EP	Public liability	100,000.00	3	11/1/73	11/1/76	648.00	216.00√	10	180.00√
Beech	BF18ET	Elevator liability	100,000.00	1	7/1/75	7/1/76	200.00∧	100.00	6	100.00√
Bi-Low	HD19SY	Steam boiler	80,000.00	1	5/1/75	5/1/76	1,200.00∧	800.00√	4	400.00√
Borkin	YY20PR	Payroll robbery	60,000.00	1	7/1/75	7/1/76	540.00∧	270.00√	6	270.00√
Bi-Low	HD21WX	Water damage	20,000.00	1	7/1/75	7/1/76	480.00∧	240.00√	6	240.00√
Franklin	F122SD	Sprinkler leakage	20,000.00	1	6/1/75	6/1/76	120.00∧	70.00	5	50.00√
Equity	E123BB	Blanket position bond	50,000.00	3	6/1/74	6/1/77	1,656.00	552.00√	17	782.00√
								$7,336.00√		$8,958.00√⊙

⊙ Agrees with general ledger.
√ Calculations verified.
∧ Examined payment data.
  Examined all policies.
Notices of premium refunds were traced to cash receipts.
Each coverage appears to be adequate.

ILLUSTRATION 18–3

STANDARD CONFIRMATION INQUIRY
FOR LIFE INSURANCE POLICIES
Developed by
AMERICAN INSTITUTE OF CERTIFIED PUBLIC ACCOUNTANTS
LIFE OFFICE MANAGEMENT ASSOCIATION
MILLION DOLLAR ROUND TABLE

ORIGINAL
To be retained by Insurance Co.

November 8, 1975

Dear Sirs:

Please furnish the information requested below in items 1 through 9 (and also in items 10 through 12 if any of those items are checked) for the policies identified on lines A, B and C. This information is requested as of the date indicated. IF THE ANSWER TO ANY ITEM IS "NONE," PLEASE SO STATE. The enclosed envelope is provided for the return of one copy of this form to the accountant named below.

(Ins. Co.) Great West Life Assurance Company

22 Tacoma Boulevard

Cincinnati, Ohio 45224

(Accountant) L. R. Moellman, C.P.A.
14 Plaza Street
Toledo, Ohio 43451

The J. C. Minton Company
(Name of owner as shown on policy contracts)

Information requested as of 10/31/75

Request authorized by
J. C. Minton, President

			Col. A	Col. B
A.	Policy number		1133797	1132899
B.	Insured		J.D. Minton	J. C. Minton
C.	Beneficiaries as shown on policies (if verification requested in item 11) Col. A— The J. C. Minton Company Col. B— Roberta Minton, wife of J. C. Minton			
1.	Face amount of basic policy		$ 50,000.00	$ 50,000.00
2.	Values shown as of (insert date if other than date requested)			
3.	Premiums, including prepaid premiums, are paid to (insert date)		6/2/76	5/8/76
4.	Policy surrender value (excluding dividends, additions and indebtedness adjustments)		$ 2,706.28	$ 2,562.90
5.	Surrender value of all dividend credits, including accumulations and additions		$ None	$ None
6.	Termination dividend currently available on surrender		$ 86.07	$ 128.61
7.	Other surrender values available to policyowner	a. Prepaid premium value	$ 212.42	$ 248.60
		b. Premium deposit funds	$ None	$ None
		c. Other	$ None	$ None
8.	Outstanding policy loans, excluding accrued interest		$ 4,130.00	$ 3,895.00
9.	If any loans exist, complete either "a" or "b" a. Interest accrued on policy loans		$ 68.70	$ 182.16
	b. 1.) Loan interest is paid to (enter date)		None	None
	2.) Interest rate is (enter rate)		5%	5%

The accountant will indicate by a check (✔) which if any of items 10-12 are to be answered

☐	**10.**	Is there an assignee of record? (enter Yes or No)		
☑	**11.**	Is beneficiary of record as shown in item C above? (enter Yes or No*)	Yes *	Yes *
☐	**12.**	Is the name of policyowner (subject to any assignment) as shown at the top of the form? (enter Yes or No) .... If No, enter name of policyowner of record.		

*If answer to 11 is No, please give name of beneficiary or date of last beneficiary change...................................

Date 11/23/75   By C. J. Fullerton   Title Treasurer
For the insurance company addressed
Additional copies of this form are available from the American Institute of CPAs, 666 Fifth Avenue, New York, N. Y. 10019

Great West Life Assurance Company

the auditor would determine the extent of the prepaid compensation and make the necessary adjustment.

Prepaid Rent and Lease Costs

The auditor should examine lease contracts and abstract therefrom all important information for inclusion in his work papers. From the lease contracts can be computed the rent expense applicable to the period under audit and the amount prepaid. The ledger accounts for prepaid rent and for rent expense must be analyzed to determine their correctness as ascertained from the computations. Rental payments are verified by examination of vouchers authorizing the rental payments.

In some contracts, the terms of the lease provide that the lessee pay the property taxes. In such cases, taxes should be charged to the Prepaid Rent account and properly prorated (if they have been prepaid) or properly accrued (if they are to be paid after incurrence).

Certain leases stipulate that an amount of money be deposited with the lessor, as a guaranty, to be returned upon the expiration of the lease, or to be applied to rentals of the final periods, or to be deducted from periodic rent payments. If the deposit is to be prorated over and deducted from periodic rent payments, it should be treated as a prepaid expense; if the deposit is to be returned at the expiration of the lease, it is not a prepaid charge but should be shown as a noncurrent asset—a nontrade receivable. If a bonus is paid to obtain a lease, a prepaid charge should be established and amortized to rent expense over the life of the lease.

In many cases, leased property or portions of it are subleased. In such instances, the auditor must examine provisions of the sublease, note the provisions in his work papers, and trace the cash receipts into the records. Some companies credit sublease revenue to rent expense, and others show the revenue from this source as a separate item.

Leased Property Improvements. Leasehold improvements are fixed assets. The cost of the improvements may be charged to a Leasehold Improvement account.

Improvements, rearrangements, and alterations to leased properties normally have been amortized over the life of the improvement or the life of the lease, whichever is shorter. In the majority of cases, the effects of remodeling and alteration revert to the landlord at the expiration of the lease. Normally, the examination of the lease will disclose the tenant's responsibility for improvements, rearrangements, and alterations, and the rights of the tenant and the landlord at the expiration of the lease. If a lease includes a renewal option clause, the improvements still may be amortized over the life of the improvement or the life of the lease, whichever is shorter, since it is not known if the lease will be renewed. However for federal income tax purposes, when the remaining term of a lease—not counting possible renewals—is less than 60 percent of the useful life of the improvements, the tenant is required to take the option period into consideration, unless he can satisfactorily show that the option probably will not be exercised.

Taxes Paid in Advance

Certain taxes are currently paid, some are paid in advance, some accrue, or are withheld. Work papers normally should include the following data:

1. The type of tax—for example, franchise, intangibles, personal property, real property, sales tax, excise taxes, income taxes, and so forth.
2. The tax period and the date the tax is payable.
3. The basis of the tax levy.
4. Amount of the tax.
5. Amount accrued.
6. Amount prepaid.
7. Tax expense for the period under audit.
8. The date when the tax, if overdue, becomes a lien on assets.

The auditor must independently verify or test tax computations, compare the amount of the tax according to the tax return or tax bill with the vouchers drawn for payment, and then vouch the payments into the disbursements records.

For the majority of taxes, the tax period does not coincide with the accounting period, thereby causing accruals and prepayments. Many taxation problems result in tax accruals, as exemplified by employer social security taxes, nonstamp excise taxes, and so forth. Other tax payments result in prepaid items, as in the case of state franchise taxes, which are ordinarily paid—in advance—for the privilege of conducting operations during the succeeding taxable year.

Real and personal property taxes may be paid in advance, or they may not, depending upon local laws; normally, they accrue and are not prepaid. Certain tax jurisdictions collect real and personal property taxes quarterly or semiannually, whereas others collect them annually. In addition, the fiscal year of certain tax jurisdictions is not the calendar year; and even if it is the calendar year, that period may not coincide with the fiscal year of the taxpayer. The American Institute has issued the following statement regarding taxes:

Unlike excise, income, and social security taxes, which are directly related to business events, real and personal property taxes are based upon the assessed valuation of property as of a given date, as determined by the laws of a state or other taxing authority. For this reason the legal liability for such taxes is generally considered as accruing at the moment of occurrence of some specific event, rather than over a period of time. It has generally been held that the taxes become a liability at the point of time when they become a lien. The Internal Revenue Service, however, holds that such taxes accrue on the assessment date.

In the accounting records, the commonly accepted method is to accrue property taxes each month for the fiscal period of the taxing authority.

An important phase of scheduling prepaid taxes is the determination of the prepaid amount in relationship to the taxable period covered. To this problem, the auditor must devote close attention, especially in view of the variation of laws among the taxing authorities.

In many instances, the client will have his various tax computations made preceding the visit of the auditors; in such cases, the auditor should verify the client's computations. The principle of offset should not be used in connection with the scheduling of taxes. In the balance sheet, it is common and acceptable practice to show prepaid taxes under one caption.

Many corporations today are recognizing accumulated income tax prepayments that arise as a result of intercompany profits in inventories and provisions for inventory obsolescence. The Accounting Principles Board in its *Opinion No. 11* concludes that the deferred method of tax allocation provides the most realistic approach to interperiod tax allocations and the proper presentation of accumulated income tax prepayments in financial statements. This interperiod tax allocation is a procedure whereby the tax effects of current timing differences are deferred currently and allocated to income tax expense of future periods. Full disclosure of this practice would require the amount being shown as the last item in the current asset section of the balance sheet plus a fully descriptive footnote explaining the nature of the account.

ILLUSTRATION. The company follows the practice of recording the full income tax effect of the investment credit in the period in which the credit is allowed as a reduction of federal income taxes payable. The investment credit for the fiscal year ended October 31, 1975, was $62,500.

The company has deferred to future periods the income tax effect resulting from timing differences between pretax income for financial statement purposes and taxable income. Accumulated income tax prepayments pertain to intercompany profits in inventories and provisions for inventory obsolescence.

Interest Deducted in Advance

Interest deducted in advance preferably should be scheduled on the work papers for notes payable, or customers' notes discounted, upon which the interest was deducted at the time of making the loan.

If interest deducted in advance is scheduled on the notes payable work papers, the prepaid amount should be cross-indexed to the schedule for prepaid expenses. In some cases, interest prepayments are scheduled separately from the notes payable work papers; and in still other cases, a work paper summarizing prepaid interest charges is prepared from the notes payable work papers and inserted along with the schedules for prepaid expenses. Regardless of the preference of the auditor in this respect, he must trace the interest entries through the original records and into the accounts. When loans from banks are confirmed, the date to which interest has been paid may also be confirmed. Interest on demand notes is on an accrual instead of a prepaid basis, owing to the indeterminate period of the note. For demand notes, periodic bills for interest are rendered the borrowers.

Commissions Paid in Advance

Commissions paid in advance arise when salesmen operating on a commission basis are permitted to draw against future earnings. In some instances, the understanding between the employer and the salesman is that all advanced commissions must be earned; in other cases, the advanced commissions are simply minimum salary amounts. In the latter situation, if the salesman does not earn the advance made during a stipulated period, the difference between the permitted advances and the actually earned commissions may be charged to current expenses and the arrangement started anew; or the difference may be carried forward as a prepaid item, to be worked out by the salesman.

To audit commissions paid in advance, the auditor must understand the arrangements covering the employment of the salesmen and the method of remuneration. Occasionally, the difference between minimum salaries and actual earnings, when the latter figure is below the minimum, is carried forward as a prepaid item, even though the salesman starts each given period with his unearned commissions canceled. A carry-forward of this nature does not constitute acceptable practice. The auditor must be certain that salesmen for whom prepaid commissions are carried forward remain employed at the balance sheet date. If the prepaid expense is for an ex-employee, it should be charged off, since collection possibilities are remote.

Salesmen's reports and commission agreements must be examined to determine the commissions earned; and this item is verified against the basis of the earnings—sales, for example—and the withdrawals of each individual to determine prepaid commissions, if they exist. If prepaid commissions are material in amount, confirmations of the amounts should be obtained directly from the salesmen.

If the commissions analysis shows accrued commissions for some salesmen, these should be shown as current liabilities and should not be offset against commissions paid in advance. After analyzing the commissions, the auditor must be certain to vouch all (or test-vouch) commissions to the accounts involved so that expenses are properly shown.

Advances to Employees

Advances to employees for company operating purposes must not be confused with loans to employees; the latter are not prepaid expenses.

Advances to employees are not cash, since the items are simply future expenses paid in advance of expense incurrence. Most companies advance lump sums of money, and some require that all unexpended amounts be returned, in which case the prepaid account should be credited upon the return. Others operate the funds on a revolving basis, in which case reimbursements are made to employees for expended portions, which will bring the fund in the control of the employee up to the original lump sum; each report is charged to expense as it is received. The auditor must test the reports and vouchers received, and he should investigate advances for which expense reports have not been received at the close of the period. In this manner, he determines the amount of the advances to be charged to expense and the amount to be treated as a prepaid item. If it is material, the advance should be confirmed. In some cases, signed receipts are required of the persons receiving the advances. If this is the case, the auditor should compare the receipts with the accounting entries. The auditor must use his judgment as to the amount of detailed work to be performed, and he must be satisfied with the results of tests. He must exercise care not to waste time on nonessentials; at the same time, he must be certain that expenses and assets are accurately portrayed.

Prepaid Selling Expenses—In General

Selling expenses should not be deferred in order to present a better-appearing income statement or a stronger balance sheet. Prepayments of selling expenses should exist only in connection with expenses incurred to obtain business for a future period, and then only when the business is definite so far as the future is concerned. As a general rule, selling costs should be charged to expense as they are incurred, because of the uncertainty of the development of the future sales. In certain businesses of a distinctly seasonal nature, selling expenses may be incurred in one season—autumn, for example—for orders to be manufactured or shipped in the following spring. If the accounts are closed in the interim, there may be some justification for deferring expenses until the specific sale is made, for which the expenses are incurred.

Prepaid Advertising Expenses

Large national advertising campaigns frequently have no effect on revenues until a later time; even in such cases, there may be no reason for deferring the advertising expense, since there may be no definite future period of benefit. Neither is there much justification for deferring advertising of an institutional nature, because this is a general advertising program.

Occasionally, there might be a reason for deferring a portion of certain advertising costs to future periods to be benefited so that current expenses are not distorted to a point where comparative figures become valueless. Specific instances are cited below.

Advertising calendar costs may be charged off in equal amounts each month of the calendar year.

Undated advertising gift materials—cigar lighters, pocket wallets, ash trays, pencils, and so forth—should be inventoried periodically and the cost (or less, if obsolescence is present) set up as a prepaid expense.

If in the last months of a fiscal period costs are incurred for the printing of catalogs, mail copy, and other advertising materials to be used in the succeeding period, those costs should be deferred to that period.

If an advertising department which prepares its own copy is maintained, the cost of usable supplies, if material, should be inventoried and deferred. If not material, the items should be charged to expense.

In all cases, the auditor should (1) analyze the expense account, (2) relate the expense to existing advertising contracts, (3) verify the prepaid expense accounts, and (4) discuss the situation with the client—if necessary—and judge the propriety of the prepaid expense.

Office and Factory Supplies

Office Supplies.   If not of significant amount, recognized accounting practice permits disbursements for office supplies to be charged to expense in the period of incurrence. If the amount of such items is material, a prepaid expense should be established on the basis of a physical inventory and pricing of the items; in this case, the auditor may test-check quantity, price, and clerical accuracy of computations on the same basis as in the verification of any inventory. In all cases, the auditor should use sound judgment regarding the practices of the client.

If stamps—postage, transfer, or tax stamps—exist in significant amount, they should be shown as prepaid items. Some concerns treat stamps as a part of their petty cash funds, in which case the fund should be reduced by the total of the stamps on hand, for balance sheet purposes. For mail-order houses, manufacturers who affix tax stamps, and companies accepting stamps in exchange for products, the total stamp volume may run to large amounts.

Factory Supplies.   Factory supplies are used as adjuncts to production and general operations of a factory and become a part of the cost of production via factory overhead charges; the remaining cost of these supplies is an asset. The same remarks, valuation principles, and auditing standards and procedures apply to factory supplies as to office supplies.

Factory supplies may be audited by comparison with the preceding year. If significant differences appear, they should be investigated. Obsolete items must be excluded from the inventory. The auditor should review the methods of controlling the physical items in order to prevent unauthorized usage of supplies.

LONG-TERM DEFERRED CHARGES

Plant Rearrangement and Alteration Costs

The objective of incurring plant rearrangement costs is to increase net income through the medium of more effective operations and a reduction of operating expenses. Plant rearrangement is either an avoidable correction of a mistake of a prior period or an unavoidable cost to meet changing conditions. In the first case, current expense should be charged; in the second case, the cost may be capitalized. At the time machinery and equipment are rearranged, there is no *assurance* that future business will benefit; consequently, deferred plant rearrangement costs become an extremely doubtful deferred charge. Recognized practice is to charge these costs to expense at the time they are incurred, if the current-period charge does not *materially* distort periodic net income.

When an auditor encounters deferred plant rearrangement costs, he must determine that charges are correct and proper. He must also ascertain that the amount deferred is being charged to expense either on the basis of an amount each year which is proportionate to the benefits or on the basis of a selected annual amount which is sufficiently large to amortize the account over a very few years.

Alterations may be revenue expenditures, or they may be capital expenditures. Often, an auditor finds it necessary to discuss the matter of alterations with the client in order to make the proper distinction; in any event, after talking with the client, the auditor must use his own judgment as to the proper classification. When property—real or personal—is purchased, certain alterations may be necessary in order to place the property in condition for proper use by the new owner. Outlays of this nature on newly acquired property should be added to the cost of the property on the theory that the cost of an asset is its purchase price plus all costs necessary to place the property in usable condition, in accordance with the wishes of the purchaser. The auditor must be certain, then, that alterations made to newly acquired assets are not charged to expense; this is ascertainable by an analysis of the asset accounts and of the repair or maintenance or other expense accounts.

If alterations are made to assets which have been owned and are in the nature of major repairs and/or part replacements which lengthen the life of the assets beyond the original estimated life, it is permissible to charge the costs to the proper depreciation accommodation.

Analogous to the deferment of plant rearrangement costs and alterations to leased properties is the cost of stripping or removing the overburden of mines before operations are begun. In such a case, it is common practice to write off the stripping costs on the basis of quantities of ores extracted.

Future Business Expenses

Business expenses incurred for future revenue and net income benefits include such items as the cost of research and development, exploitation, promotion and experimentation. Normally, the proper determination of periodic net income demands that these items be charged to expense upon incurrence.

When research and development, experimental, and exploitation costs are deferred to future periods, the auditor should be certain that the costs will benefit those future periods. If the result of research, development, experimentation, or exploitation is not a success, future years do not benefit, and the costs should have been charged to expense at incurrence. Each individual case must be studied and judgment exercised as to the propriety of the amount deferred. It is difficult to prove that a future period will be benefited by currently incurred costs of this nature; therefore, the authors believe that outlays ostensibly for future benefit should be discounted in full. The majority of business organizations agree.

An auditor must verify authorizations for the establishment of future business expenses to be deferred and trace their payment through the accounting records. Also, he must ascertain that current operating expenses are not included in the amount to be deferred. In succeeding audits, he must analyze the deferred charge accounts to ascertain that the deferred amounts are properly amortized—and to the satisfaction of the auditor. Deferring such charges permanently is not recognizable, whether or not revenue has been realized.

If a company regularly maintains a department devoted to research and development, experimental work or product development, all costs should normally be charged to expense upon incurrence, due to the recurring nature of the item, and because future revenues may not be realized.

Frequently, expenditures for research and development and experimentation are incurred in connection with the development of patents; they sometimes are deferred until patents are granted, at which time they are permanently transferred to the Patents account. If this practice is followed and if patents are not granted, the costs should be written off immediately. Often, patents are granted which have no value so far as earning capacity is concerned; in such cases, the amounts should not be transferred to the Patents account, or the Patents account should be reduced if the transfer already has been made. If the client seriously desires to carry research and development, and experimental costs forward as deferred items—and if he believes that those costs will result in valuable patents—the auditor should be certain that the items deferred are reasonable. (See further discussion of these topics in Chapter 21).

The authors believe that the best intentions of proper net income determination and safety are served if these costs (assuming they are not reimbursable) are charged to expense as they are incurred. However, for those few who do not hold to this tenet, and in cases in which the client desires to defer certain portions of such items even in the face of the auditor's objections, such costs incurred at the beginning of a business enterprise can more logically be deferred than those costs incurred for a concern that has been in operation. The FASB agrees with this position.

Public Utility Service Deposits

Public utility companies frequently require a deposit pending the granting of service, either as a condition to receive service or as a fund to assure the payment of current bills. These deposits may or may not be returned upon the discontinuance of the service. If the deposit is not refundable, it should be charged to expense at the date of disbursement; or if it is material in amount, it should be amortized over a few periods. If the deposit is refundable and is material in amount, the auditor should read the terms of the agreement; if interest is allowed, he should test the interest credits. If individual deposits are large and if the auditor suspects that liens may exist, he should confirm the deposit as of the close of the period under examination.

Unamortized Bond Discount and Issuance Costs

Bond discount and related issuance costs may be amortized by the straight-line method, the scientific method, or the bonds-outstanding method in the event of serial issues. The straight-line method is the most commonly used; the scientific method is the most accurate; and the bonds-outstanding method is employed in connection with serial bonds. When the straight-line method is used, the amortized discount plus interest equals a constant percentage of the par of the bonds. When the scientific method is used, the amortized discount plus interest equals a constant percentage of the book value of the bonds. Regardless of the method employed, the purpose is to amortize the total amount of original discount over the life of the bonds. If bonds are callable at a date preceding maturity, the discount should be amortized from the date of issue to the callable date; or if the retirement date is decided upon after the bonds have been outstanding for some time, amortization must take place from the date of decision to retire early to the call date. If bonds are to be retired at a premium, periodic charges are thereby increased.

Bonds of corporations usually are sold in entirety to a broker, bank, underwriter, or syndicate, at a price below that at which the issue will be offered for public sale. The purchaser of the entire issue then disposes of the bonds to the investors at a price above the purchase price, thereby permitting the marketing agency a profit. To the discount granted the underwriters are added legal fees, appraisal costs, and any other necessary issuance costs. The total of the issuing costs and the discount should be prorated over the bonds during their outstanding life, or in accordance with the retirement plans set forth in the preceding paragraph. Under another plan of marketing, the underwriting syndicate will agree to market the bonds at the agent of the corporation. This method avoids risk to the syndicate, since the syndicate will contract to sell the bonds for a commission expressed as a percentage of the sales price.

If bonds are issued in exchange for property, discounts do not arise unless the situation is obviously one indicating property values received substantially below the par of the bonds or when bonds of the same issue are selling for cash at a discount.

Trust indentures and underwriting syndicate contracts are examined and their contents noted for such items as retirement provisions, call dates, refunding features, conversion privileges, underwriting costs, and so forth. In the audit report, comment may be made upon the acceptability of the method of amortization. The capitalization of bond discount and issuance costs, the amortization policy, and charge-offs must be properly reflected by authorizations of the board of directors or the finance committee.

The auditor must verify the correctness of the issuing costs and the discount, and ascertain that the deferred charge account for the discount and expense has been correctly charged. He should verify the periodic amortization according to the client in order to arrive at the correctness of the remaining deferred charge.

Accountants occasionally differ as to whether unamortized bond discount and expense is a deferred charge to operations or a liability valuation account. The question of treating the bond discount and expense as a deferred charge or as a liability reduction account can be defended by each party to the controversy. See Chapter 24.

If a bond issue is retired prior to maturity date and if the bonds are *not* refunded, the remaining balance in the Unamortized Bond Discount and Expense account should be eliminated from that account. Some accountants prefer to deduct the amount of the charge-off in the income statement, as a separate nonrecurring item, so that normal net income will not be distorted, and in such a manner that it is not misleading. When bonds are partially retired, the auditor must determine that the related discount and expense are charged off, thus leaving as the unamortized balance of the account only the amount pertaining to the bonds still outstanding.

Frequently, bond issues are refunded before maturity. There is no uniformity of treatment of the amount of unamortized discount and expense, and redemption premium, on the refunded issue. In accordance with *Accounting Research Bulletin No. 43*, chapter 15, there are three methods of disposing of the unamortized balance:

1. Write off the unamortized discount issue cost and redemption premium applicable to the original issue to retained earnings or to income at the time of refunding.
2. Defer the unamortized premium or discount and other costs applicable to the original issue and amortize them over the remaining life of the original issue, just as if refunding had not occurred.
3. Defer the unamortized premium or discount and other costs applicable to the original issue, and amortize them over the life of the new bond issue.

Accounting Research Bulletin No. 43 recommends that the second alternative be followed and that when the amount written off is material, it should be charged to Retained Earnings. Since such a charge is deductible for income tax purposes in the year of refunding (*Great Western Company of California* v. *Commissioner of Internal Revenue* [297 U.S. 545]), any income tax advantage obtained from the charge-off should also be shown in the Retained Earnings account. Because the original contract is terminated upon refunding, the authors believe that all unamortized costs should be charged off at the time of refunding (item 1, above); they further believe that the charge should be to a non-recurring expense.

The Securities and Exchange Commission has refused to approve the charging of unamortized discount to a Capital Surplus account on the premise that income is thereby relieved of charges that would have been recognized had the refunding not taken place. The Commission approves of charges to income or to Retained Earnings.

Lasts, Drawings, Patterns, Molds, Templets, and so forth

If these items do not have a sufficiently long life to classify them as fixed assets, they may be classified as deferred charges. The period of amortization should not exceed the expected useful life of each item. The auditor should discuss the expected useful life of these items with the proper plant personnel and verify the cost of the items, the computation of amortization, and the reasonableness of amounts deferred.

SECTION IV: FINANCIAL STATEMENT CONSIDERATIONS

Based upon the concept of a current asset, prepaid expenses are current assets and should be presented as such in the balance sheet. Deferred charges should be separately set forth in the balance sheet.

Many people consider as sound and conservative the practice of charging prepaid expenses and deferred charges to expense when the items are acquired. To understate assets and overstate expenses is as deplorable as overstating assets and understating expenses. If not charged to the correct accounting periods as expense, prepaid and deferred items cause incorrect net income to be shown, not only for the period to which they are charged as expenses but also for subsequent periods. In this connection, the dictates of good theory and sound practice, as well as the requirements of income tax legislation and regulations, must constantly be borne in mind.

The auditor should determine that unexpired amounts of prepaid expenses and deferred charges be properly shown as assets at the balance sheet date. The only time this rule is open to exception occurs when the amount of the prepaid or deferred item is so immaterial that its treatment has practically no effect upon assets or net income, or if the amount is of annual recurrence and not material in amount and the practice is consistently followed from year to year. If financial statements are to be compared and analyzed, comparisons cannot properly be made if prepaid and deferred items are ignored or improperly and inconsistently treated. This is particularly true when financial statements are prepared once each month.

Fundamentally, unamortized bond discount is a liability valuation account, but commonly it is shown as a deferred charge.

The accounting profession recognizes the necessity for disclosing the existence of long-term leases, particularly the now widely used buy-build-sell-lease type of agreement. The requirements of Rule 3–18 (*b*) of the Securities and Exchange Commission are as follows: "Where the rentals or obligations under long-term leases are material there shall be shown the amounts of annual rentals under such leases with some indication of the periods for which they are payable, together with any important obligation assumed or guarantee made in connection therewith. If the rentals are conditional, state the minimum annual amounts." These requirements may be inadequate for proper financial reporting; additional material regarding long-term leases appears in Chapter 21.

QUESTIONS

1. You have examined the insurance policies of a client and have verified the amount of the prepaid insurance as of the date of the fiscal year-end. What procedure would you follow to prove the correctness of the insurance expense for the fiscal year under examination?

2. You are reviewing a client's entries for prepaid insurance and insurance expense. The largest (premium cost) policy for three years was purchased April 1 of the year under audit. The client charged 27 months' premium to expense and set up nine months as prepaid. What will you do? Present reasons for your answer.

(AICPA, adapted)

3. Why is it advisable to compare total prepaid expenses at the beginning and at the end of a year?

4. Explain how an examination of insurance policies might disclose:
    a) Inventory pledged as collateral to a loan.
    b) The disposition of fixed assets without entries in the records.
    c) Possible premium refunds.
    d) Inadequate insurance coverage.

5. A client has 100 individual insurance policies covering all phases and operations of its business activity. You are engaged in an audit of the financial statements of the company. An insurance department cares for all insurance matters of the company; internal control is excellent. What procedure will you follow to satisfy yourself of the accuracy of the prepaid insurance at the end of the year under examination?

6. Why should reports detailing activity of prepaid expenses and deferred charges by prepared for management?

7. National Company incurs extensive selling expenses in the late summer and early fall season of each year for equipment for spring season sale. All sales and manufacture take place according to contract, each unit being different so far as accessories and equipment are concerned; standard equipment is not manufactured in advance of contract. The company closes its records as of December 31 of each year. Order cancellation seldom occurs. The company requests your advice regarding the deferment of these selling expenses until the following year, in which the sale takes place.

8. *a*) The Golden Company operates in rented quarters. On July 1 of each year the company deposits $9,600 with the landlord. One-twelfth of the deposit is applied to each monthly rental; the gross rental per month is $2,000. You are requested to prepare the necessary journal entry for the Golden Company on August 1. If the Golden Company closed its accounts on December 31, would you classify the unused portion of the deposit as a prepaid expense or as a nontrade account receivable? Why?
    b) The Hilvers Company rents its building for $200 per month to the Gossman Company. At the beginning of the lease, which runs for five years, the Hilvers Company demanded and received from the Gossman Company a deposit of $2,000. If at the termination of the lease, the building is found to be in satisfactory order, the deposit will be returned to the Gossman Company. How should the $2,000 deposit be handled in the accounts of the Gossman Company?

9. The accounts of a clothing manufacturer include the items listed below as prepaid expenses at December 31, 1975.
    (1) Traveling expenses of salesmen incurred in 1975 but applicable to merchandise to be delivered in 1976, $10,500.
    (2) Direct-mail advertising copy to wholesalers, applicable to the 1976 line of merchandise, $27,800.
    (3) That portion of the office expense judged to be applicable to obtaining orders for 1976 delivery, $21,000.
    Should each of these items be treated as prepaid expenses? Present reasons for your answers.

10. A retail store leased its premises on January 1, 1975, for a period of 10 years at an annual rental of $25,000. The company expended $50,000 altering the store; it was estimated that the alterations would have a life of 20 years. The company charged the $50,000 to be an account entitled Leasehold Improvements and showed it as such in the balance sheet at December 31, 1975.

In January, 1976, you were summoned to audit the records of the store for the year ended December 31, 1975. What adjustments would you recommend, assuming the lease will not be renewed?

11. What action would you take in the event that in a first audit, you found an account entitled "Deferred Research and Development Costs," which is five years old and has never been credited?

12. The Farr Company issued $1,000,000 of 40-year, 6 percent bonds, at 90. The bonds were issued 25 years ago, and the company amortized $2\frac{1}{2}$ percent of the bond discount at the end of each year. At the beginning of the current year, the Farr Company purchased $300,000 of the outstanding bonds at 80 and canceled them. During the audit, you discover that the unamortized discount on the $300,000 of bonds for the remaining 15 years, amounting to $11,250 had been credited to income.

a)   What is the correct procedure with respect to the $11,250?

b)   What course would you take if the company insisted upon showing the $11,250 as income?

PROBLEMS

1. Prepare the audit adjustments and explanations for the following situations you find in the records of Rottman, Inc. who closes its accounts December 31, 1975.

a) *December 1, 1975:*

Advertising Expense	$12,000	
Cash		$12,000

Records payment of 1976 advertising contract.

b)

Balance of Office Supplies Expense at 12/31/75	$ 5,000
Balance of Office Supplies on Hand at 12/31/75	500
Inventory value of Office Supplies at 12/31/75	750

c) *June 1, 1975:*

Prepaid Insurance	$ 1,800	
Cash		$ 1,800

Records payment of 36 month policy for fire loss on inventory.

d)

Balance of Factory Supplies Expense Account at 12/31/75	$ 3,300
Physical inventory of factory supplies at 12/31/75	$ 1,100

e)   On May 1, 1975, a three-year subscription to the Professional Journal in the amount of $180 was mailed in but not paid for. Subscriptions Expense was charged for the entire amount.

f)   On September 1, 1974, paid 36 month premium of $3,600 on fire and extended coverage on building. No amortization of this premium has been recorded to date and the full amount remains in the Prepaid Insurance account.

g)   Signed a 10-year lease for a new warehouse; the closing costs of $1,200, paid on July 1, 1975, effective date of lease, was charged to Rent Expense.

   h) Paid annual dues of $1,200 on September 1, 1975, to the Chamber of Commerce and charged Dues and Subscription Expense.

   i) Subscribed to Building Reports on April 1, 1975, agreeing to pay two equal semi-annual installments of $720.00 each. The first payment was charged to Prepaid Dues and Subscriptions and the second charged to Dues and Subscriptions Expense.

   j) Vacation advances were made in the amount of $6,000 on December 15, 1975, and charged to Vacation Expense. Of this amount $3,000 applies to vacations starting January 1, 1976.

2. You are examining the financial statements of the Atlas Company, a retail enterprise, for the year ended December 31, 1975. The client's accounting department presented you with an analysis of the Prepaid Expenses account balance of $31,400 at December 31, 1975 as shown below.

   Additional information includes the following:

   (1) Insurance policy data:

Type	Period Covered	Premium
Fire	12/31/74 to 12/31/76	$1,000
Liability	6/30/75 to 6/30/76	9,500

   (2) The postage meter machine was delivered in November and the balance due was paid in January. Unused postage of $700 in the machine at December 31, 1975 was recorded as expense at time of purchase.

ATLAS COMPANY

Analysis of Prepaid Expenses Account

December 31, 1975

Description	Balance December 31, 1975
Unexpired fire insurance	$ 750
Unexpired liability insurance	4,900
Utility deposits	2,000
Loan to officer	500
Purchase of postage meter machine, one half of invoice price	400
Bond discount	3,000
Advertising of store opening	9,600
Amount due for overpayment on purchase of furniture and fixtures	675
Unsaleable inventory-entered June 30, 1975	8,300
Contributions from employees to employee welfare fund	(275)
Book value of obsolete machinery held for resale	550
Funds delivered to New Front Stores with purchase offer	1,000
Total	$31,400

   (3) Bond discount represents the unamortized portion applicable to bonds maturing in 1976.

   (4) The $9,600 paid and recorded for advertising was for the cost of an advertisement to be run in a monthly magazine for six months, beginning in December 1975. You examined an invoice received from the advertising agency and extracted the following description:

"Advertising services rendered for store opened in November 1975 . . . $6,900."

(5) Atlas has contracted to purchase New Front Stores and has been required to accompany its offer with a check for $1,000 to be held in escrow as an indication of good faith. An examination of paid checks revealed the check has not been returned from the bank through January 1976.

Assuming that you have examined acceptable underlying audit evidence, prepare a work sheet to show the necessary adjustments, corrections, and reclassifications of the items in the Prepaid Expenses account. The following column headings are suggested for your work sheet.

Adjustments and Reclassifications		Prepaid Expenses Adjusted Balance	Disposition of Adjustments and Reclassifications Accounts				
Debit	Credit	December 31, 1975	Expense Debit (Credit)	Other	Rec.– Account	Debit	Credit

(AICPA, adapted)

3. J. W. S., Inc. is a market research company and has engaged you to audit its financial statements for the fiscal year ending October 31, 1975. In reviewing the insurance program, you discover that the company carries five $25,000 life insurance policies on its chief officers. Further investigation reveals that the company is the beneficiary of these policies with the proceeds to be used to purchase each person's stock when he dies. The following information is obtained from the company records and from direct correspondence with the insurance company:

Policy No.	Insured	Annual Premium	Dividends	Period Covered
1132–899	Stockholder #1	$462.75	$184.75	6/2/75–6/2/76
1132–887	Stockholder #2	428.00	168.50	5/28/75–5/28/76
1132–954	Stockholder #3	407.50	159.75	5/28/75–5/28/76
1132–969	Stockholder #4	380.00	148.25	3/4/75–3/4/76
1133–797	Stockholder #5	439.00	173.25	3/4/75–3/4/76

An examination of the entries for payment of the premiums revealed that the company is offsetting the dividends against the premium and paying the net amount.

Correspondence with the insurance company provides the following information:

Policy No.	Cash Surrender Value	Loan @ 5%	Accrued Interest to 10/31/75
1132–899	$5,569.21	$4,130.00	$ 86.07
1132–887	5,127.20	3,775.00	80.75
1132–954	4,856.05	3,560.00	76.15
1132–969	4,462.20	3,250.00	107.31
1133–797	5,305.06	3,895.00	128.61

The general ledger of J. W. S., Inc. shows a balance of $22,787.75 in the Cash Surrender Value of Life Insurance account. The Prepaid Insurance account contains the gross annual premium, and the Dividend Income account contains the amount of the dividends on these policies. The total of the loans, $18,610.00, is found to be in the Notes Payable Bank account. No recognition has been made of the accrued interest on these policy loans.

Prepare all necessary journal entries at October 31, 1975 to correct the client's records.

4. The Jerry Company is in the construction business and has engaged you to audit its financial statements for the fiscal year ended April 30, 1976. One account you select to analyze in detail is Miscellaneous Prepaid Items. Your analysis reveals the following:

Beginning balance, 5/1/75		$ 979
Consisting of:		
Dues—U.S. Chamber of Commerce to 6/30/75	$ 25	
Dues—Tioga Chamber of Commerce to 6/30/75	16	
Dues—Greater Tioga Contractors Ass'n. to 6/30/75	15	
Dues—National Contractors Ass'n. to 11/1/75	105	
Subscription—Dun & Bradstreet Service to 9/14/75	225	
Subscription—F. W. Dodge Reports to 10/15/75	491	
Blueprint cost relating to bids	102	
Transactions for first quarter:		
Blueprint costs relating to bids		200
Subscription—Research, Inc., 5/1/75–4/30/76		24
Dues—Greater Tioga Contractors Ass'n., 7/1/75–7/1/76		96
Dues—Tioga Chamber of Commerce, 7/1/75–6/30/76		108
Dues—U.S. Chamber of Commerce, 7/1/75–6/30/76		240
Return of blueprint cost		(25)
Floor covering samples		45
Three months' amortization of prepaid items		(750)
Transactions for second quarter:		
Floor covering sample catalogs		18
Subscription—Dun & Bradstreet Service, 9/14/75– 9/14/76		840
Refund of blueprint cost		(15)
Blueprint cost relating to bids		144
Three months' amortization of prepaid items		(750)
Transactions for third quarter:		
Subscription—F. W. Dodge Reports, 10/15/75–4/15/76		504
Refund of plan cost		(110)
Dues—National Contractors Ass'n., 11/1/75–10/31/76		360
Dues—Construction Industry Ass'n., 11/1/75–10/31/76		96
Blueprint cost relating to bids		148
Three months' amortization of prepaid items		(750)
Transactions for fourth quarter:		
Refund of plan cost		(50)
Dues—Sub–Contractors Ass'n., 3/1/76–2/28/77		300
Subscription—F. W. Dodge Reports, 4/15/76–4/15/77		1,080
Subscription—Research, Inc., 5/1/76–4/30/79		120
Blueprint cost relating to bids		240
Three months' amortization of prepaid items		(750)

Further verification of the above items reveals that jobs requiring $220 of blueprint cost had been successfully bid and are in the process of construction but had not been charged with this cost. It was also determined that blueprint costs amounting to $120 relates to bids still pending. All remaining blueprint costs were not recoverable and were considered a part of the regular amortization of prepaid items. In addition, the quarterly amortization of prepaid items had been charged to the account, Dues and Subscriptions Expense.

Determine the balance of the account at April 30, 1976, and prepare the necessary adjusting entries to correctly state the balance of this account.

5. As of December 31, 1975, the Insurance Expense account on the records of the Company has a debit balance of $4,622. A Prepaid Insurance account is not carried; all premiums are charged to expense as they are incurred.

Based upon the examination of the following policies, prepare (*a*) an insurance schedule and (*b*) the adjustment entry or entries properly to set up the prepaid insurance.

Insurance Company	Policy No.	Coverage	Policy Date	Expiration Date	Total Coverage	Premium
State	101	Fire and extended, factory building	7/1/74	7/1/77	$100,000	$ 648
State	102	Fire and extended, factory building	8/16/75	8/16/78	250,000	1,728
Buckeye	103	Fire and extended, office building	2/1/71	2/1/76	25,000	300
Buckeye	104	Fire and extended, office equipment	10/1/72	10/1/77	27,000	480
Oldtown	105	Fire, merchandise	5/1/75	5/1/76	310,000	444
Mutual	106	Fire and theft, delivery equipment	8/1/75	8/1/76	24,000	240
Mutual	107	Liability, delivery equipment	8/1/75	8/1/76	50,000–100,000	360
Acme	108	Inside theft and burglary	11/1/75	11/1/78	20,000	450
Northern	109	Employee fidelity	3/1/75	3/1/78	Position–$30,000	900
State	110	Workmen's compensation	9/1/75	9/1/76	Payroll total at $0.25 per $100; payroll from 9/1/75 to 12/31/76, $82,000	Deposit of $500, made on 9/1/75

6. A client insured certain properties and purchased insurance policies containing an 80 percent coinsurance clause containing (in part) the following statement: "This Insurance Company shall be held liable for no greater proportion of any loss than the amount insured bears to 80 percent of the actual cash value of the property described herein at the time when such loss shall happen; but if the total insurance upon such property exceeds 80 percent at the time of such fire, then this Company shall

only be liable for the proportion which the sum hereby insured bears to such total insurance."

Notes: If a coinsurance clause (assume 80 percent or any other percentage) attaches it has no effect whatever when insurance is carried to the amount of 80 percent of value or more; in this case insurance pays the entire loss—but not in excess of the amount of the policy. When both insurance and loss fall below 80 percent of the value of the property, the insured becomes a coinsurer to the amount of the difference between 80 percent of the property value and the actual insurance in force at the time of loss.

From the following data obtained from your client, compute for each property (*a*) the amount to be paid by the insurance company and (*b*) the amount of the loss borne by the client.

Property	Value of Property	Insurance Required—80%	Insurance Carried	Loss
1	$10,000	$8,000	$8,000	$6,000
2	10,000	8,000	7,000	6,000
3	10,000	8,000	6,000	6,000
4	10,000	8,000	5,000	6,000

7. On July 1, 1976, a fire completely destroyed a building owned by your client. The building was insured against fire with two companies under the following three-year policies:

Insurance Company	Policy Face	Coin-surance Clause	Unexpired Premium, July 1, 1975	Date of Expiration
A	$ 80,000	80%	$ 800	8/31/76
B	120,000	80%	1,200	8/31/76

An umpire set the insurable value at the date of the fire at $260,000 and the loss at $255,000. However, there proved to be no net salvage value recoverable from the building. The building was carried at cost, $200,000, less accumulated depreciation of $30,000 to the date of the fire.

a) Compute the amount recoverable under each insurance policy and the total amount recoverable.

b) Compute the balance of the Fire Loss account after recording any of the above data that affect it. Identify the various elements entering into your computation, together with any necessary explanations.

(AICPA, adapted)

8. The audit for the year ending December 31, 1975, of the Starr Construction Company revealed that the present balance of Prepaid Insurance account consisted of the following policies. All insurance premiums were charged to this account.

Policy No.	Company	Type Coverage	Dollar Coverage	Policy Date	Expiration Date	Amount of Premium
43S7	Mutual	Fire and Extended—Bldgs.	$100,000	8–1–74	8–1–77	$1,872
65743	Clark	Fire and Extended—Bldgs.	$150,000	2–1–75	2–1–78	$2,736
2466	Eastern	Fire and Extended—Offices	$100,000	3–1–74	3–1–76	$ 720
7711T	State	Product Liability	$100,000	7–1–73	7–1–77	$ 768
0130	Exer	Fire and Theft-Inventory	$ 65,000	8–1–75	2–1–78	$ 360
5V3W	Western	Medical-Officers	$100,000	6–1–74	6–1–76	$1,200
006T	Park	Delivery Equipment	$ 50,000	11–1–75	11–1–76	$ 240
995R	Davis	Blanket Position Bond	$ 30,000	2–1–74	2–1–76	$ 480
1124	Southern	Construction Bonding*	$100,000	4–1–75	4–1–76	$ 195
W532	State	Term Insurance on Key Personnel	$ 75,000	5–1–74	5–1–78	$2,160
10010	Clark	Officer's Life†	$ 50,000	9–1–75	9–1–76	$ 120
6623	Union	Officer's Life‡	$ 50,000	9–1–75	9–1–76	$ 120

* For construction of hospital to insure that Starr will complete the project.
† Beneficiary is Company.
‡ Beneficiary is officer's wife.

(1) Prepare an Insurance Schedule for 12-31-75, showing in addition to the above information, the amount prepaid and the expense for the year.

(2) Prepare journal entries to record the proper amount of expense for 1975 and create the correct balance of Prepaid Insurance.

PRACTICE MATERIAL ASSIGNMENTS

Metalcraft, Incorporated: Audit Problem:
  Assignment 6: Prepaid Insurance and Insurance Expense.
Colby Gears, Inc.: Holmes and Moore Audit Case:
  Unexpired Insurance, Insurance Expense. Prepaid Advertising. Prepaid Interest and Interest Expense.

19

Fixed Tangible Assets and Related Expenses

Audit Objectives

The audit objectives in the examination of fixed assets are to review and evaluate the internal control of fixed assets, to verify their existence and ownership, to determine the method of recording when acquired (either at cost or other basic acquisition figure), to examine the evaluation methods used by a client, to determine the existence of any liens, and to evaluate the propriety of the depreciation or amortization program.

General Discussion

Items Included. Fixed tangible assets are capital assets used in the operation of a business. They are not purchased with the intention of reselling them, and they normally have a useful business life expectancy of more than one year. Fixed tangible assets may be classified as follows:

1. Land uses for business sites—not subject to depreciation or depletion.
2. Buildings, machinery, factory equipment, office equipment, delivery equipment, large tools, and so forth—subject to depreciation.
3. Mineral properties, oil wells, timber stands, and so forth—subject to depletion.

The propriety of the net book value of fixed tangible assets for a going concern is dependent upon the policies followed for the recording of original cost (or other basic acquisition figure), additions and improvements, replacements of parts, repairs, and deductions from and dispositions of fixed assets. The policies followed for such recording must be in accordance with accepted principles of accounting, consistently applied.

The Bases of Recording Fixed Assets

Cost Basis.   As a general rule and in accordance with recognized principles and practices, for a going concern, (1) depreciable fixed assets are carried in the records at original net acquisition costs, less separate and proper accumulations for depreciation; (2) fixed assets subject to depletion usually are carried in the records at original net cost, less accumulated depletion; and (3) nondepreciable fixed assets customarily are carried in the records at original net cost (or other basic acquisition figure).

Generally accepted accounting principles are to the effect that for fixed tangible assets, current replacement costs are not proper and historical costs are proper. The American Institute of Certified Public Accountants has expressed itself to the effect that while accounting for fixed assets normally should be based on cost and any attempt to make property accounts in general reflect current values in both impractical and inexpedient, ". . . should inflation proceed so far that original dollar costs lose their practical significance, it might be necessary to restate all assets in terms of the depreciated currency, as has been done in some countries. . . ." (*Accounting Research Bulletin No. 43*, chapter 9.)

Both the Study Group on Business Income and the Committee on Accounting Concepts and Standards of the American Accounting Association recommend strongly the preparation of *supplementary* statements to reflect fixed assets—and particularly depreciation—on some type of current-cost basis—preferably original cost adjusted to current prices. Normally, these supplementary statements are issued to management only.

Other-than-Cost Bases.   Cost is the commonly accepted basis for recording fixed assets, and depreciation charges ordinarily are based on cost. However, bases other than cost occasionally are used and may be justfied. The auditor will form an opinion and render his judgment of any procedure used by management in the valuation of fixed assets.

A few of the other-than-cost bases are (1) appraised amounts, (2) nominal amounts, (3) discovery values, and (4) pooling of interests amounts.

If *appraised* amounts are used in the accounts, the reason for the reflection of the appraised—reduced to sound value—amounts should be justifiable. Justifiable reasons might include the following: a rise in price levels over several generations when assets were acquired under conditions of very low cost; and assets acquired from a company in forced liquidation at a "bargain." Appraisals may be of importance in the event of sale, merger, refinancing, consolidation, reorganization, or quasi reorganization. If circumstances justify an appraisal and an account restatement of fixed assets, the situation is similar to that of a quasi reorganization) therefore, all other assets should be properly restated, the credits passed to a permanent capital account, and a new Retained Earnings account created and dated—to which account all net income earned subsequent to the date of quasi reorganization should be credited.

The use of *nominal* amounts occasionally is adopted particularly by nonprofit organizations. Although there is no justification for the use of far-below-cost nominal amounts—other than the classic excuse of "conservatism"—they are still found.

Discovery values often are used for extractive industries properties when the reasonable worth of the deposits is greatly in excess of the cost of acquiring the properties.

In mergers and consolidations—particularly as exemplified by the emergence of modern-day conglomerates—if the pooling of interests concept is followed, fixed assets probably will be reflected at an old and low cost and not at a realistic modern purchase price. The authors and the Accounting Principles Board are of the opinion that purchase accounting procedures reflect more realistic values and that the pooling of interests procedure generally should not be followed, except in those circumstances set forth by the APB in its *Opinion No. 16*.

When any base other than cost is used, the financial statements should clearly set forth that other base either in the statement itself or in footnotes.

Capital and Revenue Expenditures

In examining fixed asset records, an auditor must exercise care in the distinction between capital and revenue expenditures. This is often a matter of management policy or of individual preference expressed by some one person in the business organization, or it is the result of an arbitrary rule established for the guidance of associated plants. For example, one company has a rule whereby all expenditures on fixed assets in excess of $50,000 are capitalized and all expenditures on fixed assets below that figure are charged to expense. Public utilities, as well as some other companies, establish physical units of property as the basis of distinction between capital outlay and expense; an expenditure that results in the acquisition of a defined *unit of property* is capitalized by a charge to an asset account and becomes subject to depreciation accounting. Regardless of the routine followed, the auditor should make his examination sufficiently complete to be assured that the proper distinction has been made between capital and revenue charges, based on accepted principles of accounting, so that capitalized charges are not overstated (thereby presenting an overstatement of net income and an overstated asset and proprietorship position), and so that expenses are not overstated (thereby understating net income, assets, and proprietorship).

An addition to or an improvement of an asset results in a capital charge, increasing the cost of the asset. There is never much question as to what constitutes an addition to an asset, but the question of what constitutes an improvement is sometimes surrounded by controversy. The effect of an improvement is to place the asset in better condition, to make it more valuable, or to make it more productive than it was when originally purchased. If an outlay does not measure up to this test, an improvement did not take place.

Repairs to fixed assets and replacements of parts of fixed assets are divided into (1) major repairs and part replacements, which have the effect of lengthening the useful business life of the asset for a period in excess of the original life estimate; and (2) ordinary repairs and replacements, which do not lengthen the useful business life of the asset but merely maintain it in efficient operating condition. Major repairs and part replacements are charged either to asset accounts or to the proper accumulations for depreciation, thereby spreading the depreciable life over a longer period of time, although they do not make the asset more valuable or more efficient than it was when originally acquired. Major part replacement costs merely replace original costs; therefore, at the time of replacement, proper accounting theory dictates that the cost of the replaced part be removed from the asset account and that the accumulated depreciation be properly reduced. Ordinary repairs and part replacements are charged to the proper expense accounts in the period of incurrence.

Other than the cost of additions, improvements, and other expenditures which increase the estimated useful business life of an asset beyond its initially estimated life, or increase its productivity beyond its initially estimated productivity, the *only real* criterion upon which to base a distinction between minor and major repairs is the amount of the annual depreciation charge. The larger the annual charge, the lower—in terms of dollars or physical units—the amount which divides capital and revenue charges, and vice versa. For example, in a public utility, if the annual charge for depreciation and the definition of "plant unit" get out of line, they can be brought into line by changing either one. It is not possible to determine *separately* (1) the distinction between repairs and replacements and (2) the annual depreciation charge. They are interdependent and must be determined concurrently.

In an audit, it may be difficult to determine the line of demarcation between major and ordinary repairs and replacements; the auditor must use his best judgment to make the distinction or agree with acceptable management policy.

Depreciation

The following discussion assumes a sound knowledge of the principles governing depreciation and the practices of depreciating fixed assets.

Depreciation is that portion of the cost or other basic value (less estimated salvage) of a fixed asset that is systematically charged to periodic expense. The allocation is justified as a result of all factors that lead to the final disposition of the asset. These factors include wear and tear, supersession, inadequacy, obsolescence, and passage of time, and the action of the elements. However, the periodic depreciation charge does not attempt to measure or parallel physical depreciation as it occurs. If a fixed asset has an expected useful business life shorter than its physical life, the depreciable cost should be allocated over that expected shorter useful business life. If the expected useful business life is shorter than economic life, estimated salvage values must be correlated with the expected useful life of an asset.

ILLUSTRATION. An asset costing $10,000 has an estimated economic life of 10 years and an estimated salvage value of $1,000 based on that life. At the time of acquisition, the owner plans to use the asset only seven years, at the end of which time he expects to dispose of it and acquire a new one. Therefore, it is logical to assume that the estimated salvage value be increased from $1,000 to (assume) $4,000. Consequently, $6,000 is to be spread over seven years, as depreciation.

The accumulated depreciation accounts accumulate that portion of the cost of the assets which has been allocated to periodic operations during past accounting periods. To this extent, it indicates a dollar amount of assets which is equal to the costs recovered through previous depreciation expense charges and which has been retained in the business in order to maintain the basic capital position. The accumulated depreciation accounts offer no clue as to the future business usefulness of the assets so retained.

Consistency in Recording Depreciation. Although the cost of a depreciable fixed asset is systematically allocated to expense over its useful business life, the definition of depreciatin does not imply and does not state that depreciation rates and amounts cannot be changed for good cause. Consistency in recording depreciation is based on an original fair estimate of useful service life; this original fair estimate should be consistently followed until basic conditions so change that it becomes necessary to alter the estimate, because the application of the original estimate now fails to produce accurate cost allocations.

ILLUSTRATION. A new machine enters the market and thereby has the effect of radically shortening the useful life of the preceding model; the undepreciated cost of the old asset should be reapportioned over its remaining estimated service life, and the estimated salvage value should be adjusted. Also, in those instances where machinery originally estimated to operate eight hours per day is operated 24 hours per day over a period of time, physical depreciation may increase, because of the additional usage and the lack of time for maintenance and repairs; if study indicates that useful life is thereby shortened, it is proper to revise depreciation expense—and it is consistent to do so, because the depreciable cost of the asset should be allocated to expense over its useful life.

Fluctuations in market prices of assets have no relationship to cost allocation and to the fact that all depreciable fixed assets are constantly wearing out and approaching a zero value. If depreciation accounting is improper, net income cannot be properly stated. In no case is it possible to foretell precisely the expected useful business life of a fixed asset; but reasonable estimates of cost allocation can be made, based upon the cost of the asset, its estimated scrap value, and its anticipated useful business life. The anticipated useful life of the asset is based primarily upon experience and upon management policies regarding replacements. Factory buildings may be more soundly constructed than apartments and office buildings; but owing to vibration and more active physical use, the former may experience a shorter life. Periodic depreciation charges will therefore vary with local conditions of use and with income tax considerations.

For several years, the IRS has been using various accounting methods to influence the economic development of the country. One method has been the granting of an income tax credit for acquisition of depreciable personal property. A credit against the federal income tax is allowed at the rate of seven percent of the qualified investment in certain depreciable property. This credit was originally introduced in 1962, suspended between October 10, 1966 and March 9, 1967, and repealed generally after April 18, 1969, and then restored in 1971. The amount of the qualified investment is the sum of the basis of new depreciable personal property and up to $50,000 of the cost of used depreciable property. If such property has a useful life of seven years, a full seven percent of its basis or cost is allowed as a deduction. Only two-thirds of the basis or cost is taken into account if the useful life is at least five and less than seven years and one-third is taken into consideration where the useful life is at least three and less than five years. No credit is allowed if the useful life is less than three years. The manner in which this credit is handled in the financial statements must be clearly set forth in them.

Another IRS development is the Class Life Asset Depreciation Range (ADR) which is based on broad industry classes of assets. For asset classes covering buildings and land improvements, a single class life, called an asset guideline period, is given. All other classes have a range of years, called an asset depreciation range, that extend 20 percent above and below the asset guideline period. A taxpayer using ADR does not have to justify his retirement and replacement policies to the IRS. However, a depreciation period selected for an asset cannot be changed by either the taxpayer or the IRS during the remaining period of use of the asset. The ADR election is an annual one and applies to assets first placed in use after 1970. The reader is referred to related IRS publications for more detail, because this is a tax matter.

Depreciation Bases. Since depreciation is a cost recovery, the periodic depreciation charge in an income statement should be based on cost, less estimated salvage value, assuming that the assets are recorded at cost. Cost has long been recognized as the proper base by accountants, business organizations, regulatory bodies, and the United States Treasury Department in its application of the federal revenue acts.

If current replacement costs are used for fixed assets in a balance sheet, it is only logical that the income statement (not the federal income tax return) reflect depreciation charges based upon currently estimated replacement costs.

Supplementary Financial Statements. Except for those instances cited earlier, the authors do not recommend the reflection of appreciation *in the accounts.* If supplementary statements are prepared in accordance with the recommendations of the AICPA, the AAA, and the Business Income Study Group, fixed assets and related depreciation may be set forth on the basis of adjusted original cost.

Of course, when fixed assets are stated at historical costs of several years ago and when sales are made at higher current-cost prices, ratio studies become worthless—unless supplementary statements are used to adjust the original cost of fixed assets to their present depreciated replacement cost.

Methods of Depreciation

There are many methods available for the computation of depreciation charges. Several of the methods are reviewed in summary form. Each method has its advantages and disadvantages, its advocates and its opponents. Results of the application of investment tax credits (if applicable and if in existence) purposely are not considered at this point.

Proportional Methods. These methods charge off depreciable cost in proportion to elapsed time or in proportion to production. Of the proportional methods, the straight-line method is most widely used.

Straight-Line Method. This method changes depreciation in periodic equal amounts over the estimated useful business life of the asset. The theory of the method is that depreciation is proportional to expired time; wear and tear may or may not be proportional to elapsed time. Its simplicity of computation and application is its greatest advantage. The disadvantages of the method are its failure to consider fluctuations in operating conditions and the failure to equalize depreciation plus maintenance expenses over the life of an asset. Repairs and maintenance tend to increase during the later years of an asset's usefulness; if it is desired to regularize expense charges for maintenance, an equalization allowance for maintenance may be established by regular periodic expense charges and credits to the allowance.

The Working Hours Method. The working hours method implies that an asset depreciates when it is used and does not depreciate when it is not in operation. The extent to which this is correct varies with the nature of the asset. The advantages of the method are ease of application, the charging of depreciation on the basis of operations, and recognition of active use. A disadvantage is its failure to recognize the constant presence of depreciation, regardless of production, under the normal assumption that obsolescence and inadequacy are present as factors within the determination of service life.

Unit Production Method. This method is similar to the working hours method, with the simple substitution of units of production for hours of productivity. The method is based on the assumption that the asset depreciates proportionately to production.

The Composite Life Method. The use of this method involves the computation of the mean average life of a group of assets. After the composite life is computed, any method of depreciation—straight-line, a declining amount method, and so forth—may be employed.

Declining Amount Methods. There are two declining amount methods which are extensively used for financial accounting and for federal income tax purposes. Today, many corporations use a declining amount method for federal income tax reporting and the straight-line method for financial accounting and reporting. Declining amount methods charge off depreciation at a high amount in the first year of the life of an asset and at a decreasingly smaller amount in each succeeding year.

Double-Declining Amount Method. The Internal Revenue Code permits accelerated periodic depreciation expense charges for income tax purposes by approving two declining amount methods—the double-declining amount method and the sum-of-the-years-digits method. To be eligible for either accelerated depreciation method for federal income tax purposes, the fixed asset must have a useful life of at least three years; it must be a new asset; and it must have been acquired after December 31, 1953. Under the Tax Reform Act of 1969, the maximum depreciation for new buildings is limited to 150 percent of the straight-line method. The reader is urged to study related IRS publications as the Internal Revenue Code has been extended to cover residential rental property and rehabilitation of old properties rented to persons of low or moderate income.

ILLUSTRATION. In 1975, a taxpayer purchased an old building; during 1975, he made additions and alterations to it. The cost of the additions and alterations can be depreciated under any approved accelerated method, but the cost of the building cannot.

The double-declining amount method may be used for eligible fixed tangible assets, with a depreciation rate not exceeding twice the straight-line rate (except for buildings, as stated above). Salvage value may be ignored for assets acquired prior to January 1, 1962, because the full cost of the asset is not recovered. The rate is applied to the declining balance, as shown in Illustration 19–1 (to the nearest dollar). In Illustration 19–1, under the double-declining amount method, salvage value is ignored.

ILLUSTRATION 19–1

Depreciation Methods Compared

Year	Straight-Line, 20 Percent of Cost (Less Salvage) per Year	Double-Declining Amount, Rate 40 Percent of Remaining Balance per Year		Sum-of-the Years-Digits
1	$ 20,000	$ 44,000	$(5/15)$	$ 33,333
2	20,000	26,400	$(4/15)$	26,667
3	20,000	15,840	$(3/15)$	20,000
4	20,000	9,504	$(2/15)$	13,333
5	20,000	5,702	$(1/15)$	6,667
Total.	$100,000	$101,446	$(15/15)$	$100,000

Sum-of-the-Years-Digits Method. This is a declining amount method applied in a systematic manner. Under this method, the annual depreciation is computed by applying to cost less estimated salvage, a changing fraction, the denominator of which is the sum-of-the-life periods, and the numerator of which is the number of remaining years of estimated useful life as of the *beginning* of the current fiscal period. For example, if an asset has an estimated life of five years, the denominator is $1 + 2 + 3 + 4 + 5 = 15$. Depreciation for the first year would be $5/15$ of cost less estimated value; for the second year, $4/15$ of cost less estimated salvage; and so on.

Illustration 19–1 shows the annual depreciation under three methods, based upon an asset costing $110,000 new, with a scrap value of $10,000 and an estimated life of five years. Any investment tax credits (if applicable) are purposely ignored in this illustration.

For tax years ending after June 30, 1958, an additional depreciation expense charge may be taken in the year of acquisition of tangible personal property (not buildings)—acquired new or used, and having a useful business life of at least six years. The additional depreciation is limited to 20 percent per taxpayer, based upon the first $10,000 of asset cost.

In computing the additional initial provision, salvage value may be ignored. The provisions of the tax regulations may be set forth as follows: First, compute the new additional allowance on cost, but not in excess of the first $10,000 of cost. Second, compute the first-year depreciation on cost less salvage, less the first-year additional allowance. The sum of the two computations constitutes the depreciation expense for the first year for federal income tax purposes.

ILLUSTRATION.   Machinery (new) with an estimated life of 10 years, which qualifies for the double-declining amount depreciation *and* the new additional first-year provision, is acquired by one taxpayer on January 1, 1975, at a cost of $20,000. The new initial year's depreciation provision is 20 percent of $10,000, or $2,000; this reduces the base to $18,000. Salvage value is estimated at $2,000. The double-declining amount for the first year is $3,200 ($18,000 − $2,000 ÷ .10 × 2). The total first-year depreciation is $5,200.

Where declining amount methods are adopted for tax purposes, they may or may not be used for financial accounting purposes. Many persons object to accelerated depreciation on the basis that it merely offers relief from current taxes and defers until later periods larger amounts of taxes. However, if a company fairly continuously acquires new assets, taxes might be permanently deferred and capital gain advantages may accrue.

In accordance with the concepts of offering full disclosure of all material data in the presentation of financial statements and of proper and adequate financial reporting, deferred income taxes should be recognized in the accounting records. This feature is more fully treated in Chapters 22, 23, and 24.

Because of the significant effects on financial position and results of operations resulting from the depreciation method or methods used, the APB, in *Opinion No. 12* recommends that the following disclosures be made in the financial statements or in *notes* thereto:

a)   Depreciation expense for the period,
b)   Balances of major classes of depreciable assets, by nature or function, at the balance-sheet date,
c)   Accumulated depreciation, either by major classes of depreciable assets or in total, at the balance-sheet date, and
d)   A general description of the method or methods used in computing depreciation with respect to major classes of depreciable assets.

Depreciation by Revaluation.   This method is applicable to a few assets which are affected by conditions not found in the average capital asset when life and scrap value can be reasonably estimated. The difference between the estimated value of the asset at the beginning and at the end of the year equals the amount of depreciation. The method has no advantage except when applied to assets such as small tools, containers, patterns, and a few others. Its disadvantage is the encouragement to substitute a guess for an estimate.

Comments on Asset Replacement.   It must be remembered that depreciation is an allocation of cost and not a provision for asset replacement. In addition, businessmen do not care to earmark funds for specific purposes by creating depreciation funds, but they prefer to keep money in general circulation so far as the business is concerned and to trust their managerial ability to safeguard the general finances, so that fixed assets can be purchased as they are required, or so that funds may be borrowed for such acquisitions. The current assets of a profitable business normally may increase until the time arrives when certain fixed assets are replaced. At the time of replacement, current assets normally can be expected to show a pronounced decrease if fixed assets are replaced in large quantities rather than by small, periodic replacements. Ordinarily, in large business organizations with diversified assets, it is generally true that *each year*, the amounts recovered by depreciation on *all* assets are concurrently invested in the replacement of *some* of them. It is unusual if depreciation exceeds the expenditure for fixed asset replacements.

Comments on Audit Procedures for Fixed Assets

Some of the examination procedures for fixed assets depend upon whether the auditor is conducting the first audit of an established company or a recurring audit. On his first audit of an established business organization, the auditor realizes that he must render an opinion as accurate as if he had been examining the records of that client for a number of consecutive years. Because it is his first examination of an established company, the auditor's responsibility is in no way lessened. The auditor must perform a sufficient amount of analytical work to be convinced that the fixed asset figures are correct, even though this involves an examination of the records of years preceding the year under audit.

The problems with respect to fixed tangible assets in a first audit of an established organization may be classified as (1) those pertaining to the correctness of the gross carrying value of each asset and (2) those pertaining to the accuracy and reasonableness of the net carrying value of each asset.

The propriety of the gross carrying value of each asset is dependent upon the correctness of original acquisition figures, the accuracy of the distinction between capital and revenue expenditures, and the correctness of charging off fixed tangible assets which have been disposed of by sale, retirement, or otherwise.

The propriety of net carrying value is dependent upon the accuracy of the gross carrying value minus the depreciation charged off and the correctness of the charge-off of fully depreciated fixed tangible assets and those disposed of by sale or other methods. The determination of the accuracy of past accounting for gross and net carrying value of fixed tangible assets is a primary responsibility of the auditor on a first examination of an established company.

In a first audit, the auditor must display good judgment and discretion with respect to the extent of the analyses to be made in order to establish the accuracy of the asset values—gross and net—at the date of the current balance sheet. To indicate that each fixed tangible asset account must be completely analyzed from the inception of the business would be not only ridiculous but in many instances impossible. The procedures to be followed for each asset—in an initial examination—are suggested in each applicable section of this chapter and in Chapter 20.

On a repeat engagement, the auditor's problem is much simplified. He must reconcile the opening balance of the ledger figures with his preceding work paper figures and then proceed with the vouching of additions to and deductions from the fixed asset accounts during the year, with proper inspection and verification of supporting data, such as authorizations, invoices, and paid checks. The propriety of the distinction between capital and revenue expenditures must be ascertained. The auditor must be certain that his analyses result in correct figures for capitalization and that transactions, particularly deductions, are not omitted from the accounts.

When several fixed assets have been combined in one account, the auditor must attempt to separate them so that he can determine the adequacy of current depreciation, the accumulation for depreciation, and the adequacy of insurance protection. In many cases involving reorganization and group purchases, accounts appear that contain more than one type of asset. Naturally, accounts should be kept so that a controlling account with each fixed asset group is maintained—with a subsidiary ledger account for each asset in the group. Assets of a fixed nature which are not used in the business should be classified as investments or as other assets.

Management Reports

Periodically, top management should receive internally prepared reports on all fixed assets. The reports should be designed so that operating efficiency may be judged, so that decisions may be made for future capital expenditures, so that decisions may be made on the disposition of assets, and so that the effect of any decision on net income may be determined.

Management reports for proposed acquisitions of fixed assets should be designed so that at least the following questions may be answered:

1. Will the new fixed assets add an amount of net income sufficient to justify the cost?
2. Will expenses be reduced by acquiring the new assets?
3. Will new fixed assets add to diversification by adding new products?
4. In bringing new assets into normal use, what will be the dollar amount of start-up expenses?
5. How many years will be required to recover the cost of the new assets via the increase in cash flow?
6. How are the funds for the new fixed assets to be raised—from bor-

rowing, from issuance of additional capital stock, from net income and cash generated by depreciation, or from cash now in the banks?

SECTION I: INTERNAL CONTROL OF FIXED ASSETS

The objective of internal control of fixed assets is to obtain maximum operating efficiency from the money invested in those assets. The principal points of internal control over fixed assets are as follows: Fixed assets should be acquired only upon proper authorization and requisition. Fixed assets should be controlled physically and on the basis of a controlling account for each group, supported by subsidiary records. Retirements and sales of fixed assets should be properly authorized; for proper ac-

ILLUSTRATION 19–2

INTERNAL CONTROL QUESTIONNAIRE
Fixed Assets

Company_____ Period Covered_____	Yes	No	Not Appli-cable	Remarks
1. Are additions to fixed assets properly authorized and approved by the board of directors, or by the committee or person to whom the board of directors has delegated this authority?	____	____	____	_____
2. Are additions to fixed assets originated by requisition or appropriation that shows:				
a) Probable cost?	____	____	____	_____
b) Description of addition?	____	____	____	_____
c) Accounts to be charged?	____	____	____	_____
d) Reason for the addition?	____	____	____	_____
3. Do idle plant facilities exist? (See Question 2.)	____	____	____	_____
4. Are the costs of constructed fixed assets accumulated by work order?	____	____	____	_____
5. If the answer to Question 4 is "yes," are actual and probable costs compared? (See Question 2.)	____	____	____	_____
6. Is a work-order system used for major repair jobs?	____	____	____	_____
7. Is the policy sound for differentiation between capital and revenue expenditures?	____	____	____	_____
8. If the client constructs fixed assets for his own use by using his regular employees, are the costs properly controlled through:				
a) Payroll records?	____	____	____	_____
b) Disbursement records?	____	____	____	_____
9. Is each general ledger controlling account supported by detailed plant records?	____	____	____	_____
10. Are the detailed plant records balanced (at least annually) with the control accounts?	____	____	____	_____
11. Periodically, is an inventory of fixed assets compared with the detail plant records?	____	____	____	_____
12. Are individual fixed assets tagged, or otherwise identified, and related to the subsidiary ledgers?	____	____	____	_____
13. Are fixed assets priced at:				
a) Cost?	____	____	____	_____
b) Appraisal?	____	____	____	_____
c) Other?	____	____	____	_____

ILLUSTRATION 19–2 (*Continued*)

	Yes	No	Not Applicable	Remarks
14. Does the client:				
a) Use accumulated depreciation accounts?	___	___	___	_____
b) Credit the asset accounts directly?	___	___	___	_____
15. Is written approval required prior to the sale of fixed assets?	___	___	___	_____
16. Is written approval required prior to scrapping a fixed asset?	___	___	___	_____
17. When transfers of fixed assets are made from one department or plant to another department or plant:				
a) Are transfers properly authorized?	___	___	___	_____
b) Is the accounting department notified?	___	___	___	_____
18. Does the client periodically study the fixed assets for purposes of determining adequate insurance?	___	___	___	_____
19. Is the depreciation policy consistent from year to year?	___	___	___	_____
20. Are accumulated depreciation accounts:				
a) Adequate?	___	___	___	_____
b) So large as to result in a "secret" reserve?	___	___	___	_____
21. Have depreciation rates been accepted by the Internal Revenue Service?	___	___	___	_____
22. When assets are sold or otherwise retired:				
a) Are depreciation accumulations properly adjusted and charged?	___	___	___	_____
b) Are asset accounts properly credited?	___	___	___	_____
c) Is useful life properly related to the accumulated depreciation and the depreciation policy and rates?	___	___	___	_____
23. Are fully depreciated assets, still in use, included in the asset accounts?	___	___		_____
24. Are small tools properly safeguarded and kept in specific locations?	___	___	___	_____
25. Are returnable containers:				
a) Properly accounted for?	___	___	___	_____
b) Properly safeguarded?	___	___	___	_____
c) Properly inventoried?	___	___	___	_____

Prepared by_____   Reviewed by_____
Date_____   Date_____

counting entries, the accounting department must be notified of sales and retirements. Small fixed assets, easily transportable, should be under the control of as few persons as possible; and they should be allotted specific locations, if possible.

An internal control questionnaire for fixed tangible assets is shown in Illustration 19–2.

SECTION II: AUDIT PROGRAM FOR LAND AND BUILDINGS

The remaining sections of this chapter will develop audit procedures for land and buildings. Procedures for other fixed assets and the accounting and financial statement considerations are developed in Chapter 20.

Land Cost

The auditor must obtain satisfactory evidence concerning the ownership of land and should judge the propriety of valuation in conformity with the method of acquisition. In accordance with the method of acquiring land, its cost may be determined as indicated below.

Cost for improved land includes such items as the purchase price; cost of options; brokers' commissions, if paid by the purchaser; title examination fees; clearing costs; filling and drainage costs; unpaid taxes assumed; liens assumed; cost of demolishing old structures; and special assessments for improvements such as sidewalks, streets, sewers, and other permanent improvements, provided the special assessment tends to increase the value of the land. In the event of transitory special assessments to improved land, the cost should be charged to expense. Also, for many nontransitory special assessments, no criticism can be offered if the assessments are charged to expense, since the assumed increase in value is often negligible or entirely absent. For federal income tax purposes, special assessments are capital outlays.

Special assessments for improvements may be added to the Land account or carried separately in an account entitled Land Improvements. The use of the Land Improvements account is preferable, because the items therein are subject to depreciation. If special assessments are paid on an installment plan normally offered by the taxing authority, the *entire* assessment cost should be capitalized and a liability created for the unpaid portion. If interest is charged on the installment payments, it should be charged to expense as paid.

In the case of unimproved land, the purchase price only, plus commissions, title examination fees, clearing costs, and draining and filling costs, should appear as the capitalization, unless the land is definitely in a stage of current improvement, at which time assessments and taxes commonly are added to original cost. Most land-tract owners and developers charge all current carrying costs to the Land account. After productivity results, proper distinction must again be made between revenue and capital outlays. In the financial statements, the auditor should disclose the method of treating all costs incurred in the purchase and development of unimproved land.

Land and Other Assets Acquired in Noncash Transactions. If land or any other asset is required by gift, it may be recorded either at cost to the preceding owner if that figure represents a current market price, or at the current market price ascertained by *competent* appraisal. Assets acquired by gift should be set up in the accounts only after all of the requirements of the donor have been fulfilled. When assets are acquired by gift, the auditor must be certain that the client has free title to the property, not only so far as public records are concerned but also with respect to the requirements of the donor.

If assets are acquired and paid for in the capital stock of the acquiring corporation, they preferably should be capitalized at the fair market price of the capital stock so given, provided a fair market price is available—and normally, it is obtainable for a going concern. If a market price for the stock is not available, the value of the assets should first be established at their cash cost figure, if one is available. This procedure indirectly assigns a value to the stock so issued. If the par value of stock so issued exceeds the cash cost basis, the difference should be charged to the Discount on Capital Stock account. If a cash cost figure is not available for the assets, an appraisal may result in a reasonable valuation figure. In the absence of fraud, the decision of the board of directors will prevail, and the auditor is justified in accepting the reasonable conclusion of that body.

If stocks and bonds held as investments are given in exchange for fixed assets, the assets acquired should be recorded at the current market price of the securities given. A gain or loss on the disposition of the securities would be recognized at the date of the exchange.

If land has been purchased and a purchase-money mortgage given the seller as a part of the purchase price, the auditor must be certain that the land has been charged with the full contract price and that the mortgage has been credited to the proper liability account. If there is an existing mortgage when land is purchased, the buyer may either take the land subject to the mortgage or personally assume the obligation. In either case, it is necessary that the full price of the land be charged to the Land account.

Demolition Costs. If land is purchased upon which a building is located and if the building is razed immediately for the erection of a new structure, the cost of the old building and the cost of razing it are proper additions to the land cost; the realized salvage from razing reduces the land cost. In this case, the primary purpose of the purchase is to acquire the land; consequently, all costs incurred should be charged to the Land account. When land and buildings are purchased together and the decision to demolish is formed after acquisition—either due to choice or due to defective structure—the cost of demolition plus the undepreciated cost of the building is normally charged to expense.

Land held for business purposes must be segregated in the balance sheet from land held for investment or contemplated future use.

Audit Program for Land

The following subsections set forth the procedures within the audit program.

Schedule the Land. On an initial examination, the auditor's work papers should contain an analysis of the Land account from the inception

ILLUSTRATION 19–3

ACQUA FIBRE COMPANY

Land Acct. #50
December 31, 1975

	Initials	Date
Prepared By		
Approved By		

Date		Description	Amount
1974			
Oct.	10	Deposit to L. R. Anderson, broker, for offer to purchase Lots 9 and 10 in Taylor Subdivision, Anderson Township, each lot 400′ by 600′; from L. M. Doud, at a total cost of $100,000	$ 10,000√
	30	Land survey, Bevis and Associates, civil engineers	600√
Nov.	15	Balance to L. M. Doud ⊙†	90,000√
	30	C. R. Beirne, legal fees	1,000√
Dec.	31	Balance per ledger	$101,600
1975			
Aug.	1	F. W. Pressler and Associates, Inc., architects; building plans	10,000√
Nov.	8	Excavation and foundation, Diesel	34,000√
Dec.	31	Balance per ledger	$145,600
	31	Deduct: Audit adjustment 7	44,000
		Balance per Audit	$101,600

AUDIT ADJUSTMENT 7 (10)

Building	44,000	
Land		44,000
To remove the following costs to the Building account:		
Plans	$10,000	
Excavation and foundation	34,000	
	$44,000	

√ Traced to disbursements records.
⊙ Contract examined.
† Confirmed by C. R. Beirne.

of the business (if this is reasonable), as shown in Illustration 19–3. If it is not possible to revert to the inception of the Land account, that account should be reviewed for several past years and large additions and deductions should be investigated.

For the permanent file, notes should be prepared concerning the methods of acquisition, excerpts (or copies) of deeds, title guaranty policies, vouchers supporting purchase authorizations, appraisal reports, ownership confirmations, registration dates, notations of mortgages and their cancellation, and sketches of the plot or plots.

In a repeat engagement, the land schedule will include the balance at the beginning of the year, plus and minus changes made in the period under examination.

Examine Title Papers. The objective of the auditor is to determine ownership and proper valuation of the land. Land title is normally transferred by the execution of a deed, which is publicly recorded in order to assure title protection; whereas the *majority* of other assets are transferred by ordinary sale, usually unaccompanied by publicly recorded evidence of title transfer.

The auditor must ascertain that real property is recorded in the name of the client—if the client is the owner. On a first audit, therefore, the auditor should obtain a confirmation of ownership from the client's attorney or from the title guaranty company. In lieu of requesting an ownership confirmation, deeds and guaranty policies may be examined; also, tax bills prepared in the name of the owner may be examined as evidence of ownership. After determining land ownership, the process requires no repetition in subsequent engagements, unless additional land is acquired.

Normally, public records are not examined by the auditor; that is a function of a lawyer. In addition, if the auditor were to examine public records—mortgage records, lien and judgment records, and assessment records—the probabilities are that he would obtain evidence no more conclusive than that obtained from an attorney.

From his examination of title papers and confirmations the auditor should extract pertinent information for his permanent file, which will include: a description of the property; its location and size; the date of transfer to the client and the name of the preceding owner; recording data on the title papers such as date, deed book, and page number; and the lawyer's opinion of the title search.

If a title policy is also in existence, it should be compared with the deed or other title papers to determine that the date contained therein agree with the title papers.

Determine the Valuation Basis of the Land. Preferably, land should be carried at cost if it originally was acquired by purchase. The auditor should examine the original purchase contract, assuming that it still is obtainable. If available, the minutes of the board of directors authorizing the purchase, and paid checks should be examined. Copies of these records and documents should become a part of the permanent file. It may happen that none of these records is available after the expiration of years, in which event the auditor must be satisfied with the continued carrying value over the years, at a constant figure. If the land was acquired in a noncash transaction, it should be carried in the accounts in accordance with the principles set forth earlier.

If land originally was acquired by purchase at a price far below current replacement cost, it may be that after the expiration of years, an upward appraisal of the land is justifiable. In such an event, the auditor should examine appraisal reports and satisfy himself with respect to their features; examine the minutes of the board of directors for the acceptance of the appraisal, and examine the authorization to increase the carrying amount above cost; examine the capital account credited at the time of recording the appraisal; and examine the disposition, if any, of that capital account.

Vouch Charges and Credits to the Land Account. Charges and credits to the Land account should be vouched by reference to original documents—such as contracts, invoices, and deeds, and authorizations of stockholders, boards of directors, or other appropriate bodies for the incurrence of charges or credits.

Proper charges to Land accounts were set forth in the section of this chapter entitled "Land Cost." If the cost of land is to be derived, as when acquired by gift, the exchange of investment securities, or the issuance of capital stock, reference must be made back to the original basis and noted in the work papers.

Determine Liens and Assessments. An important phase of ownership verification—particularly in an initial audit—is the determination of the existence of or freedom from mortgages, taxes in arrears, judgments, and other liens. The existence of such liens should be included in the confirmation obtained from the attorney or title company. If liens do exist, they should be shown as liabilities and should not be deducted from the land value. In some cases, it has been assumed that there was clear title to land when in reality encumbrances existed.

Paid tax bills should be examined and traced to the cash disbursements records and the proper expense accounts in order to obtain added proof of the existence of or freedom from existing liens and assessments.

It occasionally happens that a deed is in the name of the equitable owner of the land, who is some person other than the client. In such cases, the auditor should mention the fact in his report.

Verify Land Revenue and Maintenance Costs. If land produces revenue, the auditor should examine the agreements and data giving rise to the revenue and should prepare appropriate notes. Entries should be traced to the accounts and the summarization of the entries therein "tied in" with the data obtainable from the agreements. Confirmation of amounts received may be requested along with confirmations for rent accruals.

ILLUSTRATION. A client informed his auditor that he had purchased a land site, for which a Land account properly appeared in the ledger. The auditor confirmed the land title and also examined the details of the Land account, and agreed with the charges for purchase price, title search cost, and so forth. The client's records contained no other data connected with the land. The auditor decided to examine the land site and discovered that it was used as a parking lot, having been rented from the client, who failed to record the rental income.

Building Cost

The principles set forth for "Land Cost" in the preceding section should be adhered to for the determination of the cost of buildings when acquired for cash, by exchange, by gift, by donation, by giving investment securities, or by giving unissued or treasury capital stock.

When acquired for cash or other items, the cost of buildings includes the contract purchase price, the cost of altering and remodeling for purposes of the new owner, unpaid taxes and accrued interest assumed by the purchaser, and legal costs of acquisition.

When buildings are constructed, the cost includes: architects' fees, permit and license costs, cost of materials, cost of construction labor, cost of construction sheds, premiums for workmen's compensation insurance, casualty insurance premiums during construction, and cost of easements.

If the view is taken that financing and certain other costs incurred during the construction period constitute costs of the structure, those items should be added. Examples include paid interest costs during construction, bond discount (or premium) amortized during the construction period, uninsured damages paid, costs of strikes, and property taxes during the construction period. The modern tendency is to consider these items

ILLUSTRATION 19-4

		Initials	Date
HIDDEN HILLS COMPANY	Prepared By		
Building Acct. #60 December 31, 1975	Approved By		

Date		Explanation	Amount
1974 Dec.	31	Balance per ledger and audit	$250,000
1975 June	30	Additions, 1975: Office addition to northwest corner, brick and concrete. Cordes Construction Co.	√ ⊙46,000
Sept.	30	Roof repairs to old structure; not a new roof	⊙ 1,000
Dec.	31	Balance per ledger	$297,000
	31	Deduct: Audit adjustment 8	1,000
	31	Balance per Audit	$296,000

AUDIT ADJUSTMENT 9 (7)

Building Maintenance 1,000
    Building 1,000
Roof repairs removed to maintenance.

√ Vouched to authorization of board of directors, dated February 19, 1975.
⊙ Vouched to invoices and cash disbursements.

as expenses—and properly so—as they are not usual and reasonable costs incurred in asset construction.

Audit Program for Buildings

The procedures to be followed in the audit program for buildings are outlined in the following subsections.

Prepare Schedules for the Building Accounts. In a repeat engagement, work papers setting forth current-period additions and deductions may be prepared, as shown in Illustration 19–4. A separate work paper may be prepared for each building if the form of Illustration 19–4 is followed; or one work paper may be used for all buildings and the data for additions and deductions spread horizontally on the sheet. Illustration 19–5 presents an analysis for the related (Illustration 19–4) accumulated depreciation of building.

ILLUSTRATION 19–5

HIDDEN HILLS COMPANY			Initials	Date
Accumulated Depreciation		Prepared By		
Building Acct. #60.1		Approved By		
December 31, 1975				

Date		Folio	Explanation	Amount
1974				
Dec.	31		Balance per ledger and per audit	$45,000
1975			Additions, 1975:	
Dec.	31	GJ 19	Added 2 percent of $297,000 for one year	5,940
	31		Balance per ledger	$50,940
	31		Deduct: Audit adjustment 9	480
				$50,460

AUDIT ADJUSTMENT 9 (7)

Accumulated Depreciation, Building 480
    Depreciation of Building   480
Correct depreciation, 1975:
    $250,000 @ 2% for 12 months $5,000
    $46,000 @ 2% for 6 months.   460
    Total depreciation, 1975 . . . . $5,460
    Recorded   5,940
    Adjustment to reduce accumulation . . . . . . $ 480

In a first examination the auditor may review the records of prior years in order to establish the propriety of the Building accounts. Work papers on a first audit of buildings may contain in addition to the customary analysis prepared in a repeat engagement, such data as the following: excerpts for authority to purchase, construct, and dispose of buildings; verification of ownership; ascertainment of proper cost; notes on contracts and other data connnected with the purchase or construction; an opinion statement of the propriety of the distinctions made between capital and revenue expenditures; an analysis of the cost of additions and improvements; computations of profits and losses in the income statements and the federal income tax returns when buildings were sold or otherwise disposed of; and computations determining the correctness of annual amortization, if buildings were erected on leased land.

Vouch and Schedule Charges and Credits.   Payments made in connection with the purchase of buildings and the expenditures made on the buildings during the audit period should be vouched. The charges and credits should be in accordance with the principles of accounting applicable to the determination of correct cost. If purchase price or construction costs have exceeded the amount authorized, approval for the excess cost should be obtained.

In a first audit, in connection with the review of the records of prior years, the auditor will verify authorizations for the purchase and/or construction of buildings. Architects' estimates, purchase orders, and contracts must be examined; and payments for the purchase or construction should be vouched as far back as necessary to establish proper cost. Normally, buildings are not so old for the present owner as to render this procedure impossible. If in a first audit the examination is limited to one year, a statement to that effect should appear in the audit report; in addition, the auditor should review major charges and credits, even if the reports of the predecessor accountant are satisfactory.

The auditor should examine expense accounts for prior years to determine the accuracy and reasonableness of the distinctions made between capital and revenue expenditures. For ordinary versus extraordinary repairs, inquiry must be made of the expectations when the repair was made, as to whether it would extend the originally estimated life.

In the event that a company is building its own plants or has contract construction work in progress at the end of the period, the auditor must ascertain that the costs of construction are not included in inventories, but are entered in fixed assets or are shown separately as "advances on contracts for fixed asset construction." The latter treatment is preferable because of the current nonproductivity of construction work in progress. All liabilities for construction work completed and not paid must be shown; an examination of invoices should determine this, accompanied by an examination of existing contracts.

ILLUSTRATION.   Assume that the contract price of a building is $500,000, that $200,000 of work is completed and paid for, and that $100,000 of work is finished and not paid for; in this case, $200,000 should appear as "advances on contracts." If the $100,000 has been billed, the advances should be shown as $300,000 and the liability thereon as $100,000. Neither during construction nor at any other time should profits in connection with the constructed buildings appear; and if any such profits have been taken up, the auditor must eliminate them by reversing the entries that placed the profit in the records.

Some accountants consider it proper to capitalize interest paid during construction and the amortization of bond discount during construction, as stated earlier. If this position is followed, premium amortization during construction should reduce total construction cost. This older practice is based upon the theory that no revenue is forthcoming during construction and that interest charges, among other expenses, must therefore be added to the cost of the construction. When construction is completed, interest charges should be shown as expenses.

Among accountants there is some difference of opinion as to whether any portion of the general factory overhead should be capitalized as a part of the cost of a fixed asset constructed. The problem is related to the correct determination of net income; some accountants contend that no portion of the overhead should be capitalized, whereas others believe that some portion should be capitalized. If a portion of the *regularly incurred* overhead were charged to the fixed asset, the goods manufactured for sale would be relieved of part of their usual costs; therefore, the cost of goods manufactured and sold would be reduced and net income for the period increased. Proprietorship would not be reduced to its correct amount until the constructed fixed asset was completely depreciated by periodic depreciation expense charges. Therefore, if the production of the fixed asset *does not* increase the factory overhead which is normally consumed by the products manufactured for sale, no portion of the regularly incurred overhead should be charged to the fixed assets. If the production of the fixed asset *does* increase the factory overhead— and it *usually does increase it*—and if the increase were absorbed by the regularly manufactured product, the cost of the regularly manufactured product would be overstated and net income during the construction period reduced. Therefore, the *increased* overhead logically should be added to the cost of the fixed assets, since these variable overhead costs are incurred because of the decision to construct. The auditor must verify material, labor, and overhead charges applicable to the constructed assets.

If a company is using a leased building, the leasehold must be examined, primarily in order to ascertain if improvements are being amortized over the life of the lease or the life of the improvement. The lease is also examined, so that the auditor is familiar with cancellation clauses and their effect upon the carrying value of the improvements made to the property. Many office buildings, department stores, specialty stores, and hotels are constructed on leased land. Most manufacturing companies own their land and buildings.

Ascertain that Buildings Are in the Name of the Client. As in the case of land, the auditor must examine the client's records and obtain other evidence to determine the ownership of buildings. Confirmations may be requested, and it may be necessary to examine public records. The examination should conclude with proof that there are no unrecorded mortgages or unrecorded liens for unpaid taxes and assessments.

Buildings owned but used for other than business purposes should be shown as investments or other assets in the balance sheet. If buildings are owned by a real estate company or by a builder, the properties should be carried as inventories and priced accordingly.

Determine Liens. Records must be investigated and proof obtained to determine the extent of liens against buildings, which must be shown as liabilities and not as reductions of the book value of the buildings; legal assistance may be required.

Investigate Proper Authorization for Appraisal Increases and Decreases. The auditor must examine appraisal reports, actions of the board of directors with respect to an appraisal, and the method of treating depreciation on the appraisal, both for account record purposes and for federal income tax purposes.

As previously mentioned, buildings preferably should be priced at cost less the accumulated depreciation. If other-than-cost figures are reflected in the accounts, the valuation should be at gross appraisal less the accumulated depreciation based on the appraisal. In the latter event, the auditor must determine that the annual depreciation charge has been correctly handled. If the reader is not familiar with the theories underlying these two methods, he should consult any recognized theory text. An illustration appears in Chapter 26.

If depreciation is based on original cost, it is necessary that the Appreciation of Fixed Assets account be reduced annually so that all accounts connected with the asset are eliminated when the asset is fully depreciated and retired. To base depreciation charges on appraisal (reproduction cost) is the preferred method, providing that the appraisal is recorded in the accounts.

Depreciation charges should be based on appraisal in order to compute net income on a basis consistent with balance sheet representations for the related assets. At the end of the life of the asset, the originally created Appreciation of Fixed Assets account will still be in the records, unless it has been permanently capitalized in the form of a capital stock dividend.

Prepare Depreciation Schedules. The responsibility of the auditor with reference to the annual depreciation provision and the total accumulated depreciation is to determine that both the annual provision and the total accumulation are created in accordance with accepted principles, consistently applied; that the annual provision is correctly computed; and that the basis of computation is proper.

A depreciation schedule may be prepared separately, as shown in Illustration 19-5, or it may be placed on the same work paper used to schedule the related asset. See the Illustrative Audit.

The auditor should verify annual charges in order to determine the propriety of the client's computations; and he must ascertain that the depreciation policy is consistently followed. The amounts of depreciation taken must be in accordance with sound practices for the particular assets involved. Net book values should be reviewed from the point of view of the general condition of the asset. He must determine to the best of his ability that the estimated life of the asset is proper and that salvage values are reasonable. The rates must be high enough to provide for obsolescence and inadequacy. The auditor then must determine that the entries for the amounts of depreciation are made in the correct manner and to the proper accounts. Determination must be made that depreciation is based upon proper cost or other basic value, less estimated salvage value, determined in accordance with the estimated useful business life of the asset.

The auditor should discuss depreciation amounts and policies with the client, especially when he is of the opinion that policies and amounts and methods fail to reflect conditions reasonably. If he believes that depreciation is materially overstated or understated, his position should be made clear in his report. He should insist that the method be sound and practical, and that it provide sufficient depreciation. Depreciation and depletion—for income tax return purposes—may differ from the book depreciation; this is proper if both are correct for their respective purposes.

The use of a blanket rate of depreciation for *all* assets constitutes unacceptable practice; each asset or related group of assets should have its own account, depreciation method and rate, and accumulated depreciation account. Proper proration of depreciation expense must be made between the manufacturing, selling, and administrative divisions.

Accumulation for depreciation accounts should be verified for entries made during the current fiscal period. The auditor must determine that book balances at the beginning of the year agree with his preceding work paper balances; and he must verify entries for the current year. In the event of a first audit, it may be necessary to analyze the accounts as far back as necessary to determine the propriety of the total balance of the account. Approval by the United States Treasury Department of federal income tax returns of past years will serve as a guide to the reasonableness at the top level of past annual depreciation. Also, on a first audit, a review should be made of all larger amounts.

Charges to accumulations for depreciation accounts should be investigated to determine their reasons and propriety. The only charges to accumulated depreciation accounts which should appear are (*a*) debits for extraordinary repairs and replacements which have the effect of lengthening the life of the asset; (*b*) debits for assets sold or otherwise disposed of, for an amount equal to the accumulated account against the asset; and (*c*) correcting entries. In connection with fixed asset retirement, the auditor must determine also that the asset is removed from the asset account to the full extent of its cost (or other basic value).

All losses or gains on asset disposition must be properly accounted for, and proper disposal must be made of the losses or gains. Income tax provisions with respect to assets carried in group accounts must not be ignored. It is therefore better to carry separate asset and accumulated depreciation accounts, so that losses may be considered as such and not appear as accumulated depreciation account charges.

The auditor must always obtain an idea of the extent of repair and replacement and general maintenance work performed in connection with fixed assets. Some companies are lax with respect to maintenance, whereas others maintain all fixed equipment in excellent operating condition.

Investigate Insurance Coverage. Insurance policies in effect on buildings must be reviewed by the auditor in order to determine the adequacy of protection. In the event of a loss from a casualty, the auditor must ascertain that the accounting has properly set forth such losses. The final net loss should, of course, be shown at its net amount after insurance adjustments have been made. When a building has been destroyed, either intentionally or by casualty, the Building account and all other accounts connected with the building must be completely closed out.

Ascertain that the Accounting for Profits or Losses on Sales Is Proper. The profit or loss on the sale of a building or any other fixed asset is the difference between the amount received and the book value of the asset sold. The profit or loss is partially affected by the method of computing depreciation from the end of the preceding accounting period to the date of the sale in the current accounting period. Variations in practice may be illustrated as follows:

A Company: Depreciation is computed from the exact date of acquisition to the exact date of disposition.

B Company: Depreciation at the annual rate is computed on the period-opening balance of the account, plus or minus one half of dispositions are not considered.

C Company: Depreciation at the annual rate is computed on the period-closing balance of the account, and acquisitions and dispositions are not considered.

D Company: Depreciation at the annual rate is computed on the period-opening balance of the account, plus or minus one half of the annual depreciation on *net* acquisitions or dispositions during the year.

E Company: Depreciation at the annual rate is computed to the nearest end of the month on assets acquired or disposed of.

The auditor should vouch disposition entries to determine that they conform to accepted principles and practice. A profit may be due to over-depreciation based on cost, or it may be due to a rise in the market price of an asset. Determination of the profit normally is made at the time of auditing the fixed asset. For federal tax purposes, the gain is taxable. If the asset is traded for a similar new asset, no gain (or loss) is recognized for taxation purposes. Any existing contracts or directors' authorizations drawn up in connection with the disposition must be examined, and notes and mortgages taken in settlement must be examined.

Verify Building Revenues and Expenses. When buildings or portions of them produce rental revenue, the auditor, by reasonable test, must verify the revenues and the expenses incurred in earning the rental revenue. Whether or not a rental agent is used, lease or other rental agreements should be examined, together with the rental schedule. The amounts called for under the lease agreements should be totaled for the year and compared with the total of the rent revenues recorded—after allowing for lost rentals caused by idle space and uncollected rents. If necessary, the auditor may request confirmations of rentals from the tenants, as well as confirmations of delinquent rents. Rental revenue may or may not be accrued; the policy for accruing expenses of the rental property should be consistent with the policy followed for the accrual of rental revenues.

The audit of the expenses connected with rented buildings should follow the same procedure as the examination of any other expense, with a sufficient examination of each type of expense to assure the accuracy of the results.

QUESTIONS

1. A CPA reviewed a random sample of 40 maintenance job orders and determined in each the dollar amount of capital items improperly expensed. He wishes to estimate this amount for the population (all maintenance job orders) with a 95 percent level of confidence. The 95 percent refers to the probability that the true population value will fall within the limits thus established for:
   a) Only this sample.
   b) All samples selected from this population.
   c) All samples of this size selected from this population.
   d) All samples of this size selected from any population.

2. While assisting Basic Products Co. in the preparation of unaudited financial statements, the CPA noted that Basic Products had increased property, plant and equipment to reflect a recent property appraisal. In this circumstance the CPA's reporting responsibility is met by:
   a) Issuing the statements on plain paper without reference to the CPA.
   b) Advising Basic's management of the deviation from generally accepted accounting principles.
   c) Describing the deviation from generally accepted accounting principles in his disclaimer of opinion.
   d) Stating in his disclaimer that Basic's financial statements are unaudited.

3. In connection with his review of plant additions, the CPA ordinarily would take exception to the capitalization of the cost of:
   a) Major reconditioning of a recently acquired secondhand floor scale.
   b) Machine operator's wages during a period of testing a new roof.

  c) Room partitions installed at the request of a new long-term lessee in the office building.

  d) Maintenance of an unused stand-by plant.

4. In connection with an audit of the fixed assets of a manufacturing company, what are the general procedures by which an auditor may satisfy himself (*a*) that all of the owned assets are recorded, and (*b*) that the amounts at which the assets are recorded are proper and in accordance with accepted accounting principles? Explain how each procedure will assist in satisfying the auditor, and whether the procedure is applicable to (*a*) or (*b*). Ignore depreciation.

5. Frost, Inc., was organized July 1, 1975, with an authorized capital of 150,000 shares of common stock. One half of the stock was sold for cash at $90 per share, and the other half of the stock was given in payment for a fully equipped building and a land site. During the course of your audit for the six months ended December 31, 1975, you noted that the fixed asset accounts involved were charged for a total of $10,000,000 and that the Common Stock account was credited for $10,000,000. In view of the fact that the board of directors may use any valuation it desires, do you consider the fixed assets correctly charged for $10,000,000?

6. As of January 1, 1975, Sons, Inc., leased ten acres of land, on a part of which it immediately constructed a building with an estimated life of 50 years. On March 31, 1975, a two-acre section was subleased to the Tremble Company, which constructed a wooden building with an estimated life of 25 years. The Sons, Inc., lease is for 40 years without renewal, and the sublease to Tremble for 30 years.

  What procedure should be followed by the auditor in his examination of the financial statements of Sons, Inc.? Prepare your answer in the form of an audit program.

7. *a*) A company built a fixed asset for its own use. It used its regular employees to construct the asset. This work was done during that period of the year when normal product manufacture was at a low point. The new asset cost $100,000, which did not include generally proratable factory overhead, but did include overhead applicable to this construction. If the asset had been built under contract, it would have cost $110,000. The company desires to put the asset on the records at $110,000 and asks your advice. Is the request reasonable and satisfactory?

  b) Assume that management insisted that the asset be placed in the records at $110,000. Prepare the entry to put the asset in the records and the entry to show depreciation at the end of the first year, assuming a scrap value of $10,000 and a life of 25 years, under the straight-line method.

8. On January 1, 1975, the Avonne Company assigned to the Brigand Company, for a bonus of $240,000, its lease on a vacant land site; the lease will run until January 1, 2000, with an option of renewal for an additional period of 20 years.

  During the year 1975, Brigand constructed a building on the land, with an estimated life of 50 years, at a cost of $800,000. On January

1, 1976, the building was ready for occupancy; and the company installed removable machinery with an estimated average service life of 20 years, at a cost of $1,400,000. Land improvements cost $180,000 and had an estimated life of 20 years.

Based upon the preceding statements, over what period should each of the items be written off in the records of the Brigand Company? Present reasons for your answers.

9. In the course of the audit of the financial statements of Detach, Inc., an analysis of the Building account showed the following debits and the reasons therefor:

   a) A fee of $10,000 paid to a firm of industrial engineers for advice and plans concerning the rearrangement of factory machinery. The advice was not followed.

   b) Title examination fees of $1,000 for a prospective land purchase in connection with a contemplated plan for acquiring a land site for another factory.

   c) Major roof construction, at a cost of $20,000. The roof was constructed of the same materials as the original roof, which also cost $20,000.

   d) Cost of moving machinery from the second floor to the first floor, $3,000.

   e) Cost of floor repairs for the places from which the machinery in (*d*) was moved, $1,000.

   What is your position with respect to the propriety or impropriety of each of the preceding entries?

10. In the course of the examination of the financial statements of the Olds Company, the following entries were discovered:

Buildings.	200,000	
Appreciation of Fixed Assets		200,000
To revalue the buildings in accordance with appraisal of the American Appraisal Company. Original cost of the buildings, 16 years ago, $1,600,000. This is the first revaluation of any asset.		
Appreciation of Fixed Assets	600,000	
Common Stock Dividend Payable		600,000
Dividend declared on common stock, payable on June 25 to stockholders of record as of June 1		
Common Stock Dividend Payable	600,000	
Common Stock.		600,000

Is the situation as recorded acceptable practice? Is the procedure legal in your state? If the dividend were a cash dividend, would you change your answers in any way?

11. The Wall Company owns a modern building which has been idle for several months. Recently, it was leased to the Street Company for four years, with an option to purchase. The terms were as follows:

   The Street Company is to pay a rental of $4,000 per month, and is also required to pay $5,000 quarterly to the lessor. The $5,000 is to be applied toward the option to purchase and against the purchase price of $500,000 if the option is exercised. If the option is not exercised, the amounts are to be considered as additional rent. The option may be exercised by the lessee at any time during the four-year period.

All improvements and additions made by Street are to revert to Wall at the end of the four-year term if the purchase option is not exercised.

The building cost the Wall Company $500,000. It was estimated to have a depreciable life of 20 years. At the date of execution of the lease, the plant was two years old, and the accumulated depreciation was $50,000.

During the first year of the lease, the Street Company spent $150,000 in improvements of a permanent nature.

Because the sales option price was equal to cost to the Wall Company, the lessor decided to omit annual depreciation of $25,000. Wall further supported its position by pointing out that depreciation on the building for four years would amount to $100,000, whereas the depreciated value of the improvements would amount to $120,000.

a) Is the Wall Company correct in omitting depreciation?

b) How should the Wall Company treat the $5,000 received quarterly?

c) How should the foregoing data be shown in the financial statements?

12. In prior years, Nott, Inc., a manufacturing company, has used an accelerated depreciation method for its depreciable assets for both Federal income tax and financial reporting. At the beginning of 1975 the Corporation changed to the straight-line method for financial reporting. As a result, depreciation expense for the year was $200,000 less for financial reporting than for income tax purposes, an amount which you consider to be material. The Corporation did not use interperiod income tax allocation in 1975. Taxable income for 1975 was $600,000. Assume that the income tax rate was 48 percent:

a) For financial statement presentation:

(1) Describe the effects of the accounting change on the Nott 1975 balance sheet, income statement and funds statement. Cite specific amounts in your answer.

(2) Explain what disclosure of the accounting change should be made in the 1975 financial statements.

b) For the audit report:

(1) Assuming that the financial statement disclosure is considered to be adequately informative, discuss the effects that the change in depreciation methods should have on the audit report.

(2) Assuming that the financial statement disclosure of the change in depreciation methods is not considered to be adequately informative, discuss the effects on the audit report.

(3) Discuss whether the audit report should indicate approval of the change in depreciation methods.

(4) Discuss the effects on the audit report of the failure to use interperiod income tax allocation.

(AICPA, adapted)

PROBLEMS

1. Waves Land Development Corporation is a closely held corporation engaged in the business of purchasing large tracts of land, subdividing the tracts, and installing paved streets and utilities. The Corporation does not construct buildings for the buyers of the land and does not have

any affiliated construction companies. Undeveloped land is usually leased for farming until the Corporation is ready to begin developing it.

The Corporation finances its land acquisitions by mortgages; the mortgagees require audited financial statements. This is your first audit of the Corporation and you have now begun the examination of the financial statements for the year ended December 31, 1975.

Your preliminary review of the records has indicated that the Corporation would have had a highly profitable year except that the president and vice president were reimbursed for exceptionally large travel and entertainment expenses.

a) The Corporation has three tracts of land in various stages of development. List the audit procedures to be employed in the verification of the physical existence and title to the Corporation's three landholdings.

b) The president of the Corporation has asked you if you will prepare a report that will contain only the balance sheet. Before you can reply, he adds that he will remove the income statement from your report before submitting it to the mortgagees if you refuse to prepare a report containing only the balance sheet.

   (1) Would generally accepted auditing standards permit the preparation of an audit report containing only a balance sheet? Discuss.

   (2) What would be your response to the president's threat to remove the income statement from your audit report? Discuss.

(AICPA, adapted)

2. On July 15, 1975, John Meents, your client, sold his apartment building to Ray Luetter. The escrow statement follows:

	John Meents, Seller		Ray Luetter, Buyer	
	Charges	*Credits*	*Charges*	*Credits*
Sales price		$250,000	$250,000	
Paid directly to seller	$ 10,000			$ 10,000
First mortgage assumed by buyer	106,000			106,000
Purchase money mortgage	84,000			84,000
Prorations:				
Real estate taxes		250	250	
Insurance adjustment.		200	200	
Interest		300	300	
Fees:				
Escrow.	100		100	
Title insurance			790	
Recording	5		10	
Attorney.	25		50	
Revenue stamps.			550	
Funds deposited in escrow account:				
July 14, 1975				52,250
Items paid from escrow account:				
Commission to Arcose Realty Co..	15,000			
Remit:				
John Meents	35,610			
Total.	$250,750	$250,750	$252,250	$252,250

Meents's accounting records are maintained on the cash basis. When you undertake the September 30, 1975 quarterly audit for your client the following information is available to you:

(1)   A "Suspense" account was opened for money received in connection with the sale of the property.

(2)   The apartment building and land were purchased on July 1, 1971, for $225,000. The building was being depreciated over a 40-year life by the straight-line method. Accumulated depreciation at December 31, 1974, was $17,500. A half year's depreciation has been consistently recorded on Meents's records for assets purchased or sold during the year. No depreciation has been recorded for 1975.

(3)   The contract of sale stated that the price for the land on which the building was built was $25,000, the cost recorded on Meents's records.

(4)   The purchase money mortgage payments are $1,000 per month plus accrued interest. The first payment was due August 1, 1975.

You are requested to prepare the audit adjustments to record the sale on Meents's records.

(AICPA, adapted)

3.   In your examination of the financial statements of Oyler, Inc., as of December 31, 1975, the contents of certain accounts and other pertinent information appear below.

Building

Date	Explanation	Debit	Credit	Balance
12–31–74	Balance. 100,000			100,000
7–1–75	New air conditioner	17,510	1,510	116,000
9–1–75	Insurance recovery		2,000	114,000

Accumulated Depreciation, Building

Date	Explanation	Debit	Credit	Balance
12–31–74	Balance: 15 years at 4% of $100,000.		60,000	60,000
12–31–75	Annual depreciation		4,440	64,440

On June 15, 1975, the company's old air conditioner was badly damaged by lightning. The air conditioner was replaced by a new and more efficient unit. The company received $2,000 as an insurance adjustment under the terms of its policy for damage to the air conditioner.

The invoice from the Crane Air Conditioning Company, dated July 1, 1975, and charged to the Building account by Oyler, Inc., follows:

List price: New air conditioner	$17,000
Sales tax: 3% of $17,000	510
Total including installation	$17,510
Less: Allowance for old air conditioner, to be removed at the expense of the Crane Air Conditioning Company.	1,510
Net Invoice price	$16,000

While examining the preceding expenditure, you ascertained that the terms included a two percent cash discount which was properly computed and taken. The sales tax is not subject to discount.

A review of subsidiary property records disclosed that the replaced air conditioner was installed when the building was constructed and was recorded at a cost of $10,000, and charged to the building account. According to its manufacturer the new air conditioner should be serviceable for 15 years.

In computing depreciation for retirements, Oyler, Inc., consistently treated a fraction of a month as a full month.

Prepare the audit adjustments for entry on the records of Oyler, Inc. The accounts have not been closed. Support your entries with computations.

4. For $200,000 Saline, Inc. purchased land upon which was located a building. Legal fees for the contract of sale and for title examination amounted to $2,000. The records of the seller showed the following:

Land $100,000
Building 200,000
Accumulated depreciation, building 180,000

Saline, Inc., immediately razed the building and realized $3,000 from the sale of building materials. Six months were necessary to construct a new building, which cost $600,000. Taxes during the construction period amounted to $2,000. In order to build the factory, it was necessary for Saline to borrow $200,000 for a period of two years, giving a first mortgage on the land and building. The interest rate on the loan was six percent. Insurance during construction was carried by Saline, Inc. Premiums were $5,000 for a five year period. An executive of the company spent the entire six months conferring with architects and contractors. His salary is $80,000 per year.

The client requests that you determine the proper cost (*a*) of the land and (*b*) of the building.

5. During the course of your audit of the financial statements of Briggs, Inc., which was organized in June, 1975, the following accounts appeared in the general ledger at the date of the audit, December 31, 1975:

Fixed Assets

Date		Item	Debits
1975			
June	1	Organization fees paid to the state	3,000
	1	Bond discount on $1,000,000 of ten-year, 6 percent bonds	6,000
	16	Land site and existing building; building value, $30,000	500,000
	30	Corporate organization costs	5,000
	30	Title clearance fees	4,000
July	31	Net cost of razing existing building	7,000
Dec.	1	Bond interest, six months	30,000
	15	Salaries of executives (no participation in construction)	50,000
	15	Stock bonus to corporate promoters; 4,000 shares at $10 par per share	40,000
	15	County real estate tax for six months ended December 31, 1975, on land only	7,000
	15	Cost of new building, paid to Arcose, Inc.	2,000,000

Prepare audit adjustments with explanations, to close out the Fixed Assets account.

6. The Beyer Company computes depreciation on its plant assets on the basis of units of production. The plant asset balance at January 1, 1975, was $2,500,000 and the accumulated depreciation at that date was $790,000, leaving a balance of $1,710,000 to be charged off through depreciation. It was then estimated that, starting on January 1, 1975, 1,900,000 units would be produced over the remaining useful life of the plant assets. In 1970, 220,000 units were produced.

No change occurred in the Plant Asset account or the Accumulated Depreciation account, except for the 1975 depreciation, until January 1, 1976. On that date, a fully depreciated item of equipment which cost $160,000 was retired and scrapped. On the same date, new equipment costing $248,000 was placed in service. It was then reestimated that, as a consequence, there would be produced 2,000,000 units over the remaining useful life of the plant assets from January 1, 1976. The production was 250,000 units in the year 1976.

Prepare journal entries, with explanations, to record the effect of the foregoing retirement and addition of equipment, and for depreciation for the years 1975 and 1976.

PRACTICE MATERIAL ASSIGNMENTS

Metalcraft, Incorporated: Audit Problem:
  Assignment 8, Section A: Land.
  Assignment 8, Section B: Buildings and Accumulated Depreciation.
Colby Gears, Inc.: Holmes and Moore Audit Case:
  Land, Buildings, Depreciation Expense, and Accumulated Depreciation.
  Machinery and Equipment Accumulated Depreciation, and Related Expenses.

20

Fixed Tangible Assets and Related Expenses (Concluded)

Machinery, Equipment, and Other Fixed Assets

The audit objectives in the examination of all fixed assets were set forth in the opening paragraph of Chapter 19. Audit procedures are similar for machinery, equipment, large tools, office equipment, and delivery equipment; consequently, one audit program is presented for all items. Special comments necessary for any one type of asset are offered where necessary.

The remarks in Chapter 19 for the determination of the original pricing base for buildings apply with equal propriety to the assets considered in this chapter. The depreciation procedures developed in the preceding chapter for buildings likewise are applicable to other fixed assets and are not repeated here.

In an initial audit of machinery and factory and other equipment, it is advisable to visit the factory in order to learn the names and functions of the assets. If a machine subsidiary record exists and if it is possible to transport subsidiary records through the factory, the machinery should be compared with the subsidiary ledger accounts in order to become familiar with the machines and to verify the records.

During an examination of machinery acquisitions of past periods, the auditor should determine the disposition of such charges as transportation costs on purchased machines, installation costs, reinstallation expenses, and the cost of machines constructed for company use. The point of this section of the examination is to be certain that only proper items for capitalization are included in the accounts and that the accounts contain all charges which should be capitalized. The deductions made from the accounts in past periods should be tested to convince the auditor that they were properly made; if any such credits are improper, the auditor must prepare the necessary corrections.

In an initial audit, the accumulations for depreciation of machinery and other fixed assets should be examined for several consecutive past years. In addition, on a first examination, the auditor should determine if his client has taken advantage of the maximum depreciation possible in accordance with Treasury Department suggestions and in accordance with usage of the assets. The depreciation policy should be consistent from year to year, and the rates should be established to provide for obsolescence and inadequacy in addition to normal wear. The general adequacy of past annual provisions may be judged by reviewing the gains or losses upon disposition. In reviewing the accumulations for depreciation, it should be borne in mind that charges to the accumulations should appear only for corrections, dispositions, retirements, and extraordinary repairs and replacements.

SECTION I: AUDIT PROGRAM FOR MACHINERY, EQUIPMENT, LARGE TOOLS, OFFICE EQUIPMENT, DELIVERY EQUIPMENT, AND OTHER FIXED ASSETS

The following audit program is presented for the assets indicated above; it is similar to the audit program for buildings.

Schedule the Accounts. A schedule for each fixed asset account may be prepared in a manner similar to that of Illustration 20–1. The auditor must be certain that asset account balances at the beginning and at the end of the period agree with the beginning and ending balance sheet balances.

The composition of the asset account (for Illustration 20–1) and its related accumulated depreciation (for Illustration 20–2) is shown below, at December 31, 1975, in accordance with the records and the audit as of that date. An annual straight-line depreciation of 25 percent of cost less salvage values based on estimated useful life is used, computed to the first of the month closest to purchase.

Vouch and Schedule Charges and Credits. Subsidiary records for machinery, furniture, and all other personal property should be reconciled with their respective controlling accounts. Subsidiary ledger accounts should be reviewed to determine that they are properly maintained.

Authorizations for fixed asset acquisitions, purchase orders, vendors' invoices, and paid checks should be traced through the records of original entry into the fixed asset accounts (or vice versa). This is necessary in order to establish the propriety of the charges. Normally, the criterion of a proper charge to a fixed asset account—for acquisition—is on the basis of a service life of more than one year.

The proper cost of a fixed asset is its net cash invoice price, plus transportation charges, installation costs, and any other costs necessary to place the asset in condition for use.

In verifying the cost of a fixed asset and vouching the charges to the fixed asset account, underlying data may consist of the following:

a)   An internal requisition for new equipment.

b)   Approval by the board of directors, a committee, or authorized person.

c)   A purchase order or contract to the vendor.

d)   A paid check, either for part or full payment. If the paid check is not for the full amount, the auditor should determine the manner of making the remaining payments.

e)   Transportation invoices if the purchaser is charged for transportation.

f)   Work orders for (1) installation costs (2) fixed assets constructed for the client's own use, and (3) improvements and major part replacements.

g)   Entries recording the acquisition.

h)   Entries for appraisals, transfers, and so forth.

If the client manufactures fixed assets for his own use, the auditor should verify charges to the asset account for material, labor, direct overhead, and general overhead prorated to the work order.

With respect to factory machinery, rearrangement and reinstallation costs are occasionally incurred. Since the original cost of arrangement

ILLUSTRATION 20–1

ABLE COMPANY

Delivery Equipment, Acct. #40
December 31, 1975

December 31, 1974: Balance per ledger and audit		$24,000
1975: Additions:		
Feb. 1 Truck No. 6, Ford (life, 4 years; salvage, $900)	VR 71√	4,500
July 9 Repairs to Truck No. 5—accident ⟨AJE 1⟩	VR 86√	600
Oct. 1 Traded Truck No. 3 for Truck No. 7—cash to boot		
(life, 4 years; salvage, $500) ⟨AJE 2–3⟩	VR 90√	3,000
		$32,100
Deductions:		
Mar. 1 Truck No. 2 sold for $1,800 cash ⟨AJE 4–5⟩	CR 36∧⊙	$ 1,800
July 18 Insurance recovery, Truck No. 5 ⟨AJE 6⟩	CR 51∧	500
Dec. 31 Balance per ledger		$29,800
Deduct: AJE 1, below	$ 600	
AJE 3, below	1,900	
AJE 5, below	2,600	5,100
		$24,700
Add: AJE 6, below		500
December 31, 1975, Balance per audit		$25,200

√ Vouchers examined.
∧ Traced to cash receipts.
⊙ Approval of sale examined.

ILLUSTRATION 20–1 (*Continued*)

AJE 1

Repairs to Delivery Equipment	600	
Delivery Equipment		600

Ordinary repairs—accident.

AJE 2

Depreciation of Delivery Equipment	450	
Accumulated Depreciation, Delivery Equipment		450

Truck No. 3, 9 months at $600 per year.

AJE 3

Accumulated Depreciation, Delivery Equipment	1,900	
Delivery Equipment		1,900

Truck No. 3, book value Oct. 1, 1975 (traded for
Truck No. 7):

Cost	$3,000
Accumulated depreciation, Oct. 1, 1975	1,900
Book value	$1,100

Carrying value of Truck No. 7:	
Cash	$3,000
Book value of Truck No. 3	1,100
Carrying value (tax method)	$4,100

AJE 4

Depreciation of Delivery Equipment	150	
Accumulated Depreciation, Delivery Equipment		150

To depreciate Truck No. 2 to the date of sale,
March 1, 1975, $3,600 for 2 months:

Total accumulation	$3,000
1975–2 months	150
Total (see AJE 5)	$3,150

AJE 5

Accumulated Depreciation, Delivery Equipment	3,150	
Delivery Equipment ($4,400–$1,800)		2,600
Profit on Sale of Fixed Assets		550

Correction for Truck No. 2 sold.

AJE 6

Delivery Equipment	500	
Repairs to Delivery Equipment		500

Removal of insurance recovery.
Composition, December 31, 1975:

Truck No. 1	$ 3,600
4	7,000
5	6,000
6	4,500
7	4,100
	$25,200

and installation has already been capitalized, the capitalization of rearrangement and reinstallation costs would be incorrect, because the asset has not been increased in capital value, even though it may be of greater productivity and general usefulness. Rearrangement and reinstallation costs (*a*) may be charged to current operations if the expense is not

ILLUSTRATION 20-2

ABLE COMPANY

Accumulated Depreciation, Delivery Equipment #40.1
December 31, 1975

December 31, 1974: Balance per ledger and audit		$ 9,900
1975 Additions:		
Dec. 31: Company addition: $24,000 @ 25%		6,000
Dec. 31: Balance per ledger		$15,900
Deduct: AJE 7, below.	$6,000	
AJE 3 (Ill. 20-1)	1,900	
AJE 5 (Ill. 20-1)	3,150	11,050
		$ 4,850
Add: AJE 2 (Ill. 20-1)	$ 450	
AJE 4 (Ill. 20-1)	150	
AJE 8, below	4,125	4,725
Dec. 31, 1975, Balance per audit		$ 9,575

AJE 7

Accumulated Depreciation, Delivery Equipment	6,000	
Depreciation of Delivery Equipment.		6,000
To remove company's computation.		

AJE 8

Depreciation of Delivery Equipment	4,125	
Accumulated Depreciation, Delivery Equipment		4,125

To depreciate the trucks as follows:*

	Cost	Salvage	Net	Rate	Time	Amount
No. 1	$3,600	$ 600	$3,000	25%	6 mo.	$ 375
No. 4	7,000	1,000	6,000	25%	12 mo.	1,500
No. 5	6,000	1,200	4,800	25%	12 mo.	1,200
No. 6	4,500	900	3,600	25%	11 mo.	825
No. 7	4,100	500	3,600	25%	3 mo.	225
Total AJE 8						$4,125

* These calculations could be prepared on a separate work paper.

Company Truck Number and Name	Date Purchased	Cost	Estimated Salvage	Depreciable Amount	Age at 1974 Dec. 31,	Accumulated Depreciation, December 31, 1974
1. Ford	June 30, 1971	$ 3,600	$ 600	$3,000	3½ years	$2,625
2. Chevrolet . . .	Aug. 20, 1971	4,400	800	3,600	3⅓ years	3,000
3. Ford	Feb. 18, 1972	3,000	600	2,400	2⅚ years	1,450
4. G.M.C.	Mar. 3, 1973	7,000	1,000	6,000	1⅚ years	2,125
5. G.M.C.	May 25, 1974	6,000	1,200	4,800	7/12 years	700
		$24,000				$9,900

an undue burden on the current period, or (*b*) may be set up as a deferred charge to operations, to be amortized over a period not in excess of the period to be benefited.

If a fixed asset charge results from an appraisal, the auditor must be satisfied with a competent appraisal report. The recording of appraisals of fixed assets other than land or buildings are not common unless a lump-sum purchase of fixed assets is made—usually of used equipment.

Credit entries to fixed asset accounts should be *completely* vouched from original evidence through the records to the accounts. Proper credit entries should appear for sales, exchanges, retirements, returns, and allowances received for defective items.

In vouching *sales* of fixed assets, evidence should be available for the authorization to sell, invoice copy, cash receipt, entries to remove the entire original cost of the asset sold, and the entire related accumulated depreciation.

In vouching *exchanges* of fixed assets, evidence should be available for the authorization to exchange, invoice copy or agreement copy, cash receipt or disbursement for a net differential, and all necessary adjusting entries.

When assets are *retired* without sale, there should exist proper authorizations for the retirement and there may be entries to remove the asset and related accumulated depreciation from the active accounts to a Retired Assets account. When a new asset is purchased to replace an existing one and if the asset accounts do not contain credit entries, the transaction must be investigated.

When fixed assets are *returned* to a vendor, entries should be supported by correspondence and credit memoranda. If the fixed asset account has been charged for transportation, installation, and other make-ready costs for the asset returned, those charges should be removed by expense debits on the normal assumption that the credit allowed by the vendor will not exceed the invoice price. If *allowances* are granted after a fixed asset has been charged to the account, the auditor should investigate to ascertain that the allowances have been credited to the proper fixed asset account and not credited to income.

Examine or Analyze Related Expense Accounts.   An examination of expense accounts related to fixed assets will more frequently disclose the inclusion of capital expenditures than will an examination of fixed asset accounts reveal the inclusion of expense charges. Entries in repair and maintenance accounts should be analyzed, since a large item in the account may be the result of several small items in original records, posted in total at the end of a month.

Complete asset acquisitions with a useful life expectancy extending beyond the current fiscal period should not be charged to expense. Frequently, small perishable hand tools are charged to Maintenance Expense at acquisition; they should be charged to a Small Tools Expense (or asset) account. The repair and maintenance accounts may properly bear charges for part replacements necessary to maintain an asset in a condition of sound operation. Some charges to repair and maintenance accounts which should be capitalized usually result from an improper desire to reduce income for tax purposes.

Ordinary repairs are periodic expenses, to be verified by the auditor. Ordinary repairs simply tend to maintain an asset in good operating condition. Although they do not make the asset more valuable or more efficient than it was when originally acquired, extraordinary repairs may have the effect of lengthening the useful business life of an asset over normal expectations and therefore may be chargeable to the accumulated depreciation. Inquiry must be made of the expectations existing when the ordinary or extraordinary repair was made; and the auditor must be guided accordingly, and in accordance with the concepts developed in Chapter 19.

Improvements are not expenses but are capitalized by adding the net improvement cost to the cost of the asset. Improvements render an asset more valuable than it was before the improvement was made. Of course, there are bound to be differences of opinion concerning the increase in the value of the asset or the lack of an increase in value. The lines of demarcation between ordinary repairs, extraordinary repairs, and improvements are not always easy to find; and the auditor must use good judgment.

Ordinary and extraordinary repairs, alterations, and improvements are not always easy to audit. Some companies consistently maintain their own equipment, whereas others do some of their own maintenance work and have some of it performed on the outside. In the latter case, no difficulties are encountered, since the expenses are usually supported by approved vouchers resulting in cash disbursements. When repairs are made by an internal staff, cost data may not be adequate. Repairs and improvements may entail labor, material, and—in some cases—overhead; and each expense element must be verified before the auditor can feel assured that the expense or capital charge is correct. If each repair or improvement has a work order prepared for it, listing the three elements of cost, both the client and the auditor are materially aided in arriving at the correct cost and proper distribution. Repair jobs should not absorb factory overhead; improvements may be permitted to absorb factory overhead to the extent that overhead is increased because of the improvement.

A company may create maintenance equalization allowances by periodic—monthly—charges to expense and credits to the allowance account. When ordinary repairs, maintenance, and part replacements are incurred, their costs are charged to the allowance account. The auditor must determine that any balance remaining in the allowance at the end of the fiscal year is closed back to the related expense account. While the theory of short-term expense equalization may be followed, expense charges of one year should not result in the distortion of net income.

Examine Data for Liabilities Related to Fixed Assets. By examining invoices and obtaining confirmations, the auditor must determine that liabilities have been recorded for all fixed asset acquisitions and construction completed and not paid for at the end of the period under examination and that the amounts are charged to the proper asset.

Purchase commitments open at the end of the period for fixed asset acquisitions should be scheduled. The total of the open commitments may be set forth in the audit report if they are abnormally large in amount and if current assets will be required in material amount early in the succeeding fiscal period.

Where any personal property fixed asset has been purchased on a deferred payment plan, the auditor should examine the installment sales contract or other documents to determine the payment provisions and the title provisions. A common method of acquisition is for the buyer to pay an initial sum and to execute several notes for the unpaid balance, the notes maturing at the end of stipulated intervals of time. The notes probably are secured by a mortgage on the asset purchased. If this is the situation, title has passed to the buyer. In some cases, title will not pass until the equipment has been completely paid for.

In any case, the equipment should be charged to the proper asset account at its *net cash* purchase price. Initial finance charges and interest charged in advance on unpaid notes should *not* be charged to the asset account but should be charged to expense or prepaid expense. A liability should be created for the *total* unpaid balance.

Depreciation on assets purchased on a deferred payment plan is to be computed on the total cost and not upon the paid portion of the contract, because the total of any asset is being used. If payments are made under a rental contract which provides for the privilege of purchase if the lessee desires, prior rental payments made by the lessee should be capitalized at the time of purchase. If the outright purchase price is less than the accumulated rentals plus the balance paid, the smaller amount should be capitalized. Furthermore, at the time of purchase, depreciation to date should be offset against the capitalized rentals.

If the use of rental or owned equipment involves royalty arrangements, the royalty payments do not attach to the equipment; the royalty liabilities should be set forth separately. If advance royalty deposits exist, the unused portion must be calculated from production, usage, or other records. The auditor's work papers should describe the conditions surrounding the royalty agreements; and if necessary, the audit report should contain necessary data and explanations.

Prepare or Verify Depreciation Schedules. Depreciation schedules may be separately prepared, or they may be prepared on the same work papers as the related asset or group. Illustration 20–2 presents an analysis of the accumulated depreciation of the fixed assets scheduled in Illustration 20–1.

If a fixed asset account is made up of a large number of related items and if a composite rate of depreciation is used, a schedule similar to Illustration 20–3 may be prepared for the assets and the related depreciation.

ILLUSTRATION 20–3

HORTON COMPANY

Office Equipment Acct. #70 and Accumulated Depreciation Acct. #70.1
December 31, 1975

Year	Assets			Accumulated Depreciation (Straight-Line)			Book Value Dec. 31
	Additions	Deductions	Balance Dec. 31	Additions	Deductions	Balance Dec. 31	
1970	$8,000	0	$ 8,000	①$ 400✓	0	$ 400	$7,600
1971	2,000	②$ 500	9,500	875✓	$ 25④	1,250	8,250
1972	1,000	0	10,500	975✓	0	2,225	8,275
1973	500	③ 1,000	10,000	1,025✓	300④	2,950	7,050
1974	800	⑤ 800	10,000	1,000✓	320④	3,630	6,370
1975	⊙ 2,000	0	12,000	1,100✓	0	4,730	7,270

① One-half year.
② Sold cash register; cost $500.
③ Sold Burroughs inventory machine; cost $1,000.
④ Accumulated depreciation on assets sold.
⑤ Sold GTI calculator; cost $800.
✓ Calculation verified.
⊙ Vouched.

The objectives of the auditor in examining depreciation rates, calculations, and accumulations are as follows:

a) To ascertain the adequacy of the accumulated depreciation.

b) To determine the accuracy of the calculations and the annual additions to the accumulation account.

c) To determine the consistency of the application of the depreciation methods in accordance with accepted principles of accounting.

d) To determine that accumulations and related asset accounts have received proper accounting entries when assets were sold, exchanged, discarded or retired.

One company may use different methods of depreciation for different assets acquired at varying dates, in accordance with the various Internal Revenue acts. The auditor must review the client's methods for determining initial-period depreciation and the method used for subsequent periods in order to be certain of consistency and tax advantages or disadvantages.

Based upon approved reasonableness of the depreciation rates used, the auditor should test the calculations of the amounts charged to expense. A composite rate—for each class of asset—may be used, or each subsidiary ledger account may have its individual applicable depreciation date. In the latter case, reasonable tests should be made of the subsidiary accounts, followed by totaling the depreciation charges for the subsidiary ledgers.

An inspection of the machinery, equipment, delivery equipment, and office equipment often results in placing the auditor in a much better position to judge the adequacy of the accumulated depreciation than if he were familiar with accounting records only.

Investigate and Schedule Insurance Coverage. The auditor must determine the amount and judge the adequacy of insurance protection carried on fixed assets. If protection appears to be inadequate, the situation should be discussed with the client.

If title to assets is not vested in the client—for rented equipment, installment purchase contracts, and so forth—the auditor should ascertain that the insurance requirements of contracts and leases are being followed.

Ascertain Correct Accounting for Profit or Loss on Disposition. The auditor should verify deductions made from fixed asset accounts during the period under examination, and he should be certain that *all* entries in connection with deductions were properly made. Also, he must ascertain the omission of any entry when assets have been retired (see the following subsection), particularly if the retired assets have not been sold or physically scrapped. The auditor's inspection of the plant and his examination of insurance policies may reveal such instances. Cash receipts for major disposals should be traced on the cash records. Verification of charges to the Accumulated Depreciation control account also are made to ascertain that the subsidiary accounts were properly reduced.

Examine Treatment of Retired Assets. By plant inspection and questions directed to the proper personnel, the auditor should search for evidence of retired assets. A retirement is not necessarily accompanied by physical disposition; an asset may be retired from active service without disposing of it or without removing it from its customary location. The accounting treatment to be accorded retired assets occurs only in the case of functional cessation; temporarily idle equipment is not included in this treatment. When an asset is retired without sale, it may or may not possess a net salvage value. An existing salvage value should be recognized in the accounts.

ILLUSTRATION. An asset costing $6,000, with a related accumulated depreciation of $4,600, is retired but not sold; the asset has an estimated salvage value of $300. The retirement entry *may* be as follows:

```
Retired (or Other) Assets . . . . . . . . . . . . . . . . .   300
Accumulated Depreciation. . . . . . . . . . . . . . . . . 4,600
Loss on Fixed Asset Retirement  . . . . . . . . . . . . . 1,100
    Fixed Asset . . . . . . . . . . . . . . . . . . . . . .        6,000
```

Fully Depreciated Assets. When the total credits in the Accumulated Depreciation account for an asset equal the total of the fully depreciable amount of that asset, naturally no further depreciation should be recorded for that asset, even though it remains in use. If the asset is continued in use, it is permissible—but not necessary—to adjust the accumulation for depreciation on the basis that the original useful life estimate was incorrect. After the accumulated depreciation is thus adjusted, depreciation at the revised rate would continue to be recorded over the remaining estimated useful life.

Comments on Small Tools. In examining perishable tools accounts, the auditor should ascertain that tools useful for more than one year are not charged to expense at the time of purchase. There is a tendency to purchase tools heavily in profitable years, charge them to expense at purchase, and then absorb them physically over succeeding years. The auditor should ascertain if an annual tool inventory has been taken, priced, and reflected in the asset account. If so, the audit proceeds in the same manner as that followed for any inventory, by test of physical quantities, testing prices, and so forth.

The verification of small tools—usually hand tools such as portable drills, sanders, files, reamers, and so forth—may be a difficult matter. The auditor should attempt to convince the client of the desirability of an annual inventory of small and perishable tools, and the establishment of a Small Tools asset account based upon the original cost less adequate amortization. In this manner, the period from the last inventory absorbs the book value of all tools broken, lost, stolen, and used up, as well as the dollar increase or decrease of those on hand.

The recommended manner of accounting for small tools is to treat them as supplies inventory, control them with proper records, and charge them to expense as they are used.

If the inventory method of accounting for tools is not followed and if they are not charged to expense at acquisition, an accumulation for depreciation may or may not be maintained; this is a matter of individual company policy—and it is not followed in the majority of factories. However, if an accumulated depreciation does exist, the auditor should analyze it to satisfy himself of the reasonableness of the account balance and the propriety of the charges and credits.

If tool purchases are small and have been charged to an expense account at acquisition, and if the tool purchases have been fairly constant in annual dollar volume, and if the omission of a tool inventory has no significant effect upon assets or income, there would be no major objection to a continuation of the practice, provided it is followed consistently.

Comments on Delivery Equipment. Because of the relatively short life of delivery equipment and because these items frequently are *exchanged* for new items, an illustration is presented setting forth the accounting procedure acceptable for federal income tax purposes when similar equipment is *exchanged*. This illustration is applicable to the exchange of any similar fixed asset. Gains or losses from such exchanges are not recognized at the time of exchange, and the basis of the newly acquired asset is the sum of the remaining net book value of the fixed asset exchanged plus the expenditure of the net asset.

ILLUSTRATION.   A delivery truck originally costing $6,400 and carrying an accumulated depreciation of $5,400 is given in exchange, plus $6,800 for a new truck with an established market price of $7,400. The journal entry would be as follows:

Truck No. 2 7,800		
Accumulated Depreciation, Truck No. 1 5,400		
Truck No. 1	6,400	
Cash	6,800	

The asset account balance of Truck No. 2, $7,800 less estimated salvage, will be depreciated over its useful life, thus allocating to expense the depreciable cost of both trucks over their combined periods of usefulness. Although the loss on such an exchange is not recognized, a gain may be realized in an amount not to exceed the amount of cash received. The auditor must examine the method of accounting used and prepare adjustments, if necessary.

Depreciation schedule preparation for delivery equipment frequently involves the use of widely varying depreciation rates because of different types of automotive equipment and a variety of operating conditions. Each item of delivery equipment preferably should be maintained in its individual subsidiary ledger account.

Comments on Returnable Containers.   Returnable containers are fixed assets, and the audit procedure applicable to them does not vary significantly from the procedure applicable to any other fixed asset. However, returnable containers may be subject to rapid depreciation, rough usage, and nonreturn.

For certain types of businesses, returnable containers represent a large investment. The auditor must obtain satisfactory proof that the container values are not overstated in the records of the client and that proper provision has been made for normal wear, breakage, and nonreturns. The proof of container quantity and valuation will differ for each type of business under audit; normally, the number of containers charged out to customers will be in excess of the number of containers on hand, exclusive of a future-use reserve supply.

Deposits may be required from customers in order to encourage the return of expensive containers, and the deposits may be at cost, above cost, or below cost. The auditor must determine that the deposit is correct and that it has been treated as a liability. Cash received for container deposits may be included as a part of the general cash available for company use, or it may be placed in a separate fund. Container deposits made by customers may be test-confirmed. In those instances where it is considered that a container will not be returned, the Container Inventory account should be credited and a charge made to the liability account which was credited when the container was sent to the customer and his deposit received; if a depreciation accumulation is used, it should be charged for the accumulated depreciation on the items. If the customer was charged at a price above the cost of the container, a profit will be realized in the event of nonreturn. The auditor should start with the container inventory as of the beginning of the period and assuming that figure to be correct as the result of the preceding audit, add the number of containers purchased and subtract the number of containers charged off because of loss, breakage, and nonreturn; the resulting figure will be the container inventory at the audit date. This figure should be verified by comparison with the client's count of the containers on hand and adding containers charged to customers.

Patterns, Drawings, etc.

Patterns, electrotypes, drawings, dies, special-job tools, and jigs are examples of assets that often present peculiar problems of valuation. The residual value of these assets is usually negligible; the problem arises in estimating the probable length of useful life and the remaining useful value. Normally, these accounts require frequent adjustment, and the assets require frequent inspection in order to prevent their overstatement. Although this class of asset will be used one time at least, many companies contemplate their repeated future use—and their expectations frequently do not materialize. Therefore, recognized practice is to the effect that the amortization of these assets be at a rapid rate—a rate so rapid that all costs are amortized against the sales of the initial manufacture, printing, reproduction, etc. The auditor may encounter opposition to his desire to eliminate the asset costs quickly; however, the costs of nonproductive assets should not be permitted to accumulate in asset accounts.

Wasting Assets

Wasting—or extractive industry—assets are composed of natural resources such as gas and oil deposits, timber stands, and deposits of iron, coal, copper, lead, sulphur, gravel, and so forth.

In auditing fixed property accounts in extractive industries, the auditor must verify title to properties owned, just as in the examination of the records for any company, by examining deeds, leases, vouchers, and other necessary evidential matter. If wasting-asset properties are carried on a basis other than cost, the auditor must rely upon expert technical estimates for quantity and consequent book valuation. From the geological reports, he should verify the computations for the estimated number of units commercially available. In many instances of mineral deposits, gas and oil deposits, and timber stands, the purchase price is insignificant; "discovery value," based upon reliable geological estimates of reserves, is used instead. When above-cost entries occur, they must be examined for propriety.

All costs of exploitation and original development should be capitalized, and these costs should be amortized on the basis of the total commercially recoverable units of product. Subsequent additional costs for shaft extensions, additional trackage and cars, and other equipment, incurred after production has begun and made for the purpose of maintaining output, frequently are charged to expense at incurrence; in most cases, they should be charged to asset accounts and depreciated.

Depletion is a cost (or discovery value) allocation to expense to reflect a decrease in the physical quantity of an attractive asset resulting from removal and use. The purchase price (or other basis) of the property, divided by the estimated number of units to be extracted from the property, equals the depletion charge per unit. In auditing wasting assets, consideration must be given to any land value remaining after the completion of operations if the land is a freehold. In the gas and oil industries, the operators commonly acquire only a leasehold, in which case the land values appear on the records of the equitable owner. Depletion charges naturally are estimates, and the auditor should attempt to convince the client of the necessity of periodic geologic estimates of the remaining quantity of the natural resource; in this way, the adequacy or inadequacy of the depletion charges may be judged.

Some extractive industry companies use an Accumulated Depletion account, whereas others credit depletion charges directly to the asset account. There is no objection to the direct credit. The auditor should determine the basis used for calculating the periodic depletion charge; as stated before, this ordinarily is an amount per unit extracted—or extracted and sold. Computations for depletion charges should be verified by the examination of production records—or production and sales records.

The accumulation of funds for the acquisition of new property must be verified on the basis of the quantity extracted and the policy of the company with respect to fund accumulation. The policy of the company with respect to the disposition of funds thus accumulated should be investigated to determine that the disposition is in accordance with the company code of regulations. Some companies may create a depletion fund for the acquisition of new properties at the termination of the present venture; other companies—organized for one venture—may return capital recoveries to the stockholders as liquidating dividends. In his report, the auditor should comment appropriately if stockholders are not advised of the nature of the dividend paid. Corporate bylaws must be examined to determine the existence of dividend provisions.

If the audit is an initial engagement, it may be necessary to verify depletion charges for several prior periods. When depletion rates are changed from time to time, based upon new quantity estimates, the changes should be investigated and commented upon in the audit report.

Buildings and other structures erected on wasting-asset land should be amortized at least by the time extractive operations terminate. For example, if a mine has an estimated life of 30 years and if a building erected on the property has an estimated life of 50 years, the building should be depreciated over 30 years. This may be accomplished by using either the straight-line, declining amounts, or units-of-output method of depreciation. Some extractive industry companies include depreciation of buildings and equipment in the depletion rate; others follow the preferred method of showing depreciation and depletion separately.

SECTION II: FINANCIAL STATEMENT CONSIDERATIONS

In income statements, depreciation of fixed assets should be shown by related groups, properly classified as manufacturing, administrative, or selling expenses. If fixed assets have been written upward or downward in the records, the depreciation in the income statement should be on the basis of the revised figures, with depreciation based on cost also indicated.

In a balance sheet, each related group of fixed tangible assets should be shown separately—preferably at cost—with the related accumulated depreciation or depletion shown as a deduction therefrom. The fixed asset controlling accounts preferably should not be combined.

Land should be separated from depreciable property, and land not used in the business should be shown separately from land used in the business. If any fixed tangible asset is being offered for sale and is not currently being used in the business, and if it is of significant amount, it should be separately set forth in the balance sheet, at an amount not in excess of its estimated net sales price.

If fixed assets are fully depreciated and in use, both their full cost (or other basic figure) and the related accumulated depreciation should be set forth in the balance sheet.

If fixed assets are in the process of construction at the balance sheet date and if their amount is segregated, they may (1) be shown separately or (2) be included with the proper group totals, with the dollar amount of the construction in process shown parenthetically.

For fixed assets purchased under an installment or conditioned sales plan, the net cash cost price should appear among the assets and the unpaid installments, plus unpaid finance charges and unpaid initial interest, should be shown among the liabilities. Even though title to the property has not passed to the purchaser, it is not acceptable accounting practice to show only the client's equity in an asset.

As previously stated, depreciation accumulations should be subtracted from the related asset or group of assets in the balance sheet. The Securities and Exchange Commission recognizes as acceptable practice—for public utilities only—the practice of showing depreciation accumulations among the liabilities, based on the theory of capital recovery.

Various additional financial statement considerations appear throughout Chapters 19 and 20.

QUESTIONS

1. Fun Development, Inc., was organized January 2, 1975, to develop a vacation and recreation area on land purchased January 2, 1975, for $200,000, and it also purchased for $80,000 an adjacent tract of land which the corporation plans to subdivide into 100 building lots. When the area is developed, the lots are expected to sell for $10,000 each.

   The corporation borrowed a substantial portion of its funds from a bank and gave a mortgage on the land. A mortgage covenant requires that the corporation furnish quarterly financial statements.

   The quarterly financial statements prepared at March 31 and June 30 by the company accountant were unacceptable to the bank. The Fun president now offers you the engagement of preparing unaudited quarterly financial statements. Because of limited funds your fee would be paid in Fun Development, Inc., common stock rather than in cash. The stock would be repurchased by Fun when funds became available. You would not receive enough stock to be a major stockholder.

   a) Discuss the ethical implications of your accepting the engagement and the reporting requirements which are applicable if you accept.

   b) Assume that you accept the engagement to prepare the September 30 statements. What disclosures, if any, would you make of your prospective ownership of Fun stock in the quarterly financial statements?

   c) The president insists that you present the 50 building lots at their expected sales price of $1,000,000 in the September 30 unaudited statements. The $1,000,000 appeared in company-prepared statements. The write-up was credited to Contributed Capital. How would you respond to the president's request?

   d) The corporation elected September 30, 1975 as its fiscal year, and you are requested to prepare the corporation's federal income tax return. Discuss the implication of signing the return and the disclosure of your stock ownership in waves (disregard the write-up of the land).

   e) After accepting your unaudited September 30 financial statements, the bank notified the corporation that the December 31 financial statements must be accompanied by a CPA's opinion. You were asked to conduct the audit and told that your fee would be paid in cash. Discuss the ethical implications of your accepting the engagement.

   (AICPA, adapted)

2. Your firm has been elected by the stockholders of the Feed Company to audit its financial statements for the year ended December 31, 1975, with a view to rendering an unqualified opinion. The company has been in operation for 20 years. The net book value of its fixed assets is $10,000,000.

   In what respects would your audit program for the fixed assets be different, if at all, under each of the following situations:

   a)   The company's financial statements have never been audited by a firm of certified public accountants?

   b)   The company's financial statements have been audited for the preceding 10 years by another reputable firm of certified public accountants which has rendered an unqualified opinion each year?

   c)   Your firm has audited the financial statements of the company for the past 10 years?

3.   What are some general principles by which you will be guided in ascertaining whether depreciation provisions have been excessive or deficient for furniture, machinery, and buildings? Would a flat rate of depreciation and a blanket accumulated depreciation account be satisfactory for these three assets?

4.   During the course of an audit of the records of a company, you discovered that fixed assets had been excessively depreciated. The company justified the practice on the basis that by overdepreciating the fixed assets, capital was protected, and as a result, dividends could be paid with regularity in profitable and unprofitable years. You are asked to certify the financial statements. What course would you pursue? Ignore tax implications.

5.   In the examination of the drawings, patterns, and dies accounts, what are two points of major importance to the auditor?

6.   A company purchased 10 milling machines at $24,000 each. The machines were purchased on the installment plan on August 1, 1975, the initial payment being $40,000; the contract stipulated that $20,000 was to be paid on the first day of each month. The buyer intends to depreciate the machinery at 10 percent per year, using the double-declining amount method. At December 31, 1975, what is the condition of all of the accounts connected with the foregoing transactions?

7.   A client is a manufacturer of electronic equipment. Total fixed assets are $20,000,000, and total assets are $75,000,000. During the audit for the current year, your analysis of the fixed assets showed total additions of $600,000 and total deductions of $200,000. You are supplied with an analysis of these additions and deductions. Some of the $600,000 additions were purchased from outside sources, and part of the work was performed by the employees of the client.

     You vouched fixed asset purchases for all amounts in excess of $4,000; you examined liabilities for unpaid amounts; and you tested small purchases and found that all fixed asset additions were reasonable and correct, and that all liabilities for unpaid amounts were correct. You examined authorizations and found that all assets purchased were correctly authorized and within the limits of the authorizations.

     In connection with assets constructed by employees, you examined shop construction order records, material requisitions, payroll distributions, and overhead distributions. You prepared work papers analyzing all construction work. You found that factory overhead normally distributed to production was not added to construction but that increases in overhead caused by construction were added. Authorizations for construction work were examined for each job and for proper approvals.

     You traced fixed asset deductions, determined that the asset accounts were credited for original cost, determined that the accumulated depreciation accounts were closed out, and traced salvage disposal realized upon the sale of the discontinued equipment. You also examined all authorizations for fixed asset disposals.

Criticize the auditing procedure.

8. A client is contemplating lending money to a corporation which is engaged in developing and operating a mining property. The client is seeking advice concerning the financial information he should obtain prior to lending the money. He has obtained an engineering report. The prospective borrower has submitted the following balance sheet of the mineral property:

ASSETS		LIABILITIES AND CAPITAL	
Fixed assets	$200,000	Liabilities	$ 50,000
		Capital	150,000
	$200,000		$200,000

   a) From the report of the engineers, what information would you expect to obtain that would be of interest and value in deciding upon the merits of the anticipated loan?

   b) What additional information would you expect the prospective borrower to furnish?

(AICPA, adapted)

9. A mining company owns its property in freehold. It also owns its mining equipment. In such a case, state how you would handle the following:

   a) Depreciation of mining equipment.
   b) Depletion of natural resources.
   c) The amortization of development expenses, assuming that they were capitalized during the pre-mining stage.

10. Silver, Inc., acquired a tract of undeveloped mineral property for $100,000 on June 12, 1971. The company has spent $300,000 additional on the property. In august, 1975, a geological survey was made of the property; the report of the geologists, submitted in December, 1975, estimated that $10,000,000 of ores were in the property, minable at profitable figures. At the December, 1975, meeting, the board of directors considered the report of the geologists and passed a resolution to place the property in the records for a total of $10,000,000. This was done by the accounting department.

   You started your annual audit on January 2, 1976. You read the report of the geologists, traced the entries for the appreciation to the accounts, and noted that the Retained Earnings account now shows a $5,600,000 credit balance; whereas, if the property revaluation had been ignored, the account would have shown a $4,000,000 debit balance. You also talked to several officials about the revaluation. A portion of the balance sheet you prepared follows:

Mineral property, at cost	$ 400,000	
Revaluation	9,600,000	$10,000,000
Common stock	$ 100,000	
Retained earnings (after revaluation credit for $9,600,000)	5,600,000	5,700,000

You certified the balance sheet and presented it to the board of directors at its January, 1976, meeting. Every director protested your presentation of the revaluation figure as a separate asset item, as well as your presentation of retained earnings.

a) Did you do sufficient work in connection with the property audit?

b) What stand would you take as to the protests raised?

11. In connection with the annual examination of the financial statements of the Loom Company for the year ended December 31, 1975, you have been assigned the audit of the Manufacturing Equipment, the Accumulated Depreciation, and Repairs to Manufacturing Equipment accounts. Your review of Loom's policies and procedures has disclosed the following information:

(1) The Manufacturing Equipment account includes the net invoice price plus freight and installation costs for all of the equipment in the plant.

(2) The Manufacturing Equipment and Accumulated Depreciation accounts are supported by a subsidiary ledger which shows the cost and accumulated depreciation for each piece of equipment.

(3) An annual budget for capital expenditures of $1,000 or more is prepared by the budget committee and approved by the board of directors. Capital expenditures over $1,000 which are not included in this budget must be approved by the board of directors and variations of 20 percent or more must be explained to the board. Approval by the production supervisor is required for capital expenditures under $1,000.

(4) Company employees handle installation, removal, repair and rebuilding of the machinery. Work orders are prepared for these activities and are subject to the same budgetary control as other expenditures. Work orders are not required for external expenditures.

a) Cite the major objectives of your audit of the Manufacturing Equipment, Manufacturing Equipment-Accumulated Depreciation and Repairs of Manufacturing Equipment accounts. Do not include in this listing the auditing procedures designed to accomplish these objectives.

b) Prepare the portion of your audit program applicable to the review of 1975 additions to the Manufacturing Equipment account.

(AICPA, adapted)

PROBLEMS

1. The Auburn Company requires a number of small machine tools to maintain its operations. Although there is great variety among the various individual tools, they cost approximately the same and have similar useful lives. The company carries a Machine Tools on Hand account in the general ledger and the account showed a balance of $2,400 (100 tools) at the end of 1973. Acquisitions, losses, and other data for two years are as follows:

Description	1974	1975
Acquisitions	50 @ $25	60 @ $26
Losses:		
Number	75	40
Scrap proceeds	$80	$40
Inventory	75 @ $23	95 @ $24

Prepare the audit adjustments for each of the two years. Show calculations.

2. The B & B Corporation showed the following data in its accounts for three presses as of the December 31, end of the current year. The company has used straight line depreciation.

	Press No.		
Description	1	2	3
Equipment, 10 year life, cost	$23,900	$51,000	$76,000
Estimated salvage value	1,900	3,000	4,000

At the beginning of the sixth year, management has decided to make the following changes:

a) Press No. 1: Change from straight line to sum-of-years'-digits depreciation to more nearly reflect the expiration of economic service value.

b) Press No. 2: Change estimated life to 15 years, based upon a careful evaluation of the physical condition of the press.

c) Press No. 3: During the fourth year, through oversight, no depreciation was recorded. The client has made no entries during the sixth year to record these decisions and you, the auditor, are expected to prepare them for the client. Show all supporting calculations.

3. You are engaged in the examination of the financial statements of West Mfg. Inc., and are auditing the Machinery and Equipment account and the related depreciation accounts for the year ended December 31, 1975.

Your permanent file contains the following schedules:

Machinery and Equipment

	Balance 12/31/73	1974 Retirements	1974 Additions	Balance 12/31/74
1961–64	$ 8,000	$2,100	–0–	$ 5,900
1965	400	–0–	–0–	400
1966	–0–	–0–	–0–	–0–
1967	–0–	–0–	–0–	–0–
1968	3,900	–0–	–0–	3,900
1969	–0–	–0–	–0–	–0–
1970	5,300	–0–	–0–	5,300
1971	–0–	–0–	–0–	–0–
1972	4,200	–0–	–0–	4,200
1973	–0–	–0–	–0–	–0–
1974	–0–	–0–	$5,700	5,700
	$21,800	$2,100	$5,700	$25,400

Accumulated Depreciation

	Balance 12/31/73	1974 Retirements	1974 Provision	Balance 12/31/74
1961-64	$ 7,840	$2,100	$ 160	$ 5,900
1965	340	-0-	40	380
1966	-0-	-0-	-0-	-0-
1967	-0-	-0-	-0-	-0-
1968	2,145	-0-	390	2,535
1969	-0-	-0-	-0-	-0-
1970	1,855	-0-	530	2,385
1971	-0-	-0-	-0-	-0-
1972	630	-0-	420	1,050
1973	-0-	-0-	-0-	-0-
1974	-0-	-0-	285	285
	$12,810	$2,100	$1,825	$12,535

A transcript of the Machinery and Equipment account for 1975 follows:

1975	Machinery and Equipment	Debit	Credit
Jan. 1	Balance forward	$25,400	
Mar. 1	Burn grinder	1,200	
May 1	Air compressor	4,500	
June 1	Power lawnmower	600	
June 1	Lift truck battery	320	
Aug. 1	Rock saw		$ 150
Nov. 1	Electric spot welder	4,500	
Nov. 1	Baking oven	2,800	
Dec. 1	Baking oven	236	
		$39,556	$ 150
Dec. 31	Balance forward		39,406
		$39,556	$39,556

Your examination reveals the following information:

(1) The company uses a 10-year life for all machinery and equipment for depreciation purposes. Depreciation is computed by the straight-line method. Six months' depreciation is recorded in the year of acquisition or retirement. For 1975 the company recorded depreciation of $2,800 on machinery and equipment.

(2) The Burn grinder was purchased for cash. The chief engineer and a used machinery dealer agreed that the machine, which was practically new, was worth $2,100 in the open market.

(3) For production reasons the new air compressor was installed in a small building that was erected in 1975 to house the machine and will also be used for general storage. The cost of the building, which

has a 25-year life, was $2,000 and is included in the $4,500 voucher for the air compressor.

(4) The power lawnmower was delivered to the home of the company president for his personal use.

(5) On June 1 the battery in a battery-powered lift truck was accidentally damaged beyond repair. The damaged battery was included at a price of $600 in the $4,200 cost of the lift truck purchased on July 1, 1972. The company decided to rent a replacement battery rather than buy a new battery. The $320 expenditure is the annual rental for the battery paid in advance, net of a $40 allowance for the scrap value of the damaged battery.

(6) The rock saw sold on August 1 had been purchased on August 1, 1962, for $1,500. The saw was in use until it was sold.

(7) On September 1 the company determined that a casting machine was no longer needed and advertised it for sale for $1,800 after determining from a machinery dealer that this was its market value. The casting machine had been purchased for $5,000 on September 1, 1970.

(8) The company elected to exercise an option under a lease-purchase agreement to buy the electric spot welder. The welder had been installed on February 1, 1975, at a monthly rental of $100.

(9) On November 1 a baking oven was purchased for $10,000. A $2,800 down-payment was made, and the balance will be paid in monthly installments over a three-year period. The December 1 payment includes interest charges of $36. Legal title to the oven will not pass to the company until the payments are completed.

Prepare the audit adjustments necessary at December 31, 1975, for machinery and equipment and the related depreciation.

(AICPA, adapted)

4. A client, Rogers, Inc., acquired a new machine in 1975 and traded in an old similar machine. The old machine was acquired in 1962 at a cost of $78,000. In 1964 it was written up $47,000 to a total of $125,000; the offsetting credit was made to Reappraisal of Fixed Assets. In the years following 1964, the appreciation had been partially amortized. Both the old and the new machine have an estimated life of 20 years each and an estimated salvage value of 10 percent. The reappraisal of the old machine did not affect its estimated life. The corporation takes one half of the annual depreciation in years of acquisition and disposition.

The terms of the purchase of the new machine provided for a trade-in allowance of $25,000 and called for a cash payment of $150,000, or 12 monthly payments of $13,000 each. The company chose the latter alternative. Other costs incurred in connection with the exchange appear in the following paragraph.

Transportation-in, new machine, $1,100; removal of old machine, $1,500; installation of new machine, $900; engineer, for supervision of installation, $600.

You are called by the client to prepare entries for the exchange on a basis acceptable for federal income tax purposes. (Show computations.)

5. The net income of the Bench Company for the year ended December 31, 1975, according to its income statement, was $300,000. The company desired a loan from its local bank and you were requested to audit the financial statements of the company. You are required to correct the reported net income, taking into consideration the following information discovered during the audit.

    (1) A profit of $30,000 was realized from the sale of capital assets and was credited directly to Retained Earnings.

    (2) Depreciation expense was understated $45,000.

    (3) Machinery costing $40,000 was manufactured by the company for its own use and was placed in the records at $45,000, the $5,000 being credited to income.

    (4) Dividends of $50,000 had been declared, charged to expense, and paid during 1975.

    (5) In order to comply with the terms of a deed of trust in connection with a bond issue, $50,000 was debited to expense and credited to a Reserve for Bond Sinking Fund.

    (6) Sales of certain investment securities had been made during the year, and a loss of $65,000 was involved, which had been debited to an extraordinary expense account.

6. The following account appears in the records of the Carr Company:

Machinery

Date		Explanation	Debit	Credit	Balance
1971					
Jan.	2	Purchased Machine No. 1	50,000		50,000
Dec.	31	Depreciation		5,000	45,000
1972					
Jan.	2	Purchased Machine No. 2	40,000		85,000
Dec.	31	Depreciation		9,000	76,000
1973					
Jan.	2	Purchased Machine No. 3	60,000		136,000
Aug.	2	Machine No. 1, ordinary repairs	2,000		138,000
	2	Machine No. 2, major repairs; originally estimated life is not extended.	4,000		142,000
Dec.	31	Depreciation		15,000	127,000
1974					
Jan.	2	Purchased Machine No. 4	44,000		171,000
	2	Machine No. 1, sold		24,000	147,000
Dec.	31	Depreciation		21,000	126,000
1975					
Jan.	2	Machine No. 2, major repairs; originally estimated life is extended.	10,000		136,000
Dec.	31	Depreciation		18,000	118,000

The accounts have not been closed for the year 1975. Prepare work papers showing the correct accounts, and prepare all necessary audit adjustments. Straight-line depreciation at 10 percent per year is to be used. For purposes of this problem, ignore salvage values.

7. Squire, Inc., manufactures chemicals and delivers its finished products in returnable drums. In order to avoid excessive losses by customer failure to return drums, a charge of $100 per drum is billed to customers. Most customers remit cash only for the price of the contents and return the drums for credit. Occasionally, the amount charged for the drums is also remitted by the customer; and in some instances, these drums are never returned for credit.

    You are summoned by the company to supply the following:

    a) In journal entry form, show how the following transactions should be recorded in the accounts of the chemical company:
    (1) Original purchase of drums.
    (2) Drums billed to customers.
    (3) Drums returned by customers.
    (4) Drums not recoverable from customers, and for which the charges cannot be collected.

    b) What accounts should be kept in the general ledger, and how should they be shown in the balance sheet?

    c) What verifications can be made to prove the balances in these ledger accounts?

8. The Internal Revenue Service requested one of your new clients, the Cobal Company, to furnish a depreciation schedule for its delivery trucks. The schedule was to set forth additions, retirements, depreciation, and other data for the three-year period ended December 31, 1975.

    The following data were compiled by the client, who immediately summoned you for assistance:

Item	Date Purchased	Cost
Truck No.:		
1	January 1, 1971	$ 4,000
2	July 1, 1971	3,600
3	January 1, 1972	2,400
4	July 1, 1972	2,000
Balance, January 1, 1973		$12,000

The Accumulated Depreciation for Delivery Equipment account, previously adjusted by a revenue agent to January 1, 1973, and entered in the ledger, had a balance on that date of $4,880, representing depreciation on the four trucks from the dates of purchase, based on a five-year life. No charges had been made to the Accumulated Depreciation account prior to January 1, 1973.

Transactions from January 1, 1973, to December 31, 1975, were as follows:

(1) Truck No. 1 was sold for $500 cash on January 2, 1973. The company debited Cash and credited Delivery Equipment, $500.

(2)   Truck No. 3 was traded for Truck No. 5 on January 2, 1974. The company paid the automobile dealer in full by giving Truck No. 3 and $760 cash. The cash market price of Truck No. 5 was $2,100. The company debited Delivery Equipment and credited Cash, $760.

(3)   On July 1, 1975, Truck No. 4 was wrecked and was sold as junk for $50 cash. The Cobal Company received $300 from the insurance company. The company debited Cash, $350; credited Miscellaneous Income, $50; and credited Delivery Equipment, $300.

(4)   Truck No. 6 was acquired new on July 1, 1975, for $6,000 cash, and was charged to the Delivery Equipment account.

Entries for depreciation had been made each December 31 as follows: 1973, $2,400; 1974, $2,150; and 1975, $2,500.

You are to prepare work papers setting forth:

a)   The accumulated depreciation, by individual trucks, at January 1, 1973. Depreciation is to be calculated by the straight-line method from the date of acquisition to the date of disposition. In order to save time in solving the problem, ignore salvage values.

b)   The correct depreciation, by individual trucks, for the years ended December 31, 1973, 1974, and 1975.

c)   A schedule of the trucks and the proper accumulated depreciation for each truck as of December 31, 1975.

d)   All entries necessary to correct the company's records from January 1, 1973, to December 31, 1975.

e)   The effect on net income for 1973, 1974, and 1975, arising from depreciation adjustments and all other errors made by the company in its truck accounting. The effect of income tax regulations on gain or loss on trades is to be taken into consideration. All trucks remaining at December 31, 1975, were in active use.

9.   The Machinery account of Hetrick, Inc., is presented below. On the basis of your examination of the entries for the period from January 1 to June 30, 1975:

a)   Prepare audit adjustments and make suggestions for whatever other corrections may be required.

b)   State the corrected balance of the Machinery account as of June 30, 1975; assume the balance at January 1 to be correct.

Notes:

(1)   Your client is modernizing production.

(2)   Entry of February 10: Milling machine cost $8,000; depreciation accrued to date of sale, $6,000.

(3)   Entry of March 3: Cost of this motor, $180; depreciation accrued to date of sale, $90; the $30 cash for which this motor was sold was credited to Other Income.

(4)   Entry of April 2: Purchase will enable the company to produce a new product.

(5)   Entry of May 17: Cost of old shelves was $320, against which depreciation of $80 had been accrued to date of sale; sold for $30 cash.

(6)   Entry of June 8: Cost of the old shop lights was $800; depreciation accumulated to date of sale, $440; sold for $130 cash.

Machinery

Date			Explanation	Debit	Credit
1975					
Jan.	1		Balance forward	1,451,000	
	25		Drill press	5,000	
	25		Installation of drill press	660	
Feb.	10		Sale of milling machine		2,600
	12		High-speed cutter	2,700	
	27		Additions to turret lathe	300	
Mar.	3		Loss on sale of 2 H.P. motor	60	
	5		Reversal of March 3 entry		60
	5		Westinghouse motor	350	
Apr.	1		Graphite lubricating service	170	
	2		New sets of small tools	740	
	9		Lubricants	300	
	15		Sundry equipment, purchased at auction	1,800	
	15		Agent's commission on above purchases	200	
May	9		Metal shelves for stock	704	
	17		Sale of lumber from old shelves		30
	17		Loss on sale of old shelves		210
	30		Wiring for new shop lights	320	
	31		Flourescent fixtures	1,000	
June	8		Sale of old shop lights		130
				1,470,704	2,850

PRACTICE MATERIAL ASSIGNMENTS

Metalcraft, Incorporated: Audit Problem:
   Assignment 8, Section C: Factory Machinery and Accumulated Depreciation.
   Assignment 8, Section D: Office Equipment and Accumulated Depreciation.
Colby Gears, Inc.: Holmes and Moore Audit Case:
   Motor Vehicles, Depreciation Expense, and Accumulated Depreciation.
   Office Equipment, Depreciation Expense, and Accumulated Depreciation.

21
Intangible Assets

Audit Objectives

An auditor must verify the nature, source, cost, appraisal figures if used, and the amortization of intangible assets. The objectives in examining intangible assets are as follows:

1. To determine the valuation base used for each intangible asset.
2. To ascertain the propriety of amortization policies.
3. To determine that evidence is proper for authorization to acquire, sell, license, or charge off any intangible.
4. To determine that revenues from intangible assets are properly accounted for and properly controlled.
5. To determine that full disclosure exists in the financial statements for intangible assets and their amortization.

A close relationship exists between the value of intangible assets and their revenue-producing ability; therefore, the problems of proper auditing and valuation of intangible assets are closely connected with the valuation of a business as a whole.

Intangible assets do not represent claims against others, nor do they represent rights in physically existent properties; they represent exclusive privileges to a product, process, or location. The exclusive privilege may be granted by a government, as in the case of patents; or it may be created, as in the case of goodwill; or it may be granted by an owner, as exemplified by a leasehold. Normally, an auditor will find documentary evidence available for inspection in connection with his intangible asset verification which will serve him as a guide to proper valuation and periodic amortization.

Intangible assets may be classified as follows:

CLASS A: Intangible assets with an existence limited by law, by regulation, by agreement, or by nature of the asset, as exemplified by the following:

1. Patents
2. Leaseholds
3. Copyrights
4. Fixed-term franchises
5. Licenses
6. Goodwill (if there is evidence of limited existence)
7. Organization costs

The cost of intangible assets of this class should be amortized by systematic charges to revenue over the period benefited.

CLASS B: Intangible assets with no limited existence and with no indication of limited life at the time of acquisition, as exemplified by the following:
1. Trademarks and trade names
2. Secret processes and formulas
3. Perpetual franchises
4. Goodwill (if there is no evidence of limited existence)

The cost of intangible assets of Class B may be carried continuously, unless it becomes reasonably evident that the term of existence of such intangible assets has become limited or that they have become worthless. If the existence of an intangible asset of Class B has become *limited*, the cost should be amortized by systematic charges to revenue over the estimated remaining period of usefulness. If such charges would distort net income, the remainder of the cost may be amortized to revenue over the remaining estimated useful life of the asset. If an intangible asset of Class B becomes *worthless*, the remaining cost should be charged to revenue.

In accordance with recognized principles of accounting, intangible assets of Class A and Class B should be stated originally at cost. If intangible assets of Class A are acquired in noncash transactions, the cost may be determined either by the fair market price of the consideration given or by the fair market price of the property acquired—whichever is more evident.

CLASS C: The excess of a parent company's investment in the capital stock of a subsidiary over its equity in the net assets of the subsidiary as shown by the latter's records at the date of acquisition, insofar as that excess would be treated as an intangible asset in the consolidated financial statements of the parent and the subsidiary. This type of asset may represent intangibles of either Class A or Class B, or be a combination of both.

When the price paid for capital stock of a subsidiary company is greater than the net assets of the subsidiary applicable thereto, the assumption is that the parent company—in effect—placed a value greater than book value on some of the assets the subsidiary company in arriving at the price paid for the investment. If possible, an allocation of such excess between tangible and intangible property should be made; and any amount allocated to intangible assets should be further allocated to determine a separate cost for each tangible asset, as indicated in Class A and Class B.

The preceding tangible asset classification and valuation are in accordance with the pronouncements of *Accounting Research Bulletin No. 43*, chapter 5.

In certain businesses, intangible assets have a much greater total revenue-producing ability than tangible assets. In these instances, an auditor must be particularly careful to determine exactly the original source of the intangible assets, the conditions under which the intangible assets were brought into the records, their original cost, subsequent appraisals, and the provisions for the amortization of their recorded amounts, if such provision is necessary or desirable. In certain cases involving intangible assets, it is difficult to assign a value to them, especially when that value is to be in excess of cost. The authors do not believe in assigning values in excess of cost to intangible assets, unless irrefutable reasons exist for the recording of appraised values; however, many cases arise in which intangible assets are so valued.

The Accounting Principles Board, in *Opinion No. 17*, provides some guidelines for amortizing intangible assets. Since the value of most intangible assets eventually disappears, the recorded costs of such assets should be amortized by systematic charges to income over the periods estimated to be benefiting from these costs. The period of amortization should not exceed forty years; however, certain factors should be considered in estimating the useful life of intangible assets. The APB recommends the auditor consider that:

a) Legal, regulatory, or contractual provisions may limit the maximum useful life.

b) Provisions for renewal or extension may alter a specified limit on useful life.

c) Effects of obsolescense, demand, competition, and other economic factors may reduce a useful life.

d) A useful life may parallel the service life expectancies of individuals or groups of employees.

e) Expected actions of competitors and others may restrict present competitive advantages.

f) An apparently unlimited useful life may in fact be indefinite and benefits cannot be reasonably projected.

g) An intangible asset may be a composite of many individual factors with varying effective lives.

Straight-line amortization is desirable and should take into consideration all pertinent factors.

SECTION I: INTERNAL CONTROL OF INTANGIBLE ASSETS

Internal control of intangible assets involves the propriety of their original recording, proper amortization, and proper retention in the accounts. Internal control may be important for certain intangible assets and of no particular significance for others. For example, in the examination of patents and any existing licensing contracts, is it important to study the system of internal control for the distribution of research and development expenses and the control over revenues arising from the licensing contracts. In the verification of goodwill, the examination of internal control may be limited to ascertaining that charges and credits

ILLUSTRATION 21–1

INTERNAL CONTROL QUESTIONNAIRE
Intangible Assets

Company_____
Period Covered_____

	Yes	No	Not Applicable	Remarks
1. Are all purchased intangibles properly recorded?				
2. Are intangible assets originally priced at cost?				
3. Are other-than-cost figures ever originally used?				
4. If acquired in noncash transactions, has the value been determined according to accepted accounting principles?				
5. If a subsidiary has been acquired through the purchase of capital stock, have separate costs been properly determined for each intangible asset?				
6. Is the amortization policy proper and adequate?				
7. Is the amortization policy consistent from year to year?				
8. Are worthless intangibles written out of the accounts?				
9. Are such write-offs recorded so that net income is not distorted?				
10. Has recognition been given to Internal Revenue requirements for the write-off of intangibles?				
11. Are additions to and deductions from intangible assets properly authorized?				
12. Do accepted accounting principles govern the recording of expenditures for additions to intangible assets?				

Prepared by_____   Reviewed by_____
Date_____   Date_____

to the account were authorized by the board of directors or some other appropriate body. Satisfactory standards of internal control are indicated in the internal control questionnaire for intangible assets in Illustration 21–1.

SECTION II: AUDIT PROGRAM FOR INTANGIBLE ASSETS

The following audit program is generally applicable to the majority of intangible assets. In succeeding sections of this chapter, the audit procedures for each intangible asset are predicated upon this program, with variations where necessary.

1. Schedule each intangible asset.
2. Examine underlying evidences of ownership privilege, validity, etc.
3. Verify valuation, which should be cost, or cost less amortization.
4. Ascertain that each intangible asset is still useful.

On a first audit of intangible assets, the principal problem is to determine the valuation originally and subsequently applied to these items in order to bring them into the accounts. There can be no debate of the statement that intangible values may become recorded in the accounts by means other than by purchase—a statement not generally applicable to fixed tangible assets. In addition, it is also true that intangible asset amounts frequently are changed after acquisition; and in many cases, these changed amounts have resulted from whim rather than from reason.

It might be mentioned at this point that the Securities and Exchange Commission requests the opinion of the accountant concerning the source and the reasonableness of the values of intangible assets. In addition, the Commission insists upon the assignment of reasonable values to intangible assets. In registration statements, intangible asset values must be given full disclosure in order to avoid a reflection of inflated asset and capital values.

Intangible Asset Schedules. In an initial engagement, in accordance with the circumstances and the audit, it may possibly be necessary and desirable to analyze each intangible asset account and verify or review the transactions back to the inception of each amount, in order to determine propriety and valuation at the time of creation, and in order to determine subsequent additions and deductions, so that values may be expressed properly at the balance sheet audit date.

If the audit is a repeat engagement, work papers setting forth the balance of each intangible asset at the beginning of the fiscal period should be prepared. Additions to each account and deductions from each account made during the audit period are then analyzed on the work papers in order to arrive at the balance at the end of the period. The audit adjustments then follow.

Examination of Underlying Evidence.   In order to establish the validity, ownership, and privilege grants of intangible assets, all underlying evidence of ownership must be studied. The underlying evidence will include purchase agreements, patent letters, franchise grants and contracts, copyright registrations, trademark registrations, formula registrations, leasehold contracts, organization cost evidence, correspondence, and other data. All necessary copies of all data become a part of the auditor's permanent file.

In connection with the verification of the origin of intangible assets, care must be exercised to be certain that the accounts were legitimately created. No intangible asset account should be the capitalized result of former operating losses, of credits to capital accounts arising from the disposition of donated capital stock originally issued for an intangible asset, or of the charge-off of unpaid capital stock subscriptions. Accounts with intangible assets have been known to serve as hiding places for expenses or for the creation or inflation of amounts and items that should not appear in a balance sheet.

Valuation Verification.   An auditor must be satisfied that the basis of carrying intangible assets is in accordance with recognized accounting principles; and he must be satisfied that the policies followed for amortization (if applicable) are in accordance with accepted principles of accounting, properly applied. A responsibility also exists for the investigation of the income productivity of each intangible asset.

As stated, intangible assets originally should be recorded at cost. Subsequent carrying value is at cost, or at cost less amortization, depending upon the class and type of intangible asset. Verification must be made of the amount and correctness of and the authority for all entries reducing intangible asset accounts during the period, and the auditor must note particularly the accounts charged to ascertain that amortization expense allocation is correct. If intangible assets are established at figures differing from cost, proper company personnel should be consulted and the basis of the valuation used discussed with them in order to determine the propriety of the amounts.

Remaining Usefulness.   If an intangible asset does not possess remaining usefulness, it should be removed from the accounts by a charge to nonrecurring expense. In order to determine usefulness, investigation and the examination of income data related to the asset will be of assistance.

ILLUSTRATION.   A company owns a patent on a certain type of machine manufactured by it and leased to others. The Patent account contains an unamortized debit balance of $20,000. Gross royalties for the past five years have averaged $150 per year, and the examination led to the conclusion that the royalties would not increase.

In addition to verifying source, cost, appraisal, and the amortization of intangible assets, an auditor's advisory duties with respect to this class of asset covers a wide field. An auditor must protect the present and future interests of present and future owners. If intangible assets are not properly treated, invested capital can be jeopardized and an investor misled.

Patents

The examination of patents accounts should include the following procedures:

1. Schedule each patent, setting forth a full description, date acquired, cost, vouched charges and credits, and the detail of the examination of the client's development costs charged to the patents accounts.
2. Examine the patent letters, and/or obtain confirmation letters from the client's patent attorney as to the validity and existence of each patent.
3. Ascertain that valuations represent purchase price or the cost research and development resulting in a successful patent.
4. Describe the amortization, and determine its propriety.
5. Prepare notes on the usefulness and productivity of each patent.
6. Prepare notes on past concluded litigation and on contemplated litigation.

A patent is an exclusive privilege granted by a government giving the right to manufacture and dispose of or otherwise benefit from the results of the invention of a product or process. In the United States, patents are granted for a period of 17 years, at the expiration of which time the monopoly ceases. A patent is registered in the name of the owner at the United States Patent Office, and this registration constitutes the true evidence of ownership of the patent.

Patent letters are issued upon the registration of the patent. These letters must be examined by the auditor; in addition to or in lieu of this examination, confirmations of the validity and existence of the patents may be obtained from the company's patent attorney. The patent letters also state the extent of the territory over which the patent is protectible; a patent issued by the United States Patent Office extends over all of the jurisdictions of the United States. Priority of application is the determining factor in the granting of a patent. If a competitor manufactures and sells the same items or uses the same process, priority of application for the patent will be the basis of decision in the litigation that may follow. Since the life of a patent extends for 17 years from the time it is granted, protection is frequently secured for a longer period because protection starts at the time of application.

The value of a patent emanates from its ability to produce income and not from the mere fact that a patent has been acquired. Patents constitute the most valuable assets of many corporations, not only from the standpoint of the cost of the patents but fundamentally from the standpoint of the earning capacity made possible by possession of the patent, which results in an income not possible for competitors. In many instances, corporations purchase patents outright from the originators. In other cases, the inventor and the manufacturer enter into a contractual relationship whereby the latter obtains the privilege, usually exclusive, of manufacturing and selling the product or of using the process covered by the patent. In such cases, the owner of the patent receives a royalty based upon production of sales. When a corporation purchases a patent, it frequently grants usage privileges to others on a royalty basis. When a manufacturer does not own a patent but manufactures under a contract with the owner, the manufacturer should not capitalize the contract on his records as a patent but should simply show his royalty costs as an expense. The comparison of debits in the Patents account with the listing of the patents owned should disclose improper charges of this nature.

Although patents may result in profits not obtainable by competitors, proper accounting practice is to record the patents at cost. If patents are appreciated in the records, the extraordinary rate of return is reduced to a normal rate, and the fact that unusual profits exist is not evident from an examination of the financial statements. If patents have been appreciated, the auditor should annotate the balance sheet, and disclose the situation in the audit report. If patents possess unusual value in excess of cost less amortization, this too may be mentioned in the report.

Vouchers and other evidence substantiating original cost should be examined and traced to the Patents account. The cost of a patent is its purchase price, if it is bought outright. If the patent is developed by the client, all research and experimental expenses, legal fees, patent fees, and other developmental items may be considered as constituting the cost of the patent. However, current expense of this nature should not be carried forward as an asset, since it is impossible to determine in advance if a patent of value will result when all work is completed. If all of these expenses were currently capitalized and if—when the patent is finally secured—it is of no value, or if it is soon superseded, or if a patent is not obtained, future periods will be forced to absorb the loss properly belonging to the developmental periods, or a current period nonrecurring expense should be charged.

Every debit in the Patents account should be "tied in" with the cost of one of the patents, and charges not allocable to a specific patent should be removed from the account. The auditor must examine contracts for purchased patents; he must verify expenses for developed patents in order to determine the legitimacy and correctness of the capitalization of the expense outlays.

A patent may be of doubtful value as an includible asset until it has withstood the test of a lawsuit brought by someone honestly interested in establishing his priority. If an infringement suit is won by a defendant, the amount spent in defense of title to the patent is a proper capitalization charge, if desired. If a lawsuit is lost, the amount spent in title defense, plus all amounts previously expended in connection with the purchase or development of the patent, should be removed from the accounts. The cost of a successful suit also may be properly capitalized if the client company is the plaintiff and had brought suit against someone allegedly infringing on its patent.

An auditor must determine the book value of patents at the balance sheet date. To do this adequately, he must of necessity discuss rates of patent amortization with management. Although the legal life of a patent is 17 years, most patents become obsolete before the expiration of that time. Consequently, the length of time during which a patent will prove to be an income-producing asset must be reasonably estimated; then, the cost of the patent should be amortized over 17 years or the estimated useful life, whichever is shorter. If there are patents that are not being used, either because of lack of demand for the product manufactured thereunder or because of the placing of the patents on an inactive status, the cost of the patents should be charged to nonrecurring expense. In amortizing patents, the auditor will discover that in many cases the credits were passed directly to the Patents account rather than to an Accumulation for Amortization of Patents account. The direct credit method is widely employed; however, the accumulation method offers certain decision-making advantages and is considered by some accountants the better method, since original cost or appraisal figures are thereby shown on the balance sheet. In many instances, a patent-owning company continues the manufacture of a patented item long after the patent has expired. In such cases, a patent does not exist, and the auditor should ascertain that no value is assigned either to a Patent account or to any other asset account after the expiration of the patent.

Sales records of patented particles and of products sold under patented processes should be examined to ascertain that excessive valuation of a patent does not exist. It may happen that a patent is correctly costed and is being amortized in proper proportion to its total legal life; investigation may prove that sales of the patented article are negligible. This simply means that the intangible asset is overvalued and must be adjusted to bring it into line with its productive probabilities.

Leaseholds

A lease represents the right to use real or personal property for the period of the contract. A lease differs from outright ownership because of the limitations imposed upon the disposal and use of the leased property and because of the limited period of occupancy or use. Office buildings, department stores, hotels, and downtown business concerns in general frequently have their owned or leased buildings constructed or leased land.

In recent years, there has been a growing practice of using long-term leases as a method of financing. A company will construct a building to its own specifications, sell the entire property (frequently to an insurance company or other financing organization), and simultaneously lease the property back for a stated number of years. This is commonly known as a "sale-and-lease-back" transaction. Normally, the lessee assumes all costs of property ownership, such as taxes, insurance, and maintenance; the lessee does not pay mortgage indebtedness on the property (assuming that the lessor has mortgaged the property).

An audit program for leaseholds may be outlined as follows:

1. Review internal control procedures for the acquisition of lease contracts and all provisions for subleases.
2. Examine leasehold authorizations.
3. Examine leasehold and sublease agreements.
4. Ascertain that leases are properly valued.
5. Verify the cost and amortization of leaseholds if advance payments have been made, or if the leases have been capitalized on the records of the lessee.
6. Verify the cost and amortization of leasehold improvements.
7. Verify rental payments.
8. Ascertain that proper disclosure of leases is presented in the financial statements.

Comments on the preceding audit program are presented in the following paragraphs.

An auditor should ascertain by reference to minutes of the board of directors or the finance committee that proper authorization exists for entering into a lease agreement or the purchase of a leasehold. The terms expressed in the authorization should be compared with the terms of the contract. In his examination of the lease contract, an auditor should extract for his work papers such data as the names of the parties; the properties involved; the exact terms of the contract; renewal features; cancellation clauses; advance deposit payments; premium payments; periodic rental; rental payment dates clauses with respect to taxes, insurance, repairs, and so forth; and improvements. If he considers it necessary, the auditor may request direct confirmation data from the lessee, the lessor, or a sublessor.

The Leasehold account should be analyzed and all entries traced to the records of original entry. If a leasehold appears as an asset, there must be verification of its valuation. If account valuation represents cost, the auditor must verify the cost computation, which should represent the present value of an annuity; and he must verify the proper annual amortization. The periodic amortization must be great enough to write off the cost of the lease and premiums paid to obtain it in conformity with the shortest time provisions of the lease contract. If account valuation represents the capitalization of the discounted value of the lease rentals payable, the auditor should verify the computations, the periodic rent and interest, and ascertain the proper distinction between current and long-term liabilities.

If a lessee makes improvements to leased properties, those improvements originally should be capitalized in a Leasehold Improvements account. The auditor should analyze this account in order to approve proper distinction between charges of a capital nature and those that represent expenses at the time of incurrence. Also, he must ascertain if the leasehold improvements are being properly depreciated. Even if a lease contains a renewal clause, improvements theoretically should be amortized over a period no longer than the period of the original lease, since there is no assurance when the improvements are made that the renewal privilege will be exercised. However, present federal income tax regulations often force amortization over the longer period, depending upon the 60 percent rule, or depending upon the business relationship existing between the lessor and the lessee. An illustrative work paper for leasehold improvements is presented in Illustration 21–2.

ILLUSTRATION 21–2

RESEARCH COMPANY

Leasehold Improvements, December 31, 1975

Explanation	Original Cost	Amortization				
		1971	*1972*	*1973*	*1974*	*1975*
1971 Improvements	144,000√	9,600	9,600	9,600	9,600	9,600
1972 Improvements	7,000√		500	500	500	500
1974 Improvements	18,000√			1,500	1,500	1,500
1975 Improvements	21,450√					1,950
Total Amortization	190,450√	9,600	10,100	11,600	11,600	13,550

√ Verified all expenditures by inspection of supporting invoices.
Lease dated January 2, 1971. Terminates December 31, 1985.
This is a 15-year lease, no option to renew.

If subleases exist, the auditor must verify not only the leasehold expenses but also the rental received from the sublessee. Premiums paid for subleases should be capitalized and systematically amortized over the life of the sublease.

With regard to proper balance sheet and income statement disclosure of long-term leases and sale-and-lease-back transactions. *Accounting Research Bulletin No. 43, Accounting Research Study No. 4,* and *Opinions of the Accounting Principles Board Nos. 5, 7, 16* and *17* of the American Institute of Certified Public Accountants should be read.

Long-term leases and "sale-and-lease-back" contracts should be given full and adequate disclosure in the financial statements of the lessee, because the lessee possesses a contract entitling him to the use of assets, and which charges him with the responsibility of making periodic rental and interest payments.

The subject of long-term leases which contain an option to purchase by the lessee, related capitalization, depreciation, and related liabilities under such leases is treated in Chapter 24.

The Securities and Exchange Commission (Rule 3–18 [b]) requirements are as follows: "Where the rentals or obligations under long-term leases are material, there shall be shown the amounts of annual rentals under such leases with some indication of the periods for which they are payable, together with any important obligation assumed or guarantee made in connection therewith. If the rentals are conditional, state the minimum annual amounts."

In general, the Securities and Exchange Commission had interpreted the disclosure required by Rule 3–18 to apply to leases extending more than three years from the balance sheet date. The Commission does not permit the showing of leases as assets and liabilities in the balance sheets of registered companies; however, it does advocate the use of footnotes and will permit the showing of leases "short," that is, as memorandum figures within the balance sheet.

If leases and their related obligations are capitalized and shown in a balance sheet, either "short" or as a part of the total dollar amount of assets and liabilities, the presentation may be as follows:

Assets
  Right to use leased building, at discounted amount of related
    rental obligations. . . . . $_____
Current Liabilities
  Current portion of lease obligation. . . . . $_____
Long-Term Liabilities
  Rental obligation under lease, discounted at _____%, payable
  in semiannual installments of $_____, through
  December, 1980, less $_____, due within one year . . . . $_____

The preceding presentation assumes that a purchase clause does not exist.

Copyrights

Copyrights are exclusive privileges granted by the federal government for the reproduction and sale of printed or otherwise produced writings, drawings, musical compositions, maps, works of art, and so forth. In the United States, copyrights are granted for a period of 28 years and are renewable once. However, most copyrighted productions do not enjoy a life of even 28 years. Therefore, the auditor must watch particularly for obsolescence of copyrights, and he also must be careful to verify copyright periods and remaining life. The safest practice is to charge the cost of the copyright against the cost of publishing a first edition or manufacturing the first production. If a copyright represents an original grant, the cost of the copyright is negligible and usually is charged to expense at the time of acquisition; if a copyright is purchased from an original holder, the auditor must verify cost and amortization, and must investigate obsolescence. Audit procedures for copyrights are similar to those for patents.

Copyrights, like patents, are often valuable possessions from the standpoint of their income-producing capacity; but as with patents, they should not be placed on the records at an amount in excess of cost. A few publishers capitalize a copyright by multiplying the annual profit resulting from the copyright by a selected number of years—often four. This is not the best practice; but if a client insists upon it, the auditor must likewise insist upon adequate amortization provisions and upon proper credit entries. In addition, the balance sheet and the audit report must fully disclose the appraisal. Publishers sometimes buy copyrighted manuscripts outright. In such cases, royalties are not paid to originators, and the Copyright account should be credited periodically for the royalties that otherwise would be paid; the charge would be to a Copyright Amortization account. Copyrights that have no value—either because they have expired or because they are not being used—and still appear as assets, should be removed from the records.

Franchises

A franchise is a contract in which the grantor permits the grantee certain usage or operating privileges. Franchises may be of limited life, or they may be perpetual. They may be revocable by the grantor, or they may be irrevocable. Also, they may be granted for a periodic fee or for a lump sum; or they may be granted gratis. Public utility commissions regulating public utilities frequently specify the expenditures chargeable to the Franchise account and the method to be followed in amortizing the account.

In auditing franchises and the related accounts, an auditor must investigate the franchise in order to be familiar with all terms of the grant, including any requirements on the part of both parties to the contract, any restrictions imposed, fees or rentals, the right of the grantor to assume operations in the event of specified contingencies, revocable features, rate clauses, service clauses, and maintenance provisions. Excerpts of these provisions become a part of the permanent file.

If the franchises were acquired by purchase, an auditor examines the franchise accounts to ascertain that they are carried at cost less proper amortization. If they have been acquired without cost, no value should appear in the accounts and annual rentals should be recorded as an operating expense. The auditor will determine the adequacy of periodic amortization charges for franchises of limited life and for franchises containing revocable clauses. If a public utility commission requires specific methods of amortization, the auditor must be certain that these legal requirements are being followed, and his report should contain appropriate comment on this matter. A franchise should be amortized at least over its legal life, if not sooner, when revocable features might lead to cancellation. Amortization is commonly on a straight-line basis, and an allowance may or may not be used.

License and Royalty Agreements

License contracts and royalty contracts may be granted under patents or copyrights. Properly, the grantee usually does not recognize as an intangible asset the cost of attorneys' fees and other costs of obtaining the license or royalty agreement, but charges these amounts to expense. If a license or royalty contract has been assigned for a consideration, it is proper to captalize the cost of obtaining the assignment. The capitalized cost should be amortized over the life of the agreement or the anticipated period of usefulness, whichever is shorter.

An auditor also must verify the licensee's payments to the grantor if payments are on the basis of production or sales.

Trademarks and Trade Names

Trademarks are recognition signs, symbols, designs, and brand names established so that identification of a product may easily be made by the purchaser. A trademark brands a product in the same manner that a signature identifies the writer of a letter or a document. Trademarks are valid under common law, based on continual usage, but ordinarily are registered with the United States Patent Office. By registration, legal protection for the use of the trademark is established, since the identification is created in the name of the registrant for his exclusive use. In order to establish the legitimate right to a trademark, it may be necessary to be able to prove priority of usage; therefore, the registration should be effected as soon as the trademark is developed. The registrant enjoys the exclusive use of the trademark; in order to continue the enjoyment of the monopoly, it is necessary that the trademark be used continuously.

The registration period with the Patent Office for trademarks and trade names is 30 years, renewable indefinitely for similar periods. Most states permit registration of trademarks and trade names; and in many states, there is no time limit to the registration. Therefore, it is not necessary to amortize their costs unless their useful productive life is limited.

Trademarks and trade names should be carried at cost but should be completely amortized by the time they are discontinued or become worthless. Costs for trademarks consist of developing outlays, design costs, or purchase price, if an insignia is purchased from a preceding owner. The cost of a trademark commonly is quite negligible if its cost is composed only of designing costs and if the trademark is considered alone and separately from promotion and advertising outlays. In many cases, trademarks are carried at a zero value. There are many cases in which a trademark is looked upon as the creator of goodwill and as a proper basis for writing up the value of the trademark or for increasing the Goodwill account. A trademark may be valuable and might lead to the element of goodwill, but that does not constitute a reason for increasing the value of the assets above cost.

A trade name differs from a trademark in that a trade name applies to a business, whereas a trademark commonly accompanies a product. Trade names are capitalized and are audited in the same manner as trademarks.

In auditing trademark accounts, the auditor should examine the registration letters and all correspondence with the client's attorney, and should verify the account charges and credits. In his report, or as a footnote to the balance sheet, the auditor should explain trademark valuations if the account is carried at a figure in excess of cost.

Secret Processes and Formulas

Secret processes and formulas are often developed which have great value to the owner and which result in a monopoly or the enjoyment of a rate of net income in excess of that of the competitive industry as a whole. So far as the accounts are concerned, it is much better to carry the formulas at their cost of development than to capitalize the additional profits. The cost of formulas constitutes all development and research costs connected with them, or the purchase price paid to obtain them. The book value of discontinued formulas should be eliminated from the records. The auditor must confer with the proper officials of a company to determine the ownership of formulas and the degree of security from discovery by outsiders, for these are vital to the general protection of the company and its profit-making possibilities. Secret formulas are similar to trademarks, with the exception of the fact that they are secret and will be of value only so long as they remain secret. The auditing procedure is the same as that applicable to trademarks.

Goodwill

The auditor should attempt to trace the history and development of goodwill appearing in the records under examination in order to clarify his understanding of this controversial asset. The major problem confronting an auditor is the determination of the basis for the existence of a Goodwill account.

There are many methods of computing the *theoretical* value of goodwill for a going concern, and approved principles should be the consistent guide in practical application. Goodwill is the least liquid of all assets, and it cannot be distributed to stockholders in the event of liquidation. Therefore (assuming purchase accounting practices), it should be placed in the accounts at the price actually paid for it upon the acquisition of a business for cash, capital stock, or other valuable consideration. The price paid for it usually is any excess of purchase price over the proprietorship of an acquired company. In a merger, goodwill is often created because of differences in earning power of the separate companies joining the merger; and capital stock in an agreed amount is issued to the stockholders of the high-profit individual companies for the greater earning power of these companies. If in these cases only no-par value capital stock is issued, it may nor be necessary to show goodwill.

If goodwill is viewed as the enjoyment of a profit by one company in excess of the normal or usual return for that industry as a whole, goodwill might exist; but if it has not been purchased, it should be omitted from the records. If the excess profit is capitalized, rates of profit over normal fall to normal, and a true return on invested capital is not shown. Therefore, the nonpurchased creation of a Goodwill account is to be discouraged; readers of the balance sheet are misled as to asset values. Investment analysts ordinarily compute rates of return on assets after excluding intangible values. Regulatory agencies, such as the Securities and Exchange Commission, discourage the showing of goodwill in excess of cost.

The first duty of an auditor in an examination of goodwill is to discover how the amount of the Goodwill account was determined by examining minutes of the board of directors, purchase contracts and cash disbursement records, and by examining the allocations made when assets were acquired in lump-sum purchases involving an amount of goodwill. In his report, the auditor should indicate the derivation of the goodwill values, a description of its method of creation, and the amortization policies, if any. He should not fail to indicate such sources of creation as arbitrary write-up, capitalized organization or development costs, unpaid capital stock subscription cancellations, discount on capital stock issuance, amounts equal to profits realized from patented products, and so on. Cost should be the maximum capitalization figure for goodwill.

Owing to fluctuations in net income, goodwill fluctuates in value from period to period just as market prices fluctuate for fixed tangible assets. The value of the goodwill when established by cost need not be altered unless the goodwill is declining, has permanently declined, or is lost.

The Securities and Exchange Commission has not adopted a rule for goodwill amortization, but the Commission investigates the statements of registrants who have indefinitely retained a Goodwill account. As the result of investigations, certain registrants amortize goodwill to income or to retained income.

The American Institute of Certified Public Accountants in its *Accounting Research Study No. 10*, entitled *Accounting for Goodwill*, provides some specific recommendations that should be carefully adhered to. It states that—

The separable resources and property rights acquired in a business combination should be recorded at fair value at the date of the purchase. The difference between the value of the consideration given and the fair value of the net separable resources and property rights acquired should be assigned to purchased goodwill.

The amount assigned to purchased goodwill represents a disbursement of existing resources, or of proceeds of stock issued to effect the business combination, in anticipation of future earnings. The expenditure should be accounted for as a reduction of stockholders' equity. The accounting can be achieved by one of two methods: (a) an immediate direct write-off to a capital surplus or retained earnings (the preferred method) or (b) showing a deduction from stockholders' equity in the balance sheet for several periods and a later write-off to capital surplus or retained earnings. The selection of method may involve significant legal and disclosure matters to be resolved by the board of directors but is not a question of accounting principle.

The recommended treatment of purchased goodwill results in balance sheet and income statement reporting for purchased goodwill which is consistent in principle with existing practices of accounting for internally developed or nonpurchased goodwill.

Research and Development Costs

Much money has been spent for R & D but there has not been total agreement as to how these expenditures should be reflected in the financial statements. As stated in Chapter 18, the Financial Accounting Standards Board is attempting to prepare guidelines for the handling of these costs. Four accounting treatments have been used and therefore must be considered by the auditor in his examination of these expenditures. The manner in which R & D costs are handled are as follows:

1. Capitalize all costs as assets when incurred and amortize when revenues are earned.
2. Treat all costs as current expenses as incurred.
3. Capitalize selectively. Predetermine the conditions that would require capitalization as well as those that would be written off as current expenses.
4. Accumulate all costs in a special intangible asset account until a determination can be made as to the degree of future benefits.

The modern trend is to follow 2, above; this is, to charge research and development costs to current period expenses.

Further complication of the situation is provided by the Internal Revenue Service. Until a recent Supreme Court decision, only an on-going business could deduct R & D costs. A new business was not permitted to deduct such costs.

With the preceding ideas in mind, an auditor might find R & D costs in many places. The Orton and Brandish survey of this topic revealed the following:

1. Not one respondent capitalized all costs and wrote them off against subsequent production.
2. Seven respondents capitalized successful R & D costs and wrote off failures to administrative expenses.
3. Twelve respondents charged R & D costs directly to cost of sales.
4. Nineteen respondents wrote off R & D costs as indirect manufacturing expenses.
5. One hundred eight respondents wrote off R & D costs as selling and administrative expenses.
6. Fifty-three respondents set forth R & D costs as an extraneous expense.
7. Nine respondents broke the costs into two categories—administrative expenses and indirect manufacturing costs.
8. Four respondents recorded basic research costs, such as central laboratory operating costs, as administrative and all other R & D costs were charged to cost of sales.

The results of this survey indicate the complex nature of R & D costs. The authors anticipate that the FASB will establish standards so that these costs will not only be properly recorded but fully disclosed in the financial statements.

Organization Costs

Organization costs are incurred by a corporation during the original formative period preceding income-producing operations. Organization costs include such charges as legal and accounting fees for incorporation, state incorporation fees, security registration and listing fees, recording fees, fees paid to promoters, and legal and accounting fees for the formation of a merger. The Organization Cost account should not include discounts on capital stock, bond discounts, or losses of early years. Rule 5–02 of Regulation S–X of the Securities and Exchange Commission suggests that stock sales commissions and other expenses involved in the issuance of capital stock be charged to Retained Earnings, and that a footnote should explain the provisions for amortization or write-off. For federal income tax purposes, organization costs incurred after 1953 may be systematically amortized to expense over a period of not less than 60 months. Thus, organization costs *might* be viewed as deferred charges—and be so classified in a balance sheet.

The major work of the auditor consists of analyzing the Organization

Cost account, tracing the charges to approved minutes of the board of directors or of the stockholders, verifying the correctness and legitimacy of all charges, and verifying amortization. He must determine that the charges represent only items applicable to original organization.

Charges to the account must be supported by authorizations and invoices, and by paid checks when cash is expended. Accountants differ as to the amortization of organization cost, some claiming that the account represents charges necessary to the permanent organization of the company and that failure on the part of management to amortize the charges therefore is proper. The preference of the authors is to charge organization cost off over a maximum period not to exceed 60 months. Most accountants now agree to a rapid write-off of organization costs because of the rather unconvincing reasons advanced in defense of carrying such costs as a permanent asset. When organization costs are amortized, the charge should be to an expense account and should be appropriately timed, or net income will be misstated. Irregular amortization will distort periodic net income.

The costs of reorganization of a capital structure—as opposed to original incorporation costs—may properly be set up as deferred charges, if material, if future periods are to be benefited, and if current earnings cannot properly absorb the charge. At the time of reorganization, any remaining balance in an original Organization Cost account should be charged off because the effect of reorganization is that of a new or fresh start.

Capital stock issuance underwriting costs incurred after a corporation has been in operation may properly be set up as deferred charges if the amount involved is significant and if current-period earnings cannot properly absorb the charge. Such costs should not be deferred for more than a few years. The auditor should examine the underwriting contract, trace the cash receipts to the records, examine entries relating to the stock issue, and examine the remittance statements from brokers or the underwriting syndicate.

SECTION III: FINANCIAL STATEMENT CONSIDERATIONS

In the discussion of each intangible asset, the financial statement considerations were set forth. In summarization, intangible assets should be shown separately classified in the balance sheet; if possible, those of limited existence should be separated from those of perpetual or unlimited existence. Usually intangible assets are the least liquid of all assets, since most of them are unsalable unless the business or a part of it is sold. Normally, intangible assets possess value only if they earn a profit over and above a fair return on tangible asset values. The basis of valuation should be stated in the balance sheet; methods of amortization should be indicated in the audit report.

QUESTIONS

1. Craven Tools, Inc., has a research and development department whose sole purpose is to carry on research and conduct experiments with the hope that a patent will be developed. Costs incurred by this department approximate $200,000 annually. On several occasions valuable patents have been developed and the company has used them as revenue-producing items. What accounting treatment would you recommend for the annual costs of operating this department?

2. If goodwill is to be reported as an asset on the balance sheet of a client, stipulate the conditions that must exist for this to be done.

3. The Grass Roots Company develops and carries out a very extensive and costly advertising campaign on behalf of new products and charges the amount above its average yearly. expense to goodwill. Do you approve?

4. When acquiring a business what should be considered in determining the existence of goodwill?

5. Prepare an internal control questionnaire for patents for a large patent-holding company. Do not follow the internal control questionnaire for intangible assets presented in the text.

6. Something New, Inc., engages extensively in research for the development of new products and processes. Expenses for research consistently have been charged to current expenses, with one exception, as follows: In 1972 a new machine development was initiated, and the company was of the opinion that it would retain the patent on the machine (when and if granted) and that the machine could be profitably marketed. Therefore, all costs incurred in the development of this machine were charged to an asset account, Special Development. Early in 1975, the development was completed and the patent was granted. The Special Development account was closed to the Patents account. Sales of the machine produced under the patent exceeded the company's best estimates, and the net income on the machine sales was excellent.

   In outline form, prepare an audit program for the patent acquired as a result of this special development, assuming that you are auditing the records of Something New, Inc., as of December 31, 1975, and assuming that the company's records were being examined for the first time.

   (AICPA, adapted)

7. The Waltz Company purchases some of its patents and develops other patents. Management is uncertain as to which costs to capitalize and which to charge to current operations. It is also uncertain where research and development costs should appear in the operating statements in those cases in which the company has been charging certain items to expense. Outline a plan for management to follow in the future.

8. A company acquires patents regularly and charges their costs to a Patents account. The account has not been amortized during the past 10 years. At the end of the 10th year you are called in to determine the present

value of the patents. What procedure will you follow in order to state properly the balance of the Patents account?

9. On July 1, 1976, your client paid $300,000 for a patent on a product; the product was in direct competition with a product of your client company. Management decided not to manufacture the product permitted under the new patent but to continue with the manufacture of its customary products. During the audit for the year ended December 31, 1976, you investigated the $300,000 as a charge to the Patents account. What would you suggest to management?

10. A obtained a patent on February 1, 1972, and immediately assigned it to B. The terms of the contract provided that B would pay A a royalty of $2 for each unit produced in accordance with the A patent and installed in B machinery delivered to any point outside the plant of the B Company.

   On February 1, 1972, B paid A $1,000 in advance royalties. Thereafter, no royalty payments or statements of royalties earned were received by A. The efforts of A to obtain information resulted in a statement by B that the $1,000 advance was in excess of the royalties earned.

   In 1975, A asked you to determine the facts. Outline a program to ascertain the amount of the royalty due or overpaid to A under his contract with B, assuming that the company granted you access to all records.

11. A company owns a patent. If it did not own the patent, the royalty cost which the company would have to pay on its sales would amount to $40,000 per year. Therefore, the board of directors of the company decides to increase its Patents account by $200,000 (five years' royalties) and to declare and pay a common stock dividend out of the appraisal increment thus created. The $200,000 increase in the Patents account is to be amortized over the remaining life of the patient. What criticisms have you to offer of the action of the board of directors of the company?

12. A company paid an annual rental of $48,000 and under the terms of its lease had the option of purchase for $500,000 at any time before the termination of the lease. The lease was for 20 years, 10 of which have expired. The appraised sound value of the property at the end of the 10th year was $700,000 owing to increased land and building values. The company is contemplating purchase of the property, and it wishes to show the value of the leasehold in its current balance sheet so that stockholders may see the desirability of purchasing the land and building for $500,000. How would you suggest showing the leasehold value?

13. How should long-term leases and sale-and-lease transactions be disclosed in the financial statements of lessees?

14. *a*) The Copyrights account of a publishing company has a debit balance of $40,000. What would be your procedure in connection with the audit of this item?

   b) In your opinion, when should copyrights appear as assets?

15. *a*) If you were auditing the records of a privately owned public utility,

to what would you devote particular attention when you were investigating the Franchise account and the franchises?

b) You were auditing the records of a local public utility for the first time. During the inspection of the franchise, you noticed a clause whereby the grantor municipality may revoke the franchise at its option. What factors would guide you in arriving at your decision as to the correct amount of periodic amortization, assuming that a lump sum had been paid for the franchise?

16. A client incurred material expenses in obtaining a trademark. He requests your advice as to whether (a) the trademark cost should be amortized over a period of years, (b) the cost should be permanently capitalized, or (c) the cost should be charged to expense at incurrence. What advice would you offer, and why?

17. During the course of a periodic audit of a beverage manufacturer you find a new account in the general ledger with the title "Formulas and Processes." This account has a debit balance of $50,000, supported by the following entry:

Formulas and Processes 50,000
  Common Stock   50,000
  To record issuance of stock at par to John Doe for secret
  formulas and processes which are not patentable.

a) Describe the procedures you would follow in connection with this new account.

b) If the only information which you could obtain was to the effect that the formula was in the safe-deposit box, that the manufacturing process was broken up so that the employees could not put the formula together in proper processes and proportions without the supervision of the factory manager, and that the $50,000 represented the value of the stock at the market, which was also par, would you be willing to issue an unqualified opinion?

18. After a newly organized corporation has started operations, may any charges be made to the Organization Cost account? Explain your answer.

PROBLEMS

1. The major cost of processing lima beans by the Fremont Canning Co. is the pressure cooking time of 38 minutes. As competition has increased, the company has carried on continuous research, over the past five years, in an attempt to improve processing of this product. Since no improvement was developed during this period, costs incurred were charged to cost of sales each year. Near the end of the fifth year, the company developed a blanching and sharp freezing process which was a patentable process.

The board of directors of the company had various suggestions as to how this patentable cost should be recognized on its financial statements. The suggestions follow:

a) The write-off of the research and development costs had resulted in material misstatement of incomes, retained earnings, and restriction of dividends over the past five years.

b) If the "cost" of the new patent is not correctly stated on the balance sheet, a valuable revenue producing asset will be concealed.

c) Failure to set up the "cost" of the new patent will cause the incorrect matching of costs and revenues.

You, the auditor, are to prepare an analysis of these proposals to be presented to the board of directors.

2. Buxton Company developed a new fishing reel that was patented. The following costs were incurred:

Materials and supplies	$ 3,000
Salaries of persons working on reel	12,000
Overhead allocation, examined and approved by you, the auditor	4,400
Market research cost incurred in determining desirable features which were built into the reel	2,700

The patent was granted on January 2, 1972. Due to the advanced design of the reel, management believes the beneficial life of the asset will be 17 years.

During the latter part of 1975, the company incurred legal fees in the amount of $4,200 in successfully protecting the patent on this reel.

On February 2, 1974, the company purchased a patent on a spinning rod for $18,000. The patent had been granted one month earlier. However, due to changing styles, management expects an improved rod to be developed within six years.

a) Prepare the journal entries, for each patent, through 1976.

b) Briefly explain your reason for the entries.

3. You are asked to prepare goodwill computations from the following data and listed approaches:

Budgeted average annual earnings expected over the next five years	$ 40,000
Budgeted average future value of net tangible assets over the next five years	300,000

Prepare calculations under each of the following assumed conditions:

a) Goodwill is to be equal to earnings capitalized at 10 percent over budgeted average of net tangible assets.

b) Goodwill will be equal to excess earnings capitalized at 20 percent; normal earnings rate for industry, 10 percent.

c) Goodwill will be equal to five years of excess earnings, normal earnings rate for industry is 10 percent.

4. Net income and net asset balances for a five-year period for Cultivator, Inc., are as follows:

Year	Net Earnings before Income Taxes	Net Assets at End of Year
1971	$ 35,000	$400,000
1972	50,000	420,000
1973	65,000	450,000
1974	100,000	500,000
1975	150,000	630,000

Plow Shares, Inc., agrees to purchase the net assets at the beginning of 1976 and make cash payment for the properties on the following basis:

10 percent is considered a normal return on Cultivator investments.

Payment for goodwill is to be calculated by capitalizing at 20 percent the average annual pre-tax earnings that are in excess of 10 percent of average year-end net assets.

If both parties agree that the net assets reported are acceptable values, compute the amount of goodwill to be recognized.

5. The following data are presented for Johnson, Inc., and Jansen, Inc., as of November 1, 1975, in connection with a proposed merger of the two companies:

	Johnson, Inc.	*Jansen, Inc.*
Net tangible assets per records, as of November 1, 1975	$328,500	$298,500
Average pre-tax earnings per records, November 1, 1970–October 31, 1975	82,000	44,000

It is agreed that the values of the respective assets contributed are to be determined on the following basis:

15 percent is to be considered a reasonable pre-tax return on the net tangible assets.

Average pre-tax earnings for the period 1970–1975 in excess of 15 percent of the net tangible assets of November 1, 1975, are to be capitalized at 25 percent in calculating goodwill.

Before determining the respective values, however, the following agreed-to adjustments must be made:

Equipment of Johnson, Inc., is estimated to be worth $40,000 more than book value. The equipment has a remaining life of five years. Jansen, Inc., wrote off all of its organization costs of $20,000 against operating revenue in 1972.

Prepare your audit working paper, supported by calculations, to show each party to the merger the determination of the amounts to be paid for (1) net tangible assets and (2) goodwill.

6. Solenoid Manufacturing Co. was incorporated January 3, 1974. The corporation's financial statements for its first year's operations were not examined by a CPA. You have been engaged to examine the financial statements for the year ended December 31, 1975, and your examination is substantially completed. The corporation's trial balance appears at the top of page 701.

The following information relates to accounts which may yet require adjustment:

(1) Patents for Solenoid's manufacturing process were acquired January 2, 1975, at a cost of $68,000. An additional $17,000 was spent in December, 1975, to improve machinery covered by the patents and charged to the Patents account. Depreciation on fixed assets has been properly recorded for 1975 in accordance with Solenoid's practice which provides a full year's depreciation for property on

SOLENOID MANUFACTURING CORPORATION

Trial Balance
December 31, 1975

	Trial Balance	
	Debit	Credit
Cash	$ 11,000	
Accounts receivable	42,500	
Provision for doubtful accounts		$ 500
Inventories	38,500	
Machinery	75,000	
Equipment	29,000	
Accumulated depreciation		10,000
Patents	85,000	
Leasehold improvements	26,000	
Prepaid expenses	10,500	
Organization expenses	29,000	
Goodwill	24,000	
Licensing agreement No. 1	50,000	
Licensing agreement No. 2	49,000	
Accounts payable		147,500
Deferred credits		12,500
Capital stock		300,000
Retained earnings, January 1, 1975	27,000	
Sales		668,500
Cost of goods sold	454,000	
Selling and general expenses	173,000	
Interest expense	3,500	
Extraordinary losses	12,000	
Totals	$1,139,000	$1,139,000

hand June 30 and no depreciation otherwise. Solenoid uses the straight-line method for all depreciation and amortization.

(2) On January 3, 1974, Solenoid purchased two licensing agreements which were then believed to have unlimited useful lives. The balance in the Licensing Agreement No. 1 account includes its purchase price of $48,000 and expenses of $2,000 related to the acquisition. The balance in the Licensing Agreement No. 2 account includes its $48,000 purchase price and $2,000 in acquisition expenses, but it has been reduced by a credit of $1,000 for the advance collection of 1974 revenue from the agreement.

In December, 1974, an explosion caused a permanent 60 percent reduction in the expected revenue-producing value of licensing agreement No. 1; and in January, 1976, a flood caused additional damage which rendered the agreement worthless.

A study of licensing agreement No. 2 made by Solenoid in January, 1975, revealed that its estimated remaining life expectancy was only 10 years as of January 1, 1975.

(3) The balance in the Goodwill account includes (a) $8,000 paid December 30, 1974, for an advertising program which it is estimated will assist in increasing Solenoid's sales over a period of four years following the disbursement; and (b) legal expenses of $16,000 incurred for Solenoid's incorporation on January 3, 1974.

(4) The Leasehold Improvements account includes (a) the $15,000 cost of improvements with a total estimated useful life of 12 years

which Solenoid as tenant, made to leased premises in January 1974; (*b*) movable assembly line equipment costing $8,500 which was installed in the leased premises in December, 1975; and (*c*) real estate taxes of $2,500 paid by Solenoid in 1975 which, under the terms of the lease should have been paid by the landlord. Solenoid paid its rent in full during 1975. A 10-year nonrenewable lease was signed January 3, 1974, for the leased building which Solenoid used in manufacturing operations.

(5)   The balance in the Organization Expenses account properly includes costs incurred during the organizational period. The corporation has exercised its option to amortize organization costs over a 60-month period for federal income tax purposes and wishes to amortize these costs for accounting purposes.

Prepare a work sheet to adjust accounts which require adjustment. Also prepare formal adjusting entries.

A separate account should be used for the accumulation of each type of amortization and for each prior period adjustment.

(AICPA, adapted)

7.   An analysis of a Patent account of a company is as follows:

Patent Account

Date	Explanation	Debits	Credits
Jan. 2, 1971	Basic patent cost	50,000	
Dec. 31, 1971	Patent cost	20,000	
Dec. 31, 1972	Patent cost	18,000	
Dec. 31, 1973	Patent cost	16,000	
Dec. 31, 1974	Patent cost	28,000	
Dec. 31, 1975	Patent cost	30,000	
		162,000	

An analysis of the Profit and Loss account shows the following net income transferred to Retained Earnings at the close of each of the following years:

1971	$ 63,000
1972	81,000
1973	99,000
1974	117,000
1975	135,000
	$495,000

No amortization has been taken on the Patent account. All expenditures since January 2, 1971, have been in connection with the basic patent.

The sales manager receives a salary of $20,000 per year plus a 10 percent commission on net income prior to the commission but after the salary.

a)   Prepare audit work papers for the adjustment of the Patent account so that it will be completely amortized by December 31, 1980.

b) Prepare audit work papers for the adjustment of the annual net income so that the sales manager will be credited with a commission of 30 percent for all years, instead of his salary and commission just indicated. In the work papers, show the adjusted net income for each of the 10 years after patent amortization and after the new arrangement for the sales manager.

8. During the course of the initial audit of the records of the Aspen Company, for the year ended December 31, 1975, the Patents account set forth below was examined. All information and data in the account has been properly audited by the examination of underlying evidence. The company does not use Provision for Amortization account.

From the data and information in the account, prepare:

a) Audit work papers for the Patents account and for the amortization of the patents.

b) Audit adjustments which you consider necessary. The accounts have not been closed for 1975.

Patents

Date	Explanation	Debit	Credit	Balance
7/1/71	Transfer from Research Expense. Application for Patent A.	55,300		55,300
7/1/72	Transfer from Legal Expense. Attorney cost for application of Patent A.	5,000		60,300
7/1/72	Legal expense in connection with Patent A, granted 7/1/72.	6,000		66,300
12/31/72	Legal expense in connection with a successful infringement suit against Patent A.	2,890		69,190
12/31/72	Transfer of 1972 research and development costs. No patent was acquired or contemplated.	22,000		91,190
2/1/73	Purchase of Patent B. This is a competitive patent, and will never be used; its remaining life is 14 years.	8,000		99,190
12/31/73	Transfer of 1973 research and development costs. No patents were applied for and none are contemplated.	20,000		119,190
7/1/74	Transfer of 1974 research and development costs, covering Patent C, applied for today.	10,000		129,190
12/31/74	Transfer of remaining 1974 research and development costs; no patent is contemplated.	6,000		135,190
7/1/75	Legal expense re Patent C, granted today.	7,000		142,190
12/31/75	Patent D received today. This is a modification of Patent A; the effect will be to extend the legal and useful life of Patent A over the legal life of Patent D.	25,000		167,190
12/31/75	Legal costs in connection with Patent D.	9,000		176,190
12/31/75	Transfer of 1975 research and development costs, not related to a patent.	23,810		200,000

9. Since your prior audit of the records of New Parts, Inc., a manufacturer of machine tools, which has a calendar-year closing, the company has undertaken a program of leasing to its customers machines which it manufactures.

The client has recorded the leased machines in a separate ledger, and the client's employees provide you with the following facts in regard to the leased machine program:
1. Term of lease—10 years.
2. Rentals due—semiannual installments in advance.
3. Expenses—lessee to pay all taxes levied, freight, and handling charges.
4. Lessee may terminate lease at end of fifth year or any year thereafter during the term of the lease by giving lessor proper written notice.
5. Lessee agrees to exercise proper care of machines and to keep them in good repair.
6. Lessee may elect to purchase machine at end of any year at the following prices: First year, 90 percent of list price; second year, 80 percent of list price; third year, 70 percent of list price; and so forth.
7. Five machines were leased during the current year.
The company has elected to apply the straight-line method of depreciation to the machines.
   a) Prepare an audit program to cover adequately this portion of the assets of the company and the related income and expense accounts.
   b) State your balance sheet treatment of the asset.
   c) Describe your recommended treatment of the rental income.

(AICPA)

10. A company purchased a 20–year lease, paying $450,000 for it at the time of purchase. The company amortized the lease on a straight-line basis and charged expense for $27,500 each year for 12 years. During the 13th year, an operating loss was incurred to the extent of $20,000 by including $27,500 as lease amortization expense. If the $20,000 loss was closed to retained earnings, that account would be almost depleted after the regular dividend was declared. The company therefore decided to charge nothing off the lease for the current year, thereby showing a $7,500 net income. Management called upon you to approve the plan. What do you suggest in view of the past amortization policy of the company?

11. A company leased a land site for 20 years, at an annual rental of $2,500. The lease does not contain a renewal clause. Immediately after negotiating for the lease, the company erected a building costing $50,000, with an estimated life of 25 years. The building was depreciated at the rate of 5 percent per year on cost. At the end of the 10th year, the original lease was canceled, and a new one was negotiated for 30 more years.
   a) What is the annual depreciation for years 11 through 40?
   b) If the original lease had contained a renewal clause for an additional 20 years, what original depreciation rate would you have used?

12. This is the initial audit for the year ended December 31, 1975, for the Skyline Company, organized January 10, 1975. The following Orga-

nization Cost account appears in the ledger. (The numbers following each item in the Explanation column are keyed to explanations appearing below the account.) Prepare proper work papers for an analysis of the Organization Cost account and draft all audit adjustments. Management agrees with your recommendation that organization costs should be amortized in accordance with the maximum provisions available for federal income tax purposes.

Date 1975		Explanation	Debit	Credit	Balance
Jan.	10	State incorporation fees (1)	2,000		2,000
	15	Legal fees (2)	5,000		7,000
	15	Cost of stock certificates (3)	500		7,500
Feb.	1	Attorney fee (4)	4,000		11,500
	1	Advertising (5)	1,000		12,500
	1	Leasehold (6)	6,000		18,500
	1	Discount on capital stock (7)	10,000		28,500
	1	Stockholders' ledgers (8)	200		28,700
	1	CPA fees (9)	4,000		32,700
	1	Brokers' commissions for stock sold (10)	3,000		35,700
	1	General accounting records (11)	300		36,000
Apr.	1	Traveling expense in connection with the establishment of a branch sales office (12)	1,000		37,000
	1	Product development costs (13)	5,000		42,000
July	1	Branch sales office opening (14)	2,500		44,500
Oct.	1	Product development costs (15)	5,000		49,500
Dec.	1	Cost of lawsuit (16)	3,000		52,500
Dec.	31	Amortization (17)		5,250	47,250

Examination of supporting documentary evidence for each charge to the Organization Cost account revealed the following information:

(1) A perpetual franchise was granted.

(2) These legal fees were solely for purposes of incorporation.

(3) First purchase of stock certificates.

(4) The amount paid the company attorney for costs involved in applying for a patent.

(5) Management stated that the advertising was for the purpose of acquainting the public with a newly formed company, prior to starting operations.

(6) The leasehold is for a period of 10 years, with an annual rental of $6,000, payable each year in advance, starting February 1, 1975.

(7) Capital stock of $100,000 was sold for $90,000 cash.

(8) Cost of stockholders' ledgers.

(9) Cost of designing and installing an accounting system—prior to the opening of business.

(10) Commission on the $100,000 of stock sold for $90,000.

(11) Cost of journals, ledgers, invoices, etc.

(12) Self-explanatory.

(13) The cost of developing products the company planned to sell in the future.

(14) Cost of prizes, entertainment, and so forth, in connection with the opening of the branch sales office.
(15) Same as (13).
(16) This is the amount paid an adjoining property owner because a newly constructed driveway of the Shebesta Company infringed on one inch of the plaintiff's property.
(17) Management originally decided to amortize the account over a 10-year period.

PRACTICE MATERIAL ASSIGNMENTS

Metalcraft, Incorporated: Audit Problem:
   Assignment 9: Research and Development Costs.
Colby-Gears, Inc.: Holmes and Moore Audit Case:
   Bring all work up to date.

22

Current Liabilities, Related
Costs and Expenses

Audit Objectives

The audit objectives for current liabilities may be expressed as follows: to evaluate the internal control over the liabilities, their processing, and their payment; to obtain satisfactory evidence that all current liabilities and related costs and expenses have been properly recorded; and to properly present the current liabilities in the balance sheet, including necessary explanatory footnotes.

Current Liabilities in General

In many respects, the audit procedures applicable to current liabilities and related costs and expenses are similar to those applicable to receivables and their related revenues. Valuations used in connection with the majority of assets are based upon original cost, amortization policies, well-established precedents, accepted principles, sound judgment, and personal opinion. Consequently, when considered as a totality, the asset side of a balance sheet represents an expression of opinion. Except for estimated accrued liabilities and cases involving a question of the existence of contingencies, liabilities are factual statements, not opinions.

Current liabilities normally are to be liquidated within a relatively short period of time. Current liabilities are those whose liquidation requires the use of current assets, or those which will create another liability.

Current liabilities normally are subdivided as follows: trade accounts payable, nontrade accounts payable, trade notes, nontrade notes, bank loans, amounts due to affiliated companies, amounts due to stockholders and officers, declared dividends payable, deposit liabilities, accrued items, amounts withheld from employees, revenues received in advance, and all other current items.

The detection of unrecorded liabilities constitutes one of the major problems in an audit. The duties of the auditor are to ascertain that all recorded liabilities are correct and also to determine that all liabilities are included which should be included at the close of the fiscal period. If current liabilities are omitted or understated, working capital may be seriously misstated and a creditor might be misled into a sale on credit or a loan of money which he would not make if a proper liability status had been presented. Furthermore, an understatement of liabilities is almost certain to involve an understatement of an asset or an expense. If management overstated liabilities, assets or expenses are overstated—and the overstatement of an expense results in a misleading concept for an investor and an improper periodic federal income tax. Therefore, an auditor must obtain satisfactory evidence that all current liabilities are properly recorded at a balance sheet date and that they are due bona fide creditors.

SECTION I: INTERNAL CONTROL OF CURRENT LIABILITIES

While the standards of examination applicable to assets are equally applicable to liabilities, the auditor must be especially watchful for unrecorded liabilities. Liabilities carry the implication of expense incurrence or of asset acquisition and internal control over these items may be weak. Therefore, when examining liabilities, the examination of internal control is important; of equal importance is the examination of the client's procedure in handling and recording liabilities.

Internal control over liabilities was set forth in Chapters 4 and 5. Summarized, the principal points of internal control over current liabilities are to ascertain (1) that unauthorized liabilities are not recorded and paid, (2) that all proper liabilities are recorded promptly and are paid properly, and (3) that period-end cutoff is proper.

Costs incurred which result in payables should be properly authorized by an internal system of requisition, purchase, receiving, purchase order and invoice approval, approval for payment, and payment.

Notes should be prenumbered by the printer and controlled physically in order to prevent unauthorized use and improper borrowing. Paid notes should be marked "Paid" and then mutilated in order to prevent date alteration and reuse. Notes payable records should be maintained by persons who cannot sign notes and who cannot disburse or accept cash. Note detail should be reconciled with control accounts at least each month. Authorizations to borrow should be set forth in the minutes of meetings of the board of directors or by proper action of the finance committee.

Accrued expenses should be approved by proper personnel. Months in advance, many concerns schedule month-end journal entries to reflect accrued expenses. Any deviation from such prescheduling should be approved in writing.

Proper internal control over contingencies demands the existence of established control procedures, proper approval, and adequate records for such items as notes receivable discounted, accounts receivable assigned, product guaranty, and contractual obligations—each of which may pass from the category of a contingency to a liability.

An internal control questionnaire for current liabilities and contingencies is shown in Illustration 22–1.

Management Reports

Periodically—at least once each month—internally prepared reports for current liabilities should be submitted to top management for review

ILLUSTRATION 22–1

INTERNAL CONTROL QUESTIONNAIRE
Accounts Payable

Company_____ Period Covered_____	Yes	No	Not Appli-cable	Remarks
1. Is there a proper system of requisitioning, purchase order placement and approval, receiving, invoice approval, and approval for payment?	____	____	____	_____
2. Are subsidiary accounts payable records or unpaid vouchers reconciled with the controlling account at frequent intervals?	____	____	____	_____
3. Are vendors' invoices verified for accuracy prior to entry?	____	____	____	_____
4. Are vendors' statements compared with recorded accounts payable?	____	____	____	_____
5. Are accounts payable adjustments properly approved?	____	____	____	_____
6. Are debit balances in Accounts Payable properly reviewed and followed?	____	____	____	_____
7. Is there a procedure whereby invoices are paid within the discount period?	____	____	____	_____
8. Are accrued expenses properly entered?	____	____	____	_____
9. Is an aging schedule prepared?	____	____	____	_____
NOTES PAYABLE				
1. Are note transactions controlled to prevent unauthorized borrowings?	____	____	____	_____
2. Does the board of directors or a committee authorize borrowing on notes?	____	____	____	_____
3. Do the records of the board or appropriate committee specify the institutions from which money may be borrowed?	____	____	____	_____
4. Do the records of the board or appropriate committee designate the officers authorized to sign notes?	____	____	____	_____
5. Are unissued notes properly safeguarded?	____	____	____	_____
6. Are notes recorded in an organized record which shows:				
a) The amount of the note?	____	____	____	_____
b) Maturity date?	____	____	____	_____
c) Interest dates?	____	____	____	_____
d) Principal payments?	____	____	____	_____
e) Interest payments?	____	____	____	_____
7. Is the person who maintains the note register authorized to sign notes or checks?	____	____	____	_____

ILLUSTRATION 22-1 (*Continued*)

	Yes	No	Not Applicable	Remarks
8. Are proper records maintained for collateral pledged as loan security?	____	____	____	_____
9. Does the client promptly meet its obligations at maturity?	____	____	____	_____
10. Are detailed note records regularly reconciled with the control account?	____	____	____	_____
11. Are paid notes properly canceled and preserved?	____	____	____	_____
12. Is accrued and/or prepaid interest correctly calculated and recorded?	____	____	____	_____
REVENUES RECEIVED IN ADVANCE				
1. Are all cash receipts entered when received?	____	____	____	_____
2. Are all coupons, tickets, merchandise orders, etc., serially numbered and properly controlled?	____	____	____	_____
3. Are used items in Question 2 properly canceled?	____	____	____	_____
4. Is there adequate review of the transfer of deferred credits to proper revenue accounts?	____	____	____	_____
CONTINGENCIES				
1. Does the client properly record possible liability for:				
a) Notes receivable discounted?	____	____	____	_____
b) Accounts receivable assigned?	____	____	____	_____
c) Accommodation endorsements?	____	____	____	_____
d) Product guarantees?	____	____	____	_____
e) Contract guarantees?	____	____	____	_____
f) Losses arising from sale and purchase contracts?	____	____	____	_____
2. Do pending or unsettled lawsuits exist?	____	____	____	_____
3. Are purchase contracts reasonable?	____	____	____	_____
4. List all known contingencies, such as pending or prospective claims for damages, defective good, etc.	____	____	____	_____

Prepared by_____   Reviewed by_____

Date_____   Date_____

and evaluation in order to indicate future cash requirements and in order to strengthen internal control over current liabilities. If a dishonest employee has visions of issuing an unauthorized payable, he will be forced to think more than once if he realizes that management will review all unpaid current liabilities.

For trade accounts, internally prepared reports may set forth the accounts payable balance of the immediately preceding report, plus the payables added and minus the payables liquidated, the available discounts lost, concluding with the current accounts payable balance. If amounts due major vendors are set forth, management's attention may be directed to the emphasis on purchasing from any one (or more) supplier.

For trade and nontrade notes payable, reports to management may be divided into sections, as indicated below:

1. The detail of outstanding notes as of the preceding report (if applicable, collateral pledged should be described).
2. Payments of principal and interest made in the current period.

3. The detail of notes issued (or renewed) in the current period.
4. The detail of notes outstanding at the close of the current period.

Interest expense for the current period and for the year to date should be compared with corresponding amounts of the prior year in order to judge the propriety of financing.

SECTION II: AUDIT PROGRAM FOR ACCOUNTS PAYABLE AND RELATED COSTS AND EXPENSES

In order to accomplish the objective of proper inclusion of all current liabilities, an auditor must be familiar with the variety of methods in operation for the original recording of current liabilities—particularly accounts payable and items resulting in accruals of expenses. The methods of accounting for accounts (vouchers) payable include not recording an invoice or other payable until payment is made, a satisfactory original record accompanied by the proper preparation of internal vouchers and the proper distribution of the related invoices to the accounts to be charged, and the employment of EDP equipment. Subsidiary payable ledgers may or may not be kept; a tickler file of payables may or may not be kept; after payment has been made, invoices commonly are filed alphabetically by creditor. There is no uniformity of practice.

A description of the operation of the various methods of recording payables is not in order in an auditing text, but a few comments for the guidance of an auditor are in order. The system which is employed by a client for processing accounts payable must be understood by the auditor—and in many instances, advisory services may be in order.

If invoices are recorded only when they are paid—a practice followed by many small business organizations—the auditor must prepare a schedule of the unpaid invoices as of the end of the period, and also prepare an audit adjustment charging the proper account and crediting the proper payable. In this situation a reversing entry should be made as of the first day of the new period in order to permit the client to record invoices in his customary manner. Obviously, this method does not adhere to satisfactory standards of internal control. If a properly includable invoice is excluded, liabilities, assets, and/or expenses will be misstated.

When a voucher system is in operation, it may or may not be accompanied by a voucher-check system. A vouchers payable system normally involves the use of a voucher register, which serves in the capacity of an invoice distribution register and an accounts payable register. Some concerns use a subsidiary creditors' ledger in connection with a voucher system, but the majority do not. Subsidiary ledgers are sometimes used in connection with a voucher system when purchases are numerous, when partial payments are commonly made, and when purchase returns take place after entry of the invoices. In general, voucher systems operate most effectively when these three conditions can be avoided.

When data processing equipment is used, normally the volume of payables invoices is large, and in order to control and forecast expenditures it is necessary to insert speed and accuracy into the recording and analysis of payables invoices. Normally, an invoice is processed so that a punched accounts payable card or tape is produced and so that a related asset or expense distribution card is produced. Periodically (at the end of each week or each month) the distribution cards or tapes are totaled to determine total charges to expenses and to assets and corresponding total credits to payables. The totaling of the accounts payable cards or tapes and their posting normally will be made in accordance with credit terms and the payment policies of the buyer.

The extent of the testing of the accuracy of accounts payable and their distribution is dependent upon the system of internal control and the accuracy indicated during the course of the audit. If the system of internal control over accounts payable is satisfactory and if the number of open items is large, a test of *not more* than 10 percent of the items should result in acceptance or rejection of the quality of the accounts payable and the accounting for them.

Regardless of the details of the operating system and regardless of the extent of the testing of payables and their related costs and expenses, the auditor must be certain that open payables are correctly shown, *that liabilities unrecorded at the end of the period are brought into the records, and that liabilities applicable to the subsequent period do not appear at the balance sheet date.*

Audit Program for Accounts Payable and Related Costs and Expenses

Procedures to be followed for accounts payable and offsetting charges are developed in the following subsections. In some examinations, certain of the items may be combined.

Prepare or Obtain Schedules of Accounts Payable. By preparing or obtaining a list of open accounts (or vouchers) payable as of the balance sheet date, a starting point is established for the procedures to be followed by the auditor. From the scheduled listing, the auditor will select those accounts chosen for further and perhaps full examination. Also, by preparing or obtaining a schedule of the open payables, proof is established that the total of the payables is in or out of agreement with the proper control account balance.

Work papers can assume innumerable forms. One work paper for accounts payable is shown in Illustration 22-2; another is shown in the Illustrative Audit. Each auditor ordinarily prepares a work paper which will be applicable to the particular situation at hand. An adding machine tape of open accounts payable may be prepared and attached to a work sheet upon which explanatory comments are placed regarding the audit procedures. Accounts payable may be aged in a manner similar to that

ILLUSTRATION 22-2

THAYER, INC.

Accounts Payable, Acct. #82
December 31, 1975

	Initials	Date
Prepared By		
Approved By		

Creditor	Refer-ence (JP or Voucher)	Account Balance		Trade Payables		Com-pany Per-sonnel	Other Non-trade Creditors	Remarks
		Dr.	Cr.	Not Due	Past Due			
Arden Co.	176		34,000√	34,000σ				
Barr Co.	244	5,000√∅						Credit for returns
Carter Co.			16,000√	15,600σ	400			$400 in dispute
A. B. Corn			8,000√			8,000		Loan from vice president
Dworn Co.			6,000√		6,000			Lawsuit in process; defective goods
Farnsworth Co.			10,000√				10,000z	Loan from customer
		5,000⊙	74,000⊙	49,600	6,400	8,000	10,000	

√ Confirmed.
⊙ Agrees with control.
∅ Not refundable in cash.
z To be liquidated by sales.
    Examined receiving records for the last seven days of 1975.
    Cash disbursements for 1975 were examined for 1976 purchases.
    Voucher record of 1976 was examined for 1975 purchases.
    The open payables (trade) were compared with invoices and receiving records.
σ Subject to discount.

used in connection with accounts receivable, in which case the work papers should conform to such an analysis.

A voucher system creates the mechanism whereby there is independent written authority for cash payments and all data for each purchase are brought together in one place. If a voucher system is in operation, the auditor must obtain or prepare a schedule showing all unpaid vouchers; and if the list was prepared for him, he must compare the items therein with the open vouchers and the uncanceled entries in the voucher register. If a voucher system is *not* used and if the listing was prepared by the client, each item in the schedule should be compared with each individual subsidiary ledger account balance and the lists footed.

Trade and nontrade accounts payable should be separated in the work papers in order to promote proper balance sheet classification. An auditor usually will have little difficulty in distinguishing between trade and nontrade items; a study of the vendors and the requirements and operations of a client company renders this distinction easy.

Adjustments must be considered in the light of their importance. Small amounts which have practically no effect upon the accounts sometimes are ignored; material amounts must be adjusted. Good judgment and accuracy of discrimination are necessary at all times.

Compare Scheduled Trial Balance with the Control Account Balance. If the total of the open accounts payable is not in agreement with the control account balance, a search must be made for the discrepancy, either by the auditor or by the client. If the two are in agreement, this does not constitute proof that errors do not exist; for example, invoices may have been received near the end of the period and not entered.

When a client prepared a list of accounts payable, the auditor should test the accuracy of the detail of the list by comparing the items therein with open items in a voucher register or account balances in subsidiary ledgers. If a voucher register is in use and if the audit is started after the end of the accounting period, the comparison with the detail of the list with the open items in the register poses the necessity of close observation because many open items may have been paid in the subsequent period—and so marked in the voucher register. Therefore, if an examination is started after the close of the period, the auditor should request the client to prepare a list of the period-end open vouchers together with sufficient descriptive data for identification purposes—such as voucher number, date, creditor, and amount.

In the event that a subsidiary ledger is operated in conjunction with a voucher system, the auditor also must reconcile the sum of the subsidiary accounts with the controlling account and must prove the subsidiary account balances against the dollar total of the vouchers applicable to each creditor. Normally, a complete voucher system does not incorporate the use of a subsidiary ledger of formal accounts; the unpaid vouchers in each creditor's file constitute the total due him.

The question of the proof of footing accuracy of each subsidiary account payable ledger account is discussed briefly here from the point of view of the testing to be performed in accepting the accuracy of the balances of the payables. Assume, in order to verify footing accuracy, that an auditor selected a representative random sample of the accounts payable ledger accounts. If the results of the tests of the footings are satisfactory, the auditor may accept those results as being representative of all footings. If the test results are not satisfactory, the testing should be continued until satisfaction is obtained, or until the decision is reached to reject the universe. Assume, however, that while the results of footing accuracy for the sample were entirely satisfactory, the total balances of the footed accounts equaled only a small percentage (say five percent) of the total dollar amount of the total payables; it might be advisable to extend the test or to select additional accounts with large balances and prove the accuracy of the footings.

Another method of testing for proof of footing accuracy may be illustrated as follows:

ILLUSTRATION. All accounts with a balance in excess of $1,000 may be selected, together with a random sample of others, so that the total sample is (say) 10 percent of the total accounts payable and at least 70 percent of the total dollar amount. The accounts whose footing accuracy is proved should be ticked. All other accounts may be accepted unless the results of the test are not satisfactory. The test should be expanded to approximately 100 percent under the following conditions:

a) If errors are too numerous to accept.

b) If the number of the accounts payable is small.

c) If the sum of the subsidiary account balances does not agree with the controlling account balance and if the auditor (not the client) is to locate the errors.

For companies with excellent internal control, as exemplified by the use of EDP equipment for the creation of payables records and independently prepared related acquisition records, footing procedures for subsidiary accounts payable accounts may be omitted.

Test Original Records and Postings to Control Accounts. As another step in establishing the accuracy of the general ledger control account for accounts payable, the following procedures are normal.

Records of original entry—voucher registers, invoice registers, and check registers—should be footed to a point whereby satisfactory results have been obtained; normally, these records or original entry will be footed for one or two months; if footing results are not satisfactory, the footing would be extended. Postings from these media to the control accounts should be traced for all corresponding months and the control account balance extracted. If postings to the Accounts Payable control account originates in the general journal, the entries should be examined in detail. Control account entries should be scrutinized for the entire audit period, and large or unusual adjustments should be verified. The proof of the footing accuracy of original records and the testing of postings may be partially performed prior to the year-end.

Postings to the subsidiary ledger accounts should be proved in accordance with the sample of those postings originally chosen.

ILLUSTRATION. The auditor noted several postings to improper subsidiary accounts, and he also noted a large number of debit balances in his schedule of accounts payable. Investigation of correspondence showed that some creditors were reporting that incorrect amounts had been received and others were complaining that their invoices were not being paid. A careless bookkeeper was responsible.

Where an EDP system is in use, the auditor may wish to compare invoices to coding sheets or print-outs. A better procedure is to test transactions and balances through the use of a retrieval package.

Vouch Credits and Debits in Accounts Payable. Tests must be made of the accuracy and genuineness of the accounts payable and accompanying internal vouchers by comparing them with original vouchers received from vendors, and tests must be made of the accuracy of vendor's invoices. Where the number of invoices is large and where internal control is satisfactory, the vouching test normally will not exceed a small percentage (assume five percent) of the items, provided that the selection is made so that a reasonable amount of the dollar volume is covered. The invoices selected may be (*a*) in accordance with the accounts selected for footing accuracy, (*b*) a block sample of one or more months' transactions, (*c*) all invoices over a selected amount plus additional invoices necessary to equal the desired percentage test, or (*d*) approximately the percentage (assume five percent) of the invoices of each creditor.

The major objectives in the examination and authentication of invoices from creditors and related internally prepared vouchers for items purchased are to determine that:

1. Purchase orders are properly originated and approved and placed in accordance with company policy.
2. Invoices are correct as to unit price, quantity, extensions, and totals.
3. Invoices and related vouchers are properly approved for payment.
4. Available discounts are taken.
5. Distributions are made to proper accounts.
6. Revenue and capital expenditures are properly distinguished.
7. All items and services purchased are for company use.

The accuracy test of the invoices may proceed as follows:

a) Compare the creditor's *name* on the invoice with the name in the client's original record and the accompanying internal voucher.
b) Compare the invoice *date* with the date of entry; duplicate entries must be investigated completely; there is no reason for them to exist.
c) Compare the *amount* of the invoice with the internal voucher and the entry in the client's original record.
d) Prove invoice *computations*.
e) Test *prices*.
f) Test *extensions*.
g) Test *footings*.
h) Scrutinize proper *approval*.
i) Scrutinize proper *mutilation*.

Each examined invoice should be ticked to indicate its proof of accuracy and its vouching, and all related original record entries should be ticked. Checks in payment of paid invoices should be compared with the invoices and related internally prepared vouchers and ticked off in the voucher register and the disbursements record. If the overall results of the test are not satisfactory, the test should be expanded beyond the test figures originally established.

In the event of discrepancies between invoices and amounts entered in the accounts, the auditor should exercise his abilities to ascertain the causes of the differences. He must be satisfied. Unreconciled accounts should be scheduled and analyzed.

Situations may be discovered wherein checks have been prepared, entered as charges to Payables and as credits to Cash, but not mailed at the balance sheet date. In such cases, an entry should be prepared, reversing the original entry. Such entries, accompanied by the nonmailing of the checks, do not represent payments but are simply attempts to reduce payables for financial statement purposes.

If a statistical sampling plan is not available, an examination of from two to 10 percent of the invoices normally should determine the quality of the universe.

Creditors' debit memoranda should be investigated to determine that proper distinction is made between returned goods and allowances for such items as transportation and defective goods not returned. The proper end-of-the-period cutoff time for debit memoranda and for inventory inclusion or exclusion should be established.

Examine Invoice Distribution.   In order to conserve time and avoid duplication of work, it is advisable (at the time of vouching) to examine the distribution of invoices to the accounts to be charged. From the point of view of internal operations, it is important to ascertain that charges are made to the proper accounts.

Compare Creditors' Statements with Accounts Payable Balances. By comparing invoices and available month-end statements with the account balances, the auditor may discover omitted items.

ILLUSTRATION.   A vendor's statement at the end of the month shows a balance due of $20,000, whereas available open invoices total only $12,000. The client's accountant withheld $8,000 of invoices received on December 29 because the goods had not been received.

In a situation such as that just illustrated, the principles indicated below should be followed:

a)   If title has passed on the basis of F.O.B. shipping point, wherein title has passed at the time of loading, the goods should be included in inventory and the invoice in accounts payable.

b)   If title has not passed to the debtor client, neither the invoice nor the liability should be included; the item is a purchase commitment.

In certain types of businesses, suppliers ship merchandise in advance of order or contract date and have no intention of billing the debtor until the proper date; in effect, the supplier is using the debtor's quarters as a warehouse. Here again, if title to the merchandise has not passed to the debtor client, the liability for the goods should be omitted along with omission from inventory. If title has passed to the client, the auditor should insist that the liability be recorded. Postdated invoices should be included in the payables, and the goods should be included in the inventory.

In certain types of businesses, title to goods may have passed to the buyer under an F.O.B. shipping point contract, with the understanding that the goods will not be shipped until instructions are received from the buyer. In many such instances, the buyer never actually receives the goods but has them shipped to another place or company. Although the buyer is not in actual physical possession, the goods belong to him and should be included in his payables.

Confirm Accounts Payable.   The confirmation of accounts payable balances is now common and is one that should be placed on the required list particularly if creditors' statements are not available or if they are not reliable, and if internal control over payables is not satisfactory. The decision to confirm or not confirm depends upon the probability of mis-statement. If collateral is given as security for accounts payable, the auditor must ascertain by confirmation the nature and value of the security held by the creditor.

All creditors circularized should be listed, (or duplicate copies of confirmation requests should be retained), and the replies should be compared with the listings (or duplicates) and ticked off. Discrepancies should be reconciled. A confirmation form similar to that shown in Illustration 22–3 may be used.

One plan of confirming accounts payable is as follows:

a)   Examine all available creditors' statements and compare them with the account balances.

b)   Circularize a selected number of other creditors requesting statements and/or confirmations. The selection may be as follows: (1) a judgment selection from the list of recorded accounts payable; and from an examination of the cash disbursements records, from which are selected regularly recurring vendor names which do not appear in the year-end open accounts payable or (2) the use of a random numbers table in making the selection of invoices or account balances to be confirmed.

Closely allied in importance to obtaining confirmations of accounts payable is the liability certificate obtained from the client (see Illustration 22–8). Such a statement will not be signed by responsible executives unless it is true. Hesitancy to sign the statement may be an indication that information is being withheld. In at least one state (Minnesota), the signing of a false statement of this nature constitutes a felony, and an injured creditor may hold the person signing it criminally liable.

Examine Debit Balances and Reclassify if Necessary.   Debit balances in accounts payable must be investigated to determine the reason for the balances; and if they are material in amount, the debit balances in accounts payable should be shown among the current assets in the balance sheet, not as a reduction of accounts payable. If debit balances exist

ILLUSTRATION 22–3

LAWNKEEPERS, INC.
Cincinnati, Ohio   45202

January 12, 1976

Lansing, Inc.
Detroit, Michigan

Gentlemen:

Please confirm directly to our auditors, Morr and Morr, Certified Public Accountants,
amounts due you on open account, as of the close of business at December 31, 1975, as
follows:

     Amount on open account, not past due . . . . $ _____
     Amount on open account, past due . . . . $ _____
     Purchase commitments. . . . . $ _____
     Security for open accounts _____

Your prompt reply will be appreciated. A reply envelope addressed to our auditors is
enclosed.

                     Very truly yours,

                     LAWNKEEPERS, INC.

---

in accounts that are not current and active, the auditor should suggest
that the client write to the vendors and request either cash or
merchandise.

Debit balances in accounts payable frequently arise in retail organizations handling a variety of small merchandise; the common cause of such
debit balances is the payment of an invoice followed by a partial return
of goods. Debit balances in accounts payable may be the result of a
debtor-creditor relationship wherein only one account is kept either in
the accounts receivable ledger or in the accounts payable ledger as a
combination receivable-payable.

Occasionally, debit balances are the result of incorrect postings; or
they may represent items that are not truly the result of liability reductions. For example, in some cases, advances are made to creditors, either
in conformity with a purchase contract or in order to finance the supplier;
such advances are not debit balances in accounts payable but are separate
assets.

ILLUSTRATION. The President of the X Company was given a blank
company check which he carried to a machine-tool manufacturers show;
he issued the check in the amount of $10,000 to one of the displaying

manufacturers. He instructed the bookkeeper to charge Accounts Payable and credit Cash for the $10,000 stating that the vendor company's invoice would follow for the *total* price of $40,000. The situation should have been shown as a contract deposit, with the footnote explanation of a $30,000 purchase commitment liability; or if the contract had been closed, the Machinery account could have been charged for $40,000, Cash credited for $10,000, and Accounts Payable credited for $30,000.

Test Invoices with Receiving and Stores Records. The purpose of comparing invoices with receiving records and stores records—especially for several days prior to the end of the period—is to ascertain that all liabilities are properly included for the period under examination.

Invoices on hand at the end of the year but not recorded must be investigated to determine the reason for the lack of entry, and the auditor must be certain that the items purchased under the *properly* unentered invoices are not included in inventories. Investigation may prove that the unentered invoices should appear as entries for the period under review.

To ascertain that all proper liabilities have been recorded, the auditor must examine purchase orders, invoices, receiving records, stores records, and monthly statements. Invoices must be compared with the purchase orders and with entries in the original records in order to ascertain that purchases made toward the close of the period have been properly entered. The liability for all goods received through the last day of the fiscal period should be recorded. Receiving and stores records should be examined to determine that liabilities for items on hand are properly included. In many cases, goods are received toward the close of the period and placed in stock, and the invoice is not received until early in the subsequent period; a liability exists as of the close of the old period.

Examine Discounts. Cash discounts should be reviewed for accuracy of computation and handling and also for the possibilities afforded by their manipulation, as pointed out in preceding chapters. If available cash discounts are not being taken, the auditor should confer with the client and point out the financial advantages of prompt invoice payment.

Some companies show their accounts payable gross; others carry them at net cost—that is, at the gross invoice price less available cash discounts. Carrying the vouchers at their net cost is recommended. The amount of the discount lost then is shown as an expense. The accounting method adopted by the client is satisfactory so long as it consistently conforms to acceptable practice. From the point of view of control over available discounts and of control over possible fraudulent manipulations, it is advisable to follow the method of recording invoices *net* and using a Discounts Lost account if the discount is not taken.

Investigate Old Unpaid Items. Accounts payable records should be examined for old unpaid items; and reasons for nonpayment investigated.

Frequently, disputes between debtor and creditor concerning allowances, returns, and discounts cause payables to remain unliquidated for long periods. Inspection of correspondence and the obtaining of confirmation replies often will clarify many points and may lead to the discovery that the recorded liability is not correct. Old unpaid items might indicate payment by note, without a record of the transaction having been made.

Accounts payable may bear interest after the expiration of a specified time. The auditor must ascertain that such interest is properly accrued.

Ascertain the Liability for Consigned Merchandise. For merchandise *received* on consignment basis, consignment contracts and accounting records must be examined to determine the existence of unpaid and unrecorded liabilities for merchandise sold. The client may have omitted the liability, without intent to deceive, by entering a sale at full price but failing to set up the liability to the consignor. Confirmation requests should be sent to all consignors, and the consignment sales and the consigned goods inventory should be reconciled with the results of the confirmations.

Examine Records of the Subsequent Period for Liabilities Not Recorded at the Balance Sheet Date. At various points in this chapter, the risk of failure to include all accounts payable has been indicated. Invoices, purchasing records, receiving records, and cash disbursements records for the early part of the subsequent period must be examined to determine the period of proper inclusion of liabilities. Entries for the new year do not belong to the period under examination.

The longer the time between the end of the accounting period and the conclusion of an audit, the better the chances of determining that all liabilities were recorded as of the end of the period under examination. Failure to include invoices in the proper period may be intentional or unintentional; but regardless of the intention, this examination must be made. Data within the subsequent period to be examined are as follows: The cash disbursements records and the Paid Bills and Unpaid Bills files are examined for two or three weeks of the new period to determine to which period the invoices underlying the disbursements are applicable. To accomplish this, trace the cash disbursements to the original invoice data and determine the applicability of the invoice. If an item included in the new period should have been in the period under examination, adjustments must be made; in these instances, the auditor must ascertain that as a result of his adjustments, the items are not included twice, once in the period under review and once in the subsequent period.

Credit memoranda data and entries should be examined and traced to the proper period of inclusion.

Examine Records for Purchase Commitment Liabilities. Purchase commitments are not liabilities at the balance sheet date but they will result in the assumption of a liability at a future date. Although there may be no effect on the balance sheet at the closing date, the immediate future effect might be detrimental in the event that assets—normally inventories—will be received under the contracts when they are not needed because of changed business conditions.

An examination of the minutes of the board of directors, minutes of finance committees, and purchasing department records frequently discloses purchase contract commitments. The contracts must be examined to ascertain their total amount, to judge their reasonableness in the light of future requirements, and to determine that the client is not defaulting on a contract. Duplicate copies of placed purchase orders open at the end of the year which have been accepted by vendors should be scheduled, priced, and totaled.

If material-amount sales contracts offset material-amount purchase contracts, if the sales contract offers proper protection, and if that is the normal method of operating, the audit report may point out the situation. If at the balance sheet date, purchase commitments exceed offsetting sales contracts, or if it appears that the client is negotiating purchase orders in an excessive amount—that is, speculatively—the balance sheet should be appropriately footnoted. When the auditor discovers sales contracts and orders for future delivery which might be canceled because of declining market activity, or contracts that might result in sales at a loss because of rising market prices, attention should be directed to the situation.

If purchase commitments without offsetting sales contracts are of normal volume and not material in total, no mention need be made of the situation; however, the audit report should set forth commitments as being normal. A market decline on a purchase commitment may result in a current liability. Contracts frequently exist for the purchase or construction of fixed assets; in such cases, a notation of the unpaid portion should be made in the balance sheet, since the effect in the near future will be a reduction of current assets if cash is used to settle the contract.

Segregate Amounts Due Officers, Affiliated Companies, etc.   One purpose of this separation is to facilitate the proper preparation of the liability section of a balance sheet. Another purpose is to emphasize the necessity of investigating amounts due personnel. Many items due official personnel may really be long-term—almost permanent—advances. The analysis of interest expense may offer a clue in this direction. Amounts due a director, stockholder, officer, or other employee should be directly confirmed for all items other than regular wages. Full notes should be prepared for each such item for possible inclusion in the audit report.

ILLUSTRATION.   A vendor requests a report on a client from a credit-rating agency. The report shows that the company owes the president $50,000 on open account. The vendor informs the company that unless the amount due the president is subordinated to its payables, additional credit will not be extended.

SECTION III: AUDIT PROGRAM FOR NOTES AND ACCEPTANCES PAYABLE

Audit Objectives

The audit objectives in examining these items are to ascertain that all outstanding notes and acceptances are recorded, that they have been properly authorized, that they are of proper amount, that related interest is proper, and that the items are properly set forth in the balance sheet. The system of internal control will guide the auditor as to the amount of work to be performed in the accomplishment of these objectives.

Compensating balances were discussed in Chapter 12.

Notes payable arise from bank loans; purchases from trade creditors; loans or purchases from nontrade creditors; commercial paper; commercial letters of credit; and notes payable to subsidiary, parent, or affiliated companies. Trade acceptances arise in the normal course of business in which the custom prevails of giving an acceptance at the time of purchase. Notes payable commonly bear interest, whereas trade acceptances do not bear interest until after maturity. The audit procedures applicable to notes, drafts, bills of exchange, and trade acceptances are the same; therefore, they are discussed together.

An internal control questionnaire for notes and acceptances payable is presented in Illustration 22–1.

Audit procedures to be followed for notes and acceptances payable are developed in the following subsections.

Prepare or Obtain Schedules of Notes and Acceptances Payable. A work paper for notes payable appears in Illustration 22–4. The form of a work paper for notes and acceptances payable should be designed to satisfy the requirements of each situation. The data for the schedule are obtainable from the notes payable register, if one is kept, or from the cash records, a Notes Payable file, the stubs of a padded notebook, or the posting medium indicated in the Notes Payable general ledger account. If the client has prepared a listing of notes payable, the auditor must compare the items therein with the data sources indicated above.

If the volume of notes is large, it is preferable to prepare separate schedules for each class of obligation. In the event that notes payable are secured, the work papers must provide space for detailing the collateral. Illustration 22–4 includes the scheduling of interest expense, prepaid interest, and accrued interest, thus saving time and work, and summarizing all related data at one point. The Illustrative Audit Papers presents additional work papers for notes payable.

The total of a notes payable schedule should be compared with the general ledger account balance sheet date. The auditor should prove the footings of controlling accounts before comparing his schedule totals

ILLUSTRATION 22–4

COOGAN COMPANY

Notes Payable, Acct. #92
December 31, 1975

	Initials	Date
Prepared By		
Approved By		

Note No.	Name of Payee	Date of Note	Maturity Date	Amount of Note	Unpaid at 12/31/75	Rate %	Total Days' Interest	Interest 1975 Expense	Interest 12/31/75 Prepaid	Interest 12/31/75 Accrual	Collateral Description	Collateral Market Price 12/31/75	Remarks
110	R Company	Sept. 1, 1976	Sept. 1, 1976	12,000 ‖ z	6,000 √	7	360	280	–0–	–0–			∅ $12,000 and interest paid 12/30/75
112	S Finance Co.	Oct. 1, 1975	Mar. 28, 1976	10,000 ⊙	10,000 √	8	180	200	200				
113	T Company	Nov. 1, 1975	Apr. 29, 1976	5,000 ‖	5,000 √	8	180	67		67	Inventory √	$15,000	
114	U Company	Nov. 1, 1975	Feb. 29, 1976	4,000 ⊙	4,000 √	8	120	53		53	U.S. bonds √	5,000	
115	Southern Bank	Dec. 1, 1975	Demand	12,000 ‖	12,000 √	5		50	–0–				Interest paid each 30 days
116	V Company	Dec. 31, 1975	Jan. 30, 1976	3,000 ‖	3,000 √	6	30	–0–	–0–	–0–			
				46,000	40,000 ∧			650	200	120			

√ Confirmed.
∧ Agrees with control.
∅ Traced to cash receipts.
⊙ Traced to cash disbursements.
‖ Traced to inventory purchased.
z $10,000—$400 interest deducted.
All notes paid during 1975 were inspected and traced to cash disbursements.
All are mutilated.
All notes are authorized by board of directors. See extract from minutes.
Note transactions for January, 1976, were examined. All proper.
Interest calculations rounded to nearest full dollar.

with the general ledger balances. If the two amounts do not agree, a search should be made for errors of the following nature:

a) Part payments not entered in the file, note register, or other medium.
b) Posting to an incorrect controlling account.
c) Incorrect entries when notes receivable are discounted.
d) Incorrect entries when notes and interest are paid.

Vouch Credits and Debits in the Accounts. The auditor must examine the minutes of the board of directors of a finance committee in order to ascertain authority to issue notes and the names of the personnel authorized to sign notes. The bylaws may stipulate the limits of indebtedness permissible by the issuance of notes.

A comparison of the detail of the note schedules and transactions with the record of the directors' meetings or appropriate committee meetings will assist in the discovery of existing irregularities.

ILLUSTRATION. A board of directors authorizes a loan of $100,000. The corresponding note entries are for $200,000; $100,000 is disbursed for the purpose indicated in the authorization, and $100,000 in the form of a non-interest bearing note, is disbursed to a senior officer who—as developments proved—was actively engaged in stock market operations.

Entries for bank notes given during the period of audit must be traced to the cash receipts records. Entries for other notes and acceptances payable are traced through the general journal, a note register, or an invoice register, depending upon the accounting system employed by the client. A client should be encouraged to use serially numbered notes with duplicate corresponding copies. All notes must be accounted for, and voided and paid returned notes should be ticked off against the copies. The total of the outstanding notes payable will equal the total of the unticked duplicates or stubs, less partial payments made.

A liability certificate (Illustration 22-7), which is obtained from the client, should contain a statement that all notes payable are recorded.

Debits to Notes Payable arise from partial and full payments, renewals, or properly authorized adjusting entries. Evidence in the form of a canceled note, a paid check, a part-payment receipts supported by a paid check, or proper authorization for an adjustment should be available for the auditor's inspection and vouching to the Notes Payable accounts. Entries corresponding to the original evidence should appear as Notes Payable debits in the cash disbursements records or in the general journal. The auditor may accept these evidences in support of account changes if they appear to be regular in all respects.

The payment entries in liquidation of notes payable should be vouched from the cash disbursements record through the notes payable record, to the debit of the Notes Payable account. The paid notes should be inspected and compared with the entries. The note record should be footed and the totals compared with general ledger account postings.

The auditor must watch for the possibility of notes that have been prepared and issued without corresponding entries made in the note records or in the cash receipts records. This situation might indicate unauthorized borrowing; in such a case, the client may have to pay the note at maturity, for a holder in due course may collect the note of a solvent debtor. To cover a fraud of this nature, a fictitious debit may be passed to some account other than Notes Payable at the time of payment, or the notes payable debits and the cash credits may be underfooted to the extent of the payments on the originally unrecorded notes. Unrecorded borrowings may be difficult to detect; the auditor should be alert to notice unusual interest payments and peculiar charges and credits to capital accounts.

Other points for which the auditor must watch during the vouching of debits and credits to the Notes Payable account include the following: credits to the Notes Payable account must be for notes actually issued; the purpose of each note payable; whether or not the notes are paid at maturity; the extent of chattel mortgages given as note security; and the extent of merchandise pledged as security and the restrictions placed on merchandise pledged, such as its separation and the use of receipts from sales to liquidate the notes. In addition, the auditor should determine if notes are subordinated to other creditor claims and if so, to what extent they are subordinated.

Confirm Notes and Collateral. Notes and acceptances payable and outstanding at the end of the period should be confirmed by direct correspondence with the holders, who should be requested to submit data pertaining to collateral and endorsements. Confirmation replies should be compared with the schedule of notes payable and should be watched for subordination of the indebtedness. Notes due to banks are confirmed at the time bank balance confirmations are requested, unless a bank account is not maintained by the client at the creditor bank. If notes are issued exclusively through a note broker, a confirmation from the broker is the only external evidence required of the amount of the notes outstanding. A notes payable confirmation form is shown in Illustration 22–5.

Examine Records for Note Renewals. General journals and notes registers should be examined for evidences of renewed notes. A clue to renewed notes is obtainable by comparing cash disbursements with the maturity dates indicated in the notes payable schedule of the preceding audit. If notes are continuously renewed, the auditor should trace the complete history of the items and render full disclosure in the audit report, if warranted.

Inspect Notes Paid during the Period. Notes fully paid during the period of examination should be obtained by the auditor, and should be examined for the simultaneous issuance dates appearing on the notes and in the records.

ILLUSTRATION 22–5
NOTES PAYABLE CONFIRMATION

SYLVAN PROPERTIES, INC.
St. Peters, Indiana

January 10, 1976

Name of Bank: Citizens National Bank
or
Name of Broker
or
Name of Other Creditor

Gentlemen:

Arden and Young, Certified Public Accountants, are now performing their periodic audit of our records.

Please confirm directly to them our indebtedness for notes due you (or sold to you, if a broker) as of __December 31, 1975__. Our liability to you as of that date stands on our records at $ 10,000 . Please list in the space provided any collateral held as security for the loan. A stamped and addressed envelope is enclosed for your convenience. Thank you.

Very truly yours,

SYLVAN PROPERTIES, INC.
J.P. Sylvan, Treasurer

. . . . DETACH HERE . . . .

January 12, 1976

Arden and Young, Certified Public Accountants
5 East Fourth Street
Cincinnati, Ohio

Gentlemen:

Amount of loan to Sylvan Properties, Inc.	$10,000
Date of loan.	November 10, 1975
Date due	February 10, 1976
Collateral held	None
Interest rate.	9%
Differences: _____	

A.L. Elmlinger
(signed) CITIZENS NATIONAL BANK

ILLUSTRATION. During this matching process, there was one note of $10,000 with no corresponding record in the cash records. The proceeds of the note had been credited to Sales; the payment of the note and interest had been charged to Sales Returns; sales invoices and credit memoranda were on file. The client company had issued unaudited interim financial statements and did not want to show a note payable.

If note transactions are voluminous, this examination will be in the form of a test of sufficient magnitude to assure the auditor of the propriety of the method of handling notes payable.

The auditor must determine that paid notes have been canceled so that they cannot be reused. In a normal situation, a paid check or bank debit memorandum should support the canceled note. Signatures on paid notes should be compared with authorized signatures.

If notes are not properly canceled, the auditor must be certain that the notes do not constitute a part of the ending balance, even though entries have been made charging Notes Payable and crediting Cash.

Verify Interest Accrued and Prepaid. Accrued interest must be verified from the last interest payment date—or the date of the note—to the end of the period under examination. When money is borrowed from financial institutions, either on direct loan or by discounting notes receivable, the financial institution may or may not deduct interest in advance. If interest is deducted in advance, the amount of the prepaid interest must be calculated from the balance sheet date to the note maturity date. The accrued interest should be tied in with the notes outstanding at the end of the examination period.

Analyze Interest Expense Accounts. Interest expense accounts must be reconciled with calculated interest on notes payable, and any other indebtedness, and must be verified and traced to the disbursements records in order to determine the correctness and promptness of the interest payments. This examination may lead to the detection of unrecorded liabilities. The interest expense appearing in the records of a client is not complete evidence of its correctness, and the auditor must test calculations. In examining interest accounts, the auditor should determine (*a*) that the liability upon which the interest was paid was properly recorded and (*b*) that the interest was promptly paid.

Examine Note Payments and Renewals Subsequent to the Balance Sheet Date. Subsequent to the balance sheet date and prior to the closing of the engagement, the auditor should compare note and interest payments with notes open at the balance sheet date in order to detect liabilities unrecorded at the balance sheet date.

ILLUSTRATION. An audit was being made for the year ended December 31, 1975. Under date of February 1, 1976, the auditor noted an interest payment to a creditor to whom a note was not shown as payable at December 31, 1975. Further examination revealed that the interest was for three months—November and December of 1975 and January of 1976. Merchandise had been purchased by giving a note; no entry was made; and the goods had been included in the December 31, 1975, inventory.

SECTION IV: MISCELLANEOUS CURRENT LIABILITIES

This section is devoted to several commonly found current liabilities represented by expense accruals, amounts withheld from employees, unclaimed wages, declared dividends, and deposits from customers.

Accrued Expenses

The objectives of auditing accrued expenses are to determine that all liabilities are recognized in the balance sheet and that all expenses applicable to the current period are properly set forth in the income statement. In auditing expense accruals, reasonableness must be exercised. It is necessary to produce accurate financial statements, but valuable time should not be wasted in verifying minutely small items wherein a difference of a few dollars will have no appreciable effect. If internal controls are satisfactory and if the accounting records are properly maintained, normally an auditor will not separately compute all accruals; he will review the methods used to recognize the accruals and then test the accuracy of client computations.

In addition, an auditor should refer to various records and documents for original information concerning accruals. Some of the sources are: the minutes, for salary, bonus, and profit-sharing agreements; patent licenses, for accrued royalties; contracts, notes, and trust indentures, for interest accruals; accounting entries made in the subsequent period to determine if any were accruable at the close of the preceding period; and applicable tax laws. If in former periods, accruals have not been brought into the records, expenses are overstated for the first period in which accrual recognition is granted. If material in amount, the change should be mentioned in the audit report.

The audit program for each accrued expense in some measure is dependent upon the item. Consequently, work papers for accrued expenses will assume a variety of forms.

Accrued Payrolls. If the end of the payroll period does not coincide with the fiscal closing date, wages, salaries, commissions, and perhaps bonuses will have accrued. Accrued salaries and wages may be verified by computation, and payments made at the first payroll date(s) of the subsequent period are examined to ascertain that an unrecorded payroll liability did not exist at the closing date.

If vacation pay is accrued by charges spread throughout the year, the vacation pay charges must be reviewed by making sufficient tests to satisfy the auditor of their accuracy. For vacation payments and accruals, the auditor should read the provision of employment contracts and obtain a copy for his work papers.

Accrued commissions should be verified from the accounts, from the reports of orders sent in by salesmen, from existing commission schedules, and from basic contracts approved by authorized personnel. If the commissions are based upon sales units or dollar volume, the verification of an accrual is simple, and the auditor may ask for confirmation from the salesmen. Also, payments made in the subsequent period should be compared with the amounts at the end of the period under audit. Debit balances in Commission accounts arising from advances made prior to earning the commission must be taken into consideration in arriving at the correct accrual of the liability. The total of individual debit balances of this nature should not be offset against the total accrual, since many individual debit balances ultimately are charged out to expense.

If there are no recorded accruals of commissions or bonuses, the auditor should inquire if contracts or other agreements exist which make necessary the recognition of these items. Also, consistency should prevail from year to year in the recognition of these liabilities. See Illustration 22–6 for a work paper for accrued payroll.

ILLUSTRATION 22–6

THE BROCK COMPANY

Accrued Payroll, Acct. #95
December 31, 1975

	Wages and Salaries	Com- missions	Bonuses	Vacation Pay	Total
Accrued, per ledger, 12/31/75	82,000*	20,000	–0–	30,000	132,000
Add unrecorded commissions†		4,000			4,000
Add unrecorded bonuses‡					
Vacation pay§			50,000		50,000
Totals	82,000	24,000	50,000	30,000	186,000

* Accrual of normal wages and salaries for four days ended December 31, 1975. Pay week ends December 27, 1975.

† Based upon firm sales and accompanying deliveries, and upon confirmations received from salesmen, $4,000 should be accrued ($100,000 Sales × 4 percent commission rate).

‡ Bonuses of $50,000 are to be accrued, based upon the examined contracts existing between the company and employees, and also in accordance with the procedures for the year ended December 31, 1974. (Approved Executive Committee minutes of 1/15/75.)

§ Vacation pay accrual was properly accumulated and allocated for the year.

AJE #27 (22)

Commissions Expense	4,000	
Bonuses Expense	50,000	
Accrued Payroll Payable.		54,000
Adjust Acct. #95 to analysis.		

Pension Plans. For employee pension plans (treated fully in Chapter 24) only the year-end liability for pension plan contributions should be shown as a current liability. The auditor must be certain that the current liability portion is properly set forth in the financial statements.

Accrued Interest. Accrued interest is more efficiently verified during the course of the examination of the obligations giving rise to the interest. In accruing interest, the practice of using the 360-day method is common. The auditor should examine minutes records for interest data on loans from officers. Also, he must be familiar with interest provisions on overdue accounts payable and overdue taxes.

Accrued Taxes. The majority of tax accruals are of major importance, such as federal, state, and city income taxes; excise taxes; social security taxes; and real and personal property taxes.

Federal, state, and city income taxes are computed on the taxable net income provided for in the federal revenue code and in the income tax acts of the various states and cities. The auditor must determine the taxable net income base for each type of income tax. Accruals of each tax for the end of the period must be brought into the records. A portion of each tax, or all of each tax, or an amount in excess of the actual tax liability may have been paid prior to the close of the period. Refundable amounts which have been approved should be shown as current assets and accruals of unpaid amounts shown as liabilities. State and city income taxes commonly are charged to expense accounts. In an initial engagement, the auditor should review copies of returns that have not been outlawed by the statute of limitations.

Prior years' tax assessments and refunds from prior years should be charged or credited to Retained Earnings in accordance with APB *Opinion No. 9;* and this is proper. Deferred federal income taxes brought into existence by investment tax credits should be shown as noncurrent liabilities; if the deferred amounts become payable, the proper sum should then be moved to the current liability category; if a deferred amount finally is earned, it should be moved to revenue.

Federal excise taxes are levied on the price or cost of the item sold or manufactured and should be accrued in accordance with the provisions of the law applicable to each tax.

Accrued social security taxes and amounts withheld from employees for both social security and income taxes are current liabilities. The auditing procedure is to adequately test the mathematical correctness of the taxes and the accruals, and of the amounts withheld from employees, using payroll and personnel records. Adequate payroll records are necessary for the correct computation of the taxes and for the reconciliation of the related liabilities. Proper distinction must be made between federal and state unemployment taxes, F.I.C.A. taxes, and so forth. See the Illustrative Audit Papers.

Real estate and personal property taxes may be prepaid, or they may accrue until payment date, depending upon the varying state laws. For example, in at least one state, the real estate taxes for the calendar year are due and payable on July 1 of that year. This provision creates accrued taxes until July 1; if the taxes are paid, prepaid taxes exist, which decline month by month. Real and personal property taxes are levied as of a certain date; however, a business organization should accrue the taxes (or write off prepayments) over the intervals between assessment dates. Reference to former tax bills and receipts, the verification of the assessed tax, and an estimate of contemplated tax rate changes provide the data from which a necessary accrual may be estimated.

Accrual Royalties. In examining royalty contracts and licensing agreements, the auditor must ascertain whether a royalty arrangement or a contract to purchase is in existence. If a contract to purchase exists, the asset price should be set up in the accounts and the remaining liability should also be set up, together with the entries for amortization of the gross cost. In cases of this nature, the payments are not expense charges but liability reductions.

For royalties based on sales, sales records must be verified, and the royalty expense and accrual verified by computation of the royalty costs applicable under the terms of the contracts.

For royalties based on production, production records and rental or lease agreements must be examined to determine the correctness of the royalty expense and the amount accrued. For this type of royalty it is advisable to obtain from the lessors of the machinery or patents confirmations of royalty amounts in accordance with the terms of the agreements. These confirmations may disclose differences in interpretation of the royalty contracts.

Amounts Withheld

Amounts withheld from employees and others are the result of laws and various private agreements. The employer or paying concern is charged with the responsibility of withholding certain amounts from the employees and other payees and of remitting to the proper authority or organization specified under the terms of the laws and agreements. The auditor must review the provisions for withholding and investigate the amounts withheld for accuracy under the terms of the applicable law or agreement. Tax returns filed with the proper tax authority and reports filed with other applicable payees must be examined, the propriety of the amounts reasonably tested, and the entries traced to the proper accounts.

Declared Dividends

Declared asset dividends are a direct liability of the issuing corporation. It is not proper to show undeclared cumulative dividends as a liability because the dividend has not been declared and a liability does not exist. It is permissible to show the accumulation as a balance sheet footnote or to segregate the amount in the stockholders' equity section as "retained earnings required for unpaid cumulative dividends."

In order to determine the liability for dividends payable at the balance sheet date, the auditor should review the minutes for dividend actions. In connection with dividends, he must be certain that declared dividends are in accordance with statute, charter, and bylaws; otherwise legal liability may result. He should be familiar with the procedure employed for stock dividends, scrip dividends, and dividends paid in assets other than cash. Stock dividends payable are not a liability but belong in the stockholders' equity section of the balance sheet. In connection with dividends in wasting-asset industries, the auditor must determine if dividends are from income or from capital—in the latter case, stockholders should be informed of the return of their investment. Small companies often disregard requirements of the law to the effect that to be legal, dividends must be declared by the board of directors. When proper action has not been taken, the attention of the client should be directed to the matter in order that appropriate action may be written into the minutes as of a prior date and the action verified by the directors.

Unclaimed Dividends. Declared dividends may be unclaimed because of inability to locate a stockholder, thus creating a liability on the records of the corporation. At the same time, if a special dividend bank account exists, a balance will remain in it. The account should be examined for unauthorized withdrawals. Good judgment must be used concerning the period for which unclaimed dividends are allowed to stand before being written off to a liability or to stockholders' equity. If a dividend bank account is used, the unclaimed balance is returned to general cash at the time the unclaimed dividends are written off.

Corporations with many stockholders employ a fiscal agent—a dividend-disbursing agent—to prepare and mail dividend checks. In general, the corporation fulfills all of its legal obligations at the time it turns over to the agent the funds necessary to pay the dividends. Therefore, the auditor is not concerned with unclaimed dividend checks, which are obligations of the agent. However, the auditor should confirm the amount of the unclaimed dividends, and he should investigate to determine that the agent periodically remits to the corporation the amounts no longer necessary because of expiration under the statute of limitations.

Unclaimed Wages

The auditor should investigate the opportunities for fraud, report upon any inadequacy in the system, and by examining payroll records be certain that the charges represent authorized payments. Unclaimed wages, either checks or currency, should be deposited in the bank and an Unclaimed Wage liability account credited. If after a reasonable time, it appears that the wages will not be claimed, the liability may be transferred to income, provided the laws of the state do not require that unclaimed wages revert to it.

LONG-TERM LIABILITIES CURRENTLY PAYABLE

Long-term liabilities maturing within the next fiscal period should be transferred from that classification into the current liability group, unless refinancing has been arranged, unless a sinking fund exists, or unless the long-term liability section of the balance sheet separately sets forth the current portion of the obligation. If there is a sinking fund, an amount of the bonds equal to the sinking fund should remain in the long-term liability classification. The auditing procedure is considered in Chapter 24 in connection with long-term liabilities.

Deposits

Companies frequently receive deposits of money from customers and from employees; the depositary company is liable for all such sums received. Examples of commonly found compulsory deposits are those required from employees for lockers, keys, and tools; and those required from customers for containers and meters. Certain deposits are of a voluntary nature, occurring when employees deposit money periodically for the ultimate purchase of stock of the company, when salesmen deposit money for the purchase of a new automobile, when amounts are withheld from employees' wages for the purchase of bonds, or when the employees save money by depositing a sum periodically with the company, which acts as a depositary in order to encourage savings. In examining deposits, the method employed to care for the deposits must be ascertained and the deposit audited by verifying the amounts received by the company with the balances shown by the deposit liability accounts. If passbooks or receipts held by depositors are easily obtainable, they should be compared with company records in order to verify balances. In many instances, deposits are never claimed, with the result that the deposit liability accounts tend to be overstated rather than understated. The estimated unclaimed balances should be transferred to a reserve or to income in order to prevent an overstatement of liabilities, provided this procedure is permissible under state laws. If the unclaimed deposits are for tangible assets such as containers, the proper asset accounts must be reduced correspondingly.

SECTION V: REVENUES RECEIVED IN ADVANCE

Revenues received in advance represent amounts received but not earned at a balance sheet date, and normally they represent liabilities for services to be performed in the future and require only the passage of time to convert to revenue. This is in contrast to current liabilities incurred for an item purchased and which will require the outlay of current assets at a future date. An auditor must familiarize himself with the class of account—revenue or liability—credited upon receipt of the advance so that he may verify the earned and unearned portions. When the revenue has been earned, a liability no longer exists and a transfer is made to the proper revenue account.

Audit Objectives

In the examination of revenues received in advance, the audit objectives are as follows: (1) to ascertain that the liability for the revenues received in advance are properly stated, (2) to ascertain that revenue has been allocated to the period in which it was earned, and (3) to ascertain that the amortization of the revenues received in advance conforms to accepted principles of accounting, consistently applied. Some revenues received in advance will be verified during the course of the audit of the related asset or revenue accounts. The following subsections discuss commonly found items of revenues received in advance.

Rent Received in Advance

Rent received in advance should be verified by determination of the rental period and by analysis of each Rental Revenue or Rent Received in Advance account. Rental leases and agreements must be examined to determine rental periods and must be compared with the cash records in order to prorate the cash received between current revenue and revenue received in advance. The advance payment should be confirmed directly to the auditor.

Interest Received in Advance

Interest received in advance is not of major importance to the majority of commercial and manufacturing companies but is an extremely important item to loan companies and to banks. The period of the loan must be determined to ascertain that the creditor has correctly determined revenue earned during the current period (1) on loans made during the current period which are repayable at some date after the close of the period and (2) on loans made in a prior period but which are still unpaid at the beginning of the current period.

Deferred Gross Profit on Installment Sales

Dealers selling on the installment plan may elect to carry forward as a deferred credit the gross profit on the uncollected portion of the sales made in any one period. This is desirable because of the possibility of large amounts of uncollectible installment accounts receivable and because of the continued cost of collection. In a year in which the collection is made, the auditor must ascertain that the gross profit percentage figure for the year in which the sale was made is applied to the collections and that the deferred credit is transferred out of the Deferred Gross Profit account to the correct current revenue account.

Collection in Advance on Contracts and on Sales

Collection in advance on contracts on which no work has been performed results in a liability which should be verified by reference to the contracts and the cash received under the contracts. When collections have been received on partially completed contracts, the proper determination of the amount earned will logically result in showing the unearned amount as a liability. The auditor must examine each contract; and if a loss has been incurred and if the amounts spent on production under a contract are shown as a current asset, then the deferred credits account should be removed by a charge and a credit to the asset.

Like collections on contracts for construction, collections on sales for future delivery should be treated as current liabilities if the materials to be delivered are included in current assets. Normally, this is not the case and a revenue received in advance exists. Correspondence and sales orders must be examined, inquiry must be made as to sales arrangements, and accounts receivable must be investigated for credit entries which precede debit entries.

Redeemable Tickets and Coupons

Most tickets and coupons are easily negotiable; and the auditor should insist upon a procedure that will result in the cancellation of presented items so that they cannot be resubmitted. Amounts collected in advance should be shown as liabilities—revenues received in advance. The number of items printed during the period should be ascertained. By test, the items redeemed during the period should be verified; and the inventory of unsold items should be determined. If a record of tickets sold is available, it must be verified to ascertain the money received or accounts receivable charged. Tickets used represent revenue for the period; and when subtracted from the total amount sold, they result in the revenue received but not earned. If tickets and coupons are loosely handled, the examination must be more extensive than if there is a satisfactory system of accounting for them.

If the method of accounting for revenue from these sources is inadequate, the situation should be discussed in a separate communication. The account balances for revenues received in advance for tickets, coupons, and similar items may have a tendency to grow, caused by a normal amount of item loss or destruction and a normal amount of items which the purchaser or receiver will never present for redemption. An auditor must be reasonable—but rigid—in this direction; and in the light of a normal percentage of claims and redemptions over several periods, he should be able to estimate the amounts that probably will remain unredeemed and transfer them to income.

Companies that credit a liability for premium coupons disbursed normally have outstanding a larger percentage of unredeemed coupons than do amusement companies or transportation companies, for example. Over a period of time, the amounts outstanding at the end of a fiscal period should bear a rather constant percentage relationship to the number of tickets sold or coupons given away.

Subscription Received in Advance

Advance subscription payments are received primarily by publishing companies dealing in periodicals. The subscription records with the individual subscribers should be examined by totaling the advance subscriptions to determine the unearned subscriptions received. The total cash received as indicated by the subscription records should be compared with the total charges (from that source) to the Cash account.

SECTION VI: CONTINGENCIES

The objectives of the audit of contingencies are to ascertain the nature and materiality of all contingencies and to determine that proper disclosure has been made in the financial statements, or accompanying footnotes, in accordance with the materiality of the items.

A contingency is an existing but uncertain situation which may *possibly* result in a future liability or loss, or asset acquisition—as a result of a related past act or a possible future act. At the balance sheet date, there is no actual liability of determinable amount because evidence does not exist to the extent necessary or possible to afford reflection in the records. If an auditor permits the omission of contingencies at the end of a fiscal period, he has failed to point out the conditions under which possible liabilities, losses, or asset acquisitions may develop as a result of prior or subsequent acts. The financial condition of a company may be as seriously affected by contingencies as by items of a real and existent nature. Extreme caution often is necessary in order to uncover contingencies because evidence of their existence may not appear in the financial records. Many of the footnotes appearing on financial statements and the prevalence of reserves for contingencies constitute ready evidence of the significance of the problem of contingencies.

Contingencies may be classified as follows:

1. Possible direct items unsettled as to the certainty of amount, such as:
    a) Additional federal income tax assessments, or rebates.
    b) Litigation involving patents, trademarks, copyright infringement suits, breaches of contract, and renegotiation refunds.
    c) Existence of future delivery contracts.
    d) Claims.
    e) Guaranties of products.
    f) Sales of mortgaged properties.
2. Secondary obligations, wherein no liability will come into existence unless a primary obligor fails to act, such as:

a)   Discounting of notes receivable.
b)   Endorsement of notes.
c)   Unused balances of outstanding letters of credit.
d)   Guaranty of obligations of others.

Class 1 contingencies which may result in possible losses or liabilities should be disclosed in the accounts if reasonably certain; and they should be disclosed in the financial statements or in accompanying footnotes. If Class 1 contingencies may result in a gain or in the acquisition of an asset, disclosure should be offered in the financial statements or the accompanying notes. The contingent gain or asset acquisition should not be reflected in the accounts in accordance with the accepted accounting principle of not reflecting a gain until it is earned and not reflecting an asset until it is acquired.

Although some auditors do not consider Class 2 contingencies to be contingencies, the fact remains that a possible direct liability may develop. Class 2 contingencies therefore should be disclosed in the financial statements or in accompanying footnotes in accordance with the canon regarding full disclosure of all *material* date.

There are many contingencies in addition to those already indicated, but those listed are most commonly encountered. The audit procedures for contingencies are directed primarily toward the detection of the items and their possible future effect on operations and financial position.

Audit Program for Contingencies

The minutes of the meetings of the board of directors and of special committees are excellent sources of information for the detection of contingencies. Special attention should be directed to contracts for the purchase and sale of unusual or nonrecurring items. Authorized commitments for the expansion of plant and plant facilities should be investigated, together with all contracts made in connection with these items. If commitments for plant expansion are material in amount, a schedule may be prepared for inclusion in the audit report, setting forth such data as the authorized expenditure, the amount completed at the date of the examination, and the balance of the uncompleted authorization.

The examination of purchase contracts, sales contracts, lease agreements, and invoices for professional services often discloses contingencies. In the event of the existence of contracts for future purchases, it may be that prices are falling at a balance sheet date and the client may be contemplating the breaking of a contract, which may give rise to a suit for breach of contract. Any possibility of such liability should be set forth—as a contingency—in the footnotes to the balance sheet.

Product and other guaranties often exist which may result ultimately in a liability, the contingency for which must be recognized as early as possible. Product quality, performance, and service guaranties may be considered as real liabilities rather than contingencies. In the case of dealers in household appliances, a portion of the sales price frequently is set aside as a liability for service and repairs. The audit work papers should set forth an analysis of the conditions under which sales are made, together with an indication of the extent of the existence of these liabilities, which may be of indefinable amount.

The client's legal division should be requested to supply information concerning possible losses from pending lawsuits—and the possibility of contemplated lawsuits. In all cases of contingencies involving litigation, final judgment has not been rendered, or appeal from judgment is contemplated. If the judgment were final, the liability would be direct not contingent. In cases of this nature where the judgment is not final, the contingency should be adequately estimated. Occasionally, clients do not wish to disclose contingencies of this nature because of final judgment to be rendered or because of interpretation by other parties to the litigation that recognition of the existence of the contingency may be at least a partial admission of the loss of the case. At all times, full disclosure should be made of every known contingency in accordance with generally accepted methods of statement presentation. This is necessary to an auditor in the event of legal action against him.

If real property subject to a mortgage has been sold and if the purchaser did not assume the mortgage, the seller may become liable for a deficiency judgment in the event that the mortgagee forecloses and the amount realized is insufficient to cover the loan.

Many contingencies are revealed from routine steps applicable to every audit. Notes and trade acceptances may be discounted, with the possibility that the primary obligor may fail to liquidate his indebtedness. If notes, acceptances, and drafts are properly handled in the records, the contingency will be automatically shown as items discounted. Endorsements may be made on notes of affiliated or other companies, either for the benefit of the endorser or as an accommodation to a third party. In the event of an accommodation endorsement of material amount, the contingency should be shown as a footnote to the balance sheet of the accommodation endorser. Normally, no record exists of accommodation endorsements, and they are difficult to detect. Therefore, the auditor should request a liability certificate stating the amount and nature of all contingencies not recorded. If the accommodation endorser has taken up the instrument, a charge to a receivable should appear, with an offsetting credit to Cash. An examination of cash disbursements showing charges to Notes or to Accounts Receivable should serve as a warning of such a transaction. Full provision should be made in the allowance for doubtful accounts for the possibility of noncollection.

Foreign drafts are often unpaid at a balance sheet date; and if the foreign importer does not honor the draft, the domestic exporter who drew the draft will become liable to the bank to which the draft was sold. Accounts receivable may be pledged or assigned, in which case the assignor will be liable in the event of nonpayment by the original debtor. In certain industries, it is customary to guarantee for subsidiary companies the payment of bond principal, bond interest, and dividends on stock; in such instances, a possible liability exists. In the event of a direct financial obligation of an indeterminate amount, there is a possibility of the development of a specific liability; and the auditor must present such conditions in footnotes to the financial statements if it is impossible to incorporate them in the statements.

If accommodation notes have been exchanged in order to assist one of the parties to the exchange, it is important that the auditor discover this transaction. In many instances, these accommodation exchanges are not recorded by the accommodating party, who normally does not discount the note he received; in such an instance, the note received in exchange will not be presented to the auditor for his examination, and it is necessary that the liability certificate indicate the existence of this circumstance.

The auditor should question responsible officials and other personnel as to the existence of contingencies and also unrecorded direct liabilities. The client must be impressed with the importance of these questions; otherwise, the existence of contingencies may not be revealed voluntarily. These failures to disclose contingencies may be due not to unwillingness but to a lack of understanding of proper financial statement preparation.

If federal income tax assessments are in dispute, the taxpayer has a contingency for assessments for which he has not provided. If adverse judgment is rendered, the contingency becomes a direct liability.

ILLUSTRATION. *Footnote Regarding Contingencies and Other Commitments.* There are various contingent liabilities and pending legal actions (including treble damage antitrust claims) which management considers routine to operations. In the ordinary course of business, the Company has incurred commitments, including employment contracts, is contingently liable as guarantor or endorser of notes and contracts, and has the usual obligations of contractors for completion of contracts and those incurred with sales of realty assets. In the opinion of management, adequate provision has been made for any losses which may reasonably be foreseen.

Liability Certificate

In order that the auditor may adequately protect himself, creditors, and stockholders, a certification of liabilities should be obtained in which responsible company executives certify that all known direct liabilities and contingencies are properly disclosed. The auditor must realize, however, that a liability certificate does not relieve him of the responsibility to do everything possible to ascertain that all liabilities and contingencies are properly displayed. A liability certificate is shown in Illustration 22–7.

ILLUSTRATION 22–7

LIABILITY CERTIFICATE

Date_____

Certen and Company
Certified Public Accountants

In connection with the audit of our records for the year ended December 31, 1975, we certify that to the best of our knowledge:

1. All direct liabilities have been recorded in the accounts, including all items in transit for which we had been billed and to which we had title.
2. As of December 31, 1975, contingencies are as noted below:
   a) Discounted notes, drafts, and acceptances . . . .$_____
   b) Accounts or notes assigned . . . .   _____
   c) Accommodation endorsements of the paper of others . . . . .   _____
   d) Lawsuits and judgments . . . .   _____
   e) Financial commitments not in the regular course of
      ordinary business . . . .   _____
   f) Open balances on letters of credit . . . .   _____
   g) Additional taxes for prior years . . . .   _____
   h) Purchase commitments at prices in excess of current
      market quotations or for quantities in excess of
      normal requirements.   _____
   i) Guarantees of debts of affiliated companies. . . . .   _____
   j) Renegotiation of government contracts . . . .   _____
3. There is subordination of liabilities in the amount of . . . . . .   _____
4. Company assets were pledged or hypothecated as liability
   security, other than as noted in 2, above, in the
   amount of. . . . .$_____
5. The contracts for construction and/or purchase of fixed
   assets amount to . . . .$_____

Signed_____ Title _____
Signed_____ Title _____

The liability certificate is not attached to the balance sheet but is retained as a part of the permanent work papers, and it may not be referred to in the audit report.

SECTION VII: FINANCIAL STATEMENT CONSIDERATIONS

In addition to the accounting and financial statement considerations developed in this chapter, the following comments are presented.

Accounts payable should be properly subdivided into trade and non-trade items. If material in amount, debit balances in accounts payable should be set forth as current assets.

Notes and acceptances payable should be properly classified in the financial statements. Common classifications are notes payable to banks; trade notes and acceptances payable; notes payable to officers; notes payable to affiliated companies; and currently maturing long-term obligations.

If any of these obligations are secured by pledged assets, that fact should be stated parenthetically in the balance sheet.

Amounts withheld from employees may be grouped in the preparation of a formal balance sheet in order to reduce detail in that statement.

Accrued expenses are classed as current liabilities because of their probable liquidation in the relatively near future. Invoices for unpaid services and inventory are not accrued expenses; they represent accounts payable.

Short-term revenues received in advance should be shown as current liabilities. Long-term deferred credits, such as unamortized bond premium, should be shown separately classified or placed in the long-term liability section of the balance sheet.

The financial statement presentation of contingencies may present rather difficult problems. The generally approved method of presenting contingencies which probably will not become actual liabilities is to append a footnote to the balance sheet. In those cases where it is possible to measure fairly accurately the amount of a possible additional liability, as exemplified by an additional tax liability or to contract adjustment, a definite provision for the possible liability should appear in the balance sheet proper, properly described. If a reserve for contingencies is set up by action of the board of directors, it should appear in the proprietorship section of the balance sheet.

QUESTIONS

1. For each of the following indicate the balance sheet classification and preferred title:
   a. Amount due trade creditors.
   b. Deposits received from customers to assure delivery of merchandise.
   c. Interest received on notes receivable due in 60 days.
   d. Employees wages earned but, not paid.
   e. Endorsed subsidiary's bank loan.
   f. Signed contract for anticipated plant rearrangement costs.
   g. Cash received from a customer, along with order, covering material cost of items to be produced to specification.
   h. Sales tax collected, to be remitted to state in 90 days.
   i. Mortgage bonds payable, 6 percent due 2001.
   j. Advanced rent received—five years in advance.
   k. One for one common stock dividend declared.
   l. Discounted customer notes receivable.
   m. Premium received on 6 percent mortgage bonds payable.
   n. Accrued estimated state income tax payable.
   o. Sinking fund cash accumulating for use to retire mortgage bonds.
   p. Appropriation of retained earnings for bond sinking fund.
   q. Appropriation of retained earnings for future plant expansion.
   r. A loan from the treasurer not supported by a note.
   s. Portion of 6 percent mortgage bonds to be retired next year.

t. Secured a 90-day loan from the bank on a discounted note payable.

u. Estimated amount of redeemable coupons.

v. Advance receipts on a construction contract that will be completed next year.

w. Federal income tax wihheld from employees.

x. Cash dividends in arrears, but not declared.

y. Interest due on mortgage bonds, but not paid.

z. Estimated three-year warranty cost on products sold this year.

aa. Cash received for concert series, half of which will be given in this year and the balance next year.

bb. Royalties due to authors, but not paid.

cc. Deposits on containers held by customers.

dd. Amount due on consigned merchandise sold by consignee.

2. Describe the audit procedure required when auditing the financial statements of a book publisher who has royalty agreements.

3. Why do bankers carefully evaluate the current liability section of a borrower's balance sheet?

4. In an audit of accounts payable, what debits and credits to the controlling account—other than cash debits and inventory acquisition credits—would you particularly investigate? Why?

5. A client requested your advice concerning the desirability of obtaining confirmation for his accounts payable. What would guide you in your answer?

6. Is the confirmation of accounts payable by direct confirmation with vendors as useful and important an audit procedure as is the confirmation of accounts receivable? Explain fully.

(AICPA)

7. When is the liability for goods purchased usually recorded by the vendee? Comment on this usage, and cite permissible exceptions to it.

8. a) Why should long-standing credit balances in accounts payable be investigated by the auditor?

   b) Why should debit balances in accounts payable be investigated by the auditor?

   c) Name all possible sources of debit balances in accounts payable and indicate the adjustment necessary for each one.

9. A client company does not record the cost of services, supplies, or materials purchased until the invoices are paid. The company only maintains distribution records which are charged for the proper amounts when cash is disbursed. How could you be certain that all liabilities were recorded at the end of the year?

10. A manufacturer of farm equipment has uniform sales contracts with all of its distributors, providing for special discounts to the distributors based upon their toal purchases during the year. At the termination of each contract year, each distributor receives a quantity discount of three percent of his total contract-year purchases which are in excess of a minimum that is uniform for all distributors. Distributor contracts are made on any day of the year.

Each month, the manufacturer provides for the total accruing liability at a percentage of the total sales for the month. The percentage is equal to the average rate of the special discount allowed in the company's preceding year on the sales in the contract years ended within that year to all distributors, including those who earned no special discount. The discounts actually allowed as each distributor's contract year expires are charged to the accrued liability account.

A current record for each distributor is not maintained by the manufacturer because the discounts accrue from month to month. The manufacturer has never attempted to determine whether the accrued liability shown on its records adequately covered the liability at any given date.

a) In a first audit, what procedure should be followed to test the adequacy of the accrued liability?

b) Outline a method whereby the liability can be determined with reasonable accuracy at the end of each month.

11. *a)* Outline a program for the verification of notes payable.

   b) Of what value is the Interest Expense account in the audit of notes payable?

12. The Kelsey Company, a subsidiary of the Wood Company, has $225,000 trade notes payable outstanding at December 31, 1975, due January 15, 1976. You started your audit of the Kelsey Company February 1, 1976, for the year ended December 31, 1975. The Kelsey Company has filed application to issue an additional $250,000 of common stock. On January 15, 1976, permission had not been received, but there is no doubt of the approval of the issue. On January 15, 1976, the Kelsey Company borrowed $100,000 from the Wood Company and used $125,000 of its own cash to pay off the $225,000 of notes payable. You were informed that the Wood Company will be given $100,000 of the new stock in payment for the $100,000 loan. Because of the proximity of the closing date to the note maturity date and because of your knowledge of the situation, how should this liability be shown on the balance sheet of the Kelsey Company at December 31, 1975? Assume that permission to issue the stock was granted on February 10, 1976, during the course of your audit.

13. During your audit of the records of a company, you discovered a debit to Notes Payable and a credit to Cash of the same amount and date. You obtained the paid check supporting the payment, but the canceled note could not be located. What course would you pursue?

14. During an audit, you discovered a posted entry charging Notes Payable and crediting Cash for $7,000. You cannot find original credit to Notes Payable which might account for the $7,000 debit. All officers were away on vacation. You examined the notes register, the Interest account, and the accounts payable and their related vouchers. You could not locate the payee of the check because all checks had been burned in an office fire. No canceled notes were on hand. Owing to the absence of the officers, you cannot send out confirmation requests. What might be some of the possibilities that resulted in the debit to the Notes Payable account?

15. As of the close of the fiscal period, the records of a client corporation show no notes payable. The bank confirmation shows notes payable to the bank of $100,000 signed by the president in the name of the corporation.

What procedure would you follow to determine (*a*) whether this discrepancy was an attempt to understand liabilities or (*b*) whether it constituted a defalcation?

16. The Acorn Company endorses the notes of its debtor companies whenever the latter request the accommodation, taking investment bonds owned by the debtor companies as security for the endorsements. The securities are taken on the basis of $110 of current market price at the time of the endorsement to $100 of endorsement. On December 31, 1975, the Acorn Company held securities (market price, $660,000) against $600,000 of note endorsements. How should this situation be shown on the balance sheet of the Acorn Company at December 31, 1975?

17. *a*) You were auditing the records of the Atlanta Company, which is the American subsidiary of a German corporation. The Atlanta Company had $400,000 of bills of exchange outstanding. Owing to the parent-subsidiary relationship, should the $400,000 be shown as a contingency on the balance sheet of the Atlanta Company? Give reasons for your answer.

b) The Arid Company endorses the notes of its debtor companies whenever any of the latter request the accommodation. On December 31, 1975, three accommodation endorsements totaled $250,000. How should this situation be shown on the balance sheet of the Arid Company?

18. The auditors of Tie, Inc., discover that purchase orders for delivery in the following year were placed in the last month of the fiscal year, which is the calendar year. The purchase contracts were not offset by sales contracts. Certain commitments were made in December, 1975; and starting early in January, 1976, the raw material market for textiles declined drastically, which meant that Tie, Inc., probably would suffer losses upon the sale of the finished products in 1976. The company does not want to show the probable loss on these commitments on its 1975 statements and asks the auditors to not mention the contingencies of the situation. The audit started on February 1, 1976, and was completed on February 15, 1976. If you were the auditor, what course would you follow?

19. *a*) Many types of equipment used in homes and in industry are sold under long-time guaranties. What provision should the manufacturer make for the possibility of noncharge repairs and replacements during the guaranty period?

b) Many home appliance manufacturers and distributors guarantee their products for a period of three years. In order to cover the cost of possible repairs and part replacements during this guaranty period, the sales price to the customer is increased, for example, by $20. The $20 service and repair charge is not specifically labeled as such to the customer but merely is a part of the total sales price. On the records of the guarantor manufacturer or distributor, how should the $20 be accounted for?

20. Tickets are sold in large quantities by the Metro Transit Company. The tickets are not totally used the day they are sold, but any time thereafter, perhaps an entire month after the sale. As auditor for the Metro Transit Company, would you recommend (*a*) a credit to a revenue account as the tickets are sold; or (*b*) a credit to a liability accounts as the sales are made, followed by a credit to a revenue account as the tickets are used? Present reasons for your answer. Which method, if either, might indicate the use of forged tickets?

21. You are examining the records of a large store. The store gives its customers stamps with every sale in excess of $0.10. The customer can save the stamps and redeem them for merchandise such as furniture and household appliances. The redemption value is approximately one percent of the sale to the customer. The store purchases the redemption merchandise from a jobber at his cost plus 10 percent. The store has a few floor samples on display. The stamps are purchased from a printer.

During the course of your annual audit of the records of this store, state what you would do in connection with the following:
a)   The propriety of the amount of stamps on hand.
b)   The floor samples purchased for display.
c)   The stamps given to customers but not redeemed.
d)   The items purchased and given to customers for redeemed stamps.

22. Describe briefly 10 steps an auditor should take to satisfy himself that as of the end of the fiscal period under examination, all liabilities and contingencies are reflected in the accounts or otherwise disclosed.

PROBLEMS

1. The College Text Publishing Company is one of your clients. An inspection of one of its author contracts reveals the following information:
a)   Two authors: main author—80 percent of royalties
                          co-author—20 percent of royalties.
b)   Royalty basis to be on text sold at various prices, net of returns.
c)   Royalty rate—Domestic sales—15 percent
                          Foreign sales—10 percent
d)   Sales for 1975 were as follows:

Domestic sales:
  7,200 @ $14.75
  3,100 @   13.50
  2,500 @   11.00
  2,200 @   10.50
Returns:
    200 @   13.50
     80 @   11.00
Foreign sales:
    800 @   13.50
    100 @   11.00
Returns:
     20 @   13.50

e) Asian translation rights have been granted and are to earn the authors ten cents per copy printed. 1,000 copies were printed in 1975.

Prepare an audit work paper setting forth your calculations which you will use to determine the accuracy of the related accounts on your client's records.

2. In the final stages of your audit of the financial statements Mills, Inc., for the year ended December 31, 1975, you were consulted by the corporation's president who believes there is no point to your examining the 1976 voucher register and testing data in support of 1976 entries. He stated that (*a*) bills pertaining to 1975 which were received too late to be included in the December voucher register were recorded as of the year-end by journal entry, (*b*) the internal auditor made tests after the year-end, and (*c*) he would furnish you with a letter certifying that there were no unrecorded liabilities.

a) Should the CPA's test for unrecorded liabilities be affected by the fact that the client made a journal entry to record 1975 bills which were received late? Explain.

b) Should a CPA's test for unrecorded liabilities be affected by the fact that a letter is obtained in which a responsible management official certifies that to the best of his knowledge all liabilities have been recorded? Explain.

c) Should a CPA's test for unrecorded liabilities be eliminated or reduced because of the internal audit tests? Explain.

d) Assume that the corporation which handled some government contracts had no internal auditor but that an auditor for a federal agency spent three weeks auditing the records and was just completing his work at this time. How would the CPA's unrecorded liability test be affected by the work of the auditor for a federal agency?

e) What sources in addition to the 1976 voucher register should the CPA consider to locate possible unrecorded liabilities?

(AICPA, adapted)

3. From the following information, prepare the current liabilities section of the balance sheet for the Drummand Company as of December 31, 1975.

(1) Notes payable arising from the purchase of raw materials, $114,000.

(2) Notes payable—bank, due in 90 days, $60,000. (Collateral on this consists of $80,000 in marketable securities.)

(3) Notes payable to officers, due on demand, $40,000.

(4) Accounts payable arising from the purchase of raw materials, $88,000.

(5) Cash balance with First Bank, $26,000; cash overdraft with College Station Bank, $35,000.

(6) Dividends in arrears on cumulative preferred stock, $48,000.

(7) City income tax withheld, $2,600.

(8) Advance receipts on special jobs being manufactured to specification for customers, $6,000.

(9) Installment notes on equipment purchased, $40,000 of which $20,000 is due in 1976 and the balance in 1977.

(10) Accounts receivable, credit balances, $3,600.

(11)   Estimated costs of meeting service requirement guarantees on products produced and sold, $14,400.

(12)   One of the company's products exploded causing injury to a customer's employee. The estimated claim is $4,800. The company has no insurance to cover a loss of this nature.

(13)   Drummond borrowed $20,000 on the cash surrender value of its officer's life insurance. Cash surrender value amounts to $80,000. Interest on this loan has been paid to the balance sheet date.

4.   The Knox Company shows net income as follows:

	Book Income	Taxable Income
1975	$42,300	$61,200
1976	60,050	55,850

The audit reveals that Knox was organized July 1, 1975, and wrote off its entire organization cost of $21,000 in that year. However, the Internal Revenue Code stipulates that a company may write off organization costs ratably over a period not to exceed 60 months. Therefore, the company, for federal income tax purposes deducted 10 percent of the cost in 1975 and 20 percent of the cost in 1976. Corporate income tax rates in 1975 and 1976 were 24 percent on the first $25,000 of profit and 50 percent on all profit in excess of $25,000.

Prepare the entries that would be made on the records of the company at the end of 1975 and 1976 to (a) recognize the income tax liability and (b) provide for proper allocation of taxes for each year.

5.   Prepare the current liabilities section of the balance sheet for the Federal Company as of December 31, 1975, from the information given below:

(1)   Additional federal income tax assessments proposed by the Treasury Department for 1974 that are being protested by the company, $13,500.

(2)   Accounts Payable—Trade, $91,500.

(3)   Notes Payable—Trade, $36,000.

(4)   Accrued interest on notes payable, $4,200.

(5)   Advance receipts from customers, $22,500. (Goods will be shipped in 1976.)

(6)   Notes Payable—Bank, $36,000. (This is a long-term note, three years, to be paid off at the rate of $1,000 per month. Inception of note 1/1/75.)

(7)   Notes Payable—Bank (due in 90 days), $60,000.

(8)   Cash dividend payable on preferred stock, $13,500.

(9)   Stock dividend payable on common stock, $4,500.

(10)   Brunemann Company has guaranteed employees' bank loans in the amount of $22,500.

(11)   Notes Payable—Officers (due in six months), $30,000.

(12)   Salaries and wages payable due to be paid 1/15/76, $3,750.

(13)   Notes receivable in the amount of $30,000 have been discounted at the bank. Company received cash of $24,000.

(14) Accrued State Unemployment and Workmen's Compensation Insurance Payable, $4,650.

(15) Subordinated notes payable to stockholders, 50 percent, due 12/31/76, $10,000.

(16) Accounts Receivable credit balance, $3,750.

(17) Provision for federal income tax, $48,000.

(18) U.S. Treasury tax anticipation bills held by the company in the amount of $30,000.

(19) Estimated future warranty costs on goods sold in 1975, $7,500.

(20) Installment notes payable on equipment purchases, one third due during 1976, $31,500.

6. *a)* On April 1, 1975, your client, The Raidonics Corporation, was licensed to manufacture a patented type of diode. The licensing agreement called for royalty payments of $0.20 for each transistor manufactured. What procedures would you follow in connection with the first annual audit as of December 31, 1975, to satisfy yourself that the liability for royalties is correctly stated?

b) After your audit was completed, you were asked to prepare a certified report for the owner of the patent on the diode, covering therein your findings as to royalty payable. Prepare the report which you would submit. Pertinent data are: 613,500 diodes were placed in production, of which 62,720 were rejected or spoiled; on July 26, 1975, a royalty payment of $6,300 was made; and on October 30, 1975, a royalty payment of $49,520 was made.

(AICPA, adapted)

7. As of January 1, 1970, Carroll leased a building for 10 years; the building was to be used as a retail store. The agreement with the owner was as follows: The annual rent was to be based on sales. On sales up to $300,000 per year the rate was to be three percent. On sales in excess of $300,000 per year, the rate was to be two percent. However, during the first five years of the term of the lease, the annual rental was to be a minimum of $8,000 per year, after which the minimum was to be increased by 12½ percent.

The lease provided that if in any one year the rent based on sales did not equal the minimum annual rental, the minimum would be payable, but the amount paid solely as a result of such minimum could be applied in reduction of the next year's rent to the extent that the next year's rent exceeded the minimum for that year. Sales by years were as follows:

1970	$192,000	1975	$282,000
1971	258,000	1976	330,000
1972	296,000	1977	284,000
1973	322,000	1978	340,000
1974	248,000	1979	394,000

a) You are to compute the amount of the rent payable each year under the terms of the lease.

b) Discuss the financial statement treatment of any amounts payable under the provision for payment of a minimum amount of rent.

(AICPA, adapted)

8. Show how you would treat and disclose each of the following items in preparing the balance sheet of a corporation as of December 31, 1975.
   (1) A note payable of $300,000, endorsed by the president of the company.
   (2) Notes receivable, discounted on August 10, 1975, and paid on January 10, 1976, amounting to $50,000.
   (3) Cash dividends payable of $160,000 declared on January 2, 1976.
   (4) The stockholders have either guaranteed or endorsed the current liabilities of the corporation.
   (5) The indebtedness due the stockholders has been subordinated to a bank.

9. During the examination of the records of the Lindsey Company as of December 31, 1975, you learned of the existence of the situations in (1), (2), and (3) below.

   What entries would you recommend, and what disclosures would you make for each of these situations in the financial statements for December 31, 1975?
   (1) The Lindsey Company has guaranteed the payment of interest on the $300,000, 10-year, first-mortgage bonds of an affiliate, the Fremont Company. The interest rate is 7½ percent, payable on June 1 and December 1 of each year. The bonds were issued by Fremont on December 1, 1973, and all interest payments have been met by that company, with the exception of the payment due on December 1, 1975. Lindsey states that it will pay the defaulted interest to the bondholders on January 15, 1976.
   (2) During the year 1975, Lindsey was named as defendant in a suit for damages for breach of contract brought by the Tiffin Company. A decision adverse to Lindsey was rendered, and Tiffin was awarded damages of $40,000. At the time of the audit, the case was under appeal to a higher court.
   (3) On December 23, 1975, Lindsey declared a common stock dividend of 1,000 shares, par $100,000, of its common stock, payable on February 1, 1976, to the common stockholders of record December 31, 1975.

   (AICPA, adapted)

10. The following data are submitted for a magazine publishing company. All subscriptions were received on July 1, 1975, to start in that month. There is no prior revenue or revenue received in advance.

Subscription for Period of—	Number of Subscriptions	Subscription Price for Period Indicated	Total Cash Received
1 year.	40,000	$12.00	$ 480,000
2 years	40,000	21.00	840,000
3 years	40,000	30.00	1,200,000
5 years	40,000	36.00	1,440,000

a) Prepare an audit program for verification of the revenue received in advance from subscriptions as of the year ended December 31, 1975.

b) Prepare work papers setting forth the revenue earned in 1975 and the amount deferred by years as of December 31, 1975.

11. The Linker Corporation requests that you compute the appropriate balance for its Provision for Product Warranty account for a balance sheet at the end of six months, June 30, 1975.

Based upon the data in the problem, prepare a work paper, including the proposed audit adjustment. Assume that proper recognition of costs for financial accounting will be allowed for federal income tax purposes.

The corporation manufactures television circuits and sells them with a six-month guaranty under which defective circuits will be replaced without charge. On December 31, 1974 the Provision for Product Warranty account had a balance of $255,000. By June 30, 1975, this account had been reduced to $40,125 by charges for the estimated net cost of circuits returned which had been sold in 1974.

At the beginning of 1975, the company expected eight percent of the dollar volume of sales to be returned. However, due to the introduction of new models during 1975, the eight percent estimated was changed to 10 percent on May 1. It is assumed that no circuits sold in a given month are returned in that month. Each circuit is stamped with a date at the time of sale so that the warranty may be properly administered. The following table of percentages indicates the probable pattern of sales returns during the six-month period of the warranty, starting with the month following the sale of circuits:

Month Following Sale	*Percentage of Total Returns Expected*
First	20
Second	30
Third	20
Fourth, fifth, sixth (10 percent each)	30
Total	100

Gross sales of circuits were as follows for the first six months of 1964:

Month	*Amount*
January	$1,800,000
February	1,650,000
March	2,050,000
April	1,425,000
May	1,000,000
June	900,000

The warranty also covers the payment of freight cost on defective circuits returned and on new circuits sent out as replacements. The freight cost is approximately 10 percent of the sales price of the circuits returned. The manufacturing cost of the circuits is 80 percent of the sales price, and the salvage value of the returned circuits averages 15 percent of their sales price. Returned circuits on hand at December

31, 1974, were thus valued in inventory at 15 percent of their original sales price.

(AICPA, adapted)

12. The Boyer Company, a manufacturer of heavy machinery, grants a four-year warranty on its products. The Estimated Liability for Product Warranty account shows the following transactions for the year:

Opening balance	$45,000
Provision	20,000
	$65,000
Cost of servicing claims.	12,000
Ending balance	$53,000

A review of unsettled claims and the company's experience indicates that the required balance at the end of the year is $80,000 and that claims have averaged 1½ percent of net sales per year.

The balance in Accrued Federal Income Taxes is $27,000, which adequately covers any additional liability for prior years' income taxes and includes a $25,000 provision for the current year. For income tax purposes only the cost of servicing claims may be deducted as an expense.

The following additional information is available from the company's records at the end of the current year:

Gross sales	$2,040,000
Sales returns and allowances.	40,000
Cost of goods sold	1,350,000
Selling and administrative expense	600,000
Net income per company before federal income taxes	50,000

Prepare the adjusting entries for the proper accounting treatment of product warranty and federal income taxes. Support each entry with detailed computations. The accounts have not been closed. The company has not allocated income taxes in the past. Assume a rate of 50 percent for income tax calculations.

(AICPA)

23

Current Liabilities, Related
Costs and Expenses
(Concluded)

Audit Objectives

The objectives in examining costs and expenses related to current liabilities may be expressed as follows: to determine the adequacy of the system of internal control of costs and expenses; to determine the purpose of the costs and expenses; to determine the correctness of item classification; to determine that the items have been properly recorded; and, to determine the correctness of the amount of the items.

When an auditor is examining current liabilities, of necessity he will be concerned with auditing related costs and expenses because these items are principally verified at the time of examining original records. The amount of additional work to be performed is dependent upon the system of internal control, the practices of the company, the use of proper account classifications, and the requirements of the engagement.

If a satisfactory system of budgetary control is in operation, the probabilities are that there will exist proper cost and expense authorization, proper incurrence, and proper account classification; also, the chances for fraud and omission of entries are greatly reduced. With a system of budgetary control in existence, top management will receive and study periodic comparative reports of operations and then will determine the causes and effects of actual cost and expense variations from the budgeted figures based upon a predetermined volume of sales. With rigid control of costs and expenses accompanied by analyses and corrective actions, the work of an auditor is expedited because he will be more confident that propriety and accuracy will exist than he would be if costs and expenses were not under proper control and administration.

Selected cost and expense accounts may be analyzed in order to determine the composition of the account, to note fluctuations therein, and to ascertain that proper distinction is being made between capital and revenue expenditures. On the other hand, many expense accounts are simply scanned and others partially tested. In some cases, authorizations of amounts appear; and if the expense charges agree with the authorizations, the auditor may be satisfied. Variations in the same expense from period to period should be investigated on the basis that any expense if not properly controlled tends to rise. Also, an analysis of variations in expense accounts may lead to the detection of fraudulent transactions.

The use of percentage figures is advisable to show points of importance and significance in a forceful manner. Percentage figures must be used with discrimination in order to avoid confusion. Consider the effectiveness of the illustration presented below:

Explanation	1975	1974	1975 Percentage of Sales	1974 Percentage of Sales	Percentage of Increase or Decrease 1975 over 1974
Sales	$4,000,000	$2,000,000	100%	100%	100%
Cost of sales	2,520,000	1,200,000	63	60	110
Gross profit	$1,480,000	$ 800,000	37%	40%	85
Selling expenses	600,000	400,000	15	20	50
	$ 880,000	$ 400,000	22%	20%	120
Administrative expenses	320,000	200,000	8	10	60
Net Income	$ 560,000	$ 200,000	14%	10%	180

Expenses may be analyzed on a comparative basis with preceding years, both as to amounts and as to percentages of totals or percentages of increase or decrease. Examine the following analysis:

Explanation	Year 1975	Year 1974	Increase or Decrease 1975 over 1974	Percentage (+ or –) 1975 over 1974
Net sales	$300,000	$200,000	+$100,000	+50%
Advertising expense	$ 10,000	$ 12,000	– 2,000	–17
Percentage of advertising to sales	3.3%	.6%		

In such an analysis, the interpretation is that sales increased by $100,000 or 50 percent in 1975 as compared with 1974, whereas advertising decreased 17 percent in 1975 as compared with 1974. In 1974, $0.06 of every sales dollar went to advertising; whereas in 1975, only $0.033 went for the same purpose. In terms of sales, advertising decreased by almost 50 percent.

An auditor must understand the judicious employment of dollar and percentage comparisons, and he should make extensive use of trends and comparisons for all major expenses for the guidance of the client and his selection of items to be audited. In all cases in which expenses are verified, the auditor must be alert to be of real service to his client so that he can suggest procedural changes, curtailments, and expansions which might result in added net income.

In an examination of expenses, the auditor should verify selected expense authorization, examine the vouchers supporting the original record entry, verify the entry, trace the entries to the accounts, and verify the expense distributions. An auditor may prefer to take each expense account and audit by analyzing it and working back to the original records and the related vouchers. Also, the auditor must remember that a paid check in itself is not necessarily good evidence of the propriety of an expense; all cash items should be paid by check, and the check plus properly approved vouchers constitute prima facie evidence of the legitimacy of an expense. All of the procedures discussed earlier in this book in connection with cash disbursements apply to expenses.

SECTION I: INTERNAL CONTROL OF EXPENSES

Internal control procedures for expenses were discussed in Chapters 4 and 5. The principal points of internal control of expenses involve approval for the incurrence of the expense, centralized points of approval, proper recording, and prompt and proper payment. An internal control questionnaire for expense appears in Illustration 23–1. Some items duplicate the questions in Illustration 22–1 showing the close relationship of current liabilities and expense considerations in an audit program.

SECTION II: AUDIT PROGRAM FOR EXPENSES

An audit program applicable to the majority of expenses is presented, followed by a brief description of several typical expenses.

Review the System of Internal Control, Internal Audit, and Budgetary Control. In starting an audit of a selected expense account, the first act is to study the entire procedure that gives rise to entries in the account. The extent to which an auditor might go in auditing the account will be partially determined by the extent of internal auditing and the dominance of the budgeting program. Every client will have his own procedures whereby expenses are incurred, and it will be the auditor's responsibility to review these procedures. Many times the auditor will find that by relating the budget figure to the actual expense account balance he will find sufficient indication of the need for auditing that account.

ILLUSTRATION 23–1

INTERNAL CONTROL QUESTIONNAIRE
Expenses

	Yes	No	Not Applicable	Remarks
Company_____				
Period Covered _____				

1. Is there centralization of approval for expenses?
2. Are all but petty cash expenses routed through the central point of approval for expenses?
3. Is a postage meter used for outgoing mail?
4. Are expense authorizations executed in writing?
5. Are expense orders and purchase orders properly approved for:
     a) Item to be acquired?
     b) Price?
     c) Quantity?
     d) Supplier?
6. Does the accounting department receive directly:
     a) A copy of the expense authorization?
     b) A copy of the purchase order?
     c) A copy of the receiving report?
7. Is there an organized purchasing department?
8. Is the purchasing department independent of:
     a) The receiving department?
     b) The shipping department?
     c) The accounting department?
9. Are all purchase orders sequentially prenumbered?
10. Are all purchase orders executed in writing?
11. Does the receiving department obtain copies of purchase orders for authority to accept goods?
12. Is the receipt of goods controlled to prevent irregularities and errors?
13. Are receiving reports sequentially prenumbered and controlled?
14. Are receiving record data matched with vendor invoice data?
15. Does the receiving department retain a copy of receiving reports?
16. Does the purchasing department receive a copy of receiving reports?
17. Is the system adequate for recording and verifying partial deliveries?
18. Is the accounting department notified of returns to vendors?
19. Are returned purchases routed through the shipping department?
20. Are shipping reports prepared for returns?
21. Does the accounting department match invoices with:
     a) Purchase orders?
     b) Receiving reports?
     c) Expense invoices?

ILLUSTRATION 23–1 *(Continued)*

	Yes	No	Not Appli- cable	Remarks
22. Are invoices and/or statements received from creditors compared—by the accounting department—with open accounts?				
23. Are invoices entered by a person who does not have access to cash and/or inventories?				
24. Are invoices properly approved for payment?				
25. Are invoices properly verified for the following:				
a) Prices?				
b) Extensions and footings?				
c) Transportation charges?				
26. Are shortages and damaged goods properly reported?				
27. Are invoices adequately stamped to prevent duplicate payment?				
28. Are all vouchers and supporting documents signed by a properly authorized person prior to authorization for payment?				
29. Prior to approval for payment, are all related documents for an invoice assembled in one place?				
30. Are items purchased for the convenience of employees routed in regular manner through the following departments:				
a) Purchasing?				
b) Receiving?				
c) Billing?				
d) Accounting?				

Prepared by_____   Reviewed by_____
Date_____   Date_____

Verify the Authority for Expense Incurrence. Regardless of size, most clients have some procedure established for the approval of expense incurrence. The minutes of the board of directors, executive committee, and official directives from other authorized parties will provide the auditor with a good basis for determining whether or not the expense has been properly incurred. Full documentation of items not properly approved must be made so that the auditor can determine the effect on the financial statements as well as forming a basis of discussion with the client.

Compare Each Expense with the Similar Item of the Prior Period. This is one way in which an auditor can objectively evaluate the variation in an expense. It then can be related to the reason for the incurrence of the expense and determined whether a material change has taken place and if the transactions relating thereto need to be tested or audited in detail.

Determine the Propriety of Expense Account Classification. Since the auditor through the financial statements is attempting to inform management, stockholders, and other interested parties of the expense involved in carrying on the business, there must be clear presentation of this information through the use of proper classification. For example, the rent paid for office space should not be confused with lease expense of the computer complex.

Analyze Selected Expense Accounts.   Many individual expense items must be shown on various tax returns and this fact will assist the auditor in selecting expense accounts to be audited. This by no means eliminates the auditing of expense accounts that may be grouped. The importance of the expense item as to its amount and nature must be determined, and this also will guide the auditor in making a valid selection of expenses to be audited.

Watch for Items Charged to Expenses Which Should Be Capitalized. Keeping this point in mind will also assist in selecting an account to be audited either by testing the entries or auditing it in detail. For example, an air conditioner, having a life expectancy of five years, is installed in the computer room. The room in which the computer is housed is leased for a period of three years. This item should be capitalized and not charged to the current year's cost of operating the computer.

Prove the Accuracy of Selected Major Invoices.   In the audit of selected expense accounts, a "material" amount should be established for each account selected. By doing this the auditor will concentrate on significant transactions and therefore will be able to completely document these transactions in his work papers in a clear and concise manner.

Examine Major Expense Accounts to Establish the Accuracy of Related Asset or Liability Accounts.   As mentioned in the earlier discussions of fixed assets and current liabilities, the need for evaluating the effect of a transaction on all financial statements must be made so that the auditor's opinion is clearly set forth. In auditing liabilities, the auditor will be looking for expenses; so when the expenses are being audited he will be looking for the related assets or liabilities. If the auditor is to be independent and objective in his work, he must carefully evaluate this interrelationship.

Ascertain that All Expenses Have Been Recorded.   Expense transactions for the early part of the subsequent period must be examined to determine the period of proper inclusion. The longer the time intervening between the end of the accounting period and the conclusion of an audit, the better the chances of determining that all expenses were recorded as of the end of the period under examination.

Verify Distribution of Expenses.   If a client has a good budgeting program, differences between actual expense and the budgeted amount may indicate incorrect distribution of an expense transaction. For example, the lease expense of a client's computer had been charged to rent expense for the office. The comparison of the actual office rent expense with the budgeted rent expense revealed a difference and upon analysis the error was found and corrected. Other errors in distribution can be found by the inspection of invoices and determining whether the item or service acquired has been properly classified. The work papers must contain full documentation of the procedures followed as well as the explanation for corrective action taken.

Ascertain the Propriety of the Contracredit for Expense Debits. This is particularly important where the client makes monthly adjusting entries. As discussed in Section IV of Chapter 22, there are many types of transactions that fall into this category and the auditor must be careful to recognize the need for accurately recognizing the propriety of the contracredit for the expense debit.

Verify the Computation of Overhead Rates. This step is of particular importance where the client is a manufacturing concern. An error in a manufacturing overhead rate will not only cause an error in the cost of goods sold but also the work in process and finished goods inventories will be erroneously stated. With more and more firms establishing overhead rates for administrative and distribution functions, the auditor may wish to review these rates with a view to determining the accuracy of monthly statements being prepared for management.

Payroll

Payroll procedure varies for almost every employer; consequently, an auditor must use ingenuity in auditing payroll records.

In starting an audit of wages, the first act is to study the entire payroll procedure from hiring through payment of the employee. This is necessary to determine the nature and operation of the system of internal control. Employment records must be inspected to determine rates of pay, effective dates of these rates of pay, as well as the termination methods. A comparison of the totals according to the periodic payroll records must be made with the cash disbursed according to the cash disbursements record. Also, tests must be made to determine that authorized persons are being paid at authorized rates. The test inspecting of authorized employment records, time tickets, and other original data will enable the auditor to establish the reliability of the records. To further satisfy himself as to the propriety of the payroll data, the auditor should test payroll footings, postings, and distributions. With the increasing number of deductions for taxes and fringe benefits, tests of individual earnings calculations should be made, the net result to be compared with the canceled check endorsed by that individual. The remitting of the deductions to the proper agency or institution should be tested in order to be certain that the client is acting as a proper custodian. A reconciliation of payroll data according to the client's records with federal and state reports must also be made by the auditor. An examination must be made to determine the status of unclaimed wages and determine what disposition is eventually made of these items. Where formal plans exist for bonus or pension plans, the auditor must not only determine if they are properly authorized and calculated, but in the case of pension plans he must determine if they abide by Treasury Department regulations. Here again the auditor must be certain of complete documentation of the work performed in his work papers.

Where labor contracts are in existence, copies of these contracts must be obtained and made a part of the auditor's work papers. In addition, a breakdown of salaries and expense allowances for officers of a corporation is mandatory for completion of the client's Federal Income tax return.

Taxes

Tax expense determination may take place during the course of the verification of current liabilities. Paid tax bills and city, county, state, and federal tax returns filed during the period must be examined to determine whether they are applicable to past, present, or future periods. An examination of paid tax bills and tax returns also indicates the amount of taxes which properly should be accrued or prepaid at the close of a fiscal period. Thus, while verifying tax liabilities, it has at the same time been necessary for the auditor to examine the related expenses. In verification of the payment of taxes, for which paid receipts and copies of tax returns are available, the auditor should examine the related entries and paid checks in support thereof. These comparisons constitute further proof that the taxes have been paid.

Tax accounts usually require analysis for proper distribution of manufacturing, selling, and administrative expenses, unless separate accounts are carried for each type of tax; even in the latter case, the auditor must examine the classification distribution so that manufacturing, selling, and administration expenses will be properly stated. The employer's portion of the Federal Insurance Contributions Act tax, applicable state unemployment taxes, and the federal unemployment tax should be prorated to the proper divisions.

In the majority of audits, the auditor prepares the federal income tax return for the client. The amount of the annual federal income tax should be charged to a separate expense account and shown as a separate item on the income statement and not part of operating expenses. Additional income tax assessments of prior years and tax refunds of prior years should be shown in the statement of retained earnings, in accordance with APB *Opinion No. 9.*

Real property taxes are verified by comparison of the tax bills with the accounting records. (Also, see page 598.) Personal property and intangible taxes, franchise taxes, state and city income taxes, processing taxes, etc., are verified by examining the returns, by computing the taxes in accordance with the audited records of the company and the applicable tax laws, and by vouching the entries through the records.

Proper auditing procedure for the Federal Insurance Contributions Act tax, the federal unemployment tax, and state unemployment taxes is to the effect that both the amount contributed by the employee and the amount contributed by the employer be verified by reconciling the payroll records to the returns and by verifying the computation of the tax.

Customs Duties. Customs duties should be verified in order to ascertain the correctness of their computations. After determining this, paid checks are compared with invoices and related entries. Customs duties preferably should be added to the cost of the item purchased.

Repairs and Maintenance

These expenses normally are analyzed at the time fixed assets are audited. Repair and maintenance charges should receive proper attention to ascertain that distribution has been made to the correct accounts and departments and that expenses and capital charges have not been confused. The verification of repairs and maintenance consists of account analyses and inspection of invoices, shop orders, and payrolls in order to determine the propriety of the charges, the correctness of the amounts, and the proper account classification. Some companies may follow the policy of capitalizing all maintenance charges in excess of a stipulated amount by charging the proper accumulated depreciation; all amounts below that figure are then charged to expense. Other concerns consider each case as it develops. In audits of large companies, only items of substantial amount need be examined. Maintenance accounts should be analyzed for the comparative data they yield between periods and between different types of fixed assets. See Illustration 23–2.

Research and Development

Research cost is the price of discovering a new idea. Development outlays are those necessary to place the research findings on a commercial basis. Many companies conduct their own research and development work, with the fundamental thought of developing patents, products, and processes that will become valuable revenue-producing adjuncts of the business. The results of research and developmental work are difficult to interpret in terms of subsequent assets. The tendency toward charging such items to expenses, as opposed to their capitalization, ordinarily prevails and is being supported by a recent opinion of the FASB. See Chapter 21 for more extensive discussion of this item. It is perfectly proper to capitalize these costs when patents of value are produced, but the optimism shown by capitalizing these items before patents are granted and proved is outside the range of good judgment. Some companies carry certain of their research and developmental costs forward as deferred charges, awaiting the time of patent, process, or product development

ILLUSTRATION 23–2

METRO COMPANY

Analysis of Machine Maintenance Expense #190
for Year Ended december 31, 1975

Month	Description	Purchases	Material	Labor	Total
January	Repair of 2 presses	$	$ 784√⊙	$ 321∧⊙	$ 1,105
February	Repair of 4 scru guns		268	444	712
March	Repair of 2 floor finishers		350	375	725
April	Repainted Dept. 4 machinery		422	206	628
May	Annual preventive maintenance on assembler		110	45	155
June	Overhaul jets on furnaces		230	320	550
July	Annual preventive maintenance of shop #2 machines		667√⊙	776∧⊙	1,443
August	New 1T lift truck	750√			
	Overhaul 4 mixers		1,175√⊙	246∧⊙	2,171
September	Repair 2 generators		202	140	342
October	Miscellaneous small items		95	165	260
November	New Selectric typewriter for factory office	600√			600
	Repainted Shop #2 machines		288√⊙	461√⊙	749
December	Set of socket wrenches	15σ			15
	Year end maintenance		230	389	619
	Total	$1,365	$4,821	$3,888	$10,074
Deduct: AJE #22		−1,350			−1,350
Adjusted Balance−12/31/75		$ 15	$4,821	$3,888	$ 8,724

√ Examined invoices and requisitions.
∧ Examined payroll distribution.
⊙ Reviewed repair work orders.
σ Client's policy to capitalize items in excess of $100.

AJE #22 (10.1)

```
Factory Equipment. . . . . . . . . . . . . . . . . . . . . . . . . . . . . .  750
Office Equipment. . . . . . . . . . . . . . . . . . . . . . . . . . . . . .  600
    Machine Maintenance Expense . . . . . . . . . . . . . . . . . . . .            1,350
    To capitalize items improperly charged to expense.
```

Transferred above charges to proper fixed asset work papers.

---

or the time when it is conclusively shown that the items should be charged to expense. If costs of this nature are treated as deferred charges, the charges should be amortized over a period no longer than the life expectancy of the developed patent, process, or product. In verifying these costs, the auditor must investigate all items either capitalized as assets or treated as deferred charges; to do this adequately, he will be forced to base his conclusions largely upon the information supplied to him by responsible officials. In any situation, he should be firmly convinced that the reasons for capitalizing or deferring the items are sound and legitimate; if he is not, he should insist upon charging them immediately to expense.

Supplies Expense

Supplies expenses for factory, office, and sales departments should be examined to the extent necessary in view of the materiality of the items and the effectiveness of internal control over physical inventories. The important point in the verification of supplies expense is to ascertain that correct differentiation has been made between the expense and the inventory elements. If the supplies inventory is correctly stated, the expense is correct. Comparisons should be made from year to year and major fluctuations investigated. Invoices should be tested and the samples should be traced to the accounts and records, and the paid checks should be examined, either at this point or at the time of examining cash disbursements. If in the examination of cash disbursements and inventories, a sufficient examination has been made of supplies expense, the only additional work necessary is to audit by comparison and to scrutinize the supplies expense accounts for large items not already examined. Proper physical control over supplies and their distribution is essential at all times. The correct distribution of supplies expense over the various divisions of a company is verified to ascertain that one division is not overburdened and another division freed of expenses properly chargeable to it.

Entertainment

Entertainment expenses may not be easy to audit. The auditor should ask for memoranda concerning the expenditures, and he should insist that a major executive approve the amounts. The auditor should test-vouch the expenditures into the proper accounts and from inquiry and investigation feel certain that the amounts designated for entertainment are not being diverted to the personal enrichment of some employee. Certain expenditures for entertainment may be disallowed as a deduction for federal income tax purposes. Illustration 23–3 sets forth a work paper analysis of Entertainment Expense.

Travel Expense

Travel expense should be investigated in order to determine its reasonableness and to ascertain whether the expense is supported by proper evidence. If supporting evidence is not available, there exists the increasing risk of disallowance for federal income tax purposes. Different companies demand reports varying in amount of detail for travel expense incurred by employees. The auditor should review the travel expense reports and note obvious items which pad the report to fictitious sums; he should discuss these matters with the proper official of the client. The expenses should be summarized and vouched to the records. Usually, an auditor can detect overstated expense reports, since certain items

ILLUSTRATION 23-3

THE AROMA G COMPANY

Analysis of Entertainment Expense #210
for the fiscal year ended October 31, 1976

Date	Paid to	Voucher Check No.	For	Amount		Comments
1975						
Nov. 15	American Express Co.	A-220	October, 1975, charges	x	$ 283⊙	On last year's Accounts Payable detail.
23	Shamois Restaurant	A-288	Entertaining customer Pres. R. Frank—discussed new contract		43N	
Dec. 23	Rights Catering	A-495	Employee party		185N	
27	Volunteer Society	A-501	Ad in monthly publication	x	22N	Advertising Expense per invoice.
1976						
Jan. 21	Downtown Eatery	A-680	District sales luncheon		200N	
28	American Express Co.	A-720	December charges		121⊙	
Mar. 22	Uptown Club	A-890	Pres. of Guiler Co. personal expense	x	120N	Family and personal friends only. No business connection.
May 14	U-Rent-A-Car	A-1200	Salesman in West Territory car rental	x	25N	Company car broke down. Needed car to complete sales calls.
June 10	Shamois Restaurant	A-1320	Employee party		130N	
Oct. 26	Uptown Club	A-2886	Entertained J. Couch, Dist. Sales Mgr., Sox, Inc. Discussed new $10,000 contract		85N	

Ledger Balance—10/31/76 . . . . $1,214

Deduct: AJE No. 25 450

Audit Balance . . . . $ 764

Above detail consists of all items in excess of $20.
N Inspected all documents supporting above. Charges and payment thereof.
⊙ Reviewed all charge tickets and had client complete all incomplete tickets.
x Incorrect charges.

AJE No. 25 (20)

110—Accounts Payable—Trade 283
209—Advertising Expense 22
10—Account Receivable—Employees 120
211—Travel Expense 25
210 Entertainment Expense 450
Correct items improperly charged to Account No. 210.

reappear with startling frequency. Naturally, an auditor has no right to demand that responsible persons submit expense reports in minute detail. Such practice may be desirable but might result in a person's devoting most of his time to preparation of reports. For purposes of federal income tax deductions, it is imperative that authentic support be given to travel expenses. If travel expenses are not properly supervised by management, unnecessary sums may be spent. Many companies want their representatives to travel in complete comfort and good style, for the effect upon customers. An auditor does not have the prerogative to set himself up as a judge as to how a person should travel and live. Many companies allow employees a flat sum per week or month for traveling; if the employee saves part of this flat amount, it belongs to him.

Interest Expense

Interest expense commonly is verified in connection with the audit of the interest-bearing payables. Interest rates must be verified in order to determine that the interest expense is not in error because of the application of an incorrect rate. The interest expense appearing in the records of a client is not complete evidence of its correctness, and the auditor must test calculations. Entries for interest are vouched through the records. Through inspection of cash disbursement records and paid checks, it should be ascertained that interest is paid when due in order to avoid penalties, if such exist. The auditor's best procedure is to prepare a schedule of interest expense based upon interest-bearing obligations covering the audit period. The interest expense is then verified for the period, not forgetting interest accruals and the amortization of interest deducted in advance.

Other Costs and Expenses

The preceding discussions are intended to be guidelines and are not all-inclusive for accounts to be audited. Such costs and expenses as idle plant, employee welfare, rent, advertising, donations, profit sharing contributions, and other items which will meet requirements of tax returns and management needs must be included if the auditor is to fully perform the audit function.

SECTION III: FINANCIAL STATEMENT CONSIDERATIONS

Preferably, income statements should be prepared in comparative form indicating changes from the preceding year. Today, many companies present stockholders with income statements for 10 consecutive years and these statements must be adjusted to reflect comparable data. In view of inflationary pressure, this presentation is becoming increasingly difficult to prepare and still be meaningful. In addition, the changes due to mergers and management philosophy can make such statements nothing more than a mass of data which is of very little use to anyone. For only modest disclosure of all material operating data, an income statement should include as a minimum sales revenues, cost of sales, selling expense, administrative expense, nonoperating revenue and expense, nonrecurring gains or losses, federal income tax, and net income.

Disagreements sometimes arise as to whether an expense should be classified as selling or administrative. In the last analysis, there may be no sharp line of demarcation between them in any given situation; the auditor may follow the practices of his client—provided these practices are proper and conform to accepted accounting principles and procedures. Normally, there is a fairly sharp line of demarcation between operating expenses, "other" expenses, and nonrecurring expenses.

QUESTIONS

1. What are the principal points of internal control over nonpayroll expenses?

2. When examining expenses, what are the audit objectives?

3. During the audit of the records of a company, you noticed the following items as of December 31, 1975:
   (1) The company set up $2,500 in a reserve for sinking fund.
   (2) The company did not provide for sales discounts on outstanding accounts receivable. The estimated discount is $500.
   (3) Bonds had been issued at a discount of $1,500, and no adjustments were made.
   (4) Factory equipment was sold at $475 over book value, and the profit of $475 was credited to Miscellaneous Income.
   (5) An error was made in computing depreciation of buildings. It was taken at five percent and should have been 2½ percent. The depreciation expense charge on December 31, 1975, was $10,000.
   (6) Accrued wages and accrued interest on notes receivable were ignored. The amounts were $400 and $200, respectively.
   (7) An account receivable for $100 is uncollectible. The allowance is adjusted every year as a percentage of net sales. No entry was made to write off this bad account.

   For each item (1)–(7) above, what is the effect on the net income for 1975? What adjustment would you recommend for each item?

4. How should an auditor verify the following:
   a) Fees of directors?
   b) Officers' salaries and commissions?
   c) Traveling expenses of officers?

   (AICPA, adapted)

5. A company manufactures a variety of products, ranging in size and price from small, inexpensive articles to large, costly items. Its operations are highly departmentalized. Its manufacturing expenses are allocated to departments, for each of which an overhead rate has been established.

How would you satisfy yourself as to the correctness of the application of the manufacturing overhead in determining the cost of sales?

6. Annually a corporation prepares a detailed advertising budget for each class of product it sells. The budgeted amounts are not spread over the months of the year. It consistently adheres to the budgets, and no important changes are allowed, although the department managers are permitted to make expenditures when they deem them advantageous. Sales budgets also are prepared.

It is desired to maintain accounts that will show, monthly, both the budgeted advertising expense and the actual advertising expenditures. How could this be done? It is understood that at the end of the year, the accounts will reflect only the actual advertising expense.

7. In each of the following cases, explain how you would proceed if irregularities were suspected in the payrolls paid in cash:

   a) Employees who have resigned have not been removed from the payroll.

   b) Casual (nonpermanent) labor is paid from an imprest fund. It is possible to reimburse the fund twice, once by repayment of cash into the fund and again through the regular payroll procedure.

   c) Unclaimed wages have been misappropriated by the paymaster.

8. A company has a contract with its sales manager whereby he receives as compensation in addition to his salary, one percent of all annual net income in excess of $100,000 before federal income taxes. In what respects would the audit of sales, bad debts, and selling expenses differ in a case of this nature from a situation in which a profit-sharing agreement was not in force?

9. In auditing traveling expenses, what procedure should be followed for a company in which both salesmen and administrative executives travel?

10. *a*) In an audit, expense accounts are examined extensively enough to result in assurance that proper distinction exists between capital and revenue charges. Would your examination in this direction be more critical if a loss for the year was incurred instead of a profit?

    b) Name a condition under which capital expenditures properly may be charged to expense upon incurrence.

11. In the examination of the records of a company, the auditor performed the following work in connection with the expense and revenue, accounts: (*a*) examined all documents and vouchers, such as sales, purchases, expense vouchers, memoranda, paid checks, and so on; (*b*) vouched each to the records of original entry and to the accounts; (*c*) verified the footings of all special-column records and traced each posting to the accounts; (*d*) footed all accounts in the general and subsidiary ledgers; (*e*) verified all adjusting entries, making all computations for accruals and deferrals; and (*f*) examined all asset and liability accounts to ascertain if any of them might hold possibilities for unrecorded revenues and expenses. His examination of all asset, liability, and capital accounts was correctly made. What did the auditor omit?

12. What factors would assist the auditor in verifying the distribution of expenses to the correct category?

13. What should be the first step in performing a payroll audit?

14. What problems does the auditor face in preparing comparative income statements for a client covering a period of ten years?

15. A company closed its accounts and discovered that a loss for the period had been incurred, whereas a satisfactory net income had been anticipated. You were called in to determine the difficulty. What items might you investigate, and how would you investigate them?

16. At the conclusion of your audit of the records of the West Company, you are confident that all expense accounts are properly stated so far as *amounts* are concerned. Should you examine the accounts further?

17. During the examination of the records of a client for the year ended December 31, 1975, you find that internal control over payrolls is not perfect because the size of the organization does not permit proper separation of duties; otherwise, there are no outstanding weaknesses in the system. Two hundred hourly employees are paid by check every two weeks. Wage rates are set forth in a union contract, which you have examined.

   a) Prepare an audit program for the examination of hourly payrolls to be performed during preliminary work period in November, 1975.

   b) What additional audit procedures, if any, would be necessary in connection with the hourly payrolls as of December 31, 1975?

18. During the course of an audit, it was considered advisable to make tests to satisfy yourself of the correctness of (a) wages, (b) sales allowances, and (c) raw material purchases. What documents would be required, and what procedure should be followed?

19. A company has sales for 1975 of $5,000,000. There is a Miscellaneous Expense account in the general ledger with a debit balance of $35,000. In an audit, to what extent should the Miscellaneous Expense account be verified?

20. For the entire current year under examination, a client corporation, in accordance with your recommendation made at the end of the prior year, charged all expenditures for research to current operating expense. Formerly, such expenditures, which are material in amount in relation to the company's operations, had been capitalized. The amounts so recorded in prior years are being amortized over five-year periods.

   a) State the additional audit procedures, if any, which should be followed.

   b) State the disclosures, if any, which should be made in the financial statements or in the accompanying footnotes.

   c) State the qualifications, comments, or references, if any, to be included in a short-form report in addition to the items in (b), above.

   (AICPA)

PROBLEMS

1. Based upon an audit (for year ended December 31, 1975) a number of adjustments must be made. In order for the client to realize the importance of these adjustments it is necessary to discuss with him the effect

on (*a*) net income (before federal income tax), (*b*) current liabilities, (*c*) net working capital, (*d*) provision for federal income tax, and (*e*) retained earnings.

Prepare an analysis which will indicate whether each of the above is increased (I), decreased (D), or no effect (N).

These are the adjusting entries:

(1)	Interest Expense..........................	$ 1,000	
	Accrued Interest Payable...................		$ 1,000
	Error in not accruing interest on note.		
(2)	Retained Earnings.......................	2,000	
	Stock Dividend Payable		2,000
	Error in recording stock dividend calculation on 6/30/75.		
(3)	Accrued Interest Payable...................	200	
	Interest Expense........................		200
	Interest due 1/1/76 recorded twice.		
(4)	Notes Payable–Trade.....................	4,000	
	Accounts Payable–Trade..................		4,000
	Payment on account recorded as payment on note payable.		
(5)	Profit Sharing Plan Expense	6,000	
	Profit Sharing Plan Payable		6,000
	Record provision of profit sharing plan approved by board of directors.		
(6)	FICA Tax Expense	4,000	
	Accrued FICA Tax Payable		4,000
	Record employer's FICA tax cost of payroll for week ended 12/31/75.		
(7)	Accrued Payroll Insurance Payable	3,000	
	Payroll Insurance Expense		3,000
	Cancel the accrual of federal unemployment insurance.		
(8)	Notes Payable–Bank	10,000	
	First Mortgage Loan Payable................		10,000
	Correct payment to bank made on short-term notes and not on the first mortgage.		
(9)	Federal Income Tax.......................	6,000	
	Provision for Federal Income Tax.............		6,000
	Record additional federal income tax due for 1975.		
(10)	Retained Earnings.......................	2,000	
	Dividend Payable		2,000
	Record cash dividend declaration to stockholders as of 12/28/75 record date.		

2. You were engaged to examine the financial statements of Spiker Corporation for the fiscal year ended June 30, 1975.

On May 1, 1975 the Corporation borrowed $500,000 from Second National Bank to finance plant expansion. The note agreement provided for the payment of principal and interest over two years. The existing plant was pledged as security for the loan.

Due to unexpected difficulties in acquiring the building site, the plant expansion had not begun at June 30, 1975. To make use of the borrowed funds, management decided to invest in U.S. short-term securities, and on May 16, 1975 the $500,000 was invested in such securities.

a) What are the audit objectives in the examination of short-term debt?

b) Prepare an audit program for the examination of the note agreement between Spiker and Second National Bank.

To illustrate the interrelationship of these transactions:

c) How could you verify the position of Spiker Corporation at June 30, 1975?

    d)   How would you verify interest income recorded?

    e)   How would you establish the authority for security purchases?

(AICPA, adapted)

3.   Prepare any necessary audit adjustments for the following audit findings of unrecorded transactions for the year ended December 31, 1975:

    a)   An invoice for an insurance premium in the amount of $18,000 dated December 31, 1975. Effective date of policy 12/1/75–11/30/78. Invoice unpaid at December 31, 1975, due to the invoice being misplaced by the client. Premium was paid on January 10, 1976 and check cleared bank on January 12, 1976.

    b)   An invoice for 10,000 computer payroll checks in the amount of $1,000 dated December 15, 1975. Checks had been received, but audit inspection confirms that none had been used by December 31, 1975. Invoice paid on January 22, 1976.

    c)   An invoice for a 3-year service contract on the client's electric typewriters in the amount of $1,800, dated December 1, 1975. Effective date of service contract, 11/1/75–10/31/78. The office manager overlooked approving this invoice until the date of payment—January 10, 1976.

    d)   The audit of the client's Form 941—Employer's Report of Federal Income Tax and FICA tax liability for the fourth quarter of 1975, revealed that the employer's share of the FICA tax, in the amount of $1,000, had not been recorded at December 31, 1975.

    e)   The return of your account payable verification letter from Research, Inc., indicated a balance due of $1,200. Comparison with the client's subsidiary ledger showed a balance of $1,800. The difference was due to a client error in crediting Dryer, Inc., for the $600 received from Research, Inc.

    f)   Your examination of the Subordinated Notes Payable account at December 31, 1975 revealed the following due dates:

$100,000 due 11/1/76
$100,000 due 11/1/77
$100,000 due 11/1/78

    g)   A review of the client's profit sharing plan revealed:

      1. No contribution if profits are $25,000 or less.

      2. When profits are in excess of $25,000, contribution is to be 10 percent of such excess, but not to exceed 20 percent of participants' annual salary.

      3. Profits are $90,000 and participants salaries are $120,000.

      No entry has been made to date.

    h)   A non-interest bearing note to the president, in the amount of $24,000, has been included in Accounts Payable—Non-trade. After a discussion of this situation with the board of directors on January 10, 1976, it was recorded in the minutes of that meeting—approval of the loan, but to be at an interest rate of 9 percent. The note was dated November 1, 1975, and due on demand.

    i)   The review of the sales bonus plan of your client revealed that no entry had been made for bonuses due at December 31, 1975. The provision of the plan stipulated the following:

No bonus on first $250,000 sales

10 percent on next $500,000 sales

5 percent on next $1,000,000 sales

2 percent on any sales in excess of $1,750,000 sales

Total audited net sales—$2,500,000 (Disregard payroll taxes).

j) Your client is in the process of obtaining a patent on a fixture it is currrently using in assembling its products. This is one of many patents the client has or will secure. The legal fees, in the amount of $2,400, incurred in the determination of the patentable nature of this item, have not been paid at December 31, 1975.

4. Philip established a business in 1973. Early in 1976, he entered into negotiations with Guy to form a partnership. You have been asked by the two men to audit Philip's records for 1973, 1974, and 1975.

According to Philip's statements, the net income by years follows:

Year ending December 31:

1973	$ 9,023
1974	10,109
1975	10,340

During the course of the audit, you discover the following:

			December 31	
Explanation		*1973*	*1974*	*1975*
1. *Omissions from the records:*				
A: Accrued expenses at end of year	$2,160	$2,904	$4,624
B: Accrued revenue at end of year	200	0	0
C: Prepaid expenses at end of year	902	1,210	1,406
D: Revenue received in advance at end of year . . .	0	600	0
Goods in transit at end of year, omitted from inventory:				
E: Purchase entry had been made.	0	2,610	0
F: Purchase entry had not been made	0	0	1,710
2. *Other points requiring consideration:*				
G: Depreciation had been recorded each month by a charge to expense and a credit to accumulated depreciation at a blanket rate of 1 percent of the end-of-the-month balances of the asset accounts. However, the sale in December, 1974, of certain assets was entered as a debit to Cash and a credit to the asset account for the sale price of	0	5,000	
(This asset was purchased in July, 1973, for $6,000.)				
H: No allowance existed for doubtful accounts. It is decided to set one up for the estimated losses as of December 31, 1975, for:				
1974 accounts	0	0	700
1975 accounts	0	0	1,500
and to correct the charge against each year so that it will show the losses (actual and estimated) relating to that year's sales. Accounts had been written off to expense as follows:				
1973 accounts	1,000	1,200	0
1974 accounts	0	400	2,000
1975 accounts	0	0	1,600

a) From the following (1–20) multiple-choice questions, you are to select the *one* correct answer for each question—that is, *Overstated, Understated,* or *No Effect.* Assume that accruals of any one year are reflected in the cash transactions of the following year and that prepayments of any year are reflected in the revenue or expense transactions of the following year.

What is the effect:

(1) On 1973 net income of the omission of accrued expenses as of the end of 1973?

(2) On 1974 net income of the omisssion of accrued expenses as of the end of 1973?

(3) On 1975 net income of the omission of accrued expenses as of the end of 1973?

(4) On 1974 net income of the omission of accrued expenses as of the end of 1973 and 1974, when considered together?

(5) On 1973 net income of the omission of accrued revenue at the end of 1973?

(6) On 1974 net income of the omission of accrued revenue at the end of 1973?

(7) On 1975 net income of the omission of accrued revenue at the end of 1973?

(8) On 1973 net income of the omission of prepaid expenses at the end of 1973?

(9) On 1974 net income of the omission of prepaid expenses at the end of 1973?

(10) On 1973 net income of the omission of prepaid expenses at the end of 1974?

(11) On 1975 net income of the omission of prepaid expenses at the end of 1974 and 1975, when considered together?

(12) On 1974 net income of the omission of revenue received in advance at the end of 1974?

(13) On 1975 net income of the omission of revenue received in advance at the end of 1974?

(14) On 1974 net income of the omission of goods in transit at the end of 1974?

(15) On 1975 net income of the omission of goods in transit at the end of 1974?

(16) On 1975 net income of the omission of goods in transit at the end of 1975?

(17) On 1975 net income of the omission of goods in transit at the end of 1974 and 1975, when considered together?

(18) On 1974 net income of the error in recording the sale of an asset?

(19) On 1975 net income of the error in recording the sale of an asset?

(20) On the cumulative three-year net income of the failure to use the "allowance" method in the annual charges for doubtful accounts?

b) What is the effect in the reported net income (*Increase, Decrease,* or

No Effect), if any, of the change from the direct charge-off method to the allowance method as outlined in item H?
(1)   For the year 1973?
(2)   For the year 1974?
(3)   For the year 1975?
c)   Compute the increase or decrease in net income for the year 1974 for each item (A through H).

(AICPA, adapted)

PRACTICE MATERIAL ASSIGNMENTS

Metalcraft, Incorporated: Audit Problem:
  Assignment 10, Section A: Trade Accounts Payable.
  Assignment 10, Section B: Notes Payable and Accrued Interest.
  Assignment 10, Section C: Accrued Rent.
  Assignment 11, Section A: Accrued Taxes and Tax Expense.

Colby Gears, Inc.: Holmes and Moore Audit Case:
  Trade Accounts Payable. Bank Loan. Accured Salaries and Wages. Accrued Vacation Pay. Accrued Interest Payable. Estimated Pension Fund Liability. State Taxes Accrued. F.I.C.A. Tax Accrual. Federal Unemployment Tax Accrual. State Unemployment Tax Accrual. Federal Taxes. Expense Accounts, other than those covered in prior assignments.

24

Long-Term Liabilities

Audit Objectives

For long-term liabilities, the audit objectives may be set forth as follows: (1) to obtain satisfactory evidence of the authority to issue long-term obligations; (2) to determine the adequacy of the system of internal control over the liabilities and the related interest expense; (3) to ascertain that all provisions of a trust indenture, lease agreements, or mortgages are followed; (4) to determine that any restrictions imposed by creditors are followed; (5) to determine that the debtor has conformed with all requirements in accordance with long-term liability contracts regarding sinking funds; (6) to ascertain that interest expense has been properly computed, including the proper amortization of bond premium or discount; (7) to determine that all long-term obligations are properly recorded and are properly classified in the balance sheet; (8) to determine that assets pledged as security to loans are properly disclosed; and (9) to determine availability of capital stock for convertible debt and debt issued with stock purchase warrants.

In auditing long-term liabilities it is normal to examine records, accounts, and entries related to the long-term liabilities, such as interest expense; premium or discount and its amortization; and entries for assets received in exchange for the issuance of the liabilities.

Long-Term Liabilities in General

The common methods used for financing a business enterprise are as follows: (1) the sale of capital stock; (2) the retention of net income in the business, resulting in the accretion of assets; and (3) short-term or long-term borrowing. Long-term liabilities are items of indebtedness with a maturity date more than one year removed from the balance sheet date. They include long-term notes payable, chattel mortgages, real property mortgages, permanent advances from affiliated companies, nontrusteed pension plans, bonds payable of all types, and long-term leases.

Business organizations resort to long-term financing for one of several reasons. First, the current debt of a company may be due or overdue, and because of the present impossibility of converting inventory and receivables, the current liabilities cannot be paid for some time. Long-term obligations may be issued and the proceeds used to liquidate the current debt. In many cases of this nature, the ultimate result may be financial difficulty caused by the initial inability to liquidate current liabilities. Second, borrowing may be advantageously promoted when a business is in need of additional funds and does not wish to increase its permanent equity capitalization. In such instances, the borrowing should take place only when the rate of interest is substantially below the estimated rate of net income to be realized by the employment of the borrowed funds. Third, long-term borrowing may be a cheaper method of financing than issuance of capital stock; of course, bond interest is a fixed charge against earnings, but the interest is a deductible expense for income tax purposes. Last, a shortage of funds needed for acquisition of fixed assets can be supplanted by long-term lease agreements.

SECTION I: INTERNAL CONTROL OF LONG-TERM LIABILITIES

Internal control features applicable to long-term liabilities primarily involve (1) control over the issued and unissued obligations, (2) control over the payment of interest of proper amount, and (3) the retirement of the long-term debt.

Long-term liabilities normally are authorized by the board of directors, or by a stipulated majority of the holders of other long-term obligations, or by a required majority of the stockholders.

One premise of internal control is the ascertainment that long-term liabilities are properly authorized. Proper internal control dictates that obligations authorized but unissued be prenumbered by the printer. They should not be signed in advance of issuance; that practice might permit the obtaining of unauthorized cash, and it would permit an unauthorized corporate indebtedness. The authorized but unissued bonds should be in the controlled possession of the properly authorized corporation officer, or in the possession of an independent bond trustee. When authorized bonds are sold, the trustee or the proper corporate official should receive and retain—from the board of directors—a written order to release the bonds.

Internal control of long-term obligations may be effected by the employment of a trust company as trustee for the obligations. Also, if there are many holders of long-term obligations in the form of bonds, a registrar, a transfer agent, and an interest-disbursing agent may be independently employed in order to add to the effectiveness of the control.

Redeemed bonds should be canceled, properly mutilated, and retained for audit in order to prevent their unauthorized reissuance.

A bond ledger should be used in which are shown the details of bonds issued, canceled, and outstanding. A subsidiary bondholders' ledger should be maintained by the issuing corporation or by the bond trustee, for bonds registered as to principal or interest. When summarized, the details of the subsidiary ledger should serve as control data for the auditor.

ILLUSTRATION 24-1

INTERNAL CONTROL QUESTIONNAIRE
Long-Term Liabilities

Company _____
Period Covered _____

	Yes	No	Not Applicable	Remarks
1. Are all long-term liabilities properly authorized by:				
a) The board of directors, and/or	___	___	___	_____
b) A required majority of the stockholders, and/or	___	___	___	_____
c) A required majority of the holders of other bonds?	___	___	___	_____
2. Does the client employ an independent transfer agent for registered bonds?	___	___	___	_____
3. Does the client employ an independent registrar for registered bonds?	___	___	___	_____
4. If the client does not employ an independent transfer agent or registrar:				
a) Are unsigned bonds properly controlled?	___	___	___	_____
b) Are bonds and other obligations signed prior to issuance?	___	___	___	_____
c) Are canceled obligations properly mutilated?	___	___	___	_____
5. Are at least two signatures necessary to validate an instrument for long-term borrowing?	___	___	___	_____
6. Does the client employ an interest-paying agent?	___	___	___	_____
7. If the client does not employ an independent interest-paying agent, is the control over coupons or interest checks proper?	___	___	___	_____
8. Are unclaimed interest amounts properly handled?	___	___	___	_____
9. Does the client have any convertible debt securities authorized?	___	___	___	_____
10. Have any convertible debt securities been issued?	___	___	___	_____
11. Does the client have any long-term debt with detachable warrants to purchase stock?	___	___	___	_____
12. Has provision for the valuation of these detachable warrants been recognized?	___	___	___	_____
13. Does the client have material rental or other obligations under long-term leases?	___	___	___	_____
14. Does the client have any sub-lease agreements?	___	___	___	_____
15. Have any amendments or changes been made in the client's lease agreements in the past year?	___	___	___	_____
16. Does the client have the right to take the investment credit on leased assets?	___	___	___	_____

Prepared by _____ Reviewed by _____
Date _____ Date _____

Proper internal control must be exercised over the payment of interest on long-term liabilities so that amounts in excess of the correct amount will not be paid. Interest on long-term liabilities either will be paid directly by the debtor or by an interest-paying agent. The use of an interest-paying agent facilitates internal control because there would be no point in issuing excess cash for interest to the agent.

Returned uncashed interest-payment checks should be set forth as a liability. If a corporation pays its own interest, proper control should be exercised over authorizing, preparing, and signing the interest checks, exactly as in the issuance of checks for the payment of any liability.

Long-term liabilities normally remain relatively unchanged from year to year; therefore, a complete evaluation of the internal controls need be made only once. In a repeat audit, a review of the internal controls is required only to the extent of ascertaining that they are continuing to operate as initially intended.

An internal control questionnaire for long-term liabilities is shown in Illustration 24–1.

SECTION II: AUDIT PROGRAM FOR BONDS PAYABLE

Bonds are issued for long periods of time and are used as a method of financing when large sums of money are desired. The amount of money wanted is normally too large to be conveniently obtained from one credit source, with the result that the bonds are issued in denominations of uniform amount. Credit risks thus are assumed by a large number of people.

A bond is an instrument under seal, promising to pay a specific sum at a determinable future date, together with interest at stated dates. Behind every secured bond issue is a mortgage known as a deed of trust or trust indenture. The trust indenture is held by the trustee, usually a trust company, which acts as the fiduciary representative of the bondholders. The mortgage conditionally transfers title in the pledged property to the trustee.

In his capacity as fiduciary representative, the trustee must maintain adequate records of all issues, records of the bond owners if the bonds are registered, records of exchanges between bondholders, and records of bond cancellations and redemptions. In some cases, a dual trust arrangement is established in which one trust company is appointed to act as registrar and another company is transfer agent. The registrar determines that bonds are not overissued and attends to registration details. The transfer agent is used only when registered bonds are issued, and he attends to the issuance of new bonds for those outstanding when bondholders buy and sell.

Authority for the issuance of bonds need not be provided for in the corporate charter. Subject to the laws of the state of incorporation, either

the board of directors or a stipulated percentage of the holders of preferred stock or the holders of voting common stock may authorize a
bond issue. The corporate code of regulations should set forth procedures
to be followed in issuing bonds; the auditor must examine the code and
understand those provisions. Most states set certain restrictions as a minimum of stockholder control, and further restrictions may be made by
the stockholders. In some states, for example, an approval of two thirds
of the stockholders is required before a prior-lien stock or a long-term
liability can be issued.

There are many types of bonds. *First-mortgage bonds* are secured
by specifically named real property and constitute a prior lien on the
pledged assets. The trust indenture stipulates the percentage of the bonds
that may be issued, based on the property values pledged. Limiting the
bond issue to a certain percentage of the value of the property protects
the bondholders in the event of necessary liquidation by giving them
a margin of safety over the bond issue. *Second-mortgage and subsequent
mortgage bonds* are secondary liens in the same property pledged under
the first mortgage. The equity in the pledged property is less in second-
mortgage bonds than in first-mortgage bonds; consequently, the risk is
greater than in the case of prior issues, with a resultant higher interest
rate. *Equipment trust bonds* are issued with property other than land
and buildings as security. Machinery, equipment, or rolling stock are
commonly used as security. *Collateral trust bonds* are issued on the basis
of investment stocks and bonds placed in the hands of the trustee as
collateral for the bond issue. The trust indenture usually stipulates the
market value of the securities which must be maintained by the borrower.
Debenture bonds are not secured by property or collateral but are issued
against the general credit of the corporation. *Income bonds,* like debentures, are issued against the general credit of the corporation; but the
payment of the interest is contingent upon its being earned. *Convertible
bonds* are those debt securities which are convertible into common stock
of the issuer or an affiliated company at a specified price at the option
of the holder. In addition, they may be sold at a price or have a value
at their issuance which is not significantly in excess of their face value.
Any type of bond may be issued on the basis of being payable or convertible at one maturity date, or the bonds may be issued to be retired
serially.

Registered bonds may be (*a*) registered as to principal and interest
or (*b*) registered as to principal only. Unregistered coupon bonds are
negotiable by transfer; endorsement is not necessary. Registered bonds
are registered on the records of the trustee in the name of the owner
and are transferable upon endorsement, assignment, and registration. All
transfers are entered in the records of the registrar and the transfer
agent if both are employed. If the bonds are registered as to principal
only, interest is paid by cashing the coupons; if the bonds are registered

as to principal and interest, interest checks—prepared by the issuing company or by the trustee—are mailed to the registered owner.

Audit Program for Bonds Payable

A description of the audit program (for bonds payable) follows:

Prepare or Obtain a Bond Schedule. Illustration 24–2 presents a schedule of bonds payable. The totals of the bonds issued and outstanding according to the ledger accounts should be compared with the authorizations of the board of directors or the stockholders.

Study the Trust Indenture. Based upon the laws of the state of incorporation and the provisions of the code of regulations, the auditor must determine that the authority to issue the bonds is proper. It is necessary to ascertain that the provisions of the trust indenture are being fulfilled, and any neglect or violation of the provisions should be brought to the attention of the client. In cases involving interpretation of trust indenture clauses, the auditor should confer with the attorneys for the company.

On the first audit or upon the issuance of new bonds, a signed copy of the trust indenture should be studied and the provisions of the instrument fully noted on work papers, or a copy of the indenture may be obtained. Important points to be found in the majority of trust indentures include:

a) The total amount of the bond issue authorized and the par value of each bond.

b) The amount of the bonds to be issued.

c) The date of the issue.

d) The maturity date of the issue.

e) Interest dates.

f) Interest rates.

g) Restrictions imposed upon the corporation as to the maintenance of the condition of pledged property, insurance, and tax requirements.

h) The provisions for retirement before maturity and the prices at which the bonds may be redeemed; decision as to which bonds may be called for retirement; the notice requirements to bondholders before the bonds are called for retirement.

i) Provisions for conversions of the bonds into capital stock.

j) A description of property pledged as security for the loan.

k) Sinking fund provisions, including such features as annual contributions; provisions for interest on sinking fund assets; and provisions for the addition or nonaddition to the fund of interest on issued bonds bought for the sinking fund.

l) Guaranty provisions for the payment of interest or principal, or both, including the names of the guarantors.

m) Provisions for such requirements as (1) the maintenance of working

ILLUSTRATION 24-2

LINDSEY CORPORATION

Analysis of Bonds Payable Account No. 242

December 31, 1975

		Initials	Date
Prepared By			
Approved By			

Period	Interest Payment or Accrual	Discount Amortization — No. of Months	Discount Amortization — Part to Be Amortized	Discount Amortization — Amount to Be Amortized	Effective Interest	Unamortized Discount	Bond Carrying Value
Dec. 1 (sales date)						$11,700	$ 88,300
Dec. 31, 1975	$ 500σ	1	1/117	$ 100	600σ	11,600√	88,400√√
Year ended Dec. 31, 1976	6,000	12	12/117	1,200	7,200	10,400	89,600
Year ended Dec. 31, 1977	6,000	12	12/117	1,200	7,200	9,200	90,800
Year ended Dec. 31, 1978	6,000	12	12/117	1,200	7,200	8,000	92,000
Year ended Dec. 31, 1979	6,000	12	12/117	1,200	7,200	6,800	93,200
Year ended Dec. 31, 1980	6,000	12	12/117	1,200	7,200	5,600	94,400
Year ended Dec. 31, 1981	6,000	12	12/117	1,200	7,200	4,400	95,600
Year ended Dec. 31, 1982	6,000	12	12/117	1,200	7,200	3,200	96,800
Year ended Dec. 31, 1983	6,000	12	12/117	1,200	7,200	2,000	98,000
Year ended Dec. 31, 1984	6,000	12	12/117	1,200	7,200	800	99,200
Jan. 1–Sept. 1, 1985 (maturity)	4,000	8	8/117	800	4,800	–0–	100,000
		117	117/117	$11,700			

On December 1, 1975, client sold $100,000 of 6 percent debenture bonds for $88,300, bonds maturing on September 1, 1985, 10 years from date of issue. Interest is payable semiannually on March 1 and September 1. Accrued interest for the period September 1–December 1 is $1,500.

σ Traced to cash disbursements and inspected canceled checks.

σ Compared to balance in Bond Interest Expense Account, 12/31/75.

√ Compared to balance in Unamortized Bond Discount Account, 12/31/75.

√√ Compared to balance in Bonds Payable Account, 12/31/75.

No adjustments necessary.

capital, (2) the proportion of bonds to capital stock at any one time, and (3) the appropriation of retained earnings.

n) Provisions concerning the use of money derived from the bond issue.

o) The trustee's name, duties, liability, and responsibility.

p) Provisions for the removal of a trustee and the appointment of another.

q) Duties of the trustee in the event of default of interest.

These duties are in conformity with the provisions for procedure after interest has not been paid for a stipulated number of interest periods; for example, a trust indenture may provide that 25 percent of the bondholders must advise the trustee to institute foreclosure proceedings.

Trace the Proceeds of Bonds Issued. When bonds are issued, they may be given in exchange for cash, fixed assets, or other liabilities. The price at which bonds are sold for cash must be determined and the cash receipts traced to the records. Also, entries for the recording of premiums and discounts must be reviewed.

If the issue was for cash to an underwriting syndicate or to an investment bank, contracts and remittance advices should be examined and compared with the entries for cash receipts, premiums or discounts, and syndicate charges. In succeeding examinations, the auditor should request a statement from the trustee of the bond indenture, showing the following data:

a) The balance of the bonds outstanding at the beginning of the period.

b) Bonds issued during the period and the premium or discount involved.

c) Bonds retired during the period, the unamortized premium or discount at the date of retirement, and the prices at which the bonds were retired.

d) The balance of the bonds outstanding at the end of the year.

e) The beginning balance, additions to and deductions from such beginning balance, and closing balance of the sinking fund.

f) The composition of the sinking fund.

g) A statement of any cash held but not in the sinking fund, as well as a statement of the accrued interest on sinking fund assets at the date of the balance sheet.

If the bonds were issued in exchange for fixed assets, the auditor must investigate the values of the properties taken in exchange and the authority to accept the properties in exchange for the bonds; and all entries must be examined.

If the bonds were issued in exchange for other liabilities, a practice found in corporate reorganizations, the entire agreement and the terms thereof should be reviewed, together with pertinent accounting entries.

Verify Recording of the Mortgage. In order to be certain that the bondholders are properly protected and in order to obtain assurance of the validity of a bond issue, the auditor must confirm the recording of the mortgage through correspondence with the company attorney; or if that is not feasible, he must personally inspect the mortgage records in the offices of the county recorder. This procedure will be followed only during a first examination or after the flotation of a new bond issue.

Confirm Pertinent Data. Confirmation should be obtained from the trustee under the bond indenture for bonds outstanding at the balance sheet date, bonds issued and retired during the year, and other necessary data, as set forth in Illustration 24–3.

ILLUSTRATION 24–3

LIBERTY TRUST COMPANY
Cincinnati, Ohio 45212

January 14, 1976

Quick and James, Certified Public Accountants
10 West Fourth Street
Cincinnati, Ohio 45202

Gentlemen:

In accordance with your request for information concerning the 6 percent, first-mortgage bond issue of the Keith Company, we hereby submit the following data, taken from our records as of December 31, 1975:

Original issue, twenty-year, 6%, first-mortgage bonds	$2,400,000
Retirements, at par bonds of $1,000	560,000
Outstanding, December 31, 1975	$1,840,000
Sinking fund balance	$ 52,000
Treasury bonds	0
Redemption fund balance	0
Uncashed interest coupons	200

Very truly yours,

LIBERTY TRUST COMPANY
John Atlas
Trust Officer

Frequently, the balance of outstanding bonds according to the trustee is not in agreement with the accounts of the client. Investigation usually will disclose that the last statement of the trustee has not been taken up in the records of the issuing corporation or that the issuing corporation has purchased its own bonds and held them and prior to cancellation charged Bonds Payable instead of Treasury Bonds; therefore, the auditor must reconcile all differences and prepare necessary audit adjustments when the bond accounts are analyzed. If a trustee is employed, his periodic reports serve as data to be used for the verification of bond transactions. If there is no trustee, the vouchers, cash receipts, and other records of the company constitute the data for verification purposes.

If there is no trustee, registered bondholders may be circularized for confirmations of their holdings; the confirmation replies should be compared with the corporation's record of its bondholders, and the total of the bonds outstanding according to the subsidiary accounts must agree with the balance of the control account. Normally, such confirmations are requested only in the event of suspicion. If the proceeds of a bond issue are fully accounted for, it is relatively easy to determine an understatement of the bond liability. In addition, if a reconciliation can be effected by starting with the bonds outstanding at the beginning of the fiscal period, adding the bonds sold, and deducting bond retirements, the balance at the close of the period is assured if proper proof of purchases and sales has been obtained.

Verify Treasury Bond Transactions.   Treasury bonds include those issued and later reacquired by the issuing corporation *and* unissued bonds of the original issue. Thus, treasury bonds differ from treasury stock. Treasury bonds are not an asset of the issuing corporation, although they may be pledged as security for other loans.

When treasury bonds are acquired by purchase in the open market or directly from bondholders, they may be charged to the Treasury Bond account at cost of acquisition. The Treasury Bond account must be adjusted to par not later than the balance sheet date, or an accurate liability balance will not be shown. Adjustments also must be made for unamortized premiums or discounts as of the acquisition date, and the loss or gain on acquisition should be closed to profit and loss.

ILLUSTRATIONS.   a) Bonds of $200,000 par value, originally issued at par, are purchased as treasury bonds, at a cost of $206,000. At the date of purchase, the entry is as follows:

Treasury Bonds	206,000	
Cash		206,000

The following entry also will be made:

Loss on Acquisition of Treasury Bonds	6,000	
Treasury Bonds		6,000

If the $206,000 were subtracted from the total bonds issued, the net liability in the balance sheet would be understated by $6,000.

b)   Par value of bonds of $200,000, carried at a net amortized issuance price of $197,000, were purchased as treasury bonds for $206,000. At the date of purchase, the entry is as follows:

Treasury Bonds	206,000	
Cash		206,000

The following entry also will be made:

Loss on Acquisition of Treasury Bonds	9,000	
Unamortized Discount		3,000
Treasury Bonds		6,000

c) Par value of bonds of $200,000, carried at a net amortized issuance price of $197,000, were purchased as treasury bonds for $192,000. At the date of purchase, the entry is as follows:

Treasury Bonds	192,000	
Cash		192,000

The following entry also will be made:

Treasury Bonds	8,000	
Unamortized Discount		3,000
Profit on Acquisition of Treasury Bonds		5,000

In the balance sheet, treasury bonds—and unissued bonds—should be deducted from the par value of the total authorized issue, and the net remaining liability should be extended. The APB, in *Opinion No. 26*, concluded that extinguishment of such type of debt before scheduled maturities should be recognized currently but should be identified as separate items.

The Treasury Bond account at the beginning of the period, plus purchased treasury bonds adjusted to par, less treasury bond credits adjusted to par, will equal the account balance at par at the end of the period. Debits and credits to the Treasury Bond account must be examined for the period under audit. Generally, credits to the Treasury Bond account are for bonds given to the trustee for cancellation. In the minutes of the meetings of the board of directors, there should be an authorization for each purchase and sale of treasury bonds. By comparing charges and credits in the Treasury Bond account with the minutes, the auditor may judge the propriety of the handling of treasury bonds. On succeeding audits, the series and number of each treasury bond should be compared with those in preceding work papers.

Treasury bonds held by the corporation should be counted, inspected, and listed in the work papers as to series and number. The custodian of the treasury bonds should be requested to sign a receipt certifying their return to him after the auditor has completed his examination of the items. Treasury bonds held by a trustee should be confirmed directly to the auditor. If treasury bonds have been pledged as collateral for loans, confirmation of the bonds should be obtained from the creditor.

ILLUSTRATION. A company treasurer prepared a certificate stating that certain treasury bonds were in the safe-deposit vault of the bank; the bank already had confirmed a loan secured by the same bonds as loan collateral; however, the treasurer did not know that this confirmation had been made.

Interest is paid on treasury bonds in some cases and is not paid in other instances; it should not be paid if the issuing company (and not a sinking fund trustee) holds its own bonds. If interest is paid on treasury bonds, a credit to Interest Income is created, and the auditor must ascertain that the net interest expense has been correctly stated.

Examine Bond Retirements. Retired bonds should be evidenced by the mutilated bond or a cremation certificate. An auditor must always be certain that the evidence for retired bonds is beyond question.

ILLUSTRATION. Failure to obtain proper evidence may be exemplified as follows: A company purchased $100,000 of its own bonds, and the treasurer stated that the bonds had been destroyed by burning. The accounting records showed a charge to Bonds Payable and a credit to Cash for the proper amount. There was no cremation certificate, but the authority for the purchase was in the minutes book of the board of directors. Three months after the conclusion of the audit, the "destroyed" bonds were presented for payment by a creditor who had loaned the chairman of the board of directors $80,000 and taken the bonds as loan security.

If retired bonds are not canceled or destroyed, there is the possibility of their being issued again—fraudulently, or in violation of the trust agreement. If a sinking fund is not in existence, the evidence of retirement is in the cash records and in the inspection of the retired bonds. All coupons subsequent to the date of retirement should be attached to the retired bonds. If the bonds have been retired by refunding, the audit procedure is substantially the same as if cash had been paid.

When bonds are retired, a profit or loss on redemption must be verified. If the bond issue has been paid in full, ascertainment must be made that the deed of trust has been canceled. All charges to the Bonds Payable account should represent retirements.

If bonds acquired by the trustee are held by him as an investment (which he may sell later), the bonds are kept alive, and interest usually is paid on them. When bonds are kept alive, a footnote should state the amount so held.

The auditor must also determine that all unamortized bond premiums and discounts applicable to retired bonds have been eliminated. Verification must be made of all entries in the unamortized premium and discount accounts to determine that proper amortization has been taken at each interest period.

Examine Sinking Fund Transactions. Sinking funds may be voluntary or may be one of the requirements of the trust indenture. If a sinking fund is in operation, a schedule must be prepared showing the charges, credits, and balance of the sinking fund; and if the sinking fund is not in the hands of a sinking fund trustee, each transaction should be verified.

The auditor must determine the accuracy of the periodic contributions to the sinking fund, must be certain that the sinking fund is adequate, must acertain that the provisions of the trust indenture are being met, and must be familiar with the terms of the sinking fund contract. Estimates of necessary sinking fund contributions are made at the time the sinking fund is started. These estimates seldom are accurate when actual interest and contributions are accumulated, thus leaving a deficiency or an excess in the fund. If a deficiency exists, it must be covered by additional contributions so that the fund is not below its theoretically computed amount at the end of any fiscal period.

Sinking fund assets are composed of stocks, bonds, cash, and accrued interest. Bonds in the fund may be those of the issuing corporation bought in conformity with the provisions of the trust indenture. If a sinking fund trustee is not used, the auditor must inspect the sinking fund assets; if a trustee exists, confirmation is obtained from him. In the majority of cases, interest on sinking fund assets is added to the fund. If a sinking fund trustee is not used, bonds of the issuing company held as sinking fund assets should be valued at par and deducted from the bonds outstanding in the same manner as treasury bonds. If the bonds are in the hands of a sinking fund trustee, the issuing company has no control over them; and the sinking fund trustee should price them at cost, with proper amortization of premium and discount. If the sinking fund is not held by a trustee, discounts and premiums on the issuing company's bonds purchased for the sinking fund should be credited or debited to the proper revenue or expense account in the same manner as when bonds are retired.

Verify Interest Expense, the Amortization of Premium or Discount and Interest Accruals. The bond interest expense for each period must be verified. Interest should be accrued to the last day of the fiscal period. To arrive at the true net interest cost, the auditor must ascertain that premiums and discounts are properly amortized. The interest expense analysis constitutes a good indication of the correctness of the bond liability. For coupon bonds, where the company *does not* retain a disbursing agent, it is common practice to deposit the periodic interest in a special bank account, which will be reduced as the coupons are cashed. The total dollar amount of the coupons cashed is determined by confirming the bank balance and reconciling it with the cashed coupons. The remaining amount of uncashed interest coupons is retained in the liability account for accrued interest payable. Cashed coupons should be mutilated to avoid presentation a second time.

For bond coupons when the company *does* retain a disbursing agent, the periodic interest is deposited with the disbursing agent who after disbursing the deposited cash returns the cashed coupons to the issuing company. The cash for the unredeemed coupons normally is retained by the disbursing agent for a reasonable period and then returned to the issuing company. The auditor should obtain a certification from the disbursing agent of the balance of cash on hand and the cashed coupons on hand, if any, and reconcile the two items to the interest accounts of the client.

Expenses of the trustee and the disbursing agents are current expenses of the bond-issuing corporation. The auditor must determine that they have been recorded as such. Expenses of the trustee are verified by examination of the trustee's report.

If a company issues its own checks in payment of bond interest, the paid checks should be compared with the list of registered bondholders at each interest date for name of the bondholder, amount, and endorsements. Unclaimed interest checks should be carefully controlled and should be listed by the auditor; if cashed prior to the subsequent audit, endorsements should be examined and the bondholders' records examined for transfers and changes in mailing addresses.

Premiums received upon the issuance of bonds should be prorated over the life of the bonds as a credit to Bond Interest. The auditor must verify the annual credit to Bond Interest arising from this source. When bonds originally sold at a premium are retired at a date preceding maturity, the remaining unamortized premium, less any redemption premiums, should be taken into income in the year of retirement. If the bonds are refunded prior to maturity, the remaining unamortized premium may be (1) credited to income in the year of retirement, (2) prorated over the life of the new bond issue as a credit to Bond Interest, or (3) prorated over the remaining life of the refunded issue just as though refunding had not occurred.

Bond issuance costs may be amortized on the same basis as bond discount, or they may be charged to expense at incurrence. If the bonds were issued at a premium, issuance costs may be deducted from the premium and the net premium amortized.

Review Insurance Coverage of Pledged Assets. Insurance coverage must be reviewed, from the standpoint of the minimum requirements of the bond indenture and also from the point of view of the adequacy of the coverage in the light of current market prices of the pledged assets.

SECTION III: AUDIT PROGRAM FOR MORTGAGES PAYABLE

The audit objectives in the examination of mortgages payable are to ascertain the authority to mortgage and that they are legal obligations of the client, to determine that the property or money received for the mortgage is properly accounted for by the mortgagor, to determine the propriety of interest and principal payments, and to ascertain the principal balance at the balance sheet date.

A mortgage is a conditional transfer of title to property, and it states that the transfer is void if the mortgage note is paid. The debt under the mortgage is evidenced by the execution of a note by the mortgagor which is held by the mortgagee until final liquidation. The lien on the property—that is, the mortgage—is security for the loan. Mortgage notes stipulate the periodic interest payments and also principal payments if the mortgage is to be paid on an installment basis. Mortgages arise from such sources as a loan, a purchase of property unencumbered, and a purchase of property with an existing mortgage which is assumed by the new owner.

Audit Program for Mortgages Payable

The procedures to be followed for the examination of mortgages payable developed in the following subsections.

Determine Authority to Mortgage. Reference should be made to the charter, code of regulations, and minutes of the meetings of stockholders and directors (or partners) to determine that the authority to mortgage is proper. In a first audit, these records and *all* contracts must be examined. In a repeat engagement, only the minutes and mortgage contracts for the year need be examined. Correspondence and agreements for the provisions of each mortgage must be examined. The work papers should contain notations for the authority for the placing of the mortgages or the assumption of mortgages on property acquired.

The auditor should determine the purpose of each mortgage. Mortgages may be placed to obtain working capital, to purchase assets outright, to finance a balance due on an asset, or to liquidate other liabilities. A statement of the purposes of mortgages placed during the period under examination should be included in the audit report. If a mortgage of a prior owner has been assumed it should be shown as a liability, and the related asset should be included at its gross cost. If property was purchased subject to a mortgage (only the vendor's equity acquired), the gross cost likewise should be shown as an asset and the liability also shown.

The auditor should be certain that mortgaged property is adequately insured and that all requirements placed on the mortgagor with respect to insurance, maintenance, and taxes are being fulfilled. Some mortgages state that if interest payments or principal installment payments are not met when due, the balance of the mortgage is immediately due. Notations of such features should be made on the work papers.

Prepare or Obtain a Mortgage Schedule. Schedules for mortgages payable may assume a variety of forms. A list of the mortgages payable may be obtained from the files of the proper official of the company; each mortgage in the list must be compared with the subsidiary records, and the total of the subsidiary balances reconciled with the balance of the controlling account. Data for the mortgage schedule may be obtained from general and subsidiary ledger accounts and from the mortgage copy. In Illustration 24–4, it should be noted that the property pledged under the mortgage is listed.

Vouch Mortgage Proceeds. Proceeds for mortgage issuance should be vouched to the credit of the mortgage accounts. As credits to the mortgage payable accounts are vouched for the year under review, the nature and purpose of each credit must be understood. Property and cash received for the mortgage given are traced to the debits of the accounts involved. If property other than cash has been obtained, the purchase contracts for the acquired assets are examined. If an existing debt has been discharged by the mortgage, the auditor must investigate the legitimacy of the debt. Cash receipts records must be watched for evidences of unreported mortgages.

Vouch Principal Payments. Charges to mortgage accounts made during the period under examination should be verified. Cash disbursements records, paid checks, and confirmations from the mortgagee are examined for these data, together with notations on the mortgage notes for principal payments.

It is not common to record payments on mortgage principal on the public records to show the reduced amount of the lien on the property. The only reason for insisting that principal payments be recorded is that if a third party acquires a mortgage and pays the original face value for it, the mortgagor can be held for that amount by the third party who was innocent of the knowledge of partial principal payments.

Confirm Mortgages and Interest. Confirmation of mortgages should be obtained from the mortgagee, requesting the amount of the mortgage, interest rate, interest dates, maturity dates, payment arrangements, principal and interest payments during the period, and the mortgage balance due. Installment agreements also should be verified. Responses must be compared with the mortgage schedule. If there are a large number of small mortgages, the confirmation requests are on a test basis.

Verify Mortgage Interest. A test of the interest payments should be made on a scale sufficient to assure their accuracy and to convince the auditor that evidences of unrecorded liens do not exist. Paid checks for interest, as well as interest receipts, should be traced through the cash disbursements records to each specific mortgage. The interest accrued from the last interest payment date to the end of the period must be verified.

Confirm Mortgage Cancellations. If a mortgage has been paid, that allegation should be verified by correspondence with the client's attorney or by investigation of the cancellation on the county records. Returned notes indicating full receipt of payment also constitute evidence of liquidation—but not evidence of record cancellation.

ILLUSTRATION 24-4

KEITH COMPANY
Analysis of Mortgages Payable Account No. 243
December 31, 1975

	Initials	Date
Prepared By		
Approved By		

Mortgagee	Property and Location	Amount of Mortgage	Date Due	Interest %	Interest Dates	Installments Prior to 1975	Installments 1975	Balance Dec. 31, 1975	Interest Paid, 1975	Accrued Interest Dec. 31, 1975	Property Value
Oldtown Bank 4 E. 10th St.	4th and Stadium Plant A	$100,000√	Oct. 1, 1977	9	4/1 10/1	$60,000	$10,000 Paid Oct. 1, 1975	$ 30,000	$3,600φ	$ 900φ 3 mos. on $30,000	$220,000
Arthur Flynn 5631 W. 3rd St.	4th and Stadium Plant B	60,000√	Jan. 1, 1979	9	1/1 7/1	None	None	60,000	5,400φ	2,700φ	100,000
First Bank & Trust Co. St. Peters, Indiana	St. Peters, Indiana, Plant E ⊙∧√	150,000√Z	July 2, 1985	10	1/2 7/2	None	7,500 Paid on Dec. 31, 1975	142,500φ	None	7,500φ	400,000
		$310,000					$17,500	$232,500W	$9,000	$11,100	

⊙ Mortgage on Plant E, St. Peters, Indiana, negotiated on July 2, 1975.
∧ Twenty (20) notes given, for $7,500 each, payable one each six months, on January 2 and July 2.
√ Proceeds used to build plant additions. Contracts examined for all work done. Records verified for payments, which totaled $153,668.76.
Z Proceeds traced to records and to the First Bank and Trust Co.
φ Interest paid and accrued verified; in agreement with company records.
W Agrees with control account.
√ Confirmed.

SECTION IV: LONG-TERM NOTES PAYABLE

Long-term notes are those that do not mature within one year. They may be analyzed on the work papers along with current notes payable annotated to indicate their life, or they may be separately analyzed and the work papers filed with the long-term liability papers. If long-term notes are for the purchase of fixed assets, they should be separated from notes due trade creditors, whether these are long-term or short-term notes. Installment contracts are examined to obtain data relative to purchase price, installments, and interest; the fixed asset accounts are examined to see that the accounts are charged at full contract price and not at the amount paid to date. Many installment contracts provide for the retention of title by the seller until the notes are paid; even so, the assets should be recorded at full cost on the records of the buyer. Payments made on the notes should be verified in the usual manner, by paid check, voucher, and accounting record examination. Notes paid in full should be on hand and canceled to prevent reissuance; these notes should be examined by the auditor. Confirmations are requested from holders of notes and compared with the balances according to the records.

SECTION V: PENSION PLANS

Pension plans assume a variety of forms, ranging from trusteed pension funds down to self-administered plans. If an employer has a liability to make current deposits into a pension fund at a balance sheet date, that obligation should be set forth as a current liability. Funds provided by the employer may be deposited periodically with a trustee (insurance company, bank, trust company, or other approved fiduciary) under an approved plan. When a pension plan has been adopted by an employer, consistency should prevail both in accounting for the plan and in its application to the employer and the employees.

Periodic premiums are expenses in the period of incurrence, and all accrued premiums should be set forth as liabilities in the balance sheet. *Accounting Research Bulletin No. 43* treats of pension plan costs which are known as annuity costs—the costs necessary to cover an employee for services performed *prior* to the adoption of the plan. Although some accountants are of the opinion that pension costs based on past services should be charged to Retained Earnings because those past services already have been rendered, *Bulletin No. 43* contains the following statement:

. . . . even though the calculation is based on past service, costs of annuities based on such service are incurred in contemplation of present and future services, not necessarily of the individual affected but of the organization as a whole, and therefore should be charged to the present and future periods benefited.

The Committee, accordingly, is of the opinion that:

a) Costs of annuities based on past service should be allocated to current and future periods; however, if they are not sufficiently material in amount to distort the results of operations in a single period, they may be absorbed in the current year.

b) Costs of annuities based on past service should not be charged to surplus.

Accounting Research Bulletin No. 47 further explores the complex nature of accounting for costs of pension plans. It points out that such items as social security benefits, employee turnover, future compensation levels, future earnings of the pension fund, and varying retirement ages complicate the problem of determining the ultimate cost of pensions. Recognizing the importance of these and other factors that can be considered, it still is desirable to have pension costs based upon actuarial calculations and the costs so determined should be systematically accrued during the expected period of active service of the covered employees. The resulting calculations will undoubtedly serve as a basis for funding the plan and will also serve for accounting purposes. *Bulletin No. 47* also calls attention to the need for recognizing costs based on past services and points out that such costs have been charged off over a 10- to 12-year period in some actual cases. This procedure would most likely affect a reasonable matching of costs and revenues.

As indicated in *Bulletin No. 43 and Bulletin No. 47*, accounting for the cost of pension plans is a very important part of an audit program. The AICPA further expressed its concern on this subject through the publication of the *Opinions of the Accounting Principles Board No. 8.* Again the many facets of the problem were explored and more direction given to the auditor to insure the proper examination of all documents as well as proper financial statement presentation of any and all types of pension plans that he might come in contact with during the course of an audit. The following are some of the opinions expressed in *APB Opinion No. 8:*

A company may limit its legal obligation by specifying that pensions shall be payable only to the extent of the assets in the pension fund.

To be acceptable for determining cost for accounting purposes, an actuarial cost method should be rational and systematic and should be consistently applied so that it results in a reasonable measure of pension cost from year to year.

Actuarial gains and losses, including realized investment gains and losses, should be given effect in the provision for pension cost in a consistent manner that reflects the long-range nature of pension cost.

All employees who may reasonably be expected to receive benefits under a pension plan should be included in the cost calculations, giving appropriate recognition to anticipated turnover.

A company that has more than one pension plan need not use the same actuarial cost method for each one; however, the accounting for each plan should conform to opinions set forth in APB No. 8.

Other opinions are expressed on such subjects as defined-contribution plans, insured plans, effect of funding, income taxes, disclosure, changes in accounting methods, and transition to recommended practices. The auditor is thus provided with comprehensive direction in the performance of that portion of the audit relating to the pension plans of a client.

In order to qualify under the Internal Revenue Code, annuity costs based on past services must be spread over the present and future periods.

If payments into the pension fund for past services are made in a lump sum and if a deferred charge to future operations is charged at that time, the allocation to future expense periods is a matter of individual judgment and expediency; for federal income tax purposes, the prepaid costs are allocable over a minimum period of 10 years if the initial past-period service cost is immediately paid in full, or approximately 12 years if 1/10 of the initial past-period service cost plus interest is paid each year.

As stated in the opening paragraph of this section, an obligation to make current deposits into a pension fund should be set forth as a current liability. If a company maintains and controls its own pension fund, how should the *total* pension fund liability be shown? In practice, there is no uniform answer to this question. Some companies show the total of the liability as a liability, some show it as a retained earnings segregation, and some show the item separately between liabilities and capital—usually accompanied by a title similar to "reserve for pension fund." The authors are of the opinion that the total is a long-term liability and should be shown as such.

Generally, in order to qualify under the Internal Revenue Code, pension funds must be deposited with an approved fund trustee. In this case, the company establishing the fund is not in possession of the fund assets and does not show fund assets or liabilities, other than currently due payments. Also, if the pension funds are trusteed, any future financial difficulty of the employer will not threaten the accumulated funds.

In the examination of the obligation of a client for the maintenance of pension agreements, the auditor's investigation should be made to ascertain that pension agreement terms are being fulfilled by the client and that the liabilities—current and long-term—under the agreement are properly stated. The auditor should include in his permanent file a copy of the pension plan agreement. Illustration 24–5 sets forth one form of work paper for pension fund plans.

If a self-administered pension plan is in existence which may be eliminated or curtailed by the employer, a liability need not be accrued, and payments may be charged to expense as they are paid—although there is no practical or theoretical objection to accruing a liability.

ILLUSTRATION 24-5

CALHOUN CORPORATION

Analysis of Pension Fund Transactions
For the Years Ended December 31

	1971	1972	1973	1974	1975
Balance at beginning of year	$ -0-	$304,400	$530,000	$ 774,000	$1,048,600
Additions:					
Company contributions	200,000	120,000	140,000	160,000	180,000
Employee contributions	100,000	120,000	140,000	160,000	180,000
Interest: 6% of average balance	4,400	12,600	20,000	28,000	36,800
Total	$304,400	$557,000	$830,000	$1,122,000	$1,445,400
Deductions:					
Benefits paid (below)	$ -0-	$ 24,000	$ 74,200	$ 66,000	$ 84,000
Refunds to employees	-0-	3,000	8,800	7,400	10,400
Total	$ -0-	$ 27,000	$ 56,000	$ 73,400	$ 94,400
Balance at end of year	$304,400	$530,000	$774,000	$1,048,600	$1,351,000
	ȡ	ȡ	ȡ	ȡ	ȡ

Schedule of Benefits Paid for Years Indicated

Date	Benefits Paid To	Type	1972	1973	1974	1975
3/1/72	Albert	Annuity	$ 6,000σ	$ 7,200σ	$ 7,200σ	$ 7,200σ
7/1/72	Bord	Death	18,000σ	-0-	-0-	-0-
3/1/73	Carl	Annuity		24,000σ	28,800σ	28,800σ
5/1/73	Dan	Annuity		16,000σ	19,200σ	19,200σ
7/1/74	Earl	Annuity			1,200σ	2,400σ
8/1/74	Ford	Death			6,200σ	-0-
9/1/74	Guy	Annuity			1,600σ	4,800σ
10/1/74	Haden	Annuity			1,800σ	7,200σ
5/1/75	Innis	Annuity				3,200σ
6/1/75	James	Annuity				4,200σ
9/1/75	Katz	Annuity				7,000σ
			$24,000	$47,200	$66,000	$84,000

ȡ Confirmed with trustees of fund—Simonds National Bank.
σ Inspected cancelled checks supporting these amounts.

SECTION VI: LEASES

Almost every business today, regardless of size, is financing some part of its operations through the leasing process. *Accounting Research Bulletin No. 43* makes two principal recommendations:

(1) . . . where the rentals or other obligations under long term leases are material in the circumstances, the committee is of the opinion that:

(a) disclosure should be made in financial statements or in notes thereto of:

    (1) the amounts of annual rentals to be paid under such leases with some indication of the periods for which they are payable and

    (2) any other important obligation assumed or guarantee made in connection therewith;

(b) the above information should be given not only in the year in which the transaction originates but also as long thereafter as the amounts involved are material; and

(c) in addition, in the year in which the transaction originates, there should be disclosure of the principal details of any important sale-and-lease transaction.

(2) . . . the committee is of the opinion that the facts relating to all such leases should be carefully considered and that, where it is clearly evident that the transaction involved is in substance a purchase, the "leased" property should be included among the assets of the lessee with suitable accounting for the corresponding liabilities and for the related charges in the income statement.

These statements clearly set forrth the facts an auditor must look for as he examines a client's lease agreements. Merely the right to use property in exchange for future rental payments does not create an equity in the property and are thus nothing more than executory contracts. *APB Opinion No. 5* further points out that the rights and obligations related to the unperformed parts of these lease agreements are not recognized as assets and liabilities in the client's financial statements. The Board further expands its opinion in *Opinion No.* 7 and recommends that the "operating method" be used and that a lessor should recognize revenue in each accounting period equivalent to the amount of rent receivable under the lease. In the same opinion, the Board recommends the use of the "financing method" when the excess of aggregate rentals over the cost of the leased property probably will be expected to compensate the lessor for the use of the funds invested. In providing guidance for the auditor who deals with the lessee, the APB in *Opinion No. 31* recommends that financial statements of lessees disclose sufficient information regarding non-capitalized lease agreements so that users of the statements can accurately determine the effect of this agreement upon the financial statements of the lessee, and spells out in detail the extent to which the auditor must go so that an unqualified opinion may be rendered.

In addition to reviewing the lease agreement to determine the nature and extent of liability, the auditor must determine who is entitled to the investment credit on the leased assets. He also must determine how this should be reflected in the financial statements. While the method of reporting the investment credit writeoff over the life of the acquired assets is considered preferable, the alternate method of treating the credit as a reduction of taxes of the year in which the credit arises is also acceptable.

Illustration 24–6 shows one form of leasing agreement. However, leases which are essentially installment purchases of property should be so recorded. The Board also indicates that where the lease agreement is "in substance" a purchase, full recording of the transaction must be made giving recognition to the acquisition of the asset and the setting-up of the related liability. Full disclosure as to the significant provisions of

ILLUSTRATION 24–6

THE TRUST LEASING COMPANY

Fourth Street, Cincinnati, Ohio   45201

February 19, 1975

R & G Incorporated
Trust Building
Cincinnati, Ohio   45275

Gentlemen:

It is a pleasure to inform you that we hereby offer to enter into a leasing transaction with you under the terms of the lease and schedule enclosed herewith and upon the following additional terms and conditions:

Equipment: One New IBM Model 370

Location: Trust Building, Cincinnati, Ohio

Cost of Equipment: $832,000

Term of Lease: Eight (8) Years

Rent: Thirty-Two (32) Quarterly Payments of $35,764.36 each

Renewal Option: $20,800 per annum

Expiration Date of This Commitment: April 30, 1975

Insurance Procedures: As set forth on the attachment incorporated herein.

ILLUSTRATION 24–6 (*Continued*)

SCHEDULE

Schedule No._____01_____

A. EQUIPMENT LEASED: As described on Indenture and Bill of Sale dated February 28, 1975, of R & G Incorporated to The Trust Leasing Company attached hereto and made a part hereof by this reference.

B. TERM: Unless sooner terminated as set forth in the lease, the term of this lease respecting each item of equipment listed on this schedule expires on March 3, 1983,

C. RENT: As rent for said equipment, lessee shall pay lessor the sum of $1,144,459.52. Except as otherwise provided in the lease or in this schedule said rent shall be payable in__32____ installments, commencing on__March 3____, 1975 as follows:

$35,764.36 per quarter, until rent is paid.

Unless sooner paid, all said rent shall be payable in any event on or before the expiration or sooner termination of this lease.

D. LOCATION: The above described equipment shall be located at Trust Building, Cincinnati, Hamilton County, Ohio and shall not be removed therefrom without the prior written consent of lessor.

E. DEPOSIT: $ None___, pursuant to paragraph 16 of the lease of which this schedule is a part.

F. RENEWAL OPTION: Lessee may renew the lease of which this schedule is a part, on a year-to-year basis, upon expiration of original term thereof, at a rental of $10,400.00 per year, and otherwise upon the same terms and conditions of the said lease. Said option may be exercised by lessee's written notice to that effect to lessor, not less than sixty (60) days before the expiration of the term of said lease. Said annual rent shall be payable in advance.

G. STIPULATED LOSS VALUE: Amount to be paid persuant to paragraph 9 of said lease for each unit lost, stolen, destroyed or damaged beyond repair during each year of the term thereof:

1st Year $704,000   2nd Year $ 693,600   3rd Year $ 653,400   4th Year $ 599,400

5th Year $540,600   6th Year $476,800   7th Year $ 407,700   8th Year $ 298,000

H. SPECIAL CONDITIONS: Personnel property and sales tax will be paid by lessee.

APPROVED AND AGREED TO this 28th day of February, 1975, as a schedule to that certain lease dated the 19th day of February, 1975, by and between the parties hereto, and made a part hereof.

TRUST LEASING COMPANY   R & G INCORPORATED

By R. J. Stenger, Pres.   By J. T. Radar, Pres.
    Title   Title

By D. L. Long, Exec. V. Pres.   By R. B. Good, V. Pres.
    Title   Title
        Lessor   Lessee
(Seal)   (Seal)
Address_____   Address_____

either situation, lease or installment acquisition, must be made in the body of the statements or footnotes thereto.

SECTION VII: FINANCIAL STATEMENT CONSIDERATIONS

As pointed out in previous sections, in the presentation of long-term liabilities in a balance sheet, it is essential that they be fully disclosed and adequately described. Each long-term liability category should be set forth under a separate title in the balance sheet, properly footnoted, if necessary, to include the exact name of the obligation, total amount authorized and issued, maturity dates, interest rates, conversion rights, restrictions on dividends, working capital maintenance requirements, a cross-reference to pledged assets, and any subordination of long-term debt to other liabilities.

Long-term liabilities are frequently subdivided into two groups, namely, long-term debt issued under an indenture or other formal agreement and long-term liabilities such as deferred credits, customers' deposits, product guaranties, and estimated liabilities for tax or other disputed claims.

Bonds payable may be carried in the balance sheet at par, together with maturity dates and interest rates; or they may be carried at par plus unamortized premium or minus unamortized discount. If the latter method is followed, the result will be to show the bond liability at its carrying value. Also, bond discount is not an asset.

If a trustee is not employed, sinking fund bonds of the issuing company, retired bonds, unissued bonds, and treasury bonds (whether or not they are kept alive) should be deducted at par from the total authorized issue and the net liability extended. Treasury bonds kept alive for resale often are shown as assets; preferably, they should be shown as deductions from the gross liability because the liability to be liquidated has been reduced by the acquisition of the bonds, in spite of intentions which—at the balance sheet date—are not fulfilled. A balance sheet should show existing conditions, not expectations.

If a bond issue—or one series of a total serial issue—is payable within one year and if a special fund is not available for the payment, the amount currently due should be moved to the current liability classification. If a special fund is available for the repayment of the amounts currently due, the fund becomes a current asset at the time the transfer is made from long-term to current liabilities. Where special payment funds are available, it is preferable to permit both the fund and the liability to remain in their usual positions; for by their removal to the current sections, the current ratio is disturbed.

In the case of convertible debt and debt issued with stock purchase warrants, the auditor must exercise extreme care in statement presentation. When stock purchase warrants are attached to debt, that portion of the proceeds which is allocable to the warrants should be accounted for as paid-in capital and the allocation should be based on the relative fair values of the two securities at time of issuance. If an entire convertible debenture note issue has been called for redemption in stock, the appropriate amounts may be included in the capital section of the balance sheet with appropriate full disclosure in a footnote. The following information briefed from Alpha Industries, Inc., 1974 Annual Report illustrates the need for full disclosure of the intricate nature of long-term liabilities.

	March 31	
	1974	*1973*
ILLUSTRATION. 6% convertible subordinated debentures (Notes A and C)	$704,000	$ 789,000
Long-term notes payable (Note B)	956,545	1,016,359
Deferred income taxes (Note D)	173,061	168,716
Deferred Income (Note A)	49,163	52,763

The accompanying notes are an integral part of these financial statements.

Note A—Reacquisition of Convertible Subordinated Debentures

In fiscal 1973, the Company changed its method of accounting for gains and losses arising from the reacquisition of its convertible subordinated debentures to conform with current generally accepted accounting principles. Such gains and losses are recognized currently in income of the period of reacquisition. In prior years gains arising from such reacquisitions were deferred and are being amortized over the period the remaining debentures are outstanding.

Note B—Long-term Notes Payable

Long-term notes payable at March 31, 1974 and 1973 are as follows:

	1974	*1973*
Mortgage note, with interest at the prime rate (which averages 9% in 1974) and payable in quarterly installments of $20,000 until November 1976 and thereafter in equal quarterly installments of $48,644 until August 1980, collateralized by property, plant and equipment with a net book value approximately $1,305,000	$ 978,302	$1,058,302
Equipment purchase contract, noninterest bearing, payable in annual installments of $15,000 until September 1976, less imputed interest at 6½% of $3,982	41,018	53,057
Other debt, payable in installments to March, 1978	45,647	–
	$1,064,967	$1,111,359
Less installments due currently	(108,422)	(95,000)
	$ 956,545	$1,016,359

Note C—Convertible Subordinated Debentures

The 6% convertible subordinated debentures are due December 15, 1987 and are convertible into common stock of the Company at $17.50 per share. Debentures may be called at prices decreasing from 104% of face value currently to 100% in 1987. The indenture provides for retirement through purchase or sinking fund redemption at $50,000 principal amount on or before each December 15, commencing in 1972. During fiscal year 1974 $100,000 principal amount of debentures previously reacquired and held in the treasury were retired to satisfy December 15, 1974 and 1973 sinking fund requirements.

Debentures outstanding as of March 31, 1974 of $704,000 are after deduction of reacquired debentures with a face value of $196,000 held in treasury for future sinking fund requirements. Such debentures were acquired for less than face value.

The indenture contains restrictions on the payment of cash dividends. At March 31, 1974 $328,053 of the Company's retained earnings were free of such restrictions.

Note D—Federal Income Taxes

The provision for income taxes consists of:

	1974	1973
Federal income taxes		
—currently payable	$253,155	$158,859
—deferred	4,345	(13,246)
State income taxes	53,894	22,942
	$311,394	$168,555

Deferred income taxes at March 31, 1974 arise principally from certain costs associated with relocating the Company's facilities in 1971 which were capitalized for financial reporting purposes but which were expensed for Federal income tax purposes.

The provision for income tax is different from that which would be obtained by applying the statutory Federal income tax rate of 48% to income before income taxes. The items causing this difference are as follows:

	1974	1973
Income tax at statutory rate of 48% less surtax exemption	$433,413	$149,020
State income taxes, net	28,025	11,930
Investment tax credit	(21,300)	(22,000)
Reduction from investment income taxed at capital gains rate	(120,845)	(3,752)
Increase due to expenses not deductible for tax purposes	6,403	29,040
Other	(14,302)	4,317
	$311,394	$168,555

The extraordinary credit in fiscal year 1974 represents the tax benefit of investment losses recorded for financial reporting purposes in prior years and not for tax purposes until 1974. The tax benefit of such losses was not recorded in prior years, since there was no assurance that it would be realized. At March 31, 1974 the Company has available additional capital loss deductions from future taxable income aggregating $771,154 which have been recorded for financial reporting purposes but for which the tax benefit will not be reflected until realization is assured.

APB Opinion No. 14, stipulates that no portion of the proceeds from the issuances of the types of convertible securities illustrated above should be accounted for as attributable to the conversion feature. The opinion is reasonably based upon the inseparability of the debt and the conversion option.

Mortgages should be shown in the balance sheet as first, second, chattel, and so forth. Each mortgage should be shown at its net payable amount. Mortgages may be current or long term, depending upon their maturity dates.

Long-term notes issued to banks and insurance companies are growing in prominence as a method of financing employed by industrial concerns.

As stated earlier, pension fund liabilities do not enjoy a uniform placement in the balance sheet. It is the opinion of the author that amounts currently due should be shown as current liabilities and that the total of the company liability under the fund should be shown as a long-term liability, regardless of the origin of the item; many business concerns place the total of the fund liability, separately, between the liability and proprietorship sections of the balance sheet. Full disclosure of pension plan liability normally requires financial statement footnotes—especially in the year in which the plan was adopted or amended. Pension costs charged to expense during a fiscal period should be disclosed, together with the actuarially determined present values of benefits vested in employees. Also, it is suggested that disclosure be given to the composition of a fund in the possession of a trustee—at market prices.

For pension plans adopted by companies subject to regulations of the Securities and Exchange Commission, Rule 3–19 of Regulation S–X provides in part:

If present in regard to the person for which the statement is filed, the following shall be set forth in the balance sheet or in notes thereto:

"*e*" Pension and retirement plans—
  (1) A brief description of the essential provisions of any employee pension or retirement plan shall be given.
  (2) The estimated annual cost of the plan shall be stated.
  (3) If a plan has not been funded or otherwise provided for, the estimated amount that would be necessary to fund or otherwise provide for the past-service cost of the plan shall be disclosed.

There are two methods available for accounting for the investment tax credit which arises from the purchase of depreciable or amortizable personal (Sec. 138) property; buildings are excluded but elevators and escalators are included. These assets must have a useful life of at least the legally specified number of years—three at present. The credit can be treated as a reduction of taxes for the year in which the credit arose or it can be reflected in net income over the productive life of the asset. Preferably the credit deferred for more than one year should be shown as a long-term liability, or separately set forth between current liabilities and long-term liabilities. If premature asset retirement occurs, that portion of the investment credit not earned should be transferred out of the long-term liabilities category to the current liability category.

QUESTIONS

1. One principle of internal control over long-term liabilities is that instruments of indebtedness be physically controlled prior to authorized issuance. Why might a company increase its liabilities by issuing long-term debt obligations if that company did not require the funds provided by such issuance?

2. During an audit of bonds payable, why is it necessary to examine the trust indenture?

3. In the examination of the liability for bonds payable, what procedures would you follow (*a*) if there is a trustee under the bond indenture, and (*b*) if there is no trustee?

4. As of December 31, 1975, the Bonds Payable account of a client contains the following entries:

    > October 1, 1974, cash . . . . 448,000 Cr.
    > April 1, 1975, cash . . . . 37,600 Dr.
    > October 1, 1975, cash . . . . 424,000 Dr.

    The bond maturity date is October 1, 1994.
    As auditor, state the examination procedures you would follow for:
    a) Confirmations, assuming a trustee.
    b) Assurance of the accuracy of the account balance of $38,000.
    c) Acceptable financial statement presentation.

5. What are the distinguishing features of convertible bonds?

6. What steps are involved in the audit of a client's treasury bonds?

7. *a*) As auditor, why would you examine redeemed interest coupons?
    b) Assuming the existence of a trustee, how would you verify the amount due as a current liability for uncashed bond interest coupons?

8. How would you verify the accuracy of charges to mortgage accounts made during the period under examination?

9. If a company maintains and controls its own pension fund, how should the total pension fund liability be shown?

10. *Accounting Research Bulletin No. 43* contains certain recommendations relating to leases. What are these recommendations?

11. The Rubel Company purchases for retirement $200,000 of its eight percent debenture bonds for $180,000 cash. The book value of the bonds is $190,000. The company calls upon you to answer the following questions:
    a) What disposition should be made of the unamortized bond discount?
    b) May the saving on the bond purchase and retirement be closed directly to Retained Earnings?
    c) May the savings be used to pay dividends?

12. *a*) How should mortgaged property be shown in a balance sheet?
    b) When will second mortgages on real estate normally be found as liabilities?

13. In an audit, what procedures could be followed to be assured that the assets of the client were not mortgaged?

14. In your audit of the records of a corporation for the year ended December 31, 1975, you discovered a mortgage payable of $40,000. You verified its existence of correspondence with the mortgagee and by an inspection of the records in the office of the local county recorder. In the course of the audit, you discovered that $10,000 had been paid on the principal of the mortgage during 1975. You traced the entry to the debit of the Mortgages Payable account. You then prepared a balance sheet, showing the mortgage at $30,000 and certified the statement. Did you proceed correctly, or did you overlook any particular procedure?

15. What method is acceptable for determining annual costs of a client's pension plan?

16. You are the auditor for an employees' profit sharing pension trust which has existed for many years. Each qualified employee has an equity in the trust which he is entitled to receive when he leaves the company. The participating employees change each year because additional employees qualify, while others are retired. The amount of equity received varies with length of service from zero for the first five years up to 100 percent with 10 years of service. The trust agreement does not state how the fund's assets should be valued.

   The trust's assets consist of the following:

	Cost	Market
Cash	$ 50,000	$ 50,000
Rental properties (building)	100,000	250,000
Stocks	1,000,000	1,250,000
Bonds	500,000	400,000

   a) You are requested to give the trustees your recommendations for the valuation of the trust's assets in certified financial statements and the reasons for your recommendations.

   b) Would your opinion be standard, or would you vary it, and if so, how?

   c) The trustees inform you that the trust has entered into a 10-year lease on the rental property. The trust is to receive annual rents of $21,000 for 10 years and the lessee has the option to purchase the building for $125,000 at the end of the lease. The lessee has installed an expensive air-conditioning system and has expended substantial sums for modernization. The trustees want your recommendations for valuing the building this year and in the future, and your suggestions for the proper accounting entries to record the yearly $21,000 payments.

   d) What disclosure, if any, of the lease should be made in the financial statements?

   (AICPA, adapted)

17. In examining the costs of pension plans, certain terms are encountered by a CPA. The elements of pension costs which the terms represent must be dealt with appropriately if generally accepted accounting princi-

ples are to be reflected in the financial statements of entities with pension plans.

a) (1) Discuss the theoretical justification for accrual recognition of pension costs.

 (2) Discuss the relative objectivity of the measurement process of accrual versus cash (pay-as-you-go) accounting for annual pension costs.

b) Explain the following terms as they apply to accounting for pension plans:

 (1) Actuarial valuations.
 (2) Actuarial cost methods.
 (3) Vested benefits.

c) What information should be disclosed about a company's pension plans in its financial statements and their notes?

(AICPA)

PROBLEMS

1. On August 1, 1975, Days' Department Store leased the use of its cosmetic section to New Perfume, Inc. for an annual rental of $6,000 payable August 1 of each year. It was agreed that New Perfume, Inc. would occupy the space at least three years and that 90-day advance notice must be given prior to moving; likewise Days' agreed to give 120 days notice if it needed the space. The accounting year ends, for each company, on December 31.

 a) What type of lease is involved? Explain.

 b) What accounting method should each party use?

2. With the ever-increasing development of pension plans as a fringe benefit, proper accounting for these costs have become of primary concern to the auditor.

 a) Briefly describe the difference between pay-as-you-go (unfunded) and funded pension plans.

 b) When a funded plan is adopted, the total cost for the first year may be apportioned to past service and current year service.

 (1) Distinguish between these two costs.

 (2) What should be the balance sheet treatment of these costs if the employer, according to the pension agreement, must accumulate in a trusteed fund enough liquid assets to guarantee the employees their benefits upon retirement?

(AICPA, adapted)

3. During the audit of a new client, Warehouse Company, for the year ended December 31, 1975, you learned of the following transactions between Warehouse Company and another client, Investors, Inc.:

 (1) Warehouse completed construction of a warehouse building on its own land in June, 1974, at a cost of $500,000. Construction was financed by a construction loan from the Uptown Bank.

 (2) On July 1, 1974, Investors, Inc. bought the building from Warehouse for $500,000 which Warehouse used to discharge its construction loan.

(3) On July 1, 1974, Investors, Inc. borrowed $500,000 from Uptown Bank to be repaid quarterly over four years plus interest at 5 percent. A mortgage was placed on the building to secure the loan, and Warehouse signed as a guarantor of the loan.

(4) On July 1, 1974, Warehouse signed a noncancellable 10-year lease of the building from Investors, Inc. The lease specified that Warehouse Company would pay $65,000 per year for 10 years, payable in advance on each July 1, and granted an option, exercisable at the end of the 10-year period, permitting Warehouse to either (a) purchase the building for $140,000 or (b) renew the lease for an additional 15 years at $25,000 per year and purchase the building for $20,000 at the end of the renewal period. The lease specified that $10,650 of the annual payment would be for insurance, taxes, and maintenance for the following 12 months; if the lease should be renewed, $11,800 of each annual payment would be for insurance, taxes, and maintenance.

(5) The building has a useful life of 40 years and is to be depreciated under the straight-line method (assume no salvage value).

(6) Warehouse and Investors, Inc. negotiated the lease for a return of 6 percent. You determine that the present value of all future lease payments is approximately equal to the sales price and that the sale-and-leaseback transaction is in reality only a financing arrangement.

For the December 31, 1975 balance sheet of Warehouse Company, prepare schedules computing the balances for the following items:

a) Prepaid insurance, taxes, and maintenance.
b) Warehouse building, less accumulated depreciation.
c) Current liabilities arising from the lease.
d) Long-term liabilities arising from the lease.

(AICPA, adapted)

4. In reviewing the accounts of the Brose Company at the beginning of 1975, you find that on January 1, 1971, it had acquired a new building in exchange for its own 6 percent First Subordinated Bonds with a par value of $400,000 that mature January 1, 1981. You determine that the bonds had a market value on the date of exchange of $368,000 however, the building was recorded at par value of the bonds and depreciation was recognized for 1971 through 1974 at the rate of 4 percent annually. What compound entry would you make to correct the accounts.

5. The Bay Company is advised by a pension consulting firm at the beginning of 1975 that the cost of establishing a certain pension plan with full recognition of past services of all present employees is $900,000. The payment needed to recognize services for 1975 is calculated at the end of 1975 to be $80,000; this amount is payable in January, 1976.

Prepare the journal entries that will appear on the records of The Bay Company in 1975 assuming that:

a) The cost of recognizing past service is paid in 1975, and such cost is to be assigned to revenue in equal installments over a 10-year period.

b) The cost of recognizing past services is to be paid in 10 equal annual installments, and The Bay Company wishes to report the full amount payable on the plan as a liability.

6. On July 1, 1971, the Loww Company issued $300,000, 5 percent, 20-year mortgage bonds. The bond indenture provided that the company deposit with the trustee on June 30, 1972, and annually thereafter, the sum necessary for the accumulation at 3 percent, compounded annually, for a sinking fund to retire the bonds at maturity. The fiscal year ends June 30.

On June 30, 1976, the balance sheet contains only the following accounts relative to the bond issued.

Bond Sinking Fund	$ 25,000
Bonds Payable	300,000

Your initial audit shows that the $25,000 was deposited on June 30, 1974, that $11,164.71 should have been set aside annually, beginning on June 30, 1972, and that $13,557.50 must be set aside annually at three percent if the fund is to be accumulated in 16 deposits. Bond interest dates are January 1, and July 1, and the interest has been paid when due.

Prepare the entries necessary to correct the records at June 30, 1976, and show account balances relative to the bond issue as they should appear on the June 30, 1976 balance sheet.

7. Your corporate client was considering the issuance of bonds as of January 1, 1975, under either of the two following plans:

Plan 1: $500,000 par value, 5 percent, first-mortgage, 20–year bonds, due on December 31, 1994, to be issued at 94 percent of par.

Plan 2: $500,000 par value, 5 percent, first-mortgage, 20-year bonds, due on December 31, 1994, to be issued at par, with provision for payment of a 6 percent premium upon maturity.

The client requests that you prepare separate sets of journal entries for each plan, with explanations:
a) At the date of issue.
b) Monthly thereafter.
c) Upon payment at the date of maturity.
d) Which plan is the more advantageous to the client?

Discounts and premiums are to be allocated to accounting periods on a straight-line basis. Insurance costs are to be ignored.

8. On July 1, 1970, the Jeffry Company issued $500,000 of 40-year, 5 percent, first-mortgage bonds at 95. During the past 10 years, the company annually has charged to expense 2½ percent of the unamortized bond discount. On July 1, 1975, the company purchased $100,000 par value of the bonds at 90 and retired and canceled them. During the course of your audit of the records of the company for the year 1975, you noted that the $10,000 of discount at the acquisition date had been credited to a nonrecurring income account. Is the transaction correctly recorded? If not, what should be the correct entry?

9. From the following data, show how the information might be set forth in an acceptable balance sheet, for Alive, Inc.

1975
July 20   Bonds authorized, first-mortgage, 20-year, 5 percent, $5,000,000.
Aug.   1   Of the bonds authorized for issuance, $4,000,000 were sold to the investment Trust Company at par.
1976
Mar. 10   Bonds of a par value of $200,000 were purchased at par and were to be held alive in the treasury.
July 18   The bonds acquired on March 10, 1976, and also $300,000 of the unissued bonds were taken to the Second Bank and pledged as collateral for a loan of $375,000.

10.   One of your clients has the following bond issues outstanding at December 31, 1974:

Series I: $15,000,000, 6 percent, due on January 1, 1997, callable at 105 until January 1, 1932, and thereafter at 103
Series II: $30,000,000, 5 percent, due on January 1, 2007, callable at 104 until January, 1987, and thereafter at 102

The company is planning to refund both issues by issuing $50,000,000 of 4 percent bonds, due January 1, 2007. The bonds are to be issued at 96. The original issue of Series I was $20,000,000; and $5,000,000 had been purchased and retired by the sinking fund trustee in accordance with the provisions of the trust indenture. On January 1, 1975, there was no cash in the sinking fund, due to purchases of the Series I bonds. Assuming that the refunding operation is to be effective on January 1, 1975, what is the total saving effected by the operation? Assume that no additional bonds will be called.

11.   Your client, a corporation, has just entered into an employee pension plan. The plan became effective January 1, 1975. During the course of your examination for the year ended December 31, 1975 you find that two entries, in connection with the pension plan, have been made as follows:

Retained Earnings. 5,000
   Cash   5,000
   To record the first of a series of five equal annual payments required to be made to an insurance company to cover the cost of pensions based on past services.

Factory Wages. 3,000
   Cash   3,000
   To record the 1975 contribution to the insurance company for pension costs based on the 1975 factory wages.

Did the two entries reflect properly the facts regarding the pension plan? Present your reasoning and describe any changes considered necessary.

PRACTICE MATERIAL ASSIGNMENTS

Metalcraft, Incorporated: Audit Problem:
  Assignment 11, Section B: Profit Sharing Plan Liability.
Colby Gears, Inc.: Holmes and Moore Audit Case:
  Complete all assigned material.

25

Owners' Equities

Audit Objectives

The objectives in auditing corporate capital are to evaluate the internal control over stock transactions and stock certificates, and to determine the propriety of the ledger accounts and balance sheet presentation of authorized capital stocks, issued and outstanding capital stocks, unissued capital stocks, treasury stocks, retained earnings, and retained earnings reservations. In addition, the auditor should determine that the privileges of each class of stockholder have been observed by the corporation and that any changes in the capital structure made during the period under audit were properly authorized and recorded. The same care must be exercised by an auditor when determining the propriety of partnership Capital and Personal accounts and the single proprietorship Capital and Personal accounts. Of course, if all assets, liabilities, expenses, and revenues are properly established and valued, the equity of the owners as a totality will be correct—but errors might exist in one or more equity accounts which could favorably or adversely affect the rights of one or more classes of the stockholders interested in the business. Therefore, it is important that each item of capital be audited. In this manner, the validity of the valuations assigned to the other accounts also is verified, since an examination of the capital accounts may disclose marked peculiarities relative to asset valuation, acquisition, and disposition. Also, the proper or improper treatment of expenses, revenues, and net income is often disclosed in the examination of owners' equities.

Owners' Equities in General

The synonymous terms "owners' equities," "capital," "proprietorship," or "net worth" represent the difference between total assets and total liabilities. These equivalent terms have no relationship to any asset, working capital, or "how much the business is worth."

808

Corporate capital is composed of the dollar amounts allocated to issued and outstanding shares of capital stock, capital contributed in excess of the par or stated value of capital stock, donated capital, appreciation of assets, retained earnings reservations, and unappropriated retained earnings.

Partnership capital is composed of the sum of the algebraic balances of the partners' Capital accounts and Personal accounts.

Single proprietorship capital is the algebra balance of the owner's Capital account and Personal account (if a Personal account is used).

For corporate capital stock, the auditor must determine the number of shares of each class of stock outstanding at the balance sheet date, the par or stated value per share, and any preferences surrounding each class. Permanent increases or decreases in authorized capital stock, rights, options, and conversion privileges granted or exercised during the period under audit must be determined in accordance with proper corporate authorization and statutory requirements.

Capital Stock Considerations

Subscriptions. Subscriptions taken prior to actual incorporation are revocable by the corporation when formed, unless the subscriptions are accepted as soon as the corporation is legally organized. Most states, by statute, have established a time period—for example, 30 days after the effective date of incorporation—in which the board of directors may accept the subscriptions. During this time, subscriptions cannot be withdrawn by the subscribers; however, the subscriptions may be specifically rejected by the board of directors.

In the event of payment default by a subscriber, most states provide that forfeited stock shall be offered for public sale, or it may be privately sold; and in either instance, the proceeds remaining after deducting the amount due, discounts allowed the new purchaser, and expenses of resale shall be refunded to the defaulting subscriber.

Capital Stock Premiums and Discounts. If capital stock is issued at an amount above par or stated value, the excess represents paid-in capital, and should be set forth in a properly named Paid-In Capital account.

In a few states original issues of par value capital stock may be sold at a discount; whereas in the majority of states, it is illegal to sell original issues below par. The legal ban on the sale of original issues of capital stock at a discount could lead (1) to possible excessive valuations when properties and services are accepted in payment of subscriptions; (2) to peculiar treasury stock transactions; (3) to failure to call for the last subscription installment by prior secret agreement; and (4) to manipulation, such as charging the discount to an asset or to an expense. In those cases subject to the regulations of the Securities and Exchange Commission, the requirements of the Commission must be met. And even if a corporation is not required to register with the Commission, an auditor will not permit subterfuges to hide discounts on capital stock.

Capital stock originally sold at a discount may be issued as "fully paid and nonassessable"; it is fully paid so far as the corporation is concerned but not so far as the creditors of the corporation are concerned. If the corporation becomes unable to pay its debts, creditors may bring action to compel stockholders to pay in the amount of the discount in complete or partial satisfaction of their claims.

Capital stock discount accounts should remain open, since a true presentation is then given of the amount paid in for the capital stock. Capital stock discounts should not be charged to income because the discount is a capital transaction, not an income statement transaction. If a corporation has written capital stock discounts off to a noncapital stock capital account, the liability of the stockholders is not thereby eliminated.

Capital Stock Given for Assets Other Than Cash. A board of directors may exercise its discretion in assigning values to noncash assets and services acquired in exchange for capital stock; and in the absence of fraud, courts will not interfere with the decisions. The requirements of the Securities and Exchange Commission are rigid, and excessive valuations in the financial statements of registrants are not permitted; they should not be tolerated in any financial statements. Outside of the jurisdiction of the Securities and Exchange Commission, there are numerous cases in which tangible and intangible assets obviously are overvalued when taken in exchange for capital stock. The amount of the excess valuation over a reasonable figure results in watered stock.

Redemption Premiums. Preferred stock is sometimes given a redemption price which is a few points in excess of the par value of the stock. The reasons for the redemption premiums are numerous, including an ostensible inducement to purchase the stock, the indirect faith shown by the issuing corporation, and the privilege of the corporation to redeem the stock without the necessity of affirmative action by the stockholders. The assignment of a redemption figure is meaningless so far as value is concerned, for in the event of liquidation and a dearth of assets to convert, the stockholders will receive less than the redemption figure. A redemption price in excess of par does reduce the value of the common stock in the event of the redemption of the preferred stock or in case of liquidation. In connection with the redemption clause, some auditors favor the establishment of a reserve to care for the redemption premium; whereas others—the authors included—do not think it necessary. The purpose of most stock issues is to raise permanent capital, and redemption is not ordinarily contemplated. If a redemption reserve has been created, the auditor should verify its correctness. If a portion of the outstanding issue has been acquired in the market at a price below the redemption price and has been retired, the redemption reserve should be adjusted downward to equal the total of the redemption premium necessary to acquire the remaining outstanding shares. In order to afford full balance sheet disclosure, a footnote or parenthetical notation should be prepared for the redemption value of preferred stock.

Premiums paid upon the redemption of preferred stock should ordinarily be charged to Retained Earnings and not to a paid-in capital account, unless that account resulted from the original sale of this same stock at a premium. This practice is in accordance with sound theory and in accordance with an opinion of the Securities and Exchange Commission, based upon the maintenance of proper distinction between capital and income. Paid-in capital should not be used to absorb expenses or charges that should be deducted from income if retained earnings exist.

Treasury Stock

Treasury stock is capital stock of a corporation which was outstanding and has been reacquired by the issuing corporation. It has not been retired or canceled and is legally available for reissuance. However, in some states where stock must be offered for purchase to the issuing corporation, such shares are considered as being retired by the Securities Division of that state and cannot be reissued. The method of acquisition by the corporation is immaterial to its creation; it may be acquired by purchase, by donation by stockholders, in settlement of a debt due the corporation, or by stock subscription forfeiture. Legally, stock once fully paid and later reacquired by the issuing corporation may be resold at a discount without the purchaser thereof being subject to discount liability. If stock once issued at a discount and later reacquired is sold at any price, in most states the original liability for the discount still holds, provided the buyer has knowledge that the stock originally sold at a discount. However, state laws vary in this respect. Most state corporation laws stipulate that capital stock cannot be originally issued at a discount.

ILLUSTRATION. In Ohio, stock cannot be issued at a discount until the corporation has been in existence for two years *and* unless good reason can be shown why the stock should be issued at a discount. A practice that smacks of subterfuge is to issue capital stock to the organizers and promoters of a corporation. This is legal, since stock may be issued for services. The stock is issued as fully paid, thereby eliminating the attachment of a liability for discount. The persons receiving the stock for services rendered then donate an agreed amount of their stock back to the corporation, which may resell it at any price, because treasury stock may be sold at a discount. Thus, the intent of the law is circumvented by unscrupulous persons.

The general corporation laws of most states consider treasury stock as issued but not outstanding; the shares reacquired are "issued" to the corporation, but they are not outstanding in the possession of a stockholder. Because treasury stock is not outstanding, it is not taken into consideration in the computation of the total number of voting shares. Treasury stock may be reissued without violating the preemptive rights requirements of the corporation laws of the states.

The majority of states that permit corporations to acquire treasury shares limit the cost of the shares acquired to the amount of the retained earnings of the corporation. This limitation restricts the retained earnings available for dividends to the amount in excess of the cost of the treasury shares. In accordance with proper accounting theory and practice, this restriction must be indicated in the balance sheet.

ILLUSTRATION.   Footnote to a published report.

Under restrictive provisions of the credit agreement mentioned under Long Term Debt, $164,416,000 of income retained in the business at December 31, 1973, was available for declaration of cash dividends and payment on account of the purchase, acquisition, redemption, or other retirement of capital stock.

The acquisition of treasury stock by a corporation has the same effect as the reduction of outstanding capital stock, with the exception that the corporate charter must be amended if a permanent reduction is to take place. The treasury shares may be held by the corporation if state laws do not prohibit the practice, for as long as the corporation desires.

Compensation Stock Options Granted Employees.   This type of option results from an agreement between the corporation and an employee that during a specified period, the corporation will issue shares of its capital stock to the employee at a stated price and upon the election of the employee; usually, certain conditions must be met by the employee. In APB *Opinion No. 25,* the AICPA recommends that the value of the stock option be determined as of the date of option is granted in order to measure compensation, because at that date, the corporation has entered into a contract to issue the shares at the stated price. In general, Rule 3-20 (d) of the SEC is in agreement with the pronouncement of the American Institute with regard to accounting for stock options. Present regulations of the United States Treasury Department provide that the value of the stock option be determined as of the date the option is exercised, to the extent that the fair value of the stock exceeds the amount paid for it. (These regulations may be changed by the passage of additional tax laws.) An auditor also must be familiar with the new "qualified" stock option plan, and the well-known "restricted" stock option.

The cost of compensation may be more properly measured if the unconditional exercisable date were used instead of the date of grant, or the date the option was exercised. Then the cost of compensation would be the excess of the market price at the exercisable date over the option price, because the unconditional exercisable date, in effect, places a contract on an operative basis.

SECTION I: INTERNAL CONTROL OF CORPORATE CAPITAL

For capital stock, the principal points of internal control revolve around the issuance of stock certificates and the proper accounting for transfers and registration of shares.

Corporations having a large number of stockholders and actively traded stocks employ a registrar who prepares stock certificates, maintains a ledger of the stockholders, approves transfers of share ownership, and issues new certificates. The corporation also employs an independent transfer agent who takes care of the details of the transfer of stock ownership. The New York Stock Exchange and other major exchanges require the maintenance of an independent registrar and an independent transfer agent for listed corporations. The NYSE requires that both the registrar and the transfer agent(s) be located in New York City.

If a corporation acts as its own registrar and transfer agent, the maintenance of individual stockholder records and of transfers of ownership normally are under the supervision of the secretary of the corporation. When a corporation acts as its own registrar and transfer agent, proper internal control demands that stock certificates be serially prenumbered by the printer or engraver, and that the authority for signing and issuance of certificates be delegated by the board of directors. As one certificate is issued, corresponding records of the certificates should be prepared containing the name and address of the stockholder and the number of shares—spelled out and in numbers. Canceled certificates should be mutilated, and any transfer tax stamps should be attached to the canceled certificate. Record entries for stock issuances and transfers should be made by a person who does not have authority to sign and issue certificates.

An internal control questionnaire for capital is shown in Illustration 25–1.

SECTION II: AUDIT PROGRAM FOR CAPITAL STOCK

The audit procedures to be followed for capital stock are developed in the following subsections.

Examine Charter, Bylaws, and Minutes. The auditor must be familiar with the state's requirements relating to incorporation procedure, qualification of securities, issuance of capital stock, minimum amount per share for which no-par-value stock may be issued, regulations pertaining to the acquisition or nonacquisition of treasury stock, requirements for the reflection of values received upon the issuance of capital stock, stockholders' records which must be maintained, imposition of transfer taxes, requirements for minimum original paid-in capital, regulations pertaining to stock dividends, and all other requirements of the state. Important, too, are the requirements of stock exchanges and of regulatory

ILLUSTRATION 25–1

INTERNAL CONTROL QUESTIONNAIRE
Corporate Capital

Company_____

Period Covered_____

	Yes	No	Not Applicable	Remarks

1. Is an independent transfer agent employed for capital stock?
2. Is an independent registrar employed for capital stock?
3. If the client does not employ an independent transfer agent or registrar:
   a) Are unissued stock certificates under the control of an officer?
   b) Are stock certificates signed in advance of issuance?
   c) Are blank stock certificates and matching stubs prenumbered by the printer?
   d) Are cancelled stock certificates properly voided?
4. Does an independent agent pay the dividends?
5. If an independent dividend-paying agent is not employed, is proper control exercised over dividend checks?
6. Are unclaimed dividend checks redeposited and set up as liabilities?
7. Is the dividend bank account regularly reconciled:
   a) By a person who does not maintain the dividend records?
   b) By a person who does not mail the dividend checks?
8. If there is no registrar, does the client regularly reconcile the number of shares outstanding— according to the stockholders' records—with the control account balance in terms of shares?
9. Are necessary tax stamps properly affixed?
10. If capital stock is exchanged for noncash assets, is proper valuation applied to the assets received?
11. Has the Securities and Exchange Commission ever rejected asset valuations referred to in Question 10?
12. Have additional authorizations been properly executed and recorded?
13. Has full consideration been given to the effect of selling treasury stock on the remaining authorized shares?
14. Have additional stock authorizations and issuances been considered in calculating earnings per share?
15. If special retained earning reserves are authorized, have they been properly established, maintained, and cancelled?
16. Have any stock dividends or stock splits been authorized?
17. Have these dividends or splits been properly executed and required entries made?
18. Have restrictions or privileges of each class of stock been properly recognized?

Prepared by_____   Reviewed by_____

Date_____   Date_____

bodies of the federal government, such as the Securities and Exchange Commission.

The auditor must examine the articles of incorporation and any amendatory certificates, and the corporate bylaws, noting all important matters which affect the client's accounting and the audit—for example, (*a*) the precise names of the various classes of stocks; (*b*) the number of authorized shares of each class; (*c*) the par value per share of each class or the stated value for no-par shares; (*d*) callable and redemption features of preferred stock; (*e*) convertible provisions for preferred stock; (*f*) the special rights of each class; (*g*) normal and liquidating dividend features; and (*h*) all other matters of importance. These data become a part of the permanent file.

Minutes of the meetings of stockholders and of the board of directors should be examined and pertinent notes made to determine policies and activities concerning authorized increases, decreases, retirements, and new issues of capital stocks, reserve creations, retirement of reserves, granting of stock options, and dividend actions. Normally, increases in capital stock (other than increases resulting from the declaration and payment of stock dividends) and retirements of capital stock must be authorized or ratified by the stockholders. After capital stock has been issued, minutes of the board of directors must be examined to ascertain that the proceeds of capital stock sales were applied in conformity with the authorizations if restrictive stipulations were inserted at the time of issuance.

An understanding must be had of the rights and privileges of each class of stockholder with respect to cumulative features of preferred stock, the participation of preferred shareholders along with the common shareholders in extra dividends, redemption fund provisions, callable features, preferred stock priority in the event of dissolution, and so forth. Inquiry must be made of existing stock options and stock warrants; balance sheet footnotes should state the conditions of each. It is a duty of the auditor to ascertain that all provisions and requirements of all capital stock issues are being fulfilled and to advise the client with respect to these matters.

Schedule Each Capital Stock Account. In an initial engagement, the auditor should prepare schedules analyzing each capital stock account for a period of time sufficient to determine the correctness of the balance at the beginning of the year under examination. This is not to be interpreted to mean that each transfer must be verified; it simply means that the analysis covers the verification of all increases in capital stock and the values received by the corporation, and all decreases and the offsetting credits. For the year under examination, the schedule should be prepared, setting forth the balance at the beginning of the year—in terms of dollars and shares—showing the increases and decreases during the year, and concluding with the balance at the end of the year.

A schedule for capital stock may be prepared as follows:

MOELMAN COMPANY

Common Stock, December 31, 1975
(Authorized to Issue, 100,000 Shares: Par, $10 per Share)

Date	Explanation	Debit	Credit	Balance in Dollars	Balance in Shares
Feb. 4, 1966	Cash		$200,000	$200,000	20,000
Mar. 3, 1971	Retained earnings; stock dividend; 50 percent		100,000	300,000	30,000
Apr. 1, 1975	Cash		200,000	500,000	50,000

This work sheet will be moved forward from year to year, and additional data will be added as changes occur in the capital stock.

Verify Entries in Capital Stock Accounts. The proceeds of capital stock sold during the year being audited must be traced through the records to the banks just as for any cash receipts. If property other than cash was received, receipt of the property must be vouched to the asset accounts. Improper valuations should be mentioned in the audit report, and the auditor's opinion should be qualified to the extent necessary under the circumstances. Charges and credits to other accounts affected when capital stock is increased or decreased must be vouched to verify the values received and parted with, and to determine the reasons for increasing or decreasing the capital stock amounts.

When no-par-value stock exists, it should be carried in the accounts at (*a*) the amount received for it; or (*b*) a stated or declared amount per share, with the excess over the stated amount being credited to a paid-in capital account—permanent capital. The laws of certain states stipulate a minimum issuance price per share for stock of a no-par value; when such laws exist, the auditor must examine the records to determine that the amounts credited to the no-par capital stock accounts have not fallen below the required minimum. If restrictive minimum-price laws do not exist, the directors may dispose of the stock at any price. The proceeds of each sale should be traced to the accounts to ascertain that the no-par stock accounts have been credited with the correct amount in accordance with regulatory laws and with the recorded actions of the board of directors.

Accounts must be inspected for the treatment of premiums received and discounts granted on the disposition of capital stock to determine that the premiums and discounts are not being amortized against income. When capital stock has been issued at a discount, has not been fully paid at any subsequent time, but is described in the records as fully paid, the auditor must be certain that laws are not thereby violated. If they are, the client's attention must be directed to the matter. Where capital stock has been issued at a discount or at a premium, the balance sheet should portray this fact, unless these discounts and premiums have been closed to a noncapital-stock capital account by authorization of the board of directors. If discounts have been charged off for one class of stock, owners' equities available to the stockholders of a different class of stock has been reduced. This may constitute unfair treatment of original stockholders of the different class who have paid par for their stock; therefore, the auditor must be certain of the legality of the transaction.

Closely connected with the discussion in the foregoing paragraph is the examination of subscription agreements and the inspection of the charges made when the Subscriptions account was credited in order to ascertain that the capital stock was being paid for and to determine that the unpaid subscriptions were carried forward and were not being written off. Directors may be personally liable for authorizing the cancellation of unpaid subscriptions in violation of original subscription contracts if authorization for the write-off does not appear in the minutes. If payments on subscriptions are in arrears, the client's attention should be directed to this condition, and it should be appropriately commented upon in the audit report.

Account for All Shares Outstanding. The auditor should account for all stock certificates. Stock certificates are (*a*) issued, (*b*) canceled, or (*c*) unissued and on hand.

If a company employs a capital stock registrar and/or a transfer agent (most corporations with capital stock listed on major exchanges employ both), the registrar or the transfer agent, or both, should be requested to confirm directly to the auditor the number of shares of each class of stock issued and outstanding at the balance sheet date. When a registrar and/or a transfer agent are employed, transfers of ownership of the stock are not requested, since the independent control is considered sufficient protection for purposes of internal control. The balance of the number of shares of each class of stock as reported by the registrar must be in agreement with the controlling accounts as shown by the client. If the two balances are not in agreement, discrepancies must be located.

If a company maintains its own capital stock records, the auditor must examine the certificate records to determine the number of shares of each class issued and outstanding. The total of the open items from the stock certificate records must be in agreement with the general ledger controlling account as to number of shares and with the sum of the subsidiary stockholders' ledger, if one is kept. There must be no overissuance of any class of stock. The auditor should ascertain whether blank stock certificates are ever presigned by the proper officials and turned over to other officers for completion and issue. Such a practice may constitute an invitation to fraud.

In addition to the use of stock certificate records, it is advisable to carry subsidiary ledger records with the stockholders; then, at the termination of each fiscal period, a trial balance work paper may be prepared which can be compared with the certificate records and the controlling account. Large companies—or their registrars—frequently will carry subscription journals, subscription ledgers, installment ledgers, transfer journals, stock ledgers, and the stock certificate records. Small companies simplify these records, many maintaining only a stock certificate book, containing a stub for each individual certificate. The verification of the transfer of shares between stockholders is not necessary if the issued and outstanding number of shares is in agreement between the controlling account, the sum of the subsidiary ledger accounts, and the sum of the open certificate stubs.

All certificate numbers should be accounted for, and missing numbers should be reported to the client. A confirmation may be obtained from the printer for the inclusive numbers preprinted on the certificates, in order to detect the issuance of certificates without entry. See Illustration 25–2.

ILLUSTRATION 25-2

THOMAS COMPANY

Common Stock Certificate Data
Year Ended December 31, 1975

Cert. No.	Stockholder Name	Balance, Dec. 31, 1974	Issued or Canceled, 1975	Balance, Dec. 31, 1975
1	T. J. Creme	100√		100
2	R. T. Waldon	50√		50
3 C	J. F. Schmidt	100√	100 C	
4	E. K. Hooper	40√		40
5 C	W. A. Hodge	60√	60 C	
6	R. T. Ball	50√		50
7	H. J. Miller		35 I√	35
8	A. F. Newton		65 I√	65
9	B. B. Boyd		30 I√	30
10	C. A. Tolson		30 I√	30
		400		400

C Canceled. Examined for mutilation.
√ Certificate stub examined. Traced to stockholders' ledger.
I Issued.

Compare Canceled Certificates and Related Records. If a company acts as its own registrar and transfer agent, certificates canceled during the year under audit must be inspected and the number of shares totaled. The stock certificate records for certificates issued during the year should be totaled; when added to or subtracted from the balance at the beginning of the year, the difference between those issued and those canceled will equal the balance at the end of the year. Canceled stock certificates should be defaced so that they cannot be used again.

ILLUSTRATION. The stock certificate books and transfer records are maintained by the company secretary. One stockholder sold his holdings to another person. When the original certificate came to the secretary for cancellation and issuance of a new certificate, the secretary issued instructions to void the old certificate and file it. The assistant to the secretary detached the power of attorney executed by the original holder; forged a power of attorney, transferring the shares to himself; and used the certificate as collateral for a personal loan. The auditor discovered the fact that there was a missing certificate number, thereby starting the investigation that led to the admission of the act by the assistant.

Canceled certificates should be inspected for endorsement by the transferor, and the transferor's signature must correspond in all respects with the name on the face of the certificate; if the assignment form on the reverse of the certificate is blank, a power of attorney transferring ownership should be attached. When a stock certificate is canceled, the name of the transferee should be inserted, either on the assignment form or on the power of attorney, if used. Frequently, neither the assignment nor the power of attorney is completed because the securities are being used for loan collateral or because they are being delivered to a broker.

Any existing stock transfer tax stamps and original-issue tax stamps are attached to the stubs or to the canceled certificates, and not to the issued certificates. The auditor must ascertain that the tax stamps have been affixed; and he should test the accuracy of the amounts so affixed, so that the client will not be subject to the penalties provided in the tax laws.

Examine Treasury Stock Transactions. In examining treasury stock transactions, the auditor must ascertain that the certificates are on hand and that they are issued in the name of the corporation. The treasury stock certificates then should be listed on a work paper, indicating the certificate numbers and the number of shares of each certificate. The certificate numbers appearing on the treasury certificates should be compared from year to year in order to detect unauthorized and unrecorded treasury stock sales and repurchases.

The subsidiary stockholders' ledger should contain an account with the treasury shares, the treasury shares being "issued" to the corporation. However, since this stock is issued but not outstanding, dividends are not paid on it, and dividend examination must be made to be certain that dividends thereon were not paid. The exclusion from income of dividends on treasury stock is in accordance with proper accounting theory and with the opinion of the Securities and Exchange Commission.

Minute records of directors should be examined for authority to acquire and dispose of treasury shares. In some states, the corporation laws specify the conditions of acquisition; in such cases, the corporation laws serve as a guide to the auditor. The method of acquiring treasury shares must be understood by the auditor so that he can be assured that true treasury stock exists and that the company has the right to acquire it and so that the reasons for acquiring it are clear. Entries must be examined for recording the acquisition and disposition of treasury shares, and these entries must follow accepted practices. Authorizations for purchases and sales of treasury stock must be traced to the Treasury Stock account and to the cash records in terms of shares and prices, not only to determine that the acquisitions and dispositions are in accordance with proper authority but also to determine gains or losses on resale.

Some auditors believe the treasury stock may be shown as an asset if the intention of the company is to resell the stock. Because treasury stock is so closely related to the capital structure of a company, the authors are of the opinion that treasury stock should not be shown as an asset.

Treasury shares should be carried in the Treasury Stock account at cost. If treasury shares are sold, the difference between purchase price and sales price is a capital account adjustment. If treasury stock of a par value is canceled and retired, it should be retired at par, and any difference between par value and cost to acquire the stock should be transferred to capital. If treasury stock of no par value is canceled and retired, one of the two following methods may be followed:

a) Charge the Capital Stock account at the original issuance price, and charge or credit the proper Paid-In Capital account for the difference between that figure and the cost to acquire the stock. Theoretically, this method is perfect; but when identification of the originally issued shares becomes impossible, the practical considerations render its use impossible.

b) Charge the Capital Stock account at the *average* issuance price, and charge or credit the proper Paid-In Capital account for the difference beween that figure and the cost to acquire the stock. This method is recommended.

Occasionally, fixed assets are acquired for treasury stock. If so, the auditor should verify the valuation placed upon the assets; he should insist that the assets be capitalized at no more than the cash realizable value of the treasury stock given in exchange, since this conforms to recognized accounting procedure. Cases involving overvaluations should be brought to light in the audit report and the opinion qualified or disclaimed if the client refuses to reduce valuations.

The majority of state corporation laws require that retained earnings be restricted to the extent of the cost of any treasury stock. This restriction of retained earnings constitutes a protection for the corporate creditors because the corporation is using its cash to pay for the treasury stock acquired. Normally, the restriction does not involve the creation of a retained earnings reserve, but it does require proper approval by the board of directors, and proper parenthetical notation following the retained earnings caption. The auditor must ascertain that the corporation has restricted its retained earnings in accordance with state requirements and that the restriction is properly handled in the owners' equities section of the balance sheet.

It should be further noted that some states consider treasury stock as canceled stock. Therefore, when these shares are sold, the company must consider the resulting shares issued as new shares and the auditor must make certain that there are enough authorized and unissued shares to cover these transactions.

Determine Adherence to Stock Option Plans, Restrictions, and Preferences. If stock option plans are in existence, the auditor must familiarize himself with the terms of the plans, and he must determine that proper disclosure is presented in the financial statements or in notes accompanying the financial statements. Also, the auditor must determine that the operation of a stock option plan is in accordance with the plan. When stock options are granted, the corporation must either acquire treasury stock or reserve unissued stock so that the corporation will be able to fulfill the option agreements when and if the eligible employees exercise their options. The auditor must verify the shares issued during the year under audit, and he must determine that the proper number of shares for future exercise are available at the balance sheet date. The following illustration is taken from the notes to the financial statements of a nationally known corporation.

ILLUSTRATION. Stockholder Equity. The prior preferred stock is being retired through annual sinking fund payments equivalent to the par value of 8,428 shares of such stock; shares outstanding have been reduced by 32,807 shares which were held by the Company at March 31, 1974 for future sinking fund requirements. Each share of Series A preferred stock is convertible, at the option of the holder, into 1–5/8 shares of common stock and is callable at $37. At March 31, 1974 and 1973, there were 5,037,877 and 5,159,843 common shares, respectively, reserved for conversion of the Series A preferred stock and the 6 percent and 5½ percent debentures.

Options, which are exercisable at various times through 1982, have been granted at quoted market to key employees to purchase common stock; options to purchase units, consisting of one share of Series A preferred stock and ¾ share of common stock, expired during 1973 and no additional options to purchase units may be granted. Option transactions (in shares) were as follows:

	Common	Series A Preferred
Outstanding, March 31, 1972	715,659	7,902
Granted	114,500	
Exercised	(7,806)	(6,854)
Cancelled	(69,560)	(1,048)
Outstanding, March 31, 1973	752,793	–
Granted	21,000	–
Cancelled	(185,818)	–
Outstanding, March 31, 1974	587,975	–

Options outstanding at March 31, 1974 were at prices ranging from $11.63 to $29.88 per share (aggregate price of $11,724,000, aggregate market value of $7,717,000) and included 144,075 shares for which became exercisable in 1974. At March 31, 1974, 673,225 common shares were reserved for issuance under stock option plans. In 1973, common stock options were exercised at prices ranging from $18.75 to $25.50; options for units were exercised at $33.38.

When a corporation has outstanding convertible preferred stock or convertible bonds, the auditor must ascertain that the corporation has in reserve the proper number of common shares to meet the elective demands of holders of the outstanding convertible bonds or convertible preferred stock.

Many preferred stocks are callable at prices a few points above par. In such cases, the auditor must investigate to determine that any existing provisions for reacquiring these shares are in conformity with the callable provisions of the preferred stock issue.

SECTION III: FINANCIAL STATEMENT CONSIDERATIONS

Capital Stock

In the balance sheet, capital stock should be shown in such a manner that there are clearly shown for each class the total authorized shares, the par or stated values, the outstanding shares, the treasury stock, and (if applicable) the dividend rates. Cumulative dividends in arrears should not be accrued in the corporate financial records, but the amounts should be indicated by a footnote to the balance sheet. The requirements of regulatory bodies, the corporate code of regulations, and the actions of the board of directors as recorded in the minutes of that body should

ILLUSTRATION 25–3

CAPITAL SECTION OF A BALANCE SHEET (Partial)

Stockholders' Equities:

Preferred stock: authorized 10,000 shares of $100 par value, of which 8,000 shares are issued and outstanding and 1,500 shares are unissued, and 500 shares are in the treasury. . . .	$ 800,000	
Common stock "A," authorized and issued, 100,000 shares of a par value of $10 per share	1,000,000	
Common stock "B," no-par-value, 1,000,000 shares authorized and issued at a stated value of $8 per share	8,000,000	
Total Capital Stock		$ 9,800,000
Paid-in capital from premium on preferred stock	$ 100,000	
Paid-in capital from the sale of "B" common stock in excess of stated value	2,000,000	2,100,000
Total Paid-In Capital.		$12,900,000

be followed in order correctly to establish capital stock in the balance sheet.

Illustration 25–3 is concluded in Chapter 26. Capital paid in from each source should be clearly, definitely, and separately set forth and explained.

Current trends for revealing maximum information in the capital stock section, together with extensive footnotes, is clearly illustrated in Illustration 25–4. The reader is urged to study reports to stockholders and note the extensive nature of the capital stock sections and the accompanying footnotes.

Subscriptions in the Balance Sheet. The balance sheet presentation of capital stock subscriptions may be briefed as follows:

1. The subscriptions receivable may be shown as a current asset, under an appropriate caption, if the subscriptions normally will be collected in the near future.
2. The subscriptions *may* be shown as a *noncurrent* asset if there is no intention of calling them in the near future; in this case, the better practice is to follow item 3, following.
3. The subscriptions *must* be deducted from the capital stock if there is no intention of ever calling them, so that total paid-in capital is not overstated.
4. The subscriptions *must* be shown as capital deductions if there is a contingency with respect to their payment, such as payment only out of dividends declared on the stock.

Treasury stock normally should be shown in the stockholders' equities section of a balance sheet at cost as a deduction from the total stockholders' equities. If treasury stock is acquired for the purpose of resale to employees under stock option plans, and if such treasury stock is shown among the assets, there must be full disclosure of the entire situation, either within the balance sheet or by appropriate footnote. If the cost of treasury shares is deducted from total stockholders' equities, definite disclosure is given to the fact that the corporation used assets to acquire the treasury stock.

Additional material regarding financial statement considerations for the equities of owners is presented in Chapter 26.

SECTION IV: AUDIT PROGRAM FOR PARTNERSHIP AND SINGLE-PROPRIETORSHIP CAPITAL

Audit Program for Partnership Capital

Examine the Partnership Agreement. Preparatory to examining the capital accounts of a partnership, the auditor must read the articles of

ILLUSTRATION 25-4

Statements of Shareholders' Equity
for the Years Ended December 31, 1974 and 1975

(expressed in thousands)

Common Shares Outstanding (Note 12)		Total Share-holders' Equity	Preferred Stock (note 12)	Common Stock (note 12)	Additional Paid-in Capital	Retained Earnings (note 12)	Treasury Stock (note 12)
31,151,862	Balance, December 31, 1973	$792,531	$5,543	$77,881	$400,648	$308,468	$ (9)
	Net loss	(170,610)				(170,610)	
	Cash dividends declared						
	Common stock at $1.25 per share	(3,892)				(3,892)	
	Preferred stock at $3.00 per share	(256)				(256)	
(3,869)	Treasury stock acquisitions	(43)					(43)
(252)	Other transactions	(10)			(10)		
31,147,741	Balance, December 31, 1974	617,720	5,543	77,881	400,638	133,710	(52)
	Net income	141,850				141,850	
	Cash dividends declared						
	Common stock at $1.25 per share	(3,788)				(3,788)	
	Preferred stock at $3.00 per share	(256)				(256)	
500	Stock options exercised, averaging $11.50 per share	6		1	5		
	Additional payment for prior acquisition	(629)			(629)		
(1,661,645)	Treasury stock acquisitions	(24,888)					(24,888)
(30)	Other transactions	115		(1)	116		
29,486,566	Balance, December 31, 1975	$730,130	$5,543	$77,881	$400,130	$271,516	$(24,940)

The accompanying notes are an integral part of these statements of shareholders' equity.

Note 12. Shareholders' Equity

Preferred Stock   At December 31, 1975, there were 85,284 Series A shares outstanding of the 10,000,000 shares authorized. The unissued shares may be issued with such voting rights, dividend rates, conversion privileges, sinking fund requirements and redemption prices as the board of directors may determine, without action by the shareholders. Each share of the Series A stock is without par value, is entitled to one vote and an annual dividend of $3.00 (cumulative), is callable at $65.00 at any time to .85 share of common stock.

There were no changes in the Company's preferred stock during the year ended December 31, 1975.

Common Stock   At December 31, 1975, there were 50,000,000 shares ($2.50 par value) authorized, 29,486,566 shares outstanding, and 1,666,076 shares held in the treasury. In 1975, the Company purchased for the treasury, through an open-market purchase plan and a tender offer, 1,661,645 shares of its common stock for $24,888,000. Of the unissued shares, a total of 1,232,423 shares are reserved for the following: 309,266 shares for conversion of convertible subordinated notes, 72,403 shares for conversion of Series A preferred stock and 850,754 shares for issuance under stock option programs. At December 31, 1975, options were outstanding for 405,467 shares at prices ranging from $9.88 to $67.38 exercisable at various times through 1980.

On various dates in 1975, the board of directors granted options to key employees to purchase an aggregate of 195,686 shares of common stock of the Company (including options to purchase an aggregate of 120,500 shares to the Company's officers and one director as a group). The exercise prices of options to purchase 168,265 of such shares, which range from $9.88 to $13.00 per share, are at the fair market value at the date of grant. The balance of such options covering 27,421 shares, were granted on the condition that the optionees consent to the cancellation of outstanding options for an equivalent number of shares granted to them during the periods from July 25, 1970, through April 30, 1972. The cancelled options were exercisable at prices ranging from $43.14 to $67.38 per share and had various expiration dates ranging from July 24, 1975 to March 9, 1978. The exercise price of each of the substitute options remains the same as the price of the corresponding cancelled option until the date when the latter would have expired; during the remainder of the term of the new options the prices range from $9.88 to $13.00 per share.

Retained Earnings   The terms of certain loan agreements restrict the payment of cash dividends on common stock to 15 percent of consolidated net income, as defined by the agreements, earned subsequent to December 31, 1974. The amount of retained earnings not restricted by these provisions at December 31, 1975 was approximately $11,500,000. The loan agreements provide for future relaxation of the dividend restrictions as the Company is able to meet certain financial ratios and earnings levels.

copartnership. On a first audit, there should be excerpted for the permanent file such data as the following:

a) The name and address of the partnership.
b) The name and address of each partner.
c) The class of each partner—that is, general, limited, silent, and so forth.
d) The duties of each partner.
e) The capital contribution of each partner.
f) The drawings or "salaries" of each of the partners.
g) Interest arrangements on Capital account balances.
h) Interest charges on drawings.
i) Dissolution arrangements.
j) Provisions in the event of withdrawal of a partner, either voluntarily or involuntarily.
k) Profit and loss sharing ratios.
l) Reciprocal life insurance arrangements.
m) The period of the partnership agreement.
n) The partnership's fiscal year.

The auditor may be supplied with a copy of the partnership agreement for his permanent files. In a repeat engagement, only the changes in the partnership contract need be excerpted.

Any violations of the partnership agreement must be reported to the partners, and it may be necessary to comment upon them in the audit report; if necessary, the audit opinion may be qualified or disclaimed. In a first audit, a search should be made for past violations of the partnership agreement. In many cases, written articles of copartnership do not exist; in such instances, the auditor must be certain that each individual partner understands the financial arrangements and practices pertaining to the Capital accounts. It may be advisable for the auditor to suggest that legally appropriate and proper articles of copartnership be drafted.

Verify Opening Entries. In an initial audit of a partnership, opening entries should be verified with respect to the assets contributed, the liabilities assumed, and the Capital account of each partner. If partners have withdrawn in the past, or if former partnerships have been dissolved and a new partnership has been formed, the accuracy of the accounting for the withdrawals, dissolutions, and new formations should be verified in order to avoid future complications. The original opening entries and all succeeding opening entries brought about by new formations should be confirmed to the auditor by all existing partners.

Verify Entries in Capital Accounts and in Personal Accounts. In a first examination, the Capital account and Personal account of each partner should be analyzed from the inception of the existing partnership, if possible; if this is considered unnecessary by the auditor, then the analyses should be made for a number of past years sufficient to result in accuracy of balance at the beginning of the year of examination.

For the period of current review, each Drawing and Capital account must be separately analyzed and each transaction therein vouched to the original records. In the vouching of the entries, particular attention should be devoted to ascertaining that in accordance with the articles of copartnership, capital contributions have been proper and withdrawals have not exceeded agreed amounts, and that the drawings have been received by the partners. Salaries also must be watched to ascertain that they are properly recorded and are in keeping with the agreement. In the absence of an agreement concerning salaries, drawings extracted by the partners cannot be treated as salary expense, even though the drawings are construed as coming from profits. Legally, partners' salaries are never expenses but are distributions of profits. When interest is credited on capital and when it is charged on drawings, the auditor must ascertain that the interest computations are in accord with the agreement. Such interest charges and credits must be tranferred to profit and loss before the final calculation of net income. The division of profits in accordance with the profit sharing ratios must be verified; if there is no agreement, profits and losses are, by law, shared equally by all partners.

After the accounts have been analyzed and the entries vouched, the auditor should have each partner approve his accounts by initialing them in the ledger or by obtaining written confirmation from each partner. Determination must be made that the periodic closing of the partnership accounts is in agreement with the articles of copartnership or that they are closed in accordance with partnership law in the absence of an agreement.

If a partner is paying his personal expenses by the issuance of partnership checks and by charges to his Personal account, it is recommended that the practice be stopped.

ILLUSTRATION. Partner A always paid his personal expenses with partnership funds and instructed the bookkeeper to charge his Personal account, which he was not in the habit of examining; the bookkeeper followed the same practice for many of his own personal expenses, charging the account of partner A.

Credits to Personal accounts normally arise from interim or year-end closings. Other credits must be carefully examined.

ILLUSTRATION. Partner A loaned the partnership $5,000 and credited his Personal account; a liability account should have been credited.

Determine that Contributions Are Not Deficient or Excessive. After vouching charges and credits to Capital accounts, the auditor must reconcile the account balances with the partnership agreement to determine that the capital is in accordance therewith or to determine whether it is deficient or excessive as indicated by the requirements of the agreement.

Deficiencies in agreed capital can work to the detriment of other partners. Excessive capital contributions by one partner can work to his financial detriment if he could use the funds elsewhere. If excessive capital does exist, investigation should be made to determine the reason for permitting the excess contribution. Is the amount in reality a loan? Is the excess contribution approved by the other partners? Because of the excess, does that partner expect a change in the profit sharing ratio? Also, the auditor must ascertain whether partnership creditors have demanded subordination of debts where amounts have been personally borrowed by partners in order to meet their individual capital contribution requirements.

In the event of dissolution of a partnership, care must be exercised to determine the amounts paid in liquidation are properly distributed to the partners. Before distribution of any amounts to the partners, all creditors must be paid in the proper order of their claims—that is, preferred debts, then fully secured debts, then partially secured debts, and, last, unsecured debts. Loans made by partners are not paid until the balances of the Capital accounts are determined; and if necessary, credits to loan accounts are offset against debit balances of Capital accounts. Following this, distributions are made to the partners. Profits and losses on liquidation of assets are apportioned in the profit sharing ratios; and after that, the distribution of the assets is made on the basis of the amounts remaining in the Capital accounts of the partners. Care must be exercised to determine that no one partner has been paid a liquidating amount to the detriment of another partner.

Capital Accounts of a Single Proprietorship

In the examination of the records of a single proprietorship, the auditor must analyze the Capital and Drawing accounts for the period under examination. It does not matter if a Drawing account is not used, since the interests of one person only are to be taken into consideration.

In a first audit of an existing single proprietorship, it usually is not reasonable or necessary to analyze the Capital account from the inception of the business. A review of the accounting records of former years and of tax returns would indicate the accuracy of prior expense charges and accepted asset charges. If a balance sheet and income statement are established for the current year-end, if the assets and liabilities in the balance sheet are worked back to the beginning of the year, and if they are properly inventoried, the accuracy of the balance sheet at the beginning of the year is established.

QUESTIONS

1. Of what items is corporate capital composed and what must the auditor determine in connection with these items?

2. What might result if the legal ban on selling original issues of capital stock at a discount were removed?

3. What is a stock option?

4. Early in the audit program of any corporation the auditor would obtain information that would become a part of the auditor's permanent file. Briefly describe the sources and nature of this material.

5. In the process of auditing the Miscellaneous Income account, you find proceeds from capital stock subscription defaults in the amount of $10,000. Would you approve this practice? Explain your answer.

6. The National Products Company has 200,000 shares of $10 par value common stock authorized. It issues half of these shares for certain patents and secret processes. This action was approved by the board of directors. In auditing the financial statements of this company, would you accept this valuation? Explain the position the auditor should take.

7. In the process of auditing the Organization Expense account, you find that the discount on common stock issued to the president has been charged to this account. Explain the position the auditor should take.

8. In the process of auditing the Retained Earnings account you find amounts representing the amount of redemption of preferred stock at less than its issuance price. Your client stipulates that this was done because a profit had been made on the transaction. How would you answer this argument?

9. For corporate capital stock, what are the principal points of internal control?

10. During the current year the authorized capital stock of a corporation had been increased and the additional shares had been sold. Outline the procedures to be followed in the verification of the capital stock if the corporation (*a*) employs a capital stock registrar and (*b*) if the company does not employ a registrar.

11. A corporation employs a registrar for its capital stock. In your annual audit of the records of the company, you requested that a confirmation be obtained from the registrar, stating the number of shares of each class of capital stock outstanding at the balance sheet date. Does the registrar's confirmation constitute final evidence of the correctness of the outstanding shares? If it does, or if it does not, would you perform additional work on the capital stock accounts in the records of the corporation?

12. During the course of the audit of the records of a company, you compared the balance of the shares in the Common Stock controlling account with the sum of the stock certificate stubs and with the share balances in the subsidiary stockholders' ledger. Three months after completion of the audit, it was discovered that all the common stock outstanding at the balance sheet date had not been properly accounted for. What are the possibilities that might lead to such a situation?

13. A company was incorporated on February 1, 1975. The authorized capital consisted of 100,000 shares of common stock of a par value of $10 per share. During the course of your audit of the records of the company

for the period ended December 31, 1975, the total of the outstanding shares, according to the certificate stubs, was 42,000 shares. The general ledger Common Stock account was as follows:

February 10, 1975, cash, 15,000 shares issued for $150,000
May 10, 1975, cash, 20,000 shares issued for   200,000

a)   Name two possibilities which may have caused the share difference.
b)   How might you detect the cause of the discrepancy?

14.   In 1975, a client contemplated a reduction in the number of shares of its authorized capital stock.

a)   You are requested to outline the procedure that the company must follow in order to effect the reduction.
b)   At the end of the year 1975, you returned to perform the annual audit of the company's records and noted that the share reduction had taken place. What are your duties with respect to the capital stock in view of this reduction?

15.   The owners of the six percent, noncumulative preferred stock of a corporation request an audit of the records of the company to ascertain whether their interests are properly protected. What three items should be particularly watched?

16.   In the examination of the records of a partnership, what steps would you take in the audit of the partners' Drawing accounts?

17.   During your audit of the records of A, B, and C, partners, what would be your guide in the following circumstances? What action would you take in each instance?

a)   In determining the division of profits.
b)   The drawings of one partner are below his permitted amount.
c)   The drawings of one partner are above his permitted amount.

18.   You were auditing the records of a partnership. You were particularly interested in determining whether each individual partner's Personal account and Capital account were correctly stated. What course of action would you follow to assure yourself that everything was in order in connection with these accounts?

PROBLEMS

1.   As the auditor, you are asked to prepare the contributed capital section of the balance sheet of National, Inc., at the end of the fiscal year, September 30, 1976. National Inc., was organized under a charter authorizing 10,000 shares of 6 percent preferred stock, the stock is cumulative, and preferred as to dividends and in liquidation. The par is $100 per share and the liquidation value is $105 per share. In addition, 20,000 shares of common stock having no par or stated value were authorized. During the first year, the following transactions occurred.

a)   Subscriptions were received for 8,000 shares of 6 percent preferred stock at $115.00 per share; a down payment of $368,000 was received, and the balance is due in two equal installments.
b)   12,000 shares of the no-par common were sold for cash at $10 per share.

c) 2,000 shares of the no-par common and 60 shares of the 6 percent preferred were issued for reimbursement for legal fees incurred in organizing the corporation.

d) The first and second installments on the preferred stock subscriptions were collected, except on 500 shares. Stock certificates were issued on fully paid shares.

e) 3,000 shares of no-par common stock and 1,000 shares of the 6 percent preferred stock, plus $50,000 cash were given in payment for a warehouse the company needed to store its finished product. The former owners had purchased the building for $80,000 and it was depreciated to a book value of $24,000 at the date of disposition.

f) 100 shares of the 6 percent preferred were sold for cash in the amount of $120,000.

g) The annual dividend was declared on the preferred stock and a $1 per share dividend was declared on the common stock. No dividends were declared on the subscribed stock.

2. Executive, Inc., is considering changing its capital structure to include the issuance of a six percent preferred stock. Using the amounts it has distributed in dividends the past three years, it requests that a schedule be prepared showing how these dividends would have been distributed assuming the following capital structures:

Dividend distribution: 1973, $25,000; 1974, $75,000; 1975, $120,000.

a) 100,000 shares of $10 common; 5,000 shares of par $100, 6 percent, noncumulative, nonparticipating preferred.

b) 100,000 shares of $10 common; 5,000 shares of $100 par, 6 percent, cumulative, fully participating preferred, dividends two years in arrears at the beginning of 1973.

c) 100,000 shares of $10 common; 5,000 shares of $100 par, 6 percent, cumulative, nonparticipating preferred, dividends two years in arrears at the beginning of 1973.

3. Capital accounts for Senate, Inc., on December 31 are as follows:

Preferred stock, $100 par, 10,000 shares issued and outstanding	$1,000,000
Premium on capital stock	100,000
Common stock, $10 par, 200,000 shares issued and outstanding	2,000,000
Premium on common stock	250,000
Retained earnings	3,000,000

Preferred stock is convertible into common stock. Prepare the entry that is made on the corporation's records assuming that all of the preferred stock is converted under each of the following assumptions:

a) Preferred shares are convertible into common on a share-for-share basis.

b) Each share of preferred is convertible into five shares of common.

4. The Filbert Company requested your advice in the following matter. The capital stock of the company has a par value of $1 per share. The market price of the stock is $12 per share. The company issues stock to its employees as partial compensation for services rendered. The compensation plans are as follows:

a) This represents a straight bonus, which is authorized by the board of directors upon the recommendation of the president. Under this plan, if an employee were voted a bonus of $1,200, he would receive 100 shares of unissued stock on the basis of a market price of $12 per share.

Should income be charged with 100 shares at $1 each, and the Capital Stock account credited at par; or should income be charged for $1,200, Capital Stock credited for $100, and Paid-In Capital credited for $1,100?

b) The sales manager has a contract with the company under which he receives a salary, and he also has the privilege of purchasing not more than 1,000 shares of unissued stock per year at $6 per share. When the contract was executed, the market price was $4 per share; it is now $12 per share.

Should Cash be charged at $6 per share, Capital Stock credited at $1 per share, and Paid-In Capital credited for $5 per share? Should Cash be charged at $6 per share and income for $6 per share with credits to Capital Stock at $1 per share and to Paid-In Capital at $11 per share?

5. During the first audit of a company, you discover a Treasury Stock account with a debit balance of $300,000. The original debit was for $500,000, and there is a credit of $270,000, representing stock disposed of in the following manner:

(1) $200,000 cash received for $430,000 of shares.
(2) $70,000 of shares delivered as payment for services in organizing the corporation; the invoice was for $30,000.

No stock was purchased as treasury stock by the corporation during the year. You are required to:

a) Adjust the accounts.
b) Explain the improper use of the term "treasury stock" by this company.

6. The capital section of the balance sheet of the Hickory Company, December 31, 1974, appears as follows:

Preferred stock, six percent, $100 par,
  5,000 shares. . . . . $ 500,000
Equity of common stock, 50,000 shares,
  no-par   3,500,000
    Total Capital $4,000,000

At December 31, 1975, the capital section appears as follows:

Preferred stock, six percent, $100 par,
  4,500 shares. . . . . $ 450,000
Equity of common stock, 60,000 shares, no-par   4,550,000
    Total Capital $5,000,000

Certain 1975 transactions follow. From the available information, and as a result of your audit, redraft the capital section of the balance sheet as of December 31, 1975.

(1) The additional 10,000 shares of no-par common stock were sold at $60 per share. The stated value of all no-par common stock is $40 per share. The first 50,000 shares were issued at $50.

(2) Net income for 1975 was $665,000.

(3) Preferred stock, 500 shares, was purchased for the treasury at $110 each.

(4) Cash dividends paid: preferred, $30,000; common, $180,000.

7. The Pecan Company was incorporated in 1975, with an authorized capital consisting of two classes of common stock: Class A, 10,000 shares, par value $50 per share; and Class B, 50,000 shares, par value $10 per share. Voting privileges were the same for both classes. Dividend stipulations differed for the two in a respect that has no significance in this problem. During 1975, 5,000 shares of Class A were sold at par, and 25,000 shares of Class B were sold at par. The Capital Stock account on the records of the company shows credits for $500,000 for the stock sold. The sum of the certificate records disclosed that 50,000 shares of both classes were issued. From the stockholders' ledger, the auditor ran an adding machine tape of the number of shares issued, and his total agreed with the 50,000 shown in the stock certificate record. He therefore assumed that everything was in proper order and proceeded to prepare a balance sheet. Did the auditor perform his proper duties? How should the stock be shown in the balance sheet? What probably was wrong with the stock certificate record?

8. James Chester, a client, owns 100 shares of the common capital stock of the Cub Corporation, which he purchased in 1973 for $15,000. Chester presents the following data and information to you, and requests:

a) The computation of the book value of a share of common stock as of October 31, 1975.

b) The theoretical value of his stock rights as of November 1, 1975.

c) The profit realized if the rights later were sold for $3,000.

Pertinent balance sheet data on October 31, 1975, for the Cub Corporation:

Current liabilities (including provisions for preferred stock dividends through October 31, 1975)	$110,000
Bonds payable	300,000
Cumulative preferred stock, 6 percent, $100 par value (entitled to $110 and accumulated dividends per share in voluntary liquidation, or to $100 per share in compulsory liquidation). Authorized, 3,000 shares; issued, 2,000 shares, of which 150 shares are in the treasury	185,000
Common stock, $100 par value (there are 10,000 shares authorized, of which 4,000 shares are issued and outstanding)	400,000
Premium on common stock	77,300
Retained earnings	341,200

The corporation proposes to issue an additional 2,000 shares of common stock. Common stockholders of record as of November 1, 1975, were notified that they will be permitted to subscribe to the new issue at $150 per share up to 50 percent of their holdings. On November

1, 1975, the market price of the stock was $225 per share. The stock is ex-rights in the market on November 3, 1975. The market price of the rights on November 3, 1975, is the same as the theoretical value computed as of November 1, 1975.

(AICPA, adapted)

9. The Logan Company has requested that you report on the capital section of its balance sheet using accepted accounting principles.

a) Prepare work papers, including adjustments, in accordance with your recommendations.

b) Dispose of noncapital section items by a brief statement in the work papers as to where they should appear.

c) Prepare a revised capital section of the balance sheet as of December 31, 1975, the date of the examination.

A balance sheet as of December 31, 1974, is presented to you; the capital section follows (assume that all items not shown are correct):

Preferred stock, $10 par; 20,000 shares authorized and issued, of which 2,000 are treasury shares costing $30,000 and shown as an asset.		$ 200,000
Common stock, no par value, stated value $4; 200,000 shares authorized, of which 150,000 are issued and outstanding.	$600,000	
Paid-in capital ($5 per share on preferred stock issued in 1960)	100,000	700,000
Provision for doubtful accounts receivable.		4,000
Reserve for depreciation . . . ·.		280,000
Reserve for fire insurance		66,000
Retained earnings.		750,000
		$2,000,000

Additional data:

(1) Of the preferred stock, 1,000 shares were sold on November 30, 1975, for $18 per share; and the $18,000 was credited to the Preferred Treasury Stock account. The shares were acquired in 1972 at $15 per share.

(2) The preferred stock carries an annual dividend of $1 per share. The dividend is cumulative. At December 31, 1974, unpaid cumulative dividends amounted to $5 per share. The entire accumulation was liquidated in September, 1975, by issuing to the preferred stockholders 18,000 shares of common stock at a stated value of $5 per share.

(3) A cash dividend of $1 per share was declared to the preferred shareholders of record December 1, 1975, payable January 1, 1976.

(4) At December 31, 1975, the Allowance for Doubtful Accounts Receivable and the Accumulated Depreciation had balances of $4,400 and $350,000, respectively.

(5) On March 15, 1975, the Reserve for Fire Insurance was increased by $20,000; Retained Earnings was debited.

(6) On December 31, 1975, the Reserve for Fire Insurance was decreased by $10,000, which is the cost less depreciation of $1,000 of one building destroyed by fire on December 1, 1975. Fire cleanup costs, estimated at $2,000, do not appear on the records.

(7) Retained earnings, as shown December 31, 1974, consisted of (*a*) land site gift in 1965, then worth $150,000; (*b*) gains of $17,000 on treasury stock transactions in 1969, and (*c*) earnings retained in the business, $483,000.

(8) Net income for the year ended December 31, 1975, according to the records of the company, was $432,500.

10. The information presented below is an analysis of the Treasury Stock account in the records of the Elm Company. The balance of the Treasury Stock account appears as an asset in the amount of $32,256 on the June 30, 1976, consolidated balance sheet.

Item	Date	Explanation	Debit	Credit
1.	Jan. 4,1971	Capital stock of Water Park, a 100 percent owned subsidiary, established in 1969	15,200	
2.	Jan. 4, 1971	Common stock, 140 shares, acquired at par and reserved for employee bonuses; 40 shares were issued in 1973 and 53 shares in 1974, leaving 47 shares on hand	14,000	
3.	May 31, 1972	Preferred stock, 38 shares (par $100), repurchased from the president at $115 per share; originally purchased by him in 1971 at the issuance price of $103 per share	4,370	
4.	Dec. 15, 1973	Common stock, 276 shares, repurchased in open market at $35	9,660	
5.	Dec. 31, 1974	Common stock, 25½ shares, representing fractional shares remaining undistributed from a stock dividend; total par value		2,550
6.	Feb. 2, 1975	Sold, for cash, 81 shares of common stock repurchased in 1973		8,424
7.	June 30, 1976	Balance		32,256
			43,230	43,230

Comment briefly on each of these items, setting forth (*a*) the corporate action which should have been taken, (*b*) the additional information required before disposing of each item, (*c*) how the accounts should be adjusted, and (*d*) how the amounts should be shown in the balance sheet of the Elm Company.

PRACTICE MATERIAL ASSIGNMENTS

Metalcraft, Incorporated: Audit Problem:
Assignment 12, Section A: Common Stock.
Colby Gears, Inc.: Holmes and Moore Audit Case:
Common Stock; Preferred Stock.

26

Owners' Equities (Concluded)

RETAINED EARNINGS: CAPITAL CONTRIBUTED IN EXCESS OF PAR OR STATED VALUE OF CAPITAL STOCK; RECORDED APPRECIATION OF ASSETS

Concepts and Terminology

This chapter will develop the audit procedures for equity capital items not credited to capital stock accounts. The excess of net assets over capital stock is divided into various accounts, and each account is created on a functional basis. For each class of noncapital stock proprietorship and for each account involved, the auditor must determine its source, legitimacy, reasonableness, accuracy, composition, and disposition. Restrictions—imposed by law or by company action—must be determined, and the propriety of all charges and credits also must be determined.

Appropriate descriptive titles must be used for items of equity capital other than capital stock, both in the records and in financial statements. Modern terminology properly involves the disappearance of the use of the old term "surplus" and the substitution of more meaningful titles. For example:

Modern Terminology	Old Terminology
Retained earnings. Retained income. Earnings retained for use in the business	Earned surplus
Capital contributed in excess of par or stated value of capital stock. Additional paid-in capital	Paid-in surplus
	Capital surplus
Retained earnings reservations (appropriations) for specific (named) purposes.	Surplus reserves (named)
Appreciation of assets. Excess of appreciation over cost.	Appreciation surplus
Excess of net assets over cost	Surplus (all above classes)

Although the new terminologies properly have increased in popularity, this chapter may—very sparingly—mention the older titles for the following reasons: (1) it is not possible to force a universal change until it has been universally accepted; (2) there is no totally preferred agreement

836

for the new titles; and (3) if one particular title is used here, many persons might prefer an alternative. A continuation of the research of recent years, dissemination of knowledge and reporting information, and the examination of noncapital stock equity titles and the methods of balance sheet presentation will lead to a better understanding of the newer terms.

General Comments

The excess of net assets over capital stock should be divided into its proper functional types and should not be grouped into one overall item. None of the accounts representing the excess of net assets over capital stock should be used to absorb charges that rightfully belong in an expense account in order that a better operating condition may be shown in the income statement; likewise, no noncapital stock equity account should receive direct normal revenue credits. These capital accounts are not substitutes for expense and revenue accounts.

When consolidated financial statements exist, the auditor must remember that the retained earnings of the subsidiary companies, which was earned before acquisition by the parent company, is not a part of the consolidated capital. The investment account in the records of the parent must be eliminated against the capital stock and the acquired retained earnings of each subsidiary company. If intercompany profits exist, they must not be taken up in the consolidated capital; if fixed assets are finally sold to a buyer who is not a part of the consolidation, then the profit or loss on the sale should be taken into the consolidated capital.

Retained Earnings. Retained earnings represents the balance of net income, and realized gains and losses of a corporation from the date of incorporation (or from the latest date when a deficit was eliminated in a quasi reorganization), after deducting distributions to stockholders and transfers to capital stock accounts or other capital accounts. If a correct amount of retained earnings is to be shown, assets, liabilities, paid-in capital, capital reserves, expenses, and revenues must be correctly handled. If the auditor is satisfied that all of these items are correct, then he is confident that the retained earnings is correct.

State laws are not particularly rigid in specifying the sources of retained earnings and its disposition. Companies not maintaining accounts with paid-in capital in excess of the capital stock accounts necessarily must charge losses on capital transactions to Retained Earnings, but gains on capital transactions should be credited to properly named paid-in capital accounts.

Assuming that other proprietorship accounts are in operation, entries in the Retained Earnings account should consist of charges for dividends, charges for retained earnings reserve creations, charges for net losses, and credits for net incomes. Debits and credits for adjustments and corrections of preceding years should appear only for adjustments of income taxes of prior years and certain other extraordinary items, as set forth in *Opinion No. 9* of the Accounting Principles Board. With respect to preceding period adjustments, the APB has concluded that those rare items which relate directly to the operations of a specific prior period or periods, which are material, should, in single-period statements, be reflected as adjustments of the opening balance of retained earnings. Where comparative statements are presented, corresponding adjustments should be made of the amounts of net income and retained earnings balance for all of the periods being reported therein, so that these statements fully disclose the retroactive application of these prior period adjustments.

The basic criteria for determining what constitutes an extraordinary item is its (*a*) unusual nature and (*b*) infrequency of occurrence.

Retained earnings may be (1) free and available for dividends or (2) appropriated for specific purposes. The propriety and adequacy of all reservations of retained earnings must be ascertained before the auditor can be confident that the amount of the retained earnings is properly stated. He must determine that similar transactions have been handled consistently each year; for instance, if a reservation for contingencies was created out of retained earnings in one year, it should be created from the same source each time it occurs; if the contingency occurs, it should be charged to expense and *not* against the appropriated amount; if profits from the sales of securities held as investments were credited to revenue one year and then closed to Retained Earnings, they should not be credited directly to Retained Earnings or any other capital account in another year. Stock dividends result in the reduction of a noncapital stock equity account, usually Retained Earnings; when this situation arises, the auditor must verify the reduction by referring to the authorization transferring a certain amount per share to the capital stock accounts. In the event that dividends are in arrears on cumulative preferred stock, or in the event that preferred stockholders participate in dividend distributions along with common stockholders, the auditor should design his statements so that the amounts of retained earnings available to each class of stockholders are shown.

In the event that a corporation has charged off a retained earnings deficit to a noncapital stock equity account, the date of the beginning of the new retained earnings should be indicated in the financial statements. The Securities and Exchange Commission and the AICPA have recommended that for a reasonable number of years, the financial statements should indicate the amount of the deficit so charged to capital. This indication serves no purpose other than that of general information.

Additional Paid-In Capital.   Additional paid-in capital accounts come into existence in many instances, several of which are considered in the following paragraphs.

Capital contributed in excess of the par or stated value of capital stock is the balance of the increases and decreases in capital which result from transactions between the corporation and its shareholders which are not entered in the capital stock accounts. The major distinction between this type of capital account and retained earnings is that the former results from transactions between the corporation and its shareholders involving the capital stock of the corporation, whereas retained earnings results from transactions between the corporation and outsiders which are based on the activities for which the corporation is organized.

Capital contributed in excess of the par or stated value (additional paid-in capital) includes the following: gains on treasury stock sold at a price in excess of acquisition cost; amounts received from stockholders when capital stock assessments are levied (if the assessments are not on stock sold at a discount and therefore to be credited to a discount account); increases brought about by the conversion of capital stock from one class to another; the amount realized upon subscription forfeiture if the amount paid in is not returned to the defaulting subscriber; devaluation of capital stock; changes from par to no-par-value stock; and amounts arising from the sale of par-value stock at a premium and the sale of no-par-value stock at a price above stated value. Additional paid-in capital represents payment capital—as permanent as the amounts received for capital stock directly and credited to the capital stock accounts.

Noncapital stock capital accounts should not be used to reduce expense charges of any year. If a deficit exists in retained earnings, there is no objection to charging it off to a noncapital stock capital account if the stockholders approve such action and if the new retained earnings is dated. This action is permissible in a quasi reorganization on the theory that a completely reorganized company would be relieved of a similar deficit. The financial statements after a quasi reorganization should include full disclosure of all actions taken.

Because additional paid-in capital amounts represent permanently invested capital, it follows that ordinary dividends should not be paid from those sources; from the standpoint of sound accounting principles, paid-in capital should be maintained intact. However, as a matter of practice, and from the standpoint of legal considerations, dividends may be and are declared from other than retained earnings, except in states that prohibit the practice or specify the kind of excess over and above the amounts credited to the capital stock accounts which is available for dividends.

When stockholders donate shares of stock to a corporation for resale by the corporation, when real or personal property is received by the corporation as a gift, or when a liability of a corporation is forgiven, the paid-in capital thus created constitutes a part of the invested capital and should not be available for dividends unless the donation was given specifically for that purpose. A Donated Capital account may be maintained, or the amounts may be credited directly to a Paid-In Capital account. At the time of donation of capital stock, there is, of course, no realized increase in the capital of the corporation; the increase takes place when the donated shares are resold. However, it is not customary to suspend the credit until the sale takes place, although, theoretically this should be done. Likewise, if property or other assets are donated contingent upon the performance of a stipulated act, the donated capital is not actually realized until the requirements are fulfilled.

Appreciation of Assets. The excess of appreciation over cost is the result of recorded appreciation—arbitrary or well founded—of some asset. Since no profit has been realized, the balance sheet should definitely segregate the excess of the appreciation over cost, and this amount should never be made available for cash dividends (stock dividends are permissible) or for the absorption of deficits, even though state laws may not prohibit the practice. Excesses arising from the appreciation of assets occasionally are created so that an existing deficit may be charged against it in order to pave the way for the declaration of dividends. In such instances, full disclosure should be made in the audit report of all matters pertaining to the appreciation, and it may be necessary for the auditor to qualify or disclaim his opinion. The general corporation acts of some states require that appreciation increments be shown separately in the balance sheet.

Based upon the assumption of sound reasons for recording an appraisal, as reflected in long-time increases in price levels or greatly increased usefulness, the authors are of the opinion that depreciation should be charged to expense on the gross reappraisal figure in order to support the appraisal and to reflect a recoupment of the higher prices as charges against revenues. For purposes of the federal income tax, of course, only cost less estimated salvage value may be recovered. Writing up an asset to appraised value to reflect a change in price level implies that the increased amount expresses the basic fixed-asset requirement in new dollars; the source of the permanent invested capital in the capital section of the balance sheet should be increased by a similar amount. This may be accomplished by permitting the Appreciation of Assets account to stand permanently or by capitalizing it in the form of a stock dividend. It is not wise to transfer the Appreciation account—either piecemeal or in total—to Retained Earnings because, as previously stated, recording the appraisal merely converts the fixed assets and capital into dollars at the higher price level prevailing at the date of the appraisal. Recording the appraisal does not realize revenue; neither does allocating the higher value figure to expense realize revenue so long as the high-price level continues.

In the face of the reasoning of the preceding paragraph, some people still advocate a periodic transfer from Appreciation of Assets to Retained Earnings equal in amount to the periodic depreciation on the amount of the appreciation. At best, such a transfer of Retained Earnings should be considered as appropriated capital, for replacement of the assets presumably will be at a higher cost. Others regard recorded appreciation as a suspended credit which should be disposed of as ultimate circumstances dictate.

SECTION I: AUDIT PROCEDURES FOR RETAINED EARNINGS AND OTHER NONCAPITAL STOCK CAPITAL ACCOUNTS

Audit Program

Auditing procedures are developed in the following subsections.

Schedule Each Account. Each noncapital stock equity account should be separately scheduled. The auditor must ascertain that entries in each account properly belong there and not in other accounts, particularly other equity accounts. The sources of each noncapital stock capital account should be explained on the work papers, and the propriety of the sources must be above question. If a quasi reorganization has been effected, any former retained earnings should not be carried forward under that title; a new account should be established and dated.

Verify Entries in Each Account. Retained Earnings. In a first audit, the entries in the Retained Earnings account should be examined for a sufficient number of prior periods to establish the accuracy of the account. Charges to the account should be properly supported by recorded actions of the board of directors for such items as dividend declarations and retained earnings appropriations.

For the year under current examination, each charge and credit should be vouched. The opening balance inserted on the work paper should agree with the work paper balance of the prior year-end; each charge and credit made during the year should be vouched by tracing each transaction to the record of original entry and by examining all supporting evidence. In verifying debits and credits, it is necessary to ascertain the reasons, propriety, mathematical correctness, and proper method of recording. Thus, it is evident that an analysis of expense and revenue accounts is essential to the determination of the correctness of the retained earnings.

Additional Paid-In Capital. Capital contributed in excess of the par or stated value of capital stock represents permanently paid-in capital. If possible, the accounts should be analyzed from their inception and entries completely vouched for the period under review. The entries in the accounts should be supported by proper authority, traced through the records, the reasons for the entries understood, and all documents examined. Capital contributed in excess of the par or stated value of capital stock should appear only upon authorization of the board of directors. The auditor should verify the source; if any additional paid-in capital account has been used to cover an operating deficit, adjustments should be made. If premiums and discounts from the sale of treasury stock or original issues of capital stock have been incorrectly carried to Retained Earnings, corrections must be made to transfer the premiums and discounts directly to the proper premium or discount account.

ILLUSTRATION. A company sold 400,000 additional shares of stock at a premium of $10 per share; the premium was properly credited to a Premium on Common Stock account; the cost of selling the stock— $131,000—was improperly charged to an existing Paid-In Capital account, the source of which was not related to the 400,000 shares issued.

The auditor must be familiar with the laws of the state of incorporation to ascertain the permissibility of recording in permanent noncapital stock equity accounts such transactions as the declaration of dividends when retained earnings are insufficient to cover the dividend; such dividends represent a return of invested capital. Many states do not prohibit dividends—cash or stock—from any noncapital stock equity account.

The auditor must verify the sources of capital excesses arising from donations, and he must prepare an analysis of the account for the period under audit or for the period of its existence in the event of a first audit. Comments must be made in the report if donated assets are overvalued, and it may be necessary to qualify or disclaim the opinion. When treasury stock donations have been credited to a separate Donated Capital account, all discounts upon the donated stock at the time of redisposal should be charged to the same account. The auditor must watch for situations wherein capital stock was given in exchange for assets and part of the stock was donated back to the corporation. In such cases, the value of the property received obviously was not the par or market price of the stock given in payment, and the assets received should be written down in accordance with the market price of the stock donated back to the company.

Recorded Appreciation of Assets. Recorded asset appreciation should be analyzed from its inception; all sources of the accounts should be verified, and each entry should be vouched. The initial examination of these accounts usually is made in connection with the examination of the assets that gave rise to the accounts.

The auditor must ascertain whether depreciation is charged (*a*) on the original asset cost or (*b*) on gross reproduction cost new.

ILLUSTRATION. An asset appraisal had been recorded. At December 31, 1975, the end of the fifth year, and after depreciation for 1975 had been recorded, the account balances were as follows:

Asset (at cost of $550,000 less estimated salvage of $50,000). $500,000
Asset (appreciation per appraisal). 100,000
Accumulated depreciation, based on cost 125,000
Accumulated depreciation on appreciation 25,000
Appreciation of assets 75,000
Reserve for replacement of asset 25,000

Age at December 31, 1975. . . . . 5 years
Estimated remaining life . . . . 15 years

If Depreciation Expense Is Based on Reproduction Cost New (*Preferred*). The entries at December 31, 1975, and for each of the following 15 years, would be as follows:

Depreciation Expense, Asset 30,000
   Accumulated Depreciation of Asset   30,000
  Annual depreciation on $600,000 at 5 percent.

At the end of the total life of 20 years, the total of the accumulated depreciation account will be $600,000, the sum of the cost less salvage plus the appraisal excess. At the end of the 20th year, the Appreciation of Assets account will still contain a credit balance of $75,000, and the Reserve for Replacement of Asset account will contain a credit balance of $25,000. These amounts should not be transferred to Retained Earnings because so long as the price level remains high, they represent a *maintenance* of invested capital and not an *increase* of invested capital. The Appreciation of Assets account may be transferred to the Reserve for Replacement of Asset account.

If Depreciation Expense Is Based on Cost. The annual entries for each of the remaining years would be as follows:

Depreciation Expense, Asset 25,000
   Accumulated Depreciation of Asset (cost less salvage).   25,000
  Annual depreciation: five percent of $500,000

Appreciation of Assets. 5,000
   Accumulated Depreciation of Asset (cost less salvage).   25,000
  Annual depreciation: $\frac{1}{15}$ of $75,000.

Retained Earnings 5,000
   Reserve for Replacement of Asset   5,000
  Retained earnings appropriated in an amount equal to the
  annual depreciation on the appreciation.

At the end of the 20th year, the sum of the two accumulated depreciation accounts will be $600,000, the sum of the depreciable amount of $500,000 plus the appraisal excess of $100,000. The Appreciation of Assets account will be eliminated, and the Reserve for Replacement of Asset will have a balance of $100,000. This method is not preferred.

Discovery Value Capital. In an extractive industry, if the excess of reasonable market price over cost is recorded by a charge to the property accounts and a credit to Discovery Value Capital, the account should be treated in the same manner as an Appreciation of Assets account.

In many instances, the discovery value of extractive industry properties may be greatly in excess of the cost of the properties; and it may appear reasonable to reflect the present values of the future incomes in the balance sheet in order to make the statement a reasonable measure of value. The balance sheet must contain a statement of original cost.

The auditor should examine the reports of geological surveys; he should then verify the accounts in order to ascertain that the discovery values reflected therein are within the limits of the quantities indicated in the survey reports. Depletion charges are verified on the basis of quantities removed.

Ascertain Restrictions on Retained Earnings.   All restrictions must be fully understood, verified, and afforded full disclosure in the financial statements and in the audit report. A footnote stating all details is highly desirable.

ILLUSTRATIONS.   Restrictions may be exemplified as follows: (*a*) A board of directors voluntarily may appropriate retained earnings for contingency reserves for specifically anticipated future contingencies; (*b*) by contact, the board of directors may be obligated to restrict retained earnings by the creation of a reserve for sinking fund; (*c*) by law, a board of directors may restrict retained earnings resulting from treasury stock purchases.

Upon the completion of the transaction for which the restriction is made, the auditor must determine that the reserve has been returned to the Retained Earnings account. A discussion of capital adjustments with the proper officers often proves enlightening.

Ascertain Authority for Noncapital Stock Capital Disbursements.   No type of noncapital stock equity should be distributed without proper action of the board of directors and/or the stockholders, with the exception of the absorption of the net loss of a current year. The auditor must ascertain that the authorized distributions do not violate the legal or contractual obligations regarding any noncapital stock equity, as illustrated above for retained earnings.

After a board of directors has provided for all restrictions, it has the discretionary power to distribute retained earnings as it desires, in the absence of fraud and discrimination. The minutes of the board of directors should always indicate the source of dividends and all other distributions.

SECTION II: DIVIDENDS

Prefatory Audit Comments

The following factors must be considered in a proposed declaration and payment of a dividend.

1. The availability of retained earnings.
2. The availability of cash for cash dividends.

3. The necessity for available cash in the future.
4. Anticipated business conditions.
5. The availability of unissued capital stock and treasury stock for stock dividends, where permissible.

Once publicly declared, a dividend payable in cash, other assets, or scrip becomes a liability of the corporation which cannot be rescinded unless the stockholders agree; and those not agreeing to the rescission must be paid. A declared stock dividend may be rescinded by the declaring board at any time prior to its distribution. If a cash dividend is legal, a dividend in any other form likewise is legal. In the United States, the majority of state laws are to the effect that dividends can be legally paid if the assets of the corporation are in excess of the liabilities and capital stock. Dividends are commonly spoken of as being declared out of net income, but it must be understood that the net income need not be currently earned. Thus, a corporation may have a net loss for any current year or years; when this loss is deducted from the previously accumulated retained earnings and there remains a credit balance, in that account, the corporation may pay a dividend. When a dividend is declared, the assumption is that it is from that portion of retained earnings representing the latest currently earned profits. The important concept is that a dividend cannot be declared and paid when capital is thereby impaired; the term "capital" is construed to mean the amount standing in the capital stock accounts. In several states, dividends may be declared from net income of the current year, even though a deficit exists.

Dividend declaration actions rest exclusively with the board of directors; and courts are extremely unwilling to interfere with this phase of management's conduct of a business, on the assumption that the corporate directors have a better knowledge of the propriety of dividend actions than any other person or group. If stockholders become dissatisfied with dividend actions or the lack of them, they have the alternatives of disposing of their stock or of electing new directors. A dividend action should be given public notice as soon as the action takes place. Most stock exchanges have a rule that the exchange must be immediately notified of dividend actions. This is done to protect minority holders. Stockholders with a knowledge of the dividend action are thereby prevented from obtaining more shares before any announced dividend action which might cause the stock to rise. Stockholders are also prevented from disposing of stock before the announcement of a dividend action which might cause the price of the stock to be driven down.

Although everyone agrees that dividends should be declared from accumulated earnings, dividend actions often indicate that the source of the dividend need not necessarily be earned; state laws vary in establishing requirements in this direction. In some states, dividends may be declared from any noncapital stock equity account. Some state laws specify that dividends may not be declared from paid-in capital created out of the proceeds of the sale of no-par stock. Most states stipulate that dividends declared from sources other than retained earnings are legal only if the source of the dividend is fully disclosed. Naturally, from the standpoint of sound accounting practice, asset dividends should not be declared from unearned increments.

All dividends except stock dividends reduce the proprietorship of the company; stock dividends simply result in a decrease in a noncapital stock capital account and an increase in a capital stock account. If a stock dividend is declared in no-par-value stock, the dividend action should always indicate the dollar or cents amount of stock per share to be removed from the Retained Earnings account or other owners' equity account and added to capital stock.

Scrip dividends bear interest and are used only when a corporation is not in a position to pay cash dividends.

While a stock dividend is not considered taxable income to the recipient, its realistic effect is to transfer a part of retained earnings to permanent capital and to distribute that transferred portion to the stockholders.

In a stock split, only the number of shares is changed. There is no transfer of accumulated earnings to permanent capital. Stock splits usually are used when it is desired to reduce the market price per share of stock, and/or when it is desired to open a larger shareholder market for the stock.

Internal Control over Dividends

Illustration 25–1, Chapter 25, included internal control over dividends. Internal control over dividends naturally differs if a corporation utilizes the services of an independent fiscal dividend-paying agent, or if a corporation directly pays the dividends to its stockholders. The employment of an independent disbursing agent strengthens internal control because of the possibilities of error and fraud are reduced. If an independent disbursing agent is employed (usually a bank or trust company serving as stock transfer agent), the dividend-paying corporation will supply it with a copy of the dividend declaration and a check for the total of the dividends. When the agent pays the dividends to the stockholders, a list of the payments is returned to the corporation.

If a corporation does not employ a dividend-disbursing agent, normally the responsibility for the payments of dividends is delegated to the corporate secretary or treasurer. The delegated corporate officer will prepare a list of the stockholders as of the record date, the number of shares owned by each stockholder, and the dividends to be paid each stockholder. By multiplying the per share dividend by the number of shares outstanding, the total according to the listing is proved; this should be the duty of a person other than the one who prepared the listing. The corporate officer (assume the secretary) who prepared the listing should submit that list and the prepared dividend checks to another corporate officer (assume the treasurer) for comparison. The checks should be mailed without rerouting back to the officer in charge of preparing the checks.

A special dividend bank account may be in use, in which case a corporation paying its dividends directly will deposit an amount equal to the total of the dividend to be paid based on any one distribution. The internal control of this dividend account must be in conformity with the internal control of any cash account.

Dividend Audit

The following procedures are presented for dividend audits:

Ascertain Dividend Dates. The dividend record dates and payment dates stated in the minutes of the board of directors should be test-compared with the corresponding dates in the accounts, cash disbursements records, and subsidiary stockholders' records. In the declaration and payment of a dividend, three dates are important: the date of declaration, the date of closing the stockholders' records so that the corporation or its disbursing agent will know to whom to issue dividend checks, and the date of payment of the dividend.

Ascertain the Amount of the Dividends. Verification of the total dollar amount of the dividends declared is made by taking the outstanding shares of stock at the record-closing date according to the general ledger accounts, computing the dividends thereon, and comparing this figure with the total paid according to the dividend list extracted from the stockholders' records.

Examine for Proper Authorization. To be legal, a dividend must be authorized by the board of directors and the action recorded in the minutes. If dividend actions do not appear and if dividends have been paid, a request should be made that the action be recorded by the secretary and ratified by the board of directors. The payment of a dividend when the claims of creditors are thereby affected, the payment of a dividend when a corporation is insolvent, and the payment of a dividend in excess of accumulated earnings of the corporation are acts that may cause the directors to be held personally liable unless state laws permit such acts.

In general, dividends are illegal in the following circumstances:

a) When dividends reduce capital below the amount of stated capital—unless they are liquidating dividends.
b) When dividends are in violation of the code of regulations.

c) When a declaration on one class of capital stock in violation of the rights of other classes of stock.

d) When dividends violate a provision of the state corporation act.

The minutes of the board of directors must be watched to ascertain whether or not there existed declared but unpaid dividends at the close of the period; these should appear as liabilities.

Determine the Source of the Dividend. The source of a dividend declaration must be determined in order to ascertain the propriety of its declaration and to verify the correctness of the accounting entries. The status of the Retained Earnings account before and after the declaration must be examined to be certain that a deficit was not created by the dividend action and that Retained Earnings was not reduced below appropriated amounts required by other actions, such as a segregation brought about by the purchase of treasury stock, or long-term debt retirement.

If stock dividends have been issued, the records must be examined to ascertain that distributions have been correctly computed and that proper entries for the dividends have been made. The auditor must be certain that the increase in the capital stock caused by the dividend does not result in an issue in excess of the total stock authorized by the charter. The AICPA Committee on Accounting Procedures in its *Accounting Research Bulletin No. 43* recommends that in those instances where the stock dividend is relatively unimportant (involving less than 20 to 25 percent of the previously outstanding stock), the fair market value of the additional shares should be transferred from retained earnings to paid-in capital. In cases where the stock dividend is so large as to be in effect a stock-split, the Committee recommends that only the par or stated value of the additional shares be capitalized.

If the dividends are those of a company engaged in an extractive industry, the records must be examined to be certain that dividends have been correctly declared so far as depletion recoveries of capital are concerned. Dividends paid by corporations operating in wasting-asset industries often include a return of capital. This is especially true in instances in which there is no intention of acquiring new properties for further operation. If dividends are declared from amounts of capital recovered through depletion charges, the dividend checks (or an accompanying notice) should indicate the portion of dividends representing profits above depletion and the portion representing a return of capital. If by the return of capital, the rights and claims of creditors are jeopardized, the directors of the corporation may be held personally liable.

Verify Dividend Payments. Paid dividend checks should be test-compared with the stockholders' records for name, amount, and endorsement. All dividend checks should be accounted for in order to complete a bank reconciliation of general cash or of a special dividend account.

Unclaimed dividend checks should be deposited in the bank and a liability account credited.

If scrip dividends have been paid, the auditor should examine the scrip records to ascertain that they are properly kept and that all matured and returned scrip has been canceled.

Determine Dividends in Arrears. When cumulative dividends on preferred stock are in arrears, they should not be included as a liability in the balance sheet but the total accumulation should be shown as a footnote.

A few companies create reserves for dividend declarations, and some concerns accumulate reserves for dividends for the dividend accrual between the last dividend and the end of the accounting period. In these remote cases, the charge should be to Retained Earnings; and the reserve should be treated as a retained earnings appropriation—not as a liability. This type of reserve may be found in connection with cumulative preferred stock dividends, since dividends on preferred stock are very close to the fixed-charge category.

SECTION III: RETAINED EARNINGS SEGREGATIONS

A true "reserve" is a segregation of appropriation of retained earnings for a specific purpose. It has no relationship to current expenses or current net income. Retained earnings reservations are established voluntarily by the board of directors or by required legal or contractual obligation— and the reserves should be placed in the stockholders' equities section of the balance sheet because they are equity restrictions.

Appropriations, if optional, are created by authorization of the board of directors; both optional and contractual reserves should be returned to the Retained Earnings account or to a permanent noncapital stock capital account by the board of directors, after fulfillment of the purposes for which the reserves were created, unless specific agreement prevents their return. Reservations of retained earnings are created in order to prevent the dissipation of net assets through the medium of dividend declarations, thereby offering protection to creditors who are interested in the maintenance of a certain amount of proprietorship or offering protection to the corporation's interests by preventing the undue depletion of capital. Contractual retained earnings appropriations are not available for dividends unless the appropriation was created for the declaration of dividends.

If a "reserve" appears in the liability section of a balance sheet, the reader thereof could make two presumptions, as follows:

1. That the "reserve" was created by proper revenue charges, and
2. That such a "reserve" might properly be used in accordance with generally accepted principles of accounting to absorb costs and expenses when expenditures therefrom are made in the future.

If a reserve is in the owners' equities section of a balance sheet, the reader thereof could make the following presumptions:

1. That an unidentified portion of the net assets had been earmarked by a proper appropriation of retained earnings, and
2. That the reserve had been established *not* to absorb future expenses, accounting-wise, but merely to put the reader of the balance sheet on notice that management considered prudent the conservation of some of its assets generally to meet a possible future event.

Auditing Retained Earnings Segregations

The audit procedures for retained earnings segregations are similar to those for any noncapital stock equity account and are discussed below.

The auditor must ascertain the authority for the retained earnings segregation, the purpose for which it was created, and whether the creation is optional or contractual. If creation of a reserve is contractual, the necessary contracts or agreements must be examined to determine that they are being followed and that the reserve is of proper amount. The reason for the creation of any reserve must still be in existence at the time of audit, regardless of whether the reserve is of proper amount. The auditor should then analyze each reserve account in the usual manner. Entries in the reserve accounts must be traced to the record of original entry, and the authority for all entries must be established. If the reasons for the amount of any particular reserve are not perfectly clear, the amount of the reserve and the reasons therefor should be discussed with the client.

In *Accounting Terminology Bulletin No. 1,* the AICPA recommends that the term "reserve" be limited to appropriations of retained earnings. The American Accounting Association Committee on Concepts and Standards Underlying Corporate Financial Statements recommends that the auditor abandon the use of the term. Such a term as appropriations would promote clarity in financial statement presentation.

Appropriations for Contingencies. Contingencies appropriations are created to provide for a specially anticipated future contingency. The auditor should ascertain the reason for the establishment of the contingency appropriation and investigate its reasonableness and adequacy. Occasionally, contingency appropriations are established with no particular idea in mind other than a rather permanent appropriation of retained earnings to take care of *any* contingency which might develop. The appropriation is created, of course, to prevent dissipation of assets that might be needed; however, if the appropriation was established merely to reduce the retained earnings balance, the action might be held to constitute fraud toward the stockholders. Contingency appropriations should be returned to retained earnings either (1) when the contingency has failed to develop or (2) when the contingency results in an actuality that reduces an asset or creates a liability by a proper charge to revenue.

Self-Insurance Appropriations. Some companies follow a program of self-insurance or partial self-insurance. The reasons advanced for self-insurance include the inadequacy of some state laws for workmen's compensation insurance ratings, the promotion of safety practices, direct cost savings, the avoidance of duplication of services, wide geographical distribution of assets, and the difficulty of purchasing certain types of coverage. The reasons advanced against self-insurance include the hazards involved, the risks of dissipating capital, and improper fund management. When a program of self-insurance is followed, retained earnings segregations may or may not be established. If a self-insurance *fund* is established, it should be large enough to provide for unexpected abnormal losses, as well as anticipated normal losses. The prerequisites to a self-insurance program include the following: The number of risks should be large, the risks should be small and uniform in size, the degree of hazard in each risk should be equal, each risk should be independent of each other risk, and the self-insurer must be financially strong. Some very large companies are capable of handling appropriations self-insurance situations. An example is a large mid-west manufacturing company with plants throughout the world, which does not carry fire insurance on all of its buildings and inventory.

As indicated, a few corporations set up appropriations for *fire loss* as a segregation of retained earnings in anticipation of a nonaccuring contingency. The loss or expense that results from a fire occurs at the date of fire and is chargeable to expense in that period. A fire loss appropriation is simply one established for a specific contingency which may occur. The fact that one fire has or has not occurred does not determine whether another fire will or will not occur. Past losses are not good guides to future risks. Thus, there apparently is little justification for charging possible fire losses to expense in piecemeal amounts. If insurance is carried, the premium paid is the expense of transferring the risk to others for stated periods of time. If insurance is not carried, the self-insurer retains the risk of having or not having a loss, and takes the risk that financial status and revenue will be sufficient to overcome the losses attendant upon a possible fire. If the reserved is disposed of, it is returned to retained earnings.

Notwithstanding this reasoning, some companies do set up appropriations for fire losses by charges to expense accounts. If losses occur, the appropriations account is charged. Under this treatment, the appropriations should not appear in the owners equity section of the balance sheet but should be separately set forth. To treat the item as a liability is incorrect, since no liability exists. When based upon what the insurance premiums would be if insurances were carried, the charges to expense are misleading, if not incorrect. When based upon formulas and experience factors, the charges to expense are hypothetical and subject to distortion by catastrophes. There is no objection to the creation of an "equalization allowance" by monthly charges to expense and the write-off of actual losses to this allowance; at the end of each fiscal year, any balance in this allowance should be closed back to expense.

Sinking Fund Appropriations for Bond Redemption. While the modern trend is away from the establishment of sinking fund appropriations for bond redemption, the appropriation *sometimes* is established in order to protect bondholders against the possibility of dividend declarations on capital stock issues when the retained earnings is not entirely adequate. There need be no necessary relationship between a sinking fund and a sinking fund appropriation unless the trust indenture so specifies. In many cases, the appropriation may be in excess of the fund, owing to periodic retirements. The bondholder receives unnecessary additional protection if both a sinking fund and a sinking fund appropriation are established; funds are definitely set aside for bond retirement, and at the same time, assets are conserved by the prevention of dividend distributions through the creation of the sinking fund appropriation. It can logically be contended that a board of directors usually can be relied upon to protect retained earnings from undue dividend distributions and that therefore an appropriation for sinking fund need not be established unless it is obligatory.

If depreciation is adequate, bondholders receive added protection, since depreciation charges have the effect of reducing retained earnings. Depreciation prevents dividend distributions in excess of actual net income, whereas sinking fund appropriations require that part of the net income be withheld from distribution as dividends. If depreciation is adequate and the amounts so withheld from profits are not required for replacements of fixed assets, it is possible that a sinking fund may be established out of these amounts; in such a case, there is no necessity for the establishment of a sinking fund appropriation if a bond indenture calls for payments to a sinking fund in excess of reasonable depreciation or depletion, and if at the same time, a sinking fund appropriation is built up, the *correct* depreciation or depletion should be charged off as an expense and the indenture appropriation amount charged to Retained Earnings and credited to the appropriation for Sinking Fund account. When excess charges of this nature are encountered, it is an indication that there is a possibility that the assets will be worn out, obsolete, or entirely depleted before the bond issue matures. The auditor should examine the trust indenture to ascertain that provisions for both funds and appropriations are not being violated, and he must report upon any matters not receiving proper attention. If a fund deficiency exists, it must be fully reported.

Appropriations for Capital Stock Redemption. Appropriations for capital stock redemptions are similar to bond redemption appropriations and are for the purpose of retiring preferred stock issues by restricting dividends on common stock particularly during a company's early life. The preferred stock issues are then retired, and the owners of the common stock derive the full benefit of the future earnings. Capital stock redemption appropriations may be voluntary or obligatory.

Short-Term Equalization Allowances

At this point, brief consideration is given to short-term equalization allowances (sometimes improperly called reservations) for strike losses, accidents, vacation pay, maintenance, and similar expense accruals. These allowances should be established by periodic (monthly) charges to expense, since it is the purpose of their establishment to equalize the charge for a year's expense within the year on the interim statements prepared. Any balances remaining at the end of a year should be closed back to the expense originally charged because the total annual expense charges should not exceed the actual expense and because these expenses do not accrue—except vacation pay. Because these items do not represent retained earnings appropriations, they should not appear in the capital section of the balance sheet but in the liability section or separately set forth, as the case may be.

Some persons still view reservations for lawsuits, patent infringement, and strike losses as retained earnings appropriations. If this fallacious theory is followed, the cost of the occurrence of the actual event for which the "reserve" is created should not be charged directly to the reservation but should be charged to expense as a nonrecurring item. The balance of the reservation or appropriation may then be returned to retained earnings.

SECTION IV: FINANCIAL STATEMENT CONSIDERATIONS

Financial statement considerations for capital stock and for amounts paid in excess of par or stated values were set forth in Chapter 25 and in Illustration 25–3. Consideration now is given to owners' equities arising from sources other than the issuance of capital stock. Proper financial statement presentation demands that capital amounts not be disguised as liabilities and that liabilities not be buried as a portion of capital. An auditor should insist that the exact status of retained earnings and appropriations of retained earnings be properly presented.

Each retained earnings appropriation should be separately set forth in the stockholders' equities section of the balance sheet and in a manner whereby they may be added to the unrestricted retained earnings.

If agreements with bondholders, banks, and other creditors restrict the use of retained earnings but do not call for the establishment of a specific appropriation these restrictions must be disclosed in the financial statements or in accompanying footnotes. Dividends in arrears on cumulative preferred stock should appear as a footnote. Short-term equalization allowances are not a part of owners' equities and therefore should not appear in the capital section of a balance sheet.

Illustration 26–1 is a continuation and conclusion of Illustration 25–3. There are other methods of presentation of the items in Illustration 26–1.

ILLUSTRATION 26–1

Total paid-in capital (from Illustration 25–3)		$12,900,000
Appreciation of fixed assets—excess over cost	$ 400,000	
Discovery value capital—excess over cost	1,000,000	1,400,000
Retained earnings appropriated for:		
Appropriations for self-insured risks	$1,200,000	
Appropriations for plant expansion	5,000,000	6,200,000
Unappropriated earnings retained for use in the business		24,500,000
Total Paid-In Capital and Retained Earnings		$45,000,000
Less: Reacquired common shares (36,400), at cost		1,108,000
Total Stockholder Equities		$43,892,000

QUESTIONS

1. What are the basic reasons for appropriation of retained earnings?
2. Explain the distinction between (a) a bond sinking fund and (b) an appropriation of retained earnings for bond sinking fund. What is the purpose of each.
3. What debits may be made to an appropriations account? Explain.
4. Explain what is meant by self-insurance.
5. How should prior period adjustments be shown if they are material and relate directly to operations of a specific prior period?
6. What conditions must be met before the auditor can be confident that the amount of retained earnings is properly stated?
7. What factors must the auditor be aware of in a proposed declaration and payment of a dividend?
8. Under what conditions might the auditor determine that dividends are illegal?
9. What audit procedures for retained earnings appropriations should the auditor follow?
10. It is desirable that the balance sheet clearly present a permanent distinction between paid-in capital and retained earnings. How is it possible to maintain such a distinction when stock dividends are declared out of retained earnings?
11. Under what conditions would the auditor find appropriations limiting the use of retained earnings?
12. Dialog Services, Inc., has appropriated retained earnings of $2,000,000 over a 10-year period for the purpose of plant expansion. In the 11th year the company completes the expansion program at a cost of

$3,000,000. The expansion was financed through company funds of $1,800,000 and borrowed funds of $1,200,000. What disposition of the appropriation for plant expansion should the auditor recommend?

13. All of the common capital stock of the Lanier Company is subscribed. This consists of 100,000 shares of a par value of $10 per share. On December 31, 1974, $5 per share had been received on all of the subscriptions. The business had been successful, and the Retained Earnings account showed a balance of $4,000,000 on December 31, 1975. At the first board meeting in January, 1976 a motion was passed to make the stock—of which $5 per share was still uncollected—fully paid. You, as auditor, were called in to offer your advice as to how the motion should be brought into the records.

14. In 1975 the Gates Company issued 10,000 shares of no-par preferred stock at 90. The stock has a preference as to assets in the event of liquidation of $100 per share, and it is convertible into common stock on the basis of 20 shares of common to one of preferred. Converted preferred stock is to be permanently retired. The par value of the common stock is $3 per share, and it originally was sold for $3 per share.

    Corporate retained earnings was large; and in December, 1975 the directors, with their action approved by the stockholders, transferred $100,000 of retained earnings to the Preferred Stock account to raise that account to its full liquidating value of $100 per share.

    In 1976 holders of 1,000 shares of preferred, now booked at $100,000, converted their holdings into 20,000 shares of common stock with a par value of $60,000. Because 1976 was the first year in which conversions had been made, the company desired to establish a definite policy for future accounting for such conversions. Three auditors are called in, and their advice is solicited. The advice of each auditor follows:

    Auditor 1: The difference of $40,000 should be credited to Retained Earnings because it was reduced when the December, 1976, action was effected.

    Auditor 2: The difference should be credited to Paid-In Capital until the full $100,000 is available for retransfer to Retained Earnings.

    Auditor 3: Retained Earnings should be credited at the rate of $10 per share of preferred converted, or a total of $10,000.

    How would you treat the situation?

15. Outline the procedure you would recommend for an audit of dividends paid.

16. The audit of Companies 1, 2, 3, 4, and 5 showed that each had cumulative preferred stock dividends in arrears at a certain date. Each company had adequate free retained earnings to cover the dividend.

    Company 1 did not show the accumulation in the balance sheet but appended a footnote thereto indicating the amount of the accumulation.

    Company 2 showed the dividend in arrears as a current liability; Retained Earnings had been debited.

    Company 3 completely ignored the dividend.

    Company 4 set up a reserve for unpaid dividends, from retained earnings.

Company 5 showed the Dividend account as a current liability; it debited Dividends, which it showed as a deduction from retained earnings in the balance sheet.

Which company or companies followed the correct procedure? Explain.

PROBLEMS

1. A corporation is starting a retirement plan for its employees; all costs are to be borne by the corporation. The plan does not involve past-period service benefits.

    The corporation will make annual payments to an insurance company for approximately 20 years; however, the corporation is not bound by agreement with either the employees or the insurance company to continue these payments. In the event that the corporation discontinues its payments, the employees are to receive all benefits of the plan; no refund will be made by the insurance company to the corporation.

    With respect to the payments to the insurance company, which of the following is correct?
    a) Charge an expense account with the payments as made.
    b) Establish a reserve by a charge to Retained Earnings for the total estimated payments to be made over the 20-year period. As annual payments are made to the insurance company, the reserve would be charged.
    c) Charge Retained Earnings with the payments as made.

2. At the regular meeting of the board of directors of the One Corporation, a dividend payable in the stock of the Two Corporation is to be declared. The stock of the Two Corporation is shown on the records at cost, $87,000; market value of the stock is $100,000.

    The question is raised whether the amount to be recorded for the dividend payable should be book value or market value.
    a) Discuss the propriety of the two methods of recording the dividend liability, including in your discussion an analysis of the circumstances under which each might be acceptable.
    b) The property dividend declaration might state that "corporate property is being distributed as a dividend," or it might state that "corporate property is being distributed in payment of the dividend liability." Discuss briefly the significance of the wording of the property dividend declaration and its effect upon the stockholder receiving the dividend.

    (AICPA)

3. You are engaged on May 1, 1975 by a committee of stockholders to perform a special audit as of December 31, 1974 of the stockholders' equity of the Major Corporation, whose stock is actively traded on a stock exchange. The group of stockholders that engaged you believes that the information contained in the stockholders' equity section of the published annual report for the year ended December 31, 1974 is not correct. If your examination confirms their suspicions, they intend to use the report in a proxy fight.

Management agrees to permit your audit but refuses to permit any direct confirmation with stockholders. To obtain cooperation in the audit, the committee of stockholders has agreed to this limitation and you have been instructed to limit your audit in this respect. You have been instructed to exclude the audit of revenues and expenses for the year.

a) Prepare an audit program for the usual examination of the stockholders equity section of the balance sheet, assuming no limitation on the scope of your examination. Exclude the audit of revenue and expense accounts.

b) Describe any special auditing procedures you would undertake in view of the limitations and other special circumstances of your examination of the Major Corporation's stockholders' equity accounts.

c) Discuss the content of your audit report for the special engagement including comments on the opinion that you would render. Do not prepare an audit report.

(AICPA, adapted)

4. Analysis of the Retained Earnings account of the Eagle Manufacturing Company revealed the following:

Appropriation for Plant Rehabilitation—lease agreement requires this appropriation.	$ 20,000
Appreciation of Building—arose as a result of authorative appraisal	100,000
Appropriation for Pensions—to meet union contract requirement	300,000
Appropriation for Self-Insurance—to meet possible losses from employee accidents or death	40,000
Appropriations for Contingencies—to meet estimated claim relating to defective products sold in current year	10,000

Which of the above items should an auditor exclude from the appropriated earnings classification? State how each item so excluded would be classified.

5. The income statement for the Arman Company for the year ended December 31, 1975, shows:

Net income before provision for federal income tax	$400,000
Less: Provision for federal income tax	180,000
Net income	$220,000
Add extraordinary gain (net of taxes) from sale of subsidiary	200,000
Net Income and Extraordinary Gain	$420,000

Calculate per-share earnings for 1975 under each of the following assumptions:

a) The company has only common stock, the number of shares outstanding totaling 200,000.

b) The company has 200,000 shares of common stock plus 100,000 shares of convertible preferred stock outstanding. The preferred stock is convertible into common stock at the rate of one preferred share for each two shares of common held.

6. The stockholders' equities accounts for the Flax Company on December 30, 1975, are as follows:

Capital stock, $50 par, 50,000 shares $2,500,000
Premium on capital stock 1,000,000
Retained earnings 5,000,000

Shares of the company's stock are selling at this time at 75. What entries would you make in each case below?

a) A stock dividend of 10 percent is declared and issued.
b) A 100 percent stock dividend is declared and issued.

7. At the conclusion of your audit of the records of the Thomas Company, you are to prepare the necessary audit adjustments and prepare the capital section of the balance sheet as of December 31, 1975.

The corporation was organized on April 1, 1970, with authorized capital consisting of the following:

Common stock, voting, no par value; 50,000 shares authorized, of a stated value of $2.50 per share.

Preferred stock, no par value, noncumulative; 75,000 shares authorized, of a stated value of $8 per share; redemption price $12 per share; annual dividend $1 per share.

The records have never been audited. As of the date of its incorporation, the Thomas Company acquired the net assets of the R & G Corporation, properly priced at $600,000, by giving 50,000 shares of preferred stock and 50,000 shares of common stock. Only one capital account is carried on the records of the Thomas Company. The analysis of this account is as follows:

Stockholders' Equities

Date	Explanation	Debits	Credits
1970			
Apr. 1	Preferred stock and common stock sold		600,000
Nov. 10	Sold for cash 25,000 shares of preferred stock		250,000
	Net income or loss:		
	1970 net loss	45,860	
	1971 net income		32,750
	1972 net income		46,200
	1973 net income		86,350
	1974 net income		85,100
	1975 net loss	50,000	
1975			
Jan. 15	Cash dividend to preferred stockholders	75,000	
25	Bought back 1,000 shares of preferred, at		
	$12 per share	12,000	
Oct. 4	Uncollectible accounts charged off	30,000	
Nov. 4	Asset scrapped, undepreciated balance	1,300	
Nov. 12	Gift of fixed asset		11,000
Dec. 31	Building revalued upward		8,000
	Balance	905,240	
		1,119,400	1,119,400

8. The New Product Company was incorporated January 2, 1971. A balance sheet in summarized form as of December 31, 1975, follows:

Summarized Balance Sheet, December 31, 1975

ASSETS

Net working capital.	$ 50,000
Fixed assets	900,000
Allowance for depreciation	(100,000)
	$850,000

CAPITAL

Common stock	$600,000
Paid-in capital	500,000
Deficit in retained earnings	(250,000)
	$850,000

The deficit in retained earnings is the result of losses for book purposes and tax purposes of $70,000, $40,000, $50,000, $60,000, and $30,000 for the years 1971 through 1975, respectively.

Effective January 2, 1976, the company concluded a quasi reorganization, eliminating the deficit in retained earnings and reducing the fixed assets from $900,000 to their appraised replacement value of $700,000. No adjustment was required for the allowance for depreciation.

In 1976 the New Product Company sold $300,000 of first-mortgage bonds at par. The bond trust indenture's definition of net income contains a provision that the depreciation deductions are to be the larger of the amount actually deducted on the financial records of the company or the amount claimed for federal income tax purposes.

Before provisions for depreciation and federal income tax, the net income for the year 1976 was $85,000 for both company and tax purposes. The estimated remaining life of the fixed assets is 20 years from December 31, 1975; the net remaining cost base is to be written off at straight-line rates for tax purposes, and the net revaluation basis is to be written off for company book purposes. On December 31, 1976, the company declared and paid cash dividends of $25,000 on the common stock.

As the auditor for the company, you are requested to prepare:

a) A summarized balance sheet (for book purposes) as of December 31, 1976.

b) Optional: A schedule setting forth the net taxable income for federal income tax purposes for the year 1976.

c) Optional: A schedule setting forth the carryforward losses for federal income tax purposes available as a reduction of 1976 and 1977 taxable income.

(AICPA, adapted)

9. On January 2, 1976, the stockholders of the Union Company authorized a stock option plan which provided for the granting of options to key employees to purchase a total of 20,000 shares of $10 par value stock of the corporation at $14 per share. On this date the market price of the stock was $16 per share.

On January 3, 1975, options to purchase 3,000 shares were granted to the president as follows: 1,000 shares for services rendered in 1974, 1,000 shares for services to be rendered in 1975, and 1,000 shares for services to be rendered in 1976. The options are exercisable during the six months following the year in which the services were rendered. On January 3, 1975, the market price of the stock was $17 per share.

The president exercised his option for 1,000 shares on April 1, 1975, when the market price was $20 per share. On September 2, 1975, he sold the 1,000 shares at $18 per share.

The president did not exercise his option in 1976. When the option lapsed on June 30, 1976, the market price of the stock was $12 per share.

You are summoned to prepare the entry or entries required in 1975 under the plan and (if necessary) to record the lapsing of the option in 1976.

(AICPA, adapted)

10.   The records of the Monroe Company have never been audited. You were requested to audit the records, and devise a plan of reorganization. As a result of the audit, you discover the following items included in the accounts:

> Debits:
> | | |
> |---|---:|
> | Land appreication . . . . | $150,000 |
> | Treasury stock (5,000 shares at cost) . . . . | 23,000 |
> | Goodwill. . . . . | 250,000 |
> | Credits: (There are no other owners' equity accounts) | |
> | Common stock, 50,000 shares, par $10 . . . . | 500,000 |
> | Retained earnings, net, after appreciation . . . . | 25,000 |

You have devised a plan, approved by the stockholders, whereby the land appreciation, treasury stock, and goodwill are to be eliminated; the treasury stock is to be canceled and retired. Because the corporate retained earnings is too small to absorb these eliminations, amounts in excess of $25,000 are to be charged against the equity of the stockholders; and new shares of a par value of $1 are to be given in exchange for the outstanding shares, on the basis of one new share for each old share.

Prepare journal entries necessary to effect the plan of reorganization.

11.   The charter of the Toms Company contains a clause that an amount of money equal to two percent of the originally issued 100,000 shares $100 par value preferred stock (issued at par) is to be turned over to a redemption fund for a period of 50 years. After the stock has been outstanding for 10 years, it may be purchased from the redemption fund at a price not to exceed $110, and retired; but premium and discounts may not be charged and credited to the redemption fund. This is considered necessary so that the fund will not be depleted if all stock is retired at a premium. In 1975, the 11th year of the existence of the fund, the company purchased 1,000 shares at $105; and later in the same year, it purchased 1,000 shares at $95. You are to prepare the entries for the two purchases and retirements.

12.   A client decided to establish an Allowance for Plant Maintenance by annual debits to Plant Maintenance and annual credits to Allowance

for Plant Maintenance. As maintenance costs are incurred, they are to be debited to the allowance. The allowance will not be closed back to expense annually.

The derivation of the amounts to be credited to the allowance each December 31 is as follows: An amount equal to the larger of the actual maintenance costs for each year or 10 percent of the annual net income prior to the amount allocated to the allowance. The following data are submitted:

Year	Actual Maintenance Costs	Net Income before Allocation to Allowance
1974	$13,200	$ 91,840
1975	10,400	113,400
1976	17,200	158,200

You are required to:

a) Prepare the journal entries for the establishment of and additions to the allowance at December 31 for each of the years indicated above.

b) Prepare the journal entries necessary to charge out the actual maintenance costs.

PRACTICE MATERIAL ASSIGNMENTS

Metalcraft, Incorporated: Audit Problem:
  Assignment 12, Section B: Retained Earnings.
Colby Gears, Inc.: Holmes and Moore Audit Case:
  Retained Earnings.

27

Closing an Audit; Post-Statement Disclosures; Financial Statements

SECTION I: CLOSING AN AUDIT

When an examination is concluded and the work papers completed, the auditor is in possession of all date necessary for adjustment of the records, analysis of the business operations, preparation of the audit report, and the rendition of an opinion—unqualified, qualified, disclaimed, or adverse. Before the auditor departs from the offices of the client, he should review the work papers and compare them with the internal control questionnaire and the audit program, in order to be certain that all material and data have been covered and accumulated.

During the examination, as the auditor prepared audit adjustments, he posted them to his working trial balance of the balance sheet and the income statement accounts. Before departing, he should close out all of his work papers, so that he possesses full information concerning the financial statements, and so that he has his records in balance, in readiness for the preparation of the audit report.

After they are reviewed, the work papers should be indexed in final form, and a table of contents prepared. The work papers should not include client's material that has been loaned to the auditor for his perusal while in the client's office, but they will contain materials prepared by the client for the auditor at his request. All materials belonging to a client should be returned to him as they were presented to the auditor.

If the auditor has followed the plans set forth in this book, all audit adjustments will be recorded in three places: (1) on the work papers for the particular account being adjusted, (2) on the working trial balance papers, and (3) on the audit adjustment work papers. The adjustments should be reviewed critically before leaving the engagement, with the following points in mind: (1) the accounting propriety and mathe-

862

matical accuracy of the adjustments, (2) the completeness and adequacy of the entry explanations, and (3) the client's probable reactions to the adjustments. In an audit, audit adjustment explanations are exceedingly important; the ideal explanation is as brief as possible and so clear that it cannot possibly be misinterpreted, either by a succeeding auditor, by the client, or by anyone else in the event of litigation.

In a new engagement, it may be difficult to anticipate the client's reaction to the audit adjustments; in a repeat engagement, the auditor can more easily interpret the attitude of the client. To omit those adjustments which may displease a client is definitely a breach of moral and technical duty. All adjustments should be made which are necessary to the fair presentation of the financial statements. If situations exist wherein a proposed audit adjustment is simply the result of a difference of opinion, neither the auditor nor the client being incorrect, the client's records should remain unadjusted.

A copy of the audit adjustments is presented to the client. These adjustments will not be shown in the audit report; only the corrected results will be shown. So that the adjustments may be understood and appreciated, the auditor should review them with the proper personnel of the client. If the accounts of the client have not been closed, standard procedure is for the client to take the audit adjustments to the indicated asset, liability, capital, expense, and revenue accounts. Very infrequently, a client may not take up the auditor's adjustments in his records.

It may happen that the accounts of a client were closed prior to the audit. In such a case, no disruption is caused if the asset and liability account adjustments are posted and postings made to an Income Summary account for all adjustments affecting expense and revenue accounts; the balance of the Income Summary account may then be closed to Retained Earnings. The individual expense and revenue accounts of the client are thus permitted to stand; but the asset, liability, and capital accounts are corrected for future periods. The income statement will reflect the proper revenues and expense and the net income as they stand corrected, since this statement is prepared from the audit work papers. If the expense and revenue adjustments are recorded through the Income Summary account—assuming that the accounts have been closed—the adjustments of the auditor may be recorded as follows:

Insurance Expense (Income Summary)	5,000	
Prepaid Insurance		5,000
Insurance expired during 1975.		
Accounts Payable	50,000	
Purchases (Income Summary)		50,000
Purchase record was not cut off promptly at		
December 31, 1975.		
Income Summary	45,000	
Retained Earnings		45,000
To close the net effect of the audit adjustments to		
Retained Earnings.		

Practices in closing an audit vary among accounting firms. Many firms follow the policy of permitting the auditor in charge of the engagement to carry all operations through to completion, with a partner or manager reviewing the work papers and the original draft of the audit report. Other firms limit the authority of the man in charge of the engagement by frequent contacts with partners or managers who conduct a review of the work as it progresses and a review of the audit adjustments before they are submitted to the client. Other firms wait until an audit is ready for closing and then have a partner or manager review the work papers and the audit adjustments before closing out the working trial balances and before submission of the audit adjustments to the client. The practices of an accounting firm often will depend upon the ability and training of the individual men on the engagement, the size of the firm, the size of the engagement, and the importance of the findings.

The following is a summary, in terms of the papers an auditor will accumulate prior to drafting an audit report:

1. A completed internal control questionnaire.
2. The audit program.
3. A balance sheet.
4. An income statement and a statement of retained earnings.
5. A statement of changes in financial position.
6. All schedules supporting the financial statements.
7. All work prepared during the course of the examination.
8. Copies of the proceedings of meetings of the board of directors, major committees, and the stockholders.
9. Copies of pension, bonus and profit sharing plans.
10. Copies of necessary contracts or notes pertaining to them.
11. Copies of bond indentures.
12. Copies of tax returns—federal, state, local.
13. Copies of all other necessary and desirable papers.
14. A copy of all audit adjustments.
15. An index of the work papers.

SECTION II: POST-STATEMENT DISCLOSURES

The reporting of material events occurring after the date of the financial statements is necessary because material events occurring after the date of the financial statements and prior to the rendition of the audit report may have an effect upon the financial statements, or the auditor (or his firm) may be accused of possessing unreported knowledge. The Securities Act requires that registration statements filed with the Securities and Exchange Commission be representative as of the date of registration. The disclosure of post-statement events is based upon three assumptions, as follows: (1) the amount is material, (2) the event is significant and is unusual, and (3) the event takes place after the balance sheet date but before the audit is closed.

Prior to drafting an audit report, the auditor should—and normally does—review the events occurring subsequent to the date of the financial statements. These reviews are made primarily to determine whether any of the events are of sufficient magnitude materially to affect the reported financial condition or operations of the client. The time required to complete an audit varies, of course; however, it is entirely possible that events have taken place after the end of the fiscal year which may affect the client's financial position or operations *subsequent thereto* and *prior to* or *subsequent to* the issuance of the audit report. However, it does not follow that a report should be delayed on the premise that such an event might occur. Also, an audit report should be completed and delivered as rapidly as possible after concluding the field work.

It must be remembered that an audit report and its accompanying financial statements primarily are historical—they are not forecasts. Also, if there is no necessity for disclosure of events occurring subsequent to the date of financial statements, the disclosure serves no purpose. Perhaps the point should be reemphasized that the work of concluding an examination and rendering the report takes place after the date of the financial statements. The auditor ordinarily determines the cutoff of cash receipts and disbursements, and expense and payable recognition; reviews the collection of receivables; and follows confirmation requests. While these procedures vary with the circumstances of each audit, the auditor nevertheless is placed in a position whereby he is able to determine the necessity for reporting events occurring subsequent to the date of the financial statements.

Post-statement events of financial importance constitute:

1. Those that directly affect the financial statements, and should be given recognition in the year-end financial statements by adjustment of those statements.
2. Those that do not require adjustment of the financial statements but may warrant comment, as footnotes to the statements or comments in the audit report.
3. Those that may fall into a questionable category between (1) and (2), in which case the decision is difficult for disclosure or nondisclosure, and wherein there may be disagreement among accountants.

In general, audit reports should include comments on post-statement events that:

1. May affect the financial statements being audited.
2. May affect future operations and subsequent financial statements.
3. Do not fall under the requirements of the Securities and Exchange Commission.
4. Do involve the Securities and Exchange Commission.

Prior to preparing the audit report, but after having completed all routine postperiod work, the auditor should:

1. Read the new-period minutes of the meetings of stockholders, the board of directors, and major committees, in order to determine if major financial events have occurred which would have an effect on the fairness of the presentation of the financial statements of the year under examination.
2. Review the client's financial statements prepared in the interim between the financial statement date and the date of submitting the audit report.
3. If applicable, study existing prospectuses.
4. Review registration statements, if applicable.
5. Discuss, with the client's officers, events that may be material.
6. Obtain a letter from the client's attorney concerning pending litigation.

In the opinion of the author, disclosure should be granted all *extraordinary events* occurring between the date of the financial statements and the date of preparing the report, whether those events affect the financial statements for the period closed or the future. The only exceptions are in those cases where *only* the interests of owners are involved *and* where the events are of a normally routine nature. The requirements for disclosure depend upon the circumstances of each case; consequently, reasoned opinion is required to judge between extraordinary and ordinary occurrences and their effect on financial position, financial operations, creditors, and investors. Both adverse and advantageous incidents should be given equal prominence in the audit report.

The following are illustrative of the items affected and the events that may take place subsequent to the date of the financial statements but prior to the rendition of the report:

Items Affected	*Post-Statement Event*
Cash:	Bank failure
	Court action impounding funds
	Robbery, burglary, or theft of money in an amount in excess of insurance
Receivables:	Bank moratorium
	Failure of major customer
	Large unforeseen note or account losses
Investments:	Drastic declines in market price
	Financial difficulties of issuing companies
	Default in interest or principal payments
	Sale of investments at prices materially above or below cost
Inventories:	Uninsured fire losses and other casualty losses
	Drastic increases or decreases in market price
	Changes in the method of pricing inventories
	Unusual use of inventory as loan collateral
Fixed Assets:	Uninsured fire and other casualty losses
	Proposed expansion or contraction plans
	Asset appraisals upward or downward
	Obsolescence caused by sudden changes in products or demand

Current Liabilities:	Unusual purchase commitments, accompanied by decreased selling prices
	Purchase contract cancellations
	Default in note payments
Long-Term Liabilities:	Large increases in funded debt
	Default in interest or principal payments
	Refunding operations
Capital Stock:	Increases or decreases in number of shares
	Unusual treasury stock transactions
	Reorganization of capital stock structure
	Conversion of convertible debt securities (see *Opinion No. 14* of the APB)
	Changes in the form of organization—that is, from a partnership to a corporation, or vice versa
Paid-In Capital:	Transfers to or from capital stock caused by changes in par or stated value
	Unusual changes in paid-in capital
Retained Earnings:	Unusual dividends that impair working capital
	Unusual appropriations
	Material losses or profits directly charged or credited (in violation of *Opinion No. 9* of the APB)
Other Items:	Changes in key executive personnel
	Changes in management policies
	Changes in laws
	Unusual additional tax assessments or refunds
	Securities and Exchange Commission requirements
	Court judgments rendered
	Actions of foreign governments (oil embargo, asset confiscation, and so forth).

The events occurring subsequent to the date of the financial statements should be of sufficient importance to warrant one or more of the following actions:

1. Amending the year-end financial statements.
2. Footnoting the financial statements.
3. Placing parenthetical notations in the financial statements.
4. Commenting in the text of the audit report. If an item is commented upon in the text of the report, the auditor should connect the financial statements and the report in a manner similar to the following: "These financial statements are an integral part of and are subject to the text comments of the accompanying report. The report text must be read in conjunction with these statements."

SECTION III: THE AUDITOR, FINANCIAL STATEMENTS, AND THE SECURITIES AND EXCHANGE COMMISSION

Requirements of the Securities and Exchange Commission—particularly those requirements pertaining to reporting—are interwoven throughout this section and other sections of this chapter. The requirements are not all-inclusive, because that subject would require a book by itself. Also, many requirements have been set forth in earlier chapters of this book.

The constantly tightening requirements of the Securities and Exchange

Commission should be followed by an auditor. As indicated in Chapter 3, the Securities and Exchange Commission administers the Securities Act, the Securities Exchange Act, the Investment Company Act, and others. The acts authorize the Commission to prescribe forms, items, and details of financial statements rendered to that body by initial registrants, those filing annual reports (10K), and by those filing a prospectus. The Securities Act of 1933 requires that a registration statement must be filed with the Commission prior to the issuance of securities for sale in interstate commerce if the issue exceeds a defined amount. Minute detail is required in a registration statement, including a complete economic history of the registrant company. The introduction to the Securities Act stipulates, in part, that the "act is to provide full and fair disclosure of the character of the securities sold in interstate and foreign commerce and through the mails." Acting under the authority conferred by the Securities Exchange Act of 1934, the Securities and Exchange Commission has held that one of its functions under the act is "to obtain an adequate disclosure of the material facts regarding corporations whose securities are registered on national security exchanges, through periodical reports. . . ."

In March, 1963, the Securities and Exchange Commission announced, in *Accounting Series Release No. 90,* that it would not accept qualified certificates filed with it in connection with a public offering of securities. Thus, the agency requires that even on a first audit, the auditor must satisfy himself with all representations in the registration statement, including year-to-year earnings, and particularly opening inventories on an initial audit.

The Securities and Exchange Commission has indicated its attitude with respect to the disclosure of events taking place after the date of the financial statements. Both the Securities Act and the Securities Exchange Act create certain possible liabilities for the accountant based upon the inclusion of an untrue statement of material fact or the failure to state a fact required to be stated or necessary to make the financial statements not misleading—not only at their effective date but also at their later date of issuance. The contention, in effect, is to say that if the responsibility of the auditor ceases at the date of the financial statements, the assumption would be that he is not required to possess knowledge of events occurring subsequent to that date.

Financial statements normally are representative *only* as of their date—not at their later date of issuance. This is not the situation with respect to financial statements incorporated in registration statements filed with the Securities and Exchange Commission, under the Securities Act; under that act, the financial statements supposedly represent conditions and operations as of the date of the registration statement. Therefore, the auditor *must* investigate nonroutine events occurring between the date of the financial statements and the effective date of the registration statement. How to meet the provisions of the act has never been conclusively interpreted by the courts or by the Commission.

Registration statements may or may not include interim financial statements, which may or may not be certified. If they are certified, information regarding the affairs of a client are disclosed up to a current date. If the financial statements are not certified, the auditor may be requested to furnish the registrant a letter setting forth the fact that an examination was not made for the interim period but that limited procedures were applied, that inquiries were made, and that the results of the application of the limited procedures and the inquiries led to the belief that the uncertified interim statements did not require amendment. Also, in the event that the securities registration does not include audited interim financial statements, the auditor may be requested to furnish a statement concerning material changes in the client's financial condition during the period between the last certified statements and the registration date. The statement of the auditor would be based upon the audit procedures and inquiries made subsequent to the date of the certified financial statements.

Except for public utility holding companies and registered investment companies, the Securities and Exchange Commission has not indicated a statement of accounting principles but prefers that statements of principles come from the accounting profession. However, the Commission is moving rapidly in the area of principle formulation—to the dismay and chagrin of the AICPA and the profession. Of course, the SEC has the power of law to aid in its attitude, while the profession is less fortunate. Where the experience of the Commission has disclosed serious discrepancies in practice as between companies and accountants, and where the Commission has felt that uniformity in practice would be of benefit, the conclusions have been expressed by rule or regulation of the Commission or in an opinion of the chief accountant of the Commission. Accounting regulations and requirements of the Commission are published in Regulations S–X, relating to the form and content of financial statements and to auditing regulations; in the Commission's *Accounting Series Releases;* and in formal Commission findings and opinions. The rules contained in Regulation S–X prescribe the method of presenting pertinent data in financial statements to be included in registration statements and reports to be filed with the Commission. The *Accounting Series Releases* were started in 1937 for the purpose of contributing to the development of uniform statements and practices in major accounting questions; these releases are now a part of the regulations (Rule 1–01[a]). Certain releases have dealt with the independence of accountants and actions against accountants which resulted in their disqualification from practice before the Commission; other releases have discussed auditing procedures. Current releases are dealing with a variety of topics—product line reporting, division reporting, material changes in the application of accounting changes in quarterly and annual reports, material charges and credits to income, and many other topics.

Under the Investment Company Act of 1940, the prescription of the form of preparing financial statements of investment companies has the effect of providing a reasonable degree of uniformity in the accounting policies and principles to be followed by the registered investment companies in maintaining their financial records.

Article 5 of Regulation S–X governs the certification, form, and content of the financial statements, including the basis for consolidation, for all companies except investment companies, insurance companies, banks, and companies in a developmental stage. Under Article 5, the balance sheet is presented in the order of "current to fixed"; the income statement shows sales, cost of sales, selling expense, general expense, administrative expense, other income, other deductions, special items, and net income before and after federal income tax provisions. An analysis of retained income is required; the income statement may be combined with the statement of retained income, provided such combination is not misleading and does not obscure annual net income.

Relating to the classification of assets as current or other than current, Rule 3.13 of Regulation S–X of the Securities and Exchange Commission states:

. . . Items classed as current assets shall be generally realizable within one year. However, generally recognized trade practices may be followed with respect to items such as installment receivables or inventories long in process, provided an appropriate explanation of the circumstances is made and, if practicable, an estimate is given of the amount not realizable within one year.

Thus, in preparing financial statements in conformity with the requirements of the Securities and Exchange Commission, the segregation indicated in the rule must be followed.

Rule 3.01 of Regulation S–X, as amended, provides that "financial statements may be filed in such form and order, and may use such accepted terminology, as will best indicate their significance and character in the light of the provisions applicable thereto." Thus, full and adequate disclosure in the financial statements reduces the necessity for reporting accounting methods in detail. In various cases decided by the Commission, it has in certain instances held that the financial statements did not result in full disclosure when the accompanying report offered explanations; and in other instances, it has held that the financial statements need not be recast when the report proper afforded disclosure. These varying decisions are caused by the circumstances in each case. "It is the philosophy of the various Securities Acts that financial statements shall be so prepared to make it possible for individuals to determine on their own account the investment of their funds to the management of a given corporation or to increase or decrease their present investments."

Section 11 (*a*) of the Securities Act of 1933 provides possible liability for false or misleading registration statements, as follows:

In case any part of the registration statement, when such part became effective, contained an untrue statement of a material fact or omitted to state a material fact required to be stated therein or necessary to make the statements therein not misleading, any person acquiring such security (unless it is proved that at the time of such acquisition he knew of such untruth or omission) may, either at law or in equity . . . sue. . . .

The possible liability may exist against

Every accountant, engineer, or appraiser, or any person whose profession gives authority to a statement made by him, who has with his consent been named as having prepared or certified any report or valuation which is used in connection with the registration statement, with respect to the statement in such registration statement, report, or valuation, which purports to have been prepared or certified by him (Section 11[*a*] [4]).

The preceding possible liabilities may not exist when

As regards any part of the registration statement purporting to be made upon his authority as an expert, (i) he had, after reasonable investigation, reasonable grounds to believe and did believe, at the time such part of the registration statement became effective, that the statements therein were true and that there was no omission to state a material fact required to be stated therein or necessary to make the statements therein not misleading (Section 11[*b*] (3) [*B*]).

Under federal security legislation, therefore, the auditor may be charged with liability for failure to protect prospective investors and present stockholders. An action to enforce a liability must be brought within one year after the discovery of the facts constituting the cause of action and within three years after such cause of action accrued. A liability may exist for carelessness and negligence, even though fraud did not exist.

As a result of federal security legislation, the accountant has been placed in the position whereby he must differentiate between the rights and privileges of the various groups interested in the financial statements—that is, the rights and privileges of the government and its agencies, preferred stockholders, common stockholders, bondholders, and so forth. These obligations of the auditor spring from the legal requirements governing the relationships existing between the various classes of financial interests; the application of these legal requirements depends upon business data, properly prepared, classified, and presented in the financial statements.

Regulation S–X, Rule 3.11, requires a statement of the policy followed for the fiscal period for which income statements are filed with respect to the following:

(1) the provisions for depreciation, depletion, and obsolescence of physical properties or reserves created in lieu thereof, including the methods and, if practicable, the rates used in computing the annual amounts; (2) the provision for depreciation and amortization of intangibles, or reserves created in lieu thereof, including the methods and, if practicable, the rates used in computing the annual amounts; (3) the accounting treatment for maintenance, repairs, renewals, and betterments; and (4) the adjustment of the accumulated reserves for depreciation, depletion, obsolescence, amortization, or reserves in lieu thereof at the time the properties are retired or otherwise disposed of.

This policy statement must be incorporated in the income statement or must accompany it. In the preparation of balance sheets for all companies, Regulation S–X requires that accumulations for depreciation, depletion, amortization, or retirements be shown as deductions from the assets to which they are applicable. Further requirements of Regulation S–X are, in part, as follows: If a director, officer, or principal stockholder, other than an affiliated company, owed the corporation at any date during the fiscal period more than one percent of the total assets, or $20,000, whichever is the lesser, such information must be filed. A schedule of indebtedness owed the registrant by each affiliated company at the beginning and at the close of the fiscal period must be filed. With respect to inventories, the regulations not only require that the basis of determining inventory values be shown but also that the method of determining the cost or the market be shown; for example, the method might be first-in, first-out; weighted average cost; last-in, first-out; or other.

The balance sheet must disclose the preferences of senior stock issues in the event of involuntary liquidation, when the excess of the preference over par value or over stated value is significant; it also must disclose any restrictions, or the absence of restrictions, upon retained earnings, resulting from the fact that the preference of the senior shares, in involuntary liquidation, exceeds its par or stated value. Noncapital stock capital items must be divided among appreciation increments, retained earnings, additional paid-in capital, and other capital items. Each significant special fund must be separately presented in the balance sheet. If significant in amount, discount on capital stock shall be shown separately and deducted from the capital stock, or treated by other proper methods. All of the requirements of Regulation S–X are minimum requirements, to which shall be added all necessary additional information and material.

Certain accounting releases of the Securities and Exchange Commission deal with the description of "surplus" following a quasi reorganization. These releases require "that a clear report be made to stockholders of the proposed restatements and that their formal consent thereto be obtained." *Release 16* indicates the disclosure considered necessary when an operating deficit has been charged off against Paid-In Capital by resolution of the board of directors, not accompanied by approval of the stockholders. The minimum disclosure is as follows:

Until such time as the results of operations of the company on the new basis are available for an appropriate period of years (at least three) any statement or showing of earned surplus should, in order to provide additional disclosure of the occurrence and the significance of the quasi-reorganization, indicate the total amount of the deficit and any charges that were made to capital surplus in the course of the quasi-reorganization which would otherwise have been required to be made against income or earned surplus.

The same release requires that the new retained earnings be dated in the balance sheets (for 10 years at a maximum) subsequent to the quasi reorganization; it also requires that full disclosure be granted the entire transaction and that an explanation be given of the possible effect on future dividends.

If, upon review by the Commission, financial statements are found to have been prepared contrary to generally accepted accounting principles, or if they otherwise fail to meet the requirements of the Commission, a deficiency letter is prepared and sent to the company allegedly at fault. The deficiency letter, followed by correspondence and/or conference with the registrants and their accountants, frequently constitute a method of resolving accounting questions which might otherwise have to be settled through formal hearings.

The Investment Company Act, which brought investment companies and their advisers under the supervision of the Securities and Exchange Commission, requires—in part—that the registered investment company file the following information:

1. A balance sheet, together with a statement of the aggregate value of investments at the date of the balance sheet.
2. A schedule setting forth the amounts and values of the securities at the balance sheet date.
3. A statement of income for the period covered by the report, which must be itemized for each revenue and expense category which is in excess of 5 percent of the total revenue or expense.
4. A statement of retained earnings, itemized for each item which is in excess of 5 percent of the total charges or credits during the period.
5. A statement of the total remuneration paid to all directors and members of the advisory board, to all officers, and to each person to whom any officer or director of the company is an affiliated person.
6. A statement of the total dollar value of purchases and sales of investment securities, other than government securities.

In addition, the same information must be transmitted to shareholders at least semiannually. The Commission has ruled that, for investment companies, the records of original entry, general ledgers, and any other important data must be retained forever.

The requirements of the Securities and Exchange Commission for the independent accountant's opinion or certificate are treated in Chapter 28.

SECTION IV: FINANCIAL STATEMENT PREPARATION

Professional accounting has become so much a matter of public interest that today the auditor is charged with responsibility for the presentation of a client's financial statements in a manner impossible of misinterpretation, regardless of the lack of technical knowledge of the person reading the statements. A client's statements are no longer prepared for the client alone—but for present stockholders, prospective stockholders, governmental agencies, creditors, the press, financial analysts, organized labor, and others who are only casually interested. The spotlight is currently focused on the income statement.

Financial statements must be prepared in accordance with recognized accounting principles and in accordance with recognized standards of preparation, and they must be prepared so that they will enhance the communication of financial data to all who may be interested. Financial statements must be adequate, and they must offer full disclosure of all material data. The physical form of financial statements may vary in accordance with (1) preference and (2) the purpose of preparation. *All financial statements should be prepared in comparative form.*

Standards of financial statement preparation may be summarized as follows:

1. Assets should be classified in a manner that will:
    a) Facilitate the accounting for their utilization.
    b) Facilitate the interpretation of the statements.
2. If assets are expressed on a basis other than cost of acquisition, that different basis should be indicated.
3. Accumulated provision for doubtful accounts, depreciation, and depletion should be deducted from the related asset basic figure in the balance sheet.
4. Assets and related liabilities should not be offset unless such offset is required by law or by contract.
5. The balance sheet should not contain a special section for reserves or for allowances. Each reserve or allowance should be identified as a subdivision of retained earnings, or as an asset reduction account, or as a liability. The position of each reserve or allowance in the balance sheet should be established accordingly.
6. Significant characteristics of long-term liabilities should be disclosed in the balance sheet, or in footnotes thereto.

7. Changes in paid-in capital and retained earnings should be disclosed in the balance sheet in the period in which the changes occur.
8. Reservations of retained earnings are to be returned to retained earnings when the need for the segregation has passed.
9. The income statement should be arranged to report in a consistent manner the detail of revenues, expenses, and periodic net income or net loss.
10. The net income or net loss in the income statement must be clearly set forth—on the basis of consistently following the all-inclusive type of income statement, as set forth in APB *Opinions Nos. 9, 15, and 30.*
11. Both the primary and the fully diluted earnings per share should be presented with equal prominence on the face of the income statement and not as footnotes to that statement.
12. The statement of changes in financial position should clearly indicate the sources and the uses of the items.

If the foregoing standards or rules are followed in the preparation of financial statements, (1) the statements will offer full disclosure; (2) they will not be misleading; (3) they will be clear in all respects; (4) they will be as concise as possible, with no sacrifice of necessary detail; (5) classifications will be clear and will not overlap; (6) the statements will indicate the specific purposes desired; and (7) they will present fairly the financial position of the company, the results of its operations, and the changes in financial position.

In an elementary accounting course, it may be wise to insist upon relative rigidity of physical form in the preparation of financial statements, so that the student is not confused, and so that he does not receive the impression that any form will suffice. As the student progresses in education, he must realize that financial statement forms have a wide range of flexibility, so that a story may be told and a picture presented in the most intelligent and enlightening manner. By the time the student has completed his organized course of study, his training should be broad enough to enable him to prepare financial statements in the most effective manner under a given set of circumstances. The important point to remember is that accounting lays down certain broad principles; and when these principles are applied, the results will be proper, regardless of minor variations in physical form.

Illustrations of financial statements appear in this chapter and in Chapter 28. It is suggested that the reader also examine available annual reports to stockholders, issued by large corporations.

SECTION V: THE BALANCE SHEET

This is not the place for a general discussion of the balance sheet, but a few comments in the nature of guides to its preparation are pre-

ILLUSTRATION 27–1

PARENT COMPANY

Statement of Financial Position
December 31, 1975, and 1974

	1975	1974
Current Assets:		
Cash	$ 81,524	$ 85,267
Marketable securities (at cost, which is approximately market)	917,960	764,020
Accounts receivable	9,252	6,922
Total Current Assets	$1,008,736	$ 856,209
Less: Current Liabilities:		
Indebtedness to companies consolidated	$ 217,205	$ 377,531
Accounts payable and accrued expenses	20,624	16,425
Income tax liability	38,066	38,223
Total Current Liabilities	$ 275,895	$ 432,179
Working Capital	$ 732,841	$ 424,030
Investments and Noncurrent Receivables, at Cost or Less:		
Stocks of companies consolidated	$1,995,630	$1,869,900
Receivables from companies consolidated	249,718	197,684
Other investments	234,333	228,777
Prepaid charges and other assets	29,704	27,462
Total Assets Less Current Liabilities	$3,242,226	$2,747,853
Deductions:		
Long-term debt	$ 444,650	$ 446,224
Deferred credits	10,240	12,685
Net Assets	$2,787,336	$2,288,944
Stockholders' Equities:		
Capital:		
Stock issued	$1,632,450	$1,428,750
Amount in excess of par value	254,220	30,460
Earnings retained in the business	900,666	829,734
	$2,787,336	$2,288,944

sented. One form of balance sheets emphasizes the working capital position and the source of the net assets, as shown in Illustration 27–1.

A balance sheet must be so prepared that it is understandable, that it fulfills the requirements of the business organization for which it is prepared, and that full disclosure is given to all material items. A balance sheet should not be so condensed that disclosures of material data are withheld.

In preparing a balance sheet, classifications should be indicated. Assets may be classified as follows:

1. Current assets (including short-term prepaid expenses).
2. Investment assets (other than current).

3. Fixed tangible assets.
4. Intangible assets.
5. Long-term deferred charges.

Liabilities may be classified as follows:

1. Current liabilities (including short-term deferred credits).
2. Long-term deferred credits.
3. Long-term liabilities.

The foregoing order is merely suggestive, and another order may be equally satisfactory. Although an interchange of this order may easily be followed, it is good practice to arrange the assets and liabilities so that the classifications coincide; that is, if the current assets are listed first, current liabilities should be listed first in the liability section. Classification must be correct at all times, since an error in shifting an asset or a liability from one classification to another can have serious consequences. Each classification of assets and liabilities must be properly subdivided so that confusion does not result from combining similar, but unrelated, items.

In order to afford adequate disclosure, explanatory footnotes regarding any items which cannot be set forth adequately in the statement proper should be appended to the balance sheet. Footnotes should never be eliminated at the sacrifice of clarity, especially in view of the modern demand for more information.

Recognized practice is to the effect that the valuation methods used should be indicated in the balance sheet whenever necessary. Fixed assets should be labeled as being included at cost or other basic figures; investments should be shown at cost, market, or the lower of cost or market, in accordance with recognized principles and consistent client practice. For credit purposes, or for purposes of showing solvency, it is more vital to present the valuation methods used in connection with current assets, particularly inventory and current investments, than for fixed assets. Consequently, if nothing is mentioned concerning the pricing of fixed assets, long-term investments, and intangible assets, the inference should be that those assets are stated at cost or other original acquisition base.

A liability should not be subtracted from a related asset and only the net difference shown. Each liability and each asset should be separately shown, even though a full equity in an asset is not owned, and even though title has not passed. If the offset habit is acquired, the true balance sheet is destroyed, and its value as a statement of condition is lost.

Balance sheet terminology is fairly well standardized so far as individual items are concerned. Each item must be captioned so that its identity and nature are fully defined and so that the terminology is not misleading.

Important comparative data should be included in the audit report, accompanied by appropriate comment. Comparative financial statements portray current changes and trends affecting the company which otherwise would not be presented. Financial statements for a series of fiscal periods increase the significance of a statement for any one period. Changes in the application of accounting principles should be pointed out in the audit report, and changes in account classifications between fiscal periods should be explained in the comparative statements. If necessary, explanations and footnotes of a preceding period should be restated or referred to in the comparative financial statements currently prepared.

Statement Standards for Individual Items

The standards of financial statement preparation briefly set forth below contain certain excerpts from the standards prepared by the American Accounting Association, and materials of the AICPA.

Cash. The net cash balance of cash funds—petty cash funds, payroll funds, and others—may be shown separately in the balance sheet, or it may be combined with the unrestricted cash in banks. The caption "cash in banks" or "cash on hand and in banks" should include only freely withdrawable and unrestricted amounts, undeposited cash, and cash items, in order to ascertain immediate debt-paying ability. Each restricted cash balance should appear in its proper balance sheet classification, accompanied by necessary explanatory notes. Cash balances restricted as to withdrawal may be the result of bid deposits, contract deposits, escrow funds, funds held in trust, deposits in closed banks, and others.

Unrestricted cash in foreign depositaries properly may be included in the caption "cash on hand and in banks" as a current asset. If the foreign funds are unrestricted by the depositor and by governmental action, the cash at foreign points should be stated in domestic dollars at the rate of exchange prevailing at the balance sheet date. If the domestic dollar is at a discount, the appreciation should be shown in the Allowance for Fluctuation of Foreign Exchange account. If the domestic dollar is at a premium, the loss may be charged to the allowance; if an allowance account does not exist, the charge should be to an expense account.

A bank overdraft may actually exist, or it may be only an apparent overdraft in the records of a client. If the latter, it probably is the result of paying liabilities in anticipation of cash collections to be deposited before the issued checks have cleared. If the prepared checks have not been mailed, they should be returned to the Cash account.

An actual bank overdraft is a current liability. If accounts are maintained in two or more banks, an overdraft in one bank theoretically should not be offset in the balance sheet by available balances in other banks. In practice, it is customary to use the principle of offset, provided available balances are freely transferable from one bank to another.

Receivables. All receivables should be shown at an amount not in excess of their cash collectible worth. Proper distinction must be made between receivables to be classified as current assets and those to be classified a noncurrent assets.

Allowances for doubtful receivables, and allowances for discounts, rebates, and transportation to be deducted, should be subtracted from the gross total of the receivables. Allowances for discounts, rebates, and transportation to be deducted are seldom used, on the basis that the amounts normally are not material and that the amounts are fairly constant from period to period. If allowances are not used or are not necessary for doubtful receivables, that fact should be indicated in the balance sheet.

In the balance sheet, the trade and nontrade accounts receivable should be separated if the nontrade receivables represent a material portion of the total receivables. Also, the nontrade accounts receivable—if material in amount—should be subdivided in a manner to disclose their origin. If the total of the nontrade accounts is not material, they may be shown together under a title such as "other accounts receivable."

Receivables of significant amount from client personnel should be segregated because of personal interests and due to the relation of these persons to a separate corporate entity.

Receivables from affiliated companies should be separately set forth because of the possibility of nonconversion to cash. The circumstances surrounding expected cash collections determine if affiliated company receivables are to be shown as current or noncurrent assets.

Receivables from capital stock subscriptions should be segregated in the balance sheet due to the relationship of the receivable to the corporate capital structure. If collection is anticipated within the operating cycle, this nontrade receivable should be included among the current assets; otherwise not.

If material in amount, credit balances in accounts receivable should be shown as such in the current liability section of the balance sheet. The gross total of the debit balances in the receivables will appear as assets. Credit balances in accounts receivable are liabilities, to be liquidated by the payment of cash or by future sales.

Drafts, notes, and acceptances receivable must be presented in accordance with recognized principles of accounting, and the presentation must offer full disclosure of all material facts. Trade and nontrade items should be separated; in accordance with circumstances, current and noncurrent items should be separated. Trade notes and acceptances not due are current assets if the collection time falls within the cycle of business operations; otherwise, they are noncurrent assets. Notes and acceptances discounted normally are not included in the assets; a footnote should set forth the amount discounted, if material.

Temporary Marketable Securities. Temporary marketable securities, classified as current assets, may be priced at the lower of cost or market;

for purposes of disclosure, the higher figure preferably should be shown parenthetically. Modern procedure is that marketable securities are carried at cost, with the higher- or lower-than-cost figure shown parenthetically.

Securities of security dealers may be priced at cost, at market, or at the lower of cost or market. Securities of investment companies may be carried at the lower of cost or market, with the other figure shown parenthetically.

Long-Term Security Investments. Long-term investments in stocks of non-controlled normally are carried at cost or at other basic acquisition figures. If market prices decline drastically and "permanently," the cost or other basic figure should be reduced. Long-term investments in bonds are carried at original cost plus amortized discount, or minus amortized premium.

Life Insurance. Either cash surrender values or loan values are used for pricing investments in life insurance. Life insurance investments are long-term investments—not current assets; the prepaid premium portion is a current asset. If there are loans outstanding against the policies, the amount of the loan may be shown among the liabilities; or it may be shown as a subtraction from the cash surrender value or the loan value, whichever is used. The audit report—and/or financial statement footnotes—should point out the loans, because the loans may defeat the purposes for which the insurance was purchased.

Investments in Funds. Investments in funds should be set forth in accordance with the intention of establishing the funds. For example, bond retirement funds and self-controlled pension funds are not current assets.

Inventories. Inventories are classified as current assets. Manufacturing supplies preferably should be included in raw materials. Supplies other than manufacturing supplies may be included with inventories or with prepaid expenses. If inventories are to be used after the normal operating cycle—as exemplified by heavy construction industry materials of significant amount—they should be removed from the current asset category. For manufacturing companies, inventories in the financial statements, or in accompanying footnotes, may be divided into raw materials, work in process, finished goods, and supplies.

The basis of pricing inventories should be clearly set forth in the financial statements. Explanatory footnotes should be included when the pricing method has been changed since the date of the preceding statements. The notes also should point out the effect of the change on net income.

If money is borrowed and inventory pledged as loan security, the loan should appear as a liability. The security for the loan should be indicated in the balance sheet.

Debits to expense for a reduction from cost to market should appear in the income statement as an expense. Otherwise, the cost of goods sold figure will be inaccurate.

Prepayments. Prepaid expenses are current assets; this is in accordance with the concept of a current asset. Long-term deferred charges should be separately disclosed. Assuming that future periods will be benefited, and in order properly to match current-period revenues and expenses, prepaid expenses and deferred charges should be neither understated nor overstated. Inconsistency of treatment from year to year defeats the objectives of proper financial statement comparison and analysis. This is especially true when financial statements are prepared each month.

Fixed Assets. In the balance sheet, each related group of fixed assets should be shown separately—preferably at cost less accumulated depreciation. Both cost and the accumulated depreciation provision should be set forth. If a basis other than cost is used, cost should be indicated parenthetically or by footnote.

In the income statement, depreciation of fixed assets should be shown by related groups, properly classified as manufacturing, administration, or selling. If fixed assets have been appraised upward or downward in the records, the depreciation in the income statement should be on the basis of the appraisal figures, with depreciation based on cost also indicated.

Land owned for business purposes should be segregated in the balance sheet from land held for investment or contemplated future use. Buildings owned but used for other than business purposes should appear in the balance sheet as investment assets or other assets.

If fixed assets are fully depreciated and are in use, both the cost (or other basic figure) and the total accumulated depreciation should appear in the accounts and in the balance sheet. The Accumulated Depreciation account should not be closed to the asset account.

The basis of pricing small perishable tools should be set forth in the balance sheet if the tools are material in total or in relationship to other fixed assets.

Intangible Assets. Intangible assets should be separately classified in the balance sheet. The basis of valuation should be fully disclosed. The methods of amortization should be disclosed.

Current Liabilities. In the financial statements, current liabilities should be properly subdivided in to trade and nontrade accounts payable; amounts due affiliated companies; declared dividends payable; trade and nontrade notes payable; bank loans payable; deposit liabilities; accrued items; amounts withheld from employees; and revenues received in advance. Amounts due company personnel—other than for wages—should be separately set forth. To reduce the detail in a formal balance sheet, related items in this paragraph frequently are grouped.

If notes or accounts payable are secured by pledged assets, that fact should be stated parenthetically in the balance sheet.

If material in amount, debit balances in accounts payable should be set forth as current assets in the balance sheet. This is unusual.

Currently maturing portions of long-term debt should be shown among the current liabilities, or they may remain in the long-term liability section of the balance sheet if accompanied by a statement of maturity date.

Unfilled purchase commitments of extraordinary amount should be disclosed by balance sheet footnote, unless the extraordinary commitments are offset by firm sales orders. Purchase commitments of normal amount need not be mentioned.

Long-Term Liabilities. Bonds payable may be shown with the premium added to par, or the discount deducted from par, thereby showing the bond liability at its carrying value. This treatment also avoids showing a premium as a "liability" or a discount as an "asset." In spite of this reasoning, practice commonly is to the effect that bond liabilities are expressed at par, with the unamortized premium shown as a deferred credit, or the unamortized discount shown as deferred charge. It is important to show interest rates if those rates are higher than the current market price of borrowing, and particularly if the bonds are not callable. If a trustee is not employed, sinking fund bonds of the issuing company, retired bonds, unissued bonds, and treasury bonds (whether or not they are kept alive) should be deducted at par from the total authorized issue and the net liability extended. Treasury bonds kept alive for resale preferably should be shown as deductions from the gross liability, because the liability to be liquidated has been reduced by the acquisition of the bonds, in spite of intentions which, at the balance sheet date, are not fulfilled. A balance sheet should show existing conditions, not expectations.

If a bond issue—or one series of a total serial issue—is payable within one year, and if a special fund is not available for the payment, the amount currently due should be moved to the current liability classification. If a special fund is available for the repayment of the amounts currently due, the fund becomes a current asset at the time the transfer is made from long-term to current liabilities. Where special payment funds are available, it is preferable to permit both the fund and the liability to remain in their usual positions, for, by their removal to the current sections, the current ratio is disturbed.

Each convertible debt security must be disclosed, and all provisions regarding conversion must be set forth in financial statement footnotes.

Mortgages should be shown in the balance sheet as first mortgages, chattel mortgages, and so on. Each mortgage should be shown at its net payable amount. Where assets are pledged as security for a mortgage, this fact should be so indicated on the asset side of the balance sheet.

Capital. The capital section of a balance sheet must be fully detailed so that each class of stock is independently presented in terms of authorized shares, par or stated values per share, shares outstanding, shares unissued, treasury shares, and dividend rates for preferred stock. Cumulative dividends in arrears on preferred stock should be shown by balance sheet footnote. Capital other than capital stock must be divided between retained earnings, various other paid-in capital amounts, and asset appreciation. Retained earnings reserves must be specifically labeled and separately shown.

The Securities and Exchange Commission (Rule 3–16 of Regulation S–X) has established the following rule for treasury stock acquired by corporations filing under the commission's jurisdiction: "Reacquired shares, if significant in amount, shall be shown separately as a deduction from capital shares, or from the total of capital shares and surplus, or from surplus, at either par or stated value or cost, as circumstances require."

Consolidated Financial Statements. When consolidated financial statements are prepared in one year in which the basis of consolidation differs from that applied in the preceding year, the auditor should indicate that accepted accounting principles have not been applied on a basis consistent with the practice of the preceding year. Consistency of financial statement preparation is a recognized standard of auditing; inconsistencies in the application of principles should be divulged.

ILLUSTRATION. An example of inconsistency in the preparation of consolidated financial statements is as follows: In the year 1970, all subsidiary companies were consolidated in the financial statements. In 1971, one subsidiary company was omitted from the consolidated financial statements. Full disclosure of the change should be expressed in the audit report.

SECTION VI: THE INCOME STATEMENT

The income statement details the periodic operations that have brought about the majority of the changes in the retained earnings. It is based on the concept of a going concern; consequently, the income statement is an interim report, since profits and losses are not fundamentally the result of short-time operations. Also, in preparing an income statement, there must be *no attempt to shift profits from one period to another* in order to *equalize* net income for a fiscal period. The net income for the year must be clearly and unequivocally set forth. Net income should be appraised not only in terms of its total amount, but also in terms of earnings per share of capital stock. One of the primary functions of a published income statement is to enable outsiders to predict the *future* course of earning capacity.

For only modest disclosure of all material operating data, an income statement should show—as a minimum—sales revenues, cost of goods sold, selling expense, administrative expense, nonoperating revenues and expenses, nonrecurring items of gain or loss (except for adjustments of *prior* years income taxes), federal income tax, and net income. Nonrecurring items of gain or loss should not be buried in sales or expense figures; if this was practiced, comparative sales and other analyses would be meaningless. Either the multistep form of income statement or the single-step form may be used; the majority of companies use the multistep form, because major items of expense are then shown by functions.

In order to afford full disclosure of all material data, the minimum requirements for the preparation of income statements, set forth in the preceding paragraph, should be expanded, and normally are expanded. The expansion may be within the income statement proper, or it may appear in supplementary date, as exemplified by separately stating total depreciation expense, the total of all types of taxes, taxes per share of

ILLUSTRATION 27–2

DIXSON, INC.

Statement of Income and Retained Earnings
For the Year Ended December 31, 1975
(in millions)

Net sales		$579,176
Less: Cost of goods manufactured and sold		330,466
Gross profit on sales		$248,710
Operating expenses:		
Selling expenses	$71,622	
Administrative expenses	73,358	
Total Operating Expenses		144,980
Net operating income		$103,730
Other expenses, net		2,117
Net income before nonrecurring items		$101,613
Less: Federal income tax applicable thereto		51,823
		$ 49,790
Nonrecurring items:		
Loss due to flood, 1975	$17,500	
Profit on sale of marketable securities	7,565	
Net nonrecurring loss		9,935
		$ 39,855
Federal income tax reduction on $9,935		5,070
Net income for the year 1975		$ 44,925
Retained earnings, December 31, 1974		40,062
		$ 84,987
Additions to retained earnings, 1975:		
Reserve for flood loss, returned to retained earnings		20,000
		$104,987
Deductions from retained earnings, 1975:		
Dividends on common stock		34,000
Retained Earnings, December 31, 1975		$ 70,987
Earnings per share of common stock:		
Primary		$0.83
Fully diluted *		0.77

* Assuming conversion of all convertible debentures to have taken place at the beginning of the period.

stock, net income per share of stock, and so forth. Most companies prefer not to show total detail in income statements, because they do not wish to divulge total information to competitors. For registered companies, the requirements of the Securities and Exchange Commission must be followed in all financial reporting.

Today, the only recognized and acceptable income statement is the "all-inclusive" type. The all-inclusive type includes charges and credits for extraordinary and nonrecurring items—gain on sale of investments, uninsured fire loss, and so forth, net of federal income taxes, even though of material amount. In the all-inclusive type of income statement, these extraordinary items must be presented in such a manner as not to distort or confuse net income. The all-inclusive type, if properly prepared, adheres to the theory of maintaining a clean retained earnings and follows the concept that the net income of a business is not accurately measurable for short periods of time. See Illustration 27–2.

Illustration 27–3 shows the type of income statement and statement of retained earnings commonly appearing in published annual reports.

The preceding illustration (27–3) conforms with *Opinion No. 30* of the APB when a client disposes of a business segment.

If the all-inclusive type of income statement is properly prepared, net income based on customary operations will not be distorted. Extraordinary items of income and expense will be fully disclosed in the income statement, will be transferred therefrom to Retained Earnings in the closing of the accounts, and will not be buried directly in retained earnings, thereby tending to equalize reported net income between years. The following arguments are set forth: First, the question of *material amount* is a matter of opinion; opinions may vary between persons, and the same person may alter his opinion from year to year. Second, all items of expense and revenue incurred or earned in a fiscal period should be reflected in the income statement of that year. Third, if an error affecting the net income of one year is corrected directly through Retained Earnings and not through an income statement in a succeeding year, the composite net income of the two years is distorted and incorrectly stated. Some persons hold that an error in the income statement of one year, if corrected in the income statement of a succeeding year, results in two incorrect income statements; however, this might be better—since it makes the sum of the two correct—than presenting one incorrect income statement and never correcting it. Fourth, the theory of maintaining a clean retained earnings avoids the possibilities of misconception in the income statement. Fifth, it is not the responsibility of the auditor to prepare financial statements so simply that the results avoid full disclosure of all revenues and expenses.

An auditor must determine that earnings per share are properly calculated and presented; see Illustratons 27–2 and 27–3. In *Opinion No. 9*, the APB recommends that earnings per share be disclosed for (a) income

ILLUSTRATION 27-3

MASON COMPANY

Consolidated Statement of Income
(Dollars in Thousands)

	Years ended December 31	
	1973	1972
Net Sales....................................	$1,555,200	$1,403,184
Cost of sales.............................	1,006,691	932,262
Selling, general and administrative expenses............	372,064	324,020
Operating income...........................	176,445	146,902
Other income, net (notes ____ and ____)	16,753	15,946
Interest expense	8,793	8,478
Income from continuing operations before income taxes.....................................	184,405	154,370
Income taxes (note _____).....................	89,841	71,504
Income from continuing operations	94,564	82,866
Discontinued operations–Gain on sale of Chicago property and loss related to writeoff of minority interest in The Newport Company (note_____).........	1,601	–
Net income	$ 92,963	$ 82,866
Per share of common stock:		
Income from continuing operations	$ 3.32	$ 2.88
Discontinued operations......................	.05	–
Net income per share.........................	$ 3.27	$ 2.88

Consolidated Statements on Retained Earnings and Capital Surplus
(Dollars in Thousands)

	Years ended December 31	
Retained Earnings	1973	1972
Balance at beginning of year......................	$171,167	$129,848
Net income	92,963	82,866
	264,130	212,714
Less cash dividends:		
Common stock: 1973, $1.46 per share; 1972, $1.415 per share	40,936	39,752
Series A preference stock, $1.00 per share Newport common stock, prior to pooling of interests......................	–	105
Balance at end of year	$221,831	$171,167
Capital Surplus		
Balance at beginning of year......................	$250,044	$245,777
Miscellaneous, net	3,524	4,267
Balance at end of year	$246,520	$250,044

before extraordinary items, (b) for extraordinary items, if any, and (c) net income. By presenting data in this manner, it will help eliminate the tendency of many users to place undue emphasis on only one amount being reported as earnings per share. It will also assist the user to place in proper perspective the calculation of cash flow per share—which is still prevalent in too many reports to stockholders. *Opinion No. 15* of the APB presents one example for the calculation of earnings per share.

During the past few years the SEC has been issuing rulings at an accelerated speed—many times without consulting professional accountants. Also see the early part of Section III of this chapter.

With regard to the all-inclusive versus the old current-operating-performance type of income statement, *Accounting Series Release No. 70* states in part:

The principal new requirement pertains to profit-and-loss or income statements and is contained in Rule 5–03 (*a*) which states:

"All items of profit and loss given recognition in the accounts during the period covered by the profit-and-loss or income statement shall be included."

The inclusion of this requirement, which states a long-established policy of the Commission, is deemed necessary because of the not always consistent practice followed by some registrants of excluding certain items from the profit-and-loss or income statements with the result that the amount shown thereon as net income or loss has been susceptible to misinterpretation by investors. Recognizing that there might be exceptional circumstances which would make it appropriate to deviate from this rule, but keeping in mind the Commission's responsibility for prohibiting the dissemination of financial statements which might be misleading to investors, Rule 5–03 was amended to read:

"Except as otherwise permitted by the Commission, the profit-and-loss or income statements filed for persons to whom this article is applicable shall comply with the provisions of this rule.

"The purpose of this revision is to make clear to registrants that they are not forestalled from giving exceptional treatment to exceptional items when both the representatives of the registrant and the Commission are convinced that such treatment is appropriate.

"Notwithstanding this provision, representatives of the executive committee of the American Institute of Accountants proposed that either Rule 5–03 (*a*) be eliminated from the regulation or the requirements with respect to the presentation of the final section of profit-and-loss or income statements be amended to permit, where appropriate, the exclusion of extraordinary items from those making up the caption net income or loss.

"To accomplish this, additional items, described in Rules 5–03 (17) and (18), were added to those previously set forth in the regulation, and the last three items of the section pertaining to profit-and-loss or income statements (Rule 5–03) now appear as follows:

"16. Net income or loss.

"17. Special items.—State separately and describe each item of profit and loss given recognition in the accounts, included herein pursuant to Rule 5–03 (*a*) and not included in the determination of net income or loss (item 16).

"18. Net income or loss and special items.

"Captions 17 and 18 are to be used in those instances where it is believed that the showing of a single unqualified figure of net income or loss might be misconstrued."

In January, 1974, the SEC issued a new proposal calling for publicly-held companies to include in their annual reports to stockholders certain additional types of information now provided to the Commission. Included in the proposal are (*a*) a general description of the company's business, (*b*) its lines of business, (*c*) a summary of operations, (*d*) identification of executive officers, (*e*) their affiliations, (*f*) information regarding liquidity, (*g*) credit policies, (*h*) financing requirements, (*i*) data regarding the company's securities, including their quoted market prices over a two-year period, and (*j*) the certification of financial statements for the last *two* years.

SECTION VII: THE STATEMENT OF RETAINED EARNINGS

The statement of retained earnings—if a separate statement is prepared—should be presented in support of the retained earnings, items appearing in the balance sheet and as a reconciliation of the changes in those accounts between the beginning and the end of a fiscal period.

One of two plans may be followed: (1) a separate statement of retained earnings may be prepared, or (2) a combined statement of income and retained earnings may be prepared. The primary purpose of a combined statement of income and retained earnings is to present, in one statement, a complete and continuing link between the balance sheet at the end of the last period and the balance sheet at the end of the current period. Earnings applicable to the current fiscal period and alterations of earnings applicable to past periods are reflected in one statement on the basis of the going-concern concept of a business; thus, it is seen that the income statement alone is not always a complete reflection of the proprietorship changes in the balance sheet. Today, a separate statement of retained earnings is disappearing; this has been brought about by the use of the all-inclusive income statement.

In the rare event that the current-operating-performance type of income statement is used, it is recommended that it be combined with the statement of retained earnings, in order to place in one statement all charges and credits affecting income over a series of years.

SECTION VIII: THE STATEMENT OF CHANGES IN FINANCIAL POSITION

The statement of changes in financial position (also known under many other titles) is now one of the major financial statements—ranking in prominence with the balance sheet and the statement of income and retained earnings. Audit reports frequently present the statement of changes in financial position before the income statement and the balance sheet. This is easily recognized if the reader will examine current annual reports to stockholders. This statement is a major statement, and it should be referred to in both the scope section and the opinion section of the audit report.

The statement of changes in financial position directs attention to the source of funds and their application during a period of time. It points out how the change in current items as a whole is related to the changes in other major (noncurrent) items in a balance sheet. The noncurrent items that increase net working capital are sources of funds; noncurrent items that decrease net working capital are called application of funds. Therefore, this statement emphasizes the net effect of the flow of funds on the current financial position—something of interest to every investor, potential investor, creditor, and financial analyst. See Illustration 27–4.

Miscellaneous Income Statement Considerations

The importance of proper income statements cannot be overemphasized; in their preparation, the principle of consistency must not be violated, and there must be proper matching of periodic revenues and related expenses. Income statements prepared in comparative form are valuable for purposes of trend studies; percentage figures can be used easily and afford the basis for valuable analyses for management purposes. In general, the percentages should be in terms of net sales as the base and/or in terms of the percentage increase or decrease in each item; comparisons must be for the same time intervals. Income statements may be prepared in long form or in short form, the latter being supported by appropriate schedules.

A few points involving differences of opinion in the preparation of an income statement are considered in the following paragraphs.

By-product sales and sales of scrap material may be considered (1) as sales, (2) as a reduction of the cost of the principal products manufactured, or (3) as other revenue. Arguments can be advanced by the proponents of each theory, and equally valid arguments can be presented by the opponents of each theory. To the author, it appears that scrap material and by-product sales are not other revenues, since the results are too closely connected with the manufacturing and sales functions of a business. Whether such revenue should be included with sales in the income statement or treated as reductions of costs depends upon the materiality of the amounts and the circumstances in each case. If the material sold is truly scrap, discarded from the manufacture of the principal product, a cost reduction should be effected; if the amount of the sale is material, and if the item is in the nature of a joint product, naturally evolved from the breakdown of the original raw material, the revenue should be treated as a sale. Reason must guide each case. After the auditor

ILLUSTRATION 27–4

THE RIDGE CORPORATION

Statement of Changes in Financial Position

	Year Ended February 28	
	1974	*1973*
Additions to Working Capital		
From operations:		
Net income for the year	$2,057,870	$1,693,009
Items recognized in net income not affecting working capital:		
Provision for depreciation and amortization	1,236,258	997,263
Increase (decrease) in noncurrent deferred income taxes	(76,200)	93,000
Equity in income of 50 percent-owned company (deduction)	(40,994)	(15,667)
Net loss of wholly-owned unconsolidated subsidiary	46,817	–
Working capital provided from operations	3,223,751	2,767,605
Net carrying amount of equipment disposals	268,949	–
Decrease in notes and accounts with officers	25,550	–
Proceeds from stock options exercised	–	11,850
Dividend received from 50 percent-owned company	5,280	9,750
Total additions	3,523,530	2,789,205
Deductions from working capital		
Additions to property, plant, and equipment	1,734,478	1,231,664
Increase in notes and accounts with officers	–	7,527
Increase in miscellaneous accounts and deposits	274,632	58,659
Increase in advances to contractors.	56,357	12,992
Cash dividends	600,839	438,274
Investment in marketable securities	710,706	225,750
Purchase of Common Shares for treasury	159,268	500,812
Investment in and advances to wholly-owned unconsolidated subsidiary	157,608	–
Advances to 50 percent-owned company	35,637	–
Total deductions	3,729,525	2,475,678
Increase (decrease) in working capital	(205,995)	313,527
Working capital at beginning of year	5,370,438	5,056,911
Working capital at end of year	$5,164,443	$5,370,438
Changes in the Components of Working Capital		
Increase (decrease) in current assets:		
Cash and certificates of deposit.	$ 208,996	($ 223,500)
Marketable securities.	1,971	590,923
Trade accounts receivable	57,233	133,599
Inventories	89,691	(309,364)
Prepaid expenses	29,199	200
Deferred income taxes applicable to allowance for returns	95,000	94,500
	482,090	286,358
Increase (decrease) in current liabilities:		
Accounts payable and accrued expenses.	363,265	(249,657)
Royalties to contractors.	74,599	79,064
Dividend payable.	(13,586)	34,643
Income taxes	263,807	232,619
Current portion of mortgage note	–	(123,838)
	688,085	(27,169)
Increase (decrease) in working capital	($ 205,995)	$ 313,527

has been firmly convinced of the soundness of his desired method in each case, he should use it consistently.

In the cost of sales section of an income statement, or in a separate statement of cost of goods manufactured and sold—both considered for a manufacturing company—practices differ, and arguments ensue in respect to the treatment of finished goods. A few accountants, in preparing a statement of cost of goods manufactured and sold, are of the opinion that the beginning and ending inventories of finished goods should not be shown in that statement, but rather in the income statement. Reasoning behind such insistence is not very forceful. The common and modern practice is to take the finished goods inventories into consideration in the statement of cost of goods manufactured and sold, if one is used, or in the cost of sales section of the income statement, if all items are shown in one statement. If finished goods inventories are omitted in the cost of sales section, then that section becomes a "cost of goods manufactured" section; it is incomplete, because gross profit is realized only upon the cost of the goods processed and actually *sold* during the accounting period.

There is no uniformity of opinion with respect to the income statement classification of bad debts expense. Some treat it as other expense, some as selling expense, and some as administrative expense. Losses from uncollectible accounts are too closely connected with the operations of the business to be considered as other expenses. To treat them as selling expenses is an indication that the sales division is responsible for the granting of credit; the selling function and the credit function should be separated, as a matter of good business policy and management. Therefore, bad debt losses should not be treated as selling expenses. To the administrative division logically belongs the duty of credit extension and collection; and bad debts expense should be charged to administrative expense. Because credits and collections are sometimes viewed as financial functions, financial expense may set up as a separate group of operating expenses.

Sales discounts are treated either as deductions from sales or as other expenses. The accounting theories advanced in support of the methods may be approximately equal in merit, and it does not matter greatly which method is employed, so long as the treatment is consistent from year to year. The trend is toward treating sales discounts as reductions of selling prices. Similar problems arise in connection with trading stamps.

Purchase discounts are treated as a reduction of the material cost or as other income. The modern—and preferred—trend is to treat purchase discounts available as cost reductions, and if a discount is not taken, to show it in the income statement as a discount lost—among the other expenses.

All auditors are in agreement that no profit should be recognized on interdepartmental or intercompany transfers or "sales." Consequently, transfers of this nature must not be shown as sales and purchases in the income statement, and eliminations must be effected prior to the preparation of the statements. When goods are transferred at a price in excess of cost, simply to keep confidential information from the transferee, the fictitious profits must be eliminated before the preparation of the income statement.

When a reserve has been created from retained earnings and the event occurs for which the reserve was created, the expense element should not be charged directly to the reserve and thereby never be shown as an expense; the expense or loss should be charged to an expense account. The reserve then may be returned to Retained Earnings. The purpose of creating the retained earnings reserve is defeated if the reserve is directly charged. Naturally, when depreciation and amortization accumulations and liability "reserves" are created by expense charges, the accumulation "reserve" is charged upon the occurrence of the event for which it was created, because expense was originally charged for the occasion.

Errors made in prior accounting periods would appear in the current-period income statement as nonrecurring items.

Multipurpose and Single-Purpose Statements

At this point, it may be well to discuss briefly multipurpose financial statements and single-purpose statements. A multipurpose financial statement is designed primarily to satisfy all general demands of the average person and is the type of statement prepared in the customary audit. A single-purpose statement is one designed to focus attention in a specific direction. The general form of a multipurpose financial statement may not vary materially from that of a single-purpose statement. But certain sections of the single-purpose statement may be presented in greater detail, accompanied by detailed explanation; for example, for short-term credit grantors, the current asset and current liability sections of a balance sheet might contain greater detail, accompanied by conversion schedules for inventories and receivables.

Some examples of single-purpose financial statements are as follows: statements prepared in conformity with blank forms supplied by banks and credit-rating agencies; liquidating statements; statements prepared for companies in bankruptcy; "pro forma" financial statements; statements prepared in accordance with the demands of protective legislation bodies, such as the Securities and Exchange Commission and the Interstate Commerce Commission; statements prepared in accordance with the requirements of state and federal taxing authorities; and statements prepared for the purpose of measuring earning power, which are of interest to investors. This last class of single-purpose financial statement—for the investor—has been the type of statement that has forced much discussion of the merits and disadvantages of special-purpose statements. For an investor, historical costs do not serve as an adequate guide for the decision to sell or acquire shares of capital stock in a company. The gravest danger of special-purpose statements lies in their possible misuse.

QUESTIONS

1. The following events occurred in the course of the audit of the financial statements of each company indicated below. Each event occurred after the end of the year under examination (December 31, 1975, in each case) but prior to the completion of the field work early in 1976.

    In your reports of examination and/or as a footnote to the financial statements, what comments would you make, if any?

    Company No. 1 incurred a loss of $5,000,000 when on January 19, 1976, fire destroyed the largest of four of the company's buildings. The gross loss was $25,000,000, and the insurance recovery was $20,000,000. Income insurance was not carried.

    Company No. 2 has a material portfolio of U.S. Treasury bonds, notes, and bills. On February 1, 1976, the company sold all the bonds, notes, and bills and invested the total proceeds in various common stocks, all listed on major stock exchanges.

    Company No. 3 has completed plans for a plant expansion program and, on March 1, 1976, an underwriting syndicate will offer for sale $50,000,000 of the company's bonds at par.

2. Survey your acquaintances who are engaged in professional public CPA practice, and ascertain from them the practices of their firms in closing an audit, with respect to the following:

    a) Does a partner or a manager review all work papers (1) at the close of an audit or (2) as the audit progresses?

    b) Who drafts the report: (1) the auditor in field charge of the engagement or (2) a partner or a manager in the office?

    c) Who reviews the adjustments with the client: (1) the auditor in field charge of the engagement or (2) a partner or a manager?

    d) Who presents the report to the client and reviews it with the client: (1) the auditor in field charge of the engagement or (2) a partner or a manager?

3. You were completing your examination of the financial statements of Rose, Inc., for the year ended December 31, 1975, when you were consulted by the corporation's president, who believes there is no point to examining the 1976 voucher register and testing data in support of 1974 entries. He stated that (*a*) bills pertaining to 1975 which were received too late to be included in December were recorded as of the year end by journal entry, (*b*) the internal auditor made tests after the year end, and (*c*) he would furnish you with a letter certifying that there were no unrecorded liabilities.

    a) Should the auditor's test for unrecorded liabilities be affected by the fact that the client made a journal entry to record 1975 bills which were received late? Explain.

    b) Should the auditor's test for unrecorded liabilities be affected by the fact that a letter is obtained in which a responsible management official certifies that to the best of his knowledge all liabilities have been recorded? Explain.

c) Should the auditor's test for unrecorded liabilities be eliminated or reduced because of the internal audit tests? Explain.

d) Assume that the corporation, which handled some government contracts, had no internal auditor but that an auditor for a federal agency spent three weeks auditing the records and was just completing his work at this time. How would the auditor's unrecorded liability test be affected by the work of the auditor for a federal agency?

e) What sources in addition to the 1976 voucher register should the auditor consider to locate possible unrecorded liabilities?

4. At the conclusion of an audit, you submitted to your client, for review purposes, pencil copies of his financial statements. The client wanted to know why the fixed assets were not in first position on the asset side of the balance sheet and why long-term liabilities were not in first position on the liability side. The client's question was based on the fact that fixed assets were larger in total dollars than any other asset classification and long-term liabilities were smaller in total dollars than were current liabilities. Answer his inquiry. The client company is not a public utility.

5. You are conducting an annual examination of the financial statements of a corporation for the purpose of rendering an opinion for use in an annual report to the stockholders.

Answer the following questions concerning events occurring subsequent to the date of the financial statements:

a) What audit procedures should normally be followed in order to obtain knowledge of post-financial statement events?

b) What is the period with which the auditor is normally concerned with regard to post-financial statement events?

c) List five different examples of events or transactions which might occur in the subsequent period.

d) What is the auditor's general responsibility, if any, for reporting such events or transactions?

e) In your audit report, how would you deal with each of the examples you listed in (*c*)?

(AICPA)

6. The following five unrelated events occurred after the date of the financial statements, but prior to drafting the audit report. For each item, (*a*) explain how each might have come to the attention of the auditor, and (*b*) discuss the auditor's responsibility to recognize each item in the preparation of the audit report.

Post-financial statement date event:

(1) A retroactive pay increase was granted.

(2) The undisputed determination by the Internal Revenue Service of additional income taxes due for a prior year.

(3) The filing of an antitrust suit by the federal government.

(4) The declaration of a 100 percent stock dividend.

(5) The sale of a fixed asset at a substantial profit.

(AICPA, adapted)

7. As of December 31, 1975, negotiations were in process between your corporate client, and one of its stockholders for the purchase and retire-

ment by the corporation of the shares owned by the stockholder at a price still to be determined. The company is a close corporation with 10,000 shares of only common stock outstanding, with a stated value of $2,500,000. The retained earnings is $4,500,000. The stockholder who desires to dispose of his stock owns 1,000 shares, and wants a price of $700 per share. The corporation has offered to purchase and retire the shares at 80 percent of book value. The corporation has adequate cash to pay the stockholder. The entire transaction and its consummation or failure to be concluded lies in the price per share. Should this matter be mentioned in the audit report for the year ended December 31, 1975? Present reasons for your answer.

8. During the course of your examination of Belmont, Inc. for the year ended December 31, 1975, your post-balance sheet examination disclosed the following items:

(1) January 3, 1976: The state government approved plans for the construction of an expressway. The plan will result in the appropriation of a portion of the land area owned by Belmont. Construction will begin in late 1976. No estimate of the condemnation award is available.

(2) January 4, 1976: The funds for a $25,000 loan to the corporation made by Mr. Belmont on July 15, 1975, were obtained by him by a loan on his personal life insurance policy. The loan was recorded in the account Loan from Officers. Mr. Belmont's source of the funds was not disclosed in the company records. The corporation pays the premiums on the life insurance policy and the wife of the president, is the beneficiary of the policy.

(3) January 7, 1976: The mineral content of a shipment of ore enroute on December 31, 1975, was determined to be 72 percent. The shipment was recorded at year end at an estimated content of 50 percent by a debit to Raw Material Inventory and a credit to Accounts Payable in the amount of $20,600. The final liability to the vendor is based on the actual mineral content of the shipment.

(4) January 15, 1976: Culminating a series of personal disagreements between Belmont, the president, and his brother-in-law, the treasurer, the latter resigned, effective immediately, under an agreement whereby the corporation would purchase his 10 percent stock ownership at book value as of December 31, 1975. Payment is to be made in two equal amounts in cash on April 1 and October 1, 1976. In December, the treasurer had obtained a divorce from his wife, who was Mr. Belmont's sister.

(5) January 31, 1976: As a result of reduced sales, production was curtailed in January and some workers were laid off. On February 5, 1976, all remaining workers went on strike. To date the strike is unsettled.

(6) February 10, 1976: A contract was signed whereby Growth, Inc., purchased from Belmont, Inc., all of the latter's fixed assets (including rights to receive the proceeds of any property condemnation), inventories, and the right to conduct business under the name "Belmont Division." The effective date of the transfer will be March 1, 1976. The sale price was $500,000 subject to adjustment following

the taking of a physical inventory. Important factors contributing to the decision to enter into the contract were the policy of the board of directors of Growth to diversify the company's activities and the report of a survey conducted by an independent market appraisal firm which revealed a declining market for Belmont products.

Assume that the preceding items came to your attention prior to completion of your audit on February 15, 1976, and that you will render a short-form report. For *each* of the above items:

a) State the audit procedures, if any, that would have brought the item to your attention. Indicate other sources of information that may have revealed the item.

b) Discuss the disclosure that you would recommend for the item, listing all details that you would suggest be disclosed. Indicate those items or details, if any, that should not be disclosed. Present your reasons for recommending or not recommending disclosure of the items or details.

(AICPA, adapted)

PROBLEMS

1. General Mag, Inc. manufactures electronic systems, which it sells to manufacturers of television sets and phonographic systems. In connection with your examination of Generals' financial statements for the year ended December 31, 1975, you completed all field work February 1, 1976, at which time you are attempting to evaluate the significance of the following items prior to drafting the audit report. Unless otherwise noted, none of the items have been disclosed in the financial statements or in footnotes.

Item 1

General stopped its policy of paying quarterly cash dividends. Dividends were paid regularly through 1974, discontinued for all of 1975 in order to finance equipment for a new plant, and resumed in the first quarter of 1976. In the annual report dividend policy is to be discussed in the president's letter to stockholders.

Item 2

A ten-year loan agreement, which the company entered into three years ago, provides that dividend payments may not exceed net income earned after taxes subsequent to the date of the agreement. The balance of retained earnings at the date of the loan agreement was $298,000. From that date through December 31, 1975, net income after taxes has totaled $360,000 and cash dividends have totaled $130,000. Based upon these data your assistant concluded that there was no retained earnings restriction at December 31, 1975.

Item 3

The company's new manufacturing plant, which cost $600,000 and has an estimated life of 25 years, is leased from the National Bank at an annual rental of $100,000. The company is obligated to pay property taxes, insurance and maintenance. At the conclusion of its ten-year non-cancelable lease, the company has the option of purchasing the property for $1. In General's income statement the rental payment is reported on a separate line.

Item 4

A major electronics company has introduced a line of products that will compete directly with General's primary line, now being produced in the specially designed new plant. Because of manufacturing innovations, the competitor's line will be of comparable quality but priced 50 percent below General's line. The competitor announced its new line during the week following completion of field work. You read the announcement in the newspaper and discussed the situation by telephone with General executives. General will meet the lower prices which are high enough to cover variable manufacturing and selling expenses but will permit recovery of only a portion of fixed costs.

For each of the preceding items, discuss:

a) Any additional disclosure in the financial statements and footnotes that you should recommend to your client.

b) The effect of the situation on the report upon General's financial statements. For this requirement assume that the client did not make the additional disclosure recommended in part (a).

Complete your discussion of each item—both parts (a) and (b)—before discussing the next item. The effects of each item on the financial statements and the audit report should be evaluated *independently* of the other items. The cumulative effects of the four items should not be considered.

(AICPA, adapted)

2. Percentages and ratios frequently are applied to test the reasonableness of the relationships existing among current financial data with similar financial data of prior periods. If an auditor can obtain prior financial relationships and a few key amounts he could prepare estimates of current financial data to test the reasonableness of data furnished by his client.

In recent years Barberry Sales Company has maintained the following relationships among the data on its financial statements:

(1) Gross profit rate on net sales . . . . 40 percent
(2) Net profit rate on net sales . . . . 10 percent
(3) Rate of selling expenses to net sales . . . . 20 percent
(4) Accounts receivable turnover . . . . 8 per year
(5) Inventory turnover . . . . 6 per year
(6) Acid-test ratio . . . . 2 to 1
(7) Current ratio . . . . 3 to 1
(8) Quick-asset composition: 8% cash, 32% marketable securities, 60% accounts receivable
(9) Asset turnover . . . . 2 per year
(10) Ratio of total assets to intangible assets . . . . 20 to 1
(11) Ratio of accumulated depreciation to cost of fixed assets . . . . 1 to 3
(12) Ratio of accounts receivable to accounts payable . . . . 1.5 to 1
(13) Ratio of working capital to stockholders' equity . . . . 1 to 1.6
(14) Ratio of total debt to stockholders' equity . . . . 1 to 2

The company had a net income of $120,000 for 1975 which resulted in earnings of $5.20 per share of common stock. Additional information includes the following:

(1) Capital stock authorized, issued (all in 1967), and outstanding: Common, $10 per share par value, issued at a 10 percent premium; Preferred, 6 percent nonparticipating, $100 per share par value, issued at 10 percent premium.
(2) Market value per share of common at December 31, 1975: $78
(3) Preferred dividends paid in 1975: $3,000
(4) Times interest earned in 1975: 33
(5) The amounts of the following were the same at December 31, 1975, as on January 1, 1975: inventory, accounts receivable, 5 percent bonds payable—due 1977, and total stockholders' equity.
(6) All purchases and sales were on open account.

a)   Prepare a condensed balance sheet and an income statement for the year ending December 31, 1975, showing the amounts you would expect to appear on Barberry's financial statements (ignoring income taxes). Major captions appearing on Barberry's balance sheet are: Current Assets, Fixed Assets, Intangible Assets, Current Liabilities, Long-Term Liabilities, and Stockholders' Equity. In addition to the accounts divulged in the problem, you should include items for Prepaid Expenses, Accrued Expenses, and Administrative Expenses. Supporting computations should be shown.

b)   Compute the following for 1975 (show computations):
(1)   Rate of return on stockholders' equity.
(2)   Price-earnings ratio for common stock.
(3)   Dividends paid per share of common stock.
(4)   Dividends paid per share of preferred stock.

(AICPA, adapted)

3.   You are concluding the audit field work of a corporate client. There is every indication that the financial statements of the client present fairly the financial position of the company as of December 31, 1975, and the results of its operations for the year then ended. As of December 31, 1975, the total assets of the company were $2,500,000; the total liabilities were $1,000,000; and the stockholders' equity was $1,500,000. The net income for 1975 was $150,000 after deducting all taxes.

The principal accounting records of the company are a general ledger, cash receipts record, invoice record, sales record, check record, and a general journal. The company prepares financial statements each month. Your field work will be completed February 20, 1976, and you plan to deliver the audit report to the client March 10, 1976.

a)   What is the purpose of a post-audit review?
b)   What period should be covered in a post-audit review for this client?
c)   For this client, outline the post-audit review program which you would follow to determine what transactions involving material amounts, if any, have occurred since the balance sheet date.

4.   You were engaged to audit the financial statements of Blair, Inc., for the year ended December 31, 1975. The company was organized on January 2, 1975, and on that date, by purchase, had acquired the assets and

had assumed the liabilities of the predecessor company. Blair did not have an organized system of accounting. The cost of the inventory acquired from the predecessor company was not definitely ascertainable from the records, because a lump sum had been paid for all assets acquired. In addition, Blair had not taken an inventory at December 31, 1975. As a result of your examination, the following information was assembled:

Net sales, 1975 . . . . $320,000
Merchandise purchased, 1975   211,840
Returned inventory purchases, 1975   19,840
Operating expenses, 1975 . . . .   20 percent of
                                                         net sales

Your investigation proved that exactly two months' inventory requirements were on hand at all times and that this condition had existed since January 2, 1975. It was also true that the inventory was turned over six times per year, equally throughout the months of the year.

Prepare an income statement for the year ended December 31, 1975. In what way, if any, would you not render an unqualified opinion of the income statement? Ignore taxes.

5. Richwell, Inc. has requested that you examine the capital section of its balance sheet and that you prepare proposals for the revision of the items contained therein, in accordance with accepted accounting principles.

   a) Prepare work papers, including audit adjustments, in accordance with your recommendations.

   b) Prepare the capital section of the balance sheet as of June 30, 1976, the date of the examination.

   A balance sheet as of June 30, 1975, is presented to you, and the capital section follows (assume that all items *not* shown are correct):

Preferred stock, $10 par; 10,000 shares authorized
  and issued, of which 2,000 are treasury shares
  costing $30,000, and shown as an asset . . . . $ 100,000
Common stock, no-par value, stated value $4.00;
  200,000 shares authorized, of which 125,000
  are issued and outstanding. $500,000
Paid-in capital ($10 per share on preferred
  stock issued in 1960).   100,000   600,000
Accumulated depreciation   280,000
Reserve for fire loss.   46,000
Retained earnings.   974,000
                                                                  $2,000,000

Additional data:

(1) Of the preferred treasury stock, 1,000 shares were sold on June 30, 1976, for $18 per share, and the $18,000 was credited to the Preferred Treasury Stock account. The shares were acquired in 1970 at $15 per share.

(2) The preferred stock carries an annual dividend of $1 per share. The dividend is cumulative. At June 30, 1975, unpaid cumulative dividends amounted to $5 per share. The entire accumulation was liqui-

dated on March 1, 1976, by issuing to the preferred stockholders 18,000 shares of common stock at a stated value of $5 per share.

(3)   A cash dividend of $1 per share was declared to the preferred shareholders of record as of June 1, 1976, payable on July 1, 1976.

(4)   At June 30, 1976, the accumulated depreciation had a balance of $350,000.

(5)   On September 15, 1975, the reserve for fire loss was increased by $10,000; retained earnings were charged.

(6)   On June 30, 1976, the reserve for fire loss was decreased by $10,000, which is the cost less depreciation of $1,000 of one building destroyed by fire on June 1, 1976. Fire cleanup costs, estimated at $2,000, do not appear in the records.

(7)   Retained earnings, as shown June 30, 1975, consisted of (*a*) a land-site gift in 1960, then worth $150,000; (*b*) gains of $17,000 on treasury stock transactions in 1968; and (*c*) earnings retained in the business, $703,000.

(8)   Net income for the year ended June 30, 1976, according to the records of the company, was $333,500.

6.   From the financial statements presented below, prepare the following:
   a)   A list of criticisms of the statements.
   b)   An acceptable balance sheet.
   c)   An acceptable combined statement of income and retained earnings.

COLDSTREAM COMPANY

Balance Sheet, December 31, 1975

ASSETS

Buildings (Note 1)	$ 9,334,000
Short-term prepaid items	75,000
Treasury stock (25,000 shares, at par)	500,000
Assets allocated to insurance fund:	
Cash in banks (including $300,000 of time deposits)	650,000
U.S. Treasury bonds, at cost.	500,000
Cash on hand and in banks	2,780,000
Accounts receivable	4,750,000
Inventories, at cost	3,411,000
	$22,000,000

LIABILITIES

Common stock; authorized and issued, 500,000 shares; par $20	$10,000,000
Accounts payable.	3,566,000
Federal income taxes.	440,000
Excess of revenue over disbursements on uncompleted contracts	690,000
Reserve for repairs of machinery (Note 2)	222,000
Reserve for self-insurance	650,000
Reserve for depreciation of buildings.	2,805,000
Appreciation capital (Note 1).	285,000
Retained earnings.	3,342,000
	$22,000,000

COLDSTREAM COMPANY

Statement of Income, Retained Earnings, and Appreciation capital
for the Year Ended December 31, 1975

Revenues.	$17,500,000
Less: Operating expenses, except depreciation	14,170,000
	$ 3,330,000
Interest on investments	22,000
Excess of provision for self-insurance charged to operations in 1975 over net losses in 1975.	360,000
Net profit before depreciation and federal income taxes.	$ 3,712,000
Gain from sale of capital assets (Note 3).	1,410,000
	$ 5,122,000
Provision for depreciation	550,000
Total profit before federal taxes	$ 4,572,000
Less: Federal income taxes	1,760,000
Net Profit	$ 2,812,000

	Retained Earnings	Appreciation Capital
Balance, December 31, 1974	$ 795,000	$610,000
Net profit, above	2,812,000	
Transfer from appreciation capital to retained earnings of depreciation on appreciation charged to income in 1974 ($270,000) and of unamortized appreciation on buildings sold.	+ 320,000	−320,000
Excess of cost of 25,000 shares of treasury stock purchased over par	− 15,000	− 5,000
	$3,912,000	
Deduct: Dividends paid in 1975	570,000	
Balance, December 31, 1975	$3,342,000	$285,000

Note 1. Buildings are stated at cost, except for three buildings recorded at appraised values when acquired in 1972. The excess of appraised values over original cost was credited to Appreciation Capital, and depreciation on appreciation has been accrued through charges to operations. On December 31, 1975, the unamortized balance of the appreciation was $290,000.

Note 2. This reserve is set up out of income in the amount of $40,000 per month; the system was started on January 1, 1975.

Note 3. Sale, in 1975, of five buildings in excess of book value; $50,000 of appreciation capital was applicable to two of the buildings acquired in 1972 and sold, above.

7. Below are presented some of the accounts appearing in the trial balance of Allan, Inc., at December 31, 1975.

	Debit	Credit
No-par common stock, issued at $5.		5,000
No-par common stock, issued at $4.		152,000
Treasury stock, no-par common, acquired at $5	15,000	
Capital stock, $100 preferred A, 500 shares		55,000
Capital stock, $100 preferred B, 500 shares		47,000
No-par common stock, authorized, 50,000 shares	0	0
Class A preferred; authorized 1,000 shares, $100 par value		100,000
Class A preferred; unissued, 500 shares	100,000	
Class B preferred; authorized, 500 shares		3,000
Class B preferred, unissued	3,000	
Reserve for 1975 federal income taxes (set up in 1975)		46,400
Reserve for loss on accounts ($6,000 added in 1975)		7,200
Reserve for reduction of December 31, 1975, inventory to market (a 1975 revenue charge)		9,100
Reserve for possible 1976 inventory declines (set up in 1975)		10,000
Reserve for preferred dividends declared (a 1975 revenue charge)		2,750
Reserve for common stock dividends to be declared (a 1975 revenue charge)		7,300
Common stock dividend of 7,300 shares declared on common of record as of January 2, 1976 (a 1975 revenue charge)		7,300
Loss on sale of fixed assets (1975)	4,000	
Organization expense unamortized	2,500	
Bond discount unamortized	3,400	
Loss on inventory decline in 1975	9,100	
Retained earnings, January 1, 1975	22,070	
Profit, 1975		162,500
The remaining accounts comprised the following:		
Cash, receivables, inventories, and fixed assets	740,430	
Accounts, notes, and bonds payable		284,950
	899,500	899,500

From the information presented, you are to prepare (1) the capital section of the December 31, 1975, balance sheet; (2) a schedule showing the changes you would make in the profit to arrive at the corrected net income for 1975 (ignore any revision of the 1975 income tax).

(AICPA, adapted)

PRACTICE MATERIAL ASSIGNMENTS

Metalcraft, Incorporated: Audit Problem:
  Assignment 13, Conclusion.

Colby Gears, Inc.: Holmes and Moore Audit Case:
  Completion of the Audit.
  Preparation of Financial Statements.

28
Audit Reports

Introduction

The objective of a customary audit is the rendition of an opinion regarding the fairness of the presentation of the financial statements of a client. The financial statements are representations of management; the opinion is that of the auditor.

There are two types of audit reports: (1) the short-form audit report and (2) the long-form audit report. The standards of reporting, as set forth in Chapter 1, apply to any audit report.

When his name is associated with financial statements, an auditor should realize the importance of setting forth a clear statement of his position. See the American Institute's *Code of Professional Ethics* (Rules of Conduct 202 and 203), which appear in Chapter 3.

As stated in Chapter 2, the short-form report contains:

1. A description of the scope of the examination—the *scope* section.
2. The auditor's opinion of the financial statements—the *opinion* section.

The long-form audit report is an expansion of the short-form report, and includes comments, data display, and various analyses. Thus, both the short-form and the long-form reports contain the same basic data.

The short-form report is used primarily for publication and issuance to stockholders. It is used in any circumstance wherein a more detailed report is not required. If issued, a long-form audit report is used primarily by management. Any report—short or long—must serve the purposes of the group to which it is directed. One report might be prepared for nonmanagement stockholders, one for management, one for a bank, and one for the Securities and Exchange Commission.

A report prepared for one purpose is not of much value for another purpose. It must be remembered that when a certified public accountant releases his report, it is out of his control—and he does not know for what purpose or by whom it may be used. Therefore, if proper reports are not issued, confusion may result, and the auditor may be blamed for that confusion.

For supplementary information regarding reports, the reader is referred to Chapters 10, 11, 12, and 13 of *Statements on Auditing Procedure No. 33*, issued by the American Institute of Certified Public Accountants, and to the pronouncements and releases of the SEC. See Chapter 27.

SECTION I: THE SHORT-FORM REPORT

A short-form audit report is made up of a statement of the scope of the examination and the auditor's opinion, and the principal financial statements and accompanying footnotes. Comments inserted between the scope and opinion paragraphs do not necessarily convert a short-form report to a long-form report. Material in addition to that presented in Chapter 2 is set forth here for the short-form report. The standard short-form report is repeated in Illustration 28–1—up-dated to include the state-

ILLUSTRATION 28–1

SHORT-FORM AUDIT REPORT OR CERTIFICATE

Date *February 10, 1976*

TO THE STOCKHOLDERS OF THE ABC COMPANY:

We have examined the balance sheet of the ABC Company as of December 31, 1975, and the related statements of income, retained earnings, and statement of changes in financial position for the year then ended. Our examination was made in accordance with generally accepted auditing standards, and accordingly included such tests of the accounting records and such other auditing procedures as we considered necessary in the circumstances.

In our opinion, the accompanying balance sheet and statements of income, retained earnings, and statement of changes in financial position present fairly the financial position of the ABC Company at December 31, 1975, and the results of its operations for the year then ended, in conformity with generally accepted accounting principles applied on a basis consistent with that of the preceding year.

(Signed)   L and M
Certified Public Accountants

---

ment of changes in financial position. As illustrated, the short-form report is unqualified. It may be qualified for any item or items, or the opinion may be disclaimed, or an adverse opinion may be rendered.

A Brief History of the Short-Form Report

Because of changing circumstances over the years, frequent alterations have been made in the short-form report or certificate. Prior to 1917, there was no uniformity in short-form reports—then commonly called "certificates"—issued by independent public accountants. This statement does not mean that the certificates were inadequate; it simply means that there was no uniformity of content.

In April, 1917, the Federal Reserve Board issued a bulletin entitled *Uniform Accounting*, in which the Board made the following reference to certificates:

The balance sheet and certificate should be connected with the accounts in such a way to insure that they shall be used only conjointly. This rule applies also to any report or memorandum containing any reservations as to the auditor's responsibility; any qualification as to the accounts, or any reference to facts materially affecting the financial position of the concern.

The certificate should be as short and concise as possible, consistent with a correct statement of the facts, and if qualifications are necessary, the auditor must state them in a clear and concise manner.

If the auditor is satisfied that his audit has been complete and conforms to the general instructions of the Federal Reserve Board, and that the balance sheet and profit and loss statement are correct, or that any minor qualifications are fully covered by the footnotes on the balance sheet, the form [shown in Illustration 28–2] is proper.

ILLUSTRATION 28–2
REPORT OF 1917

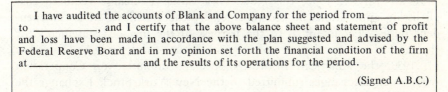

I have audited the accounts of Blank and Company for the period from _____ to _____, and I certify that the above balance sheet and statement of profit and loss have been made in accordance with the plan suggested and advised by the Federal Reserve Board and in my opinion set forth the financial condition of the firm at _____ and the results of its operations for the period.

(Signed A.B.C.)

As early as 1917, recognition was given to systems of internal control and their effect of making a testing program permissive, as indicated in the original bulletin, *Uniform Accounting*. Thus, in the two quoted certificates (Illustrations 28–2 and 28–3), there is no reference made to a detailed audit or the lack of it; the assumption was that if the suggestions of the Federal Reserve Board were followed, and if the auditor was satisfied with the results obtained, additional scope comment was not necessary.

In 1929, the Federal Reserve Board issued a bulletin entitled *Verification of Financial Statements*, in which the following statement was made: "If the auditor is convinced that his examination has been adequate and in conformity with these general instructions, that the balance sheet and profit and loss statement are correct, and that any minor qualifications are fully stated, the form (shown in Illustration 28–3) may be used."

The scope paragraph of Illustration 28–3 is extremely limited. In the opinion section, there is no reference to the fairness of presentation.

ILLUSTRATION 28–3

REPORT OF 1929

I have examined the accounts of _____ Company for the period from _____ to _____.

I certify that the accompanying balance sheet and statement of profit and loss, in my opinion, set forth the financial condition of the company at _____ and the results of operations for the period.

In 1932, the Special Committee on Cooperation with Stock Exchanges of the American Institute worked with the Committee on Stock List of the New York Stock Exchange in an effort to improve the annual reports of listed corporations and to effect "a change in the form of the audit certificate so that the auditors would specifically report to the shareholders whether the accounts as presented were properly prepared in accordance with the methods of accounting regularly employed by the company."

As of July 1, 1933, the New York Stock Exchange required that all listing applications be accompanied by the certificate of an independent public accountant as to the fairness of the financial statements for the most recent fiscal year and for each future fiscal year. At December 31, 1933, the American Institute's Special Committee on Cooperation with Stock Exchanges submitted to the New York Stock Exchange the short-form report shown in Illustration 28–4. In January, 1936, when

ILLUSTRATION 28–4

REPORT OF 1933

We have made an examination of the balance sheet of the XYZ Company as at December 31, 1933, and of the statement of income and surplus for the year 1933. In connection therewith we examined or tested accounting records of the Company and other supporting evidence and obtained information and explanations from officers and employees of the Company; we also made a general review of the accounting methods and of the operating and income accounts for the year, but we did not make a detailed audit of the transactions.

In our opinion, based upon such examination, the accompanying balance sheet and related statement of income and surplus fairly present, in accordance with accepted principles of accounting consistently maintained by the Company during the year under review, its position at December 31, 1933, and the results of its operations for the year.

Examination of Financial Statements was revised, the American Institute recommended the use of the same form.

The report in Illustration 28–4 includes a rather comprehensive scope paragraph. In the opinion section, the word "to certify" does not appear because of its association with the word "warranty." The concept of fair presentation also is introduced; and it is to be noted that the idea of consistent maintenance of the accounting records *during the year* under review is introduced, together with reference to accepted accounting principles.

On October 18, 1939, *Statements on Auditing Procedure*, No. 1, was issued, entitled "Extensions of Auditing Procedure." This statement dealt with the examination of inventories, the examination of receivables, the appointment of independent certified public accountants, and the form of the report. The certificate was changed to the form shown in Illustration 28–5.

ILLUSTRATION 28–5

REPORT OF 1939

TO THE BOARD OF DIRECTORS (OR STOCKHOLDERS) OF THE XYZ COMPANY:

We have examined the balance sheet of the XYZ Company as of April 30, 1939, and the statements of income and surplus for the year then ended, have reviewed the system of internal control and the accounting procedures of the company and, without making a detailed audit of the transactions, have examined or tested accounting records of the company and other supporting evidence, by methods and to the extent we deemed appropriate.

In our opinion, the accompanying balance sheet and related statements of income and surplus present fairly the position of the XYZ Company at April 30, 1939, and the results of its operations for the fiscal year, in conformity with generally accepted accounting principles applied on a basis consistent with that of the preceding year.

In Illustration 28–5, as compared with Illustration 28–4, internal control was mentioned; the statement pertaining to internal control was retained to emphasize testing; the reference to obtaining information from officers and employees was omitted, since it was superfluous. In the opinion paragraph, the phrase "based upon such examination" was omitted because it would be impossible to render an opinion if a proper examination was not made; consistency of the application of accounting principles with those of the preceding year was introduced because comparability of results could then be secured.

Following certain events in 1939, the Securities and Exchange Commission proceeded to study accountants' reports; and on February 5, 1941, it announced certain amendments to Rules 2.02 and 3.07 of Regulation

S–X. (See below, "Securities and Exchange Commission Requirements.")
On February 14, 1941, the American Institute changed the certificate
to the form shown in Illustration 28–6. The italicized sentence is new,
and this change was pursuant to Rule 2–02 of Regulation S–X.

In Illustration 28–6, the addition of the last sentence to the scope paragraph is an unqualified statement of the *professional* conduct of the audit;

ILLUSTRATION 28–6
REPORT OF 1941

We have examined the balance sheet of the XYZ Company as of February 28, 1941,
and the statements of income and surplus for the fiscal year then ended, have reviewed
the system of internal control and the accounting procedures of the company and, without making a detailed audit of the transactions, have examined or tested accounting
records of the company and other supporting evidence, by methods and to the extent
we deemed appropriate. *Our examination was made in accordance with generally accepted auditing standards applicable in the circumstances and included all procedures
which we considered necessary.*

In our opinion, the accompanying balance sheet and related statements of income
and surplus present fairly the position of the XYZ Company at February 28, 1941, and
the results of its operations for the fiscal year, in conformity with generally accepted
accounting principles on a basis consistent with that of the preceding year.

---

it does not mean that all audits follow the same procedures or that all
auditors would employ the same techniques of conduct for the same
type of engagement.

In 1944, the certificate was simplified. The simplification (see Illustration 28–6) consisted of the elimination of reference to the review of
the system of internal control, elimination of reference to the accounting
procedures, and elimination of the statement "by methods and to the
extent we deemed appropriate." These statements were considered superfluous (and they really are on a par with stating that "in order to prepare
a bank reconciliation, outstanding checks were taken into consideration").
The eliminations were on the proper basis that if these examination scopes
were not included, an unqualified opinion could not be rendered.

In 1948, the certificate was changed to the form shown in Illustration
28–1. These changes were made in order to correct the inconsistent expression relating to auditing standards applicable in the circumstances
and to remove all reference to the examination of the system of internal
control because one of the auditing standards includes the study of such
systems.

*It is entirely probable that the standard short-form report recom-
mended by the Institute will be revised—and expanded—in the near
future.*

SECTION II: AUDIT REPORT REQUIREMENTS AND RELATED LEGAL RESPONSIBILITY

Securities and Exchange Commission Requirements

Over the years, the Securities and Exchange Commission has revised its rules applicable to accountants' certificates and established the following requirements therefor.

RULE 2–02: ACCOUNTANTS' CERTIFICATES

a) *Technical requirements*

The accountants' certificates shall be dated, shall be signed manually, and shall identify without detailed enumeration the financial statements covered by the certificate.

b) *Representations as to the audit*

The accountant's certificate (i) shall state whether the audit was made in accordance with generally accepted auditing standards; and (ii) shall designate any auditing procedures generally recognized as normal or deemed necessary by the accountant under the circumstances of a particular case, which have been omitted, and the reasons for their omission.

Nothing in this rule shall be construed to imply authority for the omission of any procedure which independent accountants would ordinarily employ in the course of an audit made for the purpose of expressing the opinions required by paragraph (*c*) of this rule.

c) *Opinions to be expressed*

The accountant's certificate shall state clearly:
  (i)   the opinion of the accountant in respect of the financial statements covered by the certificate and the accounting principles and practices reflected therein;
 (ii)   the opinion of the accountant as to any material changes in accounting principles or practices, or adjustments of the accounts, required to be set forth by rule 3–07; and
(iii)   the nature of, and the opinion of the accountant as to, any material differences between the accounting principles and practices reflected in the financial statements and those reflected in the accounts after the entry of adjustments for the period under review.

d) *Exceptions*

Any matters to which the accountant takes exception shall be clearly identified, the exception thereto specifically and clearly stated, and, to the extent practicable, the effect of each such exception on the related financial statements given.

Rule 3–07:   Changes in Accounting Principles and Practices

a)   Any change in accounting principle or practice or in the method of applying any accounting principle or practice made during any period for which financial statements are filed which affects comparability of such financial statements with those of prior or future periods, and the effect thereof upon the net income for each period for which financial statements are filed, shall be disclosed in a note to the appropriate financial statement.

b)   Any material retroactive adjustment made during any period for which financial statements are filed, and the effect thereof upon net income of prior periods shall be disclosed in a note to the appropriate financial statement.

The Securities and Exchange Commission (1) makes a distinction between fundamental auditing standards and their methods of application, (2) directs certain recommendations to the assurance of the observation of acceptable auditing standards, (3) leaves with the accounting profession the determination of the auditing standards, and (4) recognizes varying applications of auditing procedures in conformity with the circumstances of each case. However, the SEC is altering its attitude regarding (3) and (4), above.

The requirements of the Commission relieve the auditor of no responsibility, but they do recognize that the finding of liability on the part of the auditor under the act may be affected by the scope of the audit. Thus, the representations of the auditor must be free both of negligence and of fraud. Therefore, under the act, if the accountant is innocently negligent and not guilty of fraud, his liabilities are as great as if he had knowingly misrepresented a financial condition. However, in order to defend himself on a charge of misrepresentation under the act, the accountant must not stop at proving that he had, after reasonable investigation, reasonable grounds to believe that the registrant's financial statements were true—that he was free from negligence; he must also show that he believed his representations were true, the effect of which would be to establish that he was not conscious of misrepresentation at the time of making the report and therefore was not guilty of fraud. After the auditor had proved that he was not negligent—that is, that he had reasonable grounds to believe that his representations were true—it would generally be easy to show that he believed his representations were true and that he was therefore innocent of fraud.

At this point, and in order to avoid repetition, the reader is referred back to Chapter 27 for SEC reporting proposals and requirements.

Liability for Reports Generally

In addition to the audit report requirements of the Securities and Exchange Commission, and in addition to the legal responsibilities of the accountant as set forth in Chapter 3 and throughout the text, the following comments are made concerning legal liability for audit reports.

At all times, the auditor, in his short-form or long-form report, must maintain a precise distinction between management's representations and the representations of the auditor. This is necessary in order to indicate the extent of the responsibility assumed by the auditor. Unless a statement to the contrary is included in any audit report, it may be assumed that the auditor is taking responsibility for the fairness of presentation of the financial statements *and* all other data in the report, and that these other data are fairly presented, just as are the financial statements.

If both a short-form and a long-form report are issued, supplementary data and comments in the long-form report must not lead to the possible contention that they constitute exceptions or qualifications as distinguished from report comments.

If comparative statements for a prior year or years are included in any audit report—and this is normal—and if only a long-form audit report is issued, and if the auditor examined the records for the prior year or years, he should include a statement in the opinion section setting forth the fact that he did perform the examinations in the prior year or years. If the auditor did not examine prior statements, and if he includes comparative data in the report of the current year, he should, for his protection, disclose his nonexamination of data of prior years.

When both short-form and long-form reports are prepared, they should bear the same dates and should be released simultaneously, in order to establish the fact that there are no differences in basic data. In the State Street Trust Company case (278 N.Y. 104), the suspicion of the court was aroused because of a difference in dates on the short-form report and the long-form report.

If a long-form report contains data which are omitted from a short-form report, an argument might be presented that the short-form report was misleading, because it inadequately disclosed facts known to the auditor. Therefore, care should be exercised to be certain that a long-form report is an expansion of—not an alteration of—the short-form report.

In the long-form report, supplementary financial data must be presented in such form that the argument cannot be presented that the auditor made factual representations with regard to the financial statements when he intended to present management's representations. Additional material on legal liability was presented in Chapter 3.

SECTION III: LONG-FORM AUDIT REPORTS

General Discusssion

If a long-form audit report is submitted to a client it *normally* is not passed on to others. The long-form report is presented in addition to or in lieu of the short-form report. Since an audit report is the tangible terminal result of an examination, the auditing procedures followed prior to preparing the report must be based upon auditing standards applicable in the circumstances, as set forth in this book.

Any report should be prepared promptly at the close of the audit, since delay in preparation normally will tend to dim the memory of the auditor and consequently will have an adverse effect upon the report. In addition, events subsequent to the closing of the field work might have an effect on the report. If considerable time has elapsed between the completion of the audit and the submission of the report, the client naturally will have lost some of his interest—justifiably, for possibilities of controlling unsatisfactory conditions may have passed.

The auditor must remember that the client is the person who will read and understand—or not understand—the report. Audit procedures should be de-emphasized or eliminated from the report. The client is more interested in the discoveries and comments of the auditor than in a recital of the verification procedures followed. The standard scope section indicates that the examination has been conducted in accordance with generally accepted auditing standards.

Report Drafting

The audit report is important, and highly valuable service is rendered by the auditor through his report. To be of maximum service, the auditor must use care in the compilation, drafting, and rendition of report material.

Reports may be relatively long or short, depending on several conditions. The client may desire a long report which he can study and peruse during the succeeding year, or he may be interested only in a brief report. If the report is for the guidance of management, many details with which management is familiar may be omitted; also, for managerial purposes, there might be added much material which would be omitted from a report to outsiders. If a report is for the stockholders, details may or may not be vital; today's trend is toward increasing stockholder interest in details. If the report is for prospective stockholders or for credit-extension purposes, details may be quite voluminous. If a report is for purposes of registration with the Securities and Exchange Commission, the accountant realizes in advance almost exactly how the report will be used, and he will prepare it under rules set forth by the Commission.

In any situation, everything should be included in the report that is relevant to the examination under consideration. No attempt should be made to shorten unnecessarily the text of the report, and no attempt should be made to include detail of an inconsequential nature. Also, the auditor must learn to discriminate between necessary and unnecessary statements, statistics, and other presentations. It is impossible to formulate hard and fast rules for report writing; each report must be written from the standpoint of the exigencies of the particular situation. No report should be designed so that it leads to false or doubtful conclusions, perhaps engendered by a desire to becloud an unsatisfactory situation. The ethics of an auditor must neither be forgotten nor be sacrified to the desire or to the undeserved benefit of the client.

Under no conditions should an auditor attempt to relieve himself of responsibility by disclaiming such responsibility through the medium of his certification. At all times, the auditor must perform all work necessary in order to render an adequate report. Consider the following: "We did not verify title to the company's land by the inspection of public records; we have not undertaken to pass upon the title, and we assume no responsibility for it." The auditor is avoiding a responsibility by disclaiming it. In fact, the statement might be interpreted to mean that the auditor is suspicious of the title but did nothing to confirm those suspicions. The auditor normally is not supposed to examine public records; but in a case of this nature, the auditor could (1) obtain confirmation of title from the company's attorney; (2) inspect tax bills; (3) examine cash disbursemens or tax payments, partial payments on mortgages, repairs to structures, and rent payments; and (4) analyze interest expense. If he follows these procedures, he should have a fairly conclusive idea of the ownership of the land.

In preparing a report, the auditor should be concise. He is not retained to write a dissertation; he is retained to audit. Every report should be made interesting; this is of prime importance.

A stereotyped form should not be followed, thus making all reports similar, regardless of circumstances. Factual material and a conclusion or an opinion must be distinguished. Any opinion or conclusion must be supported by facts. In commenting upon different phases of the business, the auditor should ignore mere differences of opinion engendered by personal prejudices. Every business has certain points of interest and fascination which offer excellent material for the auditor. He should use language that is forceful, clear cut, and easy to understand. Unimportant details should always be omitted. Sometimes, the distinction between important and unimportant details is difficult to make; but study, training, and experience in time will have the desired effect.

If a report is prepared for investment purposes, it should clearly set forth, among other data:

1. The amount of invested capital.
2. The sources of the capital.
3. Fixed annual charges.
4. All debts, properly classified.
5. The general policy of the company with respect to dividends and the reinvestment of earnings.

6.   Earning per share, primary, and fully diluted—before and after nonrecurring items.

If a report is prepared for credit purposes, it should show:

1.   Current assets which may be readily converted to cash.
2.   Current assets which may not be readily converted to cash.
3.   Current liabilities maturing within a short time.
4.   Ratios of current assets to current liabilities.
5.   Pledged and secured assets.
6.   Contingencies.
7.   Proposed financing.
8.   Proposed methods of liquidating an extension of credit.

Report Contents

A long-form audit report normally includes (*a*) a statement of the scope of the examination and the auditor's opinion; (*b*) the principal financial statements and accompanying footnotes; (*c*) supplementary information consisting of statistical data, comparative statements, schedules, ratios, and other accounting and financial matters of interest to the client, as well as necessary explanatory comments regarding operations and financial condition. See Audit Report I and Audit Report II, appearing later in this chapter.

The submission of a long-form report is proper and logical, because as a result of an examination an auditor obtains information and data of value to a client in the management of his business. However, every audit report need not necessarily include all of the types of materials indicated in the preceding paragraph, and many audit reports will include materials in addition to those set forth above. Additional report materials will be indicated in the following pages. Several national firms follow the report pattern indicated in the preceding paragraph; one national firm made the statement "while we follow this report pattern, we also submit to any client any additional report material he desires."

Report Comments

In the comments section, the ability of the auditor is judged by the client. The same general report form and arrangement may be followed from year to year, but the comments of one year probably are not applicable to the next year. As an audit progresses, the auditor should prepare notes pertaining to all matters upon which he desires to comment; if he does this, report preparation is facilitated. In drafting report comments, an auditor should ask himself the following three questions:

1. Is this comment of sufficient importance to direct the reader to it?
2. Am I technically qualified to comment upon this particular subject?
3. Is the comment relevant to the audit?

If these three questions can be answered affirmatively, the comment should be included in the report.

Report comments may be divided on different bases, depending upon the nature and purpose of the engagement. Report comments might contain, for example:

1. A brief history of the organization, if the audit is a first engagement, or if the report is for prospective investors, or if required by the SEC.
2. Comments on operating results, in which all important changes, their causes, and results are set forth.
3. Comments on important percentage changes and dollar changes.
4. Comments on financial statement items.
5. A general discussion of points of interest.

Other auditors arrange the text of the report by starting with comments on the most important items, regardless of their nature. Others follow the arrangement of the balance sheet and the income statement (or vice versa), regardless of the relative importance of the various items.

As stated, a detailed description of auditing procedures followed should not be included in an audit report unless a client wants such descriptions. However, a few clients desire the inclusion of audit procedures in the report; usually, the smaller the client, the greater the detail of comments on procedures. When procedural comments are placed in the report, a description of the method of item verification should be briefly included. Perhaps the most frequent type of procedural comments still placed in audit reports concerns inventory-taking observation and testing, and a reference to confirmation of receivables.

In certain instances, audit procedure comments are desired by creditors and prospective creditors who will receive a copy of the audit report from the client, by insurance companies with whom claims for insured losses have been filed, and in a few other isolated instances.

ILLUSTRATION. In its annual audit of certain trust funds administered by the trust department of a bank, one national accounting firm includes the following procedural comments between the scope section and the opinion section of the standard short-form report. "We accounted for of the securities on hand. We examined data in support of all investment the investments of the Trust Fund at September 30, 1976, by inspection transactions and determined that all income applicable to investments has been included in the income of the Trust Fund. There were no defaults of principal or income during the year. We reviewed the quarterly valuations placed on each unit for purposes of admission and withdrawal and the quarterly distributions of income to participants."

A few additional illustrative procedural comments on operations and on balance sheet items follow at this point.

SALES

On the basis of a random sample, sales invoices were examined for prices, extensions, and footings; were traced to the sales records, the accounts receivable ledger accounts, the inventory records, and the cash records; and were compared with shipping department records. Sales records were footed for one month, and the footings were traced to the classified sales accounts in the general ledger.

EXPENSES

Except for payroll, expenses for two randomly selected months were examined in detail. Expenses for the remainder of the year were reviewed. For the two selected months, expense vouchers were compared with original invoices, the voucher register, and the cash disbursements records; paid checks were inspected and traced to the check register.

For the payroll, on the basis of random selection of individual employees, an examination of 5 percent of the payroll provided an acceptable quality; each item and subitem in the sample was examined and traced to all collateral records. All W–2 forms were reconciled to the payroll totals for the year.

ACCOUNTS RECEIVABLE

Accounts receivable were verified by direct circularization. Confirmation requests were mailed to 100 percent of the customers, representing $255,000 of trade accounts receivable; replies were received from 72 percent of the customers, totaling $216,750 of accounts receivable.

INVENTORIES

Inventories were verified as follows: As to quantities, we observed the taking of the physical inventory, and we verified selected items by physical tests. As to prices, we compared cost with the latest available market quotations; all items were priced at the lower of cost or market. As to clerical accuracy, we verified extensions and footings on 50 percent of the inventory sheets selected on a random basis, and we verified the totals of all classified summaries.

LIABILITIES

To the best of our ability to ascertain, all liabilities are included in the balance sheet, and there are no unusual liabilities at December 31, 1975.

CAPITAL STOCK AND OTHER PERMANENT CAPITAL CONTRIBUTIONS

The authorized capital stock was increased from 1,000 shares to 2,000 shares on April 1, 1975. On April 10, 1975, the additional 1,000 shares were sold for $110 per share, or a total of $110,000. The $10,000 premium was credited to Paid-In Capital, thus giving rise to that account, which appears in the balance sheet for the first time.

Financial and operating ratios should be used liberally in an audit report. These can be interesting and vitalizing when correctly interpreted and discussed, and are valuable to the auditor and the client. Several ratios, turnovers, and cost apportionments which are commonly used are:

1. The working capital ratio
2. The percentage of net income to net sales
3. The percentage of net income to tangible proprietorship
4. The percentage of net income to net working capital
5. The ratio of net sales to tangible proprietorship
6. The ratio of net sales to net working capital
7. The number of days' sales in accounts receivable (collection period)
8. The ratio of net sales to inventory
9. The percentage of fixed assets to tangible proprietorship
10. The percentage of liabilities to tangible proprietorship
11. The percentage of inventory to working capital
12. The percentage of long-term liabilities to net working capital
13. The net income, after federal taxes, earned per share of common stock
14. The percentage of net income left in the business
15. Gross profit per dollar of net sales
16. Manufacturing costs per dollar of net sales
17. Selling and administrative expenses per dollar of net sales

There are many other ratios which can be used, and many of the aforementioned need not be used in every report. When ratios, turnovers, and percentage figures are used, the dollar figures should also be given; and both dollar figures and analysis figures should be presented on an annual comparative basis.

Comments included in an audit report, or separately submitted, may be divided into many classes, among which are comments on dollar increase and decrease for selected items, insurance coverage, inventory comparisons, stock option plans, sales and profits, and the general progress of the business.

Audit Report Exclusions

Items which may be transmitted verbally or by separate written communication—and which should *not* be included in an audit report unless the client wants the items covered in the report—include the following:

1. Schedules of accounts receivable and accounts payable
2. Composition of cash
3. List of outstanding checks
4. Missing vouchers
5. A list of errors
6. Audit adjustments
7. Cases of suspected fraud
8. Defects in the accounting system
9. Cost procedures
10. Production policies and factory organization
11. Sales policies
12. Dividend policies
13. Additional capital requirements
14. The capital structure
15. Personnel problems
16. Any other nonaudit comments

Report Review. Before a report is typed, it should be thoroughly reviewed. In the review of a report, there are many items to be considered. The reviewer must be certain that the financial statements fairly present the financial condition and the results of operations. In order to accomplish this, the reviewer must integrate the information in the work papers with the data in the report; for example, trade accounts payable shown in the balance sheet must be in agreement with the total of the balance of the creditors' accounts as shown in the work papers. Comparison of this nature presupposes a complete review of the work papers. Final reviews of reports are made by a manager and one or more partners of the firm.

After the report is typed, it must again be reviewed; the review copy should be marked for all corrections to be made. The report must be designed and written with the intention of making it used, useful and appreciated. The auditor should have an understanding with his client concerning the use of the comments in the report for quotation purposes by the client.

Illustrating an Audit Report. If diagrams and charts are used to illustrate a report, the story they unfold must be carefully studied before they are prepared. The purpose of a diagram or a chart is to portray information dramatically, attractively, and briefly. Charts and graphs are not used as extensively as they should be in order to build the most effective reports. If used, charts and graphs should be designed so that the meaning is clear and so that they need not be interpreted before being useful or understandable.

It is suggested that the reader examine the annual reports of several large corporations, in order to obtain ideas regarding illustrations of financial data. He will discover that the majority of illustrations are in bar charts, either single or component, and in area charts.

For the purposes of the auditor, charts are of several types, as follows:

1. *Area Charts.* These take the form of circles or maps. In the circle chart, the entire circle represents a total, or 100 percent, and the various segments represent parts of that total. The circle chart is easily adapted to graphic presentation of revenue and expense data.

2. *Bar Charts.* In a *single* bar chart, one bar is used for each item in the data to be compared, and the relationship is expressed by varying the length of the bars. In a *component parts* bar chart, one bar is divided to express proportionate relationships.

For example, a bar expressing sales may be divided into cost of sales, expenses, and net income. In a *histogram*, bars of different length and color may be placed alongside each other to form a frequency distribution; single financial statements do not contain frequency distributions; therefore, the histogram is useful for showing age distributions of employees, production per employee, wages per employee for a series of years, or similar information from *comparative* financial statements.

3. *Line Charts.* In a line chart, time or class distribution is compared by the use of lines. In a *time series* line chart, time (years) classifications are commonly used horizontally and the comparative data indicated by the movement of the line across the years. The time series line chart is very adaptable for the application of accounting data, because the items compared frequently are the result of the passage of time. In a *frequency polygon*, lines connect the midpoints of bars in the histogram. If a histogram can be used, the frequency polygon may be used, since they both are applicable to the same type of data.

SECTION IV: REPORT EXAMPLES

In Chapter 2, a standard short-form audit report was presented, together with accompanying financial statement footnotes.

Two long-form reports are submitted for study at this point. An additional audit report accompanies the *Audit Case.* It must be remembered that the form, arrangement, and content will change with the examination of each individual company and with the practices of each individual auditor—or accounting firm. With the material presented here as a basis, the expansion or contraction of any report is possible in accordance with the size of the engagement and the necessity of presentation. Each auditing firm develops its own style, and these examples are not to be considered as standards set up without possiblity of deviation. Each of the following reports is from an audit, with the names of the clients changed.

REPORT I

METRO COMPANY

Table of Contents

REPORT I (*Continued*)

LANE AND LANE
Certified Public Accountants
Cincinnati, Ohio

March 5, 1976

To the Shareholders of the Metro Company:

We have examined the balance sheets of the Metro Company as of December 31, 1975, and December 31, 1974, the related statements of income and retained earnings, and the statements of changes in financial position for the years then ended. Our examination was made in accordance with generally accepted auditing standards, and accordingly included such tests of the accounting records and such other auditing procedures as we considered necessary in the circumstances.

In our opinion, the statements mentioned present fairly the financial position of the Metro Company as of December 31, 1975 and December 31, 1974, and the results of operations, and the changes in financial position for the years then ended, in conformity with generally accepted accounting principles applied on a consistent basis.

Lane and Lane

REPORT I (*Continued*)

METRO COMPANY
Balance Sheet, December 31, 1975, and 1974

ASSETS

	1975	1974
CURRENT ASSETS:		
Cash.	$ 114,886	$ 119,801
Receivables, less allowance of $8,845 for 1975 and $8,724 for 1974	192,150	106,540
Inventories, at the lower of cost (partly Lifo) or market. . . .	281,291	274,354
Prepaid items	4,463	4,862
Total Current Assets	$ 592,790	$ 505,557
FIXED ASSETS (Note 1):		
Land.	$ 50,000	$ 45,000
Building	436,200	420,000
Machinery.	289,780	279,280
Office equipment	27,010	24,650
Total	$ 802,990	$ 768,930
Less provision for depreciation.	214,240	177,415
Fixed Assets, Net	$ 588,750	$ 591,515
OTHER ASSETS:		
Cash surrender value of life insurance	$ 5,575	$ 3,963
Sinking fund investments (Note 2).	58,250	56,525
Patents, at amortized cost	14,295	17,000
Total Other Assets	$ 78,120	$ 77,488
Total Assets	$1,259,660	$1,174,560

LIABILITIES AND STOCKHOLDER'S EQUITIES

	1975	1974
CURRENT LIABILITIES:		
Accounts payable, trade.	$ 35,183	$ 16,864
Notes payable, bank	20,000	
Other current liabilities	28,190	26,397
Debenture bonds, current portion	50,000	50,000
Federal income taxes (Note 3).	117,952	101,469
Total Current Liabilities	$ 251,325	$ 194,730
LONG-TERM LIABILITIES:		
Debenture bonds, 4% maturing after one year (Note 4)	$ 150,000	$ 200,000
Total Liabilities	$ 401,325	$ 394,730
STOCKHOLDERS' EQUITIES:		
Common stock:		
No par value; 15,000 shares authorized, of which 10,000 shares are issued and outstanding at a stated value of $40 per share (Note 5)	$ 400,000	$ 400,000
Additional paid-in capital on 10,000 shares of common stock at $10 per share	100,000	100,000
Retained earnings	358,335	279,830
Total Stockholders' Equities	$ 858,335	$ 779,830
Total Liabilities and Stockholders' Equities	$1,259,660	$1,174,560

The accompanying Notes to the Financial Statements are an integral part of the statements.

2

REPORT I (*Continued*)

METRO COMPANY
Statement of Income and Retained Earnings
For the Years Ended December 31, 1975 and 1974

	1975	1974
NET SALES.	$2,452,627	$2,083,593
Cost of sales.	1,785,148	1,492,582
Gross profit on sales.	$ 667,479	$ 591,011
Selling and administrative expenses.	422,677	399,647
NET INCOME ON OPERATIONS.	$ 244,802	$ 202,364
Interest and dividend income.	2,725	2,067
	$ 247,527	$ 204,431
Interest expense.	9,150	10,000
Net income before nonrecurring items.	$ 238,377	$ 194,431
Loss on sale of fixed assets, net of taxes.	-1,920	+700
Net income before federal income taxes.	$ 236,457	$ 195,131
Federal income taxes.	117,952	101,469
NET INCOME FOR THE YEAR*.	$ 118,505	$ 93,662
Retained earnings at the beginning of the year.	279,830	226,168
	$ 398,335	$ 319,830
Dividends declared and paid.	40,000	40,000
RETAINED EARNINGS at the end of the year.	$ 358,335	$ 279,830
*Earnings per share of common stock.	$ 11.85	$ 9.37

METRO COMPANY
Statement of Changes in Financial Position
For the Year Ended December 31, 1975

	1975	1974
Funds provided by:		
Net income for the year.	$118,505	$ 93,662
Noncash changes to income:	36,825	34,127
Depreciation.	4,765	1,700
Patent amortization.	7,500	4,000
Machinery sold (loss included in net income).	$167,595	$133,489
Funds applied to:		
Addition to land.	$ 5,000	$ -0-
Addition to building.	16,200	-0-
Addition to machinery.	18,000	14,000
Addition to office equipment.	2,360	1,254
Addition to cash surrender value of life insurance.	1,612	1,491
Addition to sinking fund investments.	1,725	1,600
Addition to patents.	2,060	-0-
Dividends on capital stock.	40,000	40,000
Reduction in long-term bonds payable.	50,000	50,000
	136,957	108,345
Increase in net working capital.	30,638	25,144

The accompanying Notes to the Financial Statements are an integral part of the statements.

3

REPORT I (*Continued*)

METRO COMPANY

NOTES TO THE FINANCIAL STATEMENTS

NOTE 1: Fixed Assets

	1975	1974
Building	$436,200	$420,000
Machinery	289,780	279,280
Office equipment	27,010	24,650
	$752,990	$723,930
Less provision for depreciation	214,240	177,415
Depreciated cost of building, machinery and office equipment	$538,750	$546,515
Land	50,000	45,000
Total Fixed Assets, Net	$588,750	$591,515

Land, building, machinery, and office equipment are originally recorded at cost of acquisition. The company uses the straight-line method in all instances. The depreciated cost of the building, machinery, and office equipment represents that portion of original cost not yet allocated as a charge against operations, and does not purport to be either a realizable value or a replacement value. Net expenditures for fixed assets in 1975 totaled $41,560; gross book values or properties sold or retired totaled $7,500.

NOTE 2: Sinking Fund Investments

Under the terms of the bond indenture (see Note 4) the company is required to maintain a sinking fund at least equal in amount to the bond installment next due for payment. The sinking fund assets are under company control.

NOTE 3: Federal Taxes on Income

In determining the amount of income subject to federal taxes, certain adjustments were made to the net income before taxes. The company is of the opinion that there are no contingencies for additional tax assessments or for tax refunds.

NOTE 4: Debenture Bonds

Debenture bonds in the amount of $500,000 were issued January 1, 1969, and are to be retired serially in the annual amount of $50,000 starting July 1, 1970. As of December 31, 1975, $200,000 of bonds are outstanding of which $50,000 is a short-term liability.

Under covenants in the bond indenture, the company is limited to $75,000 as aggregate annual payments which may be made for dividends on capital stock, or for redemption, purchase, or other acquisition of its capital stock.

NOTE 5: Common Stock

Under a restricted stock option plan, as of December 31, 1975, there were outstanding options granted to certain officers and employees to purchase 4,000 shares at the mean average market price at the date of grant, ranging from $65.50 to $81.25 per share. Options for 1,000 shares were granted during 1975. Options outstanding are not exercisable for two years, and expire ten years after date of grant, with certain exceptions due to death or disability. During 1975, options for 2,300 shares were exercised at an average price of $71.50 per share, while options for 600 shares which have expired have reverted to unissued status.

NOTE 6: Other Matters

No litigation was pending as of December 31, 1975, and none is contemplated. It is the opinion of management that contingencies do not exist for assets or liabilities.

As of December 31, 1975, commitments for property additions and improvements amounted to approximately $75,000.

As of the date of this report, March 5, 1976, to the best of our knowledge, there have been no events subsequent to December 31, 1975, which would alter the financial statements as of that date.

4

REPORT I (*Continued*)

Revenues, Expenses, and Net Income

The following summary sets forth the operations for 1975, compared with 1974:

	1975	Percent of Net Sales	1974	Percent of Net Sales	Increase (Decrease*)
Net sales	$2,452,627	100.0	$2,083,593	100.0	$369,034
Cost of sales	1,785,148	72.8	1,492,582	71.6	292,566
Gross profit on sales	$ 667,479	27.2	$ 591,011	28.4	$ 76,468
Selling expenses	167,563	6.8	158,810	7.7	8,753
Administrative expenses . . .	255,114	10.4	229,837	11.0	25,277
Net operating income	$ 244,802	10.0	$ 202,364	9.7	$ 42,438
Other expenses, net	6,425	0.3	7,933	0.4	1,508*
	$ 238,377	9.7	$ 194,431	9.3	$ 43,946
Nonrecurring items:					
Loss or gain on sale of fixed assets.	-1,920	0.1	+700	0.1	2,620*
Net income before federal income taxes	$ 236,457	9.6	$ 195,131	9.4	$ 41,326
Federal income taxes	117,952	4.8	101,469	4.9	16,483
Net income.	$ 118,505	4.8	$ 93,662	4.5	$ 24,843
Earned per share of common stock	$ 11.85		$ 9.37		$ 2.48

The sales increase in 1975 of $369,034 was caused primarily by increased volume; price changes accounted for approximately $45,000 of the increase. The cost of sales increased at a slightly faster rate of increase than did sales. In terms of the cost of sales per dollar of sales, cost of sales increased from $0.716 in 1974 to $0.728 in 1975.

After provision for federal income taxes, net income in 1975 was $118,505, compared with $93,662 in 1974. The rate of net income earned on net sales was 4.8 percent in 1975 and 4.5 percent in 1974.

REPORT I (*Continued*)

METRO COMPANY
Selling and Administrative Expenses
For the Years Ended December 31, 1975 and 1974

	1975	1974	Increase (Decrease*)
Selling Expenses:			
Transportation-out	$ 13,002	$ 11,265	$ 1,737
Sales salaries	86,900	82,141	4,759
Travel expense	4,924	6,753	1,829*
Advertising	46,416	40,230	6,186
General selling expense	16,321	18,421	2,100*
Total Selling Expenses	$167,563	$158,810	$ 8,753
Administrative Expenses:			
Administrative salaries	$179,789	$168,750	$11,039
Depreciation of office equipment	2,665	2,425	240
Uncollectible accounts expense.	6,546	4,218	2,328
Office supplies	2,324	2,675	351*
Office operating expense	7,373	6,286	1,087
Insurance expense, general	4,646	4,580	66
Professional services	8,000	6,500	1,500
Miscellaneous taxes.	17,827	11,307	6,520
F.I.C.A. tax expense	12,525	9,622	2,903
Federal unemployment tax	1,098	954	144
State unemployment tax.	9,888	8,724	1,164
Workmen's compensation insurance	1,483	1,234	249
Life insurance expense	950	2,562	1,612*
Total Administrative Expenses	$255,114	$229,837	$25,277

6

REPORT I (*Continued*)

METRO COMPANY
Statement of Cost of Sales
For the Years Ended December 31, 1975 and 1974

	1975	1974
Inventories, January 1.	$ 268,106	$ 254,610
Raw materials purchased	1,262,774	1,010,504
Transportation–inward	11,686	9,775
	$1,542,566	$1,274,889
Direct factory labor	337,051	322,861
Manufacturing overhead:		
Indirect factory labor	102,300	90,957
Depreciation of building	8,150	7,724
Depreciation of machinery	26,010	23,978
Building maintenance	7,235	6,520
Machinery maintenance	10,485	9,465
Heat and power	12,342	10,944
Factory supplies expense	12,230	11,650
Patent amortization	4,765	1,700
Total manufacturing overhead	$ 183,517	$ 162,938
	$2,063,134	$1,760,688
Inventories, December 31	277,986	268,106
Cost of sales	$1,785,148	$1,492,582

FINANCIAL CONDITION COMMENTS

Net Working Capital

The following comparative summary sets forth the changes in the net working capital, that is, the current assets and the current liabilities.

ITEM	1975	1974	Increase (Decrease*)
Current Assets:			
Cash.	$114,886	$119,801	$ 4,915*
Accounts receivable, net	154,805	84,540	70,265
Notes receivable	37,000	22,000	15,000
Accrued receivables.	345	–o–	345
Inventories	281,291	274,345	6,946
Prepaid items	4,463	4,862	399*
Total Current Assets.	$592,790	$505,557	$87,233
Current Liabilities:			
Accounts payable	$ 35,183	$ 16,864	$18,319
Notes payable.	20,000	–o–	20,000
Social security tax liability	625	365	260
Unemployment tax liability	2,692	2,299	393
Income taxes withheld.	9,624	8,214	1,410
Accrued expenses	15,249	15,519	270*
Debenture bonds, current portion	50,000	50,000	–o–
Federal income tax liability.	117,952	101,469	16,483
Total Current Liabilities	$251,325	$194,730	$56,595
Net Working Capital	$341,465	$310,827	$30,638
Dollars of current assets per dollar of current liabilities.	$ 2.36	$ 2.60	$ 0.24*

7

REPORT I (*Continued*)

Receivables
Receivables consist of the following:

Trade accounts receivable	$163,650
Less provision for doubtful accounts	8,845
Trade accounts receivable, net	$154,805
Trade notes receivable	37,000
Accrued interest receivable	345
Net receivables	$192,150

As of December 31, 1975, trade accounts receivable were summarized by invoice dates as follows:

December, 1975	$100,285
November, 1975	48,266
October, 1975	13,481
Prior to October, 1975	1,618
Total	$163,650

After adjusting for year-end sales and payments, no differences in account receivable balances were reported based upon negative confirmations sent to all customers. Based upon past experience, management is of the opinion, in which we concur, that the allowance for doubtful items is adequate.

Credit terms are net cash in thirty days; in January and February, 1976, 95 percent of the open accounts receivable, and 70 percent of the notes receivable were collected.

No differences were reported as a result of the affirmative confirmation of the notes receivable; all are trade notes and are considered to be collectible.

Inventories
Inventories, determined by physical count, are priced at the lower of cost (partly Lifo) or market, are compared below for two years:

	December 31 1975	1974	Increase (Decrease*)
Raw materials	$132,244	$129,147	$3,097
Work in process	60,302	55,606	4,696
Finished goods	85,440	83,353	2,087
Factory supplies	3,305	6,248	2,943*
Total inventories	$281,291	$274,354	$6,937
Percentage of inventories to total current assets	47.4%	54.3%	

REPORT I (*Concluded*)

Fixed Assets

Analysis of the fixed tangible assets and the related depreciation provisions is presented below:

	Asset Balance 1-1-75	Net Additions 1975	Asset Balance 12-31-75	Accumulated Depreciation 1-1-75	Depreciation 1975 RATE	Depreciation 1975 AMOUNT	Accumulated Depreciation 12-31-75	Book Value
Building	$420,000	$16,200	$436,200	$ 63,946	2%	$ 8,150	$ 72,096	$364,104
Machinery	279,280	10,500	289,780	96,976	10%	26,010	122,986	166,794
Office Equipment. .	24,650	2,360	27,010	16,493	10%	2,665	19,158	7,852
	$723,930	$29,060	$752,990	$177,415		$36,825	$214,240	$538,750

Other Liabilities

Income taxes withheld.	$ 9,624
F.I.C.A. tax liability	625
Federal unemployment tax.	1,098
State unemployment tax	1,594
Accrued compensation insurance	774
Accrued interest payable	4,150
Accrued miscellaneous taxes	10,325
Total other liabilities	$28,190

9

REPORT II

TABLE OF CONTENTS

Note: This report is designed on the basis of a type of presentation differing from Report I. Note that a statement of changes in financial position is not included.

REPORT II (*Continued*)

VICTOR AND DUNCAN
Certified Public Accountants
Cincinnati, Ohio

February 23, 1976

The Stockholders and Board of Directors of Sutton, Inc.

We have examined the balance sheet of Sutton, Inc., as of December 31, 1975, and the related statement of income and retained earnings for the year then ended. Our examination was made in accordance with generally accepted auditing standards, and accordingly included such tests of the accounting records and such other auditing procedures as we considered necessary in the circumstances.

As a part of our report, we submit the following statements:

Exhibit   I: Balance sheets at December 31, 1975, and December 31, 1974
Exhibit   II: Statements of income and retained earnings for the year ended December 31, 1975, and comparison with the year ended December 31, 1974
Schedule 1: Cost of goods manufactured and sold
Schedule 2: Selling expenses
Schedule 3: Administrative expenses
Schedule 4: Other revenues and other expenses

In our opinion, the accompanying balance sheet and statement of income and retained earnings present fairly the financial position of Sutton, Inc., at December 31, 1975, and the results of its operations for the year then ended, in generally accepted accounting principles applied on a basis consistent with that of the preceding year. We have made similar examinations in prior consecutive years.

Victor and Duncan

1

REPORT II (*Continued*)

EXHIBIT I

SUTTON, INC.

Balance Sheets, December 31, 1975, and December 31, 1974

ASSETS	1975	1974
Current Assets:		
Cash $2,298,445		$ 478,246
Accounts receivable, net of allowances 934,650		742,687
Notes receivable 159,500		136,715
Inventories (Note 1). 766,923		1,082,894
Marketable securities at cost (market $222,000)		
(Note 2) 218,583		188,200
Interest accrued 956		750
Prepaid items 11,641		9,680
Total Current Assets	$ 4,390,698	$2,639,172
Long–Term Investments:		
Bonds, at cost and par, which is approximately market . . . . . $ 50,000		$ 50,000
Stocks, at cost, which is approximately market. 400,000		800,000
Sinking fund assets. 200,000		100,000
Cash surrender value of life insurance 62,750		58,625
Pension fund assets. 350,400		290,200
Total Long–Term Investments	1,063,150	1,298,825
Fixed Assets:		
Land. . . . . $ 850,000		$ 850,000
Building, machinery, and office equipment, net		
(Note 3) 4,660,652		5,070,003
Total Fixed Assets	5,510,652	5,920,003
Patents, less amortization	35,500	42,000
Total Assets	$11,000,000	$9,900,000

LIABILITIES

	1975	1974
Current Liabilities:		
Accounts payable $1,937,546		$1,557,558
Notes payable 406,700		901,200
Taxes withheld and accrued 161,510		42,728
Other accruals 44,744		36,714
Federal income tax provision 1,340,200		130,000
Total Current Liabilities.	$ 2,890,700	$2,568,200
Long–Term Liabilities:		
First–mortgage bonds, 6% debentures	1,000,000	1,000,000
Total Liabilities	$ 3,890,700	$3,568,200
Excess of Assets over Liabilities.	$ 7,109,300	$6,331,800
Represented by ownership of:		
Preferred stock, 6 percent, $100 par; 10,000		
shares issued and outstanding $1,000,000		$1,000,000
Common stock, no–par value; stated value $10		
per share; 300,000 shares issued and outstanding 3,000,000		3,000,000
Excess of amount paid in over stated value of		
common stock 300,000		300,000
Income retained as reinvested earnings 2,809,300		2,031,800
Total Investment of Owners	$ 7,109,300	$6,331,800

NOTE 1. Inventories, in accordance with the practices of the company, are priced at the lower of cost or market of individual items on the basis of last–in, first–out, less allowances for possible losses on inactive items.

NOTE 2. Marketable securities consist of issues of the United States government, carried at the lower of cost or market on the basis of individual issues.

NOTE 3. Buildings, machinery, and office equipment are carried at cost less accumulated depreciation of $2,131,315 at December 31, 1975.

2

REPORT II *(Continued)*

EXHIBIT II

SUTTON, INC.
Statement of Income and Retained Earnings
For the Years Ended December 31, 1975, and December 31, 1974

	1975		1974	
	Dollars	Percentage	Dollars	Percentage
Net sales	$16,265,300	100	$11,934,400	100
Cost of goods sold (Schedule 1)	10,574,200	65	8,592,700	72
Gross profit on sales	$ 5,691,100	35	$ 3,341,700	28
Selling expense (Schedule 2)	$ 1,541,400	10	$ 1,192,100	10
Administrative expense (Schedule 3)	1,223,700	7	956,100	8
	$ 2,765,100	17	$ 2,148,200	18
Net operating income	$ 2,926,000	18	$ 1,193,500	10
Less: Net other expense (Schedule 4)	155,400	1	87,300	1
Net income before nonrecurring items	$ 2,770,600	17	$ 1,106,200	9
Profit on sale of securities.	62,100	0		
Loss on sale of fixed assets			76,300	1
Net income before federal income taxes	$ 2,832,700	17	$ 1,029,900	8
Federal income taxes	1,340,200	8	530,000	4
Net income.	$ 1,492,500	9	$ 499,900	4
Add: Retained earnings, Jan. 1	2,031,800		1,891,900	
Total	$ 3,524,300		$ 2,391,800	
Deductions:				
Dividends on preferred stock	$ 60,000		$ 60,000	
Dividends on common stock	600,000		300,000	
Additional federal taxes, 1973 (Note 4)	55,000		0	
Total deductions	$ 715,000		$ 360,000	
Balance of retained earnings, Dec. 31	$ 2,809,300		$ 2,031,800	
Earnings per share of common stock, after deducting $60,000 of dividends on preferred stock	$	4.78	$	1.47

NOTE 4. The additional federal income taxes of 1973
(a prior period) were charged to Retained
Earnings, in accordance with the requirements
of the AICPA.

3

REPORT II (*Continued*)

SCHEDULE 1

SUTTON, INC.

Cost of Goods Manufactured and Sold

For the Years Ended December 31, 1975, and December 31, 1974

	1975	1974
Raw material inventory, January 1.	$ 400,710	$ 350,560
Purchases of raw material	4,114,623	3,608,892
	$ 4,515,333	$3,959,452
Deduct: Raw material, December 31	238,866	400,710
Cost of raw materials used	$ 4,276,467	$3,558,742
Direct factory labor	3,384,110	2,728,461
	$ 7,660,577	$6,287,203
Manufacturing expenses:		
Supervision	$ 175,692	$ 185,610
Indirect factory labor	752,141	614,208
Factory employee pension costs	120,165	116,424
Social security taxes	73,915	71,456
Depreciation of buildings	112,563	112,563
Depreciation of machinery	295,457	289,362
Amortization of patents	6,500	6,500
Utilities	267,352	198,724
Taxes on buildings and machinery	136,864	135,729
Insurance on buildings and machinery	46,139	42,622
Cost department expense	97,450	89,761
Factory maintenance	467,828	387,246
Research and development expenses.	172,462	117,489
Employee health and recreation expense	36,780	27,451
Total Manufacturing Expense	$ 2,761,308	$2,395,145
Cost to manufacture	$10,421,885	$8,682,348
Variation of work-in-process inventory	+ 80,695	− 50,770
Cost of goods manufactured	$10,502,580	$8,631,578
Variation of finished goods inventory	+ 71,620	− 38,878
Cost of Goods Manufactured and Sold	$10,574,200	$8,592,700

4

REPORT II (*Continued*)

SCHEDULE 2

SUTTON, INC.
Selling Expense
For the Years Ended December 31, 1975, and December 31, 1974

	1975	1974
Advertising	$ 206,855	$ 135,176
Sales salaries and commissions	824,313	690,655
Sales office salaries	45,632	39,447
Social security taxes	34,572	28,614
Transportation-out	110,465	63,295
Travel expense	199,458	135,051
Sales office expense	105,837	88,601
Insurance, including pension costs	14,268	11,261
Total Selling Expenses	$1,541,400	$1,192,100

SCHEDULE 3

SUTTON, INC.
Administrative Expenses
For the Years Ended December 31, 1975, and December 31, 1974

	1975	1974
Officers' salaries	$ 619,468	$ 515,221
Office salaries	428,936	298,462
Social security taxes	38,920	28,429
Depreciation of office equipment	7,426	7,426
Telephone	13,041	10,042
Office supplies	10,460	8,649
Travel expense	17,522	21,982
Uncollectible accounts charged off	7,286	6,417
Insurance, including pension costs	25,542	23,062
Office operating expense	25,499	13,210
Professional services	29,600	23,200
Total Administrative Expenses	$1,223,700	$ 956,100

SCHEDULE 4

SUTTON, INC.
Other Revenues and Other Expenses
For the Years Ended December 31, 1975, and December 31, 1974

	1975	1974
Other expenses:		
Interest on bonds	$ 60,000	$ 60,000
Interest expense on notes	24,400	46,800
Sales discount	127,500	50,900
Market decline in inventory	16,400	
Total Other Expenses	$ 228,300	$ 157,700
Other revenues:		
Interest on bond investments	$ 2,000	$ 2,000
Interest on notes receivable	5,500	4,900
Dividends received	65,400	63,500
Total Other Revenues	$ 72,900	$ 70,400
Net Other Expense	$ 155,400	$ 87,300

5

REPORT II (*Continued*)

OPERATING COMMENTS

We reviewed revenue and expense transactions, and compared the revenues and expenses of 1975 with 1974. All material fluctuations were investigated, and satisfactory explanations were obtained in all instances. The following comments are submitted for revenues and expenses; you are referred to Exhibit II in connection with this analysis.

SALES

Net sales increased $4,330,900 in 1975 as compared with 1974, an increase of 36 percent. The increase is caused by increased volume and increased selling prices. Owing to the increased use of machinery in the plant, direct labor and manufacturing overhead increased 20 percent, or less than the percentage increase in sales.

COST OF GOODS MANUFACTURED AND SOLD

Cost of goods sold increased 23 percent in 1975, as compared with 1974. In terms of sales, cost of goods sold decreased by 7 percent in 1975, which is favorable when interpreted in terms of the net income for the year. A study of Schedule 1, Cost of Goods Manufactured and Sold, shows that the increase in cost of sales was equitably distributed over all of the items. Material costs decreased from $0.30 to $0.26 for each $1 of sales.

Controllable items of manufacturing overhead increased in 1975, with the exception of supervision, which decreased approximately $10,000. This was caused primarily by the retirement of four employees and their replacement by employees at initial salaries somewhat lower than those of their predecessors. Total manufacturing overhead constituted 17 percent of sales in 1975 and 20 percent in 1974. The increase in manufacturing overhead for 1975 was $366,163, a 15 percent increase over 1974. Manufacturing overhead increased at a lower rate of increase than sales.

Maintenance costs increased $80,582 in 1975; this condition is normal, since maintenance costs fluctuate directly with production.

GROSS PROFIT ON SALES

Gross profit increased to 35 percent of net sales in 1975 from 28 percent of net sales in 1974. The increase was primarily due to the increased sales volume.

SELLING EXPENSES

Selling expenses increased $349,300, or 29 percent. Sales increased 36 percent; selling expenses increased 7 percent. All items of selling expense increased, with the emphasis quite equally distributed.

ADMINISTRATIVE EXPENSES

Administrative expenses increased $267,600 in 1975, or 28 percent. This compares with a 36 percent increase in sales, which means that the increase in administrative expense is less than proportionate to the increase in sales. However, owing to the sales increase, administrative expenses decreased from 8.0 percent of sales in 1974 to 7.5 percent in 1975. Salaries show the greatest rise, accounting for 76 percent of the increase in adminstrative expenses.

REPORT II (*Continued*)

NET OPERATING INCOME

Net operating income was 18 percent of sales in 1975, as compared with 10 percent of sales in 1974. This increase was caused by the increase in sales and the percentage reduction in cost of sales.

NET INCOME

Net income after federal taxes increased $992,600 in 1975, or from $499,900 in 1974 to $1,492,500 in 1975, an increase of 198 percent. In terms of sales, net income for 1975 was 9.2 percent, as compared with 4.2 percent in 1974.

After deducting preferred dividend requirements from the 1975 net income, the earnings per share of common stock equal $4.78 in 1975, as compared with $1.47 in 1974.

CONDITION COMMENTS

CASH

Cash in banks was confirmed by direct correspondence with the depositories and reconciled with the balances of the cash accounts. Cash funds were verified by count.

ACCOUNTS RECEIVABLE
ALLOWANCES FOR DOUBTFUL ACCOUNTS

The accounts receivable are classified as follows:

Customers.	$867,298
Affiliated companies	76,025
Total	$943,323

We mailed confirmation requests to customers aggregating 75 percent of the total of $867,298, with the request that they notify us of any differences. The exceptions reported were minor. We reviewed the accounts with the credit department of the company in order to determine the adequacy of the allowance for doubtful accounts. The loss from uncollectible accounts is small, being less than one half of 1 percent of net sales. The allowance of $8,673 appears to be adequate.

The accounts receivable from affiliated companies represent amounts currently due from sales made, and not from advances.

The company classifies accounts receivable as to age from date of billing. We made a sufficient test of the company's classifications to determine that they are substantially correct. A summary of such classifications is as follows:

7

REPORT II (*Continued*)

Date billed:

Prior to January 1, 1975	$ 150
January, February, and March, 1975	500
April, May, and June, 1975	1,460
July, August, and September, 1975	107,200
October, November, and December, 1975	834,013
Total	$943,323

NOTES RECEIVABLE

Confirmation requests were mailed to all customers with note balances, with the request that they notify us of any differences. There were no differences reported. The notes are all taken in the normal sales operation, and the latest maturity date is July 16, 1976.

INVENTORIES

We observed the taking of the inventory, tested quantity counts, examined the inventory data for extensions and footings, and tested prices from current invoices. Management, under whose direction the inventories were taken, certified the inventories as to quantity and certified that the inventories are priced at the lower of cost or market in all instances.

All raw material has been certified to us as usable, and all finished goods as salable. Inventory was written down from cost to market to the extent of $16,400. Inventory activity was more favorable in 1975, showing a turnover for all inventories of twenty-one times in 1975, compared with eleven times in 1974.

Comparative inventories follow as of December 31:

	1975	1974	Increase or Decrease, 1975 over 1974
Raw materials. . . .	$238,866	$ 400,710	-$161,844
Work in process. . .	95,675	176,370	- 80,695
Finished goods . . .	429,728	501,348	- 71,620
Factory supplies . .	2,654	4,466	- 1,812
	$766,923	$1,082,894	-$315,971

MARKETABLE SECURITIES

Marketable securities are composed of United States Treasury notes. These securities, held in a safe-deposit box of the First National Bank, were submitted to us for examination. The December 31, 1975 market price is $222,000.

LONG-TERM INVESTMENTS

Bonds, Utilite Services, 4%, 25-year, 50 first-mortgage bonds, at cost and par of $1,000 each . . . . . . $	50,000
Common stock, Collins Company, 4,000 no-par shares, at cost	400,000
Sinking fund assets	200,000
Cash surrender value of life insurance	62,750
Pension fund	350,400
Total	$1,063,150

REPORT II *(Continued)*

The bonds of Utilite Services were examined in the safe-deposit department of the First National Bank. The bonds were purchased at par in 1973. The present market price is $1,006 per bond.

The common stock investment in the Collins Company, representing a noncontrolling interest of 4,000 shares (of a total original purchase of 8,000 shares in 1970) of no-par value, were examined in the safe-deposit department of the First National Bank. They are carried at cost and have a present market price of $396,000, which is $4,000 below cost. In February, 1975, 4,000 shares of the stock of the Collins Company were sold at a gain of $62,100.

The sinking fund of $200,000 is created for the retirement of the first-mortgage bonds of the company. The composition of the fund at December 31, 1975, as certified by the Union Trust Company, trustee under the bond indenture, was as follows:

Cash.	$ 4,658.10
Securities	195,341.90
Total	$200,000.00

In the year 1975, Sutton, Inc. remitted $44,600 to the trustee, which is the amount necessary to increase the fund $50,000 per year for twenty years.

In 1975, the cash surrender value of the life insurance increased $4,125. The policies cover three major officers in the amount of $100,000 each.

Pension fund assets, all contributed by the company, and under the investment operation of the Union Trust Company, with title vested in Baldwin, Inc., increased to $350,400 from $290,200. Company contributions to the fund in 1975 were $128,800, and payments to retired employees were $68,600.

FIXED ASSETS
ACCUMULATIONS FOR DEPRECIATION

Depreciation has been provided for the year on the straight-line method, at the same rates previously established, which have been accepted by the Internal Revenue Service for 1973 and prior years.

All fixed asset additions and deductions for the year were verified. The company exercises a conservative capitalization policy. A summary of fixed assest is presented below.

Item	Depre-ciation Rate	Cost	Total Depre-ciation	Carrying Value
Land.	0	$ 850,000	0	$ 850,000
Buildings	3	3,752,121	$1,231,092	2,521,029
Machinery.	10	2,965,584	848,331	2,117,253
Office equipment . . .	10	74,262	51,892	22,370
		$7,641,967	$2,131,315	$5,510,652

REPORT II (*Continued*)

INTANGIBLE ASSETS

Patents are amortized over a ten-year period from the time of the grant. To us, this appears proper in the light of the position enjoyed in the sale of patented products. No patents were acquired during 1975.

ACCOUNTS PAYABLE

Accounts payable were verified by the examination of supporting authorizations and evidences. We examined all sources for unrecorded liabilities as of December 31, 1975. The composition of the accounts payable is as follows:

Trade accounts payable	$862,046
Affiliated company accounts payable, regular purchases	75,500
Total	$937,546

NOTES PAYABLE

Trade notes payable, total $206,700, were confirmed by correspondence. The company regularly purchases on note from certain suppliers; therefore, these notes do not arise from the inability to meet maturing obligations. Since December 31, 1975, all have been paid and others issued.

Bank loans of $200,000 were verified by correspondence with the First National Bank. The note is due on March 29, 1976. It was made on September 30, 1975, in order to take advantage of a decline in raw material prices existing at that time, which is also the time cash funds are at their minimum. The note is subject to the terms and provisions of a loan agreement between the bank and the company relating to limitations of the right of the company to sell, assign, or pledge certain assets without the consent of the bank; maintenance of net current assets as defined; and the relationship of borrowings to net current assets.

FEDERAL INCOME TAX

The 1975 federal income tax is 1,340,200. During the year, the company paid an additional tax assessment of $55,000 levied against 1973 income.

BONDS PAYABLE

The twenty-year, 3 percent bonds of the company were issued on January 2, 1972, and constitute a first mortgage against the real properties of the company. The bonds, of a total par value of $1,000,000 were sold for cash at par. Confirmation of the outstanding bonds was obtained from the trustee at the time the sinking fund was verified.

REPORT II *(Concluded)*

CAPITAL STOCK

> Preferred, 6 percent, cumulative and nonparticipating;
> authorized, issued, and outstanding; 10,000 shares
> of a par value of $100 per share · · · · · · · · · · · · $1,000,000
> Common, no-par value; authorized, issued, and out-
> standing; 300,000 shares of a stated value of $10
> per share ·   3,000,000

The outstanding shares of preferred and common stock were confirmed by the registrar, the Central Trust Company. There were no changes in the capital stock structure in 1975.

As of May 1, 1970, the entire 10,000 shares of preferred stock are to be redeemed and retired and canceled at a premium of $5.00 per share plus dividends accumulated to that date.

WORKING CAPITAL RATIO

The current ratio of $1.51 of current assets to $1.00 of current liabilities at December 31, 1975, compares with a ratio of $1.02 to $1.00 at December 31, 1974.

RATIO OF CAPITAL TO NET FIXED ASSETS

The ratio of total capital to net fixed assets is $1.29 of capital to $1.00 of fixed assets. This compares with $1.07 of capital to $1.00 of fixed assets one year ago. The static ratio is satisfactory, and the trend is good and has been constantly increasing over the last six years.

RATIO OF SALES TO TOTAL ASSETS

Total capital employed in the business turned over 1.5 times in 1975, as compared with 1.2 times in 1974. The advantages of a better turnover of capital employed are reflected in greater net income on invested capital.

BOOK VALUE OF COMMON STOCK

The book value of the common stock at December 31, 1975, is $20.36 per share; at December 31, 1974, it was $17.77 per share, an increase of $2.59 per share.

11

Special Reports

If financial statements are prepared on a cash basis or on a partial accrual basis for other than nonprofit organizations, either the financial statements (or footnotes thereto), or the audit report should set forth the incomplete basis of the statement preparation, and the nature of omitted items of material amount.

For nonprofit organizations, *Statements on Auditing Procedure No. 33,* page 90, paragraph 8, is quoted:

If the statements are those of a nonprofit organization, they may reflect accounting practices differing in some respects from those followed by business enterprises organized for profit. In many cases generally accepted accounting principles applicable to nonprofit organizations have not been clearly defined. In those areas where the independent auditor believes generally accepted accounting principles have been clearly defined he may state his opinion as to the conformity of the financial statements either with *generally accepted accounting principles,* or (less desirably) with *accounging practices* for non-profit organizations in the particular field (e.g., hospitals, educational institutions, and so forth), and in such circumstances he may refer to financial position and results of operations. In those areas where he believes generally accepted accounting principles have not been clearly defined, the other provisions covering special reports as discussed under cash basis statements are applicable.

The other provisions referred to above deal primarily with recognized general auditing standards, standards of field work, and standards of reporting.

QUESTIONS

1. The text of the short-form audit report is said to be standard. What is meant by the word standard in this context? Does standardization mean inflexibility?

2. When an audit report is drafted there are ethical considerations that the auditor should bear in mind. Discuss.

3. *a*)   What is a footnote, as used in an audit report?
    b)   What is the similarity between footnotes to financial statements and report comments?

4. Some of the comments in an audit report are statements of fact while other comments are expressions of opinion. Explain this in terms of the balance of the cash in bank and its availability for the liquidation of current debt as compared to the collectibility of accounts receivable.

5. If management refuses to sign a liability certificate, what course of action should be followed by the auditor?

6. Why is the date used on an audit report important?

7. Refer to Report II in Chapter 28. Prepare a list of four criticisms of this report, together with very brief reasons for each criticism.

8. If a long-form report contained data which might affect the accompanying statements, taken as an entirety, should the accompanying short-form report be altered in any way from its standard form?

9. Rain, Inc. has accounts receivable which are material in amount. The management of Rain refused to permit their confirmation, and no other satisfactory means of establishing the correctness of the total is available. How would this affect the audit report?

10. What, in your opinion, are assumptions basic to every audit report?

11. It was discovered during the course of an audit that two office employees of your client were not attentive to their work, accomplished practically nothing, and spent most of their time in the office discussing matters of their own personal concern. How should this be commented on in the audit report?

12. At the beginning of your examination of the financial statements of the Atel Insurance Company, the president of the company requested that in the interest of efficiency you coordinate your audit procedures with the audit being conducted by the state insurance examiners for the same fiscal year. The state examiners audited the asset accounts of the company while you audited the accounts for liabilities, stockholders' equity, income and expenses. In addition you obtained confirmations of the accounts receivable and were satisfied with the results of your audit tests. Although you had no supervisory control over the state examiners, they allowed you to review and prepare extracts from their work papers and report. After reviewing the state examiners' work papers and report to your complete satisfaction, you are now preparing your short-form report. What effect, if any, would the above circumstances have on your short-form audit report? Discuss.

(AICPA, adapted)

13. During the course of the examination of Tomco, you recognized the following unauthorized or troublesome items which may or may not require comment in the audit report. Indicate which of the following items require a comment in the audit report and which items do not require a comment. Give reasons for your answers.
   a) Receipt of capital stock donated back to the corporation during the first year of operations
   b) General or specific office personnel inefficiency
   c) Unauthorized salary paid to treasurer
   d) A poor system of operating petty cash
   e) No contingency set up for possible additional tax assessments
   f) Overdrawn commission accounts of salesmen
   g) A factory overhead rate which obviously is too low
   h) Purchase commitments not protected by sales contracts
   i) Overprovision for insurance

14. Your client asked you to audit another company's records with the view that your client may purchase this company. You are to submit

a comprehensive report to your client. What additional comments might your report contain?

15.   The existence of fraud was suspected by the auditor; however, because of the limitations placed upon the engagement, the suspicions could not be pursued. The desirability of further work in verifying cash receipts from sales was mentioned to the treasurer of the company, who simply told the auditor to "skip it" and to confine himself to the engagement. Should the matter be mentioned in the audit report? If so, how?

PROBLEMS

1.   You are completing an examination of the financial statements of The Hill Corporation for the year ended February 28, 1976. Hill's financial statements have not been examined previously. The controller of Hill has given you the following draft of proposed footnotes to the financial statements:

NOTES TO FINANCIAL STATEMENTS
Year Ended February 28, 1976

Note 1.   Because we were not engaged as auditors until after February 28, 1975, we were unable to observe the taking of the beginning physical inventory. We satisfied ourselves as to the balance of physical inventory at February 28, 1975 by alternative procedures.

Note 2.   With the approval of the Commissioner of Internal Revenue, the Company changed its method of accounting for inventories from FIFO to LIFO on March 1, 1975. In the opinion of the company the effects of this change on the pricing of inventories and cost of goods manufactured were not material in the current year but are expected to be material in future years.

Note 3.   The stock dividend described in our May 24, 1975 letter to stockholders has been recorded as a 105 for 100 stock split. Accordingly, there were no changes in the stockholders' equity account balances from this transaction.

Note 4.   For many years the company has maintained a pension plan for certain of its employees. Prior to the current year pension expense was recognized as payments were made to retired employees. There was no change in the plan in the current year, but upon the recommendation of its auditor, the company provided $64,000, based upon an actuarial estimate, for pensions to be paid in the future to current employees.

For each Note discuss:

a)   The note's adequacy and needed revisions, if any, of the financial statements or the note.

b)   The necessary disclosure in or opinion modification of the audit report. (For this requirement assume the revisions suggested in part (*a*), if any, have been made.)

Complete your discussion of each note (both parts (*a*) and (*b*)) before beginning discussion of the next one.

(AICPA, adapted)

2. The complete opinion included in the annual report of Old Colonies, Inc., for 1975 is reproduced below:

Auditor's Certificate

More & ONN

New City, New State

To whom it may concern:

In our opinion, the accompanying balance sheet and statements of income, retained earnings and changes in financial position present fairly the financial position of Old Colonies, Inc., and the results of its operations. Our examination of these financial statements was made in accordance with generally accepted auditing standards and accordingly included such tests of the accounting records and such other auditing procedures as we considered necessary, except that we did not confirm accounts receivable, but instead accounted for subsequent collections on the accounts, and we did not observe the taking of the physical inventory because it was taken prior to our appointment as auditors.

List and discuss the deficiencies of the "Auditors' Certificate" prepared by More & Onn.

(AICPA, adapted)

3. You have completed your audit of Carter Corporation and its consolidated subsidiaries for the year ended December 31, 1975 and were satisfied with the results of your examination. You have examined the financial statements of Carter for the past three years. The corporation is now preparing its annual report to shareholders. The report will include the consolidated financial statements of Carter and its subsidiaries and your short-form auditor's report. During your audit the following matters came to your attention:

(1) The Internal Revenue Service is currently examining the corporation's 1973 federal income tax return and is questioning the amount of a deduction claimed by the corporation's domestic subsidiary for a loss sustained in 1973. The examination is still in process and any additional tax liability is indeterminable at this time. The corporation's tax counsel believes that there will be no substantial additional tax liability.

(2) A vice president who is also a stockholder resigned on December 31, 1975 after an argument with the president. The vice president is soliciting proxies from stockholders and expects to obtain sufficient proxies to gain control of the board of directors so that a new president will be appointed. The president plans to have a footnote prepared which would include information of the pending proxy fight, management's accomplishments over the years, and an appeal by management for the support of stockholders.

a) Prepare the footnotes, if any, that you would suggest for the items listed above.

b) State your reasons for not making disclosure by footnote for each of the listed items for which you did not prepare a footnote.

(AICPA, adapted)

4. On January 1, 1976, Moon, Inc. sold its 50,000 shares of authorized capital stock of $10 par value for $500,000 cash. On the same day, the corporation acquired the following assets for cash:

Raw material inventory	$100,000
Land	50,000
Buildings	150,000
Machinery	150,000
	$450,000

Land buildings, and machinery were properly priced. The corporation is under contract to acquire its raw materials from one source for as long as either the supplier or the consumer (Moon) remains in operation. As a consideration for the contract, the supplier made a "once only" concession of 50 percent in the price of the opening inventory The effect was that Moon received $200,000 of inventory at a cost of $100,000. The inventory represents a minimum amount below which the base stock of inventory should not fall.

At March 31, 1976, the following balance sheet of Moon, Inc. was prepared from the records:

ASSETS

Cash	$ 20,000
Accounts receivable, net	30,000
Raw material inventory, at contract price	205,000
Land	50,000
Buildings, net	149,500
Machinery, net	140,500
	$595,000

LIABILITIES AND CAPITAL

Liabilities	$ -0-
Common stock	500,000
Retained earnings	95,000
	$595,000

a) What adjustments should be made to the March 31, 1976 balance sheet?

b) To what extent does the balance sheet, after adjustment, call for modification within the short-form audit report?

Present two solutions. All audit requirements were satisfactorily fulfilled. Ignore taxes.

(AICPA, adapted)

5. The financial statements of Ace Manufacturing, Inc., for the fiscal year ended September 30, 1976, are presented below. The president of the company has requested you to perform the audit and render a short-form report. The report would be addressed to the board of directors and no restrictions would be placed on the scope of your audit work.

During the audit you learn that inventories of finished goods and work in process are stated at material cost alone, without including labor or overhead; that this practice has been followed for both tax and financial accounting purposes since the inception of the company in 1963; and that the elements of costs in the inventories should have been shown in the schedule shown later in the problem.

Except for the company's inventory methods, the statements are found to be acceptable in all respects. Through an examination of the previous auditor's work papers, you have been able to satisfy yourself as to the correctness of the physical count and material cost of the opening inventory.

ACE MANUFACTURING, INC.

Balance Sheet
September 30, 1976

ASSETS		LIABILITIES	
Cash	$ 6,000	Trade accounts payable	$ 18,500
Accounts receivable (net)	11,000	Salaries and wages payable	2,750
Inventories, at material cost		Taxes on income	6,500
(first-in, first-out) or market,		Common stock, par value	
whichever lower	73,000	$100 a share, authorized,	
Prepaid expenses	3,000	issued and outstanding	
Property, plant, and equipment		1,000 shares	100,000
(net)	79,000	Retained earnings	44,250
	$172,000		$172,000

ACE MANUFACTURING, INC.

Statement of Income and Retained Earnings
Year Ended September 30, 1976

Net sales of manufactured product	$375,000
Cost of materials, including freight	150,000
Gross profit on sales	$225,000
Operating expenses	192,500
Earnings from operations	$ 32,500
Other deductions, less other income	11,000
Earnings before taxes on income	$ 21,500
Taxes on income	6,500
Net earnings	$ 15,000
Retained earnings—September 30, 1975	29,250
Retained earnings—September 30, 1976	$ 44,250

	Finished Goods *September 30*		*Work in Process* *September 30*	
	1976	*1975*	*1976*	*1975*
Materials	$44,000	$37,500	$17,000	$15,500
Labor	27,500	26,000	8,000	7,000
Overhead	14,000	12,000	8,500	8,000
	$85,500	$75,500	$33,500	$30,500

Prepare an audit report addressed to the board of directors, which is justified in the circumstances. Do not submit financial statements or notes to financial statements.

(AICPA, adapted)

6. The Dot Manufacturing Company was incorporated on January 3, 1973, and began operations on that date. Consistently, the company has operated at a profit. In order to finance proposed expansion, a bank loan is contemplated. The bank has requested certified financial statements for the year ended December 31, 1975. This is the first independent audit of the company records, and you have been retained for the examination.

Following is the condensed balance sheet prepared by the company accountant as of December 31, 1975:

ASSETS		LIABILITIES AND CAPITAL	
Cash	$ 5,000	Current liabilities	$ 75,000
Accounts receivable	20,000	Mortgage on plant	50,000
Inventories	175,000	Common stock, 2,250 no-par	
Plant, machinery and		shares	225,000
equipment	250,000	Retained earnings	100,000
	$450,000		$450,000

Your examination adhered to all recognized standards and procedures. Only the following information is to be considered in answering the questions appearing at the conclusion of the problem.

(1) Early in 1975, the company started a product cost system; prior to that time, unit costs of products manufactured were not available. The inventories of $175,000 include 50 units of a certain finished product, completed before January 1, 1975, estimated at a cost of $37,500. In 1975 sales of this product amounted to 10 units at $1,000 each. Management overestimated customer demand for this product, and states that it will recover the cost of this product in its future sales. Your investigation is to the effect that this product has been superseded by a more efficient model and that management has been optimistic regarding the disposition of the 40 units on hand. You conducted tests in an effort to establish the validity of the estimated costs, but your tests did not prove of value. The balance of the inventory consists of items manufactured or purchased in 1975. Accepted auditing procedures proved that this portion of the inventory is properly priced at the lower of cost or market on a Fifo basis.

(2) On July 1, 1975, the board of directors granted stock options to certain employees to purchase 250 shares of unissued common stock at $100 per share. The options may be exercised at any time prior to December 31, 1977. At December 31, 1975, no stock had been issued under these options.

(3) The company entered into a five-year lease for a warehouse, beginning July 1, 1975. The lease calls for annual rentals of $6,000. The lease also provides for renewal for an additional five years at a rental of $7,500 per year. The Dot Company pays insurance, taxes, and maintenance on the leased property.

a) Do any of the items in (1), (2), or (3), require disclosure in the financial statements? Do any of the items require qualification of the auditor's opinion? In each case, present reasons for your answer.

b) If disclosure or opinion qualification is required, prepare a note or qualifying statement for inclusion in your audit report.

(AICPA, adapted)

7. The following comments were included in an audit report of Edwards, Inc., for the year ended December 31, 1975. (The scope, opinion, and the financial statements, are purposely omitted.) Criticize each section of the audit report, if criticism is necessary.

COMMENTS

Section 1. Cash, $31,070

Cash on hand and on deposit as of December 31, 1975, was as follows:

On hand:		
Bills	$ 1,000	
Currency.	198	$ 1,198
On deposit:		
East Coast Bank	$12,644	
West Coast Bank	17,228	29,872
Total Cash.		$31,070

We counted the cash on hand on January 2, 1976; and found it to be correct. We obtained confirmations from the East Coast Bank and the West Coast Bank, and verified the above balances. Deposits were vouched to the banks for January and December, 1975. There are no evidences of lapping or kiting. Last check number: East Coast Bank, No. 8625; West Coast Bank, No. 22216.

Section 2. Notes Receivable, $10,000

Notes receivable on hand were inspected; confirmations were obtained for those discounted. All are considered good and collectible by management.

Company A	$ 1,000
Company B	2,000
Company C	3,000
Company D	4,000
Total Notes Receivable	$10,000

Section 3. Accounts Receivable, $101,300

Accounts receivable were verified by confirmation; 65 percent of the customers responded. The credit department aged the accounts receivable and has created an allowance for uncollectible accounts of $4,000, which we consider ample after reviewing the aging prepared by the credit department. All doubtful accounts are rapidly written off. Collection attempts are continued after the accounts are written off and for a period of time sufficient to result in collectibility or the assurance of uncollectibility.

Section 4. Inventories, $160,000

Physical quantities were certified to us by the treasurer. We did not test quantities. We verified the inventory sheets for prices, extensions, and footings; prices were at the lower of cost or market. Item X appears to be slow moving; the present quantity on hand was purchased three years ago, which liquidation period is out of line with other company inventories. We have suggested depreciating item X to the extent of $10,000.

In the light of the present sales volume, it appears that December purchases are somewhat excessive. At the present rate of sales, these large purchases will not be moved for many months.

Section 5.   Land, $30,000

Buildings, $200,000

Accumulated Depreciation, $50,000

There were no changes during the year. The accumulated depreciation appears to be adequate, being four percent per year. Land and buildings are carried at cost. The present sound appraisal value of land and buildings is $300,000.

Section 6.   Machinery and Equipment, $350,000

Accumulated Depreciation, $200,000

All additions and deductions for the year were audited and were found correct. The accumulation for depreciation is adequate; and the rate of depreciation is 10 percent per year, on a straight-line basis. Subsidiary ledger accounts are carried for each machine.

Section 7.   Accounts and Notes Payable, $78,000

There is one note payable of $20,000, due the East Coast Bank, which was confirmed. The accounts payable subsidiary ledger agreed with the control. See the attached accounts payable schedule.

Section 8.   Common Stock, Par $100, $400,000

The confirmation from the registrar shows 4,000 shares of common stock issued and outstanding. During 1975, 200 shares were issued at $110 and the premium credited to Paid-In Capital. The 200 shares issued were a part of the total authorization. The proceeds of the sale were used as a part of the general cash.

PRACTICE MATERIAL ASSIGNMENTS

Metalcraft, Incorporated: Audit Problem:
  Assignment 13. Audit Report.
Colby Gears, Inc.: Holmes and Moore Audit Case:
  The Audit Report.

29

Management Advisory Services

INTRODUCTION

In the area of management advisory services the *attest function is not involved*. Therefore, a report rendered to a client for whom advisory services are performed will be totally different from an audit report, because it will be dealing with a specific area, function, information system, procedure, operation, and so forth, of a business.

The scope of the services of the certified public accountant has grown beyond the function of auditing, pure financial accounting, accounting system design and installation, and tax accounting into the broad area generally known as "management advisory services." The practice of most public accounting firms includes work in this area. In some cases management advisory services comprise as much as 30 percent of the total work of the firm. The majority of large firms of certified public accountants now maintain separately organized departments set up to handle management advisory service engagements, and this field constitutes one of great breadth and depth for a certified public accountant.

It is impossible to say just when the field of management services started; for as long as the accounting profession has existed at least some practitioners consulted with clients about general business problems and other more specialized problems outside the auditing, tax, cost, and other areas. After World Wars I and II, with the advent of business complexities, advanced management techniques, and the computer, the growth was accelerated and became recognized as a separate division of practice. The progressive public accountants have found management services a natural area of development of their practice because many of these assignments involved planning and control systems that relied heavily on accounting and related statistical information.

In recent years, responding to the increasing demands of clients for outside assistance, management advisory services have evolved and the auditors' role broadened into more complex and sophisticated business services and techniques. It is the intention of the profession to encourage extension of management services as long as these services are consistent with the members' professional competence, ethical standards, and responsibility. As expressed in *Statements on Auditing Procedure No. 33*, an auditor must acquire proficiency through education and experience. The same standards apply to those supplying management services.

The qualifications for management advisory services sometimes include special training and experience in the skills and research capabilities to apply an analytical approach to the solution of management problems. When the auditor is qualfied, he is in a position to do a better job than any other outside person because of his familiarity with a given business organization gained over the years of relationship with that business organization. Naturally, he should not attempt to furnish management advisory services of a type with which he is not familiar and of which he does not possess proper knowledge.

Management Advisory Services Described

The Committee on Management Services of the American Institute of Certified Public Accountants in *Statement on Management Services No. 1*, issued in 1969, gives the following description of management advisory services:

Management advisory services by independent accounting firms can be described as the function of providing professional advisory (consulting) services, the primary purpose of which is to improve the client's use of its capabilities and resources to achieve the objectives of the organization. This can relate to areas such as:

a) The management functions of analysis, planning, organizing, and controlling
b) The introduction of new ideas, concepts, and methods to management
c) The improvement of policies, procedures, systems, methods, and organization relationships
d) The application and use of managerial accounting, control systems, data processing, and mathematical techniques and methods, and
e) The conduct of special studies, preparation of recommendations, development of plans and programs, and provision of advice and technical assistance in their implementation.

This broad description of management advisory services has led to wide debate on the scope of management services practice. Some public accounting firms handle management services only in the area of management accounting or management information systems, while others offer management advisory services in almost every possible management requirement in which outside professional counsel is desirable or necessary.

Management advisory services involve the making of business decisions. In making decisions, there will be a choice between two or more alternatives. It must be remembered that all decisions relate to the future; and because there are no *facts* about the future, factual materials do not exist for the basis of decisions. However, there are facts concerning the past; and on the basis of the *evaluation* of those *historical* facts, and on the basis of estimates for the future, decisions are made.

Management advisory services exist—and have existed—because management may not possess the staff or have the time to do the work, *and* because management increasingly relies upon its certified public accountant for service and advice over and above that rendered through the medium of auditing, accounting services, and tax services.

At the present time there is a trend in still another direction in the management consulting field. Lately, it seems that more and more small and medium-sized businesses are looking to their auditors for help in the area of controllership. With the increasing complexity of business, top management constantly needs controllership-type advice, and lacking a full-time controller, it will attempt to employ the services of a public accountant as a "part-time controller." Before this situation can be explored thoroughly, it is necessary to relate the concept of independence to this area.

Management Advisory Services and Independence

The matter of independence has been discussed on many occasions in this text. It is necessary to reconsider the matter of independence in connection with management advisory services. When providing management advisory services, the auditor must, as in all areas of practice, give particular consideration to both independence and the appearance of independence set forth in the *Code of Professional Ethics*. The Committee on Professional Ethics in its *Opinion No. 12* states:

The Committee does not intend to suggest . . . that the rendering of professional services other than the independent audit itself would suggest to a reasonable observer a conflict of interest. . . . In the areas of management advisory services . . . , so long as the CPA's services consist of advice and technical assistance, the committee can discern no likelihood of a conflict of interest arising from such services. It is a rare instance for management to surrender its responsibility to make management decisions. However, should a member make such decisions on matters affecting the company's financial position or results of operations, it would appear that his objectivity as independent auditor of the company's financial statements might well be impaired. Consequently, such situations should be avoided.

In summary, it is the opinion of the Committee that there is no ethical reason why a member or associate may not properly perform professional services for clients in areas of . . . management advisory services, and at the same time serve the client as independent auditor, so long as he does not make management decisions or take positions which might impair that objectivity.

From the preceding it should be understood that a practitioner may render management advisory services without losing his independence, even if he renders the service for the same audit client. The offering of advice and technical assistance, per se, does not impair the accounting firm's objectivity as long as the accounting firm's role and management's role are both made quite clear; that is, the auditor offers the advice and assistance, while management has the responsibility to make the ultimate decisions.

As management advisory services are extended further and further into other areas, some members of the profession feel that there is increased pressure against independence. This depends on the nature of the role of the accountant in any one engagement.

The Auditor's Role in Management Advisory Services

The role of the auditor in the practice of management advisory services is significant because of its bearing on the type of service the auditor performs and also because of its bearing on the relationship between independent accountant and client.

Management advisory services must be discussed separately from the practice of management. The Committee on Management Services of the AICPA is explicit on the role of the independent public accountant in management advisory services. In *Statement on Management Advisory Services No. 1*, the Committee states:

The role of an independent accounting firm in performing management advisory services is to provide advice and technical assistance, and should provide for client participation in the analytical approach and process. Specifying this as the proper role recognizes both the appropriate place of management advisory services and the realities of practice. This is the only basis on which the work should be done and it is the only basis on which responsible management should permit it to be done.

In *Statement on Management Advisory Services No. 3*, the Committee states:

The propriety of this role of advisor is clear if one considers that a consultant is not in a position to carry out his recommendations since he has no authority to marshal client resources or to make management decisions. Should he attempt to do so and allow himself to be placed in such a role, he ceases to be a consultant and exercises management prerogatives—with consequent loss of the essential consulting requisites of impartiality and objectivity.

The concept of independence must be retained by the auditor in the rendition of management advisory services. Stated differently, the certified public accountant is rendering management *advisory* services—he is not *performing* a management function.

"Part-Time Controllers"

As stated earlier, more and more top managers of small and medium-sized businesses who feel that they need help in the solving of the increasingly complex problems of modern business are seeking the help of public accountants as "part-time controllers." Should the independent public accountant provide this service? To answer this question, one must again inquire as to the role of the independent accountant. If management wants controller-type help, thus allowing the public accountant to deal with every facet of the problem from the highest level, then it follows that top management will expect the public accountant to be a part of the ultimate decision-making process. Then the public practitioner has performed a management function and is no longer a consultant. Not only that, but the public accountant's independence is impaired.

This is not to state, however, that a good and much-needed service might be performed in this area. But there are important limitations and inherent dangers to be considered.

First, some people feel that management should never abdicate its responsibility of being the ultimate decision-maker; it follows that these same people feel that the accounting practitioner should never allow himself to become a decision-maker. It is very possible that the "part-time controller" may wind up making a decision on his findings by default through ignorance or lethargy on the part of top management. The danger of accepting this responsibility is that in areas subject to personal and argumentative positions, the practitioner could many times be a failure. This could result in a possible loss of the eminence the practitioner holds in the more traditional accounting fields.

Second, the controller is no longer limited to dealing with control in the financial accounting area but is involved in many allied areas and functions. This new responsibility includes such areas as statistics, operations research, mathematics, industrial engineering, and other areas not limited to accounting. The question often asked is if the public accountant as "part-time controller" should hold himself as attempting to be all things to all people? Of course this same criticism could be aimed toward management advisory services. The difference is that on any one management advisory services engagement, the practitioner is consulting in an individual area (and necessarily one in which he must be qualified) rather than an all inclusive type of engagement as "part-time controller."

Third, the "part-time controller" engagement is normally meant to be a continuous one rather than an isolated management advisory services engagement. Many times it deals directly with controls and has a direct relationship with the data audited by the independent auditor. Therefore, "part-time controlling" and auditing for the same client are incompatible. Even if no decisions are made by the "part-time controller," he would have lost the confidence of third parties, so essential to the independence of the auditor. In the rendering of management advisory services one must be on constant guard not to be put into a position such as that described above, or it may destroy his independence with the result that management advisory services and auditing would not be compatible for the same client.

Fourth, the "part-time controller" may be considered a part of the management team. Many people feel that this position creates a situation that limits the amount and quality of advice and assistance that the auditor can render. The auditor will be far more effective if his opinion is considered by all persons to be free from bias and completely objective. Management advisory services engagements should not have this obstacle.

The need for "part-time controllers" will remain. Companies that are too small for full-time help need to enlist the part-time services of some outsider. Normally the nature of the problems is such that professional accountants are the most qualified of all professionals to be called upon to answer the growing need.

The Approach to Management Advisory Services

The approach to a management advisory service engagement is somewhat different than the approach to an audit engagement. While it is true that the various auditing standards set forth in Chapter 1 apply to management advisory services, one cannot deny that a new approach as well as different techniques are involved in a management advisory service engagement.

There are certain basic philosophies underlying the new approach required for management advisory services, and these philosophies are briefly presented in the following paragraphs of this section.

The Committee on Management Services of the AICPA explains the approach as follows:

In providing this advisory service, the independent accounting firm applies an analytical approach and process which typically involve:

a)   Ascertaining the pertinent facts and circumstances
b)   Seeking and identifying objectives
c)   Defining the problem or opportunity for improvement
d)   Evaluating and determining possible solutions, and
e)   Presenting findings and recommendations, and following the client's decision to proceed, the independent accounting firm may also be involved in:
f)   Planning and scheduling actions to achieve the desired results, and
g)   Advising and providing technical assistance in implementing, in combination with knowledge and experience in such areas as:
h)   Organization and management methods
i)   Office and management functions

j) Systems and procedures

k) Data processing methods

l) Quantitative methods (mathematics, statistics, etc.), and

m) Financial management,
     to produce solutions such as:

n) A management information system

o) A sales reporting system

p) A cost accounting system

q) A work measurement program

r) Improved production control

s) An organization plan with statements of duties and responsibilities, or

t) An electronic data processing system.

In summary form the accepted approach consists of three stages of effort—analysis, design, and implementation.

Some basic philosophies underly the above approach to management advisory services. First, the psychological advantage is normally on the side of the practitioner in a management advisory services engagement. This is because most consulting is positive in nature—to make good things happen.

Second, is the concept that management advisory services are to benefit the present and the future—the past is history. It is true that accountants originally were—or are—historians; it is necessary that the historical point of view be changed. Past history may or may not be of value in determining future action and arriving at decisions for the present or the future. There should be no dependence on past accounting information except as a basis for determining or estimating corresponding figures for the future. Stated differently, decisions affect only the future; and in arriving at a decision between alternatives, only estimated future cost differentials or income differentials should be considered.

Third, if it becomes necessary to do so, all presently accepted accounting principles must be disregarded in posing and solving a management advisory problem. As a result of decisions between alternative choices, new methods, procedures, standards, and even principles may be developed. Also, as a result of decision—accompanied by disregarding accepted accounting principles—new principles may *not* be developed. A point to be remembered is that adherence to an accepted principle should not be blindly followed to the potential detriment of solving a management problem.

Fourth, because a business decision is a choice between two or more alternatives, the only costs to be considered should be those which are different for the various alternatives. Costs which are common to all alternatives logically may be ignored in arriving at a decision.

ILLUSTRATION.   A company is manufacturing an item used in production. The cost to manufacture the item is $15 per unit. The item can be purchased on the outside for $13 per unit. The decision to buy or manufacture should exclude costs common to both alternatives—that is, costs that will not be eliminated if the item is purchased, such as general overhead. The cost should include overhead that would otherwise be avoided, and lost "opportunity" cost represented by the value of space or equipment that otherwise would be available for other uses. Because present equipment might not be sold and because freed space might not be usable for other purposes, the decision might be to continue manufacturing until the present equipment is worn out, after which the item would be purchased.

Different cost and revenue information must exist or be developed for different purposes. For example, it may be necessary to develop different cost or revenue figures for the same item for different purposes. Only those costs or revenues to be affected by a decision need be considered in an advisory problem. For example, if a problem does not involve fixed costs (even though fixed costs do exist in the client's business), they should be ignored, because their existence will not affect the decision. Of course, there must be a clear distinction between fixed and variable costs (and revenues) and a complete understanding of the precise cost (and revenue) figures which are appropriate for different purposes. Marginal costs and marginal revenues, and their relationship to each other, frequently constitute the most important information in a management advisory service problem.

Guidelines for Management Advisory Service Practice

Codified guidelines for the practice of auditing have been available to the profession for years. Similar material that is generally acceptable is not available for the practice of management advisory services. However, guidelines representing a consensus of views of many practitioners in the field of management advisory services are presented in a publication of the AICPA entitled *Guidelines for Administration of the Management Advisory Services Practice* in its *Management Advisory Services Guideline Series No. 1.* Part of the material in this publication is as follows:

The publication is organized on a time cycle basis as follows:

1. Development and arrangement of engagements.
2. Problem definition and initial planning.
3. Proposal letters.
4. Engagement programs.
5. Reports.
6. Implementation of recommendations.
7. Evaluation of engagement performance.

The development of a management advisory service engagement may be externally or internally initiated. The business community many times seeks the help of a member of the profession in the solving of business problems. Further, it is the professional obligation of the CPA to inform the client of any problem areas and offer advice and assistance; of course this must be accomplished in an ethically acceptable manner. Some firms use a management advisory services questionnaire for those firms which they also audit. The client is provided with a copy of this questionnaire, which often leads to a management advisory services engagement. Other firms have the policy of making a management advisory services review with a written report in conjunction with the audit. Still other firms design internal control questionnaires in such a way to uncover any problem areas. Of course the success of one management advisory service engagement many times will result in additional work.

Once the engagement has been requested, the CPA must first decide if he should accept the assignment. Each CPA firm must make its own decision based upon the criteria for determining the scope of service mentioned earlier. If the CPA firm accepts the engagement it is important that a complete understanding is reached with the client as to the scope and objectives of the engagement. Some steps should be taken at this point to avoid possible failure later on. Among them are:

1. Do not accept the client's diagnosis of the problem but ascertain the real problem and the requirements necessary to solve it.
2. Gather and analyze all the salient facts. Extreme care must be taken that no facts are overlooked. Review and test the accumulated facts.
3. Determine the limitations and expected results of the solution.
4. Discuss the problem with the client along with the desirable course of action to be certain the client has a full understanding of the engagement.

The proposal letter is the next step. This letter covers the objectives and benefits of the engagement to the client, the scope of the work and the role of the CPA firm, the approach to the study, and fees and billing arrangements. This letter is used to minimize misunderstandings between the CPA firm and the client.

It is important that an operational plan be prepared. This plan should contain the objectives to be accomplished as well as the manpower required and personnel assigned, and the starting and completion dates. The personnel of the client should be included in the preparation of the work plan as well as in the engagement itself. The practitioner should never overestimate or underestimate the competence of the client's personnel. As the operational plan is carried out, the practitioner should constantly substantiate the facts through research, questioning, testing, and so forth. Progress reports should be submitted to the client. Proper preparation of work papers is just as important in a management advisory services engagement as in an audit.

The final report, which could in some cases be the only tangible engagement output, depends on the type of engagement and the needs of the client. It may be in the nature of a short letter, or a very long and formal report complete with applicable charts and schedules. Many times the report is supplemented by an oral presentation.

The implementation stage includes planning and scheduling actions to achieve the desired results, as well as advising and providing technical assistance. The practitioner cannot take the responsibility for making management decisions; therefore, client involvement is very important at the implementation stage. As soon as possible, client personnel should carry out the implementation on their own.

This is not to say that implementation as well as follow-up and evaluation should be ignored. It is only that in the implementation and evaluation stage, the practitioner must be careful to consider the limitations in the scope of practice and not jeopardize his objective advisory role.

Types of Management Advisory Services

Throughout the chapter, management advisory services have been described in a conceptual manner rather than in terms of areas of application. Management advisory services of the certified public accountant, working independently or in conjunction with specialists, may be classified in many ways. An itemized "list of acceptable areas of service" would be useful; however, no such list exists. The constantly changing and increasing complex business problems make an acceptable list unattainable. All management advisory service problems might be divided into three general areas, as follows:

1. Management advisory services arising directly from accounting, auditing, and taxation services. An example would be the design of a new accounting system.
2. Services arising indirectly from accounting and auditing information. An example might be the revision of a production program, based upon an audit determination that production costs were excessive.
3. Services that have small apparent relationship to accounting, auditing, or taxation. An example might be office organization.

Another method of classifying management advisory services is in terms of the various possible areas of business organization serviced. An example of such a classification appears below. The classifications and subclassifications are not totally inclusive, and they are not necessarily mutually exclusive. Many of the subclassification titles could be moved to another major classification—and perhaps classification is not even necessary, but it is presented here in order to attempt to delineate the various services.

Many of the items in the subclassifications may easily fall into the commonly used category of "special investigations." And some of the items may be in the nature of audits extended in detail for special purposes.

MANAGEMENT ADVISORY SERVICES

Type of Service	Specialists Who May Cooperate at the Request of the Client or at the Suggestion of the CPA
ACCOUNTING	
Accounting services in general.	None
Internal control procedure studies and installations	None
Development and installation of internal auditing procedures and programs	None
Accounting machine installations.	Accounting machine manufacturers
Electronic data processing equipment selection and installation	Computer equipment manufacturers
Cost accounting studies and development of cost systems	Production engineers
Budgets and their preparation	A bank, if credit is involved
Federal taxation services.	Lawyers
State and local taxation services.	Lawyers
Estate planning and tax services.	Lawyers; trust companies
Preparation of reports for the Securities and Exchange Commission	None
Information systems	Office and computer equipment manufacturers
Pro-forma statements.	None
Local, state, federal government labor reports.	None
Labor union reports	None
Special reports:	
Cash basis	None
Modified accrual basis	None
Incomplete financial presentations	None
FINANCE	
Study of working capital requirements.	None
Assistance in obtaining working capital	Banks
Study of methods of financing asset acquisitions	Banks
Development of plans for long-term financing requirements.	Banks
Credit and collection practice studies and advice	Credit investigating services
Survey of pension, retirement, and profitsharing plans	Insurance companies; trust companies; lawyers; banks
Receivership services	Lawyers
Services in determining repurchase price of shares in close corporations	Appraisal companies
Alternative methods of acquiring another company.	None
Alternative methods of financing expansion	None
ORGANIZATION	
Survey of internal organization	None
Studies of the effectiveness of employees . . .	None
Assistance for sources of capital	Banks; investment security dealers

MANAGEMENT ADVISORY SERVICES *(Continued)*

Type of Services	Specialists Who May Cooperate at the Request of the Client or at the Suggestion of the CPA
Advice regarding types of securities to be issued	Banks; investment security dealers
Preparation of organization charts	None
Preparation of flow charts	None
Advice as to form of business organization— corporation, partnership, other	Lawyers
Assistance in the reorganization of the form of business organization	Lawyers
Reorganization of financial structure	Banks
Assistance in the preparation of articles of copartnership	Lawyers

GENERAL MANAGEMENT

Survey of management policies	None
Establishment of internal reporting systems	None
Establishment of managerial cost controls	None
Assistance in preparation of reports to employees, stockholders, and others	None
Advice regarding contraction or expansion	None
Assistance in internal office organization	Specialists in office layout
Development of office operating records	Specialists in office routine
Assistance in the reorganization of a department, division, or function	None; unless special engineering is required
Measuring success of management policies	None

OFFICE MANAGEMENT

Advice regarding office equipment	Equipment manufacturers
Studies of office space utilization and space requirements	Equipment manufacturers
Studies in office organization	None
Personnel evaluation	None
Establishment of clerical work standards	Controller
Review of office paper work	Controller
Filing system surveys	Office manager
Design and operation of office forms	Form specialty companies

PERSONNEL AND INDUSTRIAL RELATIONS

Survey of accounting personnel	None
Interviewing new accounting personnel	Personnel services
Survey of nonaccounting personnel	Personnel services
Aptitude test studies	Aptitude testing services
Studies of training procedures	None
Preparation of job classifications	Engineering and job classification services
Wage-and-hour stabilization studies	None
Labor relations studies	Union representatives
Advice for pension and retirement plans	Insurance companies; trust companies; lawyers

MANAGEMENT ADVISORY SERVICES *(Continued)*

Type of Services	Specialists Who May Cooperate at the Request of the Client or at the Suggestion of the CPA
Advice for profit-sharing plans	Lawyers
Advice for wage incentive plans	Experts in incentive plans
Assistance in determining fringe benefits.	None
Arbitration	None; arbitration committees

PRODUCTION

Plant location investigations	Architects; real estate brokers; engineers
Studies of types of equipment and comparative costs	Equipment manufacturers
Development of production standards	None
Plant space-utilization studies	Production engineers
Survey of production planning	Production engineers
Survey of production records	Production engineers
Production statistics development	None
Advice in factory management	Management or engineering services
Time and motion studies	Time and motion study specialists
Survey of quality control	Quality control specialists
Waste reduction studies	Production engineers
Factory overhead studies	Engineering specialists
Material handling surveys	Production engineering specialists
Inventory control studies	Inventory control engineers

SALES MANAGEMENT

Pricing policy studies	Marketing specialists; market survey services
Development of quotas	Market research services
Market analysis	Market analysts
Studies of the profitableness of various products	None
Advice as to price establishment for items sold	Market analysts
Advice regarding outlet locations	Market analysts

ADVERTISING

Advertising control programs	Advertising agencies
Analyses of advertising methods	Advertising agencies
Productivity of advertising	Market research

SALES

Studies of marketing and merchandising methods	Market research and service specialists
Inventory control studies	Inventory control specialists
Warehousing methods and space utilization studies	Inventory control specialists; engineers
Development of distribution costs and statistics	None
Sales compensation plan development	Other companies
Development of sales training programs	Sales training services
Studies of efficiency of delivery methods and costs	Delivery service experts
Automobile fleet surveys and surveys of delivery problems	Delivery service experts; automotive company representatives

MANAGEMENT ADVISORY SERVICES *(Concluded)*

Type of Services	Specialists Who May Cooperate at the Request of the Client or at the Suggestion of the CPA
MISCELLANEOUS	
Obtaining comparative figures for comparable companies within the industry	Investment services
Advice regarding life insurance programs. . . .	Life insurance companies
Program development for fidelity, fire, and other casualty insurance	Insurance companies
Advice on general business matters	None
Advice on governmental regulations pertaining to price controls, fair trade practices, and so forth	None
Contract negotiation, renegotiation, and termination	Lawyers
Rate regulation surveys	Transportation specialists
Plan development for inventory taking.	None
Fixed asset studies involving cost, appraisals, and depreciation	Appraisal companies
Negotiations for the purchase or sale of a business	Lawyers; appraisers
Surveys for new ventures	Engineers; production specialists; market analysts
Preparation of record demolition (or retention) schedules	None
Operations research.	None

Special Reports

In 1973, the Committee on Auditing Procedure of the American Institute of Certified Public Accountants issued *Statement on Auditing Standards No. 1,* which in Sections 620 and 630, deals with the applicability of reporting standards in normal and in special circumstances. The term "special reports" has reference to reports for which the wording and content of the usual audit report is totally inappropriate because the attest function is not involved. Thus, the special types of reporting circumstances would include reports on financial statements for organizations maintaining their accounting records on a cash basis or any other incomplete basis; reports on financial statements for certain nonprofit organizations, wherein accounting practices may differ from those used by business concerns organized for profit; and "special-purpose" reports issued as a result of special studies or management services, such as the determination of rents, profit-sharing bonuses, compliance with the provisions of bond indentures, product cost analyses, capital stock purchase and sale agreements for close corporations, and all other special study report issued in accordance with the management services outlined in this chapter.

Special reports which involve no financial statements or only partial financial statements should be prepared in accordance with the special purpose—product cost analyses, profit-sharing bonuses, and so forth. The report should contain a statement of the information presented, the basis on which the report was prepared, the conclusions reached, and the opinion regarding the propriety and fairness of the presentation.

It is the opinion of the Committee that "to the extent appropriate in view of the character of the engagement, the substance of the general standards and of the standards of field work, applies to engagements involving special reports." Thus, the standards of reporting, as set forth by the American Institute, while in no way diluted, will vary with the peculiarities of each engagement not involving financial statements setting forth financial condition and the results of operations, prepared under commonly recognized principles of accounting.

APB Opinion No. 28, Interim Financial Reporting, clearly points out the need for accuracy of presentation so that this interim information can be used by interested parties. The auditor must be certain that the results of each interim period are based upon accounting principles and practices used by his client in the preparation of his latest financial statements. However, if there has been a change in an accounting practice or policy, full disclosure as to the effect of this change must be presented.

Another important advisory service rendered by CPAs is the "comfort letter" or letters for underwriters. These letters frequently refer to one or more of the following subjects:

a) The independence of the accountants
b) Compliance as to form in all material respects of the audited financial statements and schedules with the applicable accounting requirements of the various Securities Acts and published rules and regulations thereunder.
c) Unaudited financial statements and schedules in the registration statement.
d) Changes in selected financial-statement items during a period subsequent to the date and period of the latest financial statements in the registration statement.
e) Tables, statistics, and other financial information in the registration statement.

As more and more companies "go public," the importance of this management advisory service will increase markedly and will require more and more of the CPA's billable time.

Conclusion

The area of management advisory services is one of the fast growing phases of the accounting profession. As the profession becomes involved in client's affairs via the audit, it is natural to become aware of the other problems that might exist. The need for consulting services affects the entire profession, small and large firms alike. No one in the profession should think merely in terms of providing only auditing services or tax services. To ignore the challenge of management advisory services, at best, would be a failure to be in a position to play an integral part in assisting clients to improve their own profitability. A properly conducted management advisory services engagement can be a very valuable professional service and will expand the impact of the accountant upon the business community.

QUESTIONS

1. a) What are the arguments in support of the offering of management advisory services by a public accounting firm?
    b) What cautions or limitations are there in the performance of management advisory services?
    c) Do you feel that management advisory services and auditing are compatible for the same client by the same certified public accountant?

2. How can the CPA remain independent while performing management services work?

3. How should the CPA approach the providing of management services?

4. What are the basic philosophies that underly a sound approach to management advisory services?

5. What guidelines should the CPA follow in his management advisory service practice?

6. The president of a small manufacturing company has requested your services to evaluate the decision of whether or not to invest in new factory machinery. How would you approach this problem?

7. The president of a medium-sized plumbing company has asked you to become a "part-time controller" as well as audit his records at the end of the year. The plumbing company has a bookkeeper but the president would use your specialized knowledge of tax and financial matters to help him solve business problems and to help him make business decisions. Should you accept the engagement and, if so, under what conditions?

8. Your client, Nease Corporation, requested that you conduct a feasibility study to advise management of the best way the corporation can utilize electronic data processing equipment and which computer, if any, best meets the corporation's requirements. You are technically competent in this area and accept the engagement. Upon completion of your study the corporation accepts your suggestions and installs the computer and related equipment that you recommended.
    a) Discuss the effect the acceptance of this management services engagement would have upon your independence in expressing an opinion on the financial statements of the Nease Corporation.

b) Instead of accepting the engagement, assume that you recommended Mackey, of the CPA firm of Brown and Mackey, who is qualified in specialized services. Upon completion of the agreement your client requests that Mackey's partner, John Brown, perform services in other areas. Should Brown accept the engagement? Discuss.

c) A local printer of data processing forms customarily offers a commission for recommending him as supplier. The client is aware of the commission offer and suggests that Mackey accept it. Would it be proper for Mackey to accept the commission with the client's approval? Discuss.

(AICPA, adapted)

9. The president of a building and loan company has asked you to design and implement a new information system.

Answer the following questions concerning information systems:

a) What is an information system?

b) What must you consider before designing a new information system in a building and loan association?

c) What must a good information system for a building and loan association accomplish?

10. What is likely to be the composition of a "comfort" letter?

PROBLEMS

1. The local CPA chapter is planning a weekend seminar at Cedar Point Inn. The inn has adequate facilities and will turn over the entire facility for $8,000. The inn will lose estimated revenue of $4,400 and will also incur additional service and food costs of $2,200.

a) What would your recommendation be to Cedar Point Inn?

b) What intangible factors would you discuss with the Cedar Point Inn management?

2. Your client, Fashion Clothes, Inc., manufactures and sells three lines of dresses, with the following contribution margin per unit:

Bridal gowns.	$8
House dresses	1
Evening gowns	3

The following production time is required to produce one unit:

Bridal gowns.	4 hours
House dresses	15 minutes
Evening gowns	1 hour

The client's sales forecast is as follows:

Bridal gowns–as many as it can produce
House dresses–32,000 units
Evening gowns–16,000 units

The plant's productive hours are 32,000 per month. The client requests that you prepare an analysis that will assist him in maximizing his profit.

3. Construction Prefabricators, Inc., plans to renovate and update its production facilities in 1975. They have developed specifications and opened them for bids. The lowest bid, acceptable to *CPI*, is $280,000. However, due to the seasonal nature, CPI can do the work with its own employees during the slack period. After reviewing the project, the following estimates are supplied to you to determine who should do the work:

> Materials: $112,000
> Increase in labor and specific overhead costs: $76,000
> Administrative cost increase: $8,000
> Fixed overhead costs to be allocated to the renovation: $92,000

Prepare an analysis which will clearly set forth the cost comparisons of these two proposals.

4. When you had completed your audit of the Grand Junction Company, management asked for your assistance in arriving at a decision regarding the continuance of manufacturing a part or to buy it from an outside supplier. The part, which is named Stamper, is a component used in some of the finished products of the company.

From your audit work papers and from further investigation you develop the following data as being typical of the company's operations:

(1) The annual requirement for Stampers are 5,000 units. The lowest quotation from a supplier was $8 per unit.

(2) Stampers have been manufactured in the precision machinery department. If Stampers are purchased from an outside supplier, certain machinery will be sold and would realize its book value.

(3) Following are the total costs of the precision machinery department during the year under audit when 5,000 Stampers were made:

Materials	$67,500
Direct labor	50,000
Indirect labor	20,000
Light, heat, and power	8,500
Depreciation.	10,000
Property taxes and insurances	8,000
Payroll taxes (14 percent of labor cost)	9,800
Other.	5,000

(4) The following precision machinery department costs apply to the manufacture of Stampers: material, $17,500; direct labor, $28,000; indirect labor, $6,000; power, $300; other, $500. The sale of the equipment used for Stampers would reduce the following costs by the amounts indicated: depreciation, $2,000; property taxes and insurance, $1,000.

(5) The following additional precision machinery department costs would be incurred if Stampers were purchased from an outside supplier: freight, $0.50 per unit; indirect labor for receiving, handling, and so forth, $5,000. The cost of the purchased Stampers parts would be considered a precision machinery department cost.

a) Prepare a schedule showing a comparison of the total costs of the precision machinery department (1) when Stampers are made, and (2) when Stampers are bought from an outside supplier.

b) Discuss the considerations in addition to the cost factors that you would bring to the attention of management in assisting them to arrive at a decision whether to make or buy Stampers. Include in your discussion the considerations that might be applied to the evaluation of the outside supplier.

(AICPA, adapted)

5. The management of the Elkins Cotton Gin Company has engaged you to assist in the development of information to be used for managerial decisions.

The company has the capacity to process 20,000 tons of cottonseed per year. The yield of a ton of cottonseed is as follows:

Product	Average Yield per Ton of Cottonseed	Average Selling Price per Trade Unit
Oil	300 lbs.	$ 0.15 per lb.
Meal	600 lbs.	50.00 per ton
Hulls	800 lbs.	20.00 per ton
Lint	100 lbs.	3.00 per cwt.
Waste	200 lbs,	

A special marketing study revealed that the company can expect to sell its entire output for the coming year at the listed average selling prices.

You have determined the company's costs to be as follows:

Processing costs:

Variable: $9 per ton of cottonseed put into process.

Fixed: $108,000 per year.

Marketing costs:

All variable: $20 per ton sold.

Administrative costs:

All fixed: $90,000 per year.

From the above information you prepared and submitted to management a detailed report on the company's break-even point. In view of conditions in the cottonseed market, management told you that they would also like to know the average maximum amount that the company can afford to pay for a ton of cottonseed.

Management has defined the average maximum amount that the company can afford to pay for a ton of cottonseed as the amount that would result in the company's having losses no greater when operating than when closed down under the existing cost and revenue structure. Management states that you are to assume that the fixed costs shown in your break-even point report will continue unchanged even when the operations are shut down.

a) Compute the average maximum amount that the company can afford to pay for a ton of cottonseed.

b) You also plan to mention to management the factors, other than the costs that entered into your computation, that they should consider in deciding whether to shut down the plant. Discuss these additional factors.

c) The stockholders consider the minimum satisfactory return on their investment in the business to be 25 percent before corporate income taxes. The stockholders' equity in the company is $968,000. Compute the maximum average amount that the company can pay for a ton of cottonseed to realize the minimum satisfactory return on the stockholders' investment in the business.

(AICPA)

6. You have been engaged to assist the management of the TGIE Corporation in arriving at certain decisions. The TGIE Corporation has its home office in Atlanta and leases factory buildings in New York, Pennsylvania and Ohio. The same single product is manufactured in all three factories. The following information is available regarding 1975 operations:

	Total	New York	Ohio	Pennsylvania
Sales	$900,000	$200,000	$400,000	$300,000
Fixed costs:				
Factory	$180,000	$ 50,000	$ 55,000	$ 75,000
Administration	59,000	16,000	21,000	22,000
Variable cost.	500,000	100,000	220,000	180,000
Allocated home office expense	63,000	14,000	28,000	21,000
Total.	$802,000	$180,000	$324,000	$298,000
Net profit from operations	$ 98,000	$ 20,000	$ 76,000	$ 2,000

Home office expense is allocated on the basis of units sold. The sales price per unit is $10.

Management is undecided whether to renew the lease of the Pennsylvania factory, which expires on December 31, 1976, and will require an increase in rent of $15,000 per year if renewed. If the Pennsylvania factory is shut down, the amount expected to be realized from the sale of the equipment is greater than its book value and would cover all termination expenses.

If the Pennsylvania factory is shut down, the company can continue to serve customers of the Pennsylvania factory by one of the following methods:

(1) Expanding the New York factory, which would increase fixed costs by 15 percent. Additional shipping expense of $2 per unit will be incurred on the increased production.

(2) Entering into a long-term contract with a competitor who will serve the Pennsylvania factory customers and who will pay the TGIE Corporation a commission of $1.60 per unit.

The TGIE Corporation is also planning to establish a subsidiary corporation in Canada to produce the same product. Based on estimated annual Canadian sales of 40,000 units, cost studies produced the following estimates for the Canadian subsidiary:

	Total Annual Costs	Percent of Total Annual Cost That is Variable
Material	$193,600	100%
Labor	90,000	70
Overhead	80,000	64
Administration	30,000	30

The Canadian production will be sold by manufacturer's representatives who will receive a commission of 8 percent of the sales price. No portion of the United States home office expense will be allocated to the Canadian subsidiary.

a) Prepare a schedule computing TGIE's estimated net income from United States operations under each of the following procedures:

(1) Expansion of the New York factory.

(2) Negotiation of long-term contract on a commission basis.

b) Management wants to price its Canadian product to realize a 10 percent profit on the sales price. Compute to sales price per unit that would result in an estimated 10 percent profit on sales.

c) Assume that your answer to part (b) is a sales price of $11 per unit. Compute the break-even point in sales dollars for the Canadian subsidiary.

(AICPA)

Index

This book has been set in 10 and 9 point Janson, leaded 2 points. Chapter titles are 18 point Caslon Bold 79J, and chapter numbers are 36 point Caslon Bold 79J. The size of the type page is 27 × 46½ picas.